Exploring Corporate Strategy
Seventh Enhanced Media

Visit the companion website if you want to:

- *Test your knowledge and track your progress*
- *Download audio summaries of key topics*
- *Read updates on case studies and examples in the book*

Follow three steps to get more value from this Enhanced Media Edition:

1. **Visit** the *Exploring Corporate Strategy* companion website at **www.pearsoned.co.uk/ecs7**

2. **Register** your own personal account using the access codes supplied with this copy of the Enhanced Media Edition

3. **Access** valuable learning resources to help you pass your course:

   - ➤ Answer **self-assessment questions** for each chapter and save your scores to a personal gradebook

   - ➤ Listen online or download to your MP3 player: **audio summaries** of key learning points

   - ➤ Use the **online glossary** and **interactive flashcards** to check and test your understanding of key terms

   - ➤ Read recent **FT articles** to update case studies and examples in the book

   - ➤ Get guidance on **How to Analyse a Case Study**

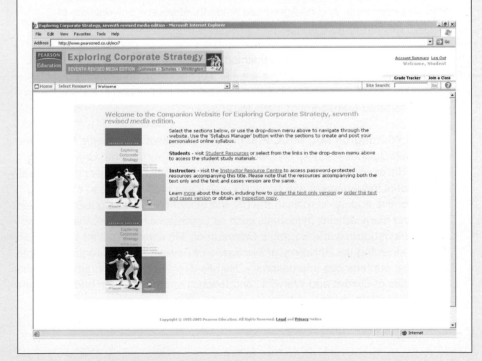

Gerry Johnson BA, PhD (left) is Professor of Strategic Management at the University of Strathclyde Graduate School of Business and a fellow of the UK Advanced Institute of Management Research. He is the author of numerous books, has published in many of the foremost management research journals and is a regular speaker at academic conferences throughout the world. He serves on the editorial boards of the *Strategic Management Journal* and the *Journal of Management Studies*. His research is in the field of strategic management practice in relation to strategy development and change in organisations. As a consultant he applies many of the concepts in *Exploring Corporate Strategy* to help management teams challenge and develop the strategies of their organisations.

Kevan Scholes MA, PhD, DMS, CIMgt, FRSA (centre) is Principal Partner of Scholes Associates – specialising in strategic management. He is also Visiting Professor of Strategic Management and formerly Director of the Sheffield Business School, UK. He has extensive experience of teaching strategy to both undergraduate and postgraduate students at several universities. In addition his corporate management development work includes organisations in manufacturing, many service sectors and a wide range of public service organisations. He has regular commitments outside the UK – including Ireland, Australia, New Zealand and Singapore. He has also been an advisor on management development to a number of national bodies and is a Companion of the Chartered Management Institute.

Richard Whittington MA, MBA, PhD (right) is Professor of Strategic Management at the Saïd Business School and Millman Fellow at New College, University of Oxford. His main research interests are in the practice of strategy and comparative international management and he works with many organisations in consulting and executive education roles in the UK and elsewhere. He has published seven books and many articles in journals such as *Organization Science*, the *Strategic Management Journal* and *Strategic Organization*. He serves on eight journal editorial boards, including the *Academy of Management Review*, and is a regular keynote speaker at conferences internationally. He has directed MBA programmes at the Universities of Oxford and Warwick, and teaches strategy at both undergraduate and postgraduate levels.

Exploring Corporate Strategy

Gerry Johnson
University of Strathclyde

Kevan Scholes
Sheffield Hallam University

Richard Whittington
Saïd Business School, University of Oxford

SEVENTH ENHANCED MEDIA EDITION

FT Prentice Hall
FINANCIAL TIMES

An imprint of **Pearson Education**
Harlow, England • London • New York • Boston • San Francisco • Toronto
Sydney • Tokyo • Singapore • Hong Kong • Seoul • Taipei • New Delhi
Cape Town • Madrid • Mexico City • Amsterdam • Munich • Paris • Milan

Pearson Education Limited
Edinburgh Gate
Harlow
Essex CM20 2JE
England

and Associated Companies throughout the world

Visit us on the World Wide Web at:
www.pearsoned.co.uk

─────────────────

Fifth edition published under the Prentice Hall imprint 1998
Sixth edition published under the Financial Times Prentice Hall imprint 2002
Seventh edition published 2005
Seventh Enhanced Media Edition published 2006

ISBN-13: 978-0-273-71018-9 (text only)
ISBN-10: 0-273-71018-4 (text only)

ISBN-13: 978-0-273-71017-2 (text and cases)
ISBN-10: 0-273-71017-6 (text and cases)

British Library Cataloguing-in-Publication Data
A catalogue record for this book is available from the British Library

Library of Congress Cataloging-in-Publication Data
A catalogue record for this book is available from the Library of Congress

10 9 8 7 6 5 4 3 2 1
10 09 08 07 06

Typeset in 9.5/13pt Stone Serif by 35
Printed and bound by Mateu Cromo, Spain

The publisher's policy is to use paper manufactured from sustainable forests.

Brief Contents

To Jenny, Maria and Phyl

Detailed Contents

Part I   INTRODUCTION

Part II   THE STRATEGIC POSITION

Part III   STRATEGIC CHOICES

7 Directions and Methods of Development

Commentary on Part III
Strategy Selection

Part V HOW STRATEGY DEVELOPS

CASE STUDIES

Companion Website Resources

Visit the *Exploring Corporate Strategy* Companion Website at **www.pearsoned.co.uk/ecs7**

Register your own personal account using the access codes supplied with this copy of the Enhanced Media Edition

Access the following teaching and learning resources:

For students

- Self-assessment questions to help test your learning
- Audio summaries of key topics
- An online glossary to explain key terms
- Interactive flashcards to test your knowledge of key terms
- FT articles to update cases and examples in the book
- Guidance on How to Analyse a Case Study

For lecturers

- Complete, downloadable Instructor's Manual
- Case Study teaching notes
- Suggested teaching plans
- Powerpoint slides that can be downloaded and used as OHTs
- Classic Case Study library
- FT articles to update cases and examples in the book
- Secure Testbank of over 350 questions

Also: This "Gradetracker" website enables students to save their scores from self-assessment questions and instructors to monitor the scores of their class.

List of Illustrations

List of Exhibits

Preface

It is now twenty-one years since the first edition of *Exploring Corporate Strategy* was published. Both the world of business and the public services have seen vast changes over that time. There have also been major changes in the subject of corporate strategy. Central to this has been a widespread recognition of the importance of the subject of strategy to practising managers in both the public and private sectors. This has been reflected in the inclusion of strategy as a subject in educational programmes at under-graduate, postgraduate and professional levels as well as its adoption in short courses and consultancy assignments. It is now accepted that an understanding of the principles and practice of strategy is not just the concern of top managers, but essential for different levels of management – though clearly emphases within the subject will vary. We have consistently argued the importance of this wider interest in strategy, so these are changes that we welcome.

The combined sales of our first six editions exceeded 650,000. This seventh edition marks a significant point in the book's development with the addition of Richard Whittington to the author team. Richard will be known to many readers through his own work and publications. Significantly Richard was known to both Gerry Johnson and Kevan Scholes as an MBA student at Aston during the development work on the first edition!

This new edition is being published at a time when most organisations are feeling the combined impact of globalisation, information technology and rapid changes in their business environment. More sectors of the economy of most countries are becoming 'knowledge based'. On the negative side there has been an increasing focus on some spectacular failures – such as Enron and WorldCom – leading to changes in corporate governance and a questioning of the motives and ethical standards of some managers and company directors. Whereas the structure of the book remains broadly the same we have tried to give more prominence to these issues.

The seventh edition also marks a step forward in terms of text layout and design. This has been made possible by the use of more colours and the incorporation of photographic materials to complement more traditional graphics and tables. The purposes of these changes are to improve clarity and 'navigation' and make reading the book an enjoyable experience. Each chapter has clear learning outcomes and a summary. Important 'definitions' are highlighted in the margins – there has been particular attention given to illustrations and case studies. The vast majority of these are new in this edition and the choice of examples reflects the issues mentioned above. All the 84 illustrations have questions, which allows them to be used as mini-cases by tutors and for students to check out their own progress on understanding the text. The case examples at the end of each chapter allow a reflection back on the range of separate issues within the chapter and help students see how they connect. We have also provided some new integrative work assignments to reinforce the connections between topics and chapters.

We have continued with the *critical commentaries* at the end of each section that were introduced for the sixth edition. The first purpose of the critical commentary is to reflect on the issues from the sections as viewed through the three strategy lenses – explained below. The commentaries are also designed to highlight the links between the separate chapter topics within a section and to take a broader view of the strategic issues in each section of the book. Together these issues are fundamental to the essence of strategy: looking at issues in more than one way and the importance of connections between issues that influence an organisation's success or failure.

Overall our aim has been to develop both the content and style of the book and we hope you will be pleased with the results of our efforts. *A guide to how to get the most from all the features and learning materials in/with* Exploring Corporate Strategy *follows this preface.*

Exploring Corporate Strategy is a conceptual book that builds on the practice of strategic management, as researchers and practitioners in the area understand it. It is a book primarily intended for students of strategy on undergraduate, diploma and master's courses in universities and colleges; students on courses with titles such as Corporate Strategy, Business Policy, Strategic Management, Organisational Policy and Corporate Policy. However, we know that many such students are already managers who are undertaking part-time study: so this book is written with the manager and the potential manager in mind.

The style of the book reflects our personal experience as active teachers, researchers and consultants for more than thirty years. It is the blending of theory with practice that is at the heart of good strategic management. It allows students both to apply concepts and theories to practical situations (for example, through case studies) and – just as important – to build their own ideas. However, it is also the case that the growing body of research and theory can be of great help in stimulating a deep understanding of strategic problems and strategic management. Our approach builds in substantial parts of such research and theory, and encourages readers to refer to more. But we also assume that readers will have the opportunity to deal with strategic problems through such means as case study work or projects, or, if they are practising managers, through their involvement in their own organisations. Our view in this respect is exactly the same as the writers of a medical or engineering text, and we encourage readers to take the same view. It is that good theory helps good practice, but that an understanding of the theory without an understanding of the practice is very dangerous – particularly if you are dealing with a patient, a bridge or, as with this book, organisations. A new feature for the seventh edition is the inclusion of a *strategy debate* as the final illustration in each chapter. These encourage readers to reflect further on a major issue from the chapter – providing contrasting views from important writers in the field.

Reinforcing this theory/practice link is one of the purposes of the section commentaries as mentioned above. The concept of the three strategy lenses is introduced in Chapter 1 and provides the framework for these reflections. As well as the 'traditional' *design* view of strategy we discuss how strategy can arise from *experience* and culture and also how it can be a product of *ideas* which emerge from the complex world within and around an organisation. The concept of lenses is used because they provide different, but complementary, ways of viewing strategy and strategic management. All three views are relevant to the study of strategy, and the text reflects this.

The structure of the book is explained in some detail in Chapter 1. However, it is useful to give a brief outline here. The book is in five parts:

Part I comprises an introduction to corporate strategy, in terms of its characteristics and the elements of strategic management (Chapter 1). The strategy lenses are also introduced.

Part II of the book is concerned with understanding an organisation's *strategic position*. Chapter 2 is concerned with understanding an organisation's position within its 'business' environment. This includes an organisation's competitive position. Chapter 3 considers the factors underpinning strategic capability – resources and competences. This includes the importance of knowledge. Chapter 4 is concerned with understanding organisational purposes. It is centred on the question of whom the organisation is there to serve and includes discussions of corporate governance, stakeholder relationships, business ethics and culture.

Part III deals with *strategic choice*. Chapter 5 deals with business-level (or competitive) strategy. The main issues are about the basis of competitive advantage and how to compete better in a fast-moving world. Chapter 6 is concerned with corporate-level and international strategy – how the corporate centre can add value to the business units (or, conversely, how it might destroy value). Chapter 7 looks at the more detailed choices of both strategic direction and method. It then looks at the criteria by which the likely success or failure of strategies could be assessed.

Part IV is about translating *strategy into action*. Chapter 8 is about organising for success and picks up recent literature about the connections between structures, organisation processes and the importance of establishing and maintaining internal and external relationships. Chapter 9 is about the relationship between an organisation's overall strategy and strategies in four key resource areas: people, information, finance and technology. Chapter 10 considers approaches to and methods of managing change and provides important links back to Chapter 4.

Part V has a single chapter (Chapter 11) which is about strategy development processes. The material in this chapter has been repositioned from Chapter 2 of previous editions. This is to allow readers to reflect more on the issues and concepts of strategy before addressing issues about the processes by which strategy is actually developed in organisations. But as a stand-alone chapter tutors and students can choose to use it at any appropriate point in their studies.

Many people have helped us with the development of this new edition. First and foremost have been the adopters of the current edition – many of whom we have had the pleasure of meeting at our annual teachers' workshops. Many of you have provided us with constructive criticism and thoughts for the new edition – we hope you are happy with the results! Also, our students and clients at Sheffield, Strathclyde and Oxford and the many other places where we teach: they are a constant source of ideas and challenge and it would be impossible to write a book of this type without this direct feedback. Our own work and contacts have expanded considerably as a result of our book and we now have important links across the world who have been a source of stimulation to us. Our contacts in Ireland, Holland, Denmark, Sweden, France, Canada, Australia, New Zealand, Singapore and the USA are especially valued.

We would like to thank those who have contributed directly to the book by providing case studies, and those organisations that have been brave enough to be written up as case studies. The growing popularity of *Exploring Corporate Strategy* has often presented these case study companies with practical problems in coping with direct enquiries from tutors and students. We hope that those using the book will respect the wishes of the case study companies and not contact them directly for further information. There are many colleagues that we need to thank for assisting us in improving our understanding of particular aspects of the subject or related area. Strategy is such a vast domain that this assistance is essential if the book is to remain up-to-date. So thank you to Julia Balogun, John Barbour, Graham Beaver, George Burt, Andrew Campbell, Frederic Frery, Royston Greenwood, Phyl Johnson, Aidan McQuade, Michael Mayer, David Pitt-Watson, Richard Schoenberg and Jill Shepherd. Special thanks are due to all those who provided and helped develop illustrations and cases – their assistance is acknowledged at the foot of those same. Thanks are also due to Christine Reid and Scott McGowan at Strathclyde for their valuable assistance with references. Melanie Scholes has also assisted with this process and with researching new academic sources and material for illustrations and cases. Our thanks are also due to those who have had a part in preparing the manuscript for the book, in particular Lorna Carlaw at Strathclyde and Jenny Scholes in Sheffield.

Gerry Johnson
Kevan Scholes
Richard Whittington

November 2004

Getting the Most from *Exploring Corporate Strategy*

Through the various editions of *Exploring Corporate Strategy* we have tried to respond to the continuing demand for more material whilst keeping the size of the text manageable for readers. These demands have included more depth in topics, more coverage of particular sectors or simply more examples and tasks for students. We have already produced additional materials and publications and improved the cross referencing to other material where it is relevant to a particular section of the text. This note gives some practical advice on how you might gain most advantage from this wide and varied range of materials.

Using *Exploring Corporate Strategy*

To get the most from *Exploring Corporate Strategy* and related materials the broad advice to students and managers is to ensure that you have achieved three things:

- you understand the concepts;
- you can apply these concepts to practical situations – if you are a manager it is particularly important to apply the concepts to your own work context;
- you read more widely than ECS.

Features of the text

- *Learning outcomes* are included at the beginning of each chapter which show what you should have achieved on completing the chapter. Check that you have understood all of these.
- *Key terms* are highlighted in the text and explained in the margins.
- *Illustration* boxes appear throughout the chapter and include questions so they can be used as 'mini'-cases. Make sure that you read and answer these to check that you understand the theory/practice connection. If you are a manager, always ask yourself an additional question: 'what are the lessons for me and my organisation from this example?' Do this for the case examples and case studies too, if you can. The best strategic managers are those who can transfer learning from one situation to another.
- *Chapter summaries* help you to recap and review the main points of the chapter.
- *Recommended key readings* are listed at the end of each chapter. Make sure that you are familiar with those that are relevant to your course of study. There are extensive references for more detailed study and in-depth research.
- *Work assignments* are organised in two levels of difficulty and are followed by integrative work assignments which reinforce the connections between topics and

chapters. Your tutors may have set some of these as course tests. In any case, you should treat these in the way you would previous examination papers – as a means of testing your own learning of both concepts and applications. If you are a manager, take the opportunity to work through these assignments for your own organisation and involve other members of your team if you can.

- A *case example* is included at the end of each chapter to help you consolidate your learning of the major themes. Answer the questions at the end of the example.

- A *section commentary* appears at the end of each major section of the book. Use them to ensure that you can see connections between issues in different chapters of that section and that you can see the section theme in more than one way (through the strategy lenses as described in Chapter 1).

- If you are using the *Case Studies* edition try to read the cases relevant to the topics on your course – even if they are not set as class work or assessments. The *Guide to Using Case Studies* on page 613 indicates the main focus of each case and the relevant chapter. Case study introductions highlight which key learning points are covered by the case.

Check the Exploring Corporate Strategy website (see below) regularly for updates and additional material and ask if your tutor has a copy of the *Exploring Corporate Strategy* videos (see details below).

Teaching and learning resources

Exploring Corporate Strategy website (www.pearsoned.co.uk/ecs7)

An outstanding resource containing a range of material for students and tutors. The website includes:

- topical material which relates to themes in the book
- updates to case studies and weblinks to the relevant company websites
- self-assessment questions
- work assignments
- tutor support material
- five additional long case studies

Exploring Corporate Strategy – video resources

There are two video resources to support the text as follows:

(a) Exploring Corporate Strategy – with the Experts (2)

The video runs for 124 minutes. It provides invaluable additional teaching material for the classroom or for private study on six separate key strategic topics from the book. Each topic presents an up-to-date coverage of the issues – assisted by leading academic or practitioner experts:

- THE THREE STRATEGY LENSES (*Gerry Johnson*)
- ORGANISATIONAL KNOWLEDGE (*Hari Tsoukas*)

- CORPORATE GOVERNANCE (*David Pitt-Watson*)
- SHAREHOLDER VALUE (*John Barbour*)
- ORGANISATIONAL STRUCTURING (*Richard Whittington*)
- STRATEGY AND INFORMATION TECHNOLOGY (*Kevan Scholes*)

The video is available in VHS/PAL format or on CD. Copies can be ordered through Claire Parkin, Scholes Associates, c/o Faculty of Organisation and Management, Stoddart Building, Sheffield Hallam University, Sheffield, S1 1WB
Tel: +44 (0) 114 2253756; Fax: +44 (0) 114 2255265; email: **c.l.parkin@shu.ac.uk**

(b) Exploring Corporate Strategy – Instructor's DVD

A new DVD will be available from June 2006. It provides material to introduce and expand upon organisations featured within cases in the text, as well as additional explanation of key topics from the authors. These include:

- Strategy in Different Contexts (Kevan Scholes)
- Five Forces and Core Competences (Richard Whittington)
- Strategic Drift and the Cultural Web (Gerry Johnson)
- Amazon: the business model
- EasyGroup: competitive strategy
- eBay: strategic capability and sustainability
- Manchester United: football club or business?
- EuroTunnel: clash of national cultures
- Marks & Spencer: two CEOs on managing the turnaround
- SAB Miller: international strategy development

This DVD is available through Pearson Education. Please contact your local representative for further information. For details of your representative, please go to **http://vig.pearsoned.co.uk/replocator**.

The Exploring Strategic Management series

This series from FT/Prentice Hall builds on readers' knowledge of *Exploring Corporate Strategy* and provides more depth by topic or sector. All these books have been written in conjunction with Gerry Johnson and Kevan Scholes. Books available are:

- V. Ambrosini with G. Johnson and K. Scholes, *Exploring Techniques of Analysis and Evaluation in Strategic Management*, 1998; ISBN: 0-13-570680-7
- T. Grundy with G. Johnson and K. Scholes, *Exploring Strategic Financial Management*, 1998; ISBN: 0-13-570102-3
- J. Balogun and V. Hope-Hailey with G. Johnson and K. Scholes, *Exploring Strategic Change*, 2nd edition, 2004; ISBN: 0-273-68327-6
- G. Johnson and K. Scholes (editors), *Exploring Public Sector Strategy*, FT/Prentice Hall, 2001; ISBN: 0-273-64687-7

A note for tutors

Instructor's manual

A comprehensive set of supporting material for tutors including:

- how to plan programmes using the text;
- classic case study library
- using the case studies;
- teaching notes for case studies;
- tutor briefs for chapter-end work assignments and questions linked to illustrations;
- a CD containing exhibits from the book and many additional PowerPoints that will be useful when preparing class sessions or presentations.

The Instructor's manual is available in both electronic and paper formats. Please contact your Pearson Education sales representative for further information.

Since the first publication of the book we have always been concerned that good-quality practical support and advice to tutors is provided. This has been one of the driving forces behind the growth of the support material. The advice above for students and managers is also likely to be relevant to tutors.

Since 1989 we have run annual one-day workshops for tutors (also in Scotland since 1995). These have proved to be very popular with both experienced tutors and those who are new to the subject.

Details of forthcoming workshops are posted on our website. We hope that the exploitation of our website will make this support more comprehensive, more universal in coverage and more consistent in terms of the support tutors can expect, irrespective of their location.

We are always happy to receive feedback from users of the book. Contact us at:

Gerry@gsb.strath.ac.uk
KScholes@scholes.u-net.com
richard.whittington@said-business-school.oxford.ac.uk

Guided Tour of the Book

Part opening pages provide a brief explanation of the topics covered in the following chapters, together with a new navigational diagram.

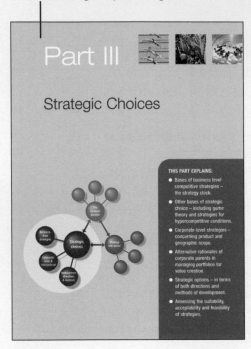

Learning outcomes list what you should have achieved or understood by the end of the chapter.

Illustrations of strategy into action appear throughout the text to highlight the connection between theory and practice. The final illustration in each chapter centres on a **key debate**, allowing you to reflect on some of the issues discussed in the chapter.

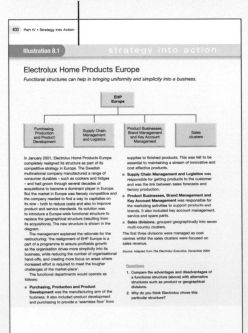

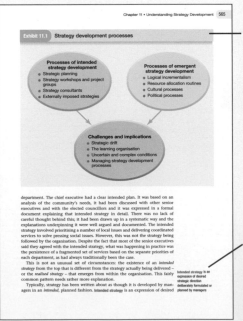

Exhibits provide a clear, visual representation of key ideas, structures and processes.

Key terms are highlighted in the text with an explanation in the margin to reinforce important terms and concepts.

Summaries recap and review the main points of the chapter.

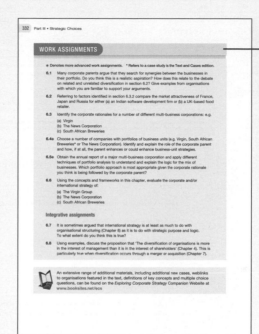

Work assignments, organised into two levels of difficulty, can be used as a means of testing your learning of theory and concepts. New **integrative assignments** test your understanding of the bigger picture.

Recommended key readings provide sources for additional study on particular topics or concepts.

Commentaries, which appear at the end of each part, highlight the connection between topics discussed within the chapters and explore the diversity of approaches to corporate strategy, allowing you to develop a deeper understanding of contemporary issues.

Case examples at the end of each chapter help consolidate your learning of the major themes.

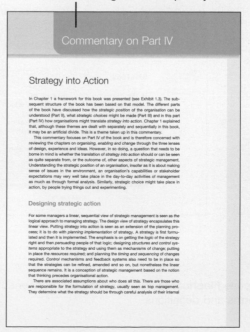

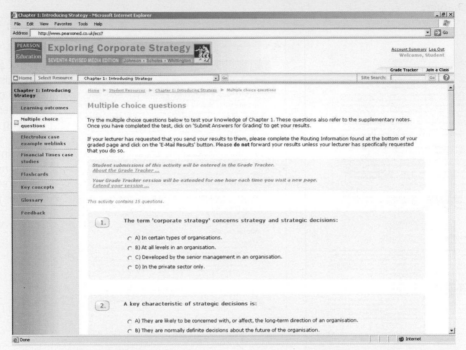

Multiple choice questions test your learning and provide helpful feedback to improve your results. Save your scores to a personal gradebook and you can track your progress.

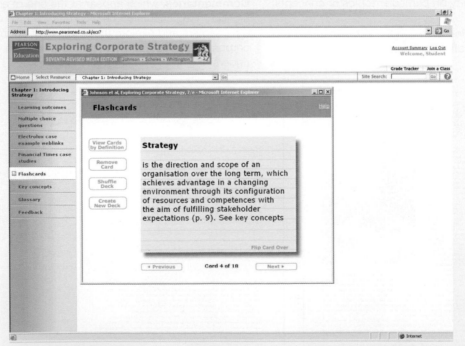

Interactive **Flashcards** and an online Glossary enable you to review and revise key terms and definitions.

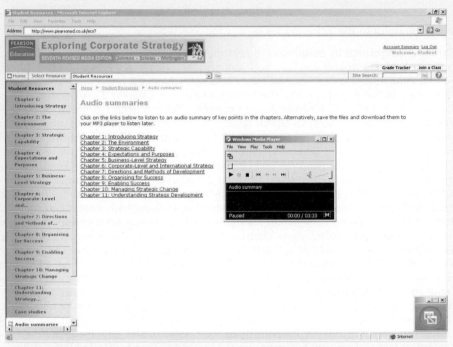

Audio summaries reinforce key topics in each chapter and allow you to study without the book. Listen online or download to your MP3 player.

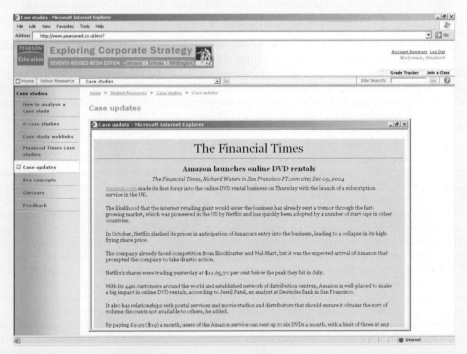

A selection of **FT articles** update and extend the case studies and examples in the book, and provide a starting point for further study.

Acknowledgements

We are grateful to the following for permission to reproduce copyright material:

Exhibit Iiii reprinted by permission of *Harvard Business Review*. Adapted from 'Strategy as simple rules' by K.M. Eisenhardt and D.N. Sull, January 2001. Copyright © 2001 by the Harvard Business School Publishing Corporation; all rights reserved; Chapter 2 case example – Tables 1,2,3 and 7 from www.brewersofeurope.org, The Brewers of Europe; Chapter 2 case example – Table 4 from Coors Brewers Ltd., UK; Chapter 2 case example – Table 6 from Euromonitor 2002; Exhibit 2.3 based on Yip, George S., *Total Global Strategy II*, 2nd edition, © 2003. Adapted by permission of Pearson Education Inc., Upper Saddle River, NJ; Exhibit 2.5 adapted with the permission of The Free Press, a Division of Simon & Schuster Adult Publishing Group, from *Competitive Strategy: Techniques for Analyzing Industries and Competitors* by Michael E. Porter. Copyright © 1980, 1998 by The Free Press. All rights reserved; Exhibit 2.7 adapted with the permission of The Free Press, a Division of Simon & Schuster Adult Publishing Group, from *Hypercompetitive Rivalries: Competing in Highly Dynamic Environments* by Richard A. D'Aveni with Robert Gunther. Copyright © 1994, 1995 by Richard A. D'Aveni. All rights reserved; Figure for Illustration 3.4 adapted from 'Understanding and using value chain analysis' by Andrew Shepherd in *Exploring Corporate Techniques of Analysis and Evaluation* in *Strategic Management*, Pearson Education Ltd (Ambrosini, V. ed. 1998); Exhibits 3.6 and 3.7 adapted with permission of the Free Press, a Division of Simon & Schuster Adult Publishing Group, from *Competitive Advantage: Creating and Sustaining Superior Performance* by Michael E. Porter. Copyright © 1985, 1998 by Michael E. Porter. All rights reserved; Exhibit 3.9 from *The Knowledge-Creating Company: How Japanese Companies Create the Dynamics of Innovation* by Ikujiro Nonaka and Hirotaka Takeuchi, copyright 1995 by Oxford University Press, Inc. Used by permission of Oxford University Press, Inc.; Chapter 4 case example – Figure 1 and Table 1 from *Annual Report*, Manchester United Plc; Exhibit 4.2 adapted from David Pitt-Watson, Hermes; Exhibit 4.5 adapted from *Proceedings of the Second International Conference on Information Systems*, Plenum Publishers, Cambridge, MA (Mendelow, A. 1991); Exhibit 6.9 from *Strategic Management Journal*, vol. 7, no. 3, © John Wiley & Sons Ltd (Montanari, J. R. and Bracker, J. S. 1986). Reproduced with permission; Exhibit 6.10d from Multinational market portfolio in global strategy development, *International Marketing Review*, Vol. 10, No. 1 (Harrel, G. D. and Kiefer, R. D. 1993) in *International Marketing Strategy*, Routledge (Phillips, C. I. and Lowe, R. eds 1994), pp. 137–8; Exhibit 6.11 adapted from *Corporate Level Strategy*, copyright © John Wiley & Sons, Inc. (Goold, M., Campbell, A. and Alexander, M. 1994). This material is used by permission of John Wiley & Sons, Inc.; Exhibit 6.12b reprinted by permission of Harvard Business School Press from *Managing Across Borders: The transnational solution* by C. A. Bartlett and S. Ghoshal. Boston, MA 1989, pp. 109–11. Copyright © 1989 by the Harvard Business School Publishing Corporation; all rights reserved; Exhibit 7.1 adapted from *Corporate Strategy*, Penguin (Ansoff, H. 1988) and matrix accompanying Exhibit 7.1 on page 377 both reprinted by permission of the Ansoff Estate; Exhibit 7.9 reprinted by permission of *Harvard Business Review*. Adapted from 'Strategy as a portfolio of real options' by T. A. Luehrman, September–October 1998. Copyright © 2001 by the Harvard Business School Publishing Corporation; all rights reserved; Exhibit 8.15 adapted from Mintzberg, Henry, *Structuring of Organizations*, 1st edition, © 1979. Reprinted by permission of Pearson Education, Inc., Upper Saddle River, NJ; Exhibit 8.16 adapted and reprinted by permission of Harvard Business School Press from *Managing Across Borders: The transnational corporation*, 2nd edition, by C. A. Bartlett and S. Ghoshal. Boston, MA 1998, Copyright 1998 by the Harvard Business School Publishing Corporation; all rights reserved; Chapter 9 case example – exhibit 3 from *NHS Direct in England*, 40th Report of the Public Accounts Committee of the House of Commons (2002) Crown copyright material is reproduced with the permission of the Controller of HMSO and the Queen's Printer for Scotland; Chapter 9 case example – exhibits 4, 5 and 6 from *NHS Direct Quarterly Stakeholder Report*, July 2003, NHS Direct Crown copyright material is reproduced with the permission of the Controller of HMSO and the Queen's Printer for Scotland; Chapter 9 case example – exhibit 7 from *Developing NHS Direct*,

April 2003, Department of Health Crown copyright material is reproduced with the permission of the Controller of HMSO and the Queen's Printer for Scotland; Exhibit 9.3 from *Strategic Human Resource Management* by Gratton, L. et al. (1999). By permission of Oxford University Press; Exhibit 9.5 adapted from *Electronic Commerce*, © John Wiley & Sons Ltd (Timmers, P. 2000). Reproduced with permission; Exhibit 9.9 abridged from *Managing Innovation: Integrating technological, market and organisational change*, 2nd edition, © John Wiley & Sons Ltd (Tidd, J, Bessant, J. and Pavitt, K. 2001). Reproduced with permission; Exhibits 9.11 and 9.12 adapted from *Managing Innovation: Integrating technological, market and organisational change*, 2nd edition, © John Wiley & Sons Ltd (Tidd, J, Bessant, J. and Pavitt, K. 2001). Reproduced with permission; Illustration 10.2 adapted from 'Mapping and re-mapping organisational culture: a local government example' in *Exploring Public Sector Strategy*, Prentice Hall (Johnson, G. and Scholes, K. eds 2001); Exhibit 10.2 adapted from *Exploring Strategic Change*, Prentice Hall (Balogun, G. and Hope Hailey, V. 1999); Exhibit 10.6 reprinted by permission of *Harvard Business Review*. Adapted from 'The way chief executives lead' by C. M. Farkas and S. Wetlaufer, May–June 1996. Copyright © 2001 by the Harvard Business School Publishing Corporation; all rights reserved; Exhibit 10.10 from 'The selection of communication media as an executive skill' in *Academy of Management Executive: The Thinking Manager's Source*, Academy of Management (Lengel, R. H. and Daft, R. L. 1998); Exhibit 11.4 from 'Strategic planning in a turbulent environment' in *Strategic Management Journal*, Vol 24 (Grant, R. 2003) © John Wiley & Sons Ltd. Reproduced with permission.

Long case studies: Airlines case study, Exhibit 1 from *The Airline Business in the 21st Century*, Routledge (Doganis, R. 2001); Allied Irish Bank case study, series of extracts from financial reports from *AIB Annual Report, 2002* (Allied Irish Bank); Amazon case study, Exhibit 5 from NASDAQ quotes on http://quotes.nasdaq.com (NASDAQ, New York); Amazon case study, Exhibit 8 from www.internetworldstats.com reproduced with the permission of www.internetworldstats.com; Amazon case study, Appendices E and F from www.cyberatlas.com copyright Jupitermedia Corporation; Barclaycard case study, Exhibit 4 courtesy of Barclays plc, Exhibits 6 and 8 courtesy of APACS; BMW case study, Exhibit 2 from Allison-Fisher Barometer of Automotive Awareness and Imagery Study (Booz Allen Hamilton); BMW case study, Exhibit 3 from 'BMW' in *Business Week*, 9 June 2003 (Edmondson, G. 2003); BMW case study, Exhibit 5 from 'Statement by H. Panke, CEO, BMW AG' on www.bmw.com (BMW AG); Coors case study, Exhibit 1 from www.beertown.org (Association of Brewers); Coors case study, Exhibits 2, 8, 9 and Appendix courtesy of Coors Brewers Ltd.; Eurotunnel case study, Tables 1, 2 and 3 from *Eurotunnel Annual Report, 2003* (Eurotunnel, 2003); Forestry Commission case study, Table 1 and Appendix from *Summary of Result from Staff Surveys* (Forestry Commission); GlaxoSmithKline case study, Exhibit 1 (Hemscott Plc, Appendix courtesy of GlaxoSmithKline); Marks and Spencer, Appendix courtesy of Marks and Spencer plc; Premier Oil case study, Exhibits 1 and 2 (Thomson Financial Datastream); Ryanair case study, Exhibits 1a, 1b, 1c and 6 from *Ryanair Annual Report* (Ryanair Holdings Plc.); Ryanair case study, Exhibits 7 and 8, British Airways data courtesy of British Airways; Ryanair case study, Exhibits 7 and 8, Lufthansa data courtesy of Deutsche Lufthansa; Ryanair case study, exhibits 7 and 8, Southwest Airlines data courtesy of Southwest Airlines; Ryanair case study, exhibits 7 and 8, Virgin Express data courtesy of Virgin Express; Salvation Army case study, Appendices 1 and 2 from *The Year Book* (Salvation Army, International Headquarters); Wimm-Bill-Dann case study, Exhibit 1 from *WBD Annual Report* (Wimm-Bill-Dann); Wimm-Bill-Dann case study, Exhibits 2 and 6 (WBD); Xelibri case study, Exhibits 1, 2, 7 and 8 courtesy of Siemens; Xelibri case study, Exhibit 5 from Gfk, *Survey in 5 major European mobile phone markets, Nov/Dec 2001* (Gfk).

AB Electrolux Sweden for Chapter 2, case example adapted from their website www. electrolux.com; J. Eppink and S. de Waal for Illustration 2.7 from 'Global influences on the public sector' published in *Exploring Public Sector Strategy* eds. Gerry Johnson and Kevan Scholes published by Pearson Education Limited; News International Newspapers for Illustration 4.4 extracted and amended from 'The man with grounds for global success' by Andrew Davidson published in *The Sunday Times* 14th September 2003; Northern Ireland Policing Board for Illustration 4.8 from *The Northern Ireland Policing Plan 2003/03*; Illustration 5.2 easyJet plc for Illustration 5.2 from *Annual Report 2002/03*; Berkshire Hathaway Inc. and Warren E Buffett for extracts in Illustration 6.2 from *Annual Report 2002*; Sage Publications London for an extract in Illustration 8.2 adapted from 'Integrating the team-based structure in the business process' by T Mullern published in *The Innovating Organisation* eds. Andrew Pettigrew and Evelyn Fenton, © Sage Publications 2000; BBC for an extract in Illustration 9.7 from *The Unlikely Heroes of the Digital Book* from the BBC News e-mail service 25th March 2003; Copyright Clearance Center Inc. for Illustration 10.1, adapted from 'Contrasts in culture: Russian and western perspectives in

Academy of Management Executive, vol. 145, no. 4, 1999; McGraw Hill Companies for an extract in Illustration 10.4 from 'Turnaround at Cisco' published in *Business Week* 24th November 2003; Administrative Science Quarterly for an extract in Illustration 11.4 from adapted from 'Architectural Innovation: the reconfiguration of existing product technology and the failure of existing firms' by R. Henderson and K. Clark published in *Administrative Science Quarterly 35*; Blackwell Publishing Limited for an extract in Illustration 11.5 adapted from 'Orchestral manoeuvres in the dark: discourse and politics in the failure to develop an artistic strategy' by S. Maitlis and T. Lawrence published in the Journal of Management Studies, vol 40, No. 1.; South African Breweries plc for extracts from their 2003 Annual Report and their website: www.sabmiller.com and the Arts Council England for extracts from their website: www.artscouncil.org.uk

We are grateful to the Financial Times Limited for permission to reprint the following material:

Illustration 1.1, Dell computers aims to stretch its way of business, © *Financial Times*, 13 November 2003; Chapter 7 Case, Tesco plots to make even more dough, © *Financial Times*, 20 September 2003; Illustration 9.8, Model seen as a case for treatment, © *Financial Times*, 4 December 2003.

Photographs:
Alamy p.107, p.380, p.797 right; Amazon.co.uk p.647; AstraZeneca UK Limited, p.621; Barclaycard, p. 886; BBC Photos, p.441; BMW, p.734; Bosch, p.339 centre; Coopers Creek, p.797; Coors Brewers Limited, p.877; Corbis p.239 bottom centre, p.275, p.333, p.503 bottom left and bottom centre, p.563 bottom left, p.617, p.673, p.761, p.833; Digital Vision p.iii, p.1 top centre and top right, p.63 bottom centre, p.115 bottom left, p.163 bottom left, p.233 top left and top right, p.239 bottom right, p.339 bottom left, p.395 bottom right, p.445 bottom right, p.559 top centre and top right, p.563 bottom centre; Dorling Kindersley p.395 bottom centre; e-Bay p.160; Eden Project Ltd/Gendall Design, p.980; Electrolux p.37; Forestry Commission (Crown Copyright), p.949; freefoto.com p.1 top left, p.5 bottom right, p.59 top centre, p.115 bottom right, p.445 bottom centre, p.503 bottom right; Getty Images p.5 bottom centre, p.59 top left, p.63 bottom right, p.115 bottom centre, p.217, p.239 bottom left, p.495, p.546; GlaxoSmithKline, p.913; Intel p.599; Marks & Spencer, p.967; Royal KPN N.V., p.863; Sabhal Mòr Ostaig/John Sitcorstri, p.1001; SABMiller, p.807; Sheffield Theatres Trust, p.704; Siemens, p.821, p.829 (all); Jeffrey Tabberner p.279 bottom left and bottom centre, Ella Towers p.59 top right, p.163 bottom right.

In some instances we have been unable to trace the owners of copyright material, and we would appreciate any information that would enable us to do so.

Part I

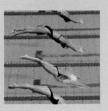

Introduction

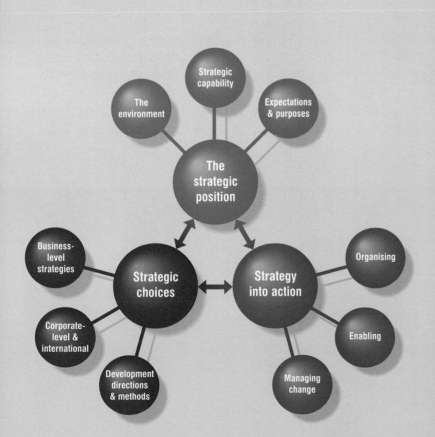

THIS PART EXPLAINS:

- The concepts and some of the main terminology necessary to understand the field of strategy and strategic management.

- The structure of this book: in particular what is meant by the strategic position, strategic choices and strategy into action, how these relate to each other and how they may differ by organisational context.

- The three strategy lenses: different explanations about how strategies develop in organisations.

Introduction to Part I

This opening part of the book is an introduction to the study of the management of strategy in organisations.

Chapter 1 explains why the study of strategic management is important, how it differs from other aspects of management and explains some of the main concepts and terms used throughout the rest of the book. It also provides a framework for thinking about strategic management in terms of understanding the *strategic position* of an organisation, *strategic choices* for the future and the ways in which strategies are *translated into action*. It goes on to show that different aspects of strategic management are likely to be important in different contexts; the small business context is, for example, very different from the multinational business; public sector organisations and not-for-profit organisations will also be different.

Chapter 1 is followed by the first of a series of commentaries that are to be found at the end of each of the parts of the book. These commentaries show how strategy development can usefully be thought of in different ways. These are introduced briefly in Chapter 1 as three strategy 'lenses' and discussed more fully in the first commentary. The first lens is strategy as *design* – which has tended to be the orthodox way in which strategy development has been explained. Here top managers design carefully thought through strategies based on extensive analysis and execute them in an orderly planned way. The second lens sees strategy moving forward in an incremental fashion building on the basis of *experience* of the past – often bases of past success. The third lens sees strategy development in terms of *ideas* that lead to innovation and change. Here strategies develop less from top-down direction and plans and more on the basis of the variety and diversity within and around organisations.

The challenge of strategic management is to be able to understand complex issues facing organisations and develop the capability for long-term organisational success. Chapter 1 and the commentary in Part I set out how this book can help readers address this challenge.

Introducing Strategy

Learning outcomes

After reading this chapter you should be able to:

● Describe the characteristics of strategic decisions and define what is meant by strategy and strategic management.

● Explain how strategic priorities vary by level: corporate, business and operational; and understand what distinguishes strategic management from operational management.

● Understand the basic vocabulary of strategy.

● Explain the elements of the *Exploring Corporate Strategy* strategic management model and understand how the relative importance of each element will vary with context and circumstances.

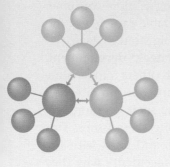

Photo: Digital Vision Ltd

Photo: Getty Images

Photo: Freefoto.com

In late 2003 Michael Dell, the founder of Dell Computers, announced that the company was planning a big push into consumer electronics. Since its foundation some 20 years earlier the company's business had been predominantly the sales of computer products to corporate customers. Now it planned to expand its direct consumer sales and extend its products beyond PCs and laptops into mainstream consumer electronics. Opportunities were arising as more consumer items became 'digitised', an area in which Dell had considerable experience. But some commentators doubted Dell's ability to make such a big strategic leap.

All organisations are faced with the challenges of strategic development: some from a desire to grasp new opportunities, such as Dell, others to overcome significant problems. This book deals with why changes in strategic direction take place in organisations, why they are important, how such decisions are taken, and the concepts that can be useful in understanding these issues. This chapter is an introduction and explanation of this theme, and deals with the questions of what is meant by 'strategy' and 'strategic management', why they are so important and what distinguishes them from other organisational challenges, tasks and decisions. In discussing these issues it will become clearer how the book deals with the subject area as a whole. The chapter draws on the Dell illustration for the purposes of discussion and, as the book progresses, other such illustrative examples are used to help develop discussion.

One other point should be made before proceeding. The term 'corporate strategy' is used here for two main reasons. First, because the book is concerned with strategy and strategic decisions in all types of organisation – small and large, commercial enterprises as well as public services – and the word 'corporate' embraces them all. Second, because, as the term is used in this book (discussed more fully in section 1.1.2), 'corporate strategy' denotes the most general level of strategy in an organisation and in this sense embraces other levels of strategy. Readers will undoubtedly come across other terms, such as 'strategic management', 'business policy' and 'organisational strategy', all of which are used to describe the same general topic.

1.1 WHAT IS STRATEGY?

Why were the issues facing Dell described as 'strategic'? What types of issues are strategic and what distinguishes them from operational issues in organisations?

1.1.1 The characteristics of strategic decisions

The characteristics usually associated with the words 'strategy' and 'strategic decisions' are these:

● Strategy is likely to be concerned with the *long-term direction* of an organisation. The transformation of Dell from a computer product company with corporate clients to a mass market provider of consumer electronic products would take a considerable period of time. Indeed in 2003 the process had already begun – about 20 per cent of its computer product sales were to consumers.

● Strategic decisions are likely to be concerned with the *scope of an organisation's activities*. For example, does (and should) the organisation concentrate on one area of activity, or should it have many? The issue of scope of activity is fundamental to strategy because it concerns the way in which those responsible for managing the organisation conceive the organisation's boundaries. This could include important decisions about product range or geographical coverage. The broadening of the scope of activities was clearly a fundamental aspect of Dell's plans.

● Strategic decisions are normally about trying to achieve some *advantage* for the organisation over competition. For example, Dell felt that the margins earned by many competitors were too high and that made them vulnerable to a strategy of lower prices and tighter margins. For other organisations advantage may be achieved in different ways and may also mean different things. For example, in the public sector, strategic advantage could be thought of as providing better value services than other providers, thus attracting support and funding from government.

● Strategy can be seen as the search for strategic fit[1] with the *business environment*. This could require *major resource changes* for an organisation in the future. For example, decisions to expand geographically may have significant implications in terms of the need to build and support a new customer base. It is important to achieve the correct *positioning* of the organisation, for example in terms of the extent to which products or services meet clearly identified market needs. This might take the form of a small business trying to find a particular niche in a market, or a multinational corporation seeking to buy up businesses that have already found successful market positions. At Dell one of the key challenges would be the building of strong consumer brands – essential for success in consumer electronics.

● However, strategy can also be seen as creating opportunities by building on an organisation's *resources and competences*.[2] This is called the resource-based view of strategy, which is concerned with exploiting the strategic capability of an organisation, in terms of the resources and competences, to provide competitive advantage and/or yield new opportunities. For example, a large multinational corporation may focus its strategies on those businesses with strong brands. A small business might try to change the 'rules of the game' in its market to suit its own capabilities – which was the basis on which many 'dot.com' companies entered established sectors. Dell's ambitions in consumer electronics were built on a belief that its knowledge of digital technologies could be exploited across a wide range of products and markets.

● The strategy of an organisation is affected not only by environmental forces and strategic capability, but also by the *values and expectations* of those who have *power* in and around the organisation. Whether an organisation is expansionist or more concerned with consolidation, or where the boundaries are drawn for the organisation's activities, may say much about the values and attitudes of those who influence strategy – the *stakeholders* of the organisation. Clearly Michael Dell as founder, chairman and CEO of Dell had a personal vision of the company's future. But Dell had relationships with many other stakeholders who were affected by the company's strategy and vice versa. First

Dell Computers aims to stretch its way of business

Managing strategy requires the consideration of a wide range of factors, which change over time.

In an interview with the *Financial Times* in November 2003, Kevin Rollins, the CEO of Dell Computers, explained how he was putting his job on the line by leading a major strategic change in the company.

The US company famous for selling PCs is planning a big push into consumer electronics. If things go according to plan, Michael Dell could eventually become the Henry Ford of the information age.

For a maker of desktop personal computers who founded his company, famously, in a University of Texas dormitory 20 years ago, this may sound unlikely. But the ambitions of Dell Inc are boundless – and thanks to a simple business idea that has proved highly adaptable, and a fearsome relentlessness . . . Consumer electronics are about to provide what could well be the biggest test of the Dell way of doing business. Until now, the company has sold mainly to corporate customers: only a fifth of its sales in the US are to consumers, and much less than that elsewhere.

. . . Dell's simple but effective idea has been to sell standardised electronic products direct to customers, usually over the internet. That removes most of the research and development that is normally required, while also cutting out retailers and other middlemen. Armed with the information it gets from taking orders directly from customers, Dell has gained two other powerful advantages. One is the ability to build products to match orders as they come in, slashing its inventory costs. The second is a highly efficient marketing machine that can adapt its message based on real-time results as orders arrive.

With its lower costs, Dell sets out to undermine profits in the markets it enters and destroy the margins that sustain its more entrenched competitors. 'Our goal is to shrink the profit pool and take the biggest slice,' says Mr Rollins. Consumer electronics companies, often with gross profit margins of more than 30 per cent, make an obvious target for this ruthless approach. 'Our gross margins are in the 18–19 per cent range: we don't need 40 per cent,' he says.

A former partner from Bain (management consultants), the Dell president applies the cool analytics and familiar jargon of the strategy consultant to this relentless expansion: search out the markets with the biggest 'profit pools' to be plundered; pick ones with close 'adjacencies' to those Dell already serves to reduce the risk of wandering into unknown territory; and apply its 'core competences' to conquering new ground. As a textbook case of applying a proven and repeatable formula, Dell takes some beating. It used the formula to move from selling PCs to businesses to selling them to consumers. Next it followed its business customers into servers, then into storage hardware. Now it wants to follow consumers into other areas of electronics as well. It has started with products closely linked to the PC, such as MP3 digital music players and 17-inch flat-panel television sets that resemble computer monitors. According to Dell's rivals, success in the PC business in the US has disguised the fact that the company has found it harder to break into other products and new geographic regions. 'Dell's success is backward-looking,' claims Jeff Clarke, head of global operations at Hewlett-Packard.

According to Steve Milunovich, technology strategist at Merrill Lynch, not all markets are as susceptible to all aspects of the Dell approach as the PC business. Yet he adds that the company has shown great discipline in attacking only those areas where its strengths still give it a clear economic and operational advantage.

Even most of the company's competitors concede that the shift in consumer electronics from analogue to digital technology plays to Dell's strengths. It is already the biggest

were the investors in the company (shareholders and banks). Even a $40bn (≈ €35bn) Fortune 500 company can make financial mistakes. The 44,000 employees clearly had an interest in Dell's success as did the communities in which Dell provided significant employment opportunities. Not least were the suppliers of components that made up a Dell product. The beliefs and values of these stakeholders will have a greater or lesser influence on the strategy development of an organisation depending on the power of each stakeholder.

purchaser of liquid crystal display screens and computer hard-drives, for instance, putting it in a strong position as these components come to play a bigger role in television sets and other household items.

'When you combine monitors and LCD televisions, we will blow away the consumer electronics guys,' says Mike George, chief marketing officer. More importantly, Dell also benefits from the standardisation that brings down the cost of components and removes the advantage once enjoyed by companies that invest in their own technology. As more of a product's functions come to reside in standardised components such as microprocessors and hard drives, the differentiation that comes from making new versions declines.

The contrast with others is stark. Sony chief Nobuyuki Idei, for instance, told the FT that the Japanese company was putting a growing emphasis on proprietary components to differentiate its products. In the past four years, 70 per cent of Sony's investment has been in silicon chips. While the digitisation of consumer electronics may have played to Dell's core strengths, though, there are at least three things about the market that are likely to test its business model. One is the fact that it will rely, at least for now, on manufacturing by other companies, reducing its ability to drive down costs. Also, the consumer electronics business is based on common products that are not configured individually for different customers: according to Mr Clarke, that removes one main advantages of Dell's build-to-order model, the ability to customise products for each buyer.

Using outside manufacturers is also likely to mean the company 'will not be able to operate on inventory that is as thin as it is in PCs,' says Charlie Kim, a consultant at Bain. Company executives suggest that once manufacturing volumes reach a high enough level, Dell is likely to start production itself.

Also, while the cost advantages may be less in 'back-end' activities such as production and sourcing, the real opportunity for Dell in consumer electronics lies in the 'front-end' marketing and sales area, says Mr. Milunovich. 'There's a big chunk of money to be taken out of distribution,' he says.

Whether Dell can take advantage of this opportunity with its direct sales system will be the second big challenge. Retail stores suit consumer products best because they bring an instant mass market and let users test the look and feel of products, says Mr Clarke. That is particularly important for products such as television sets, which buyers want to see, or handheld devices, which they want to pick up, say rivals.

Dell executives retort that similar doubts were once expressed about its efforts to sell PCs online, and that its early sales of personal digital assistants suggest that consumers familiar with the quality and style of the company's PCs are willing to buy other items online too. The third test will be whether the Dell brand and marketing approach can be adapted to suit the new market. High name-recognition helps, but will get Dell only part of the way. 'Everyone knows who Dell is – but it's still a PC-focused brand,' says Mr Kim at Bain.

For a company that still relies heavily on selling to corporate customers this will pose a big challenge. 'We're very humbled by the fact that there are virtually no other companies that are both consumer and enterprise brands,' says Mr George. He adds, though, that the basic attributes of the Dell brand – with its connotations of a certain level of value, quality and service – should extend across both types of market.

Overcoming obstacles such as these will stretch the Dell model in ways that it has never been stretched before.

Source: Richard Waters, *Financial Times*, 13 November 2003, p. 16. Reproduced with permission.

FT

Questions

1. Why were the issues facing Dell Computers described as strategic? Refer to Exhibit 1.1.
2. Identify examples of issues that fit each of the circles of the model in Exhibit 1.3.

Overall, if a *definition* of a strategy is required, the most basic might be 'the long-term direction of an organisation'. However, the characteristics described above can provide the basis for a fuller definition:

Strategy is the *direction* and *scope* of an organisation over the *long term*, which achieves *advantage* in a changing *environment* through its configuration of *resources and competences* with the aim of fulfilling *stakeholder* expectations.

Strategy is the *direction* and *scope* of an organisation over the *long term*, which achieves *advantage* in a changing *environment* through its configuration of *resources and competences* with the aim of fulfilling *stakeholder expectations*

| Exhibit 1.1 | Strategic decisions |

Strategic decisions are about:

- The **long-term** direction of an organisation
- The **scope** of an organisation's activities
- Gaining **advantage** over competitors
- Addressing changes in the **business environment**
- Building on resources and competences (**capability**)
- **Values and expectations** of stakeholders

Therefore they are likely to:

- Be **complex** in nature
- Be made in situations of **uncertainty**
- Affect **operational** decisions
- Require an **integrated** approach (both inside and outside an organisation)
- Involve considerable **change**

Exhibit 1.1 summarises these characteristics of strategic decisions and also highlights some of the consequences:

- Strategic decisions are likely to be *complex in nature*. This complexity is a defining feature of strategy and strategic decisions and is especially so in organisations with wide geographical scope, such as multinational firms, or wide ranges of products or services. For example, Dell faced complexity from several issues at the same time, such as the technical nature of the products, fast-moving markets and the need to coordinate its activities over a wide geographical area.

- Strategic decisions may also have to be made in situations of *uncertainty* about the future. For example, in Dell's case no one can really predict with much clarity where exactly digital technologies are moving – the pace of change remains relentless.

- Strategic decisions are likely to *affect operational decisions*: for example, an increased emphasis on consumer electronics would trigger off a whole series of new operational activities, such as finding new suppliers and building strong new brands. This link between overall strategy and operational aspects of the organisation is important for two other reasons. First, if the operational aspects of the organisation are not in line with the strategy, then, no matter how well considered the strategy is, it will not succeed. Second, it is at the operational level that real strategic advantage can be achieved. Indeed, competence in particular operational activities might determine which strategic developments might make most sense. For example, Dell's knowledge of internet selling was fundamental to its success.

● Strategic decisions are also likely to demand an *integrated* approach to managing the organisation. Managers have to cross functional and operational boundaries to deal with strategic problems and come to agreements with other managers who, inevitably, have different interests and perhaps different priorities. Dell's ability to exploit consumer markets requires a combination of good products supported by good marketing. Weakness in either will cause failure.

● Managers may also have to sustain *relationships and networks* outside the organisation, for example with suppliers, distributors and customers. Dell's management of its supply chain had been a pillar of its success.

● Strategic decisions usually involve *change* in organisations which may prove difficult because of the heritage of resources and because of culture. These cultural issues are heightened following mergers as two very different cultures need to be brought closer together – or at least learn how to tolerate each other. Indeed, this often proves difficult to achieve – a large percentage of mergers fail to deliver their 'promise' for these reasons (see Chapter 7).

1.1.2 Levels of strategy

Strategies exist at a number of levels in an organisation. Taking Dell as an example, it is possible to distinguish at least three different levels of strategy. The first, **corporate-level strategy**, is concerned with the overall scope of an organisation and how value will be added to the different parts (business units) of the organisation. This could include issues of geographical coverage, diversity of products/services or business units, and how resources are to be allocated between the different parts of the organisation. For Dell the push into consumer electronics was an important corporate decision because it would affect the whole company. In general, corporate-level strategy is also likely to be concerned with the expectations of owners – the shareholders and the stock market. It may well take form in an explicit or implicit statement of 'mission' that reflects such expectations. Being clear about corporate-level strategy is important: it is a *basis* of other strategic decisions.

Corporate-level strategy is concerned with the overall purpose and scope of an organisation and how value will be added to the different parts (business units) of the organisation

The second level can be thought of in terms of **business-level strategy**,[3] which is about how to compete successfully in particular markets – or how to provide best value services in the public services. This concerns which products or services should be developed in which markets and how advantage over competitors can be achieved in order to achieve the objectives of the organisation – perhaps long-term profitability or market share growth. So, whereas corporate-level strategy involves decisions about the organisation as a whole, strategic decisions here need to be related to a strategic business unit (SBU). A **strategic business unit** is a part of an organisation for which there is a distinct external market for goods or

Business-level strategy is about how to compete successfully in particular markets

A **strategic business unit** is a part of an organisation for which there is a distinct external market for goods or services that is different from another SBU

services that is different from another SBU. Dell had conceptualised its SBUs in geographical terms and decided to structure around these as three regional businesses – the Americas, Europe/Middle East/Africa and Pacific Rim. These were the primary foci for business-level strategy. But these were only SBUs if the needs of all customers within each region were very similar. This would clearly not be the case when the scope of products and customer types (corporate vs. consumer) changed with the new strategy. Dell would need to rethink its SBUs.

There should clearly be a link between strategies at an SBU level and corporate-level strategies that both assist and constrain these business-level strategies. For example, in the case of Dell, product range and internet selling were strongly dictated centrally. Marketing and customer support was regionalised. In public sector organisations a corresponding definition of an SBU might be a part of the organisation or service for which there is a distinct client group. It is important to remember that an SBU is a unit of an organisation for strategy-making purposes. It may or may not be a separate *structural* part of the organisation – such as a department or a division. Indeed SBUs will very often cross this formal structure requiring coordination in the delivery of business-level strategies as mentioned earlier.

Operational strategies are concerned with how the component parts of an organisation deliver effectively the corporate- and business-level strategies in terms of resources, processes and people

The third level of strategy is at the operating end of an organisation. Here there are **operational strategies**, which are concerned with how the component parts of an organisation deliver effectively the corporate- and business-level strategies in terms of resources, processes and people. For example, Dell had six manufacturing centres in the world operating to support all of the three regional businesses to fulfil its orders to the right standards and on time. Indeed, in most businesses, successful business strategies depend to a large extent on decisions that are taken, or activities that occur, at the operational level. The integration of operational decisions and strategy is therefore of great importance, as mentioned earlier.

1.1.3 The vocabulary of strategy

Although a definition of strategy was given at the end of section 1.1.1, in practice you will encounter many different definitions from different authors. You will also find a variety of terms used in relation to strategy, so it is worth devoting a little space to clarifying some of these. Exhibit 1.2 and Illustration 1.2 employ some of the terms that readers will come across in this and other books on strategy and in everyday business usage. Exhibit 1.2 explains these in relation to a personal strategy readers may have followed themselves – becoming fit. Illustration 1.2 shows the terminology used in practice by one organisation – British Airways.

Not all these terms are always used in organisations or in strategy books: indeed, in this book the word 'goal' is rarely used. It will also be seen, through the many examples in this book, that terminology is not used consistently across organisations. Managers and students of strategy need to be aware of this. Moreover, it may or may not be that mission, goals, objectives, strategies and so on are written down precisely. In some organisations this is done very formally; in others a mission or strategy might be implicit and, therefore, can be deduced from what an organisation is doing. However, as a general guideline the following terms are often used.

Exhibit 1.2	The vocabulary of strategy

Term	Definition	A personal example
Mission	Overriding purpose in line with the values or expectations of stakeholders	Be healthy and fit
Vision or strategic intent	Desired future state: the aspiration of the organisation	To run the London Marathon
Goal	General statement of aim or purpose	Lose weight and strengthen muscles
Objective	Quantification (if possible) or more precise statement of the goal	Lose 5 kilos by 1 September and run the marathon next year
Strategic capability	Resources, activities and processes. Some will be unique and provide 'competitive advantage'	Proximity to a fitness centre, a successful diet
Strategies	Long-term direction	Exercise regularly, compete in marathons locally, stick to appropriate diet
Business model	How product, service and information 'flow' between participating parties	Associate with a collaborative network (e.g. join running club)
Control	The monitoring of action steps to: • assess effectiveness of strategies and actions • modify as necessary strategies and/or actions	Monitor weight, kilometres run and measure times: if progress satisfactory, do nothing; if not, consider other strategies and actions

- A *mission* is a general expression of the overall purpose of the organisation, which, ideally, is in line with the values and expectations of major stakeholders and concerned with the scope and boundaries of the organisation. It is sometimes referred to in terms of the apparently simple but challenging question: '*What business are we in?*'

- A *vision* or *strategic intent* is the desired future state of the organisation. It is an aspiration around which a strategist, perhaps a chief executive, might seek to focus the attention and energies of members of the organisation.

- If the word *goal* is used, it usually means a general aim in line with the mission. It may well be qualitative in nature.

- On the other hand, an *objective* is more likely to be quantified, or at least to be a more precise aim in line with the goal. In this book the word 'objective' is used whether or not there is quantification.

- *Strategic capability* is concerned with the *resources and competences* that an organisation can use to provide value to customers or clients. *Unique resources* and *core competences* are the bases upon which an organisation achieves strategic advantage and is distinguished from competitors.

- The concept of *strategy* has already been defined. It is the long-term direction of the organisation. It is likely to be expressed in broad statements both about

Illustration 1.2

strategy into action

British Airways and the vocabulary of strategy

Company websites, annual reports and public statements contain much of the vocabulary of this book.

British Airways is a leading global airline. Privatised in 1987, the company enjoyed strong growth and profitability throughout the 1990s. After 2000 BA's fortunes dipped in the face of competition from 'no-frills' operators, government failure to establish Open Skies agreements with the US and the terror attacks in September 2001 that led to a slump in demand for air travel.

BA's website explains how it developed new strategies in this context:

Vision

'The BA Way' – Service that matters for people who value how they fly

Goals/Objectives

The BA Way outlines five over-riding goals with associated measures (in brackets)

1. Profitability, in terms of operating margin (a 10% target)
2. Customer advocacy (the number of customers who recommend BA)
3. Safety and security (the number of customers who feel safe with BA)
4. Respected company (the number of community stakeholders who respect BA)
5. Employee motivation (the number of employees who feel motivated to deliver BA's goals)

Values

The BA Way is based upon five core values:

Understanding . . . Focused . . . Cost-conscious . . . Supportive . . . Trustworthy

Strategies

The BA Way provides a high-level statement of strategies:

- To be the best UK-based network
- To understand customers better than competitors
- To develop a powerful brand that people know and trust
- To establish a competitive cost base
- To work together as one team

Competitive Strengths

Within this BA identifies its competitive strengths as:

- A 'full service' airline with a strong brand identity, associated with high standards of service, comfort and safety.
- Clearly defined and well-branded products targeting specific customer segments (e.g. Club World, developed to address the needs of long-haul business travellers).
- Membership of the One World Alliance providing customers with . . . a far more extensive network than BA could provide alone.
- Dominance of national and international slot allocations at London Heathrow airport.
- A modern, flexible and cost-effective aircraft fleet.
- As a listed company, BA must satisfy shareholder expectations, achieving profitability through a combination of service quality and operational efficiency.

Strategic initiatives

The 2002 'Future Size and Shape' (FSAS) review was designed to provide £650m of annualised cost savings, while maintaining and enhancing the high standards of customer service for which BA was renowned.

- Fleet and network Strategy: Reducing exposure to unprofitable segments – short-haul and connecting leisure passengers – while strengthening BA's position in profitable markets, which depend heavily on business travel to/from the UK.
- Product and service improvements to increase the attractiveness of BA to its core UK-based business customer base . . . including the new 'flying bed' for Club World . . . and the introduction of a premium economy product – 'World Traveller Plus'.
- Manpower reductions: A programme . . . to reduce employee headcount by 13,000 (23%).
- Improved revenue management: Yields per seat were increased by improving inventory management processes, combined with more sophisticated pricing structures.
- Customer enabled BA: An IT-based initiative designed to transform the service provided to customers.
- Gatwick: Moving away from its current hub operation, to a niche point-to-point service . . . reducing the range of long-haul destinations and developing a more focused short-haul network.
- Employee self-service: An IT-based initiative . . . to provide all employees with access . . . to personnel details, shift scheduling applications and educational materials. The result is a net reduction in administrative overhead costs.

Prepared by Neil Clark, University of Strathclyde Graduate School of Business

Source: Adapted from BA Factbook 2003 and BA Social and Environmental Report 2003/2004 (both from website: www.ba.com)

Question

Visit websites of other companies (including BA's competitors) and compare their use of strategic vocabulary. What conclusions do you draw from the similarities and differences?

the direction that the organisation should be taking and the types of action required to achieve objectives. For example, in may be stated in terms of market entry, new products or services, or ways of operating.

- A *business model* describes the structure of product, service and information flows and the roles of the participating parties. For example, a traditional model for manufactured products is a linear flow of product from component manufacturers to product manufacturers to distributor to retailers to consumers. But information may flow directly between the product manufacturer and the final consumer (advertising and market research).

- *Strategic control* involves monitoring the extent to which the strategy is achieving the objectives and suggesting corrective action (or a reconsideration of the objectives).

As the book develops, many other terms will be introduced and explained. These are the basics with which to begin.

1.2 STRATEGIC MANAGEMENT

What, then, is *strategic management*? It is not enough to say that it is the management of the process of strategic decision making. This fails to take into account a number of points important both in the management of an organisation and in the area of study with which this book is concerned. Strategic management is different in nature from other aspects of management. An operational manager is most often required to deal with problems of operational control, such as the efficient production of goods, the management of a salesforce, the monitoring of financial performance or the design of some new system that will improve the level of customer service. These are all very important tasks, but they are essentially concerned with effectively managing resources already deployed, often in a limited part of the organisation within the context of an existing strategy. Operational control is what managers are involved in for most of their time. It is vital to the success of strategy, but it is not the same as strategic management.

The scope of strategic management is greater than that of any one area of operational management. Strategic management is concerned with complexity arising out of ambiguous and non-routine situations with organisation-wide rather than operation-specific implications. This is a major challenge for managers who are used to managing on a day-to-day basis the resources they control. It can be a particular problem because of the background of managers who may typically have been trained, perhaps over many years, to undertake operational tasks and to take operational responsibility. Accountants find that they still tend to see problems in financial terms, IT managers in IT terms, marketing managers in marketing terms, and so on. Of course, each of these aspects is important, but none is adequate alone. The manager who aspires to manage or influence strategy needs to develop a capability to take an overview, to conceive of the whole rather than just the parts of the situation facing an organisation.

Because strategic management is characterised by its complexity, it is also necessary to make decisions and judgements based on the *conceptualisation* of

Exhibit 1.3   A model of the elements of strategic management

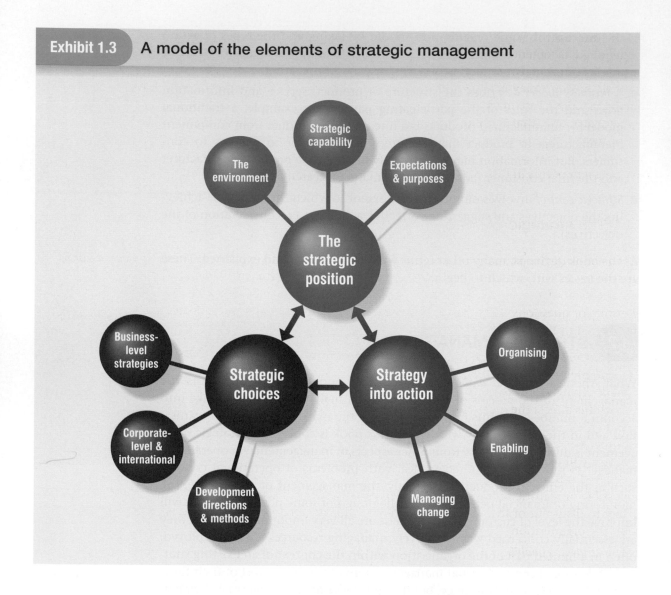

difficult issues. Yet the early training and experience of managers is often about taking action, or about detailed *planning* or *analysis*. This book explains many analytical approaches to strategy, and it is concerned too with action related to the management of strategy. However, the major emphasis is on the importance of understanding *strategic concepts* which inform this analysis and action.

Strategic management can be thought of as having three main elements within it, and it is these that provide the framework for the book. **Strategic management** includes *understanding the strategic position* of an organisation, *strategic choices* for the future and turning *strategy into action*. Exhibit 1.3 shows these elements and defines the broad coverage of this book. The next sections of this chapter discuss each of these three elements of strategic management and identifies the main issues that make up each element. But first it is important to understand why the exhibit has been drawn in this particular way. It could have shown the three elements in a linear form – understanding the strategic position preceding strategic choices, which in turn precede strategy into action. Indeed, many texts on the subject do just this. However, in practice, the elements of strategic management do not take this linear form – they are interlinked and 'inform' each other. For example, in some circumstances an understanding of the strategic position may best be built up from the experience of trying a strategy out in practice. Test marketing would be a good example. It is for structural convenience only that the subject has been divided into sections in this book; it is not meant to suggest that the process of strategic management must follow a neat and tidy path. Indeed, the evidence provided in Chapter 11 on how strategic management occurs in practice suggests that it usually does not occur in tidy ways.

1.2.1 The strategic position

Understanding the **strategic position** is concerned with identifying the impact on strategy of the external environment, an organisation's strategic capability (resources and competences) and the expectations and influence of stakeholders. The sorts of questions this raises are central to future strategies and these issues are covered in Part II of this book:

> The **strategic position** is concerned with the impact on strategy of the external environment, an organisation's strategic capability (resources and competences) and the expectations and influence of stakeholders

- The *environment*. The organisation exists in the context of a complex political, economic, social, technological, environmental and legal world. This environment changes and is more complex for some organisations than for others. How this affects the organisation could include an understanding of historical and environmental effects, as well as expected or potential changes in environmental variables. Many of those variables will give rise to *opportunities* and others will exert *threats* on the organisation – or both. A problem that has to be faced is that the range of variables is likely to be so great that it may not be possible or realistic to identify and understand each one. Therefore it is necessary to distil out of this complexity a view of the key environmental impacts on the organisation. Chapter 2 examines how this might be possible.

- The *strategic capability* of the organisation – made up of *resources and competences*. One way of thinking about the strategic capability of an organisation is to consider its *strengths* and *weaknesses* (for example, where it is at a competitive advantage or disadvantage). The aim is to form a view of the internal influences – and constraints – on strategic choices for the future. It is usually a combination of resources and high levels of competence in particular activities (in this book referred to as *core competences*) that provide advantages which competitors find difficult to imitate. Chapter 3 examines strategic capability in detail.

- Chapter 4 explores the major influences of *expectations* on an organisation's *purposes*. The issue of *corporate governance* is important. Here the question is: who *should* the organisation primarily serve and how should managers be held responsible for this? But the *expectations* of a variety of different *stakeholders* also affect purposes. Which stakeholder views prevail will depend on which group has the greatest *power*, and understanding this can be of great importance. *Cultural influences* from within the organisation and from the world around it also influence the strategy an organisation follows, not least because the environmental and resource influences on the organisation are likely to be interpreted in terms of the assumptions inherent in that culture. Chapter 4 explores how cultural influences on strategy can be examined. All of this raises *ethical* issues about what managers and organisations do and why. Chapter 4 also looks at how organisational purposes are communicated: for example, through issues like mission and objectives.

These were all important issues for Dell as it concerned itself with the next phase in the growth of the company. The decision to expand consumer electronics was influenced by a combination of market opportunities, strength in digital technologies and expectations about the company's continued financial success. So the reason for understanding the strategic position is to form a view of the key influences on the present and future well-being of an organisation, and what opportunities and threats are created by the environment, the capabilities of the organisation and the expectations of stakeholders.

1.2.2 Strategic choices

Strategic choices involve understanding the underlying bases for future strategy at both the business unit and corporate levels

Strategic choices involve understanding the underlying bases for future strategy at both the business unit and corporate levels (discussed above) and the options for developing strategy in terms of both the directions in which strategy might move and the methods of development. These issues are covered in Part III of this book:

● There are strategic choices in terms of how the organisation seeks to compete at the *business level*. This requires an identification of *bases of competitive advantage* arising from an understanding of both markets and customers and the strategic capability of the organisation. As mentioned above, Dell expected to gain advantage through its knowledge of digital technologies. These issues of business-level strategies will be discussed in Chapter 5.

● At the highest level in an organisation there are issues of *corporate-level strategy*, which are concerned with the scope of an organisation's strategies. This includes decisions about the portfolio of products and/or businesses and the spread of markets. So for many organisations international strategies are a key part of corporate-level strategy. The development of Dell had been 'guided' by key decisions on these issues of scope and Illustration 1.1 considers the impact of an important decision to extend the scope of Dell's activities. Corporate-level strategy is also concerned with the relationship between the separate parts of the business and how the corporate 'parent' adds value to these various parts. For example, the corporate parent could add value by looking for synergies between business units, by channelling resources – such as finance – or through particular competences – such as marketing or brand building. There is a danger, of course, that the parent does not add value and is merely a cost upon the business units and is therefore destroying value. There are different ways in which these issues might be resolved. For example, Dell had chosen to 'dictate' product range and selling method from the corporate centre. Other organisations devolve these decisions to their business units. These issues about the role of the centre and how it adds value are *parenting* issues and will be discussed in Chapter 6.

● Strategy may develop in the future in different *directions*. For example, Dell was progressively moving from a narrow product base (computers) and a narrow customer base (corporate clients) by extending both its product range and target markets. The development *method* used by Dell was one of internal development (growing its current business). Other organisations might develop by mergers/acquisitions and/or strategic alliances with other organisations. These options for development directions and methods are important and need careful consideration and are discussed in Chapter 7 together with a discussion of the *success criteria* that determine why some strategic choices are likely to be better than others.

1.2.3 Strategy into action

Translating **strategy into action** is concerned with ensuring that strategies are work-ing in practice. These issues are covered in Part IV of this book and include:

● *Structuring* an organisation to support successful performance. This includes organisational structures, processes and relationships (and the interaction between these elements). These issues will be discussed in Chapter 8. For example, as mentioned above, Dell was structured around three regional businesses and six manufacturing units. Therefore, the success of strategy depended on an ability to coordinate the activities of these separate units.

● *Enabling* success through the way in which the separate resource areas (people, information, finance and technology) of an organisation support strategies. The reverse is also important to success, namely the extent to which new strategies are built on the particular resource and competence strengths of an organisation. Chapter 9 considers this two-way relationship. Of course some businesses, like Dell, had transformed the way that business was conducted on their sector through developing a new business model based on their IT capabilities.

● Managing strategy very often involves *change*, and Chapter 10 looks at the various issues involved in managing change. This will include the need to understand how the context of an organisation should influence the approach to change: the different types of roles for people in managing change. It also looks at the styles that can be adopted for managing change and the levers by which change can be effected. Dell faced lots of change as it reshaped the balance of its business.

Strategy into action is concerned with ensuring that strategies are working in practice

1.2.4 Strategy development processes

Most readers of this book will either be working in organisations as managers or have plans to do so. To be effective in a management role it is important to consider the concepts, models and techniques discussed in Parts II, III and IV of the text. But it is also important to understand the *processes* through which strategies actually develop in organisations. **Strategy development processes** are the ways in which strategy develops in organisations. Part V of the book, particularly

Strategy development processes are the ways in which strategy develops in organisations

Chapter 11, does this. It considers different explanations of how strategies develop within the strategic context described by the earlier parts of the book. These processes can be grouped into two main types. First is the notion of strategy development as deliberate management intent. This is the concept of *intended strategies*. Second are explanations that place more emphasis on the emergence of strategy from the social and political processes that exist in and around all organisations. This is the concept of *emergent strategies*. The key point is that it is normal for strategy to develop through a *complex combination* of these various processes.

1.3   STRATEGY AS A SUBJECT OF STUDY

A brief explanation of the history of strategy as a subject of study is helpful in understanding how it will be presented in this book. The origins of the study and teaching of strategy can be traced to a number of major influences. The first is to do with the *task of the general manager* and, perhaps most obviously, took form in the *business policy*[4] courses run at universities such as Harvard going back to the 1960s. The continual question posed here was 'what would you do if you took over as chief executive of such and such an organisation?' The approach was based on the common-sense experience of executives and not so much on theory or research. Teaching was dominated by attempts to replicate real business situations in the classroom by the saturation exposure of students to case studies of strategic problems.

In parallel there developed in the 1960s and 1970s the influence of books on *corporate planning*.[5] Here the emphasis was on trying to analyse the various influences on an organisation's well-being in such a way as to identify opportunities or threats to future development. It took the form of highly systematised approaches to planning – incorporating techniques and concepts of operational research. This analytic approach is a dominant legacy in the study of the subject. It assumes that managers can and should understand all they possibly can about their organisational world; and that by so doing they can make optimal decisions about the organisation's future. It was a highly influential approach and, for example, gave rise to specialist corporate planning departments in organisations in the private and public sectors, especially in the 1970s.

Subsequently both of these approaches came in for considerable criticism.[6] As a result there developed a growing body of research addressing many key strategic questions. This started to become influential in how the subject was seen; how students and managers should learn about strategy and what managers should do in practice. Typically this took the form of examining *evidence* about the links between financial performance and the strategies followed by organisations on, for example, product development, market entry, diversification and associated decisions about organisational structure.[7] It was argued that managers benefit from lessons drawn from such research in order to make wiser strategic decisions. The continuing assumption was, of course, that strategic decisions should be driven by analysis and evaluation so as to make optimal decisions, but that an accumulation of research findings could provide evidence by which to do this.

Others,[8] including Quinn and Mintzberg, argued that the world was simply not that straightforward. Its complexity and uncertainty meant that it was impossible to analyse everything up front and predict the future, and that the search for optimal decisions was futile. It was necessary to accept the messiness of organisational life. This meant accepting that managers made decisions which were as much to do with collective and individual experience, organisational politics and the history and culture of the organisation as they were to do with strategy. As evidence of this, they pointed to the adaptive nature of how strategies developed in organisations.[9] They argued that it would be fruitful to spend more time understanding *managerial processes* of decision making in dealing with the complexity of strategic management in the reality of their social, political and cultural context. The orthodox view has been that such social, political and cultural constraints on managers result in suboptimal decisions, inertia and perhaps under-performance.

In parallel, starting in the 1980s, the work of Michael Porter,[10] followed in the 1990s by resource-based theories of the firm (Hamel and Prahalad),[11] became major influences around which a number of the key conceptual frameworks in strategy were built. Both were rooted in Economics.

More recently others, including Stacey and Brown and Eisenhardt, have questioned this.[12] They suggest that organisations are not so very different from living organisms. These organisms do not just plan and analyse, they live, they experience, they interpret and between them there is sufficient diversity and variety to enable them to deal with their changing environments through innovation and change. It is argued that managers are using their skills and senses within a complex world of *social interaction* in and around their organisation in much the same way. Moreover, the argument continues that this better explains how organisations cope with fast-changing environments, how new ideas and innovation come about and therefore how more significant strategic transformations occur.

This book argues that it is useful to draw on all of these views but this can be very challenging for managers. The nature of this challenge is explored in section 1.5.3 below.

1.4 STRATEGIC MANAGEMENT IN DIFFERENT CONTEXTS[13]

Dell Computers has been used in this chapter to illustrate different aspects of strategic management. To a greater or lesser extent, all these aspects are relevant for most organisations. However, it is likely that different aspects will be more important in some contexts and in some organisations than in others. For example, the need to understand rapidly developing technolgy, develop new products and exploit new market opportunities were of particular importance to Dell in the mid-2000s. This is a different emphasis from that of a steel or glass manufacturer supplying commodity-like materials into mature markets or a public sector service provider tailoring services to the needs of a local community within statutory requirements. Even within one company, different business units may face quite different market conditions – in the case of Dell resulting from the different regional markets. It would, then, be wrong to assume that all aspects of strategic management are equally important in all circumstances (see Illustration 1.3 for examples). This section reviews how the relative importance of the elements of strategy will vary with sector.

1.4.1 The small business context[14]

Small businesses are likely to be operating in a single market or a limited number of markets, probably with a limited range of products or services. The scope of the operation is therefore likely to be less of a strategic issue than it is in larger organisations. It is unlikely that small businesses will have central service departments to undertake complex analysis and market research; rather, it may be senior managers themselves, perhaps even the founder of the firm, who have direct contact with the marketplace and whose experience is therefore very influential. Indeed, in small firms the values and expectations of senior executives, who may themselves be in an ownership position, are likely to be very important, and even when current management are not owners, it may be that the values and expectations of the founders persist. It is also likely that, unless the firm is specialising in some particular market segment, it will be subject to significant competitive pressures. So the questions posed and concepts discussed about the nature of competition in Chapter 2 and bases of competitive strategy in Chapter 5 are likely to be especially relevant. Normally small firms will have to find opportunities that are well suited to the particular resources and competences of the firm. So the issues of strategic capability discussed in Chapter 3 will also be important.

Small firms are also likely to be private companies. This significantly affects their ability to raise capital. Combined with the legacy of the founder's influence on choice of product and market, this may mean that choices of strategy are limited. The firm may see its role as consolidating its position within a particular market. If it does not, and is seeking growth, then the raising of finance is crucial, so building or maintaining relationships with funding bodies such as banks becomes a key strategic issue.

1.4.2 The multinational corporation[15]

The key strategic issues facing multinationals such as Dell are substantially different from those facing the small business. Here the organisation is likely to be diverse in terms of both products and geographical markets. It may be that it has a range of different types of business in the form of subsidiary companies or divisions. Therefore, issues of structure and control at the corporate level and relationships between businesses and the corporate parent are usually a major strategic issue for multinational companies. At the business unit level, many of the competitive strategic issues will, perhaps, be similar to those faced by smaller firms – though the strength of the multinational within a given geographical area may be greater than for any small firm. However, for the multinational parent company a significant issue will be how corporate business units should be allocated resources given their different, and often competing, demands and how this is to be coordinated. The coordination of operational logistics across different business units and different countries may become especially important. For example, a multinational manufacturing company such as Toyota or General Motors has to decide on the most sensible configuration of plants for the manufacture of cars. Most have moved from manufacturing a particular car at a particular location, and now manufacture different parts of cars in different locations, bringing together such components for the assembly of a given model in a given location. The logistics problems of coordinating such operations are immense, requiring sophisticated control systems and management skills far removed from those in the smaller firm.

1.4.3 Manufacturing and service organisations

While differences exist between organisations providing services and those providing products, there is also an increasing awareness of similarities. For an organisation that competes on the basis of the services it provides – for example, insurance, management consultancy and professional services – there is no physical product. Here competitive advantage is likely to be much more related to the extent to which customers value less tangible features. This could be, for example, the soundness of advice given, the attitude of staff, the ambience of offices, the swiftness of service and so on. For manufacturing organisations the physical product itself has been regarded as central to competitive strategy and services are simply needed to support the product (such as product information, back-up service and so on). However, most have come to understand that, since physical products are often perceived by customers as very similar, other features such as service or brand image are just as important in achieving competitive advantage. For example, in the computer hardware industry it is factors like speed-to-market with new products, simplicity of the ordering process and effective helpline support that make the difference.

1.4.4 Strategy in the public sector[16]

The concepts of strategy and strategic management are just as important in the public sector as in commercial firms. Many parts of the public sector provide services to paying customers in the same way as commercial organisations – for example, postal services. However, the role of ideology in the development of strategy in the public sector is probably greater than that in commercial organisations. There is also likely to be a good deal of direct or indirect control or influence exercised from outside the organisation, by government in particular. A 'commercial' enterprise that is state controlled may find planning horizons determined more by political than by market conditions and also constraints on investment capital and sources of finance. It is for these reasons that there has been large-scale privatisation of previously state-run enterprises over the last 20 years – coal, steel, telecommunications, rail services, airlines and many more.

Other public service organisations – for example, health services and many of the amenities run by local government – have near monopoly of provision and

Illustration 1.3   strategy into action

Strategy in different contexts

Strategy can take many forms depending on the type of organisation and the circumstances in which it is operating. Below are nine examples of new strategies reported on the internet in one month. They show how widespread is the need for organisational strategies.

Bulgarian parliament approves new Bulgartabac privatisation strategy

With 112 votes 'for', 81 'against' and 18 abstainees, parliament approved the privatisation strategy for Bulgartabac Holding, under which the holding's subsidiaries will be sold individually. Representatives of tobacco heavyweights Philip Morris and British American Tobacco said the new way in which Bulgartabac will be privatised fully corresponds to their intentions and when the deals are opened they will participate in the privatisation of the companies.

Source: BTA website, Sofia, in English 10 December 2003.

Ciba to boost new product portfolio with refocused R&D strategy

The new strategy [for the Swiss pharmaceutical company] will include expansion of research activities in India and China, as well as a 15mln sfr (€1.6m) per year research fund for high risk/high reward projects, the company told analysts at today's R&D day in Basel. Chairman and CEO Armin Meyer said: 'The persistent introduction of innovative new products to the market is essential for profitable growth, higher margins and global competitiveness.' In the mid-term, the company plans for products less than five years old to make up a third of sales, compared to 26 pct in 2002.

Source: AFX Europe (Focus), 9 December 2003.

Telcordia acquires intellectual property from DAX Technologies Corporation

Telcordia(R) Technologies, Inc., a global provider of telecommunications software and services, today announced it has acquired intellectual property from DAX Technologies Corp., further extending Telcordia's wireless strategy and newly announced Elementive(TM) portfolio offerings. The technology acquisition coupled with Telcordia's own software will create two new products for wireless carriers within

Telcordia's Mobile Assurance Portfolio: Telcordia Network Vision and Telcordia Performance Vision.

Source: Business Wire, 9 December 2003.

New strategy against crime is launched

A unique new approach to fighting crime was launched yesterday by the [Kenyan] government. The approach involves encouraging the public to report criminals or planned criminal activities to the police through strategically installed boxes in Nairobi. The new approach, known as Toa Habari Kwa Polisi (give information to police), was launched yesterday by the minister for national security, Dr Chris Murungaru, at the Kencom Bus stage in the capital city.

Source: The Nation (Kenya), 6 December 2003.

New agricultural subsidy strategy to be designed

The World Bank and Turkey agreed to design a new strategy for agricultural subsidies this month during technical talks on the Country Assistance Strategy (CAS) Programmatic Financial and Public Sector Adjustment Loan (PFPSAL 3) . . . The State Planning Organization (DPT) will prepare the new agricultural assistance strategy according to the agreement reached with the World Bank, the Anatolia news agency reported on Wednesday. The World Bank will then inspect the new strategy and convey its assessment to Turkish fiscal management.

Source: Turkish Daily News, 4 December 2003.

New Motorola phone lineup will slow share erosion

Strategy Analytics recently reported a stunning 23 per cent annual increase in mobile handset sell-in in Q3 . . . Chris Ambrosio, Director of the Wireless Device Strategies service, adds, 'Strategy Analytics applauds Motorola's announcement of these six new products.

The new additions, particularly the C550, were desperately needed and long overdue. Motorola's GSM portfolio has suffered over the last year with particularly disappointing performance in Europe, the Middle East and Africa, due to antiquated product designs and a failure to tap into the MMS and cameraphone surge. The new portfolio looks to be a strong first step in recovery for Motorola in the European theatre and will add freshness to its Asian lineup as well. However, Motorola and Nokia will continue to face strong share pressure in the volatile Chinese market.'

Source: *Business Wire*, 19 November 2003.

Communists and Socialists need new strategies

[In Japan] the outcome of the Lower House election suggests the emergence of a two-party system in domestic politics. Most of the smaller parties have been left in the dust. The question is whether Japan's Communists and Social Democrats can burrow out from their disastrous showings to recover more than a marginal political presence.

The Communists focused on their opposition to raising the consumption tax and upon what they regard as 'bad constitutional amendments'. The JCP could improve its image simply by making its policy debate within the party more visible to people. It could also learn from the former Italian Communist Party, which joined a multiple-party coalition that swept itself into power.

The Social Democrats . . . campaigned solely upon the strength of pacifist, pro-Constitution planks . . . But voters rejected the Social Democrats because the party gave too little attention to coming up with realistic programmes . . . and also failed to offer a convincing plan to finance the swelling welfare spending while expressing strong objections to a consumption tax hike.

Source: *Asahi Shimbun*, 13 November 2003.

Kicking off with a new IT system

Success can bring its own problems, especially if a rapidly developing business quickly outgrows its IT capabilities. Six years ago, Fulham were an under-achieving English Third Division football club, but

three promotions, bankrolled by club chairman Mohammed Al Fayed's millions, hailed the club's return to the top echelon of English football. Off the field, it has been hard for the club to grow at the same speed. 'IT was obviously left well behind,' says Chris Holder, Fulham Football Club's IT manager. 'And in the past two years, we've had to catch up on systems and processes.' Day-to-day technology management involves two main areas: general office, such as sales, marketing and finance; and customer relations, which includes systems to run the ticket office, call centre and retail operations. 'This is a small business, but we have a world-famous brand name. Effective management of the club requires IT to run retail, ticketing, event management and stadium organisation,' says Holder.

Source: *Computing – United Kingdom*, 13 November 2003.

HP Services implementing adaptive enterprise strategy with customers across multiple industries

HP Services is delivering on the company's Adaptive Enterprise strategy globally with customers across multiple industries, including public sector, financial services, manufacturing and telecommunications/ network service providers. 'Over the past year, HP has aggressively gone after and won a number of information technology outsourcing deals that establish it as a serious player in the market,' said Traci Gere, group vice-president, US Services Research, IDC. 'Enterprises considering outsourcing deals are calling HP to the table and, increasingly, HP is making the "short list" and winning.'

Source: *Business Wire*, 9 December 2003.

Questions

1. Refer to section 1.1.1 and identify which specific issues make these examples *strategic* for the organisation involved.

2. Is this typical of the context within which each of these organisations is operating? (Refer to sections 1.4 and 1.5.)

the funding is from taxation rather than paying customers. This can put restrictions on strategic choices: for example, they may not be able to specialise on a few services or customers – they must provide a universal service. Also strategic priorities tend to be dictated by the provider of funds rather than the user of the service so the notion of competition is usually concerned with competition for *resource inputs*, typically within a political arena. The need to demonstrate *best value* in *outputs* has become increasingly important. More recently there has been a shift of emphasis to cooperation and inter-agency working in an attempt to address *outcomes* of social importance. Examples would be tackling the drugs problem, crime and disorder or mental health, all of which require cooperative efforts to improve outcomes. This means that being able to build and sustain strategic alliances is a priority – as discussed in Chapter 7.

1.4.5 The voluntary and not-for-profit sectors[17]

In the voluntary sector it is likely that underlying values and ideology will be of central strategic significance and play an important part in the development of strategy. This is particularly the case where the *raison d'être* of the organisation is rooted in such values, as is the case with organisations providing services traditionally not for profit, such as charities.

In not-for-profit organisations such as charities, churches, private schools, foundations and so on, the sources of funds may be diverse and are quite likely not to be direct beneficiaries of the services offered. Moreover, they may provide funds in advance of the services being offered – in the form of grants, for example. It is also likely that underlying values and ideology will play an important part in the development of strategy. Nonetheless the principles of competitive strategy (for funds) still hold (see Chapter 5). The fact that multiple sources of funding are likely to exist, linked to the different objectives and expectations of the funding bodies, might also lead to a high incidence of political lobbying, difficulties in clear strategic planning, and a requirement to hold decision making and responsibility at the centre, where it is answerable to external influences, rather than delegate it within the organisation.

1.5   THE CHALLENGES OF STRATEGIC MANAGEMENT

It should be clear from the discussion so far in this chapter that strategic management has many challenges. It requires managers to develop strategies that are appropriate to the specific circumstances of an organisation – but these circumstances will change over time. It also requires some clarity on which issues are more important than others and an ability to reconcile the conflicting pressures from the business environment, an organisation's strategic capability and the expectations of stakeholders. In addition this final section of the chapter looks at three sets of overarching challenges that managers face in relation to their organisation's strategies for the future:

- Preventing *strategic drift* – where strategies progressively fail to address the strategic position of the organisation and performance deteriorates. History suggests that most organisations run into difficulties because of a failure to acknowledge and address strategic drift.

- The need to understand and address *contemporary issues* that are challenging most organisations at any particular time. This section looks at four such themes: internationalisation; e-commerce; changing purposes and knowledge/learning.

- The benefit of viewing strategy in more than one way. These are the three *strategy lenses*: design, experience and ideas, as discussed below.

1.5.1 Strategic drift

Exhibit 1.4 illustrates that historical studies of the pattern of strategy development and change of organisations have shown that, typically, organisations go through long periods of relative *continuity* during which established strategy remains largely unchanged or changes *incrementally*. This can go on for considerable periods of time in some organisations. But these processes tend to create **strategic drift** – where strategies progressively fail to address the strategic position of the organisation and performance deteriorates. This is typically followed by a period of *flux* in which strategies change but in no very clear direction. There may then be *transformational* change, in which there is a fundamental change in

Strategic drift is where strategies progressively fail to address the strategic position of the organisation and performance deteriorates

---

Exhibit 1.4   The risk of strategic drift

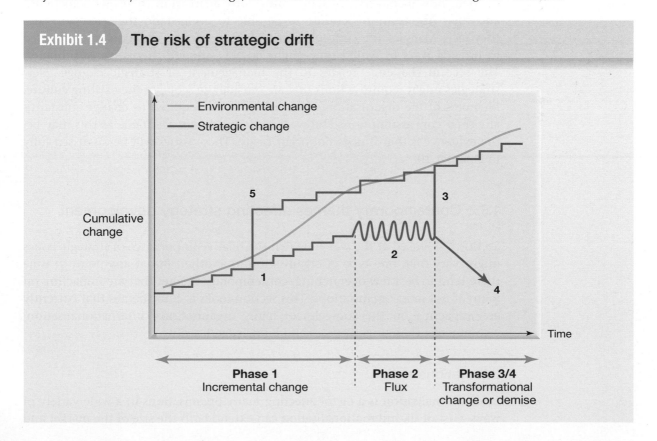

strategic direction, though this is infrequent. This pattern has become known as **punctuated equilibrium.**[18]

Punctuated equilibrium is the tendency of strategies to develop incrementally with periodic transformational change

There are strong forces at work that are likely to push organisations towards this pattern so understanding why this pattern occurs is important. This chapter has highlighted the potential complexity and uncertainty of the strategic issues that managers face. In such circumstances managers try to minimise the extent to which they are faced with uncertainty by looking for 'solutions' on the basis of current ways of seeing and doing things that are part of the existing organisational culture. For example, faced with a drop in sales enquiries advertising is increased. Or when competitors drop prices they are immediately matched and so on because this has tended to work in the past. Later parts of the book deal with this important influence of organisational culture and people's experience more fully (see section 4.5 of Chapter 4 and also Chapter 10). There are, however, dangers. Environmental change may not be gradual enough for incremental change to keep pace. If such incremental strategic change lags behind environmental change, the organisation will get out of line with its environment and, in time, need more fundamental, or transformational, change as seen in Exhibit 1.4. Indeed, transformational change tends to occur at times when performance has declined significantly. For some organisations such changes may be inadequate or too late and the organisation fails as shown in the diagram. There is another danger: that organisations become merely reactive to their environment and fail to question or challenge what is happening around them or to innovate to create new opportunities; in short, they become complacent. The first challenge is, then, how managers can stand sufficiently apart from their own experience and their organisation's culture to be able to understand the strategic issues they face. Many of the concepts and tools explained in this book are intended to provide ways in which they might do this, though this is no easy matter. The second challenge relates to the management of strategic change. New strategies might require actions that are outside the scope of the existing culture. Members of the organisation would therefore be required to change substantially their core assumptions and ways of doing things. Desirable as this may be, the evidence is that it does not occur easily. These issues will be discussed fully in Chapter 10.

1.5.2 Contemporary themes affecting strategy development

Section 1.4 looked at the way in which the relative importance of strategic issues might vary from one type of organisation to another. But at any point in time there tend to be a few overarching, contemporary themes that are impacting on many if not most organisations. This section looks at four themes that currently are impacting on the strategies of many organisations: internationalisation; e-commerce; changing purposes and knowledge/learning.

Internationalisation

Internationalisation is a factor affecting many organisations in a wide variety of ways. First of all, internationalisation can extend both the size of the market and the range of competitors, themes explored in Chapter 2. It can also raise issues of relationships with potential partners overseas (Chapter 7) and the organisation of activities across national boundaries (Chapter 8). These are issues faced everyday by a large multinational like Dell, which sources, manufactures and sells across the world and whose competitors come from Japan, Taiwan and Europe. But even small firms are now increasingly 'born global', as for instance small software companies making applications for games systems or telephone operating systems that are sold by large corporations around the world (Chapter 6). Public sector organisations too increasingly confront the opportunities and challenges of internationalisation. Patients in the UK National Health Service may now have their operations undertaken overseas, if appropriate services are not available at home. It is possible to outsource 'back-office' public sector functions to cheaper locations around the world. Police forces must cooperate across borders in the struggle against international crime and terrorism.

There is another fundamental sense in which internationalisation can affect strategy. Different countries around the world vary widely in their institutional and cultural orientations to strategic management. Many cultures give less emphasis to simple profit-maximisation than is found particularly in North American accounts of strategy. Long-term survival and the collective interests of the organisation as a whole are often given greater weight in some European and Asian cultures (see Chapter 4). The institutions that enable profit-maximisation, or penalise deviation from profit-maximisation, also differ around the world. Capital markets are highly competitive in North America and the United Kingdom, for instance. These competitive capital markets make it more dangerous for American and British managers to deviate from simple profit-maximising strategies as dissatisfied shareholders can easily permit a hostile takeover by another firm promising better results (Chapter 7). What contributes to performance also differs according to the institutional environments of various countries. As explored in Chapters 6 and 8, it can make more sense to pursue widely diversified conglomerate strategies and adopt loose holding company structures in countries where capital and labour markets are not highly efficient than in countries where such markets work well.

E-commerce

The speed at which data can be analysed and communications enacted has been transformed through the development of cheap and powerful information and communication technologies (ICT). Although most managers would accept that this is likely to impact on their own organisation they are left with considerable uncertainty about the direction and speed of those changes. In order to reduce this uncertainty managers first need to assess the impact on their current and future strategic position (see Part II of this book). This includes understanding how the *business environment* is changed by these developments: for example, the extent to which the expectations of customers are changing in relation to product features and how they 'do business' with suppliers. The relative power of buyers and suppliers is fundamentally altered in e-commerce transactions because the buyers have much easier access to information about competitive offerings. Also important is an understanding whether the organisation has the *strategic capability* to compete through e-commerce or whether it should concentrate its efforts on improving performance within its traditional business model as a way of remaining attractive to customers. The *expectations* of other stakeholders is likely to be changed by e-commerce. For example, the strategies of the organisation may be much more visible to employees, bankers and the community at large through their use of the internet.

The choices available to organisations (as discussed in Part III) are also shifted through e-commerce developments. For example, the ability to service small market segments and wider geography may be facilitated by e-commerce – particularly for many service organisations. Partnerships can also be supported and sustained over greater distances. As business units become more competent and self-sufficient through their ICT systems this raises questions of the extent of support they need from their corporate centre. This is causing many organisations to slim down the corporate centre or even abandon it altogether.

Finally, the ways in which strategy is translated into action (Part IV) need to change to support e-commerce models. Flatter structures (Chapter 8); an increased ability to integrate resources from different parts of the organisation and beyond (Chapter 9) and the need for almost constant strategic change (Chapter 10) are challenges for many organisations.

Changing purposes

There used to be a clear distinction between the purposes of the private sector and organisations in the (so-called) not-for-profit sector and/or the public sector (discussed above). The former were profit-driven organisations working to the best interests of their shareholders. The others were 'mission-driven' organisations working to increase the quality of life for a specific group of the community or society at large. Of course it was never really quite so polarised but increasingly these distinctions are becoming blurred. The private sector has seen major changes in regulations and corporate governance reforms (see Chapter 4, section 4.2) – many as a result of corporate scandals, such as Enron and WorldCom. They have also faced pressures to develop a much stronger framework of business ethics and corporate social responsibility (section 4.4). At the same time there have been opposing forces arguing for a much clearer emphasis by boards of directors on increasing shareholder value as their primary responsibility (Chapter 7).

In not-for-profit organisations and in the public sector there has been a danger of being dominated by the purposes of the 'funders' and being concerned more with resource efficiency than with service effectiveness (see Chapter 3). Awareness of such dangers has led to major efforts to make the purposes and *modus operandi* of these types of organisation more 'business like'. This has resulted in a much more prominent role for both financial targets and strategies and a major emphasis on improving the quality of service to the beneficiaries (for example, patients in hospitals). In turn this is changing the way in which strategy is managed. There is a greater need for: 'market knowledge' (Chapter 2); new competences, such as financial management (Chapter 3); an ability to work in partnerships (Chapter 7) and for less centralisation (Chapter 8), to name just a few of these changes.

Knowledge and learning

There are an increasing number of organisations that claim to depend substantially on innovation for their strategic success, and still others that argue the importance of becoming more innovatory. But this can only occur if an organisation is able to both generate and integrate *knowledge* from both inside and around the organisation to develop and deliver new product or service features. In a fast-moving world constant improvement and change become essential to survival and success. So the ability to manage *learning* is also vital. Businesses in the field of high-technology products or those dependent on research and development, for example in the pharmaceutical industry, have long experienced the extent to which innovation is important. Innovation is seen as the ability to 'change the rules of the game'. The rapid developments in information technology have thrown up opportunities for many more organisations to 'do business' in new ways – as discussed above. The success of all these innovatory organisations is likely to be built on a willingness to challenge the status quo in an industry or a market (Chapter 2) and an awareness of how the organisation's resources and competences can be 'stretched' to create new opportunities (Chapter 3). The need to see and act strategically against very short time horizons is another key feature of the innovatory context. It is likely to affect the type and quality of the people (Chapter 9), the sources of knowledge in the organisation (Chapter 3) and the extent to which the prevailing culture encourages the transfer of knowledge and the questioning of what is taken for granted (Chapter 4). Innovation will also be influenced by how people are managed and how they interact (Chapter 8). For example, organisational structures that encourage interaction and integration, rather than formal divisions of responsibility, may encourage innovation.

These four themes of internationalisation, e-commerce, changing purposes and knowledge/learning will run throughout the book both in the text and illustrations. They will be further reinforced by work assignments at the end of each part of the book. It is important to re-emphasise that these are not the only major themes that affect the strategy of many organisations. They happen to be of particular importance at the current time. But other issues will take their place in the future so it is essential that they do not become fads, fashions or obsessions for managers when thinking through strategies for their organisations.

1.5.3 The strategy lenses

In section 1.3 above it was noted that there have been many different views on how strategy should be understood, developed and implemented in organisations. All of these views have some merit. For example, the analytical tools, conceptual models, research evidence and planning systems employed by those who seek to *design* strategies are useful. They help strategists think through problems and issues so as to challenge, question and inform decision making. No doubt such an approach played a large part in the discussions in the boardroom at Dell. Kevin Rollin's background in management consultancy no doubt contributed to this. However, it is also important to understand how the *experience* of people and the culture of organisations inform and constrain the development of strategies and how they are resolved. Moreover, by understanding such phenomena, important insights can be gained into the management of strategic change. Experience and 'culture-driven' change are particularly important in organisations like Dell where the founder is still a dominant influence on strategy. There is also much to be learned from understanding how new *ideas* might emerge in organisations from the variety of experience and behaviours that are to be found across a huge corporation such as Dell. It is unrealistic to believe that all such ideas can be planned from the top.

So all these three ways of looking at strategy development are useful. They will be referred to in this book as the **strategy lenses** through which strategy in organisations can be viewed and are introduced briefly here:

The strategy lenses are three different ways of looking at the issues of strategy development for an organisation

- *Strategy as design*: the view that strategy development can be a logical process in which the forces and constraints on the organisation are weighed carefully through analytic and evaluative techniques to establish clear strategic direction. This creates conditions in which carefully planned implementation of strategy should occur. This is perhaps the most commonly held view about how strategy is developed and what managing strategy is about. It is usually associated with the notion that it is top management's responsibility to do all this and that therefore they should lead the development of strategy in organisations.

- *Strategy as experience*: here the view is that future strategies of organisations are based on the *adaptation* of past strategies influenced by the experience of managers and others in the organisation. This is strongly driven by the taken-for-granted assumptions and ways of doing things embedded in the culture of organisations. Insofar as different views and expectations exist, they will be resolved not just through rational analytic processes, but also through processes of bargaining and negotiation. Here, then, the view is that there is a tendency for the strategy of the organisation to build on and be a continuation of what has gone before.

- *Strategy as ideas*: neither of the above lenses is especially helpful in explaining innovation. So how do new ideas come about? This lens emphasises the importance of variety and diversity in and around organisations, which can potentially generate genuinely new ideas. Here strategy is seen not so much as planned from the top but as emergent from within and around the organisation as people cope with an uncertain and changing environment in their day-to-day activities. Top managers are the creators of the context and conditions in which this can happen and need to be able to recognise patterns in the emergence of such ideas that form the future strategy of their organisations. New ideas will emerge, but they are likely to have to battle for survival against the forces for conformity to past strategies (as the experience lens explains). Drawing on evolutionary and complexity theories, the ideas lens provides insights into how innovation might take place.

Viewing strategy and strategic management through only one of these lenses may result in a failure to see issues raised by the other lenses. So it helps to view something as complex as strategy in a number of complementary ways – by looking through all three lenses. This is very challenging for managers and they tend not to do so. Those readers who have an interest in a fuller description of the lenses will find this in the commentary to this part of the book. The lenses will be referred to regularly throughout the book in the commentaries at the end of each part of the book. These commentaries reflect on the issues in each part of the book and encourage readers to view them in these three different ways. This is important because all three lenses provide insights into the challenges that are faced in managing the complexity of strategy. It therefore provides a means of critically appraising most of the key strategic issues that managers face.

Illustration 1.4 shows an example of the three lenses as it might apply to decisions of individuals.

Illustration 1.4   strategy into action

Choosing a new car

The strategy lenses also apply to the personal strategies followed by individuals.

A manager was considering buying a new car. He had driven Jaguars for some time. However, he thought it would be a good idea to review the options systematically (*the design lens*). He obtained the brochures for a range of luxury car makes, identified the major factors that were important to him and considered all the performance indicators for each of the cars against these. He even allocated a weighted score to the factors that meant most to him. The analysis told him that a BMW or a Mercedes might be a better choice than a Jaguar.

This surprised him; and he didn't much like the answer. He had always driven a Jaguar, he was used to it, felt it had an especially English character and that it suited his personality (*the experience lens*). He was also looking forward to having the new model. So his inclination was to buy another Jaguar.

Actually he ended up buying an open-top Mercedes sports. This was because his wife thought he needed to liven up his image and liked the idea of driving it on holidays (*the ideas lens*). With some reluctance he bought the new Mercedes. This proved to be a good decision. They both liked the car and it depreciated in value much more slowly than a Jaguar.

So what are the lessons? The planning and analysis was there; and if it didn't end up informing the decision directly, it did indirectly. His wife justified the purchase of the Mercedes in part on the basis of

that analysis. He would have ended up with another Jaguar, a continuity of what he was used to. He actually chose what (to him) was a novel, innovative option that, in the long run, significantly changed his approach to car buying. Of course, if his wife had not intervened, his inclination to the Jaguar based on past experience would probably have prevailed. This depended on him and his circumstances – the context. Some ideas get through, some do not, depending how attractive the ideas were to him. Or it could have been that the power of analysis had been such as to overcome this. So it is with organisations. All these three lenses are likely to be there. The nature and context of the organisation are likely to determine which one prevails.

It is also difficult to say which lens was best. Who is to say that the analysis actually provided the optimal result? Maybe it was important that he should feel comfortable with his past.

Question
Choose a decision from your own personal life and consider how the three lenses impacted on the final choice that you made.

Summary

● Strategy is the *direction* and *scope* of an organisation over the *long term*, which achieves *advantage* in a changing *environment* through its configuration of *resources and competences* with the aim of fulfilling *stakeholder* expectations.

● Strategic decisions are made at a number of levels in organisations. Corporate-level strategy is concerned with an organisation's overall purpose and scope; business-level (or competitive) strategy with how to compete successfully in a market; and operational strategies with how resources, processes and people can effectively deliver corporate- and business-level strategies. Strategic management is distinguished from day-to-day operational management by the complexity of influences on decisions, the organisation-wide implications and their long-term implications.

● Strategic management has three major elements: understanding the *strategic position*, *strategic choices* for the future and translating *strategy into action*. The strategic position of an organisation is influenced by the external environment, internal strategic capability and the expectations and influence of stakeholders. Strategic choices include the underlying bases of strategy at both the corporate and business levels and the directions and methods of development. Strategic management is also concerned with understanding which choices are likely to succeed or fail. Translating strategy into action is concerned with issues of structuring, resourcing to enable future strategies and managing change.

● Strategic priorities need to be understood in terms of the particular context of an organisation. For some organisations the major challenge will be developing competitive strategy; for others it will be building organisational structures capable of integrating complex global operations. For yet others it will be understanding their competences so as to focus on what they are especially good at.

● There are a number of challenges in managing strategy successfully. First is the need to avoid *strategic drift*. Second is understanding the impact of *important contemporary themes* affecting many organisations at any one point in time. Currently these include: internationalisation, e-commerce, changing purposes and knowledge/learning. However, these will be displaced by other issues in the future. Third is the desirability of viewing an organisation's strategic issues in different ways. These are the three *strategy lenses*. A design view sees strategy in logical analytical ways. An experience view sees strategy as the product of individual experience and organisational culture. The ideas view sees strategy as emerging from ideas within and around an organisation.

Recommended key readings

It is useful to read about how strategies are managed in practice and some of the lessons that can be drawn from this which inform key themes in this book. For example:

● For a wide theoretical perspective, see R. Whittington, *What is Strategy and Does it Matter?*, 2nd edition, Thomson, 2001.

● Readers are encouraged to keep up to date with developments and strategies in organisations through newspapers, business magazines, organisations' own websites and business media websites (such as FT.com).

● For a discussion of strategy in different types of organisations, see H. Mintzberg, J. Lampel, J. Quinn and S. Ghoshal (eds), *The Strategy Process: Concepts, contexts and cases*, 4th global edition, Prentice Hall, 2003.

References

1. In the 1980s much of the writing and practice of strategic management was influenced by the writings of industrial organisations economists. One of the most influential books was Michael Porter, *Competitive Strategy*, Free Press, first published 1980. In essence, the book describes means of analysing the competitive nature of industries so that managers might be able to select among attractive and less attractive industries and choose strategies most suited to the organisation in terms of these forces. This approach, which assumes the dominant influence of industry forces and the overriding need to tailor strategies to address those forces, has become known as a 'fit' view of strategy.

2. The notion of the resource-based view of strategy is perhaps best explained in G. Hamel and C.K. Prahalad, *Competing for the Future*, Harvard Business School Press, 1994.

3. The term 'SBU' can be traced back to the development of corporate-level strategic planning in General Electric in the USA in the early 1970s. For an early account of its uses, see W.K. Hall, 'SBUs: hot, new topic in the management of diversification', *Business Horizons*, vol. 21, no. 1 (1978), pp. 17–25.

4. See for example: C. Christensen, K. Andrews and J. Bower, *Business Policy: Text and cases*, 4th edition, Irwin, 1978.

5. For example, J. Argenti, *Systematic Corporate Planning*, Nelson, 1974 or H. Ansoff, *Corporate Strategy*, Penguin, 1975.

6. See C. Hofer and D. Schendel, *Strategy Formulation: Analytical Concepts*, West, 1978.

7. One of the important books that marked this shift was: D. Schendel and C. Hofer, *Strategic Management: A new view of business policy and planning*, Little, Brown, 1979.

8. See: C. Lindblom, 'The science of muddling through', *Public Administration Review*, vol. 19 (Spring 1959), pp. 79–88; J. Quinn, *Strategies for Change*, Irwin, 1980; A. Pettigrew, *The Awakening Giant*, Blackwell, 1985; H. Mintzberg, 'Crafting strategy', *Harvard Business Review*, vol. 65, no. 4 (1987), pp. 66–75.

9. See Quinn (reference 8 above).

10. M.E. Porter, *Competitive Strategy: Techniques for analysing industries and competitors*, 1980 and *Competitive Advantage* (1985), both published by Free Press.

11. G. Hamel and C.K. Prahalad, 'The core competence of the corporation', *Harvard Business Review*, vol. 68, no. 3 (1990), pp. 79–91; G. Hamel and A. Heene (eds), *Competence-based Competition*, Wiley, 1994.

12. See: R. Stacey, *Managing Chaos: Dynamic business strategies in an unpredictable world*, Kogan Page, 1992; S. Brown and K. Eisenhardt, *Competing on the Edge: Strategy as structured chaos*, HBR Press, 1998.

13. For an extensive discussion of strategy in different types of organisations, see H. Mintzberg, J. Lampel, J. Quinn and S. Ghoshal (eds), *The Strategy Process: Concepts, contexts and cases*, 4th global edition, Prentice Hall, 2003.

14. For strategy development in small businesses, see: W. Lasher, *Strategic Thinking for Smaller Businesses and Divisions*, Blackwell, 1999.

15. There are now many books on managing strategy in multinationals. In this book we will refer often to C. Bartlett and S. Ghoshal, *Managing Across Borders: The transnational solution*, 2nd edition, Random House, 1998; and G. Yip, *Total Global Strategy II*, FT/Prentice Hall, 2003.

16. See: G. Johnson and K. Scholes (eds), *Exploring Public Sector Strategy*, FT/Prentice Hall, 2001, in particular J. Alford, 'The implications of publicness for strategic management theory' (chapter 1) and N. Collier, F. Fisnwick and G. Johnson, 'The processes of strategy development in the public sector', (chapter 2). Also;: D. McKevitt and L. Wrigley, *Managing Core Public Services*, Blackwell, 1998.

17. See: J.M. Bryson (ed.), *Strategic Planning for Public and Voluntary Services: a reader*, Pergamon, 1999.

18. The concept of punctuated equilibrium is explained in E. Romanelli and M.L. Tushman, 'Organisational transformation as punctuated equilibrium: an empirical test', *Academy of Management Journal*, vol. 37, no. 5 (1994), pp. 1141–1161.

WORK ASSIGNMENTS

✱ Denotes more advanced work assignments.   * Refers to a case study in the Text and Cases edition.   ‡ Refers to a case study on the Companion Website.

1.1   Using the characteristics discussed in section 1.1.1, write out a statement of strategy for Ministry of Sound,* Corus‡ or an organisation with which you are familiar.

1.2   Using Exhibit 1.2 and Illustration 1.2 as a guide, note down and explain examples of the vocabulary of strategy used in the annual report of an organisation of your choice.

1.3✱   Using annual reports, press articles and the internet, write a brief case study (similar to that of Dell Computers, Electrolux or Ministry of Sound*) that shows the strategic development and current strategic position of an organisation.

1.4   Using Exhibit 1.3 as a guide, note down the elements of strategic management discernible in the Ministry of Sound* or Corus‡ cases or an organisation of your choice.

1.5✱   Using Exhibit 1.3 as a guide, show how the elements of strategic management differ in:

(a) a small business (e.g. Coopers Creek*)
(b) a multinational business (e.g. Dell Computers, Electrolux)
(c) a public sector organisation (e.g. NHS Direct, BBC)

An extensive range of additional materials, including audio summaries, weblinks to organisations featured in the text, definitions of key concepts and multiple choice questions, can be found on the *Exploring Corporate Strategy* Companion Website at **www.pearsoned.co.uk/ecs7**

CASE EXAMPLE

Electrolux

By the mid-2000s Sweden's Electrolux was the world's largest producer of domestic and professional appliances for the kitchen, cleaning and outdoor use. Its products included cookers, vacuum cleaners, washing machines, fridges, lawn mowers, chain saws and also tools for the construction and stone industries. It employed over 80,000 people in more than 100 countries. Its annual sales in 2002 were 133bn Swedish Krona (about €15bn) and profits about 5.5bn Krona (≈ €600m). The company's impressive growth and development started under the leadership of Alex Wenner-Gren in 1920s' Sweden. The early growth was built around an expertise in industrial design creating the leading products in refrigeration and vacuum cleaning. By the mid-1930s the company had also established production outside Sweden in Germany, UK, France, USA and Australia.

The post-Second World War period saw a major growth in demand for domestic appliances and Electrolux expanded its range into washing machines and dishwashers. In 1967 Hans Werthén took over as president and embarked on a series of acquisitions that restructured the industry in Europe: 59 acquisitions were made in the 1970s alone followed by major acquisitions of Zanussi (Italy), White Consolidated Products (USA) and the Ganges Group (industrial products) in the 1980s. As a result by 1990 75 per cent of Electrolux's sales were outside Sweden and this increased in the 1990s as Leif Johansson expanded into Eastern Europe, Asia and South America. He also disposed of many of the 'unrelated' industrial activities. A major restructuring in the late 1990s created the shape of the group for the 2000s – with about 85 per cent of sales in consumer durables and 15 per cent in related products for professional users (such as refrigeration and laundry equipment).

Such a large company clearly had many strategic challenges and the newly appointed Chief Executive (Hans Stråberg) reflected on some of these in the mid-2000s, as follows.

Photo: Electrolux

Mission

'The Electrolux mission is to be the world leader in profitably marketing innovative product and service solutions to real problems, thereby making the personal and professional lives of our customers easier and more enjoyable. This we will achieve through a commitment to:

● driving performance throughout the entire organization;
● innovation and marketing – to products and brands;
● superior talent management;
● the Electrolux way of doing things.'

Cost and performance

'My philosophy is very clear: Before a business can grow, it needs to have its costs under control. It must be cost-efficient and profitable, and it must create value. Costs that do not add value must be contained, reduced and even eliminated.

Cost-efficiency, low complexity and profitability are always the cornerstones of building a strong business. While a strong foundation does not guarantee a solid house, it is the only basis upon which to build. So, I will continue to be dedicated to cost-efficiency and restructuring.'

Consumer insights

'We focus on really understanding consumer needs and problems related to household and garden work. By increasing our consumer insight, we are able to develop even more new products that solve these needs and problems. By being No. 1 in understanding consumers, we will strengthen the Group's position as the world's No. 1 choice.'

Brands

'Electrolux is our master brand worldwide, and will be so even more in the future. It stands for innovative, trusted solutions for an easier and more enjoyable life. To the consumer, a strong Electrolux brand is a sign of quality, dependability and leadership, giving added confidence and assurance when investing in new appliances.

Electrolux is not our only brand; in our family we have other strong brands, such as Husqvarna, AEG and Zanussi. But Electrolux is our leading brand the world over. Electrolux will not just be number one in size; it will be number one in the minds of consumers.'

Product development

'At Electrolux, product development is a core process, and innovation is the key. We will not innovate for the sake of innovation. We will provide innovative products and services that people want to buy, not focus on selling the products we currently make. I want consumers to look at our products and say: "Hey! How did Electrolux know I needed this? This is great!" We will develop products and services with innovative features and functions, making life easier for our consumers and customers.

The world's No. 1 choice is also the No. 1 innovator.'

Talent management

'Building an increasingly stronger talent base with the right attitude and enthusiasm is one of our most effective competitive weapons. We need to attract, develop, and retain top talent, which in turn, will develop Electrolux. It is absolutely vital that we succeed in this. We manage talent in the same way as we manage other key Group assets. Careers are Electrolux careers; not limited by organizational boundaries.

We, at Electrolux, consider it not only a natural development, but even more so, a career requirement to move among sectors, functions and regions.'

Social responsibility

'Electrolux is completely free of ozone-depleting CFCs [coolants for "old-style" fridges] in its worldwide operations. We can now make that statement even for recently acquired factories outside of our core European and North American markets... We've come a long way since Greenpeace blocked our front door with old refrigerators.

Recycling is a critical issue for us in Europe and in many American states. The European Union WEEE Directive places financial responsibility for end-of-life disposal of electrical appliances on manufacturers... we accept that responsibility, and applaud the EU for choosing market incentives to encourage investment in eco-design of products and efficient recycling systems. Socially responsible behaviour is central to the Electrolux corporate culture, and this year the Electrolux Group adopted a Workplace Code of Conduct. This Code defines the minimum acceptable work standards for all people in the Electrolux Group and confirms the company's commitment to act as a responsible employer and a good corporate citizen.'

Organisation

Such a complex group clearly required structures and processes through which both strategy and operations could be managed. Electrolux operations were organised into seven *business sectors*, including a total of 28 *product lines*. There were also five supporting *Group staff units*.

Business sectors

Sector heads had complete responsibility for financial results and balance sheets and each sector had its own board. The primary division of the company was between *consumer durables* and *professional products*. In turn each of these was divided into *indoor* and *outdoor* products. As consumer durables

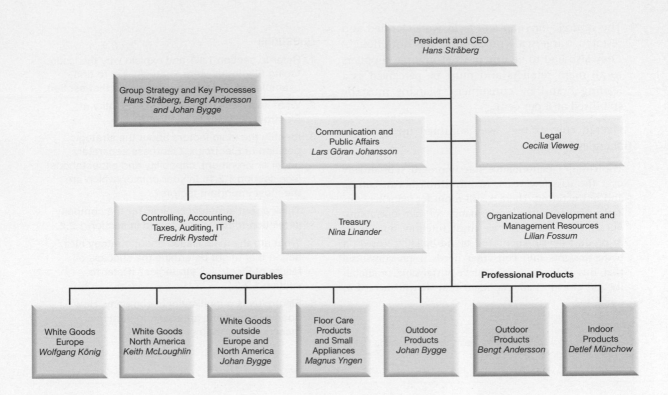

was so large it was further divided into *white goods* (larger items) and *floor products and small appliances*. White goods dominated sales and so was divided into three *geographical sectors* (Europe, North America and Rest of World).

Group staff units

These were headquarters functions supporting the business sectors covering financial, legal, organisation development and 'public relations' activities.

Six Group processes

In addition to this formal structure the Group defined six core processes within strategically import-ant areas. These processes were common for the entire group and were: purchasing, people, branding, product development, demand flow, and business support. During 2002, the President and CEO and two members of Group Management established a special working group with the task of addres-sing strategic issues and increasing cooperation between the sectors within the framework of these processes.

It should be clear from the above that Electrolux was a complex organisation in terms of both the issues it faced and the way that it operated. So it was import-

ant that the senior management were clear about their strategic priorities. The annual report explained some of Hans Stråberg's priorities and actions:

- *Profitability* still varied across the group. He identified about 50 per cent of the operations as not creating enough value owing to high manu-facturing costs and/or uncompetitive products. In contrast the successful operations were driven by a combination of strong market positions, competitive products and strong brands.

- Therefore *restructuring* was needed to improve under-performers – such as some operations in India, China and the USA. The programme was aimed at improving productivity and adjusting the cost structure.

- A *strategic review of North American operations* was undertaken resulting in accelerated product development, wider use of the Electrolux brand and some changes in organisation.

- The *position in Europe* was strengthened by increased sales in Eastern Europe, productivity improvements, a rationalisation of product vari-ants and brands and improvements in supply chain management.

● The *strategic direction and focus* were clarified and restated. Large scale production was not enough. They also had to be one of the top three suppliers to all main retailers and must be perceived as a leading brand by consumers. Margins must be stabilised at 6 per cent.

Overall the strategy was summed up by Hans Stråberg as follows:

The Group's performance has improved substantially over the past few years, mainly through cost cutting and restructuring. There is still room for reducing costs and improving the performance of our operations. But at the same time, we must intensify our efforts in product development and brand building, based on better insights into consumer needs. I am convinced that this is the way to achieve sustainable profitability and growth. I am confident that we will succeed in doing so.

Sources: Company website (www.electrolux.com); annual report 2002.

Questions

1. Refer to section 1.1.1 and explain why the issues facing Electrolux were strategic. Try to find examples of all of the items cited in that section.

2. What levels of strategy can you identify at Electrolux? (Refer to section 1.1.2.)

3. Identify the main factors about the strategic position of Electrolux. List these separately under environment, capability and expectations (see section 1.2.1). In your opinion which are the most important factors?

4. Think about strategic choices for the company in relation to the issues raised in section 1.2.2.

5. What are the main issues about strategy into action that might determine the success or failure of Electrolux strategies? (Refer to section 1.2.3.)

6. Electrolux is a multinational company. How does this affect its approach to strategic management? (See section 1.4.2.)

Strategy Lenses

Introduction

Chapter 1 has explained what is meant by strategy and strategic management. It also introduced the idea of *strategy lenses* (section 1.5.3) as different ways of viewing or understanding the subject. These three 'lenses' which employ and build on different organisational theories are used throughout this book in the commentary sections (in light blue) to interpret the content of the main chapters. The purpose of this first commentary is to introduce those lenses in more detail, building on the theory and research which underpin them.

Most people make sense of situations in more than one way, especially if they are complex. Think of everyday conversations or discussions. It is not unusual for people to say: 'But if you look at it this way. . . .' Taking one view can lead to a partial and perhaps biased understanding. A fuller picture, which might give different options or solutions, can be gained from viewing the issue in terms of multiple perspectives or, as employed here, through different lenses. The commentary sections of the book consider how the development and management of strategy can be viewed differently through:

- a *design* lens, the idea that strategy is formulated by top management through careful and objective analysis and planning and implemented down through the organisation. Looking at strategy this way can help in the *thinking through of strategic issues*;

- an *experience* lens that builds on the evidence that strategic decisions are made and strategies develop as the outcome of people's *experience and the cultural processes* in and around organisations. Looking at how strategies come about in this way can help understand the issues to be faced in *influencing decisions* in a cultural context and *managing change*;

- an *ideas* lens that helps explain why some organisations are more innovative than others and why and how some organisations seem to cope with a fast-changing environment better than others. Looking at strategy this way provides an understanding of what might be done to *foster innovation and new ideas* in organisations.

Strategy as design

The **design lens** views strategy development as the deliberate positioning of the organisation through a rational, analytic, structured and directive process. It builds

> The **design lens** views strategy development as the deliberate positioning of the organisation through a rational, analytic, structured and directive process

on two basic principles. The first is that managers are, or should be, rational decision makers. The second is that they should be taking decisions about how to optimise economic performance of their organisations. Most managers would probably agree that that is what they are there to do. Managers often defend their position, or challenge someone else's position, on the grounds that a decision is or is not rational; or is not in the best economic interests of the organisation. In many ways the principles of economics and the guidelines provided by the decision sciences help in such rational decision making; but they also support and feed the notion that this is what management – and strategic management – is all about.

In fact there are different views about what rationality actually means. For example, by *substantive rationality* is meant rationality as optimisation of outcomes given the limitations or constraints under which an organisation is operating. So this is the view that managers behave and take decisions as what economists sometimes refer to as 'rational economic men'. *Procedural rationality* is about the method or ways of making decisions. It is about whether the decision-making approach is rational. These two views of rationality are often linked when it comes to how managers may make rational decisions in organisations. So for example James March discusses rationality as a specific set of procedures for making choices, but implicitly, to achieve optimal economic output. He argues that rational choice is based on the consideration of consequences and therefore the 'anticipations of the future effects of current actions'. To do this managers need to consider four basic questions:

● The question of alternatives: what actions are possible?

● The question of expectations: what future consequences might follow from each alternative? How likely is each possible consequence, assuming that alternative is chosen?

● The question of preferences: how valuable (to the decision maker) are the consequences associated with each of the alternatives?

● The question of the decision rule: how is a choice to be made among the alternatives in terms of the values of their consequences?[1]

He makes the point that not only do these principles inform how managers should take decisions, but commentators, researchers and others interested in the economic performance of firms dissect and analyse organisations' performance based on the application of these questions in order to decide if organisational decisions make sense.

There are strong parallels here with the orthodox literature on strategic management. Tutors often start a strategy course by asking students what they mean by 'strategic management'. Typically the first few characteristics that come back from the class include: 'planning', 'setting objectives' and 'analysis'. These are words associated with a *design* view of strategy.[2] Stated more fully, the assumptions typically underpinning a design approach to strategy development are these: first in terms of *how strategic decisions are made*:

● Although the range of influences on an organisation's performance are many, *careful analysis* can identify those most likely to influence the organisation significantly. It may even be possible to forecast, predict or build scenarios about future impacts so that managers can think through the conditions in which their organisation is likely to operate. Strategy development is therefore seen as a process of *systematic thinking and reasoning.* Indeed a good deal of the early literature on strategy was to do with such systematic thinking, for example the books written by Igor Ansoff on corporate planning.[3]

- This analysis provides a basis for *strategic positioning*: that is, the matching of organisational strengths and resources with the changes in the environment of the organisation so as to take advantage of opportunities and overcome or circumvent threats. The strategy of an organisation is, therefore, the result of decisions made about the positioning and repositioning of the organisation in terms of its strengths in relation to its markets and the forces affecting it in its wider environment. Arguably the strongest influence in providing ways of doing this has been the writings of Michael Porter[4] in the early 1980s (see Chapter 2).

- This *analytic thinking precedes and governs action.* Since strategic decisions are about the long-term direction of the organisation, they are often conceived of as being taken at a point in time, resulting in a three- or five-year plan perhaps. Strategy making is also often seen as a *linear process,* very much in line with notions of procedural rationality. Decisions about what the strategy should be in terms of its content come first and are cascaded down through the organisation to those who have to make things happen. Decisions about what the strategy should be are therefore separate from the implementation of that strategy.

- *Objectives* are clear and probably explicit, there is careful and thorough *analysis* of the factors internal and external to the organisation that might affect its future and inform management about the strategic position of the organisation, and a *range of options* for future strategic direction are considered and evaluated in terms of the objectives and the forces at work on the organisation. A strategic decision is then made on the basis of what is considered to be optimal, given all these considerations.

- There are *tools and techniques* that enable managers to understand the nature and impact of the environment an organisation faces, the particular competences of that organisation, the influence of power within and around the organisation, the organisational culture and its links to strategy, the strategic choices an organisation has available to it, how decisions can be put into effect through project planning, and so on. In this book we explain many of them and discuss their usefulness.

The design lens also makes assumptions about the *form and nature of organisations*:

- *Organisations are hierarchies*. It is the responsibility of management – more specifically, top management – to plan the destiny of the organisation. It is top management who make important decisions, and lower levels of management, and eventually the population of the organisation, who carry out these decisions and implement the strategy decided at the top.

- *Organisations are rational systems*. Organisations are seen as analogous to engineered systems or, perhaps, machines. And since the complexity organisations face can be understood analytically such that logical conclusions will be reached by a rational group of top managers, the associated assumption is that people in the organisation will accept that logic.

- *Organisations are mechanisms* by which strategy can be put into effect. So how an organisation is structured (see Chapter 8) needs to be suited to the strategy.

There also need to be internal mechanisms to ensure that strategy is, indeed, being considered rationally and dispassionately. For example, the issues of corporate governance that surfaced at the beginning of this century were largely concerned with the self-interest or wrong-doings of senior executives in some organisations. However, the measures taken to address the problem focused on structured solutions such as the attempts to set up appropriate committees and the structure of boards of directors. The assumption was that structures would, or should, affect behaviour.

● This system can be controlled in a rational way too. *Control systems* (e.g. budgets, targets, appraisals) provide means by which top management can assess whether or not others in the organisation are meeting expected objectives and behaving in line with the strategy so that managers further up in the hierarchy can take corrective action.

Implications for management

Managers often talk as if strategy comes about in their organisations – or *should* come about – much as the design lens suggests. The approach is therefore seen as valuable by managers themselves. The reasons for this are as follows:

● In many respects it represents the *orthodox language of strategy.* Objective setting, planning systems and the use of analytic and evaluative tools are found in most organisations. So there are visible signs of the design lens. This is helpful, not least because it provides a way of talking about a complex set of issues. However, it should be recognised that the fact that such systems are present does not necessarily mean that they are actually the way in which strategy is developed and managed; this is explained later in this commentary and more fully in Chapter 11.

● The design lens provides the basis of an approach to managing complexity that is *logical and structured.* In this sense it helps provide a means of coping with complexity. It also provides useful *concepts, frameworks and tools* by which to analyse strategic situations.

● Important *stakeholders may expect and value such an approach*: for example, banks, financial analysts, investors and employees; so it is an important means of gaining their support and confidence.

● However, it is also to do with the *desire to feel in control and exercise control.* Quite understandably managers, particularly CEOs, need to feel in control of the complex and often challenging situations they face. The assumptions, tools and techniques of design provide them with ways in which they can feel in control.

It should also be recognised that there are other reasons managers are likely to find such an approach appealing:

● Rationality is *deeply rooted* in our way of thinking and in our systems of education. In this sense the design lens is deeply embedded in our human psyche. So, for example, even when managers do not report that strategy is actually developed in ways the design lens suggests, they often think it should be.

● Arguably and increasingly there seems to be evidence of an *all-embracing rationality* in our world. We live in a time of computer technology, global communication, space travel, advanced medicine and so on: a world in which science and reasoned solutions to the problems we face seem to surround us and provide so many benefits.

The design lens is useful in *thinking through and planning strategy*. The big question is whether this is an accurate or sufficient portrayal of strategic management. This book argues that the design lens is indeed useful but not sufficient. Other explanations help a fuller understanding of the practice of strategic management and provide insights into how the complexity of strategic management can be handled.

Strategy as experience

Much of the evidence from research on how strategies actually develop in organisations gives a different picture seen through the design lens. As early as the 1950s Herbert Simon and Charles Lindblom[5] were pointing out that rational decision-making models were unrealistic. It is not possible to obtain the information necessary to achieve the sort of exhaustive analysis required; it is not possible to predict an uncertain future; there are limits in terms of cost and time in undertaking such analysis; organisations and environments are changing continually and do not present managers with the opportunity to take decisions at a point in time. There are also psychological limitations on managers themselves which mean that they cannot be expected to weigh the consequences of options or be the objective analysts such rationality would expect – a point which is discussed more fully below. The best that can be expected is what Simon termed '*bounded rationality*' which results in managers '*satisficing*' rather than optimising: they do the best they can within the limits of their circumstances, knowledge and experience. Acknowledging this, the **experience lens** views strategy development as the outcome of *individual and collective experience* of people in organisations who influence strategy or make strategic decisions and the *taken-for-granted assumptions* most obviously represented by cultural influences.

The **experience lens** views strategy development as the outcome of individual and collective experience of individuals and their taken-for-granted assumptions

Research suggests that strategies actually tend to develop in an *adaptive and incremental* fashion building on the existing strategy and changing gradually. Strategy can therefore be seen in terms of continuity or 'momentum':[6] once an organisation has adopted a strategy, it tends to develop from and within that strategy, rather than fundamentally changing direction. Moreover such research suggests that strategies do not necessarily emanate from the top of organisations, but may *emerge* from within them. These incremental and emergent patterns of strategy development are discussed more fully in Chapter 11 which is concerned with processes of strategy development. It is, however, useful here to quote briefly from that chapter in order to explain such incremental patterns:

> An apparently coherent strategy of an organisation may develop on the basis of a series of strategic moves each of which makes sense in terms of previous moves. Perhaps a product launch, or a significant investment decision, establishes a strategic direction which, itself, guides decisions on the next strategic move – an acquisition perhaps. This in turn helps consolidate the strategic direction, and over time the overall strategic approach of the organisation becomes more established. As time goes on, each move is informed by this developing pattern of strategy and, in turn, reinforces it. (page 567)

Exhibit 11.3 shows this. Such incremental change could, of course, lead to a quite significant shift in strategy over time, but *incrementally*. In many respects, such gradual change makes a lot of sense. No organisation could function effectively if it were to undergo major revisions of strategy frequently; and, in any case, whilst change occurs in the environment, it is unlikely that it will be so great that this would be necessary. In a positive sense, incremental change could therefore be seen as adaptation to the opportunities which arise in a continually changing environment. However, it can also be seen as heavily influenced by experience.

Individual experience and bias

Human beings are able to function effectively not least because they have the cognitive capability to make sense of problems or issues they come across. They recognise and make sense of problems and issues on the basis of past experience and what they come to believe to be true about the world. More formally, **individual experience** can be explained in terms of the mental (or cognitive) models people build over time to help make sense of their situation. Managers are no exception to this. When they face a problem they make sense of it in terms of the mental models which are the basis of their experience. This has major advantages. It means they are able to relate such problems to prior events and therefore have comparisons to draw upon. It means they can interpret one issue in the light of another; they therefore have bases for making decisions based on prior experience. If they did not have such mental models they could not function effectively; they would meet each situation as though they were experiencing it for the first time.

There are, however, downsides. The same mental models, the same experience, can lead to bias. People, managers included, make sense of new issues in the context of past issues; they are likely to address a problem in much the same way as they dealt with a previous one seen as similar. Moreover, they are likely to search for evidence that supports those inclinations. So some data will be seen as more important than other data and some may not be taken on board at all. For example, a profit downturn in a business might be interpreted differently by managers with different functional backgrounds. A sales or marketing executive might see it as a result of increased competitor activity or a downturn in market demand, and may advocate increased promotional expenditure to put things right. The production manager may see it as a matter of quality or efficiency and advocate investment in more state-of-the-art manufacturing plant. The accountant may see it as matter of rising costs and advocate better cost control or reduction in expenditure. Such biases are not simply a matter of functional experience, however. They can result from any prior experience in organisational or personal terms. The important points are these:

- *Cognitive bias is* inevitable. The interpretation of events and issues in terms of prior experience is bound to take place. The idea that managers approach problems and issues of a strategic nature entirely dispassionately and objectively is unrealistic. It has been shown that whilst managers tend to see threats rather than opportunities in their environment[7] they also often exaggerate and overestimate benefits, for example when it comes to investment decisions or forecasting the outcomes of risky projects.[8]

Individual experience mental (or cognitive) is the models people build over time to help make sense of their situation

- *The future is likely to be made sense of in terms of the past.* Such interpretation and bias arise from experience of the past, not least in terms of what is seen to have worked or given rise to problems in the past. This is one explanation of why strategies tend to develop incrementally from prior strategy.

- *Bargaining and negotiation* between influential individuals as to how to interpret issues and what to do about them will arise from different interpretations according to past experience. This political explanation of how strategies develop is discussed more fully in section 11.4.4 of Chapter 11.

There now exists a good deal of research that seeks to understand the strategy of organizations and the management of strategy in cognitive and sense-making terms, more fully explained by Gerard Hodgkinson and Paul Sparrow,[9] for example.

However, managers do not operate purely as individuals; they work and interact with others in organisations, and at this collective level there are also reasons to expect similar tendencies.

Collective experience and organisational culture

Organisational culture is the 'basic *assumptions and beliefs* that are shared by members of an organisation, that operate unconsciously and define in a basic taken-for-granted fashion an organisation's view of itself and its environment'.[10] This experience is rooted, not only in individual experience, as discussed above, but also in collective (group and organisational) experience which may take form in:

Organisational culture is the 'basic *assumptions and beliefs* that are shared by members of an organisation, that operate unconsciously and define in a basic taken-for-granted fashion an organisation's view of itself and its environment'

- collective taken-for-granted assumptions, referred to in this book as the 'paradigm'[11] of an organisation;
- organisational routines, 'the way we do things around here', that become embedded in an organisation over time and therefore also become taken for granted.

This taken-for-grantedness is likely to be handed down over time within a group. Such groups might be, for example, a managerial function such as marketing or finance; an organisational unit such as a business; or more widely a professional grouping, such as accountants, an industry sector, or even a national culture. This taken-for-grantedness impacts on the strategy of organisations (discussed more fully in section 11.4.3 of Chapter 11). For example, Gerry Johnson[12] has shown how the strategy of an organisation tends to be moulded by its culture. And institutional theorists[13] who have an interest in strategy such as Royston Greenwood and Bob Hinings[14] point to the similarities between organisations in terms of the assumptions and practices common between them and the strategies they follow.

For a group or organisation to operate effectively there has to be such a generally accepted set of assumptions. In effect, it represents *collective experience* without which people who work together in an organisation would have to 'reinvent their world' for different circumstances they face. Rather like individual experience, collective experience, or the paradigm, is applied to a given situation to make sense of it. This affects what people in organisations see as important, what they respond to and therefore to how strategies develop. Exhibit I.i helps explain this.

The forces at work in the environment, and the organisation's capabilities in coping with these, are made sense of in terms of the experience of managers and the organisation's paradigm. And organisational responses tend to be in line with

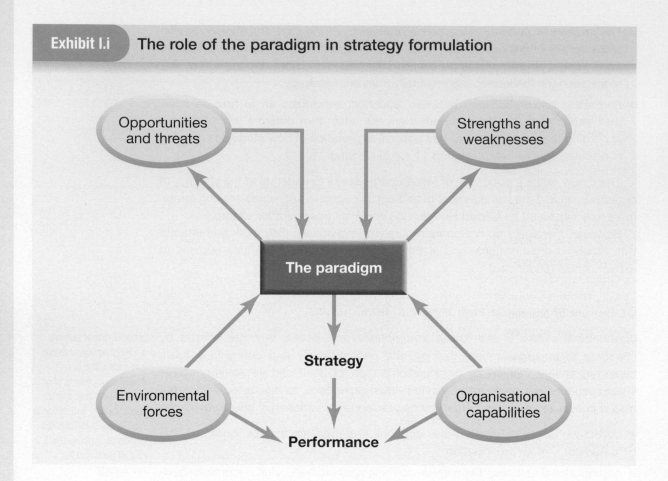

Exhibit I.i   The role of the paradigm in strategy formulation

that paradigm and embedded routines. However, environmental forces and organisational capabilities (or lack of them), while having this indirect influence on strategy formulation, nonetheless impact on organisational performance more directly. For example, many commentators suggested that the problems that beset Marks and Spencer (M&S) in the late 1990s were the result of just such a situation. Their managers were accused of being over-wedded to M&S ways of thinking and behaving, resulting in an inability to identify or take seriously changes in consumer expectations and the incursions of competitors on their traditional customer base.

Implications for management

There are important implications of the effect of individual and collective experience:

- Managers' *understanding of the strategic position* of their organisation and, indeed, the *strategy* followed by that organisation is likely to be heavily informed by such collective experience. Managers therefore need to be aware that the views of their colleagues on strategic issues – indeed their own views too – are inevitably influenced by such experience. *Questioning and challenging* such taken-for-granted experience is of key strategic importance in strategic management.

- Without such challenge, *strategic drift* (see section 1.5.1 in Chapter 1) is likely.

- Major problems can arise if significant *strategic change* is needed, precisely because such change may require a change in that which is taken for granted. It should not be assumed that the drawing up of a mission statement or the publishing of a document explaining a strategic direction will of itself change that which is taken for granted. The notion that reasoned argument necessarily changes deeply embedded assumptions or ways of doing things is flawed; readers need only think of their own experience in trying to persuade others to rethink their religious beliefs, or indeed, allegiances to sports teams to realise this.

- *Innovation* is also likely to require the questioning and challenging of basic assumptions, which can be uncomfortable for those who attempt it and threatening for those who do not welcome it. So thinking about how to build innovatory and 'learning organisations' is an important strategic consideration. This is one reason the *ideas lens*, discussed next, is important.

- However, the taken-for-grantedness of an organisation may also comprise many of the *strengths* (*or competences*) of an organisation (see section 3.4) and potentially provide bases of competitive advantage (see section 7.5.4). So this cultural dimension of organisational experience can be working both for and against the strategic development and well-being of an organisation.

In summary, the experience lens provides a view of organisations as cultures within which people make decisions about or influence strategy on the basis of their cognitive (or mental) models and established ways of doing things (or routines). It is helpful in understanding the phenomena of incremental strategic change and strategic drift. It also provides helpful insights into the challenges of developing strategy and of managing strategic change in organisations.

Strategy as ideas

The extent to which the two lenses described so far explain innovation and the generation of new ideas is rather limited. The experience lens offers an explanation in so far as new ideas might be borrowed or imitated by one organisation from another. For example, when a new CEO from a private sector company takes charge in a public sector organisation, he or she may introduce ideas 'new' to that organisation; but they may be just what he or she is familiar with from the private sector context. Notionally a design approach could result in innovation, but in fact tends to so emphasise control that it is likely to result in conformity rather than innovation. This leaves a problem: how to account for innovative strategies? How did Ericsson become a mobile phone company? Where did innovative products such as Post-Its® and the Sony Walkman® come from? How do organisations faced with highly turbulent environments and short decision horizons, such as those in high-technology businesses or e-commerce, cope with the speed of change and innovation that is required? The two lenses discussed so far do not adequately explain this. The ideas lens is helpful in explaining the sources and conditions that help generate innovation in organisations; it sees strategy as the emergence of order and innovation from the variety and diversity which exists in and around organisations.

Increasingly writers such as Richard Pascale[15] argue that there is a real danger that organisations have been built to achieve steady state growth, efficiency, and

The **ideas lens** sees strategy as the emergence of order and innovation from the variety and diversity which exist in and around organisations

control over activities inherent within what is here described as the design lens; and that this inevitably results in an 'equilibrium' eventually leading to organisational demise. Moreover that the incremental momentum inherent within the experience lens also leads either by intent or by default to the same outcomes. He is arguing that these two approaches lead to strategic drift (see section 1.5.1 in Chapter 1).

The design lens provides a view of organisations as systems or machines and the experience lens as cultures. The need, Pascale and others argue, is for another way of conceiving of organisations and their management. The ideas lens provides a view of organisations as akin to organisms living within an environment. It draws on the concepts and principles of evolutionary theory and complexity theory, both of which are well established in the natural sciences and have begun to become important in the social sciences and in organisation theory.

The importance of variety

Both complexity and evolutionary theories emphasise the importance of variety and diversity within and around organisations and place a great deal less emphasis on top-down design. Evolution explains how any living system, arguably including an organisation, evolves through natural selection acting upon that variation and diversity.[16]

Whether the concern is with species, as in the natural world, or people in societies, or indeed ideas in organisations,[17] uniformity is not the norm; there exists *variety*. If an environment changes very little – as in the Amazonian rainforest – there is more stability than in environments that change a great deal. So the birds of the Amazonian rainforest have changed little over millennia. However in other cases, where change in their environments is greater, new or changing organisms develop more rapidly. A good example is the rapid development of new strains of viruses given the advances in modern medicine to fight them. There are parallels with regard to organisations.

Variety potentially exists for all organisations at different levels and in different forms. There is an ever-changing enviromnent, there are different types of businesses, there is a variety of different groups and individuals and their experience and ideas within an organisation and there are deviations from traditional ways of doing things.

Such variety and its spawning of change at different levels mutually reinforces itself. Take the example of the micro-electronics industry. It is a fast-changing industry. This in turn has spawned many different types of businesses, from hardware manufacturers through to software boutiques and firms engaged in applications of such technology. Within these organisations in turn there develop new ideas as people interpret opportunities and potential applications differently.

People in organisations may deliberately seek to generate such variety and some of those are discussed below. However, variation may not alway, be intentionally created. In the natural world, change and newness come about because of what might appear to be *imperfections* – a mutation of a gene, for example – that may provide the basis for a 'fitter' organism in a changing environment. In organisations, ideas will also be copied imperfectly between individuals, between groups or between organisations and some of these will give rise to innovations better suited to the changing environment. An idea of the research chemist in the R&D laboratory may be taken up by a marketing executive, perhaps, but may be interpreted differently from the original idea. An organisation may seek to copy the strategy of another but will not do things in exactly the same way. Some of these imperfect copies will not be successful; but others may be. The famous exemplar of this is the Post-It®, which originated in an 'imperfect' glue being applied to paper but which resulted in a semi-adhesive for which the researcher saw market potential. There may also be surprises and unforeseen circumstances in the environment, the unexpected skills or views introduced by new appointees or unintended consequences arising from management initiatives.

Of course whilst organisations have the potential for huge variety, there may be intentional or non-intentional suppression of such variety. There are pressures for conformity, some of which have already been discussed. The culture of the organisation acts as a filter of ideas; formal processes of control, planning and evaluation act to regularise what ideas will and will not go forward; the self-interest of powerful managers may block ideas counter to their own. The historic assumptions that constitute the paradigm tend to act to resist ideas that don't 'fit'. So pressures for conformity may see off the novelty. There is also evidence that certain strategies, for example the pursuit of high levels of diversification, tend to result in low levels of innovation[18] since organisational resources and priorities are channelled towards the pursuit of that strategy rather than innovation.

Creating context

It is not possible to plan in detail or control for the 'right' amount of variety, the content of the variety or what eventually emerges. The differences arise naturally and quite likely in an unpredictable way. The evidence is that innovation comes, not from the top, but quite likely from low down in an organisation.[19] Sensing of an organisation's environment takes place throughout an organisation, not just at the top. People interpret issues in different ways according to their experience and may come up with different ideas based on personal experience. Such ideas may not be well formed or well informed and, at the individual level at least, they may be very diverse. The greater the variety of experience, the more likely there will be innovation. Organisations in industry sectors that are developing and fragmented also tend to be more innovative than those in mature and concentrated industries,[20] because of the diversity of ideas that exist in such dynamic conditions. And innovation in large organisations often comes from outside their boundaries, often from smaller businesses.[21] However, it may be possible for managers to foster new ideas and innovation by creating the context and conditions where they are more likely to emerge because there is sufficient variety within and around the organisation for them to do so. This might be achieved in different ways. First, by considering what the appropriate *boundaries* are for the organisation:

● The more the *boundaries between the organisation and its environment* are reduced, the more innovation is likely to occur. For example, for some high-technology businesses it is difficult to see quite what are their boundaries. They are networks rather than clearly bounded organisations (see section 8.4.2, Chapter 8). These are organisations intimately linked to a wider environment; and as that environment changes, so do the ideas in the network. A good example of this is Formula One motor racing where the different teams are intimately linked with the wider motor industry as well as other areas of advanced technology. Indeed they are so networked between themselves that new ideas get imitated (but changed) very rapidly.

- Similarly, within organisations what matters is *interaction and cooperation* to encourage variety and the spread of ideas. There is evidence of the 'strength of weak ties',[22] by which is meant that it is the variety of informal contacts rather than formally structured contacts that gives rise to new ideas. For example, it is not unusual to hear people say that they find the informal electronic networks they themselves set up for knowledge sharing and exchange in organisations to be more valuable than those set up formally by the organisation.

- An organisation that seeks to ensure that its people are in contact with and *responsive to a changing environment* is likely to generate a greater diversity of ideas and more innovation than one that does not. On the other hand, one that tries to insulate itself from its environment, for example by trying to resist market changes or by relying on a particular way of doing or seeing things – sometimes known as a 'strong culture' – will generate less variety of ideas and less innovation.

The *culture of and behaviour* in an organisation is also important:

- If innovation matters, *questioning and challenge* is more important than consensus. The ideas lens suggests that where an environment is complex and rapidly changing consensus may not be desirable. A diversity of ideas and views may be of benefit because innovation requires just such variety and benefits from the challenging and questioning of taken-for-granted assumptions. There are many organisations that have processes and procedures to foster such a culture. Large organisations often move executives across businesses or divisions within their portfolio with the specific intention of encouraging new ideas and challenging prevailing views.

- *Experimentation* is important. Some organisations have formal incentive programmes to encourage such experimentation. Others have established it as part of their culture. 3M is famous for its encouragement of 'skunk works' in which staff are allowed a proportion of their time to invest in their own personal ideas and develop these to the point where they can be put forward as proposals, for example, for new products. Indeed, in line with this, new ideas are likely to advance most where they are allowed and encouraged to compete with each other.

- The temptation of managers is to try to clarify and direct. In fact *ambiguity* may help foster innovation because it gives rise to the sort of latitude that may be required for people to experiment. So objectives may not always be clear, precise and detailed and action plans may allow degrees of flexibility in implementation.

- In the context of uncertainty and complexity, the *intuitive capacity* of people needs to be recognised as potentially significant.[23] People have the ability to sense changes in and appropriate responses to changes in their environment. And that the ideas that they come up with intuitively need to be taken seriously.

The *strategies* followed by organisations are also important:

- Since speed of change is important, some writers[24] have emphasised the importance of '*time pacing*' of new ideas and products. In some organisations with high rates of innovation of new products, these are not brought on stream when old products become redundant. Rather the rate of new product innovation is paced such that new products and ideas are coming to the fore even when existing ones are successful.

● 'Low-cost probes',[25] such as alliances and joint ventures, are ways in which organisations may try out possible strategic developments. They are strategic experiments.

Adaptive tension and simple rules

High levels of *control* and strict hierarchy are likely to encourage conformity and reduce variety. So the more elaborate and bureaucratic the top-down control, the less likelihood of innovation. Establishing appropriate levels of control therefore becomes crucial.

Some complexity theorists argue that innovation and creativity emerge when there is sufficient order to make things happen but not when there is such rigidity of control as to prevent such innovation. This is the idea of '*adaptive tension*' or '*edge of chaos*'.[26] Innovations are most likely to occur when the organisation never quite settles down into a steady state or equilibrium and the volatility and diversity are given sufficient rein (see Exhibit I.ii), though of course not to the extent that it cannot function. To understand what is appropriate some further explanation is needed.

Ordered patterns of behaviour can come about not just through tight control, but through '*order-generating rules*'. Taking an example from the natural sciences, the ordered pattern and direction of a flock of birds does not exist because of a plan set down by a leader and communicated through a hierarchy. The flocking of birds can be simulated on a computer with just three such rules: (i) maintain minimum distance from other birds and objects in the environment; (ii) match velocity with other birds; (iii) move towards the centre of mass of the surrounding birds.[27]

Exhibit I.ii	Conditions of adaptive tension

Richard Pascale gives an equivalent organisational example from the cement industry. A Mexican firm, Cemex, distributes its cement, not based on tight, planned scheduling, because it has realised that the construction projects it is delivering to hardly ever proceed as scheduled.

> Cemex loads its fleets of cement trucks each morning and dispatches them with no pre-ordained destination. The trick lies in how they make their rounds. Like ants scavenging a territory, they are guided to their destination by simple rules. Ants used chemical messages (called pheromones) to convey these instructions. Cemex uses an algorithm based on *greed* (deliver as much cement as rapidly as possible to as many customers as possible) and *repulsion* (avoid duplication of effort by staying as far away from the other cement trucks as possible).[28] (pp. 8–9)

In an organisational context, these order generating rules have come to be known as '*simple rules*'. The argument is that such simple rules act as guiding principles of behaviour, patterns of which form into consistent strategic directions.

Research by Kathy Eisenhardt and her colleagues is beginning to establish the nature of these simple rules.[29] Exhibit I.iii summarises the types of rules which have been identified as important in organisations facing fast-changing environments; and

Exhibit I.iii   Simple rules

Turbulent markets require strategic flexibility to seize opportunities – but flexibility can be disciplined. Different types of simple rules help.

Type	Purpose	Example
How-to rules	Spell out key features of how a process is executed – 'What makes our process unique?'	Dell focus on focused customer segments. So a Dell business must be split in two when its revenue hits $1 billion.
Boundary rules	Focus managers on which opportunities can be pursued and which should not	In Miramax movie-picking process, every movie must: i) revolve around a central human condition, such as love; ii) have a main character appealing but deeply flawed; iii) have a clear story line.
Priority rules	Help managers rank the accepted opportunities	Intel's rule for allocating manufacturing capacity: allocation is based on a product's gross margin. (See Chapter 11 case example.)
Timing rules	Synchronise managers with the pace of emerging opportunities and other parts of the company	Nortel's product development time must be less than 18 months, which forces it to move quickly into new opportunities.
Exit rules	Help managers decide when to pull out of yesterday's opportunities	In Oticon, the Danish hearing aid company, if a key team member – manager or not – chooses to leave a project for another within the company, the project is killed.

Source: Adapted from K.M. Eisenhardt and D.N. Sull, 'Strategy as simple rules', *Harvard Business Review*, January 2001, pp. 107–116.

gives some examples from such organisations of how they take form and their effects. The researchers suggest that the number of rules does not need to be many to result in consistent patterns of behaviour – perhaps between two and seven; and older, more established organisations may need fewer rules than younger organisations with less experience.

Implications for management

The implications of the ideas lens, building as it does on complexity theory and evolutionary theory as applied to innovation in the context of strategic management, are these:

- *Environmental sensitivity*: It is not possible for top management to know or understand and plan the future. The future will emerge. It does matter, however, that management need to be aware of and sensitive to the environment and encourage others to do so because it will affect the organisation and will itself throw up new ideas and challenges.

- *Creating context rather than plans*: innovation will not be achieved by determining 'tight' strategies and control systems. It is more likely to be managed by creating forms of organisation and cultures of organisation which encourage variety and informal networking. There is, then, a de-emphasis of formal planning and systems; and a greater emphasis on the day-to-day aspects of organisational life and organisation design which encourages the social interaction of people and their intuitive sensing and awareness of what is going on around them.

- *Pattern recognition*: emerging stimuli in the organisational world and ideas within the organisation are less likely to be developed through formal analysis and more likely to be developed by a reliance on 'pattern recognition' based on experience and intuition.

- *Imperfection* matters: new ideas are unlikely to emerge 'fully formed' – indeed they may be the result of 'imperfect copying'. Managers have to learn to tolerate such imperfection and allow for failures if they want innovation.

- *Simple rules and adaptive tension*: Managers may usefully generate the sort of overarching mission, intent or vision explained in Chapter 1 and provide a few guiding 'rules' or principles. However, they need to understand that too much order is dangerous; that the creation of ambiguity may be important as a means of creating adaptive tension. Insofar as top management can exercise control, this may be limited to establishing the relatively few, but absolute, simple rules and monitoring key measures linked to these.

A summary of the strategy lenses

Exhibit I.iv summarises the explanation in this commentary of the three lenses and Exhibit I.v is a more abbreviated summary. In many respects it has to be recognised that the design lens, especially in its emphasis on analysis and control, is the orthodox approach to strategy development most commonly written about in books, taught at business schools and verbalised by management when they discuss the

Exhibit I.iv   Three strategy lenses: a summary

Strategy as:

	Design	Experience	Ideas
Overview/ Summary	Deliberate positioning through rational processes to optimise economic performance	Incremental development as the outcome of individual and collective experience and the taken for granted	Emergence of order and innovation through variety, in and around the organisation
Assumptions about organisations	Mechanistic, hierarchical, rational systems	Cultures based on experience, legitimacy and past success	Complex and potentially diverse organic systems
Role of top management	Strategic decision makers	Enactors of their experience	'Coaches', creators of context and pattern recognisers
Underpinning theories	Economics; decision sciences	Institutional theory; theories of culture; psychology	Complexity and evolutionary theories

Exhibit I.v   The strategy lenses

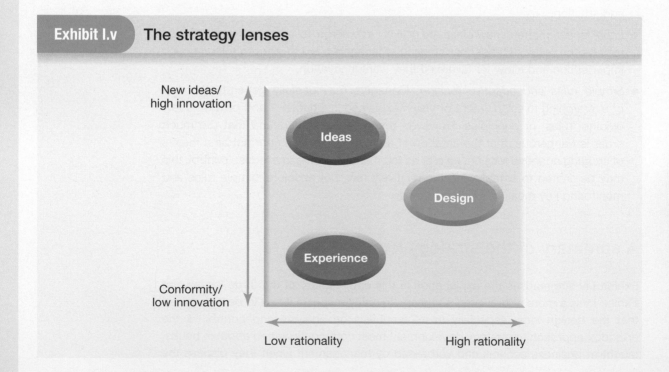

strategy of their organisations. As explained in Chapter 1, it is also a convenient lens by which to structure this book. It is high on rationality, emphasising control and order. Managers who see their role like this may be highly analytical but are unlikely to generate high levels of innovation. The other lenses are important because they raise significant challenges and insights in thinking about and managing strategy. The experience lens is rooted in evidence of how strategies develop incrementally based on experience and the historical and cultural legacy of the organisation; and suggests that it is much more difficult to make strategic changes than the design lens might imply. Organisations and managers captured by their past are likely to be reluctant to change and low on innovation. The ideas lens emphasises the potential variety of ideas that exists in and around organisations and how this might foster innovation if levels of control and the influence of past experience and culture are not too great. It therefore helps an understanding of where innovative strategies come from and how organisations cope with dynamic environments. It also poses questions about whether or not top management really have control over strategic direction to the extent the design lens suggests.

In the rest of the book the three lenses are employed in commentaries at the end of Parts II, III, IV and V in particular to examine critically the coverage of each part.

References

1. J.G. March, *A Primer on Decision Making: How Decisions Happen*, Simon & Schuster, 1994, Chapter 1, Limited Liability, pp. 1–35.
2. The design view is represented in most strategy textbooks. For example, see A.J. Rowe, R.O. Mason, and K.E. Dickel, *Strategic Management: A methodological approach*, Addison-Wesley Publishing, 1987, and R. Grant, *Contemporary Strategic Analysis: Concepts, techniques, applications*, 4th edition, Blackwell, 2002.
3. See H.I. Ansoff, *Corporate Strategy*, Penguin, 1968.
4. See M.E. Porter, *Competitive Strategy*, Free Press/Collier Macmillan, 1980, and *Competitive Advantage*, Free Press/Collier Macmillan, 1985.
5. See H.A. Simon, *The New Science of Management Decision*, Prentice Hall, 1960 and C.E. Lindblom, 'The science of muddling through', *Public Administration Review*, vol. 19 (1959), pp. 79–88.
6. The idea of strategy 'momentum' is explained more fully in D. Miller and P. Friesen, 'Momentum and revolution in organisational adaptation', *Academy of Management Journal*, vol. 23, no. 4 (1980), pp. 591–614.
7. See J.E. Dutton and S.E. Jackson, 'Categorizing strategic issues: links to organizational action', *Academy of Management Review*, vol. 12 (1987), pp. 76–90.
8. See D. Lovallo and D. Kahneman, 'Delusions of success', *Harvard Business Review*, vol. 81, no. 7 (2003), pp. 56–64.
9. For a thorough explanation of the role of psychological processes in strategy see G.P. Hodgkinson and P.R. Sparrow, *The Competent Organization*, Open University Press, 2002.
10. This definition is taken from E. Schein, *Organisational Culture and Leadership*, 2nd edition, Jossey-Bass, 1992, p. 6.
11. 'Paradigm' is a term used by a number of writers: see, for example, J. Pfeffer, 'Management as symbolic action: the creation and maintenance of organisational paradigms', in L.L. Cummings and B.M. Staw (eds), *Research in Organisational Behaviour,* JAI Press, 1981, vol. 3, pp. 1–15, and G. Johnson, *Strategic Change and the Management Process,* Blackwell, 1987.
12. See G. Johnson, *Strategic Change and the Management Process*, Blackwell, 1987.
13. For a good summary of institutional theory, see W.R. Scott, *Institutions and Organizations,* Sage, 1995.
14. For example, see R. Greenwood and C.R. Hinings, 'Understanding strategic change: the contribution of archetypes', *Academy of Management Journal*, vol. 36, no. 5 (1993), pp. 1052–1081 and 'Understanding radical organizational change: bringing together the old and the new institutionalism', *Academy of Management Review*, vol. 21, no. 4 (1996), pp. 1022–1054.
15. See R.T. Pascale, M. Millermann and L. Gioja, *Surfing the Edge of Chaos: The Laws of Nature and the New Laws of Business*, Texere, 2000.

16. For those who want to read more on evolutionary theory, see Daniel C. Dennett, *Darwin's Dangerous Idea,* Penguin, 1995 or books by Richard Dawkins such as *The Blind Watchmaker*, Penguin, 1986.

17. An excellent discussion of the development of ideas (or what the authors refer to as 'memes') and the relationship of this to the role and nature of organisations can be found in J. Weeks and C. Galunic, 'A theory of the cultural evolution of the firm: the intra-organizational ecology of memes', *Organization Studies*, vol. 24, no. 8 (2003), pp. 1309–1352.

18. See M.A. Hitt, R.E. Hoskisson and H. Kim, 'International diversification: effects of innovation and firm performance in product-diversified firms', *Academy of Management Journal*, vol. 40, no. 4 (1997), pp. 767–798.

19. See G. Johnson and A.S. Huff, 'Everyday innovation/everyday strategy', in G. Hamel, G.K. Prahalad, H. Thomas and D. O'Neal (eds), *Strategic Flexibility – Managing in a Turbulent Environment*, Wiley, 1998, pp. 13–27. Patrick Regner also shows how new strategic directions can grow from the periphery of organisations in the face of opposition from the centre; see 'Strategy creation in the periphery: inductive versus deductive strategy making', *Journal of Management Studies*, vol. 40, no. 1 (2003), pp. 57–82.

20. See Z.J. Acs and D.B. Audretsch, 'Innovation in large and small firms – an empirical analysis', *American Economic Review*, vol. 78, September (1988), pp. 678–690.

21. See E. von Hippel, *The Sources of Innovation*, Oxford University Press, 1988.

22. See M.S. Granovetter, 'The strength of weak ties', *American Journal of Sociology*, vol. 78, no. 6 (1973), pp. 1360–1380.

23. For a fuller discussion of complexity theory see R.D. Stacey, *Strategic Management and Organisational Dynamics. The Challenge of Complexity*, 3rd edition, Pearson Education, 2000.

24. See S.L. Brown and K.M. Eisenhardt, *Competing on the Edge*, Harvard Business School Press, 1998.

25. See Brown and Eisenhardt, reference 24.

26. See Brown and Eisenhardt, reference 24.

27. C.W. Reynolds, 'Flocks, herds and schools: a distributed behaviour model', *Proceedings of SIGGRAPH '87, Computer Graphics*, vol. 21, no. 4 (1987), pp. 25–34, as quoted in R.D. Stacey, reference 23, p. 277.

28. See R.T. Pascale, M. Millermann and L. Gioja, reference 15 above.

29. This discussion is based on research by K.M. Eisenhardt and D.N. Sull reported in 'Strategy as simple rules', *Harvard Business Review*, January 2001, pp. 107–116.

Part II

The Strategic Position

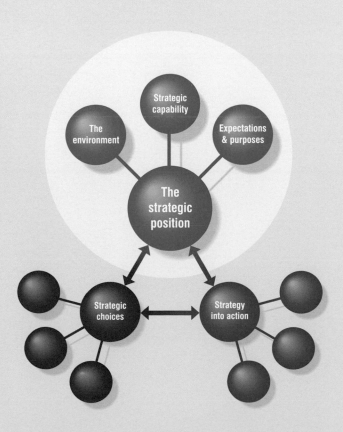

THIS PART EXPLAINS:

● The impact of the environment, organisational capabilities and expectations and purposes on strategy.

● How to understand an organisation's position in the environment.

● The determinants of strategic capability – resources, competences and the linkages between them.

● The factors that shape organisational purposes – corporate governance, stakeholder expectations, business ethics and the cultural context.

Introduction to Part II

This part of the book is concerned with understanding the forces that influence, or have to be taken into account in, the development of strategy. There are those who argue that the forces at work in an industry, sector or market are the most important: for example, that companies in more favourable environments will perform better than those in less attractive environments. So strategy development is about 'fit': that is, identifying opportunities in the environment and developing or building strategic capabilities to take advantage of such opportunities. Others argue that the strategic capabilities of organisations are what are most important because they explain differences between organisations, potential uniqueness and therefore superior performance. They take a 'resource-based view', arguing that strategies should be built on the identification of unique capabilities of an organisation. Opportunities should then be sought which allow the organisation to exploit these capabilities to achieve competitive advantage.

There are other considerations too. Organisations have different stakeholders (shareholders, customers, employees, perhaps government) who have expectations of the organisation and may exercise considerable influence and power over the strategy to be followed. The history and culture of an organisation and cultural similarities across organisations, for example professions, may also exercise an influence on strategy. Strategic management involves understanding and managing these different forces affecting the organisation and this part of the book discusses them.

- The overall theme of Chapter 2 is how managers might make sense of an uncertain and increasingly complex world around them. This is addressed by considering various layers of influence from macro-environmental issues to specific forces affecting the competitive position. However, simply identifying particular influences is not sufficient. The challenge for a strategist is to understand the interaction of these different forces and how these impact on the organisation.

- Chapter 3 is concerned with understanding an organisation's strategic capability and how this underpins the competitive advantage of the organisation or sustains excellence in providing value-for-money products or services. This is explained by considering four main issues: what is meant by 'strategic capability'; how this might provide competitive advantage for organisations; how managers might analyse capabilities; and how they might manage the development of such capabilities.

- Chapter 4 is about how expectations 'shape' organisational purposes and strategies. This is considered within four main themes. Corporate governance is concerned with understanding whom the organisation is there to serve. Stakeholder influence raises the important issue of power relationships on and in organisations. A discussion of ethics raises the question of what organisations should and should not be doing strategically. And a discussion of cultural influences helps explain how national, institutional and organisational cultures affect organisational purposes and strategy.

Although this part of the book is divided into three chapters, it should be stressed that there are strong links between these different influences on strategy. Environmental

Exhibit II.i   The business idea

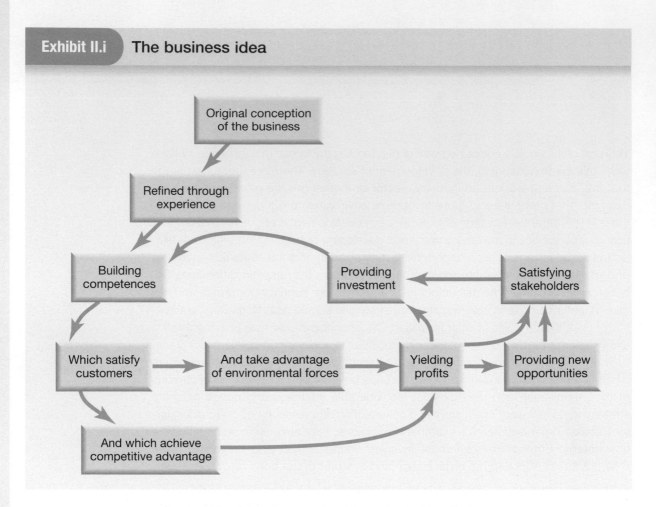

pressures for change will be constrained by the capabilities available to make changes, or by organisational culture which may lead to resistance to change. The capabilities yielding apparent opportunities will be valuable only if such opportunities can be found in the environment. The relative importance of these various influences will change over time and may show marked differences from one organisation to another. However, the ability of an organisation to find ways to respond to these different influences in an integrated way and to create value is vitally important. This notion of integration is encapsulated in the concept of the business idea.* This provides a model of why and how an organisation can be successful by reconciling the different forces and influences on strategy. This is represented in Exhibit II.i. It shows schematically how an original idea will have found a way for a successful business to operate such that environmental forces, organisational capabilities, and stakeholder expectations mutually reinforce each other. Less successful organisations would not experience the same sorts of reinforcing cycles: the different forces would be pulling in different directions rather than being mutually reinforcing. The business idea is a concept that will be revisited in the commentary at the end of Part II in order to emphasise the important lesson of integration, but also to ask how organisations might achieve such integration.

---

* The business idea is developed in *Scenarios: The art of strategic conversation,* by Kees van der Heijden, J. Wiley, 2004.

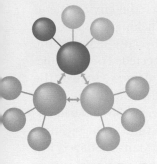

2

The Environment

Learning outcomes

After reading this chapter you should be able to:

● Describe the forces in the macro-environment of an organisation using PESTEL and other frameworks.

● Develop scenarios and explain their implications.

● Use the five forces framework to identify the sources of competition for a strategic business unit.

● Define strategic groups, market segments and critical success factors and explain how these concepts help in understanding competition at a detailed level.

● Explain the different types of strategic gap that might present opportunities or threats to organisations.

Photo: Digital Vision

Photo: Getty Images

2.1 INTRODUCTION

The theme of this chapter is how managers – whether private or public sector[1] – can make sense of an uncertain world around their organisation – the business environment. This can be difficult for several reasons. First, 'the environment' encapsulates many different influences – the difficulty is making sense of this *diversity*. Second is the problem of *complexity* which arises because many of the separate issues in the business environment are interconnected. For example, a technological development – such as information technology – changes the nature of work. In turn this changes lifestyles, which then alters consumer behaviour and purchasing patterns for many goods and services. So understanding these connections is important in building a strategic 'picture' of the business environment. Finally, there is the issue of the *speed of change*. Many managers feel that the pace of technological change and the speed of global communications mean more and faster change now than ever before.[2]

This chapter provides frameworks for understanding the environment of organisations with the aim of helping to identify key issues and ways of coping with complexity and change. These frameworks are organised in a series of 'layers' briefly introduced here and summarised in Exhibit 2.1.

Exhibit 2.1   Layers of the business environment

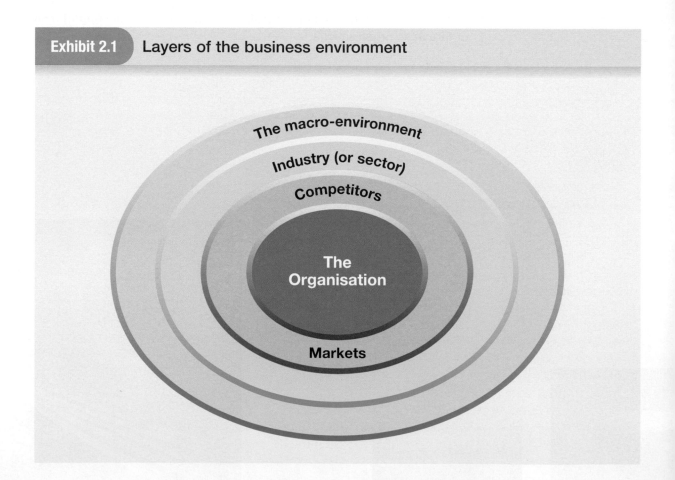

● The most general 'layer' of the environment is often referred to as the *macro-environment*. This consists of broad environmental factors that impact to a greater or lesser extent on almost all organisations. It is important to build up an understanding of how changes in the macro-environment are likely to impact on individual organisations. A starting point can be provided by the PESTEL framework which can be used to identify how future trends in the *political, economic, social, technological, environmental and legal* environments might impinge on organisations. This provides the broad 'data' from which the *key drivers of change* can be identified. These will differ from sector to sector and from country to country. Therefore they will have a different impact on one organisation from another. If the future environment is likely to be very different from the past it is helpful to construct *scenarios* of possible futures. This helps managers consider how strategies might need to change depending on the different ways in which the business environment *might* change.

● Within this broad general environment the next 'layer' is called an *industry* or a *sector*. This is a group of organisations producing the same products or services. The *five forces* framework and the concept of *cycles of competition* can be useful in understanding how the competitive dynamics within and around an industry are changing.

● The most immediate layer of the environment consists of *competitors and markets*. Within most industries or sectors there will be many different organisations with different characteristics and competing on different bases. The concept of *strategic groups* can help with the identification of both direct and indirect competitors. Similarly customers' expectations are not all the same. They have a range of different requirements the importance of which can be understood through the concepts of *market segments* and *critical success factors*.

2.2 THE MACRO-ENVIRONMENT

2.2.1 The PESTEL framework[3]

Illustration 2.1 shows some of the macro-environmental influences that might affect organisations. It is not intended to provide an exhaustive list, but it gives examples of ways in which strategies are affected by such influences and some of the ways in which organisations seek to handle aspects of their environment.[4]

Exhibit 2.2 shows the PESTEL framework, which categorises environmental influences into six main types: political, economic, social, technological, environmental and legal. As mentioned in Chapter 1 these factors are not independent of each other; many are linked. For example, technology developments change the way that people work, their living standards and their lifestyles. As any of these factors changes it affects the competitive environment in which organisations operate, as discussed in section 2.3 below. So understanding how PESTEL factors might impact on and drive change in general is only really a starting point. Managers need to understand the *key drivers of change* and also the *differential impact* of these external influences and drivers on particular industries, markets

The PESTEL framework categorises environmental influences into six main types: political, economic, social, technological, environmental and legal

Illustration 2.1   strategy into action

Examples of environmental influences

A wide range of environmental influences can affect organisational strategies and performance.

Government action

In late 2003 the Russian government froze 44 per cent of the national oil giant Yukos. This was just days after authorities had arrested chief executive Mikhail Khodorkovsky (thought to be Russia's richest man) on fraud and tax evasion charges. But many Russians believed that the case against Khodorkovsky was political. He had funded opposition groups breaking what analysts regarded as a tacit agreement to stay out of politics in return for avoiding investigations of financial affairs.

Capital markets

In 1999 and the early part of 2000 the world stock markets were driven higher and higher by investors' love affair with technology stocks. But then came the crash. Stock markets lost some 50 per cent of their value by early 2003 and technology stocks lost far more. The hardest hit were internet and telecommunications companies – many losing 90 per cent of their market valuation. This forced them to drastically scale down their development plans and many smaller companies went bankrupt.

Lobbying

Financial policy

Demographics

By the early 2000s, the trend of an ageing population was well established in the western economies. This provided challenges to those planning public service provision such as education and healthcare. It also created what was called the 'pensions timebomb' where a declining working population would have to fund pensions for a rapidly growing population of retirees. The pattern of demand for commercial goods and services was also changing – providing both opportunities and threats for the private sector.

Demographic forecasting

The Enterprise

Environmental sensing and R & D policy

Sociocultural

Growing health consciousness and social pressures on smokers in western countries have adversely affected the sales of tobacco products in these markets. Public pressure has also led to stringent regulations relating to tobacco advertising, methods of promotion, and packaging. Coupled with heavy taxes and lawsuits, which have bitten into their profits and share prices, tobacco companies have recently concentrated their marketing efforts on the developing world and diversified into other sectors.

Technology

The introduction of new multimedia mobile services such as data, entertainment and text messaging has been more than just the next level of telecommunications achievements – it has also been the driving force behind many changes in other industrial and service sectors. These new data services require secure transactions over mobile networks, more processing power and increased memory capacity. As a result, smart card manufacturers, banking applications and billing software developers had all increased their investment in R&D in order to capitalise on this technology.

Labour markets

In 2004 many IT-based service organisations in Western Europe and North America were declaring redundancies. This was a result of so-called 'offshoring' – relocating jobs overseas – many to India. The motive was major reductions in cost of running activities like customer service and call centres. Independent research (Deloitte) estimated that some 2 million jobs might migrate in a 5 year period. Deloitte also forecast that 75 per cent of the top 100 financial institutions would have offshore operations by the end of the period – saving some $138bn (€120bn) over 5 years.

Regulation of competition

In September 2003 Morrisons (the Bradford-based, medium-sized UK grocery retailer) was given permission by the UK government to mount a takeover bid for rival supermarket group Safeway. This followed a five-month investigation by the Competition Commission. Significantly its findings had prompted the government to block rival bids from the bigger Tesco, Asda and J. Sainsbury (on competition grounds). If the takeover was successful Morrisons would have to sell off about 10 per cent of the 479 Safeway stores and the other bidders could bid for these.

Labour policy
and industrial relations

Marketing
policy

The Enterprise

Economy

The World Trade Organisation (WTO) has the almost impossible task of balancing the economic interests of developed and developing economies. Through the late 1990s and early 2000s its meetings were stormy affairs. The negotiations around cotton give a flavour of the debate. A group of African countries wanted subsidies to cotton farmers in the USA, China and the EU abolished. They said that they could compete in a fair world market and cotton revenues could help tackle poverty at home. But in 2004 (a presidential election year) this was an unwelcome message in the USA with most cotton farmers based in the Southern states – Republican party strongholds.

Economic
forecasting

Environmental sensing
and R & D policy

Purchasing

Environment

In late 2003 the European Union launched its REACH initiative concerning the safety of household chemicals. The aim was to have new regulation by 2005 whereby some 30,000 chemicals would have to undergo statutory testing to prove their safety. It was targeted at substances that might cause cancer or damage genetic material. Ironically the RSPCA expressed concern about the proposals and feared a massive increase in animal testing of substances.

Suppliers

Some factors cannot be controlled but have a big impact on organisations. The weather is one of these. Unprecedented hot weather in Europe in the summer of 2003 brought mixed fortunes for Europe's farmers. In parts of continental Europe lack of rain cut harvests for wheat and cereals pushing up prices from which British farmers benefited (the British weather had produced a high-quality crop too). Most places saw early harvesting of grapes to produce a vintage year – even in Britain!

| Exhibit 2.2 | Macro-environmental influences – the PESTEL framework |

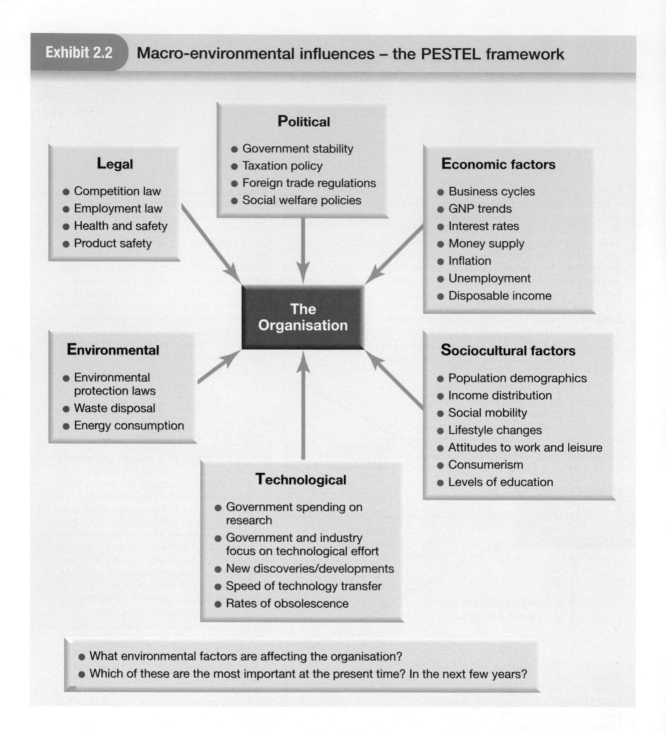

Political
- Government stability
- Taxation policy
- Foreign trade regulations
- Social welfare policies

Legal
- Competition law
- Employment law
- Health and safety
- Product safety

Economic factors
- Business cycles
- GNP trends
- Interest rates
- Money supply
- Inflation
- Unemployment
- Disposable income

The Organisation

Environmental
- Environmental protection laws
- Waste disposal
- Energy consumption

Sociocultural factors
- Population demographics
- Income distribution
- Social mobility
- Lifestyle changes
- Attitudes to work and leisure
- Consumerism
- Levels of education

Technological
- Government spending on research
- Government and industry focus on technological effort
- New discoveries/developments
- Speed of technology transfer
- Rates of obsolescence

- What environmental factors are affecting the organisation?
- Which of these are the most important at the present time? In the next few years?

and individual organisations. This will be discussed in section 2.2.2 below. The influences and drivers also vary from nation to nation (and from region to region within countries). The implications of this will be discussed in section 2.2.3 below.

It is particularly important that PESTEL is used to look at the *future* impact of environmental factors, which may be different from their past impact. Where there are high levels of uncertainty about future changes in the environment scenarios may be a useful approach and are discussed in section 2.2.4 below.

2.2.2 Key drivers of change

The PESTEL factors in Exhibit 2.2 are of limited value if they are merely seen as a listing of influences. It is important to identify a number of **key drivers of change**, which are forces likely to affect the structure of an industry, sector or market. So identifying key drivers cuts across levels in Exhibit 2.1. Although there will be many changes occurring in the macro-environment of most organisations it will be the *combined effect* of just *some* of these separate factors that will be so important, rather than all of the factors separately. Yip[5] provides a good example of the key drivers that are increasing the globalisation of some industries and markets (see Exhibit 2.3).

Key drivers of change are forces likely to affect the structure of an industry, sector or market

- There is an increasing trend to *market globalisation* for a variety of reasons. In some markets, customer needs and preferences are becoming more similar. For example, there is increasing homogeneity of consumer tastes in goods such as soft drinks, jeans, electrical items (e.g. audio equipment) and personal computers. The opening of McDonald's outlets in most countries of the world signalled similar tendencies in fast food. As some markets globalise, those operating in such markets become *global customers* and may search for suppliers who can operate on a global basis. For example, the global clients of the major accountancy firms may expect the accountancy firms to provide global services. The development of *global communication and distribution channels* may drive globalisation – the obvious example being the impact of the internet. In turn, this may provide opportunities for *transference of marketing* (e.g. global brands) across countries. Marketing policies, brand names and identities, and advertising may all be developed globally. This further generates global demand and expectations from customers, and may also provide marketing cost advantages for global operators. Nor is the public sector immune from such forces. Universities are subject to similar trends influenced by changing delivery technologies through the internet. This means, for example, that there is developing a genuinely global market for MBA students – particularly where the majority of 'tuition' is done online.

- *Cost globalisation* may give potential for competitive advantage since some organisations will have greater access to and/or be more aware of these advantages than others. This is especially the case in industries in which large-volume, standardised production is required for optimum *economies of scale*, as in many components for the electronics industry. There might also be cost advantages from the *experience* built through wider-scale operations. Other cost advantages might be achieved by central *sourcing efficiencies* from lowest-cost suppliers across the world. *Country-specific costs*, such as labour or exchange rates, encourage businesses to search globally for low cost in these respects as ways of matching the costs of competitors that have such advantages because of their location. For example, given increased reliability of communication and cost differentials of labour, software companies and call centres are being located in India, where there is highly skilled but low-cost staff. Other businesses face high *costs of product development* and may see advantages in operating globally with fewer products rather than incurring the costs of wide ranges of products on a more limited geographical scale.

Exhibit 2.3   Drivers of globalisation

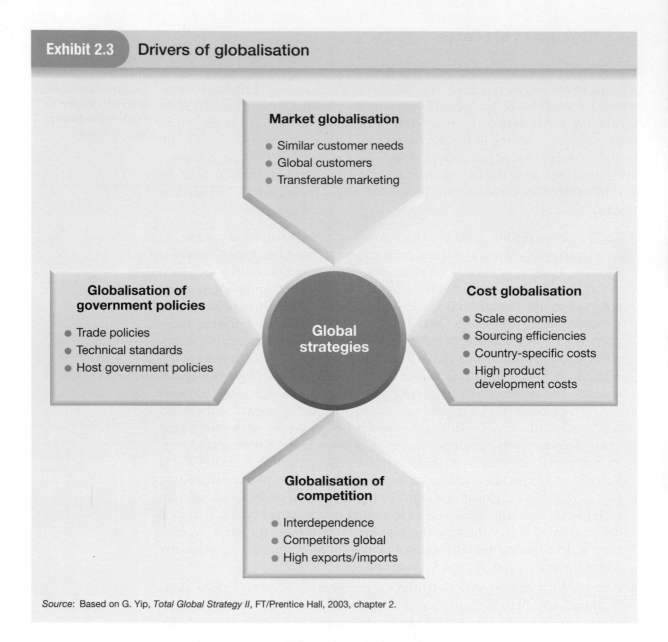

Source: Based on G. Yip, *Total Global Strategy II*, FT/Prentice Hall, 2003, chapter 2.

- The activities and policies of *governments* have also tended to drive the globalisation of industry. Political changes in the 1990s meant that almost all trading nations function with market-based economies and their *trade policies* have tended to encourage free markets between nations. Globalisation has been further encouraged by *technical standardisation* between countries of many products, such as in the automobile, aerospace and computing industries. It may also be that particular *host governments* actively seek to encourage global operators to base themselves in their countries. However, it is worth noting that in many industries country-specific regulations still persist and reduce the extent to which global strategies are possible. Also, the early 2000s have seen a rise in *citizen activism* about the impact of globalisation on developing countries – most notably at meetings of the World Trade Organisation.

● Changes in the macro-environment are increasing *global competition* which, in turn, encourages further globalisation. If the levels of *exports and imports* between countries are high, it increases interaction between competitors on a more global scale. If a business is competing globally, it also tends to place globalisation pressures on competitors, especially if customers are also operating on a global basis. It may also be that the *interdependence* of a company's operations across the world encourages the globalisation of its competitors. For example, if a company has sought out low-cost production sites in different countries, these low costs may be used to subsidise competitive activity in high-cost areas against local competitors, thus encouraging them to follow similar strategies.

Exhibit 2.3 shows the drivers of environmental change that are of particular concern to a multinational corporation. But it must be remembered that the impact of these forces may be different in different parts of the business (as shown in Illustration 2.2).

It should be remembered that Exhibit 2.3 is just an example of how key drivers of change can be identified and understood. The specific drivers will vary by industry or sector. For example, a retailer may be primarily concerned with local customer tastes and behaviour. A computer manufacturer is likely to be concerned with developments in the technological environment that lead to product innovation and obsolescence. Public sector managers are likely to be especially concerned with changes in public policy, public funding levels and demographic changes. For example, the impact of an ageing population may be a key driver. This would have several factors (as with the globalisation example), such as medical advances, social/political stability, economic advancement and so on. Also, the impact on particular parts of the public services is different – increasing (in *relative* terms) the need for health care and reducing services aimed at or driven by younger people (such as primary schools and courts).

2.2.3 Porter's Diamond

The previous section showed how key drivers of change can be identified by drawing on a PESTEL analysis and also identifying how these factors influence the more immediate competitive environment. The relative importance of these factors and their combined impact on the competitive environment will differ between countries. An example of the importance of this in the context of global competition is provided by Michael Porter in his book, *The Competitive Advantage of Nations*.[6] What has become known as **Porter's Diamond** suggests that there are inherent reasons why some nations are more competitive than others, and why some industries within nations are more competitive than others. (See Exhibit 2.4.) This is another example of how the impact of macro-environment factors on the competitive environment can be understood *strategically*.

Porter's Diamond suggests that there are inherent reasons why some nations are more competitive than others, and why some industries within nations are more competitive than others

Porter suggests that the national home base of an organisation plays an important role in creating advantage on a global scale. This home base provides factors which organisations are able to build on and extend to provide such advantage:

● There may be specific *factor conditions* that help explain the basis of advantage on a national level. These provide initial advantages that are subsequently

Illustration 2.2   strategy into action

Global forces at Pilkington

Global forces can impact differently in different parts of the same business.

The early 21st century continued to provide tough challenges for manufacturing organisations based in developed economies. This was particularly true for manufacturers of basic materials such as steel or glass as they experienced fierce competition around the world. Pilkington, based in St Helens, UK, started glass manufacturing in 1826. But the major breakthrough for the company was its development of the float glass manufacturing process, announced in 1959. This revolutionised glass manufacturing and led to a major international expansion of the company – largely through acquisitions. By the 1990s the company turnover was some £3bn (≈ €4.5bn) and it had major operations in Europe, North America, South America and Australasia.

Flat glass has two major uses – in the building industry for windows and doors in domestic and commercial properties, and for glazing systems in automobiles. Competition in the glass industry and their customers' industries was increasingly globalising the operation of glass companies. Some of these global forces impacted right across the business whilst others impacted differently in the building products and automotive sectors.

Government influence

Issues in this category included a general increase in free trade, regulations about the insulation standards in houses and office buildings, and government actions to attract inward investment – for example, in the location of manufacturing plants for automobiles. Eastern Europe had opened up as a market since the 1990s as their economies were restructured and many moved towards membership of the EU.

Market globalisation

The automobile industry was highly globalised with the major manufacturers operating in most parts of the world. Their product standardisation programmes led them to prefer suppliers who could source worldwide. In contrast, the building industry was very fragmented and building design, methods and requirements varied considerably from one continent to another. Climate was a crucial issue.

Cost globalisation

Glass was a fragile, heavy and relatively low-cost item. So shipping 'raw' glass long distances was uneconomic. However, glass manufacturing was also capital intensive – a float plant would cost some €100–150 million and needed to run at least 70 per cent of its annual capacity of 200,000 tonnes to 'pay its way'.

Global competition

As a result of some of these other forces, primary glass production had seen a progressive reduction in the number of companies. By the early 2000s there were only six major glass companies of any size, of which only three (Pilkington, Asahi and Saint Gobain) could claim to have a significant presence in the major markets worldwide – either through their own plants or through partnerships.

Source: Company publications (with permission).

Questions

1. Using Exhibit 2.3, draw up separate 'maps' for the building products and automobile glass sectors.
2. Explain how this might influence the way that the company is organised.

Exhibit 2.4 | **Porter's Diamond – the determinants of national advantage**

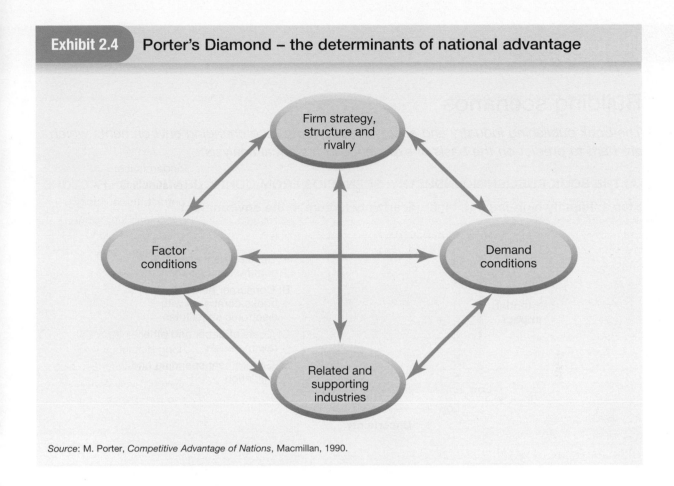

Source: M. Porter, *Competitive Advantage of Nations*, Macmillan, 1990.

built upon to yield more advanced factors of competition. For example, in countries such as Sweden and Japan, in which either legislation or custom means that it is difficult to lay off labour, there has been a greater impetus towards automation of industries. Also the linguistic ability of the Swiss has provided a significant advantage to their banking industry.

● Home *demand conditions* provide the basis upon which the characteristics of the advantage of an organisation are shaped. For example, Japanese customers' high expectations of electrical and electronic equipment have provided an impetus for those industries in Japan leading to global dominance of those sectors.

● One successful industry may lead to advantage in *related and supporting industries*. In Italy, for example, the leather footwear industry, the leather working machinery industry and the design services, which underpin them, benefit from one another. In Singapore, port services and ship repair industries are mutually advantageous.

● The characteristics of *firm strategy*, industry *structure and rivalry* in different countries also help explain bases of advantage. In Germany the propensity for systematic, often hierarchical, processes of management has been particularly successful in providing reliability and technical excellence in engineering industries. Domestic rivalry and the search for competitive advantages within a nation can help provide organisations with bases for achieving such

Illustration 2.3   strategy into action

Building scenarios

The book publishing industry and energy industry both face changing environments which are hard to predict on the basis of experience or historical analysis.

(A) THE BOOK PUBLISHING INDUSTRY: SCENARIOS FROM CONFIGURATIONS OF FACTORS

Step 1: Identify high-impact, high-uncertainty factors in the environment

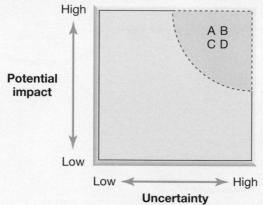

A: Development of electronic communications market

B: Consumer perceptions of books compared with electronic substitutes

C: Costs of paper and other raw materials

D: Government spending and regulation

Step 2: Identify different possible futures by factor

A: (i) Rapid change
    (ii) Measured change
B: (i) Favourable
    (ii) Unfavourable
C: (i) High and increasing
    (ii) Stabilising
D: (i) In support of books
    (ii) In support of electronic media

Step 3: Build scenarios of plausible configurations of factors

Scenario 1: no great change
Favourable consumer perceptions of books compared with electronic substitutes (B(i)) are supported by government spending and regulation (D)(i)). There is measured change in the development of electronic communications markets (A(ii)) and stable costs of paper and other raw materials (C(ii)).

Scenario 2: electronic chaos
Rapid change in the development of the electronic communications market (A(i)) is encouraged by government spending and regulation in support of electronic media (D(ii)). Furthermore, unfavourable consumer perceptions of books compared with electronic substitutes (B(ii)) are combined with high and increasing costs of paper and other raw materials (C(i)).

Scenario 3: information society
Stable consumer perceptions of books compared with

---

advantage on a more global scale. Examples are the brewing industries of The Netherlands and Denmark (see the chapter-end case example) and the pharmaceuticals industry in Switzerland.

Porter's diamond has been used in various ways. At a national level it has been employed by governments to consider the policies that they should follow to

electronic substitutes (B(ii)), measured change in the development of electronic communications markets (A(ii)) and government spending and regulation in support of books are favourable (D(i)). However, there is concern over the high and rising cost of paper and other raw materials (C(i)).

(B) THEMATIC SCENARIOS FOR THE UK ENERGY SECTOR

To demonstrate the practical application of scenario planning a workgroup was assembled at the UK Strategic Planning Society in 2003. They looked at future scenarios for the UK energy industries and developed three for the period to 2050:

Cheap future

This scenario envisaged new storage and transmission technologies reducing the emphasis on generation capacity and energy management. The future would be shaped by generation at the fuel source, energy imports and local storage. The government has an economic focus to its energy policy.

Village green

In this scenario there will be new forms of power generation but with a parochial culture of keeping production small-scale and local. The emphasis would be on providing subsidies and developing new 'green' technologies. Opportunities for local generation, renewables technologies and district heating would be explored. The government is likely to have a social focus.

Brave new world

The final scenario envisages a future with fuel cells for almost limitless storage, near-zero transmission losses and many new forms of generation (e.g. renewables, nuclear, hydrogen and local generation). The culture would be entrepreneurial, technologically advanced, consumer-driven and market-oriented. The government develops a non-interventionist economic policy.

Although the scenarios appear discrete some common themes and key drivers emerge. All scenarios envisaged a *short-term* increase in electricity prices due to increasing dependence on imported fuel. The potentially profound impact on the sector of new transmission and storage technologies was clearly critical. These are key drivers which could lead to cheaper imports reducing the need for domestic generation (affecting the gas and coal industries). Also improvements in power storage would vastly increase the attractiveness of renewables and change the rules of the energy market. All scenarios showed that if these technological breakthroughs did not occur rising costs would encourage a village environment. But in two of the scenarios the government's stance was economic – which may not be sustainable in these circumstances. A rethink about competition and access to UK markets would be essential.

Clearly the vast range of issues identified in these scenarios would have a range of effects on the industries' diverse stakeholders. These would need to be worked through in detail too.

Source: A. Shaukat and G. Ringland, 'Imagine', *Utility Week*, vol. 20, no. 11 (2003), pp. 20–21.

Question

Choose another industry with which you are familiar (or the brewing industry at the end of the chapter) and construct two or three scenarios for the future using one or both of the approaches in this illustration.

encourage the competitive advantage of their industries. Since the argument is, in essence, that domestic characteristics of competition should yield advantages on a wider basis, the implication is that competition should be encouraged at home, rather than industries being protected from overseas competition. However, governments can also act to foster such advantage by, for example, ensuring high expectations of product performance, safety or environmental standards; or encouraging vertical cooperation between suppliers and buyers on a domestic level, which could lead to innovation.

The implications of Porter's Diamond might also apply to the relative competitiveness of different regions *within* a single nation. So the discussion has been extended into a consideration of the importance of *clusters*[7] of organisations from the same industry/sector in the same location *within* countries – an important consideration for regional economic policy. But regional economic policy is also concerned with the elimination of disadvantageous circumstances and/or the attraction of investment in new sectors for economically deprived regions. The framework can help with these considerations too.

Individual organisations have also used Porter's Diamond as a way of trying to identify the extent to which they can build on home-based advantages to create competitive advantage in relation to others on a global front. For example, Dutch brewing companies – such as Heineken – have benefited from early globalisation resulting from the nature of the Dutch home market (see the chapter-end case example). Benetton, the Italian clothing company, has achieved global success by using its experience of working through a network of largely independent, often family-owned manufacturers to build its network of franchised retailers using advanced information systems.

2.2.4 Building scenarios[8]

Scenarios are detailed and plausible views of how the business environment of an organisation might develop in the future based on groupings of key environmental influences and drivers of change about which there is a high level of uncertainty

When the business environment has high levels of uncertainty arising from either complexity or rapid change (or both) it may prove impossible to develop a single view of how environment influences might affect an organisation's strategies. So a different approach will be needed to understand the future impact of the environment. **Scenarios** are detailed and plausible views of how the business environment of an organisation might develop in the future based on groupings of key environmental influences and drivers of change about which there is a high level of uncertainty. For example, in the energy industries, given lead times and costs of exploration, there is a need for views of the business environment of 20 years or even more. Whilst a whole host of environmental issues are of relevance, a number of these, such as raw material availability, transmission and storage technologies and subsequent prices and demand, are of crucial importance. Obviously, it is not possible to forecast precisely such factors over a 20-year-plus time horizon, but it can be valuable to have different views of possible futures. In other industries the level of uncertainty is very high even for much shorter time horizons and scenario planning may be valuable too. Scenario planning does not attempt to predict the unpredictable and, therefore, considers multiple, equally plausible, futures. These scenarios are not just based on a hunch; they are logically consistent but different from each other as shown in Illustration 2.3.

Sharing and debating these scenarios improves organisational learning by making managers more perceptive about the forces in the business environment and what is really important. Managers should also evaluate and develop strategies (or contingency plans) for each scenario. They should also monitor the environment to see how it is actually unfolding and adjust strategies and plans accordingly.

Illustration 2.3 shows two examples of how the scenario planning process can be undertaken. It can be seen that assumptions about the key drivers in the business environment are essential to the process of building scenarios. It is important that the number of assumptions and uncertainties is kept to just a few to avoid unmanageable complexity in the analysis. This can be done, for example, by focusing on the factors which (i) have high potential impact and (ii) are uncertain (as with the four factors identified in Illustration 2.3(a) on the book publishing industry). Each of these factors may have different futures (again see Illustration 2.3(a)). These factors may 'combine' to create scenarios of the future, such as the three in Illustration 2.3(a). If the number of factors is large, scenarios may not 'emerge' easily in this way. They may be more concerned with the 'tone' of the future – for example, (i) an optimistic future and a pessimistic future, or (ii) according to dominant themes, as in UK energy (Illustration 2.3(b)). In either case, the proponents of scenarios argue that the allocation of probabilities to factors should be avoided: it endows the scenarios with spurious accuracy, which can be unhelpful given the purpose of the scenarios.

In summary, scenarios are especially useful where it is important to take a long-term view of strategy, probably a minimum of five years; where there are a limited number of key factors influencing the success of that strategy; but where there is a high level of uncertainty about such influences.

2.3   INDUSTRIES AND SECTORS

The previous section looked at how forces in the macro-environment might influence the success or failure of an organisation's strategies. But the impact of these general factors tends to surface in the more immediate environment through changes in the competitive forces on organisations. An important aspect of this for most organisations will be competition within their industry or sector. Economic theory defines an **industry** as 'a group of firms producing the same principal product'[9] or, more broadly, 'a group of firms producing products that are close substitutes for each other'.[10] This concept of an industry can be extended into the public services through the idea of a *sector*. Social services, health care or education also have many producers of the same kinds of services. From a strategic management perspective it is useful for managers in any organisation to understand the competitive forces acting on and between organisations in the same industry or sector since this will determine the attractiveness of that industry and the way in which individual organisations might choose to compete. It may inform important decisions about product/market strategy and whether to leave or enter industries or sectors.

> An **industry** is a group of firms producing the same principal product

It is important to remember that the boundaries of an industry may be changing – for example, by *convergence* of previously separate 'industries' such as between computing, telecommunications and entertainment. **Convergence** is where previously separate industries begin to overlap in terms of activities, technologies, products and customers.[11] There are two sets of 'forces' that might drive convergence. First, convergence might be supply-led – where organisations start to behave as though there are linkages between the separate industries or sectors.

> **Convergence** is where previously separate industries begin to overlap in terms of activities, technologies, products and customers

This is very common in the public services where sectors seem to be constantly bundled and un-bundled into ministries with ever-changing names ('Education', 'Education and Science', 'Education and Employment', 'Education and Skills' etc.). This type of convergence may be driven by external factors in the business environment. For example, governments can help or hinder convergence through regulation or deregulation – a major factor in the financial services sector in many countries. The boundaries of an industry might also be destroyed by other forces in the macro-environment. For example, e-commerce is destroying the boundary of traditional retailing by offering manufacturers new or complementary ways to trade – what are now being called new 'business models'[12] – such as websites or e-auctions (as discussed in section 9.3). But the real test of these types of changes is the extent to which consumers see benefit to them in any of this supply-side convergence. So, secondly, convergence may also occur through demand-side (market) forces – where consumers start to behave as though industries have converged. For example, they start to *substitute* one product with another (e.g. TVs and PCs). Or they start to see links between complementary products that they want to have 'bundled'. The package holiday is an example of bundling air travel, hotels and entertainment to form a new market segment in the travel industry. (The importance of market segments will be discussed more fully in section 2.4.2 below.) Illustration 2.4 shows an example of how convergence was creating a whole new sector and some of the strategic challenges that this produced.

The remainder of this section looks at the forces that shape competition in an industry or sector.

2.3.1 Sources of competition – the five forces framework

Inherent within the notion of strategy is the issue of competitiveness. In business, this is about gaining advantage over competitors; in the public sector, it might be demonstrable excellence within a sector and/or advantage in the procurement of resources (the two will probably be linked). Typically managers take too parochial a view as to the sources of competition, usually focusing their attention on direct competitive rivals (as discussed below). But there are many other factors in the environment which influence this competitiveness. Porter's **five forces framework**[13] was originally developed as a way of assessing the attractiveness (profit potential) of different industries. As such it can help in identifying the sources of competition in an industry or sector (see Exhibit 2.5). Although initially used with businesses in mind, it is of value to most organisations.

The **five forces framework** helps identify the sources of competition in an industry or sector

When using this framework to understand competitive forces it is essential to bear the following in mind:

● It must be used at the level of *strategic business units* (as defined in Chapter 1 and discussed extensively in Chapters 5 and 6) and not at the level of the whole organisation. This is because organisations are diverse in their operations and markets. For example, an airline might compete simultaneously in several different arenas such as domestic and long haul, and target different customer groups such as leisure, business and freight. The impact of competitive forces may be different for each of these SBUs.

Illustration 2.4

strategy into action

Bioinformatics: convergence of health science and other technologies

Changes in the business environment can create opportunities as industries converge. But this also raises a number of other strategic issues about how these opportunities will be realised in practice.

In the mid-2000s the health science industry was increasingly interacting with other sectors such as IT, fine chemicals and agriculture. Following the finalisation of the blueprint of the human genome the industry leaders were in the process of coordinating and capitalising on the knowledge about genes, proteins and sugars. The greatest area in which convergence was occurring was with information technologies. This convergence was creating an ability to store complex human genetic information and manipulate very large-scale sets of data. This allows for improvements in understanding disease at a molecular level (for example, abnormal genes). In turn this has allowed pharmaceutical and biotechnology companies to develop IT-based techniques to discover and process drug 'targets'. Since almost $US880m (€765m) is spent each year on drug development (of which an estimated 75 per cent is associated with failed drug targets) the potential for cost reduction and faster product development is enormous.

But potential convergence was also raising some difficult strategic questions. For example, there were ethical issues about privacy for individuals and whether the extensive use of high-technology 'solutions' would further fuel the drift towards a so-called two-tier health system (haves and have-nots). There were also important public policy issues, for example about regulation and governance (both these issues are discussed in Chapter 4). The process through which convergence would occur was also unclear. Would it be through new bioinformatics companies dedicated to this new field? Or would it occur by alliances and partnerships of the current 'players' in the separate sectors? Or perhaps it would

be achieved through a process of consolidation as a few 'players' built their bioinformatics capabilities by acquisitions or mergers? (These issues are discussed in section 7.3 of Chapter 7.)

The benefits of convergence would also not be felt unless new relationships were formed with the users of these technological advances – the health-care sector. Generally the pace of change in this sector was much slower and in many countries it was predominantly a public sector near monopoly (as with the NHS in the UK). So there were issues about building relationships between two very different types of culture (the entrepreneurial bioinformatics companies and the more bureaucratic health-care system). These issues are discussed in Chapters 4 and 10.

Source: Adapted from Ernst and Young website, 2003.

Questions

1. What factors are driving the development of bioinformatics through convergence?

2. In your opinion *how* will convergence occur to develop this sector further?

3. What are the dangers for an organisation that pursues a proactive approach to becoming a bioinformatics industry leader?

Exhibit 2.5 **The five forces framework**

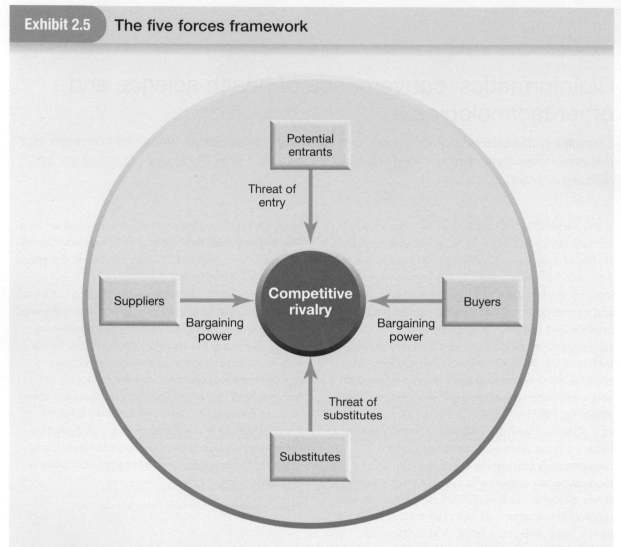

Source: Adapted from M.E. Porter, *Competitive Strategy: Techniques for Analyzing Industries and Competitors* © 1980, Free Press, 1980, p. 4. Copyright by The Free Press, a division of Simon & Schuster Inc. Reproduced with permission.

- Understanding the *connections* between competitive forces and the key drivers in the macro-environment (see section 2.1 above) is essential. For example, technological changes can destroy many of the competitive advantages and barriers that have protected organisations historically. In the public services the same could be true with political changes (such as a new government).

- The five forces are *not independent* of each other. Pressures from one direction can trigger off changes in another in a dynamic process of shifting sources of competition. For example, potential new entrants finding themselves blocked may find new routes to market by bypassing traditional distribution channels and selling directly to consumers.

- Competitive behaviour may be concerned with *disrupting* these forces and not simply accommodating them. This dynamic picture of competition will be discussed more fully in section 2.3.3.

Bearing these *caveats* in mind, the five forces is a useful starting point in understanding competitive forces.

The threat of entry

Threat of entry will depend on the extent to which there are **barriers to entry**. These are factors that need to be overcome by new entrants if they are to compete successfully. These should been seen as providing *delays* to entry and not as permanent barriers to determined potential entrants. They may deter some potential entrants but not others. Typical barriers are as follows:

Barriers to entry are factors that need to be overcome by new entrants if they are to compete successfully

- *Economies of scale.* In some industries, economies of scale are extremely important: for example, in the production of automobiles, in distribution (e.g. brewing) or in sales and marketing (e.g. advertising costs for fast-moving consumer goods). Globalisation is often driven by such global advantages as discussed above. But the economically viable scale is falling in many industries through changing 'business models'. For example, internet banking requires only 10,000 customers to be viable (particularly if they are from a profitable niche). This erodes this particular barrier to entry.

- *The capital requirement of entry.* The capital cost of entry will vary according to technology and scale. The cost of setting up a dot.com business with leased premises is minimal when compared with the cost of, for example, entering capital-intensive industries such as chemicals, power or mining. Globalisation can also leave some companies vulnerable to entrants from overseas whose cost of capital is lower.

- *Access to supply or distribution channels.* In many industries manufacturers have had control over supply and/or distribution channels. Sometimes this has been through direct ownership (vertical integration); sometimes just customer or supplier loyalty. In some industries this barrier has been overcome by new entrants who have bypassed retail distributors and sold directly to consumers through e-commerce (for example, Dell Computers and Amazon).

- *Customer or supplier loyalty.* It is difficult for a competitor to break into an industry if there are one or more established operators that know the industry well and have good relationships with the key buyers and suppliers.

- *Experience.* Early entrants into an industry gain experience sooner than others. This can give them advantage in terms of cost and/or customer/supplier loyalty. (This phenomenon is related to the concept of the 'experience curve' and is dealt with in more detail in Chapter 3 (section 3.3 and Exhibit 3.4).) Of course, this experience will be less valuable when product life cycles are shortening and may be of no value at all when a major discontinuity occurs. The opening up of the public services in many countries to competitive forces is a good example of how the accumulated experience of negotiating with the providers of funds was rapidly eroded by a lack of experience in 'customer care'.

- *Expected retaliation.* If an organisation considering entering an industry believes that the retaliation of an existing firm will be so great as to prevent entry, or mean that entry would be too costly, this is also a barrier. Entering the breakfast cereal industry to compete with Kellogg's would be unwise unless very careful attention was paid to a strategy to avoid retaliation. This dynamic interaction between incumbents and potential new entrants will be discussed more fully in section 2.3.3 below. In global markets this retaliation can take place at many different 'points' or locations.

● *Legislation or government action.* Legal restraints on competition vary from patent protection, to regulation of markets (e.g. pharmaceuticals and insurance), through to direct government action. Of course, managers in hitherto protected environments might face the pressures of competition for the first time if governments remove such protection. For example, in the 1990s many public services such as telecommunications, electricity and gas supply and rail systems, traditionally operated as state monopolies, increasingly faced deregulation and/or privatisation.

● *Differentiation.* By differentiation is meant the provision of a product or service regarded by the user as higher perceived value than the competition; its importance will be discussed more fully in Chapter 5. *Product range* can create differentiation if customers are concerned to buy a package rather than separate items. In project-based industries such as construction this can be important. However, differentiation may be eroded if competitors can imitate the offering and/or reduce customer loyalty.

Illustration 2.5 shows the barriers to entry and the other competitive forces in the mobile phone industry.

The threat of substitutes

Substitution reduces demand for a particular 'class' of products as customers switch to the alternatives

Substitution reduces demand for a particular 'class' of products as customers switch to the alternatives – even to the extent that this class of products or services becomes obsolete. This depends on whether a substitute provides a higher perceived benefit or value. Substitution may take different forms:

● There could be *product-for-product substitution* – for example, e-mail substituting for a postal service. This may be because previously different sectors are converging, as mentioned above. There may also be other organisations that are *complementors*[14] – meaning that they have products and services that make an organisation's products more competitive – and vice versa. This drives the need to substitute current products regularly with new (better) generations of product in both organisations. Intel and Microsoft would have such a relationship. More processing capability fuels demand for a better operating system and applications software which in turn creates demand for more processing speed and so on.

● There may be *substitution of need* by a new product or service, rendering an existing product or service redundant. For example, more reliable and cheaper domestic appliances reducing the need for maintenance and repair services. IT is already impacting significantly in this area – giving individuals the tools to undertake jobs themselves for which they previously needed a service provider (e.g. from secretarial services or printing, through to e-commerce transactions).

● *Generic substitution* occurs where products or services compete for disposable income; for example, furniture manufacturers compete for available household expenditure with (amongst others) suppliers of televisions, videos, cookers,

Illustration 2.5

strategy into action

The mobile phone industry

Five forces analysis provides an understanding of the competitive nature of an industry.

Competitive rivalry

By 2004 the competitive rivalry between network operators was becoming intense in most countries. In the UK numerous different packages were on offer. Initially if a customer threatened to withdraw, operators would offer a new free phone and several free months of line rental as an enticement to stay. However, as markets matured, emphasis was placed on price, coverage, general customer service and the offering of new products and services (with the advent of 3G technology).

Buying power

Buying power of consumers was high as they had so much choice. The danger for providers was confusing potential customers with over-complex offers. Independent retailers (e.g. in the UK Carphone Warehouse) competed with those owned by network operators (e.g. Vodafone). Others offered cheaper deals through newspaper adverts and the internet.

Power of suppliers

Equipment manufacturers competed for market share. Prior to 3G launch the big manufacturers – Nokia, Motorola and Ericsson – had concerns about market saturation. Supplier power was increasing as their sector consolidated through alliances (such as Casio and Hitachi in 2003). Network operators could be held back by supply difficulties as with the Hutchison (3-UK) launch of 3G services in 2003/4.

Threat of substitutes

In the 1990s the main threat of substitution was 'technological regression' where customers returned to fixed-line telephony because of high mobile call charges. By 2000 price decreases and the 'need' for everyone to have a mobile phone reduced this threat. By 2004 the greatest threat was the convergence of mobile telephony with PDAs (Personal Digital Assistants) and with the internet (e.g. MSN Messenger). This could switch both voice and text messaging onto the internet – avoiding mobile phone operator networks. Location technology in mobile phones (making the caller easy to find) might encourage this 'drift'.

Threat of entry

The threat of entrants was low because of the enormous cost in both licences (£22bn (€33bn) in the UK alone) and in the general investment needed to be a player in new 3G (broadband) technology. Power was a function of who was ahead of the game in 3G and had the licences to operate a service. There was only a threat of entrants if public policy towards this heavy regulation of the sector changed in future.

Prepared by Jill Shepherd, Graduate Business School, University of Strathclyde.

Questions

Viewing this industry through the eyes of a network operator (such as Vodaphone):

1. Which would you regard as the three most important threats to your business?
2. How could you respond to each of these to lessen their impact?
3. Answer questions 1 and 2 for an equipment manufacturer – such as Nokia.
4. What are the main benefits and limitations of five forces analysis?

cars and holidays. So some industries suffer because consumers decide to 'do without' and spend their money elsewhere. In the public sector different services (education, health, defence etc.) compete for a share of public spending.

The power of buyers and suppliers

The next two forces can be considered together because they can have similar effects in constraining the strategic freedom of an organisation and in influencing the margins (and hence financial attractiveness) of that organisation. Collectively they represent the value network within which an organisation is operating. This is an important strategic concept that will be introduced in Chapter 3 (section 3.6.1). At this stage the discussion is confined to understanding the relative power of an organisation with its buyers and suppliers. This is likely to influence the profit potential of different parts of an industry (e.g. supply, manufacture and distribution).

Buyer power is likely to be high when some of the following conditions prevail:

- There is a *concentration of buyers*, particularly if the volumes purchased by buyers are high and/or the supplying industry comprises a large number of small operators. This is the case on items such as milk in the grocery sector in many European countries, where just a few retailers dominate the market. If a product or service accounts for a high percentage of the buyers' total purchases their power is also likely to increase as they are more likely to 'shop around' to get the best price and therefore 'squeeze' suppliers than they would for more trivial purchases.

- The *cost of switching* a supplier is low or involves little risk – for example, if there are no long-term contracts or supplier approval requirements. This also occurs in e-commerce transactions where buyers are more able to shop around quickly and with no risk.

- There is a threat of the *supplier being acquired by the buyer* and/or the buyer setting up in competition with the supplier. This is called backward integration and might occur if satisfactory prices or quality from suppliers cannot be obtained. For example, a few large window manufacturers in the USA and elsewhere have decided to produce their own glass putting pressure on the glass manufacturers when negotiating with other large customers.

Supplier power is likely to be high when:

- There is a *concentration of suppliers* rather than a fragmented source of supply. This is usually the case in the provision of finance by central government to public corporations such as the National Health Service or the BBC in the UK and has been seen as a major constraint to their development. Also, suppliers' power is increased if they have a wide range of customers, which reduces their dependence on any one customer.

- The *switching costs* from one supplier to another are high, perhaps because an organisation's processes are dependent on the specialist products of a supplier, as in the aerospace industry, or where a product is clearly differentiated – such as Microsoft products. The brand of the supplier may be powerful – for example, a retailer might not be able to do without a particular brand in its range.

- There is the possibility of the *suppliers competing directly* with their buyers (this is called forward integration) if they do not obtain the prices, and hence the margins, that they seek. The glass example from above is interesting since many glass manufacturers have done just this and have business units that further process and distribute glass as a merchant. This is also the case in the steel industry.

Competitive rivalry

These wider competitive forces (the four arrows in the model) will impinge on the direct competitive rivalry between an organisation and its most immediate rivals. **Competitive rivals** are organisations with similar products and services aimed at the same customer group. There are a number of factors that affect the degree of competitive rivalry in an industry or sector:

Competitive rivals are organisations with similar products and services aimed at the same customer group

- The extent to which competitors are *in balance*. Where competitors are of roughly equal size there is the danger of intense competition as one competitor attempts to gain dominance over another. Conversely, less competitive industries tend to be those with one or two dominant organisations and where the smaller players have accommodated themselves to this situation (for example, by focusing their activities to avoid the 'attention' of the dominant companies).

- Industry *growth rates* may affect rivalry. The idea of the life cycle suggests that the stage of development of an industry or sector is important in terms of competitive behaviour. For example, in situations of growth, an organisation might expect to achieve its own growth through the growth in the marketplace; whereas when markets are mature, this has to be achieved by taking market share from competitors. Exhibit 2.6 summarises some of the conditions that can be expected at different stages in the life cycle.[15]

- *High fixed costs* in an industry, perhaps through capital intensity, may result in price wars and low margins if industry capacity exceeds demand as capacity-fill becomes a prerogative. If extra capacity can only be added in large increments (as in many manufacturing sectors, for example a steel or glass factory), the competitor making such an addition is likely to create short-term over-capacity in the industry and increased competition. For this reason in some industries competitive rivals collaborate on investment in new capacity through jointly owned plants. Sometimes rivals will collaborate to reduce fixed costs.[16] For example, if airlines are wishing to 'sponsor' a new aeroplane from Boeing or Airbus it is to their mutual advantage to create sufficient volume of potential orders to make the development viable for the plane builder.

- Where there are *high exit barriers* to an industry, there is again likely to be the persistence of excess capacity and, consequently, increased competition. Exit barriers might be high for a variety of reasons. For example, high investment in non-transferable fixed assets (very common for manufacturing companies) or high redundancy costs.

- *Differentiation* can, again, be important. In a commodity market, where products or services are undifferentiated, there is little to stop customers switching between competitors increasing rivalry.

Exhibit 2.6   The life-cycle model

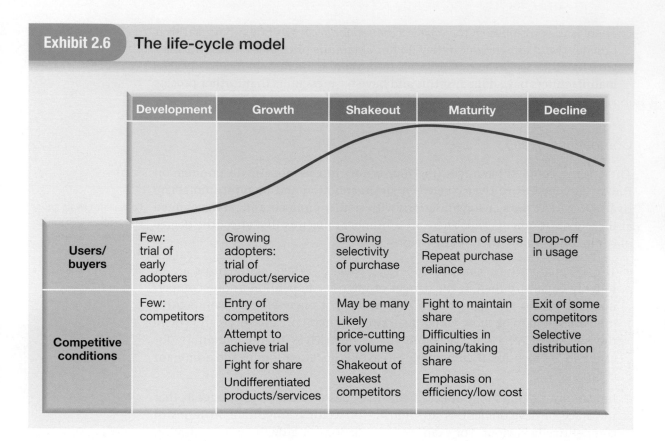

	Development	Growth	Shakeout	Maturity	Decline
Users/ buyers	Few: trial of early adopters	Growing adopters: trial of product/service	Growing selectivity of purchase	Saturation of users Repeat purchase reliance	Drop-off in usage
Competitive conditions	Few: competitors	Entry of competitors Attempt to achieve trial Fight for share Undifferentiated products/services	May be many Likely price-cutting for volume Shakeout of weakest competitors	Fight to maintain share Difficulties in gaining/taking share Emphasis on efficiency/low cost	Exit of some competitors Selective distribution

Key questions arising from the five forces framework

The five forces framework can be used to gain insights into the forces at work in the industry environment of an SBU which need particular attention in the development of strategy. It is important to use the framework for more than simply listing the forces. The following questions help focus on the *implications* of these forces:

● Are some industries more *attractive* than others? This was the original purpose of the five forces model, the argument being that an industry is attractive (in terms of profit potential) when the forces are weak. For example, if entry is difficult, suppliers and/or buyers have little power and rivalry is low.

● What are the *underlying forces* in the macro-environment that are driving the competitive forces? For example, the lower labour costs for software and service operators located in India are both an opportunity and a threat to European and US companies. So five forces needs to be linked to PESTEL as mentioned earlier.

● Is it likely that the forces will *change*, and if so, how? For example, pharmaceutical businesses built strong market positions on their expertise in marketing branded drugs to a highly fragmented set of buyers – the doctors. However, government action in many countries, such as the promotion of generic drugs and the introduction of new treatment protocols, buying procedures and price regulation, has had the effect of significantly increasing competitive pressures on such firms and forcing them to reconsider their competitive strategies.

- How do particular *competitors* stand in relation to these competitive forces? What are their strengths and weaknesses in relation to the key forces at work?

- What can managers do to *influence* the competitive forces affecting an SBU? Can barriers to entry be built, power over suppliers or buyers increased, or ways found to diminish competitive rivalry? These are the fundamental questions relating to *competitive strategy* and will be a major concern of Chapter 6.

2.3.2 The dynamics of competition[17]

The previous section has looked at how competition might arise but has not discussed the process of competition *over time*. The competitive advantage of an organisation may be eroded because the forces discussed above change and/or competitors manage to overcome adverse forces. This process of erosion may be speeded up by changes in the macro-environment such as new technologies, globalisation or deregulation. So advantage may be *temporary* – though the speed at which erosion occurs will differ between sectors and over time. Organisations may then respond to this erosion of their competitive position, creating what has been called a *cycle of competition* as shown in Exhibit 2.7 and exemplified in Illustration 2.6.

Exhibit 2.7	Cycles of competition

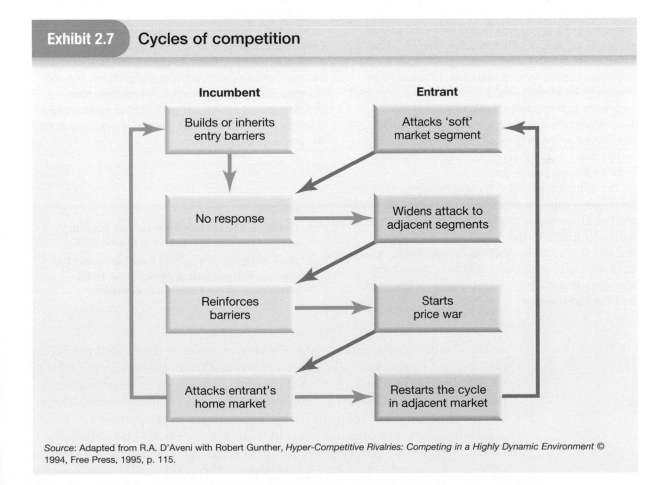

Source: Adapted from R.A. D'Aveni with Robert Gunther, *Hyper-Competitive Rivalries: Competing in a Highly Dynamic Environment* © 1994, Free Press, 1995, p. 115.

Illustration 2.6

Cycles of competition

Changes in the business environment and moves by competitors erode the competitive position of organisations which, in turn, respond by countermoves. Competition moves through cycles and any competitive advantage is temporary.

A market leader in a consumer goods sector of the French market, having achieved significant barriers to entry, was enjoying the benefits of good financial returns. This success attracted the attention of a German consumer goods company that was wishing to become a significant European-wide player (see Exhibit 2.7).

The German's first competitive move was to target a consumer age group where consumption and brand awareness were both low. The French had limited their marketing efforts to the over–25 age groups – the Germans saw a possibility of extending the market into the 18–25 group and aimed their promotional efforts at the group with some success. This first move was ignored by the French company as it did not impact on its current business. However, from this bridgehead the second move was to attack the segments (age groups) covered by the French. This triggered a competitive response to contain the entrant to the original niche. It did this by an advertising campaign reinforcing brand awareness in its traditional segments.

The entrant responded by counter-advertising and price reductions – undermining the margins earned by the French company. Competition then escalated with a counter-attack by the French into the German market. This wider competitive activity played itself out resulting in the erosion of both of the original strongholds and a progressive merger of the French and German markets.

It is possible at this stage that this whole cycle of competition could have repeated itself in an adjacent market, such as the UK. However, what happened was that the German firm saw an opportunity to move away from this *cost/quality* basis of competition by adapting the product for use by businesses. Its core competences in R&D allowed it to get the adapted product to market faster than its French rival. It then consolidated these first-mover advantages by building and defending barriers. For example, it appointed key account salesmen and gave special offers for early adoption and three-year contracts.

However, this stronghold came under attack by the French firm and a cycle of competition similar to the consumer market described above was triggered off; but the German firm had built up significant financial reserves to survive a price war, which they then initiated. It was willing and able to fund losses longer than the French competitor – which was forced to exit the business user market.

Questions

1. Could the French firm have slowed down the cycle of competition shown in Exhibit 2.7?

2. How could the French firm have prevented the German firm escalating competition, to its advantage, in the business user market?

The illustration also shows that the cycle may result in the escalation of competition on to a new basis. The various moves and countermoves on the basis of cost/quality competition (Exhibit 2.7) resulted in one player shifting the competition into adjacent markets. For large global organisations another consideration about the dynamics of competition is also illustrated in Illustration 2.6. Moves and countermoves by organisations and their competitors may take place simultaneously in several locations. So a competitive move in one arena, the German company's aggressive move into France, did not trigger off a countermove in that arena (France) but in its competitor's home territory (Germany). So the competitive dynamics between these two organisations needs to be understood as multi-point competition. There is some evidence that multi-point competition can reduce the competitive rivalry by raising the costs and risks of these moves and countermoves[18] – say in the airline industry.

It is important to understand the *speed* at which these cycles of competition might move. If the process is relatively slow then there may be significant periods of time when competition in an industry settles down to a well-established pattern. In contrast, where the speed of the cycle is very high,[19] this has been called *hypercompetition*.

Hypercompetition occurs where the frequency, boldness and aggressiveness of dynamic movements by competitors accelerate to create a condition of constant disequilibrium and change. The implications of how competition is understood and how organisations might respond are extremely important. Whereas competition in slower-moving environments is primarily concerned with building and sustaining competitive advantages that are difficult to imitate, hypercompetitive environments require organisations to acknowledge that advantages will be temporary. Competition may also be about disrupting the *status quo* so that no one is able to sustain long-term advantage on any given basis. So longer-term competitive advantage is gained through a sequence of short-lived moves. The ways in which market conditions can influence competitive moves will be discussed in section 5.5.

It should be noted that some research evidence shows that overall markets are *not* becoming more hypercompetitive[20] – although this does not diminish the benefit of understanding the concept.

> **Hypercompetition** occurs where the frequency, boldness and aggressiveness of dynamic movements by competitors accelerate to create a condition of constant disequilibrium and change

2.4   COMPETITORS AND MARKETS

An industry or sector may be a too-general level to provide for a detailed understanding of competition. For example, Ford and Morgan Cars are in the same industry (automobiles) but are they competitors? The former is a publicly quoted multinational business; the latter is owned by a British family, produces about 500 cars a year and concentrates on a specialist market niche where customers want hand-built cars and are prepared to wait up to four years for one. In a given industry there may be many companies each of which has different capabilities and which compete on different bases. This is the concept of *strategic groups*. But competition occurs in markets which are not confined to the boundaries of an industry and there will almost certainly be important differences in the expectations of different customer groups. This is the concept of *market segments*. What links these two issues is an understanding of what *customers value*. These three concepts will now be discussed.

2.4.1 Strategic groups[21]

Strategic groups are organisations within an industry or sector with similar strategic characteristics, following similar strategies or competing on similar bases.

> **Strategic groups** are organisations within an industry with similar strategic characteristics, following similar strategies or competing on similar bases

| Exhibit 2.8 | Some characteristics for identifying strategic groups |

It is useful to consider the extent to which organisations *differ* in terms of **characteristics** such as:

Scope of activities

- Extent of product (or service) diversity
- Extent of geographical coverage
- Number of market segments served
- Distribution channels used

Resource commitment

- Extent (number) of **branding**
- **Marketing effort** (e.g. advertising spread, size of salesforce)
- Extent of **vertical integration**
- Product or service **quality**
- **Technological leadership** (a leader or follower)
- **Size** of organisation

Sources: Based on M.E. Porter, *Competitive Strategy*, Free Press, 1980; and J. McGee and H. Thomas, 'Strategic groups: theory, research and taxonomy', *Strategic Management Journal*, vol. 7, no. 2 (1986), pp. 141–160.

These characteristics are different from those in other strategic groups in the same industry or sector. For example, in grocery retailing, supermarkets, convenience stores and corner shops are three of the strategic groups. There may be many different characteristics that distinguish between strategic groups but these can be grouped into two major categories (see Exhibit 2.8).[22] First, the *scope* of an organisation's activities (such as product range, geographical coverage and range of distribution channels used). Second, the *resource commitment* (such as brands, marketing spend and extent of vertical integration). Which of these characteristics are especially relevant in terms of a given industry needs to be understood in terms of the history and development of that industry and the forces at work in the environment. In Illustration 2.7, Figure 1 shows a strategic group map of the major providers of MBAs in The Netherlands in 2004.

This concept is useful in several ways:

- It helps understand who are the *most direct competitors* of any given organisation. Also it focuses on what is the basis of competitive rivalry within each strategic group and how this is different from one group to another. For example, traditional universities were competing on the value of their degrees and their research record.

● It raises the question of how likely or possible it is for an organisation to *move* from one strategic group to another. Mobility between groups depends on the extent to which there are barriers to entry between one group and another. In Illustration 2.7, Figure 2 shows examples of mobility barriers for the groupings identified in the industry. These may be substantial.

● In identifying potential opportunities and threats to organisations. Some strategic groups may be more competitively intense than others. Or, as in Illustration 2.7, Figure 3, changes in the macro-environment – particularly IT and the globalisation of companies – are creating *strategic 'spaces'*; for example, for local providers (say a polytechnic) to strike a strategic alliance with an American or British business school that provides students with content over the internet whilst receiving tutorial support locally.

2.4.2 Market segments

The concept of strategic groups discussed above helps with understanding the similarities and differences in the characteristics of 'producers' – those organisations that are actual or potential competitors. However, the success or failure of organisations is also concerned with how well they understand customer needs and are able to meet those needs. So an understanding of markets is crucial. In most markets there is a wide diversity of customers' needs, so the concept of market segments can be useful in identifying similarities and differences between groups of customers or users. A **market segment**[23] is a group of customers who have similar needs that are different from customer needs in other parts of the market. It will be seen in Chapter 3 that this understanding of what customers (and other stakeholders) value and how an organisation and its competitors are positioned to meet these needs is a critical element in understanding strategic capability.

*A **market segment** is a group of customers who have similar needs that are different from customer needs in other parts of the market*

The concept of market segments should remind managers of several important issues:

● *Customer needs* may vary for a whole variety of reasons – some of which are identified in Exhibit 2.9. Theoretically, any of these factors could be used to identify market segments. However, in practical terms it is important to consider which bases of segmentation are most important in any particular market. For example, in industrial markets, segmentation is often thought of in terms of industrial classification of buyers – such as 'we sell to the domestic appliance industry'. However, it may be that this is not the most relevant basis of segmentation when thinking about the future. Segmentation by buyer behaviour (for example, direct buying versus those users who buy through third parties such as contractors) or purchase value (for example, high-value bulk purchasers versus frequent low-value purchasers) might be more appropriate in some markets. Indeed, it is often useful to consider different bases of segmentation in the same market to help understand the dynamics of that market and how these are changing. Illustration 2.8 shows three different examples of how companies have concentrated on particular segments in order to get a dominant position.

Illustration 2.7

Strategic groups in Dutch MBA education

Mapping of strategic groups can provide insights into the competitive structures of industries or sectors and the opportunities and constraints for development.

In the mid-2000s there were three kinds of institutions offering MBA courses in The Netherlands: traditional universities, for-profit business schools (FPBSs), and polytechnics.

● Traditional universities offered a wide range of subjects, carried out research, and attracted students both nationally and internationally. Their programmes were more academic than vocational. A university degree was generally valued more highly than that of a polytechnic.

● FPBSs were relatively new, and provided MBA degrees only. Usually they were located close to the centre or capital of the country. MBA education at FPBSs was generally more of the action learning type, which made it attractive for practising managers. Many students already had diplomas from a university or polytechnic. Several of these schools received accreditation from the Dutch Validation Council.

● Polytechnics (in The Netherlands named HogeScholen) often attracted students from the region and provided education more aimed at application of theory than at developing conceptual

thinking. Some of the polytechnics provided MBA degrees, in some cases in cooperation with universities in the UK.

Figure 1 gives an indication of how these three types of institution were positioned in terms of geographical coverage and 'orientation'. Figure 2 shows the barriers confronting organisations who wished to move from one group to another (they show the barriers *into* a group). For example, if the FPBSs tried to 'enter' the strategic group of traditional universities they would need to build up a reputation in research or innovation. They may not be interested in doing research, since there would be high costs and little pay-off for their effort. In reverse, for traditional universities to move in the direction of the FPBSs may be difficult since the faculty may not have skills in action learning and may be inexperienced at working with older students.

Figure 3 shows where 'strategic space' might exist. These spaces are created by changes in the macro-environment – particularly globalisation and information technology. This could provide opportunities for Dutch business schools to seek more international business. However, the reverse

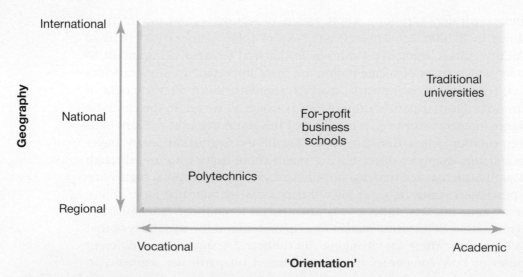

Figure 1 Strategic groups in MBA education in The Netherlands

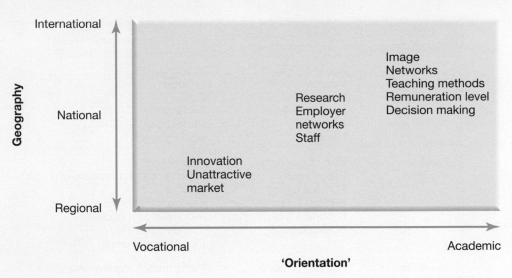

Figure 2 Mobility barriers

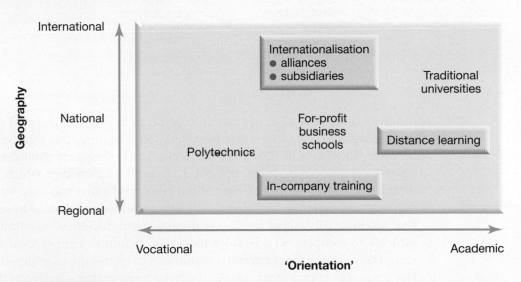

Figure 3 Strategic space

threat of international competitors entering the Dutch market was a major concern. Information and communication technology helps students study at their own place of work or at home, and also enables them to tap into an international network. So an American or British school could provide content over the internet and local student support through partnerships with Dutch institutions. Indeed the University of Phoenix had already made efforts to do just this.

Source: This is an updated version of J. Eppink and S. de Waal, 'Global influences on the public sector', in G. Johnson and K. Scholes (eds), *Exploring Public Sector Strategy*, FT/Prentice Hall, 2001, chapter 3.

Question

How might this analysis influence the next strategic moves by each of the three types of institution?

Exhibit 2.9	Some bases of market segmentation

Type of factor	Consumer markets	Industrial/ organisational markets
Characteristics of people/ organisations	Age, sex, race Income Family size Life-cycle stage Location Lifestyle	Industry Location Size Technology Profitability Management
Purchase/use situation	Size of purchase Brand loyalty Purpose of use Purchasing behaviour Importance of purchase Choice criteria	Application Importance of purchase Volume Frequency of purchase Purchasing procedure Choice criteria Distribution channel
Users' needs and preferences for product characteristics	Product similarity Price preference Brand preferences Desired features Quality	Performance requirements Assistance from suppliers Brand preferences Desired features Quality Service requirements

- *Relative market share* (that is, share in relation to that of competitors) within a market segment is an important consideration. Organisations that have built up most experience in servicing a particular market segment should not only have lower costs in so doing, but also have built relationships which may be difficult for others to break down. What customers value will vary by market segment and therefore 'producers' are likely to achieve advantage in segments that are especially suited to their particular strengths. They may find it very difficult to compete on a broader basis. For example, a small local brewery competing against the big brands on the basis of its low prices underpinned by low costs of distribution and marketing is confined to that segment of the local market that values low price.

- How market segments can be *identified and 'serviced'*[24] is influenced by a number of trends in the business environment already discussed in this chapter. For example, the wide availability of consumer data and the ability to process it electronically combined with increased flexibility of companies' operations allow segmentation to be undertaken at a micro-level – even down to individual consumers. So internet shopping selectively targets consumers with special offers based on their past purchasing patterns. The emergence of more affluent, mobile consumers means that geographical segmentation may be much less effective than lifestyle segmentation (across national boundaries).

Illustration 2.8 strategy into action

Bases for identifying market segments

Markets can be segmented in many different ways but this must always relate to customer need.

OnScreen™ displays

In November 2003 New Millennium Media International announced the details of a market segmentation analysis undertaken by Principia Partners. The company was an advertising-media company specialising in motion display advertising based on LED technology. It was about to launch an advanced new product called OnScreen™. The analysis suggested segmentation by customer use and identified the following major segments: retail signage/billboards, transportation (large-scale displays in airports, rail stations etc.), indoor arenas, outdoor events, financial exchanges and rental and mobile markets. These were all sub-categories of the overall signage/display markets – but represented the segments where the particular features of OnScreen™ would be especially valued by customers.

Saga

Founded in 1951 Saga gained national attention by providing affordable holidays and tours for British pensioners – particularly offering 'off-season' deals. This was so successful that the company soon developed into a full-service travel company aiming at the older customer (the over-50s). The holidays on offer were described as for those who are 'mature in years but young at heart'. Saga opened up in Boston, USA, in 1979.

Progressively the company expanded its portfolio of activities as it became clear that this group was growing in size and also becoming more affluent. By the mid-2000s, as well as its travel services the company offered a wide range of insurance services, a credit card, share dealing and investments and provided information and products relating to health – such as medical insurance and food supplements.

You could buy a new car online with Saga. It also provided a telephone service and was an Internet Service Provider. It had a long established magazine and even its own radio station in several parts of the UK.

ICI

In 2003 Imperial Chemical Industries (ICI) was a £6bn (≈ €8.5bn) business manufacturing paints and speciality chemical products (e.g. flavours, fragrances, starches, adhesives). The company had about one third of its sales in each of the UK and USA. Of the remaining third the company had a growing presence in Asia. In a 'strategic update' published in late 2003 the company indicated that the balance and development of its business was to be determined by market opportunities – both by product group and by geography. It categorised these market opportunities into four types using two dimensions (grow/maintain and aggressively/selectively) – which indicated the strategy to be followed. Importantly the geographical segmentation showed major opportunities for aggressive growth in Asia for most product groups.

Sources: Business Wire, 12 November 2003: Saga website; *Regulatory News*, 30 October, 2003: ICI website.

Questions

1. What was the basis of identifying market segments in each of the three examples and why was it useful?

2. What were the dangers of each company's approach?

2.4.3 Identifying the strategic customer

Bringing goods and services to market usually involves a range of 'players' performing different roles. In Chapter 3 this will be discussed in more detail through the concept of the value network. For example, most consumers purchase goods through retail outlets. So the manufacturers have two 'customers' – the shops and the shops' customers. Although both customers influence demand usually one of these will be more influential than the others – this is the strategic customer. The **strategic customer** is the person(s) at whom the strategy is primarily addressed because they have the most influence over which goods or services are purchased. Unless you are clear on who the strategic customer is, you end up analysing and targeting the wrong people because in many markets the strategic customer acts as a 'gatekeeper' to the end user. So there has to be an understanding of what is valued by that strategic customer as a starting point for strategy. This does not mean that the requirements of the other customers are unimportant – they have to be met. But the requirements of the strategic customer are of paramount importance. Returning to the example, it should be clear that for many consumer goods the retail outlet is the strategic customer as the way it displays, promotes and supports products in store is hugely influential on the final consumer preferences. But internet shopping may change this pattern putting the final consumer back as the strategic customer. There are many instances where the strategic customer does not use the product themselves. Purchasing of gifts is an obvious example. Also within organisations managers are buying plant, equipment, software on behalf of those who use them in organisations – they are the strategic customer – but not the user. In the public sector the strategic customer is very often the 'body' who controls the funds or authorises use rather than the user of the service. So family doctors are the strategic customers of pharmaceutical companies and so on.

> The **strategic customer** is the person(s) at whom the strategy is primarily addressed because they have the most influence over which goods or services are purchased

2.4.4 Understanding what customers value – critical success factors

Although the concept of market segments is useful, managers may fail to be realistic about how markets are segmented and the strategic implications of that segmentation. It will be seen in the next chapter that an understanding of customer needs and how they differ between segments is crucial to developing the appropriate strategic capability in an organisation. However, customers will value many product/service features to a greater or lesser degree. From the potential providers' viewpoint it is valuable to understand which features are of particular importance to a group of customers (market segment). These are known as the critical success factors. **Critical success factors** (CSFs) are those product features that are particularly valued by a group of customers and, therefore, where the organisation must excel to outperform competition.

> **Critical success factors** (CSFs) are those product features that are particularly valued by a group of customers and, therefore, where the organisation must excel to outperform competition

   The extent to which the offerings of different providers address the factors valued by customers can be visualised by creating a strategy canvas[25] (see Exhibit 2.10). It is a simple but useful way of comparing differences between customers (market segments) with differences between providers (strategic groups), both of which have been discussed above. The exhibit relates to one segment of

| Exhibit 2.10 | A strategy canvas – perceived value by customers in the electrical engineering industry |

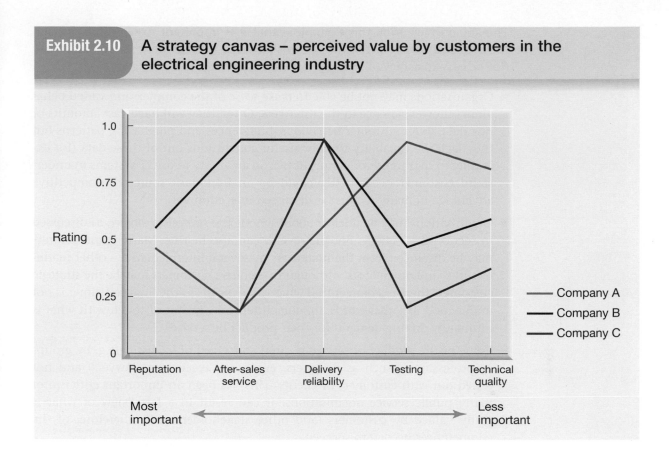

the electrical engineering industry – company-based buyers of electrical engineering equipment – and illustrates the following:

- In this market segment there were many factors valued by customers, most of which were taken for granted (for example, that the product is fit for its purpose). These are the *threshold* product features which would be expected from any provider into this segment.

- The factors shown in Exhibit 2.10 (the reputation of a producer, after-sales service, delivery reliability, testing facilities and technical quality) were seen as particularly important by customers. They were the factors which would determine which provider was preferred (from amongst those that met the threshold requirements). Indeed, reputation, after-sales service and reliable delivery were *especially* valued by customers in this segment. So from the potential providers' viewpoint these are the *critical success factors*.

- The exhibit profiles *different providers* against these factors that customers value. For example, it is clear that the particular strengths that company A possesses are not the factors *most* valued by customers; whereas B's strengths appear to have a better match.

- This provides a link into the issues of *strategic capability* discussed in Chapter 3. For example, company A needs to consider if it should attempt to switch its resources to improve customer service and delivery. Alternatively, it might focus on a different market segment in which customers value technical features more.

The key message from this example is that it is important to see value through the eyes of the customer. Although this might be a self-evident statement, it may not be easy to achieve this for several reasons:

- Organisations may not be able to *make sense* of the complex and varied behaviours they experience in their markets. Often they will have vast amounts of raw data about customer behaviour, preferences and purchasing patterns but they lack the capability to draw useful conclusions out of these data (for example, to spot trends or connections). So an ability to use IT systems to understand customer needs better could be an important source of competitive advantage in many sectors (as discussed in section 9.3).

- Organisations may be unclear about who is the *strategic customer*, as discussed in section 2.4.3 above. But the reverse can also be true. Many manufacturers may be distanced from the final users by several intermediaries – other manufacturers and distributors. Although these direct customers may be the strategic customers there is a danger that what value means to the final consumer is not understood. In other words, manufacturers may be out of touch with what is ultimately driving demand for their product or service.

- Value of the product or service is often conceived of *internally* (e.g. by groups of professionals such as designers, engineers, teachers or lawyers) and not tested out with customers or clients. This has been an important criticism of many public service organisations. It can result in a false view of what is really valued by customers (and other stakeholders) and, therefore, of the competences needed to succeed.

- Customers' concept of value *changes over time* – either because they become more experienced (through repeat purchase) or because competitive offerings become available which offer better value. The concept of the product life cycle discussed earlier (see Exhibit 2.6) also suggests that conditions in markets change over time in terms of customer behaviour.

2.5 OPPORTUNITIES AND THREATS

The concepts and frameworks discussed above should be helpful in understanding the factors in the macro-, industry and competitor/market environments of an organisation. However, the critical issue is the *implications* that are drawn from this understanding in guiding strategic decisions and choices. There is usually a need to understand in a more detailed way how this collection of environmental factors might influence strategic success or failure. This can be done in more than one way. This identification of opportunities and threats can be extremely valuable when thinking about strategic choices for the future (see Chapters 5, 6 and 7). (Illustration 2.9 outlines a key debate: just how much do such industry and market factors affect successful strategic outcomes?)

2.5.1 Strategic gaps

Kim and Mauborgne[26] have argued that if organisations simply concentrate on competing head-to-head with competitive rivals this will lead to competitive convergence where all 'players' find the environment tough and threatening. They have encouraged managers to seek out opportunities in the business environment which they call strategic gaps. A **strategic gap** is an opportunity in the competitive environment that is not being fully exploited by competitors. By using some of the frameworks described in this chapter, managers can begin to identify opportunities to gain competitive advantage in this way:

A **strategic gap** is an opportunity in the competitive environment that is not being fully exploited by competitors

Opportunities in substitute industries

Organisations face competition from industries that are producing substitutes, as discussed in section 2.3.2 above. But substitution also provides opportunities. In order to identify gaps a *realistic* assessment has to be made of the relative merits of the products/technologies (incumbent and potential substitutes) *in the eyes of the customer*. An example would be software companies substituting electronic versions of reference books and atlases for the traditional paper versions. The paper versions have more advantages than meet the eye: no hardware requirement (hence greater portability) and the ability to browse are two important benefits. This means that software producers need to design features to counter the strengths of the paper versions; for example, the search features in the software. Of course, as computer hardware develops into a new generation of portable handheld devices, this particular shortcoming of electronic versions might be rectified.

Opportunities in other strategic groups or strategic spaces

It is also possible to identify opportunities by looking across strategic groups – particularly if changes in the macro-environment make new market spaces economically viable. For example, deregulation of markets (say in electricity generation and distribution) and advances in IT (say with educational study programmes) could both create new market gaps. In the first case, the locally based smaller-scale generation of electricity becomes viable – possibly linked to waste incineration plants. In the latter case, geography can be 'shrunk' and educational programmes delivered across continents through the internet and teleconferencing (together with local tutorial support). New strategic groups emerge in these industries/sectors.

Opportunities in the chain of buyers

Sections 2.4.3 and 2.4.4 above emphasised that identifying who is the strategic customer is critically important. It was also noted that this can be confusing, as there may be several people involved in the overall purchase decision. The user is one party but they may not buy the product themselves. There may be other influencers on the purchase decision too. Importantly, each of these parties may

Illustration 2.9 key debate

How much does industry matter?

A good start in strategy must be to choose a profitable industry to compete in. But does simply being in the right industry matter more than having the right kinds of skills and resources?

This chapter has focused on the role of the environment in strategy-making, with particular regard to industries. But the importance of industries in determining organisational performance has been challenged in recent years. This has led to a debate about whether strategy-making should be externally-orientated, starting with the environment, or internally-orientated, starting with the organisation's own skills and resources (the focus of Chapter 3).[1]

Managers favouring an external approach look primarily *outside* the organisation, for example building market share in their industries through mergers and acquisitions or aggressive marketing. Managers favouring an internal approach concentrate their attention *inside* the organisation, fostering the skills of their people or nurturing technologies, for example. Because managerial time is limited, there is a real trade-off to be made between external and internal approaches.

The chief advocate of the external approach is Michael Porter, Professor at Harvard Business School and founder of the Monitor Consulting Group. An influential sceptic of this approach is Richard Rumelt, a student at Harvard Business School but now at University of California Los Angeles. Porter, Rumelt

and others have done a series of empirical studies examining the relative importance of industries in explaining organisations' performance.

Typically, these studies take a large sample of firms and compare the extent to which variance in profitability is due to firms or industries (controlling for other effects such as size). If firms within the same industry tend to bunch together in terms of profitability, it is industry that is accounting for the greater proportion of profitability: an external approach to strategy is supported. If firms within the same industry vary widely in terms of profitability, it is the specific skills and resources of the firms that matter most: an internal approach is most appropriate.

The two most important studies in fact find that more of the variance in profitability is due to firms rather than industries – firms account for 47 per cent in Rumelt's study of manufacturing (see the figure).[2] However, when Porter and McGahan included service industries as well as manufacturing, they found a larger industry effect (19 per cent).[3]

The implication from this work is that firm-specific factors generally influence profitability more than industry factors. Firms need to attend carefully to their own skills and resources. However, the greater

value different aspects of the product or service. These distinctions are often quite marked in business-to-business transactions, say with the purchase of capital equipment. The purchasing department may be looking for low prices and financial stability of suppliers. The user department (production) may place emphasis on special product features. Others – such as the marketing department – may be concerned with whether the equipment will speed throughput and reduce delivery times. By considering who is the 'most profitable buyer' an organisation may shift its view of the market and aim its promotion and selling at *those* 'buyers' with the intention of creating new strategic customers.

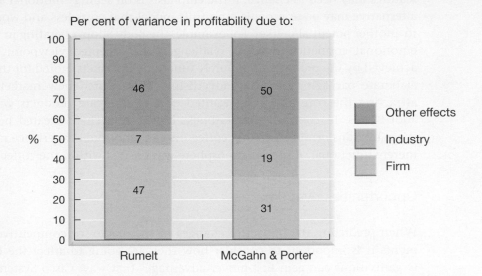

Per cent of variance in profitability due to:

industry effect found in Porter and McGahan's study of both manufacturing and services suggests that industry's importance varies strongly by industry. External influences can matter more in some industries than others.

Notes:
1. E.H. Bowman and C.E. Helfat, 'Does corporate strategy matter?', *Strategic Management Journal*, vol. 22, no. 1 (2001), pp. 1–14.
2. R.P. Rumelt, 'How much does industry matter?', *Strategic Management Journal*, vol. 12, no. 2 (1991), pp. 167–185.
3. M.E. Porter and A.M. McGahan, 'How much does industry matter really?', *Strategic Management Journal*, vol. 18, Summer Special Issue (1997), pp. 15–30; M.E. Porter and A.M. McGahan, 'The emergence and sustainability of abnormal profits', *Strategic Organization*, vol. 1, no. 1 (2003), pp. 79–108.

Question

Porter and McGahan's study suggests that some industries influence member firms' profitabilities more than others: in other words, their profitabilities bunch together. Why might some industries have a larger influence on their members' profitability than others?

Opportunities for complementary products and services

This involves a consideration of the potential value of complementary products and services. For example, in book retailing the overall 'book-buying experience' is much more than just stocking the right books. It also includes an ambience conducive to browsing (such as reading areas or coffee bars) and opening hours to suit busy customers. Crucially it could also be concerned with employing staff who are themselves 'book oriented' and can provide a book recommendation service.

Opportunities in new market segments

Looking for new market segments may provide opportunities but product/service features may need to change. If the emphasis is on selling emotional appeal, the alternative may be to provide a no-frills model that costs less and would appeal to another potential market. For example, the Body Shop, operating in the highly emotional cosmetics industry, challenged the accepted viewpoint. This was achieved by the production of purely functional products, noted for their lack of elaborate packaging or heavy advertising. This created new market space by attracting the consumer who wanted quality skin-care products without the added frills. In contrast, the Starbucks coffee-shop chain created new market space by transforming drinking coffee into an emotional experience rather than merely functional. A special atmosphere was created within the coffee bars.

Opportunities over time

When predicting the impact of changes in the macro- or competitive environments it is important to consider how they are going to affect the consumer. Organisations can gain first-mover advantages that way. Cisco Systems realised that the future was going to create a significant need for high-speed data exchange and was at the forefront of producing equipment to address this future need. It identified new market space because no one else had assessed the likely implications of the internet boom. This meant that it could offer specially designed products well ahead of its rivals, giving it an important competitive edge.

2.5.2 SWOT[27]

A **SWOT** analysis summarises the key issues from the business environment and the strategic capability of an organisation that are most likely to impact on strategy development

The key 'strategic messages' from both the business environment (this chapter) and concerning strategic capability (Chapter 3) can be summarised in the form of a SWOT analysis. A **SWOT** analysis summarises the key issues from the business environment and the strategic capability of an organisation that are most likely to impact on strategy development. This can be useful as a basis against which to judge future strategic choices, as seen in Chapters 5, 6 and 7. The aim is to identify the extent to which the current strengths and weaknesses are relevant to, and capable of, dealing with the threats or capitalising on the opportunities in the business environment. SWOT analysis will be discussed in section 3.6.4.

Summary

- *Environmental influences* and trends can be thought of as *layers* around an organisation. The most general layer is the macro-environment where an understanding of political, economic, social, technological, environmental and legal influences (PESTEL) can provide an overall picture of the variety of forces at work around an organisation. This can also cast light on the *key drivers of change* and provide the basis for examining the future impact of environmental forces on both industries (or sectors) and organisations within industries.

- When there are long-term strategic horizons but high levels of uncertainty around key environmental forces, *scenarios* can be a useful way of understanding the implications of these influences on strategy. This includes the need for organisations to be ready to face more than one situation in their future environment.

- Within the more general environment are *industries* or *sectors*. However, the boundaries of these are not sharp and change over time – for example, through the convergence of previously separate industries.

- *The five forces framework* helps with understanding the sources of competition within and around an industry especially in terms of barriers to entry, the power of buyers and suppliers, the threat of substitutes and the extent of competitive rivalry.

- The basis of competition within an industry is *dynamic*. The way in which competition is played out varies over time – sometimes changing very rapidly. This is called the *cycle of competition*. Some industries and sectors are characterised by rapid pace of change to the extent that competitive advantage on any particular basis will not last for any significant period of time. This is *hypercompetition* and the implications for organisations are significant. Since advantages may be temporary and quickly eroded, it is essential continuously to find new bases for competing. Long-term advantage may be sustained through a series of temporary advantages.

- Within an industry or sector *strategic groups* are usually found. These are organisations with similar strategic characteristics, following similar strategies or competing on similar bases. The success or failure of organisations is also concerned with how well they understand customer needs and are able to meet those needs. So an understanding of markets is important. The concept of *market segments* can be useful in understanding similarities and differences between groups of customers or users. It is especially important to understand what different customer groups particularly value – the *critical success factors*.

- *Opportunities* and *threats* arise in the environment for many different reasons. The frameworks and concepts in this chapter can help build up a picture of the competitive position of an organisation and how it might change in the future.

Recommended key readings

- Good general texts on international business and global organisations are: C. Hill, *International Business: Competing in the global marketplace*, 3rd edition, McGraw-Hill, 2000; A. Rugman and R. Hodgetts, *International Business*, 3rd edition, FT/Prentice Hall, 2003; while G. Yip, *Total Global Strategy II*, 2nd edition, FT/Prentice Hall, 2003, chapter 2, explains in more detail the forces for globalisation in industries.

- To understand scenarios in detail see: K. van der Heijden, R. Bradfield, G. Burt, G. Cairns and G. Wright, *The Sixth Sense: Accelerating organisational learning with scenarios*, John Wiley, 2002.

- M.E. Porter, *Competitive Strategy: Techniques for analysing industries and competitors*, Free Press, 1980, is essential reading for those who are faced with an analysis of an organisation's competitive environment.

- R. D'Aveni (with R. Gunther), *Hypercompetitive Rivalries*, Free Press, 1995, is an authoritative source on the dynamics of competition and hypercompetition.

- Most marketing textbooks have useful chapters on market segmentation. For example, P. Kotler, G. Armstrong, J. Saunders and V. Wong, *Principles of Marketing*, 3rd European edition, FT/Prentice Hall, 2002, chapter 9.

References

1. For a discussion on how environmental forces – particularly *global forces* – impact on the public sector see: J. Eppink and S. de Waal, 'Global influences on the public sector', in G. Johnson and K. Scholes (eds), *Exploring Public Sector Strategy*, Financial Times/Prentice Hall, 2001, Chapter 3.

2. Henry Mintzberg argues that environmental change is not now faster than it was: see *The Rise and Fall of Strategic Planning*, Prentice Hall, 1994, Chapter 4.

3. Previous editions of this book have used the PEST framework. However, this can lead to an under emphasis on ('green') environmental issues. This is the reason for the change to PESTEL.

4. A useful student text on the business environment is: I. Worthington and C. Britton, *The Business Environment*, FT/Prentice Hall, 2003.

5. See G. Yip, *Total Global Strategy II*, 2nd edition, FT/Prentice Hall, 2003, Chapter 2. Useful general texts on international business and global organisations are: C. Hill, *International Business: Competing in the global marketplace*, 3rd edition, McGraw-Hill, 2000; A. Rugman and R. Hodgetts, *International Business*, 3rd edition, FT/Prentice Hall, 2003.

6. M. Porter, *Competitive Advantage of Nations*, Macmillan, 1990.

7. See: M. Porter, 'Clusters and the new economics of competitiveness', *Harvard Business Review*, vol. 76, no. 6 (1998), pp. 77–90. The evidence for the importance of clusters has been challenged by others. For example: R. Martin and P. Sunley, 'Deconstructing clusters: chaotic concept or policy panacea', *Journal of Economic Geography*, vol. 3, no. 1 (2003), pp. 5–35.

8. K. van der Heijden, R. Bradfield, G. Burt, G. Cairns and G. Wright, *The Sixth Sense: Accelerating organisational learning with scenarios*, Wiley, 2002; P. Schwartz, *The Art of the Long View: Planning the future in an uncertain world*, Currency Doubleday, 1996; G. Ringland, *Scenario Planning*, Wiley, 1998; P. Schoemaker, *Profiting from Uncertainty: Strategies for succeeding no matter what the future brings*, Free Press, 2002. Also G. Price's chapter, 'The why and how of scenario planning', in V. Ambrosini with G. Johnson and K. Scholes (eds), *Exploring Techniques of Analysis and Evaluation in Strategic Management*, Prentice Hall, 1998.

9. D. Rutherford, *Routledge Dictionary of Economics*, 2nd edition, Routledge, 1995.

10. See M.E. Porter, *Competitive Strategy: Techniques for analysing industries and competitors*, Free Press, 1980, p. 5.

11. See: L. Van den Berghe and K. Verweire, 'Convergence in the financial services industry', *Geneva Papers on Risk and Insurance*, vol. 25, no. 2 (2000), pp. 262–272; A. Malhotra and A. Gupta, 'An investigation of firms' responses to industry convergence', *Academy of Management Proceedings*, 2001, pp. G1–6.

12. In business books the term 'business model' has traditionally been used to refer to the types of framework and concepts discussed in this book and shown in the exhibits. In the e-commerce world it is used more narrowly to describe the relationships and information flows in an 'industry' or sector. This is often described in terms of a 'value network' as discussed in section 3.6.1 of Chapter 3. Changing business models as a result of IT are described more fully in section 10.3 and readers can refer to the references given there.

13. Porter (reference 10 above), Chapter 1. C. Christensen, 'The past and future of competitive advantage', *Sloan Management Review*, vol. 42, no. 2 (2001), pp. 105–109 provides an interesting critique and update of some of the factors underlying Porter's five forces.

14. A. Brandenburger and B. Nalebuff, 'The right game: use game theory to shape strategy', *Harvard Business Review*, vol. 73, no. 4 (1995), pp. 57–71 identify 'complementors' as key players in the 'strategy game'.

15. A useful article about the life cycle of industries is: A. McGahan, 'How industries evolve', *Business Strategy Review*, vol. 11, no. 3 (2000), pp. 1–16.

16. See Brandenburger and Nalehbuff (reference 14 above).

17. For a full discussion of the dynamics of competition see: R. D'Aveni (with R. Gunther), *Hypercompetitive Rivalries*, Free Press, 1995.

18. J. Gimeno and C. Woo, 'Hypercompetition in a multi-market environment: the role of strategic similarity and multi-market contact on competition de-escalation', *Organisation Science*, vol. 7, no. 3 (1996), pp. 323–341.

19. This definition is from D'Aveni (reference 17 above) p. 2. In his later book, R. D'Aveni, *Strategic Supremacy: How*

industry leaders create spheres of influence, Simon and Schuster International, 2002, he gives examples of strategies that can help defend a strong position in conditions of hypercompetition.

20. G. McNamara, P. Vaaler and C. Devers, 'Same as ever it was: the search for evidence of increasing hypercompetition', *Strategic Management Journal*, vol. 24 (2003), pp. 261–278.

21. The early work on strategic groups is reported in : J. McGee and H. Thomas, 'Strategic groups, theory, research and taxonomy', *Strategic Management Journal*, vol. 7, no. 2 (1986), pp. 141–160. For a review of the research on strategic groups see: J. McGee, H. Thomas and M. Pruett, 'Strategic groups and the analysis of market structure and industry dynamics', *British Journal of Management*, vol. 6, no. 4 (1995), pp. 257–270. For an example of the use of strategic group analysis see: C. Flavian, A. Haberberg and Y. Polo, 'Subtle strategic insights from strategic group analysis', *Journal of Strategic Marketing*, vol. 7, no. 2 (1999), pp. 89–106. A paper covering the theoretical roots of strategic group analysis is: H. Thomas and T. Pollock, 'From I-O economics' S-C-P paradigm through strategic groups to competence-based competition', *Journal of Management*, vol. 10, no. 2 (1999), pp. 127–140.

22. The characteristics listed in Exhibit 2.8 are based on those discussed by Porter (reference 10 above), J. McGee and H. Thomas and Flavian, Haberberg and Polo (both reference 21 above).

23. A useful discussion of segmentation in relation to competitive strategy is provided in M.E. Porter, *Competitive Advantage*, Free Press, 1985, Chapter 7. See also the discussion on market segmentation in P. Kotler, G. Armstrong, J. Saunders and V. Wong, *Principles of Marketing*, 3rd European edition, FT/Prentice Hall, 2002, Chapter 9. For a more detailed review of segmentation methods see: M. Wedel and W. Kamakura, *Market Segmentation: Conceptual and methodological foundations*, 2nd edition, Kluwer Academic, 1999.

24. M. Wedel, 'Is segmentation history?', *Marketing Research*, vol. 13, no. 4 (2001), pp. 26–29.

25. The term strategy canvas was introduced by: C. Kim and R. Mauborgne, 'Charting your company's future', *Harvard Business Review*, vol. 80, no. 6 (2002), pp. 76–82. The example shown in Exhibit 2.10 pre-dates the use of that terminology but is a similar approach. It is dealt with more extensively in G. Johnson, C. Bowman and P. Rudd's chapter, 'Competitor analysis', in V. Ambrosini with G. Johnson and K. Scholes (eds), *Exploring Techniques of Analysis and Evaluation in Strategic Management*, Prentice Hall, 1998.

26. See: W. Kim and R. Mauborgne, 'Creating new market space', *Harvard Business Review*, vol. 77, no. 1 (1999), pp. 83–93.

27. The idea of SWOT as a common-sense checklist has been used for many years: for example, S. Tilles, 'Making strategy explicit', in I. Ansoff (ed.), *Business Strategy*, Penguin, 1968. See also T. Jacobs, J. Shepherd and G. Johnson's chapter on SWOT analysis in V. Ambrosini with G. Johnson and K. Scholes (see reference 25 above); E. Valentin, 'SWOT analysis from a resource-based view', *Journal of Marketing Theory and Practice*, vol. 9, no. 2 (2001), pp. 54–69. SWOT will be discussed more fully in section 3.6.4 and Illustration 3.7.

WORK ASSIGNMENTS

✱ Denotes more advanced work assignments.   * Refers to a case study in the Text and Cases edition.   ‡ Refers to a case study on the Companion Website.

In the assignments that follow, an example of an industry is normally required. For this purpose, the European brewing industry, the pharmaceutical industry,* the ICT industry (see Dell, bioinformatics, mobile phones), or an industry of your choice could be useful.

2.1   Using Illustration 2.1 and Exhibit 2.2 as a guide, undertake an audit of the macro-environment of a chosen industry or sector. What are the key environmental influences on organisations in that industry? What are the main drivers of change?

2.2   Identify the main future changes likely in an industry of your choice. Following the guidelines in section 2.2.4 and Illustration 2.3, construct scenarios for the industry for an appropriate time period.

2.3   Assume you have just become personal assistant to the chief executive of a major pharmaceutical company. She knows you have recently undertaken a business management degree and asks if you would prepare a brief report summarising how scenario planning might be useful to a company in the pharmaceutical industry.

2.4✱   Drawing on section 2.3 use five forces analyses to compare two organisations in different industries or sectors in terms of the key environmental influences and competitive forces which they face. Is one competitive environment more favourable than the other?

2.5✱   Compare two industries in terms of the key environmental influences and competitive forces in them. Assess and compare the entry barriers, and the extent of competitive rivalry in the two industries.

2.6✱   Building on section 2.4.1 and Illustration 2.7:

(a) Identify the strategic characteristics that most distinguish organisations in an industry or sector of your choice. Construct one or more strategic group maps on these bases.

(b) Assess the extent to which mobility between strategic groups is possible. (If you have constructed more than one map for the industry, do the mobility barriers you identify differ amongst them? What does this signify?)

(c) Identify any vacant strategic spaces in the maps. Do any represent viable strategic positions? What would be the characteristics of an organisation competing in such a space?

2.7   Read sections 2.4.2 to 2.4.4. For an industry or sector of your choice identify one or more market segments into which the products or services are offered. Then identify the strategic customer and the critical success factors for each segment. Which providers' offerings are best matched with these market requirements?

2.8   To what extent are the models discussed in this chapter appropriate in the analysis of the environment of a public sector or not-for-profit organisation? Give examples to support your arguments.

2.9   Read section 2.5.1 and then identify strategic gaps in the environment of an organisation with which you are familiar.

2.10* Using the concepts and frameworks in this chapter, write a report for an organisation (e.g. a brewing company (see chapter-end case example), Corus,‡ Thorntons,* Amazon*) which assesses its business environment and its competitive position within that environment.

Integrative assignments

2.11 For a specific industry or sector of your choice consider how the factors shown in Exhibit 2.3 might drive globalisation. Then think about how this might require both changes in international strategy (Chapter 6) and international structures (Chapter 8).

2.12 As public sector organisations become more 'business-like' it requires them to have better knowledge of their 'customers' and 'markets'. Explain how this knowledge might influence the *method* by which strategy improvement is achieved (Chapter 7) and the way in which the organisation is managed (particularly the issue of centralisation or devolution of decision making – Chapter 8).

 An extensive range of additional materials, including audio summaries, weblinks to organisations featured in the text, definitions of key concepts and multiple choice questions, can be found on the *Exploring Corporate Strategy* Companion Website at **www.pearsoned.co.uk/ecs7**

Global forces and the European brewing industry

Mike Blee

This case is centred on the European brewing industry and examines how the increasingly competitive pressure of operating within global markets is causing consolidation through acquisitions, alliances and closures within the industry. This has resulted in the growth of the brewers' reliance upon super brands.

In the mid 2000s the major centre for production of beer in the world was Europe; its production was twice that of the USA, which in 2003 was the world's largest beer-producing country. In the alcoholic drinks sector beer sales are dominant: total sales across the world accounted for 74 per cent of all alcoholic purchases (Euromonitor 2002).

Although the European market as a whole is mature, with beer sales showing slight falls in most markets, Datamonitor 2003 reported that the alcoholic beverage sector grew at an annual rate in

Photo: Alamy

Table 1 European beer consumption by country and year (000 hectolitres)

Country	1980	1997	1998	1999	2000	2001	2002
Austria	7651	9145	8736	8810	8762	8627	8734
Belgium	12945	10243	10011	10203	10064	9986	9901
Denmark	6698	6165	5707	5562	5452	5282	5202
Finland	2738	4170	4084	4087	4024	4085	4136
France	23745	21655	22663	22833	21420	21331	20629
Germany‡	89820	107679	104550	104629	103105	100904	100385
Greece	N/A	3940	4211	4354	4288	4181	4247
Ireland	4174	5406	5592	5699	5594	5625	5536
Italy	9539	14535	15501	15675	16289	16694	16340
Luxembourg	417	466	452	474	472	445	440
Netherlands	12213	13475	13225	13309	13129	12922	11985
Norway*	7651	2330	2203	2305	2327	2290	2420
Portugal	3534	6318	6494	6475	6453	6276	5948
Spain	20065	26238	26677	27772	29151	31126	30715
Sweden	3935	5459	5077	5258	5011	4932	4998
Switzerland*	4433	4249	4277	4212	4194	4141	4127
UK	65490	61114	58835	58917	57007	58234	59384
Total‡	269358	302587	298295	300574	296742	297081	295127

* Non-EU countries; ‡1980 excludes GDR. Figures adjusted.

Source: www.Brewersofeurope.org

Table 2 Annual consumption per capita by country and year (litres)

Country	1980	1997	1998	1999	2000	2001	2002
Austria	101.9	113.3	108.1	108.9	108.1	107.0	108.5
Belgium	131.0	101.0	98.0	100.0	99.0	98.0	96.0
Denmark	130.7	116.7	107.7	104.6	102.2	98.6	96.7
Finland	56.6	84.0	80.0	80.1	77.9	80.2	79.5
France	44.3	37.0	38.6	38.7	36.2	35.9	34.7
Germany	145.9	131.2	127.5	127.5	125.3	122.4	121.5
Greece	N/A	39.0	42.0	43.0	40.0	39.0	39.0
Ireland	121.7	123.7	124.2	126.0	125.0	125.0	125.0
Italy	16.7	25.4	26.9	27.1	28.1	28.9	28.2
Luxembourg	115.8	112.0	107.0	110.0	108.2	100.9	98.5
Netherlands	86.4	86.4	84.3	84.4	82.8	80.5	79.2
Norway*	48.1	52.9	49.7	51.7	52.0	51.0	53.7
Portugal	35.0	63.6	63.3	64.9	64.6	61.3	58.6
Spain	53.7	66.7	66.9	69.1	72.0	75.7	73.4
Sweden	47.4	61.7	57.3	59.3	56.4	55.4	55.9
Switzerland*	69.5	59.5	59.9	58.8	58.3	57.2	56.6
UK	118.3	103.6	99.3	99.0	97.2	99.0	100.6
Total	82.5	78.6	77.2	77.6	75.9	75.9	76.8

* Non-EU countries.

Source: www.brewersofeurope.org

value terms by 2.6 per cent per year between 1997 and 2002.

The Interbrew market trend report 2002 states that within Europe the on-trade market (sold through licensed premises) beer accounts for 59 per cent of all alcoholic beverage sales by volume, while in the take-home market this figure increases to 72 per cent.

Two key trends within Europe were the rapid growth in leisure spending and the consumers' increased awareness of health and fitness. These factors had resulted in a drop in the volumes of beer consumed.

Another current trend across Europe is towards drinking a wider range of alcoholic beverages. There has been a growth in demand for flavoured alcoholic beverages, with wine consumption having shown large increases. Within the UK alone wine sales had grown from 14 per cent of the market in 1980 to 26 per cent of the market in 2002. Meanwhile there has been a negative trend in the overall consumption of spirits.

Acquisition, licensing and strategic alliances have all occurred as the leading brewers battle to control the market. There are global pressures for consolidation due to over capacity within the industry and this has resulted in a focus upon cost containment and brand reinforcement (see Table 5). Interbrew's market trend survey 2002 shows that the consolidated global share of the top 20 brewers increased from 51 per cent in 1990 to 65 per cent in the year 2000. The report suggests that consolidation will further increase and compares brewing with the cigarette industry. In 2002 the five largest global brewers accounted for 30 per cent of production volume, whereas in the cigarette industry the five leading players had a 60 per cent market share.

Table 3 European production by country and year (000 hectolitres)

Country	1990	1997	1998	1999	2000	2001	2002
Austria	7606	9366	8830	8869	8750	8588	8731
Belgium	14291	14014	14105	14575	14734	14966	15696
Denmark	8169	9181	8075	8024	7460	7233	8534
Finland	2823	4804	4697	4700	4612	4631	4797
France	21684	19483	19807	19866	18926	18866	18117
Germany‡	92342	114800	111700	112800	110000	108500	108400
Greece	N/A	3945	4022	4359	4500	4454	4443
Ireland	6000	8152	8478	8648	8324	8712	8113
Italy	8569	11455	12193	12179	12575	12782	12592
Luxembourg	729	481	469	450	438	397	386
Netherlands	15684	24701	23988	24502	25072	25232	24898
Norway*	2001	2299	2169	2222	2223	2216	2300
Portugal	3557	6623	6784	6760	6451	6554	7121
Spain	20027	24773	24991	25852	26414	27741	27860
Sweden	3759	4858	4568	4673	4495	4449	4376
Switzerland*	4127	3563	3586	3599	3630	3551	3494
UK	64830	59139	56652	57854	55279	56802	56672
Total‡	276198	321637	315114	319932	313883	315674	316530

* Non-EU countries; ‡ 1980 excludes GDR.

Source: www.brewersofeurope.org

Consolidation trends are indeed continuing: Interbrew had purchased in 2001 parts of the old Bass Empire, Becks and Whitbread and in 2004 announced a merger with Am Bev, the Brazilian brewery group. Meanwhile Scottish and Newcastle had acquired the Danone French brewing operations as well as Bulmer cider. In 2003 it targeted Eastern Europe and China, acquiring Finland's biggest brewery, Hartwall, for £1.2bn (€1.8bn) together with a purchase in December 2003 of a 20 per cent shareholding in a leading Chinese brewery. It is interesting to note that Bass contradicted this trend prior to the sale of the company in 2001, when a disposal took place of its interests in Northern China and some of its operations in the Czech Republic.

In 2003 Anheuser-Busch was the world's largest brewer ranked by sales volume but with limited overseas operations. It had invested in a Mainland Chinese brewery and had a significant shareholding in Modelo of Mexico. However, its European operations were limited to just one brewery in the UK at Mortlake. In 2004 its world no. 1 position was to be challenged by the Interbrew/Am Bev merger. This gave Interbrew 14 per cent global market share which made it no. 1 (by volume but not by value).

Coors, another large American brewer, had gained European market entry by the purchase from Interbrew in 2002 of the Carling Brewing Company. This sale was forced upon Interbrew by the UK regulatory authorities as they felt the dominant position held by Interbrew within the UK's lager market was against the consumers' interest.

South African Breweries has also been extremely active. In early 2002 there were market rumours of a merger with Interbrew; these were unfounded, however 2002 resulted in two major acquisitions – the Miller Group (USA) and Pilsner Urquell in the Czech Republic.

These large global brewers (Table 4) control a range of key brands with which they will start to achieve large cost savings with the premium lagers leading the way. Volume sales will help to contain costs and should lead to increased economies of scale. However, differences will occur in the various local country markets. Where there are significant taste and product differentials potential savings are limited. The large groups, however, hope to utilise increased knowledge management systems and linked technologies across these combined brands to improve performance.

During 2003, due to the activity highlighted above, there were major changes to the world market shares of the leading brewers (Table 4) with an ever-increasing domination of global brands (Table 5). Trends within Western Europe (Table 6) reinforced

Table 4 The world's top 10 brewery companies by volume: 2003

Position	Company	Country of Origin
1	Anheuser–Busch	USA
2	South African Breweries/Miller	South Africa
3	Heineken	Netherlands
4	Interbrew	Belgium
5	Carlsberg	Denmark
6	Am Bev	Brazil
7	Scottish & Newcastle	United Kingdom
8	Coors	USA
9	Modelo	Mexico
10	Kirin	Japan

Source: Coors Brewers Limited UK

the dominance of the key players and the importance of the lager market in branding terms.

The two largest Western European markets

Germany

At nearly twice the size of the UK market in consumption terms, the German beer market is very different to that of the UK. It is highly fragmented, having in excess of 1,200 breweries. However, acquisition has happened in this market with Becks going to Interbrew in 2002 and Holsten being acquired by Carlsberg in 2004. German beer drinkers are used to strict German purity laws and therefore generally trust and drink German beer as against imports. This has resulted in large numbers of regional breweries satisfying the home market. Exports from Germany

Table 5 Top exported lager brands (world), 2001

Brand Name	Ownership	Export sales (million hectolitres)	Percentage of global sales
Heineken	Heineken	17.7	82
Carlsberg	Carlsberg	8.9	87.6
Amstel	Heineken	8.5	78.7
Budweiser	Anheuser-Busch	8	17.1
Corona Extra	Groupo Modelo	7.7	32
Stella Artois	Interbrew	6.8	88.5
Fosters	Fosters	5.7	68.7
Skol	Carlsberg	5.2	18
Tuborg	Carlsberg	3.3	63.3
Becks	Interbrew	2.7	62.5

Source: Impact/Interbrew SA/Industry Estimates/Company reports

Table 6 European beer market: top companies, 2001, by market share by volume

Company	Home Country	Market Share	Leading Brand
Heineken	Netherlands	11.7%	Heineken
Interbrew	Belgium	10.4%	Stella Artois
Carlsberg	Denmark	6.9%	Carlsberg
Scottish & Newcastle	United Kingdom	6.9%	Kronenbourg
Mahou SA	Spain	2.9%	San Miguel
Holsten Brauerei	Germany	2.6%	Konig
Diageo PLC	United Kingdom	2.2%	Guinness
Binding-Brauerei	Germany	2.1%	Radeberger
SA Damm	Spain	2.1%	Super Bock
Brau & Brunnen	Germany	1.9%	Jever

Source: Euromonitor 2002

Table 7 **Imports and exports of beer by country (2001)**

Country	Imports (% of Consumption)	Exports (% of Production)
Austria	5.3	4.8
Belgium	19	39
Denmark	1.7	34.1
Finland	1.9	6
France	25.5	12.4
Germany	3.2	10
Greece	4	10
Holland	6.1	51.9
Ireland	11.9	28
Italy	26.4	3.9
Luxembourg	37.6	–
Norway*	4.1	0.8
Portugal	4.7	11.2
Spain	13	2.3
Sweden	11.6	–
Switzerland*	14.8	0.6
United Kingdom	8.6	5.6
Total	9.3	14.1‡

Note: Import figures do not include beers brewed under licence in home country; export figures do not include licensed brews produced elsewhere.

* excludes Sweden; ‡ Non-EU countries.

Source: www.brewersofeurope.org

are nearly double that of the UK in volume percentage terms (Table 7).

Packaging in Germany differs from many major markets with 60 per cent of all beer produced being sold in bottles. Due to a deposit scheme being introduced on cans in 2003 the sales of bottled beers have grown significantly.

Discount own-label beers have increased the off-trade to 70 per cent of total beer volume. However, sales in Germany during 2002 dropped at their highest annual rate in the previous decade and sales since 1998 have declined overall by 7 per cent. The outlook for the later part of the decade is that there will be declining consumption and a gradual drop in the number of breweries, with increases in merger and acquisition as the market consolidates to contain costs. This follows the trends being experienced already in the majority of European markets.

The fastest growing niche in 2003 was within the youth market. Sales of flavoured beer mixed with either lemon-lime soda or cola, available in draught and bottles, had an increasing market share, up

30 per cent in 2002. These accounted for 3 per cent of the total annual beer consumption. Pilsner-type beers in 2002 still dominated the market holding a 67 per cent market share.

United Kingdom

Beer sales were fairly mature and although there was a steady decline in the 1990s the market has begun to stabilise at around 55 million hectolitres per year. However, there are some definite market trends. The major change in the UK industry has been the disposal of the tied pub chains by the national breweries. Scottish and Newcastle became the last of the large companies to dispose of their chains in 2003.

These public house chains are now independently managed separate companies and this has increased the distribution chain access to a much wider variety of brewers. These large independent chains of public houses exert high buyer power on the brewing industry.

Meanwhile ownership of breweries within the UK had rapidly changed. Foreign multinationals have targeted and entered the industry. The Keynote Report 2003 shows three foreign multinationals, Interbrew, Coors and Carlsberg, control 53 per cent of the market. The leading brewer is Scottish and Newcastle with 27 per cent of the market. There are a number of large regional brewers with well-known speciality brands but the trend by the majors in the market has been to consolidate production, closing down plants and containing costs.

Lagers and premium lagers dominate the home market and many are brewed under licence arrangements. Consumption of lager has grown from just over 50 per cent of the total UK market in 1990 to 62 per cent in 2002. In 2003 60 per cent of UK beer was packaged in draught form. As the UK market switches more towards production of lager the trend will be for increasing sales through supermarkets resulting in a reduction of draught beer demand. There is limited export of traditional UK beers as demand is relatively limited and therefore the reliance is on the internal market.

As supermarkets within the UK sell high volumes of beer, they exert high buyer power over the supplying breweries and are in a position to dictate terms for the supply of product. As a result there is heavy discounting and brand value destruction as the brewers find themselves operating in an over capacity market with low profit margins. The market is moving more and more towards increased sales in the off-trade. BBPA data 2003 reported that the wholesale price of beer had declined by 16 per cent from the level that was obtained in 1992.

However, home sales are additionally hindered by the 'booze cruise'. Excise duties on alcohol are much lower in France and importation of alcoholic beverages for personal use is legal. These cruises have almost become a feature of daily life with large quantities of beer carrying low excise duties being imported both legally for personal use and illegally for onward sale.

Four brewing companies

Heineken (The Netherlands)

In 2004 Heineken was by far the biggest and most global of the European brewery businesses. It remains a family business and its brands are available in more than 170 countries. It owns more than 110 breweries in over 50 countries and exports all over the world. In the UK its licence agreement with Whitbread ceased in 2003 and this was followed by the introduction of its full-strength range. Heineken is now sold as a premium beer in all markets except its home market.

Heineken has become Europe's favourite brand of beer and the most international beer in the world, with sales increasing annually. Founded in Amsterdam in 1963, the company's other brands include Amstel and Murphys. Heineken had been acquiring other brewing groups since 1991 and in 2003 announced its biggest acquisition to date: the Austrian brewery BBAG. Of Heineken's turnover, 76.5 per cent is European based.

The four major strategic objectives for Heineken were to:

● remain one of the top global brewers;
● be more profitable per hectolitre than other international brewers;
● build the most valuable brand portfolio with Heineken as the international flagship brand;
● remain independent.

By the utilisation of its key brands the company aims for a broad leadership position with a target of being no. 1 or no. 2 in its local markets. Achieving this in production, marketing and distribution brings economies of scale. The local breweries give it market access from which they can sell their high-premium Heineken and Amstel beers.

Grolsch (The Netherlands)

In 2004 Royal Grolsch NV is a medium-size international brewing group – less than one-tenth the size of Heineken, with overall sales in 2002 of 3.27 million hectolitres. The group's strategy calls for this to increase to 4.6 million hectolitres by the end of 2006. Its key products include Grolsch premium lager and new flavoured beers (Grolsch lemon and Grolsch pink grapefruit). In The Netherlands Grolsch holds the rights for the sale and distribution of the valued US Miller brand. The Grolsch Brewery has been established since 1615 and has been exporting since 1946. The brand is available in over 50 countries; however, in certain territories, including the UK and Poland, the brand is brewed under licence. In the five years to 2002 the group turnover had increased by 20 per cent with net profits increasing by more than 30 per cent. Although the home market for beer is declining, The Netherlands is still the company's most important market and accounts for over 50 per cent of its sales volume. Export sales are increasing, with the UK, USA and Canada being the most important overseas territories.

Grolsch has two main breweries that are situated in Enschede and Groenio. From 2005 production is situated within a single new site at Bokelo. Efficiency is the key driver behind this relocation: by concentrating brewing on one site, Grolsch will gain ultimate cost control and will also increase volume capacity significantly. Grolsch's drive to optimise costs has included the outsourcing of its distribution and a move within The Netherlands to use inland shipping rather than road.

Interbrew (Belgium)

Interbrew is one of the oldest beer companies in the world. It has operations in 21 countries and Interbrew's beers are sold in more than 120 countries. The company strategy is to build strong local brand reputation as well as to market its international labels. These include Becks, Stella Artois, Bass, Hoegaarden and Labatts. Interbrew has been on the acquisition and organic growth trail as a determined strategy since 1993. In the five years to 2003 the company had made over 20 acquisitions and 35 per cent of the operating income during 2002 was derived from this acquisition programme. 2004 saw the merger between Interbrew and Brazil's largest brewer Am Bev. Interbrew's philosophy is reinforced by its claim to be 'The World's Local Brewer'.

In 2001 the company acquired Bass (UK), Whitbreads (UK) and Becks (Germany). At the time of acquisition Bass brands accounted for 24 per cent of the UK market. The acquisition from Bass was unconditional and when the UK regulatory authorities challenged the decision to acquire Bass, Interbrew was forced into a sale situation. Due to this forced sale the stock market at that time formed the view that Interbrew had overpaid for the company.

On appeal to the High Court Interbrew managed to overturn the competition authority decision agreeing as a result to sell the Carling Brewing Company to Coors but retaining much of the Bass Empire. Between 2000 and 2002 net turnover for the Interbrew company increased in excess of 20 per cent. In 2002 Interbrew invested heavily in the growth market of China and in 2004 Interbrew became the largest brewer in Germany, following a partnership with Spaten giving them an 11 per cent market share.

Scottish and Newcastle (UK)

Scottish and Newcastle is an international brewing group with leading positions in 13 European countries. These countries include the UK, France, Finland and Russia. Its strategy is to be a major force within the global brewing industry with a concentration of effort upon expanding a number of leading positions in the Western European market. In 2003 the company disposed of its retail and leisure businesses, which had been significant in the company's past. In the year 2000 this business alone had accounted for £1.1bn of turnover and £246m of profits.

The company's expansion strategy is to enter high-growth emerging markets. This will be achieved by working through alliances with experienced local breweries that hold strong market positions. Its key brands include John Smiths, Kronebourg, Kanterbrau and Baltika and it brews Fosters under licence for the UK market. In 2003 turnover had increased by 17 per cent, with profits up 8 per cent

and overall volume up 2.4 per cent. The brands of Kronebourg, Fosters and Newcastle Brown all showed substantial volume growth in the year 2003. Acquisitions in the early 2000s have included Hartwell, Kronebourg from Danone in France, Bulmers Cider and investments in Mainland China and India.

The Hartwell acquisition is particularly important as this gives the group a 50 per cent investment in Baltic Beverages. This results in exposure to the high growth markets of Russia, Ukraine and the Baltic countries. The growth rate of the Russian market was such than in 2002 it was bigger than any Western European country's home market other than Germany.

The future

Forecasts from Euromonitor 2002 conclude that the world market for beer between 2002 and 2007 will increase by 35 per cent in Eastern Europe and the Asian Pacific region by 28 per cent whilst Canadean's latest annual global beer report forecasts sales of 1.5bn hectolitres in 2005.

The Interbrew market report 2002 concludes that most beer markets in Europe are now relatively mature with limited potential for growth resulting in the focus now moving towards Asia and Eastern Europe.

Questions

1. Using the data from the case, what are the major trends in the European brewing industry?

2. For the four breweries outlined above (or breweries of your own choice) explain:
   (a) how these trends will impact differently on these different companies; and
   (b) how you think the strategy of each company should change.

3

Strategic Capability

Learning outcomes

After reading this chapter you should be able to understand:

● What is meant by strategic capability and how this contributes to the competitive advantage of organisations.

● The strategic importance of resources, competences, core competences and dynamic capabilities.

● The importance of continual improvement in cost efficiency.

● The characteristics of strategic capabilities to provide sustainable competitive advantage, including rarity, robustness and non-substitutability of strategic capabilities.

● The relationship of organisational knowledge to strategic capability.

● Ways of diagnosing strategic capability including the analysis of value chains and networks, activity systems, the role of benchmarking and SWOT analysis.

● Ways in which managers may develop strategic capabilities of organisations.

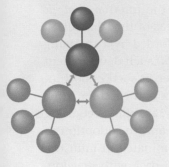

3.1 INTRODUCTION

Chapter 2 outlined how the external environment in which an organisation is operating can create both strategic opportunities and threats. But successful strategies are also dependent on the organisation having the internal *strategic capability* required for survival and success, which is the focus of this chapter.

Strategy development can be driven by opportunities afforded by a changing environment. Sometimes known as the search for *strategic fit*, such development implies the change of internal strategic capabilities to better fit such opportunities. The major upheavals in many manufacturing industries in the last ten years or so have been examples of such adjustments in strategic capability, requiring the search for major improvements in labour productivity and the adoption of new technologies. The early twenty-first century is also dominated in industry, commerce and the public services by the struggle to keep pace with developments in IT even just to stay in business.

However, understanding strategic capability is also important from another perspective. An organisation's strategic capability may be the leading edge of strategic development. New opportunities may be created by *stretching* and exploiting capabilities either in ways which competitors find difficult to match or to create quite new market opportunities, or both. For example, to continue the IT theme, stretching IT capabilities has been the basis on which organisations have sought to create new services and areas of economic activity.

In either case, be it through strategic fit or stretch, a key concept to bear in mind is that if an organisation is to achieve competitive advantage over others, it will do so because it has capabilities that the others do not have or have difficulty in obtaining. These capabilities could be the resources the organisation has. They could also be the way these resources are used or deployed and this is known as the organisation's competences. This explanation of competitive advantage in terms of strategic capabilities is sometimes called the **resource-based view** of strategy:[1] that the competitive advantage of an organisation is explained by the distinctiveness of its capabilities. In turn this helps explain how some businesses are able to achieve extraordinary profits or returns compared with others. They have resources or competences that permit them to produce at lower cost or generate a superior product or service at standard cost in relation to other businesses with inferior resources or capabilities.[2]

This chapter therefore focuses on the strategic capabilities of organisations: what they are, how they can be understood, analysed and managed. The chapter has six sections as follows:

*The **resource-based view** of strategy: the competitive advantage of an organisation is explained by the distinctiveness of its capabilities*

- Section 3.2 discusses the *foundations of strategic capability*. Specifically, it considers what is meant by *tangible and intangible resources* and what is meant by *competences*. It then explains the importance of *threshold capabilities* both in terms of resources and competences. It concludes by introducing the concepts of *unique resources* and *core competences* that are central to an understanding of bases of competitive advantage.

- Section 3.3 is concerned with a vital basis of strategic capability of any organisation: namely the ability to achieve and continually improve its *cost efficiency*.

- Section 3.4 considers what sort of capabilities might allow organisations to *sustain competitive advantage* over time (in a public sector context the equivalent concern is how organisations might sustain 'demonstrable excellence'). The section discusses the criteria regarded as vital to achieve this. The importance of *value* to customers is briefly revisited. Uniqueness or *rarity* of resources or competences is discussed. So too is the importance of *robustness* or *non-imitability*; and here the concept of *core competences* is discussed more fully. The section also considers the criterion of *non-substitutability* of strategic capability by competitors. There is then a consideration of the extent to which these explanations of strategic capability to achieve sustainable competitive advantage are suited to organisations in fast-changing business environments. The argument is made that in such situations *dynamic capabilities* that allow the organisation to learn and adapt to new conditions may become more significant.

- Section 3.5 discusses how the concept of *organisational knowledge* relates to strategic capability and how it might contribute to competitive advantage of organisations.

- Section 3.6 moves on to consider the ways in which strategic capability might be analysed. First it considers the concept of the *value chain and value network* as ways of understanding which activities add value and which do not. The section then moves on to explain how managers might seek to understand strategic capabilities through *activity mapping*. This is followed by considering how managers might monitor the extent and comparability of their strategic capability through *benchmarking*. The section concludes by revisiting *SWOT* (see Chapter 2, section 2.5.2) from the point of view of understanding strategic capability in relation to competitors.

- The chapter concludes in section 3.7 by discussing how managers might be able to *develop the strategic capability* through internal and external development, the management of people and the building of dynamic capabilities.

3.2   FOUNDATIONS OF STRATEGIC CAPABILITY

This chapter employs some important concepts that need to be defined. This is not only to make it easier to follow the argument in the rest of the chapter, but also because different writers, managers and consultants use different terms and concepts in explaining the importance of strategic capability: so, given such differences, it is important to understand how the terms are used here. Overall, **strategic capability** can be defined as the adequacy and suitability of the resources and competences of an organisation for it to survive and prosper. Exhibit 3.1 shows the elements of strategic capability that are employed in the chapter to explain the concept.

Strategic capability is the adequacy and suitability of the resources and competences of an organisation for it to survive and prosper

3.2.1 Resources and competences

Perhaps the most basic concept is that of *resources*. **Tangible resources** are the physical assets of an organisation such as plant, labour and finance. In contrast,

Tangible resources are the physical assets of an organisation such as plant, labour and finance

Exhibit 3.1	Strategic capabilities and competitive advantage

	Resources	Competences
Threshold capabilities	**Threshold resources** ● Tangible ● Intangible	**Threshold competences**
Capabilities for competitive advantage	**Unique resources** ● Tangible ● Intangible	**Core competences**

Intangible resources are non-physical assets such as information, reputation and knowledge

intangible resources[3] are non-physical assets such as information, reputation and knowledge. Typically, an organisation's resources can be considered under the following four broad categories:

- *Physical resources* – such as the number of machines, buildings or the production capacity of the organisation. The nature of these resources, such as the age, condition, capacity and location of each resource, will determine the usefulness of such resources.

- *Financial resources* – such as capital, cash, debtors and creditors, and suppliers of money (shareholders, bankers, etc.).

- *Human resources* – including the number and mix (e.g. demographic profile) of people in an organisation. The intangible resource of their skills and knowledge is also likely to be important. This applies both to employees and other people in an organisation's networks. In knowledge-based economies people do genuinely become the most valuable asset.

- *Intellectual capital* is an important aspect of the intangible resources of an organisation. This includes patents, brands, business systems and customer databases. There should be no doubt that these intangible resources have a value, since when businesses are sold part of the value is 'goodwill'. In a knowledge-based economy intellectual capital is likely to be a major asset of many organisations.

Such resources are certainly important; but what an organisation does – how it employs and deploys its resources – matters at least as much as what resources it has. There would be no point in having state of the art equipment or valuable knowledge or a valuable brand if they were not used effectively. The efficiency and effectiveness of physical or financial resources, or the people in an organisation, depends on not just their existence but how they are managed, the

Exhibit 3.2	Strategic capability – the terminology	

Term	Definition	Example (athletics)
Strategic capability	The ability to perform at the level required to survive and prosper. It is underpinned by the resources and competences of the organisation.	Athletic ability suited to a chosen event.
Threshold resources	The resources needed to meet customers' minimum requirements and therefore to continue to exist.	A healthy body (for individuals). Medical facilities and practitioners. Training venues and equipment. Food supplements.
Threshold competences	Activities and processes needed to meet customers' minimum requirements and therefore to continue to exist.	Individual training regimes. Physiotherapy/injury management. Diet planning.
Unique resources	Resources that underpin competitive advantage and are difficult for competitors to imitate or obtain.	Exceptional heart and lungs Height or weight World-class coach
Core competences	Activities that underpin competitive advantage and are difficult for competitors to imitate or obtain.	A combination of dedication, tenacity, time to train, demanding levels of competition and a will to win.

cooperation between people, their adaptability, their innovatory capacity, the relationship with customers and suppliers and the experience and learning about what works well and what does not. The term **competences** is used to mean the activities and processes through which an organisation deploys its resources effectively. In understanding strategic capability, the emphasis is, then, not just on what resources exist but on how they are used.

Competences are the activities and processes through which an organisation deploys its resources effectively

Within these broad definitions, other terms are commonly used and are now explained. As the explanation proceeds, it might be useful to refer to the two examples provided in Exhibit 3.2: one relating the concepts to a business and the other to sport.

3.2.2 Threshold capabilities

An extension of these concepts relates to the search for competitive advantage. An important distinction here is between capabilities (resources or competences) that are at a threshold level and those that might help the organisation achieve competitive advantage. **Threshold capabilities** are those essential for the organisation to be able to compete in a given market. Without these an organisation is unlikely to be able to survive in the market. The first two basic questions are:

Threshold capabilities are those capabilities essential for the organisation to be able to compete in a given market

● What are the *threshold resources* needed to support particular strategies? If an organisation does not possess these resources it will be unable to meet customers' minimum requirements and therefore be unable to continue to exist. For example, the increasing demands by modern multiple retailers made on their suppliers means that those suppliers have to possess quite sophisticated IT infrastructure simply to stand a chance of meeting retailer requirements.

● Similarly what are the *threshold competences* required to deploy resources so as to meet customers' requirements and support particular strategies? Using the same example, a powerful retailer does not simply expect its suppliers to have the required IT infrastructure, but to be able to use it effectively so as to guarantee the required level of service.

Arising from these are other important issues:

● *Threshold levels of capability will change* and will usually rise over time as critical success factors change (see section 2.4.4 of Chapter 2) and through the activities of competitors and new entrants. So there is a need continuously to review and improve this resource and competence base just to stay in business. Some industries or sectors have seen progressive shakeout of suppliers as the processes of competition make resource requirements an increasingly difficult barrier to achieve. The way in which the Premier Football League in England developed during the 1990s created a gulf between those who were able to spend money on expensive squads of players and ground improvements and those who could not. The latter group tended to be relegated to lower divisions. (See the Manchester United case example at the end of Chapter 4.)

● One of the challenges that firms face is the *trade-offs* that they may need to make in order to achieve a level of threshold capability required for different sorts of customers. For example, many firms have found it difficult to compete in market segments that require large quantities of standard product as well as market segments that require added value specialist products. The first might require high-capacity, fast-throughput plant, standardised highly efficient systems and a low-cost labour force. The second might require a skilled labour force, flexible plant and a more innovative capacity. The organisation may have to make some difficult choices here with the danger that it fails to achieve the threshold capabilities required for either segment.

● A problem for established organisations is the *redundancy of capabilities* they may experience as step changes in the business environment take place. Unless an organisation is able to dispose of those redundant resources or competences it may be unable to free up sufficient funds to invest in the new ones that are needed and their cost base will be too high. For example, traditional banks continue to struggle with their legacy of a vast array of branches in a world where new competitors do not have branches and have invested heavily in call centres and online internet banking.

● It is important to recognise that the threshold level required is likely to involve *complementary resources and competences*. There is little point in meeting threshold levels in resource terms if the threshold levels are not met with regard to competences. For example, having an excellent intangible resource such as an historically powerful brand is not much use without the marketing competences to exploit it.

Identifying these threshold resources and competences is therefore important. If organisations do not pay attention to them they cannot even expect to be 'in the game'. They do not have the capability to be competitive.

3.2.3 Unique resources and core competences

While threshold capabilities are fundamentally important they do not of them-selves create competitive advantage. Competitive advantage is more likely to be created and sustained if the organisation has distinctive or unique capabilities that competitors cannot imitate. This may be because the organisation has some *unique resources*. **Unique resources** are those resources that critically underpin com-petitive advantage and that others cannot imitate or obtain. It is, however, more likely that an organisation is able to achieve competitive advantage because it has distinctive, or core, competences. The concept of core competences was developed in the 1990s, most notably by Gary Hamel and C.K. Prahalad. While various definitions exist, in this book **core competences**[4] are taken to mean the activities and processes through which resources are deployed in such a way as to achieve competitive advantage in ways that others cannot imitate or obtain. For example, a supplier that achieves competitive advantage in a retail market might have done so on the basis of a unique resource such as a powerful brand, or by finding ways of providing service or building relationships with that retailer in ways that its competitors find difficult to imitate, a core competence. Section 3.3 of this chapter is particularly concerned with the role played by unique resources and core competences in contributing to long-term competitive advantage, and therefore discusses these concepts in a good deal more depth.

Unique resources are those resources that critically underpin competitive advantage and that others cannot easily imitate or obtain

Core competences are the activities and processes through which resources are deployed in such a way as to achieve competitive advantage in ways that others cannot imitate or obtain

Putting these concepts together, the summary argument is this. To survive and prosper an organisation needs to address the challenges of the environment that it faces discussed in Chapter 2. In particular it must be capable of delivering against the critical success factors that arise from demands and needs of its customers, discussed in section 2.4.4 of Chapter 2. The strategic capability to do so is dependent on the resources plus the competences it has. These must reach a threshold level in order for the organisation to survive. The further challenge is to achieve competitive advantage (discussed more fully in Chapter 5). This requires it to have strategic capabilities that its competitors find difficult to imi-tate or obtain. These could be unique resources but are more likely to be the core competences of the organisation.

3.3 COST EFFICIENCY

An important strategic capability in any organisation is to ensure attention is paid to achieving and continually improving cost efficiency. This will involve having both appropriate resources and the competences to manage costs. Customers can benefit from cost efficiency in terms of lower prices or more prod-uct features for the same price. In some public services the key stakeholder may be the budget provider who wishes to maintain levels of service provision and quality but at reduced cost. The management of the cost base of an organisation could be a basis for achieving competitive advantage (see sections 3.4.1 and 3.4.2). However, for many organisations in many markets this is becoming a threshold strategic capability for two reasons:

Exhibit 3.3   Sources of cost efficiency

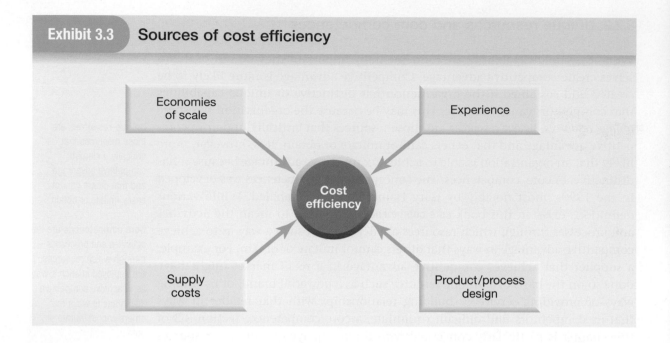

- First, because *customers do not value product features at any price*. If the price rises too high they will be prepared to sacrifice value and opt for a lower priced product. So the challenge is to ensure that an appropriate level of value is offered at an acceptable price. This means that costs have to be kept as low as possible commensurate with the value to be provided; and everyone is forced to do so. Not to do so invites customers to switch products or invites competition.

- Second, *competitive rivalry* will continually require the driving down of costs because competitors will be trying to reduce their cost so as to underprice their rivals while offering similar value. In this context cost efficiency does not become a basis of competitive advantage: it becomes a requirement for survival in a market – a threshold capability.

Cost efficiency is determined by a number of *cost drivers* (see Exhibit 3.3), as follows.

Economies of scale may be an important source of cost advantage in manufacturing organisations, since the high capital costs of plant need to be recovered over a high volume of output. Traditionally manufacturing sectors in which this has been especially important have been motor vehicles, chemicals and metals. In other industries, such as drinks and tobacco and food, scale economies are important in distribution or marketing. In other sectors such as textiles and leather goods, economies of scale have been less significant.[5]

Supply costs influence an organisation's overall cost position. Location may influence supply costs, which is why, historically, steel or glass manufacturing was close to raw material or energy sources. In some instances, ownership of raw materials gave cost advantage too. How supplier relationships are fostered and maintained is of major importance in sustaining this position. Supply costs are of particular importance to organisations which act as intermediaries, where the value added through their own activities is low and the need to identify and manage input costs is critically important to success. For example, in commodity or currency trading, the key resource is knowledge of how prices might move and hence competitive advantage can be gained through competences that maintain higher-quality information than that of competitors. Traditionally, this was concerned with personal contacts and networks that were often difficult to imitate. But now information technology capability is critical to success. Since all traders now have access to similar information systems, ensuring that such technology is up-to-date has become a threshold competence and attempts to innovate to create advantage are likely to be eroded. Achieving competitive advantage is more likely to be about innovative ways in which systems are exploited – and these may also be short-lived.

Product/process design also influences the cost position. Efficiency gains in production processes have been achieved by many organisations over a number of years through improvements in *capacity-fill, labour productivity, yield* (from materials) or *working capital* utilisation. The important issue is having the knowledge to understand the relative importance of each item to maintaining a competitive position. For example, managing capacity-fill has become a major competitive issue in many service industries: an unfilled seat in a plane, train or theatre cannot be 'stocked' for later sale. So marketing special offers (while protecting the core business) and having the IT capability to analyse and optimise revenue are important competences. In contrast, much less attention has been paid to how product *design* may contribute to the overall cost competitiveness of an organisation. Where it has been undertaken, it has tended to be limited to the production processes (e.g. ease of manufacture). However, product design will also influence costs in other parts of the value system – for example, in distribution or after-sales service. Canon gained advantage over Xerox photocopiers in this way – Canon eroded Xerox's advantage (which was built on the Xerox service and support network) by designing a copier that needed far less servicing. The ability to conceive of the design/cost relationship in this more holistic way and to gain the information needed for such an understanding requires successful organisations to have good knowledge of where and how cost is added throughout the value chain (see section 3.6.1).

Experience[6] can be a key source of cost efficiency and there is some evidence it may provide competitive advantage. There have been many studies concerning the important relationship between the cumulative experience gained by an organisation and its unit costs – described as the *experience curve*. This is represented in Exhibit 3.4. The experience curve suggests that an organisation undertaking any activity learns to do it more efficiently over time, and hence develops core competences in this activity. Since companies with higher market share have more 'cumulative experience', it is clearly important to gain and hold market share, as discussed in Chapter 2. It is important to remember that it is the *relative market share* in definable market segments that matters. There are important implications of the experience curve concept that could influence an organisation's competitive position:

● *Growth is not optional* in many markets. If an organisation chooses to grow more slowly than the competition, it should expect the competitors to gain cost advantage in the longer term – through experience.

● Organisations should expect their real *unit costs to decline year on year*. In high-growth industries this will happen quickly, but even in mature industries this

| Exhibit 3.4 | The experience curve |

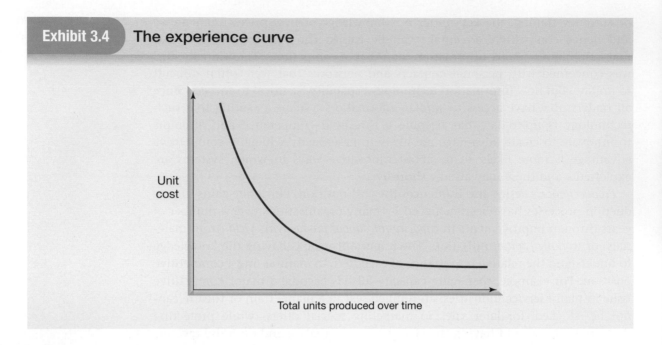

decline in costs should occur. Organisations that fail both to recognise and to have the competence to respond to this are likely to suffer.

● *First mover advantage* can be important. The organisation that moves down the experience curve by getting into a market first should, on the face of it, be able to reduce its cost base because of the accumulated experience it builds up over its rivals by being first.

● However, the likelihood of *sustained advantage through experience curve benefits are not high*. It would be likely to require very high market share advantages not available to most firms.

● The implication of this is that *continual reduction in costs is a necessity* for organisations in competitive markets. Even if it is not able to provide competitive advantage, it is a threshold competence for survival.

● It may be possible to reduce cost by *outsourcing* (see section 3.6.1) those activities where an organisation is not very experienced and other organisations are. Historically, one of the criticisms of public services was that their quasi-monopoly status had tended to shield them from the pressures to push down unit costs, resulting in a preference to keep everything in-house even where experience was low and costs high.

3.4 CAPABILITIES FOR SUSTAINABLE COMPETITIVE ADVANTAGE

All of the factors discussed in sections 3.2 and 3.3 are important. If the capabilities of an organisation do not meet customer needs, at least to a threshold level, the organisation cannot survive. If it cannot manage its costs efficiently and continue to improve on this, it will be vulnerable to those who can. However, if the aim is to achieve *competitive advantage* then this itself is not enough. The question then becomes, what resources and competences might provide competitive advantage in ways that can be sustained over time? If this is to be achieved, then strategic capability has to meet other criteria. These are now reviewed.[7]

3.4.1 Value of strategic capabilities

It is important to emphasise that if an organisation seeks to build competitive advantage it must meet the needs and expectations of its customers. The importance of value to the customer may seem to be an obvious point to make but in practice it is often overlooked or ignored. Managers may argue that some distinctive capability of their organisation is of value simply because it is distinctive. Having capabilities in terms of resources or competences that are different from other organisations is, of itself, not a basis of competitive advantage. There is little point in having capabilities that are 'valueless' in customer terms; the strategic capabilities must be able to deliver what the customer values in terms of product or service. So the discussion in section 2.4.4 of Chapter 2 and the lessons it draws are important here too. Given this fundamental requirement, there are then other key capability requirements to achieve sustainable competitive advantage.

3.4.2 Rarity of strategic capabilities

Clearly, competitive advantage cannot be achieved if the strategic capability of an organisation is the same as other organisations. It could, however, be that a competitor possesses some unique or rare capability providing competitive advantage. This could take the form of *unique resources*. For example, some libraries have unique collections of books unavailable elsewhere; a company may have a powerful brand; retail stores may have prime locations. Some organisations have patented products or services that give them advantage – resources that may need to be defended by a willingness to bring litigation against illegal imitators. Mining companies may own a particular outcrop of minerals. For service organisations unique resources may be intellectual capital – particularly talented individuals. Illustration 3.1 shows how the Ordnance Survey was able to exploit its intellectual capital to advantage. All of these may be rare resources that provide competitive advantage.

Competitive advantage could also be based on rare competences such as the years of experience in, for example, brand management or building relationships with key customers; or perhaps the way in which different parts of a global business have learned to work together harmoniously. Other examples help make important points about the extent to which rarity might provide sustainable competitive advantage:

● Rarity may depend on who owns the competence and how *easily transferable* it is. For example, the competitive advantages of some professional service organisations are built around the competence of specific individuals – such as a doctor in 'leading-edge' medicine. Or the reputation of a fashion house may

Illustration 3.1   strategy into action

The Ordnance Survey

Some organisations have unique resources in their intellectual capital – but these still need to be exploited.

The Ordnance Survey (OS) has existed in the UK for over 200 years as the national mapping agency. Its core functions have included producing, maintaining and marketing maps and managing computer data and geographical information. These are used for leisure, educational and administrative purposes. Its activities were progressively commercialised during the 1990s, and in 1999 the government changed its status from a government body to a trading fund – it then had to run its own finances and make a 9 per cent return on capital. The OS earned income from selling products and services, including issuing licences for others to utilise copyright material. As a result, in 2000 OS made a profit of £12.7m (€19m) on a turnover of £99.6m (€149.4m).

Although the public perception of OS had been as a provider of maps, OS had kept ahead in the market by utilising technology, as computers replaced the need for drawing by hand, and quicker and more accurate revisions could be made. It realised the importance and potential of geographical information systems, which allow a wide variety of information to be synthesised more rapidly. This had the effect of making maps more interactive, and therefore more responsive to consumer needs.

Competitive advantage had been gained by OS being able to license its data. OS had worked with several private sector partners who incorporated OS data into their software products. Innovation had been crucial, as OS attempted to provide a comprehensive service via its Solution Centre, which operated as a consultancy. Computerised data evolved into the biggest part of the business and OS utilised its experience in data collection by providing services to many public and private organisations. This included aiding the police in mapping crime patterns, locating derelict land for development, targeting marketing efforts, calculating insurance risks, and managing property portfolios. OS had also benefited from the growing telecom industry and adopted an e-strategy to turn its maps into digital data for use in mobile phones, mapping websites, and in-car navigation systems.

OS also ensured that it maintained its leading position in the market by capitalising on and investing in new technology and developments – some 3,000 changes were entered into its database daily, ensuring consistent relevance and accuracy. The National Topographic Database, which recorded over 2 million features of the UK landscape, proved to be a successful product. OS was also fiercely protective of its copyright – in March 2001 the Automobile Association agreed to pay OS £20m for alleged copyright infringement.

Sources: Adapted from *Financial Times*, 19 August 2000, 3 October 2000 and 22 December 2000; *Computer Weekly*, 5 October 2000.

Questions

1. What are the unique resources that OS possesses?
2. What competences are needed to exploit these resources?
3. How might a competitor undermine these unique resources?

be built on a top designer. But since these individuals may leave, as Tom Ford did from Gucci in 2003, or join competitors, this resource may be a fragile basis of advantage. More durable advantage *may* be found in the organisation's competences that exist for recruiting, training, motivating and rewarding these rare individuals – so ensuring that they do not defect to 'competitors'. Or a core competence may be embedded in the culture that attracts them to work for the particular organisation.

- An organisation may have secured *preferred access* to customers or suppliers – perhaps through an approval process or by winning a bidding process (as with broadcasting or mobile phone licences). This may be particularly advantageous if this approval for access cannot be obtained without a specified history of operation or having followed a specified development programme – say with pharmaceutical products. This means that a competitor cannot find a short-cut to imitation.

- Some competences are *situation dependent* and not transferable because they are only of value if used in a particular organisation. For example, the systems for operating particular machines are not applicable to organisations that do not use those same machines. It might also be the case that the transfer costs of moving competences from one organisation to another are too high. This is a problem that global companies face when trying to bring the performance of all of their locations up to the standards of the best.

- Sometimes incumbent organisations have advantage because they have *sunk costs* (say in set-up) that are already written off and they are able to operate at significantly lower overall cost. Other organisations would face much higher costs to set up to compete. However, there is always the possibility that a competitor could find some new way of competing dependent on a different resource or competence base. This has often happened in manufacturing, where existing firms reliant on long-established manufacturing technologies have found themselves facing competitors utilising different technologies.

Whilst rarity of strategic capabilities can, then, provide the basis of competitive advantage, there are dangers of redundancy. Rare capabilities may come to be what Dorothy Leonard-Barton refers to as '*core rigidities*',[8] difficult to change and damaging to the organisation and its markets. Managers may be so wedded to these bases of success that they perceive them as strengths of the organisation and 'invent' customer values around them. So, for many years, the managers of Marks & Spencer remained convinced that their customers wanted the sort of merchandise and service that they had been uniquely providing and that the reason for the decline in the fortunes of the firm in the late 1990s was solely to do with market factors outside their control. Clearly this is a contributory reason for the phenomenon of *strategic drift* introduced in Chapter 1 (section 1.5.1).

3.4.3 Robustness of strategic capabilities

It should be clear by now that the search for strategic capability that provides sustainable competitive advantage is not straightforward. It involves identifying capabilities that are likely to be durable and which competitors find difficult to imitate or obtain. Indeed the criterion of *robustness* is sometimes referred to as 'non-imitability'.[9]

At the risk of over-generalisation, it is unusual for competitive advantage to be explainable by differences in the tangible resource base of organisations since over time these can usually be imitated or traded. Advantage is more likely to be determined by the way in which resources are deployed to create competences in the organisation's activities. For example, as suggested earlier an IT system itself will not improve an organisation's competitive standing: it is how it is used that matters. Indeed what will probably make most difference is how the system is used to bring together customer needs with areas of activities and knowledge both inside and outside the organisation. It is therefore to do with linking sets of competences. So, extending the earlier definition, *core competences* are likely to be the *linked* activities or processes through which resources are deployed in such a way as to achieve competitive advantage. They create and sustain the ability to meet the critical success factors of particular customer groups better than other providers and in ways that are difficult to imitate. In order to achieve this advantage, core competences therefore need to fulfil the following criteria:

- They must relate to an activity or process that underpins the value in the product or service features – as seen through the eyes of the customer (or other powerful stakeholder). This is the value criterion discussed earlier.

- The competences must lead to levels of performance that are significantly better than competitors (or similar organisations in the public sector).

- The competences must be robust – that is, difficult for competitors to imitate.

There are several ways in which these conditions might be achieved. These are now reviewed and summarised in Exhibit 3.5. Illustration 3.2 also gives a business example that this discussion refers to.

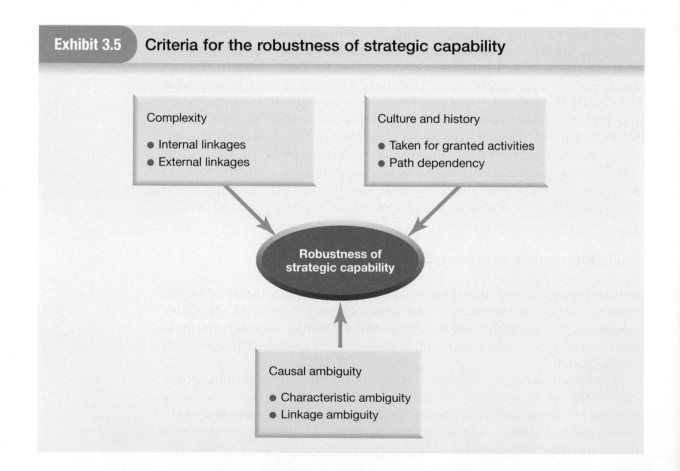

Exhibit 3.5   **Criteria for the robustness of strategic capability**

Complexity
- Internal linkages
- External linkages

Culture and history
- Taken for granted activities
- Path dependency

Robustness of strategic capability

Causal ambiguity
- Characteristic ambiguity
- Linkage ambiguity

Illustration 3.2

Strategic capability for Plasco

Strategic capability underpinning competitive success may be based on complex linkages rooted in the history and culture of an organisation.

Plasco, a manufacturer of plastics goods, had won several major retail accounts from competitors. Managers were keen to understand the bases of these successes as a way of understanding strategic capabilities better. To do this they started with an analysis of customer value (as explained in section 2.4.4). From this they identified that the major retailers with whom it had been successful particularly valued a powerful brand, a good product range, innovation, good service and reliable delivery. In particular, Plasco was outperforming competitors when it came to delivery, service and product range.

They then undertook an activity mapping exercise, as explained in section 3.6.2 of this chapter (see Exhibit 3.8). Some of what emerged from this the senior management knew about; but they were not aware of some of the other explanations for success that emerged.

When they analysed the bases of reliable delivery, they could not find reasons why they were outperforming competitors. The logistics of the company were no different from other companies. They were essential but not unique – threshold resources and competences.

When they examined the activities that gave rise to the good service they provided, however, they found other explanations. They were readily able to identify that much was down to their having a more flexible approach than their competitors, the main one of which was a major US multinational. But the explanations for this flexibility were less obvious. The flexibility took form, for example, in the ability to amend the requirements of the retailers' orders at short notice; or when the buyers in the retailers had made an error, to 'bale them out' by taking back stock that had been delivered. What was much less obvious were the activities underpinning this flexibility. The mapping surfaced some explanations:

- The junior manager and staff within the firm were 'bending the rules' to take back goods from the major retailers when, strictly speaking, the policies and systems of the business did not allow it.

- Plant utilisation was relatively lower and less automated than competitors, so it was easier to change production runs at short notice. Company policy, on the other hand, was to improve productivity through increased utilisation and to begin to automate the plans. Lower levels of production management were not anxious to do this, knowing that if they did, it would reduce the flexibility and therefore diminish their ability to provide the service customers wanted.

A good deal of this was down to the knowledge of quite junior managers, sales representatives and staff in the factory as to 'how to work the system' and how to work together to solve the retailers' problems. This was not a matter of company policy or formal training; but it was custom and practice that had built up over the years. The end result was a relationship between sales personnel and retail buyers in which buyers were encouraged to 'ask the impossible' of the company when difficulties arose.

Sound logistics and good quality products were vital, but the core competences which underpinned their success were the result of linked sets of activities built up over the years which it was difficult, not only for competitors but also for people in the organisation, to clearly identify.

Questions

1. Why might it be difficult for a large, automated US plastics manufacturer to deal with retailers in the same way as Plasco?

2. How should Plasco senior managers respond to the explanations of strategic capability surfaced by the mapping?

Complexity[10]

The core competences of an organisation are unlikely to be one clearly discernible activity. Core competences are more likely to be the linked set of activities and processes that, together, deliver customer value. These may be within the organisation or between the organisation and customers, suppliers or other key stakeholders. Managers may refer to such linked activities with a 'shorthand' explanation. The managers in Plasco (see Illustration 3.2) talked about 'flexibility' and 'innovation'; but 'flexibility' or 'innovation' are themselves made up of and dependent on sets of related activities as Illustration 3.2 shows. Section 3.6.2 and Exhibit 3.8 below show how such linked sets of activities might be mapped so that they can be better understood. However, even if a competitor possessed such a map in great detail as a graphic representation of how a given organisation achieved 'flexibility', it is unlikely that it would be able to replicate the sort of complexity it represents. Indeed in the company described in Illustration 3.2 the management of Plasco were not clear about it themselves.

External interconnectedness of competences is also important. Firms can make it difficult for others to imitate or obtain their bases of competitive advantage by developing competitive advantage together with the customer. In this way they build an intimate relationship on some aspect of the customer's business on which the customer is dependent on them. This is sometimes referred to as *co-specialisation*. For example, an industrial lubricants business moved away from just selling its products to customers and coming to agreements with those customers about managing the applications of lubricants within the customers' sites against agreed targets on cost savings. The more efficient the use of lubricants, the more both parties benefited. Similarly software businesses can achieve advantage by developing computer programs that are distinctively beneficial to specific customer needs. The customers benefit, but in turn are likely to be dependent on that software business for such service and are unlikely to switch readily to a competitor.

Culture and history

In most organisations such competences are likely to become embedded in their culture. Indeed, managers within an organisation may not understand them *explicitly* themselves. So coordination between various activities occurs 'naturally' because people know their part in the wider picture or it is simply 'taken for granted' that activities are done in particular ways. For example, in the plastics business described in Illustration 3.2 the experience in rapid changes in production runs and the close links between sales personnel, production and despatch were not planned or formalised: they were the way the firm had come to operate over the years.

Linked to this cultural embeddedness, therefore, is the likelihood that such competences have developed over time and in a particular way. This historic path by which competences have arisen in an organisation is, itself, difficult to discern and imitate. This is referred to as *path dependency*.[11] It is simplistic to assume that if the competences in one organisation have taken decades to develop, another can imitate them quickly or easily. High levels of service to customers, the encouragement of innovation or keeping costs to a minimum may seem straightforward, but if they have been built into an organisation's culture over years, perhaps decades, they will be difficult to imitate. Again, however, it should be noted that there is a danger that culturally embedded competences built up over such periods of time become so embedded that they are difficult to change; that is, they become core rigidities.

Causal ambiguity[12]

Another reason why competences might be robust is that competitors find it difficult to discern the causes and effects underpinning an organisation's advantage. This is called *causal ambiguity*. So, high levels of uncertainty can exist on how to imitate a successful strategy because competitors are unclear as to just what gives rise to what. This uncertainty could relate to any or all of the aspects of strategic capability discussed in the preceding sections of this chapter. Causal ambiguity may exist in two different forms:[13]

- *Characteristic ambiguity*: this is where the significance of the characteristic itself is difficult to discern or comprehend, for example because it is based on tacit knowledge or rooted in the organisation's culture. For example, it is quite possible that the 'rule bending' in Plasco would have been counter-cultural for its US rival and therefore not readily identified or seen as relevant or significant.

- *Linkage ambiguity*: where managers themselves, let alone competitors, find it difficult to explain which activities and processes are dependent on which other activities and processes to form the linkages that create the competences that give rise to competitive advantage. It would be very difficult for the competitors of Plasco to understand the cause and effect linkages in Plasco when the management of the company did not fully comprehend them themselves.

Competitors may, then, see that one of their rivals is outperforming them in terms of service to customers. They may be able to see all manner of activity relating to customer service – the way customers are dealt with on the telephone or when problems arise; face-to-face relationships between customers and sales people; the flexibility in deliveries or return policies of goods. The list could be very long and they may, in any case, miss how rooted such activities are in the culture and heritage of the organisation let alone its HR policies and training. Much the same point is made about the way in which competitors find it difficult to copy Dell (see the case example at the end of Chapter 1). As was recorded in the *Financial Times* (13 November 2003):

> Talk to senior Dell executives and before long the phrase crops up: 'maniacal focus'. A ferocious attention to detail applied to a tried and tested business model. They see no end to the continual adjustments that can be made to speed the company's processes and bring down costs. Dell's way of doing business is no secret but the years of maniacal focus on fine tuning the system make it difficult for others to catch up.

The point is that it is difficult for a competitor to see how it all works. Moreover even if that were possible it would be difficult for competitors to replicate it in their own culture and structure.

3.4.4 Non-substitutability[14]

Achieving sustained competitive advantage also means avoiding the risk of sub-stitution. Providing value to customers and possessing competences that are complex, culturally embedded and causally ambiguous may mean that it is very difficult for organisations to copy them. However, the organisation may still be at risk from substitution. Substitution could take different forms:

● It could take the form already discussed in Chapter 2 in relation to the five forces model of competition. In other words the product or service as a whole might be a victim of substitution. To take one example in the world of business, e-mail systems have substituted for postal systems. No matter how complex and culturally embedded were the competences of the postal service, it could not avoid this sort of substitution.

● Substitution might, however, not be at the product or service level. It could be at the competence level. For example, it may be that the success of a business has been based on a charismatic leader and the way that individual has developed the management systems in the organisation. But alternative ways of managing may be a substitution for that approach. Similarly task-based industries have often suffered because of an over-reliance on the undoubted competences of skilled craftsmen that have been replaced by expert systems and mechanisations.

So managers need to be aware of the extent to which their competence base is vulnerable to substitution.

In summary and from a resource-based view of organisations, sustainable compet-itive advantage might be achieved by organisations having strategic capabilities which are (a) valuable to buyers, (b) rare, (c) robust, and (d) non-substitutable.

3.4.5 Dynamic capabilities

Implicit within a good deal of what is written in the resource-based view of strategy is that sustainable competitive advantage can be achieved by develop-ing strategic capabilities that provide advantage over time. They are durable. However, managers often claim that the hypercompetitive conditions discussed in section 2.3.2 of Chapter 2 are becoming increasingly prevalent. Environments are changing faster. Technology is giving rise to innovation at a faster rate and therefore greater capacity for imitation and substitution of existing products and services. Customers have more choice and the chances of establishing a sustain-able competitive advantage based on a set of durable competences become less likely. Nonetheless, in such circumstances, some firms do achieve competitive advantage over others. The point is that more emphasis has to be placed on the organisation's capability to change, innovate, be flexible and to learn how to

Dynamic capabilities are an organisation's abilities to develop and change competences to meet the needs of rapidly changing environments

adapt to a rapidly changing environment.

How firms achieve competitive advantage in such circumstances has been the subject of study of academics such as David Teece.[15] The term most often used to describe the strategic capabilities that achieve competitive advantage in such dynamic conditions is *dynamic capabilities*. Here **dynamic capabilities** are taken to mean an organisation's ability to develop and change competences to meet the needs of rapidly changing environments.[16] These capabilities may be relatively formal, such as the organisational systems for new product development or standardised procedures for agreement for capital expenditure. They may also take the form of major strategic moves, such as acquisitions or alliances by which new skills are learned by the organisation. Or they may be more informal such as the way in which decisions get taken or, perhaps, how decisions can get taken faster than usual when fast response is needed. They could also take the form of embedded 'organisational knowledge' (see section 3.5 below) about how to deal with particular circumstances the organisation faces, or how to innovate. Indeed, it is likely that dynamic capabilities will have both formal and informal, visible and invisible, characteristics associated with them. For example, Kathy Eisenhardt[17] has shown that successful acquisition processes that bring in new knowledge to the organisation depend on high-quality pre- and post-acquisition analysis of how the acquisition can be integrated into the new organisation so as to capture synergies and bases of learning from that acquisition. However, hand-in-hand with these formal procedures will be more informal ways of doing things in the acquisition process built on infomal personal relationships and the exchange of knowledge (see below) in more informal ways.

The bottom line is that, whereas in more stable conditions competitive advantage might be achieved by building core competences that may be durable over time, in more dynamic market conditions competitive advantage has to be developed by building the capacity to change, innovate and learn – to build the capacity for dynamic capability. And arguably the more such dynamic capabilities of learning become important, the more the concept of organisational knowledge, explained in the next section, becomes important.

3.5 ORGANISATIONAL KNOWLEDGE[18]

Knowledge can be defined as the awareness, consciousness or familiarity gained by experience or learning. However, in the context of organisations, it is not just individual knowledge that matters, but the knowledge of groups of people in the organisation, or the organisation as a whole. **Organisational knowledge** is the collective and shared experience accumulated through systems, routines and activities of sharing across the organisation.

Peter Drucker[19] and others have referred to the growth of a 'knowledge-based economy'. There are various reasons organisational knowledge has been highlighted as important. First, as organisations become more complex and larger the need to share and pool what people know becomes more of a challenge. Second, because information systems have started to provide more sophisticated ways of doing this. And third, because there is an increasing realisation that many of the lessons discussed already in this chapter are true. It is less likely that organisations will achieve competitive advantage through their physical resources and more likely that they will achieve advantage through the way they do things and the experience that they have accumulated. And therefore that knowledge about how to do things which draws on that experience becomes crucially important.

Organisational knowledge is the collective and shared experience accumulated through systems, routines and activities of sharing across the organisation

The concept of organisational knowledge therefore closely relates to some of the ideas discussed in the chapter so far because it can be the basis of strategic capability. There are resources that underpin knowledge. For example, acquiring or developing adequate hardware and software for information systems infrastructure is a threshold capability for most organisations in the twenty-first century. Some knowledge will be a *rare resource* – for example, the knowledge of a particularly talented individual, such as a research scientist, or the intellectual property of an organisation (e.g. its patents). Knowledge is captured by formal organisational systems, processes (such as market research or procurement processes), and day-to-day activities which draw on people's experience. So it is likely to be a *complex* and *causally ambiguous* strategic capability made up of *linked competences*. It is also concerned with the capacity of an organisation to learn and is therefore central to the *dynamic capability* of an organisation to adapt to changing conditions.

In the context of explaining strategic capability there is, then, only a fine line between organisational knowledge and the linked concepts of intangible resources, competences and dynamic capabilities. A number of useful insights arise here:

● The evidence is that the sharing of knowledge and experience is an essentially social process relying on *'communities of interest'*[20] developing and sharing information because they see it as mutually beneficial. This could happen through formal systems such as the internet (and indeed does) but is also facilitated by social contact and trust. Organisational knowledge therefore highlights the social and cultural aspects of strategic capability.

● Exchange of knowledge is more likely to occur in *cultures of trust* without strong hierarchical or functional boundaries, than in organisations heavily dependent on such hierarchies or demarcation of roles. Think about this in personal terms: who do you most readily share your experiences with and in what circumstances?

● Knowledge takes different forms. Nonaka and Takeuchi[21] distinguish between two types of knowledge. *Explicit knowledge* is codified; and 'objective' knowledge is transmitted in formal systematic ways (e.g. through codified information systems or formal language). In contrast, *tacit knowledge* is personal, context-specific and therefore hard to formalise and communicate. As for individuals, organisational competence usually requires both kinds of knowledge. For example, a driving instructor can drive a car through tacit knowledge, but to teach others requires explicit knowledge of the driving process and this is what is first of all communicated to the learner driver. The learner must use this explicit knowledge to develop his or her tacit knowledge on how to drive a car. The tacit knowledge is, however, achieved through practice and feedback on performance.

● Not surprisingly, organisations have tried to improve the sharing of knowledge by setting up *IT-based systems* to do it. Some of these have been heavily promoted by consultancy firms in the form of knowledge management systems. When this began they were little more than computerised data gathering and information systems. It took some time to realise that while some of this knowledge and competence can be codified and built into computer-based systems, it is very difficult to codify the sharing of such knowledge where it relies

Illustration 3.3   strategy into action

Road mending and the management of organisational knowledge

Formal knowledge management systems may be useful to the point where they facilitate better sharing of knowledge; but they can also reduce knowledge sharing.

A local government department responsible for road mending had a manual system of job allocation it had used for many years. The road menders would pick up their job sheets every morning. These identified which roads needed repairing, which 'gangs' should work on which roads and where the specific locations of jobs were. In fact the road menders had come to employ a somewhat different system. Each morning, after picking up the job sheets, they all met in a local café for breakfast. Here they discussed the jobs and reallocated the job sheets according to their own experience. Moreover they added other jobs based on what they had seen locally. For example, on the way to work one road mender may have identified a small-scale job that needed doing near to one of the specified jobs. The end result was, by the time they had left the café, they had reallocated a lot of the work and added in new jobs.

This informal system of knowledge sharing was known to the management of the department responsible for road maintenance, but they had also come to accept it. However, an increasing pressure to reduce costs and improve productivity caused management to review the situation and they became concerned that its informality was inefficient. They therefore brought in management consultants to advise what should be done. The management consultants advised that a more formal computer-based job allocation system should be introduced which would more carefully record information on required repairs, inform the planning and logistics of the jobs to be done, update information about road repairs completed and monitor the work progress of the gangs. They also observed that the time spent in the café was costly and

inefficient. So, after negotiations with the union, this practice was ended and the new system introduced.

The management of the department were shocked to find that productivity on road repairs declined after the computer-based knowledge management system was introduced. They had failed to realise that the job reallocation in the café was actually an efficient way of sharing the very localised, experience-based knowledge of the road menders. This knowledge had been largely lost, though not entirely. Informal knowledge sharing still persisted. Although breakfasts in the café had ceased, the road menders themselves had set up a separate knowledge-sharing system which comprised a notebook in the café so that any of the road menders calling in during the day could record where they had seen other jobs that needed doing adjacent to current jobs that were being done. The problem was that this notebook wasn't working well because the identification of such jobs was not being picked up early enough by the gangs already out on the road and the men, resenting the new system, were not as motivated as they had been with their 'own' system.

Questions

1. How might the management have tried to improve efficiency differently?

2. Think of a situation where you share knowledge with others. Identify what components of this sharing could be systematically captured and where it would be difficult to do so.

on, or benefits from, the social interaction and trust between people, as shown in Illustration 3.3. Indeed organisations found that people with common interests often bypassed the formal systems and set up their own systems in order to share experience amongst people they trusted and from whose knowledge and experience they thought they could benefit. Some researchers[22] have argued that attempts to over-formalise such knowledge systems in organisations can be harmful because it actually reduces the social aspects of knowledge sharing. Arguably, such codified knowledge-based systems may be useful up to the point where they facilitate better sharing of knowledge; but not beyond that point.

● Arguably, the more formal and systematic the system of knowledge, the greater is the *danger of imitation* and therefore the less valuable the knowledge becomes in competitive strategy terms. If knowledge can be codified, then there is more of a chance of it being copied. Non-imitatable competitive advantage is much more likely to exist where knowledge is lodged in the experience of groups of indiuals.

3.6   DIAGNOSING STRATEGIC CAPABILITY

So far this chapter has been concerned with explaining strategic capability and the associated concepts that help this explanation. However, strategists need to go beyond the concepts to understand more specifically how strategic capabilities underpinning competitive advantage can be examined. This section provides some ways in which this can be done.

3.6.1 The value chain and value network

If organisations are to achieve competitive advantage by delivering value to customers, they need to understand how that value is created or lost. The value chain and value network concepts can be helpful in understanding how value is created or lost in terms of the activities undertaken by organisations.

The value chain

The value chain describes the activities within and around an organisation which together create a product or service. It is the cost of these *value activities* and the value that they deliver that determines whether or not best value products or services are developed. The concept was used and developed by Michael Porter[23] in relation to competitive strategy. Exhibit 3.6 is a representation of a value chain. **Primary activities** are *directly* concerned with the creation or delivery of a product or service and can be grouped into five main areas. For example, for a manufacturing business:

Primary activities are directly concerned with the creation or delivery of a product or service

● *Inbound logistics* are the activities concerned with receiving, storing and distributing the inputs to the product or service. They include materials handling, stock control, transport, etc.

Exhibit 3.6	The value chain within an organisation

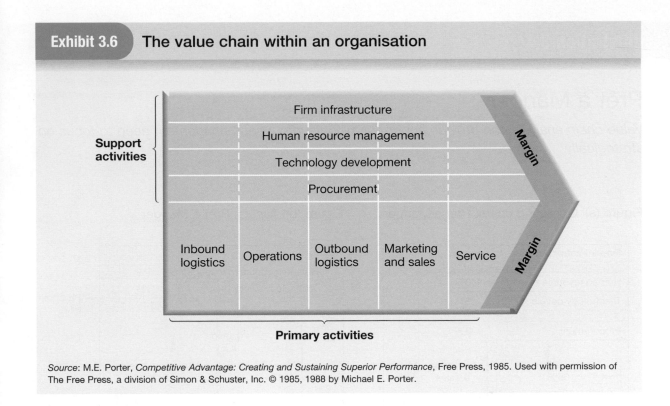

Source: M.E. Porter, *Competitive Advantage: Creating and Sustaining Superior Performance*, Free Press, 1985. Used with permission of The Free Press, a division of Simon & Schuster, Inc. © 1985, 1988 by Michael E. Porter.

- *Operations* transform these various inputs into the final product or service: machining, packaging, assembly, testing, etc.

- *Outbound logistics* collect, store and distribute the product to customers. For tangible products this would be warehousing, materials handling, distribution, etc. In the case of services, they may be more concerned with arrangements for bringing customers to the service if it is a fixed location (e.g. sports events).

- *Marketing and sales* provide the means whereby consumers/users are made aware of the product or service and are able to purchase it. This would include sales administration, advertising, selling and so on. In public services, communication networks which help users access a particular service are often important.

- *Service* includes all those activities which enhance or maintain the value of a product or service, such as installation, repair, training and spares.

Each of these groups of primary activities is linked to support activities. **Support activities** help to improve the effectiveness or efficiency of primary activities. They can be divided into four areas:

Support activities help to improve the effectiveness or efficiency of primary activities

- *Procurement.* This refers to the *processes* for acquiring the various resource inputs to the primary activities. As such, it occurs in many parts of the organisation.

- *Technology development.* All value activities have a 'technology', even if it is just know-how. The key technologies may be concerned directly with the product (e.g. R&D, product design) or with processes (e.g. process development) or with a particular resource (e.g. raw materials improvements). This area is fundamental to the innovative capacity of the organisation.

Illustration 3.4

Prêt à Manger

Value chain analysis can provide important insights into what management need to focus on strategically

Figure (a) Operating costs: Prêt à Manger

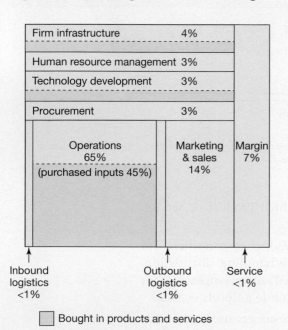

Figure (b) Assets: Prêt à Manger

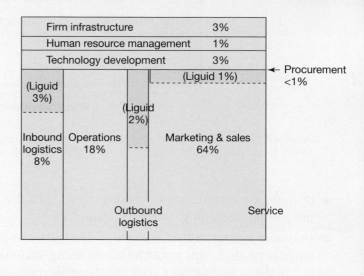

- *Human resource management.* This is a particularly important area which transcends all primary activities. It is concerned with those activities involved in recruiting, managing, training, developing and rewarding people within the organisation.

- *Infrastructure.* The systems of planning, finance, quality control, information management, etc. important to an organisation's performance in its primary activities. Infrastructure also consists of the structures and routines of the organisation which are part of its culture (see Chapter 4, section 4.5.3).

These descriptions of different activities within the firm can be thought of in at least two ways such that they can contribute to the analysis of the strategic position of the organisation.

First, they can be seen as *generic descriptions of activities* that might be mapped in an activity system. So managers might be able to see if there is a cluster of

The two figures represent the value chains of Prêt à Manger based (a) on their cost and (b) on their assets. Consider some of the implications.

From a breakdown of operating costs (a), the importance of Prêt à Manger managing its purchased inputs is clear as is the criticality of production level setting. If the forecast for lunchtime sales is, say, 10 per cent too high, then the morning's sandwich making consumes 10 per cent more purchased inputs than it should, resulting in wastage of 4.5 per cent of sales and wiping out over 60 per cent of the day's profits.

Translating assets into a value chain framework can be just as enlightening. What is interesting is the contrasting position of 'Marketing and Sales' versus 'Operations'. The source of this can be traced to an imbalance in property leasehold assets, even though half the floor area of a typical Prêt à Manger outlet is kitchen and half is shop. Simple accounting would have allocated the leasehold cost equally, but the value chain framework prompts deeper questions: Why is the property leasehold cost this high? Is it mostly the need for operating space or is it the need for marketing and sales space? The answer is that sandwich making could take place in a low-cost factory unit, but selling needs high-value retail locations.

The marketing and sales portion of the asset value chain is high because the retail locations are expensive. Perhaps the single most important aspect of Prêt à Manger's strategic management support layer is ensuring that these high-cost sites are also high value to the company and its clientele. Prêt à Manger wants to sell sandwiches, not newspapers or jewellery, so local market research that enables a site's sandwich revenue potential to be closely predicted is extremely valuable. Look at the asset map again; if an outlet's sales turned out to be half the level expected when the site was acquired, would the asset cost change? Hardly at all – the liquid element is tiny, and the bulk of the spend for fixtures and fittings is not transferable to another site.

Source: Adapted from Andrew Shepherd, 'Understanding and using value chain analysis', in *Exploring Corporate Techniques of Analysis and Evaluation in Strategic Management*, edited by Veronique Ambrosini, Prentice Hall, 1998, pp. 20–44.

Questions

1. How might understanding of Pret a Manger's value chain inform decisions on its future strategy?

2. Draw up a value chain for another business in terms of the activities within its component parts.

3. Estimate the relative costs and/or assets associated with these activities.

4. What are the strategic implications of your analysis?

activities providing particular benefit to customers located within particular areas of the value chain. Perhaps the firm is especially good at outbound logistics linked to its marketing and sales operation and supported by its technology development. It might be less good in terms of its operations and its inbound logistics. So this might raise questions as to what the firm should be concentrating on and what, perhaps, it might be de-emphasising or outsourcing. The categorisation of activities also requires managers to think about the role such activities play. For example, in a local family-run sandwich bar, is sandwich making best thought of as 'operations' or as 'marketing and sales', given that its reputation and appeal may well rely on the social relations and banter between customers and sandwich makers? Arguably it is 'operations' if done badly but 'marketing and sales' if done well.

These various activities can also be examined in terms of the *cost and value of activities*.[24] Illustration 3.4 shows this in relation to the value chain of Prêt à Manger. It shows how, by identifying the cost base and base of elements of the value chain, important insights are provided about what management need to focus on in relation to their strategy.

The value network

In most industries it is rare for a single organisation to undertake in-house all of the value activities from the product design through to the delivery of the final product or service to the final consumer. There is usually specialisation of role and any one organisation is part of the wider *value network*. The **value network**[25] is the set of inter-organisational links and relationships that are necessary to create a product or service (see Exhibit 3.7). It is this process of specialisation within the value network on a set of linked activities that can underpin excellence in creating best-value products. So an organisation needs to be clear about what activities it ought to undertake itself and which it should not and, perhaps, outsource. However, since much of the cost and value creation will occur in the supply and distribution chains, managers need to understand this whole process and how they can manage these linkages and relationships to improve customer value. It is not sufficient to look at the organisation's internal position alone. For example, the quality of a consumer durable product (say a cooker or a television) when it reaches the final purchaser is not only influenced by the linked set of activities which are undertaken within the manufacturing company itself. It is also determined by the quality of components from suppliers and the performance of the distributors.

It is therefore critical that organisations understand the bases of their strategic capabilities in relation to the wider value network. Some of the key questions they need to address are these:

> The **value network** is the set of inter-organisational links and relationships that are necessary to create a product or service

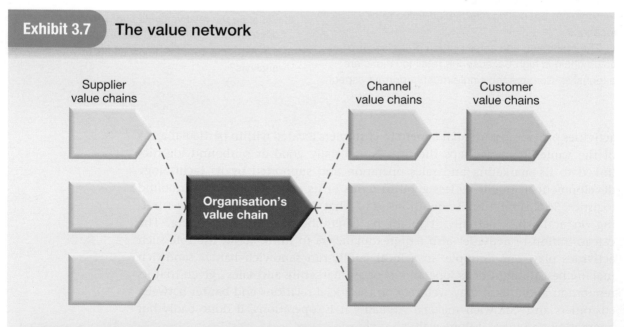

Exhibit 3.7   The value network

Supplier value chains

Channel value chains

Customer value chains

Organisation's value chain

Source: M.E. Porter, *Competitive Advantage: Creating and Sustaining Superior Performance*, Free Press, 1985. Used with permission of The Free Press, a division of Simon & Schuster Inc. © 1985, 1988 by Michael E. Porter.

- *Where cost and value are created.* Here the sort of analysis explained in relation to the cost and value of activities in the value chain (see above) can help.

- *Which activities are centrally important* to their own strategic capability and which are less central. A firm may, for example, decide that it is important to retain direct control of centrally important capabilities, especially if they relate to activities and processes that it believes are core competences. On the other hand, another firm in a highly competitive market may require to cut costs in key areas and may decide it can only do so by outsourcing to lower cost producers.

- *Where the profit pools*[26] *are.* **Profit pools** are defined here as the potential profits at different parts of the value network. The point is that some parts of a value network are inherently more profitable than others because of the differences in competitive intensity. For example, historically in the computer industry microprocessors and software have been more profitable than hardware manufacture. The strategic question becomes whether it is possible to focus on the areas of greatest profit potential? Care does have to be exercised here however. It is one thing to identify such potential; it is another to be successful in it given the competences the organisation has. For example, in the 1990s many car manufacturers recognised that greater profit potential lay in services such as car hire and financing rather than manufacturing but found they did not have the relevant competences to succeed in such sectors.

  Profit pools are the potential profits at different parts of the value network

- *The 'make or buy'* decision for a particular activity or component is therefore critical. This is the *outsourcing* decision. There are businesses that now offer the benefits of outsourcing (as Illustration 3.5 shows). Of course, the more an organisation outsources, the more its ability to influence the performance of other organisations in the value network may become a critically important competence in itself and even a source of competitive advantage.

- Who might be the *best partners* in the various parts of the value network? And what kind of *relationships* are important to develop with each partner? For example, should they be regarded as suppliers or should they be regarded as alliance partners? Some businesses have seen the benefit of moving closer in their relationships with suppliers such that they are cooperating more and more on such things as market intelligence, product design, and research and development.

3.6.2 Activity maps

As has already been explained, managers often find it difficult to identify with any clarity the strategic capability of their organisation. Too often they highlight capabilities that are not valued by customers but are seen as important within the organisation, perhaps because they were valuable in the past. Or they highlight things that are, in fact, critical success factors (product features particularly valued by customers) like 'good service' or 'reliable delivery' when, as has been shown, strategic capability is about the resources, processes and activities that underpin the ability to meet these critical success factors. Or they identify capabilities at too generic a level. This is not surprising given that strategic capability

Illustration 3.5   strategy into action

Agility through outsourcing with British Telecom

The benefits suggested for outsourcing are extensive.

British Telecom (BT) promotes its outsourcing business with the strap-line 'Agility through Outsourcing'.

> Many organisations both in the public and private sector have reviewed their internal processes and found that they lack the necessary resources to meet the increasing challenges put on them by changing demands of their customers. . . . They have turned to companies whose core competences fill the gaps in their internal structure. They hand over the running of whole business functions, such as payroll or training, gaining the expertise they need to meet that step change requirement forced on them by the expectations of their customers, but at a predictable cost.

BT offers its clients the opportunity to outsource its information, communication and technology (ICT) functions to provide them with 'freedom from technology':

> Making an investment in technology requires a great deal of expert knowledge to ensure that it becomes an enabler for business rather than a barrier to it. Often organisations find they don't have that expertise in-house. The solution is either buying that expertise in, further raising the level of investment, or handing over the responsibility of managing their ICT systems to a third party like BT that has the relevant skills at its core.

BT has such skills, it argues, because in its own transformation from a public sector organisation to a private company, it placed ICT processes and management at its core, reducing its own cost base and focusing on competitive advantage and customer care by aligning its people, processes and technology. The result is that it believes it can offer a:

> Totally integrated approach to IT infrastructure, software systems and applications which enables us to manage more effectively on behalf of our customers . . . BT can take some or all of the operational responsibility on behalf of the clients' ICT departments. We are able to provide a customised communication service that involves taking over the customer's existing network, including services from other carriers. All solutions are tailored to meet the specialised needs of each customer . . . our services will

> go to the extent of transferring assets including staffing resources. We buy the assets from our customers that we need to serve their top technology needs. As a result they get a capital injection by removing those assets from the balance sheet . . . these organisations can then plough the money they saved into products that benefit their core competences, focused on giving a high quality service to their customers.

BT suggests further benefits to potential clients. Its services:

> Greatly benefit organisations that have a specific process or service, which depends greatly on leading edge technology, but for which there is little in-house expertise. The benefits include:

- Achieving costs savings and predictable costs, improving piece of mind through reduced risk.
- Gain access to funds which otherwise would not be available for potential large scale projects.
- Reduce the risk of business change by involving economies of scale from BT.
- Increased agility to reach new markets or new geographies.
- Increased agility to change your business in line with changes in the environment.
- Take advantage of access to resources in expertise not available internally.
- Improve access to technology, innovation and scarce technical skills.
- Reduce management overheads and supplier interfaces.
- Achieve productivity gains leading to lower costs.

Source: The Sunday Times Enterprise Network website (www.enterprisenetwork.co.uk)

Questions

1. Other than ICT, what other areas of business operations might benefit from outsourcing? Specify some of the benefits that might be gained.

2. Given the benefits stated in this illustration, why might businesses choose to keep their ICT or other business operations in-house?

is likely to be rooted in a complex, causally ambiguous set of linked activities (see section 3.4.2). But if they are to be managed proactively, finding a way of identifying and understanding them is important.

One way of undertaking such diagnosis is through the mapping of activities. An activity map tries to show how the different activities of an organisation are linked together. Illustration 3.2 described the search by Plasco's management for the company's strategic capabilities using activity mapping. There are computer programs in existence that can be used;[27] or they may be done more basically, for example by drawing network diagrams, as shown in Exhibit 3.8.[28] This map was generated by groups of managers from within the organisation, working with a facilitator, mapping the activities of their organisation on a large blank wall initially by using Post-its®.[29]

They began by undertaking the sort of competitor analysis explained in section 2.4.4 of Chapter 2. The aim here was to identify, first, the *critical success factors* in relation to their customers; and second, on which of these their own business outperformed competitors. This identified the CSFs of brand reputation, product range, innovation, excellence of service and reliability of delivery, and the fact that Plasco was seen as particularly successful in terms of its level of service and its product range in relation to competitors delivered these CSFs. Managers were relatively easily able to identify what Michael Porter refers to as *higher order strategic themes*.[30] In Plasco's case these were that a good deal of the benefits it offered were to do with flexibility and rapid response. But the reasons why the organisation outperformed competitors did not emerge until these themes themselves were 'unpacked' by identifying the resources and competences that underpinned these items. To do this a facilitator worked with the managers to encourage them to keep questioning just what activities existed in the company that 'delivered' the customer benefits. Exhibit 3.8 is only a selection of these activities. The eventual map covered most of a wall and consisted of hundreds of Post-its®, each one representing an activity in some way contributing to strategic capability. The activity-based competences described in Illustration 3.2 and summarised in Exhibit 3.8 emerged from this diagnostic process.

General lessons that can be drawn from such maps about how competitive advantage is achieved and the relationship between competences and competitive advantage include:

- *Consistency*. Most basically because the different activities that create value to customers are consistent with each other. They are pulling in the same direction rather than opposing each other.

- *Reinforcement*. Because the different activities may be reinforcing each other (e.g. in Plasco an open management style facilitated rule bending).

- *Difficulties of imitation*. It is more difficult for a competitor to imitate a mix of such activities than to imitate any given one. It is robust in that it represents linked activities built up over years, culturally embedded, complex and causally ambiguous – the lessons of section 3.4.3. If the multinational competitor of Plasco decided to try to compete on the same basis of flexibility it would have no comparable experience to draw on to do this.

- *Trade-offs*. Even if imitation were possible it could in any case pose another problem for competitors. For example, Plasco's international competitor might

Exhibit 3.8   An activity system map*

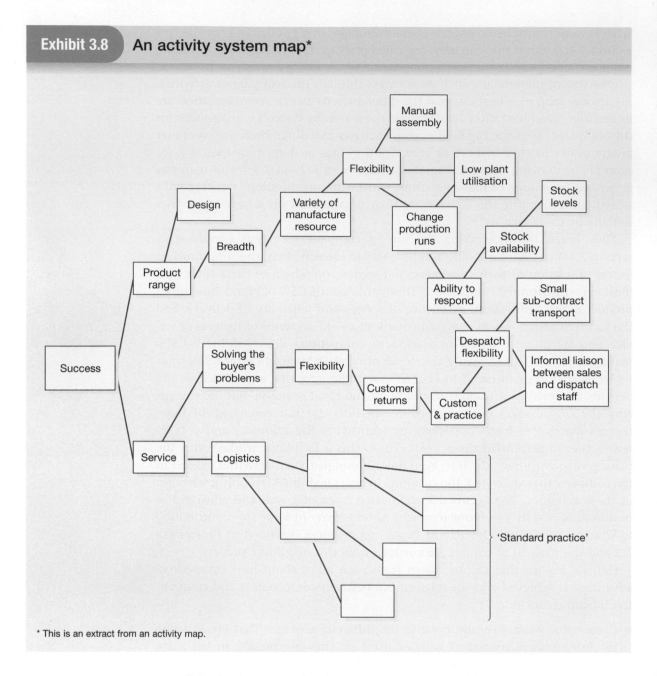

* This is an extract from an activity map.

well find it has jeopardised its existing position with the existing customers it has set out to satisfy by means of more standardised mass production.

Such maps can also be helpful in informing managers what they can do to preserve and develop strategic capability. This is discussed in section 3.7 below.

3.6.3 Benchmarking[31]

An organisation's strategic capability has to be assessed in relative terms since it concerns the ability to meet and beat the performance of competitors. There are different ways in which relative performance might be understood. Section 2.4 in Chapter 2 has already discussed the importance of competitor analysis, including understanding how one organisation compares with another in terms of their overall strategic characteristics and in terms of how customers view them. This section examines the value of *benchmarking* which is now widely used to further inform the relative standing of organisations.

Types of benchmarking

There are a number of different approaches to benchmarking, some more useful than others.

- *Historical benchmarking*. It is common for organisations to consider their performance in relation to previous years in order to identify any significant changes. The danger with historical comparison alone, however, is that it can lead to complacency since it is the rate of improvement compared with that of competitors that is important.

- *Industry/sector benchmarking*. Insights about performance standards can be gleaned by looking at the comparative performance of other organisations in the same industry sector or between similar public service providers. These industry norms compare the performance of organisations in the same industry or sector against a set of performance indicators. Illustration 3.6 shows such comparisons in the form of league tables (often the case in the public sector in the UK). Some public sector organisations have, in effect, acknowledged the existence of strategic groups by benchmarking against similar organisations rather than everybody. So local government services and police treat 'urban' differently from 'rural' in their benchmarking and league tables. School league tables acknowledge the difference between comprehensive and selective and so on. While it may make sense to compare like with like, an overriding danger of industry norm comparisons (whether in the private or public sector) is that the whole industry may be performing badly and losing out competitively to other industries that can satisfy customers' needs in different ways. So a benchmarking regime should probably look wider than a particular industry or sector, as discussed below. Another danger with benchmarking within an industry is that the boundaries of industries are blurring through competitive activity and industry convergence. For example, supermarkets are (incrementally) entering retail banking and their benchmarking needs to reflect this (as does the benchmarking of the traditional retail banks).

- *Best-in-class benchmarking*. The shortcomings of industry norm comparisons have encouraged organisations to seek comparisons more widely through the search for best practice wherever it may be found. The potential for change is enhanced by (benchmarking) partnerships established across industries or sectors. Best-in-class benchmarking compares an organisation's performance against 'best in class' performance – wherever that is found. The real power of this approach is not just 'beyond industry/sector' comparisons. It is concerned with shaking managers out of the mindset that improvements in performance will be gradual as a result of incremental changes in resources or competences, which is not the reality that many organisations face in the twenty-first

Illustration 3.6

Benchmarking UK hospitals

Benchmarking against 'industry norms' is commonly used to assess standards of performance

In 2004 the UK Labour government was pursuing a policy of establishing a number of 'foundation hospitals'. Whilst these would be funded by the state and remain part of the National Health Service, they would have a greater degree of independence of decision and strategy making. It was a contentious policy with many Labour supporters themselves opposing it.

The government had proposed that in order to gain foundation status a hospital would have to gain a '3 star status' within the benchmarking exercise undertaken by the Commission for Health Improvement (CHI) that examined all major UK hospitals. The ratings were based on a system of grading against targets and measures of clinical capability and service. Targets included:

- Waiting times: including the number of patients (a) waiting for more than 12 hours for admission to accident and emergency, (b) waiting for admission to hospital, within this (c) waiting for cancer care and (d) outpatients waiting for treatment.

- The number of patients not readmitted within 28 days of a cancelled operation.

- The achievement of financial plans.

- Hospital cleanliness.

- The total time spent waiting for treatment in accident and emergency.

In addition to measures such as these, hospitals were also rated on the basis of factors taken into consideration during visits made by the CHI.

In July 2003 the 'league tables' for such performance were published. The *Guardian* reported: 'Four of the 29 NHS hospitals being groomed by ministers for foundation status were forced out of the running last night when the health inspectorate decided they were no longer good enough to qualify for the top 3 star grading. However, the government was pleased that 50 of the hospitals had improved their rating status during the year compared with 35 that had lost stars and 81 that had stayed the same.'

There were, however, many criticisms of the system. The *Guardian* raised questions about the volatility of the gradings year on year which 'cast doubt on the theory underpinning the government's foundation policy'.

James Johnson, Chairman of the British Medical Association, claimed that the star ratings: '. . . measure little more than a hospital's ability to meet political targets, and take inadequate account of clinical care or factors such as social deprivation. It is grossly unfair on staff working in low rated trusts – the public's confidence in them is being undermined.' The Chief Executive of the Newcastle Hospitals Trust, marked down for excessive waiting times, pointed out that it should not be penalised for the number of patients referred to the hospital, which was outside its control.

John Reid, the Labour government's Health Secretary, said that 'the purpose of this exercise is not to condemn or shame those trusts who fail to make the grade on any particular indicator but to help them overcome local difficulties and offer better services for patients in the future'. However, Liam Fox, the Conservative Party spokesman on health, said 'the star ratings system is ludicrous and should be scrapped. The ratings bear no relation to the quality of care that patients are receiving.'

Source: NHS performance ratings; *Guardian*, 16 July 2003.

Questions

1. If you were the chief executive of a hospital (e.g. the Newcastle Hospital), what would you prioritise in order to score well in the benchmarking exercise?

2. What are your conclusions about the benefits and drawbacks of benchmarking exercises of this type? Use other examples to support your case.

3. What might the bases of comparison be for 'best-in-class' benchmarking of hospitals?

century. They face threats from other organisations that achieve dramatic improvements in performance on particular value activities or through how activities are linked together. But benchmarking can only provide the 'shock' that in turn should encourage managers to understand better how to improve their competences. They will then need to observe how activities might be performed better. For example, British Airways improved aircraft maintenance, refuelling and turnround time by studying the processes surrounding Formula One Grand Prix motor racing pit stops.[32] A police force wishing to improve the way in which it responded to emergency telephone calls studied call centre operations in the banking and IT sectors.

For service organisations in particular, the critical issue is that improved performance in one sector – particularly on issues like speed and reliability – shifts the *general level* of expectations in customers about speed or reliability from all companies and public sector organisations. So benchmarking these issues could 'break the frame' within organisations about the performance standards to be achieved. Of course, organisations can view this in a positive rather than a threatening light. Benchmarking can be used to spot opportunities to outperform dramatically the incumbent providers by organisations which may not be current competitors but which are particularly competent at certain activities or business processes. This is an example of stretching core competences to exploit opportunities in different markets or arenas.

The value of benchmarking

The importance of benchmarking is not in the detailed 'mechanics' of comparison but in the impact that these comparisons might have on behaviours. It can be usefully regarded as a process for gaining momentum for improvement and change. But it has dangers too:

● One of the major criticisms of benchmarking is that it leads to a situation where '*you get what you measure*'; and this may not be what is intended strategically. The mechanics of the process can take over and cloud the purpose of the exercise and it can also result in changes in behaviour that are unintended and certainly dysfunctional. For example, the university sector in the UK has been subjected to rankings in league tables on research output, teaching quality and the success of graduating students in terms of employment and starting salaries. This has resulted in academics being 'forced' to orientate their published research to certain types of academic journals that may have little to do directly with the quality of the education in universities. The general point is that if the basis of benchmarking is flawed it can set off a reorientation of strategies that are flawed – in the sense that they do not lead to genuinely better performance.

● Since benchmarking compares inputs (resources), outputs or outcomes it is also important to remember that it will *not identify the reasons for the good or poor performance* of organisations since the process does not compare competences directly. For example, it may demonstrate that one organisation is less good at customer service than another; but it will not show the underlying reasons. However, if it is well directed it could encourage managers to seek out these reasons and hence understand how their competences could be improved. Managers would need to observe and understand how top-performing organisations undertook their activities and to assess if these could be imitated or improved upon.

3.6.4 Strengths and weaknesses[33]

The issues discussed in the preceding sections provide insights into the strategic capability of an organisation. The key 'strategic messages' from both the business environment (Chapter 2) and this chapter can be summarised in the form of an analysis of strengths, weaknesses, opportunities and threats (SWOT). A **SWOT analysis** summarises the key issues from the business environment and the strategic capability of an organisation that are most likely to impact on strategy development. This can also be useful as a basis against which to generate strategic options (see Chapter 7, section 7.2.5) and assess future courses of action (see Chapter 7, section 7.4).

A **SWOT analysis** summarises the key issues from the business environment and the strategic capability of an organisation that are most likely to impact on strategy development

The aim is to identify the extent to which the current strengths and weaknesses are relevant to and capable of dealing with the changes taking place in the business environment. However, in the context of this chapter, if the strategic capability of an organisation is to be understood it must be remembered it is not absolute but relative to its competitors. So SWOT analysis is really only useful if it is comparative – if it examines strengths, weaknesses, opportunities and threats relative to those of competitors. Illustration 3.7 takes the example of a pharmaceuticals firm (Pharmcare). It assumes that key environmental impacts have been identified from the sort of analyses explained in Chapter 2. It also assumes that major strengths and weaknesses have been identified using the sorts of analytic tools explained in this chapter. A scoring mechanism (plus 3 to minus 3) is used as a means of getting managers to assess the interrelationship between the environmental impacts and the strengths and weaknesses of the firm. A positive (+) denotes that the strength of the company would help it take advantage of, or counteract a problem arising from an environmental change or that a weakness would be offset by that change. A negative (–) score denotes the strength would be reduced by such a change or that a weakness would prevent the organisation from overcoming problems associated with that change.

Pharmcare's share price was taking a dip because investors were concerned that its strong position in the market was under threat. Were management becoming too complacent, even arrogant, they wondered? The pharmaceutical market was changing with new ways of doing business often driven by new technology or the quest to provide medicines at lower cost to more people, politicians forever trying different ways of coping with soaring healthcare costs and an ever more informed patient, but was Pharmcare keeping pace? The strategic review of the firms's position (Illustration 3.7a) confirmed its strengths of a flexible sales-force, well-known brand name and new healthcare department but identified a major weakness, namely competence in information and communication technology (ICT). When the impact of environmental forces on competitors was analysed (Illustration 3.7b) it showed that Pharmcare was indeed outperforming

Illustration 3.7 strategy into action

SWOT analysis of Pharmcare

A SWOT analysis explores the relationship between the environmental influences and the strategic capabilities of an organisation compared to its competitors.

(a) SWOT analysis for Pharmcare

	Environmental change (opportunities and threats)					
	Healthcare rationing	Complex and changing buying structures	Increased integration of healthcare	Informed patients	+	–
Strengths						
Flexible salesforce	+3	+5	+2	+2	12	0
Highly innovative R&D	0	0	+3	+3	+6	0
Strong brand name	+2	+1	0	–1	3	–1
Healthcare education department	+4	+3	+4	+5	+16	0
Weaknesses						
Limited competences in biotechnology and genetics	0	0	–4	–3	0	–7
No imminent product launch	0	–2	–2	–2	0	–6
Weak ICT competences	–2	–2	–5	–5	0	–14
Over-reliance on leading product	–1	–1	–3	–1	0	–6
Environmental impact scores	+9	+9	+9	+10		
	–3	–5	–14	–12		

(b) Competitor SWOT analyses

	Environmental change (opportunities and threats)				
	Healthcare rationing	Complex and changing buying structures	Increased integration of healthcare	Informed patients	Overall impact
Pharmcare *Big pharma, global player which investors are worrying is becoming too arrogant*	+6 A flexible salesforce combined with a new h/c ed department creates synergy in this area	+4 A flexible salesforce combined with a new h/c education department creates synergy in this area	–5 Weak ICT, limited activity in new technologies and over-reliance on one product outweigh strengths	–2 h/c ed department weakened by patients lobbying against branding and, once again, lack of ICT competence	+3 Could do better considering starting in a position of strength but reasonable alignment with the changing times
Company W *Big pharma losing ground in new areas of competition*	–5 Focus is on old style promotional selling rather than helping doctors control costs through drugs	–5 Traditional salesforce not helped by marketing which can be insensitive to national differences	+0 Alliances with equipment manufacturers but little work done across alliance to show dual use of drugs and new surgical techniques	–4 Has yet to create web presence or consider patients to be a customer, albeit indirect	–14 Needs to modernise to remain powerful in industry with new business models
Company X *Biotech niche vaccine start-up*	+4 Specialising in vaccines considered too low margin for big pharma gives company an edge	–3 Niche vaccines are voluntary, meaning start-ups suffer from not having big salesforce and no alliance with big pharma. Govt is hot on vaccines at the moment for security but in the future?	+1 Little integration in this area currently but there could be in the future	+1 Disease prevention becoming fashionable but vaccine scares possible, as are panics regarding new diseases – biotech firms can produce vaccines against very rapidly	+3 If the environment plays into its hand could be a very profitable game to play
Company Y *New global player operational in new drugs and off patent biotech generics*	+4 Biotech generics hot area as although prices lower than patented versions, markets unsaturated, but can the company overcome regulatory hurdles to launch drugs before Pharmcare?	–2 Yet to develop worldwide salesforce but making the right moves having bought into a US salesforce	+3 Very innovative use of web to show how products fit into healthcare processes	+1 Innovative use of web but currently only in local markets	+6 Could become a strong player in the future if learning in generics market transferred to new drugs

Questions

1. Are the items with hightest scores (+ or –) in the right-hand columns of (a) the principal strengths and weaknesses of the company?
2. How readily can executives identify the strengths and weaknesses of competitors?
3. Identify the benefits and dangers (other than those identified in the text) of a SWOT analysis such as that in the illustration.

Prepared by Jill Shepherd, Simon Fraser University, Vancouver, Canada.

its traditional competitor (Company W), but was potentially vulnerable to changing dynamics in the general industry structure courtesy of niche players (Company X) and a new combination of competences, including ICT, within a firm increasingly similar to itself (Company Y).

Overall, a SWOT analysis should help focus discussion on future choices and the extent to which an organisation is capable of supporting these strategies. There are, however, some dangers in undertaking a SWOT analysis. The main ones are these:

● A SWOT exercise can generate very *long lists* of apparent strengths, weaknesses, opportunities and threats. What matters, however, is to be clear about what is really important and what is less important.

● There is a danger of *over-generalisation*. Remember the lessons of sections 3.6.1 and 3.6.2. Identifying a very general explanation of strategic capability does little to explain the underlying reasons for that capability. So SWOT analysis is not a substitute for more rigorous, insightful analysis.

3.7   MANAGING STRATEGIC CAPABILITY

The previous section has been concerned with diagnosing strategic capability. This section considers what managers might do, other than such diagnosis, to manage and hopefully improve the strategic capability of their organisation, either because they are unable to meet threshold requirements, or because they have identified possible bases of achieving competitive advantage. This is considered in terms of (a) the limitations of managing strategic capabilities; (b) stretching and adding capabilities; (c) managing people for capability development and (d) building dynamic capabilities.

3.7.1 The limitations of managing strategic capabilities

One of the lessons that emerges from an understanding of strategic capabilities is that, quite often, the most valuable bases of strategic capability lie in aspects of the organisation that are very difficult to discern or be specific about. This raises some tricky questions for managers. How is it possible to manage directly that which it is not always easy to be clear about? For example, in the Plasco illustration, a good deal of the capabilities of that organisation were to be found in activities that the top management were not directly managing. Should they seek to manage these directly or should they not? Research by Veronique Ambrosini[34] has explored this with regard to the sources of causal ambiguity (see section 3.4.2). She argues that it is important to understand what managers might be able to do and what they cannot do according to how much they understand and value the bases of strategic capability in terms of causal ambiguity. Consider some different circumstances:

● *Competences are valued but not understood.* Managers may know that there are activities and processes in their organisation that have a positive impact and they may value these. But they may not understand just how this positive impact arises. For example, the delivery of value may be dependent on highly specialised local skills; or on complex linkages far down in the organisation. The lesson here is that managers may have to be careful about disturbing the bases of such capabilities whilst, at the same time, ensuring that they monitor the benefits created for customers.

- *Competences are not valued.* Here managers know about activities and processes in the organisation but do not recognise their positive impact or value such activities. There are real dangers here that managers take the wrong course of action. For example, they may end up cutting out areas of activity that create actual or potential competitive advantage. This often happens in organisations where top management are intent on cutting costs without a sufficient understanding of how value is created. It would be wise to understand the value-creating capabilities better before such decisions.

- *Competences are recognised, valued and understood.* This might be the sort of situation that was the outcome of the sort of analysis undertaken by Plasco. Here managers may be able to act to nurture and further develop such competences, for example by ensuring that overall company policies support and enhance such capabilities. The danger can be that top management may seek to preserve such capabilities by over-formalising or codifying them such that they become 'set in stone'.

3.7.2 Stretching and adding capabilities

There may be situations where decisions and actions can be taken that relate to the development of strategic capabilities from within the organisation and by external development. For example:

- *Extending best practices.* It might be that management identify strategic capabilities in one area of the business, perhaps customer service in some of the geographic business units of a multinational, that are not present in other business units. They might seek to extend such best practice throughout all the business units. Whilst this seems straightforward, studies[35] find it is not. The capabilities of one part of an organisation might not be easily transferred to another because of the problems of managing change (see Chapter 10).

- *Adding and changing activities.* Could activities be added, or existing activities be changed so that they become more reinforcing of outcomes that deliver against critical success factors? For example, in Plasco, could even faster internal ways of responding to customer needs be found?

- *Stretching competences.* Managers may also see the opportunity to build new products or services out of existing competences. For example, a chemicals business that undertook an activity mapping exercise to identify its bases of competitive advantage learned that it was not its expertise in chemicals that mattered so much as its competences in meeting and servicing varied and specific customer needs. Managers began to realise that these competences might allow them to develop what amounted to an industrial services business rather than seeing the business in terms of chemicals. Indeed building new businesses on the basis of such competences is the basis upon which related diversification is built as explained in section 6.2.1 of Chapter 6.[36]

- *Building on apparent 'weaknesses'*. Danny Miller's research[37] showed that firms, faced with a situation of being unable to match rivals' strategic capability, may develop competitive advantage by developing what might historically have been seen as valueless resources or activities, for example historically unproductive teams, underperforming businesses or difficult client relationships. They did so by recognising and relating potential benefits in such areas to potential market opportunities and then developing and fostering them through experimentation within supportive cultures and, possibly, outside the mainstream organisational structures.

- *Ceasing activities*.[38] Could activities currently undertaken but not central to the delivery of value to customers be done away with, outsourced or reduced in cost? This could have a number of benefits. It could reduce the cost base of the company, conceivably help reduce the price to the customer and reduce the amount of time spent by people in the organisation on activities that do not deliver customer value.

- *Trade-offs*. Does the organisation face trade-off decisions? For example, could the activity system of the organisation be improved to the benefit of customers by structuring the organisation in such a way as to avoid overlapping or inconsistent activity systems? It can be the case that within a given business, customers in different market segments have different requirements with the business trying to deal with them through the same business unit. Might it be that different business units are required when different activity systems are necessary for different sorts of customers?

- *External capability development*. There may also be ways of developing capabilities by looking externally. For example, managers may seek to develop capabilities by building external relationships with other organisations or by acquisition. One of the major reasons firms enter into alliances and joint ventures (see Chapter 7, section 7.3.3) is to learn new ways of doing things. For example, Sir George Mathewson of the Royal Bank of Scotland[39] has argued that, given its original position as a 'relatively small bank at the edge of Europe', its succesful growth in Europe and its acquisition of NatWest might not have been possible had it not been for its alliance with Banco Santander. It was an important way of giving managers in the bank exposure to the European context. Similarly acquisitions may be about trying to acquire new skills and competences (Chapter 7, section 7.3.2).

3.7.3 Managing people for capability development

One of the lessons of this chapter is that strategic capability often lies in the day-to-day activities that people undertake in organisations, so developing the capability of people to recognise the importance of what they do in terms of the strategic capability of the organisation is important.

- *Targeted training and development* may be possible. Often companies design training and development programmes that are very general. For strategic purposes it may be important to target much more specifically on the development of competences which can provide competitive advantage. For example, an engineering business, whilst acknowledging the undoubted abilities its personnel had in the technical aspects of engineering products, recognised that these were attributes that competitors had too and that there was a need to develop people's abilities to innovate more around value adding customer service. The business therefore changed its training and development programmes to emphasise these requirements.

- *HR policies* might be employed to develop particular competences. For example, in the 1990s KPMG, the accountancy firm, realising that it needed to develop more general business and management skills in its future partners, changed its HR policies on recruitment and assessment to favour those individuals with such aptitude; and an oil company that sought to build its competitive advantage around the building of close customer relationships in markets for industrial oils did so by ensuring that senior field managers with an aptitude for this were promoted and sent to different parts of the world that needed to be developed in such ways.

- More generally, it may be important to *develop people's awareness* of how what they do can matter at the strategic level. It is a common complaint in organisations that 'no one values what I do'. One lesson of this chapter is that what people do on a day-to-day basis may not be labelled 'strategic' but can be so. Helping people see how their work relates to the bigger strategic picture can both enhance the likelihood that they will, indeed, contribute positively to helping achieve competitive success and increase their motivation to do so.

3.7.4 Building dynamic capabilities

Particularly in fast-changing conditions successful firms may be those that have grown the dynamic capabilities (see section 3.4.4) to continually readjust required competences. In effect their competence becomes that of learning and development. In this context, the characteristics of what has become known as a *'learning organisation'* may become especially important. These include:

- the recognition of the significance of the *intuition* of people in the organisation;

- the acceptance that different, even *conflicting ideas* and views are to be welcomed;

- and that *experimentation* is the norm and becomes part of the learning process.

Managers need to consider how to protect and foster such behaviour. For example, it may be that those within the organisation who show most ability to contribute to such learning are the least powerful, perhaps quite junior in the hierarchy. They may need the protection of more powerful people.

Managers also need to consider what *additional activities* might be helpful to support such learning, the way the organisation should be organised (see Chapter 8) to facilitate learning and what strategies the organisation should be following that might add to the dynamic capabilities. For example, an organisation

| Exhibit 3.9 | Knowledge creation processes |

		To	
		Tacit knowledge	Explicit knowledge
From	Tacit knowledge	Socialisation (sympathised knowledge)	Externalisation (conceptual knowledge)
	Explicit knowledge	Internalisation (operational knowledge)	Combination (systematic knowledge)

Source: I. Nonaka and H. Takeuchi, *The Knowledge-Creating Company*, Oxford University Press Inc., © 1995. Reprinted by permission of Oxford University Press.

might choose to set up internal 'venturing' business units or projects to provide a base for its more adaptable, innovative staff.

Lessons from the *management of organisational knowledge* are relevant in such a context. The point has been made earlier in the chapter (see section 3.5) that formal systems tend only to capture formalised organisational knowledge and that this is only a partial basis for achieving strategic capability, certainly in dynamic conditions. So those who have studied organisational knowledge point to the importance of establishing the right sort of culture and strucuture for the organisation to encourage sharing and learning. Moreover they point out that the more the emphasis is on establishing formal systems, the more that may inhibit and constrain dynamic capabilities.

Extending this argument, Nonaka and Takeuchi[40] argue that truly innovative companies are ones that can modify and enlarge the knowledge of individuals to create a '*spiral of interaction*' between tacit and explicit knowledge through the four processes shown in Exhibit 3.9:

● *Socialisation* is a process of sharing experiences between individuals and thereby allowing them to acquire tacit knowledge from others without a formal system or the use of language. The apprenticeship model in craft industries is a good example.

● *Externalisation* is the process of articulating tacit knowledge into explicit concepts. This can be very difficult. It may require a combination of different methods such as model building, metaphors or analogies.

● *Combination* is the process of systematising concepts into a 'knowledge system', for example by linking separate bodies of explicit knowledge. Individuals achieve this through formal methods of meetings, documents or computer networks.

● *Internalisation* is the process of embodying explicit knowledge into tacit knowledge. It is closely related to 'learning by doing'.

Illustration 3.8

key debate

The resource-based view of competitive advantage: is it useful to managers?

The view that the management of strategic capability is central for achieving competitive advantage has been questioned.

Since the early 1990s, the resource-based view (RBV) of strategy has become highly influential. Much academic research is carried out on it, a good deal of which has been used in this chapter, and managers increasingly talk about the importance of building on core competences to gain competitive advantage. However, two US academics, Richard Priem and John Butler, have raised questions about the value of RBV.[1]

The critique

In the context of this chapter, 2 of Priem and Butler's observations are especially significant:

- *The risk of tautology.* The underlying explanation of RBV is that the resource characteristics (or capabilities) that lead to competitive advantage are those that are valuable and rare. Yet competitive advantage is defined in terms of value and rarity. This verges on tautology. Others argue that, to say that a business performs better than another because it has superior resources or is better at some things than other businesses is a statement of the obvious. It can only be helpful if it is possible to be specific about what capabilities are important and why.

- *The lack of specificity.* However, there is typically little specific in what is written about RBV. And some would say the same is true when managers talk about capabilities or competences. 'Top management skills', 'innovation' or 'organisational culture' mean little without being specific about the activities and processes that comprise them. Priem and Butler suggest this is particularly so with regard to the argued importance of tacit knowledge in bestowing competitive advantage. 'This may be descriptively correct, but it is likely to be quite difficult for practitioners to effectively manipulate that which is inherently unknowable.' (The problem raised at the beginning of section 3.6.2.)

The result, argue Priem and Butler, is that 'Simply advising practitioners to obtain rare and valuable resources in order to achieve competitive advantage and, further that those resources should be hard to imitate and non-substitutable' is not very helpful in providing practical help.

The response

Jay Barney,[2] one of the main proponents of RBV, acknowledges that some of this critique is useful. For example, he accepts the argument that there is a need to understand more about how resources are used or how people behave in bestowing competitive advantage. However, he defends the managerial relevance of RBV because he believes it highlights that managers need to identify and develop the most critical capabilities of a firm.

Others try to be more specific. For example, Anne Marie Knott[3] studied franchising as a way of understanding how capabilities might be managed and transferred between organisations. She shows that competences in the form of activities and processes from a franchisor can be passed to franchisees without them being imitated by firms outside the franchise operation. She concludes that managers must be able to identify such competences and establish ways of transferring them and suggests that competitive advantage therefore lies in the management skills of franchisors in helping franchisees learn the necessary skills. To which Priem and Butler would, presumably, respond by pointing out that 'management skills' is a non-specific category that fails to identify the activities involved!

Notes:

1. R. Priem and J.E. Butler, 'Is the resource-based "view" a useful perspective for strategic management research?', *Academy of Management Review*, vol. 26, no. 1 (2001), pp. 22–40.
2. J. Barney, 'Is the resource based "view" a useful perspective for strategic management research? Yes', *Academy of Management Review*, vol. 26, no. 1 (2001), pp. 41–56.
3. A.M. Knott, 'The organizational routines factor market paradox', *Strategic Management Journal*, vol. 24, Special Issue (2003), pp. 929–943.

Questions

1. How specific would the identification of strategic capabilities need to be to permit them to be managed to achieve competitive advantage?

2. If it were possible to identify specifically the management skills of successful franchisors, (a) might they be deliberately fostered but (b) would it then be likely they could be imitated?

Managers should also ask whether there are inherent *dangers in the current bases of competitive* success. For example, it could be that the activities that provide bases of success become too embedded in the organisation's way of doing things and therefore become difficult to change: they can become *core rigidities*.[41]

Illustration 3.8 summarises a key debate that writers on strategic capabilities are pursuing.

Summary

- Strategic capability is concerned with the adequacy and suitability of resources and competences required for an organisation to survive and prosper. Competitive advantage is achieved by organisations that are able to develop strategic capabilities more appreciated by customers and in ways that competitors find difficult to imitate.

- Strategic capabilities comprise tangible and intangible resources and competences – the way such resources are used and deployed. Organisations require such resources and competences at least to a threshold level in order to be able to compete. If they are to achieve competitive advantage, they require resources and competences which are both valuable to customers and difficult for competitors to imitate (such competences are known as core competences).

- The continual improvement of cost efficiency is a vital strategic capability if an organisation is to continue to prosper.

- The sustainability of competitive advantage is likely to depend on strategic capabilities being valuable to customers, rare, robust (i.e. difficult to imitate) or non-substitutable.

- In dynamic conditions, it is unlikely that such strategic capabilities will remain stable. In such circumstances dynamic capabilities are important, i.e. the ability to continually change strategic capabilities.

- Analysing an organisation's value chain and value network can be an important basis of understanding how value to a customer is created and how it can be developed.

- The activities which underpin the strategic capabilities of an organisation may be understood by activity mapping.

- Benchmarking can be a useful way of understanding the relative performance of organisations and challenging the assumptions managers have about the performance of their organisation.

- A SWOT analysis can be a useful way of drawing together an understanding of strengths, weaknesses, opportunities and threats an organisation faces.

- Managers need to think about how and to what extent they can manage the development of the strategic capabilities of their organisation. They may do this by stretching such capabilities, managing people in the organisation and, in fast-changing environments, building dynamic capabilities.

Recommended key readings

- For an understanding of the resource based view of the firm, an early and much cited paper is by Jay Barney: 'Firm resources and sustained competitive advantage', *Journal of Management*, vol. 17 (1991), pp. 99–120. The paper by D.J. Teece, G. Pisano and A. Shuen: 'Dynamic capabilities and strategic management', *Strategic Management Journal*, vol. 18, no. 7, also provides a good summary as well as dealing with the concept of dynamic capabilities.

- Papers that prompted the interest in core competences and the search for competitive advantage are by G. Hamel and C.K. Prahalad: 'The core competence of the corporation', *Harvard Business Review*, vol. 68, no. 3 (1990), pp. 79–91, and 'Strategy as stretch and leverage', *Harvard Business Review*, vol. 71, no. 2 (1993), pp. 75–84.

- Michael Porter explains how mapping what he calls 'activity systems' can be important in considering competitive strategy in his article 'What is strategy?', *Harvard Business Review*, Nov–Dec (1996).

- An interesting paper discussing the management of strategic capabilities and in particular how apparent weaknesses may be converted to bases of advantage is: D. Miller, 'An asymmetry-based view of advantage: towards an attainable sustainability', *Strategic Management Journal*, vol. 24 no. 10 (2003), pp. 961–976.

References

1. The concept of resource-based strategies was introduced by B. Wernerfelt, 'A resource-based view of the firm', *Strategic Management Journal*, vol. 5, no. 2 (1984), pp. 171–180. There are now many books and papers that explain and summarise the approach. See for example the beginning of D.J. Teece, G. Pisano and A. Shuen: 'Dynamic capabilities and strategic management', *Strategic Management Journal*, vol. 18, no. 7 (1997), pp. 509–534, and the introductory paper by D. Hoopes, T. Madsen and G. Walker to the special issue of the *Strategic Management Journal*, 'Why is there a resource based view?' (vol. 24, no. 10 (2003), pp. 889–902).

2. Extraordinary profits as defined here are also sometimes referred to by economists as rents. For an explanation related to strategy see R. Perman and J. Scoular, *Business Economics*, Oxford University Press, 1999, pp. 67–73.

3. Intangible resources have become increasingly recognised as being of strategic importance. See: T. Clarke and S. Clegg, *Changing Paradigms: The transformation of management knowledge for the 21st century*, Harper Collins, 2000, p. 342 (this outlines Arthur Andersen's classification of intangible assets); R. Hall, 'The strategic analysis of intangible resources', *Strategic Management Journal*, vol. 13, no. 2 (1992), pp. 135–144; and 'A framework linking intangible resources and capabilities to sustainable competitive advantage', *Strategic Management Journal*, vol. 14, no. 8 (1993), pp. 607–618.

4. Gary Hamel and C.K. Prahalad were the academics who promoted the idea of core competences. For example: G. Hamel and C.K. Prahalad, 'The core competence of the corporation', *Harvard Business Review*, vol. 68, no. 3 (1990), pp. 79–91. The idea of driving strategy development from the resources and competences of an organisation is discussed in G. Hamel and C.K. Prahalad, 'Strategic intent', *Harvard Business Review*, vol. 67, no. 3 (1989), pp. 63–76, and G. Hamel and C.K. Prahalad, 'Strategy as stretch and leverage', *Harvard Business Review*, vol. 71, no. 2 (1993), pp. 75–84. Also see G. Hamel and A. Heene (eds), *Competence-based Competition*, John Wiley, 1994.

5. Perman and Scoular discuss economies of scale and differences between industry sectors in pages 91–100 of their book (see reference 2 above).

6. P. Conley, *Experience Curves as a Planning Tool*, available as a pamphlet from the Boston Consulting Group. See also A.C. Hax and N.S. Majluf, in R.G. Dyson (ed.), *Strategic Planning: Models and analytical techniques*, John Wiley, 1990.

7. The headings used in this chapter are similar, but not identical, to those used most commonly by writers in academic papers on RBV. These are sometimes referred to as VRIN. This stands for Valuable, Rare, difficult to Imitate (we use 'robust') and non-Substitutable and they were first identified by Jay Barney; see 'Firm Resources and Sustained Competitive Advantage', *Journal of Management*, vol. 17 (1991), pp. 99–120.

8. For a full explanation of 'core rigidities' see D. Leonard-Barton, 'Core capabilities and core rigidities: a paradox in managing new product development', *Strategic Management Journal*, vol. 13 (Summer 1992), pp. 111–125.

9. See reference 7 above.

10. We use the word 'complexity'; others use the word 'interconnectedness'. See for example K. Cool, L.A. Costa and I. Dierickx, 'Constructing competitive advantage' in A. Pettigrew, H. Thomas and R. Whittington (eds), *The Handbook of Strategy and Management*, edited by pp. 55–71, Sage Publications, 2002.

11. For a fuller discussion of path dependency see the paper by Teece, Pisano and Shuen (reference 1 above).

12. The seminal paper on causal ambiguity is S. Lippman and R. Rumelt, 'Uncertain imitability: an analysis of interfirm differences in efficiency under competition', *Bell Journal of Economics*, vol. 13 (1982), pp. 418–438.

13. The distinction between and importance of characteristic and linkage ambiguity is explained in detail by A.W. King and C.P. Zeithaml in 'Competencies and firm performance: examining the causal ambiguity paradox', *Strategic Management Journal*, vol. 22 (2001), pp. 75–99.

14. The importance of non-substitutability and ways of identifying possible bases of substitution are discussed in M.A. Peteraf and M.E. Bergen, 'Scanning dynamic competitive landscapes: a market and resource-based framework' *Strategic Management Journal*, vol. 24, no. 10 (2003), pp. 1027–1042.

15. David Teece has written about dynamic capabilities in the paper referred to in reference 1 above. Different writers have different views on what dynamic capabilities are but tend to emphasise relatively formal organisational processes such as product development, alliances and particular ways of taking decisions in firms (e.g. K. Eisenhardt and J. Martin, 'Dynamic capabilities; what are they?', *Strategic Management Journal*, vol. 21 (2000), pp. 1105–1121; M. Zollo and S. Winter, 'Deliberate learning and the evolution of dynamic capabilities', *Organization Science*, vol. 13, no. 3 (2002), pp. 339–351). A different view is that dynamic capabilities are about organisational learning (see section 11.6.2 of chapter 11) which places more emphasis on the way the organisation is run, on the capacity of its culture to allow for or facilitate learning and adaptation.

16. This definition is the one Teece, Pisano and Shuen use; see reference 1 above.

17. See K. Eisenhardt and J. Martin (reference 15 above).

18. The importance of analysing and understanding knowledge is discussed in I. Nonaka and H. Takeuchi, *The Knowledge Creating Company*, Oxford University Press, 1995 and V. von Krogh, K. Ichijo and I. Nonaka, *Enabling Knowledge Creation: How to unlock the mystery of tacit knowledge and release the power of innovation*, Oxford University Press, 2000. There are also collections of articles on organisational knowledge: e.g. the Special Issue of the *Strategic Management Journal* edited by R. Grant and J.-C. Spender, vol. 17 (1996), and the *Harvard Business Review on Knowledge Management*, HBR Press, 1998.

19. See P. Drucker, *Management Challenges for the 21st Century*, Butterworth-Heinemann, 1999.

20. E.C. Wenger and W.M. Snyder, 'Communities of practice: the organisational frontier', *Harvard Business Review*, Jan–Feb (2000) and E.C. Wenger, *Communities of Practice: Learning, Meaning and Identity*, Cambridge University Press, 1999.

21. See reference 18 above.

22. The danger that formal systems of knowledge sharing can reduce social aspects of knowledge sharing is shown in: S. Newell, H. Scarbrough and J. Swan, 'From global knowledge management to internal electronic fences: contradictory outcomes of intranet development', *British Journal of Management*, vol. 12 (2001), pp. 97–111.

23. An extensive discussion of the value chain concept and its application can be found in M.E. Porter, *Competitive Advantage*, Free Press, 1985.

24. For an extended example of value chain analysis see A. Shepherd, 'Understanding and using value chain analysis', in Veronique Ambrosini (ed.), *Exploring Techniques of Analysis and Evaluation in Strategic Management*, Prentice Hall, 1998.

25. P. Timmers, *Electronic Commerce*, John Wiley, 2000, pp. 182–193, provides an interesting discussion of how value networks are being created and changed by IT.

26. The importance of profit pools is discussed by O. Gadiesh and J.L. Gilbert in 'Profit pools: a fresh look at strategy', *Harvard Business Review*, May–June (1998), pp. 139–147.

27. A good example of such computer-based systems for analysing organisational capabilities can be found in a paper by C. Eden and F. Ackermann, 'Mapping distinctive competencies: a systemic approach', *Journal of the Operational Society*, vol. 51 (2000), pp. 12–20.

28. For a more comprehensive account of the use of such network mapping see V. Ambrosini, *Tacit and Ambiguous Resources as Sources of Competitive Advantage*, Palgrave Macmillan, 2003.

29. The paper by Phyllis and Gerry Johnson, 'Facilitating group cognitive mapping of core competencies' (in *Mapping Strategic Knowledge*, edited by Anne Huff and Mark Jenkins, Sage, 2002) explains some of the problems of undertaking such mapping.

30. Michael Porter explains how mapping what he calls 'activity systems' can be important in considering competitive strategy in his article 'What is strategy?', *Harvard Business Review*, Nov–Dec (1996).

31. Benchmarking is used extensively in both private and public sectors. S. Codling, *Benchmarking Basics*, Gower, 1998, is a practical guide to benchmarking. Also see J. Holloway, *Identifying Best Practices in Benchmarking*, Chartered Institute of Management Accountants, 1999. And for a review of the use of benchmarking in the public sector see: M. Wisniewski, 'Measuring up to the best: a manager's guide to benchmarking', in G. Johnson and K. Scholes (eds), *Exploring Public Sector Strategy*, Financial Times/Prentice Hall, 2001, Chapter 5.

32. See A. Murdoch, 'Lateral benchmarking, or what Formula One taught an airline', *Management Today*, November (1997), pp. 64–67. See also the Formula One case study in the case study section of this book (Text and Cases version only).

33. The idea of SWOT as a common-sense checklist has been used for many years: for example, S. Tilles, 'Making strategy explicit', in I. Ansoff (ed.), *Business Strategy*, Penguin, 1968. See also T. Jacobs, J. Shepherd and G. Johnson's chapter on SWOT analysis in V. Ambrosini (ed.), *Exploring Techniques of Strategy Analysis and Evaluation*, Prentice Hall, 1998.

34. See reference 28.

35. See C.A. Maritan and T.H. Brush, 'Heterogeneity and transferring practices: implementing flow practices in multiple plants', *Strategic Management Journal*, vol. 24, no. 10 (2003), pp. 945–960.

36. In their 1990 paper, Hamel and Prahalad (see reference 4 above) discuss the stretching of competences as the basis of related diversification.

37. See D. Miller, 'An asymmetry-based view of advantage: towards an attainable sustainability', *Strategic Management Journal*, vol. 24, no. 10 (2003), pp. 961–977.

38. The evidence for this is provided in the paper by D. Miller (see reference 37).

39. From a speech by Sir George Mathewson at the British Academy of Management in Edinburgh in 2000 also recorded in the case study on the Royal Bank of Scotland Group in the 6th edition of *Exploring Corporate Strategy* (2002).

40. See reference 18 above.

41. See reference 8 above.

WORK ASSIGNMENTS

✷ Denotes more advanced work assignments.   * Refers to a case study in the Text and Cases edition.

3.1 Using Exhibits 3.1 and 3.2 identify the resources and competences of an organisation with which you are familiar. You can answer this in relation to Amazon* or Formula One* if you so wish.

3.2 Undertake an analysis of the strategic capability of an organisation with which you are familiar in order to identify which capabilities, if any, meet the criteria of (a) value, (b) rarity, (c) robustness and (d) non-substitutability (see section 3.4). You can answer this in relation to Amazon* or Formula One* if you so wish.

3.3 Explain how the organisation you have analysed in assignment 3.2 does or does not gain competitive advantage. Is this based on specific capabilities or linked capabilities? (If you have not undertaken an activity map analysis in 3.2, do so here.)

3.4 Use Exhibits 3.6 and 3.7 to map out the key value activities for Amazon* or a Formula One team* or an organisation of your choice, both within the organisation and in the wider value network in which it operates.

3.5✷ Take any industry and public service and sketch out a map of how core competences have changed over time. Why have these changes occurred? How did the relative strengths of different companies or service providers change over this period? Why?

3.6✷ For a benchmarking exercise which you have access to, make a critical assessment of the benefits and dangers of the approach that was taken.

3.7 Prepare a SWOT analysis for an organisation of your choice and in relation to competitors (see Illustration 3.7). Explain carefully why you have chosen each of the factors you have included in the analysis; in particular their relationship to other analyses you have undertaken in Chapters 2 and 3. What are the conclusions you arrive at from your analysis?

An extensive range of additional materials, including audio summaries, weblinks to organisations featured in the text, definitions of key concepts and multiple choice questions, can be found on the *Exploring Corporate Strategy* Companion Website at **www.pearsoned.co.uk/ecs7**

Listening at eBay

Jill Shepherd, Simon Fraser University, Vancouver, Canada

At least 30 million people will buy and sell well over $20bn in merchandise (in 2003) – more than the gross domestic product of all but 70 of the world's countries. More than 150,000 entrepreneurs will earn a full-time living selling everything from diet pills and Kate Spade handbags to £30,000 BMWs and hulking industrial lathes. More automobiles, of all things, sell on eBay than even no. 1 US dealer AutoNation. So what does this add up to? 'This is a whole new way of doing business,' says Whitman. 'We're creating something that didn't exist before.

It wasn't planned, but as users plunged into consumer electronics, cars, and industrial gear, eBay followed. Today, eBay has 27,000 categories, including eight with gross sales of more than £1 billion each.

Source: eBay

eBay's business model

Value in eBay is created by providing a virtual world-wide market for buyers and sellers and collecting a tax on transactions as they happen. The business model of eBay relies on its customers being the organisation's product-development team, sales and marketing force, merchandising department, and the security department.

The organisation, headed by Meg Whitman, was founded in 1995, when Pierre Omidyar launched a basic site called Auction Web. His girlfriend wanted to trade her collection of Pez dispensers, but Omidyar had a broader vision in mind, namely empowering everyday consumers to trade without the need for large corporations. He even wanted traders to be responsible for building the community and deciding how to build the website. It worked; soon he found himself answering e-mails from buyers and sellers during the day and rewriting the site's software at night to incorporate their suggestions, which ranged from fixing software bugs to creating new product categories. Some 100,000 messages from customers are posted per week in which tips are shared, system glitches are pointed out and changes are lobbied for. The COO, Brian Swette, is quoted as saying, 'The trick is to keep up with what buyers and

sellers want. We've had to constantly change how we run. We start from the principle that if there's noise, you better listen.' Currently the technology allows every move of every potential customer to be traced, yielding rich information.

Structurally, the business model is realised through 5,000 employees, roughly half of whom are in customer support and a fifth in technology. A key role in eBay is 'category manager', a concept Whitman brought to eBay from her days in marketing giant P&G. Category managers direct the 23 major categories as well as the 35,000 subcategories, from collectibles to sports gear, to jewellery and watches, and even jet-planes.

Conventional companies might spend big money on getting to know their customers and persuading them to provide feedback, but for eBay such feedback is often free and offered without the need for enticement. Even so some of the company's most effective ways of getting user input do not rely on the Net and do not come free. eBay organises Voice of the Customer groups, which involve flying in a new group of about 10 sellers and buyers from around the country to its San Jose (Californian) headquarters every few months to discuss the company in depth. Teleconferences are held for new features and policies, however small a change they involve. Even workshops and classes are held to teach people how to make the most of the site. Participants tend to double their selling activity on eBay after taking a class.

The company is governed from both outside and within. The eBay system has a source of automatic control in the form of buyers and sellers rating each other on each transaction, creating rules and norms. There's an educational system that offers classes around the country on how to sell on eBay. Both buyers and sellers build up reputations which are valuable, in turn encouraging further good behaviour in themselves and others. When that wasn't quite enough, eBay formed its own police force to patrol the listings for fraud and kick out offenders, the Trust and Safety Dept, now staffed by several hundred eBay employees worldwide. They do everything from trolling the site for suspicious listings to working with law enforcement agencies to catch crooks. eBay also has developed software that recognises patterns of behaviour common to previous fraud cases, such as sellers from Romania who recently started selling large numbers of big-ticket items.

eBay's management

Meg Whitman's style and past has heavily influenced the management of eBay. When she joined the company in 1998, it was more of a collection of geeks, handpicked by the pony-tailed Omidyar, than a blue-chip – something which underpinned Omidyar's recruitment of Meg. Meg, an ex-consultant, filled many of the senior management roles including the head of the US business, head of international operations and vice-president of consumer marketing with consultants. The result: eBay has become data and metric driven. 'If you can't measure it, you can't control it', Meg says. Whereas in the early days you could touch and feel the way the organisation worked, its current size means it needs to be measured. Category managers are expected to spend their days measuring and acting upon data within their fiefdom.

Some measures are standard for e-business and include how many people are visiting the site, how many of those then register to become users, how long each user remains per visit, how long pages take to load and so on. A measure Meg likes is the 'take rate', the ratio of revenues to the value of goods traded on the site (the higher the better). She measures which days are the busiest, directing when to offer free listings in order to stimulate the supply of auction items. Noise on the discussion boards is used to understand whether the community is in 'supportive' or 'ready to kill you mood' on a scale of 1 to 10. Normal for eBay is around 3.

Category managers in eBay, unlike their counterparts in Procter and Gamble, can only indirectly control their products. They have no stock to reorder once levels of toothpaste or washing-up liquid run low on the supermarket shelves. They provide tools to buy and sell more effectively. 'What they can do is endlessly try to eke out small wins in their categories – say, a slight jump in scrap-metal listings or new bidders for comic books. To get there, they use marketing and merchandising schemes such as enhancing the presentation of their users' products and giving them tools to buy and sell better.' Over and above this unusual existence, the work environment can be tough and ultracompetitive, say ex-eBayers. Changes often come only after PowerPoint slides are exchanged and refined at a low level, eventually presented at a senior level and after the change has been approved in a sign-off procedure which includes every department. An advance in the ways shoes could be searched for took ten months to happen. Aware that analysis can mean paralysis, Meg commissioned consultants (who else) to benchmark the rate at which change is indeed implemented in eBay. eBay was rated as average amongst the companies surveyed.

Over time eBay has upgraded its ability to ensure the technology does not rule. Until the late 1990s, the site was plagued with outages, including one in 1999 which shut the site down for 22 hours courtesy of software problems and no backup systems. Former Gateway Inc. Chief Information Officer Maynard Webb, who joined as president of eBay's technology unit, quickly took action to upgrade systems. Now the site is down for less than 42 minutes a month, despite much higher traffic.

Meg is a leader who buys into the company in more ways than one. Having auctioned some $35,000 worth of furnishings in her ski condo in Colorado to understand the selling experience, she became a top seller among the company's employees and ensured that her learning from the experience was listened to by fellow top execs. Meg is also known for listening carefully to her employees and expects her managers to do the same. As the business is as much, if not more, its customers, any false move can cause revolts within the community that is eBay.

Most of all eBay tries to stay aware and flexible. Nearly all of its fastest-growing new categories emerged from registering seller activity in the area and quietly giving it a nudge at the right moment. For example, after noticing a few car sales, eBay created a separate site called eBay Motors in 1999, with special features such as vehicle inspections and shipping. Some four years later, eBay expects to gross some $1 billion worth of autos and parts, many of which are sold by professional dealers.

The democratic underpinning of eBay, whilst easily embraced by customers, can, however, take some getting used to. New managers can take six months to understand the ethos. 'Some of the terms you learn in business school – drive, force, commit – don't apply', says former PepsiCo Inc. exec William C. Cobb, now senior vice-president in charge of eBay's international operations. 'We're over here listening, adapting, enabling.'

Sources: Robert D. Hof, 'The People's Company', *Business Week*, (e-biz), 3 December (2001), pp. 11–17 and 'The eBay economy', *Business Week*, 25 August (2003), pp. 87–90; Adam Lashinsky, 'Meg and Machine', *Fortune*, 9 January (2003), pp. 48–55.

Questions

1. How do you think Meg Whitman would describe eBay's strategic capabilities?

2. Undertake your own analysis of eBay's strategic capabilities, e.g. by activity mapping (section 3.6.2).

3. Give your own explanation of eBay's strategic capabilities with particular emphasis on:

   (a) identifying linkages of activities;
   (b) identifying core competences.

   How might eBay manage the future development of its strategic capabilities?

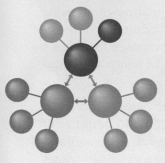

4

Expectations and Purposes

Learning outcomes

After reading this chapter you should be able to understand:

● The importance of corporate governance, the governance chain and the different corporate governance arrangements in different countries.

● The meaning of organisational stakeholders and how their expectations shape strategy.

● Stakeholder mapping – the importance of stakeholder power and interest.

● Ethical issues and their impact on strategy.

● How culture can help or hinder strategy development.

● How to use the cultural web to diagnose culture.

● How organisational purposes can be communicated.

Photo: Digital Vision

Photo: Digital Vision

Photo: Ella Towers

4.1   INTRODUCTION

The previous two chapters have looked respectively at the influence of the environment and resources on an organisation's strategic position. However, this fails to recognise the complex role that people play in the evolution of strategy. Strategy is also about what people *expect* an organisation to achieve and, therefore, what influence people can have over an organisation's purposes. Exhibit 4.1 shows that there are four main types of expectations – each of which will influence an organisation's purposes to some degree:

● The most fundamental expectations are concerned with *whom should* the organisation be there to serve and *how should* the direction and purposes of an organisation be determined? This is the province of *corporate governance* and the *regulatory framework* within which organisations operate. This relates not only to the power to influence purposes, but also to the processes of

Exhibit 4.1   Expectations and purposes

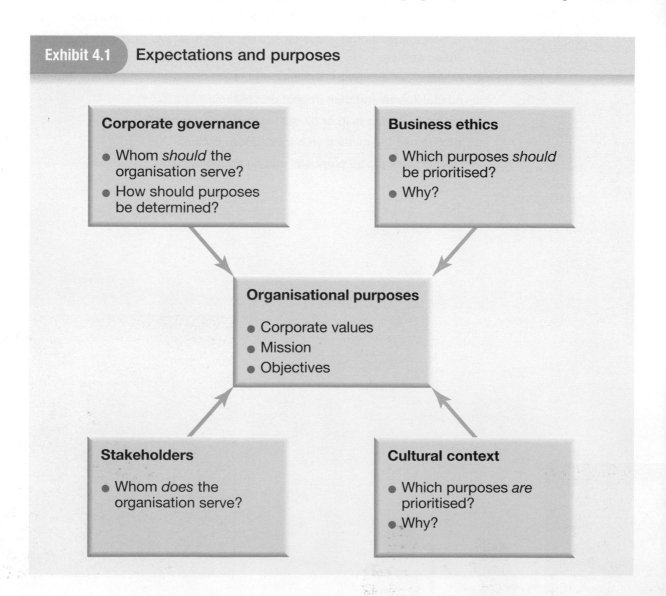

supervising executive decisions and actions, and the issues of *accountability*. So these are the *formal* expectations of organisations. There are significant differences in the approach to corporate governance in different countries and these will be discussed. Corporate scandals in the early 2000s – such as Enron and WorldCom – have raised the issue of corporate governance high on the agenda in many countries.

- *Whom* the organisation *does actually* serve in practice is not always the same as whom they should serve. This is because the expectations of powerful individuals and groups are likely to have more influence on organisational purposes than those of weaker 'players'. This will be addressed through the concept of *organisational stakeholders*. Stakeholders are those individuals or groups who depend on the organisation to fulfil their own goals, and on whom, in turn, the organisation depends. This requires an understanding of both the *power* and *interest* of different stakeholder groups.

- There are also expectations about *which purposes* an organisation *should* fulfil. This is an *ethical* consideration concerned with the expectations of society at large. At the broadest level, these issues impinge on corporate governance – particularly in relation to the accountability of organisations. At a more detailed level the ethical agenda is also concerned with expectations about *corporate social responsibility* to the various stakeholders – particularly those with little formal power. It is also concerned with the *behaviour of individuals* within organisations.

- *Which purposes are actually* prioritised above others is related to a variety of factors in the *cultural context* in which an organisation is operating. This is because expectations are also influenced by history and experience which become 'enshrined' in culture as explained below. The concept of the *cultural web* will be used as a means of understanding how culture at several 'levels' might influence expectations and organisational purposes. This will include the broader issues of *national cultures*, right through to the expectations of the various *subcultures* within an organisation.

4.2   CORPORATE GOVERNANCE[1]

The **governance framework** describes whom the organisation is there to serve and how the purposes and priorities of the organisation should be decided. This concerns how an organisation should function and the distribution of power among different stakeholders. This section will discuss a number of issues relating to corporate governance and the implications to strategic management. It will be seen that there are different traditions and frameworks in different countries.[2]

*The **governance framework** describes whom the organisation is there to serve and how the purposes and priorities of the organisation should be decided*

4.2.1 The governance chain

Corporate governance has become an increasingly important issue for organisations for two main reasons. First, the need to separate *ownership* and *management control* of organisations (which is now the norm except with very small

Exhibit 4.2   The chain of corporate governance: typical reporting structures

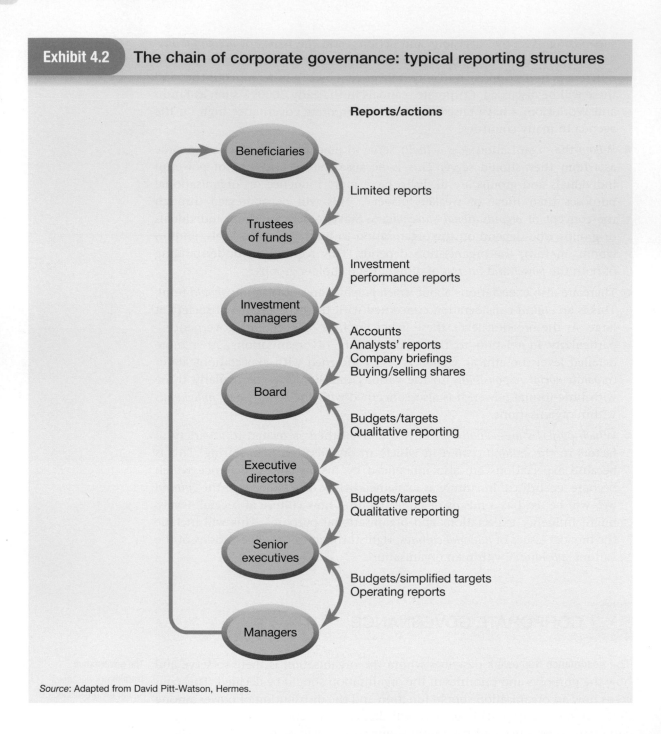

Reports/actions

Beneficiaries

Limited reports

Trustees of funds

Investment performance reports

Investment managers

Accounts
Analysts' reports
Company briefings
Buying/selling shares

Board

Budgets/targets
Qualitative reporting

Executive directors

Budgets/targets
Qualitative reporting

Senior executives

Budgets/simplified targets
Operating reports

Managers

Source: Adapted from David Pitt-Watson, Hermes.

businesses), means that most organisations operate within a hierarchy, or chain, of governance. This chain represents all those groups that have influence on an organisation's purposes through their direct involvement in either ownership or management of an organisation. Although the details of the chain will vary from one organisation to another, Exhibit 4.2 illustrates a typical chain of governance for a publicly quoted company in the UK. Second, there has been an increasing tendency to make organisations more visibly accountable and/or responsive, not only to those 'owners' and 'managers' in the governance chain but to a wider range of stakeholders – including the community at large. The rights and influence of these other stakeholders will be discussed later in this section and extensively in section 4.3.

The governance chain can be helpful in understanding how organisational purposes and strategy might be influenced by the various groups in the chain. Specifically, the principal–agent model[3] can be useful in explaining how each of these relationships in the corporate governance chain operates. In the simplest chain (for example, in a small family business) the board are the direct 'agent' for the shareholders (the 'principal'). There may be a small number of family share-holders, some of whom will be elected as board members and also run the company day-to-day. Non-executive shareholders (the beneficiaries) directly scrutinise the performance of the board in providing them with financial returns. In larger organisations the situation is more complicated as there is a need to employ professional managers to run the organisation without being either share-holders or board members. So in the more complex chain shown in Exhibit 4.2 there are extra links in the chain since these managers are 'agents' for the board – indeed there will be several layers of management as shown. In larger publicly quoted companies the chain will also have additional links on the shareholder side since there are now thousands of individual shareholders. But most of these beneficiaries will not have invested directly in companies (see Exhibit 4.2). Most will hold financial investments – particularly in pension funds that are investing in a whole range of companies. These funds are controlled by trustees and the day-to-day investment activity is undertaken by investment managers. So the final beneficiaries may not even know in which companies they have a financial stake and have little power to influence the companies' boards directly. The prin-cipal–agent relationships on the shareholder side are therefore as shown in the exhibit. The board are the agents for investment managers who in turn are agents for trustees and eventually the ultimate beneficiaries. Interestingly, as shown in the diagram, the beneficiaries of companies' performance are employees of firms whose pensions are dependent on a competitive and successful private sector in the economy. So the governance chain is, in theory, a circle – starting and finish-ing with many millions of individual employees and their dependants.

Principal–agent theory assumes that there is an incentive for each of these 'agents' to work diligently in the best interests of the 'principal' at each point in this chain. But it can be seen from Exhibit 4.2 that the executives and other man-agers who are driving strategy in an organisation are likely to be very remote from the ultimate beneficiaries of the company's performance. So there has been an increasing need to scrutinise the activities of each 'agent' in the chain to safe-guard the interests of the final beneficiaries. The exhibit highlights the informa-tion typically available to each 'player' in the chain to judge the performance of others. Since the power of any 'player' will be influenced by their access to information, disclosure has become an increasingly important requirement on directors and managers (as discussed below). This is because the agent at each point in the chain will be working in their own self-interest too, which will be reflected in their day-to-day decisions. Managers will be striving for promotion and/or increased earnings, investment managers will be seeking to increase their bonuses and so on. This may not result in decisions that are in the best interests of the final beneficiary. For example, in the UK/USA-type economies the normal way in which investment managers exert their influence on boards of directors is simply through decisions about the buying and selling of shares. This process, in turn, is influenced by analyst's reports and company briefings rather than an in-depth engagement with the company on strategic issues.

The governance chain helps highlight some important considerations for managers when thinking about organisational purposes and strategies:

- *Conflicts of interest* are likely to arise both between different groups in the governance chain and for individual managers or directors as they try to balance these various interests. This is a particular issue for boards of directors fulfilling their 'agency' role where there has been much criticism of directors acting in their own self-interest at the expense of shareholders. This is often shown dramatically in major issues like mergers and acquisitions and has resulted in important developments in both the role of the board and the disclosure of information to other stakeholders (see sections below for more detail).

- *Directors' responsibilities to shareholders* is an issue. A very important question in large publicly quoted corporations is whether directors and managers should regard themselves as *solely* responsible to shareholders and, if so, which shareholders? Or should they have a wider responsibility as 'trustees of the assets of the corporation' on behalf of a wider range of stakeholders?[4] The guiding principle in the UK[5] is that boards of directors are responsible *to* shareholders but must also be responsible *for relationships with* other stakeholders and *take into account* their interests. This will be discussed more fully in section 4.4 below when looking at the ethical stance of organisations.

- This issue of *accountability to stakeholders* (both in the governance chain and beyond) clearly has a major influence on the processes through which strategies are developed. For example, in public sector organisations, where a wide range of stakeholder interests need to be taken into account *explicitly*, strategy development usually involves a major process of consultation with stakeholders with the lengthening of time scales for the adoption of new strategies. So managers need to ensure that they plan sufficient time for this to happen. In contrast, where shareholdings are dispersed amongst a large number of shareholders, and/or investment managers for major institutional shareholders intervene only through buying/selling shares as is common in the UK/USA system (see above), managers tend to determine purposes and strategies themselves with little consultation with shareholders. The stock market becomes the judge of their actions through share price movements. However, Illustration 4.1 shows that there has been a growing tendency for shareholder activism[6] requiring boards to be more overtly responsive to shareholder opinion. This activism is often expressed through shareholder resolutions – again slowing down the pace at which strategic changes can be made. So those driving strategy may need to reassess both their time scales and the processes through which they keep shareholders involved (or at least are kept informed).

- *Within* organisations the principal–agent model applies to the way in which *targets*, *budgets and rewards* are structured. This will affect the way in which managers and other people behave and, in turn, will determine the extent to

Illustration 4.1   strategy into action

Shareholder power on the march

Boards of directors have been accused of pursuing their own interests rather than the best interests of their shareholders. But in some companies shareholders are fighting back.

Michael Green at ITV

In October 2003 the board of Carlton TV withdrew its support for their current chairman, Michael Green, becoming the chairman of the new ITV company to be created by the merger of Carlton with its major rival Granada. This was instigated by a group of disgruntled investors who owned big stakes in both Carlton and Granada. They argued that he was the wrong man – having lost Carlton about £800m (€1.2bn) in the spectacular failure of ITV Digital. More importantly they argued that the new company needed an independent, non-executive chairman from outside either Carlton or Granada.

Pay and rewards at GSK

In May 2003 the board of GlaxoSmithKline (GSK) suffered an unprecedented defeat at their AGM when the recommendations of their remuneration committee were rejected. The chairman, Sir Christopher Hogg, agreed to refer the matter for independent advice to ensure that they were in line with best practice. The revolt started with institutional shareholders who were opposed to several aspects of the directors' remuneration arrangements. Of particular concern was the controversial 'golden parachute' pay package for chief executive Jean-Pierre Garnier. This massive severance payment for the CEO (estimated at about €30m) would even apply if he was forced to resign for poor performance.

Conrad Black at Hollinger

Despite owning 73 per cent of the newspaper publisher Hollinger International, the Canadian Conrad Black suffered a humiliating defeat in November 2003. He had founded the company which included titles such as the *Daily* and *Sunday Telegraph* (UK), the *Chicago Sunday Times* (USA) and the *Jerusalem Post* (Israel).The campaign to unseat him as chief executive was led by Tweedy Browne, a New York-based institutional shareholder that owned 18 per cent of Hollinger. The battle centred on $154m (€134m) of management fees paid to Lord Black and other executives. Things heated up when the publisher's auditor (KPMG) forced the company to post a warning in its annual report that Black's ownership of the company could represent a conflict with shareholders' interests.

BSkyB and the Murdochs

In November 2003 James Murdoch, 30-year-old son of Rupert Murdoch, was appointed as CEO of BSkyB where his father was chairman. James became the youngest CEO of a FTSE 100 company by a considerable margin. The appointment was criticised by many shareholders concerned about nepotism and the possible creation of a publicly quoted company run like a family firm. Members of the appointments committee stated that the appointment process had been rigorous and that James Murdoch was the best candidate with a track record at Star TV as evidence.

Sources: Adapted from *BBC e-mail service 2003, FT.com*

Questions

1. Refer to Exhibit 4.2. For each of the four examples above list for each of the 'players' in the corporate governance chain:
   (a) the pros and cons of the issues from their point of view;
   (b) (therefore) what outcome they would have preferred.

2. What are your own views about the benefits and dangers of institutional investors having as much power as described in the first three examples?

3. Would you feel differently about the BSkyB issues if it were a Murdoch-owned family company or if the Murdoch family owned a majority share?

which the owners' best interests are being pursued. This has been an area where there has been much concern and on which many of the corporate governance reforms have centred (see below).

Overall the concept of the governance chain challenges directors and managers to be knowledgeable about the expectations of the beneficiaries, to actively work on their behalf and to keep them informed. But the principal–agent model is a reminder that 'agents' will tend to work in their own self-interest and need to be 'encouraged' to work in the interests of the 'principal'. This can be achieved in two broad ways. Either this can be achieved by 'contracting' particular outcomes (such as financial performance) and using performance-related incentives. Alternatively regulations and corporate governance mechanisms can be extended to more closely monitor the 'agent's' behaviour. This latter issue will now be discussed in relation to corporate governance reforms.

4.2.2 Corporate governance reforms

It should be clear from above that the governance chain usually operates imperfectly – because of unequal division of power between the different 'players' and with each 'agent' in the chain pursuing their own self-interest. Very different levels of access to information make these problems worse. In addition they have been magnified and made public by major changes in the structure of local and global economies such as privatisation, the increasing importance of private pension funds and some high-profile cases of fraud or poor governance in global companies (such as Enron[7] and WorldCom). So during the last ten years many governments have felt a need to be seen to be proactive in reforming various aspects of corporate governance. They have tended to do this by 'sponsoring' committees to advise on specific issues of corporate governance.[8] Initially they concentrated on internal financial controls and external disclosure of information.[9] Later committees focused on the broadening of internal control requirements beyond simply financial controls and looked at the role and effectiveness of non-executive directors.[10] The public sector in the UK picked up a similar agenda and also showed a particular interest in *risk management* of their organisation's strategies – a traditionally weak area.[11] This is concerned with demonstrating (in advance) that the risks associated with any strategy have been properly identified and, where possible, there are contingencies to cover these risks. More widely for the public sector in Europe there have been concerns to review and change the governance arrangements of the EU in anticipation of a major expansion in member states.[12] In turn these changes will affect the business environment within which European companies and public sector organisations are developing and delivering their strategies.

So there has been no shortage of initiatives for improvements in the corporate governance framework even though it has been criticism of the approach to reforms. In particular there have been concerns that reform has generally been driven by responses to high-profile failures of governance resulting in a tendency to concentrate on the wrong issues and/or the wrong solutions.[13] For example, although changes in the structure of board committees might be useful, the really important issue is the behaviour within the board. An important implication to policy makers (in government) is that a more strategic approach is needed to corporate governance reform. Specifically this means only sponsoring governance changes that will demonstrably encourage or require directors and managers (as 'agents') to behave in ways and pursue strategies that are in the interests of 'principals' in their governance chain as discussed above.

The implication to directors and managers is that they must be both familiar with these governance reforms and more proactive in addressing the interests of the 'principals' in the governance chain. This could require major changes in behaviour for many managers and directors, a large number of whom are focused on building big empires, climbing up through the hierarchy and increasing their personal financial rewards – often disregarding the consequences of their behaviour on the final beneficiaries of the company's performance (Exhibit 4.2). The following sections will review this governance agenda in more detail.

4.2.3 The role of the governing bodies

The primary statutory responsibility of the governing body of an organisation is to ensure that the organisation fulfils the wishes and purposes of the 'owners'. In the private sector, this is the board of directors working on behalf of shareholders. In the public sector, the governing body is accountable to the political arm of government – possibly through some intermediate 'agency' such as a funding body. A self-evident, but much neglected question is 'what is the purpose of a board and their deliberations on strategy?' There are important differences between countries in the form of ownership of companies, which lead to differences regarding the role, composition and *modus operandi* of the board of directors.[14] In turn, these have a considerable influence on how the purposes of an organisation are shaped and the ways in which strategies are developed.

Different ownership structures

In the UK, the USA and Australia, the wide spread of shareholdings tends to limit the power of the individual shareholders and heighten that of intermediaries (such as pension fund managers). In most other European countries (e.g. Belgium, The Netherlands and France), shareholding is more closely held and often minority led – perhaps by the founding family, financial institutions or other interests either acting together or using protective mechanisms such as preference shares. The board are strongly controlled by these particular shareholder interests. In Japan, the board tend to be viewed as just one part of a multi-layered corporate decision-making process, and hence are usually dominated by corporate executives. Japanese banks tend to have shareholdings in organisations, as against simply providing loan capital. There is also likely to be a complex web of cross-shareholdings between companies. These latter two factors tend to reduce the pressure for short-term results[15] as against longer-term performance, in marked contrast to US/UK companies.

Understanding these differences is particularly important when developing the international strategies of an organisation. It raises important questions:

- Will the governance arrangements *help or hinder the investment* needed to pursue the strategy? This may influence the choice of location for new ventures. For example, it has been argued that one reason why the UK gets more than its 'fair share' of inward investment to the EU is because the ownership structures are more open to new investors than elsewhere.

- How will governance affect the *speed* at which developments can take place? For example, this is often cited as a barrier or disincentive for investing in Japan. The decision-making process is thorough but slow.

- Which *relationships* will be crucial to the acceptance of new strategies? For example, in continental Europe considerable power will be held by a small number of shareholders who will need to be persuaded of the need for strategy changes.

- How quickly will *pay-offs* from the strategy be expected? Whereas in Japan a long-term view of 'pay-off' will be taken, in the UK/USA institutional investors will be looking for short-term pay-offs (dividends and share price). This could influence the detailed sequence of activities and operational tactics. Indeed a major criticism of UK/US boards is that this short-termism is further reinforced by the incentive packages for directors (particularly share options).

How governing bodies operate

These different traditions bring with them different structures and compositions of the board. In the UK and USA, the single-tier board usually incorporate both executive and non-executive directors. The board supervise the activities and performance of managers. Many organisations have adopted a subcommittee structure (for example, on especially important issues such as technology development or marketing), which allows for a more detailed involvement of the board with the work of the managers of the organisation.

In many other European countries (notably Germany, The Netherlands and France), the *two-tier board* are either mandatory or prevalent. In Germany, the 'upper-tier' or supervisory board oversee the work of the 'lower-tier' board, which are entrusted with the day-to-day management of the organisation. Importantly, the composition of this supervisory board is built around the principles of *co-determination* – half of the members being elected by shareholders, the other half by employees. However, the shareholders maintain the final say through the chairman's casting vote. In France, the two-tier system remains optional rather than mandatory. The main potential benefit of the two-tier form of governance is the counter-balancing of the power of managers, which is often a feature of management-dominated unitary boards in the UK and the USA – particularly where non-executive directors are weak or ineffective or not being given sufficient information. The European form of governance means that the purposes and strategies of an organisation are subject to wider consultation than is typically the case in UK/US companies. This may, of course, result in slower decision-making. In Sweden employees exert control through employee-controlled pension funds.

In Japan, the composition of the board is heavily weighted towards executive members. The entry of executives on to the board is controlled by the chairman, who will frequently take external advice (for example, from bankers) before a manager is promoted to director. In Japanese corporate culture a prerequisite of a good director is someone who is able to continue to promote the interests of employees. So, in contrast to Germany, employees in Japan have power through cultural norms (trust and the implicit 'duties' of directors) rather than through the legal framework of governance.

The public services have a wide variety of arrangements for governing bodies, but there are some commonalities. Governing bodies are often 'representational' of key stakeholders, in practice even if not by regulation. This particularly applies to the place of employees and unions on governing bodies. There has been a move in many countries to increase the proportion of (so-called) independent members on governing bodies. These independent members are the nearest equivalent of the non-executive director in the private sector.

Again it is important for directors and managers to understand the impact of these different arrangements on the strategy-making processes in the organisation:

- The success of a strategy is dependent on *context* (e.g. country). Strategies that would work in one country may not work in another. This can be a particular problem for multinational businesses or with international strategic alliances. This was dramatically illustrated in Corus (the Anglo/Dutch steel company) in 2002 when the supervisory board in The Netherlands vetoed the British proposals to dispose of the company's aluminium business to fund losses in UK steel-making plants.

- The more *'closed' governance models* of Germany and Japan[16] discussed above are under pressure to change as a result of the increased globalisation of capital markets and cross-country mergers and acquisitions. So policy-makers and managers in those countries need to consider whether corporate governance changes may be needed to reflect this trend.

- The *combining of the chairman and CEO roles* remains a considerable difference between US practice and most other countries. The combined role is common in the USA, unusual in the UK and banned in most Nordic countries. The arguments centre on the need for the chairman to actively represent the interests of the shareholders and to scrutinise the activities of the company executives. There are concerns that this cannot happen if the roles are combined and may not happen if CEOs are routinely promoted to chairmanship of their own company.

The different corporate governance traditions and frameworks in different countries tend to result in a different prioritisation of many of the corporate governance issues discussed in this section of the book, as shown in the critique given in Exhibit 4.3.

How governing bodies influence strategy

As discussed above the ultimate responsibility for the success or failure of strategy and the benefits which owners receive lies with the governing body (e.g. the board) of the organisation. So the board must be concerned with how strategy is managed in the organisation. The board have two broad choices on how they influence strategy:

Exhibit 4.3   Strengths and weaknesses of governance systems

Anglo-Saxon Model (US, UK, etc.)

Strengths
- Dynamic market orientation
- Fluid capital investment
- Extensive internationalisation

Weaknesses
- Volatile instability
- Short-termism
- Inadequate governance structures

Rhine Model (Germany, Switzerland, Austria, The Netherlands)

Strengths
- Long-term industrial strategy
- Very stable capital investment
- Robust governance procedures

Weaknesses
- Internationalisation more difficult
- Lack of flexibility
- Inadequate investment in new industries

Latin Model (France, Italy, Spain)

Strengths
- Long-term state-oriented industrial strategy
- Very stable capital investment (public sector, institutional investors, cross participations)
- Consistency between political, economic and administrative goals

Weaknesses
- Involvement of the government (potential conflicts between economic goals and political necessities)
- Lack of capital
- Risk of collusion between executives, members of the board, politicians and civil servants

Japanese Model

Strengths
- Very long-term industrial strategy
- Stable capital investment
- Major overseas activity

Weaknesses
- Financial speculation
- Secretive, sometimes corrupt, governance procedures
- Weak accountability

Source: Adapted from T. Clarke and S. Clegg, *Changing Paradigms: The transformation of management knowledge for the 21st century*, HarperCollins Business, 2000, Table 6.5, p. 324.

- Strategic management can be entirely *delegated to management* – with the board receiving and approving plans/decisions. In this situation the 'stewardship' role of the board requires processes that ensure that purposes and strategies are not 'captured' by management at the expense of other stakeholders – particularly the owners.

- The board can *engage with management* in the strategic management process. But this has many practical problems concerning the time and knowledge-level of (particularly) non-executive directors to perform their role this way.

Fuller discussions of these 'styles' will be found in Chapter 6 (section 6.5) and Chapter 8 (section 8.4.1).

The need for boards to be more clearly engaged in, and influencing, the strategic management of their organisation came to public prominence following the failures of Enron and WorldCom in the early 2000s. There was considerable discussion as to whether the boards of companies were really exercising their stewardship role (as 'independent' monitors of an organisation's activities on behalf of shareholders). Governments also responded in terms of changes to the governance framework for companies[17] to ensure that boards developed strategies that were in the interests of their shareholders and beneficiaries. The implications on how board members engage in an organisation's strategy are important:

● They must be seen to be *operating 'independently' of the management* of the company. So the role of non-executive directors is heightened.

● They must be *competent* to scrutinise the activities of managers. So the collective experience of the board, their training and the information at their disposal are crucially important.

● They must have the *time* to do their job properly. So limitations on the number of directorships that an individual can hold are also an important consideration.

● It is the *'softer' issues* that will distinguish effective from ineffective boards[18] and the success or failure of strategy. For example: respect, trust, 'constructive friction' between board members, fluidity of roles, individual as well as collective responsibility and rigorous evaluation of individual director and collective board performance.

But it is important to remember from the earlier discussion about the principal–agent model that the board as 'agent' are likely to operate in their members' own self-interests at the expense of shareholders – as the corporate scandals have shown. Hence the emphasis from governments on extending and tightening corporate governance arrangements (see section 4.2.2 above).

4.2.4 Rights of creditors and lenders

One of the reasons why corporate governance varies so much from one country to another is the differing arrangements for corporate finance. There are the different 'traditions' regarding *debt/equity* ratios and the extent to which the *relationship* with bankers is regarded as one of partnership or simply a buyer/supplier contract in a free market. In the USA and UK, equity is the dominant form of long-term finance and commercial banks provide debt capital. So relationships with bankers are towards the contractual (customer–supplier) end of the spectrum. In contrast, in Japan (and to a lesser extent Germany), banks often have significant equity stakes and may be part of the same parent company, and the lead banks may organise the activities of other banks. The power of lenders in these two extremes is very different and exercised in different ways. UK and US banks may exercise their power through *exit* (i.e. withdrawing funds) even if this liquidates the company. Japanese banks are more concerned to steer the longer-term strategy of the organisation and to use their power to make their voice heard. It is important that managers understand how these corporate governance arrangements will have an impact on purposes and strategies. For example, the contractual relationships of the US/UK system put the burden of financial risk onto the company and therefore limit the gearing that is regarded as prudent. This means that more equity is needed for major strategy developments. It also means that the company itself has a higher degree of influence over purposes and strategies – since the banks are not seeking a strategic involvement with the company. However, when strategies start to fail the organisation becomes increasingly dependent on the bank as its key stakeholder. This happens frequently in family-owned small businesses.

Since in most countries the trade creditor is the least protected stakeholder in the trading process organisations need to assess and/or mitigate their risk when contracting with *their* customers. This would, for example, influence who they 'appoint' as distributors It also explains why in most economies there is an important service sector providing assessment and/or mitigation of credit risks – particularly crucial for the promotion of exports to developing economies.

4.2.5 Relationships with customers and clients

The legal framework of many countries enshrines the principle of *caveat emptor*, placing the burden of risk on the customer and giving the balance of power to the company. However, there have been some significant moves to change this. Legislation to protect consumers' interests grew substantially from the 1960s onwards. In situations of natural monopolies, many governments created 'watchdog' bodies to represent the customers' interests. In the case of the privatised utilities in the UK and elsewhere, this has become enshrined in the office of the regulator (Oftel, Ofwat, etc.). Their powers of regulation set them up as a surrogate for the market and they exert control over prices and services through a set of performance targets. This has important implications for how companies in these regulated sectors construct their competitive strategies.

Even without the use of a legally binding framework, there have been other attempts to give more rights and voice to individual consumers. In the 1990s the *Citizen's Charter Initiative* in the UK public services was an early attempt to raise performance standards on 'customer service'. This impetus was maintained through the *Best Value Framework*, which placed a duty on public service organisations to identify and move towards the standards reached by the best providers. Crucially, this benchmarking had to be made beyond the public services (see section 3.6.3). Following the UK Local Government Act (1999) this process was extended by the Audit Commission, which developed a process of Corporate Governance Inspection[19] for local government authorities with the aim of further improving the services that local people receive. They define corporate governance as '. . . the way in which local councils lead, direct and control their functions and relate to their communities and partners'. Such a broad definition is essentially about a review of strategic management in the organisation. Not surprisingly these reviews are fairly wide-ranging, as can be seen in Illustration 4.2. So a substantially enhanced corporate governance framework for public services is requiring managers and politicians to pay far more attention to the needs of

Illustration 4.2   strategy into action

Corporate governance audits in the public sector

Corporate governance is a key issue for the public sector too.

Corporate governance audits are undertaken for local government authorities in the UK. The audits assess the way in which local councils lead, direct and control their functions and relate to their communities and partners. The audits and recommendations are published on the Audit Commission's website which has open access. Extracts from the summary points of one audit give a flavour of the process:

1. '. . . The previous audit found significant weaknesses in the council's political and managerial processes. . . . this inspection has found a very different picture.'

2. ' (the council) now has taken strong leadership . . . to make difficult decisions and change the way it works'.

3. '. . . however the council still has much work to do in embedding cultural change, new systems and processes and maintaining momentum.'

4. 'The council has made dramatic progress in risk management and financial control. . . . resources are now being proactively matched to priorities.'

5. '(there has been) significant improvement in standards of (personal) conduct . . . Stakeholders have recognised real changes and councillors are less inclined to fight political battles at every meeting or in the local media.'

6. 'The council has made some progress in improving structures and processes. This includes clarifying roles, responsibilities and accountabilities at senior management and cabinet level.'

7. 'The council's scrutiny committees have not yet effectively established their roles.'

8. 'In terms of the quality of service delivery, some progress has been made but more is needed before the impact of this work is translated into outcomes for the (citizens).'

9. '. . . the council has been successful implementing a project management approach to resolving difficult issues . . . such as performance management, procurement, communications, integrated planning and e-government.'

10. 'The council's least progress has been made on community focus . . . the council has not yet provided the appropriate leadership expected by such a key player (in local partnerships).'

11. 'The council is aware of the need to involve the local public more in influencing its decisions and a number of consultation exercises have taken place . . . but there remains a high level of public apathy and scepticism towards the council.'

Source: UK Audit Commission website (www.audit-commission.gov.uk).

Questions

1. What are the differences in scope and emphasis between this public sector view of corporate governance and what would be typical in the private sector?

2. Why do these differences occur?

their customers and communities when deciding their purposes, priorities and strategies.

4.2.6 Forms of ownership

The form of ownership can have a fundamental effect on the purposes of an organisation and the strategies that are pursued. There may also be issues as to whether the form of ownership is appropriate to the strategic purposes of an organisation.

● *Private or public ownership of equity* is an issue for commercial organisations. As they develop and grow, many organisations – for example, a family business – move from private ownership to a publicly quoted corporation. Such a decision might be made because the owners decide that increased equity is required to finance the growth of the business. The family members who own the business need to recognise that their role will change. They become answerable to a much wider group of shareholders and to institutions acting for those shareholders.

● *Sale of all or part of the company* may be recommended by the board of directors of a business who have a responsibility to provide shareholders with a return on their investment. It may be that the board arrive at the view that a different corporate parent would better achieve this primary purpose. For example, the company may not be able to compete because it is trading nationally within increasingly global markets. The sale of the business might therefore make sense.

● Businesses become the *targets for acquisitions* and a board might decide that such an offer is more attractive to shareholders than the returns they can promise in the future. Mergers and acquisitions have such a fundamental impact on an organisation's purposes and performance that specific corporate governance measures have been developed (see section 4.2.6 below).

● *Mutual ownership* by their members has been the tradition in some sectors – for example, insurance companies and building societies. Customers (for example, those with savings accounts and/or mortgages) are members of the organisation in place of shareholders and this clearly has a major impact on purposes and strategies. As many UK building societies became banks in the late 1990s they changed their form of ownership by de-mutualising and issuing windfall shares to members. This changes the governance arrangements for the organisation to be more similar to companies.

● *Privatisation* of public sector bodies has occurred in many countries.[20] Historically, most public sector bodies were tightly controlled by their 'owners', the central or local government departments. Governments took such decisions in order to require organisations to face up to market forces, to become more aware of customer needs and competitive pressures and to provide access to private sector capital. In turn, managers found more latitude in terms of strategic choice – what they could provide in terms of product or services; the ability to diversify, raise capital for expansion and so on. In some other countries (for example, Ireland and New Zealand), governments retained ownership but created state-owned enterprises with considerable commercial freedom.[21]

4.2.7 Mergers and acquisitions

Mergers and acquisitions often result in dramatic changes in the purposes of the organisations involved with the resultant impact on a wide range of stakeholders. For this reason the topic has attracted considerable attention and specific corporate governance measures have been put in place. The impact of corporate governance on strategy, and the differences between the USA and UK, and Continental European countries such as Germany, are shown clearly in the area of acquisitions (particularly hostile take-overs). In the USA and UK, the exposure of managers to the threat of take-over (i.e. a market-pressure-based system) is regarded as a primary means of ensuring the good performance of organisations. In contrast, in Germany institutional mechanisms are used as the primary means of influencing the performance of companies. These include equity ownership by banks, two-tier boards and co-determination (see section 4.2.3 above).

But in countries where hostile bids are common, questions have been raised as to whether this market-based system actually is in the best interests of shareholders. Most mergers and expectations fail to deliver the promised benefits to shareholders and, at least in the short/medium term, they are likely to lead to loss of shareholder value. The criticism has tended to focus on the *conflict of interest* for a board of directors between their *personal* positions and careers (as executives) and the best interests of shareholders. The directors may pursue mergers because it would enlarge their empire, improve their financial rewards or because they feel that investment analysts will expect acquisitive growth. There are sometimes the reverse criticisms that directors launch defensive measures against take-over offers even if this is in the longer-term interests of the shareholders and positively beneficial to other stakeholders, such as employees or customers. This raises difficult ethical issues for managers, as will be discussed below (section 4.4.3). Mergers and acquisitions are discussed more fully in Chapter 7 (section 7.3.2).

4.3   STAKEHOLDER EXPECTATIONS[22]

The corporate governance framework provides the formal requirements and boundaries within which strategy is being developed. It relates to the relationships and responsibilities within the governance chain shown earlier in Exhibit 4.2. But alongside this it is also important to understand the expectations of other groups who are not in the corporate governance chain – such as suppliers, customers or local communities. For *all* of these groups (both inside and outside the governance chain) it is important to understand their expectations in detail, how these might differ from each other and the extent to which they are likely to seek influence over an organisation's purposes and strategies. Collectively these groups are called organisational stakeholders and exist both outside and inside an organisation as this section will explain.

Stakeholders are those individuals or groups who depend on an organisation to fulfil their own goals and on whom, in turn, the organisation depends. Important external stakeholders would usually include financial institutions, customers, suppliers, shareholders and unions. Inside an organisation few individuals have sufficient power to determine unilaterally the strategy of the organisation. Influence is likely to occur only because individuals share expectations with others by being a part of a stakeholder group, which may be departments, geographical locations or different levels in the hierarchy. Individuals may belong to more

Stakeholders are those individuals or groups who depend on the organisation to fulfil their own goals and on whom, in turn, the organisation depends

than one stakeholder group and stakeholder groups will 'line up' differently depending on the issue or strategy in hand.

External stakeholders can be usefully divided into three types in terms of the nature of their relationship with the organisation and, therefore, how they might affect the success or failure of a particular strategy:[23]

● Stakeholders from the *'market' environment* such as suppliers, competitors, distributors, shareholders (who can be identified using the five-forces framework from Chapter 2 (Exhibit 2.5) and the governance chain above). These stakeholders have an economic relationship with the organisation and influence the value-creation process as 'members' of the value network discussed in Chapter 3.

● Stakeholders from the *social/political environment* such as policy makers, regulators, government agencies who will influence the 'social legitimacy' of the strategy.

● Stakeholders in the *technological environment* such as key adopters, standards agencies and owners of competitive technologies who will influence the diffusion of new technologies and the adoption of industry standards (as discussed in section 9.5 of Chapter 9).

These three sets of stakeholders are rarely of equal importance in any specific situation. For example, the 'technological group' are clearly crucial for strategies of new product introduction whilst the 'social/political' group are usually particularly influential in the public sector context.

Some of these external stakeholders may seek to influence strategy through their links with internal stakeholders. For example, customers may pressurise sales managers to represent their interests within the company. Even if external stakeholders are passive, they may represent real constraints on the development of new strategies.

For these reasons, the stakeholder concept is valuable when trying to understand the political context within which specific strategic developments (such as the introduction of a new product or extension into a new geographical area) would take place. In this sense it is also concerned with strategic choice, as will be seen in Chapter 7.

Since the expectations of stakeholder groups will differ, it is quite normal for conflict to exist regarding the importance or desirability of many aspects of strategy. In most situations, a compromise will need to be reached between expectations that cannot all be achieved simultaneously.

Exhibit 4.4 shows some of the typical stakeholder expectations that exist and how they might conflict. Large global organisations may have added complications as they are operating in multiple arenas. For example, an overseas division is part of the parent company, with all that implies in terms of expectations about behaviour and performance. But it is also part of the local community, which has different expectations, and these two 'worlds' may not sit comfortably alongside each other.[24] Back at head office the division is expected to behave like 'any other division' even though this may conflict with the ability to meet local expectations of behaviour. For example, in recent years, overseas outlets of McDonald's have often been targeted in anti-capitalist protests.

Exhibit 4.4	Some common conflicts of expectations

- In order to grow, short-term profitability, cash flow and pay levels may need to be sacrificed.

- 'Short-termism' may suit managerial career aspirations but preclude investment in long-term projects.

- When family businesses grow, the owners may lose control if they need to appoint professional managers.

- New developments may require additional funding through share issue or loans. In either case, financial independence may be sacrificed.

- Public ownership of shares will require more openness and accountability from the management.

- Cost efficiency through capital investment can mean job losses.

- Extending into mass markets may require a decline in quality standards.

- In public services, a common conflict is between mass provision and specialist services (e.g. preventative dentistry or heart transplants).

- In large multinational organisations, conflict can result because of a division's responsibilities to the company and also to its host country.

4.3.1 Stakeholder mapping[25]

Stakeholder mapping identifies stakeholder expectations and power and helps in understanding political priorities. It underlines the importance of two issues:

- How *interested* each stakeholder group is to impress its expectations on the organisation's purposes and choice of specific strategies.

- Whether stakeholders have the *power* to do so (see section 4.3.3 below).

Stakeholder mapping identifies stakeholder expectations and power and helps in understanding political priorities

Power/interest matrix

The power/interest matrix can be seen in Exhibit 4.5. It seeks to describe the political context within which an individual strategy would be pursued. It does this by classifying stakeholders in relation to the power they hold and the extent to which they are likely to show interest in supporting or opposing a particular strategy. The matrix indicates the type of relationship which organisations typically might establish with stakeholder groups in the different quadrants. Clearly, the acceptability of strategies to *key players* (segment D) is of major importance. Often the most difficult issues relate to stakeholders in segment C (institutional shareholders often fall into this category). Although these stakeholders might, in general, be relatively passive, a disastrous situation can arise when their level of

Exhibit 4.5   Stakeholder mapping: the power/interest matrix

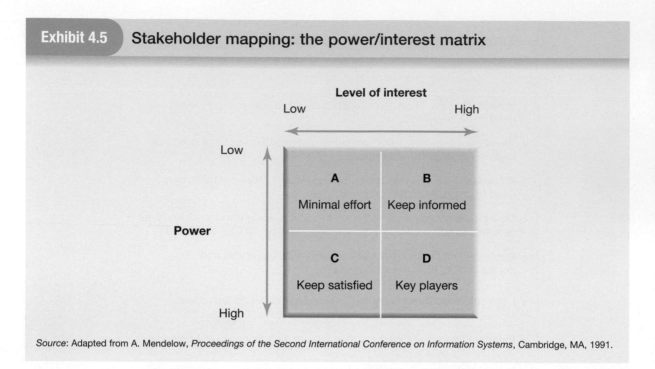

Source: Adapted from A. Mendelow, *Proceedings of the Second International Conference on Information Systems*, Cambridge, MA, 1991.

interest is underrated and they suddenly *reposition* to segment D and frustrate the adoption of a new strategy. A view might be taken that it is a *responsibility* of strategists or managers to raise the level of interest of powerful stakeholders (such as institutional shareholders), so that they can better fulfil their expected role within the corporate governance framework. This could also be concerned with how non-executive directors can be assisted in fulfilling their role, say, through good information and briefing.

Similarly, organisations might address the expectations of stakeholders in segment B through information – for example, to community groups. These stakeholders can be crucially important 'allies' in influencing the attitudes of more powerful stakeholders: for example, through *lobbying*.

Stakeholder mapping might help in understanding better some of the following issues:

● Whether the *actual levels of interest and power* of stakeholders properly reflect the corporate governance framework within which the organisation is operating, as in the examples above (non-executive directors, community groups).

● Who the key *blockers* and *facilitators* of a strategy are likely to be and how this could be responded to – for example, in terms of education or persuasion.

● Whether *repositioning* of certain stakeholders is desirable and/or feasible. This could be to lessen the influence of a key player or, in certain instances, to ensure that there are more key players who will champion the strategy (this is often critical in the public sector context).

● *Maintaining* the level of interest or power of some key stakeholders may be essential. For example, public 'endorsement' by powerful suppliers or customers may be critical to the success of a strategy. Equally, it may be necessary to discourage some stakeholders from repositioning themselves. This is what is meant by *keep satisfied* in relation to stakeholders in segment C, and to a lesser extent *keep informed* for those in segment B. The use of *side payments*[26] to stakeholders as a means of securing the acceptance of new strategies has traditionally been regarded as a key maintenance activity. For example, a 'deal' may be done with another department to support them on one of *their* strategies if they agree not to oppose *this* strategy.

These questions raise some difficult ethical issues for managers in deciding the role they should play in the political activity surrounding strategic change. For example, are managers really the honest brokers who weigh the conflicting expectations of stakeholder groups? Or are they answerable to one stakeholder – such as shareholders – and hence is their role to ensure the acceptability of their strategies to other stakeholders? Or are they, as many authors suggest, the real power behind the throne, constructing strategies to suit their own purposes and managing stakeholder expectations to ensure acceptance of these strategies? These issues will be addressed in section 4.4 below.

Illustration 4.3a shows some of the practical issues of using stakeholder mapping to understand the political context surrounding a new strategy and to establish political priorities. The example relates to a German bank with headquarters in Frankfurt (Germany) and providing corporate banking services from head office and a regional office in Toulouse (France). It is considering the closure of its Toulouse office and providing all corporate banking services from Frankfurt. The example illustrates several issues.

- Stakeholder groups are *not usually 'homogeneous'* but contain a variety of subgroups with somewhat different expectations and power. In the illustration, *customers* are shown divided into those who are largely supportive of the strategy (customer X), those who are actively hostile (customer Y) and those who are indifferent (customer Z). So when using stakeholder mapping, there is clearly a balance to be struck between describing stakeholders too generically – hence hiding important issues of diversity – and too much subdivision, making the situation confusing and difficult to interpret.

- Most stakeholder groups consist of *large numbers of individuals* (such as customers or shareholders), and hence can be thought of largely independently of the expectations of individuals within that group. With some stakeholder groups this is not the case: they consist of a small number of individuals or even single individuals (e.g. the chairman of the company or the minister of a government department).

- The *role and the individual* currently undertaking that role need to be distinguished. It is useful to know if a new individual in that role would shift the positioning. Serious misjudgements can be made if proper care is not paid to this point. In the example, it has been concluded that the German minister (segment C) is largely indifferent to the new development – it is very low in her priorities. However, a change of minister might shift this situation overnight. Although it will be impossible for the bank to remove such uncertainties entirely, there are implications for the political priorities. For example, those permanent officials who are advising the minister need to be kept satisfied, since they will outlive individual ministers and provide a continuity which can diminish uncertainty. It is also possible, of course, that the German minister's level of interest will be raised by lobbying from her French counterpart. This would have implications for how the company handles the situation in France.

Illustration 4.3a   strategy into action

Stakeholder mapping at Tallman GmbH

Stakeholder mapping can be a useful tool for determining the political priorities for specific strategic developments or changes.

Tallman GmbH was a German bank providing both retail and corporate banking services throughout Germany, Benelux and France. There were concerns about its loss in market share in the corporate sector which was serviced from two centres – Frankfurt (for Germany and Benelux) and Toulouse (for France). It was considering closing the Toulouse operation and servicing all corporate clients from Frankfurt. This would result in significant job losses in Toulouse, some of which would be replaced in Frankfurt alongside vastly improved IT systems.

Two power/interest maps were drawn up by the company officials to establish likely stakeholder

reactions to the proposed closure of the Toulouse operation. Map A represents the likely situation and map B the preferred situation – where support for the proposal would be sufficient to proceed.

Referring to map A it can be seen that, with the exception of customer X and IT supplier A, the stakeholders in box B are currently opposed to the closure of the Toulouse operation. If Tallman was to have any chance of convincing these stakeholders to change their stance to a more supportive one, the company must address their questions and, where possible, alleviate their fears. If such fears were overcome, these people might become important

Map A: The likely situation

A	B Shareholder M (−) Toulouse office (−) Customer X (+) French minister (−) Marketing (−) IT supplier A (+)
C Customer Z German minister	D Customer Y (+) Frankfurt office (+) Corporate finance (+)

Map B: The preferred situation

A French minister	B Shareholder M (−) Toulouse office (−) Marketing (−) IT supplier A (+)
C Customer Z German minister	D Customer X (+) Customer Y (+) Frankfurt office (+) Corporate finance (+)

Stakeholder mapping may produce 'typical' maps in the sense that the political context commonly occurs for organisations. In these circumstances the political dangers and priorities are well understood and managers can learn from the experience of others.[27]

4.3.2 Power[28]

The previous section was concerned with understanding stakeholder expectations and highlighted the importance of power. Power is the mechanism by which expectations are able to influence purposes and strategies. It has been seen that,

allies in influencing the more powerful stakeholders in boxes C and D. The supportive attitude of customer X could be usefully harnessed in this quest. Customer X was a multinational with operations throughout Europe. They had shown dissatisfaction with the inconsistent treatment that they received from Frankfurt and Toulouse.

The relationships Tallman had with the stakeholders in box C were the most difficult to manage since, whilst they were considered to be relatively passive, largely owing to their indifference to the proposed strategy, a disastrous situation could arise if their level of interest was underrated. For example, if the German minister were replaced, her successor might be opposed to the strategy and actively seek to stop the changes. In this case they would shift to box D.

The acceptability of the proposed strategy to the current players in box D was a key consideration. Of particular concern was customer Y (a major French manufacturer who operated only in France – accounting for 20 per cent of Toulouse corporate banking income). Customer Y was opposed to the closure of the Toulouse operation and could have the power to prevent it from happening, for example by the withdrawal of its business. The company clearly needed to have open discussions with this stakeholder.

By comparing the position of stakeholders in map A and map B, and identifying any changes and mismatches, Tallman could establish a number of tactics to change the stance of certain stakeholders to a more positive one and to increase the power of certain stakeholders. For example, customer X could be encouraged to champion the proposed strategy and assist Tallman by providing media access, or even convincing customer Y that the change could be beneficial.

Tallman could also seek to dissuade or prevent powerful stakeholders from changing their stance to a negative one: for example, unless direct action were taken, lobbying from her French counterpart may well raise the German minister's level of interest. This has implications for how the company handles the situation in France. Time could be spent talking the strategy through with the French minister and also customer Y to try to shift them away from opposition at least to neutrality, if not support.

Question

To ensure that you are clear about how to undertake stakeholder mapping, produce your own complete analysis for Tallman GmbH against a different strategy, i.e. *to service all corporate clients from Toulouse*. Ensure that you go through the following steps:

1. Plot the most likely situation (map A) – remembering to be careful to *reassess* interest and power for each stakeholder in relation to this *new* strategy.

2. Map the preferred situation (map B).

3. Identify the mismatches – and hence the political priorities. Remember to include the need to *maintain* a stakeholder in its 'opening' position (if relevant).

4. Finish off by listing the actions you would propose to take and give a final view of the degree of political risk in pursuing this new strategy.

---

in most organisations, power will be unequally shared between the various stakeholders. For the purposes of this discussion, **power** is the ability of individuals or groups to persuade, induce or coerce others into following certain courses of action. This is the mechanism by which one set of expectations will dominate strategic development or seek compromise with others.

There are many different sources of power. On the one hand, there is power that people or groups derive from their position within the organisation and through the formal corporate governance arrangements. But stakeholders may have power by other means, as summarised in Exhibit 4.6. This exhibit can be used to understand how powerful each stakeholder is in influencing a particular strategy (as part of stakeholder mapping).

Power is the ability of individuals or groups to persuade, induce or coerce others into following certain courses of action

Exhibit 4.6   Sources and indicators of power

Sources of power	
Within organisations	**For external stakeholders**
<ul><li>Hierarchy (formal power), e.g. autocratic decision making</li><li>Influence (informal power), e.g. charismatic leadership</li><li>Control of strategic resources, e.g. strategic products</li><li>Possession of knowledge and skills, e.g. computer specialists</li><li>Control of the human environment, e.g. negotiating skills</li><li>Involvement in strategy implementation, e.g. by exercising discretion</li></ul>	<ul><li>Control of strategic resources, e.g. materials, labour, money</li><li>Involvement in stategy implementation, e.g. distribution outlets, agents</li><li>Possession of knowledge or skills, e.g. subcontractors, partners</li><li>Through internal links, e.g. informal influence</li></ul>

Indicators of power	
Within organisations	**For external stakeholders**
<ul><li>Status</li><li>Claim on resources</li><li>Representation</li><li>Symbols</li></ul>	<ul><li>Status</li><li>Resource dependence</li><li>Negotiating arrangements</li><li>Symbols</li></ul>

It should be noted that the relative importance of these sources will vary over time. Indeed, major changes in the business environment – such as deregulation or the advent of cheap and powerful IT – can drastically shift the power balance between organisations and their stakeholders. For example, consumers' knowledge of different companies' offerings through internet browsing has increased their power considerably as they compare different offerings and reduce their traditional loyalty to a particular supplier. Deregulation and 'citizen empowerment' have required public service organisations to adopt more customer-focused strategies.

Since there are a variety of different sources of power, it is useful to look for *indicators of power*, which are the visible signs that stakeholders have been able to exploit one or more of the sources of power listed in Exhibit 4.6. There are four useful indicators of power: the *status* of the individual or group (such as job grade or reputation); the *claim on resources* (such as budget size); *representation* in powerful positions; and *symbols* of power (such as office size or use of titles and names).

No single indicator is likely fully to uncover the structure of power within a company. However, by looking at all four indicators, it may be possible to

Illustration 4.3b   strategy into action

Assessment of power at Tallman GmbH

Assessing the power of stakeholders is an important part of stakeholder mapping.

The corporate finance department is seen as powerful by all measures, and the marketing department universally weak. Equally, the Frankfurt operation is particularly powerful compared with Toulouse. This analysis provides important data in the process of stakeholder mapping, since the strategic importance of power is also related to whether individuals or groups are likely to exercise their power. This assessment thus helped in deciding where to locate the stakeholders on the power/interest maps.

Combining the results of this analysis with the stakeholder mapping exercise, it can be seen that Toulouse's only real hope is to encourage supplier A to reposition by convincing it of the increased IT opportunities which a two-centre operation would provide. Perhaps shareholder M could be helpful in this process through lobbying the supplier.

Internal stakeholders

Indicators of power	Corporate finance	Marketing	Frankfurt	Toulouse
Status				
Position in hierarchy (closeness to board)	H	L	H	M
Salary of top manager	H	L	H	L
Average grade of staff	H	M	H	L
Claim on resources				
Number of staff	M	H	M	M
Size of similar company	H	L	H	L
Budget as per cent of total	H	M	H	L
Representation				
Number of directors	H	None	M	None
Most influential directors	H	None	M	None
Symbols				
Quality of accommodation	H	L	M	M
Support services	H	L	H	L

H = high   M = medium   L = low

External stakeholders

Indicators of power	IT supplier A	Customer Y	Shareholder M
Status	M	H	L
Resource dependence	M	H	H
Negotiating arrangements	M	H	L
Symbols	M	H	L

H = high   M = medium   L = low

understand which people or groups appear to have power by a number of these measures. It should be remembered that the distribution of power will vary *in relation to the particular strategy under consideration*. For example, a corporate finance function will be more powerful in relation to developments requiring new capital or revenue commitments than in relation to ones which are largely self-financing or within the financial authority of separate divisions or subsidiaries. Illustration 4.3b shows these indicators of power in the bank from the previous illustration. The corporate finance department was seen as powerful by all indicators and the marketing department as universally weak. Equally, Frankfurt was particularly powerful in relation to Toulouse.

A similar understanding of the power held by external stakeholders can be useful. The indicators of power here are slightly different:

● The *status* of an external stakeholder can often be inferred by the speed with which the company responds.

● *Resource dependence* in terms of the relative size of shareholdings or loans, or the proportion of a company's business tied up with any one customer, or a similar dependence on suppliers. A key indicator could be the ease with which a supplier, financier or customer could switch or *be switched* at short notice.

● *Symbols* are also valuable clues about power. For example, whether the management team wines and dines a customer or supplier, or the level of person in the company who deals with a particular supplier.

Again, no single indicator will give a full understanding of the extent of the power held by external stakeholders. Illustration 4.3b shows these indicators of power for the bank from the previous illustration. It can be seen that Toulouse's only real hope of survival is to encourage supplier A to 'reposition' by convincing it of the increased IT opportunities that a two-centre operation would provide. Perhaps shareholder M could be helpful in this process through lobbying the supplier.

4.4 BUSINESS ETHICS AND SOCIAL RESPONSIBILITY[29]

The previous sections have discussed the formal obligations of organisations imposed through the regulatory and corporate governance frameworks and also the expectations of those stakeholders who are most interested and powerful. However, there has been little discussion so far about the societal expectations of organisations and how these impact on an organisation's purposes. Governments have increasingly taken the view that these expectations cannot be achieved through regulation alone.[30] This is the province of *business ethics* and exists at three levels:

● At the *macro* level, there are issues about the role of businesses and other organisations in the national and international organisation of society. Expectations range from laissez-faire free enterprise at one extreme to organisations as shapers of society at the other. There are also important issues of international relationships and the role of business on an international scale. This is the first issue – the broad *ethical stance* of an organisation, which is concerned with the *extent* to which an organisation will exceed its minimum obligations to stakeholders and society at large. Managers need to understand the factors that influence these societal expectations of organisations – particularly in relation to how inclusive or exclusive they are expected to be to the interests of the various stakeholders discussed in the previous section.

● Within this macro framework, *corporate social responsibility* is concerned with the *specific ways* in which an organisation will move beyond the minimum obligations provided through regulation and corporate governance, and how the conflicting demands of different stakeholders will be reconciled.

● At the *individual* level, it concerns the behaviour and actions of individuals within organisations. This is clearly an important issue for the management of organisations, but it is discussed here only insofar as it affects strategy, and in particular the role of managers in the strategic management process.

4.4.1 The ethical stance

The regulatory environment and the corporate governance arrangements for an organisation determine the minimum obligations of an organisation towards its various stakeholders. The **ethical stance** is the *extent* to which an organisation will exceed its minimum obligations to stakeholders and society at large. Different organisations take very different stances and there is likely to be a strong relationship between the ethical stance, the character of an organisation and how strategy is managed.

> The **ethical stance** is the *extent* to which an organisation will exceed its minimum obligations to stakeholders and society at large

Exhibit 4.7 outlines four *stereotypes*[31] to illustrate these differences. They represent a progressively more inclusive 'list' of stakeholder interests and a greater breadth of criteria against which strategies and performance will be judged.

Exhibit 4.7   Four possible ethical stances

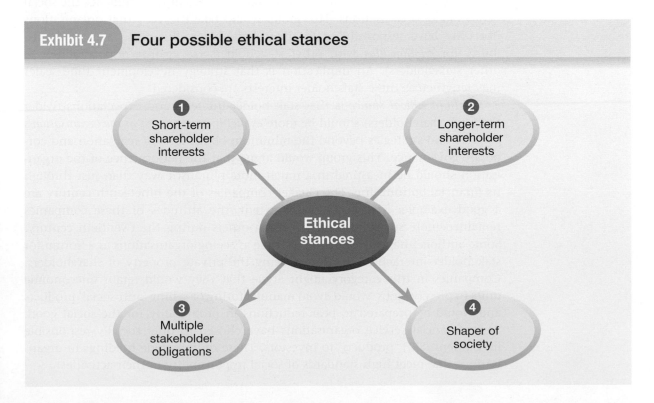

Type 1 represents one extreme stance where organisations take the view that the only responsibility of business is the short-term interests of shareholders. Their stance is that it is the domain of government to prescribe, through legislation and regulation, the constraints which society chooses to impose on businesses in their pursuit of economic efficiency (i.e. the legal and regulatory environment and the arrangements for corporate governance). The organisation will meet these minimum obligations but no more. It is also argued that expecting companies to exercise social duties can, in extreme cases, undermine the authority of government and give business organisations even more power: for example, multinationals operating in developing countries. Although strategic management is dominated by managers pursuing strategies where financial outcomes exclude other considerations it has been argued[32] that there are some 'social' actions that can be justified in terms of improving short-term profitability. This might occur, for example, if social obligations were imposed as a requirement for gaining contracts (e.g. if equal opportunities employment practices were required from suppliers to public sector customers).

The second type of ethical stance is similar to that of the previous group, but it is tempered with recognition of the *long-term financial benefit to the shareholder* of well-managed relationships with other stakeholders. This has been called a stance of *enlightened self-interest*. The justification for social action is that an organisation's *reputation*[33] is important to its long-term financial success and there is some evidence that links these two together.[34] For example, external sponsorships, corporate philanthropy[35] or welfare provision might be regarded as sensible expenditures akin to any other form of investment or promotion expenditure. The avoidance of 'shady' marketing practices is necessary to prevent the need for yet more legislation in that area. The position of many governments is that this kind of 'business case' must be the basis on which *they* attempt to influence the social behaviour of organisations. This group would take the view that organisations not only have responsibility to their shareholders but also have a responsibility for *relationships* with other stakeholders (as against responsibilities *to* other stakeholders). An implication is that strategy development time scales may lengthen as these stakeholder interests are considered.

The third ethical stance is that stakeholder interests and expectations (wider than just shareholders) should be more *explicitly incorporated in the organisation's purposes* and strategies beyond the minimum obligations of regulation and corporate governance. This group would argue that the performance of the organisation should be measured in a much more pluralistic way than just through its financial bottom line. The Quaker companies of the nineteenth century are a good example: to a considerable extent, the attitudes of these companies remained more socially progressive than others during the twentieth century. Some authors[36] have described this stance as seeing organisations as a 'forum for stakeholder interaction' as against being the private property of shareholders. Companies in this category might argue that they would retain uneconomic units to preserve jobs, would avoid manufacturing or selling 'anti-social' products and would be prepared to bear reductions in profitability for the social good. Some financial service organisations have chosen to offer socially responsible investment (SRI) 'products' to investors. These only include holdings in organisations that meet high standards of social responsibility in their activities.

However, there are clearly important but difficult issues of balance between the interests of different stakeholders. For example, many public sector organisations are, rightly, positioned within this group as they are subject to a wide diversity of expectations and unitary measures of performance are often inadequate in reflecting this diversity. There are also many family-owned small firms that are in this category through the way that they operate. They will balance their own self-interest with that of their employees and local communities even where this might constrain the strategic choices they make (e.g. overseas sourcing vs. local production). Organisations in this category inevitably take longer over the development of new strategies as they are committed to wide consultation with stakeholders and with managing the difficult political trade-offs between conflicting stakeholders' expectations as discussed in section 4.3.

The final, fourth group represent the *ideological* end of the spectrum. They have purposes that are concerned with *shaping society*, and the financial considerations are regarded as of secondary importance or a constraint. The extent to which this is a viable ethical stance clearly depends upon issues of regulation, corporate governance and accountability. Arguably, it is easier for a privately owned organisation to operate in this way, since it is not accountable to external shareholders. Some would argue that the great historical achievements of the public services in transforming the quality of life for millions of people were largely because they were 'mission driven' in this way, and supported by a political framework in which they operated. In many countries there has been a major challenge to the legitimacy of this mission-driven stance within public services and a reassertion of the rights of citizens (as taxpayers) to expect demonstrable best value from their public services. This has severely curtailed the ability of public services – particularly at the local level – to be proactive shapers of society.

Charitable organisations face similar dilemmas – it is often fundamental to their existence that they have zeal to protect and improve the interests of particular groups in society. But they also need to remain financially viable, which can bring problems with their image – sometimes being seen as over-commercial and spending too much on administration or promotional activities.

Illustration 4.4 describes the view of the chairman of a company about the ethical stance of the company.

4.4.2 Corporate social responsibility[37]

Within this broad ethical stance **corporate social responsibility** is concerned with the *ways* in which an organisation exceeds the minimum obligations to stakeholders specified through regulation and corporate governance.* This includes considerations as to how the conflicting demands of different stakeholders will be reconciled. As mentioned in section 4.3 above, the legal and regulatory frameworks pay uneven attention to the rights of different stakeholders. Therefore it is useful[38] to distinguish between contractual stakeholders – such as customers, suppliers or employees – who have a legal relationship with an organisation, and

Corporate social responsibility is concerned with the *ways* in which an organisation exceeds the minimum obligations to stakeholders specified through regulation and corporate governance

---

* It should be noted that the term '**corporate social responsibility**' often is used to include *both* the ethical stance and the specific issues discussed in this section.

Illustration 4.4   strategy into action

Starbucks, the benevolent capitalist?

Can making profits be combined with a social conscience?

In September 2003 *The Sunday Times* interviewed Howard Schultz, the chairman of Starbucks, the multinational chain of coffee stores. From its small beginnings in Seattle in 1971 Starbucks (by 2003) had 7,000 stores and 70,000 employees worldwide. The following are extracts in which Schultz explains the 'ethical stance' of Starbucks:

Schultz . . . has a commitment to worker-friendly employment practices. His motivation to create an employee-centric company were based on his experience growing up poor in New York [he says]: 'One of the things I remember as a young boy was how my father's self-esteem was linked to how he was treated as an uneducated blue collar worker, who was disrespected in the workplace . . . That's why I wanted to build the kind of company that did not leave its people behind, that would value people whether they were well educated or not and that would give everyone an opportunity and a clean slate'. Schultz has also promoted an interest in fair-trade issues [and] . . . he is immensely proud of his firm's environmental and social awareness policies, its drive to integrate its stores into local communities and, especially, its innovative share-option scheme for employees. 'When we created that it was the first time in the history of America that a programme like that was created for part-time workers and we've brought it to the UK'. Schultz claimed that it paid off with low rates of people leaving for other jobs. Despite these claims for its progressive social policies some still see Starbucks as an evil empire – alongside the more aggressive American multinationals such as MacDonalds or Wal-Mart. It is regularly attacked by anti-globalisation protestors and has drawn criticism from a range of opponents. Schultz himself has been targeted by fair-trade activists and Starbucks reception in Europe has been chillier than elsewhere. Schultz countered these accusations: 'I'm not concerned with Starbucks becoming the most profitable company in the world. That's a very shallow goal, to achieve profitability at all costs. That isn't a zero-sum game for me or anyone else at Starbucks. It's very important that we do something that hasn't been done before, to build a different kind of company that does achieve the fiscal issues . . . but demonstrates its heart and its conscience in giving back to our employees, to the communities we serve, to the coffee-growing regions, and then to reward our shareholders.'

Source: The text has been amended and extracted from an article that was originally published in *The Sunday Times,* 14 September 2003, p. 3.7.

Questions

1. Looking at Exhibit 4.7 how would you characterise Schultz's view of Starbucks' ethical stance?

2. Do other stakeholders see Starbucks in the same way?

3. If there are differences between these views does it matter to the success or failure of Starbucks' strategies?

community stakeholders – such as local communities, consumers (in general) and pressure groups – who do not have the protection of the law to the same extent as the first group. Therefore the corporate social responsibility policies of companies will be particularly important to these community stakeholders.

Exhibit 4.8 outlines a number of these issues, both internal and external to the organisation, and provides a checklist against which an organisation's actions on corporate social responsibility can be assessed. Although a large number of companies produce guidelines on some or all of the issues, a significant number have no programme at all. *Social auditing*[39] is a way of ensuring that these issues of corporate social responsibility get systematically reviewed and has been championed by a number of progressive organisations. This can take several forms ranging from social audits undertaken by independent external bodies, through aspects

| Exhibit 4.8 | Some questions of corporate social responsibility |

Should organisations be responsible for . . .

INTERNAL ASPECTS

Exployee welfare
. . . providing medical care, assistance with housing finance, extended sick leave, assistance for dependants, etc.?

Working conditions
. . . job security, enhancing working surroundings, social and sporting clubs, above-minimum safety standards, training and development, etc.?

Job design
. . . designing jobs to the increased satisfaction of workers rather than just for economic efficiency? This would include issues of work/life balance?

Intellectual property
. . . respecting the private knowledge of individuals and not claiming corporate ownership?

EXTERNAL ASPECTS

Environmental issues
. . . reducing pollution to below legal standards if competitors are not doing so?
. . . energy conservation?

Products
. . . dangers arising from the careless use of products by consumers?

Markets and marketing
. . . deciding not to sell in some markets?
. . . advertising standards?

Suppliers
. . . 'fair' terms of trade?
. . . blacklisting suppliers?

Employment
. . . positive discrimination in favour of minorities?
. . . maintaining jobs?

Community activity
. . . sponsoring local events and supporting local good works?

Human rights
. . . respecting human rights in relation to: child labour, workers' and union rights, oppressive political regimes? Both directly and in the choice of markets, suppliers and partners?

of the social agenda that are now mandatory in company reporting (e.g. some environmental issues) to voluntary social accounting by organisations themselves. Indeed it has been acts of *corporate irresponsibility* that have triggered changes in both the regulatory and corporate governance arrangements for organisations – such as those triggered by the Enron and WorldCom collapses of the early 2000s (discussed in section 4.2 above).

Illustration 4.5

strategy into action

Ethical dilemmas

Managers face a range of different ethical dilemmas that need to be resolved.

Conflicting objectives

You are a Dutch manager in charge of the mining operations of your multinational company in Namibia. You employ mainly local workers on very low wages. Your operation provides livelihood for 1,000 families and is the mainstay of the local economy. There is no other local work other than subsistence farming. You have discovered many safety problems with the mine but the company engineer has advised that the cost of upgrading facilities would make the mine uneconomic. Closing the mine would cause a major political stir and harm the parent company's reputation. But keeping it open risks the chance of a major disaster.

Performance data

You are the recently appointed head teacher of a school that is now improving following a period of very poor performance under your predecessor. It has been made clear that one important performance indicator is pupil attendance levels – that must be brought up to the national average (95 per cent). You have now collected all the data for your regular statistical return and notice to your disappointment that your attendance record has fallen just below your required target. On discussing this with your deputy she asks if you would like her to 're-examine and correct' the attendance data before submission.

Bribery

You are the newly appointed manager in charge of a new sales office in New York set up following extensive market research by your British company. After a few months you discover that none of the company's products can be sold in New York without code approval from an obscure New York authority that is controlled by Local 4 of the electricians' union. Further investigation reveals that Local 4 had Mafia connections.

Shortly afterwards you are visited by Local 4 representatives who offer you a deal. If the company pays an annual 'consultative fee' of $12,000 (€10,400) (with escalation clauses as sales grew) you will secure approval in six months. The alternative is to attempt to secure approval alone, which informed sources say is unlikely to succeed.

Company policy is opposed to bribery. But the project is a make-or-break for the company's ventures in the USA and your own career. Given the potential gains $12,000 is a small amount and would probably be approved if presented 'appropriately'.

Rationing

Rationing is one of the most important issues in many public sector organisations. You are a Swedish doctor working on secondment in charge of a local hospital in rural Nigeria. The medical facilities are poor, particularly supplies of medicines and blood. A bus leaving town has collided with a tourist vehicle. Apart from several fatalities there are four seriously injured survivors. Two are local children (both age 2), one is an elderly leader of a local tribe and the fourth is a German tourist. They all have the same blood group and need transfusions. There is only enough blood for two patients.

Questions

You are the 'player' faced with each of these dilemmas:

1. **What choices of action do you have?**
2. **List the pros and cons of each choice to your organisation, the external parties and yourself.**
3. **Explain what you would do and justify your actions from an ethical point of view.**

In a globalising world companies may need to develop an approach to corporate social responsibility which will have universal elements whilst also being applicable to many very different localities. The Caux Round Table[40] exists with the purpose of defining and promoting standards in business that should have universal acceptance. Since the actions of companies in one country may have an impact on other countries (e.g. pollution control or trading practices) there is an increasing need to look at the global impact of an organisation's strategies. These *Principles for Business* include the much larger issue as to whether companies and governments collectively are concerned with the global sustainability[41] of their strategies in terms of the environmental impact (e.g. global warming) or the exhaustion of finite resources. In turn these have produced responses from governments that regulate the actions of companies when developing strategies – for example, new regulations on recycling.

4.4.3 The role of individuals and managers

It should be clear from the preceding discussion that business ethics – as part of strategic management – raises difficult dilemmas for individuals and managers within organisations. Some examples are shown in Illustration 4.5. These raise questions about the responsibility of an individual who believes that the strategy of his or her organisation is unethical (for example, its trading practices) or is not adequately representing the legitimate interests of one or more stakeholder groups. Should the individual report the organisation; or should he or she leave the company on the grounds of a mismatch of values? This has often been called *whistleblowing*.[42] The Public Interest Disclosure Act (1998) gives protection in law to whistleblowing employees in the UK.

Managers are usually in a powerful position within organisations to influence the expectations of other stakeholders. They have access to information and channels of influence which are not available to many other stakeholders. With this power comes an ethical responsibility to behave with *integrity*. Given that strategy development can be an intensely political process, managers can find real difficulties establishing and maintaining this position of integrity. As has been seen, there is a potential conflict for managers between what strategies are best for their own career and what strategies are in the longer-term interests of their organisation and the shareholders. Integrity is a key ingredient of professional management and is included in the code of conduct of professional bodies, such as the Chartered Management Institute. Best practice is shared through the international links between these professional bodies. Perhaps the biggest challenge for managers is to develop a high level of self-awareness of their own behaviour in relation to the issues raised above.[43] This can be difficult because behaviour is deep-rooted and driven by unconscious beliefs – a key theme of the following section on culture.

4.5 THE CULTURAL CONTEXT

Section 4.3 about stakeholder expectations sought to explain why differences in expectations might arise between stakeholders. It would be easy to conclude that such political pressures would result in a vast variation in the types of strategy individual organisations would be pursuing – even in the same industry or market. But this is rarely the case, as has already been observed in Chapter 2 in the discussion of strategic groups. In practice there is a much higher level of commonality between the strategies of different organisations in the same sector than might be expected. In some instances this may be deemed necessary to protect the interests of particular stakeholders and becomes enshrined in regulation or in corporate governance (for example, in pharmaceuticals or financial services). However, this uniformity is more often explained in cultural terms.

Organisational culture
is the 'basic *assumptions and beliefs* that are shared by members of an organisation, that operate unconsciously and define in a basic taken-for-granted fashion an organisation's view of itself and its environment'

Schein defines **organisational culture** as the 'basic *assumptions and beliefs* that are shared by members of an organisation, that operate unconsciously and define in a basic taken-for-granted fashion an organisation's view of itself and its environment'.[44] So expectations and strategy are rooted in 'collective experience' (group and organisational) and become reflected in organisational routines that accumulated over time. In other words culture is about the collective behaviours in an organisation and strategies can be seen as the outcome of the collective taken-for-granted assumptions, behaviours and routines of organisations. This taken-for-grantedness is likely to be handed down over time within a group and so organisations can be 'captured' by their culture. It can be seen in Illustration 4.6 that within a newspaper company it might be taken for granted that it is in the business of 'news' – despite the fact that the financial viability of the organisation is actually determined by the ability to sell advertising space. This could result in some difficult conflicts in strategy – for example, about the space devoted to stories as against advertisements or even the nature of some of the advertising. The assumptions and behaviours of individuals within organisations are also influenced by assumptions and behaviours in the parts of the business environment with which those individuals and the organisation as a whole 'impinge'. These are called cultural frames of reference and are shown in Exhibit 4.9[45] and

---

Exhibit 4.9   Cultural frames of reference

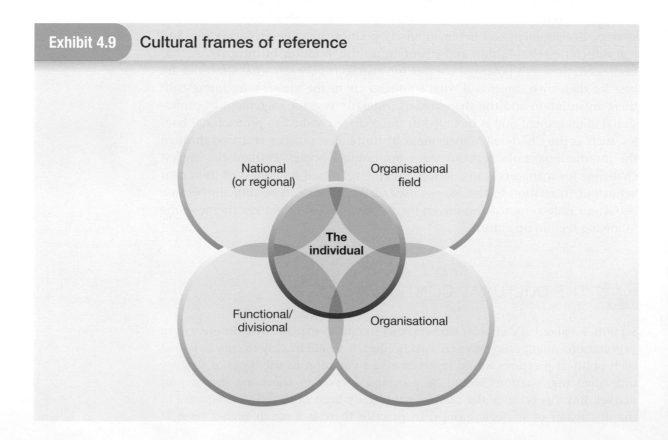

discussed below. The exhibit also shows that there are normally subcultures in parts of an organisation – which have different assumptions, behaviours and expectations. This may be the differences between business functions, geographical locations or even different informal groups (perhaps by age or length of service).

The sections that follow will identify the important factors and issues in each of the cultural frames of reference and then show how organisational culture can be *characterised* as a means of understanding the influences of culture on both current and future organisational purposes and strategies.

4.5.1 National and regional cultures[46]

The national cultural context influences the expectations of stakeholders directly. For example, Hofstede and Schneider and Barsoux showed how attitudes to work, authority, equality and a number of other important factors differ from one location to another.[47] In turn these have been shaped by powerful cultural forces concerned with history, religion and even climate. Organisations that operate internationally have the problem of coping with the very different standards and expectations of the various countries in which they operate.[48] Illustration 4.6 shows how this can create issues and difficulties in mergers between British and French companies.

Although they are not shown separately in Exhibit 4.9 (for reasons of simplification), it may be necessary to identify important *subnational* (usually regional) cultures. For example, attitudes to some aspects of employment, supplier relationships and, certainly, consumer preferences may differ significantly at a regional level even in a relatively small and cohesive country like the UK, and quite markedly elsewhere in Europe (e.g. between northern and southern Italy). There are usually big differences between urban and rural locations too. There also are developing aspects of *supranational* culture beyond a single nation. For example, moves towards a 'Euro-consumer' with converging tastes and preferences are of crucial strategic importance to many organisations in planning their product and distribution strategies. On a lesser scale Nordic countries would be seen as similar on many dimensions and different from the 'Latin' European countries.

4.5.2 The organisational field[49]

Culture is also shaped by 'work-based' groupings such as an industry (or sector) or a profession. This cultural influence is better understood as the influence of the organisational field. The formal academic definition of an **organisational field** is a community of organisations with a common 'meaning system' and whose participants interact more frequently with one another than with those outside the field.[50] Organisations within a field tend to share a common business environment such as a dominant technology, regulation or education and training. In turn this can mean that they tend to cohere around common norms and values. For example, there are many organisations in the organisational field of 'justice' (such as lawyers, police, courts, prisons and probation services). Although, as specialists, their roles are different and their detailed prescriptions as to how justice should be achieved differ, they are all tied together into the

An **organisational field** is a community of organisations that partake of a common meaning system and whose participants interact more frequently with one another than with those outside the field

Illustration 4.6   strategy into action

Culture and strategy

Culture will inform and drive strategy. This can underpin success or cause difficulties.

Newspapers are about news

The top management team of a newspaper business had spent the morning in small groups analysing the changes in the business environment they faced. They concluded that they faced many major challenges, including changing demographics, electronic media and the growth in free newspapers. Also over 70 per cent of their revenue was from the sale of advertising space rather than the newspaper itself. Indeed there seemed to be so many threats that one group decided that 'the end of the world is nigh!'

In the afternoon they turned their attention to the future strategy of the organisation. This quickly became a series of proposals about how they could improve the coverage of news and sport and the physical presentation of the newspaper itself. One of the younger members of the team suggested that they might consider a more fundamental question: '. . . whether we are really in the news business or if we are an advertising medium?' He was met with astonished silence from his colleagues.

So, in the morning, these managers were quite able to undertake a 'rational' analysis which raised questions about the traditional role of a newspaper. But, in the same afternoon, when it came to what they should do, the paradigm 'newspapers are about news' drove their thinking.

IKEA

In the mid-2000s the Swedish company IKEA was the leader in the European 'flat-pack' householder furniture business. It had a presence in some 30 countries and was famous for its good-quality products marketed at low prices. This had been achieved by the vision of the founder, Ingvar Kamprad, and an almost obsessive attention to every item that would add to cost – so much so that cost reduction became ingrained in the company culture. Kampard himself drove an old Volvo and bought fruit and vegetables in the afternoons at markets when they were cheap. IKEA staff always travelled economy class and took buses not taxis. There were wall stickers urging staff to turn off lights, taps and computers. There were prizes for the store or office that saved most electricity.

Cross-border mergers

French and British companies approach business in different ways – strongly shaped by the different national cultures. This can be an important impediment to successful mergers unless managers are aware of these differences and able to manage their impact within the merged companies. The impact of national culture is seen in the day-to-day ways that companies function. The French are much more committed to rational, analytical approaches to decision making whereas the British tend to get straight to the point and rely more on 'gut feel'. Meetings in France are held mainly to rubber stamp what has already been decided by 'the boss'. The British expect to go to meetings to influence decisions. The membership of meetings tends to reflect these different purposes. The French have more people involved – since it is part of the education and communication process. In Britain the membership is usually confined to those who have a 'right' to influence the decision.

Sources: *Financial Times*, 24 November 2003; A. Senter, 'Cross Channel culture club', *Management Today*, February 1999, pp. 73–5.

Questions

1. For each of the three examples make lists of advantages and disadvantages of the (four) corporate cultures described.
2. Imagine that you work for a French company that is considering a merger with a British company. Write a short executive report to your CEO listing the cultural clashes that might arise and how they could be handled.

same 'politico-economic system'. They are all committed to the principle that justice is a good thing which is worth striving for and they interact frequently on this issue. An organisational field, therefore, is both the organisations comprising it and the assumptions they adhere to. This shared set of assumptions will be referred to in this book as the recipe.

A **recipe**[51] is a set of assumptions held in common within an organisational field about organisational purposes and a 'shared wisdom' on how to manage organisations. Such cultural influences can be advantageous – say to customers – in maintaining standards and consistency between individual providers. The danger is that managers become 'institutionalised' and do not see the lessons that can be learnt from outside their organisational field. Professions, or trade associations, often attempt to formalise an organisational field where the membership is exclusive and the behaviour of members is regulated.

> A **recipe** is a set of assumptions held in common within an organisational field about organisational purposes and a 'shared wisdom' on how to manage organisations

Because the dominant culture varies from one field to another, the transition of managers between sectors can prove quite difficult. A number of private sector managers were encouraged to join public services during the 1990s in an attempt to inject new cultures and outlooks into the public sector. Many were surprised at the difficulties they experienced in adjusting their management style to the different traditions and expectations of their new organisation (for example, in issues like consensus building as part of the decision-making process).

The practical implication of these comments is that *legitimacy* is an important influence on an organisation's purposes and strategies. **Legitimacy** is concerned with meeting the expectations within an organisational field in terms of assumptions, behaviours and strategies. Strategies can be shaped by the need for legitimacy in several ways. For example, through *regulation* (e.g. standards of behaviour), *normative expectations* (what society expects), or simply that which is taken for granted as being appropriate (e.g. the *recipe*). Over time, there tends to develop a consensus amongst managers in an organisational field about strategies that will be successful – so strategies themselves become legitimised. Stepping outside that strategy may be risky because important stakeholders (such as customers or bankers) may not go along with it. Therefore, organisations tend to mimic each other's strategies. There will be differences in strategies between organisations but within bounds of legitimacy.[52] This is discussed in Chapter 5 (section 5.3.6). Of course, some fringe players may actually represent successful future strategies (e.g. Virgin in financial services), but *initially* this may not be seen – for example, customers may remain loyal to established providers or bankers may be reluctant to fund these ventures.

> **Legitimacy** is concerned with meeting the expectations within an organisational field in terms of assumptions, behaviours and strategies

4.5.3 Organisational culture

It is useful to conceive of the culture of an organisation as consisting of four layers[53] (see Exhibit 4.10):

● *Values* may be easy to identify in an organisation, and are often written down as statements about the organisation's mission, objectives or strategies (which will be as discussed in section 4.6 below). However, they tend to be vague, such as 'service to the community' or 'equal employment opportunities'.

Exhibit 4.10   Culture in four layers

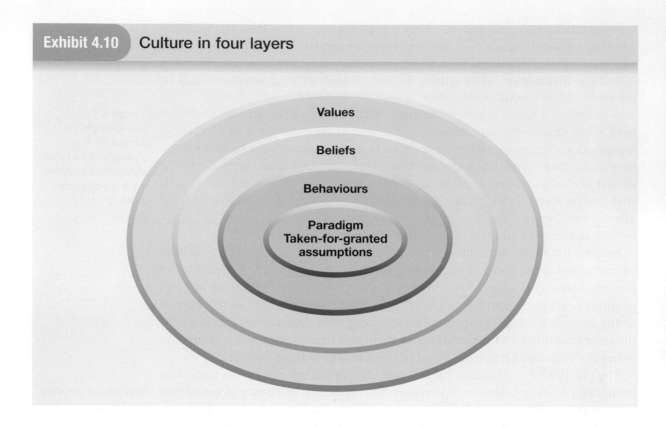

- *Beliefs* are more specific, but again they are issues which people in the organisation can surface and talk about. They might include a belief that the company should not trade with particular countries, or that professional staff should not have their professional actions appraised by managers.

- *Behaviours* are the day-to-day way in which an organisation operates and can be seen by people both inside and outside the organisation. This includes the work routines, how the organisation is structured and controlled and 'softer' issues around the symbolic behaviours.

- *Taken-for-granted assumptions* are the core of an organisation's culture. They are the aspects of organisational life which people find difficult to identify and explain. Here they are referred to as the organisational paradigm. The **paradigm** is the set of assumptions held in common and taken for granted in an organisation. For an organisation to operate effectively there has to be such a generally accepted set of assumptions. As mentioned above, these assumptions represent *collective experience* without which people would have to 'reinvent their world' for different circumstances that they face. Illustration 4.6 showed how the paradigm both informs and drives strategy (the newspaper example). It can underpin successful strategies (IKEA) and constrain the development of new strategies (cross-border mergers).

A **paradigm** is the set of assumptions held relatively in common and taken for granted in an organisation

As organisations increasingly make visible their carefully considered public statements of their values, beliefs and purposes – for example, in annual reports, mission or values statements and business plans – there is a danger that these are seen as useful and accurate descriptions of the organisational behaviours and paradigm. But this is likely to be at best only partially true, and at worst misleading. This is not to suggest that there is any organised deception. It is simply that the statements of values and beliefs are often statements of the aspirations of a particular stakeholder (such as the CEO) rather than accurate descriptions of the 'real' culture (behaviours and assumptions about 'how you run an organisation like this' and 'what really matters around here'). For example, an outside observer of a police force might conclude from its public statements of purpose and priorities that it had a balanced approach to the various aspects of police work – catching criminals, crime prevention, community relations. However, a deeper probing might quickly reveal that (in cultural terms) there is the 'real' police work (catching criminals) and the 'lesser work' (crime prevention, community relations). Section 4.5.5 below will show how these behaviours and assumptions can be surfaced and understood using the cultural web.

4.5.4 Functional and divisional subcultures

In seeking to understand the relationship between culture and an organisation's strategies, it may be possible to identify some aspects of culture that pervade the whole organisation. However, as mentioned above, there may also be important *subcultures* within organisations. These subcultures may relate directly to the structure of the organisation. For example, the differences between geographical divisions in a multinational company, or between functional groups such as finance, marketing and operations, can be very powerful. Differences between divisions may be particularly evident in organisations that have grown through acquisition. Also different divisions may be pursuing different types of strategy and these different market positionings require or foster different cultures. Indeed, it will be seen later (Chapter 10) that aligning strategic positioning and organisational culture is a critical feature of successful organisations. Differences between business functions also can relate to the different nature of work in different functions. For example, whether work tasks are routine or complex; short or long cycle times; inward or outward focused. So an engineering department developing major new manufacturing plants is vastly different from the public relations department responding to external scrutiny.

4.5.5 The cultural web[54]

Trying to understand the culture at all of these levels is clearly important, but it is not straightforward. For example, it has already been noted that even when a strategy and the values of an organisation are written down, the underlying assumptions which make up the paradigm are usually evident only in the way in which people behave day-to-day. These behaviours not only give clues about the paradigm, but are also likely to reinforce the assumptions within that paradigm. The concept of the **cultural web** is a representation of the taken-for-granted assumptions, or paradigm, of an organisation and the behavioural manifestations of organisational culture (see Exhibit 4.11). It is the inner two ovals in Exhibit 4.10. The cultural web can be used to understand culture in any

The **cultural web** is a representation of the taken-for-granted assumptions, or paradigm, of an organisation and the physical manifestations of organisational culture

Exhibit 4.11   The cultural web

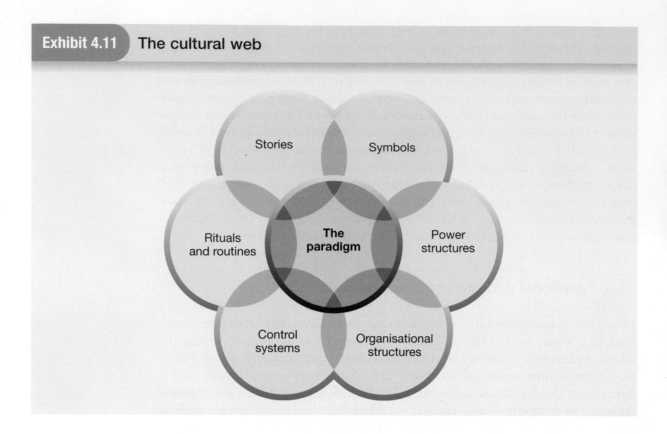

of the frames of reference discussed above but is most often used at the organisational and/or functional/divisional levels in Exhibit 4.9.[55]

Illustration 4.7 shows a cultural web drawn up by health care managers in the National Health Service in the UK.[56] It would be similar to many other state-owned health care systems in other countries. It should, however, be borne in mind that this is the view of managers – clinicians might well have quite different views.

Exhibit 4.12 outlines some of the questions that might help build up an understanding of culture through the elements of the cultural web:

● The *routine behaviours* that members of the organisation display both internally and towards those outside the organisation make up 'the way we do things around here' on a day-to-day basis. At its best, this lubricates the working of the organisation, and may provide a distinctive organisational competence. However, it can also represent a taken-for-grantedness about how things should happen which is extremely difficult to change.

● The *rituals* of organisational life are particular activities or special events through which the organisation emphasises what is particularly important and reinforces 'the way we do things around here'. Examples include training programmes, interview panels, promotion and assessment procedures, sales conferences and so on. An extreme example, of course, is the ritualistic training of army recruits to prepare them for the discipline required in conflict. However, rituals can also be informal activities such as drinks in the pub after work or gossiping around photocopying machines. A checklist of rituals is provided in Chapter 10 (see Exhibit 10.8).

Exhibit 4.12	The cultural web: some useful questions

Stories
- What core beliefs do stories reflect?
- How pervasive are these beliefs (through levels)?
- Do stories relate to:
  - strengths or weaknesses?
  - successes or failures?
  - conformity or mavericks?
- Who are the heroes and villains?
- What norms do the mavericks deviate from?

Symbols
- Are there particular symbols which denote the organisation?
- What status symbols are there?
- What language and jargon are used?
- What aspects of strategy are highlighted in publicity?

Routines and rituals
- Which routines are emphasised?
- Which would look odd if changed?
- What behaviour do routines encourage?
- What are the key rituals?
- What core beliefs do they reflect?
- What do training programmes emphasise?
- How easy are rituals/routines to change?

Power structures
- How is power distributed in the organisation?
- What are the core beliefs of the leadership?
- How strongly held are these beliefs (idealists or pragmatists)?
- Where are the main blockages to change?

Stories — Symbols — Routines and rituals — **The paradigm** — Power structures — Control systems — Organisational structures

Control systems
- What is most closely monitored/controlled?
- Is emphasis on reward or punishment?
- Are controls related to history or current strategies?
- Are there many/few controls?

Organisational structures
- How mechanistic/organic are the structures?
- How flat/hierarchical are the structures?
- How formal/informal are the structures?
- Do structures encourage collaboration or competition?
- What types of power structure do they support?

Overall

- What do the answers to these questions suggest are the (four) fundamental assumptions that are the paradigm?
- How would you characterise the dominant culture?
- How easy is this to change?

- The *stories* told by members of an organisation to each other, to outsiders, to new recruits and so on, embed the present in its organisational history and also flag up important events and personalities. They typically have to do with successes, disasters, heroes, villains and mavericks (who deviate from the norm). They are devices for telling people what is important in the organisation.

Illustration 4.7   strategy into action

The cultural web of the NHS

The cultural web can be used to identify the behaviours and taken-for-granted assumptions of an organisation.

The diagram shows a cultural web produced by managers in the NHS.

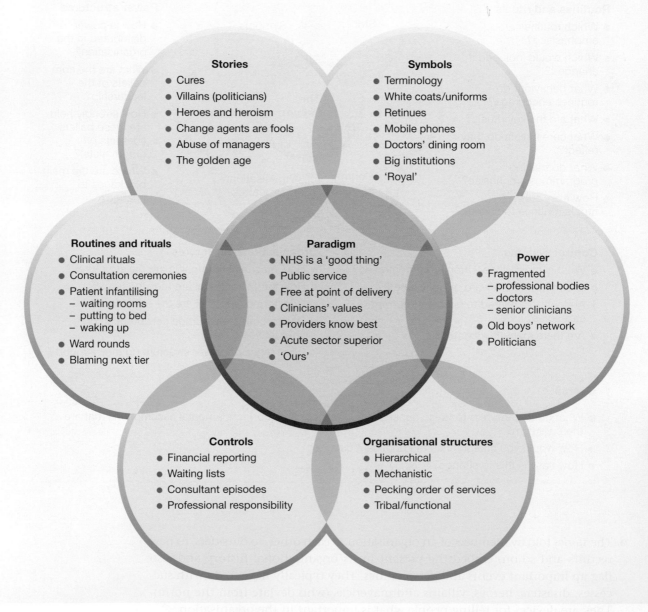

Stories
- Cures
- Villains (politicians)
- Heroes and heroism
- Change agents are fools
- Abuse of managers
- The golden age

Symbols
- Terminology
- White coats/uniforms
- Retinues
- Mobile phones
- Doctors' dining room
- Big institutions
- 'Royal'

Routines and rituals
- Clinical rituals
- Consultation ceremonies
- Patient infantilising
  – waiting rooms
  – putting to bed
  – waking up
- Ward rounds
- Blaming next tier

Paradigm
- NHS is a 'good thing'
- Public service
- Free at point of delivery
- Clinicians' values
- Providers know best
- Acute sector superior
- 'Ours'

Power
- Fragmented
  – professional bodies
  – doctors
  – senior clinicians
- Old boys' network
- Politicians

Controls
- Financial reporting
- Waiting lists
- Consultant episodes
- Professional responsibility

Organisational structures
- Hierarchical
- Mechanistic
- Pecking order of services
- Tribal/functional

Routines and rituals

This took the form, for example, in *routines* of consultation and of prescribing drugs. *Rituals* had to do with what the managers termed 'infantilising', which 'put patients in their place' – making them wait, putting them to bed, waking them up and so on. The subservience of patients was further emphasised by the elevation of clinicians with ritual consultation ceremonies and ward rounds. These are routines and rituals which emphasise that it is the professionals who are in control.

Stories

Most of the stories within health services concern developments in curing – particularly terminal illnesses. The heroes of the health service are in curing, not so much in caring. There are also stories about villainous politicians trying to change the system, the failure of those who try to make changes and of heroic acts by those defending the system (often well-known medical figures).

Symbols

Symbols reflected the various institutions within the organisation, with uniforms for clinical and nursing staff, distinct symbols for clinicians, such as their staff retinues, and status symbols such as mobile phones and dining rooms. The importance of the size and status of hospitals was reflected, not least, in the designation of 'Royal' in the name, seen as a key means of ensuring that it might withstand the threat of closure.

Power structures

The power structure was fragmented between clinicians, nurses and managers. However, historically, senior clinicians were the most powerful and managers had hitherto been seen as 'administration'. As with many other organisations, there was also a strong informal network of individuals and groups that coalesced around specific issues to promote or resist a particular view.

Control systems

In hospitals the key measure has been 'completed clinical episodes', i.e. activity rather than results. Control over staff is exerted by senior professionals. Patronage is a key feature of this professional culture.

Organisation structures

Structures were hierarchical and mechanistic. There was a clear pecking order between services with the 'caring' services low down the list – for example, mental health. At the informal level there were lots of 'tribalism' between functions and professional groups.

The paradigm

The assumptions which constitute the *paradigm* reflect the common public perception in the UK that the NHS is a 'good thing': a public service which should be provided equally, free of charge at the point of delivery. However, it is medical values that are central and that 'medics know best'. This is an organisation concerned with curing illness rather than preventing illness in the first case. For example, pregnancy is not an illness, but pregnant women often argue that hospitals treat them as though they are ill. It is the acute sector within hospitals which is central to the service rather than, for example, care in the community. Overall, the NHS is seen as belonging to those who provide the services.

Questions

1. Read through section 4.5.5 of the text and ensure that you understand what are the elements of the cultural web (using this NHS managers example).
2. From all the detail in this web, develop up to four statements, which together you feel would encapsulate the culture of the NHS at that time.
3. What are the implications of this analysis in terms of the ease or difficulty with which new strategies might be developed?

- *Symbols*[57] such as logos, offices, cars and titles, or the type of language and terminology commonly used, become a shorthand representation of the nature of the organisation. For example, in long-established or conservative organisations it is likely that there will be many symbols of hierarchy or deference to do with formal office layout, differences in privileges between levels of management, the way in which people address each other, and so on. In turn this formalisation may reflect difficulties in changing strategies within a hierarchical or deferential system. The form of language used in an organisation can also be particularly revealing, especially with regard to customers or clients. For example, the head of a consumer protection agency in Australia described his clients as 'complainers'. In a major teaching hospital in the UK, consultants described patients as 'clinical material'. Whilst such examples might be amusing, they reveal an underlying assumption about customers (or patients) which might play a significant role in influencing the strategy of an organisation.

  Although symbols are shown separately in the cultural web, it should be remembered that many elements of the web are symbolic, in the sense that they convey messages beyond their functional purpose. Routines, control and reward systems and structures are symbolic.

- *Power structures* are also likely to influence the key assumptions. The most powerful groupings within the organisation are likely to be closely associated with the core assumptions and beliefs. For example, although accountancy firms may offer a whole range of services, typically the most powerful individuals or groups have been qualified chartered accountants with a set of assumptions about the business and its market that are rooted in the audit practice. It should be remembered that there are many sources of power in organisations (see section 4.3.3 above).

- The *control systems*, measurements and reward systems emphasise what is important to monitor in the organisation. For example, public service organisations have often been accused of being concerned more with stewardship of funds than with quality of service. This is reflected in their procedures, which are more about accounting for spending rather than with quality of service. Reward systems are important influences on behaviours, but can also prove to be a barrier to success of new strategies. For example, an organisation with individually based bonus schemes related to volume could find it difficult to promote strategies requiring teamwork and an emphasis on quality rather than volume.

- *Organisational structure* is likely to reflect power and show important roles and relationships. Formal hierarchical, mechanistic structures may emphasise that strategy is the province of top managers and everyone else is 'working to orders'. Highly devolved structures (as discussed in Chapter 8) may signify that collaboration is less important than competition and so on.

- The *paradigm* of the organisation encapsulates and reinforces the behaviours observed in the other elements of the cultural web. The illustration shows that the overall picture of the NHS was of a 'producer-driven' culture dominated by medical practice, fragmented in its power bases historically, with a division between clinical aspects of the organisation and its management. It is a culture in which management had traditionally been seen as relatively unimportant.

The detailed 'map' produced by the cultural web is a rich source of information about an organisation's culture. But in understanding the influence of culture on organisational purposes, it is important to be able to characterise the culture which the information conveys. Sometimes it is possible to capture the essence of an organisation's culture in a simple graphic descriptor. For example, the NHS cultural web in Illustration 4.7 could be summed up as 'The National Sickness Service'. Sometimes this can be done to define the dominant culture of different strategic groups within a sector. For example, comparing cultural webs for old and new universities in the UK, they might be characterised as 'Boffins and Gurus' and 'Teaching Factories' respectively. The cultural webs of even large companies sometimes would deserve the cultural characterisation of 'The Family Firm'. Although this approach is rather crude and unscientific, it can be very powerful in terms of organisational members seeing the organisation as it really is – which may not be immediately apparent from all of the detailed points in the cultural web. The importance of this is in getting people to understand that culture drives strategies – for example, a 'national sickness service' would clearly prioritise strategies that are about spectacular developments in curing sick people above health promotion strategies. So those favouring health promotion strategies need to understand how they can gain support in such a cultural context rather than assuming that rational processes like planning and resource allocation will be enough.

4.6 COMMUNICATING ORGANISATIONAL PURPOSES

The previous sections have looked at the factors that influence organisational purposes – the corporate governance framework, stakeholder relationships, ethical standards and culture. This section will look at ways in which organisations attempt to explicitly communicate purposes, for example through statements of *corporate values*, *vision*, *mission* and *objectives*. In some instances such statements may be a formal requirement of corporate governance. In others they may be expected of the organisation by one or more stakeholders. Illustration 4.8 is an example for the Northern Ireland Police Service. Despite this, it must be remembered that these statements may not be an accurate reflection of the priorities within the organisation, for the political and cultural reasons discussed above.

4.6.1 Corporate values[58]

Increasingly organisations have been keen to develop and communicate a set of corporate values that define the way that the organisation operates. Of particular importance are the organisation's **core values** – these are the 'principles' that guide an organisation's actions. For example, emergency services such as ambulance and fire fighters have an overriding commitment to saving life even to the extent that they would break strike action to attend emergencies when life is threatened. Some authors have argued that the success of many US corporates – such as

Core values are the principles that guide an organisation's actions

Illustration 4.8

strategy into action

Organisational purposes for the Northern Ireland Police Service

Organisations are finding it useful to publish a statement of their purposes. This is usually done at several levels of detail.

As part of its Policing Plan for 2003/04 the Police Service of Northern Ireland (PSNI) outlined its mission, overarching aims and priorities. It also reported on performance in previous years against the key performance targets and indicators for each priority. The following are extracts from the report:

1. Mission statement

In partnership making Northern Ireland safer.
Achieving effective and professional policing in partnership with the community, helping to secure a safe and just society in which human rights and responsibilities are properly respected and balanced.

2. Overarching aims

- To promote safety and reduce disorder
- To reduce crime and fear of crime
- To contribute to delivering in a way which secures and maintains public confidence in the rule of law.

The emphasis and importance placed on each area are flexible and open to change in order to meet the needs and demands of the local community.

3. Priorities (examples)

Priorities to 'reduce crime and the fear of crime'

- To work in partnership with other relevant agencies to help reduce the incidence of crime, including organised crime
- To disrupt the illegal supply of controlled drugs and to work in partnership with other agencies in tackling the problem of drug misuse
- To uphold the rule of law, counter the terrorist threat and bring to justice those responsible for crime

4. Targets to 'reduce crime and the fear of crime' (examples)

- Reduce the number of domestic burglaries by 5 per cent (annually)

- Reduce the number of vehicle crimes by 5 per cent (annually)
- Establish an accurate baseline of the number of crimes and incidents of a racist or homophobic nature
- To demonstrate police contribution towards delivery of the Northern Ireland Community Safety Strategy
- To report the number of domestic incidents and domestic violence offences and develop a strategy for monitoring disposal of incidents
- To increase the number of seizures of illicit drugs
- To achieve a detection rate for violent crime of 55 per cent

5. Indicators (examples)

- Number of persons charged with terrorist offences
- Number of deaths occurring as a result of the security situation
- Number of shooting and bombing incidents
- Number of casualties arising from paramilitary-style attacks

Source: Police Service of Northern Ireland, Policing Plan 2003/04.

Questions

1. How useful are these various statements of purpose to the shaping and implementation of PSNI strategy? In answering the question ensure that you give a critique of each of the various 'levels' of statement in order to establish:
   (a) what it is meant to achieve;
   (b) whether you feel that it does so;
   (c) any improvements you would suggest.
2. Comment on the extent to which these various levels of purpose are consistent with each other.

Disney, General Electric or 3M – can be attributed (at least in part) to strong core values.[59] However, there are potential downsides to public statements of corporate values if an organisation demonstrably fails to live them out in practice. Whereas *core values* should be an expression of the way the organisation *is*, there are other corporate values to which the organisation is wishing to *aspire*. Unless this distinction is clear there is room for considerable misunderstanding and cynicism about statements of corporate values. In many organisations there are also corporate values which are the basic minimum (*threshold*) values to which all stakeholders must 'subscribe'. These could, for example, be concerned with aspects of corporate social responsibility as discussed in section 4.4.2 above. Many public sector organisations will refuse to deal with suppliers who do not meet these threshold standards.

4.6.2 Mission statements

Whereas corporate values may set a back cloth and boundaries within which strategies are developed, a **mission statement** is a statement of the overriding direction and purpose of an organisation. It can be thought of as an expression of its *raison d'être*. Some organisations use the term 'vision statement' – some even have both vision and mission statements. If there is substantial disagreement within the organisation or with stakeholders as to its mission (or vision), it may well give rise to real problems in resolving the strategic direction of the organisation. Although mission statements had become much more widely adopted by the early 2000s, many critics regard them as bland and wide-ranging.[60] However, this may be necessary given the political nature of strategic management, since it is essential *at that level* to have statements to which most, if not all, stakeholders can subscribe. They need to emphasise the common ground amongst stakeholders and not the differences.

A **mission statement** is a statement of the overriding direction and purpose of an organisation

4.6.3 Objectives

Objectives are statements of specific outcomes that are to be achieved. Objectives – both at the corporate and business unit level – are often expressed in financial terms. They could be the expression of desired sales or profit levels, rates of growth, dividend levels or share valuations.[61] But organisations also have market-based objectives, many of which are quantified as targets – such as market share, customer service, repeat business and so on.

Objectives are statements of specific outcomes that are to be achieved

Many writers[62] have argued that objectives are not helpful unless they are capable of being measured and achieved, i.e. unless they are closed. This view is not taken here. There may be some objectives which are important, but which are difficult to quantify or express in measurable terms. An objective such as 'to be a leader in technology' may be highly relevant in today's technological environment, but it may become absurd if it has to be expressed in some measurable way. It is nonetheless valid as an objective.

However, there are times when specific objectives are required. These are likely to be when urgent action is needed, such as in a crisis or at times of major

Illustration 4.9   key debate

Are managers just unprincipled agents?

Can senior managers be trusted to run their organisations in the interests of their shareholders? Is the remedy to untrustworthiness worse than the problem?

Section 4.2 introduced agency theory, the notion of a division between the interests of principals (for example, the shareholders of a business) and their agents (the managers that shareholders hire to run their businesses). Harvard Business School professor Michael Jensen, one of the key proponents of agency theory, warns that there are no 'perfect agents' in the real world.[1] Nobody can so thoroughly embody the wishes of somebody else that he or she can be that person's perfect agent. Either through their own self-interest, or perhaps by error, managers cannot be trusted to maximise shareholders' interests.

This agency perspective offers a dire warning with regard to strategy. Surplus cash that should be paid back directly to shareholders is liable to be wasted by managers on self-aggrandising acquisitions, indulgent research initiatives and pet investment projects. In this view, a good deal of strategy serves managers more than shareholders.

According to Michael Jensen, the best safeguard against such managerial agency problems is to align managers' interests unambiguously with the shareholder goal of long-run value maximisation. This alignment should be financial, through the use of stock options and other performance-related pay. Managers should become rich if they make their shareholders rich. Managers should be punished by pay-cuts or dismissal if they fail.

Here Jensen warns against stakeholder theory. For him, managers' focus should be exclusively on value maximisation. Stakeholder theory, by introducing other interests such as those of customers or employees, risks only confusing managerial objectives. Without a single clear objective, managers are hard to motivate and control. Besides, long-run value maximisation requires treating employees and customers appropriately too.

The trouble with this exclusively financial view of managers and organisations, according to Sumantra Ghoshal, is that it can easily be self-defeating.[2] Treat managers as untrustworthy, and they will behave untrustworthily. The challenge is not so much protecting value from being wasted by managers as encouraging managers to create value in the first place. Value creation in an organisation relies on trust, mutuality and enough space in the system to allow for experimentation and risk-taking. Managers, indeed all employees, should be encouraged to exchange information and try out risky innovations without constant regard to their selfish financial interests. Shareholders' interests will best be served if managers are treated as value-creators rather than value-cheats.

There is real-world support for both views. A scandal such as Enron shows that professional managers such as Enron's Chief Executive Officer Jeff Skilling can indeed pursue projects and hide losses contrary to shareholder interests, just as Michael Jensen would expect. On the other hand, Sumantra Ghoshal might respond by saying that Enron's excesses were driven precisely by the huge financial incentives offered to top executives. Instead of aligning managerial and shareholder interests, these incentives just gave top Enron executives a good reason to cheat. It might be no coincidence that Jeff Skilling had obtained his MBA from Jensen's Harvard Business School.

Sources:
1. M.C. Jensen, 'Value maximisation, stakeholder theory and the corporate objective function, *European Financial Management*, vol. 7, no. 3 (2001), pp. 297–317; M.C. Jensen and K.J. Murphy, 'CEO Incentives – it's not how much you pay, but how', *Harvard Business Review*, May–June (1990), pp. 138–149.
2. S. Ghoshal, C.A. Bartlett and P. Moran, 'A New Manifesto for Management', *Sloan Management Review*, Spring (1999), pp. 9–20.

Questions

To what extent should senior managers' pay be according to financial performance and are there alternative mechanisms available for ensuring appropriate managerial behaviour that would have fewer undesirable side-effects?

transition, and it becomes essential for management to focus attention on a limited number of priority requirements. An extreme example would be in a *turnaround* situation. If the choice is between going out of business and surviving, there is no room for latitude through vaguely stated requirements and control.

A recurring problem with objectives is that managers and employees 'lower down' in the hierarchy are unclear as to how their day-to-day work contributes to the achievement of higher level of objectives. This could, in principle, be addressed by a 'cascade' of objectives – defining a set of detailed objectives at each level in the hierarchy. Many organisations attempt to do this to some extent.

Summary

- Expectations and purposes are influenced by four main factors: corporate governance, stakeholder expectations, business ethics and culture.

- The *corporate governance* arrangements determine whom the organisation is there to serve and how the purposes and priorities should be decided. Corporate governance has become more complex for two main reasons: first, the separation of ownership and management control, and second, the increasing tendency to make organisations more visibly accountable to a wider range of stakeholders.

- Stakeholders differ in terms of the power that they hold and the extent to which they are actively interested in the strategies that an organisation is pursuing. Although they may be in agreement about the broad purposes of an organisation, at a more detailed level there are usually differing expectations amongst stakeholders. *Stakeholder mapping* can help with understanding these differences.

- Purposes are also influenced by the *ethical stance* taken by the organisation about its relationships with the wider society within which it operates. This stance may vary from a narrow view that the short-term interests of shareholders should be paramount, through to some organisations that would see themselves as shapers of society. Within this broad stance, specific issues of *corporate social responsibility* will be important. There can also be ethical *dilemmas for individuals* within organisations if their personal values come into conflict with the ethical standards and behaviours in the organisation.

  (Governance, managers' expectations as shareholders and ethics are all related to the agency issue which is the subject of the key debate in Illustration 4.9.)

- Purposes are strongly influenced by cultural frames of reference at various 'levels'. This ranges from the national culture, through the organisational field to the organisational culture and subcultures. All of these 'cultural arenas' influence whether strategies are regarded as legitimate.

- Culture consists of 'layers' of values, beliefs, behaviours and taken-for-granted assumptions in organisations. The *cultural web* is a useful concept for understanding how these latter two layers connect and influence strategy.

- Organisational purposes can be communicated at different levels of detail, from overall statements of corporate values and mission through to detailed operational objectives for the various parts of the organisation.

Recommended key readings

- R.I. Tricker, *International Corporate Governance: Text, cases and readings*, Prentice Hall, 1999, remains the most comprehensive book on corporate governance. Also useful are A. Davies, *A Strategic Approach to Corporate Governance*, Gower, 1999; R. Monks and N. Minow (eds), *Corporate Governance*, 2nd edition, Blackwell, 2002.

- For more about the stakeholder concept read K. Scholes' chapter in V. Ambrosini with G. Johnson and K. Scholes (eds), *Exploring Techniques of Analysis and Evaluation in Strategic Management*, Prentice Hall, 1998. Readers should be familiar with the political context of strategic decision making by reading J. Pfeffer, *Managing with Power: Politics and influence in organisations*, HBS Press, 1994 or D. Buchanan and R. Badham, *Power, Politics and Organisational change: winning the turf game*, Sage, 1999.

- Readers can gain some useful insights into business ethics by reading: P. Werhane and R.E. Freeman, 'Business ethics: the state of the art', *International Journal of Management Research*, vol. 1, no. 1 (1999), pp. 1–16. A useful book on corporate social responsibility is: W. Frederick, J. Post and K. Davis, *Business and Society: Management, public policy, ethics*, 7th edition, McGraw-Hill, 1992.

- E. Schein, *Organisation Culture and Leadership*, Jossey-Bass, 1997 and A. Brown, *Organisational Culture*, FT/Prentice Hall, 1998 are useful in understanding the relationship between organisational culture and strategy. The influence of national culture on strategy can be found in G. Hofstede, *Culture's Consequences*, 2nd edition, Sage, 2001 and S. Schneider and J.-L. Barsoux, *Managing Across Cultures*, 2nd edition, Financial Times/Prentice Hall, 2003.

- A full explanation of the cultural web can be found in G. Johnson's chapter 'Mapping and re-mapping organisational culture' in V. Ambrosini with G. Johnson and K. Scholes (eds), *Exploring Techniques of Analysis and Evaluation in Strategic Management*, Prentice Hall, 1998.

References

1. Useful general references on corporate governance are: A. Davies, *A Strategic Approach to Corporate Governance*, Gower, 1999; R. Monks and N. Minow (eds), *Corporate Governance*, 2nd edition, Blackwell, 2002 and R.I. Tricker, *International Corporate Governance: Text, cases and readings*, Prentice Hall, 1999 (which remains the most comprehensive book on the subject). Also, *Harvard Business Review on Corporate Governance*, HBS Press, 2000, is a collection of eight papers published in the journal during the 1990s. CIMA, *Corporate Governance: History, Practice and Future*, 2000, is a guide for practising managers. Those interested in an annual research update can find this in 'Corporate governance digest', *Business Horizons* (usually the May issue).

2. These differences between countries are discussed in the general books (reference 1 above) and also in: T. Clarke and S. Clegg, *Changing Paradigms: The transformation of management knowledge in the 21st century*, HarperCollins, 2000, Chapter 5.

3. The principal–agency model is part of agency theory which developed within organisational economics but is now widely used in the management field as described here. Two useful references are: K. Eisenhardt, 'Agency theory: An assessment and review', *Academy of Management Review*, vol. 14, no. 1 (1989), pp. 57–74; J.-J. Laffont and D. Martimort, *The Theory of Incentives: The Principal–Agent Model*, Princeton University Press, 2002.

4. This issue of to whom corporate managers should be accountable is discussed by J. Charkham, *Keeping Good Company: A study of corporate governance in five countries*, Clarendon Press, 1994, and J. Kay, 'The stakeholder corporation', in G. Kelley, D. Kelly and A. Gamble, *Stakeholder Capitalism*, Macmillan, 1997.

5. This principle was established by the Hampel Committee on Corporate Governance, 1997.

6. An interesting review of the issues raised by shareholder activists can be found in: S. Graves, K. Rehbien and S. Waddock, 'Fad and fashion in shareholder activism: the landscape of shareholder resolutions, 1988–1998', *Business and Society Review*, vol. 106, no. 4 (2001), pp. 293–314.

7. For a review of the Enron collapse see: C.W. Thomas, 'The rise and fall of Enron', *Journal of Accountancy*, vol. 193, no. 4 (2002), pp. 41–47. An assessment of the wider strategic lessons is: R. Whittington et al., 'Taking strategy seriously: responsibility and reform for an important social practice', *Journal of Management Enquiry*, vol. 12, no. 4 (2003), pp. 396–409.

8. The contribution of each of these reports is neatly summarised by G. Vinten, 'Corporate Governance: the need to know', *Industrial and Commercial Training*, vol. 32, no. 5 (2000), pp. 173–178.

9. The Treadway (1987) and the COSO (1992) reports in the USA and the Cadbury reports (1992 and 1996) in the UK.

10. For example, in the UK the Hampel (1998), Turnbull (1999) and Higgs (2003) reports.

11. The importance of risk management in the public sector was addressed in: 'Supporting innovation: managing risk in government departments', *Report by the Comptroller and Auditor General*, The Stationery Office, July 2000.

12. *Governance White Paper*, European Commission, July 2001.

13. D. Norburn, B. Boyd, M. Fox and M. Muth, 'International corporate governance reform', *European Business Journal*, vol.12, no. 3 (2000), pp. 116–133.

14. See reference 2 above and J. Charkham (reference 3 above).

15. Short-termism as an issue in the Anglo-American tradition is contrasted with the 'Rhine model' more typical of Germany, Switzerland, Benelux and northern European countries by M. Albert, 'The Rhine model of capitalism: an investigation', in W. Nicoll, D. Norburn and R. Schoenberg (eds), *Perspectives on European Business*, Whurr Publishers, 1995.

16. See: A. Fliaster and R. Marr, 'Change of the insider-oriented corporate governance in Japan and Germany: between Americanisation and tradition', *Journal of Change Management*, vol. 1, no. 3 (2001), pp. 242–256.

17. In the USA: the Sabanes–Oxley Act (2002). In the UK: D. Higgs, 'Review of the role and effectiveness of non-executive directors', UK Department of Trade and Industry, 2003.

18. See Norburn et al. (reference 13 above); J. Sonnenfeld, 'What makes great boards great', *Harvard Business Review*, vol. 80, no. 9 (2002), pp. 106–113.

19. See: *Changing Gear: Best Value Annual Statement*, UK Audit Commission, 2001.

20. The privatisation of public utilities is discussed in P. Jackson and C. Price, *Privatisation and Regulation: A review of the issues*, Longman, 1994, Chapter 3.

21. E. Doyle, 'Implications of ownership for strategy: the example of commercial semi-state bodies in Ireland, in G. Johnson and K. Scholes (eds), *Exploring Public Sector Strategy*, Financial Times/Prentice Hall, 2001, Chapter 10.

22. The early writings about stakeholders are still worthy of note. For example, the seminal work by R.M. Cyert and J.G. March, *A Behavioural Theory of the Firm*, Prentice Hall, 1964; I.I. Mitroff, *Stakeholder of the Organisational Mind*, Jossey-Bass, 1983; R.E. Freeman, *Strategic Management: A stakeholder approach*, Pitman, 1984.

23. Details on how these three groups interact with organisations *in detail* can be found in: J. Cummings and J. Doh, 'Identifying who matters: mapping key players in multiple environments', *California Management Review*, vol. 42, no. 2 (2000), pp. 83–104.

24. T. Kostova and S. Zaheer, 'Organisational legitimacy under conditions of complexity: the case of the multinational enterprise', *Academy of Management Review*, vol. 24, no.1 (1999), pp. 64–81.

25. This approach to stakeholder mapping has been adapted from A. Mendelow, *Proceedings of 2nd International Conference on Information Systems*, Cambridge, MA, 1991. See also K. Scholes' chapter, 'Stakeholder analysis', in V. Ambrosini with G. Johnson and K. Scholes (eds), *Exploring Techniques of Analysis and Evaluation in Strategic Management*, Prentice Hall, 1998. For a public sector explanation see K. Scholes, 'Stakeholder mapping: a practical tool for public sector managers', in G. Johnson and K. Scholes (eds), *Exploring Public Sector Strategy*, Financial Times/Prentice Hall, 2001, Chapter 9 and J. Bryson, G. Cunningham and K. Lokkesmoe, 'What to do when stakeholders matter: the case of problem formulation for the African American men project of Hennepin County, Minnesota', *Public Administration Review*, vol. 62, no. 5 (2002), pp. 568–584.

26. See Cyert and March (reference 22 above).

27. K. Scholes in Ambrosini (1998) and K. Scholes in Johnson and Scholes, eds (2001) (both reference 25 above) describe nine typical stakeholder maps and the political implications of each map.

28. J. Pfeffer, *Managing with Power: Politics and influence in organisations*, HBS Press, 1994 (particularly part II, pp. 69–165); S.R. Clegg, *Frameworks of Power*, Sage Publications, 1989; D. Buchanan and R. Badham, *Power, Politics and Organisational Change: Winning the turf game*, Sage, 1999 and C. Hardy (ed.), *Power and Politics in Organisations*, Ashgate, 1995, provide a useful analysis of the relationship between power and strategy.

29. There is a prolific flow of literature on business ethics. Readers can gain some useful insights into the field by reading: P. Werhane and R.E. Freeman, 'Business Ethics: the state of the art', *International Journal of Management Research*, vol. 1, no. 1 March (1999), pp. 1–16. This is a useful summary of recent publications on business ethics. Practising managers might wish to consult: B. Kelley, *Ethics at Work*, Gower, 1999, which covers many of the issues in this section and includes the Institute of Management guidelines on ethical management.

30. See for example how government in the UK viewed these issues in: 'Business and society: corporate social responsibility report', *Department for Trade and Industry*, 2002. The Department of Trade and Industry also have a website devoted to the promotion of corporate social responsibility: www.societyandbusiness.gov.uk. The European Union has also published a Green Paper on these issues: 'Promoting a European framework for corporate social responsibility', *European Union Green Paper*, 2001.

31. Some authors propose more categories. For example, Marcus (reported in M. Jones, 'The institutional determinants of social responsibility', *Journal of Business Ethics*, vol. 20, no. 2 (1999), pp. 163–179) suggests five categories: narrow, financial, utilitarian, social justice and social harmony.

32. See: A. McWilliams and D. Seigel, 'Corporate social responsibility: a theory of the firm perspective', *Academy of Management Review*, vol. 26 (2001), pp. 117–127.

33. See S. Macleod, 'Why worry about CSR', *Strategic Communication Management*, Aug/Sept (2001), pp. 8–9.

34. K. Schnietz and M. Epstein, 'Does a reputation for corporate social responsibility pay off?', *Social Issues in Management Conference Papers*, Academy of Management Proceedings, 08967911, 2002. This paper shows that the Fortune 500 firms that were also in the Domini Social Index outperformed the others in terms of stock return.

35. See: M. Porter and M. Kramer, 'The competitive advantage of corporate philanthropy', *Harvard Business Review*, vol. 80, no. 12 (2002), pp. 56–68.

36. H. Hummels, 'Organizing ethics: a stakeholder debate', *Journal of Business Ethics*, vol. 17, no. 13 (1998), pp. 1403–1419.

37. Two useful books on corporate social responsibility are: W. Frederick, J. Post and K. Davis, *Business and Society: Management, public policy, ethics*, 7th edition, McGraw-Hill, 1992; B. Allen, *Getting to Grips with Corporate Social Responsibility: A compendium of CSR experience with contributions from a wide range of business gurus*, Kingshall Solutions, 2003. Also see: S. Cook, 'Who cares wins', *Management Today*, January (2003), pp. 40–47.

38. J. Charkham, 'Corporate governance lessons from abroad', *European Business Journal*, vol. 4, no. 2 (1992), pp. 8–16.

39. A. Wilson, 'Social reporting: developing theory and current practice' in: M. Bennett and P. James (eds), *Sustainable Measures – Evaluation and Reporting of Environmental and Social Performance*, Greenleaf Publishing, 1999; R. Gray, 'Thirty years of social accounting, reporting and auditing: what

(if anything) have we learnt?', *Business Ethics: A European Review*, vol. 10, no. 1 (2001), pp. 9–15; D. Clutterbuck, 'Corporate responsibility audit', in V. Ambrosini with G. Johnson and K. Scholes (eds), *Exploring Techniques of Analysis and Evaluation in Strategic Management*, Prentice Hall, 1998, Chapter 11.

40. Details of the Caux Round Table can be seen on their website: www.cauxroundtable.org.

41. For example, see: P. Shrivastava, 'The role of corporations in achieving ecological sustainability', *Academy of Management Review*, vol. 20, no. 4 (1995), pp. 936–960.

42. See: T.D. Miethe, *Tough Choices in Exposing Fraud, Waste, and Abuse on the Job*, Westview Press, 1999; G. Vinten, *Whistleblowing. Subversion or Corporate Citizenship?*, Paul Chapman, 1994; R. Larmer, 'Whistleblowing and employee loyalty', *Journal of Business Ethics*, vol. 11, no. 2 (1992), pp. 125–128.

43. M. Banaji, M. Bazeman and D. Chugh, 'How (UN)ethical are you?', *Harvard Business Review*, vol. 81, no. 12 (2003), pp. 56–64.

44. This definition of culture is taken from E. Schein, *Organisational Culture and Leadership*, 2nd edition, Jossey-Bass, 1997, p. 6.

45. A similar categorisation is used in Chapter 3 of: S. Schneider and J.-L. Barsoux, *Managing Across Cultures*, 2nd edition, Financial Times/Prentice Hall, 2003.

46. One of the earlier works on the influence of national culture was G. Hofstede. His book is now updated: G. Hofstede, *Culture's Consequences*, Sage, 2nd edition, 2001. Another comprehensive coverage of this topic can be found in R. Mead, *International Management: Cross-cultural dimensions*, Blackwell, 1994.

47. See Schneider and Barsoux (reference 45 above) – differences between national cultures are explained – particularly in Chapters 4 and 5; T. Jackson, 'Management ethics and corporate policy: a cross-cultural comparison', *Journal of Management Studies*, vol. 37, no. 3 (2000), pp. 349–370 looks at how national culture influences management ethics and provides a useful link to section 4.4 of this book.

48. See R. Lewis, *When Cultures Collide: Managing successfully across cultures*, 2nd edition, Brealey, 2000, a practical guide for managers. It offers an insight into different national cultures, business conventions and leadership styles. C. Buggy, 'Empathy is the key to cultural communication', *Professional Manager*, vol. 8, no. 1 (1999) argues that understanding cultural differences is crucial to success.

49. A useful review of research on this topic is: T. Dacin, J. Goodstein and R. Scott, 'Institutional theory and institutional change: introduction to the special research forum', *Academy of Management Journal*, vol. 45, no. 1 (2002), pp. 45–57.

50. This definition is taken from W. Scott, *Institutions and Organizations*, Sage, 1995.

51. The term 'recipe' was introduced to refer to *industries* by J. Spender, *Industry Recipes: The nature and sources of management judgement*, Blackwell, 1989. We have broadened its use by applying it to *organisational fields*. The fundamental idea that behaviours are driven by a collective set of norms and values remains unchanged.

52. D. Deephouse, 'To be different or to be the same?: It's a question (and theory) of strategic balance', *Strategic Management Journal*, vol. 20, no. 2 (1999), pp. 147–166.

53. E. Schein, *Organisation Culture and Leadership*, 2nd edition, Jossey-Bass, 1997, and A. Brown, *Organisational Culture*, FT/Prentice Hall, 1998 are useful in understanding the relationship between organisational culture and strategy. S. Cartright, C. Cooper and C. Earley, *Handbook of Organisational Culture (and Climate)*, Wiley, 2001 also has a wide range of material on this topic.

54. A fuller explanation of the cultural web can be found in G. Johnson, *Strategic Change and the Management Process*, 1987, and G. Johnson, 'Managing strategic change: strategy, culture and action', *Long Range Planning*, vol. 25, Blackwell, no. 1 (1992), pp. 28–36.

55. A practical explanation of cultural web mapping can be found in G. Johnson, 'Mapping and re-mapping organisational culture', in V. Ambrosini with G. Johnson and K. Scholes (eds), *Exploring Techniques of Analysis and Evaluation in Strategic Management*, Prentice Hall, 1998.

56. A detailed public sector example of cultural web mapping can be found in G. Johnson, 'Mapping and re-mapping organisational culture: a local government example', in G. Johnson and K. Scholes (eds), *Exploring Public Sector Strategy*, Financial Times/Prentice Hall, 2001, Chapter 17.

57. The significance of organisational symbolism is explained in G. Johnson, 'Managing strategic change: the role of symbolic action', *British Journal of Management*, vol. 1, no. 4 (1990), pp. 183–200.

58. P. Lencioni, 'Make your values mean something', *Harvard Business Review*, vol. 80, no. 7 (2002), pp. 113–117.

59. See J. Collins and J. Porras, *Built to Last: Successful habits of visionary companies*, Harper Business, 2002.

60. For example, see: B. Bartkus, M. Glassman and B. McAfee, 'Mission statements: are they smoke and mirrors?', *Business Horizons*, vol. 43, no. 6 (2000), pp. 23–28.

61. Communicating effectively with the investing community is essential as discussed by: A. Hutton, 'Four rules', *Harvard Business Review*, vol. 79, no. 5 (2001), pp. 125–132.

62. For example, I. Ansoff, *Corporate Strategy*, Penguin, 1968, p. 44, argued that objectives should be precise and measurable.

WORK ASSIGNMENTS

✱ Denotes more advanced work assignments.   * Refers to a case study in the Text and Cases edition.

4.1✱ For an organisation of your choice, map out a governance chain that identifies all the key players through to the beneficiaries of the organisation's good (or poor) performance. To what extent do you think managers are:

(a) knowledgeable about the expectations of beneficiaries?
(b) actively pursuing their interests?
(c) keeping them informed?

How would you change any of these aspects of the organisation's operations? Why?

4.2✱ Undertake a critique of the different traditions of corporate governance in the UK/USA, Germany and Japan in terms of your own views of their strengths and weaknesses. Is there a better system than any of these? Why?

4.3 Choose any organisation which does not operate a two-tier board (or the public sector equivalent).

(a) Would a two-tier board be a better form of governance? Why?
(b) What would you need to do to move to a two-tier system?
(c) Is this likely to be possible?

4.4✱ Write a discussion paper explaining how a change in ownership of an organisation with which you are familiar (private or public sector) might benefit shareholders or other stakeholders.

4.5 Using Illustration 4.3 as a worked example, identify and map out the stakeholders for Manchester United, Sheffield Theatres,* or an organisation of your choice in relation to:

(a) current strategies;
(b) a number of different future strategies of your choice.

What are the implications of your analysis for the management?

4.6 For an organisation of your choice, use Exhibit 4.7 to establish the *overall stance* of the organisation on ethical issues.

4.7✱ Identify the key corporate social responsibility issues which are of major concern in an industry or public service of your choice (refer to Exhibit 4.8). Compare the approach of two or more organisations in that industry, and explain how this relates to their competitive standing.

4.8 Use the questions in Exhibit 4.12 to plot out a tentative cultural web for Marks and Spencer* or an organisation of your choice.

4.9✱ By using a number of the examples from above, critically appraise the assertion that 'culture can only really be usefully analysed by the symptoms displayed in the way the organisation operates'. Refer to Schein's book in the recommended key readings to assist you with this task.

Integrative assignments

4.10 Using specific examples explain how changes in corporate governance and in expectations about corporate social responsibility are requiring organisations to develop new

▶

competences (Chapter 3) and also creating dilemmas in the pursuit of shareholder value (Chapter 7).

4.11 By using examples discuss the proposition that 'changing to e-commerce business models may be necessary to gain competitive advantage in a changing business environment but the change is made difficult because of organisational culture'. Refer to Chapters 2, 5, 9 and 10 in your answer.

 An extensive range of additional materials, including audio summaries, weblinks to organisations featured in the text, definitions of key concepts and multiple choice questions, can be found on the *Exploring Corporate Strategy* Companion Website at **www.pearsoned.co.uk/ecs7**

CASE EXAMPLE

Manchester United, brand of hope and glory

Bob Perry, University of Wolverhampton Business School

Brand it like Beckham

'Beckham-mania' hit Spain in the summer of 2003 with the arrival of the world's most recognisable footballer. David Beckham's medical and subsequent contract-signing ceremony attracted the world media including Japanese television who beamed it back during peak viewing time. Beckham's former club Manchester United had earlier accepted a £30m (€45m) transfer bid from Barcelona but the player had chosen instead the club's most fierce rival, Real Madrid.

Constantly in the media, some regarded Beckham as too interested in self-promotion. When United manager Sir Alex Ferguson did not choose him for some key games it seemed that Beckham might leave the club he had supported as a boy and played for since school. Beckham had no part in the United/ Barcelona discussions, and it was rumoured that he had already signed a pre-contract deal with Madrid. Undoubtedly his agent, the company SFX, would have negotiated this on his behalf. SFX were acting for Beckham the England captain, celebrity and biggest 'brand' in football, connecting different audiences from sports, fashion and style. With few other clubs with the status and financial wherewithal to afford him, and with Beckham determined on a move to Real Madrid, there was only one 'acceptable' buyer. Madrid squeezed the transfer fee down to a maximum of £25m and consistent with club policy, Beckham agreed to sign over 50 per cent of his image rights and new personal sponsorship deals. (Even his personal terms, a four-year contract worth £18m, represented a slight pay cut for him.)

Barcelona had estimated that the Beckham 'brand' would bring an additional annual £18m to the club. Beckham now belonged to Real Madrid and they were quick to maximise the returns on their latest acquisition. Advertising revenue from the signing ceremony alone raised £2m, and pre-orders for the number 23 Beckham replica shirt were estimated at

Photo: Getty Images

£2m. Beckham's ability to sell more merchandise than any other footballer, especially in the Far East, was undisputed. Madrid hoped to break into the Asian market with Beckham's help and analysts felt that the outlay in getting Beckham could be recouped in a few years.

Manchester United: super club

The reigning English Champions Manchester United were renowned for their business acumen, but had they been out manoeuvred? They appeared content with the deal; Beckham had cost no transfer fee and had given several years' good service. Sir Alex Ferguson was responsible for all football matters and once he decided that Beckham should be sold, the board of directors supported him. Asked about the loss of Beckham on merchandising income, a spokesperson pointed to the fact that 'Van Nistelrooy' not 'Beckham' shirts were the club's best-sellers. Further, the chief executive made clear that dealings in players were for football reasons alone; using players to exploit particular markets would be 'cheating the fans'.

This case study is intended as a basis for class discussion and not intended as an illustration of either good or bad management practice.

The club may have lost a component of their brand but still boasted a strong squad of players. Further, their impressive financial credentials made them the world's largest club (generating £100m revenue 'before a ball is kicked'). Financial performance reflected fast growth and increasing profitability for their shareholders (see Figure 1 below).

At the height of the stock market boom in March 2000, with the club's share prices of 402p the market valuation had reached the 'magical' £1bn. Inevitably, with the stock market cooling the price had fallen but by October 2003 shares hit a two-year high of 200p with a reported 22 per cent increase in pre-tax profits. Shareholders received an increased basic dividend for the 12th consecutive year and a special dividend, thanks in part to strong operating results.

This impressive financial performance was set against a background of a recession in the football industry. Turnover for 2003 had reached a record £173m, meaning that the club had nearly doubled in size over a five-year period. The debt-free balance sheet showed a massive bank and cash position of £28.6m and United had invested over £4m in capital projects.

On the playing side rewards for their players were considerable and although payroll costs increased by £8.7m during the year they still only represented a cautious 46 per cent of turnover. The club made clear it intended to use profits from player sales to strengthen the playing squad still further in the future.

Manchester United had a set-up many aspired to and a unique brand upon which to trade (Table 1).

Table 1   Manchester United's financial performance

	2002 (£m)	2003 (£m)	Annual increase (%)	Five-year increase (%)
Group turnover	146.1	173	18	97
Pre-tax profit	32.3	39.3	22	41
Earnings per share	9.6p	11.5p	20	
Basic dividend per share	2.1p	2.5p	19	
Special dividend per share	1.0p	1.5p	50	
Wages to turnover ratio(%)	48	46	12	
Analysis of turnover:*(%)				
Match day	38	41		
Media	36	32		
Commercial	26	27		
	100	**100**		

*(Financial year to 31 July)

*Match day includes revenues generated from 'home' games in the league, cup and European competition.

Media includes television income that increase with progress to later stages of the UEFA Champions' League. It also includes pay per view games and income from *MU Interactive* website.

Commercial includes all other income sources such as merchandising, sponsorship and non-match conference and catering revenues.

Source: All information extracted from Manchester United plc Annual Reports

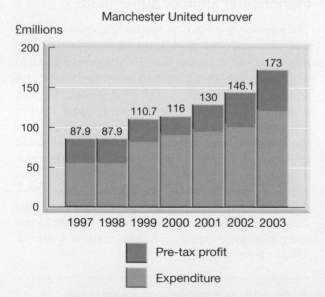

Manchester United turnover
£millions

Figure 1 **Manchester United annual growth**

Manchester United's transformation

The basis of United as a global brand rather than provincial English football club is built upon the club's history, partly triumphal and partly tragic. In 1958 the Munich air disaster shook the football world. The plane crash resulted in death and injury to several of the club's and country's best players. With loaned players, youngsters and crash survivors United showed dogged determination to continue to compete at the very highest level of international football, thus attracting many admirers – some far outside the Manchester region. United were one of the first to boast supporters far beyond their geographical base and their name and something of their history became known in every country with an interest in football. Teams that comprised exciting flair players enhanced United's attraction and playing success was taken to a new level when they became the first English team to win the European Cup in 1968.

In the boardroom the financial value of the brand was also being recognised. By 1989 majority shareholder Martin Edwards was ready to accept a bid of £10m but the deal fell through. Two years later, the club was floated on the stock exchange at a price of 32p per share and with a valuation of £40m. Further share issues followed in 1994 and 1997. (Edwards reduced his stake in the club by selling some shares for £71m.) By 1997 Manchester United had become the world's wealthiest club, exceeding the turnover of others by some distance, and Edwards' wealth had grown accordingly.[1]

In September 1998 the board wanted to accept an offer of £623m from the broadcasting company BskyB, but when the news of this negotiations 'leaked' there was an uprising of supporters and others. Their concerns were that media ownership would ruin the football club as they had known and loved it for generations. In April 1999, the government blocked the plan, ruling the proposal against the public interest.

The new ethos

New lucrative possibilities continued to present themselves. Speculation concerning the formation of a European super league involving leading clubs definitely including Manchester United emerged. If clubs left their national leagues this was a clear threat not only to the quality of national league football but also to UEFA (the European football body), who had always organised the European Cup/Champions' League competition. UEFA managed to avert the proposed development by offering major concessions to clubs through a doubling of the Champions League to 32 clubs. More matches meant greater revenue and UEFA had now directed £330m to Europe's richest clubs.

A group called the G14 clubs[2] formed and backed by the ultimate threat of a breakaway collectively pressed for more concessions from UEFA. The clubs believed they could obtain more for the Europe-wide television rights without UEFA and were frustrated at having to release key players for international duty. United stayed well briefed with their Chief Executive becoming the G14 vice president.

United's 2003 financial accounts revealed that competing in the UEFA Champions' League earned

£28m as compared with £8.5m from the domestic FA Cup.

Some resented the way in which the traditionally working-class game had evolved. Subdued and seated, rich corporate guests now spectated. Standing chanting males had previously supported their team.

At the forefront of the change were United with a more business-like approach and an expanding list of commercial partners and corporate sponsors. United no longer represented Manchester in the same way, some supporters travelled from far and wide for home games and the club was owned by big business. Additionally, the issue of constantly changing replica kit caused resentment amongst parents of young fans who felt pressured into spending large amounts. (A television programme once revealed that replica kits often had a mark-up as high as 200 per cent.) Shirt sales were however very lucrative and thanks to a tie-up with Nike, United can expect to sell 2.5m replica shirts worldwide every year.

Despite the misgivings of traditionalists, United showed no signs of shifting direction. Former *Umbro International* sportswear chief executive Peter Kenyon joined the board in 1997 with a brief to broaden United's supporter base. The commercial logic was faultless: the greater the support, the greater the potential to sell club merchandise and a clinical brand marketing campaign began.

As if to prove they had a warmer side too, during 2000 United established a partnership to raise £1m for Unicef, the United Nations children's fund. This was perceived as fitting the ethos of Manchester United as reaching out to 'global children' and involved visits by players and officials to some of the poorest communities in the world. (In Mongolia, Brazil and Uganda, United encountered some families surviving on less than £200 a year.) Some local school children and disabled groups were also offered use of some of the facilities at the club's breathtaking training centre.

In August 2000 Kenyon succeeded Edwards as Chief Executive. Edwards was not always at one with the manager Sir Alex Ferguson and was unpopular with the fans for his attempts to sell the club. Kenyon promised a more communicative, people-centred change of style and made great play of his loyalty to the club as local boy made good and supporter of long standing. Kenyon's strategy rested on:

● success on the pitch;
● developing media rights in terms of both content and ownership;

'Football clubs are marketing brands, not teams . . . it is no longer a case of doing well on the pitch; the more merchandise you sell, the better.'

A Real Madrid spokesperson at the time of the Beckham transfer

'Famous players after all come and go.'

A Manchester United director at the time of the Beckham transfer

'Running a football club is easy; all you've got to do is to make enough profit year after year to do three things: develop your team, develop your stadium and – if you're a quoted company – to pay a dividend. If you can do all these things, year on year, then life is good.'

Former Manchester United Finance Director

'Football used to be about glory, romance, loyalty and the national game, and not about exploitation and multinational corporations. But that is exactly what Manchester United now is.'

A journalist

'We strive to ensure that shareholders, loyal supporters, customers and key commercial partners alike benefit from our performance.'

Extracted from a Manchester United plc Annual Report

Figure 2 Some interesting quotations

- developing the international brand;
- turning more fans into customers (see Figure 2).

United in a new century

Under Sir Alex Ferguson's continued management the club achieved outstanding on-field successes in the FA Cup, Premiership and the Champions' League. Old Trafford, the club's ground since 1910, had thanks to capital investment increased its capacity to 67,500 (the largest in Britain) and developed a club museum. Despite sell-out crowds and a waiting list for season tickets, the club attempted to 'peg' admission prices and of twenty Premiership clubs only six charged less. The ground hosted home games, European finals, internationals, pop concerts and developed a museum. It became a tourism destination from Scandinavia, Australia and China.

Despite the increased revenue from Old Trafford, United had become less dependent upon gate receipts alone. Merchandising and related activities had expanded rapidly with over 1,500 items in the on-site *Megastore* shop and hundreds of outlets throughout the world. (In March 2000 a 15,000-square-foot store and internet-related Red Café in the heart of Asia.) There was Manchester United mail order and a deal with BSkyB saw the launch

of Manchester United satellite channel (MUTV). October 2000 saw the premiere of a movie: another portfolio item along with Manchester United Insurance credit cards, savings accounts, hotel and leisure facilities, and weddings at the ground. The *Red Cinema* was launched in August 2003 in nearby Salford Quays.

Data analysis using United's Customer Relationship Management System allowed them to build buying profiles of the 1.9m UK members. A target of achieving a database of 3.5m fan details by 2006 was set. Even this represented the tip of the iceberg: a commissioned survey of the supporter base calculated over 40m people worldwide and growing. For organisations wishing to associate themselves with Manchester United, sponsorship did not come cheaply. *Vodafone* paid £30m for a four-year deal for the privilege of shirt sponsorship.

United's marketing drive, particularly into so-called 'new media', continued. Future investment plans were well advanced in new-media technology, principally the internet and mobile telephone potential. United's strategy had been to enter robust business partnerships and harness the benefits of new technology. The official website was launched in August 1998, with a modest number of hits a month initially recorded. By the time the site was relaunched in July 2002 it was achieving a staggering 600,000 unique visitors per month. The club were said to be looking forward to the possibilities of relaying matches live across the globe using the site as a platform.

The early years of the new century saw football in something of a recession. Now less popular with investors, television companies felt that they had over paid in the past for coverage and looked to renegotiate less generous deals. Meanwhile, top players and their agents continued to press for large financial personal rewards from the game when previously transfer fees between clubs had led to a circulation of money within the game. Some clubs meanwhile had been destabilised financially through spending a dangerous proportion of their turnover on players' costs in a quest to compete with the top clubs such as United.

This growing financial rift between the top few clubs and the rest dismayed smaller clubs in the English Football League, many of whom were struggling to survive. One club chairman remarked:

> 'Matches can be rescheduled at short notice to suit satellite stations and their exclusive audiences. There is a disregard for the little clubs. The gap between the haves and the have-nots is too great. Manchester United is now marketed as the national team – which has taken it away from its roots and its local community. Football should be a love affair otherwise you are just a business. The big clubs have forgotten their roots and are isolating themselves.

There were also concerns that not enough money was recycled to schools and junior football – from where the next generation of players would come.

Despite these concerns and the perilous state of some clubs' finances, Manchester United appeared to grow stronger, exhibiting awesome negotiating 'muscle'. A long-term deal with Nike in 2002 guaranteed £303m over 13 years in a 50/50 partnership whereby kit could be accessed in over 60 countries worldwide. United also announced a unique marketing alliance with the world's wealthiest baseball team, the New York Yankees. This involved agreement on shared market information, joint sponsorship and promotional programmes and the sale of goods. United now used the Yankees' huge merchandising network to target the elusive North American market. (United concede that their players might be mobbed in Kuala Lumpur but could be unknown in the States.) In January 2003 it was announced that delayed television coverage of games featuring United would be screened on the Yankees' club channel network reaching 5m New

Yorkers. (In return, the Yankees got access to Europe and the Far East.) United's involvement in a summer tournament in the USA during 2003 was broadcast live on MUTV channel, whilst building on the North American fan base and partner relationships.

In April 2003 Kenyon announced that in future the club intended to develop and control its own media rights by getting back the content of collectively negotiated TV deals.

On the field, players continued to benefit from the best training facilities money could buy at the purpose-built, multi-million pound Trafford Training Centre, Carrington, set in 70 acres. Potentially they could also enjoy huge salaries. Six of the top ten *Sunday Times* top earners from UK football in 2002 were on Manchester United's payroll. The club was better placed than any to pay the top dollar in terms of transfer fees[3] and wage demands and at the same time keep operating expenses within their safety ceiling of 50 per cent of revenues. The first team itself represented a combination of expensive buys and players who have progressed through thanks to the club's youth policy, and the average age of the talented professional playing staff was a youthful 25 years old.

United, like others, were relieved that approvals of plans to further modify the transfer system in accordance with European Union law were modest. The European Commission had expressed concern that by tying players to clubs the transfer system restricts players' freedom of movement hence the need for some reform. UEFA/Fifa, the game's two leading governing bodies, responded by outlining a plan including a new type of playing contract, protection of 'poaching' of players by other clubs, and compensation for clubs for developing young players. United could continue to buy new players and keep them contracted to the club.

An FA ruling that a club cannot sign players under the age of 16 unless they live within a 90-minute drive of that club could have proved a hindrance. Instead United set about developing links with clubs elsewhere in the country including First Division Walsall in England and Newport in Wales. In addition United have a number of feeder clubs abroad including clubs in Australia, Belgium, Norway, Ireland and Sweden.

Factors influencing United's future

Financial analysts believed that the club has only exploited the more obvious income streams and more lucrative yet there were areas offering themselves, particularly in countries late to embrace the game such as the USA. In China an estimated 20m potential customers are accustomed to televised English football and the United brand has 79 per cent 'name awareness'. The challenge lies in converting this potential into revenue flows.

In December 2002 Edwards stepped down as chairman but of greater surprise was the resignation of Chief Executive Peter Kenyon in September 2003. Kenyon was rumoured to have been lured away by a huge financial package from Premiership rivals Chelsea. Funded by the personal fortune of new owner Roman Abramovich, Chelsea soon spent £100m in transfer fees to improve their team's competitiveness. Now apparently they also sought to emulate United's financial success and needed Kenyon's managerial talent.

Various key questions relating to United's future readily arise including:

- Would United's commercial operations suffer as a result of Kenyon's departure?

- How much longer would an aging Sir Alex continue as manager and would the team be as successful if he retired?

- Would predators eye United's cash-rich position and seek to gain ownership possibly with the intention of diluting the current emphasis on investing on the playing side of the business?

The frantic pace of change in the global sport, leisure and entertainment industries continued throughout the 1990s. Manchester United perhaps epitomised this change more than most. With other clubs overstretching themselves, United remained hugely impressive both on and off the field. Now in a new decade, and even with the loss of key figures, they were better placed to balance their responsibilities both as a football club and as an organisation with shareholder responsibilities, but were they getting that balance right?

Notes

1. In 2002 *The Sunday Times* named 53 people who were top earners from the UK football industry with Edwards by far the biggest earner, thanks to still more share sales.
2. The G14 Europe's most powerful clubs originally comprised (highest turnover first): Manchester United (England); Real Madrid (Spain); Bayern Munich (Germany); Juventus (Italy); Barcelona (Spain); AC Milan, Internazionale (both Italy); Liverpool (England); Borussia Dortmund (Germany); Paris St-Germain (France); PSV Eindhoven, Ajax (both Holland); Marseilles (France) and Porto (Portugal). Arsenal, Bayer Leverkusen, Olympique Lyonnais and Valencia joined this group in September 2002.
3. Juan Sebastian Veron (£28m), Ruud van Nistelrooy (£19m) and Rio Ferdinand (£30m) were big money buys during 2001 and 2002.

Sources: D. Conn, 'Europe's richest clubs launch power play', *Independent*, 14 September 2000; S. Curry, 'Netting a billion', *Sunday Times*, 12 March 2000; I. Hawkey, 'Transfers face shake-up', *Sunday Times*, 29 October 2000; J. Hunt, 'He knows the score but still sold Beckham', *Sunday Express*, 6 July 2003; G. Otway, 'Gold Trafford expanding to cash in on the dream', *Sunday Times*, 30 May 1999; T. Rich, 'Real cash in by beaming Beckham's medical to Japan', *Independent*, 1 July 2003; T. Rich, 'Why £25m for David Beckham plc could be a Real steal', *Independent*, 19 June 2003; J. Rowley, 'Can Man U save the world?', *Sunday Times*, 6 August 2000; M. Walker, 'Real take half of Beckham's private deals', *Guardian*, 19 June 2003; J. White, 'Transfer tied up "weeks ago"', *Guardian*, 19 June 2003; Soccer investor weekly (various issues); Company annual financial reports; Other corporate data (including www.manutd.com); Industry data, e.g. Deloitte and Touche's football analysis (www.deloitte.co.uk); Financial and sports media; *Without Walls*, Channel 4, 1995 and *Panorama*, BBC, December 1997.

Questions

1. Do you feel that the various aspects of corporate governance discussed in section 4.2 are appropriate for a football club? What changes in governance would you like to see?

2. Using section 4.3.1 and Exhibit 4.5, undertake a stakeholder mapping exercise for any strategic development that is likely to be under consideration by the board (for example, 'The formation of a European super league of major clubs'). How would you use this analysis if you were:
   (a) a board member wishing to support the strategy?
   (b) an opponent of the strategy?

3. Refer to Exhibit 4.7 and decide which ethical stance you feel best describes Manchester United now and how you would wish to see the club. Justify your own position.

4. Refer to section 4.5.3 and decide what you feel were the key cultural characteristics of Manchester United in terms of values, beliefs and taken-for-granted assumptions:
   (a) pre-1990, and (b) today.
   What are the implications of these changes to current and future strategies?

Coping with Complexity: The 'Business Idea'

The management of strategy involves coping with uncertainty, change and complexity. This is evident from the discussion in the preceding three chapters which have reviewed many of the forces at work on the strategies of organisations, from macro-environmental trends, to forces of competition, internal capabilities, organisation culture and stakeholder influences. These different forces do not tend to act singly on organisations; they are likely to be interdependent. They may also exert influence in different directions. Shareholders may require year on year increasing profit returns, the government may be demanding increasing expenditure on environmental protection, competitive pressures may be demanding heavy investment in more efficient plant and more attention to customer service, whilst the capabilities of the organisation may historically lie in its technical excellence. Clearly this is a complex problem. How organisations – especially successful ones – and their managers cope with this complexity is the theme for this commentary.

This commentary uses the three lenses of design, experience and ideas, introduced in section 1.5.3 of Chapter 1 and the Commentary to Part I, to consider this key issue. It does so first by briefly revisiting the concept of the 'business idea' presented in the introduction to Part II. It then discusses what each of the three lenses has to say about that concept. Finally it draws the insights from the three lenses together to help provide an understanding of how managers might handle such complexity.

The business idea

In the introduction to this part of the book, the business idea[1] was introduced as a model of why an organisation might be successful (see Exhibit II.i on page 62). The key point is that some organisations have found ways of reconciling the complexity of the different forces they face such that these become positive feedback loops which provide for success. To take an example, Exhibit II.ii is a representation of the business idea for Kindercare. Its business idea underpinned its growth and success as a child care centre in the USA.[2] The exhibit shows how Kindercare was built around the concept of 'innovative child care'. More innovative child care leads to more teacher satisfaction, which leads to retention of motivated ex-schoolteachers and in turn to more innovative child care. It also gives parents good feelings such that they are prepared to pay rather more for the services. In turn this leads to the sorts of revenues which allow the setting up of professional management services at the

Exhibit II.ii | **The business idea at Kindercare**

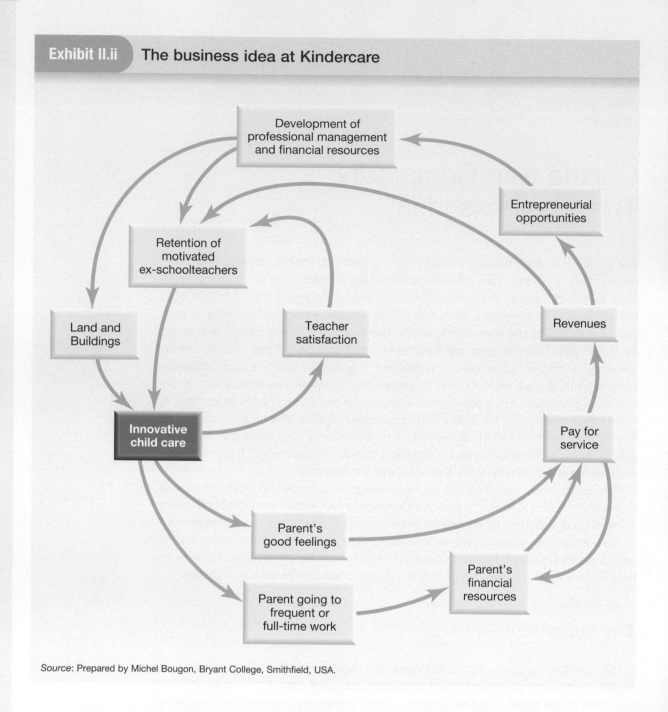

Source: Prepared by Michel Bougon, Bryant College, Smithfield, USA.

centre, thus freeing up teachers to concentrate on teaching and further innovation, as well as funds for acquiring land and buildings. Less successful organisations would not be experiencing the same sort of positive feedback. The different forces would be pulling in different directions rather than being mutually reinforcing.

However, as it stands this is no more than a description of why a business is successful. It does not explain *how* such a self-reinforcing business idea comes about; and as an extension of this, what managers might do about it, if anything. The different lenses are now used to explore this.

Complexity and design

Chapters 2, 3 and 4 have shown that the organisational world is, indeed, a complex place, but have presented concepts and frameworks by which managers can unpack this complexity. The design view suggests that such analysis also allows managers to go further. It suggests that such analytic understanding allows managers to build a sufficiently clear picture to deliberately position and direct their organisation in such a way as to benefit from environmental opportunities, circumvent threats, build on or develop capabilities and proactively manage the sometimes conflicting interests and influences of stakeholders.

Most of the frameworks discussed in these chapters could, for example, be used to provide data based on analysis for more or less formalised strategic decision making to feed into a corporate planning exercise or a strategy workshop, for example. Indeed, the sequencing of the chapters might be used as a logical way of doing this. A design view of strategic management is that this complex organisational world is sufficiently stable, predictable or at least discernible for such analysis to be useful for the purposes of strategy design.

The design lens therefore suggests that managers can and should analyse and plan the integration of the different forces represented by the business idea. A starting point for such analysis might be historical. Over time, all organisations must have developed a business idea that accounts for their current or past success. So analysing what this business idea is could be very useful in order to understand the basis for success that exists (or existed), but also to understand ways in which it might be built on. Systems thinking can help such analysis. The components of the business idea can be broken down in a systematic, analytic way, much as has been done in Exhibit II.ii. This could further draw on much of the discussion in Chapters 2, 3 and 4: for example, to identify the capabilities of the organisation, key drivers in the environment, key stakeholders and their influences, and aspects of organisational culture.

Managers might then ask questions such as:

- What are the core elements of the business idea that must be protected and defended?

- What is there within the business idea that is difficult for other organisations to copy and therefore provides distinctiveness and might be the basis of competitive advantage?

- Is the business idea likely to be relevant in the future, for example in terms of scenarios that have been built?

- What are the strengths and weaknesses inherent in the current business idea?

- Is the business idea capable of extension, for example as a basis for new strategic directions (e.g. entry into new markets) or methods of strategy development such as acquisitions (see Chapter 7)?

- If not, is it possible to conceive of other mutually reinforcing cycles developed from or extending the existing business idea that might be suited to the challenges and opportunities of the future? This would entail designing new activities and processes complementary but additive to those that currently exist.

Looking at the complexity of integrating different forces and influences on strategy through this lens, the business idea becomes manageable; indeed it becomes a planning tool. It could be used as part of a strategic planning process, a strategy workshop by managers or, indeed, a project assignment by students.

Complexity and experience

The second lens, strategy as experience, begins from a different starting point, emphasising the influence of the personal experience of individuals, the culture of organisations and the institutional norms in which those organisations exist.

Beginning first with managers as individuals, it is important to understand that they have to simplify the complexity they face: it is not possible for them to operate in terms of 'perfect knowledge'. Understanding the effect of such *simplification processes* is important. Research shows that, even if managers have a very rich understanding of their environment, for example, it is unlikely that they will bring that complex understanding to bear for all situations and all decisions. They will access part of that knowledge.[3] This is called *selective attention*: selecting from total understanding the parts of knowledge which seem most relevant. Managers also use *exemplars* and *prototypes* as a way of making sense of, for example, competition. It is not unusual for managers to refer to a dominant competitor rather than a list of competitive characteristics: 'We compete against the Japanese . . .' or 'The service on Singapore Airlines . . .' are ways of encapsulating quite complex sets of characteristics. Over time, this partial representation of reality can become fixed. The Japanese become a generic competitor; Singapore Airlines *is* competition. The risk is that the 'chunk' of information most often used becomes the only information used and that stimuli from the environment are selected out to fit these dominant representations of reality. Information that squares with Singapore Airlines being the main competitor is taken on board, whilst information counter to this is not. Sometimes this distortion can lead to severe errors as managers miss crucial indicators because they are, in effect, scanning the environment for issues and events that are familiar or readily recognisable.[4] Managers also tend to exaggerate their own (or their organisation's) influence or control over events (known as 'attribution error'), discount luck and inflate the capabilities of their organisation whilst discounting or reducing the potential of competitors.[5]

In terms of the experience lens, then, the business idea can also be thought of as a mental model of what an organisation is about. As such, it is both useful, because it provides managers with short-cuts in their making sense of complexity, but also potentially dangerous because the evidence is that such mental models become fixed, begin to dictate how new stimuli are made sense of and bias responses to such stimuli.

Much the same can be said at the level of organisational culture. There also exists an organisational way of doing things akin to the business idea. The business idea may have originated in the mind of an entrepreneur and been developed over many years through trial and error as that entrepreneur grew the business and experienced success and failure. Some initiatives worked; others did not. Some skills proved to be important; others were not. Opportunities arose suited to the skills of the business and were adopted; other opportunities less suited were not. How the business idea was delivered gradually became embedded in organisational processes and routines around which people learned to cohere. The integration of the different forces and influences on strategy were not developed by design but through the experience of individuals and groups of people working together, gradually building into a culture, reinforced by success. The organisation's paradigm and culture web (see Chapter 4) are, in effect, the business idea in taken-for-granted form. What are the consequences?

First, the business idea and the potential for *strategic drift.* The culturally embedded business idea becomes a ready-made solution to circumstances that arise. However, there may – some would argue there must – come a time when this business idea becomes less and less relevant to the environment. This is what is referred to in Chapter 1, section 1.5.3, as strategic drift. This is because the business idea becomes so routinised that it leads to myopia. To continue the example above, the organisation's systems become so attuned to understanding and dealing with *the* competition of Singapore Airlines and educating major stakeholders – shareholders, analysts, staff, the press – that this is what matters, that there is a danger that other key forces at work are overlooked or ignored.

Second, *the importance of questioning and challenge.* The embeddedness of this 'cultural business idea' may mean that it is very difficult to change. If strategies are to be developed effectively there must, therefore, be means of questioning and challenging that which is taken for granted. The experience lens suggests that the major role of the frameworks of analysis described in Chapters 2, 3 and 4 is to do just this. It may be at least as important to surface the assumptions that managers have as to undertake careful economic analysis, because it is likely to be these assumptions that are driving strategic decisions. Indeed, there are those[6] who argue that strategy discussions between managers should be largely about identifying such assumptions and using the agenda that emerges for the purposes of debate.

However, there is a *challenge and a paradox* here. The taken-for-grantedness of the business idea helps explain why some organisations achieve competitive advantage which is difficult for others to copy. Imitation of the bases of advantage is difficult because those bases are difficult to identify, precisely because they are embedded in the culture (see section 3) in the form of routines, control systems and so on.

- The *challenge* is that raised in the key debate at the end of Chapter 3 (Illustration 3.8). Is it really conceivable that the deeply embedded, taken-for-granted, perhaps everyday routines that make up the bases of success can be readily analysed? Outsiders would have difficulty identifying them; and so too might senior executives who are unlikely to be involved in such activities. For example, whilst the sort of mapping of capabilities described in Illustration 3.2 did get to a level of detail far greater than that shown in this book, it took managers two days; and that within a culture of openness and trust.

- The *paradox* is this: if one of the reasons that competences lodged in an organisation's culture yield advantage is because they are so natural to the organisation concerned and so difficult for others to see, does trying to manage them mean that there is a risk that they lose their advantage? To manage them might mean simplifying them; potentially codifying them. In this way they become more visible internally, but arguably less taken for granted, less complex, less causally ambiguous and more visible and potentially more imitable by others.[7]

The message from the experience lens is that a reliance on analysis and planning for making sense of complexity might well under-estimate the problems of managing the business idea. Surfacing and challenging the taken-for-granted components of that idea may well be an important way of understanding the strategic situation the organisation is in and deliberating on ways to go forward. However, it needs to be recognised that it will not be easy to do. Executives who wish to do so will need to invest substantial time, not only of their own and other senior executives, but also of people in the organisation whose day-to-day lives are engaged with such processes.

Complexity and ideas

Whereas the experience lens emphasises the embeddedness of the business idea in the culture of organisation and therefore uniformity and conformity, the ideas lens helps to explain innovation and how new business ideas come about. It emphasises the importance of variety and diversity at different levels, across and within organisations as the source of innovation and new ideas.

First, at the level of a population of organisations, for every successful business idea there were probably many unsuccessful ones. The successful ones proved to be more attractive to the conditions of their environment – to buyers in the market, to investors, to communities, to potential and actual employees and so on. However, for every successful entrepreneur there are many who do not succeed. In the market for cheap flight airlines, easyJet and Ryanair have succeeded but others have not. Firms compete with other firms; in this sense one business idea competes with the business ideas of competitors; some survive and some do not. This is the position taken by 'population ecologists'[8] who study strategy in terms of the births and deaths of populations of businesses, and who tend to emphasise a good deal less the centrality, influence and control of managers on all of this than do adherents of the design school of thinking.

The importance of trial and error behaviour, with particular emphasis on the importance of imperfect copying, is also highlighted by the ideas lens. Remember the institutionalist view described in the Commentary to Part I and Chapter 4 (section 4.5). A successful business idea, evident in the strategy of an organisation, will tend to be imitated by others. However, it will not be imitated perfectly. Organisations will have an imperfect notion of the components of the business idea of competitors. They will copy parts of the strategy of successful organisations and add their own dimensions based on their own business idea. The result could be success or it could be failure. Arguably this is just what has happened with the success of Virgin Air. Richard Branson copied the basics of transcontinental flights but introduced his own version of it. The important point to understand is that, through such imperfect copying, ideas are always recombining to produce new ideas; and in this way successful innovatory strategies may develop. Here is an explanation of how successful organisations lose out and others take over from them. However, the explanation is not founded so much on the design capabilities of managers as on the results of imperfect copying and the resulting variety of new business ideas eventually giving rise to a winning strategy.[9]

Another level at which the ideas lens sheds light on the business idea is within an organisation itself. Whilst organisations are cultures which embed a business idea and around which people cohere, there will also be elements of diversity and variety. There will be some individuals or groups within the organisation who have different ways of doing things or who see things differently. Or they will be networked with others outside their organisation who do. This accounts for why new ideas, in effect amendments to the dominant business idea, develop within the organisation. This could happen quite low down in the organisation. The routine of taking back unwanted goods from major retailers in the company in Illustration 3.2 was not originated at the top of the organisation but by a junior despatch manager seeking to help a sales executive, who in turn was trying to satisfy a concern of a buyer in a major retailer. The lessons drawn from studies of strategic innovations emphasise the importance of this variety and diversity of ideas within organisations rather than a reliance on top-down strategic planning.[10]

There are lessons here for managers.

- *The 'two-edged sword'.* Any successful organisation will have a 'business idea' that has developed with that success and, in turn, supports it. But it is a 'two-edged sword'. It may eventually become so embedded that it constrains the organisation from changing and innovating. The ideas lens shows that managers have to work proactively to create the context that allows for the variety and diversity that might prevent this happening. To do so they have to recognise some of the lessons already suggested in the Commentary to Part I. These include:

- *Tolerating deviance.* There needs to be a recognition that innovation could come from anywhere in the organisation and is likely to take form, at least initially, in deviations from the prevailing norms. That is likely to mean deviations from the apparently positive feedback loops that might represent the successful business idea of the past. This may not be comfortable and the experience lens suggests that it is likely to be resisted. The strategic manager who seeks innovation is likely to have to be tolerant of such deviations and allow the sort of latitude that permits and facilitates it.

- *Vision and simple rules.* The ideas lens suggests that creating this latitude may not be helped by a detailed prescription or specification of the business idea, as the design lens suggests. Rather there is a need to create an overarching vision of what the organisation is about, or is seeking to achieve. It may also be helped by developing the few 'simple rules' that are needed to establish organisational coherence but which are sufficiently flexible to allow and encourage variety and diversity. And some would say that these need to be sufficiently ambiguous to create the sort of 'adaptive tension' required for innovation (see page 45 in the Commentary to Part I).

- *Continual change.* For managers in organisations that rely on innovation it is also important to accept that the knowledge and understanding of their bases of success can never be perfect, and that they cannot gain advantage by trying to make it so. Rather, advantage lies in continually transforming what they have faster than their competitors.

The key point is that the ideas lens sheds light on the sources and bases of variety and diversity, and therefore innovation and change in the business ideas of organisations, and suggests ways in which managers may facilitate this.

Our view

This section commentary has addressed an important challenge that strategic managers face: the integration of different influences and forces on strategy development, here referred to as the 'business idea'. It is accepted that successful organisations have found ways to integrate such forces in such a way as to achieve the sort of positive feedback shown in Exhibit II.ii. However, what the lenses show is that this can be understood in different ways. We argue that these different ways are not incompatible but are usefully complementary.

The experience lens recognises that the complexity of an organisation's business idea has very likely developed over time through people's experience, experimentation and its gradual embeddedness in culture. It represents the basis of success of the organisation; but it also potentially contains the seeds of downfall because it becomes so embedded that it cannot easily be changed. In this respect it provides explanations of strategic drift and the Icarus paradox.[11]

The design lens argues that these complex, mutually reinforcing interactions can be understood, analysed and planned. We would argue that that may be more problematic than some adherents to this school of strategy would admit. However, this does not mean that the tools of analysis are wasted, because they also provide a basis upon which managers can challenge and question taken-for-grantedness and thus help manage the development of the business idea, or at least question it.

The ideas lens suggests that it is not just a matter of top-down management. There will be variety within and between business ideas. Imperfect copying and deviation from the business idea will throw up new ideas. The challenge is for managers to accept that they cannot expect to control all this; that they themselves are one of the forces that select for and against new ideas; but that they can and should cultivate the potentially positive effects of the imperfection and deviation that will exist in and around their organisations through the way in which they design and control their organisations.

Brown and Eisenhardt[12] argue that organisations potentially face two opposite problems. Some managers and some organisations may be too wedded to one view of the future – they call this the Foresight Trap – based on their experience or a detailed plan which results in a rigidity of views. For other managers or organisations there is too little attention to the forces that will affect the future, leading to no view at all about what it might be like; and therefore chaos. They suggest that managers need to avoid falling into either of these traps and accept the inevitability of the ambiguity and uncertainty of the complexity they face. The lessons they draw are these:

● *An adaptive business* idea. Rather than trying to identify a definitive future, managers need to have an overall view of the environment of their organisation, broad enough to accommodate different futures, and a vision about the identity of their organisation which they can adjust as the future unfolds. In terms of the business idea, this suggests that it is indeed important to have views about how different forces, internal and external to the organisation, interlink and are integrated; but not a view which is over-rigid. Rather than seeing the business idea as a fixed system, it needs to be seen as an adaptive one.

● *Constant* scanning. Managers need to avoid major one-off exercises looking at their environment and likely futures. There should be 'constant but thin' attention to the future. In other words, managers should constantly keep in touch with their environment and how it is changing; and should challenge assumptions about this in their organisation. But they should not assume that such attention can take the form of one-off analytic exercises. It was to be an ongoing process.

● *Experimentation*. The future will be understood through action, through doing. Organisations need to try out new ideas and see if they work and in so doing learn about the future as it changes; so encouraging the variety within the organisation that gives rise to such ideas is important.

References

1. For a full explanation of the business idea see Kees van der Heijden, *Scenarios: The Art of Strategic Conversation*, Wiley, 2004.
2. This example is adapted from M.G. Bougon and J. Komocar, 'Directing strategic change: a dynamic holistic approach', in A. Huff (ed.), *Managing Strategic Thought*, Wiley, 1990.
3. For a review of these points see the introduction to J. Dutton, E. Walton and E. Abrahamson, 'Important dimensions of strategic issues: separating the wheat from the chaff', *Journal of Management Studies*, vol. 26, no. 4 (1989), pp. 380–395.
4. See A. Tversky and D. Kahnemann, 'Judgements under uncertainty: heuristics and biases', *Science*, vol. 185 (1975), pp. 1124–1131.
5. See D. Lovallo and D. Kahneman, 'Delusions of success', *Harvard Business Review*, vol. 81, no. 7 (2003), pp. 56–64.
6. This is the approach taken by C. Eden and F. Ackerman in *Making Strategy: The journey of strategy*, Sage Publications, 1998.
7. This argument is similar to that taken by J.B. Barney, 'Organizational culture: can it be a source of sustained competitive advantage?', *Academy of Management Review*, vol. 11, no. 3 (1986), pp. 656–665.
8. The approach taken by the population ecologists can be found in M.T. Hannan and J. Freeman, *Organizational Ecology*, Harvard University Press, 1988. For an example of how a population ecology perspective might provide strategic insights see B.S. Silverman, J.A. Nickerson and J. Freeman, 'Profitability, transactional assignment and organizational mortality in the US trucking Industry', *Strategic Management Journal*, vol. 18 (special issue) (1997), pp. 31–52.
9. Imperfect copying or 'mutation' is explained by J. Weeks and C. Galunic, 'A theory of the cultural evolution of the firm: the intra-organizational ecology of memes', *Organization Studies*, vol. 24, no. 8 (2003), pp. 1309–1352.
10. See S.L. Brown and K.M. Eisenhardt, *Competing on the Edge*, Harvard Business School Press, 1998.
11. See D. Miller, *The Icarus Paradox*, HarperCollins, 1990.
12. See reference 10.

Part III

Strategic Choices

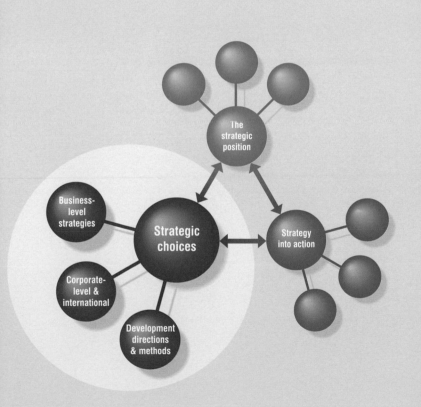

THIS PART EXPLAINS:

● Bases of business-level competitive strategies – the strategy clock.

● Other bases of strategic choice – including game theory and strategies for hypercompetitive conditions.

● Corporate-level strategies – concerning product and geographic scope.

● Alternative rationales of corporate parents in managing portfolios for value creation.

● Strategic options – in terms of both directions and methods of development.

● Assessing the suitability, acceptability and feasibility of strategies.

Introduction to Part III

Strategic choices are concerned with decisions about an organisation's future and the way in which it needs to respond to the many pressures and influences discussed in Part II of the book. In turn, the consideration of future strategies must be mindful of the realities of translating strategy into action which, in turn, can be significant constraints on strategic choice.

Chapter 1 (section 1.1.2) explained different levels of strategy and strategic decisions. Here the concern is with the business and corporate levels. At both these levels managers are faced with choices as to how to meet the competing expectations of a range of different stakeholders. For example:

- Business-level managers must take decisions about how to satisfy the needs of customers or users in such a way as to meet the economic expectations of stakeholders, for example shareholders or, in the public sector, government. In so doing they are likely to face competition, so the search for competitive advantage becomes centrally important.

- Managers also have to take decisions about the scope of the organisation's activities. This includes decisions about which businesses it makes sense to have in their portfolio and how they can add more value to those businesses in comparison with other corporations which might seek to own them. And where they should operate geographically: in their home market or by developing internationally?

- In turn, managers face decisions about how they deliver these strategies in terms of the products and markets they might develop. Does it make sense to launch new products, enter new markets and should this be done through organic development, alliances or mergers and acquisitions?

There are, then, common themes in the choices that have to made to do with *satisfying expectations* of stakeholders by *creating value* in the context of actual or potential *competition* and decisions about product and market scope.

The overall challenge, which is the theme of Part III as a whole, is the extent to which these different levels of strategic choice are consistent with each other. For example, competitive strategy at the business unit level seeks to achieve competitive advantage so that an organisation might both provide value to customers and achieve above average profits. How then might such value creation be enhanced at the corporate level?

The discussion of strategic choice has been divided into three chapters as shown in Exhibit III.i.

Chapter 5 is concerned with business-level or competitive strategy. How might business units compete successfully in markets so as to meet the needs of customers (or users) and create value for stakeholders, of which one may well be a corporate parent? This is first considered by examining generic choices of the bases of competitive strategies: these are the fundamental choices available by which competitive advantage in markets might be achieved. Questions are also raised,

Exhibit III.i   Strategic choices

Strategic choices

Business or competitive strategy
- Bases of competitive strategy
- Sustainability of competitive advantage
- Strategies in hypercompetitive conditions
- Competition and collaboration
- Game theory

Corporate and international strategy
- Product/market diversity
- International diversity and strategy
- Value creation and the corporate parent
- Corporate parenting rationales
- Managing corporate portfolios

Directions and methods of development
- Protect and build
- Product development
- Market development
- Diversification through
- Internal development
- Mergers and acquisitions
- Strategic alliances and
- Success criteria of strategies

building on Chapter 3, about the extent to which sustainable competitive advantage is possible to achieve and when it makes sense to choose collaborative rather than competitive strategies. The chapter also considers the implications of turbulent, fast-changing 'hypercompetitive' environments on choices of competitive strategy. The contribution of game theory to ways of thinking about competitive strategy is then discussed.

Chapter 6 is concerned with corporate-level and international strategy. First, the extent of corporate diversity is discussed in terms of both product and international diversity. In particular the extent and nature of such diversity is considered in terms of the reasons for diversity and the effects on performance. Second, the question is posed as to how corporate parents, who manage multiple business units, might create or destroy the value created by those businesses. Different rationales of corporate parenting are discussed, as are different logics for the management of the portfolio of businesses within a corporation.

Chapter 7 deals with choices of both strategic direction and method. This includes considerations of how directions of strategic development can be built around market opportunities; developments of products or services; development of competences and the various combinations of these three parameters. Development methods ranging from internal development, through strategic alliances to acquisitions and mergers are also explained. The chapter then moves on to discuss why some strategies might succeed better than others. It does this by introducing the concepts of suitability, acceptability and feasibility:

- *Suitability* is a broad criterion concerned with whether a strategic option addresses the circumstances in which the organisation is operating – the strategic position as discussed in Part II.

- *Acceptability* is concerned with the expected performance outcomes (such as return or risk) of a strategic option, and the extent to which these would be in line with expectations.

- *Feasibilty* is concerned with whether a strategy could be made to work in practice, and therefore with the practicalities of resourcing and strategic capability.

Different approaches to evaluating strategic options are also explained and discussed in the context of these concepts.

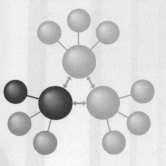

5

Business-Level Strategy

Learning outcomes

After reading this chapter you should be able to explain:

- How to identify strategic business units (SBUs) in organisations.
- Different bases of achieving competitive advantage in terms of 'routes' on the strategy clock:
  - price-based strategies;
  - differentiation strategies;
  - hybrid and focus strategies.
- The factors influencing the sustainability of competitive advantage.
- The relationship between competition and collaboration.
- The principles of game theory in relation to competitive strategy.

5.1   INTRODUCTION

This chapter is about the competitive strategies of organisations and the choices that can be made to gain competitive advantage. The equivalent issues in the public services are the choices that underpin best value in service provision. The previous three chapters have reviewed the many forces at work in the business environment, the internal capabilities of organisations and the expectations and influences of stakeholders. All of these are potentially important influences on the development of business-level strategy.

It is important to remember that competitive strategy in an organisation is created in the separate business units of the organisation. Most organisations have a number of business units, which are competing in different markets, where customers or clients have different needs and require different products or services. So to understand business-level strategy it is important to be able to identify the SBUs in an organisation. The chapter begins with this issue. However, it should be remembered that an SBU is a part of an organisation for strategy-making purposes and the organisation may not be structured around SBUs. Exhibit 5.1 then shows the three main elements that constitute business-level strategy and which provide the structure for the rest of the chapter:

Exhibit 5.1   Business-level strategies

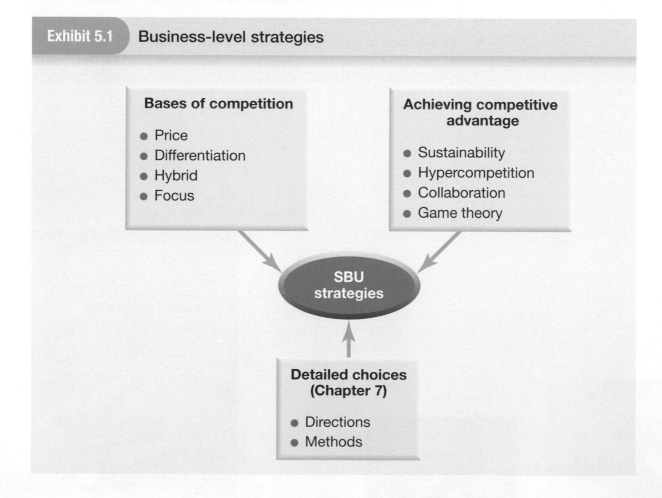

Bases of competition

- Price
- Differentiation
- Hybrid
- Focus

Achieving competitive advantage

- Sustainability
- Hypercompetition
- Collaboration
- Game theory

SBU strategies

Detailed choices (Chapter 7)

- Directions
- Methods

- First is the issue of the broad *bases of competition* 'available' to SBUs. These include price-based strategies, differentiation strategies, hybrid and focus strategies.

- The later sections look at ways of *achieving competitive advantage*. This starts in section 5.4 with issues about the *sustainability of strategy over time*. However, in a fast-changing and uncertain world the sustainability of competitive advantage can be problematic. The idea of *hypercompetition* (introduced in Chapter 2, section 2.3.2) is revisited in section 5.5 to consider lessons for strategic choices. The potential benefits of *cooperative* strategies with competitors are also discussed in section 5.6 as are the dynamics of competition and the interdependence of competitors' actions (*game theory*) in section 5.7.

- The third element in Exhibit 5.1 is the *detailed choices* of development directions and methods within the more generic choices considered. This is discussed in detail in Chapter 7, which looks at choices of direction such as new products or new markets and methods such as acquisitions or strategic alliances.

5.2 IDENTIFYING STRATEGIC BUSINESS UNITS

A **strategic business unit** is a part of an organisation for which there is a distinct external market for goods or services that is different from another SBU. As mentioned above, the identification of an organisation's strategic business units is essential to the development of business-level strategies since these will vary from one SBU to another. There are two opposing pitfalls that need to be avoided:

> A **strategic business unit** is a part of an organisation for which there is a distinct external market for goods or services that is different from another SBU

- If each product and each geographical branch (and so on) is considered to be an independent SBU such immense variety of competitive strategies for a single organisation would create a lack of focus and inefficiency. This would make the development of corporate-level strategy (see Chapter 6) almost impossible.

- On the other hand, the concept of the SBU is important in properly reflecting the diversity of products and markets that actually exist.

There are two broad criteria which can help in avoiding these two pitfalls and, therefore, in identifying SBUs that are useful when developing business-level strategies.

- *External criteria* for identifying SBUs are about the nature of the marketplace for different parts of the organisation. Two parts of an organisation should only be regarded as the same SBU if they are targeting the same *customer types*, through the same sorts of *channels* and facing similar *competitors*. For example, a 'unit' tailoring products/services to specific local needs cannot belong to the same SBU as another that offers standardised products or services globally. Nor are units that offer the same products to a customer group through exclusively different channels (retail or mail-order/internet).

- *Internal criteria* for identifying SBUs are about the nature of an organisation's strategic capability – its resources and competences. Two parts of an organisation should only be regarded as the same SBU if they have similar products/

services built on similar technologies and sharing a similar set of resources and competences. This usually means that the cost structure of the 'units' will be similar. So within a company like Kodak the units offering film-based products are not in the same SBU as those offering digital photography products – even though they are addressing the same customers through the same channels.

The identification of SBUs impacts on the choices of generic competitive strategies (see section 5.3 below); corporate-level issues about relationships between SBUs (Chapter 6) and issues of organisation design (Chapter 8).[1] These decisions occur in the public sector too. The frequent 're-packaging' of activities into and within ministries in central government shows how difficult these judgements can be. For example, in the UK over the last few decades 'Education' has been partnered with 'Science', then 'Employment' and then with 'Skills'. It is important to review the definition of SBUs as the business environment and/or an organisation's capabilities change. For example, the development of mobile telephony created new SBUs for telecom companies – many of which were floated off as independent companies.

5.3 BASES OF COMPETITIVE ADVANTAGE: THE 'STRATEGY CLOCK'

Competitive strategy is concerned with the basis on which a business unit might achieve competitive advantage in its market

This section reviews different ways in which managers in an organisation might think about **competitive strategy**, the bases on which a business unit might achieve competitive advantage in its market. For public service organisations, the concern is with an equivalent issue: the bases on which the organisation chooses to sustain the quality of its services within agreed budgets, i.e. how it provides 'best value'.

Porter[2] pioneered thinking in this field when he proposed that there were three different 'generic' strategies by which an organisation could achieve competitive advantage. These were: 'overall cost leadership', 'differentiation' and 'focus'. Over the following 20 years there was much debate as to exactly what each of these categories meant. In particular many confused Porter's 'cost leadership' with low prices. To remove any such confusions the discussion in this book will present 'market-facing' generic strategies similar to those used by Bowman and D'Aveni.[3] These are based on the principle that organisations achieve competitive advantage by providing their customers with what they want, or need, better or more effectively than competitors. This is a proposition with which Porter would agree and the strategy clock (Exhibit 5.2) enshrines Porter's categories of differentiation and focus alongside price – as discussed in the sections below.

Assuming that there are a number of providers customers will choose which offering to accept on their perception of value-for-money. This consists of the combination of price and customer-perceived product/service benefits of each offering. Since the positions on the 'strategy clock' represent different positions in the market where customers (or potential customers) have different 'requirements' in terms of value-for-money they also represent a set of generic strategies for achieving competitive advantage. Illustration 5.1 shows an example in the

Exhibit 5.2	The strategy clock: competitive strategy options

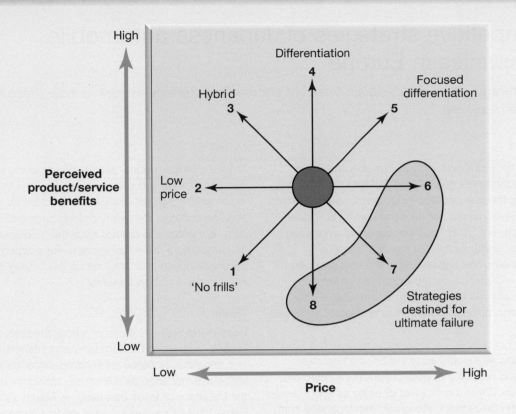

		Needs/risks	
1	'No frills'	Likely to be segment specific	
2	Low price	Risk of price war and low margins; need to be cost leader	
3	Hybrid	Low cost base and reinvestment in low price and differentiation	Differentiation
4	Differentiation (a) Without price premium	Perceived added value by user, yielding market share benefits	Differentiation
	(b) With price premium	Perceive added value sufficient to bear price premium	Differentiation
5	Focused differentiation	Perceived added value to a particular segment, warranting price premium	Differentiation
6	Increased price/standard value	Higher margins if competitors do not follow; risk of losing market share	Likely failure
7	Increased price/low value	Only feasible in monopoly situation	Likely failure
8	Low value/standard price	Loss of market share	Likely failure

Note: The strategy clock is adapted from the work of Cliff Bowman (see D. Faulkner and C. Bowman, *The Essence of Competitive Strategy*, Prentice Hall, 1995). However, Bowman uses the dimension 'Perceived Use Value'.

Illustration 5.1   strategy into action

Competitive strategies of Japanese automobile companies in Europe

The strategy clock helps explain bases of competitive strategy as well as how these might change over time.

Route 1

During the 1960s and early 1970s, the Japanese car manufacturers entered the European market by targeting the low-cost/low-added-value sector, which they believed would not be defended by European manufacturers. Their 'no frills' products were seen as cheap, and bought with few added-value expectations. The sales volume that this produced and the experience gained from this market entry strategy allowed them to form a bridgehead into Europe and develop other, more profitable, strategies.

Route 2

By the late 1970s and early 1980s, the improved quality and reliability of their products changed the perception of their cars to that of being as good as their European competitors. However, the Japanese cars continued to be sold at a cheaper price than their rivals, which allowed them to increase sales volume further.

Route 3

Following their earlier success, the Japanese further advanced their position in the late 1980s by producing competitively priced cars that were more reliable and of better quality than their rivals. Competitors followed the Japanese and attempted to maintain their position by improving the quality and reducing the relative prices of their own cars.

Route 4

By the mid-1990s, the main Japanese manufacturers, in common with other automobile companies, were seeking ways to differentiate their products on the basis of providing extra features such as air-bags, air conditioning and longer-term warranties. For much of this period the Japanese lead times for such innovations were less than most of their competitors'. However, by 2000, competitors were catching up and sustainable differentiation was becoming more difficult.

Route 5

Toyota's Lexus model – which stands alone from the rest of its range and does not use the Toyota name – is competing against manufacturers such as Jaguar and Mercedes in the luxury market segment. Because, as a new entrant, it did not have the 'pedigree' of its competitors, advertising campaigns aimed to persuade buyers that they should be buying cars not on name, but on features.

Route 8

Despite having high levels of labour productivity Nissan experienced falling sales and financial losses in Europe due to fierce price competition. Its product range was not seen as sufficiently attractive to hold market share or trade profitably. In March 1999 Renault bought a controlling stake in Nissan and embarked on a programme of product development. One successful outcome was the new Micra, which had a successful launch in early 2003.

Source: Updated from original prepared by Tony Jacobs, Bristol Business School.

Questions

1. Why do new entrants to industries often enter 'through' route 1 on the strategy clock?

2. Why did the incumbent market leaders not respond to the Japanese 'trading up' through routes 2 and 3 on the clock?

3. Would it be feasible to enter the market through route 5 and then move to other positions?

4. Nissan was trying to address its route 8 positioning. To where on the strategy clock were Nissan re-positioning?

context of the history of Japanese car firms in the European automobile market. The consideration of each of these strategies will also acknowledge the importance of an organisation's costs – particularly relative to competitors. But it will be seen in the subsequent discussions that cost is a strategic consideration for all strategies on the clock – not just those where the lead edge is low price.

Since these strategies are 'market-facing' it is important to understand the critical success factors for each position on the clock. Customers at positions 1 and 2 are primarily concerned with price – but only if the product/service benefits meet their threshold requirements as discussed in Chapter 2 (section 2.4.3). This usually means that customers emphasise functionality over service or more aesthetic issues such as design or packaging. In contrast, customers at position 5 on the clock require a customised product or service and are prepared to pay a price premium for that 'privilege'. Of course, in any particular market the volume of demand is unlikely to be evenly spread across the positions on the clock. In commodity-like markets demand is substantially weighted towards positions 1 and 2. Many public services are of this type too. Other markets have significant demand in positions 4 and 5. Historically professional services were of this type. However, markets change over time. Commodity-like markets develop value-added niches which may grow rapidly as disposable incomes rise. For example, this has occurred in the drinks market with premium and speciality beers (see the case example at the end of Chapter 2) and in many sectors of retailing. Customised markets may become more commodity-like particularly where IT can de-mystify and routinise the professional content of the product – as in financial services (as discussed in Chapter 9).

So the strategy clock is an important concept in helping managers understand the changing requirements of their markets and the choices they can make about positioning and competitive advantage. Each position on the clock will now be discussed in more detail.

5.3.1 Price-based strategies (routes 1 and 2)

Route 1 is the **'no frills' strategy**, which combines a low price, low perceived product/service benefits and a focus on a price-sensitive market segment. These segments might exist for a number of reasons:

A 'no frills' strategy combines a low price, low perceived product/service benefits and a focus on a price-sensitive market segment

- The products or services are *commodity-like*. Customers do not discern or value differences in the offering of different suppliers. So price becomes the key competitive issue. Basic foodstuffs – particularly in developing economies – are an example.

- There may be *price-sensitive customers*, who cannot afford, or choose not, to buy better-quality goods. The grocery retail chains Aldi and Netto in Europe follow this strategy. Their stores are basic, their merchandise range is relatively limited with few speciality or luxury products, and their prices are very low. In the public services many decisions are made by the funders irrespective of what the users might ideally like. As they are working within tight budgets they may decide to fund only a basic-level provision (for example, in subsidised spectacles or dentistry).

● The buyers have *high power and/or low switching costs* – so building customer loyalty is difficult – for example, with petrol retailing. So providers try to buy loyalty in other ways, such as loyalty cards.

● Where there are a *small number of providers with similar market shares*. So the cost structure is similar and new product/service features are quickly imitated. Price becomes the key competitive weapon.

● Where the major providers are competing on a non-price basis the low-price segment may be an opportunity for smaller players to *avoid the major competitors*. A regionally based corporate law firm may gain business in this way. Or a new entrant may seek to achieve market entry through route 1 and use this as a bridgehead to build volume before moving on to other strategies.

A **low-price strategy** seeks to achieve a lower price than competitors whilst trying to maintain similar perceived product or service benefits to those offered by competitors

Illustration 5.2 shown an example of one company's no-frills strategy. Route 2, the **low-price strategy**, seeks to achieve a lower price than competitors whilst trying to maintain similar perceived product or service benefits to those offered by competitors. In the public sector the 'price' of a service to government as the provider of funds is essentially the unit costs of the organisation receiving the budget. Here the expectation may, indeed, be that there will be year-on-year efficiency gains and that these will be achieved without loss of perceived benefits.

If a business unit aims to achieve competitive advantage through a low-price strategy it has two basic choices. The first is to try to identify and focus on a market segment that is unattractive to competitors and in this way avoid competitive pressures to erode price. A more challenging situation is where there is competition on the basis of price. This is a common occurrence in the public sector and for commodity-like markets. There are several potential pitfalls when competing on price:

● *Margin reduction*. Although tactical advantage may be gained by reducing price it is likely to be followed by competitors.

● This can lead to an *inability to reinvest* to develop the product or service and result in a loss of perceived benefit of the product. In the public sector this can result in a drift towards being the 'provider of last resort' serving only those parts of the community who cannot afford to purchase better services from the private sector. This has been a central concern for those involved in public sector housing provision.

● So clearly, in the long run, a low-price strategy cannot be pursued without a *low-cost base*. However, low cost in itself is not a basis for advantage. Managers often pursue low-cost strategies that do not give them competitive advantage. The key challenge is how costs can be reduced in ways which others cannot match such that a low-price strategy might give sustainable advantage. The evidence is that this is difficult to achieve, but some ways in which it might be possible are discussed in section 5.4.1 below.

A **differentiation strategy** seeks to provide products or services benefits that are different from those of competitors and that are widely valued by buyers

5.3.2 Differentiation strategies (route 4)

The next option is a broad **differentiation strategy** which seeks to provide products or services that offer benefits different from those of competitors and that are

Illustration 5.2

easyJet's 'no frills' strategy

Multiple bases for keeping costs down can provide a basis for a successful no-frills strategy.

Launched in 1995, easyJet was seen as the brash young upstart of the European airline industry and widely tipped to fail. But by the mid-2000s this Luton-based airline has done more than survive. From a starting point of six hired planes working one route, by 2003 it had 74 aircraft flying 105 routes to 38 airports and carrying over 20 million passengers per annum.

Beneath the surface of easyJet's cosmetic cost savings of not offering free in-flight refreshments or different first, business and economy classes, was a philosophy of cost saving that permeated through the whole company. The 2002/03 annual report reconfirmed this business model for the airline:

'Our overriding commitment is to safety and customer service, rooted in a strong and dynamic culture that can accommodate our continuing rate of growth. The business model is:

● Dense point-to-point network
  – Linking major airports with large catchment areas
  – High levels of frequency
  – Attractive to business and leisure travellers
● Strong, visible brand
  – Extremely high levels of awareness with consumers
  – Supported by innovative and effective advertising
● Dynamic fares
  – Simple fare structure; the earlier you book, the less you pay
  – Aim to be the lowest fare on the route
  – Demand led, with proprietary yield management system
● 100 per cent direct sales
  – easyJet does not pay commissions to intermediaries
  – over 90 per cent of sales are online
● Highly utilised fleet
  – A large, modern, efficient and relatively environmentally friendly fleet
  – The introduction of Airbus A319 aircraft, combined

with the retirement of 'old generation' Boeing 737 aircraft, will result in a two-type 'new technology' fleet, which will increase commonality and lessen complexity
  – High levels of asset utilisation reduce unit costs
● Scaleable
  – The key to sustaining high levels of growth is the scaleability of the operations
  – This also reduces the marginal cost of incremental growth
  – Increasing scale brings valuable economies.

Despite impressive financial results (£96m profit on £932m revenue ($\approx$ €144m on $\approx$ €1.4bn)) the report also acknowledged that the company had to continue its efforts:

'Our first priority continues to be increasing frequency on existing routes as this brings economies in terms of the operations and increases the attractiveness of easyJet's service to consumers – particularly in the business sector. It is also the lowest risk route to growth and in the year to September 2003 this accounted for approximately two thirds of the net growth in capacity.

Our second priority is to add flights between existing destinations, known as joining the dots, which benefits from synergies with existing operations and customer relationships at each destination.

Our third priority is to add new destinations to the network. These [latter two] collectively accounted for the other one third of the net growth in capacity in 2003.

Source: easyJet annual report 2002/03.

Questions

1. Read sections 5.3.1 and 5.4.1 and identify the bases of easyJet's no-frills strategy.

2. How easy would it be for larger airlines such as BA to imitate the strategy?

widely valued by buyers.[4] The aim is to achieve competitive advantage by offering better products or services at the same price or enhancing margins by pricing slightly higher. In public services, the equivalent is the achievement of a 'centre of excellence' status, which could attract higher funding from government (for example, universities try to show that they are better at research or teaching than other universities).

The extent to which a differentiation approach will be successful is likely to be dependent on a number of factors:

- Has the organisation clearly identified *who is the strategic customer*? This is not always straightforward, as discussed in section 2.4.3 of Chapter 2. For example, for a newspaper business, is the customer the reader of the newspaper, the advertiser, or both? They are likely to have different needs and be looking for different benefits. Public sector organisations face a similar issue. It may be very important that they offer perceived benefits, but to whom? Is it the service user or the provider of funds? These are difficult questions to answer but the concept of the strategic customer can be helpful. The extent to which the organisation understands *what is valued* by the strategic customer can be dangerously taken for granted by managers. This is a reminder of the importance of identifying critical success factors (Chapter 2, section 2.4.2).

- It is important to be clear *who are the competitors*. For example, is the business competing with a wide competitor base or with a much narrower base, perhaps within a particular market segment? In the latter case, a strategy of focused differentiation may be appropriate (position 5 on the clock – see section 5.3.4 below). In the case of broad-based differentiation, it is likely that the business will have to concentrate on bases of differentiation commonly valued by customers in that market. For example, in the automobile mass market reliability is a key customer requirement (critical success factor) and those manufacturers who are able to demonstrate high levels of reliability have advantage over others.

Some of these problems of identifying appropriate bases of differentiation are demonstrated in Illustration 5.3.

5.3.3 The hybrid strategy (route 3)

A **hybrid strategy** seeks simultaneously to achieve differentiation and a price lower than that of competitors

A **hybrid strategy** seeks simultaneously to achieve differentiation and a price lower than that of competitors. Here the success of the strategy depends on the ability to deliver enhanced benefits to customers together with low prices whilst achieving sufficient margins for reinvestment to maintain and develop the bases of differentiation.[5] It might be argued that, if differentiation can be achieved, there should be no need to have a lower price, since it should be possible to obtain prices at least equal to competition, if not higher. However, the hybrid strategy could be advantageous in the following circumstances:

- If much *greater volumes* can be achieved than competitors then margins may still be better because of a low cost base.

Illustration 5.3

Crinkly biscuits as competitive advantage?

In building a competitive strategy, executives need to be wary of spurious bases of competitive advantage.

Senior executives of an international food manufacturing company were taking part in a strategy workshop, discussing bases of competitive advantage for their strategic business units. The issues of competitive advantage based on perceived customer needs was raised, and one of the executives, the quality assurance manager for a biscuit business, commented as follows:

> I totally agree. In our business we know what customers want and we have invested to provide it. Our research shows that customers care a lot about the crinkles on the edges of their biscuits. They like neat regular crinkles. We have just invested £1 million in equipment that will deliver just that with very little wastage. We are the leader in this field.

In the discussion which followed, it became clear that there were at least three flaws in what the manager had said. First, his point of reference for considering his strategy was the end user, the consumer. In fact, the company referred to grocery retailers as 'competitors' because such retailers sold own-brand goods. Yet if the major retailers, which controlled 50 per cent of the distribution of biscuits, did not stock the product, it never reached the consumer. Whilst consumers were, of course, very important, the strategic customer was the retailer; but the business had no clear strategy for achieving competitive advantage with regard to retailers.

Second, it became clear that the identification of customer need was based on a survey which had pre-specified certain characteristics of biscuits, one of which was 'regular crinkles'. The quality assurance manager's colleagues were of the opinion that the fact that 'consumers had ticked a few boxes to do with ideas thought up by some guys in the R&D department' was a spurious basis upon which to build a strategy, let alone invest large amounts of capital.

Third, when challenged, the manager had to admit that there was nothing to stop a competitor buying similar equipment and achieving just the same quality of crinkles. If there was any competitive advantage – and this was dubious – it was easily imitable.

Questions

This example illustrates three common shortcomings in differentiation strategies:

(a) Value-for-money is incorrectly assessed by focusing on the wrong customer (or 'stakeholder').

(b) Inappropriate research to identify benefits.

(c) Easy imitation of the supposed sources of differentiation.

Bearing in mind these shortcomings identified in the claim for differentiation made in the illustration:

1. What *might have been* sustainable bases of differentiation for this biscuit business?

2. Do the bases of differentiation explained in (the later) Illustration 5.5 on the Australian wine industry overcome these shortcomings?

● If an organisation is clear about the *activities on which differentiation can be built* (i.e. potential core competences) it may then be able to reduce costs on other activities. IKEA recognised that it could achieve a high standard of product, but at a low cost, whilst concentrating on building differentiation on the basis of its marketing, range, logistics and store operations. Also low customer expectations on service levels allow cost reduction because customers are prepared to transport and build its products (see Illustration 5.4).

Illustration 5.4   strategy into action

IKEA's hybrid strategy

Combining perceived low price with perceived added value can be a highly successful strategy but one which requires innovative thinking.

Since IKEA began in 1953 it has grown into a highly successful global network of stores but retained the same retailing concept: 'to offer a wide range of furnishing items of good design and function at prices so low that the majority of people can afford to buy them'.

The product offering was clearly different. The products were simple, high-quality Scandinavian design. They were also provided in knock-down furniture kits that the customers transported and assembled themselves, thus saving the often lengthy time that other stores required for delivery. The huge suburban stores had plenty of parking and amenities such as cafés, restaurants, wheelchairs and supervised childcare facilities. The customers expected styling and quality readily available at reasonable prices. IKEA met this expectation by encouraging customers to create value for themselves by taking on certain tasks traditionally done by the manufacturer and retailer, for example the assembly and delivery of the products. Of course, this also reduced cost. So too did the fact that customers were supplied with tape measures, pens and notepaper when they visited the stores; thus reducing the number of sales staff required.

To deliver low-cost yet high-quality products consistently, IKEA had buying offices around the world whose prime purpose was to identify potential suppliers. Designers at headquarters then reviewed these to decide which would provide what for each of the products, their overall aim being to design for low cost and ease of manufacture. The most economical suppliers were always chosen over traditional suppliers, so a shirt manufacturer might be employed to produce seat covers. Although the process through which acceptance to become an IKEA supplier was not easy, it was highly coveted, for, once part of the IKEA system, suppliers gained access to global markets and received technical assistance, leased equipment and advice on how to bring production up to world-quality standards. But IKEA had always been frugal in its approach. In its early years it had relocated to Denmark to escape Swedish taxation. Indeed the whole philosophy of keeping costs down ran through the company – it was ingrained in its culture (see Illustration 4.6).

Source: Company data; *Financial Times*, 24 November 2003.

Questions

1. Which other businesses can you think of that follow a hybrid strategy?
2. Why might businesses find it difficult to follow a hybrid strategy and how can these be overcome?

● As an *entry strategy* in a market with established competitors. This is often used when developing a global strategy. Organisations search for the 'loose brick'[6] in a competitor's portfolio of businesses – perhaps a poorly run operation in a geographical area of the world – then enter that market with a superior product and, if necessary, a lower price. The aim is to take market share, divert the attention of the competitor, and establish a foothold from which they could move further. However, in following such a strategy it is important to ensure that (a) the overall cost base is such that low margins can be sustained, and (b) a clear follow-through strategy has been considered after entry has been achieved.

5.3.4 Focused differentiation (route 5)

A **focused differentiation** strategy seeks to provide high perceived product/service benefits justifying a substantial price premium, usually to a selected market segment (niche). In many markets these are described as premium products and are usually heavily branded. For example, in the alcoholic drinks market premium beers, single malt whiskies, wines from particular chateaux, all compete to convince customers that their product is sufficiently differentiated from their competitors' to 'justify' significantly higher prices. In the public services national or international centres of excellence (such as a specialist museum) achieve unit levels of funding significantly higher than the more generalist providers. However, focused differentiation raises some important issues:

A focused differentiation strategy seeks to provide high perceived product/ service benefits justifying a substantial price premium, usually to a selected market segment (niche)

- A *choice* may have to be made between a focus strategy (position 5) and broad differentiation (position 4) if sales are to grow. This may take on global proportions, as managers have to make decisions in increasingly global markets. Growth may be achieved by targeting new sales into the same niches in more countries/markets (i.e. maintaining position 5 on the strategy clock in all markets) rather than by broadening the appeal in a single country/market (i.e. moving from 5 to 4 on the strategy clock).

- Pursuing a focus strategy may be difficult when it is only *part* of an organisation's overall strategy – a very common situation. For example, department stores attempt to sell a wide range of products in one store. In so doing they may try to appeal to a range of different customer types. So a focus strategy for a particular range of goods may run into problems because the store itself, the fixtures and fittings, the decor and store ambience, and the staff, may not be appropriate to the needs of the target group of customers for that range of goods. This practicality puts limitations on the degree of diversity of positioning that an organisation can sustain. This is an important issue for corporate-level strategy that will be discussed in Chapter 6.

- Focus strategies may *conflict with stakeholder expectations*. For example, a public library service could probably be run more cost-efficiently if it were to pull out of low-demand parts of its community and put more resources into its popular branch libraries. It might also find that concentrating its development efforts on IT-based online information services would prove popular with some parts of the community. However, the extent to which these strategies would be regarded as within the library's remit might be hotly debated – particularly in relation to its purpose of social inclusion.

- *New ventures* often start in very focused ways – for example, new 'leading-edge' medical services in hospitals. It may, however, be difficult to find ways to grow such new ventures. Moving from route 5 to route 4 will mean a lowering of price and therefore cost, whilst maintaining differentiation features. On the other hand, maintaining a highly focused (route 5) approach may not be easy because users may not be prepared to pay the price or, in the public sector, provide funding for such projects.

- The *market situation* may change such that differences between segments may be eroded, leaving the organisation open to much wider competition. Customers may become unwilling to pay a price premium as the features of the 'regular' offerings improve. Or the market may be further segmented by even more differentiated offerings from competitors. Sometimes these changes will happen simultaneously. For example, some of the more 'up-market' restaurants offering a general menu have been hit by rising standards elsewhere and by the advent of specialist 'niche' restaurants that specialise on particular ethnic foods or by type of food (e.g. seafood or vegetarian).

5.3.5 Failure strategies (routes 6, 7 and 8)

A **failure strategy** is one that does not provide perceived value-for-money in terms of product features, price or both

A **failure strategy** is one which does not provide perceived value-for-money in terms of product features, price or both. For example, the strategies suggested by routes 6, 7 and 8 are probably destined for failure. Route 6 suggests increasing price without increasing product/service benefits to the customer. This is, of course, the very strategy that monopoly organisations are accused of following. However, unless the organisation is protected by legislation, or high economic barriers to entry, competitors are likely to erode market share. Route 7 is an even more disastrous extension of route 6, involving the reduction in product/service benefits whilst increasing relative price. Route 8, reduction in benefits whilst maintaining price, is also dangerous, though firms have tried to follow it. There is a high risk that competitors will increase their share substantially. Although the logic of routes 6, 7 and 8 might suggest withdrawal from the market many public service providers stumble on because there is no market mechanism to punish poor value-for-money and/or there is a lack of political will to close down the services.

Arguably there is another basis of failure, which is for a business to be unclear as to its fundamental generic strategy such that it ends up being 'stuck in the middle' – a recipe for failure.

5.4   SUSTAINING COMPETITIVE ADVANTAGE

If the lessons of searching for competitive advantage as discussed in section 5.3 above are to be taken seriously, the issue of sustainability is important. Is it possible to achieve competitive advantage in such a way that it can be preserved over time? There may be some circumstances where sustainability is possible – at least for a period of time – and this is addressed in this section. In contrast, section 5.5 looks at competitive strategy in circumstances where sustainability is not possible or at least extremely difficult.

A good deal of what follows builds on the earlier discussion in Chapter 3 (section 3.3.2) on the robustness of core competences.

5.4.1 Sustaining price-based advantage

Competitive advantage through low prices might be sustained in a number of ways (see Exhibit 5.3):

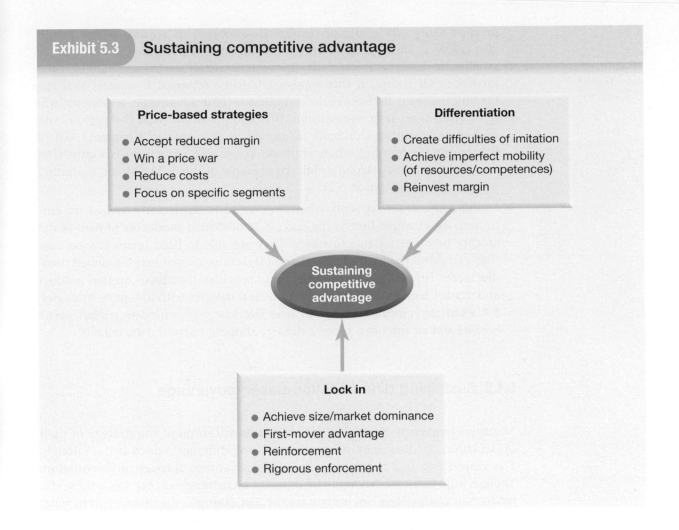

Exhibit 5.3   Sustaining competitive advantage

Price-based strategies
- Accept reduced margin
- Win a price war
- Reduce costs
- Focus on specific segments

Differentiation
- Create difficulties of imitation
- Achieve imperfect mobility (of resources/competences)
- Reinvest margin

Sustaining competitive advantage

Lock in
- Achieve size/market dominance
- First-mover advantage
- Reinforcement
- Rigorous enforcement

- An organisation pursuing low-price strategies may be prepared to accept the (previously mentioned) *reduced margin* either because it can sell more volume than competitors or it can cross-subsidise that business unit from elsewhere in its portfolio (see Chapter 6 for further discussion of portfolio strategies).

- An organisation may be prepared to sustain and win a *price war*[7] with competitors either because it has a lower cost structure (see below) or it has 'deeper pockets' to fund short- to medium-term losses with the aim of driving out competitors in the longer term. Supermarkets have been accused of pursuing such strategies. Price wars are becoming more prevalent as consumers use the internet to compare prices and 'shop around'.

- An organisation has cost advantages through *organisationally specific capabilities* driving down cost throughout the value chain.[8] Porter comments on cost leadership as '*the* low-cost producer in its industry . . . [who] must find and exploit all sources of cost advantage'.[9] (See Chapter 3, section 3.3 and Exhibit 3.3.) For example, cost advantage might be achieved because a business is able to obtain raw materials at lower prices than competitors, or to produce more efficiently, or because it is located in an area where labour cost is low, or because its distribution costs provide advantages. Or it may be possible to reduce substantially the costs of activities by outsourcing their provision. Of course, if this approach is to be followed it matters that the operational areas it chooses do truly bestow cost advantages to support real price advantages over competition. It is also important that competitors will find these advantages difficult to imitate as discussed in Chapter 3. All of this requires a mindset where innovation (in cost reduction) is regarded as essential to survival. An international example of this is McDonald's; another is easyJet (see Illustration 5.2).

- *Focusing on market segments* where low price is particularly valued by customers. An example here is the success of dedicated producers of own-brand grocery products for supermarkets. They are able to hold prices low because they can avoid the high overhead and marketing costs of major branded manufacturers. However, they can only do so provided they focus on that product and market segment. But there are some real dangers with low-price strategies. For example, customers start to *associate low price with low product/service benefits* and an intended route 2 strategy slipping to route 1 by default.

5.4.2 Sustaining differentiation-based advantage

Managers frequently claim that differentiation is central to the strategy of their organisation but they may simply mean 'being different' which is not enough. The concern of this section is sustainable advantage through differentiation. There is little point in striving to be different if customers do not value those differences or competitors can imitate readily. For example, the investment in state-of-the-art production equipment by the biscuit manufacturer in Illustration 5.3, even if it were really meeting an important customer need, could be imitated readily by a competitor who could make the same investment. Or a firm of accountants which carries out a relatively standardised audit procedure will find it difficult to differentiate its services based on variations of those procedures. Even if it can develop such variations, they are likely to be copied rapidly by others. This is not to say that such actions are not important. These improvements may be vital to compete effectively – but that is not the same as *sustainable differentiation*.

Conditions to sustain advantage through differentiation[10] include the following (see Exhibit 5.3 and Illustration 5.5):

- *Create difficulties of imitation.* Section 3.4 of Chapter 3 discussed the factors that can make strategies difficult to imitate.
- *Imperfect mobility* of the resources and/or competences that are sustaining differentiation is another reason why sustainability may be possible. This is concerned with whether or not the resources and competences of an organisation could be *traded*. For example, a pharmaceutical firm may gain great benefits from having top research scientists, or a football club from its star players, but these valuable assets may be poached by competitors: they are tradable. On the

Illustration 5.5   strategy into action

Differentiation in the wine industry: an Australian success story but the French fight back

Successful differentiation needs to be based on what customers value.

By 2001 the traditional dominance of French wines in the UK had ended, with sales of Australian wine outstripping them for the first time. Australian wines accounted for 19.5 per cent of UK wine sales in terms of value (up 25 per cent over 1999), with French wines showing a steady decline. And for wines over £5.00 (≈ €7.5), Australian wine had already overtaken French wines. The success of Australian wines with retailers was put down to several factors. The quality was consistent, compared with French wines that could differ by year and location. Also, whilst the French had always highlighted the importance of the local area of origin of the wine within France, Australia had, in effect, 'branded' the country as a wine region and then concentrated on the variety of grape – a Shiraz or a Chardonnay, for example. This avoided the confusing details of the location of vineyards and the names of chateaux that many customers found difficult about French wines. There was so much concern in France that in 2001, the French government appointed a six-man committee to study the problem. The committee's proposals – that France should fight a war on two fronts, by improving the quality of its appellation wine and by creating an entirely new range of quality, generic wines – shocked the purists. The intention was to strengthen, and parallel, the system of Appellation d'Origine Contrôlée, not to weaken or abandon it. The proposals amounted, nevertheless, to a radical change, not just in the labelling of French wine, but in the official French mythology of wine.

The system of Appellation d'Origine Contrôlée (AOC) is the legal expression of 'terroir'. The individual wine-grower is a custodian of the terroir and its traditions. But the same appellation can produce both wonderful and terrible results – hence the unpredictability of French wine, which is charming to the connoisseur, but infuriating to the dinner-party host, who expects to get what he or she paid for. The New World approach to the production of wine of all qualities, however, originates from the consumer, not the soil. The makers of middle-range Australian wines base their product on a popular grape variety, such as Chardonnay, rather than a single vineyard. The company decides the style, quality and taste of the wine that it wants to achieve, based on consumer demand, and buys the grapes it needs – from wherever it can find them – to create a reliable, standardised product. It is just this approach – creating so-called 'vins de cepage' (wines based on a grape variety) that the French committee were proposing. A half-dozen new, readily identifiable French labels would be created, to rival the Jacob's Creeks and the Rosemounts of Australia.

Sources: Adapted from *Financial Times*, 11 February and 3/4 March 2001; *Independent*, 4 August 2003.

Questions

1. What were the reasons for the success of Australian wines? Were these sustainable (see section 5.4.2)?

2. What else would you advise French wine producers to do to counter the Australian success?

other hand, some bases of advantage are very difficult to trade and imperfect mobility will be more likely. For example:

– Many *intangible assets* such as brand, image or reputation are difficult for a competitor to obtain. Even if the competitor acquires the company to use the brand, the reputation of the brand may not readily transfer given new ownership.

> – *Switching costs* are the actual or perceived cost for a buyer of changing the source of supply of a product or service. The buyer might be dependent on the supplier for particular components, services or skills; or the benefits of switching may simply not be worth the cost or risk.
>
> – *Co-specialisation* may also help achieve imperfect mobility: for example, if one organisation's resources or competences are intimately linked with the buyers' organisation. It could be, for example, that a whole element of the value chain for one organisation, perhaps distribution or manufacturing, is undertaken by another.

● An organisation that is able to achieve and sustain a *lower cost position* may have a better margin than competitors which can be reinvested into differentiated products or services. For example, Kellogg's or Mars may well be the lowest cost operators in their markets, but they reinvest their profits into branding and product and service differentiation. In reverse there is a real danger that cost reductions for their own sake may result in an inability to sustain a differentiation strategy. For example, many public and private organisations now outsource their IT systems for reasons of cost efficiency. This means that there is no one in the organisation who is taking a strategic view of how the organisation's competitive strategy might be transformed through IT rather than just being more efficient (see section 9.3 in Chapter 9 for a full discussion of this issue).

5.4.3 The delta model and lock-in

Hax and Wilde[11] have presented another approach to thinking about sustainability, whether it be for price-based or differentiation-based strategies – the idea of 'lock-in'. **Lock-in** is where an organisation achieves a proprietary position in its industry; it become an industry standard. For example, IBM, Microsoft and Pentium (Intel) all became industry standards – but they were not necessarily the best products. For example, technically speaking, many argue that the Apple Macintosh had a better operating system than Microsoft but this did not stop Microsoft becoming the industry standard by achieving a lock-in position. Lock-in means that other businesses have to conform to or relate to that standard in order to prosper. The 'architecture' of the industry is built around this dominant player. For example, software applications by other businesses are written around the Microsoft standard for Pentium processors, making it very difficult for other organisations to break into the market. In the public sector in the UK, reference is made to the 'gold standard', by which is meant an exemplar organisation – setting the 'business model' for the sector against which the activities and performance of others are judged. If other organisations choose to provide services significantly differently they run the risk of a loss of credibility.

The achievement of lock-in is likely to be dependent on a number of factors (see Exhibit 5.3):

● *Size or market dominance.* It is unlikely that other organisations seek to conform to such standards unless they perceive the organisation that promotes it to be dominant in its market.

Lock-in is where an organisation achieves a proprietary position in its industry; it becomes an industry standard

Illustration 5.6   strategy into action

Lock-in at Dolby and Visa

Becoming the industry standard requires a strong brand, close relationships with other companies and a willingness to protect the brand.

Dolby

Dolby was the creator of specialist audio technologies whose name appears on screen credits in most cinemas. Dolby was privately owned and in the mid-2000s the profit levels were 'thought to be substantial'. Most of Dolby's business came from licensing related audio technologies to around 500 consumer goods companies, including most of the large Japanese electronics manufacturers. In the past 20 years, these businesses had sold about 800 million products that relied on Dolby's audio ideas. Their value to much larger companies began by Dolby feeding them its own technology – backed by strong branding and patent protection. One-third of Dolby's revenue came from making systems used in production studios and cinemas as part of projection machinery. Dolby argued that this gave 'an ability to follow trends in areas such as film or video content creation' and to pick up ideas relevant to the consumer side of the business. As these relationships became successful and well established they began to be used by other firms, so Dolby became a conduit for related technologies.

Visa

In late 2003 MasterCard International filed a legal action in the USA in an attempt to block enforcement of Visa's so-called 'Settlement Service Fee'. This settlement fee imposed coercive and prohibitive fines on the top 100 Visa issuers if they made a change in brand strategy and reduced their Visa debit volume. 'Visa's intentions are clear: instead of developing value-added programmes and solutions that benefit issuers, merchants and consumers, they seek to lock in their dominant position in off-line debit by penalising members who want to change brands,' said MasterCard's lawyer. 'Visa is changing the rules mid-stream and bullying its members so it becomes virtually impossible for them to switch brands. It's like telling airline passengers halfway through a flight that if they want to fly on another carrier any time over the next 10 years, they'll have to pay a huge fee to get off the plane. This is nothing more than a thinly-veiled effort to block competition and cling to business they might otherwise lose,' the MasterCard lawyer said. 'The rule, which aims at unfairly stifling Visa debit issuers' freedom of choice, is not based on legitimate brand dedication concerns, and, by undermining competition, will ultimately hurt consumers. Financial institutions who issue MasterCard and Visa cards should have the ability to make brand decisions based on their best judgment about strength of brand, quality of service and other competitive factors that benefit their cardholders. Instead, Visa's rule sets up prohibitive fines and contrived exit barriers which sharply limit issuers' options,' the lawyer claimed.

Source: Adapted from *Financial Times*, 6 February 2001; *Business Wire*, 18 September 2003.

Questions

1. Using the checklists in sections 5.4.2 (on sustaining differentiation) and 5.4.3 (on lock-in), identify the ways in which Dolby and Visa attempt to sustain competitive advantage.
2. What could their competitors do to undermine the 'lock-in' position of Dolby and Visa?

- It is likely that such standards will be set *early in life cycles of markets*. In the volatility of growth markets it is more likely that the single-minded pursuit of lock-in by the *first movers* will be successful than when the market is mature. This was the case for Microsoft and Intel. Similarly, it was the same for the dominance of Sky over its rivals. Sky, with the financial support of the News Corporation, was able to undercut and invest heavily in technology, sustaining substantial losses over many years, in order to achieve that target. This is not to say it had an inherently better product. But what it had was management and investors with a more single-minded drive and commitment to get to market fast and achieve dominance.

- Once this position is achieved, it may be *self-reinforcing* and escalating. When one or more firms support the standard, then more come on board. Then others are obliged to and so on.

- There is likely to be rigorous *insistence on the preservation* of that lock-in position. Rivals will be seen off fiercely; insistence on conformity to the standard will be strict. This can of course lead to problems, as Microsoft found in the American courts when it was deemed to be operating against the interests of the market.

Illustration 5.6 shows how two companies set out to achieve and retain a lock-in position in their industry.

5.5 COMPETITIVE STRATEGY IN HYPERCOMPETITIVE CONDITIONS[12]

As section 2.3.2 of Chapter 2 made clear, many organisations in both the public and private sectors face turbulent, fast-changing, uncertain business environments and increased levels of competition. This sort of environment is called *hypercompetitive*. In slower-moving environments competitive strategy may be primarily concerned with building and sustaining competitive advantages that are difficult to imitate – as discussed in section 5.4 above. However, in hypercompetitive environments organisations need to acknowledge that advantage will be temporary. Competitive advantage will relate to organisations' ability to change, speed, flexibility, innovation and disruption of markets. This section highlights the kind of moves that competitors are likely to make and the ways in which these can be overcome (see Exhibit 5.4).

5.5.1 Repositioning

One strategy to cope with these competitive pressures is that of *repositioning* on the strategy clock (Exhibit 5.2). For example, an organisation positioned at positions 1 or 2 may attempt to stave off competitors through establishing some degree of differentiation without any increase in price (i.e. a move to position 3 on the strategy clock). As this is imitated new sources of differentiation will need to be sought. So agility is essential.

| Exhibit 5.4 | Competitive strategies in hypercompetitive conditions |

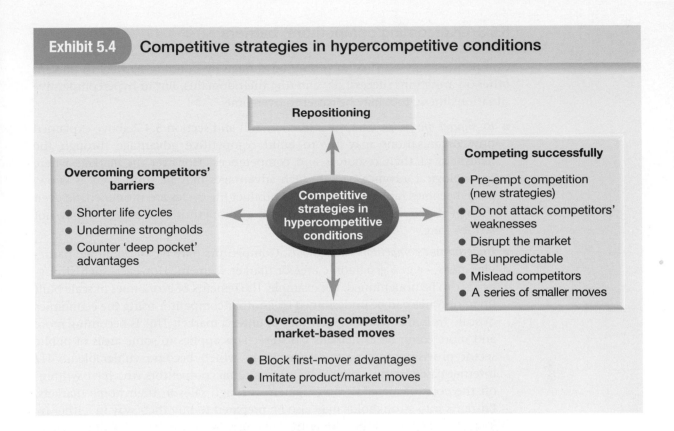

5.5.2 Overcoming competitors' market-based moves

There are a number of market-based strategic moves that may work in slower changing environments but can be purposefully undermined in hypercompetitive situations:

● *Blocking first-mover advantages.* A competitor may try to achieve advantage as a *first mover* (perhaps attempting to achieve 'lock-in' as mentioned in section 5.4.3 above). It is important that organisations realise the importance of not allowing a competitor to establish a dominant product or design before they make a response. Many organisations have learnt how to achieve advantage over the first mover. Instead of launching an imitation product, they may launch a product with enhanced features, seeking to further differentiate and thus leapfrog or outflank the first mover. Or it could be that they attack a particular segment, eroding the market power of the first mover. Or they may pursue a 'no frills' strategy to capture a downmarket segment with a cheaper product before moving into the main market of the first mover.

● *Imitate competitors' product/market moves.* Competitors may seek to achieve advantage by developing new products or entering new markets. This is discussed more fully in Chapter 7 (section 7.2). In fact, such moves may be relatively easily imitated. The competitor is then faced with exactly the same problems of sustaining advantage as it would in its original product/market arena.

5.5.3 Overcoming competitors' barriers

Competitors may also try to sustain advantage by building barriers to prevent other organisations successfully entering their domains. But in hypercompetitive situations these, too, may be easier to overcome:

● *By shorter life cycles*. Chapter 3 (section 3.3) and section 5.4.2 above explained how organisations may try to build competitive advantage through the *robustness* of their resources and competences. However, in markets where technological advance is rapid such advantages may be short-lived as knowledge becomes rapidly outdated and product life cycles are shortened. So even though it may be difficult to overcome a competitor's advantage it may not last for long.

● *Undermining competitors' strongholds*. Competitors may try to dominate particular areas – e.g. a geographic area or market segment. However, such strongholds can be undermined. For example, the benefits of economies of scale built up in one area can be undermined by another competitor using the economies of scale from its own home territory to enter a market. This is becoming more and more common as markets globalise. This applies to some areas of public sector provision too, such as education, which become vulnerable to IT/internet-based training offered by international competitors who have written-off the costs of materials development through sales in their home markets. Entrants into strongholds may also be prepared to buy their way in, either by low price, or even by providing their services free for a period of time. Where competitors have built strongholds by tying up distribution channels entrants may be able to get round this too, for example by using different distribution channels such as mail order or e-business rather than retailing. Acquisition may also be a route into a stronghold.

● *Countering competitors' deep pockets*. Some competitors may have substantial surplus resources (sometimes called '*deep pockets*') which they can use to withstand an intensive competitive war (as mentioned in section 5.4.1 above). Global reach also may allow for the moving of resources to wherever they are necessary either to preserve the interests of the company itself or to tackle competition. So organisations need to find ways around competitors' deep pocket advantages. For example, smaller firms may *avoid direct competition* by concentrating on market niches. They might *merge or build alliances* so that they can compete with larger firms. For example, retail organisations such as SPAR are a way of bringing together smaller retailers to combat the power of major retailers.

5.5.4 Ingredients of successful hypercompetitive strategies

The previous sections have given examples of how traditional bases of competitive advantage may be overcome in hypercompetitive situations. In summary the argument[13] is that managers need to rethink their approach to business-level strategy. It is argued that it may no longer be possible to plan for sustainable positions of competitive advantage. Indeed, planning for long-term sustainability will destroy competitive advantage because it will slow down response. In the hypercompetitive environment, competing increases the speed of hypercompetition and makes winning more difficult. However, there may be no alternative. Managers have to learn to be better at doing things faster than competitors. Some important principles emerge:

● An organisation has to be prepared to *pre-empt imitation by others by competing in new ways*. Sustaining old advantages can be a distraction from developing new advantages. An organisation's willingness to cannibalise the basis of its own success could be crucial.

● *Attacking competitors' weaknesses can be unwise* as they learn about how their strengths and weaknesses are perceived and build their strategies accordingly.

● A *series of smaller moves may be more effective than a bigger one-off change*. The longer-term direction is then not as easily discernible by competitors and smaller moves create more flexibility and give a series *of temporary advantages*.

● *Disruption of the* status quo *is strategic behaviour, not mischief*. The ability constantly to 'break the mould' could be a core competence.

● *Predictability is dangerous*. So surprise, unpredictability and apparent irrationality may be important. If competitors come to see a pattern in the behaviour of an organisation they can predict the next competitive moves and quickly learn how to imitate or outflank the organisation. At the least managers must learn ways of appearing to be unpredictable to the external world whilst, internally, thinking strategies through carefully.

● *Misleading signals of strategic intentions may also be useful*. In this the strategist may draw on the lessons of game theory (see section 5.7 below) to signal moves which competitors may expect but which are not the surprise moves that actually occur.

5.6 COMPETITION AND COLLABORATION[14]

So far the emphasis of the discussion of business-level strategy has been on competition and competitive advantage. However, the concept of the organisational field (see Chapter 4, section 4.5.2) is a reminder that advantage may not always be achieved by competition alone. Chapter 7 (section 7.3.3) also discusses the importance of strategic alliances. Collaboration between organisations may be a crucial ingredient in achieving advantage or avoiding competition. Also, organisations simultaneously may compete in some markets and collaborate in others.

In general collaboration between potential competitors or between buyers and sellers is likely to be advantageous when the combined costs of purchase and buying transactions (such as negotiating and contracting) are lower through collaboration than the cost of operating alone. Such collaboration also helps build switching costs. This can be illustrated by briefly returning to the five forces framework from section 2.3.1. For example (see Exhibit 5.5):

Exhibit 5.5   Competition and collaboration

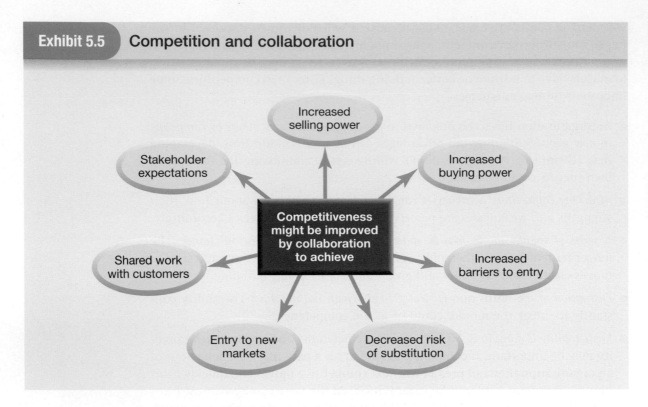

- *Collaboration to increase selling power.* Component manufacturers might build close links with customers – for example, in the aerospace industry. This can help in research and development activities, in reducing stock and in joint planning to design new products. Crucially collaboration is used by the buyer to ensure high levels of product quality in an industry where product failure usually has catastrophic consequences. This means that achieving accredited supplier status is tough – which increases seller power once achieved.

- *Collaboration to increase buying power.* Many organisations are now able to tie suppliers into their enterprise resource planning (ERP) system (as discussed in section 8.3.2). Indeed, many manufacturers have actively sought out suppliers who are able to collaborate in these ways and in many cases made it an essential requirement to become an accredited supplier. For many years the power and profitability of pharmaceutical companies were aided by the fragmented nature of their buyers – in the main, individual doctors. But now many governments have promoted, or required, collaboration between doctors and centralised government drug-specifying agencies, the result of which has been more coordinated buying power.

- *Collaboration to build barriers to entry or avoid substitution.* Faced with threatened entry or substitute products, organisations in an industry may collaborate to invest in research and development or marketing. For example, trade associations have been established to promote an industry's generic features such as safety standards or technical specifications in order to speed up innovation and pre-empt the possibility of substitution. These efforts to prevent entry may be frustrated by the collaborative efforts of other organisations seeking to gain entry.

Illustration 5.7   strategy into action

Business–university collaboration in the creative and cultural industries

Public/private sector collaboration may bring benefits to both parties.

In 2003 the UK government set up a committee (The Lambert Committee) to report on business–university collaboration in the UK and to propose how it might be improved. The first stage was to seek ideas from a wide range of stakeholders. The following is an extract from the Arts and Humanities Research Board (AHRB), which supported work that was fundamental to a range of creative and cultural industries.

We are in the early stages of exploring a range of partnerships and possible strategic interventions (see below). In collaboration with the Department for Culture, Media and Sports (DCMS) and others, a Creative Industries/Higher Education Forum has been established. This group will seek to bring together the supply and demand side of this relationship to foster stronger links and new activities.

Creative and cultural industries: a role for creative clusters

Many universities have developed links with businesses in the creative and cultural industries . . . However, many of the companies in the creative industries are small (SMEs) . . . An organic development in recent years has been the creation of a number of 'creative clusters' bringing together local or regional HEIs with business for the generation of new ideas, products and processes. Examples exist from around the country, including, Scotland, Sheffield, London, Bristol, Nottingham. Such creative clusters supported by business enterprise and support services could provide the basis for supporting small-scale individual entrepreneurship.

Working with Regional Development Agencies (RDAs)

Both the Research Councils and RDAs are channels to their respective communities, and work has already commenced on identifying ways in which jointly they can be both a catalyst for new ideas and a facilitator of knowledge transfer. Such activities might cover individual projects, jointly-sponsored schemes, and facilitation of sector clusters, such as creative clusters.

Embedding practitioners and professionals in HEIs

Many traditional models of the relationship between HEIs and business describe a linear process in which knowledge is passed to industry. However, it can be argued that, increasingly, knowledge transfer is not a process, but an interaction based on access to people, information, data and infrastructure. In the creative and performing arts the concept of portfolio careers is not uncommon. Individuals can hold part-time research or teaching positions alongside other forms of employment or self-employment, including artistic performance. In addition, it is not uncommon for businesses and other non-private sector organisations to provide visiting professorships or lectureships.

Widening the definition of knowledge transfer in a knowledge economy

Increasingly a large number of people are trading their knowledge, expertise and experience through non-conventional employment means. However, in looking for evidence of knowledge transfer from academia to business the focus tends to be on the numbers of patents, spin-outs and companies created. These are undoubtedly important indicators to industrial performance, but a wider evidence base looking at employment patterns and self-employment would give a wider perspective.

Charting this new landscape

It is the role of bodies such as the AHRB to provide an environment that enables the ideas and creativity of the academic community to be unlocked and developed. Working with analogous bodies in other sectors, such as the RDAs, the aspiration is to find ways to improve the links out from academia to the wider society and economy.

Source: AHRB response to the Lambert Committee, ukonline.gov.uk website, 2003 © Crown Copyright 2003.

Questions

1. Look at section 5.6 and then identify the potential benefits from business–university collaboration to a number of the important stakeholders.

2. What are the risks of collaboration to each of these stakeholders (as against 'going it alone')?

● *Collaboration to gain entry and competitive power.* Organisations seeking to develop beyond their traditional boundaries (for example, geographical expansion) may need to collaborate with others to gain entry into new arenas. The only way of gaining local market knowledge may be to collaborate with local operators. Indeed, in some parts of the world, governments require entrants to collaborate in such ways. Collaboration may also be advantageous for purposes of developing required infrastructure such as distribution channels, information systems or research and development activities. It may also be needed for cultural reasons: buyers may prefer to do business with local rather than expatriate managers.

● *Collaboration to share work with customers.* An important trend in the public services is a move towards more *co-production* with clients,[15] for example self-assessment of income tax. The motives may be varied but include cost efficiency, quality/reliability improvement or increased 'ownership/responsibility' from the clients. E-commerce allows more organisations to take this approach on board. For example, websites can be designed to assist customers with self-service (the virtual shopping basket is an example) or to allow them to design/customise a product or service to their own specification (for example, when ordering a new computer or the decoration and furnishing of a room).

● In the public sector *collaboration may be required* in order to gain more leverage from public investment, to raise the overall standards of the sector or to address social issues that cross several professional fields (such as drugs or community safety). One key difference from the private sector is that sharing of knowledge and dissemination of best practice is regarded as a duty (or at least set out as a requirement). This can be difficult for managers in the era of a market-driven public sector judging their performance through benchmarking and publishing league tables. Collaborating with competitors is not as easy as it sounds. Illustration 5.7 looks at public/private sector collaboration in one sector.

5.7 GAME THEORY

Game theory is concerned with the interrelationships between the competitive moves of a set of competitors

The origins of game theory can be traced back to the study of war. **Game theory** is concerned with the interrelationships between the competitive moves of a set of competitors. The central idea is that the strategist has to anticipate the reaction of competitors. There are three core assumptions in this. First, that a competitor will behave rationally and always try to win to their own benefit. Second, that the competitor is in an interdependent relationship with other competitors. So all competitors are affected by what other competitors do; one competitor's move will galvanise response from another competitor, and the outcome of choices made by one competitor is dependent on the choices made by another. Third, that to a greater or lesser extent competitors are aware of the interdependencies that exist and of the sorts of move that competitors could take. Arguably, this is especially so within strategic groups (see section 2.4.1) where competitors are following similar strategies or have similar characteristics or where competitors are targeting the same market segments.

There are two key principles to guide the development of successful strategies of competition that flow from these assumptions:

● Strategists, as game theorists, need to put themselves in the position of the competitor or competitors. They can then take an informed, rational, view about what that competitor is likely to do and choose their best course of action in this light.

● To do this it is important to identify if there is any strategy that could be followed by a competitor that would lead to the strategist's own organisation being dominated in the market. If there is then the priority is to take the necessary steps to eliminate that strategy.

These principles seem simple enough, but the study of game theory based on them has become very complex and elaborate. Readers who wish to follow this up may wish to do so separately.[16] The practical application of game theory can have major impacts. To take a spectacular example, many of the government auctions around the world for third-generation mobile phone licences in the early 2000s were based on game theory principles. In the UK auction the revenue raised was £22 billion after more than 100 rounds of bidding.[17] In the sections below the basic assumptions and guiding principles of game theory are explained and illustrated so as to allow the reader to consider their value in developing competitive strategy.

5.7.1 Simultaneous games

A simultaneous game is where the players involved – for example, competitors – are all faced with making decisions at a point in time. Perhaps the most famous example of game theory is a simultaneous game, the Prisoner's Dilemma, represented in Exhibit 5.6. This is usually shown in terms of individuals, but here as companies, that have to choose whether or not to cooperate. Suppose, for example, that two firms dominate a market and have to decide whether to try to gain market share through spending heavily on marketing. They may know

Exhibit 5.6   A 'Prisoner's Dilemma'

		Competitor A	
		Heavy marketing spend	Low marketing spend
Competitor B	Heavy marketing spend	B = 5 A = 5	B = 12 A = 2
	Low marketing spend	B = 2 A = 12	B = 9 A = 9

that the returns from such heavy expenditure would not offset its cost. Therefore, the logical course of action would be for both parties to keep marketing expenditure at the current low level to preserve their current shares: in a sense to collude tacitly to keep the situation as it is for mutual benefit. If both players select this strategy, the pay-off to each firm is represented in the bottom right-hand quadrant of Exhibit 5.6. However, there is likely to be a temptation by one or the other competitor to try to steal an advantage over the other. Each knows that if they alone spent more on marketing they would achieve substantial returns. This is represented in the top right and bottom left quadrants. The danger is, of course, that, knowing this, both parties decide they must spend heavily on marketing to ensure that the other competitor does not get an advantage. The result is the top left quadrant which is a much worse return to both firms than would have happened had they both decided to keep marketing expenditures at the current level. The Prisoner's Dilemma model therefore suggests that the incentives open to both parties (in this case to spend heavily on marketing) may lead to a pay-off which is much worse for both.

In practice this 'lose–lose' outcome is not likely if there are a limited number of competitors, as will be seen later. But something very similar often occurs when there are many competitors jostling for position in a fragmented market. In such circumstances, whilst it might be most logical for all competitors to hold prices at a relatively high level, no one expects anyone else to do so, and price wars result.

Nonetheless, the example of the Prisoner's Dilemma illustrates some important principles. It may well be that the end result is a lesser pay-off than could logically be achieved: but it is the *dominant strategy*. A **dominant strategy** is one that outperforms all other strategies whatever rivals choose, so it makes sense to use it if it exists. In the Prisoner's Dilemma example it would be much better for cooperation to exist between the two parties. However, the fact is that if either of the competitors breaks rank on this the other one will suffer badly. So the dominant strategy is to spend heavily on marketing.

In the above example the competitors were equal – they started from the same position. However quite likely this won't be so. Competitors will have different resource bases and competences. Suppose for example that two such competitors – Innova and Dolla in the market for computer games – face a decision on investment in research and development. Suppose too that Innova has a dominant strategy and Dolla does not. If an organisation does not have a dominant strategy, it is important to identify whether it faces a **dominated strategy**, that is, a competitive strategy that, if pursued by a competitor, is bound to outperform the company. If such a dominated strategy exists, the aim should be to try to eliminate the possibility of that situation occurring. And if there is not a dominant or dominated strategy, it is necessary to look for an equilibrium. In game theory, **equilibrium** is a situation where each competitor contrives to get the best possible strategic solution for themselves given the response from the other. An example here will help.

Innova is known to have highly innovative designers but is short of the finance required to invest heavily in rapid development of products. Dolla is strong financially but relatively weak in terms of its research and design. In terms of the crucial choice of investing in research and design or not, investing heavily would

---

A **dominant strategy** is one that outperforms all other strategies whatever rivals choose

A **dominated strategy** is a competitive strategy that, if pursued by a competitor, is bound to outperform the company

In game theory, **equilibrium** is a situation where each competitor contrives to get the best possible strategic solution for themselves given the response from the other

Exhibit 5.7   A simultaneous move game

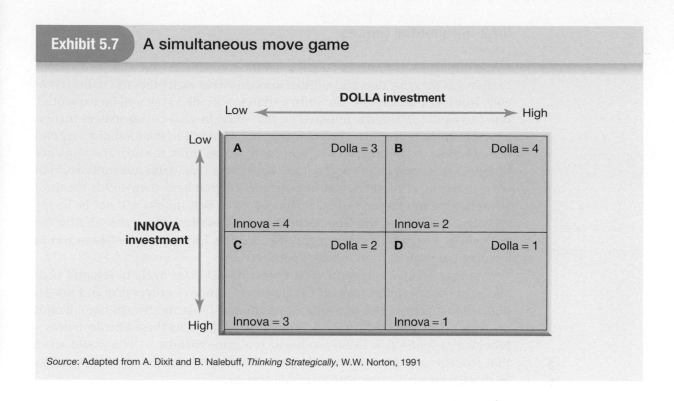

Source: Adapted from A. Dixit and B. Nalebuff, *Thinking Strategically*, W.W. Norton, 1991

shorten the development time but would incur considerable costs. These choices can be thought of in terms of the sort of matrix shown in Exhibit 5.7.

Each of the competitors probably regards high levels of investment by both as the worst outcome: Innova because its financial position is weak and it could be a risky route to follow; Dolla because if it can raise the finance, Innova has better chances of winning given its design capabilities. This is represented by a low pay-off (Box D) in Exhibit 5.7.

Innova has a dominant strategy, which is to keep its investment low. If Dolla were to invest low, Innova would get a better pay-off by also investing low (Box A). On the other hand, if Dolla were to go for a high level of investment, Innova would suffer, but not as much by keeping investment on the low side as it would if it went for a high level of investment (Box B is better than Box D for Innova).

Dolla, on the other hand, does not have a dominant strategy. However, it knows that Innova does and therefore probably expects that Innova will keep levels of investment down. Dolla also knows that if it goes for a low level of investment, it loses whether or not Innova adopts the same strategy or goes for a high level of investment (Boxes A and C). So it does not make sense for Dolla to go for a low level of investment; it is a *dominated strategy*. In the knowledge of this the likelihood is that Dolla will decide to go for high levels of investment.

This is not what Innova ideally wants – but the best it can do is follow its dominant strategy of investing low which results in the least worst pay-off – the *equilibrium* solution (Box B). It does not result in high pay-off but a high pay-off for Innova is only possible if Dolla invests low. Of course, the temptation would be to imitate Dolla but this would result in a worse pay-off.

5.7.2 Sequential games

In the simultaneous games discussed so far the competitors were making decisions or moves at the same time and without knowing what each other was doing. However, this is not usually the case since a strategic decision may well be sequential, one party making a move, followed by the other. In such circumstances there is a need to think differently. The guiding principle here is to *think forwards and then reason backwards*. In other words, start by trying to think through the sequence of moves that competitors might make based on a reasonable assumption about what that competitor desires as the outcome. On that basis then decide the most advantageous moves you can make. Indeed given that Innova will not be happy with the outcome of the simultaneous game described above considering the problem as a sequential game might help. Exhibit 5.8 sets out possible moves in a sequential manner from Innova's point of view.

If Innova decides to invest low, it knows that Dolla is likely to respond high and gain the advantage (pay-off C). However, if Innova moves first and invests high, then it places Dolla in a difficult position. If Dolla also invests high, it ends up with a low pay-off as well as Innova (pay-off A). In these circumstances – provided of course that Dolla's strategist is a game theorist – Dolla would reject that strategy as a *dominated strategy* and choose to invest low (with pay-off B). In this (sequential) game, this is the *equilibrium*.

Exhibit 5.8   **A sequential move game**

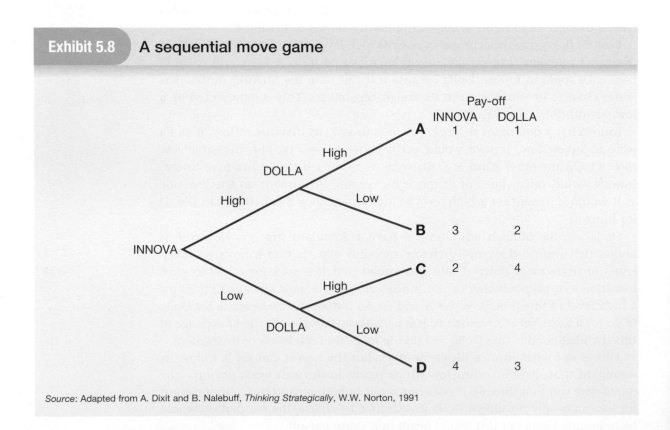

Source: Adapted from A. Dixit and B. Nalebuff, *Thinking Strategically*, W.W. Norton, 1991

By working through these different game logics, Innova comes to realise that if it waits for Dolla to make a move, it is bound to lose out; if it moves first and invests high, then it stands a chance of winning the competitive game. Of course there are risks here, not least the financial risks for Innova. There are also risks in that Dolla may not believe that Innova will really invest high; so Innova needs to recognise the importance of being credible in its move. If it appears to waver in its decision, perhaps by delaying, or by not making a substantial enough investment, very likely Dolla will invest high too and both lose out (pay-off A). Of course, if there is some way of Innova appearing to be credible in a decision to invest high, whilst actually investing low, thus persuading Dolla to invest low too, then Innova achieves its *dominant strategy* (pay-off D). So game theory is also about bluff and counter-bluff in which some important strategic lessons need to be recognised, in particular the importance of:

- identifying dominant and dominated strategies;
- the timing in strategic moves;
- the careful weighing of risk;
- establishing credibility and commitment: for example, in the illustration here Innova could not achieve its desired outcome unless it had a reputation for sticking to its decisions.

5.7.3 Repeated games[18]

The above examples ended up with both parties sub-optimising the outcome. In fact, if there were only two competitors involved this would probably be unlikely because, over time, they would learn to ensure a better outcome. In repeated games, competitors interact repeatedly and it has been shown that in such circumstances the equilibrium outcome is much more likely to favour cooperation or accommodation of both parties' best interests. This is not necessarily because of explicit collusion, but because they learn to do so through experience. The presence or absence of implicit cooperation will, however, be dependent upon a number of factors. These include:

- The *number of competitors* in a market. If it is low, there is likely to be cooperation. The greater the number of competitors the more it is likely that someone will break rank.
- If there are *small competitors* competing with larger competitors it is quite possible that the smaller competitors will gain disproportionately by breaking rank. Larger competitors may not be hurt too much by this and be prepared to tolerate it.
- Where there are *substantial differences between organisations*, for example in terms of cost structures, quality, market shares etc., cooperation is less likely, not least because the bases of competition differ.
- If there is a *lack of transparency* on bases of competition within the market, then again cooperation is difficult. For example, implicit cooperation on price is difficult in situations of tendering.

5.7.4 Changing the rules of the game

Another lesson that comes out of game theory is that, by thinking through the logic of the game, a competitor might find that they are simply not able to compete effectively within the rules as they exist. This will be especially important if that competitor needs to eliminate a dominated strategy. For example, a competitor might find that competitors are always battling it out on price and that their cost structure is such that they cannot hope to compete effectively. Or, as with the examples given here, that competition always seems to be played out on the basis of heavy marketing expenditure or heavy investment in research and development; and these are battles they cannot win. An alternative approach for a competitor who decides they cannot win on such bases is to try to change the rules of the game. For example, in a market dominated by price-based strategies, a competitor might try to shift the rules of the game towards:

- *Bases of differentiation* based on clearer identification of what customers value (see section 5.3.2 above).

- Making *pricing more transparent*, for example by trying to get published price lists established as the norm in the industry. The internet is making price information much more transparent to both customers and competitors. On the face of it, this may not seem to avoid price competition, but the principles of game theory would suggest that greater transparency is likely to encourage cooperative behaviour amongst competitors.

- Building *incentives for customer loyalty*. The growth in the use of loyalty cards in the retailing sector is a good example. The principles of differentiation suggests that this might be a weak strategy because competitors will imitate it and did. However, the pressure on competition through price can be reduced for all competitors.

Game theory does of course rely on the principle of rationality; and it may well be that competitors do not always behave rationally. However, it does provide a useful way of thinking through the logic of interactive competitive markets and, in particular, when it makes sense to compete, on what bases, and when it makes sense to cooperate.

An underlying theme in this chapter is the search for competitive advantage and the need for distinctiveness and strategies of differentiation to achieve this. The key debate in Illustration 5.8 reconsiders this theme and questions the extent to which differentiation does provide competitive advantage.

Illustration 5.8

key debate

To be different or the same?

Can differentiation strategies rebound, making an organisation seem dangerously eccentric rather than delivering competitive advantage?

This chapter has introduced the potential value of differentiation strategies, in which the organisation emphasises its uniqueness. This is consistent also with the argument of the resource-based view (Chapter 3) in favour of the distinctiveness and inimitability of an organisation's resources. But how far should an organisation push its uniqueness, especially if there is a danger of it beginning to be seen as simply eccentric?

McKinsey & Co. consultant Philipp Natterman makes a strong case for differentiation.[1] He tracks the relationship between profitability and differentiation (in terms of pricing and product features) over long periods in both the personal computer and mobile phone industries. He finds that as differentiation falls over time, so too do industry profit margins. Natterman blames management techniques such as benchmarking (Chapter 3), which tend to encourage convergence on industry 'best practices'. The trouble with best practices is that they easily become standard practices. There is no competitive advantage in following the herd.

However, 'institutional theorists' such as Paul DiMaggio and Water Powell point to some advantages in herd-like behaviour.[2] They think of industries as 'organisational fields' in which all sorts of actors must interact – customers, suppliers, employees and regulators. The ability of these actors to interact effectively depends upon being legitimate in the eyes of other actors in the field. Over time, industries develop institutionalised norms of legitimate behaviour, which it makes sense for everybody to follow. It is easier for customers and suppliers to do business with organisations that are more or less the same as the others in the industry. It is reassuring to potential employees and industry regulators if organisations do not seem highly eccentric. Especially when there is high uncertainty about what drives performance – for example, in knowledge-based industries – it can be a lot better to be legitimate than different. To the extent that customers, suppliers, employees and regulators value conformity, then it is valuable in itself. Being a 'misfit' can be costly.

This institutionalist appreciation of conformity makes sense of a lot of strategic behaviour. For example, merger waves in some industries seem to driven by bandwagons, in which organisations become panicked into making acquisitions simply for fear of being left behind. Likewise, many management initiatives, such as business process re-engineering, e-business or outsourcing, are the product of fads and fashions as much as hard objective analysis. The insight from institutionalist theory, however, is that following the fashion is not necessarily a bad thing.

Thus institutional theory and the resource-based view appear to have opposing perspectives on the value of differentiation. David Deephouse has investigated this apparent trade-off between differentiation and conformity in the American banking industry and found a curvilinear relationship between differentiation and financial performance.[3] Strong conformity led to inferior performance; moderate differentiation was associated with improved performance; extreme differentiation appeared to damage performance.

Deephouse concludes in favour of 'balance' between differentiation and conformity. He also suggests that the value of differentiation depends on the extent to which key actors in the industry – customers, suppliers, employees and so on – have converged on institutionalised norms of appropriate strategy. It seems that strategies can be too differentiated, but that how much 'too differentiated' is depends on the kind of industry that one is in.

Sources:
1. P.M. Natterman, 'Best practice does not equal best strategy', *McKinsey Quarterly*, no. 2 (2000), pp. 22–31.
2. P. DiMaggio and W. Powell, 'The iron cage revisited: Institutional isomorphism and collective rationality in organizational fields', *American Sociological Review*, vol. 48 (1983), pp. 147–160.
3. D. Deephouse, 'To be different or to be the same? It's a question (and theory) of strategic balance', *Strategic Management Journal*, vol. 20 (1999), pp. 147–166.

Questions

1. To what extent do (a) universities, (b) car manufacturers compete by being different or the same?

2. Considering the nature of their industries, and key actors within them, why might these organisations adopt these approaches to conformity or differentiation?

Summary

- Business-level strategy is about competing better or, in the public services, providing best value services. Organisations consist of a number of strategic business units (SBUs) and business-level strategy needs to be developed for each of these SBUs. So identifying an organisation's SBUs is an important prerequisite to developing business-level strategic choices.

- Generic (market-facing) choices of strategies to achieve *competitive advantage* include:

  - A *'no frills'* strategy, combining low price and low perceived added value.

  - A *low-price* strategy providing lower price than competitors at similar added value of product or service to competitors.

  - A *differentiation* strategy, which seeks to provide products or services which are unique or different from competitors.

  - A *hybrid* strategy, which seeks simultaneously to achieve differentiation and prices lower than competitors.

  - A *focused differentiation* strategy, which seeks to provide high perceived value justifying a substantial price premium.

- Sustaining bases of competitive advantage is likely to require a linked set of organisational competences which competitors find difficult to imitate and/or the ability to achieve a 'lock-in' position to becoming the 'industry standard' recognised by suppliers and buyers.

- In hypercompetitive conditions sustainable competitive advantage is difficult to achieve. Speed, flexibility, innovation and the willingness to change successful strategies are important bases of competitive success. In such circumstances the competences of the organisation required for success are likely to be found in organisational cultures and structures.

- Strategies of collaboration may offer alternatives to competitive strategies or may run in parallel.

- Game theory provides a basis for thinking through competitors' strategic moves in such a way as to pre-empt or counter them.

Recommended key readings

- The foundations of the discussions of generic competitive strategies are to be found in the writings of Michael Porter, which include *Competitive Strategy* (1980) and *Competitive Advantage* (1985), both published by Free Press. Both are recommended for readers who wish to understand the background to discussions in sections 5.3 and 5.4 of this chapter on competitive strategy and competitive advantage.

- Hypercompetition, and the strategies associated with such conditions, are explained in Richard D'Aveni, *Hypercompetitive Rivalries: Competing in highly dynamic environments*, Free Press, 1995.

- A useful book on collaborative strategies is: Y. Doz and G. Hamel, *Alliance Advantage: The art of creating value through partnering*, Harvard Business School Press, 1998.

- There is much written on game theory but a good deal of it can be rather inaccessible to the lay reader. An exception is the book by A.K. Dixit and B.J. Nalebuff, *Thinking Strategically*, W.W. Norton, 1991.

References

1. For a detailed discussion as to how organisational structures might 'address' an organisation's mix of SBUs see: M. Goold and A. Campbell, *Designing Effective Organisations: How to create structured networks*, Jossey Bass, 2002; K. Eisenhardt and S. Brown, 'Patching', *Harvard Business Review*, vol. 77, no. 3 (1999), p. 72.

2. M. Porter, *Competitive Advantage*, Free Press, 1985.

3. D. Faulkner and C. Bowman, *The Essence of Competitive Strategy*, Prentice Hall, 1995. A similar framework is also used by Richard D'Aveni, *Hypercompetitive Rivalries: Competing in highly dynamic environments*, Free Press, 1995.

4. B. Sharp and J. Dawes, 'What is differentiation and how does it work?', *Journal of Marketing Management*, vol. 17, no. 7/8 (2001), pp. 739–759 reviews the relationship between differentiation and profitability.

5. See, for example: D. Miller, 'The generic strategy trap', *Journal of Business Strategy*, vol. 13, no. 1 (1992), pp. 37–42; and C.W.L. Hill, 'Differentiation versus low cost or differentiation and low cost': a contingency framework', *Academy of Management Review*, vol. 13, no. 3 (1998), pp. 401–412.

6. See G. Hamel and C.K. Prahalad, 'Do you really have a global strategy?', *Harvard Business Review*, vol. 63, no. 4 (1985), pp. 139–148.

7. For a detailed discussion of price wars see: A. Rao, M. Bergen and S. Davis, 'How to fight a price war', *Harvard Business Review*, vol. 78, no. 2 (2000), pp. 107–115.

8. Cost advantage is discussed in R. Grant, *Contemporary Strategy Analysis*, 4th edition, Blackwell, 2002, Chapter 8.

9. These quotes concerning Porter's three competitive strategies are taken from his book *Competitive Advantage*, Free Press, 1985, pp. 12–15.

10. There is much written on the issue of sustainability of competitive advantage. For an early contribution see C.K. Prahalad and G. Hamel, 'The core competence of the corporation', *Harvard Business Review*, May–June, 1990. Also see

D. Collis and C. Montgomery, 'Competing on resources: strategy in the 1990s', *Harvard Business Review*, July–August, 1995.

11. The Delta Model is explained and illustrated more fully in A.C. Hax and D.L. Wilde II, 'The Delta Model', *Sloan Management Review*, vol. 40, no. 2 (1999), pp. 11–28.

12. This section is based on the work of Richard D'Aveni, *Hypercompetitive Rivalries: Competing in highly dynamic environments*, Free Press, 1995. For readers who want to read more on the topic, there is a special edition of *Organization Science* (vol. 7, no. 3, 1996) devoted to it.

13. This is the radical conclusion reached by D'Aveni (see reference 12 above).

14. Useful books on collaborative strategies are: Y. Doz and G. Hamel, *Alliance Advantage: The art of creating value through partnering*, Harvard Business School Press, 1998; *Creating Collaborative Advantage*, ed. Chris Huxham, Sage Publications, 1996 and D. Faulkner, *Strategic Alliances: Co-operating to compete*, McGraw-Hill, 1995.

15. See: J. Brudney and R. England, 'Towards a definition of the co-production concept', *Public Administration Review*, vol. 43, no. 10 (1983), pp. 59–65, and J. Alford, 'A public management road less travelled: clients as co-producers of public services', *Australian Journal of Public Administration*, vol. 57, no. 4 (1998), pp. 128–137.

16. For readings on game theory see: A.K. Dixit and B.J. Nalebuff, *Thinking Strategically*, W.W. Norton, 1991; A. Brandenburger and B. Nalebuff, *Co-opetition*, Profile Books, 1997 and J. McMillan, *Games, Strategies and Managers*, Oxford University Press, 1992.

17. A specialist in the field of auction design is Paul Klemperer of Oxford University. Material related to the subject can be accessed on his website: www.nuff.ox.ac.uk/economics/people/klemperer.htm

18. To understand more on repeated games, see R. Axelrod, *The Evolution of Cooperation*, Penguin, 1990.

An extensive range of additional materials, including audio summaries, weblinks to organisations featured in the text, definitions of key concepts and multiple choice questions, can be found on the *Exploring Corporate Strategy* Companion Website at **www.pearsoned.co.uk/ecs7**

WORK ASSIGNMENTS

✱ Denotes more advanced work assignments.   * Refers to a case study in the Text and Case edition.

5.1 Using Exhibit 5.2, the strategy clock, identify examples of organisations following strategic routes 1 to 5. If you find it difficult to be clear about which route is being followed, note down the reasons for this, and consider if the organisations have a clear competitive strategy.

5.2✱ Michael Porter argues that a business must have a clear competitive strategy. Assess the extent to which any, or all, of the following have a clear competitive strategy:
  (a) Barclaycard*
  (b) Marks & Spencer* (throughout its existence)
  (c) an organisation of your choice.

5.3 You have been appointed personal assistant to the chief executive of a major manufacturing firm, who has asked you to explain what is meant by 'differentiation' and why it is important. Write a brief report addressing these questions.

5.4✱ How appropriate are bases of competitive advantage explained in section 5.3 for considering the strategies of public sector organisations? Illustrate your argument by reference to a public sector organisation of your choice.

5.5 Applying the lessons from section 5.4, consider how sustainable are the strategies of any of:
  (a) Ryanair*
  (b) Thorntons*
  (c) an organisation of your choice.

5.6 Discuss the view that hypercompetitive conditions and hypercompetitive strategies are relevant in only a few industries or sectors.

5.7✱ Choose an industry or sector which is becoming more and more competitive (e.g. financial services or fashion retailing). How might the principles of hypercompetitive strategies apply to that industry?

5.8 Drawing on sections 5.6 (on collaborative strategies) write a report for the chief executive of a business in a competitive market (e.g. pharmaceuticals* or Formula One*) explaining when and in what ways cooperation rather than direct competition might make sense.

5.9✱ Follow up the key reading on game theory (Dixit and Nalebuff). To what extent and how do you consider game theory approaches useful in developing competitive strategy for organisations?

Integrative assignments

5.10 Use examples to show how organisations might develop core competences (Chapter 3) to gain competitive advantage through either a low price or a differentiation strategy. Explain how a determined competitor might be able to undermine this advantage by using IT to destroy core competences (Chapter 9).

5.11 Refer to section 5.4.3 and Exhibit 5.3. If the achievement of 'lock-in' was to be the basis of an international strategy (Chapter 6) explain how this might influence the choices around both the direction and methods of strategy development (Chapter 7).

CASE EXAMPLE

Madonna: still the reigning queen of pop?

Phyl Johnson, Graduate School of Business, University of Strathclyde

The music industry is full of one-hit wonders and brief careers. Pop stars that remain at the top for decades are very few. Madonna is one such phenomenon; the question is, after over twenty years at the top, how much longer can it last?

Described by billboard magazine as the smartest business woman in show business, Madonna, Louise Ciccone, began her music career in 1983 with the hit single 'Holiday' and in 2003 once again enjoyed reasonable chart success for her album 'American Life'. In the meantime she had consistent chart success with her singles and albums, sell-out world tours, major roles in six films, picked up eighteen music awards, been the style icon behind a range of products from Pepsi and Max Factor to the Gap and became a worldwide best-selling children's author.

The foundation of Madonna's business success was her ability to sustain her reign as the 'queen of pop' since 1983. Along with many others, Phil Quattro, the President of Warner Brothers, has argued that 'she always manages to land on the cusp of what we call contemporary music, every established artist faces the dilemma of maintaining their importance and relevance, Madonna never fails to be relevant.' Madonna's chameleon-like ability to change persona, change her music genre with it and yet still achieve major record sales has been the hallmark of her success.

Madonna's early poppy style was targeted at young 'wannabe' girls. The image that she portrayed through hits such as 'Holiday' and 'Lucky Star' in 1983 was picked up by Macy's, the US-based department store. It produced a range of Madonna-lookalike clothes that mothers were happy to purchase for their daughters. One year later in 1984, Madonna then underwent her first image change and, in doing so, offered the first hint of the smart cookie behind the media image. In the video for her hit 'Material Girl', she deliberately mirrored the glamour-based, sexual pussycat image of Marilyn Monroe whilst simultaneously mocking both the growing materialism of the late 1980s and the men fawning after her. Media analysts Sam and Diana Kirschner com-

Photo: © Rune Hellestad/Corbis

mented that with this kind of packaging, Madonna allowed the record companies to keep hold of a saleable 'Marilyn image' for a new cohort of fans, but also allowed her original fan base of now growing-up wannabe girls to take the more critical message from the music. The theme of courting controversy but staying marketable enough has been recurrent throughout her career, if slightly toned down in later years.

Madonna's subsequent image changes were more dramatic. First she took on the Catholic Church in her 1989 video 'Like a Prayer' where, as a red-dressed 'sinner', she kissed a black saint easily interpreted as a Jesus figure. Her image had become increasingly sexual whilst also holding on to a critical social theme: e.g. her pointed illustration of white-only imagery in the Catholic Church. At this point in her career, Madonna took full control of her image in the $60m (€52m) deal with Time-Warner that created

Releases	Year	Image	Target Audience
Lucky Star	1982	Trashy pop	Young wannabe girls, dovetailing from fading disco to emerging 'club scene'
Like a Virgin Like a Prayer	1984	Originally a Marilyn glamour image, then became a Saint & Sinner	More grown-up, rebellious fan base, more critical female audience and male worshippers
Vogue Erotica Bedtime Stories	1990 1992 1994	Erotic porn star, sadomasochistic, sexual control, more Minnelli in *Cabaret* than Monroe	Peculiar mix of target audiences: gay club scene, 90s women taking control of their own lives, also pure male titillation
Something to Remember Evita	1995	Softer image, ballads preparing for glamour image of *Evita* film role	Broadest audience target, picking up potential film audiences as well as regular fan base. Most conventional image. Max Factor later used this mixture of Marilyn and Eva Peron to market their glamour image
Ray of Light	1998	Earth mother, eastern mysticism, dance music fusion	Clubbing generation of the 90s, new cohort of fans plus original fan base of now 30-somethings desperately staying trendy
Music	2000	Acid rock, tongue in cheek Miss USA/cow girl, cool Britannia	Managing to hit the changing club scene and 30-something Brits
American Life	2003	Militaristic image Che Guevara Anti-consumerism of American dream	Unclear audience reliant on existing base

her record company Maverick. In 1991, she published a coffee-table soft porn book entitled 'Sex' that exclusively featured pictures of herself in erotic poses. Her image and music also reflected this erotic theme. In her 'Girlie' tour, her singles 'Erotica' and 'Justify my Love' and her fly-on-the-wall movie 'In bed with Madonna' she played out scenes of sadomasochistic and lesbian fantasies. Although allegedly a period of her career she would rather forget, Madonna more than survived it. In fact, she gained a whole new demography of fans who not only respected her artistic courage, but also did not miss the fact that Madonna was consistent in her message: her sexuality was her own and not in need of a male gaze. She used the media's love affair with her, and the *cause célèbre* status gained from having MTV ban the video for 'Justify my Love', to promote the message that women's sexuality and freedom is just as important and acceptable as men's.

Changing gear in 1996, Madonna finally took centre stage in the lead role in the film *Evita* that she had chased for over five years. She beat other heavyweight contenders for the role including Meryl Streep and Elaine Page, both with more acceptable pasts than Madonna. Yet she achieved the image transition from erotica to saint-like persona of Eva Peron and won critical acclaim to boot. Another vote of confidence from the 'establishment' came from Max Factor, who in 1999 signed her up to front their re-launch campaign that was crafted around a glamour theme. Proctor and Gamble (owners of the Max Factor make-up range) argued that it saw Madonna as 'the closest thing the 90s has to an old-style Hollywood star . . . she is a real woman'.

With many pre-release leaks, Madonna's keenly awaited album 'Ray of Light' was released in 1998. Radio stations worldwide were desperate to get hold of the album being billed as her most successful musical voyage to date. In a smart move, Madonna had teamed up with techno pioneer William Orbit to write and produce the album. It was a huge success, taking Madonna into the super-trendy techno sphere, not the natural environment for a pop star from the early 80s. Madonna took up an 'earth mother/spiritual' image and spawned a trend for all things eastern in fashion and music. This phase may have produced more than just an image, as it is the time in Madonna's life where she locates the beginning of her continued faith in the Kabbalah tradition of eastern spiritual worship.

By 2001, her next persona was unveiled with the release of her album 'Music'. Here her style had moved on again to 'acid rock'. With her marriage to British movie director Guy Ritchie, the ultimate 'American Pie' had become a fully-fledged Brit babe, even earning the endearing nickname of 'Madge' in the British press.

However, by 2003 some commentators were suggesting that an interesting turn of events hinted that perhaps Madonna 'the cutting edge', Madonna 'the fearless', was starting to think about *being part of* rather than *beating* the establishment. Still in recovery from the flop of her movie *Swept Away* (directed by her husband), Madonna launched her new Che Guevara-inspired image. Instead of maximising the potential of this image in terms of its political and social symbolism during the Gulf War, in April 2003 she withdrew her militaristic image and video for the album 'American Life'. Her press release expressed her wish to be sensitive and not risk offence in light of the armed combat under way in Iraq. She then moved on to publish her Kabbalah-inspired children's fiction in summer 2003. *The English Roses*, based on the themes of compassion and friendship, became an immediate best-seller. Questions in the press revolved around the theme 'Has Madonna gone soft?'

Subsequent evidence could have suggested that, no, Madonna hadn't gone soft at all and that after a temporary blip, she's solidly a material girl at heart after all. By late 2003 she'd wiped the military image from the West's collective memory with a glitzy high profile ad campaign for Gap, the clothing retailer, in which she danced around accompanied by rapper Missy Elliot to a retrospective re-mix of her 1980s

track 'Get into the Grove'. Here Madonna was keeping the 'thirty-somethings' who remembered the track from first time around happily purchasing jeans for themselves and their newly teenage daughters, whilst also purchasing the re-released CD (on sale in store) for them to share and a copy of *The English Roses* (also promoted in the Gap stores) for perhaps the youngest member of the family. Madonna was managing to cover all the demographics in a one-stop shop. But Madonna the rebel was still around for a new generation of music fans. After snogging Britney Spears and Christina Aguilera live on stage at the MTV music awards in autumn 2003 and starring in strongly suggestive lesbian scenes in Britney's new video, Madge was back on the front pages for all the right record-selling reasons. However, the interesting question being asked was, can a mellower Madonna really still pull in the record sales with a younger generation of fans who don't know her rebellious past and to whom a Britney-Kiss doesn't raise much of an eyebrow?

Sources: 'Bennett takes the reins at Maverick', *Billboard Magazine*, 7 August 1999; 'Warner Bros expects Madonna to light up international markets', *Billboard Magazine*, 21 February 1998; 'Maverick builds on early success', *Billboard Magazine*, 12 November 1994; A. Jardine, 'Max Factor strikes gold with Madonna', *Marketing*, vol. 29 (1999), pp. 14–15; Kirschner, S. and Kirschner, D. 'MTV, adolescence and Madonna: a discourse analysis', in *Perspectives on Psychology and the Media*, American Psychological Association, Washington, DC, 1997; 'Warner to buy out maverick co-founder', *Los Angeles Times*, 2 March 1999; Why Madonna is back in Vogue', *New Statesman*, 18 September 2000; 'Madonna & Microsoft', *The Financial Times*, 28 November 2000.

Questions

1. Describe and explain the strategy being followed by Madonna in terms of the explanation of competitive strategy given in Chapter 5.

2. Why has she experienced sustained success over the past two decades?

3. What might threaten the sustainability of her success?

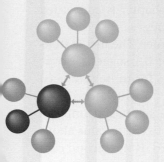

6

Corporate-Level and International Strategy

Learning outcomes

After reading this chapter you should be able to:

● Understand why organisations might increase their product and geographic diversity.

● Understand what is meant by related and unrelated diversification.

● Explain factors that organisations might consider in comparing the attractiveness of different geographic markets and locations of elements of their value chain internationally.

● Understand the difference between multi-domestic and global strategies.

● Explain how different extents of product and geographic diversity might affect performance.

● Explain the different rationales for value creation of corporate parents.

● Explain different frameworks for managing corporate portfolios.

Photo: Jeffrey Taberner

Photo: Jeffrey Taberner

Photo: Getty Images

6.1 INTRODUCTION

Chapter 5 was concerned with how value might be created as business units interact with customers in their markets. However, many organisations comprise many such units and operate across many markets. This chapter is concerned with the challenges managers face in dealing with these issues.

In this context, there are two central concerns in the chapter. The first is strategic decisions about the *scope of an organisation*. As Exhibit 6.1 suggests, scope decisions are about the *diversity of products* (and the markets for those products) and the *international or geographic diversity* of the business units in a corporate portfolio. These are important decisions because they raise significant implications about how such scope and diversity are to be managed to create value above and beyond that created at the business unit level. This, then, is the second central concern of the chapter: how is *value added* (or destroyed) *at the corporate level* as distinct from the business level in organisations? This requires an understanding of the different *parenting roles* the corporate level might play and how it might seek to *manage its portfolio* of interests.

The focus is, then, on corporate-level, as distinct from business-level strategy. Here the view is that anything above the business-unit level represents corporate-level activity and is the subject of the discussion in this chapter. Exhibit 6.2 represents a simplified multi-business company structure. It shows a number of business units grouped within divisions and above those a corporate centre. Above the business units, managers are usually providing services and, quite

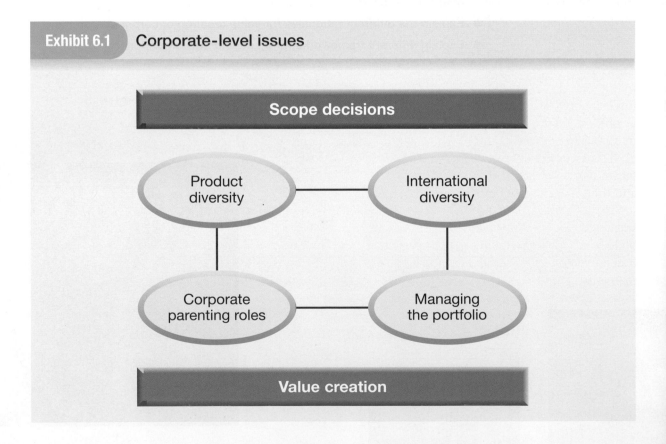

Exhibit 6.1   **Corporate-level issues**

| Exhibit 6.2 | The multi-business organisation |

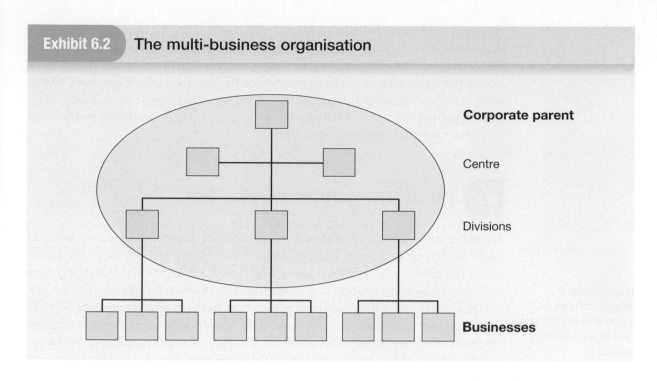

likely, strategic guidance to business units as well as acting to control or coordinate business-level activities. They will also take decisions that may affect many business units; for example, which to invest in and which not to invest in; and sometimes which to divest. In all these roles they are, at least in theory, seeking to add value to that created at the business-unit level.

In this chapter these levels of management above that of business units are referred to as the **corporate parent**. So, a corporate centre or the divisions within a corporation which look after several business units act in a corporate parenting role. Of course it could be that there are parts of the corporate centre that do interact with customers: a central call centre or a customer service department in a commercial organisation; or a special crime squad or specialist helicopter unit in a police force, for example. But where this is the case the same lessons apply as discussed in Chapter 5 relating to the development of customer-facing business-level strategy. This chapter is concerned with corporate-level strategy and therefore the corporate parenting role.

The **corporate parent** refers to the levels of management above that of the business units and therefore without direct interaction with buyers and competitors

This discussion does not only relate to large conglomerate businesses. Even small businesses may consist of a number of business units. For example, a local builder may be undertaking contract work for local government, work for industrial buyers and for local homeowners. Not only are these different market segments, but the mode of operation and capabilities required for competitive success are also likely to be different. Moreover, the owner of that business has to take decisions about the extent of investment and activity in each segment. Public sector organisations such as local government or health services also provide different services, which correspond to business units in commercial organisations. So corporate-level strategy is relevant to them too.

The discussion on corporate-level strategy in this chapter begins in section 6.2 by considering issues of scope related to *product/market diversity* in terms of the extent of relatedness and unrelatedness of the portfolio and the effects of this on corporate performance. Section 6.3 then discusses scope in terms of the *international diversity* of organisations; and again the effects of this on performance. In the context of these discussions of scope, section 6.4 turns to the question of how a corporate parent might or might not be able to *create* or *add value* to the business units within it through different *corporate parenting roles* it might play. Finally section 6.5 explains the logic of different ways of *managing portfolios* of businesses within diversified organisations.

6.2 PRODUCT/MARKET DIVERSITY

Diversification is a strategy that takes the organisation into both new markets and products or services

An underpinning issue related to how a corporate parent may or may not add value to that created by its business units is the extent and nature of the diversity of the products or services it offers. The concern here, then, is with the nature of the diversification strategy it is following. **Diversification** is typically defined as a strategy which takes the organisation into new markets and products or services and therefore increases the diversity that a corporate parent must oversee. Diversification might be undertaken for a variety of reasons, some more value-creating than others. Three potentially value-creating reasons for diversification are as follows.

First, there may be efficiency gains from applying the organisation's existing resources or capabilities to new markets and products or services. These are often described as *economies of scope*, by contrast to economies of scale.[1] If an organisation has under-utilised resources or capabilities that it cannot effectively close or dispose of to other potential users, it can make sense to use these resources or capabilities by diversification into a new activity. In other words, there are economies to be gained by extending the scope of the organisation's activities. For example, many universities have large resources in terms of halls of residence, which they must have for their students but which are under-utilised out of term-time. These halls of residence are more efficiently used if the universities expand the scope of their activities into conferencing and tourism during vacation periods. Likewise, there are economies of scope to be had for cable television companies if they use their expensive but high-capacity networks for telephone services as well. Economies of scope may apply to both tangible resources, such as halls of residence or cable networks, and intangible resources and capabilities, such as brands or skills. Sometimes these scope benefits are referred to as the benefits of **synergy**,[2] by which is meant the benefits that might be gained where activities or processes complement each other such that their combined effect is greater than the sum of the parts. Illustration 6.1 shows how a French company, Zodiac, has diversified following this approach.

Synergy refers to the benefits that might be gained where activities or processes complement each other such that their combined effect is greater than the sum of the parts

Second, there may also be gains from applying *corporate managerial capabilities* to new markets and products and services. In a sense, this extends the point above, but highlights skills that can easily be neglected. At the corporate parent level, managers may develop a capability to manage a range of different products and services which, although they do not share resources at the operational unit level, do draw on similar kinds of overall corporate managerial skills. Prahalad and Bettis have described this set of corporate skills as the 'dominant

Illustration 6.1   strategy into action

Zodiac: inflatable diversifications

An organisation may seek the benefits of synergies by building a portfolio of businesses through related diversification.

The Zodiac company was founded near Paris, France, in 1896 by Maurice Mallet just after his first hot-air balloon ascent. For 40 years, Zodiac manufactured only dirigible airships. In 1937, the German Zeppelin *Hindenburg* crashed near New York, which abruptly stopped the development of the market for airships. Because of the extinction of its traditional activity, Zodiac decided to leverage its technical expertise and moved from dirigibles to inflatable boats. This diversification proved to be very successful: in 2004, with over one million units sold in 50 years, the Zodiac rubber dinghy (priced at approximately €10,000) was extremely popular worldwide.

However, because of increasing competition, especially from Italian manufacturers, Zodiac diversified its business interests. In 1978, it took over Aerazur, a company specialising in parachutes, but also in life vests and inflatable life rafts. These products had strong market and technical synergies with rubber boats and their main customers were aircraft manufacturers. Zodiac confirmed this move to a new market in 1987 by the takeover of Air Cruisers, a manufacturer of inflatable escape slides for airplanes. As a consequence, Zodiac became a key supplier to Boeing, McDonnel Douglas and Airbus. Zodiac strengthened this position through the takeover of the two leading manufacturers of airplane seats: Sicma Aero Seats from France and Weber Aircraft from the USA. In 1997, Zodiac also took over, for €150m, MAG Aerospace, the world leader for aircraft vacuum waste systems. Finally, in 1999, Zodiac took over Intertechnique, a leading player in active components for aircraft (fuel circulation, hydraulics, oxygen and life support, electrical power, flight-deck controls and displays, systems monitoring, etc.). By combining these competences with its traditional expertise in inflatable products, Zodiac launched a new business unit: airbags for the automobile industry.

In parallel to these diversifications, Zodiac strengthened its position in inflatable boats by the takeover of several competitors: Bombard-L'Angevinière in 1980, Sevylor in 1981, Hurricane and Metzeler in 1987.

Finally, Zodiac developed a swimming-pool business. The first product line, back in 1981, was based on inflatable structure technology, and Zodiac later moved – again through takeovers – to rigid aboveground pools, modular in-ground pools, pool cleaners and water purification systems, inflatable beach gear and air mattresses.

In 2003, total sales of the Zodiac group reached €1.48bn with a net profit of €115m. Zodiac was a very international company, with a strong presence in the USA. It was listed on the Paris stock exchange and rumours of takeovers from powerful US groups were frequent. However, the family of the founder, institutional investors, the management and the employees together held 55 per cent of the stocks.

Far above the marine and the leisure businesses, aircraft products accounted for almost 75 per cent of the total turnover of the group. Zodiac held a 40 per cent market share of the world market for some airline equipment: for instance, the electrical power systems of the new Airbus A380 were Zodiac products. In 2004, Zodiac even reached Mars: NASA Mars probes *Spirit* and *Opportunity* were equipped with Zodiac equipment, developed by its US subsidiary Pioneer Aerospace.

Prepared by Frédéric Fréry, ESCP-EAP European School of Management.

Questions

1. What were the bases of the synergies underlying each of Zodiac's diversifications?

2. What are the advantages and potential dangers of such a basis of diversification?

general management logic', or 'dominant logic' for short.[3] Corporate managers can still add value to businesses that are distinct operationally – using different technologies, distribution channels or brands, for instance – so long as they require similar parenting skills. The acquisitive French conglomerate LVMH built up by Bernard Arnault includes a wide range of businesses – from champagne, through fashion and perfumes, to financial media – that share very few operational resources or capabilities, but which all require the nurturing of their individual brands and the highly idiosyncratic skills of their creative people. Arnault is able to create value for the specialised companies he bought by adding his skills in parenting such businesses to the operational advantages that they already had.

Third, having a diverse range of products or services can *increase market power*. With a diverse range of products or services, an organisation can afford to cross-subsidise one product from the surpluses earned by another, in a way that competitors may not be able to. This can give an organisation a competitive advantage for the subsidised product, and the long-run effect may be to drive out other competitors, leaving the organisation with a monopoly from which good profits can then be earned. While profitable for the organisation, this may be less good for consumers. This was the reasoning behind the European Commission's refusal to allow General Electric's $43bn (€37bn) bid for electronic controls company Honeywell in 2001.[4] General Electric might be able to bundle its jet engines with Honeywell's aviation electronics in a cheaper package than rival jet engine manufacturers United Technologies and Rolls-Royce could possibly match. As aircraft manufacturers and airlines increasingly chose the cheaper overall package, the European Commission feared that United Technologies and Rolls-Royce would eventually be driven out of business, leaving General Electric able to put up its prices again without threat from competition.

There are several other reasons that are often given for diversification, but which are less obviously value-creating and sometimes serve managerial interests more than shareholders'.

Organisations often *diversify to respond to environmental change*. Sometimes this can be justified at least for defending existing value, for instance where markets or technologies are converging. For instance, Microsoft has invested enormously in developing its XBox electronic games package ($500m (€415m) in marketing alone), as it sees increasingly sophisticated games machines as potentially encroaching on its traditional domain of computing.[5] However, sometimes diversification out of declining markets into growth markets is motivated more by corporate managers wanting to save their jobs. When during the 1980s American oil companies responded to declining growth by acquiring new businesses in high-tech areas such as computing, they were straying far from their dominant logic and ended up destroying a great deal of value. In this case, it might have been more profitable for shareholders if the managers had simply let their oil businesses decline gracefully, even if it meant that there would be fewer jobs for them.

Organisations might *diversify in order to spread risk* across a range of businesses. Conventional finance theory is very sceptical about risk as a driver for diversification. It argues that investors can diversify more effectively themselves by investing in a diverse portfolio of companies. While managers might like the security of a diverse range of businesses, investors do not need each of the companies they invest in to be diversified as well; they would prefer managers to concentrate on managing their core business as well as they can. However, this logic might not apply so well to private businesses, where the owners have a large proportion of their assets tied up in the business and cannot diversify their investment easily. For private businesses, it can make sense to diversify risk across a number of distinct activities, so that if one part is in trouble, the whole business is not pulled down.

Organisations sometimes diversify because of the *expectations of powerful stakeholders*, including top managers. Under pressure from Wall Street analysts to deliver continued revenue growth, in the late 1990s the US energy company Enron diversified beyond its original interest in energy trading into trading commodities such as petrochemicals, aluminium and even bandwidth.[6] By satisfying the analysts in the short term, this strategy boosted the share price and allowed top management to stay in place, while privately selling their shares at over-inflated prices. However, it soon transpired that very little of this diversification had been profitable, and in 2001 Enron collapsed in the largest bankruptcy in history.

In order to decide whether or not such reasons make sense and help organisational performance, it is important to be clear about different forms of diversification, in particular the degree of relatedness (or unrelatedness) of business units in a portfolio. The next sections consider related and unrelated diversification.

6.2.1 Related diversification

Related diversification can be defined as strategy development beyond current products and markets, but within the capabilities or value network of the organisation (see sections 3.4 and 3.6.1). For example, Procter and Gamble and Unilever are diversified corporations, but virtually all of their interests are in fast-moving consumer goods distributed to retailers, and increasingly in building global brands in that arena. They therefore benefit from capabilities in research and development, consumer marketing, building relationships with powerful retailers and global brand development.

Drawing on the idea of the value network, one way of thinking of different forms of related diversification is shown in Exhibit 6.3:

- **Vertical integration** describes either backward or forward integration into adjacent activities in the value network. **Backward integration** refers to development into activities concerned with the inputs into the company's current business (i.e. they are further back in the value system). For example, raw materials, machinery and labour are all important inputs into a manufacturing company, so the acquisition by a car manufacturer of a component manufacturer would be related diversification through backward integration. **Forward integration** refers to development into activities which are concerned with a company's outputs (i.e. are further forward in the value system), such as transport, distribution, repairs and servicing.

- **Horizontal integration** is development into activities which are complementary to present activities. For example, many organisations have realised that there are

Related diversification is strategy development beyond current products and markets, but within the capabilities or value network of the organisation

Vertical integration is backward or forward integration into adjacent activities in the value network

Backward integration is development into activities concerned with the inputs into the company's current business

Forward integration is development into activities which are concerned with a company's outputs

Horizontal integration is development into activities which are complementary to present activities

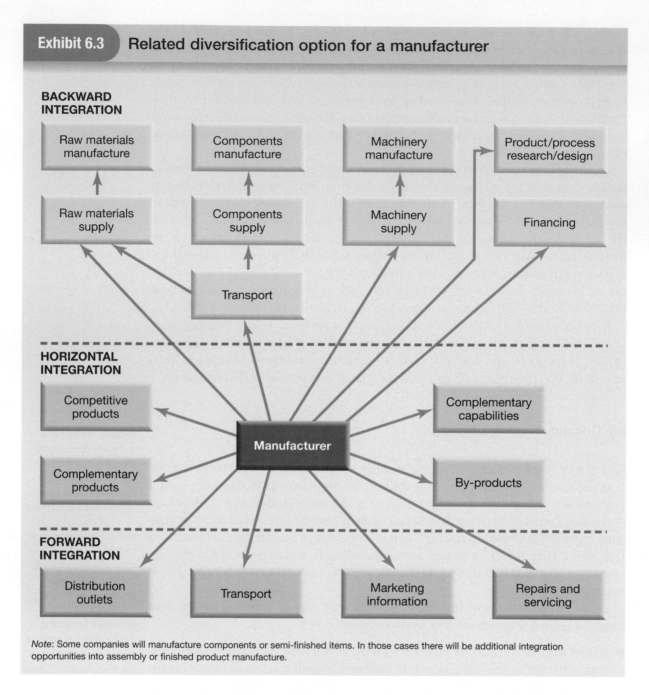

Exhibit 6.3 **Related diversification option for a manufacturer**

BACKWARD INTEGRATION

Raw materials manufacture

Components manufacture

Machinery manufacture

Product/process research/design

Raw materials supply

Components supply

Machinery supply

Financing

Transport

HORIZONTAL INTEGRATION

Competitive products

Complementary capabilities

Manufacturer

Complementary products

By-products

FORWARD INTEGRATION

Distribution outlets

Transport

Marketing information

Repairs and servicing

Note: Some companies will manufacture components or semi-finished items. In those cases there will be additional integration opportunities into assembly or finished product manufacture.

opportunities in other markets for the exploitation of the organisation's strategic capabilities – perhaps to displace the current providers as a new entrant. For example, the Automobile Association (AA) was founded as a members' club for motorists in the UK and extended into providing rescue services for breakdowns. As this market came under attack from specialist breakdown organisations, the AA extended into new markets by exploiting its expertise in rapid response to crisis. It launched a home service for electrical and plumbing emergencies, a development pioneered by similar motoring organisations in Australia. Other organisations have seen opportunities to diversify into what they see as complementary products and services (again for example, Zodiac – see Illustration 6.1).

It is becoming clear that distinguishing bases of relatedness in terms of the value network and strategic capabilities is of strategic importance. To continue the example given above: which is more useful, to conceive of Unilever's related diversification in terms of moves into products and markets within the value network of the fast-moving consumer goods industry, or in terms of moves into companies in which competences such as marketing, global brand development and research and development are crucial? In the case of Unilever these may go hand in hand, but for other organisations they may well not. For example, in the late 1990s some car manufacturers began to integrate forward into repairs and servicing following a value network logic, but rapidly realised that this involved quite different capabilities and began to withdraw from these ventures. Indeed, there have been many instances of large conglomerates choosing to de-merge to form more focused corporations around more related capabilities; a tendency which appears to have improved profits, net worth and reduced risk of being taken over.[7] This has also led to the questioning of just what is meant by synergies and synergistic benefits. These are often exaggerated by managers trying to justify their existing scope or new acquisitions. Synergies are often harder to identify and more costly to extract in practice than managers like to admit.[8]

The 'ownership' of more value activities within the value system through vertical or horizontal integration does not therefore guarantee improved performance for the organisation, or better value for money for the consumer or client. There has, however, been increasing emphasis on improving performance within the value system through external linkages and the management of relationships with the various parties in the supply and distribution chains rather than through diversifying into such businesses. Arguably, the ability to manage this well could itself be a core competence at the business or corporate level. It would include the need to ensure that innovation and improvement of value for money are occurring within other organisations in the value system on which the organisation depends, such as suppliers and distributors.

Related diversification is often seen as superior to unrelated diversification, in particular because it is likely to yield economies of scope. However, it is useful to consider reasons why related diversification can be problematic. Some have already been raised. Others include:

- the time and cost involved in top management at the corporate level trying to ensure that the benefits of relatedness are achieved through sharing or transfer across business units;
- the difficulty for business-unit managers in sharing resources with other business units, or adapting to corporate-wide policies, especially when they are incentivised and rewarded primarily on the basis of the performance of their own business alone.

In summary, a simple statement such as 'relatedness matters' has to be questioned.[9] Whilst there is evidence that it may have positive effects on performance (see section 6.3.3) more careful thought needs to go into just what relatedness means and what gives rise to performance benefits. The balance of argument is that what really matters is relatedness to strategic capability.

6.2.2 Unrelated diversification

Unrelated diversification is the development of products or services beyond the current capabilities or value network

If related diversification involves development within current capabilities or the current value system, **unrelated diversification** is the development of products or services beyond the current capabilities or value network. Unrelated diversification is often described as a 'conglomerate strategy'. Because there are no obvious economies of scope between the different businesses, but there is an obvious cost of the headquarters, unrelated diversified companies' share prices often suffer from what is called the 'conglomerate discount' – in other words, a lower valuation than the individual constituent businesses would have if standalone. In 2003, the French conglomerate Vivendi-Universal, with interests spreading from utilities to mobile telephony and media, was trading at an estimated discount of 15–20 per cent. Naturally, shareholders were pressurising management to break the conglomerate up into its more highly valued parts.

However, the case against conglomerates can be exaggerated and there are certainly instances where unrelated diversification seems to pay:

- Conglomerates may succeed by *exploiting dominant logics*. As at Berkshire Hathaway, a skilled investor such as Warren Buffet, the so-called Oracle of Omaha and one of the richest men in the world, may be able to add value to diverse businesses within his dominant logic.[10] Berkshire Hathaway includes businesses in different areas of manufacturing, insurance, distribution and retailing but Buffet focuses on mature businesses that he can understand and whose managers he can trust. During the e-business boom of the late 1990s, Buffet deliberately avoided buying high-technology businesses because he knew they were outside his dominant logic. (See Illustration 6.2.)

- Conglomerates may be *effective in countries with underdeveloped markets*. Conglomerates can work effectively as internal markets for capital and managerial talent where the external capital and labour markets do not yet work well. For example, Korean conglomerates (the chaebol) have been successful in part because they are able to mobilise investment and develop managers in a way that standalone companies in South Korea have traditionally not been able to. Also, the strong cultural cohesion amongst managers in these chaebol reduces the coordination and monitoring costs that would be necessary in a Western conglomerate, where managers would be trusted less.[11]

It is important also to recognise that the distinction between related and unrelated diversification is often a matter of degree. As in the case of Berkshire Hathaway, although there are very few operational relationships between the constituent businesses, there is a relationship in terms of similar parenting requirements (see section 6.4.4). As in the case of the car manufacturers diversifying forwards into apparently related businesses such as repairs and servicing, the relationships can turn out to be much less substantial than at first they appear. The blurred boundary between related and unrelated diversification will be important for considering the performance consequences of diversification and is raised in the key debate in Illustration 6.8.

Illustration 6.2   strategy into action

Berkshire Hathaway Inc.

A portfolio manager may seek to manage a highly diverse set of business units on behalf of its shareholders.

Berkshire Hathaway's chairman is Warren Buffett, one of the world's richest men, and Charles Munger is vice-chairman. The businesses in the portfolio are highly diverse. There are insurance businesses, including GEICO, the sixth largest automobile insurer in the USA, manufacturers of carpets, building products, clothing and footwear. There are service businesses (the training of aircraft and ship operators), retailers of home furnishings and fine jewellery, a daily and Sunday newspaper and the largest direct seller of housewear products in the USA.

The annual report of Berkshire Hathaway (2002) provides an insight into its rationale and management. Warren Buffett explains how he and his vice-chairman run the business.

> Charlie Munger and I think of our shareholders as owner-partners and of ourselves as managing partners. (Because of the size of our shareholdings we are also, for better or worse, controlling partners.) We do not view the company itself as the ultimate owner of our business assets but instead view the company as a conduit through which our shareholders own the assets . . . Our long term economic goal . . . is to maximise Berkshire's average annual rate of gain in intrinsic business value on a per-share basis. We do not measure the economic significance or performance of Berkshire by its size; we measure by per-share progress.
>
> Our preference would be to reach our goal by directly owning a diversified group of businesses that generate cash and consistently earn above average returns on capital. Our second choice is to own parts of similar businesses, attained primarily through purchases of marketable common stocks by our insurance subsidiaries . . . Charlie and I are interested only in acquisitions that we believe will raise the per-share intrinsic value of Berkshire's stock.
>
> Regardless of price we have no interest at all in selling any good businesses that Berkshire owns. We are also

very reluctant to sell sub-par businesses as long as we expect them to generate at least some cash and as ong as we feel good about their managers and labour relations . . . Gin rummy managerial behaviour (discard your least promising business at each turn) is not our style. We would rather have our overall results penalised a bit than engaged in that kind of behaviour.

Buffett then explains how they manage their subsidiary businesses:

> . . . we delegate almost to the point of abdication: though Berkshire has about 45,000 employees, only 12 of these are at headquarters . . . Charlie and I mainly attend to capital allocation and the care and feeding of our key managers. Most of these managers are happiest when they are left alone to run their businesses and that is customarily just how we leave them. That puts them in charge of all operating decisions and of despatching the excess cash they generate to headquarters. By sending it to us, they don't get diverted by the various enticements that would come their way were they responsible for deploying the cash their businesses throw off. Further more, Charlie and I are exposed to a much wider range of possibilities for investing these funds than any of our managers could find in his/her own industry.

Questions

1. In what ways does Berkshire Hathaway conform (and not conform) to the archetypal portfolio manager described in section 6.4.2?

2. Using the checklist explained in section 6.4 suggest how and in what ways Berkshire Hathaway may or may not add value to its shareholders.

6.2.3 Diversification and performance

Because most large corporations today are diversified, but also because diversification can sometimes be in management's self-interest, many scholars and policy-makers have been concerned to establish whether diversified companies really perform better than undiversified companies. After all, it would be deeply troubling if large corporations were diversifying simply to spread risk for managers, to save managerial jobs in declining businesses or to preserve the image of growth, as in the case of Enron.

Early research[12] suggested that firms which developed through *related diversification* outperformed both those that remained specialised and also those which developed through *unrelated diversification*. These findings were later questioned.[13] In the research work on diversification and performance since then the most generalisable finding is that the diversification–performance relationship follows an inverted U-shape[14] as in Exhibit 6.4. In other words, related and limitedly diversified companies perform better on average than *both* undiversified companies and heavily diversified companies or conglomerates. Some diversification is good for you – but not too much.

However, these are the averages, and some scholars have found exceptions:

● Conglomerates in developing economies often perform well, indicating the capacity for internal markets for labour and capital to do better than external markets.[15]

● Conglomerates have tended to perform better since the early 1970s, indicating the potential for improving managerial skills in managing unrelated diversification.[16]

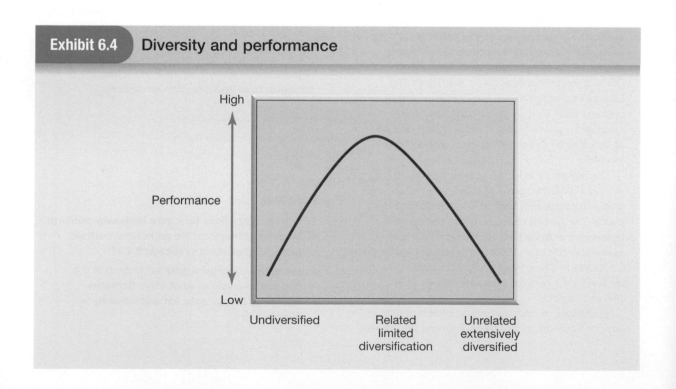

Exhibit 6.4 **Diversity and performance**

● Conglomerates can perform well for short periods of time, but then tend to decline and break up, particularly when the founding generation of top managers retire.[17]

Overall, then, it seems that related and limited diversification is good for performance. However, the case for unrelated diversification is rather more ambiguous and such strategies need rigorous questioning.

6.3 INTERNATIONAL DIVERSITY AND INTERNATIONAL STRATEGY

Section 6.2 was concerned with the diversity of an organisation in terms of its products or services. This section is concerned with the international diversity of an organisation. The reasons why organisations might pursue a strategy of international diversification are reviewed. Then two dimensions of international diversity are discussed. The first relates to the markets in which an organisation offers its products and/or services. The second relates to the location of an organisation's value-adding activities which occurs, for instance, when an organisation sets up manufacturing operations in a foreign country. The implication in terms of the resulting generic types of international strategy are then discussed as well as the implications for performance.

6.3.1 Reasons for international diversity

There are many reasons for organisations to follow a strategy of internationalisation. First, there may be *market-based reasons*:

● The *globalisation of markets and competition* can be seen as both cause and consequence of the internationalisation of individual organisations. There is evidence of homogenisation in some markets; for example, the international success of consumer products such as the Sony PlayStation and the worldwide reach of sports-clothing manufacturers such as Nike and Adidas-Solomon. Globalisation thereby relates not only to contextual factors such as worldwide homogenisation of consumer demand but also to the *adoption of global strategies* in which activities are tightly integrated and coordinated on a cross-national basis and the whole world is seen as a potential area of operation (see section 6.5.6 for a more detailed discussion). Companies such as Boeing not only offer their products on a global basis but are ready and able to exploit the unique advantages associated with particular countries and locations on a worldwide basis.

● Firms acting as suppliers to industrial companies may *follow their customers* when these internationalise their operations. When BMW set up a manufacturing site in Spartanburg, South Carolina, USA, for example, it continued purchasing transmission systems from its established German suppliers. Similarly, it may be necessary for organisations to have a presence in the home market of global customers (i.e. organisations with a global reach such as Boeing) to gain access to, or credibility with, their global divisions or subsidiaries.

● By expanding its markets internationally a firm can *bypass limitations in its home market*. An example of such market seeking international expansion is the French Bank BNP Paribas that accelerated the search for possible acquisitions in the USA after considering the French banking sector close to consolidation. Often it is those organisations with small home markets which lead internationalisation (as can be seen in the chapter-end case example in Chapter 3 about the European brewing industry – where Heineken (The Netherlands), Carlsberg (Denmark) and Guinness (Ireland) are the most internationalised companies.

● There may also be opportunities to *exploit differences between countries and geographical regions*. For example:[18]

  – The exploitation of *differences in culture*. The success of US-based fast food chains of the 1990s in particular largely exploited the general popularity of American culture at that time and French firms have cashed in on home-based cultural specifics associated with French cuisine, wines and perfumes.

  – *Administrative differences* allow firms to take advantage, for example, of tax differentials. The News Corporation has placed many of its US acquisitions into holding companies in the Cayman Islands and has therefore reaped tax benefits in its expansion in the USA.

  – It is not always the case that global reach makes sense. Exploiting *geographically specific differences* can help at times. Telephone company Cable and Wireless has focused on exploiting regional differences and regional specificity in smaller countries around the world.

  – The exploitation of *specific economic factors*. This could include, for example, labour or the costs of capital. A significant part of the success of Embraer, the Brazilian producer of regional jets, has been labour costs, which in 2002 were half those of its main rival, the Canadian firm Bombardier.

The underlying message is that organisations can look for and exploit differences just as they can look for and exploit global reach.

Strategies of internationalisation may also be pursued to build on and *take advantage of strategic capabilities*:

● By internationalising companies are able *to broaden the size of the market* so as to *exploit strategic capabilities*. For example, the American online retailer Amazon.com and coffee retailer Starbucks were able rapidly to gain strong competitive positions in countries such as the United Kingdom by leveraging their existing strategic capabilities in this new market.

● The *internationalisation of value-adding activities* allows an organisation to access and develop resources and capabilities in ways not possible in its 'home' country thereby enhancing its competitive advantage and competitive position. In order to improve its cost efficiency General Electric, for example, employs a workforce of more than 11,000 in India who conduct back-office activities such as analysing credit risks and analysing insurance claims, for services provided in other countries around the globe.

- Companies may also seek to *enhance their knowledge base* by entering markets that are strategically important as a source of industry innovation – for example, the USA for computer software, Germany for industrial control equipment, or the UK for popular music.

There may also be *economic benefits* in strategies of internationalisation:

- International diversification allows firms to reap *economies of scale* by expanding the size of the market they serve. The opportunity for exploiting economies of scale are likely to be highest in markets characterised by cross-nationally *homogenous consumer tastes* and needs. In such markets products can be developed and produced in centralised manufacturing operations without need for substantial adaptation to local demand.

- *Stabilisation of earnings across markets*: for example, in the automobile industry, the presence of Toyota in all three of the major 'arenas' (North America, Europe and Asia Pacific) allows it to balance reduced sales in one arena due to stagnating economic conditions by sales in an arena with more positive economic growth rates. And the recovery in the Asian markets in the early years of this century allowed firms such as Canon, Sony and Matsushita Electric to expand production of mobile phones, digital cameras and flat-screen televisions despite continued stagnation in Europe.

Illustration 6.3 explains some of the reasons for Deutsche Post's increasing international diversity after 1997.

6.3.2 Market selection and entry

The process of market entry requires an organisation to select attractive and profitable national markets and to identify the appropriate entry mode. The selection of national markets involves considerations at the macro level and in terms of competitive and market conditions already discussed in Chapter 2. Accordingly, countries can initially be compared along the dimensions identified in the PESTEL framework (see section 2.2.1 in Chapter 2) before the industry- and market-specific conditions are evaluated (sections 2.3 and 2.4 in Chapter 2).

Some factors that require particular attention in comparing the attractiveness of national markets are these:

- *Macro-economic conditions* reflected in indicators such as the GDP and levels of disposable income which help in the estimation of the potential size of the market. Companies must also be aware of the stability of a country's currency which may affect its income stream.

- The *political environment* may create significant opportunities for organisations. It is common for regional development agencies in the United Kingdom to provide investment incentives to foreign investors. For example, Scottish Enterprise provided a subsidy in order to attract the 2003 MTV music awards to the Scottish capital Edinburgh, while political and regulatory changes can create opportunities for international expansion as with Deutsche Post (see Illustration 6.3).

Illustration 6.3   strategy into action

Deutsche Post's increasing international diversity

Globalising markets and political and regulatory change are amongst the reasons for an organisation's increasing international diversity.

The internationalisation of Deutsche Post is closely linked to the opportunities and pressures resulting from the deregulation of national and international markets and the associated globalisation of the transport and logistics industries. The foundation was laid by the 'big bang' reform of the German postal system in 1990. The 'Law concerning the Structure of Posts and Telecommunication' retained Deutsche Post as a public company but aimed to prepare the company for gradual privatisation (the firm went public in 2000 with an initial sale of 29 per cent of share capital). In the following years the company went through a period of consolidation and restructuring which saw the integration of the former East German Post. By 1997, a year which saw a liberalisation of the German postal market, the company had put into place the groundwork for a period of rapid international expansion.

The subsequent globalisation of Deutsche Post's activities was largely driven by the demands of a growing number of business customers for a single provider of integrated national and international shipping and logistics services. Over the next five years Deutsche Post responded by acquiring key players in the international transport and logistics market, notably Danzas and DHL, with the aim of 'becoming the leading global provider of express and logistics services'. This international expansion enabled Deutsche Post – renamed Deutsche Post World Net (DPWN) in order to highlight its global ambitions – to, for example, gain a major contract with fellow German company BMW for the transport, storage and delivery of cars to its Asian dealerships. As part of its so-called 'START' programme DPWN initiated, in 2003, a programme aimed at harmonising its products and sales structures, creating integrated networks and implementing group-wide process management in order to realise the benefits of the economies of scale resulting from its global operations. At the same time DPWN implemented its 'One brand – One face to the customer' motto by making the DHL brand its global 'public face' with the expectation that this 'familiar and trusted brand name will aid us as we continue to develop globalised services'.

Deregulation and wider political changes, reflected in the elimination of trade restrictions, continued to drive international expansion. China's entry into the World Trade Organisation enhanced the potential for growth in its international postal market. Accordingly, DPWN strengthened its commitment to this increasingly important market and was rewarded with a 35 per cent growth rate over the period from 2002 to 2004 and, through a joint venture with Sinotrans, gained a 40 per cent market share of Chinese cross-border express services. DPWN aimed to exploit regulatory changes closer to home as well. With its subsidiary Deutsche Post Global Mail (UK) gaining a long-term licence for unlimited bulk mail delivery from the British regulator 'Postcomm', DPWN saw further opportunity for growth in the UK and continued to expand its presence in the British postal market through the acquisition of postal operator Speedmail.

Sources: www.dpwn.de/en_de/press/news; DPWN Annual Report 2002.

Prepared by Michael Mayer, Edinburgh University.

Questions

1. Evaluate the political risks associated with DPWN's strategy.

2. To what extent might cultural issues be a factor in the further development of DPWN's quest to become an integrated global player?

- The *infrastructure* of national markets will also be an important factor in assessing the attractiveness of national markets for entry, in particular:
  - *existing transport and communication infrastructure*;
  - availability of necessary *local resources* such as appropriately skilled labour;
  - *tariff and non-tariff barriers to trade*: a key factor in deciding between exporting and local production. The higher these barriers are, the more attractive local production will be.

- The similarity of *cultural norms and social structures* with the organisation's home country can provide an indicator of any changes to established products, processes and procedures which may be required.

- The extent of *political and legal risks* that an organisation might face when doing business in the country. In broad terms political risk relates to the effect that political and social events or conditions may have on the profitability of a firm's activities and the security of its investments. Key types of political risks include:[19]
  - *Sovereign risks* arise from the policies and decisions of host governments, including changes in tax laws and restrictions on expatriate employment and, in increasingly rare instances, from the expropriation of an organisation's investments.
  - Notably, risks can arise not only from governmental intervention but also from the absence of effective regulation and control.[20] For example, Microsoft has been engaged in an ongoing effort to ensure the *protection of its intellectual property* in the face of product piracy in China, while the lack of consistent legislation and effective law enforcement has led to serious contractual and financial problems for Canadian oil exploration companies in Russia. Similarly, *corruption* remains a serious problem in a number of countries, with often negative effects on direct foreign investment.
  - *International risks* are linked to developments in the international political economy and include the effects of economic sanctions. For example, US strategic interests have had an important effect on the construction and routing of oil pipelines in the Caspian region.[21]
  - *Security risks* to employees arising from civil unrest, violent crime and the threat of kidnapping are of concern to organisations operating in countries as diverse as South Africa, Russia and the Yemen.

Once a particular national market has been selected for entry, an organisation needs to choose which, if any, value-adding activities are to be located in that market. Entry modes differ in the degree of resource commitment to a particular market and the extent to which an organisation is operationally involved in a particular location. The key entry mode types are: exporting, contractual arrangement through licensing and franchising, joint ventures and alliances and foreign direct investment which may involve the acquisition of established companies (the route explored by BNP Paribas) and 'greenfield' investments, the development of facilities 'from scratch'. These alternative methods of strategy development are explained further in section 7.3 of Chapter 7 but the specific advantages and disadvantages for international market entry are summarised in Exhibit 6.5.

Exhibit 6.5   Market entry modes: advantages and disadvantages

Exporting

Advantages

- No operational facilities needed in the host country
- Economies of scale can be exploited
- By using Internet small/inexperienced firms can gain access to international markets

Disadvantages

- Does not allow the firm to benefit from the locational advantages of the host nation
- Limits opportunities to gain knowledge of local markets and competitors
- May create dependence on export intermediaries
- Exposure to trade barriers such as import duties
- Incurs transportation costs
- May limit the ability to respond quickly to customer demands

Joint ventures and alliances

Advantages

- Investment risk shared with partner
- Combining of complementary resources and know-how
- May be a governmental condition for market entry

Disadvantages

- Difficulty of identifying appropriate partner and agreeing appropriate contractual terms
- Managing the relationship with the foreign partner
- Loss of competitive advantage through imitation
- Limits ability to integrate and coordinate activities across national boundaries

Licensing

Advantages

- Contractually agreed income through sale of production and marketing rights
- Limits economic and financial exposure

Disadvantages

- Difficulty of identifying appropriate partner and agreeing contractual terms
- Loss of competitive advantage through imitation
- Limits benefits from the locational advantages of host nation

Foreign direct investment

Advantages

- Full control of resources and capabilities
- Facilitates integration and coordination of activities across national boundaries
- Acquisitions allow rapid market entry
- Greenfield investments allow development of state of the art facilities and can attract financial support from the host government

Disadvantages

- Substantial investment in and commitment to host country leading to economic and financial exposure
- Acquisition may lead to problems of integration and coordination
- Greenfield entry time-consuming and less predictable in terms of cost.

Internationalisation brings organisations into new and often unknown territory, requiring managers to learn new ways of doing business – managerial practices appropriate in the home country may require adaptation and modification elsewhere.[22] Internationalisation is therefore typically seen as a sequential process whereby companies gradually increase their commitment to newly entered markets, accumulating knowledge and increasing their capabilities along the way. Consequently **staged international expansion** suggests that firms initially use entry modes that allow them to maximise knowledge acquisition whilst minimising the exposure of their assets. Once the initial decision for market entry has been made they then sequentially increase their exposure and thereby their commitment to a particular market over time. An example is the entry of automobile manufacturer BMW into the American market. After a lengthy period of exporting from Germany to the USA, BMW set up a manufacturing plant in Spartanburg, South Carolina in order to strengthen its competitive position in the strategically important American market. Such sequential market entry allows firms to gradually increase their understanding of the local market while limiting their economic exposure.[23]

> **Staged international expansion**: firms initially use entry modes that allow them to maximise knowledge acquisition whilst minimising the exposure of their assets

In contrast to such gradual internationalisation followed by many large and established firms, there is evidence that some small firms are internationalising rapidly at early stages in their development using multiple modes of entry to several countries. For firms such as medical systems producer Heartware International,[24] headquartered in the USA but with product development located in The Netherlands and early sales in the USA, the UK, Italy, Spain and Brazil, the emphasis has been less on the gradual accumulation of international competence but rather on their ability to enter foreign markets at a stage where they are still fledgling enterprises. In so doing they need to manage simultaneously the process of internationalisation and develop their wider strategy and infrastructure whilst often lacking the usually expected experiential knowledge to do so.[25]

6.3.3 The international value network

As is clear from the above discussion, internationalisation relates to much more than the development of new markets. It also includes decisions about the *location of elements of an organisation's value chain* (see section 3.6.1 of Chapter 3). As Bruce Kogut has explained, an organisation can improve the configuration of its value chain and network[26] through such internationalisation. It can do this by selectively exploiting differences between countries and locating each element of the value chain in that country or region where it can be conducted most effectively and efficiently. This may be achieved both through foreign direct investments and joint ventures but also through **global sourcing** by purchasing services and components from the most appropriate suppliers around the world, regardless of their location. For example, in the UK the NHS has been sourcing medical personnel from overseas to offset a shortfall in domestic skills and capacity.

> **Global sourcing**: purchasing services and components from the most appropriate suppliers around the world regardless of their location

Different locational advantages can be identified:

● Although *cost advantages* are based on a combination of factors ranging from transportation and communications costs, to taxation and investment incentives, labour costs are often a crucial element in the locational decision. American and European firms, for example, are increasingly moving software programming tasks to India where a computer programmer costs an American firm about one-quarter of what it would pay for a worker with comparable skills in the USA. Such cost advantages are not static, however. Estimates suggest that in about 15 years the cost of employing top software engineers will be at similar levels in India as in the USA. Indian IT firms have already begun moving work to even more low-cost locations such as China with some predicting that subsidiaries of Indian firms will come to control as much as 40 per cent of China's IT service exports.

● The existence of *unique capabilities* may allow an organisation to enhance its competitive advantage. A reason for Accenture to locate a rapidly expanding software development office in the Chinese city of Dalian was that communication with potential Japanese and Korean multinational firms operating in the region was easier than if an equivalent location in India or the Philippines had been chosen. Organisations may also seek to exploit advantages related to specific technological and scientific capabilities. Boeing, for example, located its largest engineering centre outside of the USA in Moscow to help it access Russian know-how in areas such as aerodynamics. Organisations such as Boeing are thus increasingly leveraging their ability selectively to exploit locational advantages with a view to building on and enhancing their existing strategic capabilities. Put differently, internationalisation is increasingly, not only about exploiting existing capabilities in new national markets, but about developing strategic capabilities by drawing on the capabilities elsewhere in the world.

● The *characteristics of national locations* can enable organisations to develop differentiated product offerings aimed at different market segments. American guitar-maker Gibson, for example, complements its US-made products with often similar, lower-cost alternatives produced in South Korea under the Epiphone brand. Gibson's competitor Fender similarly offers less costly 'Mexican-made' alternatives to its range of US-made products.

Of course one of the consequences of organisations trying to exploit the locational advantages available in different countries' organisations can be that they create complex networks of intra- and inter-organisational relationships. Boeing, for example, has developed a global web of R&D activities through its subsidiaries and partnerships with collaborating organisations (see Illustration 6.4). Take also the example of General Motor's Pontiac Le Mans, the design, development and production of which drew on a full range of locational options available to the American firm. The car was designed at the firm's German subsidiary Opel, while the development of the advertising strategy was outsourced to an agency located in the United Kingdom, drawing on the creative talent available at that location. Many of the more complex components were produced in countries such as Japan, exploiting sophisticated manufacturing and technological capabilities, while the car was assembled in South Korea, a location where a lower-cost, yet skilled, labour force was available. In order to benefit from the international dispersal of key value-adding activities an organisation therefore needs to develop the capability to coordinate effectively such networks of relationships. Each

Illustration 6.4

strategy into action

Boeing's global R&D network

Organisations may seek to exploit locational advantages worldwide.

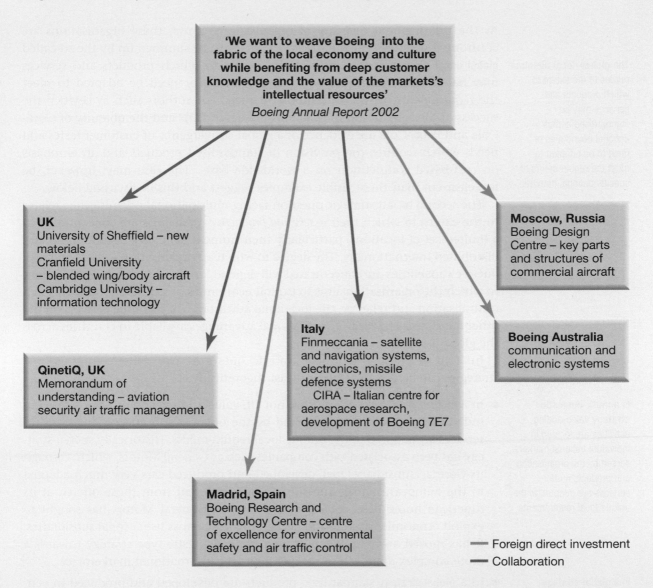

'We want to weave Boeing into the fabric of the local economy and culture while benefiting from deep customer knowledge and the value of the markets's intellectual resources'
Boeing Annual Report 2002

UK
University of Sheffield – new materials
Cranfield University – blended wing/body aircraft
Cambridge University – information technology

QinetiQ, UK
Memorandum of understanding – aviation security air traffic management

Italy
Finmeccania – satellite and navigation systems, electronics, missile defence systems
   CIRA – Italian centre for aerospace research, development of Boeing 7E7

Madrid, Spain
Boeing Research and Technology Centre – centre of excellence for environmental safety and air traffic control

Moscow, Russia
Boeing Design Centre – key parts and structures of commercial aircraft

Boeing Australia
communication and electronic systems

— Foreign direct investment
— Collaboration

Source: Boeing.com, Boeing Annual Report 2002, Aviation International News Online.

Prepared by Michael Mayer, Edinburgh University.

Questions

1. What reasons might be driving the internationalisation of Boeing's R&D activities?

2. What challenges might Boeing face as it internationalises its R&D activities?

international investment decision therefore needs to be evaluated, in relation to not only specific locational advantages, but the wider organisational and managerial implications. Increased costs of coordination and control, for example, might offset possible cost savings (see also section 8.3 in Chapter 8).

6.3.4 International strategies

As the international diversity of organisations grows, these organisations are confronted with two key questions. The first can be summed up by the so-called **global–local dilemma** and relates to the extent to which products and services may be standardised across national boundaries or need be adapted to meet the requirements of specific national markets. For authors such as Levitt,[27] the success of McDonald's on the Champs Elysées in Paris and the ubiquity of Coca-Cola and Pepsi-Cola are evidence of a global convergence of customer tastes and needs which requires the provision of standardised products and an emphasis on cost-based competition on a worldwide basis. The case may, however, be less clear-cut than these visible examples suggest and this is discussed below.

The **global–local dilemma** relates to the extent to which products and services may be standardised across national boundaries or need to be adapted to meet the requirements of specific national markets

The second broad strategic question facing multinational organisations relates to the extent to which their *assets and productive capabilities* are concentrated in a limited set of locations, particularly their home base, or are decentralised and distributed internationally. The degree to which an organisation's assets and productive capabilities are concentrated will depend, on the one hand, on the extent to which the organisation aims to exploit economies of scale achievable through centralisation and relies on the locational advantages of its home base or, on the other hand, seeks to access the locational advantages available in countries across the globe (see section 6.3.3).

In light of these two broad strategic questions two generic international strategies can be distinguished, at least theoretically.

In a **multi-domestic strategy** value-adding activities are located in individual national markets served by the organisation and products and/or services are adapted to the unique local requirements

● In a **multi-domestic strategy** most, if not all, value-adding activities are located in individual national markets served by the organisation and products and/or services are adapted to the unique local requirements. Historically such a strategy has been associated with companies such as General Motors, which, through its German subsidiary Opel, developed and produced cars very much adapted to the European market and substantially different from those offered at its American home base. Increasingly, however, General Motors has sought to exploit economies of scale and deepen linkages across its national subsidiaries. It has moved away from following a multi-domestic type strategy towards a more complex approach of competing in the international marketplace.

In a **global strategy** standardised products exploiting economies of scale and value-adding activities are typically concentrated in a limited set of locations

● In a **global strategy** standardised products are developed and produced in centralized locations. With a greater emphasis on exploiting economies of scale, value-adding activities are typically concentrated in a more limited set of locations than for multi-domestic strategies. This strategy has traditionally been associated with companies such as Boeing with its US-based manufacturing and R&D capabilities. As was discussed in section 6.3.3 and shown in Illustration 6.4, Boeing is, however, increasingly expanding its global 'reach' and knowledge base by locating R&D capabilities in an increasingly wide range of countries whilst retaining a close linkage and integration of its disparate activities with a view to sustaining its strategic focus and cohesiveness.

In practice, then, organisations rarely, if ever, fall neatly into the basic categories of pure global or multi-domestic strategies. Instead they seek to develop their own specific ways of balancing on the one hand the tension between standardisation and adaptation of products and/or services and, on the other hand, exploiting the opportunities provided by unique locational characteristics and economies of scale. Requirements for adaptation may be minimal, such as the fitting of appropriate national keyboards to laptop computers, or more substantial such as development of different language versions of software interfaces. Cross-national differences can be very substantial, however, requiring the provision of significantly different product or service offerings. The success of sports utility vehicles in the USA, for example, is unlikely to be matched in European markets because of the different social and cultural conditions as well as the differently developed road networks. Certainly to a greater or lesser extent most large multinational organisations face the need to tailor their product or service offering to local needs to some degree. The challenge is to identify what parts of that offering can be standardised globally and what needs to be tailored locally. Illustration 6.5 shows how Hindustan Lever has adapted its products and services to the local conditions of Indian rural markets. This balancing of local responsiveness with the benefits of global scale can also result in complex challenges to the organisation of multinational organisations, a matter addressed in Chapter 8 (section 8.3).

6.3.5 International diversity and performance

Just as for product/service diversity discussed in section 6.2.3 the relationship between international diversification and performance has been extensively researched. Some of the main findings from such research are these:

● While the potential performance benefits of internationalisation are substantial, in that it allows firms to realise economies of scale and scope and benefit from the locational advantages available in countries around the globe, the combination of diverse locations and diverse business units gives rise to levels of complexity beyond which benefits are not gained and costs begin to exceed benefits.[28] Accordingly, the balance of evidence again suggests an inverted U-shaped relationship between international diversification and performance (similar to the findings on product/service diversification shown in Exhibit 6.4 and reported in section 6.2.3 above) where moderate levels of international diversity lead to the best results.[29]

● A number of studies have suggested that, in contrast to firms in the manufacturing sector, international diversity may not lead to improved performance for service sector firms. There are three possible reasons for such an effect. First, the operations of foreign firms remain more tightly regulated and restricted in many countries; second, due to the intangible nature of services these are often more sensitive to cultural differences and require greater adaptation than manufactured products which may lead to higher initial learning

Illustration 6.5   strategy into action

Strategic innovation at Hindustan Lever Ltd

Large multinational corporations may still need to tailor their products and services to local market needs.

Unilever is one of the world's biggest consumer products companies. It seeks to establish its brands on a global basis and support them with state of the art research and development (see Illustration 6.7). However, it is acutely aware that markets differ and that, if it is to be global, it has to be prepared to adapt to local market conditions. It also recognises that if it is to have global reach, it has to be able to market its goods in poorer areas as well as richer areas. Indeed it estimates that by 2010 half of its sales will come from the developing world – an increase of over 30 per cent from the equivalent figure in 2000.

In the rural areas of India Hindustan Lever is setting about marketing Unilever's branded goods in ways suited to local conditions.

Much of the effort goes into marketing branded goods in local haats or market places, where Unilever representatives sell the products from the back of trucks using loudspeakers to explain the brand proposition. Local executives argue that, poor as people are, they 'aren't naturally inclined to settle for throwaway versions of the real deal – if the companies that make the real deal bother to explain the difference'.

To help develop the skills to do this Lever management trainees in India begin their career by spending weeks living in rural villages where they eat, sleep and talk with the locals: 'Once you have spent time with consumers, you realise that they want the same things you want. They want a good quality of life.'

The same executives have innovated further in the way goods are marketed. They have developed direct sales models where women, belonging to self-help groups that run micro credit operations, sell Lever products so as to make their collectives' savings grow. Where television viewing is uncommon Hindustan Lever marketing executives have also mounted thousands of live shows at cattle and trade markets, employing rural folklore. The aim here is not just to push the Lever brands, it is to explain the importance of more frequent washing and better hygiene. Indeed sales personnel attend religious festivals and use ultraviolet light wands on people's hands to show the dangers of germs and dirt.

But it is not just the way the goods are marketed that is tailored to rural India. Product development is also different. For example, Indian women are very proud of the care of their hair and regard hair grooming as a luxury. However, they tend to use the same soap for body washing as for washing their hair. So Lever has dedicated research and development efforts into finding a low-cost soap that can be used for the body and for the hair and which is targeted to smaller towns and rural areas.

As Keki Dadiseth, a director of Hindustan Lever, puts it: 'Everyone wants brands. And there are a lot more poor people in the world than rich people. To be a global business . . . you have to participate in all segments.'

Source: Rekha Balu, 'Strategic innovation: Hindustan Lever Ltd', *FastCompany.com* (www.fastcompany.com/magazine), Issue 47, June 2001.

Questions

1. What are the challenges a multinational such as Unilever faces in developing global brands whilst encouraging local responsiveness?

2. What other examples of local tailoring of global brands can you think of?

3. Multinationals have been criticised for marketing more expensive branded goods in poorer areas of developing countries. What are your views of the ethical dimensions to Hindustan Lever's activities?

costs; third, the simultaneity of production and consumption requires a significant local presence and reduces the scope for the exploitation of economies of scale in production compared to manufacturing firms.[30]

● An important question to consider is the interaction between international diversification and product/service diversification. Compared to single business firms it has been suggested that product-diversified firms are likely to do better from international expansion because they have already developed the necessary skills and structures for managing internal diversity.[31] At the other end of the spectrum there is general consensus that firms that are highly diversified both in terms of product and internationally are likely to face excessive costs of coordination and control leading to poor performance. As many firms have not yet reached levels of internationalisation where negative effects outweigh possible gains[32] and because of current scepticism with regard to the benefits of high levels of product diversification, many companies currently opt for reducing their product diversity whilst focusing in international scope; for example, see Illustration 6.7 on Unilever.

6.4 VALUE CREATION AND THE CORPORATE PARENT

In one major multinational corporation the Finance Director claimed that no business within its portfolio, having been divested, had not done better on its own or with another corporate parent. His point was that the value-adding activities of the corporate parent should not be taken for granted. In the absence of clarity about how it adds value to its business units, it is in danger of merely being a cost to them and therefore reducing or destroying the value created by them. It is the role of any corporate parent to ensure it does add value rather than destroy it.

Indeed how corporate parents create value is central not only to the performance of companies but also to their survival. Investors and potential investors are continually seeking ways to achieve better returns. In so doing they make choices between one corporation and another on the basis of many of the issues discussed in this chapter. In this sense competition takes place between corporate parents for the right to own businesses.

6.4.1 Value-adding and value-destroying activities of corporate parents[33]

There are those who argue that corporate parents should, indeed, be able to add value and there are those who argue that generally they do not. These differing views are now summarised.

The value-adding activities

A primary role is that of *envisioning* the overall role and expectations of the organisation; or, in the phrase of Hamel and Prahalad,[34] establishing a clear corporate-level *strategic intent*. Being clear about this is important for three main reasons.

- *Focus*: because in the absence of such clarity it is likely that the corporate parent will undertake activities and bear costs that have nothing to do with adding value to the business units, and are therefore just costs which diminish value.

- *Clarity to external stakeholders*: because corporate managers need to make clear to stakeholders what the corporation as a whole is about. In the absence of doing so, investors (and this might be the government for public sector organisations) can become confused, for example, about why certain businesses are within a portfolio, or how a corporate parent might add value to them and their judgement will affect share price or investment decisions.

- *Clarity to business units*: internally, if business unit managers are not able to make sense of what their corporate parent is there for, they inevitably feel as though the corporate centre is either little more than a cost burden, or that corporate executives lack clarity of direction. In either case they are likely to become demotivated. They will also wish to know if their business is seen as central to corporate aspirations or not. If they are not clear, it is unlikely that they will manage the business in ways to enhance the overall aspirations of the corporation. Indeed, strategic decisions at the business level could run counter to corporate strategy. Of course, the reverse is the case. Clarity at the corporate level can provide a basis on which strategic choice is made at the business level. It also helps in the setting of clear *expectations* and *standards* so that business units know what is expected of them.

A second role is that of *intervening* within business units to improve performance or to develop business unit strategy. For example:

- by regularly monitoring the *performance* of business units and their senior executives against the standards they have been set;

- by taking action to *improve business-unit level performance*, for example by replacing managers, selling off businesses or ensuring turnaround of poorly performing divisions or businesses;

- actively seeking to *challenge and develop the strategic ambitions* of the business unit. This might, for example, include helping to internationalise a traditionally domestic business;

- *coaching and training* of people and managers in business units;

- helping *develop the strategic capabilities* of business units;

- achieving *synergies* across business units and encouraging *collaboration* and *coordinating* across business units which could result in products or services which a single unit could not deliver.

Third, the corporate parent may be able to offer *central services and resources* to help business units such as:

- *Investment*, particularly during the early days of new ventures.

- *Scale advantages* from resource sharing, particularly in the use of infrastructure, support services and other overhead items.

- *Transferable managerial capabilities* that can be used across business units. In a multinational corporation such as Shell or Unilever this will include moving executives from business unit to business unit across the world to gain experience of different international markets and operations.

The corporate parent may also have *expertise* of its own that can be helpful to business units. For example:

● Providing *expertise* and *services* not available within smaller units – for example, personnel and financial services, estates management and IT infrastructure. Some of the most successful corporate parents have competences in market analysis, or cost analysis, which help to reassess the role and future of divisions or subsidiaries. Human resource, management development and succession planning may be ways in which the parent could add value.

● *Knowledge creation and sharing processes* that might help foster innovation and learning. Centrally organised knowledge management systems have become commonplace in large corporations for example (but see section 3.5 in Chapter 3).

● *Leverage*, for example in access to markets or in purchasing, by combining the purchasing power of the business units.

● Skills in *brokering* external linkages or collaborations and accessing *external networks*.

Advocates of the benefits of multi-business corporations would say that the alternative to corporate parents undertaking such roles is for business units to be reliant on market forces, not least the mechanisms of the financial markets. However, they would argue that this is inefficient. Typically, given the poor performance of a firm, financial markets have done little more than have the effect of reducing share price and waiting for takeovers to occur in the hope that improvement might take place because of new management. So, on the face of it the costs of achieving such benefits should be less within a corporate structure and the efficiencies much greater. After all, the corporate parent should have ready access to internal information within the businesses and have the cooperation of the managers in the business units in taking action since the managers work for the corporation.

Value-destroying activities[35]

There are, however, contrary arguments. It is argued that corporate parents tend to destroy value and that businesses would be better off on their own subject to financial market mechanisms. Here the argument is that the sometimes very large financial cost of the centre is rarely offset by the benefits the corporate parent provides. Further, the corporate parent may also create diseconomies. More specifically:

● Corporate parents can add cost with systems and hierarchies that delay decisions, create a '*bureaucratic fog*' and hinder market responsiveness. Not least this is because there may be several levels of corporate parent above the business unit, each with executives who have a decision-making influence over the business units.

● Corporate parents may buffer the executives in businesses from the realities of financial markets by providing a *financial 'safety net'* that means that executives are not truly answerable for the performance of their businesses.

Illustration 6.6

Wrong numbers for France Telecom

A key issue of corporate-level strategy is the value-adding role of the corporate parent.

Michel Bon became CEO of state-owned France Telecom in 1995. Two years later, the French government floated 45 per cent of what was until then a department of the Ministry of Telecommunications. Over 4 million people – among them 70 per cent of the company's 220,000 employees – bought shares at an initial price of €32.8. In March 2000, the share price reached its peak at €219. At the peak of the internet bubble, France Telecom was multiplying its international acquisitions through an ambitious expansion strategy. More than €70bn were dedicated to acquisitions in Europe, in the USA, in Asia, or in Latin America.

Two years later, in June 2002, the share price had fallen to €8.6. France Telecom announced an historic €8.28bn loss for a global €43bn turnover. Debts exceeded €61bn – the equivalent of one quarter of the French government's budget.

Investors were concerned by the consequences of four extremely risky operations:

- In order to take an 18.3 per cent stake in NTL – a cable operator which was supposed to obtain a 3G licence in the UK – France Telecom had spent €4.58bn. Unfortunately, NTL had not received a licence and France Telecom was trying to sell off its shares – which were virtually valueless – to any possible buyer.

- The French and the German governments had forced their national operators, France Telecom and Deutsche Telekom, to make a nonaggression pact. However, Deutsche Telekom had broken this alliance in 1999, forcing France Telecom to take a 28.5 per cent stake in MobilCom. MobilCom, the smallest German mobile phone operator, had paid the exorbitant sum of €8.4bn – without infrastructure investments – in order to obtain a 3G licence in Germany. In 2002, it was going bankrupt.

- In the USA, France Telecom had invested €4.8bn in November 2000 to take over Equant, a company providing large corporations with telecommunication services. The goal was to merge Equant with France Telecom's subsidiary Global One. However, the merger appeared problematic and Equant added €2bn to France Telecom's debt.

- The most ambitious acquisition had been the takeover of the British mobile phone operator Orange, bought from Vodafone for €43.2bn in August 2000 and floated on the Paris and London stock exchanges in February 2001. In 2002, Orange was the leader on the French and British mobile phone markets, with over 40 million subscribers, but its market value had fallen to €33.5bn. France Telecom was committed to pay Vodafone a share price of €130, whereas the actual value was only €30.

- Far from having a clear overall vision of what is trying to be achieved, the *diversity and size* of some corporations make it very difficult to see what they are about.

- Corporate hierarchies provide a *focus for managerial ambition*. Managers aspire to be at the top of the corporate ladder, rather than performing the value creation role of the business-unit level. The corporate centre is rather more seen as a vehicle for empire building in which executives seek to grow the number of businesses and the size of the corporation for motives of personal ambition.

Analysts and commentators continue to raise questions about the extent to which corporate parents really do add value.[36] An example of the questions raised about the value-adding capabilities of France Telecom as a corporate parent is

Analysts disagreed on Michel Bon's responsibility. Almost all operators had suffered heavy losses in 2001, after the burst of the internet bubble: €21.8bn for Vodafone, €7.5bn for KPN, €3.5bn for Deutsche Telekom, €2.8bn for BT and bankruptcy for WorldCom. Moreover, France Telecom had been forced by its majority shareholder – the French government – to pay its acquisitions in cash and not in equity, in order to avoid 'creeping privatisation'. It was also possible that some of these acquisitions would eventually be profitable, especially Orange and Equant, but France Telecom had failed to become a world leader like Vodafone (which had taken over Mannesmann in Germany, AirTouch in the USA and Japan Telecom in Japan).

Even if France Telecom was compelled to sell off some of its most profitable investments in order to reduce its debt (for example, its stake in the chip manufacturer ST Microeletronics, in the French television broadcaster TDF or in the Italian mobile phone operator Wind), banks and financial analysts were still confident in its future, as long as it was backed by the French government. At the end of 2001, France Telecom issued a 4.5 per cent bond for €2.5bn, which was sold in only 48 hours, for a total amount of €5bn.

In September 2002, France Telecom announced that its debt had reached €70bn – seven times Eurotunnel's debt, a new world record. Even if its operational profit was excellent (one of the highest in the industry, thanks to mobile phones and broadband internet), because of its financial burden, the company suffered a half-yearly €12.2bn loss. Its equity capital had fallen from €21bn to minus €440m in only six months. Michel Bon was forced to resign, but the French government – which announced a €15bn increase in capital – confirmed that it had always approved the strategy along the past seven years.

In September 2003, after a drastic cost-cutting plan, the new CEO, Thierry Breton, decided to buy back all Orange shares (the most profitable subsidiary), to sell all operations in Argentina and Salvador, and announced the first net profit in two years (€2.5bn in the first semester of 2003). The €15bn increase in capital had reduced the debt to less than €50bn and the government's stake to 50.01 per cent. The share price was above €20.

Sources: *Les Echos*, 2 September 2003 and 16 September 2002; N. Brafman and G. Fontaine, 'Le rêve brisé de France Telecom', *Capital*, no. 128, May 2002, pp. 38–42; T. Gadault, 'France Telecom: pourquoi Bon a raison', *L'Expansion*, no. 662, April 2002, pp.126–129.

Prepared by Frédéric Fréry, ESCP-EAP European School of Management.

Questions

1. What do you think of Michel Bon's expansion strategy?
2. What should be the future strategy for France Telecom?

given in Illustration 6.6. In both private and public sector organisations similar questions about the value-adding capabilities of parents arise. In the UK there has been much questioning of the extent to which it makes sense for local government authorities to control many services that, historically, they had within their portfolios. For example, in the UK traditionally schools were managed through local education authorities (LEAs) who allocated government funds and provided certain services. However, both central government and many head teachers and governing bodies of schools began to question the value-adding role of this level of management. Central government, wishing to improve education standards, began to centralise education policy; and the schools themselves wanted more flexibility in decision making. The result was that many schools opted out of LEA control and for direct funding from central government.

There are, then, questions as to the benefits of diversified corporations, as the key debate in Illustration 6.8 shows. The view taken in this chapter is that, indeed, there is a real risk that corporate parents will destroy value, but that this is not inevitable. If parents do have the information about business units such that they can provide the sorts of benefit identified above, then a well-managed parent should be able to add value. The real issue is, then, not whether a business unit should have a parent or be independent, but whether the corporate strategy of the parent is such that it does enhance value created at business-unit level; and in turn which parent suits which business and vice versa? Bearing in mind these issues and in the context of the international and diversified nature of many large organisations, an underlying theme of this chapter is now addressed: what is the strategic rationale of the corporate parent? What is it there for? What role in value creation does it see for itself? In what ways might it add value to its business units? The discussion which follows considers three corporate rationales,[37] summarised in Exhibit 6.6.

6.4.2 The portfolio manager

A **portfolio manager** is a corporate parent acting as an agent on behalf of financial markets and shareholders

The **portfolio manager** is, in effect, a corporate parent acting as an agent on behalf of financial markets and shareholders with a view to enhancing the value attained from the various businesses in a more efficient or effective way than financial markets could. Its role is to identify and acquire under-valued assets or businesses and improve them. It might do this, for example, by acquiring another corporation, divesting low-performing businesses within it and encouraging the improved performance of those with potential. Such corporations may not be much concerned about the relatedness (see sections 6.2.1 and 6.2.2) of the business units in their portfolio and may only play limited roles within those business units. For example, they may be adept at identifying restructuring opportunities in businesses or to intervene if performance in those business units is declining. Or they may divert those businesses. To do this they may have specialists at the centre who move into businesses for limited periods of time.

Portfolio managers seek to keep the cost of the centre low, for example by having a small corporate staff with few central services, leaving the business units alone so that their chief executives have a high degree of autonomy, but setting clear financial targets for those chief executives with high rewards if they achieve them and the expectation of low rewards, or loss of position, if they do not.

Such corporate parents could, of course, manage quite a large number of such businesses because they are not directly intervening in the product/market strategies of those businesses. Rather they are setting financial targets, making central evaluations about the well-being and future prospects of such businesses and investing or divesting accordingly.

Internationally, the role of the corporate parent as a portfolio manager would be compatible with a strategy where only financial relationships between markets are exploited: businesses in different countries are left to manage themselves in other respects. In effect, an extreme form of a multi-domestic international strategy (see section 6.7).

Exhibit 6.6   Portfolio managers, synergy managers and parental developers

	Portfolio managers	Synergy managers	Parental developers
Logic	• 'Agent' for financial markets • Value creation at SBU level limited	• The achievement of synergistic benefits	• Central competences can be used to create value in SBUs
Strategic requirements	• Identifying and acquiring undervalued assets • Divesting low-performing SBUs quickly and good performers at a premium • Low level strategic role at SBU level	• Sharing activities/resources or transferring skills/competences to enhance competitive advantage of SBUs • Identification of appropriate bases for sharing or transferring • Identification of benefits which outweigh costs	• SBUs not fulfilling their potential (a parenting opportunity) • The parent has clear and relevant resources or capabilities to enhance SBU potential • The portfolio is suited to parent's expertise
Organisational requirements	• Autonomous SBUs • Small, low cost corporate staff • Incentives based on SBU results	• Collaborative SBUs • Corporate staff as integrators • Overcoming SBU resistance to sharing or transferring • Incentives affected by corporate results	• Corporate managers understand SBUs ('sufficient feel') • Effective structural and control linkages from parent to SBUs • SBUs may be autonomous unless collaboration is required • Incentives based on SBU performance

A parallel situation in the public sector is that the parent would be acting on behalf of the government in the allocation of financial resources. For example, the Higher Education Funding Council in the UK is responsible on behalf of government for the allocation of research funds to universities in England and Wales. It sets criteria and establishes procedures by which to evaluate universities' research activities, and funds are allocated according to the ratings which result. But it does not intervene in the universities themselves with regard to the strategies they choose to follow.

Some argue that the days of the portfolio manager are gone. They are certainly not popular with financial analysts not least because financial analysts and investors have become more adept at analysing for themselves the opportunities presented by under-performing businesses. There are now many fewer such corporations than there used to be. However, some do remain and are successful. Illustration 6.2 includes a description of the corporate parenting approach of Warren Buffet at Berkshire Hathaway.

The **synergy manager**: a corporate parent seeking to enhance value across business units by managing synergies across business units

6.4.3 The synergy manager

Synergy is often seen as *the raison d'être* of the corporate parent. Indeed it is often given as a reason by corporate managers for product/service or international diversification (see sections 6.2 and 6.3).[38] In terms of corporate parenting, the logic is that *value can be enhanced across business units* in a number of ways:[39]

- *Resources or activities* might be shared: for example, common distribution systems might be used for different businesses; overseas offices may be shared by smaller business units acting in different geographical areas; common brand names may provide value to different products within different businesses.

- There may exist common *skills or competences* across businesses. For example, on the face of it there may be diverse products or technologies within an industrial products business; but the value-adding capabilities of service offered to industrial customers may be a common thread through such businesses. If this is so, then the skills and competences learned in one business may be shared by another, thus improving performance. Or there may exist expertise built up, for example, in marketing or research, which is transferable to other businesses within a portfolio less capable in such ways, again enhancing their performance.

However, the problems in achieving such synergistic benefits are similar to those in achieving the benefits of relatedness (see sections 6.3.1 and 6.3.2). Specifically:

- *Excessive costs*: the benefits in such sharing or transference of skills need to outweigh the costs of undertaking such integration – whether financial or in terms of opportunity cost. Often these are not achieved.

- *Overcoming self-interest*: managers in the business units have to be prepared to cooperate in such transference and sharing; and there are reasons they may not wish to do so, not least of which is that such sharing detracts from focusing on the primary concerns they have for their own businesses. Also, for managers in the businesses to be collaborative in achieving such synergistic benefits, rewards may have to be tailored to encourage such sharing. The problem is that rewards to business managers are typically on business-unit performance, whereas under this strategy they are being asked to cooperate in sharing activities between businesses. The business-unit manager will respond by asking 'what's in it for me?' and may conclude that there is very little.

Other problems include:

- The *illusion of synergy*: skills or competences on which argued synergy is supposed to be based may not really exist or, if they do, may not add value. It is not unusual for managers to claim, either at the business level or the corporate level, that particular competences exist, are important and are useful to share, when they are little more than the inherited myths in the business, or are not really valued by customers.

- *Compatibility between business-unit systems and culture*: a business may have been acquired with the logic of gaining synergistically from an existing business in a firm's portfolio, only to find that the two businesses are quite different in cultural terms such that sharing between the two is problematic.

- *Variations in local conditions*: for example, universities in the USA, UK and Australasia have sought to internationalise their operations, particularly into Asian markets. In so doing they may have difficulties in reconciling their own approaches to education and teaching with the norms in local markets.

- *Determination*: finally, the corporate parent needs to be determined to achieve such synergies. The need here, at a minimum, is for central staff to act as integrators, and therefore to understand the businesses well enough to do so. The parent may also need to be prepared to intervene at the business level in terms of strategic direction and control to ensure that such potential synergies bear fruit. However, in turn this raises questions as to whether such detailed understanding of businesses and hands-on directive influence from the corporate centre makes sense for other reasons. This relates to the sorts of issues discussed in section 8.3 of Chapter 8.

The notion of synergy has become less taken for granted. It has been realised that synergistic benefits are not as easy to achieve as would appear. However, it continues to be a dominant theme in corporate-level strategy, as Illustration 6.1 on Zodiac exemplifies.

6.4.4 The parental developer[40]

The **parental developer** seeks to employ its own competences as a parent to add value to its businesses. Here, then, the issue is not so much about how it can help create or develop benefits across business units or transfer capabilities between business units, as in the case of managing synergy. Rather parental developers have to be clear about the relevant resources or capabilities they themselves have as parents to enhance the potential of business units. Suppose, for example, the parent has a great deal of experience in globalising domestically based businesses; or a valuable brand that may enhance the performance or image of a business; or perhaps specialist skills in financial management, brand marketing or research and development. If such parenting competences exist, corporate managers then need to identify a '*parenting opportunity*': a business or businesses which are not fulfilling their potential but where improvement could be made by the application of the competences of the parent – for example, a business which could benefit by being more global, by brand development or by central R&D support.

The competences that parents have will vary. Royal Dutch Shell would argue that it is not just its huge financial muscle that matters but also that it is adept at negotiating with governments, as well as developing high-calibre internationally mobile executives who can work almost anywhere in the world within a Shell corporate framework. These competences are especially valuable in allowing it to develop businesses globally. 3M is single-mindedly concerned with inculcating a focus on innovation in its businesses. It tries to ensure a corporate culture based on this, set clear innovation targets for its businesses and elevate the standing of technical personnel concerned with innovation. Unilever has increasingly sought to focus on developing its core expertise in global branding and marketing in the fast-moving consumer goods company, with supporting state-of-the-art research and development facilities to back it up. It would argue

> The **parental developer**: a corporate parent seeking to employ its own competences as a parent to add value to its businesses and build parenting skills that are appropriate for their portfolio of business units

that this is where it can add greatest value to its businesses, and that it has significantly affected the shape of the corporation over the years (see Illustration 6.7).

Managing an organisation on this basis does, however, pose some challenges. For example:

- *Identifying capabilities of the parent*: a big challenge for the corporate parent is being sure about just how it can add value to business units. If the value-adding capabilities of the parent are wrongly identified then, far from the businesses benefiting, they will be subject to interference from the centre in ways which are counter-productive. There needs to be some hard evidence of such value-adding capabilities.

- *Focus*: if the corporate parent identifies that it has value-adding capabilities in particular and limited ways, the implication is that it should not be providing services in other ways, or if it does they should be at minimal cost. For example, some corporate parents have decided to outsource a great many services that were once seen as a traditional role of the centre: legal services, payroll services, training and development and so on. One firm, following such a course of action, claimed that by reducing the head office workforce in such ways by over 50 per cent it would save over 60 per cent of the costs of the centre. Just as significantly it would focus the attention and management time of corporate executives on activities that really could add value as distinct from merely administrative functions. Following the same logic in the public sector can create a dilemma. On the one hand, keeping such central services in the public sector ensures political control over social purposes – for example, ensuring service coverage to all sections of the community. On the other hand, a private sector company might be a better parent, in the sense that it might be more skilled at providing the service or doing it more efficiently.

- *The 'crown jewel' problem*: the corporate parent may realise that there are some business units within its portfolio where it can add little value. This may help identify businesses that should not be part of the corporate portfolio. More uncomfortably, however, such business units could be high-performing businesses, successful in their own right and not requiring the competences of the parent. The parent may argue that other businesses in the portfolio can learn from them; but this is the logic of synergy management rather than parental development. The question the parental developer has to ask is how it is adding value to *that* business. The logic of the parental development approach is that since the centre cannot add value, it is a cost and is therefore destroying value; that the parent should therefore consider divesting such a business, realising a premium for it and reinvesting it in businesses where it can add value. Logical as this may seem, it is unlikely to find favour, not least because the executives at the centre might be indicted by their own shareholders for selling the 'crown jewels'.

- *Mixed parenting*: this, in turn, raises the question as to whether the parent could adopt multiple rationales in its parenting. For example, could it simultaneously act as a parental developer for some of its businesses with a hands-off, almost portfolio approach, for those in which it cannot add further value? Or could it be both a synergy manager and a parental developer? The dangers are, of course, that the rationale becomes confused, the centre unclear as to what it is trying to achieve, the business unit managers confused as to their

| Exhibit 6.7 | Value-adding potential of corporate rationales |

Value-adding activities (see section 6.4.1)	Portfolio manager	Synergy manager	Parental developer
Envisioning			
Developing strategic intent/mission		●	●
Clear external image		●	●
Setting expectation/standards	●		
Intervening			
Monitoring performance	●		
Improving business and performance			●
Challenging/developing strategy		●	●
Coaching and Training			
Developing strategic capabilities		●	
Achieving synergies		●	
Central Services			
Investment	●	●	●
Scale advantages		●	
Transferring managerial capabilities		●	
Expertise			
Specialist expertise			●
Knowledge sharing		●	
Leverage		●	
Brokering		●	

role in the corporation and the cost of the centre escalates. A multiple approach also raises the issue of multiple control styles in corporate bodies (see section 6.6 below), and in particular whether this is feasible.

● *Sufficient 'feel'*: if the logic of the parental developer is to be followed then the executives of the corporate parent must also have 'sufficient feel' or understanding of the businesses within the portfolio to know where they can add value and where they cannot: this is an issue taken up in section 6.5.3 below in relation to the logic of portfolios.

The three roles of the parent can be considered in terms of the possible value-adding roles of corporate parents suggested in section 6.4.1 above. Exhibit 6.7

identifies how the main value-adding roles of corporate parents might differ in line with the discussion in sections 6.4.2–4 (though it should be noted that other value-adding roles may be performed as well).

Clearly much of the above also has implications for how a multi-business corporation is organised and managed. In particular there are implications about the way in which the corporate parent interacts with and seeks to exercise more or less control over the businesses. Much of this has already been intimated above. A portfolio manager is likely to exert minimal strategic control, leaving business-level strategy to chief executives of the businesses, and exercising control more through clear and challenging financial targets. On the other hand, the synergy manager and parental developer may be intervening a good deal in the businesses in order to achieve synergies across the business units or provide parental benefits. What would be very counterproductive is for the means of control to be inconsistent with the logic of the corporate parent. For example, if a portfolio manager were to have a diverse portfolio but try to intervene in the strategies of the businesses, it would very likely lead to disaster. Conversely, if a synergy manager tried to make transferences between business units without having an understanding of those businesses and involving themselves in the strategy of those businesses, it could be chaos. In Chapter 8 (section 8.3.2) this issue of corporate control is discussed more fully.

6.5 MANAGING THE CORPORATE PORTFOLIO

The discussion in section 6.4 was about the rationales that corporate parents might adopt for the management of a multi-business organisation. It should be seen that each of these rationales has implications in terms of the number and nature of the business units within such a group; or vice versa, the number and nature of business units will have implications for the rationale the parent might adopt. To take two examples: a parent acting as a portfolio manager might be able to manage a very diverse set of businesses with no particular similarities between them, largely by setting financial targets, whereas a synergy manager needs to understand the businesses well and can therefore probably only cope with a limited number of related-type businesses. The converse of this argument is also important; the extent of diversity of a corporate portfolio should inform the role played by the corporate parent. For example, it would be foolish for managers of a highly diverse portfolio to try to adopt the role of a synergy manager, unless of course they chose to change the portfolio radically.

This section is to do with the models managers might use to make sense of the nature and diversity of the business units within the portfolio, or businesses they might be considering adding given the different rationales described above.

A number of tools have been developed to help managers choose what business units to have in a portfolio. Each tool gives more or less focus on one of three criteria:

● the *balance* of the portfolio, e.g. in relation to its markets and the needs of the corporation;

- the *attractiveness* of the business units in the portfolio in terms of how profitable they are or are likely to be and how fast they are growing; and

- the degree of '*fit*' that the business units have with each other in terms of potential synergies or the extent to which the corporate parent will be good at looking after them.

6.5.1 The growth share (or BCG) matrix[41]

One of the most common and long-standing ways of conceiving of the balance of a portfolio of businesses is in terms of the relationship between market share and market growth identified by the Boston Consulting Group (BCG). Exhibit 6.8 represents this approach and shows the terms typically used to refer to the types of businesses in such a portfolio.

- A **star** is a business unit which has a high market share in a growing market. The business unit may be spending heavily to gain that share, but experience curve benefits (see page 123 and Exhibit 3.4) should mean that costs are reducing over time and, it is to be hoped, at a rate faster than that of competitors.

A **star** is a business unit which has a high market share in a growing market

- A **question mark** (or problem child) is a business unit in a growing market, but without a high market share. It may be necessary to spend heavily to increase market share, but if so, it is unlikely that the business unit is achieving sufficient cost reduction benefits to offset such investments.

A **question mark** (or problem child) is a business unit in a growing market, but without a high market share

---

Exhibit 6.8   **The growth share (or BCG) matrix**

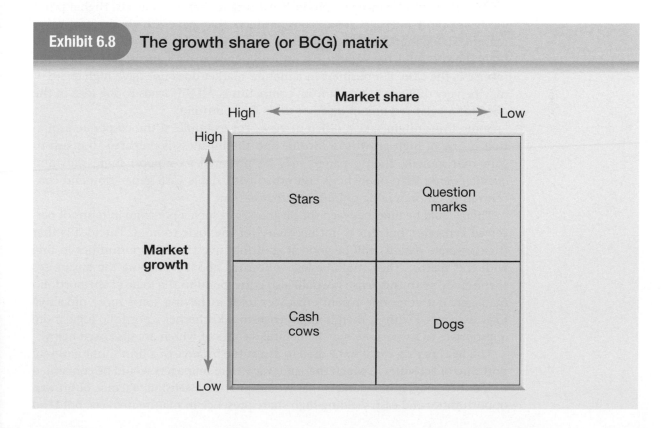

A **cash cow** is a business unit with a high market share in a mature market

- A **cash cow** is a business unit with a high market share in a mature market. Because growth is low and market conditions are more stable, the need for heavy marketing investment is less. But high relative market share means that the business unit should be able to maintain unit cost levels below those of competitors. The cash cow should then be a cash provider (e.g. to finance stars or question marks).

Dogs are business units with a low share in static or declining markets

- **Dogs** are business units with a low share in static or declining markets and are thus the worst of all combinations. They may be a cash drain and use up a disproportionate amount of company time and resources.

The growth share matrix permits business units to be examined in relation to (a) market (segment) share and (b) the growth rate of that market and in this respect the life cycle development of that market. It is therefore a way of considering the balance and development of a portfolio.

It is argued that market growth rate is important for a business unit seeking to dominate a market because it may be easier to gain dominance when a market is in its growth state. So 'stars' are particularly attractive. But if all competitors in the growth stage are trying to gain market share, competition will be very fierce. So it will be necessary to invest in that business unit in order to gain share and market dominance. Moreover, it is likely that such a business unit will need to price low or spend high amounts on advertising and selling, or both. These businesses are 'question marks' or 'problem children'. They have potential but can eat up investment and are likely to be yielding low margins in seeking to beat competition and gain share. Investing here is high risk unless this potentially low-margin activity is financed by products earning higher profit levels. Higher profit levels are most likely to come from products that have a high share in more mature, stable markets. This is where competition is likely to be less fierce and high share should have given rise to experience curve benefits. Of course the reverse is the case; if a business in a mature market does not have high share, it may be very difficult to take it from competitors. All this leads to the idea of the need for a balanced mix of business units in a portfolio.

Some firms might take a different view. For example, if the corporate aspiration is one of high growth in income and the business is prepared to invest to gain that growth, then a parent may be prepared to support more *stars* and *question marks* than one who is concerned with stable cash generation and concentrating on preserving or building its *cash cows*.

There could be links between the businesses in such a portfolio in terms of perceived synergies; but this is not necessary for the logic to hold. The idea is that the corporate parents will be good at spotting investment opportunities in line with this matrix. They could be less concerned about managing the businesses themselves; so in this sense it would also correspond to the logic of the portfolio manager. If a corporate parent envisages itself as having some more proactive logic associated with it, then it might wish to ask whether a portfolio logic more appropriate to its purpose may be helpful – some of which are discussed below.

The BCG matrix can also be used to assess the balance of a firm's international portfolio of activities in much the same way. Here managers would be concerned to identify geographic markets that would provide a sensible balance of growth opportunities and cash yielding high share presence in mature markets, but tend to shift their efforts away from those countries where they had a low market share in static or declining markets.

However, some caution needs to be exercised in the use of the BCG matrix:

- There can be practical difficulties in deciding what exactly 'high' and 'low' (growth and share) can mean in a particular situation.

- The analysis should be applied to *strategic business units*, not to products or to broad markets (which might include many market segments).

- In many organisations the critical resource to be planned and balanced will not be cash, but the innovative capacity, which consists of the time and creative energy of the organisation's managers, designers, engineers, etc. *Question marks* and *stars* are very demanding on these types of resource.

- The position of *dogs* is often misunderstood. Certainly, there may be some business units which need immediate deletion. However, other dogs may have a useful place in the portfolio. They may be necessary to complete the product range and provide a credible presence in the market. They may be held for defensive reasons – to keep competitors out. They may also be capable of revitalisation.

- Little is said about the behavioural implications of such a strategy. How does central management motivate the managers of *cash cows*, who may see all their hard-earned surpluses being invested in other businesses? There may be political difficulties if the decision is taken to delete 'dogs' that are the brainchild of people with power within the organisation. Indeed, perhaps the single factor which makes the creation and management of a balanced port-folio difficult in practice is the jealousy that can arise between the various strategic business units.

In addition to these general limitations of the model three points are of particular relevance to its use in an international context.

- The model does not account for possibly different mechanisms of market entry that may be required, i.e. in some countries the opportunity for full equity ownership may be limited.

- Different levels of economic and political risk are not accounted for: countries with potentially very attractive growth rates – such as China – may carry with them higher levels of risk.

- For product-diversified firms the model does not take into account the shared use of resources, for example sales and distribution facilities.[42]

6.5.2 Balance in a public sector portfolio

The different services offered by public sector organisations can also be considered in terms of the balance of a portfolio, as seen in Exhibit 6.9. Here the key judgements are concerned with (a) the organisation's 'ability to serve effectively' by providing perceived value for money with the resources which are available to it, and (b) the political attractiveness of its services in terms of the extent to which it can gain stakeholder and public support for funding.[43] Not all services

Exhibit 6.9   Public sector portfolio matrix

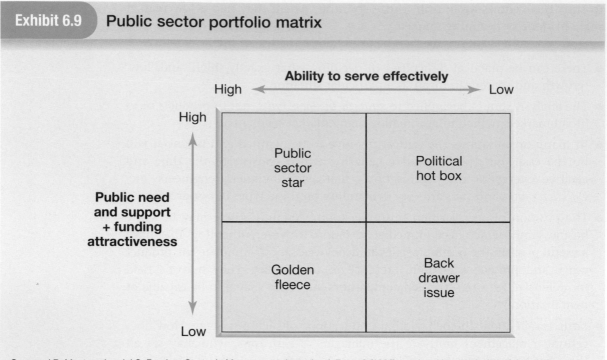

Source: J.R. Montanari and J.S. Bracker, *Strategic Management Journal*, vol. 7, no. 3 (1986), reprinted by permission of John Wiley & Sons Ltd.

will be public sector 'stars' in this respect. Some may be services required politically or because of public need, but for which there are limited resources – the 'political hot box'. In many respects this is where the National Health Service in the UK finds itself. Similarly – and a point often forgotten by public sector managers when reviewing their portfolio of activities – a provider of public services may be mandated to provide some statutory services and find resources 'locked up' in so doing. There are still other services that a public sector provider may have undertaken effectively for many years but for which there is little popular public support or funding attractiveness: these are referred to as the 'golden fleece' in the matrix. 'Back drawer issues' are the equivalent of dogs in the BCG matrix; they have neither political (or public) support, nor sufficient resources. In a review of the public sector portfolio, they are the sorts of service which, if possible, should be dropped.

Another problem may arise for managers in public sector organisations. They may find it difficult to develop services with real growth potential or generate surpluses to be reinvested, because this may not be their brief from government. They may be expected to manage services which cannot make money, but which are public necessities. Further, if they seek to develop services which can grow and make money, these may be privatised or put out to private tender. It may be seen as legitimate for a local government leisure department to manage public parks and recreation grounds, but the development of indoor tennis and swimming pools with profit potential may be seen as an inappropriate activity. The definition of the appropriate portfolio of activities therefore requires a clarity of corporate purposes and aspirations.

6.5.3 The directional policy matrix

Another way to consider a portfolio of businesses is by means of the *directional policy matrix*,[44] which categorises business units into those with good prospects and those with less good prospects. Sometimes known as the *attractiveness matrix*, it provides a way of considering a portfolio of business units by directing attention to the attractiveness of both the environment for SBUs and their competitive position. Specifically, the **directional policy matrix** positions business units according to (a) how attractive the relevant market is in which they are operating, and (b) the competitive strength of the SBU in that market. Each business unit is positioned within the matrix according to a series of indicators of attractiveness and strength. The factors typically considered are set out in Exhibit 6.10(a). However, these should not be thought of as pre-ordained. The factors should be those most relevant to the organisation and its market: for example, as identified by PESTEL or five forces analyses for attractiveness and through competitor analysis to identify business unit strength. Some analysts also choose to show graphically how large the market is for a given business unit's activity, and even the market share of that business unit, as shown in Exhibit 6.10(b). For example, managers in a firm with the portfolio shown in Exhibit 6.10(b) will be concerned that they have relatively low shares in the largest and most attractive market, whereas their greatest strength is in a market with only medium attractiveness and smaller markets with little long-term attractiveness.

The **directional policy matrix** positions SBUs according to (a) how attractive the relevant market is in which they are operating, and (b) the competitive strength of the SBU in that market

The matrix also provides a way of considering appropriate corporate-level strategies given the positioning of the business units as shown in Exhibit 6.10(c). It suggests that the businesses with the highest growth potential and the greatest strength are those in which to invest for growth; and those that are the weakest and in the least attractive markets should be divested or harvested (i.e. used to yield as much cash as possible before divesting or closure). The difficult decisions relate to those businesses in the middle ground; and in the example in Exhibit 6.10(b) there are a number of these. Where the matrix helps in this respect is in getting managers to identify the reasons for the positions in the matrix such that they can ask questions about whether it is possible to grow such businesses. Further, if choices of investment have to be made between the businesses, which look most likely to show a pay-off on the basis of such evidence.

The directional policy matrix can also be used to consider and compare international investment opportunities. Here the matrix focuses on a company's competitive position in the same product market across different national markets (see Exhibit 6.10(d)). In addition to standard considerations such as market size, growth and competitive conditions, the assessment of the attractiveness of a national market needs to include a consideration of existing tariff and non-tariff barriers to trade, government regulations such as price controls and local content requirements, and national economic and political stability.[45] While the model thus overcomes some of the limitations of the BCG matrix in international portfolio planning, again it does not take into account possible resource linkages between product groups in organisations that are diversified both internationally and in terms of product/service range.

This portfolio logic is essentially about understanding the relative strength of a business in the context of its markets so as to make decisions about investment,

Exhibit 6.10a Indicators of SBU strength and market attractiveness

Indicators of SBU strength compared with competition	Indicators of market attractiveness
• Market share • Salesforce • Marketing • R&D • Manufacturing • Distribution • Financial resources • Managerial competence • Competitive position in terms of, e.g. image, breadth of product line, quality/reliability, customer service	• Market size • Market growth rate • Cyclicality • Competitive structure • Barriers to entry • Industry profitability • Technology • Inflation • Regulation • Workforce availability • Social issues • Environmental issues • Political issues • Legal issues

Exhibit 6.10b Market attractiveness/SBU strength matrix

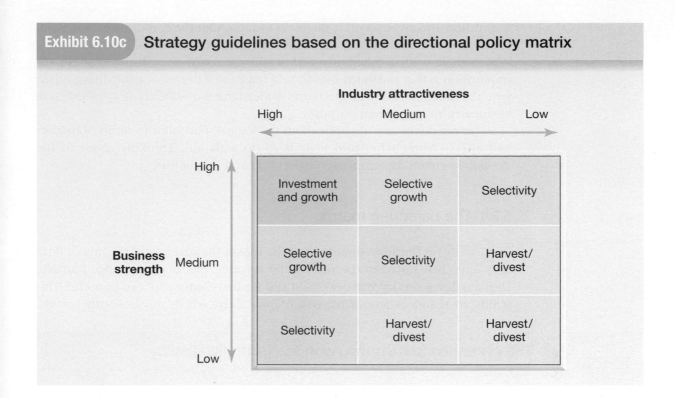

Exhibit 6.10c   Strategy guidelines based on the directional policy matrix

Industry attractiveness

	High	Medium	Low
High	Investment and growth	Selective growth	Selectivity
Business strength — Medium	Selective growth	Selectivity	Harvest/divest
Low	Selectivity	Harvest/divest	Harvest/divest

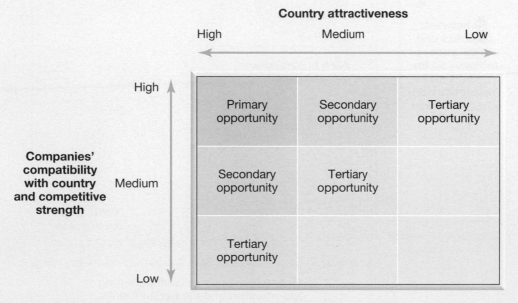

Exhibit 6.10d   International investment opportunities based on the directional policy matrix

Country attractiveness

	High	Medium	Low
High	Primary opportunity	Secondary opportunity	Tertiary opportunity
Companies' compatibility with country and competitive strength — Medium	Secondary opportunity	Tertiary opportunity	
Low	Tertiary opportunity		

Source: Harrel, G.D. and R.D. Kiefer (1993), 'Multinational market portfolio in global strategy development', *International Marketing Review* 10 (1); Phillips, C., I. Duole, and R. Lowe, *International Marketing Strategy*, Routledge 1994, pp. 137–8.

acquisition and divestment. It therefore assumes that the corporate parent needs to have an understanding of the businesses, their strategies and bases of success. Whilst there is little inherently within this matrix to do with relatedness, the implication is that the businesses should have some degree of relatedness, otherwise the parent would be expected to understand too wide an array of different businesses for investment purposes.

So far the discussion has been about the logic of portfolios in terms of balance and attractiveness. The third logic is to do with 'fit'. Thinking about fit has developed around two concepts – parenting and capabilities.

6.5.4 The parenting matrix

In deciding on the appropriateness of the role of the parent and the mix of business units best suited to the parent, the *parenting matrix* (or Ashridge Portfolio Display) developed by Michael Goold and Andrew Campbell[46] can be useful. This builds on the ideas set out in section 6.4.4 above which discussed the *parental*

Exhibit 6.11   **The parenting matrix: the Ashridge Portfolio Display**

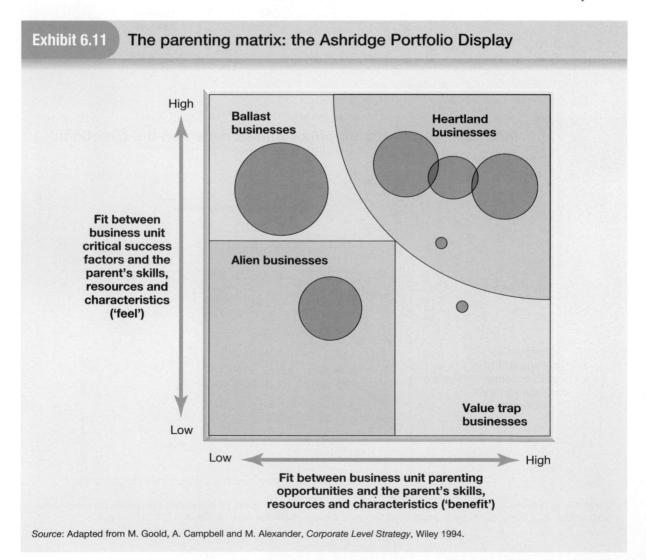

Source: Adapted from M. Goold, A. Campbell and M. Alexander, *Corporate Level Strategy*, Wiley 1994.

developer corporate rationale. It suggests that corporations should seek to build portfolios that fit well with their corporate centre parenting skills and that the corporate centre should in turn build parenting skills that are appropriate for its portfolio. By juggling these two principles, corporations should be able to move towards greater fit in terms of two dimensions (see Exhibit 6.11):

- The extent to which the corporate parent has sufficient *'feel'* for the businesses in the portfolio. In effect this is the fit between the *critical success factors* of the business units (see Chapter 2, section 2.4.4) and the capabilities (in terms of competences and resources) and characteristics of the corporate parent.

- The fit between the *parenting opportunities* of business units (see below) and the capabilities and characteristics of the parent. So this is about how the businesses might *benefit* from the parent.

The logic for using these two dimensions of fit is as follows. If the critical success factors of the business unit fit badly with the capabilities and characteristics of the parent, then parent managers are likely to misunderstand the business and inadvertently do it harm. So the first measure of fit is about avoiding problems. For example, when BAT, a tobacco company, acquired Eagle Star, a financial services company, in the 1990s there was low *critical success factor fit*: the critical success factors of insurance did not fit well with the skills and characteristics of BAT managers. The result was problematic. BAT encouraged Eagle Star to gain market share (a normal strategy in tobacco) with the consequence that Eagle Star took on inappropriate insurance risks, incurring some big losses a few years later. The lack of fit was partly the cause of these subsequent losses. Fit between critical success factors of the business and the characteristics of the parent is therefore about downside risk. High fit means low risk of problems. Low fit means high risk of problems.

Fit between the parenting opportunities of the business and the characteristics of the parent is about benefit and opportunity. High fit means high potential for added value. Low fit means low potential. A 'parenting opportunity' is an opportunity for the business to improve that which can be better exploited with help from a parent organisation. For example, the business may need to cut costs and could be helped by a parent organisation with experience of doing this; the business may need to expand in Asia and would be helped by a parent with good Asian contacts; the business may need to improve its marketing skills and could be helped by a parent with strong marketing skills; and so on.

Exhibit 6.11 shows what a resulting portfolio might look like.

- *Heartland* business units are ones to which the parent can add value without danger of doing harm. They should be at the core of future strategy.

- *Ballast* business units are ones the parent understands well but can do little for. They would probably be just as successful as independent companies. If they are part of a future corporate strategy, they need to be managed with a light touch and bear as little cost of the corporate bureaucracy as possible.

- *Value trap* business units are dangerous. They appear attractive because there are opportunities for the parent to add value. But they are deceptively attractive, because there is a high danger that the parent's attentions will result in more harm than good. Value trap businesses should only be included in the future strategy if they can be moved into the heartland. Moreover, some adjustments to the skills, resources or characteristics of the parent will probably be necessary.

● *Alien* business units are clear misfits. They offer little opportunity to add value and they rub awkwardly with the normal behaviour of the parent. Exit is the best strategy.

This approach to considering corporate portfolios therefore places the emphasis firmly on asking how the parent benefits the business units, and this results in a number of challenges.

● *Value or cost of the corporate parent.* If the parent is not enhancing the performance of the business units, what is its role? A corporate body has a role to play with regard to purely corporate affairs, such as dealing with financial institutions and negotiating with governments. But if its role is limited to this, the cost of delivering these functions should be low to the business unit. A large and costly corporate headquarters that does little to enhance the strategies of its business units can be a great cost burden to them, thus undermining potential market-based competitive advantage, and so reducing the overall returns for shareholders.

● *Understanding value creation at the business-unit level.* An overall pattern has emerged in the past decade or so which suggests that organisations throughout the world are attempting to drive responsibility for strategic decisions nearer and nearer to markets. There is an attempt to ensure that business-specific competences are directed at developing successful competitive strategies. The trend towards deregulation and privatisation of public utilities and government authorities, increasing throughout the world, has a similar rationale underlying it. The aim is to give the responsibility for developing strategic capability and achieving competitive advantage in markets to the business-unit level – to managers who are most closely in touch with their markets. The role of the parent has therefore been increasingly seen as one of facilitation, or of taking a hands-off approach as far as possible.

● *Understanding value creation at the corporate level.* If the corporate parent seeks to enhance the strategies of the businesses it must be very clear where and how it can add value. It must also avoid undertaking roles that do not enhance strategies at the business-unit level. For example, the corporate parent may impose cumbersome strategic planning more to do with providing information to the centre than with aiding the strategic development of the units; it may retain a large head office staff which duplicate the roles of executives in business units; or it may make demands on business-unit strategy that are not sensible in terms of competitive strategy at that level.

● *Sufficient feel.* If the corporate parent does, indeed, seek to enhance business strategies, it needs to consider the number of business units for which it can sensibly do so. For this the parent has to have sufficient feel for the businesses, so the number cannot be great unless they are similar businesses in terms of technology, products or capabilities; or in similar markets.

● *Reviewing the portfolio.* The corporate parent should also assess which businesses should most sensibly be within its portfolio given these considerations. Illustration 6.7 shows how Unilever reviewed its role as a corporate parent and, in consequence, its portfolio.

Illustration 6.7

strategy into action

Unilever's parenting

If the role of the parent is to add value to business units, it needs to be clear about how it can do this for which businesses.

Unilever, the consumer products company, involved in food, detergents and personal products, has built skills, resources and characteristics which make it an effective parent of certain kinds of business, but a less effective parent of others.

Unilever developed as a decentralised organisation, traditionally setting great store in the country or regional manager. It had a strong technology base and centralised corporate research laboratories; a strong marketing focus, built around skills in product development and branding for mass market consumers; and an unusual human resource management process, monitoring the progress of 20,000 managers, a large portion of whom were expatriates.

These skills, resources and characteristics fitted well with the parenting opportunities and critical success factors of Unilever's main businesses. Food businesses have traditionally been regional or local businesses that can benefit from access to product and market knowledge from around the globe. They can also leverage central research laboratories and Unilever's pool of management talent without compromising their local focus. Detergent and personal product businesses also gain from Unilever's global coverage, central research, pool of managers and central policies, but they gain less than the food businesses. The detergent and personal products businesses, now called Home and Personal Care (HPC), are less local and more global. This means that some of Unilever's parenting behaviour, such as the company's bias toward decentralisation, has some negative side-effects. Moreover, Unilever's approach to sharing know-how across borders through working groups means that some of the benefits of centralised knowledge management are missed.

The trade-off that Unilever has historically made between centralisation and localisation suits the food businesses better than the HPC businesses, resulting in the different positioning on the parenting matrix. Because of these differences, Unilever divided the company into two divisions – foods and HPC. The purpose of the reorganisation was to allow HPC to become more centralised. However, since both food and HPC are becoming more global and less local, even the food division has had to give more attention to international brands and become more centralised

itself. So there are those who argue that this common trajectory may justify keeping the two divisions together: food being able to learn from HPC how to become more global while HPC learns from food how to retain local responsiveness.

This trend to focus more on those businesses and products that best suit Unilever's unique combination of centralisation and localisation has been going on for the last 25 years. Businesses such as tea plantations and animal feeds were disposed of in the 1980s. These businesses had critical success factors that were very different from the main food and detergents businesses and did not fit well with Unilever's consumer marketing bias. Moreover, they were benefiting very little from Unilever's global reach, central research and pool of product managers.

In the 1990s, Unilever also exited speciality chemicals. This business had been retained because of some synergies in the research area. However, its critical success factors (plant optimisation, technology sale, technology service and global manufacturing) were very different to branded foods and, like tea plantations and animal feeds, it was gaining little from Unilever's unique strengths.

Major acquisitions have been made within the area of focus as well. Best Foods, a US-based food company, has dramatically increased Unilever's presence in the USA and worldwide. Moreover, Unilever has announced an intention of focusing on a few hundred international brands, dropping many of its local brands.

Prepared by Andrew Campbell, Ashridge Strategic Management Centre.

Questions

1. How might the results of this parenting matrix exercise differ from a portfolio exercise using the growth share matrix?

2. What are the benefits and disadvantages of keeping the two divisions set up in 2000 in one company? Should Unilever consider a de-merger?

The concept of fit has equal relevance in the public sector. The implication is that public sector managers should control directly only those services and activities that fit services and activities for which they have special managerial expertise. Other services should be outsourced or set up as independent agencies. Whilst outsourcing, privatising and setting up independent agencies is driven as much by political dogma as by corporate-level strategy analysis, the trend has been in this direction.

6.5.5 Roles in an international portfolio

As Chris Bartlett and Sumantra Ghoshal have highlighted, the complexity of the strategies followed by organisations such as Boeing and General Motors can result in highly differentiated networks of subsidiaries with a range of distinct strategic roles. Subsidiaries may play different roles according to the level of local resources and capabilities available to them and the strategic importance of their local environment (see Exhibit 6.12).[47]

- '**Strategic leaders**' are subsidiaries that not only hold valuable resources and capabilities but are also located in countries that are crucial for competitive success because of, for example, the size of the local market or the accessibility of key technologies.

- '**Contributors**', subsidiaries with valuable internal resources but located in countries of lesser strategic significance, can nevertheless play key roles in a multinational organisation's competitive success. The Australian subsidiary of

Strategic leaders (in the context of international strategy) are subsidiaries that not only hold valuable resources and capabilities located in countries that are crucial for competitive success

Contributors are subsidiaries with valuable internal resources but located in countries of lesser strategic significance, which nonetheless play key roles in a multinational organisation's competitive success

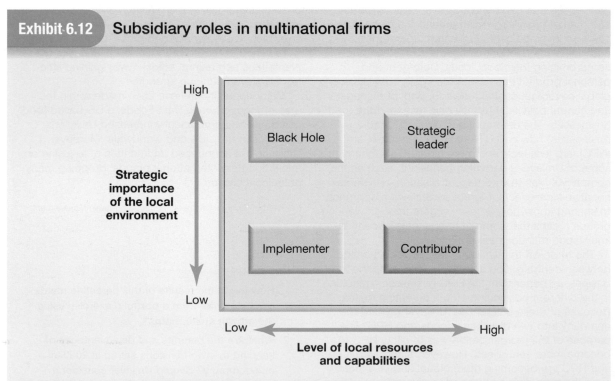

Exhibit 6.12   Subsidiary roles in multinational firms

Source: Bartlett, C.A. and S. Ghoshal, *Managing Across Borders: The Transnational Solution*, Boston: The Harvard Business School Press, 1989, pp. 105–111.

the Swedish telecommunications firm Ericsson played such a role in development of systems important for the firm's development.

- **Implementers**, though not substantially enhancing competitive advantage, help generate financial resources.
- **'Black holes'** are subsidiaries located in countries that are crucial for competitive success but with low-level resources or capabilities. This is a position many subsidiaries of American and European firms found themselves in over long periods in Japan. Possibilities for overcoming this unattractive position include the development of alliances and the selective and targeted development of key resources and capabilities.[48]

Black holes are subsidiaries located in countries that are crucial for competitive success but with low-level resources or capabilities

Again this does, of course, in turn relate to how these subsidiaries are controlled and managed and this is discussed in section 8.3 of Chapter 8.

6.5.6 Trends in portfolio management

The trend in management thinking has been to move away from focusing mainly on the balance and attractiveness criteria (i.e. sections 6.5.1 and 6.5.3 above) towards focusing more on the fit criterion (i.e. 6.5.4 above). In other words, the challenge the corporate parent increasingly faces is to justify how a portfolio of businesses achieves greater value than the sum of its parts because of either the synergistic fit between the businesses, or the fit between business needs and parental competences, or both. Many companies diversified in the 1970s and 1980s in order to get into more attractive businesses and balance their portfolios. Most of these initiatives failed and from the 1990s there has been a period of unbundling, break-ups, and de-mergers of portfolios that had, at best, spurious relatedness. Corporate parents sought to achieve greater focus on technologies or markets they could understand and in which there were greater chances of achieving such fit.

The increasing sophistication of the capital markets has, in turn, encouraged this trend. As explained at the beginning of the chapter, shareholders no longer need corporate managers in conglomerates to act on their behalf to smooth earnings over a portfolio of businesses because they can smooth their returns themselves by investing in a selection of companies with different earnings profiles. Moreover, shareholders can move money into attractive sectors, such as health care or emerging technologies, more easily than corporate parents can. The argument is that corporate parents should stop doing tasks that shareholders can more easily do for themselves and focus on creating additional value from the application of management expertise.

There has been a parallel trend in the public sector, with increasing political pressure by governments to challenge what large and often bureaucratic bodies have to offer to more local delivery of services. Here the driving forces have been the combination of a desire to reduce the cost of central government and the demand for more local accountability for services.

Underlying much of this debate and wider issues raised in this chapter is the debate on the nature and benefits of the corporation as a whole. This is the theme of this chapter's key debate in Illustration 6.8.

Illustration 6.8   key debate

Why have corporate strategies anyway?

Do we really need multinational and diversified corporations?

The notion of corporate strategy assumes that corporations own and control businesses in a range of markets or countries. But 'transaction cost' economist Oliver Williamson believes that such diversified corporations should only exist in the presence of 'market failures'.[1] If markets worked well, there would be no need for business units to be coordinated through managerial hierarchies. Business units could be independent, coordinating where necessary simply by transacting in the marketplace. The 'invisible hand' of the market could replace the 'visible hand' of managers at corporate headquarters. There would be no 'corporate strategy'.

Market failures favouring the corporation occur for two reasons:

- *'Bounded rationality'*: people cannot know everything that is going on in the market, so perfectly rational market transactions are impossible. Information, for instance on quality and costs, can sometimes be better inside the corporate fold.

- *'Opportunism'*: independent businesses trading between each other may behave opportunistically, for example by cheating on delivery or quality promises. Cheating can sometimes be policed and punished more easily within a corporate hierarchy.

According to Williamson, activities should only be brought into the corporation when the 'transaction costs' of coping with bounded rationality (gaining information) and opportunism (guarding against cheats) are lower inside the corporate hierarchy than they would be if simply relying on transactions in the marketplace.

This comparison of the transaction costs of markets and hierarchies has powerful implications for trends in product and geographical diversification:

- Improving capital markets may reduce the relative information advantages of conglomerates in managing a set of unrelated businesses. As markets get better at capturing information there will be less need for conglomerates, something that may account for the recent decline in conglomerates in many economies.

- Improving protection of intellectual property rights internationally may increase the incentives for multinational corporations to license out their technologies to companies abroad, rather than trying to do everything themselves. If the prospect of collecting royalties improves, there is less advantage in multinationals keeping everything in-house.

Thus fewer market failures also mean narrower product and geographical scope.

Williamson's 'transaction cost' view puts a heavy burden on corporations to justify themselves. Two defences are possible. First, knowledge is hard to trade in the market. Buyers can only know the value of new knowledge once they have already bought it. Colleagues in sister business units within the same corporation are better at transferring knowledge than independent companies are in the open market.[2] Second, corporations are not just about minimising the costs of information and cheating, but also about maximising the value of the combined resources. Bringing creative people together in a collective enterprise enhances knowledge exchange, innovation and motivation. Corporations are value creators as well as cost minimisers.[3]

Notes:
1. O.E. Williamson, 'Strategy research: governance and competence perspectives', *Strategic Management Journal*, vol. 12 (1998), pp. 75–94.
2. B. Kogut and U. Zander, 'What firms do? Coordination, identity and learning', *Organization Science*, vol. 7, no. 5 (1996), pp. 502–519.
3. S. Ghoshal, C. Bartlett and P. Moran, 'A new manifesto for management', *Sloan Management Review*, Spring (1999), pp. 9–20.

Question

Consider a multinational diversified corporation such as Cadbury Schweppes or Unilever: what kinds of hard-to-trade knowledge might it be able to transfer between product and country subsidiaries and is such knowledge likely to be of increasing or decreasing importance?

Summary

- Many corporations comprise several, sometimes many, business units. Decisions and activities above the level of business units are the concern of what in this chapter is termed the corporate parent.

- Corporate strategy is concerned with decisions of the corporate parent about (a) the product and international scope; and (b) how they seek to add value to that created by their business units.

- Product diversity is often considered in terms of related and unrelated diversification. Increasingly relatedness is being considered in terms of relatedness of strategic capabilities.

- Benefits of international scale and scope may be achieved through the careful selection of (a) which markets might be entered internationally, (b) which elements of the organisation's value chain might be located in different parts of the world and (c) the extent to which products and services or assets are standardised or locally specific.

- Both in relation to product and international scope, performance suffers if organisations become very diverse.

- Corporate parents may seek to add value by adopting different parenting roles: the portfolio manager, the synergy manager or the parental developer.

- Several portfolio models exist to help corporate parents manage their business portfolios, the most common of which are: the BCG box, the directional policy matrix, the parenting matrix and models relating to public sector and internationally diversified organisations.

Recommended key readings

- The chapter by M. Goold and G. Luchs, 'Why diversify: four decades of management thinking', in D.O. Faulkner and A. Campbell (eds), *The Oxford Handbook of Strategy*, vol. 2, Oxford University Press, 2003, pp. 18–42, is a useful discussion on diversification. The challenge of building and managing diversified organisations is also the focus of the paper by M. Goold and A. Campbell, 'Desperately seeking synergy', *Harvard Business Review*, vol. 76, no. 2 (1998), pp. 131–145.

- A seminal and award-winning article on the development of multinational firms is B. Kogut and U. Zander, 'Knowledge of the firm and the evolutionary theory of the multinational enterprise', *Journal of International Business Studies*, vol. 24, no. 4 (1993), pp. 625–645.

- An article which provides a balanced account of the evidence on globalisation and international economic integration is: P. Ghemawat, 'Semiglobalization and international business strategy', *Journal of International Business Studies*, vol. 34, no. 2 (2003), pp. 138–152.

- The issue of parenting is covered in detail with many examples in M. Goold, A. Campbell and M. Alexander, *Corporate Level Strategy*, Wiley, 1994.

- A summary of different portfolio analyses, their benefits and limitations is provided in D. Faulkner, 'Portfolio matrices', in V. Ambrosini (ed.) with G. Johnson and K. Scholes, *Exploring Techniques of Analysis and Evaluation in Strategic Management*, Prentice Hall, 1998.

References

1. On economies of scope, see D.J. Teece, 'Towards an economic theory of the multi-product firm', *Journal of Economic Behavior and Organization*, vol. 3 (1982), pp. 39–63.

2. See A. Campbell and K. Luchs, *Strategic Synergy*, Butterworth/Heinemann, 1992.

3. See C.K. Prahalad and R. Bettis, 'The dominant logic: a new link between diversity and performance', *Strategic Management Journal*, vol. 6, no. 1 (1986), pp. 485–501; R. Bettis and C.K. Prahalad, 'The dominant logic: retrospective and extension', *Strategic Management Journal*, vol. 16, no. 1 (1995), pp. 5–15.

4. See L. Cohen, 'How United Technologies lawyers outmaneuvred GE', *Wall Street Journal*, 2 July 2001.

5. See M.A. Schilling, 'Technological leapfrogging: lessons from the U.S. video games console industry', *California Management Review*, vol. 45, no. 3 (2003), pp. 6–33.

6. P.C. Fusaro and R.M. Miller, *What Went Wrong at Enron*, Wiley, 2002 is a good account of the situation that developed at Enron in the late 1990s.

7. This is usefully discussed by P. Comment and G. Jarrell, 'Corporate focus and stock returns', *Journal of Financial Economics*, vol. 37 (1995), pp. 67–87, and C.C. Markides, *Diversification, Refocusing and Economic Performance*, MIT Press, 1995.

8. M. Goold and A. Campbell, 'Desperately seeking synergy', *Harvard Business Review*, vol. 76, no. 2 (1998), pp. 131–145.

9. This question is raised in the discussion on synergy by Campbell and Luchs (see reference 2 above).

10. See A. Serwer, 'The oracle of everything', *Fortune*, 11 November 2002.

11. See C. Markides, 'Corporate strategy: the role of the centre', in A. Pettigrew, H. Thomas and R. Whittington (eds), *Handbook of Strategy and Management*, Sage, 2002.

12. The classic study here is by R.P. Rumelt, *Strategy, Structure and Economic Performance*, Harvard University Press, 1974.

13. C.A. Montgomery, 'The measurement of firm diversification: some new empirical evidence', *Academy of Management Journal*, vol. 25, no. 2 (1982), pp. 299–307; and R.A. Bettis, 'Performance differences in related and unrelated diversified firms', *Strategic Management Journal*, vol. 2 (1981), pp. 379–393.

14. L.E. Palich, L.B. Cardinal and C. Miller, 'Curvilinearity in the diversification-performance linkage: an examination of over three decades of research', *Strategic Management Journal*, vol. 21 (2000), pp. 155–174.

15. T. Khanna and K. Palepu, 'The future of business groups in emerging markets: long-run evidence from Chile', *Academy of Management Journal*, vol. 43, no. 3 (2000), pp. 268–285.

16. R. Grant, A. Jammine and H. Thomas, 'Diversity, diversification and profitability among British manufacturing companies, 1972–1984', *Strategic Management Journal*, vol. 17 (1988), pp. 109–122.

17. R. Whittington and M. Mayer, *The European Corporation: Strategy, Structure and Social Science*, Oxford University Press, 2000.

18. For a fuller explanation see P. Ghemawat, 'The forgotten strategy', *Harvard Business Review*, November 2003, pp. 76–84.

19. This discussion is based on B. Burmester, 'Political risk in international business', in M. Tayeb (ed.), *International Business*, Prentice Hall, 2000, pp. 247–272.

20. See M.E. Bergara, W.J. Henisz and P.T. Spiller, 'Political institutions and electric utility investment: a cross-national analysis', *California Management Review*, vol. 40, no. 2 (1998), pp. 18–35.

21. J. Imle, 'Multinationals and the new world of energy development: A corporate perspective', *Journal of International Affairs*, vol. 53, no. 1 (1999), pp. 263–280.

22. See J.W. Lu and P.W. Beamish, 'Internationalisation and performance of SMEs', *Strategic Management Journal*, vol. 22 (2001), pp. 565–586; and K.L. Newman and S.D. Nollen, 'Culture and congruence: the fit between management practices and national culture', *Journal of International Business Studies*, vol. 27, no. 4 (1996), pp. 753–779.

23. For detailed discussions of the role of learning and experience in market entry see: M.F. Guillén, 'Experience, imitation, and the sequence of foreign entry: wholly owned and joint-venture manufacturing by South Korean firms and business groups in China, 1987–1995', *Journal of International Business Studies*, vol. 83 (2003), pp. 185–198; and M.K. Erramilli, 'The experience factor in foreign market entry modes by service firms', *Journal of International Business Studies*, vol. 22, no. 3 (1991), pp. 479–501.

24. R.D. Hisrich, *Cases in International Entrepreneurship*, Irwin, 1997.

25. M.V. Jones, 'The internationalization of small high-technology firms', *Journal of International Marketing*, vol. 7 (1999), pp. 15–41. See also B.M. Oviatt and P.P. McDougall, 'Toward a theory of new international ventures', *Journal of International Business Studies*, vol. 25 (1994), pp. 45–64.

26. B. Kogut, 'Designing global strategies: comparative and competitive value added chains', *Sloan Management Review*, vol. 27 (1985), pp. 15–28.

27. T. Levitt, 'The globalization of markets', *Harvard Business Review*, vol. 61 (1983), pp. 92–102.

28. A useful review of the international dimension is: M. Hitt and R.E. Hoskisson, 'International diversification: effects on innovation and firm performance in product-diversified firms', *Academy of Management Journal*, vol. 40, no. 4 (1997), pp. 767–798.

29. See L. Gomes and K. Ramaswamy, 'An empirical examination of the form of the relationship between multinationality and performance', *Journal of International Business Studies*, vol. 30 (1999), pp. 173–188. J. Geringer, S. Tallman and D.M. Olsen, 'Product and international diversification among Japanese multinational firms', *Strategic Management Journal*, vol. 21 (2000), pp. 51–80.

30. See N. Capar and M. Kotabe, 'The relationship between international diversification and performance in service firms', *Journal of International Business Studies*, vol. 34 (2003), pp. 345–355; F.J. Contractor, S.K. Kundu and C. Hsu, 'A three-stage theory of international expansion: the link between multinationality and performance in the service sector', *Journal of International Business Studies*, vol. 34 (2003), pp. 5–18.

31. M. Hitt and R. Hoskisson, 'International diversification: effects on innovation and firm performance', *Academy of Management Journal*, vol. 40, no. 4 (1997), pp. 767–798.

32. S. Tallman and J. Li, 'Effects of international diversity and product diversity on the performance of multinational firms', *Academy of Management Journal*, vol. 39 (1996), pp. 179–196.

33. The opening chapters of M. Goold and K.S. Luchs, *Managing the Multibusiness Company*, Routledge, 1996, provide a good introduction to the theories underpinning the value-adding capabilities of multi-product firms.

34. For a discussion of the role of a clarity of mission, see A. Campbell, M. Devine and D. Young, *A Sense of Mission*, Hutchinson Business, 1990. However, G. Hamel and C.K. Prahalad argue in Chapter 6 of their book, *Competing for the Future*, Harvard Business School Press, 1994, that mission statements have insufficient impact for the competence of a clarity of 'strategic intent'. This is more likely to be a brief but clear statement which focuses more on clarity of strategic direction (they use the word 'destiny') than on how that strategic direction will be achieved. See also Hamel and Prahalad on strategic intent in the *Harvard Business Review*, vol. 67, no. 3 (1989), pp. 63–76.

35. M. Goold, A. Campbell and M. Alexander, *Corporate Level Strategy*, Wiley, 1994, is concerned with both the value-adding and value-destroying capacity of corporate parents.

36. The extent and means of the value-adding capabilities of corporate parents is the theme of M. Goold, A. Campbell and M. Alexander (see reference 35).

37. The first two rationales discussed here are based on a paper by Michael Porter, 'From competitive advantage to corporate strategy', *Harvard Business Review*, vol. 65, no. 3 (1987), pp. 43–59.

38. See A. Campbell and K. Luchs, *Strategic Synergy*, Butterworth/Heinemann, 1992.

39. Here the rationales of the 'synergy manager' and 'skills transferer' described by Porter (see reference 37 above) have been combined.

40. The logic of parental development is explained extensively in Goold, Campbell and Alexander (see reference 35 above).

41. For a more extensive discussion of the use of the growth share matrix see A.C. Hax and N.S. Majluf in R.G. Dyson (ed.), *Strategic Planning: Models and analytical techniques*, Wiley, 1990; and D. Faulkner, 'Portfolio matrices', in V. Ambrosini (ed.), *Exploring Techniques of Analysis and Evaluation in Strategic Management*, Prentice Hall, 1998; for source explanations of the BCG matrix see B.D. Henderson, *Henderson on Corporate Strategy*, Abt Books, 1979.

42. See Y. Wind and S. Douglas, 'International portfolio analysis and strategy', *Journal of International Business Studies*, vol. 12 (1981), pp. 69–82; G. Albaum, J. Strandskov, E. Duerr and L. Doud, *International Marketing and Export Management*, Addison-Wesley, 1989.

43. For a fuller explanation of this matrix see J.R. Montanari and J.S. Bracker, 'The strategic management process at the public planning unit level', *Strategic Management Journal*, vol. 7, no. 3 (1986), pp. 251–266.

44. See A. Hax and N. Majluf, 'The use of the industry attractiveness–business strength matrix in strategic planning', in R. Dyson (ed.), *Strategic Planning: Models and analytical techniques*, Wiley, 1990.

45. G. Albaum, J. Strandskov, E. Duerr and L. Dowd, *International Marketing and Export Management*, Addison-Wesley, 1989.

46. The discussion in this section draws on M. Goold, A. Campbell and M. Alexander, *Corporate Level Strategy*, Wiley, 1994, which provides an excellent basis for understanding issues of parenting.

47 C.A. Bartlett and S. Ghoshal, *Managing Across Borders: The Transnational Solution*, The Harvard Business School Press, 1989, pp. 105–111; A.M. Rugman and A. Verbeke, 'Extending the theory of the multinational enterprise: internalization and strategic management perspectives', *Journal of International Business Studies*, vol. 34 (2003), pp. 125–137.

48. For a more far-reaching exploration of the role of subsidiaries in multinational corporations see: J. Birkinshaw, *Entrepreneurship and the Global Firm*, Sage, 2000.

WORK ASSIGNMENTS

✱ Denotes more advanced work assignments.   * Refers to a case study in the Text and Cases edition.

6.1   Many corporate parents argue that they search for synergies between the businesses in their portfolio. Do you think this is a realistic aspiration? How does this relate to the debate on related and unrelated diversification in section 6.2? Give examples from organisations with which you are familiar to support your arguments.

6.2   Referring to factors identified in section 6.3.2 compare the market attractiveness of France, Japan and Russia for either (a) an Indian software development firm or (b) a UK-based food retailer.

6.3   Identify the corporate rationales for a number of different multi-business corporations: e.g.

   (a) Virgin
   (b) The News Corporation
   (c) South African Breweries

6.4✱   Choose a number of companies with portfolios of business units (e.g. Virgin, South African Breweries* or The News Corporation). Identify and explain the role of the corporate parent and how, if at all, the parent enhances or could enhance business-unit strategies.

6.5✱   Obtain the annual report of a major multi-business corporation and apply different techniques of portfolio analysis to understand and explain the logic for the mix of businesses. Which portfolio approach is most appropriate given the corporate rationale you think is being followed by the corporate parent?

6.6   Using the concepts and frameworks in this chapter, evaluate the corporate and/or international strategy of:

   (a) The Virgin Group
   (b) The News Corporation
   (c) South African Breweries

Integrative assignments

6.7   It is sometimes argued that international strategy is at least as much to do with organisational structuring (Chapter 8) as it is to do with strategic purpose and logic. To what extent do you think this is true?

6.8   Using examples, discuss the proposition that 'The diversification of organisations is more in the interest of management than it is in the interest of shareholders' (Chapter 4). This is particularly true when diversification occurs through a merger or acquisition (Chapter 7).

An extensive range of additional materials, including audio summaries, weblinks to organisations featured in the text, definitions of key concepts and multiple choice questions, can be found on the *Exploring Corporate Strategy* Companion Website at **www.pearsoned.co.uk/ecs7**

The Virgin Group

Aidan McQuade, Strathclyde University Graduate School of Business

Introduction

The Virgin Group is one of the UK's largest private companies, with an annual turnover estimated at £5bn (€7.2bn)[1] per annum in 2002. Virgin's highest-profile business was Virgin Atlantic, which had developed to be a major force in the international airline business. However, by 2002, the group included over 200 businesses spanning three continents and including financial services, planes, trains, cinemas and music stores. (Figure 1 indicates the breadth of the group's activities.) Its name was instantly recognisable. According to a 1996 survey 96 per cent of UK consumers were aware of the brand Virgin and 95 per cent were able to name Richard Branson as the Virgin Group's founding member. Research also showed that the Virgin name was associated with words such as 'fun', 'innovative', 'daring' and 'successful'. The personal image and personality of the founder, Richard Branson, were high profile: in the 1997 'Think different' advertisements for Apple Computers, Branson was featured together

Photo: © Reuters/Corbis

with Einstein and Gandhi as a 'shaper of the 20th century'; a survey of students in 2000 found that Branson was their no. 1 role model. Branson's taste for publicity has led him to stunts as diverse as appearing as a cockney street trader in the US comedy 'Friends', to attempting a non-stop flight around the world in a balloon.

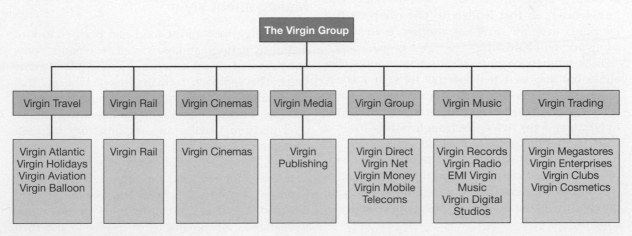

Figure 1 The Virgin Group

This case was based on the original case study by Urmilla Lawson.

Origins and ownership

Virgin was founded in 1970 as a mail-order record business and developed as a private company in music publishing and retailing. In 1986 the company was floated on the stock exchange with a turnover of £250m (€359m). However, Branson became tired of the public listing obligations. Compliance with the rules governing public limited companies and reporting to shareholders were expensive and time-consuming and he resented making presentations in the City to people whom, he believed, did not understand the business. The pressure to create short-term profit, especially as the share price began to fall, was the final straw: Branson decided to take the business back into private ownership and the shares were bought back at the original offer price, which valued the company at £240m (€344.4m).

Virgin had grown fast, becoming profitable and entering and claiming a significant share of new markets without the traditional trappings of the typical multinational. There was little sense of management hierarchy and there seemed to be a minimum of corporate bureaucracy. There was no 'group' as such; financial results were not consolidated either for external examination or, so Virgin claimed, for internal use. Its financial operations were managed from Geneva.

In 2001 Branson described the Virgin Group as 'a branded venture capital house',[2] investing in a series of brands and ventures to expand them at the expense of profits. The use of partners provided flexibility and limited risk. Each business was 'ring-fenced', so that lenders to one company had no rights over the assets of another, even if that company went bankrupt.

Each business or group of businesses ran its own affairs but they were tied together through a degree of shared ownership and shared values. Some argued that Virgin's ownership structure enabled it to take long-term views, free from investors' fixation with short-term returns. Branson argued that, as he expanded, he would rather sacrifice short-term profits for long-term growth and the capital value of the various businesses. Others argued that financing purely through equity slowed the group's ability to expand.

Corporate structure

The structure of Virgin Group was so opaque that the true financial position of Virgin Group was unclear.

Due to its status as a private company, the complex group structure, and unavailability of consolidated accounts, it was difficult to arrive at accurate figures for the group's collective turnover and profit. Companies within the group did not even share a common accounting year-end.

Virgin has been described as a 'keiretsu' organisation – a structure of loosely linked autonomous units run by self-managed teams that use a common brand name. Branson's philosophy was that if a business got to a certain size, he would spin off a new business from the existing one. Branson argued that, as Virgin almost wholly comprised private companies, the running of the group must be fundamentally different from that of a public limited company which must keep shareholders, stakeholders and analysts happy, and must pay attention to short-term goals of high taxable profits and healthy dividends. He argues that the advantage of a private conglomerate was that the owners could ignore short-term objectives and concentrate on long-term profits, reinvesting for this purpose. By 2003, though, Branson seemed to have thought again about the relative merits of public limited companies. In December there was a public offering of shares in his low-cost Australian airline, Virgin Blue, valued on offering at £983m (€1.4bn). This was used partly to fund Virgin's expansion into North America. January 2004 also saw rumours that Branson would float Virgin Mobile, with an estimated worth of about £1bn (€1.42bn) in the course of that year.

Management style

Historically, the Virgin Group had been controlled mainly by Branson and his trusted lieutenants, many of whom had stayed with him for more than twenty years. The approach to management was one that decentralised decision making, keeping head-office cost low, with an emphasis on autonomous business-level decision making and responsibility for their own development.

With businesses scattered across a wide range of industries and markets, the approach was largely hands-off. Until he was needed to finalise big deals or to settle strategy, Branson ruled by delegating to managers and giving them leeway to use their initiative. However, when it came to marketing and promotion, he would take a more involved role. Regarding the financing of the group and its deals, Branson's operating style was expressed in his autobiography: 'In the early 1970s I spent my time juggling different banks and suppliers and creditors in order to play one off against the other and stay solvent. I am now juggling bigger deals instead of the banks. It is only a matter of scale.'

Within the business units, Branson adopted his own personal style of management, priding himself on actively involving employees and seeking their ideas on ways of further adding value to his customers. Employees were still held accountable for their performance and human resource management systems were in place to keep people committed by stock options, bonuses and profit sharing, and wherever possible, there was promotion from within.[3]

Corporate rationale

The name Virgin was chosen to represent the idea of the company being a virgin in every business it enters. Virgin's rationale for expansion was 'based upon a fierce external diversification strategy . . . fueled by Richard Branson's constant need to be creative in his approach to new challenges'.[4] For him 'The brand is the single most important asset that we have; our ultimate objective is to establish it as a major global name. That means that we heed to have a number of core businesses with global potential.'

Virgin's expansion into new markets had been through a series of joint ventures whereby Virgin provided the brand and its partner provided the majority of capital. For example, Virgin's stake in Virgin Direct required an initial outlay of only £15m (€21.5m), whilst its partner, AMP, ploughed £450m (€645.8m) into the joint venture. Virgin Group's move into clothing and cosmetics required an initial outlay of only £1,000 (€1,435), whilst its partner, Victory Corporation, invested £20m (€28.7m). With Virgin Mobile, Virgin built a business in the wireless industry by forming partnerships with existing operators to sell mobile services under the Virgin brand name. The carriers' competences lay in network management, not branding. Virgin set out to differentiate itself by offering innovative services such as no line rentals, no monthly fees and cheaper prepaid offerings. Although it did not operate its own network, Virgin won an award for the best wireless operator in the UK.

While not all of Virgin's businesses are joint ventures, some commentators argued that Virgin had become an endorsement brand that could not always offer real expertise to the businesses with which it was associated. However, Will Whitehorn, Director of Corporate Affairs for Virgin, stated, 'At Virgin we know what the brand means and when we put our brand name on something we are making a promise.' So before entering a new market, it was thoroughly researched to decide whether Virgin could offer something truly different. The aim was to extend the brand name at a low cost into selected areas where its reputation could be used to shake up a relatively static market. Based on a set of attributes and values rather than a market sector, it was about being the consumer's champion. But this was underpinned by its public relations and marketing skills; its experience with greenfield start-ups; and its understanding of the opportunities presented by 'institutionalised' markets. Virgin saw an 'institutionalised' market as one dominated by few competitors, not giving good value to customers because they had become either inefficient or preoccupied with each other; and Virgin believed it did well when it identified complacency in the marketplace and offered more for less.

Branson and his business development team reviewed about 50 business proposals a week, with about four new projects under discussion at any one time. Good prospects would then be those that fitted the Virgin brand, could respond to the Virgin method of treatment, offered an enticing reward-to-risk ratio and had a capable management team.

Corporate performance

By 2003 Virgin had, with mixed results, taken on one established industry after another, from British Airways to Coca-Cola and railways, in an effort to shake up 'fat and complacent business sectors'. Virgin Atlantic was a great success and described by Branson as a core business which he would never sell. Virgin Blue, a low-cost airline established as a joint venture with an Australian logistics company, Patrick, has also been a success. Some analysts worried that such success could not be sustained given the cyclical nature of the airline industry and the prospect of increased competition with deregulation. Indeed other Virgin airline interests were more problematic. The Brussels-based Virgin Express airline had been dogged by losses in its early days before a turnaround was accomplished. However, in early 2003, a Belgian Parliament report highlighted the apparently irregular sale of landing slots by Sabena to Virgin Express in 1996, a deal which contributed to the demise of Sabena. While 2003 saw Virgin Express in profit, these had slumped in the third quarter to €1.7m, from €4.5m for the same period the previous year. Virgin Express blamed this on what it described as 'illegal' government aid to low-cost competitors.

In 2000, Branson folded his loss-making UK clothing line, Virgin Clothing. By 2003 he consolidated Virgin Cola and Virgin Vodka into one business – Virgin Drinks. The most public problem was Virgin Trains, whose Cross Country and West Coast lines were ranked 23rd and 24th out of 25 train operating franchises, according to the Strategic Rail Authority's Review in 2000. By 2003 Virgin West Coast was the 20th most punctual rail operator out of 26, with 73.5 per cent of its trains arriving on time. Virgin Cross Country was the least punctual operator in the country. At the end of 2000 Virgin Rail failed to win the East Coast main line franchise. The loss of rail passengers in 2001, following rail disasters and the consequent national disruption to rail traffic as a result of emergency upgrading of track, did nothing to help its business prospects.

It was estimated that Virgin needed to double passenger numbers and spend £750m (€1.08bn) on new rolling stock and service improvements. A £2.2bn (€3.17bn) investment on a fleet of 75 new high-speed trains was aimed at achieving this. By 2002 Virgin Rail was reporting profits, though it had received its last government subsidy of £56.5m (€81m), in 2001. In 2002 it paid its first premium of £4.2m (€6m), with £1.35bn (€1.94bn) to pay the British government over the subsequent nine years.

International expansion

The beginning of the twenty-first century saw further expansion by Virgin into telecoms in Europe, Branson indicating interest in expansion of financial services and announcement in 2002 of plans for a US$1bn (€788m) investment programme in the USA. The US expansion was dependent on the partial flotation of a raft of existing businesses and the success of a joint venture with Sprint, the fourth biggest mobile telecom operator in the USA. The flotation of Virgin Blue was the first of the anticipated public offerings. The return to public flotation, albeit on this occasion of individual businesses rather than the group as a whole, was accompanied by rumours that it signified a cash crisis for Virgin, reported by some journalists.[5] Branson denied this. Selling chunks of some businesses to fund new and existing businesses had become a familiar story at Virgin – it had sold off its UK and Irish cinema houses, sold Virgin Music, sold a

49 per cent stake in Virgin Atlantic to Singapore Airlines and in 2001 sold Virgin Sun, a short-haul package holiday business, to First Choice, a larger rival of that business, for £5.9m (€8.5m).

In an interview in 2001 Branson appeared sanguine about such sales. 'Every year I suspect we'll sell five businesses in a given country, but we'll replace five. We don't buy companies, we start them from scratch. The way we manage to grow companies is by selling those we have built and established over the years.' He also said that if his expectations were correct then Virgin would trade companies far more actively than in the past.

According to Branson, however, one of the companies that would not be up for sale was Virgin Atlantic. Despite the 49 per cent stake in the company owned by Singapore Airlines the rest would not be sold. 'It's a key company. We would never sell it. There are some businesses you preserve, which wouldn't ever be sold, and that's one.'

A challenging future

To many commentators Virgin's mixed results highlighted a risk with its approach: 'The greatest threat [is] that . . . Virgin brand, its most precious asset, may become associated with failure.'[6] This point was emphasised by a commentator[7] who noted 'a customer enjoying a nice massage on a Virgin Atlantic flight may be predisposed into drinking Virgin Cola or staying in a Virgin hotel,[8] but a customer who has a bad enough experience with any one of the product lines may shun all the others'. For example, in the UK the tension between the excellent reputation of Virgin's airlines and the appalling reputation of rail remained unresolved by 2004. Given Branson's foray into so many diverse products and services increasingly on a global scale some critics argued that the risk of such an eventuality was further increased. However, Virgin argues that its brand research indicates that people who have had a bad experience will blame that particular Virgin company or product but will be willing to use other Virgin products or services, due to the very diversity of the brand.

There were also issues directly related to Branson himself. He was so high-profile and so closely linked to the Virgin brand, there was also a risk he could undermine Virgin's value if some of his high-publicity personal ventures failed spectacularly. And what would happen to Virgin and its brand 'after Branson'?

Notes

1. January 2004 exchange rate.
2. R. Hawkins, 'Executive of Virgin Group outlines corporate strategy', *Knight Rider/Tribune Business News*, 29 July 2001.
3. C. Vignali, 'Virgin Cola', *British Food Journal*, vol. 103, no. 2 (2001), pp. 131–139.
4. ibid.
5. R. Hawkins, 'Branson in new dash for cash', *Sunday Business*, 29 July 2001; A. Rayner, 'Virgin in push to open up US aviation market', *The Times*, 5 June 2002.
6. *The Times* 1998, quoted in Vignali, 2001.
7. M. Wells, 'Red Baron', *Forbes Magazine*, vol. 166, no. 1 (2000).
8. By 2004 Virgin no longer had a hotel operation.

Sources: *The Economist*, 'Cross his heart', 5 October 2002; 'Virgin on the ridiculous', 29 May 2003; 'Virgin Rail: tilting too far', 12 July 2001; P. McCosker, 'Stretching the brand: a review of the Virgin Group', *European Case Clearing House*, 2000; 'Virgin push to open up US aviation market', *The Times*, 5 June 2002; 'Branson plans $1 bn US expansion', *The Times*, 30 April 2002; 'Branson eyes 31bn float for Virgin Mobile', *Observer*, 18 January 2004; 'Virgin Flies High with Brand Extensions', *Strategic Direction*, vol. 18, no. 10 (October 2002); 'Virgin shapes kangaroo strategy', *South China Morning Post*, 28 June 2002.

Questions

1. What is the corporate rationale of the Virgin Group?

2. Are there any relationships of a strategic nature between businesses within the Virgin portfolio?

3. Does the Virgin Group, as a corporate parent, add value to its businesses? If so how?

4. What are the main issues facing the Virgin Group and how should they be tackled?

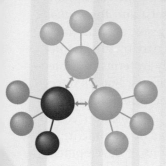

7

Directions and Methods of Development

Learning outcomes

After reading this chapter you should be able to understand and explain:

- The various strategy development *directions* open to an organisation.
- Three *methods* of strategy development (internal, acquisition and alliances).
- Different *forms of strategic alliance* and conditions for successful alliances.
- The three *success criteria* for strategic choices: suitability, acceptability and feasibility.
- How different *techniques* can be used to evaluate strategic options.

Photo: Digital Vision

Photo: Bosch

Photo: Digital Vision

7.1   INTRODUCTION

Chapter 5 was concerned with the broad issues of strategic choices at the business unit level. Within this broad 'steer' there are a number of specific options concerning both the *direction* (e.g. new products, new markets) and the *method* (e.g. internal, merger/acquisition, alliances) of developing an organisation's strategies, as previously indicated in Exhibit 5.1. The first part of the chapter looks at development directions for an organisation – mainly in terms of strategic options concerned with market coverage and product features. But whatever the broad strategy and development direction, there will be different *methods* by which a strategy might be pursued. For example, the organisation could pursue the development through its own efforts alone (*internal* development); or through *strategic alliances* with one or more other organisations or development may be achieved by *acquisition* of another organisation. The middle part of the chapter considers the issue of development methods.

It should also be clear from Part II of this book that the survival of organisations and the success of strategies are influenced by the ability to respond to the competing pressures from the business environment (Chapter 2), strategic capability (Chapter 3) and the cultural and political context (Chapter 4). These three pressures create *motives* for pursuing some strategies and not others:

- *Environment-based motives* – fitting new strategies to a changing business environment.

- *Capability-based motives* – stretching and exploiting the resources and competences of an organisation.

- *Expectations-based motives* – meeting the expectations created by the cultural and political context.

These motives will be used to describe and explain both the development directions and methods commonly found in organisations. In particular the identification of development directions (section 7.2) builds on much of the detailed discussions in Part II of the book. Additionally these motives will be used in the final part of the chapter to introduce the *success criteria* by which strategies can be judged. The aim of this final part of the chapter is to help readers understand these criteria and some of the techniques that can be used to evaluate strategic options.

7.2   DIRECTIONS FOR STRATEGY DEVELOPMENT

Development directions are the strategic options available to an organisation, in terms of products and market coverage

The identification of possible development directions builds on an understanding of an organisation's strategic position – as discussed in Part II of the book. This section uses one main approach (see Exhibit 7.1) which is an adaptation of Ansoff's product/market matrix[1] used for identifying *directions* for strategic development. Section 7.2.5 will briefly review other ways of generating these options. **Development directions** are the strategic options available to an organisation

Exhibit 7.1	Strategy development directions

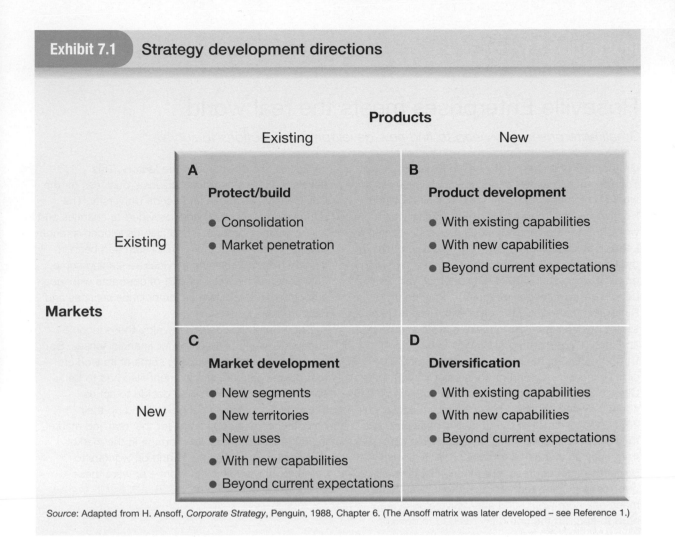

Source: Adapted from H. Ansoff, *Corporate Strategy*, Penguin, 1988, Chapter 6. (The Ansoff matrix was later developed – see Reference 1.)

in terms of products and market coverage, taking into account the strategic capability of the organisation and the expectations of stakeholders. Although this section will look separately at the directions represented by the four boxes in Exhibit 7.1 it should be remembered that, in practice, a combination of development directions is usually pursued if organisations are to develop successfully in the future. For example, development into new markets usually requires some product changes too. Illustration 7.1 underlines this point. Many of the points discussed in this section are summarised in Exhibit 7.5 later in the chapter, which will be used when exploring success criteria in section 7.4.

7.2.1 Protect and build on current position

Box A in Exhibit 7.1 represents strategies which are concerned with protecting, or building on, an organisation's current position. Within this broad category there are a number of options.

Illustration 7.1   strategy into action

Roseville Enterprises meets the real world

Small enterprises may need to find new development directions to survive.

On the face of it Leeds (UK)-based Roseville Enterprises had a level of security in its business that would be the envy of many small business owners. Roseville was established in 1986, originally as a workshop for the blind. By 2003 it was still owned by Leeds City Council. It was one of 100 enterprises in the UK classed as a 'supported business' receiving a grant of some £300,000 to help unemployed disabled people get and keep a job (some 75 per cent of Roseville employees were disabled). Despite its public sector ownership it had to make a profit to survive and in 2001/2 operating profit was £400,000 on £11.5m (≈ €16m) turnover. However, some 80 per cent of the work came from one contract with Leeds City Council, renewing windows and doors in 70,000 council-owned houses. This contract would run until 2008. Also because of the durability of its products they did not need replacing or maintaining as frequently as those that it replaced. A 'typical' business might address this situation by downsizing – but Roseville felt a real obligation to its workforce, many of whom would find alternative employment hard to find. So the company needed to develop new income streams to replace this potential loss of some £9m. One possibility was to offer a window replacement service to the 34,000 employees of Leeds City Council. The company admitted that costs would have to be stripped out if it was to compete more widely in the commercial market. There were also some uncertainties as to whether commercial profits would reduce the level of grant that it received in the future. Despite its dependence on the single contract Roseville had already broadened its range of activities. In 1994 it began a computer-refurbishing

service to use downtime in the factory. This developed into a computer disposal business for the City Council, hospitals and Leeds University. The refurbished computers were provided to charities and disadvantaged groups. It had also developed a range of pine furniture. Another growth area had been in laundry hire and cleaning services – cleaning some 35,000 items per week as part of contracts with local-authority residential homes, ambulance services and restaurants.

But if Roseville couldn't develop these income streams it would be heading for financial losses. So the alternative of encouraging some of its workers to enter mainstream employment also had to be considered. In effect it could decide to act as a 'bridge' for disabled people to build up their competence and confidence for the 'real' job market. In 2003 there was a skills shortage in the market so perhaps Roseville could hand on workers to commercial window fabricators – or were these its competitors?

Source: Adapted from *The Sunday Times*, 9 February 2003.

Questions

1. Referring to Exhibit 7.1, classify the various development direction for Roseville mentioned above.

2. What business is it in?

3. How would your answer to question 2 influence your view on the suitability of each of these development directions?

Consolidation

Consolidation is where organisations protect and strengthen their position in their current markets with current products

Consolidation is where organisations protect and strengthen their position in their current markets with current products. Since the market situation is likely to be changing (e.g. through improved performance of competitors or new entrants) consolidation does not mean standing still. Indeed, it may require considerable reshaping and innovation to improve the value of an organisation's products or services. In turn, this will require attention to how an organisation's resources and competences should be adapted and developed to maintain the competitive position of the organisation:

● Consolidation may require reshaping by *downsizing or withdrawal from some activities*. For example:

  – The concept of the *product life cycle* (see Exhibit 2.6) is a reminder that demand for any product or service has a finite life. Even where demand remains strong, the ability to compete profitably will vary through the stages of the life cycle. Knowing when to withdraw from markets can be crucial.

  – In some markets, the *value* of a company's products or assets is subject to changes over time, and a key issue may be the astute acquisition and disposal of these products, assets or businesses. This is particularly important for companies operating in markets that are subject to *speculation*, such as energy, metals, commodities, land or property.

  – The company has serious *competitive disadvantages*, e.g. it is unable to secure the resources or achieve the competence levels of the leaders in the market overall or the niches or segments of the market.

  – *Prioritisation* of activities is always necessary. So downsizing or withdrawal from some activities releases resources for others. The shift in a local government authority's range of services over time is a good example of such a policy.

  – The *expectations* of dominant stakeholders may be a reason for downsizing or withdrawal. For example, the objective of a small entrepreneur may be to 'make a million' and then retire. This would lead to a preference for strategies that make the company an attractive proposition to sell, rather than being guided by longer-term considerations of viability or growth.

● Consolidation may also be concerned with the *maintenance of market share* in existing markets. The link between performance and relative market share was emphasised by the experience curve work (see Chapter 3, section 3.3). High-share organisations have a number of advantages over their competitors. For example, asset turnover, purchase/sales ratios and R&D/sales ratios are all likely to benefit from economies of scale. The increased ability to spend on R&D means that high-share organisations are more able to develop strategies of higher price/higher quality than low-share competitors and this may be self-sustaining. Also the ability to invest in improved quality of service, building and sustaining brands and/or to incur higher levels of marketing expenditure can bring real advantages to high-share companies that their competitors may be unable to match. However, it must be remembered that high market share and size are not always the same. There are large firms which do not dominate the markets in which they operate – such as Sainsbury in UK grocery retailing. There are also small firms that dominate market segments – such as Dolby in sound systems (Illustration 5.6) or Pure Digital in digital radios (Illustration 9.7). An implication is that gaining and holding market share during the growth phase of the product life cycle is important since it may give advantages during the maturity phase.

Market penetration

Within the broad category of protecting and building an organisation's position, there may be opportunities for **market penetration**, which is where an organisation gains market share. The previous discussion is relevant to this direction, since, for example, competences that sustain or improve quality or innovation or increasing marketing activity could all be means of achieving market penetration. So, too, are the arguments concerning the long-term desirability of obtaining a dominant market share. However, it needs to be noted that the ease with which an organisation can pursue a policy of market penetration may be dependent on:

● *Market growth rate.* When the overall market is growing, or can be induced to grow, it is easier for organisations with a small market share, or even new entrants, to gain share. This is because the absolute level of sales of the established organisations may still be growing, and in some instances those companies may be unable or unwilling to meet the new demand. Import penetration into some industries has occurred in this way. In contrast, market penetration in static markets may be much more difficult to achieve. In declining markets opportunities to gain share through the acquisition of failing companies (or those wishing to withdraw) may arise. Some companies have grown quickly in this way. For example, in the steel industry LNM moved rapidly in the early 2000s to become no. 2 in Europe through acquisitions of Eastern European state-owned plants (see the Corus case study in the case study section of the Text and Cases edition).

● There may be *resource issues* driving or preventing market penetration. Building market share can be a costly process for weakly positioned businesses. Short-term profits are likely to be sacrificed, particularly when trying to build share from a low base. E-commerce companies such as Amazon who set out to gain share from traditional retailers had to wait seven years before making a profit (see the Amazon case study in the case study section).

● Sometimes the *complacency of market leaders* can allow lower share competitors to catch up because they are not regarded as serious competitors (i.e. they are not like the current competitors). But the growth and development of markets redefines the 'definition' of a credible player. Virgin's extensions into airlines and financial services are good examples (see case example at the end of Chapter 6). Also, a low-share competitor may build a reputation in a market segment of little interest to the market leader, from which it penetrates the wider market. The development of no-frills airlines such as easyJet (Illustration 5.2) and Ryanair (case study section) illustrates this process.

7.2.2 Product development

Changes in the business environment may create demand for new products or services at the expense of established provision. **Product development** is where organisations deliver modified or new products to existing markets. At a minimum, product development may be needed to survive but may also represent a considerable opportunity. Sometimes this may be achieved *with existing capabilities*. For example:

- Retailers tend to follow the *changing needs of their customers* by introducing new product lines; and public services shift their pattern of services as the needs of their communities change.

- When *product life cycles are short* – as with software or consumer electronics – product development becomes an essential requirement of an organisation's strategy. An organisation's advantage might lie in the processes of knowledge creation and integration as discussed in section 3.5 of Chapter 3.

- An organisation may have developed a *core competence* in market analysis that it is able to exploit. With the advent of cheap and powerful IT, those organisations which are good at data-mining[2] may gain advantage in this way, as discussed in section 9.3. Successful product development requires high-quality information about changing customer needs and the creativity to know how better to provide for these needs.

However, product development may require the *development of new capabilities*:

- There may be a need to respond to a *change of emphasis* amongst customers concerning the importance of product/service features. This can occur because customers become more experienced at judging value for money – for example, through repeat purchase, because new choices become available in the market or because the internet makes search and comparison so much easier.

- The *critical success factors* (CSFs – see section 2.4.3) may change if the previous CSFs can be met by many providers. The focus of competition shifts to meeting new CSFs and advantage will be gained by those organisations that are competent to deliver these other aspects of the customer experience. For example, functionality of the product may become a threshold requirement (which all providers must meet) and other factors such as the quality of information provided to clients, the clarity of billing, the ease of payment methods and so on may become the CSFs. Many consumer durables such as televisions, washing machines or cookers now face markets of this type.

Despite the attractiveness of product development, it may not always be in line with *expectations* and may raise uncomfortable dilemmas for organisations:

- Whilst new products may be vital to the future of the organisation, the process of creating a broad product line is *expensive*, *risky* and potentially *unprofitable*, because most new product ideas never reach the market; and of those that do, there are relatively few that succeed. Product development may require a commitment to high levels of spending on R&D. Whilst high-market-share companies may benefit in profit terms from relatively high levels of R&D expenditure, companies in a weak market position with high expenditure may suffer because they cannot really afford that level of investment. Profitability can be depressed by over-rapid rates of new product introductions, as organisations struggle to learn new competences needed to debug production, train salespeople, educate customers and establish new channels.

- New products may need to be developed because the *consequences of not developing* new products could be unacceptable. It is possible that performance may become so poor in relation to that of competitors or other providers that the organisation becomes a target for acquisition by organisations which have core competences in *corporate turnaround*.

7.2.3 Market development

Normally organisations will be selective in their market coverage. This may lead to a situation where there are no further opportunities within the current market segments. In these circumstances an organisation may develop by **market development**, where existing products are offered in new markets. Both *capability and market considerations* might drive an organisation's development into new markets. For example:

Market development is where existing products are offered in new markets

- Whether products can be exploited in other *market segments*, where similar critical success factors exist. For example, this was one reason for allowing public service providers 'commercial freedom' to seek out paying customers to complement the publicly funded provision.

- Development of *new uses* for existing products. For example, manufacturers of stainless steel have progressively found new applications for existing products, which were originally used for cutlery and tableware. Nowadays the uses include aerospace, automobile exhausts, beer barrels and many applications in the chemical manufacturing industry.

- *Geographical* spread, either nationally or internationally, into new markets. Chapters 2 and 6 discussed how in many industries there are increasing market and/or financial pressures for globalisation and that companies need to know how to respond and have the capability to do so (readers may wish to refer back to the extensive section on international strategy in Chapter 6, section 6.3). Illustration 7.2 below is an example. It is not unusual for organisations with small home markets to be the 'leaders' of globalisation (as can be seen in the chapter-end case example in Chapter 2 about the European brewing industry – where Heineken (Netherlands), Interbrew (Belgium), Carlsberg (Denmark) and Guinness (Ireland) were the most globalised companies).

In reality market development usually requires some degree of both product development and capability development. For example, a manufacturer of branded grocery products for the premium market may enter the mainstream market through own-brand sales to supermarkets. This will require the development of new capabilities in (for example) key account selling.

Organisations also may encounter some difficulties around credibility and *expectations* as they attempt to enter new markets or market segments. A specialist may not be seen as a credible 'mainstream' supplier. The reverse may be even more problematic where a mainstream provider attempts to develop sales in specialist niches. For example, some engineering companies selling capital equipment to manufacturers have tried to develop a consultancy role advising on manufacturing and/or engineering practice in competition with independent consultants. They have found it difficult to compete at the fee levels of the independents as their customers tend to see them as engineers not consultants and assume the advice is all part of the package that comes with the equipment purchase.

Diversification is defined as a strategy that takes an organisation away from both its current markets and products

7.2.4 Diversification[3]

Diversification is defined as a strategy that takes the organisation away from both its current markets and products (i.e. box D in Exhibit 7.1). Diversification will increase the diversity that a corporate centre must oversee and Chapter 6 discussed the various forms of related and unrelated diversification and the reasons why they might make sense in terms of corporate-level strategy. Even small (single SBU) organisations may find themselves in circumstances where diversification may be a real option – or even a necessity. The motives for diversification, the advantages and disadvantages of diversification and the impact on performance were all discussed in section 6.2 of Chapter 6 so the arguments will not be repeated here.

It should be remembered that if a single SBU diversifies it is likely to create a new set of management challenges akin to those dealt with by a corporate centre in larger organisations (as discussed in Chapter 6). So diversification may lead to a decline in performance if an organisation does not have the parenting capabilities to manage a more diverse set of operations.

7.2.5 The TOWS matrix

The discussion so far in this section has used the amended Ansoff matrix (Exhibit 7.1) as the framework by which strategy development direction options can be 'generated'. In doing so there has been extensive reference back to the insights that should be available about an organisation's strategic position (from the frameworks presented in Part II of this book). A complementary way of generating options from this knowledge of an organisation's strategic position is known as the TOWS matrix and is shown in Exhibit 7.2. This builds directly on the information about the strategic position that is summarised in a SWOT analysis (see section 3.6.4 and Illustration 3.8 in Chapter 3). Each box of the TOWS matrix is used to identify options that address a different combination of the internal factors (strengths and weaknesses) and the external factors (opportunities and threats). For example, the top left-hand box should list options that use the strengths of the organisation to take advantage of opportunities in the business environment. An example might be the extension of sales into an adjacent

---

Exhibit 7.2   The TOWS matrix

		Internal factors	
		Strengths (S)	**Weaknesses (W)**
External factors	**Opportunities (O)**	**SO Strategic options** Generate options here that use strengths to take advantage of opportunities	**WO Strategic options** Generate options here that take advantage of opportunities by overcoming weaknesses
	Threats (T)	**ST Strategic options** Generate options here that use strengths to avoid threats	**WT Strategic options** Generate options here that minimise weaknesses and avoid threats

geographical market where demand is expected to grow quickly. In contrast the bottom right-hand box should list options that minimise weaknesses and also avoid threats. An example might be the avoidance of major competitors by focusing activities on the specialist niches in the market that the organisation is capable of servicing successfully. In this sense the TOWS matrix not only helps generate strategic options it also addresses their suitability – as discussed in section 7.4.1 below.

7.3 METHODS OF STRATEGY DEVELOPMENT

The previous section of this chapter reviewed the directions in which organisations might develop. However, for any of these directions there are different *methods of development*. A **development method** is the *means* by which any strategic direction will be pursued. These methods can be divided into three types: internal development, acquisition (or disposal) and joint development (or alliances). Many of the points discussed in this section are summarised in Exhibit 7.5 later in the chapter, which will be used when discussing success criteria in section 7.4.

> A **development method** is the *means* by which any strategic direction will be pursued

7.3.1 Internal development

> **Internal development** is where strategies are developed by building on and developing an organisation's own capabilities

Internal development is where strategies are developed by building on and developing an organisation's own capabilities. For many organisations, internal development (sometimes known as 'organic development') has been the primary method of strategy development, and there are some compelling *capability* reasons why this should be so:

● For products that are *highly technical* in design or method of manufacture, businesses may choose to develop new products themselves, since the process of development is seen as the best way of acquiring the necessary capabilities to compete successfully in the marketplace. Indeed, it has been seen above that these competences may also spawn further new products and create new market opportunities.

● A similar argument may apply to the development of *new markets* by direct involvement. For example, many manufacturers choose to forgo the use of agents, since they feel that the direct involvement gained from having their own sales force is of advantage in gaining a full understanding of the market. This market knowledge may be a core competence creating competitive advantage over other organisations that are more distant from their customers.

● Although the final *cost* of developing new activities internally may be greater than that of acquiring other companies, the *spread of cost over time* may be more favourable and realistic. This contrasts with acquisitions that may require a major expenditure at one point in time. This is a strong motive for internal development in small companies or many public services that may not have the resources available for major one-off investments. The slower rate of change which internal development brings may also minimise the disruption to other activities.

There may also be issues relating to the business *environment* which would create a preference for internal development:

● An organisation may have *no choice* about how new ventures are developed. In many instances those breaking new ground may not be in a position to develop by acquisition or joint development, since they are the only ones in the field.

● This problem is not confined to such extreme situations. Organisations wishing to develop by acquisition may not be able to find a suitable target for acquisition. For example, this is a particular difficulty for foreign companies attempting to enter Japan.

Internal development also may avoid the often traumatic political and cultural problems arising from post-acquisition integration and coping with the different traditions and incompatible *expectations* of two organisations.

7.3.2 Mergers and acquisitions[4]

Acquisition is where strategies are developed by taking over ownership of another organisation. Worldwide merger and acquisition activity takes place on a major scale. Globally the number of completed acquisitions tripled between 1991 and 2001. Nor were these confined to deals *within* countries: for example, in 1998 there were 3,000 *cross-border* acquisitions[5] in Europe, valued at $220bn (€190bn) (representing 45 per cent of the total value of European mergers and acquisitions). But the worldwide announced deals declined rapidly after 2000 (falling by nearly 30 per cent in 2002 to about 25,000 deals). In 2002 North America showed its lowest level of activity since 1994. None-the-less worldwide announced deals in 2002 were valued at $1.2trillion (≈ €1trillion). Not only does development by acquisition tend to go in waves[6] it also tends to be selective in terms of industry sector. For example, in the UK, the 1990s saw a wave of mergers in professional service organisations, such as law firms, property services, accountancy firms and financial services. This was followed by mergers in pharmaceuticals, electricity and information technology sectors. In 2000, 25 per cent of the takeovers involving British companies were in the IT sector – amounting to almost 900 deals.[7]

Similarly, international developments through acquisition have been critically important in some industries, such as newspapers and media, food and drink, many sectors of the leisure industries and, in the late 1990s, in the telecommunications sector. In the early 2000s the most active sectors worldwide were Healthcare, Energy and Financial services. Global activity in mergers is dominated by North America (about 42 per cent of the total world value in 2002) and Western Europe (37 per cent). This contrasts sharply with Japan (4 per cent). Within Europe the UK continues to show the highest activity (12 per cent of world value in 2002) compared to France (6 per cent) and Germany (5 per cent). These differences between countries are a reminder of the different corporate governance and ownership arrangements in different parts of the world (as discussed in section 4.2 of Chapter 4).

Acquisition is where strategies are developed by taking over ownership of another organisation

Motives for acquisitions and mergers[8]

There are many different motives for developing through acquisition or merger. These can be usefully grouped under the three headings of *environment*, *strategic capability* and *expectations* that have been used earlier in the book to explore the strategic position of an organisation. The need to keep up with a changing *environment* can dominate thinking about acquisitions:

- A compelling reason to develop by acquisition is the *speed* with which it allows the company to enter new product or market areas. In some cases the product or market is changing so rapidly that acquisition becomes the only way of successfully entering the market, since the process of internal development is too slow. This remains a key motive in many e-commerce businesses.

- The *competitive situation* may influence a company to prefer acquisition. In markets that are static and where market shares of companies are reasonably steady, it can be a difficult proposition for a new company to enter the market, since its presence may create excess capacity. If, however, the new company enters by acquisition, the risk of competitive reaction is reduced. In some cases the motive is industry consolidation by shutting down the acquired company's capacity to restore a better balance between supply and demand. This is clearly more likely to happen in industries that have low levels of concentration.

- *Deregulation* was a major driving force behind merger and acquisition activities in many industries such as telecommunications, electricity and other public utilities. This was because regulation (or the process/type of deregulation) created a level of fragmentation that was regarded as sub-optimal. So this was an opportunity for acquisitive organisations to rationalise provision and/or seek to gain other benefits (for example, through the creation of 'multi-utility' companies offering electricity, gas, telecommunications and other services to customers).

There may be *financial motives* for acquisitions. If the share value or price/earnings (P/E) ratio of a company is high, the motive may be to spot and acquire a firm with a low share value or P/E ratio. Indeed, this is one of the major stimuli for the more opportunistic acquisitive companies. An extreme example is asset stripping, where the main motive for the acquisition is short-term gain by buying up undervalued assets and disposing of them piecemeal.

There may be *capability considerations* too:

- An acquisition may provide the opportunity to *exploit an organisation's core competences* in a new arena, for example through global expansion. In contrast it can also be a means of addressing a *lack of resources or competences* to compete successfully. For example, a company may be acquired for its R&D expertise, or its knowledge of a particular type of production system or business processes.

- *Cost efficiency* is a commonly stated reason for acquisitions and/or, in the public sector, for merging units or rationalising provision (by cutting out duplication or by gaining scale advantages).

- *Learning* can be an important motive. For example, an established company may already be a long way down the experience curve and have achieved efficiencies or expertise that would be difficult to match quickly by internal development. The necessary innovation and organisational learning would be too slow.

Acquisition can also be driven by the *expectations* of key stakeholders:

● Institutional shareholders may expect to see *continuing growth* and acquisitions may be a quick way to deliver this growth. But there are considerable dangers that acquisitive growth may result in value destruction rather than creation – for some of the reasons discussed in Chapter 6. For example, the 'parent' does not have sufficient feel for the acquired businesses and, accidentally, destroys value. This is clearly more likely where acquisition is the method of pursuing diversification.

● Growth through acquisitions can also be very attractive to *ambitious senior managers* as it speeds the growth of the company. In turn, this might enhance their self-importance, provide better career paths and greater monetary rewards.

● There are some stakeholders whose motives are *speculative* rather than strategic. They favour acquisitions that might bring a short-term boost to share value. Other stakeholders are usually wary of the speculators since their short-term gain can destroy longer-term prospects.

Illustration 7.2 shows one company's acquisition plans as part of a strategy of international market development.

Acquisitions and financial performance

Many of the findings about the impact of acquisitions on financial performance[9] act as a reminder that acquisition is not an easy or guaranteed route to improving financial performance. Indeed in the majority of cases it leads to poor performance or even serious financial difficulties. The most common mistake is in paying too much for a company – possibly through lack of experience in acquisitions or poor financial advice (for example, from the investment bank). An acquisition will probably include poor resources/competences as well as those which were the reason for the purchase. For this reason many acquirers attempt to buy products or processes rather than whole companies if possible. At the very best it is likely to take the acquiring company some considerable time to gain any financial benefit from acquisitions, if at all. As many as 70 per cent of acquisitions end up with lower returns to shareholders of both organisations. Many studies confirm the importance of non-economic factors in determining post-acquisition performance. These will be discussed in the next section.

Making acquisitions work[10]

It should be remembered that the detailed implementation agenda following an acquisition or merger will vary considerably depending on the strategic direction for which that development method is being used.[11] Nonetheless there are some frequently occurring issues that can spell success or failure for an acquisition/merger and therefore need to be managed:

Illustration 7.2

General Electric focuses on Europe

Globalisation may be essential for organisations with high market shares at home. Could acquisitions be a quick way to achieve this?

In October 2003 Jeff Immelt, the chairman and CEO of General Electric, the giant American conglomerate (whose annual sales of some $130bn (≈ €115bn) spanned aircraft engines, financial services, lighting, locomotives, medical instruments, plastic, TVs and more), made an offer of £5.7bn for Amersham, the British healthcare sector company. Amersham supplied the chemicals used in X-ray and other forms of medical imaging and had a turnover of about £1bn (≈ €1.5bn) per year. Only the previous day he had concluded the acquisition of Finland's Instrumentarium, a medical instruments business. GE already had a strong presence in Europe (particularly in the UK) in its more 'mature' businesses that stretched back to the 1930s. The UK was GE's third biggest market after the USA and Japan and it employed 15,000 people in the UK generating $5bn of sales. But Immelt had a desire to expand more quickly in Europe than in the USA. A section of the annual report was entitled 'small where we should be big'. The logic was built on the fact that in most sectors GE generally had half the market share in Europe than it did in the USA. Also market enlargement and regulatory convergence between European countries was viewed favourably.

But in expanding operations in Europe GE had an eye to the most attractive sectors – hence its interest in healthcare. Before he became GE chairman Immelt used to run GE's medical operations. He had a vision for healthcare which he very much shared with Sir William Castell, Amersham's CEO for 14 years. The plan was to combine Amersham with GE Medical systems (which made MRI and CT scanning equipment) to form GE Healthcare (with an estimated turnover of $13bn). The hope was to capitalise on the emergence of 'personalised medicine' – therapies that take advantage of increased genetic understanding of disease (for example, see Illustration 2.4 in Chapter 2).

Despite the fact that Amersham was only one third the size of GE medical systems the business was to be headed by Castell. Unusually he was also to be appointed to the GE board as a vice-president.

Nor were the Amersham shareholders likely to be disappointed by the offer of GE stock worth 800p (€12) – analysts had valued Amersham at 720p and potential rivals, such as Siemens or Philips, would struggle to match the price. GE's willingness to pay the price probably reflected the need to keep the GE earnings machine moving ahead in a weak home economy. Healthcare was thought to offer rosier profit prospects than the more mature businesses. Amersham was unlikely to be GE's last development in the healthcare sector or in Europe. Shortly before Amersham and Instrumentarium GE had made European acquisitions in financial services – buying the First National loans company for £848m from Abbey National in the UK and had also announced plans for a wind farm in the Irish Sea. For GE's operations to match (proportionately) those in the USA it would need to increase annual sales by $25bn – a gap equivalent to 30 Amershams.

Source: Adapted from *The Sunday Times*, 12 October 2003.

Questions

1. Why was GE choosing to develop into Europe?
2. By referring to section 7.3.2 explain the advantages and disadvantages of market development by *acquisition*.
3. How could GE avoid some of the disadvantages?

- The acquirer may find difficulty in *adding any value* to its purchases (the parenting issue as discussed in Chapter 6). There will be a need to be decisive about key roles (post-merger). Middle managers also need to be brought on board quickly to remove the internal uncertainties and ensure that there is no loss of external focus (e.g. on service to customers).

- An inability to *integrate the new company* into the activities of the old means that the expected synergistic benefits, which are often the cited reasons for acquisitions, are not realised. There will be inevitable decisions on whether to remove or retain executives of the acquired company.

- Where the motive was about *organisational learning* through the transfer of knowledge it can be difficult to know exactly which knowledge to transfer. Managers themselves in the acquired organisation may be unclear about the reasons for their success (or failure).

- Under-achievement often results from problems of *cultural fit*. This can be particularly problematic with cross-country acquisitions[12] (see Illustration 4.6 in Chapter 4). This 'clash of cultures' may simply arise because the business models and/or organisational routines are so different in each organisation.

7.3.3 Strategic alliances[13]

A **strategic alliance** is where two or more organisations share resources and activities to pursue a strategy. This kind of joint development of new strategies has become increasingly popular. This is because organisations cannot always cope with increasingly complex environments (such as globalisation)[14] from internal resources and competences alone. They may see the need to obtain materials, skills, innovation, finance or access to markets, and recognise that these may be as readily available through cooperation as through ownership. Many companies rely on alliances for up to 25 per cent of their activities and the top 500 global companies have an average of 60 alliances each.[15] Despite this about half of alliances will fail. Alliances vary considerably in their complexity, from simple two-partner alliances co-producing a product to one with multiple partners providing complex products and solutions.[16]

A **strategic alliance** is where two or more organisations share resources and activities to pursue a strategy

Motives for alliances[17]

There are many detailed motives for alliances but they tend to be of three main types:

- The need for *critical mass*, which alliances can achieve by forming partnerships with either competitors or providers of complementary products. This can lead to cost reduction and an improved customer offering.

- *Co-specialisation* – allowing each partner to concentrate on activities that best match their capabilities. For example, alliances are used to enter new geographical markets where an organisation needs local knowledge and expertise in distribution, marketing and customer support. Similarly alliances with organisations in other parts of the value chain (e.g. suppliers or distributors) are very common.

- *Learning* from partners and developing competences that may be more widely exploited elsewhere. For example, first steps into e-commerce may be achieved with a partner that has expertise in website development. However, the longer term intention might be to bring those activities in-house.

Strategic alliances are also important in the public sector[18] – as a means of addressing particular social outcomes. For example, Illustration 7.3 shows how the problem of drug abuse was tackled by collaborative arrangements between the different agencies involved (health, police, social services and education). There have also been many public/private partnerships in the UK; for example, the Public Finance Initiative (PFI) was established to allow public sector organisations to gain advantage through partnerships for the development and maintenance of capital items – particularly property.

Types of alliance

There are a variety of types of strategic alliance (see Exhibit 7.3). Some may be formalised inter-organisational relationships. At the other extreme, there can be loose arrangements of cooperation and informal networking between organisations, with no shareholding or ownership involved:

- *Joint ventures* are arrangements where organisations remain independent but set up a newly created organisation jointly owned by the parents. The joint venture often is a favoured means of collaborative ventures in China. Local firms provide labour and entry to markets; western companies provide

---

Exhibit 7.3 **Types of strategic alliance**

	FORM OF RELATIONSHIP		
Examples	**Loose (Market)** ● Networks ● Opportunistic alliances	**Contractual** ● Licensing ● Franchising ● Subcontracting	**Ownership** ● Consortia ● Joint ventures
INFLUENCING FACTORS			
The Market ● Speed of market change	Fast change ⟶		Slow change
Resources ● Asset management	Managed separately by each partner ⟶		Managed together
● Partner's assets	Draws on 'parent's' assets ⟶		Dedicated assets for alliance
● Risk of losing assets to partner	High risk ⟶		Low risk
Expectations ● Spreading financial risk	Maintains risk ⟶		Dilutes risk
● Political climate	Unfavourable climate ⟶		Favourable climate

Illustration 7.3   strategy into action

UK anti-drug strategy

The ability to coordinate the activities of different public and voluntary sector agencies can be the key to successful 'social welfare' strategies.

In the mid-2000s, Britain, like most western countries, was facing growing social problems from the misuse of drugs. The government's strategy to tackle this issue (first published in 1998) had four objectives:

1. Young people are to be helped to resist drug use in order to achieve their full potential in society.

2. Communities are to be protected from drug-related anti-social and criminal behaviour.

3. Treatment should enable people with drug problems to overcome them and live healthy and crime-free lives.

4. Stifle the availability of illegal drugs on the streets.

But the practical question was how to organise to meet these objectives as the responsibilities were split across several 'agencies':

- *Health* was responsible for diagnosing and treating patients of drug abuse.

- *Criminal justice* (police, prisons, probation and customs/excise) was responsible for enforcing the law and the rehabilitation of offenders.

- *Social services* were responsible for the social care and protection of drug users and their families.

- *Education* was responsible for drug education.

- *Voluntary sector* (mainly charities) ran services alongside and in partnership with many of these public sector agencies – such as information, counselling and support.

The following structures and processes were put in place to promote and support the collaborative working that was necessary if the drug problems were to be contained or reduced:

- At ministerial level in central government there was a cabinet sub-committee devoted to the issue including ministers from the main 'involved' departments.

- Initially, Keith Hellawell, the ex-chief constable of West Yorkshire Police, was appointed as a full-time 'drugs czar' to spear-head efforts and reported to this committee. But this role was terminated in the early 2000s.

- At local levels, *Drug Action Teams* were established comprising senior people from the local public and voluntary agencies concerned. They advised on and informed strategies and actions that were taken in local areas.

The overall approach to tackling drugs was emphasised in a comment by South Yorkshire Police:

> Whenever we take a dealer out we simply create a void, an opportunity for someone else to move in and take over his pitch. The only realistic chance we have of making any long-term inroads into the problem is to work in partnership to change the culture and attitudes of society, and so to reduce demand. We can only do that through better education and by providing treatment services for those suffering.

Sources: Adapted from UK Anti-Drug Co-ordination Unit; South Yorkshire Police.

Questions

1. What are the alternative ways in which the anti-drug strategy could be delivered other than this particular approach of alliances?

2. Compare the benefits and problems of these various approaches.

technology, management expertise and finance. *Consortia* may well involve two or more organisations in a joint venture arrangement, and will typically be more focused on a particular venture or project. Examples include large civil engineering projects, or major aerospace undertakings, such as the European Airbus. They might also exist between public sector organisations where services (such as public transport) cross administrative boundaries.

● At the other extreme, *networks* are arrangements whereby two or more organisations work in collaboration without formal relationships where there is mutual advantage in doing so. Networks have been created in the airline industry (such as 'One World') – largely for marketing purposes but with some cross-equity involvement between (some) partners in the alliance. *Opportunistic alliances* might also arise around particular ventures or projects.

● Many intermediate arrangements exist. One such is *franchising*, perhaps the best-known examples of which are Coca-Cola and McDonald's. Here the franchise holder undertakes specific activities such as manufacturing, distribution or selling, whilst the franchiser is responsible for the brand name, marketing and probably training. *Licensing* is common in science-based industries, where, for example, the right to manufacture a patented product is granted for a fee. With *subcontracting*, a company chooses to subcontract particular services or part of a process: for example, increasingly in public services responsibility for waste removal, cleaning and IT services may be subcontracted (outsourced) to private companies. All these intermediate arrangements are likely to be contractual in nature, but are unlikely to involve ownership.

● Some parts of the public services organisations (such as the PAYE system for tax collection) involves the customer (or employer) in *co-production*.[19] Co-production is increasingly possible with modern IT in the private sector too. Many e-commerce companies are trying to move beyond customisation of products/services (which assumes a prior knowledge of customer needs) to customerisation[20] where the customer 'designs' the product/service online.

Factors influencing the types of alliance

Exhibit 7.3 shows the factors that can influence the type of alliance:

● *Speed of market change* will require strategic moves to be made quickly. So an opportunistic alliance will be more appropriate than a joint venture, which would take too long.

● A major issue of *strategic capability* is how resources will be managed. If a strategy requires separate, dedicated, resources then a joint venture will be appropriate. In contrast many strategies can be supported by the current resources of the partners probably favouring a looser contractual relationship.

● Some organisations will operate in situations where there are *expectations* that alliances should be the preferred development method. Some stakeholders may prefer alliances as a means of spreading their financial risk. Many public sector ventures either require or 'prefer' alliances – often with the private sector.[21] So alliances suit the political climate.

Ingredients of successful alliances[22]

Although organisations may see many of the benefits of alliances (outlined above), it is not necessarily easy to make alliances work. The success of alliances is dependent on how they are managed and the way in which the partners foster the evolution of the partnership. For example, the following are likely to be important:

- A clear *strategic purpose* for the alliance together with *senior management support* are important since alliances require a wider range of relationships to be built and sustained. This can create cultural and political hurdles which senior managers must help to overcome.

- *Compatibility* at the operational level requiring efforts by partners to achieve strong interpersonal relationships at these lower levels too and not just between senior managers. In cross-country partnerships this will include the need to transcend national cultural differences (see Illustration 4.6 in Chapter 4).

- Defining and meeting *performance expectations*. This requires the willingness to exchange performance information. This would include clear *goals, governance and organisational arrangements* – concerning activities that cross or connect the partners. However, it can also be important to keep the alliance *simple and flexible* and allow the alliance to *evolve and change* rather than prescribing it too rigidly at the outset.

- *Trust* is probably the most important ingredient of success and a major reason for failure if it is absent. But trust has two separate elements. Trust can be *competence based* in the sense that each partner is confident that the other has the resources and competences to fulfil their part in the alliance. Trust is also *character based* and concerns whether partners trust each other's motives and are compatible in terms of attitudes to integrity, openness, discretion and consistency of behaviour.

7.4   SUCCESS CRITERIA

This section of the chapter looks at why some strategies might succeed better than others by introducing the concept of **success criteria** by which strategic options can be judged.[23] There are three main *success criteria*:

Success criteria are used to assess the likely success of a strategic option

- *Suitability* is concerned with whether a strategy addresses the circumstances in which an organisation is operating – the *strategic position* as discussed in Part II of this book.

- *Acceptability* is concerned with the expected *performance outcomes* (such as the *return* or *risk*) of a strategy and the extent to which these would be in line with the *expectations* of stakeholders.

- *Feasibility* is concerned with whether a strategy could be made to work in practice. Assessing the feasibility of a strategy requires an emphasis on more detailed practicalities of *strategic capability*.

Each of these criteria will now be discussed in more detail.

7.4.1 Suitability

Suitability is concerned with whether a strategy addresses the circumstances in which an organisation is operating – the strategic position

Suitability is concerned with whether a strategy addresses the circumstances in which an organisation is operating – the strategic position. This relates back to the discussions in Part II of the book. It requires a broad assessment of the extent to which new strategies would fit with the future trends and changes in the *environment*, exploit the *strategic capability* of an organisation and meet the *expectations* of stakeholders. Each of these factors is addressed in more detail in the other two success criteria. Suitability can be thought of as the *rationale* of a strategy and whether it 'makes sense' in relation to the strategic position of an organisation. So the concepts and frameworks already discussed in Chapters 2 to 4 can be helpful in understanding suitability. Some examples are shown in Exhibit 7.4.

The discussions in sections 7.2 and 7.3 above about development directions and methods were concerned with not only understanding what directions and methods were 'available' to organisations but also explaining some reasons why each might be preferred. So the various examples in those sections illustrated why strategies might be regarded as *suitable* from the point of view of the

Exhibit 7.4	Understanding the suitability of strategic options by using concepts about the strategic position

Concept	Exhibit Illustrations	Helps with understanding	Suitable strategies must address (examples)
PESTEL	Ex. 2.2 III. 2.1	Opportunities for growth/decline Changes in industry structure	Industry convergence (through vertical integration?)
Scenarios	III. 2.3	Extent of uncertainty/risk	Need for contingency plans
5-forces	Ex. 2.5 III. 2.5	Competitive forces	Development of barriers to new entrants
Strategic groups	III. 2.7	Attractiveness of groups Mobility barriers Strategic spaces	Need to reposition to a more attractive group
Core competences	Ex. 3.1	Industry threshold standards Basis of competitive advantage	Eliminating weaknesses Exploiting strengths
Value chain	Ex's. 3.6 and 3.7	Opportunities for vertical integration or outsourcing	How vertical integration would be achieved (e.g. merger or alliance)
Stakeholder mapping	Ex. 4.5 III. 4.4 a&b	Acceptability of strategies to stakeholders Power and interest	How each stakeholder will be affected. How this political (power/interest) situation could be managed
Cultural web	Ex. 4.11 III. 4.7	'Real' acceptability Impact on feasibility	How culture clash would be 'managed' in a merger or alliance

Exhibit 7.5 Some examples of suitability

Strategic option	Why this option might be suitable in terms of:		
	Environment	Capability	Expectations
Directions			
Consolidation	Withdraw from declining markets Sell valuable assets (speculation) Maintain market share	Build on strengths through continued investment and innovation	Better returns at low risk by exploiting current strategies
Market penetration	Gain market share for advantage	Exploit superior resources and competences	
Product development	Exploit knowledge of customer needs	Exploit R&D	Better returns at medium risk by exploiting current strengths or market knowledge
Market development	Current markets saturated New opportunities for: geographical spread, entering new segments or new uses	Exploit current products	
Diversification	Current markets saturated or declining	Exploit core competences in new arenas	Better returns at higher risk by 'sweating the assets'
Methods			
Internal development	First in field Partners or acquisitions not 'available'	Learning and competence development Spread of cost	Cultural/political ease
Merger/acquisition	Speed Supply/demand P/E ratios	Acquire competences Scale economies	Returns: growth or share value Problems of culture clash
Joint development	Speed Industry norm	Complementary competences Learning from partners	'Required' for entry Dilutes risk Fashionable

environment, capability and expectations. Exhibit 7.5 summarises these points from the earlier sections and provides a checklist of typical reasons why specific directions or methods of development might be regarded as suitable.

Section 7.2.5 introduced the TOWS matrix as a method of identifying strategic options directly from a SWOT analysis. So this, too, provides an assessment of suitability by 'justifying' options by the extent to which they address the strategic position of the organisation.

It is also important to understand why strategies might be *unsuitable* (particularly if managers might prefer these strategies). For example:

● The choice would be *biased* in the sense that it would not properly address all (three) of the above factors about an organisation's strategic position. For

Exhibit 7.6 Understanding the relative suitability of strategic options

Method	Capability
Ranking	● Options are assessed against key factors in the environment, resources and expectations ● A score (and ranking) is established for each option
Decision trees	● Options are 'eliminated' by progressively introducing further requirements to be met
Scenarios	● Options are matched to different future scenarios

instance, the desire to chase market opportunities without the necessary competences or funding or the pursuit of a strategy against the wishes of a powerful stakeholder would be examples.

● It is the *relative suitability* of options that matters. There may be options 'available' to an organisation that are *more suitable*. There are some useful frameworks that can assist in understanding better the relative suitability of different strategic options:

 – *Ranking* strategic options against a set of factors concerning an organisation's strategic position (as shown in Exhibit 7.6). See Illustration 7.4 for a detailed example.

 – *Decision trees*, which also assess strategic options against a list of key factors (from Exhibit 7.4). However, preferred options emerge by progressively introducing requirements which must be met (such as growth, investment or diversity). See Illustration 7.5.

 – *Scenarios*, which attempt to match specific options with a range of possible future situations and are particularly useful where a high degree of uncertainty exists (as discussed in section 2.2.4 – see Illustration 2.3). Suitable options are ones that fit the various scenarios – so several need to be 'kept open' – perhaps in the form of contingency plans.

● The elements of the strategy are not *internally consistent*. The *competitive strategy* (such as low price or differentiation), the development *direction* (such as product development or diversification) and the development *method* (internal, acquisition or alliances) need to be consistent. Strategies are unlikely to succeed if these three elements do not work together as a 'package'. Since organisations are likely to be developing and changing elements of a strategy incrementally over time, it is quite probable that strategies will become internally inconsistent resulting in declining performance.

For example, suppose that a manufacturer of consumer durable goods was competing on the *basis* of commodity products (position 1 on the strategy clock – Exhibit 5.2). Its concern was to grow market share in the home market (*market penetration*), gain scale economies and fight off the threat of cheap imported goods. It was pursuing this by *acquisitions* of smaller-share companies. This strategy was working well until there were no more small players left to acquire and the threat of cheap imports remained significant unless costs could be further reduced. In consequence the *method* of gaining market share had to switch to *internal* efforts to win customers from competitors and a major cost reduction programme commencing with the rationalisation of the production facilities the manufacturer had inherited from the acquisitions. So the search for internal consistency is a continuous not a one-off process.

7.4.2 Acceptability

Acceptability is concerned with the expected performance outcomes of a strategy. These can be of three broad types: *return*, *risk* and *stakeholder reactions*. Exhibit 7.7 summarises some frameworks that can be useful in understanding the acceptability of strategies together with some of the limitations of each of these. In general, it is helpful to use more than one approach in building up a picture of the acceptability of a particular strategy.

> **Acceptability** is concerned with the expected performance outcomes of a strategy

Return

Returns are the benefits which stakeholders are expected to receive from a strategy. So an assessment of the financial and non-financial returns likely to accrue

> **Returns** are the benefits which stakeholders are expected to receive from a strategy

Exhibit 7.7	Some criteria for understanding the acceptability of strategic options

Criteria	Used to understand	Examples	Limitations
Return			
Profitability	Financial return of investments	Return on capital Payback period Discounted cash flow (DCF)	Apply to discrete projects Only tangible costs/ benefits
Cost–benefit	Wider costs/benefits (including intangibles)	Major infrastructure projects	Difficulties of quantification
Real options	Sequence of decisions	Real options analysis	Quantification
Shareholder value analysis (SVA)	Impact of new strategies on shareholder value	Mergers/acquisitions	Technical detail often difficult
Risk			
Financial ratio projections	Robustness of strategy	Break-even analysis Impact on gearing and liquidity	
Sensitivity analysis	Test assumptions/robustness	'What if?' analysis	Tests factors separately
Stakeholder reactions	Political dimension of strategy	Stakeholder mapping Game theory	Largely qualitative

Illustration 7.4

Ranking options: Churchill Pottery

Ranking can usefully build on a SWOT analysis by comparing strategic options against the key strategic factors from the SWOT analysis.

In the 1990s Churchill Pottery, based in Stoke-on-Trent, UK, was one of the subjects of a BBC series entitled *Troubleshooter*, where the management teams of a number of companies were invited to discuss their organisation's strategic development with Sir John Harvey-Jones (ex-Chairman of ICI). Like many traditional manufacturing companies at the time, Churchill found itself under increasing pressure from cheaper imports in its traditional markets, and was considering whether to move 'up market' by launching a new range aimed at the design-conscious end of the market. The ranking exercise below was done by a group of participants on a management programme having seen the Churchill Pottery video.

The results of the ranking are interesting. First, they highlight the need to do *something*. Second, the radical departures in strategy – such as moves into retailing or diversification – are regarded as unsuitable. They do not address the problems of the core business, do not fit the capabilities of Churchill and would not fit culturally. This leaves related developments as the front runners – as might be expected in a traditional manufacturing firm like

Churchill. The choice boils down to significant investments in cost reduction to support an essentially 'commodity' approach to the market (options 2 and 5) or an 'added value' attack on the growing 'up-market' segments. The company chose the latter and with some success – presumably helped by their wide television exposure through the *Troubleshooter* series.

Source: Based on the *BBC Troubleshooter* series.

Questions

1. Has option 4 been ranked above the others because:
   (a) it has the most ticks?
   (b) it has the least crosses?
   (c) a combination of these?
   (d) other reasons?
   Justify your answer.

2. List the main strengths and limitations of ranking analysis.

Ranking exercise

Strategic options	Key strategic factors						
	Family ownership	Investment funds	Low price imports	Lack of marketing/ design skills	Automation low	Consumer taste (design)	Ranking
1. Do nothing	✓	?	✗	?	✗	✗	C
2. Consolidate in current segments (investment/ automation)	✓	✗	✓	?	✓	?	B
3. Expand overseas sales (Europe)	✗	✗	✗	✗	✗	?	C
4. Launch 'up-market' range	✓	✓	✓	✗	?	✓	A
5. Expand 'own-label' production (to hotel/ catering industry)	✓	✓	✓	?	✗	?	B
6. Open retail outlets	✗	✗	?	✗	?	?	C
7. Diversify	✗	✗	?	?	?	✓	C

✓ = favourable; ✗ = unfavourable; ? = uncertain or irrelevant.

A = most suitable; **B** = possible; **C** = unsuitable.

Illustration 7.5

A strategic decision tree for a law firm

Decision trees evaluate future options by progressively eliminating others as additional criteria are introduced to the evaluation.

A law firm had most of its work related to house conveyancing where profits had been significantly squeezed. Therefore, it wanted to consider a range of new strategies for the future. Using a strategic decision tree it was able to eliminate certain options by identifying a few key criteria which future developments would incorporate, such as growth, investment (in premises, IT systems or acquisitions), and diversification (for example, into matrimonial law which, in turn, often brings house conveyancing work as families 'reshape').

Analysis of the decision tree reveals that if the partners of the firm wish growth to be an important aspect of future strategies, options 1–4 are ranked more highly than options 5–8. At the second step, the need for low investment strategies would rank options 3 and 4 above 1 and 2, and so on.

The partners were aware that this technique has limitations in that the choice at each branch of the tree can tend to be simplistic. Answering 'yes' or 'no'

to diversification does not allow for the wide variety of alternatives which might exist between these two extremes, for example *adapting the 'style' of its conveyancing service* (this could be an important variant of options 6 or 8). Nevertheless, as a starting point for evaluation, the decision tree provides a useful framework.

Questions

1. Try reversing the sequence of the three parameters (to diversification, investment and growth) and redraw the decision tree. Do the same eight options still emerge?

2. Add a fourth parameter to the decision tree. This new parameter is development by *internal methods* or by *acquisition*. List your sixteen options in the right-hand column.

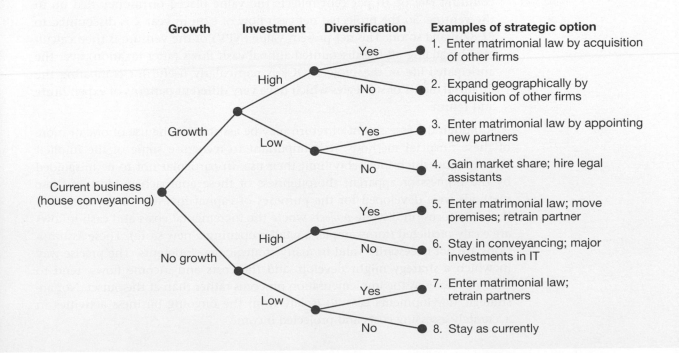

Growth	Investment	Diversification	Examples of strategic option

- Current business (house conveyancing)
  - Growth
    - High
      - Yes → 1. Enter matrimonial law by acquisition of other firms
      - No → 2. Expand geographically by acquisition of other firms
    - Low
      - Yes → 3. Enter matrimonial law by appointing new partners
      - No → 4. Gain market share; hire legal assistants
  - No growth
    - High
      - Yes → 5. Enter matrimonial law; move premises; retrain partner
      - No → 6. Stay in conveyancing; major investments in IT
    - Low
      - Yes → 7. Enter matrimonial law; retrain partners
      - No → 8. Stay as currently

from specific strategies could be a key criterion of acceptability of a strategy – at least to some stakeholders. There are a number of different approaches to understanding return. This section looks briefly at three of these approaches. It is important to remember that there are no absolute standards as to what constitutes a good or poor return. It will differ between industries, countries and also between different stakeholders. There are also arguments as to which measures give the best assessment of return, as will be seen below.

Profitability analyses[24]

Traditional financial analyses have been used extensively in assessing the acceptability of strategies. Three of the more commonly used approaches are as follows (see Exhibit 7.8):

● Forecasting the *return on capital employed* (ROCE) a specific time after a new strategy is implemented (e.g. the new strategy will result in a return on capital of 15 per cent by year 3). This is shown in Exhibit 7.8(a).

● *Payback period* has been used where a significant capital injection is needed to support a new venture. In Exhibit 7.8(b), the payback period is calculated by finding the time at which the cumulative net cash flow becomes zero – in the example, three and a half years.

   The judgement is whether this is regarded as an adequate outcome and if the organisation is prepared to wait that long for a return. This will vary from one industry to another. Major public sector ventures such as bridge building may well be assessed on a payback period of up to 60 years.

● *Discounted cash flow* (DCF) is a widely used investment appraisal technique, and is essentially an extension of the payback period analysis. Once the net cash flows have been assessed for each of the years (see Exhibit 7.8c), they are discounted progressively to reflect the fact that funds generated early are of more real value than those in later periods (years). In the example, the discounting rate of 10 per cent reflects the value placed on money tied up in the venture. So the projected net cash flow of €2m in year 2 is discounted to €1.82m and so on. The net present value (NPV) of the venture is then calculated by adding all the discounted annual cash flows (after taxation) over the anticipated life of the project. DCF is particularly useful for comparing the financial merits of strategies which have very different patterns of expenditure and return.

Although the assessment of return may be assisted by the use of one or more of these financial methods, it is important to recognise some of the implicit assumptions which inevitably limit their use. In particular not to be misguided by the tidiness or apparent thoroughness of these approaches. Most of these methods were developed for the purposes of capital investment appraisal and therefore focus on discrete *projects* where the incremental costs and cash inflows are easily predicted (for example, a retailer opening a new store). These assumptions are not necessarily valid in many strategic developments. The precise way in which a strategy might develop, and the costs and income flows, tend to become clearer as the implementation proceeds rather than at the outset. Nor are strategic developments easy to isolate from the ongoing business activities in accurately assessing costs and projected income.

Exhibit 7.8   Assessing profitability

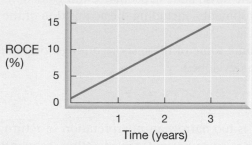

(a) Return on capital employed

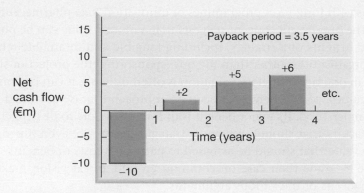

(b) Payback period

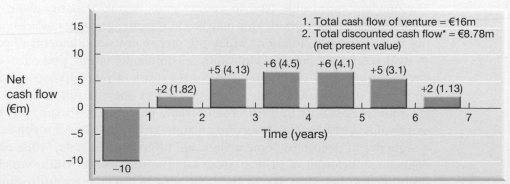

* Using a discounting rate of 10%.
Figures in brackets are discounted by 10% annually.

(c) Discounted cash flow (DCF)

Additionally, financial appraisals tend to focus on the direct *tangible* costs and benefits, and do not set the strategy in its wider context. For example, a new product launch may look unprofitable as an isolated project, but may make strategic sense through the market acceptability of other products in the company's portfolio. Or, in reverse, the intangible cost of losing *strategic focus* through new ventures is readily overlooked. These were certainly the views of Sir George Mathewson, chairman of the Royal Bank of Scotland, and guided his approach to the bank's successful development – including the acquisition of the much larger NatWest bank in 2000.

In an attempt to overcome some of these shortcomings, other approaches to assessing return have been developed.

Cost–benefit[25]

In many situations, profit is too narrow an interpretation of return, particularly where intangible benefits are an important consideration, as mentioned above. This is usually the case for major public infrastructure projects, such as the siting of an airport or a sewer construction project, as shown in Illustration 7.6, or in organisations with long-term programmes of innovation (e.g. pharmaceuticals or aerospace). The *cost–benefit* concept suggests that a money value can be put on all the costs and benefits of a strategy, including tangible and intangible returns to people and organisations other than the one 'sponsoring' the project or strategy.

Although in practice monetary valuation is often difficult, it can be done, and, despite difficulties, cost–benefit analysis is an approach that is valuable if its limitations are understood. Its major benefit is in forcing people to be explicit about the various factors that should influence strategic choice. So, even if people disagree on the value that should be assigned to particular costs or benefits, at least they are able to argue their case on common ground and decision makers can compare the merits of the various arguments.

Real options[26]

The previous approaches tend to assume some degree of clarity about the outcomes of a strategic option. This may be OK for slow-growing mature companies but there are many situations where the precise costs and benefits of particular strategies tend to become clear only as implementation proceeds. In these circumstances the traditional Discounted Cash Flow approaches discussed above will tend to undervalue a 'project' because they do not take into account the value of flexibility in the decision-making process. Luehrman[27] says that this extra value arises because 'executing a strategy almost always involves making a sequence of decisions. Some actions are taken immediately, while others are deliberately deferred. . . . The strategy sets the framework within which future decisions will be made, but at the same time it leaves space for learning from ongoing developments and for discretion to act based on what is learnt.' So the flexibility can be used to expand, extend, contract, defer or close down a project. This suggests that a strategy should be seen as a *series* of 'real' options (i.e. choices of direction at particular points in time as the strategy takes shape, as a result of the previous choices that were made). The benefit of this approach is that it can provide a clearer understanding of both strategic and financial return and

Illustration 7.6

strategy into action

Sewerage construction project

Investment in items of infrastructure – such as sewers – often requires a careful consideration of the wider costs and benefits of the project.

Britain's privatised water companies were monopolies supplying water and disposing of sewage. One of their priorities was investment in new sewerage systems to meet the increasing standards required by law. They frequently used cost–benefit analysis to assess projects. The figures below are from an actual analysis.

Cost/Benefit	£m	£m
Benefits		
Multiplier/linkage benefits		0.9
Flood prevention		2.5
Reduced traffic disruption		7.2
Amenity benefits		4.6
Investment benefit		23.6
Encouragement of visitors		4.0
Total benefits		42.8
Costs		
Construction cost	18.2	
Less: Unskilled labour cost	(4.7)	
Opportunity cost of construction	(13.5)	
Present value of net benefits (NPV)	29.3	
Real internal rate of return (IRR)	15%	

Note: Figures discounted at a *real* discount rate of 5% over 40 years.

Benefits

Benefits result mainly from reduced use of rivers as overflow sewers. There are also economic benefits resulting from construction. The following benefits are quantified in the table:

- The multiplier benefit to the local economy of increased spending by those employed on the project.

- The linkage benefit to the local economy of purchases from local firms, including the multiplier effect of such spending.

- Reduced risk of flooding from overflows or old sewers collapsing – flood probabilities can be quantified using historical records, and the cost of flood damage by detailed assessment of the property vulnerable to damage.

- Reduced traffic disruption from flooding and road closures for repairs to old sewers – statistics on the costs of delays to users, traffic flows on roads affected and past closure frequency can be used to quantify savings.

- Increased amenity value of rivers (e.g. for boating and fishing) can be measured by surveys asking visitors what the value is to them or by looking at the effect on demand of charges imposed elsewhere.

- Increased rental values and take-up of space can be measured by consultation with developers and observed effects elsewhere.

- Increased visitor numbers to riverside facilities resulting from reduced pollution.

Construction cost

This is net of the cost of unskilled labour. Use of unskilled labour is not a burden on the economy, and its cost must be deducted to arrive at opportunity cost.

Net benefits

Once the difficult task of quantifying costs and benefits is complete, standard discounting techniques can be used to calculate net present value and internal rate of return, and analysis can then proceed as for conventional projects.

Source: G. Owen, formerly of Sheffield Business School.

Questions

1. What do you feel about the appropriateness of the listed benefits?

2. How easy or difficult is it to assign money values to these benefits?

Exhibit 7.9   Real options framework

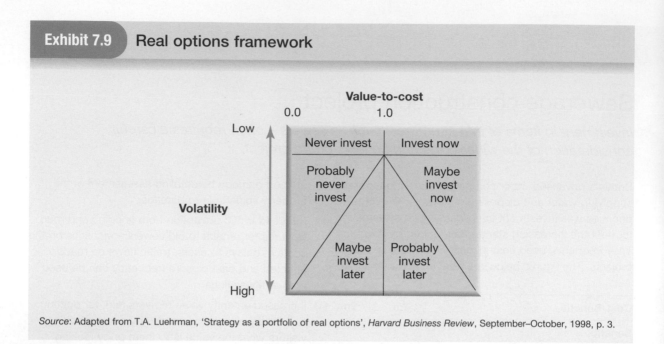

Source: Adapted from T.A. Luehrman, 'Strategy as a portfolio of real options', *Harvard Business Review*, September–October, 1998, p. 3.

risk of a strategy by examining each step (option) separately as it 'occurs'. For example, the value that will accrue from investing in a technology that creates a 'platform' from which several products or process improvements may spring is not clear at the outset. However, as the project develops learning will occur as to which directions the development should progress or even if it should be terminated early. This philosophy has been enshrined in the stage-gate approach to major R&D projects (as discussed in section 9.5.4 of Chapter 9). The degree of volatility surrounding a strategy will change over time as a result of this partial implementation (i.e. the previous steps (options)). So strategic and financial evaluations are brought more closely together than is usually the case. Real options bridge the somewhat rigid Discounted Cash Flow approach and the intuitive approaches (such as scenarios discussed above).

Exhibit 7.9 shows that high levels of volatility should have two effects. Firstly, to defer decisions as far as possible because (secondly) the passage of time will clarify the expected returns – even to the extent that apparently unfavourable strategies might prove viable at a later date (the category 'maybe invest later' in the exhibit). This can help in deciding whether to pursue the strategy at all and whether it should be pursued immediately or deferred to a later date.

Shareholder value analysis[28]

For many years there have been attempts to address many of the limitations and criticisms of traditional financial analyses. Historically based accounting measures – such as operating profit – ignore the cost of capital completely and, therefore, may give misleading signals about where value is being created or destroyed. This can produce completely misleading views about the acceptability of specific strategic options. Another reason was a continuing concern about the need for company directors to pay attention to their primary legal responsibility, namely the creation of value and benefits for the shareholders. Also progressive waves of mergers and acquisitions caused both corporate raiders and victims alike to look at how corporate strategies were, or were not, generating shareholder value. Together, these factors spawned *shareholder value analysis* (SVA) – a field of study initially led by Rappaport. Later this was extended into 'managing for shareholder value' (MFV) (see section 9.3 of Chapter 9). A number of well-known companies from around the world now claim to have taken various steps towards managing for value. These include Coca-Cola, Cadbury Schweppes, Lufthansa, Reuters and Telstra.

The shareholder value measure used most commonly is total shareholder returns (TSRs), which in any year is equal to the increase in the price of a share over the year plus the dividends per share earned in the year, all divided by the share price at the start of the year. This can be used to assess the financial acceptability of specific strategies. More widely value-based businesses use this measure to set themselves overall performance goals (e.g. to earn TSRs of 20 per cent each year, or for TSRs to be in the top quartile of a peer group of companies, or to double the value of the business in four years). They also use TSRs to reward managers – typically the most senior managers – for the performance the business has achieved for its owners. Used effectively, TSR goals align the interests of owners and managers.

Although shareholder value analysis has done much to address the shortcomings of traditional financial analyses, it does not remove many of the inherent uncertainties surrounding strategic choices. It has also been criticised for overemphasising short-term returns.[29] Nevertheless, the idea of valuing a strategy may serve to give greater realism and clarity to otherwise vague strategies. It is an important way in which business and financial strategies should overlap and is discussed further in section 9.4.

Risk

The likely return from a particular strategy is an important aspect of the acceptability of that strategy. However, another aspect of acceptability is the *risk* that an organisation faces in pursuing a particular strategy. **Risk** concerns the probability and consequences of the failure of a strategy. This risk can be particularly high for organisations with major long-term programmes of innovation or where high levels of uncertainty exist about key issues in the environment. There has been a progressive move to incorporate a *formal* risk assessment in regular business plans as well as with the investment appraisals of major projects. Importantly risks other than ones with immediate financial impact are included such as 'risk to corporate or brand image' or 'risk of missing an opportunity'. Risk should be seen as an opportunity as well as a threat. This development has been important in the public sector in the UK and in industries where there are high levels of public concern about new developments – such as Genetically Modified Crops.[30] This approach to risk assessment defines risk quite broadly as '. . . something happening that may have an impact on the achievement of objectives as this is most likely to affect service delivery for citizens'.[31] So developing a good understanding of an organisation's strategic position (Part II of this book) is at the core of good risk assessment. But it also requires an ability to manage risk.

Risk concerns the probability and consequences of the failure of a strategy

Some of the concepts below can be used to establish the detail within a risk assessment.

Financial ratios[32]

Although risk assessment should be broader than just financial numbers these numbers usually *are* important. The projection of how key financial ratios might change if a specific strategy were adopted can provide useful insights into risk. At the broadest level, an assessment of how the *capital structure* of the company would change is a good general measure of risk. For example, strategies that would require an increase in long-term debt will increase the gearing of the company and, hence, its financial risk.

At a more detailed level, a consideration of the likely impact on an organisation's *liquidity* is important in assessing risk. For example, a small retailer eager to grow quickly may be tempted to fund the required shop-fitting costs by delaying payments to suppliers and increasing bank overdraft. This reduced liquidity increases the financial risk of the business. The extent to which this increased risk threatens survival depends on the likelihood of either creditors or the bank demanding payments from the company – an issue that clearly requires judgement.

Sensitivity analysis[33]

Sensitivity analysis is sometimes referred to as *what if?* analysis. It allows each of the important assumptions underlying a particular strategy to be questioned and challenged. In particular, it seeks to test how sensitive the predicted performance or outcome (e.g. profit) is to each of these assumptions. For example, the key assumptions underlying a strategy might be that market demand will grow by 5 per cent p.a., or that the company will stay strike-free, or that certain expensive machines will operate at 90 per cent loading. Sensitivity analysis asks what would be the effect on performance (in this case, profitability) if, for example, market demand grew at only 1 per cent, or by as much as 10 per cent? Would either of these extremes alter the decision to pursue that particular strategy? A similar process might be repeated for the other key assumptions. This can help develop a clearer picture of the risks of making particular strategic decisions and the degree of confidence managers might have in a given decision. Illustration 7.7 shows how sensitivity analysis can be used.

Stakeholder reactions

In Chapter 4, s*takeholder mapping* (Exhibit 4.5) was presented as a way of understanding the political context and prioritising the 'political agenda' for an organisation. Therefore, stakeholder mapping can be useful in understanding the likely reactions of stakeholders to new strategies, the ability to manage these reactions, and hence the acceptability of a strategy.

There are many situations where judgements of stakeholder reactions could be crucial. For example:

● A new strategy might require a substantial issue of *new shares*, which could be unacceptable to powerful groups of shareholders, since it dilutes their voting power.

- Plans to *merge* with other companies or to *trade* with new countries could be unacceptable to unions, government or some customers.

- A new e-commerce business model might cut out *channels* (such as retailers), hence running the risk of a backlash, which could jeopardise the success of the strategy.

- Attempts to gain market share in static markets might upset the status quo to such an extent that competitors will be forced to retaliate in a way that is damaging to all parties, for example by instigating a price war.

Since an important issue may be the likely reactions of competitors to particular strategic changes, *game theory* could be useful in understanding risk (see Chapter 5, section 5.7). Both governments and telecom companies allegedly used game theory to guide their bidding for the so-called third-generation mobile telephone licences in Europe in the early 2000s. The 'winners' were governments as licences brought in £22bn (≈ €33bn) in the UK alone.

7.4.3 Feasibility

Feasibility is concerned with whether an organisation has the resources and competences to deliver a strategy. A number of approaches can be used to understand feasibility.

> **Feasibility** is concerned with whether an organisation has the resources and competences to deliver a strategy

Financial feasibility

A useful way of assessing financial feasibility is *funds flow forecasting*, which seeks to identify the funds which would be required for any strategy and the likely sources of those funds, as shown in Illustration 7.8.

It should be remembered that funds flow forecasting is subject to the difficulties and errors of any method of forecasting. However, it should highlight whether a proposed strategy is likely to be feasible in financial terms and the *timing* of new funding requirements. It can normally be undertaken using a spreadsheet. This issue of funding strategic developments is an important interface between business and financial strategies and is discussed more fully in section 9.4.

Financial feasibility can also be assessed through break-even analysis,[34] which is a simple and widely used approach to assessing the feasibility of meeting targets of return (e.g. profit) and, as such, combines a parallel assessment of acceptability. It also provides an assessment of the risk of various strategies, particularly where different strategic options require markedly different cost structures.

Resource deployment[35]

Although financial feasibility is important, a wider understanding of the feasibility of *specific* strategies can be achieved by identifying the resources and competences needed for that strategy. For example, geographical expansion in the home market might be critically dependent on marketing and distribution

Illustration 7.7   strategy into action

Sensitivity analysis

Sensitivity analysis is a useful technique for assessing the extent to which the success of a preferred strategy is dependent on the key assumptions which underlie that strategy.

In 2004 the Dunsmore Chemical Company was a single-product company trading in a mature and relatively stable market. It was intended to use this established situation as a 'cash cow' to generate funds for a new venture with a related product. Estimates had shown that the company would need to generate some £4m (≈ €6m) cash (at 2004 values) between 2005 and 2010 for this new venture to be possible.

Although the expected performance of the company was for a cash flow of £9.5m over that period (the *base case*), management was concerned to assess the likely impact of three key factors:

● Possible increases in *production costs* (labour, overheads and materials), which might be as much as 3 per cent p.a. in real terms.

● *Capacity fill*, which might be reduced by as much as 25 per cent owing to ageing plant and uncertain labour relations.

● *Price levels*, which might be affected by the threatened entry of a new major competitor. This could squeeze prices by as much as 3 per cent p.a. in real terms.

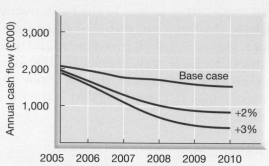

(a) Sensitivity of cash flow to changes in real production costs

It was decided to use sensitivity analysis to assess the possible impact of each of these factors on the company's ability to generate £4m. The results are shown in the graphs.

From this analysis, the management concluded that its target of £4m would be achieved with *capacity utilisation* as low as 60 per cent, which was certainly going to be achieved. Increased *production costs* of 3 per cent p.a. would still allow the company to achieve the £4m target over the period. In contrast,

expertise, together with the availability of cash to fund increased stocks. In contrast, a different strategy of developing new products to sell to current customers is dependent on engineering skills, the capability of machinery and the company's reputation for quality in new products.

A resource deployment assessment can be used to judge two things (as shown in Exhibit 7.10). First, the extent to which an organisation's current capabilities (resources and competences) would need to change to reach or maintain the *threshold* requirements for a strategy. Second, how unique resources and/or core competences can be developed to sustain competitive advantage. The issue is whether these changes are *feasible* in terms of scale, quality of resource or time-scale of change.

The next section of the book (Chapters 8 to 10) will look at the practical issues of translating strategy into action. In practice, the implementation of strategies may throw up issues that might make organisations reconsider whether particular strategic options are, in fact, feasible. This may lead to a reshaping, or even abandonment, of strategic options.

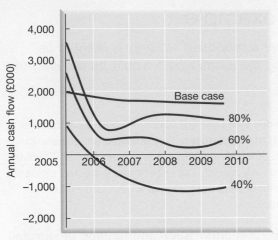

(b) Sensitivity of cash flow to changes in plant utilisation

(c) Sensitivity of cash flow to reductions in real price

price squeezes of 3 per cent p.a. would result in a shortfall of £2m.

The management concluded from this analysis that the key factor which should affect its thinking on this matter was the likely impact of new competition and the extent to which it could protect price levels if such competition emerged. The management therefore developed an aggressive marketing strategy to deter potential entrants.

Source: The calculations for the sensitivity test utilise computer programs employed in the Doman case study by Peter Jones (Sheffield Business School).

Question

What should the company do if its marketing campaigns fail to stop real price erosion:

(a) Push to achieve more sales volume/capacity fill?
(b) Reduce unit costs of production?
(c) Something else?

Exhibit 7.10   Resource deployment – some important questions

Staying in business

- Do we lack any necessary resources?
- Are we performing below threshold on any activity?

Competing successfully

- Which unique resources already exist?
- Which core competences already exist?
- Could better performance create a core competence?
- What new resources or activities could be unique or core competences?

Illustration 7.8

strategy into action

Funds flow analysis: a worked example

A funds flow analysis can be used to assess whether a proposed strategy is likely to be feasible in financial terms. It does this by forecasting the funds which would be required for the strategy and the likely sources of those funds.

Kentex plc (a UK electrical goods retailer) was considering pursuing a strategy of expansion which in the immediate future would involve opening new stores in the Irish Republic. To evaluate the financial feasibility of this proposal and establish what funds would be required and how these funds may be sourced, the company decided to undertake a funds flow analysis.

Stage 1: Identification of sources

Opening of the new stores was estimated to increase the sales revenue from the current £30m (≈ €45m) to £31.65m per annum over the following three years. This was expected to generate funds from operations totalling £15m over the three years. This was the estimate of future profits corrected for non-fund items such as depreciation and represents real flow of funds into the company for a three-year period.

Stage 2: Identification of uses

There would be a number of costs associated with the new stores. First, Kentex decided to purchase rather than lease property so there would be the direct costs of the capital investment required for purchasing and fitting out the stores. This was forecast to be £13.25m. Also there will be additional working capital costs to cover stock, etc. This was not calculated by separate consideration of each element, e.g. stock increases, increased creditors; instead the forecasts were based on a simple pro rata adjustment. On the

previous sales level of £30m, a working capital level of £10m was required, so the expected increase in sales of £1.65m would require an additional £0.55m in working capital. Tax liability and expected dividend payments were estimated at £1.2m and £0.5m respectively.

Stage 3: Identification and funding of shortfall

These calculations show a shortfall in funds of £0.5m. The company then finalised the forecast by looking at alternative ways of funding the shortfall. Whilst it could raise funds through the issue of new share capital, it chose to seek a short-term loan of £0.65m. It should be noted that this in turn would incur interest payments of £0.15m over the three-year period assuming simple interest at 7.5 per cent per annum, hence leaving a net income of £0.5m.

Questions

1. Which parts of this assessment are likely to have the greatest probability of error?

2. What are the implications of your answer to question 1 on how the analysis should be presented to the decision-makers?

3. How might this uncertainty influence the management of the implementation phase if approval is given?

Sources	£	Uses	£
Funds from operations	15,000,000	New fixed assets	13,250,000
		Working capital	550,000
		Tax	1,200,000
		Dividends	500,000
Subtotal	15,000,000	**Subtotal**	15,500,000

Note: Shortfall between sources and uses amounting to £500,000.

Illustration 7.9

key debate

Merger madness?

Mergers and acquisitions involve huge sums of money, but how wisely is it being spent?

This chapter has introduced the importance of mergers and acquisitions as a method of development, but also pointed to some challenges. There have been some spectacular failures. When in 2001 media company Time Warner merged with internet company AOL, Time Warner shares were worth a total of $90bn (€78bn). Just under three years later, Time Warner investors' holdings in the merged company were worth only $36bn, a loss of over $50bn (in the same period, media companies' valuations had fallen on average 16 per cent).

Harvard Business School professor Michael Porter has been a prominent sceptic of mergers and acquisitions, noting that half of all acquired companies are sold off again within a few years.[1] The figure shows the aggregate dollar return (i.e. the change in stock price associated with the acquisition announcement) of acquiring companies in the United States between 1996 and 2001.[2] In 2000, acquiring firms' shareholders lost, in all, more than $150bn. The authors of this study calculate that in the whole period 1991 to 2001, acquiring firms' shareholders lost more than $7 for every $100 spent on acquisitions.

One interpretation of these large losses is that mergers and acquisitions represent a reckless waste of money by managers who are careless of investors' interests. It might be appropriate therefore to make mergers and acquisitions more difficult by legislating to help target companies resist or refuse hostile bids. If the law restricted hostile bids, wasteful acquisitions could be cut.

There are some drawbacks to restricting mergers and acquisitions, however.[3] Even if acquiring companies often fail to make money for their shareholders, they can improve the profitability of the system as a whole in at least two ways:

- The threat of being taken over if they do not satisfy their shareholders helps keep managers focused on performance. In 2004, American cable company Comcast launched a hostile bid for Disney, attacking the poor performance of Chairman and Chief Executive Officer Michael Eisner.

- Mergers and acquisitions can be an effective way of restructuring stagnant firms and industries. The absence of hostile takeovers in Japan is often blamed for the slow restructuring of Japanese industry since the early 1990s.

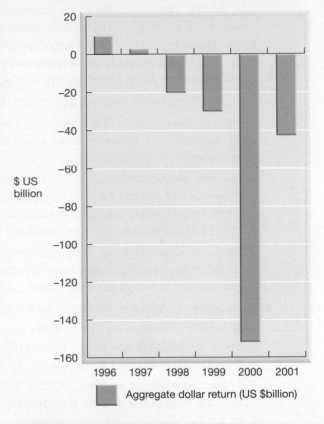

$ US billion

Aggregate dollar return (US $billion)

Sources:
1. M. Porter, 'From competitive advantage to corporate strategy', *Harvard Business Review*, May–June (1987), pp. 43–60.
2. S.B. Moeller, F.P. Schlingman and R.M. Stulz, 'Wealth destruction on a massive scale? A study of acquiring firm returns in the recent merger wave', http://www.cob.ohio-state.edu/fin/dice/papers/2003/ and forthcoming *Journal of Finance*, 2004.
3. 'Hostile bids are back again: who should rejoice?', *The Economist*, 21 February 2004.

Question

For a recent large merger or acquisition, track the share prices of the companies involved (using www.bigcharts.com, for instance), for several weeks both before and after the announcement. What do the share price movements suggest about the merits of the deal?

Summary

- A strategic choice has three elements: the broad *competitive strategy* (discussed in Chapter 5), the *direction* of development and the *method* of development. These three elements must be compatible with each other.

- Development directions can be identified in four broad categories by using an amended Ansoff matrix: *protect* and *build* (current products in current markets); *product development* (for existing markets); *market development* (with existing products); and *diversification* (away from existing products and markets). An organisation's *competences* and the *expectations* in and around the organisation will also create (or limit) development directions. The TOWS matrix is a complementary way of generating stray options directly from a SWOT analysis of an organisation's strategic position.

- There are three broad *methods* of strategy development:

  - Internal development has the major benefit of building organisational competences through learning. However, it can result in overstretched resources and the loss of the advantages of specialisation.

  - Mergers and acquisitions may have advantages of speed and the ability to acquire competences not already held 'in-house'. However, the track record of acquisitions is not good, largely owing to cultural differences and a failure of the 'parent' to understand (and influence) the businesses it has acquired. (See the key debate in Illustration 7.9.)

  - Strategic alliances have many different forms. The most successful alliances appear to be those where partners have positive attitudes to managing and developing the partnership. In particular, where there is trust between partners.

- The success or failure of strategies will be related to three main *success criteria*:

  - Suitability is concerned with whether a strategy addresses the circumstances in which the organisation is operating – the strategic position as discussed in Part II of this book. It is about the *rationale* of a strategy.

  - The acceptability of a strategy relates to three issues: the expected *return* from a strategy, the level of *risk* and the likely *reaction of stakeholders.*

  - Feasibility is concerned with whether an organisation has the resources and competences to deliver a strategy. Feasibility is also informed by implementation of a strategy. So strategies may need to be reshaped as implementation proceeds.

  There are a range of analytical techniques that help to evaluate strategic options against these three criteria.

Recommended key readings

- A comprehensive book on mergers and acquisitions is: P. Gaughan, *Mergers, Acquisitions and Corporate Restructurings*, 2nd edition, Wiley, 2000.

- A useful book on strategic alliances is Y. Doz and G. Hamel, *Alliance Advantage*, Harvard Business School Press, 1998.

- A companion book which explores techniques more fully is V. Ambrosini with G. Johnson and K. Scholes (eds), *Exploring Techniques of Analysis and Evaluation in Strategic Management*, Prentice Hall, 1998.

- A useful text on financial analyses for both strategic analysis and strategy evaluation is: A.N. Grundy with G. Johnson and K. Scholes, *Exploring Strategic Financial Management*, Prentice Hall, 1998.

References

1. This figure is an extension of the product/market matrix: see H. Ansoff, *Corporate Strategy*, Penguin, 1988, Chapter 6. The Ansoff matrix was later developed into the one shown below.

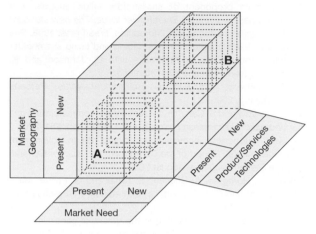

Source: H. Ansoff, The New Corporate Strategy, Wiley, 1988.

2. Data-mining is discussed in: B. Gates, *Business @ the Speed of Thought*, Penguin, 1999, pp. 225–233. For more detail see: C. Carmen and B. Lewis, 'A basic primer on data mining', *Information Systems Management*, vol. 19, no. 4 (2002), pp. 56–60 and J. Hall and P. Owen, 'Mining the store', *Journal of Business Strategy*, vol. 22, no. 2 (2001), pp. 24–27.

3. References on diversification can be found in section 6.2 of Chapter 6.

4. A comprehensive book on mergers and acquisitions is: P. Gaughan, *Mergers, Acquisitions and Corporate Restructurings*, 2nd edition, Wiley, 2000. A good discussion of the practicalities can be found in: D. Carey, 'Making mergers succeed', *Harvard Business Review*, vol. 78, no. 3 (2000), pp. 145–154.

5. R. Schoenberg and R. Reeves, 'What determines acquisition activity within an industry?', *European Management Journal*, vol. 17, no. 1 (1999), pp. 93–98.

6. G. Muller-Stewens, 'Catching the right wave', *European Business Forum*, issue 4, Winter 2000, pp. 6–7, illustrates the major waves of mergers over the last 100 years. Gaughan (reference 4) describes the five major merger waves in the USA.

7. *The Sunday Times*, 7 January 2001 ('Top deals in 2000').

8. Useful discussions of the reasons for, and problems with, mergers and acquisitions can be found in P. Haspeslagh, 'Maintaining momentum in mergers', *European Business Forum*, issue 4, Winter 2000, pp. 53–56: B. Savill and P. Wright, 'Success factors in acquisitions', *European Business Forum*, issue 4, Winter 2000, pp. 29–33; R. Schoenberg, 'Mergers and acquisitions: motives, value creation and implementation', *The Oxford Handbook of Corporate Strategy*, Chapter 21, Oxford University Press, 2003; R. Schoenberg, 'Knowledge transfer and resource sharing as value creation mechanisms in inbound continental European acquisitions', *Journal of Euromarketing*, vol. 10, no. 1 (2001), pp. 99–114; R. Larsson and S. Finkelstein,

'Integrating strategic, organisational and human resource perspectives on mergers and acquisitions: a case study survey of synergy realisation', *Organisation Science*, vol. 10, no. 1 (1999), pp. 1–26. A practical guide for managers is: T. Galpin and M. Herndon, *The Complete Guide to Mergers and Acquisitions*, Jossey-Bass, 2000.

9. For example, see: M. Zey and T. Swenson, 'The transformation and survival of Fortune 500 industrial corporations through mergers and acquisitions, 1981–1995', *Sociological Quarterly*, vol. 42, no. 3 (2001), pp. 461–486.

10. See: D. Carey (reference 4 above); J. Birkinshaw, H. Bresman and L. Hakanson, 'Managing the post-acquisition integration process: how the human integration and task integration processes interact to foster value creation', *Journal of Management Studies*, vol. 37, no. 3 (2000), pp. 395–425; Haspeslagh, and Savill and Wright (both from reference 8 above); R. Schoenberg, 'The influence of cultural compatibility within cross-border acquisitions: a review', *Advances in Mergers and Acquisitions*, vol. 1 (2000), pp. 43–59; A. Gregory, 'An examination of the long term performance of UK acquiring firms', *Journal of Business Finance and Accounting*, vol. 24 (1997), pp. 971–1002.

11. J. Bower, 'Not all M&As are alike', *Harvard Business Review*, vol. 79, no. 3 (2001), pp. 93–101.

12. See: J. Child, D. Faulkner and R. Pitkethly, *The Management of International Acquisitions*, Oxford University Press, 2003.

13. Useful books on strategic alliances are: Y. Doz and G. Hamel, *Alliance Advantage: The art of creating value through partnering*, Harvard Business School Press, 1998. For a detailed theoretical insight see Y. Doz, D. Faulkner and M. de Rond, *Co-operative Strategies: Economic, Business and Organisational Issues*, Oxford University Press, 2001. A practical guide for managers is: E. Rigsbee, *Developing Strategic Alliances*, Crisp, 2000. See also: D. Ernst and T. Halevy, 'When to think alliance', *McKinsey Quarterly*, no. 4 (2000), pp. 46–55.

14. For a consideration of the special issues of global strategic alliances see: G. Yip, *Total Global Strategy II*, 2nd edition, FT/Prentice Hall, 2003, pp. 82–85.

15. J. Dyer, P. Kale and H. Singh, 'How to make strategic alliances work', *Sloan Management Review*, vol. 42, no. 4 (2001), pp. 37–43 and D. Ernst, 'Give alliances their due', *McKinsey Quarterly*, no. 3 (2002), pp. 4–5.

16. Doz and Hamel (reference 13 above), p. 6.

17. See: Doz and Hamel (reference 13 above), Chapters 1 and 2; Ernst and Halevy (reference 13 above); M. Koza and A. Lewin, 'The co-evolution of strategic alliances', *Organisation Science*, vol. 9, no. 3 (1998), pp. 255–264.

18. G. Kelly, 'Providing public services', *New Economy*, vol. 7, no. 3 (2000), pp. 132–137.

19. See: J. Alford, 'A public management road less travelled: clients as co-producers of public services', *Australian Journal of Public Administration*, vol. 57, no. 4 (1998), pp. 128–137.

20. See: J. Wind and V. Mahajan, *Digital Marketing: Global strategies from the world's leading experts*, Wiley, 2001.

21. S. Hill, 'Public sector partnerships and public/voluntary sector partnerships: the Scottish experience', in G. Johnson and K. Scholes (eds), *Exploring Public Sector Strategy*, Financial Times/Prentice Hall, 2001, Chapter 12. R. Butler and J. Gill, 'Formation and control of public–private partnerships: a

stakeholder approach', in G. Johnson and K. Scholes (eds), *Exploring Public Sector Strategy*, Financial Times/Prentice Hall, 2001, Chapter 11.

22. See Doz and Hamel (reference 13 above); T. Pietras and C. Stormer, 'Making strategic alliances work', *Business and Economic Review*, vol. 47, no. 4 (2001), pp. 9–12; N. Kaplan and J. Hurd, 'Realising the promise of partnerships', *Journal of Business Strategy*, vol. 23, no. 3 (2002), pp. 38–42; A. Parkhe, 'Interfirm diversity in global alliances' *Business Horizons*, vol. 44, no. 6 (2001), pp. 2–4.

23. For a companion book which explores techniques more fully, see V. Ambrosini with G. Johnson and K. Scholes (eds), *Exploring Techniques of Analysis and Evaluation in Strategic Management*, Prentice Hall, 1998.

24. A useful book on financial analyses for both strategic analysis and strategy evaluation is: A.N. Grundy with G. Johnson and K. Scholes, *Exploring Strategic Financial Management*, Prentice Hall, 1998.

25. Cost–benefit analysis is discussed in A. Williams and E. Giardina, *Efficiency in the Public Sector: The theory and practice of cost–benefit analysis*, Edward Elgar, 1993. (Despite the title, the book covers the private sector too.) A detailed example in the water industry can be found in: N. Poew, 'Water companies' service performance and environmental trade-off', *Journal of Environmental Planning and Management*, vol. 45, no. 3 (2002), pp. 363–379.

26. Real options evaluation can get lost in the mathematics so readers wishing to gain more detail of how real options analysis works can consult one of the following: T. Copeland, 'The real options approach to capital allocation', *Strategic Finance*, vol. 83, no. 4 (2001), pp. 33–37; T. Copeland, T. Koller and J. Murrin, *Valuation: Measuring and managing the value of companies*, 3rd edition, Wiley, 2000; T. Copeland and V. Antikarov, *Real Options: A practitioner's guide*, Texere Publishing, 2001; L. Trigeorgis, *Managerial Flexibility and Strategy in Resource Allocation*, MIT Press, 2002; P. Boer, *The Real Options Solution: Finding total value in a high risk world*, Wiley, 2002.

27. T. Luehrman, 'Strategy as a portfolio of real options', *Harvard Business Review*, vol. 76, no. 5 (1998), pp. 89–99.

28. The main proponent of shareholder value analysis was A. Rappaport, *Creating Shareholder Value: The new standard for business performance*, 2nd edition, Free Press, 1998. See also R. Mill's chapter, 'Understanding and using shareholder value analysis', in V. Ambrosini with G. Johnson and K. Scholes (see reference 23), Chapter 15.

29. A. Kennedy, *The End of Shareholder Value*, Perseus Publishing, 2000.

30. L. Levidow and S. Carr, 'UK: precautionary commercialisation', *Journal of Risk Research*, vol. 3, no. 3 (2000), pp. 261–270.

31. See: 'Supporting innovation: managing risk in government departments', *Report of the Comptroller and Auditor General*, The Stationery Office, August 2000.

32. See C. Horngren, A. Bhimani, S. Datar and G. Foster, *Management and Cost Accounting*, 2nd edition, FT/Prentice Hall, 2002, Chapter 19.

33. For those readers interested in the details of sensitivity analysis see: A. Satelli, K. Chan and M. Scott (eds), *Sensitivity Analysis*, Wiley, 2000. A briefer description can be found in: C. Horngren et al. (reference 32 above), pp. 233–234. Computer spreadsheets are ideally suited for sensitivity analysis.

34. Break-even analysis is covered in most standard accountancy texts. See, for example, Horngren et al. (reference 32 above) pp. 229–232.

35. This relates to the idea of 'resource-based strategies' discussed in Chapter 3. See that chapter for references.

An extensive range of additional materials, including audio summaries, weblinks to organisations featured in the text, definitions of key concepts and multiple choice questions, can be found on the *Exploring Corporate Strategy* Companion Website at **www.pearsoned.co.uk/ecs7**

WORK ASSIGNMENTS

✱ Denotes more advanced work assignments.   * Refers to a case study in the Text and Cases edition.

7.1   Identify possible development strategies in terms of their combination of *direction* and *method* of development in one of the following:

(a) Barclaycard*
(b) Coopers Creek*
(c) an organisation of your choice.

7.2✱   Referring to sections 7.3.2 and 6.4 (Chapter 6) and using additional examples of your own, criticise the argument that 'synergy is a sound basis for acquisition'.

7.3   Write a short (one paragraph) statement to a chief executive who has asked you to advise whether or not the company should develop through mergers/acquisitions. Write a similar statement to the chief executive of a hospital who is considering possible mergers with other hospitals.

7.4✱   'Strategic alliances will not survive in the long term if they are simply seen as ways of "blocking gaps" in an organisation's resource base or competences.' Discuss this in relation to any alliances which have recently featured in the business or public sector press.

7.5   Undertake a ranking analysis of the choices available to Coopers Creek,* Barclaycard* or an organisation of your choice similar to that shown in Illustration 7.4.

7.6✱   Bearing in mind your answers to the questions in Illustration 7.6:

(a) what is your feeling about the overall 'validity' of cost–benefit analysis?
(b) how could it be improved?

7.7   Using Illustration 7.7 as an example, what would you propose as the most important parameters to include in a sensitivity analysis in the case of each of the following organisations?

(a) Thorntons*
(b) Sheffield Theatres*
(c) Barclaycard*
(d) an organisation of your choice.

7.8✱   Using examples from your answer to previous assignments, make a critical appraisal of the statement that 'Strategic choice is, in the end, a highly subjective matter. It is dangerous to believe that, in reality, analytical techniques will ever change this situation.' Refer to the commentary at the end of Part III of the book.

Integrative assignments

7.9   Explain how the success criteria (see section 7.4) might differ between public and private sector organisations. Show how this relates to both the nature of the business environment (Chapter 2) and the expectations of stakeholders (Chapter 4).

7.10   Referring to Exhibit 7.1 choose examples that explain how pursuing the strategic development direction of 'international market development' will require organisations to understand their business environment (Chapter 2), change their capabilities (Chapter 3) and consider how they will gain competitive advantage (Chapter 5). Also refer to section 6.3 of Chapter 6 in your answer.

Tesco plots to make even more dough

Susanna Voyle

Following an interview with Sir Terry Leahy, the Chief Executive of Tesco in September 2003, an article in the *Financial Times* explained how the company had managed to dominate grocery retailing in the UK and described what strategies such a successful organisation could pursue in the future:

The figures speak for themselves. Last year Tesco sold 57,855 tonnes of its cheapest own-brand bread, 14m toothbrushes and enough liquid soap to wash 26m people from head to toe.

More than 1,600 trucks criss-cross the UK every day to supply its 800-plus stores, while 1,000 vans are delivering internet orders.

And its home market is just the start. Tesco has pushed into 10 other countries and next week Sir Terry Leahy, the group's chief executive, is off to China to see if he can find ways to make it number 11.

It has more than 307,000 staff worldwide, 227,000 of those in the UK, making it easily the country's biggest private sector employer.

As if all that was not enough, this week the group upped the ante. Sir Terry unveiled record half-year results that were well above the City's forecasts and left many seasoned Tesco observers gasping for superlatives. But then he said that was not good enough.

Instead of talking about Tesco as just a supermarket force, Sir Terry positioned the group as part of the wider general retail scene squaring up for a fight with anybody and everybody.

While the group has about 20 per cent of the grocery market, he said, it only had 5 per cent of non-food – and would be targeting its over-priced high street rivals. 'Our share of the total retail market is just 12.3 per cent and there is a lot left to go for,' said Tesco in its statement.

Sir Terry admits that he took a conscious decision to reposition the group. 'We used that measure in order to indicate that we see the opportunities in terms of broad retailing,' he said.

The lure of non-food is easy to understand. For a mature low-margin business like grocery, areas such as health and beauty, books and entertainment, electrical products and clothing offer untapped new markets with higher margins.

The group has already built scale in some mass markets. It sells more top 100 chart CDs than anybody else, with just over 16 per cent of the market. It sells more Harry Potter titles than anybody else.

But in spite of such obvious success, Sir Terry clearly

Photo: Alamy

feels there is a lot further to go. To understand why – and why capturing that growth is so important – you have to understand how Tesco got to its pre-eminent position.

The scale of the Tesco story is made more amazing by the transformation that the group has had to undergo. Started as a pile-it-high, sell-it-cheap grocery chain, Tesco has gradually reinvented itself. In the words of senior Tesco insiders, it is now a 'broad church' retailer, with more formats than others – from hypermarkets to convenience stores; and wider ranges – from cheap and cheerful Value to its up-market Finest selection.

The journey has not always been straightforward. There was a serious wobble 10 years ago when the group was suffering – with falling underlying sales, slowing profits growth and investors worried about the depressed share price as a new breed of discount food retailers from continental Europe entered the UK.

That pain led to the three big developments which became the building blocks for the new Tesco – a redefined marketing focus, the Value range and the Clubcard loyalty scheme. Growth has been pretty consistent since, and in 1995 Tesco overtook Sainsbury to become market leader. It has never really looked back.

Today Tesco's strategy is clear, with growth pursued from four areas – the core UK grocery business, non-food, international expansion and retailing services such as financial services, the dotcom business and telecommunications packages. Basically, Tesco is using its strong and stable core to keep the business ticking over while it forges new and riskier areas of growth. Pushing further into non-food is the next phase.

But that is really all about extending the time until the UK business hits real maturity – because Sir Terry hopes that by then the international business will be so well established that it can take over as the main growth engine.

So who stands to lose out if Tesco, along with Asda, ends up becoming a general retailer? The obvious victims are small independents – corner shops and bookshops.

But fears about supermarket growth have hit the share prices of lots of the larger specialists – Dixons in electricals, Boots in health and beauty and HMV Media in entertainment, for example. According to the doom-mongers, all are facing a long slow death, in spite of their claims that moving further up the quality chain would give them protection.

More general retailers are also suffering. Woolworths is losing market share in all sorts of categories. WH Smith is suffering as well. But not everyone agrees with the apocalyptical view of the effects of supermarket growth. From the other side of the Channel, where he has lived with hypermarkets for decades, the chief executive of Kesa Electricals, the business spun out of Kingfisher this year, dismisses British hysteria on the subject.

Jean-Noel Labroue says Britain is only worried about the threat to specialists because we have not lived with the phenomenon long enough to know that their market shares will naturally plateau after a few years, leaving them pegged at the commodity end. 'Nearly 40 years ago two retail concepts started to be born in France – Castorama and Darty,' he says, referring to the country's biggest hypermarket operator and the leading electrical chain that is part of his group. 'Now we are both still there and when you go to a shopping centre you will find that wherever there is a Carrefour there is usually a Darty as well. There is space for both.'

French hypermarkets have between 20 and 25 per cent of the market for electricals – a share they quickly built up but which has held steady for some time now.

And he has a warning for British supermarkets. 'Food is what really drives their customer traffic,' he says. 'If they start to forget what they are on earth for . . . they will have real difficulties.'

So there was no change of strategy from Tesco this week. But there was a change of tone and the type of language used. And the timing of the move was fascinating, coming just ahead of the government's expected ruling on the Safeway bid battle, possibly due next week.

That is expected to give the green light to the bid from Wm Morrison Supermarkets and in effect block the bigger rivals Tesco, Asda and Sainsbury.

Just a couple of months ago, when the outcome of the Safeway situation looked less certain, Tesco might not have been so triumphalist. It has been perceived wisdom in the world of supermarkets that – short of some disastrous unforeseen own-goal – the only thing that could knock Tesco off-track was an Asda deal to buy Safeway. Asda is understood to have argued strongly in its case to the Competition Commission that it should be allowed to buy Safeway because it was the only chain which could restrain the Tesco giant. It appears, however, that this view has been dismissed by the commission, who were more worried about creating an all-powerful duopoly if it let Asda bid.

Many people feel that Wal-Mart's move into the UK was not just about securing good European growth. It was as much an attempt to undermine Tesco in its home market so it would be less of a threat internationally.

So with record-breaking growth and the Asda threat pegged back, Tesco must be set fair. Sir Terry, for one, is not complacent. He knows that, in spite of its success, it would be very easy for Tesco to stumble. 'There are all sorts of things that could knock us off course. Customers vote every day and you are punished very quickly in this market if you get it wrong. Size is no protection – and the past is not a useful guide to the future.'

Source: Financial Times, 20 September 2003, p. M3.

Questions

1. Using Exhibit 7.2 identify the development directions available to Tesco. Assess the relative suitability of each of these options by ranking them (using Illustration 7.4 as an example).

2. For each of the top four development directions in your ranking compare the relative merits of each development method (internal, acquisition or strategic alliance).

3. Complete your evaluation of the options that now appear most suitable by applying the criteria of acceptability and feasibility (see section 7.4).

4. If you were the Chief Executive of Tesco which options would you prefer? Explain why these might be different from *your* favoured options.

Strategy selection

The theme of the chapters in Part III has been 'strategic choices'. The chapters have discussed the sorts of strategic choices that organisations have to make and what evidence there is about which lead to success. However, there has been little mention of *how* such choices are made. Just how does a particular strategy end up being the one followed by an organisation? This commentary takes this question as its theme and uses the three different lenses to offer explanations of what might, therefore, be termed *strategy selection*.

A design view of strategy selection

Those who take a highly rational approach to strategic management tend to take a linear and top-down view of strategy selection. The organisation's objectives, quantified where possible, are used as yardsticks by which options are assessed (for example, whether strategies are likely to meet pre-determined targets such as return on capital or market share). Options are made explicit and cases made for them on the basis of an analysis of the environment (Chapter 2) and capabilities of the organisation (Chapter 3). They are then systematically evaluated by examining the relative merits of such options using, perhaps, criteria such as suitability, feasibility and acceptability explained in Chapter 7 (section 7.4). The strategy that best meets these criteria and is most likely to achieve the specified objectives is then chosen. Here, then, strategy selection is an entirely rational matter. The assumption also tends to be that it is top management doing this, or people appointed by them to do it, for example consultants or specialist strategic planners.

This view is appealing. It is logical, analytical and should give rational and informed answers. However, the problems discussed so far in the commentaries remain. Managers do not have access to perfect information, they cannot know the future, objectives are rarely unambiguous because there are multiple stakeholders, and managers themselves are not merely dispassionate analysts. It is probably more realistic to see strategy selection by design in a more moderated form.

Formal planning and systematic analysis and evaluation of strategies should not be regarded as exclusive processes through which strategies are selected, but they can be valuable tools. So the critical issue for strategic managers is to ensure that an organisation's planning and evaluation activities assist how strategy selection takes place. For example, *sensitivity analysis* (section 7.4.2 above) is a useful technique for allowing decision makers to understand the risks and uncertainties surrounding specific strategies, but it does not select strategies for those decision makers. Formal planning systems used appropriately can be helpful. They might help involve people in the organisation in thinking through strategy and therefore act as a means of *raising the level of debate* amongst a wider group of decision makers or people who may influence decisions about the eventual strategy followed. *Scenario planning* can promote not only thinking about uncertain futures, but the challenging of preconceptions people might have about what strategy their organisation should follow in the future. *Option theory* (section 7.4.2) provides means of evaluating and monitoring strategic options as they develop – it quite literally allows organisations to keep options open. *Game theory* (section 5.7) requires people to put themselves in the place of their competitors and think options through from their point of view as well as their own, again potentially challenging preconceptions about the strategy to follow. *Strategy workshops* (see section 11.3.2 of Chapter 11) that employ tools of strategy analysis can fulfil a similar purpose and allow people in the organisation to contribute to the quality of thinking about future strategies.

Much of what has been discussed in Chapters 5, 6 and 7 are, then, concepts, models and tools which allow and encourage rational, analytic thinking. However, they are not just about top-down planning of strategy. They are as much to do with enriching discussions and debates about the strategy of organisations and therefore about strategic thinking and learning. However, if this moderated view about the contribution of such approaches is taken, the question of how strategies are actually selected still remains. So it is useful to look at different explanations of this.

Strategy selection and experience

The experience lens sees organisations in terms of individual and collective experience. It positions individual judgement and the influence of organisational culture as more central and sees political processes as ways in which such differences may be reconciled.

Selection by doing: the logical incrementalist view

If selection does not take place as part of a formal planning process or by means of a particular evaluative device, this does not, of itself, necessarily mean there is an absence of rationality. Managers in organisations know well enough that it is impossible to plan everything up-front. Strategy selection often occurs 'in the doing'. For example, a retailer introduces a new range of products in some stores and monitors their success. If they succeed they are extended to other stores: if they fail, they are dropped. E-commerce businesses do not try to plan up-front all possible new developments. It would be impossible in the turbulent world in which they exist. But managers of such businesses might, for example, look for acquisition opportunities of new start-up businesses with the very rational purpose of developing new options for the future. The corporate centre of a multinational may monitor local initiatives for ones which might be potential winners internationally. This may then be followed by a geographical region being encouraged to test the wider acceptability of the innovation with modifications required for different local circumstances. If this proves successful, the innovation could then be adopted internationally. The selection of these strategies has not necessarily been the result of a detailed formal planning process but of experimentation and learning by doing. What works is developed further; what does not, is not. It is, however, considered and intentional, corresponding to what is referred to in Chapter 11 as *logical incrementalism*.[1] Furthermore, it could be that analytic tools are used as part of the selection process at any of the stages in the experimentation process as a way of checking *why* a strategy might be worth following or developing. Of course, it is also possible that a strategy developed in such a way might eventually be built into a formal strategic plan, which is a statement of the future direction of the organisation.

The role of cultural and political processes

Studies that have traced how particular strategic decisions are made in organisations[2] show how cultural and political processes also play an important part in strategy selection. They also show that it is difficult to separate out selection as a distinct process as it occurs in practice (see Exhibit III.ii). Selection needs to be seen as part of an iterative process much more based on experience and cultural and political processes in organisations.

The *awareness* of strategic issues is not necessarily an analytical process; rather, people get a 'gut feeling' based on their previous experience or received wisdom. This awareness 'incubates' as various stimuli help build up a picture of the extent to which circumstances deviate from what is normally to be expected, perhaps in terms of internal performance measures such as turnover or profit performance, or perhaps

Exhibit III.ii   **Phases of strategic decision making**

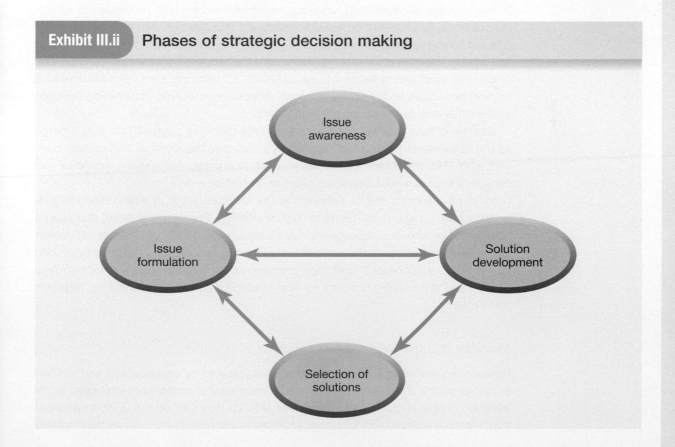

customer reaction to the quality and price of service or products. This accumulation of stimuli eventually reaches a point where the presence of a problem cannot be ignored. Typically, a *triggering point* is reached when the formal information systems of the organisation highlight the problem: a variance against budget becomes undeniable or a number of sales areas consistently report dropping sales. At this stage, however, issues may still be ill-defined.

Issue formulation involves information gathering, but not always in a highly structured, objective manner. Information is gathered on a verbal and informal basis, perhaps supplemented by more formal analysis. However, making sense of information draws heavily on *experience* – individual and collective – and the assumptions encapsulated in the paradigm. The role of information generated from analysis is often to post-rationalise or legitimise managers' emerging views of the situation.

Through *debate and discussion* there may be an attempt to reach an organisational view on the problem to be tackled. An emerging view therefore takes shape in terms of both individual and collective experience, with different views resolved through political processes of negotiation. It may also be that these processes of issue formulation trigger a different problem. So the process tends to be iterative.

In *developing solutions*, managers typically 'search' for known, existing or tried solutions; or wait for possible solutions to emerge, drawing on their experience. Managers begin with a rather vague idea of a possible solution and refine it by recycling it through selection routines (see below) back into problem identification or through further search routines. The process is again based on debate and discussion and collective management wisdom and experience.

The process of developing solutions therefore overlaps with processes of *selecting solutions*. A number of potential solutions get reduced until one or more emerges. It is not formal analysis which plays the major role, but judgement, negotiation and bargaining. It should also be remembered that the process might well be taking place below the most senior levels of management, so referring possible solutions to a higher hierarchical level may be required; indeed, another way of selecting between possibilities may be to seek such *authorisation*.

Studies of how strategic decisions are made therefore suggest that they emerge as the *outcome* of managerial experience within a social, political and cultural context, even if formal planning procedures exist. And in this process the individual and collective experience of managers plays an important role.

In some respects, this is reflected in the different ways in which many organisations now set about the development of strategy. For example, there has been a substantial growth of *strategy workshops* (see section 11.3.2 of Chapter 11). Whilst such events may employ the sorts of techniques of analysis and planning described in this book, a successful workshop process works through issues in face-to-face debate and discussion, drawing on and surfacing different experiences, interests and views.

Mimicry and the institutionalisation of strategies

Researchers who look at patterns of strategies followed by organisations add a different dimension to this. They point out that a great deal of similarity of strategies exists between organisations within organisational fields (see section 4.5.2); strategies become institutionalised. For example, professional service firms such as accountants and lawyers follow similar strategies; retailers follow similar strategies, as do universities, and so on. A number of observations arise.

First, this may be because the individual and collective experience of managers in organisations tends to be from within those organisational fields; they have common experience, compete according to the same sorts of 'rules', and therefore follow similar strategies.[3] Second, it may make a lot of sense for one organisation to mimic a successful strategy of another; so there develops an 'orthodoxy' of strategy. Third, mimicry may not be so much to do with imitating success as striving for 'legitimacy'. Universities strive for research excellence because it is commonly accepted that that is what universities are about. The major firms of accountants have all been trying to develop globally. No doubt there are argued economic reasons for this, but there is also the fear that without doing so they would cease to be taken seriously as 'a major player'.

Another explanation for such similarities of strategies being followed across organisations is the faddish nature of strategic logic. In the 1980s the emphasis, for example, was on competing on the basis of finding suitable markets in which to do so. This was the result of a marketing orthodoxy of the time and also Michael Porter's highly influential work on competitive forces at work in markets. From the 1990s the emphasis has swung towards the importance of strategic capabilities upon which competitive advantage can be built. In the 1980s everyone was sure of the wisdom of the former; since the 1990s they have become convinced of the wisdom of the latter.

All of this suggests that it is the tendency of organisations to conform, to follow the strategy being followed by others, especially if that is successful; that strategy selection is to do with mimicry and organisational legitimacy. Of course those involved in strategic management in organisations may employ the rhetoric of competitive strategy and differentiation and use tools of analysis and evaluation as part of that rhetoric.[4] But in the end for many organisations the strategy selected will be on the basis of conformity.

The ideas lens: strategy selection or evolution?

Much of what has been said so far suggests the strong influence of forces for conformity. As researchers in institutional theory point out, innovation is not common; similarity is. And there is little evidence that the formal planned design of strategies gives rise to innovation. When it occurs, how then do more innovative strategies get selected? The discussion above describing how experimentation and logical incrementalism occur is a useful starting point. Seeing strategy development through both the experience lens and the ideas lens, there is less emphasis on selection at a point in time or, indeed, formal evaluation, and more emphasis on the emergence of 'strategic ideas' from within the organisation rather than planned strategy from the top.

This then leaves the question as to how these 'strategic ideas' get to become organisational strategies. Of course, it may be that in any organisation very few of such strategic ideas do come to take form as a coherent organisational strategy, or even part of such a strategy. For every one that does, there may be many that do not. However, this is what the ideas lens (and evolutionary theory in particular) suggests, given its emphasis on the importance of variety. Variety will spawn innovation;

but not all innovatory ideas will come to fruition. Evolutionary theorists[5] draw on the concepts of *selection* and *retention* to explain how such strategic ideas might come to be adopted in organisations. Some of these are similar to those explained in terms of the other lenses: but some are not.

Selection might take place through what Weeks and Galunic[6] refer to as *function*, *fit* and *form*.

- By *function* they mean that a strategic idea is perceived to have a functional benefit. For example:
  - Most obviously, does it address the *needs of market forces*? Strategy will develop and prosper according to whether it is relevant to customer needs. This is of course a conventional view of strategic success to do with competitive strategy (see Chapter 5).
  - A variant on this, of course, is that it may come to be adopted because it is *perceived* to have such functional benefits by managers in the organisation, whether it actually does so or not.
  - Or it may be that it has the function of serving the *interests of individuals* within the organisation; for example, in furthering their political ends or career aspirations.

- By *fit* they mean that a strategic idea is likely to be more successful in competing with other strategic ideas if it *aligns with other successful strategic ideas*. This could happen at two levels. Just as the institutional theorists point out, a strategic idea could be adopted because it is seen to make sense in terms of what other organisations are doing. Or it could be that it fits with the culture and experience of the organisation itself. For example, a manufacturing firm may see itself as an expert in its field and therefore pursue a strategy of diversification through backward or forward integration, by acquisitions. It may not be economic logic so much as the perceived fit with the organisation's know-how and ways of doing business that drive this. Of course, the reverse is also the case. In well-established, often successful organisations, it can be difficult to get new ideas accepted because they are not seen as desirable in terms of 'the way we do things around here'.

- By *form* they mean that some strategic ideas, by their very nature, are *more or less attractive than others*. For example, it appears that those ideas that are essentially altruistic tend to spread and get adopted most.[7] In line with this, complexity theory emphasises the need for sufficient support or 'positive feedback'; and some ideas are more likely to attract this than others. For example, a new product idea in a science-based research-intensive company received widespread support because it addressed 'green' issues. Research scientists were attracted to the idea that their work was being put to good use. And senior managers, who were also scientists by background, admitted that it was also attractive because, unusually for their business, its application and potential benefits were the sort of thing that interested their colleagues in other divisions, their friends and their families. The new product idea persisted despite strong evidence of its lack of commercial viability. Of course, in time this positive feedback at this level would probably not be enough for it to persist because it would run into market selection mechanisms; but emotional attraction had carried the idea forward within the organisation.

As well as processes of selection, there are processes of retention. '*Retention* occurs when selected variations are preserved, duplicated or otherwise reproduced'[8] leading to their future repetition. This may depend on a number of conditions and processes:

- It is unlikely that an innovation at whatever level will initially find widespread support; so it may matter that there exists *sufficient initial support*. The extent to which this may happen is likely to depend, at least initially, on the role of *communities of interest* – groups with similar interests – for the promotion of ideas and initiatives. This might apply, for instance, to the scientific community in the above example. In the marketplace this might take the form of a niche market. For the innovative entrepreneur, it may be the backing of a risk-taking venture capitalist. For the innovative scientist in the R&D lab, it may be sufficient support from a senior manager as champion of the idea against the objections of other senior management colleagues.

- At whichever level, however, the idea of retention suggests that there may be a *struggle for survival*; so it may well be that conflict is inevitable in the organisation or in the marketplace, between individuals or between ideas. Retention depends on the survival of such conflict.

- There are many processes at work in organisations that may lead to the *replication of activities* as they develop such that they become routinised and thus retained. These vary from formal procedures (e.g. job descriptions), accounting and control systems, management information systems, organisation structuring, to the formal or informal standardisation of work routines and the eventual embedding of such activities and routines in the culture of the organisation.

- Retention will also depend on the extent to which the new idea or activity is *legitimated*. For example, the ways of doing things associated with the emerging strategic idea become seen as the 'right way' to do things, or best practice, in an organisation. Excellence of customer service, where it exists, may now be replicated by formal training. But its origins most often were in new practices being selected for by market forces and then coming to be seen as the way to do things.

- Retention may also depend on the extent to which the emerging *strategy becomes owned* by powerful or influential people. Most obviously this could be senior executives, but it could also be important stakeholders, or those who heavily influence the replication of activities in the organisation; so it could, for example, be influential sales executives in their dealings with customers.

What, within all this, is the role of senior managers, traditionally seen as the planners and selectors of strategy? Remember, underpinning the ideas lens is the observation that innovation is likely to be dependent on variety and that ideas will emerge rather than be planned from the top. So if the organisation is to be innovative it is important that such variety is encouraged. Managers need to recognise that, whilst formal selection processes (e.g. project and financial evaluation) are important, three factors need to be borne in mind:

- Care has to be taken that such formal systems do not prematurely curtail initiatives or discourage the necessary variety of ideas that underpin such initiatives.

- If the lessons about 'simple rules' (see commentary to Part I) have been taken on board, it is important that selection procedures criteria emphasise such rules, but not too many of them.

● The role and relevance of the more informal processes in organisations need to be recognised. For example, ideas and their selection and retention may depend on the extent to which they are attractive to and fostered by a community of interest. Such communities of interest are likely to be social, not just formal, groups in an organisation. Their importance and preservation needs to be recognised.

Our view

As in the commentary to Part II, our view is that these different lenses shed light and provide guidance on the issue of strategy selection in usefully different but complementary ways.

It is important to be realistic about how strategies develop and how they are selected. Strategic choice based on, or strongly influenced by, experience and cultural and political processes is the norm. This does suggest that strategies are probably better thought of as emerging rather than being selected at a point in time. It also suggests that the strong influence of experience and organisational culture can lead to problems of strategic drift (see section 1.5.1). This explanation also makes it difficult to explain how more innovative strategies come to exist, and this is where explanations are helpful from evolutionary and complexity theory since they focus attention on the generation of ideas and see cultural and political processes as selection retention mechanisms. Formal planning and evaluation processes can play an important part too. Not only are they another selection mechanism, but they can be means of raising challenging, analytic and evaluative questions which perform the role of changing minds, not just making plans.

References

1. See J.B. Quinn, *Strategic Change: Logical Incrementalism*, Irwin, 1980.
2. This section brings together the work of a number of researchers. For a thorough discussion of the problem of awareness and diagnosis stages of the decision-making process, see M.A. Lyles, 'Formulating strategic problems: empirical analysis and model development', *Strategic Management Journal*, vol. 2, no. 1 (1981), pp. 61–75; H. Mintzberg, O. Raisinghani and A. Theoret, 'The structure of unstructured decision processes', *Administrative Science Quarterly*, vol. 21, no. 2 (1976), pp. 246–275; and L.M. Fahey, 'On strategic management decision processes', *Strategic Management Journal*, vol. 2, no. 1 (1981), pp. 43–60.
3. The classic account of institutionalisation is by P. DiMaggio and W. Powell, 'The iron cage revisited: institutional isomorphism and collective rationality in organizational fields', *American Sociological Review*, vol. 48 (1983), pp. 147–160.
4. See D. Barry and M. Elmes, 'Strategy retold: toward a narrative view of strategic discourse', *Academy of Management Review*, vol. 22, no. 2 (1997), pp. 429–452.
5. See for example chapter 2 of *Organizations Evolving* by Howard Aldrich (Sage, 1999).
6. The selection and retention of strategic ideas, or 'memes', is discussed in J. Weeks and C. Galunic, 'A theory of the cultural evolution of the firm: the intra-organizational ecology of memes', *Organization Studies*, vol. 24, no. 8 (2003), pp. 1309–1352.
7. The role of altruism and other bases of attraction is discussed by Susan Blackmore in *The Meme Machine*, Oxford University Press, 1999.
8. See Aldrich, p. 30 (reference 5 above).

Part IV

Strategy into Action

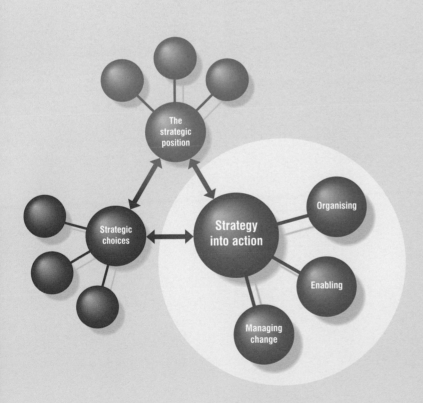

THIS PART EXPLAINS:

● The way in which organisational structures, organisational processes and the management of relationships are important in organising for strategic success.

● The relationship between an organisation's overall strategy for the resource areas of people, information, finance and technology.

● The importance of understanding organisational context and, in particular, the barriers to strategic change in considering the management of change.

● Different approaches to managing change including the styles and roles of management and the levers they may employ in managing change.

Introduction to Part IV

Understanding the strategic position of an organisation and considering the strategic choices open to it are of little value unless the preferred strategies can be turned into organisational action. Such action takes form in the day-to-day processes and relationships that exist in organisations so, if strategic action is to be in line with the intended strategy, these need to be managed. This is likely to mean, as a minimum, that thought needs to be given to the way the organisation is designed in terms of its structure, but also in terms of how people might work with each other in terms of more informal relationships. Such processes will very likely be within resource areas or functions of the organisation; so how these relate to the overall strategy is therefore important. The development of a new strategy may also require significant strategic change for the organisation. Such change does not take place simply because it is considered to be desirable; it takes place if it can be made to work and put into effect by members of the organisation. Part IV deals with the vital issues of translating strategy into action and the difficulties and methods of managing strategic change. This discussion includes a range of related issues:

- Chapter 8 is about *organising* for success. It looks at three separate strands of this topic and how they can contribute to successful strategies. These strands are organisational structures, organisational processes, and the management of relationships. The chapter reviews the various types of organisational structure and looks at the advantages and disadvantages of each one. Organisational processes are concerned with different forms of 'control' within organisations, ranging from direct supervision and centralised planning to self-control and the personal motivation of staff. The section on relationships looks at the important issue of centralisation or devolution of both strategic and operational decision making. It is also concerned with the boundaries of an organisation and how external relationships need to be established and maintained. So it includes issues such as networking, outsourcing and alliances. In discussing these topics the chapter highlights the importance in organising for success of how these various elements work together to create configurations that are well matched to an organisation's strategies.

- Chapter 9 looks at the relationship between an organisation's overall strategy and the strategies in four key resource areas: people, information, finance and technology. The two questions that are pursued through the chapter are these. First, whether the separate resource areas of an organisation are capable of *enabling* strategies to be executed successfully. For example, if the management of information is adequate to support a move into e-commerce activities. Or whether the competences of staff and the organisational culture are in line with new strategies – perhaps a strategic alliance in a new country. The second question is whether the strategies of an organisation are being shaped to capitalise on the expertise in a particular resource area. For example, an organisation may have access to funds that its competitors do not. Or perhaps it has developed new technologies that could transform product features or reduce the cost of operational processes. Importantly, success or failure of strategies will also depend on how these separate resource areas are integrated together – for example, to support a new product launch.

● Chapter 10 examines more specifically how *strategic change* might be managed. This is done in several ways. First, by acknowledging that it is important for the means of managing change to suit an organisation's specific needs. Therefore that it is important to understand organisational change contexts and organisational barriers to change. Second, by looking at the different approaches to managing change, including the styles of management and roles that managers and others play in managing strategic change. Finally, by considering a range of levers that might be employed to help manage change in organisations. The levers specific to urgent turnaround contexts are discussed. Then other levers, including changes to organisational routines, the management of political and symbolic processes, the importance of communication, and other specific tactics for managing change, are discussed.

8

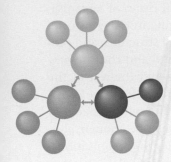

Organising for Success

Learning outcomes

After reading this chapter you should be able to understand:

● Key challenges in organising for success, such as ensuring control, managing knowledge, coping with change and responding to globalisation.

● The main structural types of organisations and their strengths and weaknesses.

● The most important organisational processes (such as planning systems and performance targets) and the circumstances where they will be most appropriate.

● How the management of internal and external relationships can help or hinder success.

● How the three strands of structure, processes and relationships should reinforce each other in organisational configurations.

● The implications of configurations for organisational performance and change.

8.1   INTRODUCTION

Perhaps the most important resource of an organisation is its *people*. So the roles people play, the processes through which they interact and the relationships that they build are crucial to the success of strategy. These are all issues of 'organisation design'. Views about designing organisations are changing in today's world. Traditionally management scientists have emphasised formal structures and processes.[1] These formal approaches suited a top-down, command-and-control view of strategy, where managers at the top made the decisions and the rest of the organisation simply implemented them. However, in a world where key knowledge is held by employees at all levels in the organisation, and where change is constant, relying on formal top-down structures may no longer be enough.

A fast-moving, knowledge-intensive world raises two issues for organisations. First, a static concept of formal structure is less and less appropriate. Organisations are constantly having to reorganise themselves in response to changing conditions. For this reason some authors suggest that we should use the *verb* 'organising' more than the *noun* 'organisation'.[2] Second, harnessing the valuable knowledge that lies throughout the organisation requires more than top-down formal hierarchies. Informal relationships and processes are vital to generating and sharing the in-depth knowledge that is now often fundamental to competitive advantage.

This chapter takes on board new thinking about organisation design both by emphasising change and by including informal processes and relationships alongside the formal. An important idea here is that formal structures and processes need to be aligned with informal processes and relationships into coherent *configurations*. An organisation's **configuration** consists of the structures, processes and relationships through which the organisation operates[3] – as shown in Exhibit 8.1. Configuring the organisation so that all these elements fit both together and with key strategic challenges is crucial to organisational success.

> An organisation's **configuration** consists of the structures, processes and relationships through which the organisation operates

Exhibit 8.1 shows the three strands of an organisation's configuration, locking together into a coherent 'virtuous circle'. These three strands provide the structure for the first parts of the chapter, addressing in turn:

● The *structural design* (describing roles, responsibilities and lines of reporting) in organisations. Structural design can deeply influence the sources of an organisation's advantage, particularly with regard to knowledge management; failure to adjust structures appropriately can fatally undermine strategy implementation. But good structure alone is not enough for success.

● The *processes* that drive and support people within and around an organisation. These processes too can have a major influence on success or failure, defining how strategies are made and controlled and the ways that managers and other employees interact and implement strategy in action.

● The *relationships* that connect people both within and outside the organisation, in particular:

  – relationships between organisational units and the centre (this relates to discussions in Chapter 5 about the role of corporate parents);

  – relationships outside the firm, including issues such as *outsourcing* (raised in Chapter 3) and *strategic alliances* (raised in Chapter 7).

| Exhibit 8.1 | Organisational configurations: structure, processes and relationships |

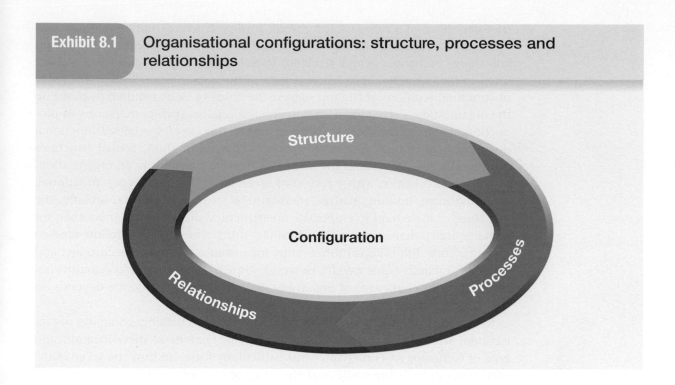

The various structures, processes and relationships will be considered in the light of three key challenges for organisations in the twenty-first century:

● The *speed of change* and the increased levels of *uncertainty* in the business environment, as discussed in Chapter 2. As a result, organisations need to have flexible designs and be skilled at reorganising.

● The importance of *knowledge creation* and *knowledge sharing* as a fundamental ingredient of strategic success, as discussed in Chapter 3. Organisational designs should both foster concentrations of expertise and encourage people to share their knowledge.

● The rise of *globalisation,* as discussed in Chapter 2. Organising for a globalising world has many challenges: communicating across wider geography, coordinating more diversity and building relationships across diverse cultures are some examples. Globalisation also brings greater recognition of different kinds of organising around the world.

After considering each of the three strands separately, the chapter will examine how structures, processes and relationships can be fitted together into coherent configurations, and some of the implications of this for change and performance.

8.2 STRUCTURAL TYPES

Managers often start describing their organisation by drawing an organisation chart, mapping out its formal structure. These structural charts define the 'levels' and roles in an organisation. They are important to managers not just because they describe who is responsible for what. Formal structures matter in at least two more ways. First, structural reporting lines shape patterns of communication and knowledge exchange: people tend not to talk much to people much higher or lower in the hierarchy, or in different parts of the organisation. Second, the kinds of structural positions at the top suggest the kinds of skills required to move up the organisation: a structure with functional specialists such as marketing or production at the top indicates the importance to success of specialised functional disciplines rather than general business experience. In short, formal structures can reveal a great deal about the role of knowledge and skills in an organisation.

This chapter begins with a review of seven basic structural types: functional, multidivisional, holding, matrix, transnational, team and project. Broadly, the first three of these tend to emphasise one structural dimension over another, for instance functional specialisms or business units. The four that follow tend to mix structural dimensions more evenly, for instance trying to give product and geographical units equal weight. However, none of these structures is a universal solution to the challenges of organising. Rather, the right structure depends on the particular kinds of challenges each organisation faces.

Researchers propose a wide number of important challenges shaping organisational structure, including organisational size, extent of diversification and type of technology.[4] This chapter will particularly focus on how the seven structural types fit both the traditional challenge of control and the three new challenges of change, knowledge and globalisation. This implies that the first step in organisational design is deciding what the key challenges facing the organisation actually are. As we shall see later, the configurational approach stresses that whatever structure is chosen should also be aligned with matching processes and relationships.

8.2.1 The functional structure

A **functional structure** is based on the primary activities that have to be undertaken by an organisation such as production, finance and accounting, marketing, human resources and research and development

Once an organisation grows beyond a very basic level of size and complexity, it has to start dividing up responsibilities. One fundamental kind of structure is the **functional structure**, which divides responsibilities according to the organisation's primary roles such as production, research and sales. Exhibit 8.2 represents a typical organisation chart for such a business. This structure is usually found in smaller companies, or those with narrow, rather than diverse, product ranges. Also, within a multidivisional structure (see below), the divisions themselves may be split up into functional departments (as in Illustration 8.1).

Exhibit 8.2 also summarises the potential advantages and disadvantages of a functional structure. There are advantages in that it gives senior managers direct hands-on involvement in operations and allows greater operational control from the top. The functional structure provides a clear definition of roles and tasks, increasing accountability. Functional departments also provide concentrations of expertise, thus fostering knowledge development in areas of functional specialism.

However, there are disadvantages, particularly as organisations become larger or more diverse. Perhaps the major concern in a fast-moving world is that senior managers focus on their functional responsibilities, becoming overburdened with routine operations and too concerned with narrow functional interests. As

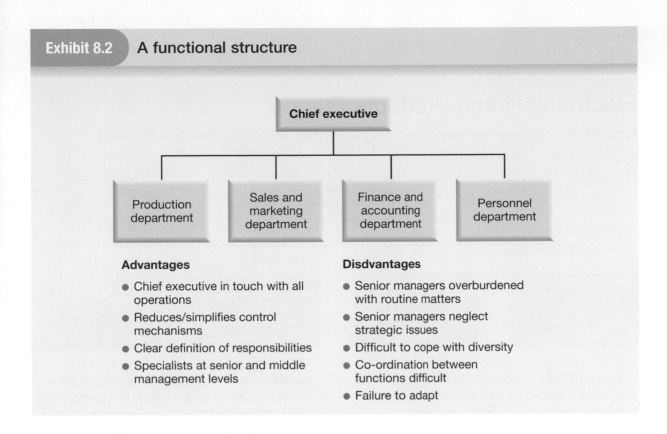

Exhibit 8.2 — A functional structure

Chief executive

- Production department
- Sales and marketing department
- Finance and accounting department
- Personnel department

Advantages

- Chief executive in touch with all operations
- Reduces/simplifies control mechanisms
- Clear definition of responsibilities
- Specialists at senior and middle management levels

Disdvantages

- Senior managers overburdened with routine matters
- Senior managers neglect strategic issues
- Difficult to cope with diversity
- Co-ordination between functions difficult
- Failure to adapt

a result, they find it hard either to take a strategic view of the organisation as a whole or to deliver a coordinated response quickly. Functional organisations can be inflexible. Separate functional departments tend also to be inward looking – so-called 'functional silos' – making it difficult to integrate the knowledge of different functional specialists. Finally, because they are centralised around particular functions, functional structures are not good at coping with product or geographical diversity. For example, a central marketing department may try to impose a uniform approach to advertising regardless of the diverse needs of the organisation's various SBUs around the world (notice that, in Illustration 8.1, Electrolux introduces a functional structure within just its European business).

8.2.2 The multidivisional structure

A **multidivisional structure** is built up of separate divisions on the basis of products, services or geographical areas (see Exhibit 8.3). Divisionalisation often comes about as an attempt to overcome the problems that functional structures have in dealing with the diversity mentioned above.[5] Each division can respond to the specific requirements of its product/market strategy, using its own set of functional departments. A similar situation exists in many public services, where the organisation is structured around *service departments* such as recreation, social services and education.

There are several potential advantages to divisional structures. They are flexible in the sense that organisations can add, close or merge divisions as

A **multidivisional structure** is built up of separate divisions on the basis of products, services or geographical areas

Illustration 8.1

Electrolux Home Products Europe

Functional structures can help in bringing uniformity and simplicity into a business.

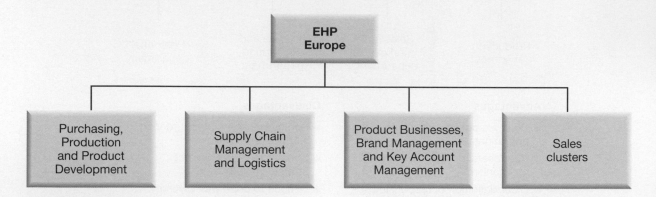

In January 2001, Electrolux Home Products Europe completely realigned its structure as part of its competitive strategy in Europe. The Swedish multinational company manufactured a range of consumer durables – such as cookers and fridges – and had grown through several decades of acquisitions to become a dominant player in Europe. But the market in Europe was fiercely competitive and the company needed to find a way to capitalise on its size – both to reduce costs and also to improve product and service standards. Its solution was to introduce a Europe-wide functional structure to replace the geographical structure (resulting from its acquisitions). The new structure is shown in the diagram.

The management explained the rationale for the restructuring: 'the realignment of EHP Europe is a part of a programme to ensure profitable growth as the organisation drives more simplicity into its business, while reducing the number of organisational hand-offs, and creating more focus on areas where increased effort is required to meet the tougher challenges of the market-place'.

The functional departments would operate as follows:

● **Purchasing, Production and Product Development** was the manufacturing arm of the business. It also included product development and purchasing to provide a 'seamless flow' from supplies to finished products. This was felt to be essential to maintaining a stream of innovative and cost effective products.

● **Supply Chain Management and Logistics** was responsible for getting products to the customer and was the link between sales forecasts and factory production.

● **Product Businesses, Brand Management and Key Account Management** was responsible for the marketing activities to support products and brands. It also included key account management, service and spare parts.

● **Sales divisions**, grouped geographically into seven multi-country clusters.

The first three divisions were managed as cost centres whilst the sales clusters were focused on sales revenue.

Source: Adapted from *The Electrolux Executive*, December 2000.

Questions

1. Compare the advantages and disadvantages of a functional structure (above) with alternative structures such as product or geographical divisions.

2. Why do you think Electrolux chose this particular structure?

Exhibit 8.3 A multidivisional structure

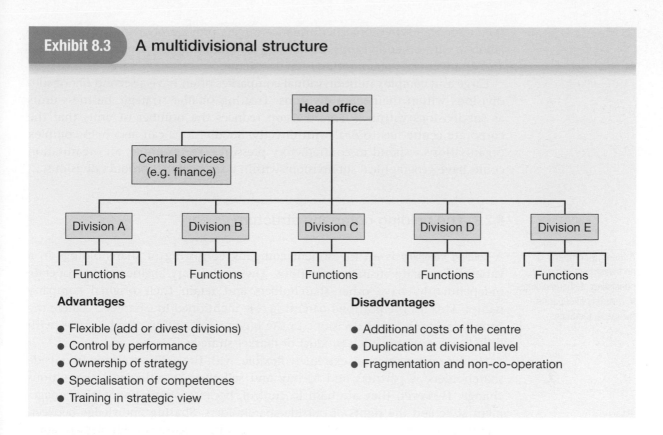

Advantages

- Flexible (add or divest divisions)
- Control by performance
- Ownership of strategy
- Specialisation of competences
- Training in strategic view

Disadvantages

- Additional costs of the centre
- Duplication at divisional level
- Fragmentation and non-co-operation

circumstances change. As self-standing business units, it is possible to control divisions from a distance by monitoring business performance. Divisional managers have greater personal ownership for their own divisional strategies. Geographical divisions – for example, a European division or a North American division – offer a means of managing internationally. There can be benefits of specialisation within a division, allowing competences to develop with a clearer focus on a particular product group, technology or customer group. Management responsibility for a whole divisional business is good training in taking a strategic view for managers expecting to go on to a main board position.

However, divisional structures can also have disadvantages of three main types. First, divisions can become so specialised and self-sufficient that they are *de facto* independent businesses – but carrying the costs of the corporate centre of the company. So it may make more sense to split the company into independent businesses, and de-mergers of this type have been very common. Paradoxically, the second type of problem may occur for the opposite reason. Divisions have created their own 'corporate centres' without having all the parenting skills needed to add value to their business units. For example, the division may be weak in functional expertise in finance, marketing, human resources or IT. The result is that the business units carry the costs of this divisional centre but are not as well supported as they would be by the 'real' corporate centre of the company where these skills do exist. Here the solution might be to revert to a direct reporting of business units to the corporate centre. Finally, divisionalisation tends to get in the way of cooperation and knowledge sharing between business units: divisions can quite literally divide. Expertise is fragmented and divisional performance targets provide poor incentives to collaborate with other divisions. Exhibit 8.3 summarises these potential advantages and disadvantages of a multidivisional structure.

Large and complex multidivisional companies often have a second tier of subdivisions within their main divisions. Treating smaller strategic business units as subdivisions within a large division reduces the number of units that the corporate centre has to deal with directly. Subdivisions can also help complex organisations respond to contradictory pressures. For example, an organisation could have geographical subdivisions within a set of global product divisions.

8.2.3 The holding company structure

A **holding company** is an investment company consisting of shareholdings in a variety of separate business operations

A **holding company** is an investment company consisting of shareholdings in a variety of separate business operations. These subsidiary businesses may operate independently, have other shareholders and retain their original company names. This fits the portfolio parenting role mentioned in Chapter 5, where the parent company limits decisions to the buying and selling of subsidiaries with little involvement in their product or market strategy.

Holding companies are extremely flexible, with the ability to bring in outside shareholders as partners and to buy and sell their subsidiaries as conditions change. However, they are hard to control, because of the hands-off management style and the rights of outside shareholders. Sharing knowledge between highly autonomous subsidiaries is very difficult. Because subsidiaries are autonomous and often operate in unrelated areas, there is little scope for synergy. For these reasons, holding companies have fallen out of favour in Western economies. Traditional holding companies such as Lonhro and the Anglo-American conglomerate Hanson plc were broken up during the 1990s.

However, in many emerging economies, such as India, Russia and South America, holding companies still play a prominent role.[6] Where capital markets and markets for managerial labour do not work very well, holding companies fill a useful gap. Subsidiaries can gain access to investment capital and talented managers from inside the holding company in a way they could not do on the open market. In emerging economies, therefore, holding companies can add value by making up for the failings of external markets for capital and labour.

8.2.4 The matrix structure

A **matrix structure** is a combination of structures which could take the form of product and geographical divisions or functional and divisional structures operating in tandem

A **matrix structure** combines different structural dimensions simultaneously, for example product divisions and geographical territories or product divisions and functional specialisms. Exhibit 8.4 gives examples of such a structure.

Matrix structures have several advantages. They are effective at knowledge management because they allow separate areas of knowledge to be integrated across organisational boundaries. Particularly in professional service organisations, matrix organisation can be helpful in applying particular knowledge specialisms to different market or geographical segments. For example, to serve a particular client, a consulting firm may draw on people from groups with

| Exhibit 8.4 | Two examples of matrix structures |

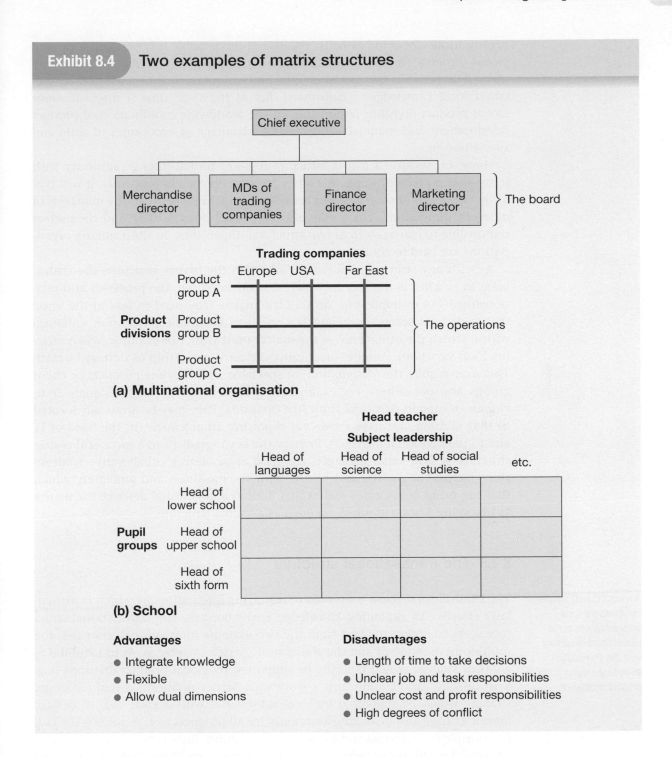

(a) Multinational organisation

(b) School

Advantages

● Integrate knowledge
● Flexible
● Allow dual dimensions

Disadvantages

● Length of time to take decisions
● Unclear job and task responsibilities
● Unclear cost and profit responsibilities
● High degrees of conflict

particular knowledge specialisms (e.g. strategy or organisation design) and others grouped according to particular markets (industry sectors or geographical regions). Exhibit 8.4 shows how a school might combine the separate knowledge of subject specialists to create programmes of study tailored differently to various age groups. Matrix organisations are flexible, because they allow different dimensions of the organisation to be mixed together. They are particularly attractive to organisations operating globally, because of the possible mix between local and global dimensions. For example, a global company may prefer geographically defined divisions as the operating units for local marketing (because of their specialist local knowledge of customers). But at the same time it may still want global product divisions responsible for the worldwide coordination of product development and manufacturing, taking advantage of economies of scale and specialisation.

However, because a matrix structure replaces formal lines of authority with (cross-matrix) relationships, this often brings problems. In particular, it will typically take *longer to reach decisions* because of bargaining between the managers of different dimensions. There may also be *conflict* because staff find themselves responsible to managers from two structural dimensions. In short, matrix organisations are hard to control.

As with any structure, but particularly with the matrix structure, the critical issue in practice is the way in which it is operated (i.e. the processes and relationships). For example, one 'arm' of the matrix may need to *lead* in the sense that it dictates some key parameters (such as economic production volumes) within which the other 'arm' of the matrix must work (for example, when offering local variation). Another practicality concerns ownership of strategy by staff. This may require the 'designation' of specialist staff to some products or client groups and not others. For example, the IT department may designate individuals to support particular front-line divisions. They may be physically located in that division and have a two-way reporting arrangement (to the head of IT and to the divisional manager). Perhaps the key ingredient in a successful matrix structure is that senior managers are good at sustaining collaborative relationships (across the matrix) and coping with the messiness and ambiguity which that can bring. It is for this reason that Bartlett and Ghoshal describe the matrix as involving a 'state of mind' as much as a formal structure.[7]

8.2.5 The transnational structure

A **transnational structure** combines the local responsiveness of the international subsidiary with the coordination advantages found in global product companies

The **transnational structure** is a means of managing internationally which is particularly effective in exploiting knowledge across borders. The transnational structure seeks to obtain the best from the two extreme international strategies, the multidomestic strategy and the global strategy (see Chapter 5). As in Exhibit 8.5, a global strategy would typically be supported by global product divisions (e.g. a worldwide cars division and a worldwide lorries division); a multidomestic strategy would be supported by local subsidiaries with a great deal of design, manufacturing and marketing autonomy for all products (e.g. AutoCorp UK Ltd, responsible for both cars and lorries). In the exhibit, international divisions refer to standalone divisions tacked alongside the structures of the major home-based business, as was often the case with American corporations as they started to internationalise in the 1950s and 1960s (e.g. AutoCorp North America would have its local car and lorry divisions, while its overseas businesses would all be handled by the Autocorp International Division). The transnational structure, however, attempts to achieve both high local responsiveness and high global coordination.

Exhibit 8.5 Multinational structures

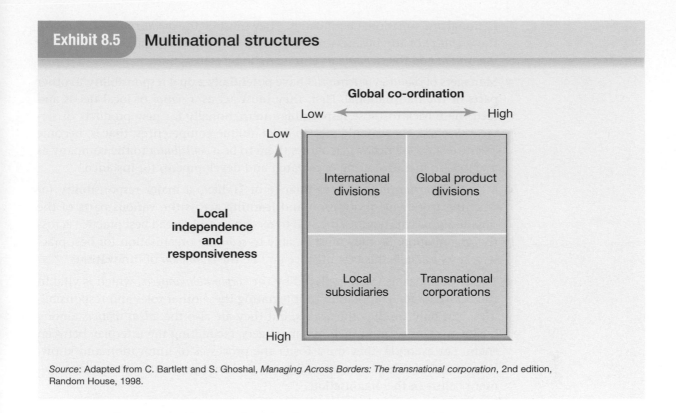

Source: Adapted from C. Bartlett and S. Ghoshal, *Managing Across Borders: The transnational corporation*, 2nd edition, Random House, 1998.

As Bartlett and Ghoshal describe it, the transnational is like a matrix but has two specific features: first, it responds specifically to the challenge of globalisation; second, it tends to have more fixed responsibilities within its cross-cutting dimensions.[8] The transnational has the following detailed characteristics:

- Each national unit operates independently, but is a source of ideas and capabilities for the whole corporation. For example, in Unilever, the centre for innovation in hair-care products worldwide is in France.[9]

- National units achieve greater scale economies through specialisation on behalf of the whole corporation, or at least large regions. Unilever in Europe has replaced its web of small national food manufacturing units with a few specialised larger factories that export its products to other European countries.

- The corporate centre manages this global network by first establishing the role of each business unit, then sustaining the systems, relationships and culture to make the network of business units operate effectively. Unilever has established a system of 'forums' bringing managers together internationally to help them swap experience and coordinate their needs.

The success of a transnational corporation is dependent on the ability *simultaneously* to achieve global competences, local responsiveness and organisation-wide innovation and learning. This requires clarity as to boundaries, relationships and the roles that the various managers need to perform. For example:

- Those responsible for *global products or businesses* have the overriding responsibility to further the company's global competitiveness, which will cross both national and functional boundaries. They must be the *product/market strategist*, the *architect* of the business resources and competences, the *driver of product innovation* and the *coordinator* of transnational transactions.

● Managers of *countries or territories* have potentially a dual responsibility to other parts of the transnational. First, they must act as a *sensor* of local needs and feed these back to those responsible internationally for new products or services. Second, they should seek to *build* unique competences: that is, become a centre of excellence which allows them to be a *contributor* to the company as a whole, in manufacturing or research and development, for instance.

● Managers of *functions* such as finance or IT have a major responsibility for ensuring worldwide innovation and learning across the various parts of the organisation. This requires the skill to recognise and spread best practice across the organisation. So they must be able to *scan* the organisation for best practice, *cross-pollinate* this best practice and be the *champion* of innovations.

● The critical issue is the role played by the *corporate managers*, which is vital in the transnational corporation in integrating these other roles and responsibilities. Not only are they the *leaders*, but they are also the *talent spotters* among business, country and functional managers, facilitating the interplay between them. For example, they must foster the processes of innovation and knowledge creation. They are responsible for the *development* of a strong management centre in the organisation.

There are some disadvantages to a transnational structure. It is very demanding of managers in terms of willingness to work not just at their immediate responsibilities but for the good of the transnational as a whole. Diffuse responsibilities also make for similar complexities and control problems to those of the matrix organisation. The Swiss–Swedish engineering giant ABB was often used as a model for the transnational during the 1990s, but in 1998 the company restructured along clearer product divisional lines.[10] Strengthening the product divisions over the country managers was intended to reduce internal politics and simplify international coordination.

8.2.6 Team-based structures[11]

A **team-based structure** attempts to combine both horizontal and vertical coordination through structuring people into cross-functional teams

Another way of trying to integrate knowledge in a flexible fashion is using team-based structures. A **team-based structure** attempts to combine both horizontal and vertical coordination through structuring people into cross-functional teams – often built around business processes. For example, an information systems company might have development teams, product teams and applications teams who, respectively, are responsible for: (a) new product development, (b) service and support of standard products, and (c) customising products to particular customers (or customer groups). Each of these teams will have a mix of specialists within it – particularly software engineers and customer service specialists so they are able to see the issues holistically. Bringing all these specialists together has great benefits for knowledge sharing and knowledge development. Illustration 8.2 shows an example of a team-based structure.

Illustration 8.2

Team-based structures at Saab Training Systems

A change in structure may be needed to improve competitive performance.

In the 1990s Saab Training Systems was a high-tech company working in the defence industry. It was a fully owned subsidiary of the Swedish company Saab. In 1997 the company had 260 employees and a turnover of about £52m (≈ €78m). It sold computer-aided equipment for military training – for example, laser-based simulators. The market was characterised by long, complicated and politicised negotiations with clients, fierce global competition and overcapacity as defence budgets reduced as a result of the 'peace dividend'. This high degree of uncertainty and need for flexibility had forced the company to react. It shunned external alliances, which were common in the industry, and focused on exploiting its core competence in laser-based simulation. But it also needed to drastically speed up throughput times in both development and production to get new product to commercialisation faster and then to shorten delivery times.

The company decided to abandon its traditional functional structure in favour of a more flexible team-based structure and a more business-process-oriented way of doing business. Before these changes the company was organised into functions (production, development, marketing and purchasing). Each function had its own internal hierarchy. This structure created problems with cross-functional coordination and communication. In the new structure 40 teams were created that reported directly to the senior management team. Team sizes were between six and eight. If they got bigger they were split. The teams were built around the business processes. There were five *business teams* who negotiated contracts with customers and monitored contracts. Each team was responsible for one or more products

and particular geographical markets. When a contract was signed it became a 'project' to which other teams were assigned: a *delivery team* (who planned production and tested products prior to shipping); a *purchasing team* (responsible for sourcing materials and components); and an *applications team* (who adapted the company's 'standard' products to the need of particular customers). Finally, production was assigned to one of 14 *product teams* (who were also responsible for product development). In addition to these 'front-line' teams there were central functions such as personnel and finance.

Coordination of the various teams involved in a customer's order was very important since the particular mix of teams assigned to that order was temporary. It was dissolved as soon as the order was delivered to the customer. Also, product teams were working on more than one project at any time. The responsibility for coordination of any project was shared between the business team (commercial responsibility) and delivery teams (production planning).

Source: Adapted from T. Mullern, 'Integrating the team-based structure in the business process', in A. Pettigrew and E. Fenton (eds), *The Innovating Organisation*, Sage, 2000, Chapter 8.

Questions

1. Why did the functional structure not suit the company's strategy?

2. How did the team-based structure help?

3. What problems could the team-based approach create?

Team-based structures can also help organisations respond flexibly to diverse customers. For example, in a university department different teams of lecturers and administrators may be created to support separately the undergraduate and postgraduate students. But lecturers are still connected to their academic subject group too. In many public services there are concerns that traditional structures (into separate professional departments or organisations such as social services, health and education) hinder the ability to address major strategic issues of social concern. For example, mental health requires professional expertise from each of these areas. So *cross-cutting* (diagonal slice) teams may be created to tackle these major issues. Another example is drug abuse (police, social services and health care). Small *self-managed teams* are often highly motivated and adaptable, and therefore can provide better value products or services than a traditional organisation with strict division of labour and extensive formal controls. However, the complexity of an organisation working with many small teams can lead to difficulties of control and raises problems of scaling-up if the organisation aims to work on, for example, a global scale.

8.2.7 Project-based structures[12]

A **project-based structure** is one where teams are created, undertake the work and are then dissolved

For some organisations, teams are built around projects that have a finite life span. A **project-based structure** is one where teams are created, undertake the work (e.g. internal or external contracts) and are then dissolved. This can be particularly appropriate for organisations that deliver large, expensive and durable goods or services (civil engineering, information systems) or those delivering time-limited events – such as conferences, sporting events or even management development programmes. The organisation structure is a constantly changing collection of project teams created, steered and glued together loosely by a small corporate group. Many organisations use such teams in a more ad hoc way to complement the 'main' structure. For example, *taskforces* are set up to make progress on new elements of strategy or to provide momentum where the regular structure of the organisation is not effective.

The project-based structure can be highly flexible, with projects being set up and dissolved as required. Because project teams should have clear tasks to achieve within a defined life, accountability and control are good. As project team members will typically be drawn from different departments within the firm, projects can be effective at knowledge exchange. Projects can also draw members internationally and, because project life spans are typically short, project teams may be more willing to work temporarily around the world. There are disadvantages, however. Without strong programme management providing overarching strategic control, organisations are prone to proliferate projects in an ill-coordinated fashion. The constant breaking up of project teams can also hinder the accumulation of knowledge over time or within specialisms.

Overall, team-based and project-based structures have been growing in importance because of their inherent flexibility. Such flexibility can be vital in a fast-moving world where individual knowledge and competences need to be redeployed and integrated quickly and in novel ways.

8.2.8 Choosing structures

At the beginning of this chapter we stressed the challenges of control, change, knowledge and globalisation for organisation design today. From our discussion so far, it should be clear that functional, multidivisional, holding, matrix, transnational, team and project structures each have their own advantages and

Exhibit 8.6   Comparison of structures

Challenge	Functional	Multidivisional	Holding	Matrix	Transnational	Team	Project
Control	★★★	★★	★	★	★★	★	★★
Change	★	★★	★★★	★★★	★★★	★★	★★★
Knowledge	★★	★	★	★★★	★★★	★★★	★★
Globalisation	★	★★	★★	★★★	★★★	★	★★

★ Stars indicate typical capacities to cope with each challenge, with three stars indicating high, two stars indicating medium, and one star indicating poor.

disadvantages with regard to these four challenges. Organisational designers, therefore, have to choose structures according to the particular strategic challenges they face.

Exhibit 8.6 summarises how the seven basic structures meet the challenges of control, change, knowledge and globalisation introduced at the beginning of the chapter. No structure scores high across all the four challenges. Organisational designers have to choose. If they seek control, but are less concerned for flexibility in response to change or global reach, then they might prefer a functional structure. If they want to foster knowledge and flexibility on a global scale, then they might consider a matrix or transnational structure. Structural choice depends on the strategic challenges the organisation faces.

In reality, few organisations adopt a structure that is just like one of the pure structural types discussed above. Structures often blend different types (see section 8.5 below) and have to be tailor-made to the particular mix of challenges facing the organisation. Goold and Campbell provide *nine design tests* against which to check specific tailor-made structural solutions.[13] The first four tests stress fit with the key objectives and constraints of the organisation:

● *The Market-Advantage Test*: this test of fit with market strategy is fundamental, following Alfred Chandler's classic principle that 'structure follows strategy'.[14] For example, if coordination between two steps in a production process is important to market advantage, then they should probably be placed in the same structural unit.

● *The Parenting Advantage Test*: the structural design should fit the 'parenting' role of the corporate centre (see Chapter 5). For example, if the corporate centre aims to add value as a synergy manager, then it should design a structure that places important integrative specialisms, such as marketing or research, at the centre.

● *The People Test*: the structural design must fit the people available. It is dangerous to switch completely from a functional structure to a multidivisional structure if, as is likely, the organisation lacks managers with competence in running decentralised business units.

● *The Feasibility Test*: this is a catch-all category, indicating that the structure must fit legal, stakeholder, trade union or similar constraints. For example, after scandals involving biased research, investment banks are now required by financial regulators to separate their research and analysis departments from their deal-making departments.

Goold and Campbell then propose five tests based on good general design principles:

- *The Specialised Cultures Test*: this test reflects the value of bringing together specialists so that they can develop their expertise in close collaboration with each other. A structure fails if it breaks up important specialist cultures.

- *The Difficult Links Test*: this test asks whether a proposed structure will set up links between parts of the organisations that are important but bound to be strained. For example, extreme decentralisation to profit-accountable business units is likely to strain relationships with a central research and development department. Unless compensating mechanisms are put in place, this kind of structure is likely to fail.

- *The Redundant Hierarchy Test*: any structural design should be checked in case it has too many layers of management, causing undue blockages and expense. Delayering in response to redundant hierarchies has been an important structural trend in recent years.

- *The Accountability Test*: this test stresses the importance of clear lines of accountability, ensuring the control and commitment of managers throughout the structure. Because of their dual lines of reporting, matrix structures are often accused of lacking clear accountability.

- *The Flexibility Test*: in a fast-moving world, an important test is the extent to which a design will allow for change in the future. For instance, divisional domains should be specified broadly enough to allow divisional managers to follow new opportunities as they emerge. As Kathleen Eisenhardt puts it, structures should also have enough 'modularity' (i.e. standardisation) to allow easy 'patching' of one part of the organisation on to another part of the organisation, as market needs change.[15]

Goold and Campbell's nine tests provide a rigorous screen for effective structures. But even if the structural design passes these tests, the structure still needs to be matched to the other strands of the organisation's configuration, its processes and relationships. Each strand will have to reinforce the others. The following two sections introduce processes and relationships in turn.

8.3   PROCESSES

Structure is a key ingredient of organising for success. But within any structure, what makes organisations work are the formal and informal organisational processes.[16] These processes can be thought of as controls on the organisation's operations and can therefore help or hinder the translation of strategy into action.

Control processes can be subdivided in two ways. First, they tend to emphasise either control over inputs or control over outputs. Input control processes concern

Exhibit 8.7	Types of control processes

	Input	**Output**
Direct	Direct supervision Planning processes	Performance targeting
Indirect	Cultural processes Self-control	Internal markets

themselves with the resources consumed in the strategy, especially financial resources and human commitment. Output control processes focus on ensuring satisfactory results, for example the meeting of targets or achieving market competitiveness. The second subdivision is between direct and indirect controls. Direct controls involve close supervision or monitoring. Indirect controls are more hands-off, setting up the conditions whereby desired behaviours are achieved semi-automatically. How the six processes we shall consider emphasise either input or output controls or direct or indirect control is summarised in Exhibit 8.7.

Organisations normally use a blend of these control processes, but some will dominate over others according to the strategic challenges. Again, capacities to cope with change, knowledge and globalisation are important. As we shall see, input measures tend to require that the controllers have high levels of knowledge of what the controlled are supposed to do. In many knowledge-intensive organisations, especially those generating innovation and change, controllers rarely have complete knowledge of what their expert employees are doing, and tend to rely more on output controls. At least they can know when a unit has made its revenue or profitability targets. Direct control relies heavily on the physical presence of management, although now surveillance through information technology can substitute. For this reason, global organisations may make use of indirect controls for their geographically dispersed subsidiaries. On the other hand, direct control processes can be very effective for small organisations on a single site.

8.3.1 Direct supervision

Direct supervision is the direct control of strategic decisions by one or a few individuals, typically focused on the effort put into the business by employees. It is a dominant process in small organisations. It can also exist in larger organisations where little change is occurring and if the complexity of the business is not too great for a small number of managers to control the strategy *in detail* from the centre. This is often found in family businesses and in parts of the public sector with a history of 'hands-on' political involvement (often where a single political party has dominated for a long period).

Direct supervision is the direct control of strategic decisions by one or a few individuals

Direct supervision requires that the controllers thoroughly understand what is entailed by the jobs they supervise. They must be able to correct errors, but not cramp innovative experiments. Direct supervision is easiest on a single site, although long-distance monitoring (for instance, of trading strategies in banking) is now possible through electronic means. Direct supervision can also be effective during a *crisis*, when autocratic control through direct supervision may be necessary to achieve quick results. The appointment of receivers to companies in financial difficulty by their creditors is a good example.

8.3.2 Planning processes

Planning processes plan and control the allocation of resources and monitor their utilisation

Planning processes are the archetypal administrative control, where the successful implementation of strategies is achieved through processes that plan and control the allocation of resources and monitor their utilisation. The focus is on controlling the organisation's inputs, particularly financial. A plan would cover all parts of the organisation and show clearly, in financial terms, the level of resources allocated to each area (whether that be functions, divisions or business units). It would also show the detailed ways in which this resource was to be used. This would usually take the form of a *budget*. For example, the marketing function may be allocated €5m but will need to show how this will be spent, e.g. the proportions spent on staff, advertising, exhibitions and so on. These cost items would then be monitored regularly to measure actual spend against plan.

One strength of this planned approach to strategic control is the ability to monitor the implementation of strategy (planning's strengths and weaknesses will be further discussed in Chapter 11). The detailed way in which planning can support strategy varies:

- Planning can be achieved by *standardisation of work processes (such as product or service features)*. Sometimes these work processes are subject to a rigorous framework of assessment and review – for example, to meet externally audited quality standards (such as ISO 9000). In many service organisations such 'routinisation' has been achieved through IT systems leading to de-skilling of service delivery and significant reductions in cost. This can give competitive advantage where organisations are positioning on low price with commodity-like products or services. For example, the cost of transactions in internet banking are a fraction of transactions made through branches.

- *Enterprise resource planning (ERP) systems*,[17] supplied by software specialists such as SAP or Oracle, use sophisticated IT to achieve planning type control. These systems aim to integrate the entire business operations, including personnel, finance, manufacturing operations, warehousing etc. This started with the use of EPOS (electronic point of sale) systems in retail outlets, which linked back into stock control. Further advantage may be gained if these systems can stretch more widely in the value-system beyond the boundaries of the organisation into the supply and distribution chains – for example, in automatic ordering of supplies to avoid 'stockout'. E-commerce operations are taking the integrative capability further (this is discussed more fully in Chapter 9). Illustration 8.3 shows an example of enterprise resource planning.

- Centralised planning approaches often use a *formula* for controlling resource allocation within an organisation. For example, in the public services, budgets might be allocated on a per capita basis (e.g. number of patients for doctors).

Planning processes work best in simple and stable conditions, where a budget or a formula can apply equally well to all the units in the organisation and where assumptions are likely to hold good for the whole of the budget or formula period. Where there is diversity in the needs of business units, standard budgets or formulae are likely to advantage some units, while handicapping others. Thus in the UK some argue that the government should no longer treat all hospitals and universities the same way: each has its own challenges and opportunities. Also budgets and formulae can be inflexible where changing circumstances contradict original assumptions. Organisations can be penalised unfairly for adverse changes in circumstances, or denied the resources to respond to opportunities unforeseen in the original budget.

Because of the dangers of insensitivity to diverse needs in the organisation, or possible changing circumstances, it is often helpful to involve those most directly involved in *bottom-up* planning. It will be seen in section 8.3.2 below that in these situations 'bottom-up' planning from business units is an important process – but within central guidelines (see Exhibit 8.8). If this approach is to work there need to be processes of *reconciliation* to ensure that the sum total of business unit plans can be resourced. This may be resolved through processes of *bargaining* and hopefully a revisiting of some of the central policies and guidelines, which should be regarded as movable (to a greater or lesser extent) through these planning processes. There may need to be several iterations of this process, as shown in Exhibit 8.8. The danger of bottom-up planning is that cross-cutting aspects of strategy are not addressed in the plans of individual business units; for example, the need to invest in integrative infrastructure such as common information technology systems.

8.3.3 Self-control and personal motivation

With rapid change, increasing complexity and the need to exploit knowledge, employee motivation is increasingly important to performance. Under these pressures, promoting self-control and personal motivation can be an effective means of control, influencing the quality of employee input without direct intervention.

Firstly, processes of **self-control** achieve the integration of knowledge and co-ordination of activities by the direct interaction of individuals without supervision.[18] The contribution of managers to this process is to ensure that individuals have the *channels* to interact (perhaps by improving the IT and communications infrastructure), and that the social processes which this interaction creates are properly *regulated* to avoid the rigidities mentioned in section 8.3.2 above. So managers are concerned with shaping the *context*[19] in which others are working – particularly to ensure that knowledge creation and integration is working. If individuals are to have a greater say in how they perform their work and achieve the organisation's goals, they need to be properly *supported* in the way in which

*Processes of **self-control** achieve the integration of knowledge and coordination of activities by the direct interaction of individuals without supervision*

Illustration 8.3   strategy into action

Enterprise resource planning (ERP) at Bharat Petroleum

ERP systems were at the heart of Bharat Petroleum's strategic transformation as it prepared for deregulation in the Indian oil industry.

Bharat Petroleum is one of India's top three refining and distribution companies. It has 4,854 gas stations, some 1,000 kerosene dealers, and 1,828 liquid petroleum gas (LPG) distributors scattered all over the vast country that is India. Facing deregulation of its markets, and possibly partial privatisation, Bharat Petroleum embarked upon enterprise integration through the implementation of a SAP R/3 ERP system. The aim was to gain control over the company's operations through improved information in areas such as inventory and product despatch, all working to support better customer service and satisfaction. The new system was to cover 200 sites and include a wide range of processes from financial accounting, to personnel administration, quality management, maintenance, plant management, and sales. The Finance Director projected cost savings alone of £5m (€7.5m) per year.

The implementation of the ERP system was not conceived simply as an information systems project. It built upon a previous delayering and restructuring of the company around six new strategic business units. The ERP implementation itself was named project ENTRANS, short for Enterprise Transformation. The head of the project team was not an information systems specialist, but a human resource professional. Only ten members of the 60-person project team were from information systems. A project steering group, meeting at least monthly, oversaw the whole process, with the heads of all six strategic business units, Finance, Human Resources and Information Technology represented. The head of IT at Bharat Petroleum commented himself: 'The unique thing about Bharat Petroleum's ERP implementation is that, right from its conception, it has been a business initiative. We (IT) just performed the necessary catalytic role.'

Implementation was carried out with assistance from PriceWaterhouseCoopers, 24 SAP consultants, a team of 70 in-house SAP qualified consultants and six full-time change coaches. All users were involved in training, focused on improving 'organisational learning' and Visionary Leadership and Planning Programmes. Bharat Petroleum's chairman declared there would be no reduction in the workforce as a direct result of ERP, even though lower staff costs were included in the benefits case.

Implementation was scheduled over 24 months, with pilots selected carefully on the basis of proximity to the project team (based in Mumbai), salience of the processes involved, and business and IT-readiness. Many initial teething problems were encountered. Informal processes were not always fully incorporated into the new SAP system, with awkward consequences. However, plant managers felt that ERP's formalisation of processes did eventually contribute greatly to increasing discipline amongst staff. In the year after completion of the implementation, Bharat Petroleum achieved 24 per cent sales growth. SAP itself rated Bharat Petroleum as in the top quartile of SAP ERP implementations.

Source: A. Teltumbde, A. Tripathy and A. Sahu, 'Bharat Petrolem Corporation Limited', *Vikalpa*, vol. 27, no. 3 (2002), pp. 45–58.

Questions

1. What is the significance of the ERP implementation not being headed by an information systems expert?

2. What possible dangers might there be in the formalisation and embedding of detailed business processes in an ERP system?

3. What should a company like Bharat Petroleum do with the large team of specialised in-house consultants and coaches once the ERP implementation project is completed?

Exhibit 8.8 'Bottom-up' business planning

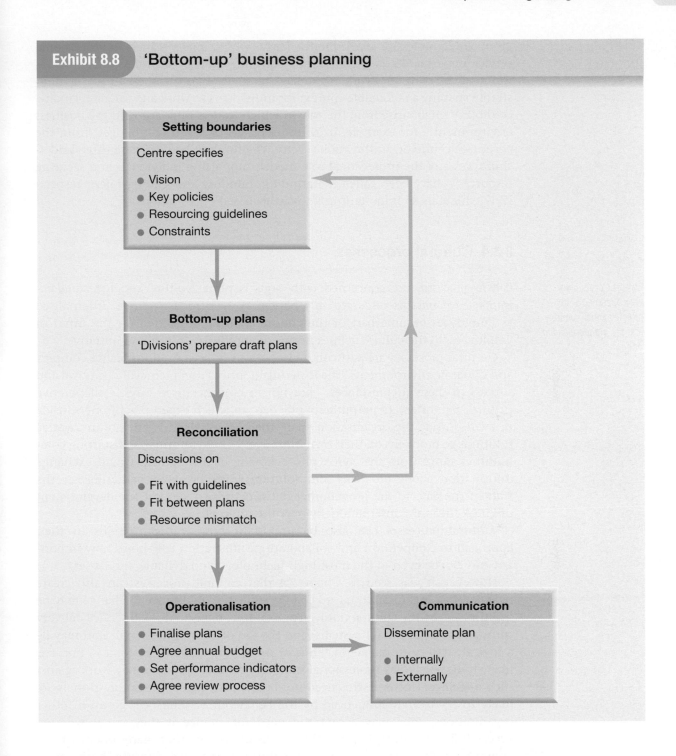

resources are made available to them. One of these key resources is likely to be information, and it will be seen in Chapter 9 that an organisation's IT strategy is a critical ingredient in this process of supporting individuals.

Secondly, the type of *leaders and leadership style* strongly influence personal motivation. The credibility of leaders is important and can be built in more than one way. For example, credibility may arise from being a member of the peer group – as a professional role model. This is why so many leaders in professional service departments or organisations continue their own professional work as well as overseeing the work of others. Credibility may also be built by demonstrably shaping a favourable context for individuals to work and interact. Finally, credibility might arise from the way in which leaders interface with the business environment – for example, in winning orders or securing a budget (from the corporate centre or, in the public sector, the funding body). These three leadership roles – of the professional role model, supporting individuals and securing resources – have been called the grinding, minding and finding roles[20] respectively which are so important in knowledge-based organisations.

8.3.4 Cultural processes

Cultural processes
are concerned with
organisational culture
and the *standardisation*
of norms

Cultural processes are concerned with organisational culture and the *standardisation of norms* (as discussed in Chapter 4). Control is indirect, internalised as employees become part of the culture. Control is exerted on the input of employees, as the culture defines norms of appropriate effort and initiative.

Cultural processes are particularly important in organisations facing complex and dynamic environments. The fostering of innovation is crucial to survival and success in these circumstances – but not in bureaucratised ways. Collaborative cultures can foster 'communities of practice', in which expert practitioners inside or even outside the organisation share their knowledge to generate innovative solutions to problems on their own initiative.[21] These informal, self-starting communities range from the Xerox photocopying engineers who would exchange information about problems and solutions over breakfast gatherings at the start of the day, to the programmer networks which support the development of Linux 'freeware' internationally over the internet.

Cultural processes can also be important *between* organisations in their approach to competition and collaboration. Illustration 8.4 shows how important this can be even in the most high-technology and dynamic industries.

However, it was seen in Chapter 4 that cultural processes can also create *rigidities* if an organisation has to change strategy.[22] Resistance to change may be 'legitimised' by the cultural norms. For example, plans to de-skill service delivery through routinisation (IT systems) and the use of 'non-professional' staff may be a logical strategy to pursue in terms of improving value to customers, but it is likely to be resisted by professional staff. The cultural processes may work against such a change. However, this need not be the case. Since these professionals are likely to be strongly influenced by the behaviour of their peer group in other organisations, they may accept the need for change if they see it working successfully elsewhere. It is for these sorts of reasons that many organisations commit significant resources to maintaining *professional networks*, both inside and between organisations, as a method of keeping in touch with best practice.

Training and development is another way in which organisations invest in maintaining the cultural processes within an organisation. It provides a common set of reference points (norms) to which people can relate their own work and priorities, and a common language with which to communicate with other parts of the organisation.

Illustration 8.4   strategy into action

Networking in Silicon Alley

Many major international cities are developing new media districts, where large firms and a mass of small firms and entrepreneurs collaborate effectively through dense social networks.

With the internet boom of the 1990s, New York developed a rival industrial district to West Coast Silicon Valley, the so-called Silicon Alley. Silicon Alley emerged along a stretch of Broadway running from the Flatiron District, through Greenwich Village and into SoHo. These areas were full of young creative people attracted by New York University and the relatively cheap space of the old factory lofts. During the 1990s, these creatives began to experiment with the new media technologies such as CD-ROMs, electronic bulletin boards and the World Wide Web. Close to New York's huge advertising and publishing industries, they began to forge relationships not only between each other but also with large corporations.

The new media businesses interchanged through local networks. For example, Echo (East Coast Hang Out) – an electronic bulletin board that became a virtual community of 3,500 members – organised get-togethers in local bars. Other organisers of face-to-face interactions included the Silicon Alley Jewish Center and Webgrrls, an association for new media women. The New York New Media Association (NYNMA) grew to 8,000 members, bringing together entrepreneurs, consultants, venture capitalists, musicians, graphic artists and lawyers. The NYNMA organized beer-bashes for new media people to mix together and help 'newbies' enter the industry.

Big business got involved as well. A coalition of large companies such as McGraw-Hill, Time Warner, Forbes, and IBM advanced the idea of a new media centre, providing subsidised wired office space,

equipment and research facilities for new start-ups. Multinational telecommunications giant Ericsson established a Cyberlab, which enabled participants to connect into the company's resources and networks. Ericsson's ambition was to encourage Silicon Alley firms to apply its technologies in order to establish them as industry standards.

At the height of the internet boom, Silicon Alley had 4,000 firms and 138,000 workers. But then came the internet bust, and many of the businesses failed. Silicon Alley responded in characteristic networking mode. Consultancy company thehiredguns.com launched monthly 'pink slip parties' (named after the colour of the redundancy notices), where redundant workers could network about new business and job opportunities.

Sources: M. Indergaard, 'The webs they weave: Malaysia's multimedia super-corridor and New York City's Silicon Alley', *Urban Studies*, vol. 40, no. 2 (2003), pp. 379–401; *Business Week*, 7 March 2002.

Questions

1. Why are face-to-face interaction and geographical proximity so important, even in industries such as new media where electronic communications are prevalent?

2. What can large firms get from networking with start-ups and small new media businesses that they cannot provide themselves?

8.3.5 Performance targeting processes

Performance targets focus on the *outputs* of an organisation (or part of an organisation), such as product quality, revenues or profits. These targets are often known as Key Performance Indicators (KPIs). The performance of an organisation is judged, either internally or externally, on its ability to meet these targets. However, within specified boundaries, the organisation remains free on how

Performance targets relate to the *outputs* of an organisation (or part of an organisation), such as product quality, prices or profit targets should be achieved. This approach can be particularly appropriate in certain situations:

● *Within large businesses*, corporate centres may choose performance targets to control their business units without getting involved in the details of how they achieve them. These targets are often cascaded down the organisation as specific targets for sub-units, functions and even individuals.

● In *regulated markets*, such as privatised utilities in the UK and elsewhere, government-appointed regulators increasingly exercise control through agreed *performance indicators* (PIs), such as service or quality levels, as a means of ensuring 'competitive' performance.[23]

● In *the public services*, where control of resource inputs was the dominant approach historically, governments are attempting to move control processes towards outputs (such as quality of service) and, more importantly, towards outcomes (for example, patient mortality rates in health care, as previously seen in Illustration 4.7).

Many managers find it difficult to develop a useful set of targets. One reason for this is that any particular set of indicators is liable to give only a partial view of the overall picture. Also, some important indicators (such as customer satisfaction) tend to get neglected because they are hard to measure, leaving the focus on easily available data such as financial ratios. Recently, *balanced scorecards*[24] have been used as a way of widening the scope of performance indicators. **Balanced scorecards** combine both qualitative and quantitative measures, acknowledge the expectations of different stakeholders and relate an assessment of performance to choice of strategy (as shown in Exhibit 8.9 and Illustration 8.5). Importantly, performance is linked not only to short-term outputs but also to the way in which processes are managed – for example, the processes of innovation and learning which are crucial to long-term success.

Exhibit 8.9 is an example of a balanced scorecard for a small start-up company supplying standard tools and light equipment into the engineering industry. The owner-manager's financial perspective was simply one of survival during this start-up period, requiring a positive cash flow (after the initial investments in plant, stock and premises). The strategy was to compete on customer service for both initial delivery and maintenance back-up. This required core competences in order processing and maintenance scheduling underpinned by the company's IT system. These core competences were open to imitation, so, in turn, the ability to improve these service standards continuously was critical to success.

Balanced scorecards combine both qualitative and quantitative measures, acknowledge the expectations of different stakeholders and relate an assessment of performance to choice of strategy

8.3.6 Market processes[25]

Market processes are the dominant way in which organisations relate to their external suppliers, distributors and competitors in capitalist economies. It is not surprising that managers (and even politicians) have attempted to use *internal markets* to control their own organisations.[26] Market processes involve some formalised system of 'contracting' for resources or inputs from other parts of an

Market processes involve some formalised system of 'contracting' for resources

---

Exhibit 8.9 **The balanced scorecard: an example**

Financial perspective	
CSF*	**Measures**
Survival	Cash flow

Customer perspective	
CSF*	**Measures**
Customer service (standard products)	• Delivery time • Maintenance response time

Internal perspective	
CSF*	**Measures**
IT systems development • Features • Cost	Performance per £ invested (vs. competitors)

Innovation and learning perspective	
CSF*	**Measures**
Service leadership	• Speed to market (new standards) • Speed of imitation (robustness)

* CSF = critical success factor

---

organisation and for supplying outputs to other parts of an organisation. Control focuses on outputs, for example revenues earned in successful competition for contracts. The control is indirect: rather than accepting detailed performance targets determined externally, units have simply to earn their keep in competitive markets.

Internal markets can be used in a variety of ways. There might be *competitive bidding*, perhaps through the creation of an internal investment bank at the corporate centre, for 'top-sliced' resources to support particular products or services. Also, a customer–supplier relationship may be established between a central service department, such as training or IT, and the operating units. In practice, though, internal markets are rarely entirely free, with some direct interventions common. For example, the corporate centre might set rules for *transfer prices* between internal business units to prevent exploitative contract pricing, or insist on *service-level agreements* to ensure appropriate service by an essential internal supplier, such as IT, for the various units that depend on it.

Internal markets work well where complexity or rapid change make impractical detailed direct or input controls. But they can create problems as well. First, they can increase bargaining between units, consuming important management time. Second, they may create a new bureaucracy monitoring all of the internal transfers of resources between units. Third, an overzealous use of market

Illustration 8.5

The balanced scorecard: Philips Electronics

Balanced scorecards attempt to reflect the interdependence of different performance factors – which together will determine success or failure.

Philips Electronics, with more than 250,000 employees in 150 countries, uses the balanced score card to manage its diverse product lines and divisions around the world. The company has identified four critical success factors (CSFs) for the organisation as a whole:

- competence (knowledge, technology, leadership and teamwork);
- processes (drivers for performance);
- customers (value propositions);
- financial (value, growth and productivity).

Philips uses these scorecard criteria at four levels: the strategy review; operations review; business unit; and the individual employee. Criteria at one level are cascaded down to more detailed criteria appropriate at each level. This helps employees understand how their day-to-day activities link ultimately to the corporate goals. At a business unit level, for example, each management team determines the local critical success factors and agrees indicators for each. Targets are then set for each indicator based on the gap between present performance and desired performance for the current year plus two to four years into the future. These targets are derived from an analysis of the market and world-class performance. Targets must be specific, measurable, ambitious, realistic and time-phased.

Examples of indicators at the business unit level include:

Financial
Economic profit

Income from operations
Working capital
Operational cash flow
Inventory turns

Customers
Rank in customer survey
Market share

Repeat order rate
Complaints
Brand index

Processes
Percentage reduction in
    process cycle time
Number of engineering changes
Capacity utilisation
Order response time
Process capability

Competence
Leadership competence
Percentage of patent-protected
    turnover
Training days per employee
Quality improvement team
    participation

Source: A. Gumbus and B. Lyons, 'The balanced scorecard at Philips Electronics', *Strategic Finance*, November (2002), pp. 45–49.

Questions

1. Imagine yourself as the chief executive of Philips Electronics and draw up a table that shows the various ways that the balanced scorecard could be used in managing your organisation.

2. Imagine yourself as an ordinary employee of Philips Electronics and list possible pros and cons of the balanced scorecard as applied to you individually.

3. What possible disadvantages or dangers might the balanced scorecard technique have for organisations?

mechanisms can lead to dysfunctional competition and legalistic contracting, destroying cultures of collaboration and relationships. These have all been complaints made against the internal markets and semi-autonomous Foundation Hospitals introduced in the UK's National Health Service. On the other hand, their proponents claim that these market processes free a traditionally over-centralised health service to innovate and respond to local needs, while market disciplines maintain overall control.

8.4   RELATIONSHIPS

A key aspect of an organisation's configuration is the ability to integrate the knowledge and activities of different parts of an organisation (both horizontally and vertically) and with other organisations (particularly within the value chain, as discussed in Chapter 3). Structures and processes are an important part of this, as discussed in the previous sections. However, there are basic issues too around how both internal and external *relationships* are built and maintained, especially in ways that are fluid enough to respond to an uncertain environment. This section looks at the following issues (see Exhibit 8.10):

● Relating internally, especially with regard to where responsibility and authority for operational and strategic decisions should be vested inside an organisation.

● Relating externally, for example through outsourcing, alliances, networks and virtuality.

8.4.1 Relating internally

Relating to the centre

One of the important continuing debates in both public[27] and private sector organisations has been concerned with *devolution*. **Devolution** concerns the extent to which the centre of an organisation delegates decision making to units and managers lower down in the hierarchy.

Devolution concerns the extent to which the centre of an organisation delegates decision making to units and managers lower down in the hierarchy

Devolution is particularly effective where important knowledge is dispersed throughout the organisation and where responsiveness to the changing needs of different customer segments is important. In these conditions, top managers can be too remote from the 'sharp-end' to really understand the organisation's

---

Exhibit 8.10   Relating internally and externally

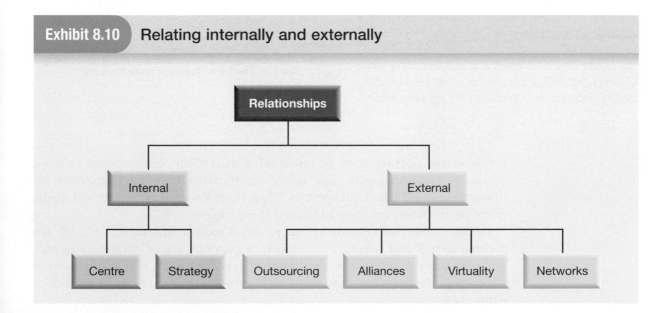

Illustration 8.6   strategy into action

Bertelsmann devolves with new strategy

The German media giant's reappraisal of its adventurous online publishing strategies has also seen more decision making devolved to its divisions.

In 2002, Dr Thomas Middelhoff, the innovative and audacious chairman and chief executive of German media group Bertelsmann, was forced to resign under pressure from family shareholders. His replacement, Gunther Thielen, embarked on a strategic retrenchment and reduction of headquarters control.

The Bertelsmann group comprised principally: RTL, Europe's largest broadcaster; Random House, the world's largest book publisher; Gruner & Jahr, Europe's biggest magazine publisher; BMG, a leading company in the music industry; arvato, involved in media services; and the DirectGroup, involved in media distribution through clubs and the internet. Thomas Middelhoff had greatly expanded the company – including the acquisition of RTL – since his appointment as chairman and chief executive in 1998. The major strategic thrust was the transformation of a traditional German conglomerate into an integrated, global media giant. Content could be shared between different parts of the group; the same content could be transmitted via different distribution channels within the group. Middelhoff had controlled the businesses through three divisions (content, media services and direct-to-consumer), and established the position of Chief Operating Officer to manage them directly. Middelhoff also had a 'corporate executive council' and a 15-strong 'office of the chairman' supporting his initiatives from the centre. Unfortunately, Middelhoff's strategy was overwhelmed by mounting debt and the difficulties of some of the new online ventures.

The new chairman and chief executive, Gunther Thielen, reversed much of Middelhoff's strategy. He declared that the period of large acquisitions was over, and that the future lay in innovation and organic growth. He embarked on selective divestments, cost-cutting and reorganisation. The post of Chief Operating Officer was abolished, as were the 'corporate executive council' and the 'office of the chairman'. The three divisions were split into six divisions based on the main businesses. Thielen declared that he would encourage decentralisation 'to ensure our business divisions continue to have as much creative and decision-making autonomy as possible'.

Sources: www.bertelsmann.com; *Financial Times*, 23 August 2002; *Financial Times*, 21 November 2003.

Questions

1. Explain how centralisation fitted with Thomas Middelhoff's strategy and devolution fitted with Gunther Theilen's strategy.

2. What possible disadvantages or problems might Gunther Theilen's devolved style have for Bertelsmann?

---

resources and opportunities. In fast-moving markets, it is often better to place decision-making authority *close to the action* rather than force decisions up through slow and remote hierarchies. Illustration 8.6 shows how German media group Bertelsmann has been addressing these issues.

Despite these reasons why increased devolution might make sense, it can become a 'fad' and simply a reaction to a previous era of overcentralisation. To avoid this risk the issue of centralisation vs. devolution needs to be seen as a *continuum* from highly centralised to highly devolved and not as a black or white choice.

Relating over strategy

Section 6.4 looked at the question of whether and in what ways a corporate parent can add value to its constituent business units or departments. An important determinant of organising for success is clarity around how responsibilities for strategic decision making are to be *divided* between the centre and the business units. Goold and Campbell[28] provide three *strategy styles* describing typical ways of dividing these responsibilities. The organisational processes and the way that relationships work are very different in each case.

Strategic planning

The **strategic planning style** (Exhibit 8.11) is the most centralised of the three styles. Here strategic planning refers not to planning in general but to a particular style of relationship between the centre and business units. The centre is the *master planner* prescribing detailed roles for departments and business units, whose role is confined to the operational delivery of the plan. In the extreme form of this style, the centre is expected to add value in most of the ways outlined in Exhibit 6.7. The centre orchestrates, coordinates and controls all of business unit activities through the extensive use of the formal planning and control systems (as discussed in section 8.3.2 above) shown in Exhibit 8.11. The centre also directly manages the infrastructure and provides many corporate services. This is the classic bureaucracy familiar to many managers in large public sector organisations.

The strategic planning style is well-suited to the synergy manager or parental developer roles adopted by corporate centres, as discussed in section 6.4. It is

> In a **strategic planning style** of control, the relationship between the centre and the business units is one of a parent who is the *master planner* prescribing detailed roles for departments and business units

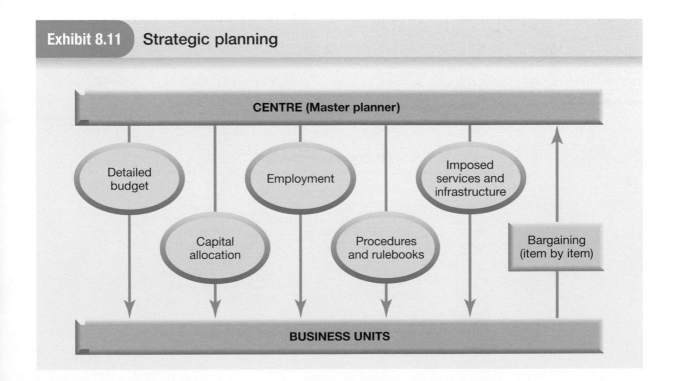

Exhibit 8.11   Strategic planning

CENTRE (Master planner)

- Detailed budget
- Capital allocation
- Employment
- Procedures and rulebooks
- Imposed services and infrastructure
- Bargaining (item by item)

BUSINESS UNITS

particularly appropriate where corporate managers have a detailed working knowledge of each business unit and where business unit strategies are of a size or sensitivity that can have major ramifications for the corporate whole. Where the corporate centre does not have detailed working knowledge, the strategic planning style can be dysfunctional. Corporate managers may hold back the development of business areas that they do not understand or steer them in inappropriate directions. There are also the bureaucratic costs of centralisation and demotivating effects on business unit managers who may feel little personal commitment to strategies handed down from the centre. Goold and Campbell and others have found many private sector organisations abandoning this style.[29]

Financial control

In **financial control** the role of the centre is confined to setting financial targets, allocating resources, appraising performance and intervening to avert or correct poor performance

Financial control (Exhibit 8.12) is the most extreme form of devolution, dissolving the organisation into highly autonomous business units. The relationship between the centre and the business units is as a parent who is a *shareholder or banker* for those units. As the name suggests, the relationship is financial and there is little concern for the detailed product/market strategy of business units – even to the extent that they can compete openly with each other provided they deliver the financial results. They might even have authority to raise funds from outside the company. This style is typically managed through a holding company structure, as discussed in section 8.2.3, and is suited to the portfolio manager or restructurer roles of a corporate centre, as discussed in section 6.4.

In financial control the role of the centre is confined to setting financial targets, allocating resources, appraising performance and intervening in the case of poor performance. Importantly, these interventions would usually be replacing business unit managers rather than dictating changes in strategy. So the dominant processes are performance targets as discussed in section 8.3.5 above. Business units managers are held strictly accountable for meeting these targets.

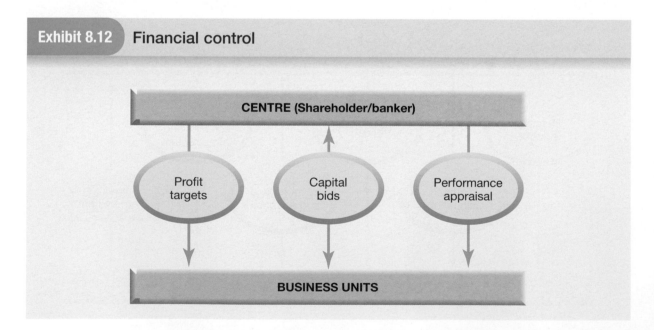

Exhibit 8.12   Financial control

In the public sector, such extreme devolution is rarely found for reasons of political accountability: the minister is ultimately responsible. In the private sector, however, the style can be appropriate to organisations operating in stable markets with mature technologies and where there is only a short time lag between management decisions and the financial consequences: for example, organisations trading commodities or dealing with basic products. It is also appropriate where the diversity of business units is great – since the other two styles require some measure of relatedness between business units. A major concern with financial control can be the dominance of short-termism. No one has responsibility for fostering innovation and organisational learning. The business units are focused on meeting tough short-term targets set by a centre that does not have the resources or the competences to manage the knowledge creation and integration processes. So competence development can only really happen through acquisitions and disposals.

Strategic control

Strategic control (Exhibit 8.13) lies between the two extremes of strategic planning and financial control and is the style most organisations operate. The relationship between the centre and the business units is one of a parent who behaves as a *strategic shaper*, influencing the *behaviour* in business units[30] and forming the *context* within which managers are operating. Like strategic planning, this is a style suited to the synergy manager or parental developer roles of a corporate centre as discussed in section 6.4. However, because it allows more discretion lower down, it is more suitable where the centre has little knowledge about business unit operations and business unit strategies are unlikely to make major

Strategic control is concerned with shaping the *behaviour* in business units and with shaping the *context* within which managers are operating

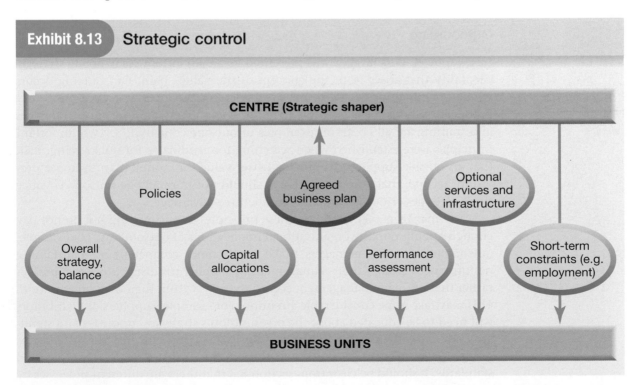

Exhibit 8.13 Strategic control

impacts on the corporation as a whole. Referring back to Exhibit 6.7, the centre would expect to add value by:

- Defining and shaping the *overall* strategy of the organisation.
- Deciding the *balance* of activities and the role of each business unit.
- Defining and controlling organisational *policies* (on employment, market coverage, interaction between units etc.).
- Fostering *organisational learning* between units.
- Defining standards and assessing the *performance* of the separate business units and intervening to improve performance (i.e. the processes of performance targeting discussed in section 8.3.5 above).

However, the centre does not fulfil these roles through an imposed master plan. Rather, strategic control is built through the processes of agreeing strategies with business units (perhaps through their business plans) – but within central boundaries and guidelines. Perhaps the biggest risk with this style is that the centre tries to shape strategy in these ways without being clear about the 'corporate logic' or having the competences to actually add value in these ways.

8.4.2 Relating externally

Organisations have important relationships outside their boundaries as well, for example with customers, suppliers, subcontractors and partners. This section will look at four of the most important such relationships, all of which have seen a good deal of change in recent years.

Outsourcing

In Chapter 3, outsourcing was presented as an important issue about strategic capability that arises from the concept of the value chain. Outsourcing occurs where organisations decide to buy in services or products that were previously produced in-house. For example, payroll, component manufacture, IT services and training are all common examples of outsourced activities. Two important principles were established when searching for candidates for outsourcing: first, that an outside supplier can provide better value for money than in-house provision; second, that core competences should not normally be outsourced since these activities critically underpin competitive advantage.

Many managers take on board these principles of outsourcing but do not pay enough attention to the organisational implications of outsourcing. For example, outsourcing requires managers to be much more competent at maintaining performance through their management of supplier (or distributor) *relationships* rather than through management control systems within their own organisation. This may take some considerable attention. For example, suppliers or distributors will need to be educated about the organisation's strategies, priorities and standards and how their work influences the final performance of the product or service. They need to be motivated to perform consistently to these required standards. It should be clear from section 8.3 that there are different processes by which this might be achieved. At one extreme, suppliers might be 'tied in' through enterprise resource planning systems. This might be possible and desirable where the requirements of the supplier are clear and unlikely to change quickly. At the other extreme, the relationship may be maintained through cultural processes and norms – for example, working with suppliers who know the company well and are tuned into the cultural norms. This would be important where suppliers are adding creative input to the product or service (such as designers) where the two-way interaction needs to be much more fluid. Between these extremes, market mechanisms could be used if a contractual approach to the relationship is felt to be appropriate – for example, for one-off projects or where there is a range of potential suppliers.

Illustration 8.7 shows how the UK railway system – which had been a single company (British Rail) running the railways through a 'command and control approach' – was divided into smaller specialist companies separately responsible for the infrastructure (Railtrack), service provision (Train Operating Companies) and rolling stock (ROSCOs). This arrangement was blamed for the disastrous situation in 2000–2004 (see Illustration 8.7).

Strategic alliances

This issue of managing relationships with other organisations (or other parts of the same organisation) surfaced in Chapter 7 in the discussion about strategic alliances. The organisational concerns are similar to those with outsourcing except that a strategic alliance may be much more overtly relational in the way the alliance is constructed (as against the contractual nature of many supplier–customer relationships). Readers are referred to Exhibit 7.3, which shows the spectrum of strategic alliance types from entirely contractual to essentially relational. The important organisational issue is finding the balance between the best sources of specialist knowledge (which would suggest many members of an alliance) and the competence to integrate these strands of specialist knowledge to create a best-value product or service to customers. The more members of an alliance, the more complex this integration task becomes and the more effort that needs to be put into the ingredients of successful alliances, as discussed in section 7.3.3 – such as trust. This will be discussed further below when considering networks and the ability of some organisations to achieve a nodal position in a network of multiple partners.

Networks[31]

Outsourcing, alliances and virtuality are particular cases of a general trend to rely on network relationships outside the organisation's boundaries. Taken together, they mean that more organisations have become dependent on internal and external networks to ensure success. So *cooperation* has become a key aspect of organising for success. Other important networks include:

● *Teleworking*, where people carry out their work *independently* but remain connected to key corporate resources (such as databases and specialist advice) and to colleagues, suppliers and clients through the telecommunications and computing infrastructure. Since the exploitation of the internet remains a

Illustration 8.7

British railways in crisis

Sometimes a command and control system might be the best way to deliver reliable service.

In January 2004 the UK government announced an urgent review of how Britain's railways were run. The purpose was to make changes that would drastically improve the quality of service, stuck at unacceptable levels. The Railways Act of 1993 had privatised the previously public sector British Rail that ran an integrated nationwide rail service. The major changes on privatisation were to divide responsibility for these separate aspects of the railway as described below. This was very 'fashionable' in public sector thinking at the time.

But in the autumn of 2000 the British railway system nearly reached 'melt down'. The aftermath of a fatal accident caused by poor track maintenance and the worst autumn rainfall for 400 years together created chaos. Many suggested that this was an inevitable result of privatisation and the way in which the previously managed 'command and control' system had been split into a 'quasi market' with more than 100 service providers tied together through legal contracts, performance measures and penalty payments. It was felt to be impossible to cope with crisis when management, ownership and operation of the industry were divided between numerous uncooperative companies and institutions that had contractual relationships with each other.

Indeed an outsider often had difficulty understanding how the industry was structured. At privatisation the previously integrated functions of the railway were divided into:

- *Railtrack* – who owned and ran the infrastructure and directly managed 14 major stations.
- Train operating companies (*TOCs*) – 28 companies that ran the trains under a renewable franchise.
- Rolling stock companies (*ROSCOs*) – who owned the trains and leased them to the TOCs.
- *Maintenance companies* – who undertook most of the track maintenance under contract to Railtrack.
- There were also several *regulatory* and similar bodies who were involved in railways: The Office of Rail Regulation (ORR), who regulated the activities of Railtrack and the TOC's, and Passenger Transport Executives (PTEs) (in seven major urban conurbations) who specified service levels and provided subsidies.
- Earlier criticism of the fragmented system had led to government creating the *Strategic Rail Authority* (SRA) to provide a focus and direction for Britain's railways and take over the function of awarding franchises.

This crisis of 2000 eventually led to the closure of Railtrack as a private company and its re-emergence as 'Network Rail' – a company limited by guarantee (i.e. charitable status). But service performance did not improve. By 2004 both experts and press acknowledged the need for further changes. For example, David Begg, chair of the Commission for Integrated Transport, wrote:

> . . . The review is not about creeping re-nationalisation. . . . Nor is the announcement a prelude to ministers or civil servants running our railways. They do not want to and they would not be very good at it. . . . What the government's review must look for is simplicity, clarity and performance. We need to break down some of the artificial barriers that privatisation created and the legalistic regime that obstructs cooperation. At the top we need a simplified structure that unites the regulatory, safety, operational and contractual framework. On the ground we need operational integration, so that the train operator has some say over the track his trains run on, the signals they pass and the maintenance and investment programme.

In July 2004 the government announced its intention to close the SRA.

Sources: *The Times*, 30 November 2000; *Financial Times*, 20 January 2004.

Questions

1. What problems does a 'quasi-market' structure create?
2. What were the key structural changes needed in 2004 to make significant improvements to service performance?

major strategic issue for many organisations (see Chapter 9), new ways of organising will be essential. The internet allows many formal structures to be dismantled and replaced with well-functioning networks supported by this information infrastructure.

- *Federations* of experts who voluntarily come together to integrate their expertise to create products or services. In the entertainment business, musicians, actors and other creative artists sometimes come together in this way as well as through the more formal processes of agents and contracts. Some organisations make their living by maintaining databases of resources (people) in the network and possibly facilitating social contact through organising networking events.

- *One-stop shops* are a solution to the problem of coordinating diverse network members so that the customer experiences a coherent, joined-up service. The one-stop shop creates a physical presence through which all customer enquiries are channelled (see Exhibit 8.14). The function of the one-stop shop is to put together a complete package of products or services from various network members. A 'turnkey' contractor (say, in civil engineering) might operate in this way – using their own expertise in project management and managing a network of suppliers, but not actually undertaking any of the detailed work themselves. With the growth of e-commerce, the one-stop shop may, in fact, be *virtual* in the sense that clients enter via a 'gateway' (say a website) but the physical services or products that are being integrated into the customer's product or service are

---

Exhibit 8.14   **'Joined-up' services: smoothing the network**

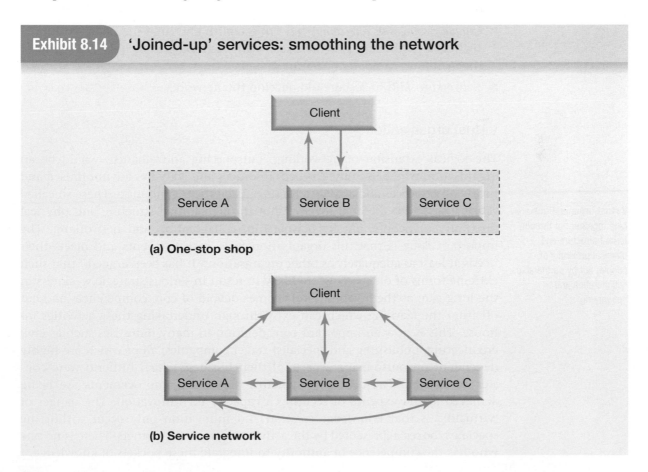

(a) One-stop shop

(b) Service network

actually dispersed (in physical terms). The critical issue is that it feels joined-up to the customer whose needs can be satisfied through this one gateway.

● In a *service network* the client may access all of the services of the network through any of the constituent members of the network. A well-functioning service network may not be easy to achieve, since it requires all members of the network to be fully informed, capable and willing to 'cross-sell' other people's products and to act collaboratively. Above all else, it requires *trust and respect* between members of the network. Some service networks also have a one-start shop facility. For example, Best Western is an international network of independent hotels, where customers can receive information or make bookings at any hotel in the network or through central booking points. This facility has the clear advantage of encouraging travellers to 'book on' their next destination with Best Western.

It can be seen that coordination in a network is a crucial activity. It can also be well rewarded. Organisations that achieve a *nodal position* in the network, connecting many nodes in the network, are potentially highly valuable.[32] To achieve a nodal position, organisations should have three strengths:

● A *compelling vision* that legitimises the need for the network and entices in partners. In the public sector this may be a vision of politicians who then set up the network to deliver – for example, on drugs, crime and disorder, social exclusion and so on.

● *Unique resources or core competences* to establish and hold the nodal position – such as a proprietary system as seen with technologies such as VHS video or the Windows computer operating system.

● *Networking skills* to sustain and develop the network.

Virtual organisation[33]

The logical extension of networking, outsourcing and alliances would be an organisation where in-house (owned) resources and activities are minimised and nearly all resources and activities reside outside the organisation. These so-called **virtual organisations** are held together not through formal structure and physical proximity of people, but by partnership, collaboration and networking. The important issue is that this organisation feels 'real' to clients and meets their needs at least as adequately as other organisations. It has been argued[34] that such extreme forms of outsourcing are likely to result in serious strategic weakness in the long run, as the organisation becomes devoid of core competences and cut off from the learning which can exist through undertaking these activities in-house. This is now an important consideration in many industries such as civil engineering, publishing and specialist travel companies, all of which are highly dependent on outsourcing aspects of their business which hitherto were considered as core. The concern is whether short-term improvements are being achieved at the expense of securing a capacity for innovation. The danger of 'virtuality' is that knowledge creation and innovation only occur within the specialist 'boxes' represented by the activities of separate partners. There is no one who has the competence or authority to integrate these pockets of knowledge.

Virtual organisations are held together not through formal structure and physical proximity of people, but by partnership, collaboration and networking

8.5   CONFIGURATIONS

This chapter has so far treated structure, processes and relationships separately. But Exhibit 8.1 at the outset of this chapter was a reminder that organising for success is not achieved through structures, processes and relationships independently, but by the way in which the elements work together consistently. This interdependence is reflected in an organisation's *configuration*.

Research by Andrew Pettigrew, Richard Whittington and colleagues[35] supports the view that integration of key organising elements into a coherent configuration is critical to success. For example, an organisation will not work well if trying to mix a bureaucratic culture with a fluid project structure and wide external networks. To a certain extent these configurations can be designed. However, these configurations often also *emerge* over time as an organisation finds ways of adjusting to the context in which it is operating. This final section will look at the following issues about configurations and strategy:

- stereotypical configurations;

- reinforcing cycles and the implications for change;

- managing dilemmas in configurations.

8.5.1 Stereotypical configurations

Because structures, processes and relationships work best when matching each other, organisations generally tend towards one of only a limited set of configurations. Mintzberg suggests there are six pure configurational stereotypes, each fitting particular situational factors to do with either the environment or the nature of the organisation itself. Each of these stereotypes has a different but reinforcing mix of structures, processes and relationships, as summarised in Exhibit 8.15.

- The *simple* configuration may have no formal structure, but be dominated by the chief executive or founder. The organisation is driven by the chief executive's vision and personality, mostly through direct supervision and personal relationships. This combination works well in small entrepreneurial organisations where flexibility to changing circumstances is critical to success.

- The *machine bureaucracy* is typically structured around functional departments. It has strict planning systems to standardise work routines. The machine bureaucracy tends towards centralisation. This configuration is very appropriate to organisations producing commodity products or services where cost is critical (postal services for example).

- The *professional bureaucracy* is bureaucratic in terms of standardising core knowledge and competences, but is less centralised than the machine bureaucracy. Cultural processes such as training and self-control through professional responsibility keep work to standard while allowing enough discretion to respond to particular client or customer needs. Hospitals often adopt this configuration.

Exhibit 8.15 Mintzberg's six organisational configurations

	Situational factors		Design parameters		
Configuration	Environment	Internal	Typical structure	Key processes	Typical relationships
Simple	Simple/dynamic Hostile	Small Young Simple tasks	CEO-control	Direct supervision	Centralised
Machine bureaucracy	Simple/static	Old Large Regulated tasks Technocrat control	Functional	Planning systems	Centralised Strategic planning
Professional bureaucracy	Complex/static	Simple systems Professional control	Functional	Cultural processes Self-control	Devolved
Divisionalised	Simple/static Diversity	Old Very large Divisible tasks Middle-line control Often young	Multidivisional	Performance targets Markets	Devolved Financial or strategic control
Adhocracy	Complex/dynamic	Complex tasks Expert control	Projects	Cultural processes Self-control	Devolved Networks and alliances
Missionary	Simple/static	Middle-aged Often 'enclaves' Simple systems Ideological control	Teams	Cultural processes	Networks

Source: Adapted from H. Mintzberg, *The Structuring of Organizations*, Prentice Hall, 1979.

- The *divisionalised* configuration combines a multidivisional structure with devolved relationships with divisional general managers. Divisions are controlled through processes of target setting and relate to the centre typically through strategic control or financial control relationships. Market processes would be used between divisions if they have customer–supplier relationships. This configuration works best for large or diverse organisations.

- The *adhocracy* is found in organisations faced by constant innovation and change. It is good at ad hoc solutions to specific problems. Adhocracies use project structures and make many relationships inside and outside the organisation. They rely on cultural processes and self-control to keep things together. Consulting organisations often configure themselves this way.

- *Missionary* organisations rely more on cultural processes than formal structures, though there will often be extensive use of teams. Networks between people sharing similar ideologies within and outside the organisation are important. Many voluntary organisations operate in this way.

Although few organisations fit perfectly into just one of these stereotypes, they can be used to think through how the configuration matches the situation and how far the design parameters of structure, processes and relationships fit each other. Poor performance might be the result of an inappropriate configuration for the situation or inconsistency between structure, processes and relationships.

8.5.2 Reinforcing cycles

Part II of the book introduced the *business idea* as an explanation of how the elements of an organisation's strategic position (environment, resources and expectations) were interconnected and reinforced each other. This idea of a reinforcing cycle of related factors is useful here too. Whereas an organisation's configuration may be thought of as 'following' strategy either in a planned or incremental way, in reality the relationship also works in the opposite direction: that is, organisations operating with particular configurations tend to seek out strategies that best fit that configuration and 'reject' those which require change. Also, the fact that it is possible to identify a limited number of stereotypes for organisational configurations, as described above, is a reminder that the separate organisational strands (structure, processes and relationships) are not independent variables – they tend to occur in particular groupings. Indeed, configurations found in practice tend to be very *cohesive, robust* and *difficult to change.*[36] The explanation of this draws together the issues which have been discussed above.

Reinforcing cycles are created by the *dynamic interaction* between the various factors of environment, configuration and elements of strategy. Reinforcing cycles tend to preserve the status quo. Exhibit 8.16 shows two examples from the stereotypes in section 8.5.1 above. The machine bureaucracy is a configuration often adopted in stable environmental conditions and can help create a position of cost leadership. This can underpin a positioning of 'low price' (or cost efficiency in the public services), requiring standardised work processes which, in turn, are well supported by a defensive culture. This culture *seeks out* stable parts of the environment and the whole cycle is self-perpetuating. A similar reinforcing cycle can occur with the adhocracy, as seen in the same exhibit.

None of this may be a problem for an organisation – in fact, the matching of these various organisational issues to each other may prove to be a source of great strength to the organisation. However, the interdependence between these elements can also cause *strategic drift*. Changing just one of the factors on its own will break the virtuous circle of reinforcement and the result will be declining performance. Virtuous circles can become vicious circles. Only when all the factors are realigned into a new reinforcing cycle will it be possible to achieve higher levels of performance.

The implications of these reinforcing cycles are captured in the *change and performance J-curve.*[37] The shape of the J-curve describes a typical trajectory of performance during configurational change. Early in the change process, performance falls beneath the starting point as change in some factors disrupts the original reinforcing cycle (the bottom of the J). Managers must reassemble all the factors into a new reinforcing cycle before performance can start climbing up the J-curve to beyond the starting point. In other words, things usually get worse before they get better.

Reinforcing cycles are created by the *dynamic interaction* between the various factors of environment, configuration and elements of strategy; they tend to preserve the status quo

Exhibit 8.16   Reinforcing cycles: two examples

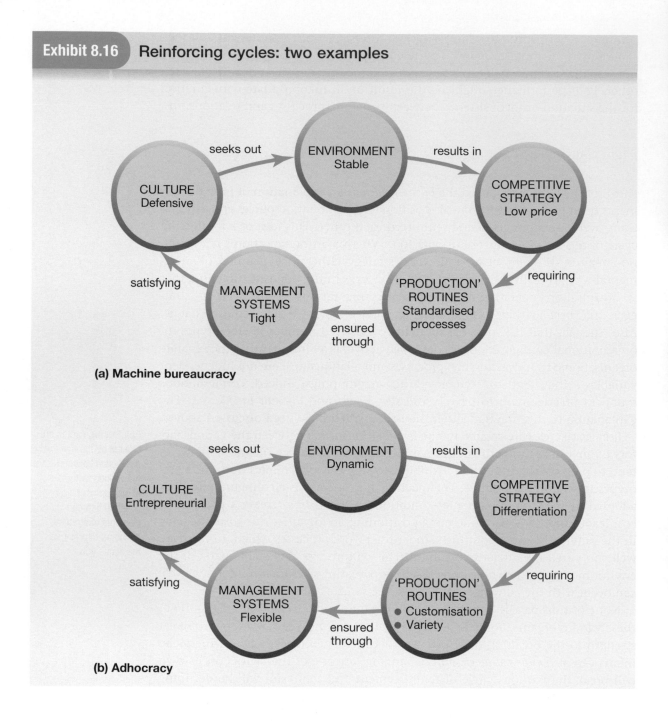

(a) Machine bureaucracy

(b) Adhocracy

An example of this change and performance J-curve is BP in the 1990s. Chief Executive Bob Horton initiated major changes in strategy, structure and relationships. Thus the company became strategically more focused on its core oil business, many non-essential services were subcontracted and the structure was delayered. What Horton failed to do was change the cultural processes in line with these strategic, structural and relationship changes. Morale and performance both declined and Horton was forced to resign. Only when his successors instituted the requisite cultural changes did BP's performance rise above the levels before Horton's initial changes.[38] Given the risks of underestimating the extent of change required, it is not surprising that organisational leaders need a great deal of courage and persistence to break out of old reinforcing cycles and build new ones. Managing change will be discussed more fully in Chapter 10.

8.5.3 Configuration dilemmas

A theme of this chapter, and especially the discussion of configurations, is that successful organising requires fitting key elements to each other and to key strategic challenges and circumstances. In practice, it is often hard to find perfect fits across all these dimensions, and there can be major trade-offs between optimising on one element and optimising on another. The chapter concludes by considering some of these practical dilemmas (sometimes called *dualities*)[39] and the ways in which they can be addressed.

Exhibit 8.17 summarises some dilemmas in organising. Hierarchies are often necessary to ensure control and action, but they can sit uneasily with networks that foster knowledge exchange and innovation. Vertical accountability promotes maximum performance by subordinates, but can lead managers to maximise their own self-interest, at the expense of horizontal relationships. Empowerment of employees lower down the organisation gives scope for initiative, but over the long term can lead to incoherence. Centralisation might be needed for standardisation, but this can be at the cost of the initiative and flexibility fostered by devolution. Having the best practice on a particular element of the organisation, for instance financial controls, may actually be damaging if it does not fit with the needs of the organisation as a whole.

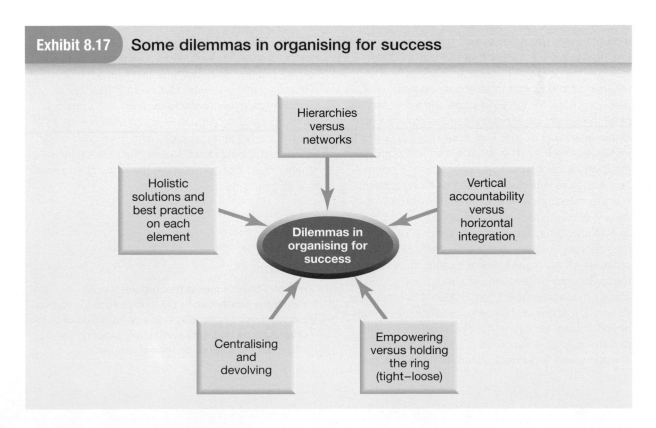

Exhibit 8.17   Some dilemmas in organising for success

Illustration 8.8

Does structure follow strategy?

A key message of this chapter is that strategy and structure should fit together. But which determines which?

Alfred Chandler, Professor of Business History at Harvard Business School, proposes one of the fundamental rules of strategic management: 'unless structure follows strategy, inefficiency results'.[43] This logical sequence fits the 'design' lens for strategy, but does assume that structure is very much subordinate to strategy: structure can easily be fixed once the big strategic decisions are made. But some authors warn that this dangerously underestimates structure's role. Sometimes strategy follows structure.

Chandler's rule is based on the historical experience of companies like General Motors, Exxon and DuPont. DuPont, for example, was originally an explosives company. During the First World War, however, the company anticipated the peace by deliberately diversifying out of explosives into new civil markets such as plastics and paints. Yet the end of the war plunged DuPont into crisis. All its new businesses were loss-making; only explosives still made money. The problem was not the diversification strategy, but the structure that DuPont used to manage the new civil businesses. DuPont had retained its old functional structure, so that responsibilities for the production and marketing of all the new businesses were still centralised on single functional heads. They could not cope with the increased diversity. The solution was not to abandon the diversification strategy; rather it was to adopt a new structure with decentralised divisions for each of the separate businesses. DuPont thrives today with a variant of this multidivisional structure.

Hall and Saias accept the importance of strategy for structure but warn that the causality can go the other way.[44] An organisation's existing structure very much determines the kinds of strategic opportunities that its management will see and want to grasp. For instance, it is easy for a company with a decentralised multidivisional structure to make acquisitions and divestments: all it has to do is add or subtract divisions, with few ramifications for the rest of the

business. On the other hand, it can be very hard for the top managers of a decentralised multidivisional organisation to see opportunities for innovation and knowledge-sharing within the operations of the divisions: they are too far away from the real business. In other words, structures can shape strategies.

Amburgey and Dacin tested the relative impact of strategy and structure on each other by analysing the strategic and structural changes of more than 200 American corporations over nearly thirty years.[45] They found that moves towards decentralised structures were often followed by moves towards increasingly diversified strategies: here, structure was determining strategy. Overall, however, increased diversification was twice as likely to be followed by structural decentralisation as the other way round. In other words, structure does follow strategy, but only most of the time.

Henry Mintzberg concludes that 'structure follows strategy as the left foot follows the right'.[46] In other words, strategy and structure are related reciprocally rather than just one way. Mintzberg warns that a simple 'design' approach to strategy and structure can be misleading. Structure is not always easy to fix after the big strategic decisions have been made. Strategists should check to see that their existing structures are not constraining the kinds of strategies that they consider.

Question

Hall and Saias suggest that organisational structures can influence the kinds of strategies that management teams will pursue. What kinds of organisations might be particularly susceptible to structural constraints on their strategies?

Managers should recognise that any organisational design is likely to face dilemmas of these kinds and is unlikely to optimise on all dimensions. However, they may be able to manage these dilemmas in three ways:

● by *subdividing* the organisation, so that the one part of the organisation is organised optimally according to one side of these dilemmas, while the rest responds to the other. Thus for example IBM created the PC in a specialised new venture division, kept separate from the traditional mainframe activities which were dominated by principles of hierarchy and vertical accountability highly antagonistic to radical innovation;[40]

● by *combining* different organising principles at the same time, for instance networks and traditional hierarchies. Managing simultaneously according to contradictory principles is obviously very demanding. However, it has been argued that organisations such as ABB and Unilever are now 'networked multidivisionals', combining network principles emphasizing horizontal integration with divisional structures ensuring vertical accountability;[41]

● by *reorganising* frequently so that no one side of the dilemma can become too entrenched. The rate of major reorganisation for large UK companies increased from once every four years to once every three years in the last decade.[42] Given this pace of reorganising, many organisations are like pendulums, constantly swinging between centralisation and devolution, for example, without resting long on one side or another.

A final dilemma arising from the interconnectedness of configurations is which element drives the others. The extent to which strategic elements drive structural elements is the subject of the key debate in Illustration 8.8.

Summary

- Organising for success is about an organisation's configuration. This is built up of three related strands: structures, processes and relationships.

- Successful organising means responding to the key challenges facing the organisation. This chapter has stressed control, change, knowledge and globalisation.

- There are many *structural types* (such as functional, divisional, matrix). Each structural type has its own strengths and weaknesses and responds differently to the challenges of control, change, knowledge and globalisation.

- There is a range of different organisational *processes* to facilitate strategy. These processes can focus on either inputs or outputs and be direct or indirect.

- Relationships are also important to success. Internally, key issues are *centralisation versus devolution* and *strategy style*. Externally, there are choices around outsourcing, alliances, virtuality and networks which may help or hinder success.

- The separate organisational strands should come together to form a coherent organisational configuration. Mintzberg's stereotypical configurations show a common relationship between the organisation's situation and the three strands of structure, processes and relationships. But coherence is not easy to design and often involves hard dilemmas.

- The value of configurations lies in the *reinforcing cycles* that they set up. But these reinforcing cycles also raise challenges for change.

Recommended key readings

- A comprehensive review of structuring issues in the modern economy is A. Pettigrew and E. Fenton (eds), *The Innovating Organisation*, Sage, 2000.

- M. Goold and A. Campbell, *Designing Effective Organisations*, Jossey-Bass, 2002, provides a practical guide to organisational design issues and particularly nine tests of effective organisation.

- For a discussion of issues of structuring in the public sector context see: K. Scholes, 'Strategy and structure in the public sector', in G. Johnson and K. Scholes (eds), *Exploring Public Sector Strategy*, Financial Times/Prentice Hall, 2001, Chapter 13.

- Organisational configurations are covered comprehensively in H. Mintzberg, *The Structuring of Organizations*, Prentice Hall, 1979. The related idea of organisational complementarity is discussed in A. Pettigrew, R. Whittington, L. Melin, C. Sanchez-Runde, F. van den Bosch, W. Ruigrok and T. Numagami (eds), *Innovative Forms of Organizing*, Sage, 2003.

- Configurations in multinational corporations are covered in C. Bartlett and S. Ghoshal, *Managing Across Borders: The transnational corporation*, 2nd edition, Random House Business Books, 1998, and G. Yip, *Total Global Strategy II*, Prentice Hall, 2002.

References

1. Some of these early writings are to be found in D. Pugh, *Organisation Theory*, Penguin, 1984.

2. The point has been argued by E. Fenton and A. Pettigrew, 'Theoretical perspectives on new forms of organising', in A. Pettigrew and E. Fenton (eds), *The Innovating Organisation*, Sage, 2000, Chapter 1, and also by R. Whittington and L. Melin, 'The challenge of organizing/strategizing', in A. Pettigrew, R. Whittington, L. Melin, C. Sanchez-Runde, F. van den Bosch, W. Ruigrok and T. Numagami (eds), *Innovative Forms of Organizing*, Sage, 2003.

3. This idea of configuration is similar to that of *Strategic Architecture*, as discussed by G. Hamel and C.K. Prahalad, *Competing for the Future*, Harvard Business School Press, 1994, Chapter 10, and *complementarities*, as discussed by R. Whittington, A. Pettigrew, S. Peck, E. Fenton and M. Conyon, 'Change and complementarities in the new competitive landscape', *Organization Science*, vol. 10, no. 5 (1999), pp. 583–600.

4. The view that organisations should fit their structures to key challenges ('contingencies') is associated with the long tradition of research on contingency theory: see L. Donaldson, *The Contingency Theory of Organizations*, Sage, 2001 or R. Whittington, 'Organisational structure', in *The Oxford Handbook of Strategy*, Volume II, Oxford University Press, 2003, Chapter 28, for summaries.

5. This view of divisionalisation as a response to diversity was originally put forward by A.D. Chandler, *Strategy and Structure*, MIT Press, 1962. See R. Whittington and M. Mayer, *The European Corporation: Strategy, Structure and Social Science*, Oxford University Press, 2000, for a summary of Chandler's argument and the success of divisional organisations in contemporary Europe.

6. T. Khanna and K. Palepu, 'The Right Way to Restructure Conglomerates in Emerging Markets', *Harvard Business Review*, July–August (1999), pp. 125–134.

7. Matrix structures are discussed by C. Bartlett and S. Ghoshal, 'Matrix management: not a structure, more a frame of mind', *Harvard Business Review*, vol. 68, no. 4 (1990), pp. 138–145.

8. C. Bartlett and S. Ghoshal, *Managing Across Borders: the Transnational Solution*, 2nd edition, Random House, 1998.

9. For background on Unilever, which adopted some important elements of the transnational structure, see A. Pettigrew and R. Whittington, 'Complementarities in action: organizational change and performance in BP and Unilever 1985–2002', in A. Pettigrew, R. Whittington, L. Melin, C. Sanchez-Runde, F. van den Bosch, W. Ruigrok and T. Numagami (eds), *Innovating Forms of Organizing*, Sage, 2003.

10. For ABB as a model of the transnational, see C. Bartlett and S. Ghoshal in above; on ABB's subsequent divisionalisation, see W. Ruigok, L. Achtenhagen, M. Wagner and J. Rüeg-Stürm, 'ABB: beyond the global matrix, toward the network multidivisional organisation', in A. Pettigrew and E. Fenton (eds), *The Innovating Organisation*, Sage, 2000, Chapter 4.

11. T. Mullern, 'Integrating the team-based structure in the business process: the case of Saab Training Systems', in A. Pettigrew and E. Fenton (eds), *The Innovating Organisation*, Sage, 2000, Chapter 8.

12. See reference 7, page 238.

13. M. Goold and A. Campbell, *Designing Effective Organisations*, Jossey-Bass, 2002. See also M. Goold and A. Campbell, 'Do you have a well-designed organisation?', *Harvard Business Review*, vol. 80, no. 3 (2002), pp. 117–224.

14. A.D. Chandler, *Strategy and Structure: Chapters in the History of American Enterprise*, MIT Press, 1962.

15. This practice of 'patching' parts of the organisation on to each other according to changing market needs is described in K. Eisenhardt and S. Brown, 'Patching: restitching business portfolios in dynamic markets', *Harvard Business Review*, vol. 25, no. 3 (1999), pp. 72–80.

16. For example, this is the theme that runs through Pettigrew and Fenton's book – see reference 2.

17. For readers who would like to read more about ERP the following are useful: P. Bingi, M. Sharma and J. Godla, 'Critical issues affecting an ERP implementation', *Information Systems Management*, vol. 16, no. 3 (1999), pp. 7–14; T. Grossman and J. Walsh, 'Avoiding the pitfalls of ERP

system implementation', *Information Systems Management*, vol. 21, no. 2 (2004), pp. 38–42.

18. H. Mintzberg, *The Structuring of Organizations*, Prentice Hall, 1979.

19. The idea of top managers as 'shapers of context' is discussed in S. Ghoshal and C. Bartlett, 'Linking organisational context and managerial action: the dimensions of the quality of management', *Strategic Management Journal*, vol. 15 (1994), pp. 91–112; C. Bartlett and S. Ghoshal, 'Changing the role of top management: beyond strategy to purpose', *Harvard Business Review*, vol. 72, no. 6 (1994), pp. 79–88.

20. This description of the three roles in professional service organisations was originally introduced by: D.H. Maister, 'Balancing the professional service organisation', *Sloan Management Review*, vol. 24, no. 1 (1982).

21. E.C. Wenger and W.M. Snyder, 'Communities of practice: the organizational frontier', *Harvard Business Review*, vol. 78, no. 1 (2000), pp. 139–146.

22. For example, D. Leonard-Barton, 'Core capabilities and core rigidities: a paradox in managing new product development', *Strategic Management Journal*, vol. 13 (Summer 1992), pp. 111–125.

23. D. Helm and T. Jenkinson, *Competition in Regulated Industries*, Clarendon Press, 1999, provides a number of in-depth case studies of competitive implications of deregulation. See also A. Lomi and E. Larsen, 'Learning without experience: strategic implications of deregulation and competition in the international electricity industry', *European Management Journal*, vol. 17, no. 2 (1999), pp. 151–164.

24. See R. Kaplan and D. Norton, 'The balanced scorecard: measures that drive performance', *Harvard Business Review*, vol. 70, no. 1 (1992), pp. 71–79; for a recent development, see R. Kaplan and D. Norton, 'Having trouble with your strategy? Then map it', *Harvard Business Review*, vol. 78, no. 5 (2000), pp. 167–176.

25. Market mechanisms of several types were introduced into many large organisations, particularly previously administered monopolies in the public sector in many countries: see Helm and Jenkinson (reference 23 above).

26. Companies like Royal Dutch Shell have been experimenting with internal markets to stimulate innovation. See Gary Hamel, 'Bringing Silicon Valley inside', *Harvard Business Review*, vol. 77, no. 5 (1999), pp. 70–84.

27. For a discussion of these issues in the public sector context see: K. Scholes, 'Strategy and structure in the public sector', in G. Johnson and K. Scholes (eds), *Exploring Public Sector Strategy*, Financial Times/Prentice Hall, 2001, Chapter 13, and T. Forbes, 'Devolution and control within the UK public sector: National Health Service Trusts', ibid., Chapter 16.

28. M. Goold and A. Campbell, *Strategies and Styles*, Blackwell, 1987.

29. See M. Goold, A. Campbell and K. Lucks, 'Strategies and styles revisited: strategic planning and financial control', *Long Range Planning*, vol. 26, no. 6 (1993), pp. 49–61; and R. Grant, 'Strategic planning in a turbulent environment: evidence from the oil majors', *Strategic Management Journal*, vol. 24, no. 6 (2003), pp. 491–517.

30. C. Bartlett and S. Ghoshal, 'Changing the role of top management: beyond strategy to purpose', *Harvard Business Review*, vol. 72, no. 6 (1994), pp. 79–88.

31. See W. Ruigrok, L. Achtenhagen, M. Wagner and J. Ruegg-Sturm, 'ABB: beyond the global matrix towards the network organisation', in A. Pettigrew and E. Fenton (eds), *The Innovating Organisation*, Sage, 2000, Chapter 4. Also J.C. Jarillo, *Strategic Networks: Creating the borderless organisation*, Butterworth-Heinemann, 1993.

32. Y. Doz and G. Hamel, *Alliance Advantage*, Harvard Business School Press, 1998, p. 235.

33. Virtual organisations and the extensive use of subcontracting have been widely discussed. For example, W. Davidow and M. Malone, *The Virtual Corporation*, Harper Business, 1992. For a cautious view, see H. Chesborough and D. Teece, 'Organising for innovation: when is virtual virtuous?', *Harvard Business Review*, vol. 80, no. 2. (2002), pp. 127–136.

34. See Jarillo, reference 31.

35. See Pettigrew and Fenton – reference 3 above. A summary of the research project (INNFORM) can be found in A. Pettigrew, R. Whittington, L. Melin, C. Sanchez-Runde, F. van den Bosch, W. Ruigrok and T. Numagami (eds), *Innovating Forms of Organizing*, Sage, 2003.

36. This idea of configurations being cohesive is discussed in D. Miller, 'Organisational configurations: cohesion, change and prediction', *Human Relations*, vol. 43, no. 8 (1990), pp. 771–789. For the related notion of complementarities, see R. Whittington, A. Pettigrew, S. Peck, E. Fenton and M. Conyon, 'Change and complementarities in the new competitive landscape', *Organization Science*, vol. 10, no. 5 (1999), pp. 583–600.

37. R. Whittington, A. Pettigrew, S. Peck, E. Fenton and M. Conyon, 'Change and complementarities in the new competitive landscape', *Organization Science*, vol. 10, no. 5 (1999), pp. 583–600.

38. For a short account of BP and Unilever's configurations, see A. Pettigrew and R. Whittington, 'How to join-up change', *People Management*, vol. 7, no. 20 (2001), pp. 52–55; for a more detailed account, see A. Pettigrew and R. Whittington, 'Complementarities in action: organizational change and performance in BP and Unilever 1985–2002', in A. Pettigrew, R. Whittington, L. Melin, C. Sanchez-Runde, F. van den Bosch, W. Ruigrok and T. Numagami (eds), *Innovating Forms of Organizing*, Sage, 2003.

39. A. Pettigrew and E. Fenton, 'Complexities and dualities in innovative forms of organising', in A. Pettigrew and E. Fenton (eds), *The Innovating Organisation*, Sage, 2000, Chapter 10.

40. R.A. Burgelman, 'Managing the new venture division: implications for strategic management', *Strategic Management Journal*, vol. 6, no. 1 (1985), pp. 39–54.

41. See Whittington and Mayer in reference 5 above and Ruigrok et al. in references 10 and 22 above.

42. R. Whittington and M. Mayer, *Organising for Success: A Report on Knowledge*, CIPD, 2002.

43. A. Chandler, *Strategy and Structure: Chapters in the History of American Enterprise*, MIT Press, 1962, p. 314.

44. D.J. Hall and M.A. Saias, 'Strategy follows structure!', *Strategic Management Journal*, vol. 1, no. 2 (1980), pp. 149–163.

45. T. Amburgey and T. Dacin, 'As the left foot follows the right? The dynamics of strategic and structural change', *Academy of Management Journal*, vol. 37, no. 6 (1994), pp. 1427–1452.

46. H. Mintzberg, 'The Design School: reconsidering the basic premises of strategic management', *Strategic Management Journal*, vol. 11 (1990), pp. 171–195.

WORK ASSIGNMENTS

✱ Denotes more advanced work assignments.

8.1   Draw up organisation charts for a number of organisations with which you are familiar and/or any of the case studies in the book. Why are the organisations structured in this way?

8.2   Referring to section 8.2.2 on the multidivisional structure, consider the advantages of creating divisions along different bases – such as product, geography or technology. Do this for an organisation with which you are familiar or one of the case organisations (to be specified).

8.3✱ Referring to Illustration 8.3, write a short executive brief to the CEO of a multidivisional organisation explaining how balanced scorecards could be a useful management process to monitor and control the performance of divisions. Be sure you present your critique of both the advantages and pitfalls of this approach.

8.4✱ Make a critical appraisal of the importance of the centre/division relationship in underpinning the strategic development of organisations (see Exhibits 8.11 to 8.13). Illustrate your answer by describing (with justification) the relationships which you feel would be most appropriate for the following organisations:

(a) the BBC (Case Example)
(b) Bertelsmann (Illustration 8.6)
(c) Electrolux (Illustration 8.1)
(d) an organisation of your choice.

8.5✱ Referring to Exhibits 8.11 to 8.13, choose an organisation with which you are familiar and discuss the following two situations: (i) increasing centralisation, (ii) increasing devolution. In each case, explain and justify:

(a) examples of the circumstances in which you would recommend each change;
(b) how the change would assist the organisation to improve its performance;
(c) any potential dangers of the change and how these might be avoided.

8.6   By referring to Exhibit 8.15, explain which of Mintzberg's organisational configurations best fits the situation of each of the organisations in assignment 8.4. To what extent is the actual configuration of the organisation in line with this expectation, and what are the implications of any mismatches?

8.7✱ By referring to the elements of organising for success (structures, processes and relationships), compare the key difference you would expect to find in an organisation operating in a relatively simple/static environment and another organisation operating in a complex/dynamic environment (see Exhibit 8.16).

 An extensive range of additional materials, including audio summaries, weblinks to organisations featured in the text, definitions of key concepts and multiple choice questions, can be found on the *Exploring Corporate Strategy* Companion Website at **www.pearsoned.co.uk/ecs7**

CASE EXAMPLE

Building One BBC

In April 2000, Greg Dyke, the new Director-General of the BBC, announced a major reorganisation of one of the world's most famous broadcasters. His proposed management delayering was welcomed enthusiastically by many creative and journalistic staff in the organisation. Four years later, however, Greg Dyke was forced to resign, after a doubtful BBC news story set off a train of events that led to the suicide of government scientist Dr David Kelly. Still popular internally, Dyke's resignation prompted demonstrations of support inside the BBC, but some said that the earlier reorganisation was in part to blame for the events that led to his downfall.

The BBC had been founded in 1922 as a public service broadcaster of radio and, subsequently, television. It is independent of government and overseen by a board of governors. At the beginning of Greg Dyke's office, the BBC had an income of some £2 billion (≈ €3 billion) derived from a licence fee paid by 22 million households in the UK. As such the BBC remained one of the few large broadcasters in the world which did not carry advertising, although it did derive commercial income of almost £100 million from the sale of programme rights and branded products worldwide. In the UK, and to some extent in other parts of the world, the BBC was seen more as an institution than a company. Its broadcasts reached over 50 million people domestically each week and almost 300 million worldwide. It had a global reputation for the diversity, depth and quality of its programming – particularly in drama, documentaries and news.

Not surprisingly, such a prominent institution was constantly in the public eye – not only in terms of its broadcasting output but also in how it was financed and managed. The appointment of Greg Dyke as Director-General, combining the role of Chief Executive and Editor-in-Chief, was something of a shock to many people. He did not fit the 'establishment figure' image of most of his predecessors. He had a background in commercial television and was more flamboyant and 'streetwise'. Like many new leaders, his first steps in stamping his brand on the BBC was to review its structure and management processes and this is what was announced in April 2000 and published in the booklet *Building One BBC*.

Photo: BBC

Structure prior to 2000

John Birt's structure for the BBC was built on the principles being adopted by many parts of the public sector at the time. Birt created an internal market by separating the management responsibilities into divisions covering the three major aspects of broadcasting: Resources (such as studios, outside broadcast equipment etc.), Programme Production and Programme Broadcasting (see Figure 1).

Each of these divisions had its own 'headquarters', several business units[1] and traded with each other in an internal market and also with third parties outside the BBC. For example, those broadcasting programmes would commission services both internally and from external production companies. The programme producers would hire infrastructure from BBC resources but also use external studios and equipment. They would sell their programmes both internally and to other broadcasters. BBC Resources would hire its facilities externally as well as to the BBC programme producers. This structural arrangement was designed to bring some 'market discipline' to the organisation and to ensure that each of these three major areas was delivering value for money when tested against its competitors. In this BBC internal market John Birt saw the role of the centre as the regulator of the market – defining the 'rules' and setting up the systems and procedures to

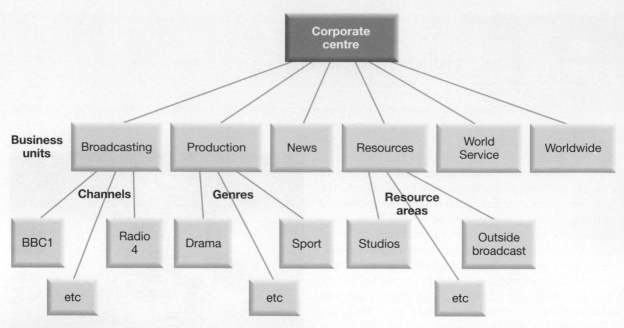

Figure 1 John Birt's structure (pre-2000; simplified)

manage this internal market. This included targets and transfer prices between the 'customers' and 'suppliers'. But most things that might be centralised in other organisations were devolved and duplicated, such as financial management. Significantly, because of the very fast nature of news, that area of the BBC's activities was excluded from this internal market and both production and broadcast were managed as a single unit. Indeed, live news was broadcast as it was produced.

New goals for the future – Building One BBC

In his introduction to *Building One BBC*, Greg Dyke explained the background to the structural changes:

> Our aim is for the BBC to be a place where people work collaboratively, enjoy their job and are inspired and united behind a common purpose – to create great television programmes and outstanding on-line services. If the BBC is to be a magnet for the best talent in Britain, then it must be an exciting and creative place to work.
>
>   . . . People are proud to work for the BBC, but want to see change. They believe that the BBC has taken bold steps towards a strong position in the digital age, but think it has too many managerial layers and costly processes, and that too much time is spent on negotiating within the BBC. As a result, as an organisation, we simply move too slowly. People also comment on a culture of division and of internal – rather than audience – focus.

He then went on to list five goals that the changes were designed to address:

- *To put audiences first [and] creativity and programme making at the heart of the BBC.* This was seen as the only way in which the BBC could win and retain its audiences in the digital age – where there would be vast choice for consumers.

- *Over time to raise the proportion of BBC funding that is spent on programmes from 76 per cent to 85 per cent.* Put another way, this meant reducing management overhead from 24 per cent to 15 per cent.

- *Create a culture of collaboration, in which people work together to make great programmes.* The implication was that the current structure bred a divisive culture.

- *To change the way the organisation works so that we can take decisions quickly and act decisively, while retaining sufficient checks and balances to avoid damaging mistakes.* This was contrasted with the way in which the digital world was spawning new entrants who acted decisively (such as Microsoft or AOL).

- *To make sure that the BBC is properly equipped with the skills it needs to compete effectively in the digital world.* New skills were needed in things like cross-media brand-building, distribution, gateway and rights management.

Greg Dyke's changes

Building One BBC went on to explain the nine changes that would help achieve these goals:

- *A flatter structure would be introduced* in which BBC Broadcast and BBC Production headquarters would disappear, bringing programme and channel interests closer to the centre of the BBC and resulting in a substantial reduction in overhead. This structure was symbolically depicted as a flower (see Figure 2). One layer of senior management was cut, so that 17 directors would in future report direct to the Director-General.

- *A more inclusive top-team would be created* where the number of programming and broadcasting people on the Executive Committee[2] will rise from four to nine. The top 50–60 managers will join them in a Leadership Group. The purpose of this was to raise the strategic importance of programming and broadcasting issues and to gain more ownership of BBC strategies.

- *BBC Production would be replaced* by three programming divisions: Drama, Entertainment and Children (DEC); Factual and Learning (FL); and Sport. They would report directly to the Director-General and be represented on the Executive Committee.

New Structure

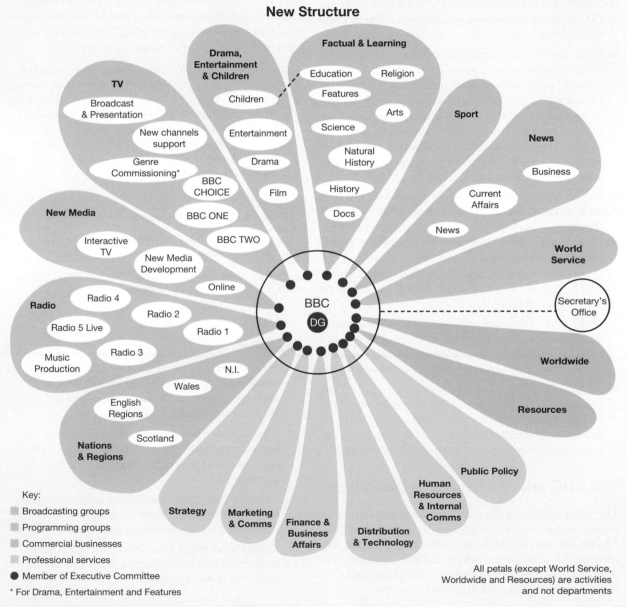

Key:
- ▢ Broadcasting groups
- ▢ Programming groups
- ▢ Commercial businesses
- ▢ Professional services
- ● Member of Executive Committee

* For Drama, Entertainment and Features

All petals (except World Service, Worldwide and Resources) are activities and not departments

Figure 2 Greg Dyke's new structure (2000)

● *In Sport, Children and Education*[3] *commissioning and programme making would be reintegrated to create a single BBC division for each area.* Previously it was only News that was integrated in this way. The reason for this change was that Sport was similar to News in having a high proportion of live coverage. Children and Education were felt to be two market segments where integrated management of all the products for that segment would be beneficial and give the managers 'cross-media capability'. For example, Sport would manage the online sports service as well as broadcasting of events.

● Similar arguments were used to justify *the reintegration of music commissioning and production in radio* (for Radios 1, 2, and 3).

● Over the whole corporation *a more collaborative commissioning process would be introduced, with programme guarantees in most areas.* This meant that broadcasters and programme-makers would work more closely together in planning their activities over a sensible time period – such as a season or a year. It was an attempt to eliminate the worst of the internally competitive behaviour that the internal market had generated.

● *A* New Media *division would be set up.* BBC On-line and interactive television would be brought together, as well as 'blue skies' developments. This was a response to merging technologies and a desire to ensure that the BBC had an integrated vision about new technologies and, more importantly, would develop and deliver a coherent rather than fragmented strategy.

● *Duplication of central and support functions would be eliminated (e.g. Marketing, Strategy, Finance and Human Resources).* If divisions needed support they would draw on resources provided centrally.

● *Internal trading would be simplified* with a reduction in business units from 190 to about 40. This would vastly simplify and reduce the cost of internal financial transactions between internal customers and suppliers in the internal market.

The BBC and the suicide of David Kelly

The years following Greg Dyke's reorganisation were prosperous ones for the BBC, with income reaching £2.7bn (€4.1bn) in 2003. But then came the crisis following BBC journalist Andrew Gilligan's contentious reporting of the scientist Dr David Kelly's remarks on the government case for the 2003 Iraq War.

Lord Hutton's official inquiry into the circumstances surrounding the death of David Kelly was prompted not only by the sad suicide of the government scientist, but also by the serious implications of Andrew Gilligan's claim that the government had knowingly led the United Kingdom into war on a false premise. When he reported in early 2004, Lord Hutton was critical of both Andrew Gilligan's reporting and the BBC's response to government accusations of inaccuracy. Greg Dyke was found not to have read Andrew Gilligan's report for a month after the broadcast, even while the BBC was vigorously defending it. Procedures in the newsroom appeared sloppy, and warning signs about Gilligan's professionalism had been ignored. Parts of the BBC news team had become over-concerned with sensationalist reporting. *The Economist* magazine commented:

> Mr Dyke cannot be expected to know about everything that happens in the BBC's sprawling 3,400 news empire. Furthermore, he is a television executive rather than an experienced journalist. But complacency followed by naivity was precisely not what the BBC needed at such a moment. . . . Ten times the size of a well-staffed broadsheet newspaper, the BBC's news team is too huge for hands-on editing from the top.

Notes

1. For example, Programme Broadcasting included the various radio and television channels.
2. The Executive Committee had 18 members.
3. The latter two are units within DEC and FL respectively.

Sources: BBC Annual Reports; *Building One BBC* – April 2000 (by permission); *The Economist*, 20 September 2003.

Questions

1. What would you see as the strengths and weaknesses of John Birt's structure? Why were there exceptions within the internal market structure (particularly News)?

2. Discuss how the role of the corporate centre had changed between John Birt and Greg Dyke and compare it with Goold and Campbell's stereotypes.

3. How had Greg Dyke modfied the internal market and why? Why didn't Greg Dyke choose to dismantle the internal market completely?

4. In what ways might Greg Dyke's reorganisation have contributed to the sequence of events that finally led to his resignation?

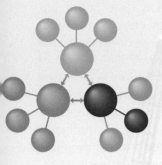

9

Enabling Success

Learning outcomes

After reading this chapter you should be able to:

● Explain why resource management issues are important in enabling strategic success.

● Describe how the management of people can enable successful strategies. This includes the development of people's competences, the management of their behaviour and the appropriate organisational structures and processes.

● Explain how developments in access to and processing of information can enable success through building or destroying capabilities, creating new business models and changing management processes.

● Understand how the management of finance can enable strategic success by: developing strategies to create financial value; providing for the different funding needs of different strategies and addressing the differing financial expectations of stakeholders.

● Describe how technology can: change the competitive forces on an organisation; affect strategic capability and influence management processes.

● Understand how a variety of resources and competences need to be integrated across resource areas to enable the success of a strategy.

Photo: Freefoto.com

Photo: Freefoto.com

Photo: Digital Vision

9.1 INTRODUCTION

Since very few individuals sit at the very top of organisations, their experience of, and contribution to, strategic success is from 'below'. They will operate in parts of an organisation where their day-to-day work is dominated by issues about that function, department, division or project team. It should be clear from discussions earlier in this book that in all organisations except the very smallest, this type of *specialisation* is usually a key factor underpinning success. This specialisation might be reflected in the formal structures of the organisation as discussed in Chapter 8 or it might be concerned with the different contributions that individuals make within teams. In either case, managers and individuals lower down in organisations may control resources, activities and business processes that are crucial in *enabling* strategic success. They are also likely to be the most knowledgeable about changes in parts of the business environment with which they interface. For example, HR specialists should understand the labour market, finance managers the money markets, marketing the customers and so on. So, many of the issues in the parts of an organisation will be strategic too. In fact, with the continuing move to flatter structures and the adoption of new organisational forms – such as networks and project teams – more 'responsibility' for strategy is found at lower levels, as discussed in Chapter 8. So more managers now have responsibility for integrating resources to deliver strategies – perhaps in their division or geographical location. So they, too, need to understand how the capabilities in separate resource areas contribute to the overall success of organisational strategies and be capable of managing those resources (such as people, information etc.) *strategically*. The efforts, decisions and priorities of all these managers in the parts of the business are crucial to success or failure of the overall strategies as will be seen in Chapter 11.

The purpose of this chapter is to help readers to understand better the crucial role that managers and individuals in the parts of an organisation play in *enabling* the success of strategies. The chapter will look at four key resource areas: people, information, finance and technology and the ways in which they might enable strategic success. In each case two related questions will be considered (see Exhibit 9.1):

● Are the separate resource areas capable of *enabling* overall business strategies to be executed successfully? This will include the need for those managing resources to make sense of the business strategy and change capabilities and behaviours accordingly.

But also . . .

● Are the business strategies of the organisation being shaped to *capitalise on the expertise* in each resource area? This requires senior managers to make sense of strategies that might emerge from strengths in specific resource areas. The resource-based view of strategy introduced in Chapter 3 is particularly concerned with this issue.

So, in summary, **enabling success** is concerned with the two-way relationship between overall business strategies and strategies in separate resource areas such

Enabling success is concerned with the two-way relationship between overall business strategies and strategies in separate resource areas such as people, information, finance and technology

Exhibit 9.1	Enabling strategic success

as people, information, finance and technology. To take one example to illustrate this point at the outset, many organisations at the beginning of the 21st century are rightly concerned about whether they are 'missing the boat' in terms of the use of IT and the exploitation of information in their business. Clearly there are concerns as to how information processing capability might be 'grafted' into the business to improve the competitiveness of current strategies. But to understand properly this relationship between information and business strategy it is also important to ask how the whole business process might be transformed by IT. The danger of asking only the first question is that strategy moves forward as a set of adjustments to an old business idea – to perform things a little better, a little cheaper and a little faster. It does not ask the radical question as to changing the business idea to capitalise on the new capabilities that IT offers. These same two-way considerations apply to the other resource areas too, as will be seen below. Chapter 11 will look at how the processes of managing change need to reflect these two-way considerations too.

9.2   MANAGING PEOPLE[1]

The knowledge and experience of people can be the key factors enabling the success of strategies. But they can also hinder the successful adoption of new strategies too. So people-related issues are a central concern and responsibility of most managers in organisations and are not confined to a specialist human resource function. Indeed, although formal HR systems and structures may be vitally important in supporting successful strategies, it is quite possible that they may hinder strategy if they are not tailored to the types of strategies being pursued

---

Exhibit 9.2   Strategy and people

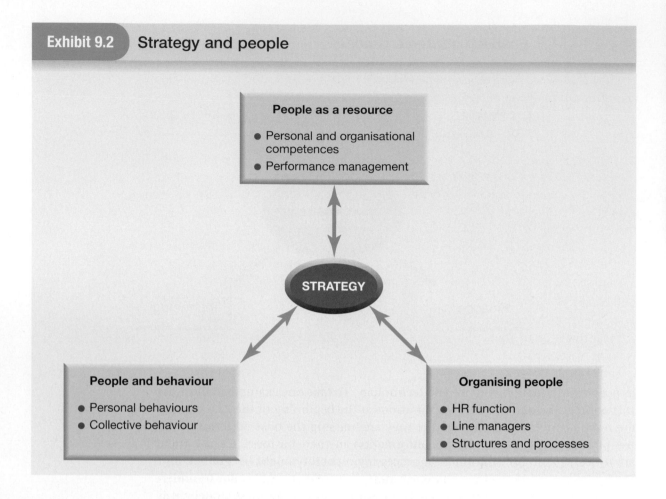

Also, the relationship between people and successful strategies goes beyond the traditional agenda of the HR function and is concerned with behaviours as much as competences. The ability to change behaviours may be the key ingredient for success. Creating a climate where people strive to achieve success and the motivation of individuals are crucial roles of any manager and are a central part of their involvement in their organisation's strategy. It is helpful to think about the people dimension of strategy as being concerned with three related issues (see Exhibit 9.2):

● people as a *resource* (which relates to Chapter 3);
● people and *behaviour* (which relates to Chapter 4);
● the need to *organise* people (which relates to Chapter 8).

9.2.1 People as a resource[2]

An important message from Chapter 3 of this book is that the possession of resources (including people) does not guarantee strategic success. Strategic capability is concerned with how these resources are deployed, managed, controlled and, in the case of people, motivated to create competences in those activities and business processes needed to run the business. This is a tough agenda in a rapidly changing world since the performance standards are constantly shifting in an upward direction. Much of this 'hard' side of human resource management is concerned with these issues of performance management. So traditional HR activities can help enable successful strategies in the following ways:

- *Audits* to assess HR requirements to support strategies and/or identify people-based core competences on which future strategies might be built.

- *Goal-setting and performance assessment* of individuals and teams. Most organisations will expect line managers to undertake these tasks, usually within a centrally designed appraisal scheme. This improves the chances of appraisals being linked to strategy. Also, there has been a move towards so-called 360° appraisals. These assess an individual's performance from multiple perspectives – not just the line manager but also from other parts of the organisation on which the work of the individual and/or their team impacts. This is an attempt to assess the full impact of an employee's work on the success of strategy.

- In many organisations the planning of *rewards* has had to take on board the reality of more teamworking in delivering strategy. Highly geared individual incentives (often found in salesforces) may undermine this teamwork. But team incentives tend to have complemented individual incentives rather than replaced them.

- *Recruitment* is a key method of improving strategic capability in many organisations. For example, many public sector organisations have needed to recruit people with marketing and IT skills as they try to get closer to their customers and exploit IT. Similarly, *redeployment* and *redundancy* planning are important in all organisations facing change. *Succession planning* has had to be refocused away from preparing people for particular jobs in a hierarchy to simply ensuring that a sufficiently large pool of talented individuals exists to meet future leadership requirements.

- The existence of uniquely *competent individuals* in an organisation, such as a top surgeon in a hospital, a criminal lawyer or a leading academic in a university, will not be a robust source of long-term strategic advantage since those individuals may leave or retire or die. So if excellence is to be sustained, a major concern should be how those persons' *knowledge can be spread* in the organisation, for example through using them in mentoring roles or by 'codification' of their knowledge into work routines. However, these processes of spreading knowledge may educate competitors too (for example, as employees move organisations). So innovation and creativity must be continuously nurtured in the organisation.

- In *training and development* there has been a reduction in the use of formal programmes and more coaching and mentoring to support self-development. These are important skills for individuals if their organisation's strategies are changing and developing constantly.

In order to put in place and execute HR strategies in all these areas, managers and HR professionals need to be familiar with the organisation's strategies, how these might be changing in the future and the implication to people's competences. Illustration 9.1 shows how many companies might attempt this alignment

Illustration 9.1   strategy into action

Performance management systems

One way of aligning business and HR strategies is through performance management.

Founded in 1997 and based in California, Saba was a leading provider of human capital development and management (HCDM) solutions, which are designed to increase organisational performance through the implementation of an IT-based management system for aligning, developing and managing people. The company's literature explained how their products assisted managers in performance assessment:

Far more robust than basic employee appraisal offerings, Saba Enterprise Performance delivers deep employee assessment capabilities, along with support for strategic initiatives, goal alignment, employee action plans and competency management. Saba Enterprise Performance supports an organization's strategies and goals by helping to communicate and align people's activities with their objectives. Additionally, it reduces the costs associated with performance appraisals. It also moves beyond other performance management solutions because of its tight integration with Saba Enterprise Learning – the industry-leading management system for the development and management of people. Business strategy execution and improved workforce performance are some of the key benefits provided by the rich features included with Saba Enterprise Performance.

Innovative features in this release include:

Initiative management
Saba Enterprise Performance helps organizations execute on their business strategy by focusing people on strategic initiatives, such as responding to new competitors, launching a product or investing in a new line of business. When an initiative is identified, organizations can rapidly define corresponding goals and required competencies, and assign and select cross-functional team members, all while maintaining visibility over the entire initiative process.

Goal alignment
Saba Enterprise Performance allows top-down visibility for executives to understand in real-time how well their organization is executing. Saba Enterprise Performance is designed to proactively notify people of trends or exceptions, such as goals not being achieved on time. It also allows people to view how their own goals impact and contribute to the strategic goals of the organization. Additionally, the product includes a time-bound Action Plan feature that supports assigned goals, prior accomplishments and required learning activities.

Goals in the Action Plan are prescriptive and can be based on the person's role or on a strategic initiative.

Performance assessments
Saba Enterprise Performance offers powerful performance assessment capabilities designed to increase the productivity of individuals and the overall organization. Assessments can be deployed across the extended enterprise of suppliers, customers and partners, allowing management to accurately assess people's performance and suggest improvements. Using Saba Enterprise Performance, organizations can improve the quality and effectiveness of their performance review process by measuring performance against established criteria and reviewing user feedback. For example, multi-rater assessments (MRAs) help organizations grow their talent by providing people with a 360-degree assessment of their competencies from their managers, peers, customers and direct reports.

Enterprise learning
Unlike performance management systems that do not deliver learning interventions to help people achieve their goals, Saba Enterprise Performance can be seamlessly integrated with Saba Enterprise Learning on the new Saba 5 platform. Together, Saba Enterprise Performance and Saba Enterprise Learning help organizations focus learning resources on organizational and competency goals, and maximize the return on investment of learning efforts. Using both Saba solutions, organizations can plan and create personalized development plans to meet individual needs, and deliver learning designed to close competency gaps and improve individual performance.

Source: *Business Wire* Philadelphia, 8 October 2003.

Questions

1. What are the advantages in systematising performance management in the ways described above?
2. What are the dangers and pitfalls?
3. Give examples of organisations where you think systems like Saba's would be either particularly appropriate or particularly inappropriate. Give your reasons.

through formalised approaches to performance management – assisted by IT-based systems. But many would argue that it may be better to go further and expect employees *themselves* to understand and 'manage' these issues. If these things do not happen it is likely that business strategies will fail because either the HR strategies and/or people's competences are 'out of line' with the business strategy.

However, it is not enough simply to adjust the performance management processes to support changing strategies. Managers need to be able and willing to envisage a future where the strategies and performance of the organisation are transformed by exploiting the performance management capabilities of the organisation better than their competitors. For example, a capability in mentoring and coaching could provide an environment that will attract creative people who like to be challenged and to learn. In turn, this creates a workforce that is much more able than competitors to 'think out of the box' and to produce innovative product features and new ways of competing in the market. This will require organisation structures and processes to support these behaviours, as mentioned in Chapter 8 and discussed further below.

9.2.2 People and behaviour[3]

People are not like other resources. They influence strategy both through their competence (section 9.2.1) but also through their behaviour as discussed in Chapter 4. Chapter 10 will also emphasise that many of the problems of managing change result from a failure to understand, address and change behaviours. This 'soft' side of human resource management is concerned with the behaviour of people – both individually and collectively. It is very often neglected in favour of the 'harder' issues discussed in the previous section. So people's behaviour is an area where the day-to-day actions of individual managers can contribute significantly in enabling the success of business strategies. This will require managers to be clear about this link between their actions and the organisation's strategies. For example:

- Seeing their role as people-oriented *'shapers of context'*[4] and not just as analytically driven 'masterplanners'. This will require an understanding of how these 'softer' aspects of strategy help or hinder strategic success – as discussed in Chapter 4 (particularly the cultural web (Exhibit 4.11) and stakeholder mapping (Exhibit 4.5)).

- Understanding *the relationship between behaviours and strategic choices*. This is crucial if managers are to properly prioritise their efforts in managing organisational behaviours. For example, since behaviours (culture) may hinder particular types of strategy decisions will be needed on how culture (behaviours) can be changed (as discussed in Chapter 4). However, it may make more sense not to pursue those particular strategies but concentrate on strategies that are particularly suited to an organisation's culture. Indeed, there may be some strategies where an organisation's culture gives unique advantage over other organisations.

- Being realistic about the *difficulty and time scales* in achieving behaviour changes. Culture change is a long process of changing behaviours. The hard change tools (structures and systems) if used alone are unlikely to deliver, as seen in Chapter 10.

● Being able to vary their *style* of managing change with different circumstances, as will be discussed in Chapter 10. So a manager's relationship and leadership skills with both internal and external stakeholders are important. Also, *teams* in organisations must be capable of operating different styles simultaneously. Therefore, a manager's ability to build and maintain teams of different personality types is just as important as the mix of competences in those teams.[5]

Illustration 9.2 shows how important is the behaviour of front-line staff – particularly in service organisations. In this example their behaviour was clearly out of line with the stated business strategy of 'customer care'. So the intended strategy and the actual (realised) strategies were not the same (this issue will be discussed more fully in Chapter 11). Whereas the company's policies could play a role in keeping front-line behaviours in line with strategy they are not sufficient. Fundamentally it is the day-to-day actions of managers that will shape and change the behaviour of front-line staff. But HR policies and frameworks can help with these softer-side issues. For example, in the high-technology sector the ability of staff and managers to build internal and external networks of personal contacts can be crucial in keeping at the leading edge of knowledge. These behaviours can be supported by 'hard-side' HR activities such as mentoring and rewards.[6]

9.2.3 Organising people[7]

Chapter 8 was concerned with the issues of organising for success with particular emphasis on how the balance of this agenda is changing in the 21st century. It is not the intention to repeat that detail here but to highlight some of the implications to how people might enable strategic success in the modern world.

The HR function

There are a number of important considerations concerning the HR function in organisations. The most challenging question is whether a specialist HR function is needed at all, or at least whether its traditional scale and functions are appropriate. In principle (and in practice in many organisations), people can be managed strategically without a specialist HR function. Readers may expect that in a faster-moving world there might be a movement away from specialist HR teams. This may make sense for many items – for example, the dismantling of across-company grades and pay scales as organisations globalise – to reflect the much greater diversity in the labour markets. But for other aspects the reverse might be true. For example, a major problem of highly devolved organisations is the failure of the devolved units to understand and put in place competence development (through training, mentoring etc.) that matches overall business strategies. This may be because managers at that level are unfamiliar with corporate-level strategies, are extremely busy and may not have the professional HR knowledge.

If an HR function is felt to be valuable against these measures then the expectations as to its role must be clear and consistent with the discussion above. There

Illustration 9.2

strategy into action

Customer relations at KLM: the reliable airline

What people do in providing customer services needs to be aligned with an organisation's strategy.

Cityhopper Flight KL1481 was due to leave Amsterdam for Glasgow at 19:55 on 25 November 2003. As the time approached for boarding, passengers were informed that they would not be boarding that plane, though they were given no clear explanation as to why. They later found that it had been diverted to Leeds. They were, however, informed that there would be another plane departing at 21:30. The plane arrived at 21:00 and at 21:20 they began to board. This took 30 minutes. At 22:00 the pilot announced that this plane had a fault with the hydraulics. He went on to explain: 'We have had a bad day: five of our Cityhoppers have developed faults so we are short of planes.' Passengers wondered quite what this said about the maintenance standards of KLM. Some minutes later they were told that no replacement plane could be found and they would have to stay in Amsterdam that night.

When they disembarked it became clear there would be further problems. Passengers were asked to move to a transfer desk where they would be informed of what would happen to them. When they arrived there were only five KLM ground staff and long queues developed. There was no announcement of what would happen the next day. One of the ground staff was heard to say that further of their colleagues would soon be arriving, so the back end of the queues moved to set up new lines. Additional staff did arrive but they could not deal with the passengers because their computer screens did not work. So whilst people queued, numerous ground staff stood around exchanging increasingly heated and acrimonious comments with passengers. One passenger was heard to say 'I'm being made to feel this is my fault!' Eventually a supervisor arrived. He also made no announcement to the passengers or engaged with them. After about 15 minutes he went away. It emerged but was never announced that KLM had not laid on another flight to Glasgow, but were filling vacant seats on various other flights going to Scotland.

It was after midnight when the last passengers went on their way to hotels around the airport. Muttering passengers were heard to say they would never fly with KLM again.

The Director Customer Relationship Management at KLM, commented:

> We regret the problems encountered by our passengers on this particular flight.
>
> In this case, we certainly learn that despite the fact that technical problems occur in our business, both to airplanes and computer systems, the number of ground handling staff was not sufficient to satisfy the needs of our customers at this particular moment. Consequently the attitude of our staff towards customers was not appropriate and communication was not managed properly.
>
> We learn everyday from our customers' negative travel experience by transforming this information into knowledge and action to prevent these things happening again to other passengers. Our product and services at all customer contact points, like for instance reservations, ground, transfer and inflight is regularly monitored and measured by a set of standard survey and measurement tools. The process behind this information flow is organised in such a way that: the cause of the problem is notified; a correction is requested and implemented and the situation is monitored through regular surveys.

Questions

1. In what ways were KLM's HR policies and systems adequate or not to deliver the promise of The Reliable Airline?

2. How did the behaviour of front-line staff influence the actual service delivery?

3. What could be changed to improve the consistency of service delivery?

are four broad roles that an HR function could fulfil in enabling successful business strategies:[8]

- As a *service provider* (for example, undertaking recruitment or arranging training) to line managers who are carrying the strategic responsibility for the HR issues.

- As a *regulator* 'setting the rules' within which line managers operate, for example on pay and promotions.

- As an *advisor* on issues of HR strategy to line managers ensuring that HR policies and practice are in line with the best organisational practice.

- As a *change agent* moving the organisation forward.

The determinant of the most appropriate role for an HR function is the organisation's context. The type of staff, the nature of the strategy and the broad structural arrangements in the organisation are all important. For example, some aspects of HR strategy need to be controlled centrally because they are crucial to the delivery of corporate-wide strategies, whilst other aspects can be usefully devolved since they need to be interpreted differently in different parts of the organisation.

Middle (line) managers

It has been mentioned above that there has been a significant move towards line managers being centrally involved in managing people issues themselves. This has the clear advantage of more ownership and a better chance of blending people-related issues with business strategies. But there are also worries – some of which have already been mentioned above. Research[9] confirms the concerns as to whether the circumstances in which line managers operate are conducive to their doing a good job on people management issues and hence the risk that strategic success is not enabled as well as it could be:

- Whether it is realistic to expect line managers to be *competent HR professionals*. Handled badly, this could be a formula for mediocrity. This same concern could equally be applied to other areas such as information management (discussed in section 9.3 below).

- The *short-term pressures* to meet targets do not help line managers in taking a more strategic view of people-related issues. Downsizing and delayering have left the remaining managers too busy.

- Trade unions and professional associations have tended to *resist a dispersion of responsibility* for HR strategies. From a union's point of view it is much easier to deal with a single, centralised authority. Professional bodies may take a similar view.

- Managers may lack the *incentive* to take on more of the formal HR activities, either directly in their pay or grade or indirectly in their judgement as to which competences make them more marketable outside the company.

- There has been criticism of middle managers as the 'gatekeepers' who maintain the status quo and block strategic change whereas, in reality, their active involvement in change programmes is crucial. It has been suggested that it is

better to think of their management role more as a *change relayer*[10] or an inter-
mediary as discussed in Chapter 10 (section 10.3.2).

Despite these concerns it is important to recognise the crucial influence of middle
managers on the day-to-day performance and behaviour of people in their organisation. The implication for top managers is not to bypass middle managers in
the strategy development process, otherwise the changes may not stick with the
people in the organisation.

Structures and processes

People may be held back from enabling strategic success because the traditional
structures and roles do not match future strategies. Also as circumstances and
strategies change, organisations may need to change the processes and relationships discussed in Chapter 8. For example, the development of new product features may require more collaborative working between separate departments and
with suppliers or distributors. This change in behaviour might be supported by a
reduction in departmentally based targets and the creation of a cross-departmental
development budget. More generally a movement towards devolved structures
will require people to improve their relationship management skills if they are
to retain the 'business' of other internal 'customers' who now have the choice
to source from an external third party. They need to spend more time with managers in the operating divisions in order to understand their needs better and
to improve the service levels to the best that could be provided by an external
supplier.

Another challenge is whether some HR issues (e.g. recruitment, training) should
reside in the organisation or be bought in from specialist suppliers (e.g. consultants). External agencies will have the advantage of a wider experience and
knowledge of best practice but the disadvantage of being unfamiliar with the
detailed circumstances of specific organisations.

9.2.4 Implications for managers

The various separate points about the relationship between business strategies
and people have been brought together and summarised in the model shown in
Exhibit 9.3. This model has important implications both to managers and those
responsible for HR strategies in organisations on how an organisation gains
competitive advantage from people:

● There must be activities to ensure the *maintenance* of competitiveness. This is
  about ensuring that people are able to support the strategies of an organisation in the short term: for example, objective setting, performance appraisal,
  rewards and training.

● Simultaneously there must be activities to provide a *platform on which new
  strategies can be built* in the longer term: for example, leadership, culture, competences and organisation development. The management of these longer-term
  issues might create opportunities for significant *transformations* in strategy and
  competitiveness.

Exhibit 9.3   Competitive advantage through people

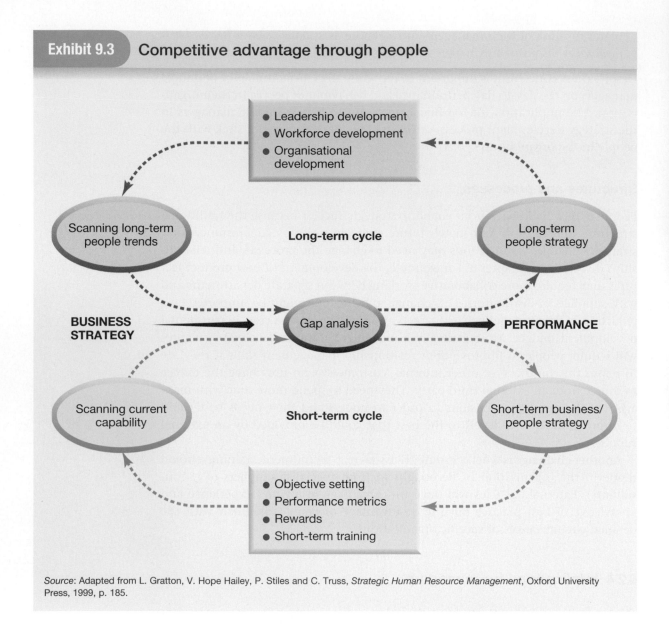

Source: Adapted from L. Gratton, V. Hope Hailey, P. Stiles and C. Truss, *Strategic Human Resource Management*, Oxford University Press, 1999, p. 185.

● These two 'cycles' of activities must be *linked*. Achieving short-term delivery goals must not be at the expense of longer-term capability. For example, using reward systems as the main tool to stimulate short-term success – say, through individual bonus schemes – may compromise the ability to take more radical and strategic interventions, such as the creation of new roles and relationships to enable a more innovative organisation. It is also important to connect these activities to a particular strategy. In these ways, the feedback processes and redirection of both business and people-related issues can occur.

● Those organisations that are *competent in managing these processes* are likely to gain competitive advantage. Others run the risk of failing to deliver successful business strategies for one or more of the following reasons:

   – The *HR strategies* are out of line with the overall business strategy.

- *People's competences and/or behaviours* are out of line with either HR strategies and/or business strategies.
- *Business strategies* are failing to capitalise on the strengths of an organisation's capabilities (Chapter 3) and/or culture (behaviours) (Chapter 4).

9.3   MANAGING INFORMATION[11]

In the early 21st century, knowledge creation and information management are issues at the front of managers' minds as potential sources of improved competitiveness, as discussed in Chapter 3 and in the introduction to this chapter. Within this wider agenda, considerations have naturally focused on IT and the extent to which it can transform competitiveness. But therein lies the danger that was flagged up in the introduction to this chapter. IT and information systems start to take on a purpose of their own – disconnected from the organisation's strategies. From a strategic point of view the issue is the extent to which improvements in information processing capability (through IT and information systems) can improve and assist the way in which knowledge is created and shared both

---

Exhibit 9.4   Strategy and information

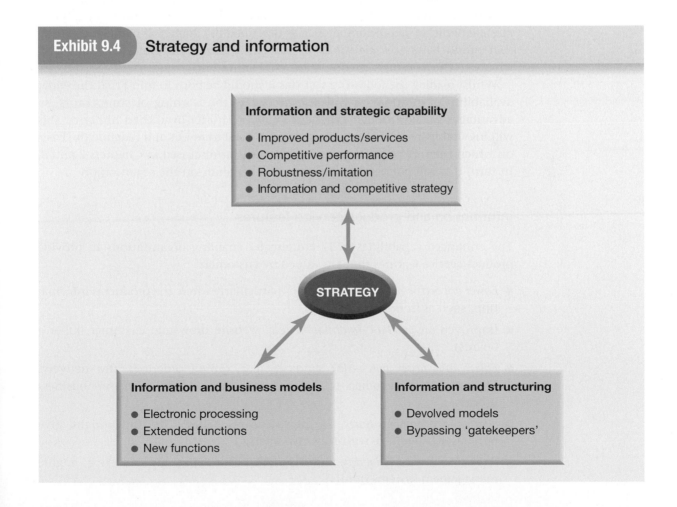

Information and strategic capability

- Improved products/services
- Competitive performance
- Robustness/imitation
- Information and competitive strategy

STRATEGY

Information and business models

- Electronic processing
- Extended functions
- New functions

Information and structuring

- Devolved models
- Bypassing 'gatekeepers'

within and around an organisation. Chapter 3 made the important point that not all of this knowledge will be captured in systems. Indeed, the tacit knowledge embedded in organisations is difficult to capture yet is usually the basis on which competitive advantage is built. This will be reflected in the discussions in this section, which will look at three main connections between information, IT developments and strategy (see Exhibit 9.4):

- information and *strategic capability* – particularly the impact of IT and information systems developments on core competences (as discussed in Chapter 3);
- information and changing *business models* within and across industries and sectors;
- information and *structures/management processes* (as discussed in Chapter 8).

9.3.1 Information and strategic capability

Chapter 3 explained the concept of strategic capability and the way in which it might depend on organisational competences. Information strategies can have a profound influence on creating and destroying the core competences that underpin competitive advantage (see Illustration 9.3). This will be demonstrated by looking at examples of how information and IT might impact on three important 'elements' of a core competence as described in Chapter 3, namely: ensuring that products/services *are valued by customers*, *outperform competitors* and contribute to the *robustness* of competences (to imitation).

Whilst reading the following sections it should be born in mind that the wider availability of information will also accelerate the learning of competitors, so advantages gained through experience may be shorter-lived than hitherto. This will inevitably mean that organisations will need to revisit and redefine the basis on which they are competing more frequently, as discussed in Chapters 2 and 5. In turn, this will put yet more information demands on the organisation.

Information and product/service features

The enhanced capabilities of IT are already enabling organisations to provide product/service features that are valued by customers:

- *Lower prices* (through reduced costs) – particularly where the product is information, such as in financial services.
- Improved *pre-purchase information* (e.g. website browsing, customer bulletin boards).
- *Easier and faster purchasing processes* (e.g. online ordering) and delivery. This can allow customers to move closer to just-in-time with *their* business processes.
- *Shorter development times* for new features. These, in turn, might give purchasers advantage with *their* customers.
- *Product or service reliability* and diagnostics are being improved (e.g. engine management systems in cars).

- *Personalised products* or services are increasingly being offered without price premium (e.g. customising computer architecture for each purchaser).
- Improved *after-sales service* can be provided by better information systems (e.g. automatic service reminders).

The strategic importance of this list is that if customers value some or all of these improved features and if competitors learn quickly how to provide them by exploiting information and IT, then the threshold standards that need to be achieved to survive in a market will rise rapidly. So providers who are unable to deliver these higher standards will fall out of the market.

Information and competitive performance

Chapter 3 reminded readers that competitiveness and standards of performance are determined not just within a particular industry or sector. Customer expectations of service standards, for example on speed or reliability, become the universal benchmarks crossing all industries and public services. So, for example, public service providers become 'compelled' to develop websites because the expectations of the general public have been raised through their dealings with the private sector.

One of the most important implications of the IT revolution for organisations producing or distributing physical products is that, in future, competitive advantage is more likely to be achieved through service performance (e.g. speed and reliability of delivery or maintenance) than in product features *per se*. So managers need to conceive of their business not as a product company with support services but as a service company which supplies a product. This is a profound mind-set shift for some managers when considering which competences are most crucial to competitive performance. Their ability to process information and to build their market knowledge becomes much more important than previously.

Paradoxically there are lessons in reverse to be learnt from the high mortality rate of 'dot.com' start-up companies in the early 2000s. Competence in information management is not enough. A capability in the logistics of both the supply and distribution chains is also an essential requirement – particularly for companies dealing in tangible products. Since this will usually require premises this phenomenon has been dubbed the need for both 'bricks and clicks'.[12]

Another implication of enhanced information processing capability is that, at least for a period of time, competitive advantage might be gained by organisations that are able to use this capability to build a much more detailed knowledge of the market. This knowledge results from competences in analysing the subtle differences between customer needs in different parts of the market and building product or service features to meet these needs (as mentioned in Chapters 2 and 5). Most organisations now have colossal amounts of raw data about these issues and the IT processing capacity to analyse the data (both of which are necessary). But they are not good at this data-mining process, which will convert data into market knowledge. **Data mining**[13] is the process of finding trends, patterns and connections in data in order to inform and improve competitive performance. For example, building up individual customer purchasing history as a basis

Data mining is the process of finding trends, patterns and connections in data in order to inform and improve competitive performance

Illustration 9.3   strategy into action

Dabs.com takes on the high street retailers

E-commerce can allow small companies to compete with the major names in their sector.

In October 2003 Dabs.com won the e-trading award in *The Sunday Times* e-commerce awards – for businesses with less than 250 employees. Dabs.com was an electrical goods retailer based in Bolton, UK, which began in 1987 as a mail order supplier. But soon after launching its e-commerce website in 2000 it wound down its telephone-sales team and moved to 100 per cent online trading. In three years sales tripled to £151m (about €200m) – all financed from its own earnings and without increasing staff numbers from 230. The company aimed to continue this rapid growth at the expense of the high street retailers (such as Dixons) and through expansion into mainland Europe's online markets. This was a big challenge. Online purchases held only 5 per cent of the market and they received less generous terms from manufacturers who were worried about fuelling a major price war for their goods.

But Dabs felt that its e-commerce model had advantages that high street shops would find difficult to match. Its website allowed for almost instant changes in price to reflect market conditions. The site also allowed for 'streaming' of video images to provide the potential purchaser with demonstrations of products. This was popular with manufacturers as it ensured that a product was always presented in the way Dabs wanted rather than relying on half-hearted efforts from shop assistants. In 2004 Dabs was going a step further with the launch of its own technology TV channel on the Sky Network. Manufacturers would fund the programming and consumers could place orders through their TV sets. This gave access to a wide range of customers who had either cable or

satellite TV but not the internet on a computer. Search engines (such as Google) were also another major driver of growth – accounting for about 25 per cent of Dabs' business. These engines used a 'pay per click' charging model.

The plans for European expansion included a target of €100m of sales in France alone within three years. The risks were higher than UK expansion but start-up costs were a fraction of the equivalent 'bricks and mortar' development. Perhaps the biggest surprise to observers of Dobs' impressive growth was that for the very first time it did open a retail outlet – at Liverpool airport. Since brand awareness was crucial the firm argued that the shop was designed for this purpose. 4.5 million people passed through Liverpool airport each year. Dabs had plans for five more stores which had to break even, engage with passers-by and, most importantly, give consumers an incentive to buy online.

Source: *The Sunday Times*, 12 October 2003.

Questions

1. List the relative advantages and disadvantages of purchasing online as against through a shop *from the consumer's perspective*.
2. What is Dabs doing to increase the advantages and reduce the disadvantages compared to retail shops?
3. What else could it do?

for targeting promotional offers (as many websites are now doing); identifying connected purchases (for example, readers of particular newspapers or magazines have similar purchasing patterns for other goods and services); or simply finding underlying drivers of demand (such as demographic factors as discussed in Chapter 2). Data mining can also help with profitability analysis as a basis for creating priorities for customer retention. In financial services data mining can also help with credit risk assessment, customer attrition forecasts and detection of fraud.

Information and robustness

Chapter 3 (section 3.4.3) considered several reasons why resources or competences might be robust. Information processing capability can have an influence on any of these factors – hence changing the vulnerability of an organisation to imitation of its core competences.

- First, a resource or competence might be *rare*. When IT infrastructure costs were high this used to be a reason why a few larger organisations gained advantage over others through their IT infrastructure and competences. Others could not afford the capital costs. On the whole, this is no longer true. IT is now pervasive even in very small companies. However, information itself might be rare – whether this be about product, processes or markets.

- Core competences may also be difficult to imitate because they are *complex*. Here the situation has moved on. The mastery of the hardware and standard software needed to build information systems used to be complex – now it is not. The current areas of complexity are more in data-mining activities (discussed above) and the activities which underpin speed to market. Managing relationships in the value network (see Chapter 3, section 3.6.1) is an area where 'e-relationship management'[14] with customers can be particularly important (i.e. joining up all the different routes through which customers interface with a company).

- Core competences may be robust because of *causal ambiguity* – competitors find it hard to understand the reasons why an organisation is successful. This is because the competences are embedded in the way the organisation works and are not explicit. Many IT developments – particularly intelligent systems – are essentially concerned with attempting to codify the tacit knowledge in organisations to make it explicit. For example, helplines use every customer query and its solution to progressively build up knowledge as to what can go wrong with a product and how it is solved. This ability to codify previously tacit knowledge removes barriers to imitation and undermines core competences. Of course, some types of organisational knowledge are difficult to codify – such as intuition and experience which is shared knowledge based on interactions across many parts of an organisation – the 'ways of doing things'. As mentioned in the introduction to this section, there is a danger in becoming over-dependent on systems and ignoring tacit knowledge simply because it is difficult to codify and build into the system. But this is the very reason why it is difficult to imitate and may be crucial to competitive advantage.

Information and competitive strategy

The strategic role of information in organisations will need to be different depending on the way in which the organisation is positioning its products or services in the market (as described by the strategy clock from Chapter 5 – Exhibit 5.2). Competence in information management also might be the platform for new bases of competition through the creation of different product/service features. Since larger organisations will tend to have a collection of strategic business units pursuing different strategies, there must be the information capability to support all SBUs but in different ways. The role of information in enabling different competitive strategies could be as follows:

- *Routinisation* (positions 1 and 2 on the strategy clock) – where the role of information, usually through IT systems, is to reduce drastically the cost of transactions with customers, suppliers or channels. For example, by moving the customer towards self-service (e.g. websites replacing face-to-face selling).

- *Mass customisation* (position 3 on the strategy clock) – where information systems can create more product features that are valued (as discussed above) at the same or lower price. This is a major battleground in many sectors at the present time – such as consumer electronics.

- *Customisation* (positions 4 and 5 on the strategy clock) – where information can be provided to customers (say, through websites) in advance of any face-to-face or telephone contact, which is reserved for advising a much more knowledgeable potential customer.

- *The IT laggards* – who do not value the features that IT-based systems can offer and will remain significant parts of the market in most sectors. This provides a continuing opportunity for those providers who are especially good at providing information in more traditional ways, for example personal face-to-face service.

9.3.2 Information and changing business models

A **business model** describes the structure of product, service and information flows and the roles of the participating parties

The impact that information processing capability has on the competences to undertake activities and business processes (as exemplified above) is transforming the way in which organisations build their relationships with others in their value network (as discussed in section 3.6.1). This is concerned with how business models[15] are changing in both the private and public sectors. A **business model** describes the structure of product, service and information flows and the roles of the participating parties. This includes potential benefits and sources of revenue to each of the parties. The value chain framework discussed in section 3.6.1 can be used to identify many traditional business models. For example, the linear supply chain from component manufacturers, to finished product assemblers, primary distributors, retailers and finally the consumer. Even in this case – where the product 'flows' in a linear fashion through the chain – information and other services may exist in branches of the chain. For example, market research and after-sales service may be undertaken by other parties from outside this linear chain. Exhibit 9.5 shows how e-commerce models are emerging out of traditional business models based on the degree of *innovation* from traditional approaches and the *complexity* (mainly the level of integration of activities). It can be seen that IT is impacting in three main ways:

- By *replacing physical or paper-based processes with electronic processes*. For example, *e-shops* move marketing and 'display' to websites. *E-procurement* moves tendering, negotiation and purchasing processes to websites. In both cases the advantages are in reduced costs and wider choice. An *e-mall* takes the concept a little further by creating a collection of e-shops with a common umbrella – such as a brand.

Exhibit 9.5	New business models

		Degree of innovation		
		Same as before	Extended	New
Degree of integration	Single function	E-shop E-procurement	E-auction Value chain services (e.g. payment systems, logistics) Trust services	Information brokerage (e.g. search engines)
	Integrated functions	E-mall	Third-party marketplace (e.g. web hosting)	Virtual communities Collaboration platforms Value chain integrator

Source: Adapted from P. Timmers, *Electronic Commerce*, Wiley, 2000, Chapter 3.

- By significantly *extending the functions* that traditional business models can offer. For example, sourcing or selling through *e-auctions* is both easy and cheap and can lead to significantly reduced purchasing costs or increased revenues. *Trust services* (such as supplier or customer certification or vetting) extend the types of information services available to members of trade associations. Other information functions in the value chain can be provided more efficiently or effectively by *value chain service specialists* – such as payments or logistics. Some organisations see benefits in leaving a number of value chain activities to specialists who create *third-party marketplaces* and may offer web-based marketing, branding, payment systems, logistics and so on. This could be viewed as a complementary route to market rather than a complete replacement.

- Models which are *transformational* in the sense that business can only be done this way electronically. So it could be argued that the first two categories above are little more than the exploitation of IT to enable improvements in the efficiency and effectiveness of information processing within 'old' business models. Perhaps the most well-established example of transformational changes is the *information brokerage* role of companies like Yahoo! or Google with their search engines. *Virtual communities* can be sustained by IT – as Amazon tries to do in bringing authors, readers and publishers into dialogue on their website. Sometimes IT can provide a *collaboration platform*, for example allowing customers and suppliers to work together on product design using specialist IT design tools. *Value chain integration* may be made possible through IT if separate activities can be knitted together by faster and more reliable information flows. For example, sales staff can discuss requirements with customers using both 'real-time' information about manufacturing capability, availability and production scheduling and also 'straight-through' information about the same issues in the supply chain. Sometimes integration allows customers to change their specification and delivery schedules themselves – which then automatically reconfigures requirements back in the supply chain.

From a strategic point of view the important considerations of any of these e-commerce business models is the extent to which they are able to create better value for money for customers. In doing so they will threaten the position of some organisations and provide opportunities to others – including new entrants. For example, Dell Computers'[16] success (see Illustration 1.1) was built on its ability to act more quickly and more flexibly than competitors. This was possible through its 'choice' of business model – direct sale and build-to-order hence cutting out a number of intermediary roles in the value chain. But to suggest that IT will always lead to the demise of intermediaries is not true. Some intermediary roles will be redundant, as customers are able to gather information more freely and 'talk' directly to potential suppliers. At the same time, new intermediary roles will be spawned if they add value or reduce cost. Many of the roles discussed above have that potential, such as third-party marketplaces, virtual communities or information brokerage.

Illustration 9.4 uses the five forces framework from Chapter 2 (Exhibit 2.5) to summarise some of the impacts of these changing business models on the competitive position of organisations.

9.3.3 Information and structuring

Chapter 8 was concerned with organising to create and support successful strategies. Improvements in information processing capability are making a significant contribution to better ways of organising. But how information is managed needs to fit the organisational approach and vice versa. A few examples illustrate this point:

- Organisations configured as a centralised bureaucracy (close to Goold and Campbell's *strategic planning* – see Exhibit 8.11) must deliver routinised business processes, which reduce cost whilst maintaining threshold quality levels. It has already been pointed out in the previous chapter that organisations competing with low-price strategies (positions 1 or 2 on the strategy clock, Exhibit 5.2) may find a centralised bureaucratic configuration to be appropriate. As mentioned above, IT can facilitate this cost reduction through routinisation whilst also enabling quite complex coordination.

- At the corporate centre of highly devolved organisations (operating close to Goold and Campbell's *financial control* – Exhibit 8.12) there is less concern with complex coordination and a requirement for accurate and timely information about the performance of business units against pre-agreed targets. This is the core of the relationship between the corporate centre and the business units.

- In the middle ground of *strategic control* (see Exhibit 8.13) information may assist in a number of ways. First, bottom-up business planning from business units is likely to be important and the corporate centre needs to be able to

Illustration 9.4 · strategy into action

Information technology and the five competitive forces

Information technology can transform the competitive forces in an industry.

In Chapter 2, the five forces framework was introduced as a way of mapping out the competitive forces in an industry.

New entrants

Barriers to entry may be raised because of the up-front investment needed to operate and compete – although this continues to decline. More importantly, incumbents may have tied suppliers and/or customers into their particular systems, creating inertia to change. Barriers may be lowered for a number of the reasons mentioned below, such as better-informed consumers leading to less customer loyalty.

Power of suppliers

A major threat for many organisations is that their suppliers are able to forward integrate using IT and take over some or all of the functions undertaken by the organisation. This is particularly threatening for intermediaries – such as travel agents – where IT is increasing the number of companies dealing directly with the end customers. But suppliers may have power without forward integration, in particular where they own the 'technology platform' around which a business's systems and operations are built. Microsoft's Windows operating system is still hugely powerful in this respect.

Power of buyers

It has been claimed that one of the most important social impacts of the internet is to empower consumers by giving them easy access to market information and, therefore, making them more knowledgeable and discerning consumers. The same would apply to business-to-business transactions – e-auctions being an obvious example.

Substitutes

IT is impacting at all three levels of substitution. It is creating direct product-for-product substitution (e.g. internet vs. branch banking). But it is also substituting the need for certain products and services as consumers are able to undertake those tasks themselves using IT software packages (e.g. some legal services) or satisfy the need in a different way (e.g. teleconferencing instead of business travel). At the level of generic substitution, IT hardware, software and IT-related services are capturing a growing percentage of consumer spending – at the expense of sectors whose products/services are seen as less exciting.

Competitive rivalry

As consumers become more knowledgeable about the offerings of different providers it is driving many markets to be commodity-like – in the sense that consumers regard the offerings as much the same. Of course, IT can assist providers in their attempts to differentiate themselves from competitors – largely in terms of improved service. But IT software and systems are widely available to competitors – so they may catch up quickly. So IT is fuelling hypercompetition, as discussed in Chapters 2 and 5.

Questions

1. Choose an organisation with which you are familiar (or one of the case studies in this book) and analyse how IT will impact on each of the five forces in its industry.

2. What are the implications for the organisation's future strategies?

coordinate and reconcile these plans. High-quality reliable information is needed to support those processes. Second, it may be that parts of the organisation have customer–supplier relationships with each other – perhaps in an internal market. This too requires high-quality information. Finally, information is required about the performance of business units and of the corporate centre.

Gatekeepers are
individuals or groups who
gain power from their
control of information

- Better information can allow managers and external stakeholders to bypass some of the traditional **gatekeepers**, who gained power from their control of information. Within organisations, many middle management roles have been as information conduits between the senior managers and the front line. IT-based systems can create direct communication between the top and the bottom of an organisation and many chief executives are introducing their own websites for that purpose. (Readers are reminded that middle managers play other important roles in the strategy of their organisation as well as being information gatekeepers (see section 9.2.3 above).) The same issues also apply to the bypassing of unions as information conduits to employees. Also externally the salesforce is no longer the primary route through which customers gain their product knowledge or even place orders. Their role will move from 'closing deals' to relationship management and advice. In the public sector politicians are able to put in place two-way communication with their communities rather than relying on managers as the conduit and filter. There are already challenging implications for the whole way in which the political and service provision processes work.

In summary, IT is creating a world with fewer 'gatekeepers' – so flattened structures, with more direct communication of strategy to and from the front line and more direct interaction at much lower levels across the organisation (and with external stakeholders). But this interaction is informed by a common database and 'regulated' by guidelines or rules within these information systems. It is also a world where the key decision makers are much better informed about the impact of past strategies and outside influences through the accumulation of knowledge from the front line on day-to-day issues like customer queries (for example, on help lines).

9.3.4 Implications for managers[17]

There are two main implications of these previous discussions for managers and those responsible for information strategy in organisations, as follows:

- Managers need to realise that information processing capability can *transform* the organisation, not just fine-tune current strategies and processes. They need to move away from seeing information management as a support function and place it on a par with other business functions.
- Information managers need to understand the *full potential of IT* from their professional knowledge and external networks (i.e. be the company benchmarker). They need to understand the limitations of IT too – for example, it cannot replace certain types of knowledge (such as intuition). Nor can it replace knowledge sharing that depends on social contact. They need to be involved in and credible on business strategy as part of the corporate team (and not sit on the sidelines) and to see new business opportunities that IT could open up. They also need to have the influencing skills to educate and persuade senior colleagues about these opportunities.

9.4 MANAGING FINANCE[18]

Finance and the way that it is managed can be a key determinant of strategic success. From a shareholder's point of view, what matters is the cash-generating capability of the business since this determines the ability to pay dividends in the short term and to reinvest for the future (which, in turn, should enable a future flow of dividend payments). The public sector equivalent is the need to deliver best value within financial limits. However, as highlighted in previous sections in this chapter, strategic success – in this case enabled through good financial management – cannot be achieved through a set of 'rules' and priorities which apply in equal measure to all organisations and at all times. The relationship between finance and strategic success is dependent on context. Nonetheless, there are three broad issues that organisations of all types face (see Exhibit 9.6):

Exhibit 9.6   **Strategy and finance**

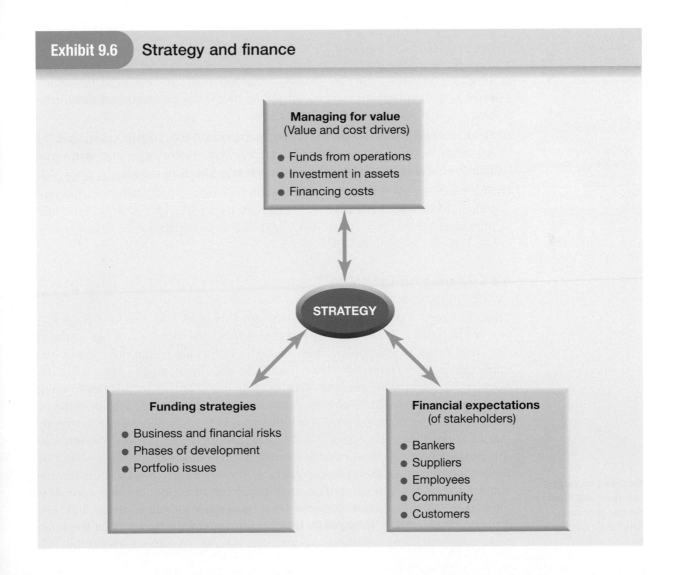

Exhibit 9.7	The determinants of value creation

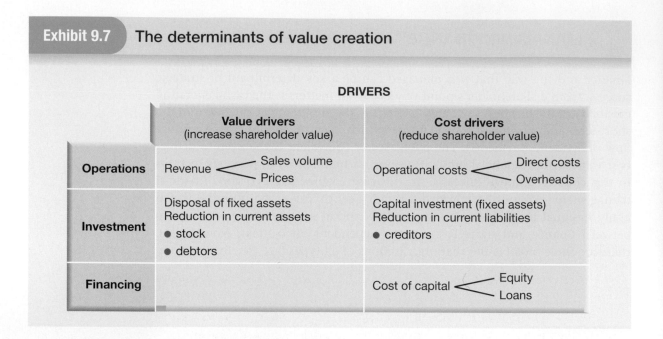

> ● *Managing for value*, whether this is concerned with creating value for share-holders or ensuring the best use of public money, is an important considera-tion for, and responsibility of, managers.
>
> ● *Funding* strategic developments is clearly important too: in particular, that the nature of the funding is appropriate for the type of strategy – and vice versa. This is concerned with balancing business and financial risks.
>
> ● The *financial expectations* of stakeholders will vary – both between different stakeholders and in relation to different strategies. This should influence managers in both strategy development and implementation.

9.4.1 Managing for value[19]

There has been a continuing theme through this book that the long-term suc-cess of strategies is determined by the extent to which they deliver best value in the eyes of major stakeholders. Two examples of this are competitiveness in the marketplace (i.e. value to customers) and the ability to provide value to share-holders (through the returns they receive in dividend and share price movement – see section 7.4.2). In competitive markets these two issues are likely to be closely linked in the long term since the returns to shareholders are driven by market success. However, this broad connection between competitiveness and shareholder value needs exploring further. Shareholder value is determined by the long-term cash-generating capability of the organisation which, in turn, is determined by the ways in which a wide number of factors are managed. It is important that managers understand what 'managing for value' means and how it might be achieved.[20] **Managing for value** is concerned with maximising the long-term cash-generating capability of an organisation. As shown in Exhibit 9.7,

Managing for value is concerned with maximising the long-term cash-generating capability of an organisation

value creation is determined by three main issues: funds from operations, investment in (or disposal of) assets, and financing costs.

- *Funds from operations* are clearly a major contributor to value creation. In the long term, this concerns the extent to which the organisation is operating profitably. This is determined by:
  - Sales revenue – made up of sales volume and the prices that the organisation is able to maintain in its markets.
  - 'Production' and selling costs – both made up of fixed and variable elements.
  - Overhead or indirect costs.
- *Investment in assets* – the extent to which assets and working capital are being stretched is also a key consideration. Some organisations have developed competences in supporting much higher levels of business from the same asset base than others. This will affect value creation as follows:
  - The costs of capital investment or, in some cases, the disposal of redundant assets.
  - The management of the elements of working capital such as stock, debtors and creditors will increase or decrease shareholder value as indicated.
- *Financing costs* – the mix of capital in the business – between debt (requiring interest payments) and equity will determine the cost of capital (and also the financial risk).

The issues in the public sector are very similar. The problem for most public sector managers is that their financial responsibilities are usually confined to managing their budget (i.e. the cash outflows of operations). They will usually be doing this with little understanding of the other financial issues from the diagram, which will be managed by the corporate financial function. There is a real need for managers to be much more familiar with the impact of their day-to-day management decisions on the wider financial health of the organisation; for example, the use of fixed assets or the incurring of bad debts.

Key value and cost drivers

It is not the intention in this book to discuss the detailed issues concerning the management of each of the separate items shown in Exhibit 9.7. From a business strategy point of view the critical issue is to understand what are the **key value and cost drivers**. These are the factors that have most influence on the cash generation capability of an organisation. The value chain concept (section 3.6.1) is important in helping managers understand how and where value may be created within an organisation and in the wider value network. Importantly, it is likely that costs and value creation are spread *unevenly* across the activities in the value chain and value network. So some activities are more crucial to value (or cost) creation than others. However, this will vary with the type of business and with the circumstances in which it is operating, as will be seen below. Financial analysis can sharpen up an understanding of the significance of this by quantification of *value drivers* (which drive cash inflows) and *cost drivers* (which drive cash outflows).

Key value and cost drivers are the factors that have most influence on the cash generation cabability of an organisation

Some examples illustrate the importance of this identification of key cost and value drivers:

● *Sources of capital* are usually of major importance, for two reasons. The cost of capital is a major cost driver and will vary with source. So the relative cash outflows which result from servicing loans as against equity would be an important strategic consideration. However, debt and equity also bear different levels of risk. So the gearing of an organisation should also be determined by the financial and business risks. This will be discussed more fully in section 9.4.3 below.

● *Capital expenditure* (capex) can be a major cash outflow that can destroy shareholder value unless it contributes to improving the revenues or reducing the costs elsewhere in Exhibit 9.7. In principle, the business cases for capex items should address this issue before expenditure is approved. Commonly the case for expenditure would relate to *enhanced product features* leading to increased sales and/or better prices; or *reduced costs* (for example, through increased labour productivity) or *decreased working capital* (for example, through stock reduction by streamlining production or distribution). New capital expenditure increases the *capital intensity* of the business, which will affect both the fixed asset turnover and the ratio of fixed to variable costs and hence the relative importance of sales volume.

● The detailed *cost structure* of businesses varies considerably from sector to sector and hence the relative importance of specific cost items. As mentioned above, cost and value creation are spread unevenly through the activities in the value chain. For example, service organisations are generally more labour intensive than manufacturing – underlining the importance of wage levels. Retailers are concerned with stock turnover and sales volume per square metre – reflecting two major cost drivers.

● Sometimes the crucial cost or value drivers are *outside the organisation* (in the supply or distribution chain). The strategic implication is that organisations need to be competent in maintaining the performance of key suppliers or distributors. This means the ability to select, motivate and 'control' suppliers and distributors. It may also mean a reconsideration as to whether any of these activities should be taken 'in house' if they are so critically important to cost and value creation. This was discussed in Chapters 3 and 8 (outsourcing). Since suppliers' prices are the buyers' costs, there may also be an unevenness in the shareholder value creation being achieved by different organisations in the value network. This may be a result of the relative *bargaining power* of suppliers and buyers (as discussed in the five forces framework – section 2.3.1). For example, a manufacturer simultaneously facing a scarcity of supply of a raw material and powerful distributors for their product will find it difficult to maintain shareholder value creation. Since supply costs and product prices may be dictated by others, shareholder value creation will need to centre on managing the costs of in-house activities and/or the other items listed above (cost of capital and investment costs).

● The *type of strategy* being pursued is also important since this shifts the 'mix' of cost and value needed to support a competitive product or service. It may be that an organisation is successfully differentiating itself from its competitors by extra spending in selected areas (e.g. advertising). Provided this spending results in added value (possibly through prices) or relative cost reductions elsewhere (say in production costs through greater volume from increased sales), this may well be a defensible cost.

● The key cost and value drivers may change *over time*. For example, during the introduction of a new product, the key factor may be establishing *sales volume*; once established, *prices and unit costs* might be most important; during decline, improving cash flow through *stock and debtor reduction* may be essential to support the introduction of the next generation of products.

Overall, the message is that managers can benefit considerably from a detailed understanding of the value creation processes within their organisation and the wider value network – it can help them be more strategic in how they prioritise their efforts for performance improvement. Illustration 9.5 shows how one organisation did just this.

9.4.2 Funding strategy development[21]

In all organisations managers need to decide how the organisation will be financed and strategic developments supported. These decisions will be influenced by ownership – for example, whether the business is privately held or publicly quoted – and by the overall corporate goals of the organisation. For example, there will be a different financial need if a business is seeking rapid growth by acquisition or development of new products compared with if it is seeking to consolidate its past performance. This section uses the growth/share matrix (see Exhibit 6.8) to illustrate how financial strategies need to vary for the different 'phases' of development of a business unit – see Exhibit 9.8.

This is just one example of how financial and business strategies need to match and is concerned with the relationship between financial risk and financial return to investors. The greater the risk to shareholders or lenders, the greater the return these investors will require. Therefore, from an organisation's point of view, the important issue is how they should balance the business risk with the financial risk to the organisation. Debt brings greater financial risk than equity since it carries an obligation to pay interest. As a generalisation, the greater the business risk the lower should be the financial risk taken by the organisation, and the growth/share matrix is a convenient way of illustrating this:

● *Question marks* (or *problem children*)[22] are clearly high business risk. They are at the beginning of their life cycle and are not yet established in their markets; moreover, they are likely to require substantial investment. For those who wish to invest in them, therefore, there is a need to understand the nature of risk and a desire to seek high returns. A stand-alone business in this situation might, for example, seek to finance such growth from specialists in this kind of investment, such as venture capitalists who, themselves, seek to offset risk by having a portfolio of such investments. The 'dot.com' boom and bust of the late 1990s showed that major mistakes can be made by both investors and start-up companies themselves. The major lessons for investors were that new

Illustration 9.5

strategy into action

Managing for shareholder value at Cadbury Schweppes plc: the journey continues

Companies use 'managing for value' as a platform for improving their performance.

In 1996, Cadbury Schweppes set out an explicit corporate objective of delivering superior returns to shareowners. Between then and 2000 there was a concerted push across the company to embed the core financial, strategic and operational disciplines required by value-based businesses. These developments produced significant improvements in performance for shareowners. However, it became clear to the management team that they needed to find and exploit new opportunities for profitable growth in order to sustain and expand their success.

At the heart of their hunt for profitable growth lay a belief that managing for value is '20 per cent about the numbers and 80 per cent about the people'. Bob Stack – the Group Chief HR Officer – and his team were central in the creation and delivery of a number of programmes aimed at driving up performance by improving the understanding, capability and motivation of the top 200 managers across the company. Their key programmes included:

● 'Unlocking Good Growth' – which helped managers to develop deep insights about consumers and about how consumer-focused innovation could help Cadbury to serve those consumers more effectively.

● A 'Sales and Marketing Academy' was introduced. It educated managers in the use of consistent, value-based tools and techniques for improving and leveraging commercial capabilities. It set common standards for performance across the business.

● A 'Cadbury Purpose and Value' statement was developed and communicated widely. This set out a clear framework for the strategic intent of the company and how it wanted to conduct its business. This included re-designing the corporate imagery and communication materials to align them better with the core corporate purpose of 'working together to create brands people love'.

Two additional organisational initiatives were essential parts of the overall package. These were the seamless transition to a new CEO and the move to a more global organisation structure. This reorganisation was driven – in part – by the need to integrate a number of corporate acquisitions, including that of the Adams confectionery business, a global business based in the USA. It also gave rise to a global cost and efficiency initiative, 'Fuel for Growth', which was established to exploit the growth and synergy benefits that became accessible with a more global organisation.

The work by Cadbury is a fine example of 'using structure and HR to drive business behaviour'. Top line growth increased to an average of 14 per cent during the period 2000–2003; and Total Returns to Shareholders were significantly above the average for the FTSE 100.

Prepared by Professor John Barbour, Corporate Value Improvement Ltd.

Questions

1. If managing for value is indeed '20 per cent about the numbers and 80 per cent about the people' then why do many companies focus their efforts in managing for value on the analysis of data?

2. Why don't more companies use their HR functions as key drivers of the business?

3. How should managing for value be seen in the context of broader corporate imperatives and responsibilities?

Exhibit 9.8   **Funding strategies in different circumstances**

GROWTH (Stars)		LAUNCH (Question marks)	
Business risk:	*High*	Business risk:	*Very high*
Financial risk needs to be:	*Low*	Financial risk needs to be:	*Very low*
Funding by:	*Equity* (growth investors)	Funding by:	*Equity* (venture capital)
Dividends:	*Nominal*	Dividends:	*Zero*
MATURITY (Cash cows)		**DECLINE (Dogs)**	
Business risk:	*Medium*	Business risk:	*Low*
Financial risk can be:	*Medium*	Financial risk can be:	*High*
Funding by:	*Debt and equity* (retaining earnings)	Funding by:	*Debt*
Dividends:	*High*	Dividends:	*Total*

Source: Adapted from K. Ward, *Corporate Financial Strategy*, Butterworth/Heinemann, 1993, Chapter 2.

types of business need to be judged on their own merits and realistic time scales for returns on investment should be set. The lessons for companies were that they should be realistic about the investment requirements and payback periods and not be stampeded into excessive short-term spending (e.g. on marketing) in an attempt to show short-term results that are not sustainable. Many business start-ups are also wary of venture capital companies fearing that they will lose control of their company and/or sensitive information will be leaked to competitors. Schemes for private investors (so-called 'business angels') have become popular for these reasons.

● In the case of *stars* the degree of business risk remains high in these high-growth situations even though relatively high market shares are being achieved. The market position here remains volatile and probably highly competitive. It could be that a business has been financed on the basis of venture capital initially, but as it grows and becomes established it needs to seek other financing. Since the main attractions to investors here are the product or business concept and the prospect of future earnings, equity capital is likely to be appropriate; a business might seek to raise equity by public flotation.

● Businesses that operate in mature markets with high shares (*cash cows*) should be generating regular and substantial surpluses. Here the business risk is lower and the opportunity for retained earnings is high, and in the case of a portfolio of businesses, the corporation may be seeking to recycle such a surplus into its growth businesses. In these circumstances, it may make sense to raise finance through debt capital as well as equity, since reliable returns can be used to service such debt and, in any case, the return expected by lenders is likely to be less than that expected by those providing equity. (Since interest on debt has to be repaid, the financial risk for the business itself is higher than with equity finance, so it is also reasonable for the business to expect the cost of debt to be lower than with equity.) Provided increased debt (*gearing* or *leverage*) does not lead to an unacceptable level of risk, this cheaper debt funding will in fact increase the residual profits achieved by a company in these circumstances. The danger is that an organisation overstretches itself, takes on too much debt, increases its financial risk by so doing, suffers a downturn in its markets and is unable to service its interest payments.

● If a business is in decline, in effect a *dog*, then equity finance will be difficult to attract. However, borrowing may be possible if secured against residual assets in the business. At this stage, it is likely that the emphasis in the business will be on cost cutting, and it could well be that the cash flows from such businesses are quite strong. These businesses may provide relatively low-risk investments.

Illustration 9.6 shows how funding sources need to match circumstances.

Exhibit 9.8 also shows that dividend policy might need to change with the nature of the business. In the launch phase investors may be mainly concerned with growth potential and cash will be limited for dividend payments. This would still be largely true during growth – though some dividend payments may be needed. During maturity the cash flow of the business should be strongly positive; opportunities for reinvestment to create further value may be limited so shareholders might receive most value by dividend payments. During decline the argument for providing shareholder value through dividends is even stronger.

At the corporate level in *diversified* companies there can be a problem in developing a financial strategy for a portfolio with a mix of businesses growing at different rates and in high- or low-share positions. The organisation needs to consider its *overall* risk/return position. For example, organisations that have sought high growth through an acquisitive diversification strategy have suffered because they may be perceived by the investing community as a high (business) risk organisation and they have not been able to put in place appropriate financial strategies; they may have difficulty raising debt capital, and those who provide equity may expect high returns. As a result they have been either unable or unwilling to attract equity investment and have sought to finance growth out of borrowings, in effect relying on ever-growing cash to finance such borrowing. A decline in growth means that debt cannot be serviced and could lead to bankruptcy. The crucial point is that financial strategy of conglomerates should be driven by the nature of the portfolio strategy. For example:

● A company focusing on a portfolio of *high-growth, high-risk investments* in emerging industries would need to have more equity and less debt, as is common with venture capital funded companies.

● A company focusing on a portfolio of *mature cash cow businesses* with reliable cash flows would need the opposite – more debt and less equity.

● A company seeking to develop *new and innovative businesses* on a regular basis might, in effect, be acting as its own venture capitalist, accepting high risk at

Illustration 9.6   strategy into action

High-technology companies struggle for funding

The mix of funding in a business must reflect the nature of the industry 'life cycle'.

Telecommunications

In early 2001 the stock markets around the world had a major 'shakeout' of technology shares. Some companies saw their market valuation drop by 90 per cent from a year before. The companies who really struggled were the smaller operators – such as Kingston Communications, Atlantic and Redstone Telecom in the telecom section and many smaller internet and 'dot.com' companies too. These smaller companies were finding it difficult, if not impossible, to raise debt finance to offset this dramatic fall in their stock market valuation and inject much-needed cash to fund developments in their fiercely competitive sectors. These developments were crucial to their future strategies and included laying infrastructure (such as fibre-optic cables) and brand building.

The chairmen of these small companies were trying to reassure potential investors that they were not building their businesses beyond their capabilities. They had been reshaping their businesses to cut overheads. But most companies were suffering from a drastic change in attitude from their financiers as market conditions changed. In particular, they became especially nervous about the high level of debt being carried by companies – raising questions as to whether the interest payments on this debt could be met. But the owners of the smaller companies were fiercely protective about their independence and were trying to avoid any possibility of being swallowed up by the major telecom companies such as British Telecom. So the speed of business development was dependent on how much finance was available – even to the extent that developments had to come into positive cash flow before services could be extended further.

Computer games

By the mid-2000s the development of computer games had become a major international industry –

dominated by companies in Britain, North America and Japan. But at the beginning of the industry (in the late 1980s) it was largely driven by individual developers writing programs in their bedrooms – it was a cottage industry. Then games cost as little as €6,000 to develop and required just a couple of people – a programmer and an artist. By the early 2000s there were more than 300 games companies in the UK alone. However, by 2004 new titles were costing €3m to develop, needing teams of 30 or more programmers, artists, sound engineers and producers. This clearly had a major impact on the structure of the industry and how games companies were funded. Firms needed to be big to survive. Many of the company founders were choosing to sell out to corporate organisations or go public through share flotations. The Department for Trade and Industry in the UK published a report in 2002 that concluded that the financial sector and government bodies had failed to understand the importance of the games sector and its funding needs. Some companies, such as Rock Star, had been founded in Britain but moved to the USA.

Sources: Adapted from *The Sunday Times*, 18 March 2001; *The Sunday Times*, 12 October 2003

Questions

1. Referring to section 9.4.2 and Exhibit 9.8, explain why many companies ended up with the financial difficulties described above.

2. If you were managing one of these companies, how would you ensure that there was a closer match between company strategy and funding?

the business level and seeking to offset such risk by encouraging new and innovative ideas. If it does so, it should consider whether it has a role to play as those businesses mature, or whether it needs to consider selling them on to other organisations, not least to raise capital for further investment.

Finally, it should be remembered that although the discussion in this section has been concerned with how funding should match strategy, the reverse is a key consideration too. This concerns how strategic developments might be driven by the funding circumstances of the organisation. A number of examples have appeared earlier in this book:

● The *ownership* of an organisation – in particular, whether it is privately owned, publicly quoted, a charity or a public sector organisation will dictate the sources and amounts of funding available. It has previously been seen (Chapter 4) that a common motive for changing the form of ownership is the need to open up new funding sources. Given the tendency for investors to seek short-term returns from publicly quoted companies, private ownership may provide a less pressured environment for investments that are likely to have long pay-back periods. However, ownership may in reality be a limitation on strategic development by dictating the funding environment within which strategy will *actually* develop.

● Although the potential *motives* for an acquisition are varied (as outlined in Chapter 7), often the driving force can be financial rather than strategic; for example, the need to reinvest excess funds or to show continuing growth to hold up share price. So an organisation may get driven into 'unholy alliances' creating all sorts of strategic problems (such as cultural clash) because of this shorter-term financial prerogative. The longer-term result is declining performance and destruction of shareholder value.

9.4.3 The financial expectations of stakeholders

Section 9.4.1 looked at how business strategies might create or destroy value for shareholders of a business. The public sector equivalent is the extent to which politicians (as the owners or guardians of public money) would regard public money to have been well spent. But it was seen in Chapter 4 that the owners are not the only ones who have a stake in organisations. So other stakeholders will have financial expectations of organisations. The issue is the extent to which business strategies should address these considerations and how they can be squared with creating value for the owners. For example:

● Chapter 4 made the point that *institutional shareholders* such as asset managers of pension funds usually represented the interests of the real beneficiaries of a company's performance. This is the concept of the governance chain. So strategy is strongly influenced by the financial expectations of these intermediaries who can become the key players on major strategic changes – such as mergers or take-overs. There is a continuing concern that managers are distorting the long-term strategies of their companies as they respond to the shorter-term pressures on earnings exerted by stock market analysts and institutional shareholders.[23]

● *Bankers* and other providers of interest-bearing loans are concerned about the *risk* attached to their loans and the competence with which this is managed. A consistently good track record in managing that risk could be regarded (in itself) as a reason for bankers to invest further with some companies and not others. The risk would be influenced by the capital structure of the company – particularly the gearing ratio (of debt to equity), which determines how sensitive the solvency of the company is to changes in its profit position. Interest cover is a similar measure that relates interest payments to profit.

● *Suppliers* and *employees* are likely to be concerned with good prices and wages but also the *liquidity* of the company, which is a measure of its ability to meet short-term commitments to creditors and wages. Bankers will share this concern because a deteriorating liquidity position may require correction through additional loans and the increased risk profile discussed above. Again, a track record in this area could be a competence underpinning good supplier relationships, resulting in discounts or improved credit.

● The *community* will be concerned with jobs but also with the *social cost* of an organisation's strategies, such as pollution or marketing. This is rarely accounted for in traditional financial analyses, but it is an issue of growing concern. Matters of business ethics were discussed in Chapter 5 (section 5.4). Failure to pay proper attention to these issues could be a source of strategic weakness.

● *Customers* are concerned about best-value products or services. This assessment is rarely made in traditional financial analyses, the implication being that companies that survive profitably in a competitive environment *must* be providing value for money. However, as mentioned above, cost and value creation tends to be distributed unevenly across the various activities and 'players' in the value chain. The relative 'winners' and 'losers' at any time are determined by circumstances that change the relative bargaining power of buyers and suppliers in the chain (as discussed in the five forces framework – section 2.3.1). Commodity-like industries (such as oil, steel or glass) show this very clearly in the way that prices swing with market conditions (supply/demand). In turn, this creates large swings in the shareholder value creation between peaks and troughs in demand. Where competitive pressures have not existed, such as in many public services, there have been attempts to develop performance measures more related to best value. However, many management information systems are not geared to such a detailed analysis of separate value activities, making this process difficult. In the UK in the late 1990s, political weight was put behind this process through the *Best Value Initiative* which defined a range of performance indicators and set standards against a benchmark of best performance (beyond the public sector).

Overall, managers need to be conscious of the financial impact on various stakeholders of the strategies they are pursuing or planning to pursue. They also need to understand how these expectations could enable the success of some strategies whilst limiting the ability of an organisation to succeed with other strategies.

9.5 MANAGING TECHNOLOGY[24]

This section is about the relationship between technology and strategic success. As with previous sections of this chapter, it is important to start with a warning. It is easy for organisations to get distracted by technology development without relating it to overall strategy and asking how the creation and sharing of knowledge about the technology will be managed in the organisation. Crucial is the question as to how this process will provide competitive advantage. As mentioned in Chapter 3, the technology itself may be easy to acquire by competitors so is not necessarily a source of advantage. The ways in which the technology is exploited are where advantage may be created.

Technological development can take several forms, each of which might give organisations advantage in a particular way, as shown in Exhibit 9.9. As with the other issues in this chapter, the link between business strategy and technology is likely to be *dependent on context*.[25] So factors such as company size, industry sector, product type and county will shape the relationship. However, it is useful to identify a number of different types of technology development where the strategic implications are different. These are called **technological paths** or trajectories:[26]

A **technological path** identifies the major factors that are influencing technological developments

- *Supplier-dominated developments* – such as in agriculture, with advances in machinery, fertilisers and pesticides. The strategic issue for an agricultural

Exhibit 9.9 Strategic advantage through technology development

Mechanism	Strategic advantage	Examples
Novelty in product or service	Offering something no one else can	Introducing the first . . . Walkman®, fountain pen, camera, dishwasher . . . to the world
Novelty in process	Offering it in ways others can't match – faster, lower cost, more customised, etc.	Pilkington's float glass process, Bessemer's steel process, Internet banking, online bookselling, etc.
Complexity	Offering something which others find difficult to master	Rolls-Royce and aircraft engines – complex machining and metallurgy
Legal protection of intellectual property	Offering something which others cannot do unless they pay you a licence or other fee	Blockbuster drugs like Zantac®, Viagra®, etc.
Robust design	Offering something which provides the platform on which other variations and generations can be built	Boeing 737 – over thirty years old the design is still being adapted and configured to suit different users
Rewriting the rules	Offering something which represents a completely new product or process which makes the old ones redundant	Typewriters vs. computer word processing Ice vs. refrigerators Electric vs. gas or oil lamps

Source: Abridged version from J. Tidd, J. Bessant and K. Pavitt, *Managing Innovation: Integrating technological, market and organisational change*, 2nd edition, Wiley, 2001.

producer is rapid learning on how these new technologies might transform business processes in 'their' part of the value network. Capitalising on this type of supplier-led development remains the current challenge for organisations in many different sectors in exploiting computer hardware and software developments (as discussed in section 9.3 above).

● *Scale-intensive developments* – such as complex manufacturing systems in automobiles and other sectors – where advantage is gained from economies of scale and learning results from that scale, as discussed in Chapter 3. Here the strategic challenge is to ensure that incremental learning *does* occur and best practice is diffused through the organisation.

● *Information-intensive developments* – such as in financial services, retailing or travel – where the exploitation of IT is the central strategic issue. This has already been discussed in section 9.3 above.

● *Science-based developments* are still important in many sectors such as pharmaceuticals, electronics, materials and engineering. The strategic challenges are to monitor academic research, develop products and acquire the resources to achieve commercial-scale production. An associated task is the assessment and management of risk.

Bearing in mind these introductory comments about the types of technology development, this section of the chapter will now look at the following issues about the relationship between business strategy and technology and how technology can enable strategic success (see Exhibit 9.10):

● how technology changes the *competitive situation*;

● technology and *strategic capability*;

● *organising* technology to achieve advantage.

9.5.1 Technology and the competitive situation

In Chapter 2, the five forces framework was used as a checklist for understanding the competitive forces within an industry and how they might determine the competitive position of different organisations. Technology can have a significant impact on these forces – particularly in industries that are globalising[27] – and this should influence how the strategies of individual organisations develop in the future, as the following examples illustrate:

● *Barriers to entry* for potential new entrants may be lowered by reducing the economies of scale, for example in publishing, or the capital requirements for set-up, e.g. in computing. In some cases, barriers may be raised as technologies become more difficult to master and products more complex, for example in the aerospace industry.

● *Substitution* may be assisted by technology at several levels. New products may displace old, e.g. DVDs for videotape. The need may be displaced, for example using video conferencing rather than travelling to meetings. Or technological developments in other sectors may 'steal' consumer demand through an array of exciting products, e.g. electronic goods displacing consumer spending on

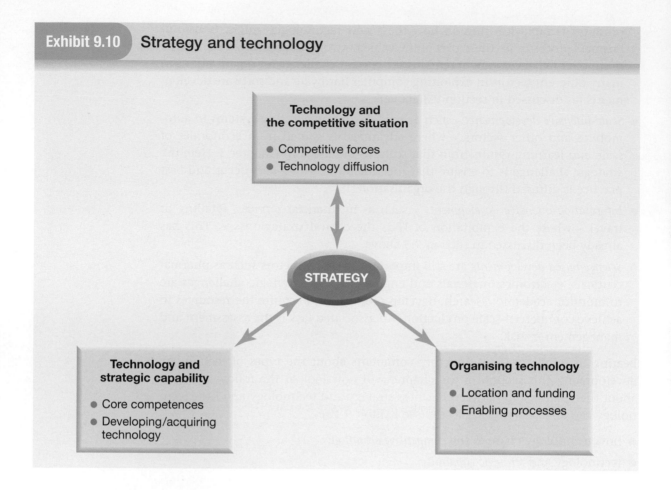

Exhibit 9.10   Strategy and technology

household durables such as kitchens and carpets. Sometimes technology can stop substitution, for example by tying the usage of one product to another – the 'debate' about Microsoft's success in tying software developments into the Windows operating system is an example.

● The *relative power of suppliers and buyers* can also be changed by technology. The Microsoft example applies here too since the issues raised in the court cases were about the extent to which Microsoft (as a supplier to most businesses and households) had unreasonably high levels of power over its customers. But technological developments can work in the favour of buyers by freeing them from a single source of supply. This often happens when international specifications and standards are agreed (say for steel).

● *Competitive rivalry* amongst organisations can be raised through this process of generic specifications or diminished if one firm develops a new product or process which it is able to patent. The level of competitive rivalry in generic pharmaceutical products as against ethical (proprietary) pharmaceutical products is markedly different.

The strategic issues raised for individual organisations through these examples are two-fold. First, some organisations may be technological leaders and trying to gain advantage in some of the ways outlined above. Second, many other organisations may need to assess the likely impact on their competitive position of technological developments led by current or potential competitors.

9.5.2 The diffusion of innovation[28]

Since technological development can be expensive, its commercial attractiveness can hinge on the extent and pace at which a market is likely to adopt new products – or the improved performance of existing products. This is called the **diffusion** of innovations. Diffusion is influenced by a number of factors to do with two main issues: the *nature* of the innovation and the *processes* of bringing the innovation to market. Clearly these are issues which should strongly link business strategy and technology strategies together. Research on the pace of diffusion centres on two sets of issues that determine the pace of diffusion:

> **Diffusion** is the extent and pace at which a market is likely to adopt new products

- *Supply-side issues* concerned with product features such as:
  - *Degree of improvement* in performance above current products (from a customer's perspective) – to provide sufficient incentive to change; for example, whether wide-screen television will encourage TV set replacement by consumers earlier than otherwise.
  - *Compatibility* with other factors, e.g. wide-screen TV is more attractive when the broadcasting networks change more of their programmes to that format.
  - *Complexity* can discourage uptake. This can be complexity in the product itself or in the marketing methods being used to commercialise the product (e.g. unduly complex pricing structures as with mobile phones or many financial service products).
  - *Experimentation* – the ability to test products before commitment to a final decision – either directly or through the availability of information about the experience of other customers. This is why new product marketing often features satisfied customers and/or endorsements from suitable role models such as sports or pop celebrities.
  - *Relationship management* – how easy it is to get information, place orders and receive support. This relates to the choice of business model as described in section 9.3.2 above.
- *Demand-side issues* – processes that exist in markets that drive adoption of new products or new product features:
  - *Market awareness* is the basic requirement. Many potentially successful products have failed through lack of consumer awareness – particularly when the promotional effort of the manufacturer has been confined to 'push' promotion to its intermediaries (e.g. distributors).
  - *Observability* (to potential adopters) of the benefits of the product or service in use. This is an important determinant in spreading adoption – for example, through creating a 'band wagon' effect. For some products this can be difficult if the benefits are intangible or do not accrue immediately (e.g. financial investments). Intermediaries (such as distributors) also need to observe that there is benefit to them too. This could be observed if they see *their* competitors gaining commercial advantage from the new product.

– Customers are *different from each other* and range from innovators (the first to adopt) through to laggards (the last to adopt). Also, the likelihood and extent of adoption by the slower groups is influenced by the response of the faster groups. This requires a sophisticated approach to new product launch – particularly where a company is introducing a new-generation product and wishing simultaneously to win new customers whilst progressively moving its current customers from old to new product or service.

The practical importance of the various factors listed above is as a checklist against which the technology strategies (for product/service improvements) can be matched to the market conditions in which the new or improved products will need to compete. This integration of these two sets of knowledge is of critical importance to the commercial success of technological developments. For example, a manager writing a 'business case' to secure funds for improving particular product features would need to address many of the issues listed above. It would start by showing why the improved features might be *valued by customers* sufficiently to switch purchase or upgrade. It might also address issues of *compatibility* with other equipment that the consumer or distributor uses in conjunction with the product. In other words at a minimum it is essential that the product or service matches the threshold requirements of both consumers and intermediaries. This may entail considerable effort to allay some of their concerns about switching to the new product. Adoption would be more likely if the product matches the *critical success factors (CSFs)* of consumers and intermediaries (see Chapter 2, section 2.4.3). The marketing plan would address how these attributes would be *communicated* and who would be the initial *target audiences*. It would address how initial adoptions would then be *'rolled out'* into wider uptake in the market.[29]

A **tipping point** is where demand for a product or service suddenly takes off or declines – sometimes dramatically

A final and crucial observation about diffusion is that demand tends not to increase steadily. There may be a slow process of adoption and then a **tipping point** where demand for a product or service suddenly takes off or declines – sometimes dramatically.[30] This phenomenon is also observed in public health in the progress of an epidemic. It is equally relevant to decline as well as growth – which is of interest to many public sector organisations – for example, reductions in crime. It appears that it is the combination of three factors that accelerates adoption at a tipping point: the influence of a *few important people* (e.g. high-profile early adopters); a memorable *message* (usually about benefits) and small changes in *context* (usually the business environment). Illustration 9.7 shows how technology diffusion occurred in one sector.

9.5.3 Technology and strategic capability

Core competences

Chapter 3 underlined the importance of identifying core competences as the basis of an organisation's competitive advantage. As mentioned in the introduction to this section, technology itself is usually easy to imitate by competitors and is, therefore, not usually a unique resource or a core competence. There

Illustration 9.7

Pure Digital's Evoke-1 digital radio

New product adoption is driven by issues of both supply and demand.

In July 2002 Imagination Technologies, a small firm of engineers and scientists, launched the UK's first sub-£100 (€150) digital radio – the Evoke-1 through its subsidiary company Pure Digital. This was pretty impressive for a company that had never been in radios. Indeed it normally just focused on technologies, which it then licensed to others for manufacture, marketing and distribution (which it regarded as the risky issues). Even more surprisingly the Evoke sold 40,000 during the 2002 Christmas rush, more than most radios do in their lifetimes. By mid-2003 Evokes were still in short supply and John Lewis on Oxford Street in London said it had 3,000 customer orders unfilled.

Digital broadcasting uses the radio spectrum more efficiently, allowing more data to be broadcast. This results in a strong signal, and potential for more channels. The technology offers the possibility of combining text, pictures or other interactive services with audio output. By 2003 the UK had up to 50 digital channels, including digital versions of existing broadcasters and coverage of the population was 85 per cent and rising. UK analogue radio (the old system) will be switched over to digital some time after 2010. In early 2003 the Digital Radio Development Bureau expected digital radio ownership to treble to half a million by the end of the year, and to double again in 2004.

Although this was a major change in its approach Mr Yassaie, who ran the firm, argued that it would have been crazy not to have launched into digital radio. First, the company had built up such levels of expertise in a few key areas of technology that products could be developed at double-quick speed. So when it decided to launch a sub-£100 product, it

took just 18 months to bring it to market – a fraction of the time it would take any other company. Second, it did not take a wild gambler to see that the UK digital radio market was due to grow – admittedly from around zero. 'Usually you create a technology, and there's no content for it,' Mr Yassaie said. 'With digital radio, there were 30–40 channels already, but no one had reasonably priced kit to listen to them on.' But the firm would not have the digital market to itself. A host of consumer-savvy competitors, including Bush, Goodmans and Alba, were planning to launch rivals to the Evoke in 2003. Pure Digital itself was expanding the range and bringing out a handheld digital radio. For Christmas 2003 it had a major radio advertising campaign through a joint promotion with Classic FM – a very successful UK classical music station. But if it wanted to remain competitive, it had to do something about its production processes – the three-month lead time needed by its Chinese manufacturers had contributed to the patchy supply of the Evoke. Having waiting lists at John Lewis is all very flattering – but consumers' patience would run out sooner rather than later.

Source: Extracts from *BBC e-mail service* 25 March 2003.

Questions

Read section 9.5.2 and:

1. Explain the reasons why the Evoke-1 radio had been such a success.

2. Think of any new product or service that has failed and explain why the product was not widely adopted.

---

are, of course, exceptions to this, where technological breakthroughs have been carefully patented. However, from a strategic point of view the importance of technology lies in the potential both to create and to destroy core competences (as seen in the case of IT in section 9.3.1 above). So if technology is to enable success there are some important implications for business and technology strategies:

- To tie future developments to a *single technology* that an organisation has mastered can be both inappropriate and unduly risky. So allowing future strategic choices to be dominated by opportunities (for market development or new uses or diversification) only based on that technology could be imprudent. For example, stainless steel was the wonder material of the 1960s, substituting for other materials in many consumer and industrial applications. But, in turn, it has been substituted in some applications by developments in polymers, ceramics and composite materials.

- Core competences may be found in the processes of *linking technologies* together rather than the technologies *per se*. Indeed, many advances in manufacturing are concerned with how computerised process control can be grafted to the technologies of the plant and machinery – not in being excellent in just one or other technology.

- *Dynamic capabilities* (as discussed in Chapter 3) may be important in a rapidly changing and competitive world. The fruits of any particular development are likely to be shorter-lived than hitherto. So competitive advantage needs to be underpinned by the processes that ensure a constant flow of improvements and in the ability to bring improvements to market quickly. This can lead to first-mover advantages. However, there is also evidence that in some circumstances commercial advantages of technological developments may accrue to follower companies rather than the pioneers.[31] In either case the way in which technology development is organised is likely to be of strategic importance, and this will be discussed below in section 9.5.4.

Developing or acquiring technology

An important strategic decision for many organisations is whether technology is developed 'in house' or acquired externally. This can be a key determinant in the success or failure of strategies. This is a complex subject given that many different variables could influence these decisions.[32] However, for the purposes of illustrating the link between business and technology strategies a few general principles are useful (see Exhibit 9.11):

- *In-house development* may be favoured if the technology is key to competitive advantage and an organisation has expectations of gaining first-mover advantages. This will be feasible if the organisation already has a good knowledge of both the technology and the market opportunities and the complexity is not too great – it is within current fields of organisational knowledge. It is also important that the organisation is willing to take commercial and financial risk.

- *Alliances* are likely to be appropriate for 'threshold' technologies rather than ones on which competitive advantage is to be built. For example, a manufacturer of branded drinks may seek a partner to improve bottling and distribution processes. These are both important activities but competitive advantage is concerned with the product itself and brand maintenance. Alliances might also be appropriate where there is an intention to follow and imitate rather than lead. This would be particularly the case where the complexity of product or market knowledge is beyond the current knowledge base – so organisational learning is an important objective. Alliances also help to limit financial risk.

| Exhibit 9.11 | Developing or acquiring technology |

Influencing factors

Method		Importance of the technology	Prior knowledge and reputation	Complexity	Willingness to take risk	Desire to lead or follow	Speed
	In-house	Key	High	Low/Medium	High	Lead	Slow
	Alliances	Threshold	Low	High	Medium	Follow	Medium
	Acquisition	Key or threshold	Very Low	High	Low	Follow	High

Source: Adapted from J. Tidd, J. Bessant and K. Pavitt, *Managing Innovation: Integrating technological, market and organisational change*, 2nd edition, Wiley, 2001.

● *Acquisition of current players or rights* may be particularly appropriate if speed is important and there is no time for learning. It may also be essential if the level of complexity, both in technology and market application, is beyond current organisational knowledge and where credibility of the technology is essential to business success – so the source of the technology matters. So production under licence of an established technology may be more successful than developing an alternative. Organisations acquiring technology need to have a good understanding of the technology needs of their product lines, an ability to identify and evaluate appropriate external technologies and the competence to negotiate an appropriate deal with the owners of the technology rights.[33]

The choice between in-house development, alliances and acquisition will also vary through the technology life cycle[34] as companies move from issues of product functionality and market share, through establishing industry quality standards to further developments in the technology. Long-term survivors will need to use all of these methods as they move through the life cycle.

Illustration 9.8 shows how one company developed through a combination of these processes.

9.5.4 Organising technology development

The location and funding of technology development

An important debate in many larger organisations is who within the organisation should be driving technology development and who should be funding it.[35] This is part of the wider strategic debate about how strategic responsibilities could be divided between the corporate centre and divisions/departments of an organisation – discussed in section 6.4 and expanded in section 8.4. Decisions on this could be important in enabling strategic success through technology.

Illustration 9.8

Merck and new drug development

The development of new technologies and products and their commercialisation cannot always be done alone.

The following is an article from the *Financial Times* in December 2003 that tried to explain some of the reasons for a major pharmaceutical firm's financial difficulties.

Merck has long been proud of its reputation as a scientific innovator. But for many investors and analysts, the deeply ingrained culture of the US pharmaceuticals group has become a millstone around the neck. While most other companies in the drugs industry have done endless deals to keep growing, Merck has clung to its core belief that a drugs group should back its own scientists to produce the new and exciting products that will drive revenues . . . After a stream of disappointing news over the past two years, the impression that the Merck model has come unstuck was exacerbated in recent weeks when it pulled two of the four products it had in late-stage clinical trials – substance 'p', also called aprepitant, for depression, and then MK-767 for diabetes. The shares have fallen 25 per cent over the past year, a period when many pharmaceuticals stocks have rallied after a miserable 2002. With Merck's best-selling drug, cholesterol treatment Zocor, losing US patent protection in 2006, the pressure is now on to explain where medium-term growth will come from. Speculation about a merger or acquisition has revived . . . [but] such a big shift in strategy, however, would require a new chief executive to replace Raymond Gilmartin, who has consistently set himself against a big merger . . . 'M&A disrupts the research process,' he said in an interview before the two late-stage failures. 'I do not see any fundamental shift in the industry's ability to innovate.'

For other observers, Merck's problems derive from its reluctance to do small deals with the biotechnology industry to take advantage of the wealth of innovation taking place outside the company. Too much faith has been placed on the company's own scientists, they say. 'Merck was unwilling to take the plunge and partner with other companies,' says Matthew Emmens, a former Merck executive who is now chief executive of Shire Pharmaceuticals in the UK. 'And in my view the company's performance has gone down because of that.' Mr Gilmartin recognises that this was a problem at Merck, but said the culture had changed significantly since the late 1990s when it re-examined its approach to product licensing. 'We did have a reputation for being hard to access and for not doing much outside,' he said. 'But we have had a step-function change in our relationships with the outside world.' While Merck did 10 deals with biotech companies in 1999, Mr Gilmartin said, it completed 48 deals last year. About a third of sales now come from products that were in-licensed. Nor is everyone prepared to write off the Merck model. The plan to lay off 4,400 people has convinced some investors that the company is realistic about short-term prospects. And with pricing pressures growing in the US and Europe, especially for so-called 'me-too drugs' that differ little from existing products, Merck's emphasis on innovative, new drugs has supporters. 'Kudos to Merck for continuing to pursue novel, albeit higher-risk, drugs,' says Timothy Anderson, analyst at Prudential Securities.

Source: Financial Times 4 December 2003.

Question

Read section 9.5.3. What are the advantages and disadvantages of the (so-called) Merck model of technology development bearing in mind the influencing factors in Exhibit 9.11?

Exhibit 9.12 shows that different arrangements are likely to be suitable for different aspects of technology development. For example, at one extreme, new technologies are best assessed and funded corporately whilst at the other, incremental product and process improvements are best undertaken and funded locally. Between these extremes, the commercialisation of new technologies is often best done locally but funded corporately since others will learn and benefit from the first moves. Experimentation with new technologies might remain corporate but be funded by divisions who see commercial potential in their arena.

Exhibit 9.12   Funding and location of R&D

		Located at	
		Corporate	**Divisional**
Funded by	**Corporate**	Assessing new technologies	Commercialising new technologies
	Divisional	Exploratory development of new technologies	Incremental product or process improvements

Source: Adapted from J. Tidd, J. Bessant and K. Pavitt, *Managing Innovation: Integrating technological, market and organisation change*, 2nd edition, Wiley, 2001.

These same principles might lead to conclusions that some technology development activities might be outsourced[36] where the technological expertise is inadequate in both divisions and the corporate centre but the particular technology development is crucial to securing current and future business. Also the different stages of development might be developed in different ways: for example, the ideas generation and early research might be undertaken internally whilst external organisations might be used to develop prototypes and/or undertake test marketing.[37]

Sometimes the technological expertise of an organisation might be greater than the current business can exploit – leading to considerations of spin-off of R&D (in whole or in part) to allow new commercial opportunities to be exploited (by licensing technology to third parties).

Enabling processes

Chapter 8 underlined the importance of organisational processes in enabling the success of strategies. This is particularly true in technology development where there are real dangers that an organisation's competence in technology fails to be exploited commercially. Since these processes are often difficult to manage, they may prove to be core competences that underpin competitive advantage, as mentioned above. Some of the following processes may be of crucial importance in enabling success through technology:

● *Scanning the business environment* (both technology and market developments) and spotting the opportunities for gaining advantage and the potential threats to current business. Related to this is the ability to select projects or developments that have a good strategic fit with the business. But this is not as easy as it sounds. It may mean giving preference to transformational technologies – which could be very challenging in terms of both competences and culture of the organisation.

● *Resourcing developments adequately*, but not over-generously, so as to ensure a good return for the investment. This is much easier to see in hindsight than in advance, but past experience, good benchmarking and a willingness to use appropriate approaches to investment appraisal[38] can help. This also includes the ability to monitor and review projects through their various stages – many organisations now use **stage-gate processes** to good effect.[39] This is a structured review process to assess progress on meeting product performance characteristics during the development process and ensuring that they are matched with market data. These processes must also include the ability to terminate and accelerate projects, to capture the learning from both successes and failures, and to disseminate results and best practice.

A **stage-gate process** is a structured review process to assess progress on meeting product performance characteristics during the development process and ensuring that they are matched with market data

Of course, behind these processes is a set of much more detailed activities which will determine their success or failure. This would include activities ranging from forecasting, concept testing and option screening to communication, negotiation and motivation.

Implications to managers[40]

The preceding sections were intended to underline the importance of 'aligning' business and technology strategies in organisations as a way of enabling strategic success. Successful organisations will be those where there is a strong commitment to innovation from senior management and a business acumen based on an understanding of the business strategy and technology relationship.

There needs to be a creative climate where innovation is fostered, communication is extensive and where there is a culture of a learning organisation. Structures and processes must facilitate the creation of this environment and provide a commitment to individual and team development. In particular, it must support key individuals who will champion and facilitate the exploitation of technology for strategic success.

9.6 INTEGRATING RESOURCES

The sections above have looked at how separate resource areas need to support an organisation's strategies and may also provide the basis on which new strategies can be built. However, there is a third issue that has only partly emerged from the consideration of the separate resource areas above. As discussed in Chapter 3, most organisational strategies not only require competences in separate resource areas, but require an ability to pull a range of resources and competences together – both inside the organisation and in the wider value network. For example, Exhibit 9.13 shows some of the resources and activities that need to be integrated by an organisation hoping to gain competitive advantage through bringing new products to the market more quickly than competitors. This can be a complex matter and, therefore, may be the basis of competitive advantage. Competence in new product launch requires an ability to integrate and coordinate the separate activities of R&D, manufacture, etc. – each of which, in turn, involves bringing together a complex mixture of resources. It is not sufficient

Exhibit 9.13   Resource integration in a new product launch

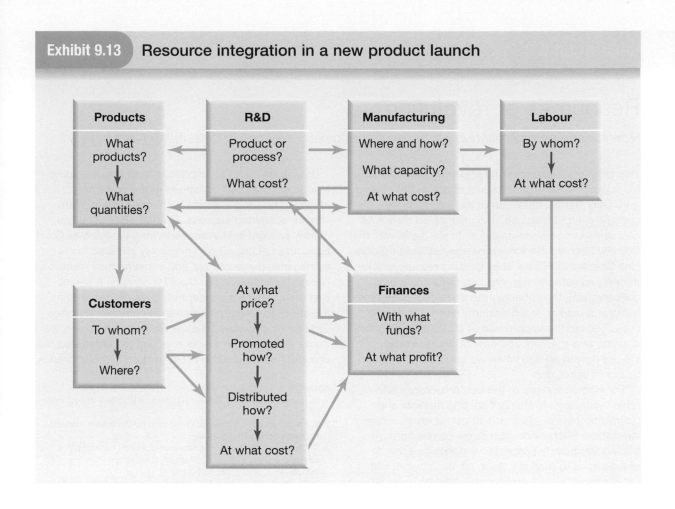

simply to own these resources or to be competent in these separate activities. It is the ability to link these together effectively and quickly that determines the success or failure of the strategy.

The concluding message of the chapter as a whole is the same as for the separate resource areas. Systems developments have made important contributions to the performance of many organisations – for example, the way in which enterprise resource planning (ERP) has helped with resource integration, as discussed in section 8.3.2 (see also Illustration 8.3). However, it is not sufficient to regard resource management and resource integration as being solely about the systems and procedures of an organisation's business functions. It has been seen above that although these systems and procedures may be vitally important in all resource areas, they can hold back strategic change and will not, by themselves, achieve resource integration. Integration also results from people's behaviours and 'the way things are done' in an organisation. This is likely to be a potential benefit, since this embedded knowledge will be difficult to imitate. However, it can also prove to be the Achilles heel of an organisation as managers find it difficult to challenge and change this knowledge and behaviours in the organisation and fail to respond to change. This lesson is highlighted is different parts of the book and is the theme of the key debate in Illustration 9.9.

Illustration 9.9

Resources or revolution

How far can an organisation go beyond its original resources in determining its strategy?

This chapter emphasises the importance of resources for supporting an organisation's strategy. For strategy guru Gary Hamel, chairman of the international consulting firm Strategos, this reliance on resources can easily become too cautious. In the same way that Dorothy Leonard-Barton warns against 'core rigidities' (see Chapter 3), Hamel sees existing resources and markets as liable to trap organisations into a fatal conservatism. Incumbency, the sheer fact of already being in a market, is increasingly worthless. Hamel urges instead the importance of strategic 'revolutions', creating new markets and new business models.[1,2] We are now in an age when we need only be limited by our imaginations.

For Hamel, survival in the contemporary world of rapid technological change, shifting markets and global competition demands constant revolutionary innovation. Such innovation rarely comes from traditional strategy processes emphasising the 'fit' of resources to markets. As in his earlier work with CK Prahalad, Hamel emphasises 'stretch' over 'fit', and now 'revolutionaries' over 'planners'.

As an example, Hamel cites Pierre Omidyar, founder in 1995 of what rapidly became the world's premier internet auction site, eBay. Omidyar's starting point was not the fit of resources to markets, but a desire to help his fiancée with her collection of Pez sweet dispensers. Starting on his own while retaining his day job, Omidyar had none of the resources of a traditional auction house. Far from fitting a market, he was creating a new kind of market. Traditional strategy processes would never have allowed eBay to happen.

A reminder of the importance of resources, however, comes from another of Hamel's exemplars of revolution, Enron. Enron is applauded by Hamel for its revolutionary capacity to create and trade in markets for gas, electricity, broadband and commodities. But it was inadequacies in unique and hard-to-imitate resources that contributed to Enron's ultimate failure. In the competitive markets that Enron created and traded in, Enron had few sources of sustainable advantage.[3] The result was losses that led to the largest bankruptcy in corporate history at that time. Here resources did matter.

Hamel points to an important truth about existing resources: they can constrain. At the same time, however, building a strong resource-base appears vital for sustained success. Even at eBay, Omidyar quickly brought in Harvard MBA Meg Whitman as Chief Executive Officer, who immediately invested in the managerial, measurement and infrastructural resources necessary to take it into the 21st century. It seems that David Teece's concept of 'dynamic capabilities',[4] the ability to develop and change competences (see Chapter 3), provides an essential bridge between the constraints of current resources and the unfettered but unsupported imagination of Gary Hamel's revolutionaries.

Notes:
1. G. Hamel, *Leading the Revolution*, Harvard Business School Press, 2000.
2. G. Hamel and C.K. Prahalad, *Competing for the Future*, Harvard Business School Press, 1994.
3. S. Chatterjee, 'Enron's incremental descent into bankruptcy: a strategic and organisational analysis', *Long Range Planning*, vol. 36, no. 2 (2003), pp. 133–149.
4. D. Teece, G. Pisano and A. Shuen, 'Dynamic capabilities and strategic management', *Strategic Management Journal*, vol. 18, no. 7 (1997), pp. 509–533.

Questions

In his book *Leading the Revolution*, Gary Hamel notes that the current coffee bar fashion was created by Starbucks, a small Seattle coffee company founded in 1971, which only opened its first of more than 7,500 coffee bars in 1984. Hamel asks: why wasn't the coffee bar fashion launched by multi-billion dollar multinational Nestlé, owner of Nescafé, the best-selling coffee in the world?

1. Compare the resources of Nestlé and Starbucks in the late 1980s and early 1990s (see www.nestle.com and www.starbucks.com, and Illustration 4.4). Why didn't Nestlé lead in the creation of the coffee bar fashion?

2. What implications does the failure of Nestlé have for other powerful incumbents in their present markets?

Summary

- Managers and individuals who are *below senior managers* in organisations usually control resources, activities and business processes that are crucial in *enabling* strategic success. They are also likely to be the most knowledgeable about changes in the parts of the business environment with which they interface. So understanding the relationship between resource management and strategic success is important. This is a two-way relationship. Resource management must support an organisation's business strategies. But the development of unique resources and core competences in parts of an organisation may provide the 'springboard' from which new business strategies are developed.

- The *'hard' side* of resource management – systems and procedures – is vitally important in enabling success. But in all resource areas the critical question is how these systems contribute to the creation and integration of knowledge. Only part of this knowledge can be captured in systems. Indeed, competitive advantage is more likely to be gained from knowledge that cannot be codified since it will be more difficult to imitate by competitors.

- Understanding the way in which *people* might enable success concerns both the formal systems and procedures and the informal ways in which people behave. Also important are the ways in which people can be organised for success – the structures and processes discussed in Chapter 8.

- *Information* is a key resource which is of particular attention at the moment with the continuing rapid advances in information technology. This increased ability to access and process information can build or destroy an organisation's core competences, so it is crucial to competitive advantage. IT is also spawning new business models – where traditional 'value networks' are being reconfigured. This is a serious threat to some organisations and an opportunity for others. Changing capability in access to and processing of information also has important implications for the structures and processes within and between organisations.

- *Finance* is a resource of central importance in all organisations. So it is particularly important to understand whether and how business strategies might deliver financial value to shareholders or owners. Most strategic developments need funding which, in turn, creates risk. So the types of funding need to vary with strategy. Stakeholders other than owners have financial expectations that will also influence an organisation's business strategies.

- The final resource area considered in this chapter is *technology* development. This will affect the competitive forces on an organisation and also its strategic capability. So the ways that technology is developed, exploited, organised and funded will all influence the success or failure of strategy.

- Organisations need to be able to *integrate resources and competences across resource areas* to support current strategies or to develop new strategies. Capability in separate resource areas is not enough.

Recommended key readings

- Good general reference books on human resource management: L. Mullins, *Management and Organisational Behaviour*, 6th edition, FT/Prentice Hall, 2002; T. Watson, *Organising and Managing Work*, FT/Prentice Hall, 2002.

- Good general references on information management are: J. Ward and J. Peppard, *Strategic Planning for Information Systems*, 3rd edition, Wiley, 2002 and D. Chaffey, *e-Business and e-Commerce Management*, 2nd edition, FT/Prentice Hall, 2004.

- T. Grundy (with G. Johnson and K. Scholes), *Exploring Strategic Financial Management*, Prentice Hall, 1998, and K. Ward, *Corporate Financial Strategy*, Butterworth/Heinemann, 1993, explore the relationship between financial and business strategies.

- The relationship between technology and strategy is extensively reviewed in: J. Tidd, J. Bessant and K. Pavitt, *Managing Innovation: Integrating technological, market and organisational change*, 2nd edition, Wiley, 2001.

References

1. Good general reference books on human resource management: L. Mullins, *Management and Organisational Behaviour*, 6th edition, FT/Prentice Hall, 2002; T. Watson, *Organising and Managing Work*, FT/Prentice Hall, 2002. Two useful papers are: J. Pfeffer and J. Veiga, 'Putting people first for organisational success', *Academy of Management Executive*, vol. 13, no. 2 (1999), pp. 37–50 and B. Becker and M. Huselid, 'Overview: Strategic human resource management in five leading firms', *Human Resource Management*, vol. 38, no. 4 (1999), pp. 287–301.
2. See Mullins (chapters 19, 20 and 21); Watson (chapters 6 and 11) (reference 1 above).
3. See Mullins (chapters 4, 13 and 14); Watson (chapters 4, 8 and 10) (reference 1 above).
4. C. Bartlett and S. Ghoshal, 'Building competitive advantage through people', *Sloan Management Review*, vol. 43, no. 2 (2002), pp. 34–41.
5. The seminal work on this issue of balanced teams was: R. Belbin, *Management Teams: Why they succeed or fail*, Heinemann, 1981.
6. See: C. Collins and K. Clark, 'Strategic human resource practices, top management team social networks and firm performance: the role of human resource practices in creating organisational competitive advantage', *Academy of Management Journal*, vol. 46, no. 6 (2003), pp. 740–751.
7. See Mullins (chapters 6, 15 and 16); Watson (chapter 7) (reference 1 above).
8. J. Storey, *Developments in the Management of Human Resources*, Blackwell, 1992, used this categorisation of the roles of HR functions. D. Ulrich, *Human Resource Champion*, Harvard Business School Press, 1997, presents a slightly different categorisation based on the two dimensions of change vs. maintenance *and* people vs. processes.
9. For example, downsizing creates problems in this respect. See R. Thomas and D. Dunkerley, 'Careering downwards? Middle managers' experience in the downsized organisation', *British Journal of Management*, vol. 10 (1999), pp. 157–169.
10. J. Balogun and V. Hope Hailey (with G. Johnson and K. Scholes), *Exploring Strategic Change*, Prentice Hall, 1999, p. 218.
11. A good general reference on information management is: J. Ward and J. Peppard, *Strategic Planning for Information Systems*, 3rd edition, Wiley, 2002. Two books have been used as background on the issues of information management and the power of IT: P. Timmers, *Electronic Commerce*, Wiley, 2000, and D. Chaffey, *e-Business and e-Commerce Management*, 2nd edition, FT/Prentice Hall, 2004. Readers might also find the following to be useful: C. Prahalad and M. Krishnan, 'The dynamic synchronisation of strategy and information techology', *Sloan Management Review*, vol. 43, no. 4 (2002), pp. 24–31; B. Gates, *Business@the Speed of Thought*, Penguin, 1999; M. Porter, 'Strategy and the internet', *Harvard Business Review*, vol. 79, no. 2 (2001), pp. 63–78; J. Brown and J. Hagel, 'Does IT matter?', *Harvard Business Review*, vol. 81, no. 7 (2003), pp. 109–112; G. Carr, 'IT doesn't matter', *Harvard Business Review*, vol. 81, no. 5 (2003), pp. 41–50.
12. See Prahalad and Krishnan (reference 11 above).
13. The details of how data mining is done are discussed in: C. Carmen and B. Lewis, 'A basic primer on data mining', *Information Systems Management*, vol. 19, no. 4 (2002), pp. 56–60 and J. Hall and P. Owen, 'Mining the store', *Journal of Business Strategy*, vol. 22, no. 2 (2001), pp. 24–27.
14. The need to join up the different customer interfaces (such as salesforce, websites, call centres) is discussed in: *Customer Essentials*, CBR Special Report, 1999, pp. 7–20.
15. See Timmers (reference 11 above), chapter 3.
16. See: K. Kraemer, J. Dedrick and S. Yamashiro, 'Refining and extending the business model with information technology: Dell Computer Corporation', *Information Society*, vol. 16, no. 1 (2000), pp. 5–26. Dell computers is also the subject of Illustration 1.1 in chapter 1 of this book.
17. Readers should find the following article useful: G. Rifkin and J. Kurtzman, 'Is your e-business plan radical enough', *Sloan Management Review*, vol. 43, no. 3 (2002), pp. 91–95.
18. Readers may wish to consult one or more standard texts on finance. For example: J. Samuels and F. Wilkes, *Financial Management and Decision Making*, Thomson, 1998, or M. Glautier and B. Underdown, *Accounting Theory and Practice*, 7th edition, Pearson Education, 2000.
19. The seminal work on managing for shareholder value has been updated: A. Rappaport, *Creating Shareholder Value*, 2nd edition, Free Press, 1998. T. Grundy (with G. Johnson and K. Scholes), *Exploring Strategic Financial Management*, Prentice Hall, 1998, chapter 2, is also a useful reference on managing for value.
20. J. Martin and W. Petty, 'Value based management', *Baylor Business Review*, vol. 19, no. 1 (2001), pp. 2–3 review the arguments briefly.

21. For readers who wish to follow up the discussion in this section, see K. Ward, *Corporate Financial Strategy*, Butterworth/Heinemann, 1993, and T. Grundy and K. Ward (eds), *Developing Financial Strategies: A comprehensive model in strategic business finance*, Kogan Page, 1996.

22. There have been a great deal of research and publication around the funding of this start-up phase. For example: D. Champion, 'A stealthier way to raise money', *Harvard Business Review*, vol. 78, no. 5 (2000), pp. 18–19; Q. Mills, 'Who's to blame for the bubble?', *Harvard Business Review*, vol. 79, no. 5 (2001), pp. 22–23; H. Van Auken, 'Financing small technology-based companies: the relationship between familiarity with capital and ability to price and negotiate investment', *Journal of Small Business Management*, vol. 39, no. 3 (2001), pp. 240–258; M. Van Osnabrugge and R. Robinson, 'The influence of a venture capitalist's source of funds', *Venture Capital*, vol. 3, no. 1 (2001), pp. 25–39.

23. See: A. Kennedy, *The End of Shareholder Value: Corporations at the crossroads*, Perseus Publishing, 2000 and H. Collingwood, 'The earnings game', *Harvard Business Review*, vol. 79, no. 6 (2001), pp. 65–72.

24. The major source for this section is: J. Tidd, J. Bessant and K. Pavitt, *Managing Innovation: Integrating technological, market and organisational change*, 2nd edition, Wiley, 2001.

25. S. Collinson, 'Developing and deploying knowledge for innovation: British and Japanese corporations compared', *International Journal of Innovation Management*, vol. 5, no. 1 (2001), pp. 73–103. This paper shows how contextual issues such as culture, power, and motivation have a major influence over the processes of innovation.

26. K. Pavitt, 'What we know about the strategic management of technology', *California Management Review*, vol. 32 (1990), pp. 17–26.

27. A useful international comparison of R&D strategies can be found in: E. Roberts, 'Benchmarking global strategic management of technology', *Research Technology Management*, vol. 44, no. 2 (2001), pp. 25–36.

28. There are a number of useful sources regarding diffusion of technology and/or the adoption of new products: E. Rogers, *Diffusion of Innovations*, Free Press, 1995; C. Kim and R. Mauborgne, 'Knowing a winning business idea when you see one', *Harvard Business Review*, vol. 78, no. 5 (2000), pp. 129–138 and J. Cummings and J. Doh, 'Identifying who matters: mapping key players in multiple environments', *California Management Review*, vol. 42, no. 2 (2000), pp. 83–104 (the section on the technological context is about diffusion, pp. 91–97).

29. Cummings and Doh, reference 28 above.

30. M. Gladwell, *The Tipping Point*, Abacus, 2000.

31. W. Boulding and M. Christen, 'First mover disadvantage', *Harvard Business Review*, vol. 79, no. 9 (2001), pp. 20–21.

32. See Tidd *et al.* (reference 24 above) p. 222, and J. Tidd and M. Trewhella, 'Organisational and technological antecedents for knowledge acquisition', *R&D Management*, vol. 27, no. 4 (1997), pp. 359–375.

33. For example see: G. Slowinski, S. Stanton, J. Tao, W. Miller and D. McConnell, 'Acquiring external technology', *Research Technology Management*, vol. 43, no. 5 (2002), pp. 29–35.

34. E. Roberts and W. Lui, 'Ally or acquire? How technology leaders decide', *Sloan Management Review*, vol. 43, no. 1 (2001), pp. 26–34.

35. R. Buderi, 'Funding central research', *Research Technology Management*, vol. 43, no. 4 (2000), pp. 18–25 gives some useful examples including Siemens, NEC, Hewlett-Packard and IBM.

36. See: C. Kimzey and S. Kurokawa, 'Technology outsourcing in the US and Japan', *Research Technology Management*, vol. 45, no. 4 (2002), pp. 36–42.

37. E. Kessler and P. Bierly, 'Internal vs. external learning in product development', *R & D Management*, vol. 30, no. 3 (2000), pp. 213–223.

38. A. Lloyd, 'Technology, innovation and competitive advantage; making a business process perspective part of investment appraisal', *International Journal of Innovation Management*, vol. 5, no. 3 (2001), pp. 351–376.

39. The stage-gate process is discussed in: R. Thomas, *New Product Development: Managing and forecasting for strategic success*, Wiley, 1993; R. Cooper, S. Edgett, J. Kleinschmidt and J. Elko, 'Optimising the stage-gate process: what best practice companies do', *Research Technology Management*, vol. 45, no. 5 (2002), pp. 21–26 and vol. 45, no. 6 (2002), pp. 43–49.

40. See Tidd *et al.* (reference 24 above), p. 306.

An extensive range of additional materials, including audio summaries, weblinks to organisations featured in the text, definitions of key concepts and multiple choice questions, can be found on the *Exploring Corporate Strategy* Companion Website at **www.pearsoned.co.uk/ecs7**

WORK ASSIGNMENTS

✱ Denotes more advanced work assignments.

9.1 Choose a strategic development for an organisation with which you are familiar and list the key human resource changes that will be needed to enable success (refer to Exhibit 9.2 as a checklist).

9.2✱ Write an executive report to your CEO advising on whether or not the HR function should be closed and the work devolved to middle (line) managers. Centre your arguments on the impact on the strategic performance of the organisation.

9.3✱ (a) Choose an organisation which is shifting its generic competitive strategy from low price to differentiation. Describe how the information strategies will need to change to support this new strategy.

(b) Choose an organisation which is attempting the opposite shift (differentiation to low price) and undertake the same analysis.

9.4 Find examples of all of the business models outlined in Exhibit 9.5. Explain in which sectors you feel each business model is most likely to have particular impact. Why?

9.5 Referring to Exhibit 9.7, give as many reasons as you can why profitable companies might be destroying shareholder value (with examples). Now repeat the exercise for organisations with poor levels of profitability that are nonetheless creating shareholder value (with examples).

9.6✱ Write an executive report on how sources of funding need to be related to the nature of an industry and the types of strategies that an organisation is pursuing.

9.7 Choose an industry or sector with which you are familiar and describe the ways in which new technologies and products have diffused into the market (refer to section 9.5.2). Who have been the winners and losers? Why?

9.8✱ By referring to Exhibit 9.11, write a report advising your CEO how technology should be acquired by your organisation. Remember to justify your conclusions.

9.9 Refer to the new product launch example in Exhibit 9.13. If you were project managing this launch, identify the specific ways in you would ensure integration between the various resource areas. Remember to identify both 'hard' and 'soft' ways in which you would achieve this integration.

Integrative assignments

9.10 Using examples discuss the proposition that 'IT is seen as the servant of current strategies and business models rather than as a way of revolutionising the way an organisation does business and gains advantage'. Support your answer by references to both the value chain (Chapter 3) and culture (Chapter 4).

9.11 The knowledge of an organisation is dispersed throughout the major resource areas discussed in this chapter. So how does an organisation manage to integrate and gain advantage from this knowledge? Refer to Chapters 3 and 4 to support your answer.

CASE EXAMPLE

NHS Direct – a fast-moving and developing service

Alex Murdock, London South Bank University

'NHS Direct Online wins one of the first ever e-Europe, e-Health awards – for Empowering Citizens in the Management of Health and Wellbeing.'[7]

When Mr Bob Gann stepped up to receive this award in 2003 he must have reflected that he would little have thought that his background as a librarian would have put him in a key position in the delivery of UK Health Services. As Director of NHS Direct Online he was a key person in the further development of the original NHS Direct concept.

NHS Direct itself provides people at home or at work with help and advice over the telephone in respect of health matters. It also has set up internet-based services and has started to also cover emergency out-of-hours services. The original model of a telephone helpline has been extended and the service has major aspirations.

Each month NHS Direct and NHS Direct Online now each handle 500,000 telephone calls and online visits respectively. This probably makes it the largest e-health service in the world.

The service has grown in both remit and complexity. There are differences in both operation and governance of the service in England, Wales and Scotland. The service has to interact in an increasingly diverse environment with (in the case of England) some 22 partner organisations.

However the service needs to function on a national level in respect of policies, networks, systems, performance and planning. The Government regards it as a national 'brand' and as contributing to wider developments in the NHS. The devolution associated with Wales and Scotland has meant variations in service development.

The introduction of NHS Direct[1]

NHS Direct represented the first step in a process that sought to radically reconfigure the delivery of

Photo: Getty Images

health care services and health care information. It provided both opportunities and challenges to all the actors in the health care environment. The UK Government had hoped that NHS Direct would become a well-used and well-regarded '24x7' gateway to the NHS in people's own homes.

The speed of growth of the service had concerned a number of doctors. GPs in the pilot areas had reported local concerns that NHS Direct was adding to doctors' workload by advising patients to contact their doctor for further advice. The doctors were also concerned over a diversion of nurses away from direct care in hospitals. In the professional medical journals NHS Direct was variously accused of being 'a cosmetic front', 'parasitic and destructive of the NHS' and based on 'political dogma'. A common thread was a concern that it might be used to mask a shortage of doctors.

The phone service was run through call centres and employed experienced nurses. NHS Direct call centres had successfully recruited nurses who had a wide variety of nursing experience including both hospital and community settings. About 60 per cent of the nurses worked part-time for the service – often combining it with work elsewhere in the NHS. The provision of flexible hours and, in one case, a workplace crèche also had a positive impact on staff recruitment. A national competency framework had been developed together with a planned rotation of staff between call centres and walk-in centres.

There were some concerns that planned expansion might impact negatively on other employers of nurses (both within and outside the NHS). The inducements offered to attract nurses to NHS Direct may be insufficient to retain them – especially if their image was of 'protocol-driven call centre workers' rather than trained health care professionals. There were also issues of how NHS Direct nursing staff were kept up to date on developments within the hospital and community care settings.

NHS Direct was supported by a considerable amount of technology including extensive use of diagnostic software which had prompted the nurses staffing the service to ask particular questions of callers and suggested possible diagnoses and recommend appropriate action.

The National Health Service and NHS Direct: size, finance and growth projections

The UK National Health Service (NHS) is one of the largest public sector organisations in Europe. In September 2002 there were over 1.2 million staff in the NHS Hospital and Community Health Services. Within this there were over 603,000 professionally qualified clinical staff in the NHS, including 103,350 doctors, 367,520 qualified nursing, midwifery & health visiting staff (including practice nurses), 116,598 qualified scientific, therapeutic & technical (ST&T) staff and 15,609 qualified ambulance staff. Government plans envisaged an increase in clinical staff up to the year 2006.

The NHS across the UK spent over £65bn (≈ €100bn) in 2002–03, which made it the second biggest area of government spending after social security. Of the £65.4bn allocated to the UK NHS in 2002–03, the NHS in England received £53.4bn. The health service in Wales received £3.4bn and Scotland's NHS received £6.7bn. Increases meant

Total NHS spending
£ billion, UK

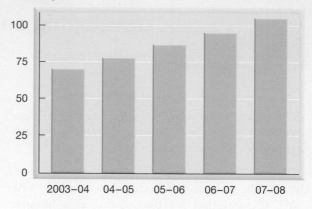

Source: HM Treasury

Health's share of GDP
% of GDP, UK

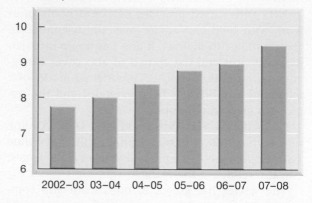

Source: HM Treasury

Figure 1 **Projected NHS spending and share of gross domestic product (GDP)[2]**

the NHS budget was more than £25bn higher than it was in 1999–2000. Furthermore NHS spending was planned to further increase to over £100bn in 2007–8 (see Figure 1).

NHS spending amounted to approximately 6.6 per cent of national income and was planned to increase thus converging on the (higher) proportion of GDP spent on health spent by most other European countries.

The unit costs of NHS Direct were comparable with other NHS services. In May 2000 the Royal College of Nursing reported that an NHS Direct call cost £8 (≈ €12) while an attendance at an Accident & Emergency department cost £42. The cost per contact with a GP was £10.55.

Figure 2 NHS Direct (England): costs and usage of various primary care services[3]

	Cost without calling NHS Direct	Cost including call to NHS Direct	Usage without NHS Direct advice	Usage with NHS Direct advice
Self care		£15.11	17%	35%
GP in-hours contact	£15.70	£30.81	29%	19%
GP out of hours (urgent) contact	£22.66	£37.77	22%	15%
Accident and Emergency Hospital attendance	£64.96	£80.77	3%	3%
Ambulance journey	£141.54	£156.65	8%	8%

However later (in 2001) a university study reassessed the costs of an NHS Direct call and a calculation was made of the impact of NHS Direct usage on subsequent usage of other services. This suggested that NHS Direct saved about 45 per cent of its running costs through reduced usage of other services. In 2000–01 the running costs of NHS Direct in England had been calculated at £80m.

NHS Direct: implementation and service relationships

The implementation of NHS Direct has generally been regarded as successful. There have been searching reports by various UK bodies including the National Audit Office and the Public Accounts Committee of the House of Commons. These have been complimentary of the service. The Public Accounts Committee Report noted that:

> NHS Direct has quickly established itself as the world's largest provider of telephone healthcare advice, and is proving popular with the public. It has a good safety record, with very few recorded adverse events. Departments should consider what wider lessons they could learn from the successful introduction of this significant and innovative service on time.[4]

The importance of the relationship to other aspects of the NHS and related services is shown by Figure 3 below which sets out how NHS Direct functioned as a gateway to various services. The concept of triage whereby callers are categorised in terms of seriousness and urgency has been used in health care for some time and has been used in both accident and emergency services and increasingly in primary care settings.

The original perception that NHS Direct would have a significant impact upon reducing the demands upon GP (family doctor), accident and emergency hospital and ambulance services has not been entirely

fulfilled. So far the demands upon ambulance and accident and emergency services have not been significantly reduced. Figure 2 above suggests that the main impact might be upon the family doctor services.

However the Public Accounts Committee noted the challenge of integration of the service with other NHS services. It cautioned the Department of Health to set a clear strategic direction for the service in order to avoid it becoming a victim of its own success by trying to do too many things at once. Callers were seen as waiting for too long and the service needed to improve both its capacity and technical competence.

Initially a Special Health Authority was set up to oversee the English part of NHS Direct. Strategic Health Authorities manage the delivery of local health services, develop health strategies and ensure that national health priorities are translated into local plans. In April 2004 a Special Health Authority was set up to deliver all NHS Direct services. The NHS Direct Special Health Authority is working with Primary Care Trusts to ensure locally relevant services are delivered. Strategic Health Authorities are facilitating PCTs to form consortias to commission NHS Direct services. The UK Government has major aspirations riding on the future success of the service. In the official documentation setting up the Authority the following statement was made:

> NHS Direct has been a leading example of the new modernised NHS based around the needs of patients. In five years it has grown from a small pilot scheme to a unique national service.[5]

NHS Direct Online

The growth of the internet-based service has been particularly significant. The increase in access to this online web-based service is shown by Figure 4.

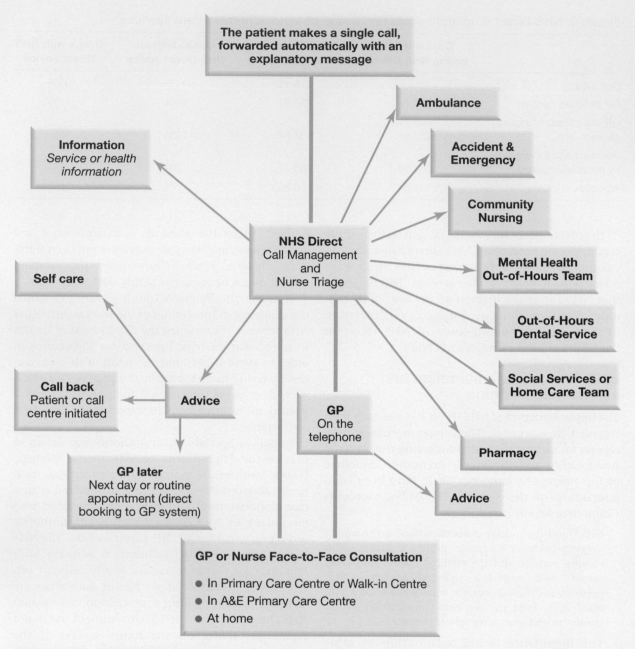

Figure 3 The NHS gateway to services[6]

NHS Direct Online forms one element of the NHS's new National Knowledge Service. NHS Direct Online is aimed primarily at patients and the public, whereas the National electronic Library for Health is aimed at health professionals.

The users of the online service are not necessarily the same as the users of NHS Direct. It is probable that the service may be reaching a more sophisticated and IT-literate user. It was quite likely (though NHS Direct does not provide any data) that the user group may have included professionals involved in service delivery and health promotional and educational services.

The extension of the service and ability to address challenge

The UK is a multi-cultural and multi-lingual society. NHS Direct (at least in England) has demonstrated an ability to reach users whose first language is not English through the creation of specialist language services. Figure 5 shows the breakdown for the 10 most used

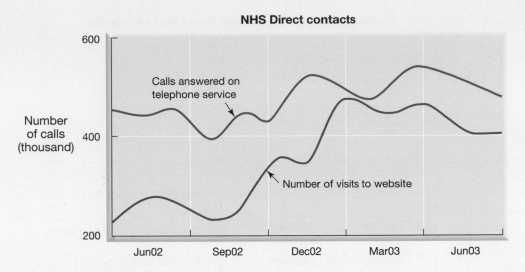

NHS Direct contacts

Calls answered on telephone service

Number of visits to website

Number of calls (thousand)

Source: Health Intelligence Unit, June 2003

Figure 4 **Growth of telephone and website services**[7]

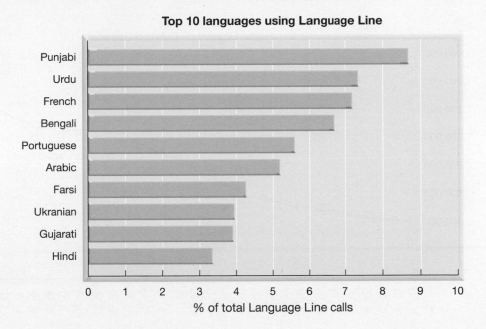

Top 10 languages using Language Line

% of total Language Line calls

Source: Language Line, June 2003

Figure 5 **NHS Direct and language provision (England)**[8]

languages. In Wales the service is provided in Welsh though the actual usage of this facility was relatively limited accounting for some 1.5 per cent of total calls.

The experience of the past years with a number of health scares about infectious disease and other risks to the general public has not been lost on NHS Direct. It regards a part of its role to serve as a source of information, advice and reassurance. This has been seen as both a local and national function of the service. Figure 6 shows the number and type of such alerts that the service handled over a three-month period.

The further development of NHS Direct

The success of the service has led to the Dept of Health to project an ambitious programme for future expansion of the service. Figure 7 shows the plan to

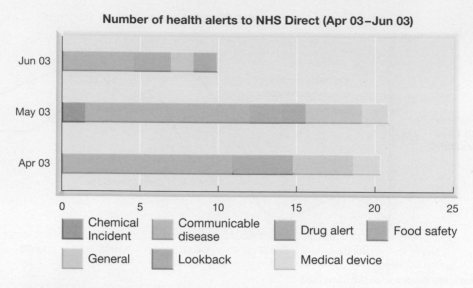

Source: Health Intelligence Unit, June 2003

Figure 6 NHS Direct: health alerts[9]

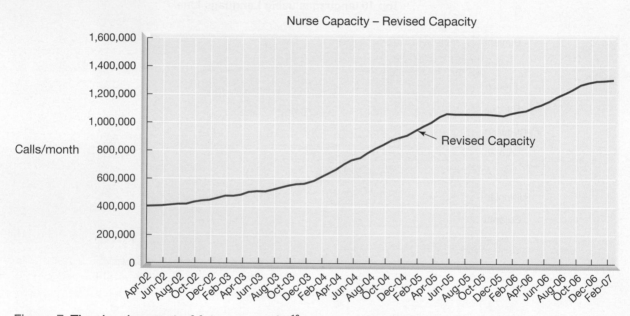

Figure 7 The development of future capacity[10]

increase capacity to a point in 2007 when it is envisaged that the service will have a capacity of 1.3 million calls per month (in England).

The review of the service in England by the National Audit Office also focused upon the need to address three key areas:

● Capacity – to meet the new demands the service will have to develop new human resource strategies, develop networks to deal with variations in

demand between centres and be able to provide a justification for additional funding.

● Safety – to maintain or even improve on the current safety record whilst expanding services.

● Integration – to link with other health care providers to prevent duplication and inefficiencies and promote joint working. This will involve the need to develop further communication strategies and IT systems.

From April 2004, Primary Care Trusts (the bodies which manage non-hospital based health services in England) are to be given the funding to commission NHS Direct services from a new special health authority. It is planned that funding for NHS Direct in England may be increased to £182m in 2005/6.

Variations in national development

There were variations in the development of the service throughout the United Kingdom. In particular these related to differences in both the governance and in the way that the service was developing. The growth of devolution in the UK with a National Assembly in Wales and a separate Parliament in Scotland had created the potential for different service developments.

Wales
In Wales the service was managed from one health authority (Swansea) on behalf of all of Wales. The majority of the advice was for home care, suggesting that the service was more likely to advise callers to pursue this option than in England. The service had also developed a significant role in the area of Dental advice. The NHS Direct service had been used by over 10 per cent of the population of Wales in 2002. This was a high population usage of the service. The service had also spearheaded relationships with voluntary organisations such as Samaritans (suicide prevention) and Childline (child abuse).

The service was also very aware of the health plan priorities for Wales and had sought to integrate its service strategy with them. The fact that the service was managed from within a particular health authority may well have encouraged this.

Scotland
In Scotland the development path taken by the service had shown some variations. It had adopted a different name – using the term NHS24. This could be seen as a departure from the UK government image of developing a 'brand' for the service which would almost certainly have implied a common title. It had also integrated the service into existing provision using a number of sites (as opposed to Wales). Close collaboration with health agencies and doctors had been a major focus of the service development with the service being heavily 'nurse led'.

The development of the service also had involved a close partnership between four agencies:

- NHS24 operated the systems and employed the staff;
- CAPGemini provided strategic consultancy;
- BT Consultancy contributed system consultancy and provision;
- AXA was the supplier of triage software systems, i.e. priority management.

Furthermore Scotland had pioneered the extension of the service into a new area – that of lower priority ambulance calls (known as Category C calls). The fact that there was one ambulance service for the whole of Scotland had meant that this was easier to develop than elsewhere in the UK. The ambulance service in Scotland referred calls which were seen as neither life-threatening nor serious (defined as Category C) to NHS24. This had required close collaboration between the two services and the development of a high level of trust and mutual understanding. Other agencies in Scotland, such as the police, are closely monitoring the NHS24 model and there is a possibility of further service integration taking place.

Both Wales and Scotland have been undertaking evaluations of their services. However that of Scotland had involved bringing in independent academic and medical experts whereas Wales had involved the Commission for Health Improvement – a government agency. It is quite likely that the evaluations may take slightly different paths as a consequence. The Scottish evaluation team had started by publishing a magazine to promote their evaluation activities, for example.

The future?

NHS Direct has undoubtedly been a success story so far. However a warning note was sounded by a manager quoted in an article in *Primary Care* in June 2003. He noted:

> NHS Direct has achieved a 20 per cent growth in capacity with the same number of staff. And there is more of that to come. But being a telephone service, the demand is there and then. When we've got the capacity we give a good service but if the capacity isn't there, then you can quickly cross the line, so it's going to be challenging.[11]

As the service expands into new areas such as dentistry, management of patient appointments and emergency service cover, it is going to prove more complicated to deliver the prompt, safe and integrated service set for it by key government reports. The increasingly complex and fast-moving technological milieu within which it has chosen to move is not always conducive to consolidation and reflection.

Notes

1. The author acknowledges J. Munro *et al.*, 'Evaluation of NHS Direct first wave sites', 2nd interim report to Dept of Health, March 2000, as a background source.
2. Derived from HM Treasury sources reported in *the Guardian*, October 2003.
3. Derived from National Audit Office Report, *NHS Direct in England*, January 2002 HC 505.
4. 40th Report of Public Accounts Committee of House of Commons, *NHS Direct in England*, 2002.
5. Recruitment material for NHS Direct.
6. Figure taken from 40th Report of Public Accounts Committee, ibid.
7. NHS Direct Quarterly Stakeholder Report, July 2003.
8. Ibid.
9. Ibid.
10. *Developing NHS Direct*, Dept of Health, April 2003.
11. *Primary Care*, June 2003.

Questions

1. What are the human resource implications of the further extension of NHS Direct services?
2. What are the major benefits and difficulties of extending the 'business model' of NHS Direct into further areas such as emergency services?
3. From the government (tax payers') perspective what are the arguments for and against NHS Direct being a good *financial* investment?
4. How might the current differences in service provision and governance between the different parts of the UK be managed?
5. What are the issues that will help or hinder the diffusion of information technology in the NHS as shown by the development of NHS Direct Online?

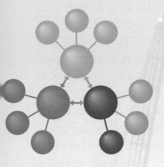

10

Managing Strategic Change

Learning outcomes

After reading this chapter you should be able to:

- Understand differences in the scope of strategic change.

- Explain how different aspects of organisational context might affect the design of strategic change programmes.

- Undertake a forcefield analysis to identify forces blocking and facilitating change.

- Explain the role of different change agents and the main styles of managing change they may apply.

- Explain steps required in turnaround strategies.

- Explain how different levers might be employed to influence strategic change, including the management of organisational routines, political and symbolic processes, forms of communication and other change tactics.

- Understand the unintended consequences that could result from change programmes.

Photo: © Steve Chenn/Corbis

Photo: Corbis

Photo: Freefoto.com

10.1   INTRODUCTION

This chapter is concerned with the management tasks and processes involved in changing strategies. Chapters 8 and 9 have already addressed important issues to do with the structuring of organisations and the role of enabling activities and processes important in effecting strategic change. However, designing a structure and processes to put a strategy into effect does not in itself mean that people will make it happen. In fact there is an assumption in most of what is written about strategic change that there will be a tendency towards *inertia* and *resistance to change*;[1] people will tend to hold on to existing ways of doing things and existing beliefs about what makes sense. As explained in Chapter 1 (section 1.5.1) this often leads to *strategic drift*.[2] Discussion of the 'experience lens' in the commentaries to the different parts of the book and explanations of how strategies develop in Chapter 11 also emphasise the same tendency. Managing strategic change therefore poses a major challenge for managers.

The assumption in much of what is written on the subject of strategic change is also that it happens in a *top-down* manner; that top managers decide strategy, plan how it will be implemented and then somehow effect the changes required. It is, of course, a major role of top managers to influence the strategic direction of the organisation. However, it is unrealistic to suppose they can control everything. Chapter 11 (section 11.4) will make it clear that strategies often emerge from lower down in the organisation in any case and, certainly, there are many others in the organisation – middle managers and below – who play a major role in managing change. This chapter takes this into account in explaining how strategic change might be managed.

If change is to be successful it also has to *link the strategic and the operational* and everyday aspects of the organisation. This emphasises the importance not only of translating strategic change into detailed resource plans, key tasks and the way the organisation is managed through control processes (Chapter 9), but also of how change is communicated through the everyday aspects of the organisation discussed in this chapter.

The approach taken to managing strategic change will also need to be *context dependent*. Managers need to consider how to balance the different approaches to managing strategic change according to the circumstances they face as well as trying to create the sort of organisational context that will facilitate change.

These themes provide a background to the content of this chapter. Exhibit 10.1 provides a structure for the chapter. Section 10.2 begins by explaining important issues that need to be considered in *diagnosing the situation* an organisation faces when embarking on strategic change, in terms of the *types of change* required, the variety of *contextual and cultural factors* that need to be taken into account and the *forces blocking or facilitating change*. Section 10.3 then discusses the management of strategic change in terms of the *styles of management* and the roles played by *strategic leaders* and other *change agents* in managing strategic change. Section 10.4 then goes on to consider in more detail the means they might employ for *managing change*. The steps commonly used for rapid '*turnaround strategies*' are discussed first. Then *levers for change* are reviewed including changes in *structure and control*, organisational *routines*, *symbols*, as are the roles of *political*

Exhibit 10.1   Key elements in managing strategic change

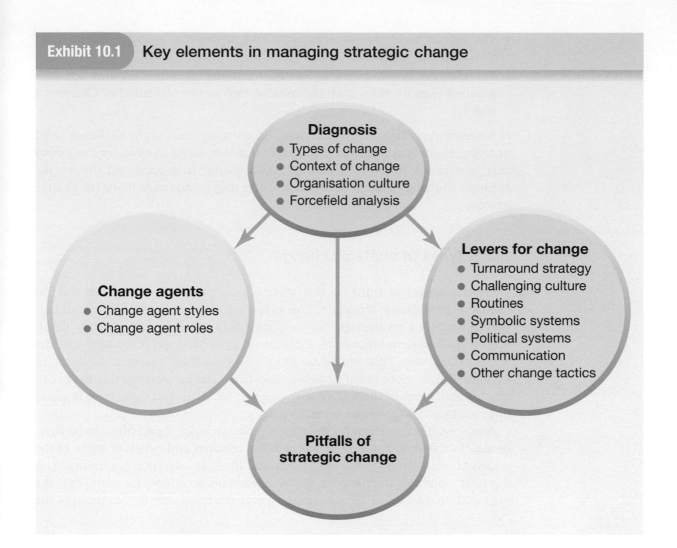

Diagnosis
- Types of change
- Context of change
- Organisation culture
- Forcefield analysis

Change agents
- Change agent styles
- Change agent roles

Levers for change
- Turnaround strategy
- Challenging culture
- Routines
- Symbolic systems
- Political systems
- Communication
- Other change tactics

Pitfalls of strategic change

---

activity, different forms of *communication* and more specific *tactics* for managing change. Finally section 10.4 considers some of the *pitfalls* that have been found to be common in change programmes in organisations.

10.2 DIAGNOSING THE CHANGE SITUATION

It is important to remember that in managing strategic change much of what has been written in previous chapters in this book is usually seen as an essential precursor in identifying the need for and direction of strategic change. It will not be repeated in any detail here, but it is important to remember the need to understand:

- Why strategic change is needed (discussed in Chapters 2, 3 and 4).
- The basis of the strategy in terms of strategic purpose, perhaps encapsulated in the form of a clear statement of strategic intent and bases of competitive advantage (discussed in Chapters 5 and 6).

- The more specific possible directions and methods of strategy development (discussed in Chapter 7).

- The changes in structures, processes, relationships, resources and activities required to move from strategic thinking into action (discussed in Chapters 8 and 9).

However, there is also a need to understand the magnitude of the challenge faced in trying to effect strategic change. To do this it is useful to consider the *type* of change required, the wider *context* in which change is to occur and the specific *blockages* to change that exist and what forces might exist to *facilitate* the change process.

10.2.1 Types of strategic change

There is a danger in thinking that there is only one way, or one best way, to change organisational strategies. This is not so. As was suggested in the discussion in Chapter 1 on strategic drift (section 1.5.1), quite typically strategy development is *incremental* in nature. It builds on prior strategy; it is *adaptive* in the way it occurs, with only occasional more *transformational* changes.[3] (Chapter 11 explains this in more detail.) Balogun and Hope Hailey[4] develop this further to identify four types of strategic change (see Exhibit 10.2), and these have implications for how change might be managed.

Arguably, it is beneficial for the *nature of change* in an organisation to be *incremental*. In this way it will build on the skills, routines and beliefs of those in the organisation, so that change is efficient and likely to win their commitment. A *'big bang'* approach to change might be needed on occasions, for example if the organisation is facing crisis or needs to change direction very fast. In terms of the

---

Exhibit 10.2   Types of change

	Scope of change	
	Realignment	**Transformation**
Nature of change — Incremental	Adaptation	Evolution
Nature of change — Big Bang	Reconstruction	Revolution

Source: Adapted from J. Balogun and V. Hope Hailey, *Exploring Strategic Change*, Prentice Hall, 1999.

scope of the change process, the issue is whether it can occur within the current paradigm (i.e. current organisational beliefs and assumptions – see Chapter 4, section 4.5.5). This can be thought of as a *realignment* of strategy rather than a fundamental change of strategic direction. Or does it require paradigm change? This is more *transformational* change. Combining these two axes shows that there are four types of strategic change:

● *Adaptation* is change which can be accommodated within the current paradigm and occur incrementally. It is the most common form of change in organisations.

● *Reconstruction* is the type of change which may be rapid and could involve a good deal of upheaval in an organisation, but which does not fundamentally change the paradigm. It could be a *turnaround* situation where there is need for major structural changes or a major cost-cutting programme to deal with a decline in financial performance or difficult or changing market conditions. This is discussed in section 10.4.1 in this chapter.

● *Evolution* is a change in strategy which requires paradigm change, but over time. It may be that managers anticipate the need for transformational change, perhaps through the sorts of analytical technique described earlier in the book. They may then be in a position of planned evolutionary change, with time in which to achieve it. Another way in which evolution can be explained is by conceiving of organisations as 'learning systems', continually adjusting their strategies as their environment changes. This has given rise to the idea of the *learning organisation*, which is discussed in section 11.6.2 in Chapter 11 and the commentary to Part IV.

● *Revolution* is change which requires rapid and major strategic and paradigm change. This could be in circumstances where the strategy has been so bounded by the existing paradigm and established ways of doing things in the organisation that, even when environmental or competitive pressures might require fundamental change, the organisation has failed to respond. This might have occurred over many years (see the discussion of strategic drift in section 1.5.1 of Chapter 1) and resulted in circumstances where pressures for change are extreme – for example, a take-over threatens the continued existence of a firm.

It is therefore helpful to have a view about the type of change required. The sort of cultural analysis explained in section 4.5.5 of Chapter 4 can be useful here to consider a central question. This is whether or not the change required could be accommodated within the bounds of the culture as it is; or whether it would require a really significant shift in this regard. For example, a retailer may launch quite new products without requiring fundamental changes in the assumptions and beliefs of the organisation. On the other hand, some changes in strategy, even if they do not take the form of dramatic product changes, may require fundamental changes in core assumptions in the organisation. For example, the shift from a production focus for a manufacturer to a customer-led, service ethos may not entail the visible output of the firm in the form of its products to be changed, but will very likely require significant culture change (see section 10.2.3 below).

10.2.2 The importance of context

There is no one right 'formula' for the management of change. The success of any attempt at managing change will be dependent on the wider context in which that change is taking place. Take an obvious example. Managing change in a small, perhaps relatively new, business, where a motivated team are themselves driving change, would be quite different from trying to manage change in a major corporation, or perhaps a long-established public sector organisation, with established routines, formal structures and perhaps a great deal of resistance to change. The contexts are completely different and the approach to managing change therefore needs to be different.[5]

Balogun and Hope Hailey[6] build on this point to highlight a number of important contextual features that need to be taken into account in designing change programmes. One of these is, indeed, the scope of change required and this has been discussed in section 10.2.1 above. Exhibit 10.3 also summarises others. It is useful, then, to consider these contextual characteristics before embarking on a programme of change. Illustration 10.1 gives an example of Russian firms as a context in which such understanding has been shown to be very important.

Consider some examples of how the contextual features shown in Exhibit 10.3 might require different approaches to change:

Exhibit 10.3 **Contextual features and their influence on strategic change programmes**

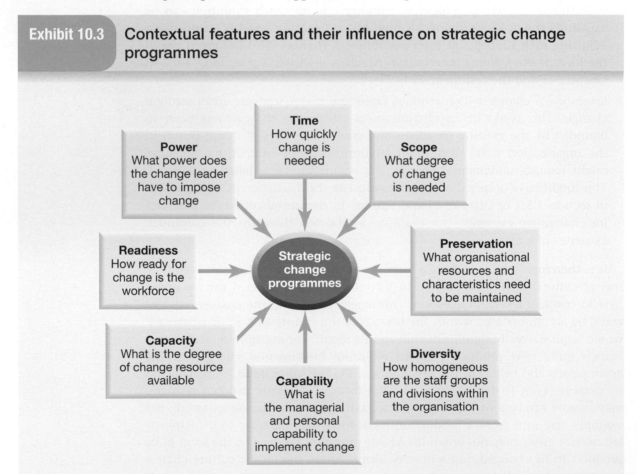

Illustration 10.1   strategy into action

The change context for western ventures in Russian companies

Westerners working in alliances with companies in other parts of the world frequently fail to understand the importance of cultural context.

The challenge for Russian firms of moving from a centrally planned economy with state-controlled production units to a market-based economy is huge in scope. Russian firms have often looked to the west for the injection of capital and as alliance partners to help with this. How western managers might engage with such a challenge needs to bear the Russian context in mind.

Perhaps paradoxically for a once centrally planned economy, Russian managers have tended not to take the idea of long-term plans very seriously. Time horizons can be very limited; a Russian manager is quite likely to think of time horizons in days or weeks. Moreover, the notion of five-year plans has, of itself, connotations of the central planning and unfulfilled promises of the Communist past.

Russian managers also tend to emphasise continuity and tradition more than westerners. Their orientation is towards history and the preservation of what they have, rather than the necessity for changes. Hand in hand with this goes an emphasis on conformity. They are wary of independent thinking or openness, regarding such behaviour as potentially anti-social and promoting conflict. There is also a mistrust of change which can be explained, not least, as a result of their aversion to risk and uncertainty.

Managers in Russia have traditionally been concerned with the development and maintenance of rules and procedures, rather than the management of change. The role of senior managers, in particular, has been seen as exercising a top-down, directive style with an expectation of high degrees of clarity and a dislike of ambiguity. Formal bureaucratic control rather than feedback is expected. The experience and capability in change management is limited. The extent to which resources are available to put change into practice may also be dependent upon whether external investment, often from the west, can be obtained. However, western managers may be seen in just that role: as investors rather than as agents of, or role models for, change.

There are also differences between Russian and western cultural assumptions both in business and personally. In business there remains a disquiet about the primacy of profits and of market forces; and also of the western emphasis on efficiency, professionalism and modernity. Russians tend to emphasise fate, destiny and faith in the Russian context.

All this can raise problems for western managers who may see themselves as trying to change the system, introduce a market focus, longer-term strategic thinking, establish western systems of control and feedback and more participative styles of management.

Source: Adapted from S. Miichailova, 'Contrasts in culture: Russian and western perspectives on organisational change', *Academy of Management Executive*, vol. 145, no. 4 (2000), pp. 99–111.

Questions

1. Use the discussion of context in section 10.2.2 to identify key contextual issues which need to be taken into account in influencing change in Russian firms.

2. What problems do you think western managers might face?

3. Read the rest of the chapter and suggest the approach to change that western managers might follow, bearing in mind the Russian context.

● The *time* available for change could be dramatically different. For example, a business facing immediate decline in turnover or profits from rapid changes in its markets has a quite different context for change compared with a business where the management may see the need for change coming in the future, perhaps years away, and have time to plan it carefully as a staged incremental process.

● No matter how significant the change, it may be that there is a need for the *preservation* of certain aspects of the organisation, in particular those that are to do with the competences on which changes need to be based. Suppose, for example, that a fast-growing computer business needs to become more formally organised because of its growth. This could well upset technical experts who have been used to rapid access to senior management: but it could be vital to preserve their expertise and motivation.

● Change may be helped if there is a *diversity* of experience, views and opinions within an organisation: but suppose that organisation has followed a strategy for many decades, leading to a very homogeneous way of seeing the world. Change could be hampered by this. So gauging the nature and extent of diversity so as to utilise and build on it could be important.

● To what extent is there any experience or *capability* in managing change in the organisation? It could be that one organisation has managers who have managed change effectively in the past, or a workforce that has been used to and has accepted past changes in their work practices, whilst another has little experience of change.

● Does the organisation have the *capacity* for change in terms of available resources? Change can be costly, not only in financial terms, but in terms of management time.

● In some organisations there could be a *readiness* for change throughout. In others there could be widespread resistance or pockets or levels of resistance in some parts of the organisation and readiness in others.

● Is there anyone in the organisation who has the *power* to effect change? Too often it is assumed that the chief executive has such power, but in the face of resistance from below, or perhaps resistance from external stakeholders, this may not be the case. It may also be that the chief executive supposes that others in the organisation have the power to effect change when they do not.

Pulling this together, the questions that emerge are these:

● Does the organisation in question have the capacity, capability, readiness and power structures to achieve the scope of change required? For example, in a study of attempts to manage change in hospitals[7] it was found that their governance and organisational structures prevented any clear authority to manage change. This, combined with the resource constraints they laboured under, meant that major one-off change initiatives were not likely to succeed.

● How does the context inform the choices about the means by which change can be managed? These choices about means are reviewed later in the chapter.

● Does the context need to be changed before the strategic change itself can occur? For example, it could be that new management with experience of managing change need to be introduced to enhance the capability and readiness for change to get the organisation to a point where it is ready to embark on a more significant strategic change programme. Or that people with a greater diversity of experience in line with the future strategic direction need to be brought in.

● Or perhaps it needs to be recognised that in some contexts change has to be managed in stages. The researchers in the hospital study reported above found that change tended to take place by one initiative making limited progress, then stalling, followed by a later one making further advances.

10.2.3 Using the cultural web to diagnose organisational context

Chapter 4 introduced the idea of the cultural web (see section 4.5.5 of Chapter 4) as both a useful concept in explaining organisational culture and as a diagnostic tool to understand the culture of a particular organisation. It can also be used to consider the problems and requirements of strategic change. It is useful in this respect, not least because it embraces the softer aspects of culture such as organisational symbols and the routine 'ways of doing things around here', as well as political processes and the harder aspects of organisations such as structures and control systems. The cultural web can also be used to analyse the current culture of an organisation and consider the differences that would be needed if the desired future strategy were to be put into effect successfully.

Illustration 10.2 shows the cultural webs produced as part of a strategic change workshop by managers in the technical services department of a local government authority in the UK.[8] What emerged from this analysis was that the organisation's current culture was largely unsuited to desired future strategy. Indeed departments had their own strategies, each reflecting the high professional standards so highly valued but not always emphasising the needs of the users of the services. This was not compatible with the strategy the chief executive had been trying to develop. He wanted a strategy to address key local issues which crossed department responsibilities and therefore required cooperation across departments. However, the organisation described in Illustration 10.2 was not just inherently departmental and functional, but that functionalism was preserved and legitimated by a professional ethos, protected by powerful departmental heads. Whilst these departmental heads did take part in discussions on overall local government strategy and might agree to the logic of such a strategy, back in their departments their focus was on preserving service standards strongly influenced by professional norms and established procedures. The strategy was on paper only whilst there was a continuation of departmental strategies driven by the long-established culture and powerful individuals dedicated to its preservation.

Managers who undertook the analysis came to see that it was unrealistic to believe that significant strategic change could occur if major change did not occur to many aspects of the organisation encapsulated in the web. However, they could use their analysis of the current and required future cultural web to inform their discussions about what changes were required. Here the forcefield analysis explained in the next section can help.

Illustration 10.2   strategy into action

Understanding the cultural context for change in local government

The cultural web can be used as a way of understanding current organisational culture and desired future culture.

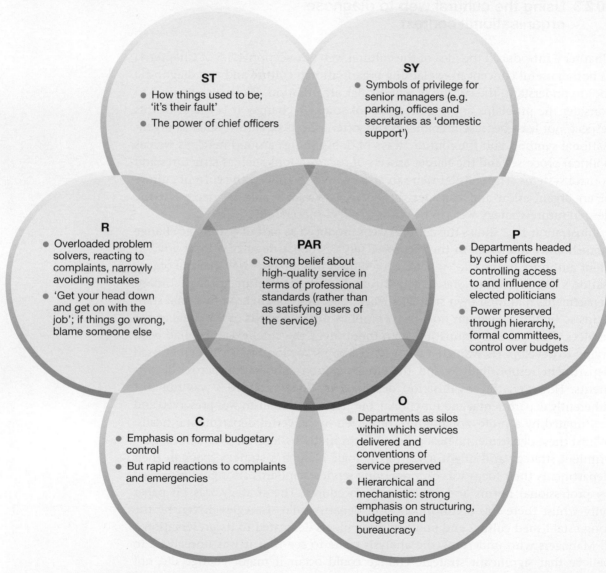

ST
- How things used to be; 'it's their fault'
- The power of chief officers

SY
- Symbols of privilege for senior managers (e.g. parking, offices and secretaries as 'domestic support')

R
- Overloaded problem solvers, reacting to complaints, narrowly avoiding mistakes
- 'Get your head down and get on with the job'; if things go wrong, blame someone else

PAR
- Strong belief about high-quality service in terms of professional standards (rather than as satisfying users of the service)

P
- Departments headed by chief officers controlling access to and influence of elected politicians
- Power preserved through hierarchy, formal committees, control over budgets

C
- Emphasis on formal budgetary control
- But rapid reactions to complaints and emergencies

O
- Departments as silos within which services delivered and conventions of service preserved
- Hierarchical and mechanistic: strong emphasis on structuring, budgeting and bureaucracy

Figure 1 **Technical Services – current**

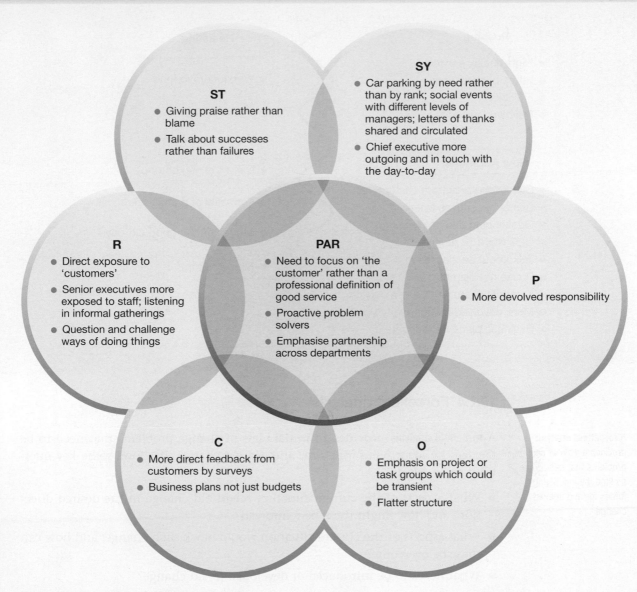

ST
- Giving praise rather than blame
- Talk about successes rather than failures

SY
- Car parking by need rather than by rank; social events with different levels of managers; letters of thanks shared and circulated
- Chief executive more outgoing and in touch with the day-to-day

R
- Direct exposure to 'customers'
- Senior executives more exposed to staff; listening in informal gatherings
- Question and challenge ways of doing things

PAR
- Need to focus on 'the customer' rather than a professional definition of good service
- Proactive problem solvers
- Emphasise partnership across departments

P
- More devolved responsibility

C
- More direct feedback from customers by surveys
- Business plans not just budgets

O
- Emphasis on project or task groups which could be transient
- Flatter structure

Figure 2 **Technical Services – future**

Source: Adapted from G. Johnson, 'Mapping and re-mapping organisational culture: a local government example', in G. Johnson and K. Scholes (eds), *Exploring Public Sector Strategy*, Prentice Hall, 2001.

Questions

1. How might a change manager use the cultural web to help manage change?

2. What are likely to be the main problems in making changes indicated by the future web?

Exhibit 10.4   Forcefield analysis

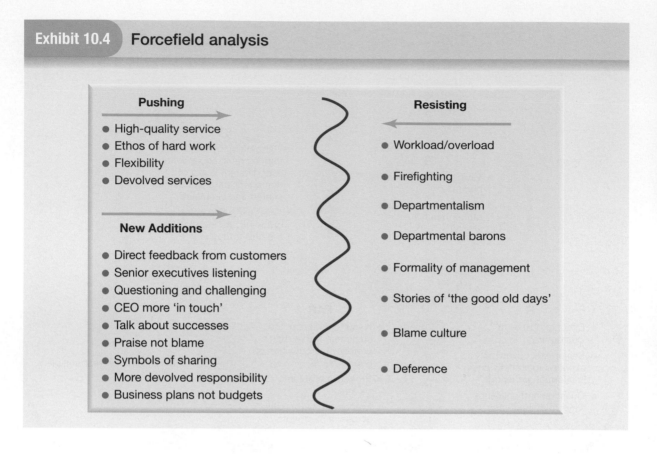

10.2.4 Forcefield analysis

A **forcefield analysis** provides a view of change problems that need to be tackled, by identifying forces for and against change

A **forcefield analysis** provides an initial view of change problems that need to be tackled, by identifying forces for and against change. It allows some key questions to be asked:

- What aspects of the current situation might aid change in the desired direction, and how might these be reinforced?
- What aspects of the current situation would block such change, and how can these be overcome?
- What needs to be introduced or developed to aid change?

Exhibit 10.4 is a representation of the sorts of blockage to change in the example given in Illustration 10.2, Figure 1. Whilst the blockages identified constituted a significant problem, the forcefield analysis also identified aspects of the organisation and its culture that might facilitate change. The managers saw the dedication to good service, the ethos of hard work and the flexibility in service delivery that had developed as potentially positive, if only some of the blockages could be overcome. Moreover, the devolved nature of some services (to local offices) might be harnessed positively in a different culture.

Conceiving of what the organisation would need to look like if a different strategy were being followed is also useful and the cultural web can be used for this too (see Illustration 10.2, Figure 2). This helps identify what needs to be added or introduced if change is to occur. What typically emerges from such an exercise in diagnosing a change situation is that the routines, control systems, structures, symbols and power or dependency relationships can be both important blockages and facilitators to change. Deciding which are blockages and which are facilitators is a helpful diagnostic basis for managing change.

Changes in the structure, design and control systems of organisations have already been reviewed in Chapter 8. In the next two sections (10.3 and 10.4), different styles and roles in the change process and other levers for managing change are discussed.

10.3 CHANGE MANAGEMENT: STYLES AND ROLES

This section of the chapter is concerned with the role people play in managing strategic change; and how they do it. It begins by considering different *styles of managing change* that might be employed. It then goes on to examine the role in strategic change played by *strategic leaders*; the role *middle managers* have in effecting change; and the influence of *outsiders* such as consultants and external *stakeholders*.

10.3.1 Styles of managing change

Whoever is in the position of managing change needs to consider the style of management they adopt. Different styles are likely to be more or less appropriate according to organisational context. These styles are summarised in Exhibit 10.5.[9]

- **Education and communication** involve the explanation of the reasons for and means of strategic change. It might be appropriate if there is a problem in managing change based on misinformation or lack of information and if there is adequate time to invest in persuading people and give them the chance to assimilate the information. However, there are problems here. Assuming that reasoned argument will overcome perhaps years of embedded assumptions about what 'really matters' could be naïve especially if there is a lack of mutual trust and respect between managers and employees. Relying on processes of communication in a top-down fashion may also be problematic. Change is typically likely to be more effective if those affected by it are involved in its development and planning.

  Education and communication involve the explanation of the reasons for and means of strategic change

- **Collaboration** or *participation* in the change process is the involvement of those who will be affected by strategic change in the change agenda; for example, the identification of strategic issues, the strategic decision-making process, the setting of priorities, the planning of strategic change or the translation of stated strategy into routine aspects of organisational life. Such involvement fosters a more positive attitude to change; people see the constraints the organisation faces as less significant[10] and are likely to feel increased ownership of and commitment to a decision or change process. It may therefore be a way of building readiness and capability for change. However, there is the inevitable

  Collaboration or participation in the change process is the involvement of those who will be affected by strategic change in the change agenda

Exhibit 10.5	Styles of managing strategic change

Style	Means/context	Benefits	Problems	Circumstances of effectiveness
Education and communication	Group briefings assume internalisation of strategic logic and trust of top management	Overcoming lack of (or mis)information	Time consuming Direction or progress may be unclear	Incremental change or long-time horizontal transformational change
Collaboration/ participation	Involvement in setting the strategy agenda and/or resolving strategic issues by taskforces or groups	Increasing ownership of a decision or process May improve quality of decisions	Time consuming Solutions/outcome within existing paradigm	
Intervention	Change agent retains co-ordination/control: delegates elements of change	Process is guided/controlled but involvement takes place	Risk of perceived manipulation	Incremental or non-crisis transformational change
Direction	Use of authority to set direction and means of change	Clarity and speed	Risk of lack of acceptance and ill-conceived strategy	Transformational change
Coercion/edict	Explicit use of power through edict	May be successful in crises or state of confusion	Least successful unless crisis	Crisis, rapid transformational change or change in established autocratic cultures

risk that solutions will be found from within the existing culture so anyone who sets up such a process may need to retain the ability to intervene in the process.

Intervention is the coordination of and authority over processes of change by a change agent who delegates elements of the change process

● **Intervention** is the coordination of and authority over processes of change by a change agent who delegates elements of the change process. For example, it might be that particular stages of change, such as ideas generation, data collection, detailed planning, the development of rationales for change or the identification of critical success factors are delegated to project teams or taskforces (see section 11.3.2 in Chapter 11). Such teams may not take full responsibility for the change process, but become involved in it and see their work building towards it. The sponsor of the change ensures the monitoring of progress and that change is seen to occur.[11] An advantage here is that it involves members of the organization, not only in originating ideas, but also in the *partial implementation* of solutions. For example, those who originate ideas might be given responsibility for coordinating or overseeing the implementation of such aspects of the strategic change. This involvement is likely to give rise to greater commitment to the change.

Direction involves the use of personal managerial authority to establish a clear future strategy and how change will occur

● **Direction** involves the use of personal managerial authority to establish a clear future strategy and how change will occur. It is essentially top-down management of strategic change. It may be associated with a clear vision or strategic intent developed by someone seen as a leader in the organisation; but it may also be accompanied by similar clarity about the sorts of critical success factors and priorities discussed in Chapter 9.

- In its most extreme form, a directive style becomes **coercion**, involving the imposition of change or the issuing of edicts about change. This is the explicit use of power and may be necessary if the organisation is facing a crisis, for example.

> **Coercion** is the imposition of change or the issuing of edicts about change

There are some overall observations that can be made about the appropriateness of these different styles in different contexts (see section 10.2.2):

- Different stages in a change process may require different styles of managing change. Clear direction may be vital to motivate a desire or create a *readiness* to change, whilst participation or intervention may be more helpful in gaining wider commitment across the organisation, and developing *capabilities* to identify blockages to change and plan and implement specific action programmes.

- In terms of *time and scope*, participative styles are likely to be most appropriate for incremental change within organisations, but where transformational change is required, directive approaches may be more appropriate. It is also worth noting that even where top management see themselves adopting participative styles, their subordinates may perceive this as directive and, indeed, may welcome such direction.[12]

- In organisations with hierarchical *power structures* a directive style will be typical and it may be difficult to break away from it, not least because people expect it. On the other hand in 'flatter' power structures (or if the organisation corresponds to the sort of adhocracy, network or learning organisation described elsewhere in this book), it is likely that collaboration and participation will be not only desirable but inevitable. This can of course lead to difficulties if there is disagreement about what is required; and such organisations have found that here too there may be times when stronger direction is needed in some form.

- Different styles suit different managers' personality types. However, these observations suggest that those with the greatest *capability* to manage change may have the ability to adopt different styles in different circumstances. Indeed, there is evidence for this when it comes to the effectiveness of strategic leaders (see section 10.3.2 below).

- Styles of managing change are not mutually exclusive in a change programme. To a greater or lesser extent, there will be a *diversity* of views about change within the organization and amongst its different stakeholders. Education and communication may be appropriate for some stakeholders, such as financial institutions; participation may be appropriate for groups in parts of the organisation where it is necessary to build *capability and readiness*; whereas if there are parts of the organisation where change has to happen fast, *timing* may demand a more directive style.

Illustration 10.3 shows how chief executives may use different styles in different contexts.

Illustration 10.3   strategy into action

Styles of managing change

Executives use different styles of managing change.

Start with the truth

Carly Fiorina is chairman and CEO of Hewlett-Packard in Palo Alto, California:

> I remember my first meeting with 700 of our senior leaders, when we underwent this very realistic self-appraisal . . . You can't do your own interpretation of what's wrong and beat people up; to motivate them to change, you have to show them a mirror. . . . I wrote down comments these managers had themselves made two years earlier about the company, including the comment that HP was too slow and indecisive. I also wrote down things customers had said about us, both good and bad. When confronted with the inescapable facts of what they had said about themselves and what customers had told us, managers accepted the truth.
>
> Once you have the truth, people need aspirational goals. To cross that uncomfortable gap between the truth and the goal, you must set very achievable, step-by-step measures. The process of doing begets progress; along the way, you must remind people of how far they've come already and how much closer they are to achieving the goal. That's when you see the light in their eyes.

Set different incentive levels[1]

Lui Chuanzhi is chairman of Legend Group of Beijing:

> Our executive team needs a sense of ownership in the company. Many state-owned enterprises in China face a special challenge: They cannot give their senior executives stock. But we took an untraditional approach; we reformed our ownership structure to make Legend a joint stock company, enabling us to give all our executive team members stock. In addition, senior executives need recognition, so we provide them with opportunities to speak to the media. . . .
>
> Midlevel managers want to become senior managers, so they respond best to challenges – to opportunities to display and hone their talents. We set very high performance standards for our middle managers, and we let them participate in strategic processes, in designing their own work, and in making and executing their own decisions. If they get good results, they are handsomely rewarded.
>
> Line employees need a sense of stability. If they take responsibility and are conscientious, they earn a predictable bonus. We also tie team performance to company or unit performance, and individual performance to team performance.

Build on the key influencers[2]

William Bratton was the police commissioner of New York City responsible for the Zero Tolerance campaign that reduced crime in the city.

Bratton's belief is that once 'the beliefs and energies of a critical mass of people are engaged, conversion to another idea will spread like an epidemic, bringing about fundamental change very quickly'. This involves putting key managers face-to-face with detailed operational problems so that they cannot evade reality. He puts these 'under a spotlight'. For example, he brings together senior policemen and, with only two days' notice, requires them to face questions from senior colleagues about the performance of their precinct and how the detailed operations of that precinct contribute to the overall strategy for the force. The aim is to introduce a 'culture of performance' such that failings cannot be covered up. However, 'the meetings gave high achievers the chance to be recognised both for making improvements . . . and for helping (their colleagues)'. The effect is to allow success to be applauded but to make it very clear that underperformance is not tolerated.

1. 'Moving mountains', *Harvard Business Review*, January 2003, pp. 41–47.
2. W.C. Kim and R. Mauborgne, 'Tipping point leadership', *Harvard Business Review*, April 2003, pp. 60–69.

Questions

Read section 10.3.1 of the text and Exhibit 10.5, then answer the following questions in relation to each of the three examples above.

1. Does the style match the circumstances? In what circumstances would it not be appropriate?

2. What might be the problems of each of the styles?

3. Only some stakeholders are specifically mentioned in the examples. Does this mean that the style should be the same towards all stakehoders of the organisation?

10.3.2 Roles in managing change

When it comes to considering strategic change, there is too often an over-emphasis on individuals at the top of an organisation. It is useful to think of *change agency* more broadly. A '**change agent**' is the individual or group that helps effect strategic change in an organisation. For example, the creator of a strategy may, or may not, also be the change agent. He or she may need to rely on others to take a lead in effecting changes to strategy. It could well be that a middle manager is also change agent in a particular context. Or it may be that there is a group of change agents from within the organisation or perhaps from outside, such as consultants, who have a whole team working on a project, together with managers from within the organisation. So change agency does not necessarily correspond to one individual.

> A **change agent** is the individual or group that effects strategic change in an organisation

Strategic leadership

The management of change is, however, often directly linked to the role of a strategic leader. **Leadership** is the process of influencing an organisation (or group within an organisation) in its efforts towards achieving an aim or goal.[13] Within this definition, a leader is not necessarily someone at the top of an organisation, but rather someone who is in a position to have influence. They are often categorised in two ways:

> **Leadership** is the process of influencing an organisation (or group within an organisation) in its efforts towards achieving an aim or goal

- *Charismatic leaders*, who are mainly concerned with building a vision for the organisation and energising people to achieve it, and are therefore usually associated with managing change. The evidence suggests that these leaders have particularly beneficial impact on performance when the people who work for them see the organisation facing uncertainty.[14]

- *Instrumental or transactional leaders*,[15] who focus more on designing systems and controlling the organisation's activities, and are more likely to be associated with improving the current situation.

A more specific set of approaches is helpful, however, in understanding how leaders manage strategy and change. The evidence is that they attend more to some aspects of strategic management than to other aspects. This is shown in Exhibit 10.6. In some respects these different approaches correspond to the different change management styles discussed in the previous section of the chapter. The approaches vary. Charismatic leaders take a personal responsibility in the search for future opportunities and the development of overall strategy (*the strategy approach*) or on *strategic change* and the continual reinvention of the organisation. Others focus on developing people who can take responsibility for strategy at the market interface (*the human assets approach*) or on a particular area of *expertise* that will be a source of competitive advantage. The transactional leader's focus is on development, communication and monitoring of a set of *controls* to ensure uniform organisational behaviour and standards (a so-called box approach). A distinctive focus on strategic change is certainly one of these approaches, but only one.

Exhibit 10.6	Strategic leadership approaches

	Strategy	Human assets	Expertise	Control (box)	Change
Focus of attention	Strategic analysis and strategy formulation	Developing people	Disseminating expertise as source of competitive advantage	Setting procedures and measures of control	Continual change
Indicative behaviour	Scanning markets, technological changes etc.	Getting the right people; creating a coherent culture	Cultivating and improving area of expertise through systems and procedures	Monitoring performance against controls to ensure uniform, predictable performance	Communicating and motivating through speeches, meetings etc.
Role of other managers	Day-to-day operations	Strategy development devolved	Immersion in and management of expertise area	Ensure uniform performance against control measures	Change agents; openness to change
Implications for managing change	Delegated	Recruiting/ developing people capable of managing strategy locally	Change in line with expertise approach	Change carefully monitored and controlled	Change central to the approach

Source: Reprinted by permission of Harvard Business Review. Adapted from C.M. Farkas and S. Wetlaufer; 'The ways chief executives lead', *Harvard Business Review*, May–June 1996, pp.110–123. Copyright © 1996 by the Harvard Business School Publishing Corporation; all rights reserved.

Faced with the need for change, each of the approaches has implications for how change might be managed by such strategic leaders, as also shown in Exhibit 10.6. The strategic leader who takes personal responsibility for the formulation of strategy may well delegate responsibility for managing specific change processes, whereas another for whom change is *the* approach will see it as a personal responsibility. The strategic leader who focuses on control or a particular area of expertise may seek to manage change through those control mechanisms or on the back of that expertise. The human assets approach may lead to extensive involvement, even leadership of change, by local managers. Indeed here the strategic leader may be more of a facilitator of change generated from below, encouraging strategic debate, building on a diversity of views and synthesising a clarity of strategic direction from that debate.

There is a debate as to whether the approaches described above are a function of the personality of individual strategic leaders or not. Ideally what is required is the ability to tailor the strategic leadership approach to context. There is evidence[16] that the most successful strategic leaders are able to do just this. Indeed with regard to the management of change, it would seem to be a problem if they cannot. After all, some approaches are more to do with creating strategy, or with control rather than the management of change, and might well lead to approaches to change not suited to the particular needs of the specific change context.

Middle managers

A top-down approach to managing strategy and strategic change sees middle managers as implementers of strategy. Their role is to put into effect the direction established by top management by making sure that resources are allocated and controlled appropriately, monitoring performance and behaviour of staff and, where necessary, explaining the strategy to those reporting to them. Those who take such an approach often tend to view middle managers not so much as facilitators of the strategy, but as blockages to its success. Indeed, this is sometimes seen as one reason for reducing the numbers and layers of management, so as to speed up communication between top management and organisational members, and to reduce potential blockages and filters.

However, Steve Floyd and Bill Wooldridge have shown that middle managers can and do provide a real benefit in both the development and the implementation of strategy especially as organisations become larger, more complex and yet reduce hierarchical structures.[17] Middle managers' wider involvement in strategic management has been discussed in Chapter 9 (section 9.2.4). In the context of managing strategic change it is important to emphasise five important roles they play:

- The first is the systematic role of *implementation and control*: this does reflect the idea of top-down change in which they are monitors of that change.

- The second is as '*translators*' of strategy when it is established by more senior management. Top management may set down a strategic direction; but how it is made sense of in specific contexts (e.g. a region of a multinational or a functional department) may, intentionally or not, be left to middle managers. If misinterpretation of that intended strategy is to be avoided, it is therefore vital that middle managers understand and feel an ownership of it.

- Similarly, middle managers are likely to be involved in the *reinterpretation and adjustment* of strategic responses as events unfold (e.g. in terms of relationships with customers, suppliers, the workforce and so on) – a vital role they are uniquely qualified for because they are in day-to-day contact with such aspects of the organisation and its environment.

- They are therefore a crucial *relevance bridge* between top management and members of the organisation at lower levels. Because they are in touch with the day-to-day routines of the organisation which can so easily become blockages to change and the climate for change that can help or hinder change, they are in a position to translate change initiatives into a locally relevant form or message. (See the key debate in Illustration 10.8.)

- They are also in a position to be *advisors* to more senior management on what are likely to be the organisational blockages and requirements for change; an example is that of the technical services managers given in Illustration 10.2.

Middle managers may therefore contribute substantially either to galvanising commitment to strategy and the change process, or to blocking it. Such involvement could help to achieve a positive role of commitment. Lack of commitment can result in serious blockages and resistance. The involvement of middle management in strategy development, the planning of and implementation of strategic change programmes and feedback on strategic change can therefore be very important.

Outsiders

Whilst existing managers have important roles to play, 'outsiders' are important in the change process. Outsiders may take different forms.

- A *new chief executive* from outside the organisation may be introduced into a business to enhance the capability for change. This is especially so in turnaround situations (see 10.4.1 below). He or she changes the context for change by bringing a fresh perspective on the organisation, not bound by the constraints of the past, or the everyday routines and ways of doing things that can prevent strategic change. *Hybrid* new chief executives seem to be especially successful. These are chief executives who are not part of the mainline culture of the organisation, but who have experience and visible success from within the same industry or even the same company. For example, they might have been a successful change agent with a competitor or some other part of a conglomerate.

- The introduction or arrival of *new management from outside the organisation* can also increase the diversity of ideas, views and assumptions which can help break down cultural barriers to change; and they may help increase the experience of and capability for change. The success of introducing outsiders in middle and senior executive positions is, however, likely to depend on how much explicit *visible backing* they have from the chief executive. Without such backing they are likely to be seen as lacking authority and influence. With such backing, however, they can help galvanise change in the organisation.

- *Consultants* are often used in change processes. This may be to help formulate the strategy or to plan the change process. However, consultants are increasingly used as facilitators of change processes: for example, in a coordinating capacity, as project planners for change programmes, as facilitators of project teams working on change, or of strategy workshops used to develop strategy and plan the means of strategic change. The value of consultants is threefold. First, they too do not inherit the cultural baggage of the organisation and can therefore bring a dispassionate view to the process. Second, as a result they may ask questions and undertake analyses which challenge taken for granted ways of seeing or doing things. Third, they signal symbolically the importance of the change process, not least because their fees may be of a very high order.

- It should also be remembered that there are likely to be key influencers of change external to an organisation within its *stakeholder network*. Government, investors, customers, suppliers and business analysts all have the potential to act as change agents on organisations.

10.4 LEVERS FOR MANAGING STRATEGIC CHANGE

So far the chapter has looked at differences in the type of change required, the importance of understanding other aspects of the change context and the management styles and roles in effecting change. The rest of the chapter examines different 'levers' that can be employed to manage strategic change. It is worth noting that many of these levers correspond to the elements of the cultural web. The implication is that the forces that act to embed and protect current ways of doing things and the current paradigm (see section 5.5.5) can also be levers for changing the ways things are.

10.4.1 Turnaround: managing rapid strategy reconstruction

As explained in section 10.2.1 strategic change can be of different types. Whilst many change programmes require cultural change and need to be transformational, there are circumstances where the emphasis has to be on rapid reconstruction where, in its absence, a business could face closure, enter terminal decline or be taken over. This is commonly referred to as a **turnaround strategy**, where the emphasis is on speed of change and rapid cost reduction and/or revenue generation. Managers need to be able to prioritise the things that give quick and significant improvements. Some of the main elements of turnaround strategies are as follows:[18]

> In a **turnaround strategy** the emphasis is on speed of change and rapid cost reduction and/or revenue generation

- *Crisis stabilisation.* The aim here is to regain control over the deteriorating position. There is likely to be a short-term focus on cost reduction and/or revenue increase and these typically involve some of steps identified in Exhibit 10.7. There is nothing novel about these steps: arguably many of them are good management practice. The difference is the speed at which they are carried out, the focus of managerial attention on them. Studies[19] have shown that the most successful turnaround strategies focus more on reducing direct operational costs and on productivity gains, whereas less effective approaches pay more attention to the reduction of overheads.

Exhibit 10.7   **Turnaround: revenue generation and cost reduction**

Increasing revenue	Reducing costs
• Ensure marketing mix tailored to key market segments	• Reduce labour costs and reduce costs of senior management
• Review pricing strategy to maximise revenue	• Focus on productivity improvement
• Focus organisational activities on needs of target market sector customers	• Reduce marketing costs not focused on target market
• Exploit additional opportunities for revenue creation related to target market	• Tighten financial controls
• Invest funds from reduction of costs in new growth areas	• Tighten control on cash expenses
	• Establish competitive bidding for suppliers; defer creditor payments; speed up debtor payments
	• Reduce inventory
	• Eliminate non-profitable products/services

However, too often turnarounds are seen as no more than cost-cutting exercises when, in fact, a wider alignment between causes of decline and solutions is an important consideration. For example, in a situation where the decline is principally a result of changes in the external environment it may be folly to expect that cost-cutting alone can lead to renewed growth. Other elements of turnaround strategies are important.

- *Management changes*. Changes in management are usually required, especially at the top level. This usually includes the introduction of a new chairman or chief executive, as well as changes in the board, especially in marketing, sales and finance, for three main reasons. First because the old management may well be the ones that were in charge when the problems developed and be seen as the cause of them by key stakeholders. Second because it may be necessary to bring in management with experience of turnaround management. Third because, since the new management are likely to come from outside the existing organisation, they may bring quite different approaches to the way the organisation has operated in the past. It also appears that these situations are times when more directive approaches to change (see section 10.3.1) are required.

- *Gaining stakeholder support*. It is likely that, as decline has occurred, there has been less and less good quality of information to key stakeholders. In a turnaround situation it is vital that key stakeholders, perhaps the bank or key shareholder groups, as well as employees are kept clearly informed of the situation as it is and improvements as they are being made. It is also likely that a clear assessment of the power of different stakeholder groups (see section 4.3.1 in Chapter 4) will become vitally important in managing turnaround.

- *Clarifying the target market(s)*. Central to any turnaround success is ensuring clarity on the target market or market segments most likely to generate cash and grow profits and focusing revenue generating activities on those key market segments. Indeed it may be that a reason for the demise of the organisation is because it had this wrong in the first place. Consequently the turnaround strategy, while involving cost-cutting, may require the business to reconceptualise and reorient itself to the market. There is also evidence that a successful turnaround strategy involves getting much closer to customers and improving the flow of marketing information, especially to senior levels of management.

- *Re-focusing*. Clarifying the target market is also likely to provide the opportunity to discontinue products and services that are either not targeted on those markets, eating up management time for little return or not making sufficient financial contribution. There may also be opportunities to outsource such peripheral areas of activity.

- *Financial restructuring*. The financial structure of the organisation may need to be changed. This typically involves changing the existing capital structure, raising additional finance or renegotiating agreements with creditors, especially banks.

- *Prioritisation of critical improvement areas*. All of this requires the ability of management to prioritise those things that give quick and significant improvements.

Illustration 10.4　　strategy into action

Turnaround at Cisco

Turnaround strategies typically emphasise speed of change and rapid cost reduction and revenue generation.

In March 2001 Cisco announced 8,500 job losses (18 per cent of the payroll) as a result of a major downturn in its market. On top of this there were changes in almost every aspect of the business. *Business Week* (24 November 2003) reported as follows:

Engineering

In the boom, engineers followed their 'geek muses' . . . In 2001, Cisco centralised engineering and top execs starting getting the tech roadmap . . . Since then Cisco has cut its product line 27 per cent to 24,000 models to focus on the most successful. That has helped win volume discounts worth hundreds of millions of dollars.

Operations

Cisco had carried on buying parts . . . 'it had mountains of inventory that was obsolete. [Chief Finance Officer Larry Carter] recommended moving quickly to take a roughly $2bn write-off – 20 per cent of Cisco's accumulated profits since it was formed in 1984.'

> In the past each unit [could] choose its own suppliers and manufacturers. Now a committee overseas all such decisions . . . [The result]: . . . more than 3000 resellers and 800 suppliers were squeezed out as Cisco reduced its partnerships to cut costs. Cisco has cut its suppliers and manufacturers and productivity is surging [by 2003]. . . . Outsourcing of production was increased from 45 per cent to 90 per cent by 2003 in order to lower costs. . . . Sales per worker has risen 24 per cent to $548,000 [by 2003].

The company also 'began playing hardball with suppliers to keep profits up. The CEO of one supplier said Cisco wanted to take 90 days to pay for his products instead of the normal 30 (and) extend the warrantee on its goods to 3 years from 1.' The supplier was told that if it did not agree Cisco managers would be told not to use their products.

Acquisitions

'Cisco had long been a binge buyer of even unproven start ups with no profits. Now it focuses on established companies that can contribute to earnings. Midlevel managers with the authority to invest $10m in a promising start up saw the open cheque book snapped shut. The result: acquisitions tumbled from 23 deals in 2000 to 2 in 2001. And . . . Linksys, which Cisco bought in March (2003) contributed to earnings from day 1.'

Culture

'The old Cisco was known for its *carpe diem* culture – with little coordinated planning. Now teamwork is emphasised. The result: . . . top executives are collaborating – partly because of new compensation policies that tie 30 per cent of their annual bonuses to their ability to work with peers.'

Growth strategy

'Cisco focused almost exclusively on networking gear. Now it's pursuing six new markets, including security and net phones. Over 50 per cent of its $3.3bn R & D budget in 2002 is for emerging markets.'

By November 2003 when Cisco announced its quarterly results, its market share of the communications equipment business had risen to 16 per cent from 10 per cent in 2001. The company had earned $3.6bn . . . 'nearly $1bn dollars more than its previous best in 2000. And with no long term debt and $19.7bn in cash and investments, Cisco's balance sheet is among the strongest in the tech industry'.

Source: *Business Week*, 24 November 2003.

Questions

1. Which of the elements of turnaround strategies identified in section 10.4.1 are to be found in the Cisco turnaround?

2. Which of these elements do you consider to be most important in the Cisco turnaround, and why?

3. As Cisco returned to a healthy position should any of the measures taken in the turnaround be relaxed or done away with? If so, why?

A more general comment about successful turnaround strategies, as distinct from less successful ones, is that the focus of action tends to be on getting the existing business right rather than looking for new opportunities in quite different markets or new businesses that managers may not understand.

Illustration 10.4 describes Cisco's turnaround from 2001 to 2003.

10.4.2 Challenging the taken for granted

As has already been explained, one of the major challenges in achieving strategic change can be the need to change often longstanding mindsets or taken for granted assumptions – the paradigm. There are different views on how this might be achieved.

There are those who believe that sufficient evidence, perhaps in the form of careful strategic analysis, will itself serve to challenge and therefore change the paradigm. However, the evidence is that where longstanding assumptions have persisted, they will be very resistant to change. People will find ways of questioning, reconfiguring and reinterpreting such analysis to bring it in line with the existing paradigm. It may take much persistence to overcome this. One chief executive, who had clear evidence of a declining market demand for the company's main product, faced persistent denial of this by his senior team. He spent six months repeatedly challenging their plans for growth in the light of this evidence before he gained their acceptance that a strategy less dependent on that product was necessary.

Others argue that such taken-for-grantedness could be challenged by unpacking in an analytic fashion just what people do take for granted, bringing this into the open and debating it. For example, it might be done through workshop sessions with senior management, where they systematically question and challenge each other's assumptions and the received wisdom in the firm.[20] The idea is that making visible such assumptions means that they are more likely to be questioned. Indeed strategy workshops of this sort have become more and more common as an instrument of change (see section 11.3.2 in Chapter 11).

Others argue that managers need to be brought closer to the realities of changing circumstances before they can overcome existing ways of seeing things. For example, scenario planning is advocated as a way of overcoming individual biases and cultural assumptions by getting people to see possible different futures and the implications for their organisations.[21] Still others argue that senior managers are often too far removed from the realities of their organisations and need to be brought face-to-face with it. They may rarely speak to customers directly or experience themselves the services offered by their own firms. A senior executive of a rail company explained that in the past senior executives in the organisation had always travelled first class or by chauffeur-driven cars. Hardly any of them had ever travelled in a crowded railway carriage. He introduced a policy that all senior executives should travel economy class wherever possible.

Whichever the mechanism, there is likely to be a need to get the people responsible for managing change to see the realities of the circumstances they face and to challenge the taken for granted that they inherit; a lesson evident is the different styles adopted by the executives quoted in Illustration 10.3.

10.4.3 Changing organisational routines

Routines are the organisationally specific 'ways we do things around here'[22] which tend to persist over time and guide people's behaviour. As has been seen in the discussion in Chapters 3 and 5, it may be that an organisation which becomes especially good at carrying out its operations in particular ways achieves real competitive advantages. However, well-established routines can also be serious blockages to change; as Dorothy Leonard-Barton[23] points out, they can become '*core rigidities*'. Managers can make the mistake of assuming that because they have identified a strategy that requires operational changes in work practices and explained what such changes are, the changes will necessarily take place. They may find that the reasons why such changes are delayed or do not occur have to do with the persistent influence of longstanding organisational routines. It is unrealistic to suppose that because people have a strategy explained to them, even if they agree with it, that they will change the way they have been doing things, maybe over many years.

If a planned, top-down approach to change is adopted, it is important to identify the critical success factors and competences underpinning these factors. In so doing, the planning of the implementation of the intended strategy can be driven down to operational levels, and it is likely this will require changes in the routines of the organisation. It is at this level that changes in strategy become really meaningful for most people in their everyday organisational lives. Moreover, as mentioned above, routines are closely linked to the taken-for-grantedness of the paradigm, so changing routines may have the effect of questioning and challenging deep-rooted beliefs and assumptions in the organisation. There are different views on this, however. Richard Pascale argues: 'It is easier to act your way into a better way of thinking than to think your way into a better way of acting';[24] in other words, that it is easier to change behaviour and thus change taken-for-granted assumptions than to try to change taken-for-granted assumptions as a way of changing behaviour. If this advice is to be taken seriously, it would argue that the style of change employed (see section 10.3.3 above) needs to take this into account; that education and communication to persuade people to change may be less powerful than involving people in the activities of changing; and that changing routines to change behaviour may itself help change people's beliefs and assumptions.

Even when change is not planned in detail, change agents may experiment with changing routines as a way of changing strategy. They may begin tentatively by *extending* existing ways of doing things such that there is hardly any discernible difference. When this becomes acceptable they may go further and '*bend the rules of the game*'. This could give rise to resistance, but persistent *extending* and *bending* may eventually achieve enough support from different stakeholders such that new routines become acceptable. When sufficient questioning of the status quo is achieved, change agents may actively *subvert* existing ways of doing things so as to make clear a fundamental change from the past. This could well be an approach adopted by middle managers in seeking to carry with them both more senior managers and people who work for them, both of whom may be resistant to change. It is an incremental, experimental process that is likely to suffer setbacks and require persistence and political acumen.[25]

Routines are the organisationally specific 'ways we do things around here' which tend to persist over time and guide people's behaviour

The overall lesson is that changes in routines may appear to be mundane, but they can have significant impact. Illustration 10.5 gives some examples of changes in routines linked to strategic change.

10.4.4 Symbolic processes[26]

Change levers are not always of an overt, formal nature: they may also be symbolic in nature. Chapter 4 (section 4.5.5) explained how symbolic acts and artefacts of an organisation help preserve the paradigm, and how their relationship to culture and strategy can be analysed. Here the concern is their role in managing change.

Symbols are objects, events, acts or people which express more than their intrinsic content. They may be everyday things which are nevertheless especially meaningful in the context of a particular situation or organisation. It is argued that changing symbols can help reshape beliefs and expectations because meaning becomes apparent in the day-to-day experiences people have of organisations. This is one reason why changes in routines (discussed above) are important, but other such everyday or 'mundane' aspects include the stories that people tell, the status symbols such as cars and sizes of office, the type of language and technology used, and organisational rituals. Consider some examples.

- Many of the *rituals*[27] of organisations are implicitly concerned with effecting or consolidating change. Exhibit 10.8 identifies and gives examples of such rituals as well as suggesting what role they might play in change processes.[28] New rituals can be introduced or old rituals done away with and, arguably, these are ways of signalling or reinforcing change.

- Symbolic significance is also embedded in the *systems and processes* discussed elsewhere in this chapter and in Chapter 8. Reward systems, information and control systems, and organisational structures that represent reporting relationships and status are also symbolic in nature. For example, changes that have occurred from manual accounting procedures in banks to electronic information-based systems have not only signalled an era of technological change, but also highlighted to staff that their prime responsibility is dealing with customers, rather than dealing with forms.

- Changes in *physical aspects* of the work environment are powerful symbols of change. Typical here is a change of location for the head office, relocation of personnel, changes in dress or uniforms, and alterations to offices or office space.

- Perhaps the most powerful symbol of all in relation to change is the *behaviour of change agents* themselves, particularly strategic leaders. Their behaviour, language and the stories associated with them can signal powerfully the need for change and appropriate behaviour relating to the management of change. Having made pronouncements about the need for change, it is vital that the visible behaviour of change agents is in line with such change because, for most people in an organisation, their organisational world is one of behaviours and actions, not of abstractions.

- Also important in effecting change is the *language* used by change agents.[29] Either consciously or unconsciously, change agents may employ language and

Symbols are objects, events, acts or people which express more than their intrinsic content

Exhibit 10.8	Organisational rituals and culture change	

Types of ritual	Role	Examples
Rites of passage	Consolidate and promote social roles and interaction	Induction programmes Training programmes
Rites of enhancement	Recognise effort benefiting organisation Similarly motivate others	Awards ceremonies Promotions
Rites of renewal	Reassure that something is being done Focus attention on issues	Appointment of consultants Project teams
Rites of integration	Encourage shared commitment Reassert rightness of norms	Christmas parties
Rites of conflict reduction	Reduce conflict and aggression	Negotiating committees
Rites of degradation	Publicly acknowledge problems Dissolve/weaken social or political roles	Firing top executives Demotion or 'passing over'
Rites of sense making	Sharing of interpretations and sense making	Rumours Surveys to evaluate new practices
Rites of challenge	'Throwing down the gauntlet'	New CEO's different behaviour
Rites of counter-challenge	Resistance to new ways of doing things	Grumbling Working to rule

metaphor to galvanise change. Some examples are included in Illustration 10.5. In this context, language is not simply concerned with communicating facts and information. Of course, there is also the danger that change agents do not realise the power of language and, whilst espousing change, use language that signals adherence to the status quo, or personal reluctance to change. Those involved in change need to think carefully about the language they use.

● *Stories* may also be managed to some extent. The use of corporate newsletters and newspapers is an example. There are, however, more subtle examples. One chief executive claimed that the most effective way of spreading a story in his business was to get his secretary to leave a memo from him marked 'strictly confidential' by the photocopier for ten minutes: 'Its contents would be all over the office in half an hour.'

There is an important qualification to the idea that the manipulation of symbols can be a useful lever for managing change. The significance and meaning of symbols are dependent on how they are interpreted. So a change agent's intentions in the use of symbolic levers may not be interpreted as intended (see the nursing example in Illustration 10.5). So, whilst symbolic changes are important, their impact is difficult to predict.

Illustration 10.5 gives other examples of such symbolic signalling of change.

Illustration 10.5   strategy into action

Changes in routines and symbols

Changes in organisational routines and symbols can be a powerful signal of and stimulus for change.

Changes in routines

- A drug can only be promoted on launch on the basis of claims substantiated by clinical data, so how pharmaceutical firms conduct clinical trials is strategically important. The traditional approach has been to base extensive data collection on a scientific research protocol and then to write a report explaining why all these data had been collected: a highly time-consuming and costly process. Some firms changed their procedures to ensure that scientific tests addressed regulatory and medical need. They created ideal claims statements and drafted the report they would need. Only then did they create research protocols and data collection forms, specifying the data required from the trials to support the claims.

- In a retail business with an espoused strategy of customer care, the chief executive, on visiting stores, tended to ignore staff and customers alike: he seemed to be interested only in the financial information in the store manager's office. He was unaware of this until it was pointed out; and his change in behaviour afterwards, insisting on talking to staff and customers on his visits, became a 'story' which spread around the company, substantially supporting the strategic direction of the firms.

Language that challenges and questions

- The chief executive of a retailing firm facing a crisis addressed his board: 'I suggest we think of ourselves like bulls facing a choice: the abattoir or the bull ring. I've made up my mind: what about you?'

- In another company, the chief executive described the threat of a takeover in terms of pending warfare: 'We've been targeted: they've got the hired guns [merchant bankers, consultants, etc.] on board. Don't expect chivalry: don't look for white knights; this is a shoot-out situation.'

Physical objects as symbols of change

- In a textile firm in Scotland, equipment associated with the 'old ways of doing things' was taken into the yard at the rear of the factory and physically dismantled in front of the workforce.

- The head nurse of a recovery unit for patients who had been severely ill decided that, if nurses wore everyday clothes rather than nurses' uniforms, it would signal to patients that they were on the road to recovery and a normal life; and to nurses that they were concerned with rehabilitation. However, the decision had other implications for the nurses too. It blurred the status distinction between nurses and other non-professional members of staff. Nurses preferred to wear their uniforms. Whilst they recognised that uniforms signalled a medically fragile role of patients, they reinforced their separate and professional status as acute care workers.

Sources: M.G. Pratt and E. Rafaeli, 'The role of symbols in fragmented organisations: an illustration from organisational dress', presented at the Academy of Management Meeting, Atlanta, GA, 1993 and 'Organisational dress as a symbol of multi-layered social idealities', *Academy of Management Journal*, vol. 40, no. 4 (1997), pp. 862–898.

Questions

For an organisation with which you are familiar:

1. Identify at least five important routines, symbols or rituals in the organisation.

2. In what way could they be changed to support a different strategy? Be explicit as to how the symbols might relate to the new strategy.

3. Why are these potential levers for change often ignored by change agents?

10.4.5 Power and political processes[30]

In order to effect change powerful support is required from an individual or group combining both power and interest, as described in Chapter 4 (see section 4.3.3). This may be the chief executive, a powerful member of the board or an influential outsider. To achieve this a reconfiguration of *power structures* may be necessary, especially if transformational change is required.

Chapter 4 discussed the importance of understanding the political context in and around the organisation. Having established this understanding, there is also a need to consider the implementation of strategy within this political context. Exhibit 10.9 shows some of the mechanisms associated with power which can be used for change or building a context for change (see section 10.2.2). The manipulation of *organisational resources*, the relationship with powerful *stakeholder groups* and *elites*, activity with regard to *subsystems* in the organization and, again, *symbolic activity* may all be used to: (a) build a power base; (b) encourage support or overcome resistance; and (c) achieve commitment to a strategy or course of action.

Exhibit 10.9   Political mechanisms in organisations

Activity areas	Mechanisms				Key problems
	Resources	Elites	Subsystems	Symbolic	
Building the power base	Control of resources Acquisition of/identification with expertise Acquisition of additional resources	Sponsorship by an elite Association with an elite	Alliance building Team building	Building on legitimation	Time required for building Perceived duality of ideals Perceived as threat by existing elites
Overcoming resistance	Withdrawal of resources Use of 'counter-intelligence'	Breakdown or division of elites Association with change agent Association with respected outsider	Foster momentum for change Sponsorship/ reward of change agents	Attack or remove legitimation Foster confusion, conflict and questioning	Striking from too low a power base Potentially destructive: need for rapid rebuilding
Achieving compliance	Giving resources	Removal of resistant elites Need for visible 'change hero'	Partial implementation and collaboration Implantation of 'disciples' Support for 'Young Turks'	Applause/reward Reassurance Symbolic confirmation	Converting the body of the organisation Slipping back

- Acquiring additional *resources* or being identified with important resource areas or areas of expertise, and the ability to withdraw or allocate such resources, can be a valuable tool in overcoming resistance or persuading others to accept change and therefore building readiness.

- Association with powerful *stakeholder groups*, or their supporters, can help build a power base. This may be necessary for the change agent who does not have a strong personal power base from which to work. Similarly, association with a change agent who is respected or visibly successful can help a manager overcome resistance to change. Indeed change agents facing resistance to change may deliberately seek out and win over someone who is highly respected from within the very group resistant to change.

- It may be necessary to *remove individuals or groups* resistant to change. Who these are can vary – from powerful individuals in senior positions, to loose networks within the organisation and sometimes including external stakeholders with powerful influence, to whole layers of resistance perhaps in the form of senior executives in a threatened function or service.

- Building up *alliances* and *networks* of contacts and sympathisers, even though they may not be powerful themselves, may be important in overcoming the resistance of more powerful groups. Attempting to convert the whole organisation to an acceptance of change is difficult – it is likely that there will be parts of the organisation or individuals in it more sympathetic to that change than others. The change agent might sensibly concentrate on these to develop momentum, building a team strongly supportive of the activities and beliefs of the change agent. He or she may also seek to marginalise those who are resistant to change. However, the danger is that powerful groups in the organisation may regard the building of such a team, or acts of marginalisation, as a threat to their own power, and this may lead to further resistance to change. An analysis of power and interest similar to the stakeholder mapping described in Chapter 4 can, therefore, be useful to identify bases of alliance and likely political resistance.

- To build power, the manager may initially seek to identify with the very *symbols* which preserve and reinforce the paradigm – to work within the committee structures, become identified with the organisational rituals or stories that exist and so on. On the other hand, in breaking resistance to change, removing, challenging or changing rituals and symbols may be a very powerful means of achieving the questioning of what is taken for granted.

Political aspects of management in general, and change specifically, are unavoidable; and the lessons of organisational life are as important for the manager as they are, and always have been, for the medieval prince or the modern politician (see Illustration 10.6).

However, the political aspects of management are also difficult, and potentially hazardous. Exhibit 10.9 also summarises some of the problems. In overcoming resistance, the major problem may simply be the lack of power to be able to undertake such activity. Attempting to overcome resistance from a lower power base is highly problematic. There is a second major danger: in the breaking down of the status quo, the process becomes so destructive and takes so long

Illustration 10.6

strategy into action

Machiavelli on political processes

'. . . There is nothing more difficult to handle, more doubtful of success and more dangerous to carry through than initiating change . . .'.

Nicolo Machiavelli, a court advisor in 16th-century Florence, wrote about the possession of *power* and use of *political skill*. Rather than advocating a singular approach, he argued the need to vary tactics according to the situation; at times leniency and at others a brutal approach based on fear. His consideration of the deliberate use of 'fear' as well as 'love' as political devices earned the label 'Machiavellian'.

Although Machiavelli's concern was a prince's state craft, many have seen his lessons as relevant to today's managers of change. Amongst the situations he considered are these:

Succession

The challenge here is to change things sufficiently that *eventually* the members of the organisation are loyal to the successor and their strategic direction rather than to the memory of the previous leader. A tricky situation on which Machiavelli's view was: change things but not too much and not too quickly; maintain the institutions of predecessors and gradually make changes as events unfold. On personal style, if you are the natural successor, 'there is no need to use fear, simply do not give offence, be assiduous and one should increasingly be loved'.

Merger

One of Machiavelli's starkest warnings to leaders is to be wary of old alliances (e.g. prior to a merger). They cannot satisfy all the expectations of those who put them there but equally cannot be too harsh on those to whom a debt is owed. Therefore Machiavelli argues 'be wary of your friends'. As for the new population that once had its own ways of working, in order to bring them around to a new way of working (a new culture) there are only two political routes to go. First: wipe out the old ways (the old culture) swiftly and harshly: 'Whoever becomes the master of a city accustomed to (its own) freedom, and does not

destroy it, may expect to be destroyed himself.' Second, be present and be frequently visible.

Conqueror/take-over

Whereas in a merger there has been negotiated agreement in the hope of improvement for all parties involved, a take-over (especially a hostile one) has been executed with the advantage of one population in mind over and above another. Machiavelli sees the new leader as the conqueror. If the leader has self-doubt they should mask it. He suggests imitation. Imitate the manner in which others have executed the task before in an outstanding manner: 'if his own prowess fail, . . . at least it has an air of greatness about it'. In this situation a leader has automatic enemies – those who prospered under the old order – who are likely to be resistant to change, lukewarm supporters at best and probably lacking confidence. Machiavelli argues that there are two approaches to gain compliance: use force or use persuasion. He argues those who try the latter always come to grief whereas those who use force are 'seldom endangered'. He suggests that those leaders who can survive the 'dangerous time' of a take-over 'will begin to be venerated and if they have forcefully destroyed those envious of their abilities, they will stay powerful, secure, respected and . . . happy'.

Prepared by Phyl Johnson, University of Strathclyde.

Source: Nicolo Machiavelli, *The Prince*, Pengion Classics, 1999.

Questions

1. To what extent do you agree with Machiavelli's advice in relation to 21st-century organisations? If you do not, what would you advise in the circumstances identified?

2. How might the political mechanisms outlined in Exhibit 10.9 be used to put such guidelines into effect?

that the organisation cannot recover from it. If the process needs to take place, its replacement by some new set of beliefs and the implementation of a new strategy is vital and needs to be speedy. Further, as already identified, in implementing change the main problem is likely to be carrying the body of the organisation with the change. It is one thing to change the commitment of a few senior executives at the top of an organisation; it is quite another to convert the body of the organisation to an acceptance of significant change.

10.4.6 Communicating and monitoring change

Managers faced with effecting change typically underestimate substantially the extent to which members of the organisation understand the need for change, what it is intended to achieve, or what is involved in the changes. Some important points to emphasise are as follows.

- It is argued that effective communication may be the single most important factor in overcoming resistance to change.[31] In particular open communication that builds trust is important in times of change.

- The importance of clarity of *vision* and *strategic intent* explained in Chapters 4 and 6 therefore needs to be emphasised again. The reasons for a change in strategic direction may be complex, and the strategy itself may therefore embrace complex ideas. However, to be effective it is important that the strategic purpose of the change is clear.

- There are *choices of media* by which to communicate the strategy and the elements of the strategic change programme.[32] Exhibit 10.10 summarises some of the choices and the likely effectiveness of these in different circumstances. Choices of media richness vary from face-to-face, one-to-one communication through to routine bulletins on noticeboards and circulars sent round the organisation. The extent to which these different forms of media are likely to be effective depends on the extent to which the nature of the change is routine or complex. To communicate a highly complex set of changes, it would be inappropriate to use standardised bulletins and circulars with no chance of any feedback or interaction. In situations of strategic change, members of the organisation not involved in the development of the strategy may see the effects of change as non-routine even when senior executives regard them as routine. So communication which provides interaction and involvement is likely to be desirable.

- The *involvement* of members of the organisation in the strategy development process or the planning of strategic change is also, in itself, a means of communication and can be very effective. Those who are involved might be used to cascade information about the change programme into the organisation, in effect becoming part of the change agency process themselves. This is an important element of the *intervention* style described in section 10.3.3 above.

- Communication needs to be seen as a two-way process. *Feedback* on communication is important, particularly if the changes to be introduced are difficult to understand or threatening or if it is critically important to get the changes

---

Exhibit 10.10   **Effective and ineffective communication of change**

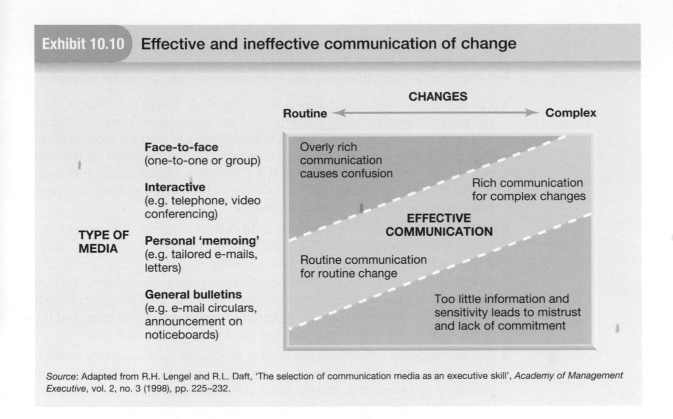

Source: Adapted from R.H. Lengel and R.L. Daft, 'The selection of communication media as an executive skill', *Academy of Management Executive*, vol. 2, no. 3 (1998), pp. 225–232.

---

right. It is rare that changes have been thought through in ways that have meaning or can be put into effect at lower levels in the organisation. In addition, the purpose of the changes may be misunderstood or misconstrued at such levels.

● *Emotional* aspects of communication are especially important for the change agent since emotions can so readily induce negative or positive responses. Researchers in the field[33] suggest that it is important to use appropriate messages, symbols (see section 10.4.5) and language (words such as 'danger' or 'risk') to describe the negative situation that needs changing and positive language associated with pleasure and progress to describe the desired future.

● Executives are used to *monitoring* of performance for all sorts of organisational activities. Yet too often change programmes, whilst fundamental to the future of the organisation, are not subject to the same monitoring. Some researchers have noted that in change programmes they have observed such monitoring is of key importance. They argue that it may be unrealistic to change core values and that, more effective, seems to be close monitoring of required changes in behaviour and the threat of sanctions if this is not done.[34]

10.4.7 Change tactics

There are also some more specific tactics of change which might be employed to facilitate the change process.

Timing

The importance of timing is often neglected in thinking about strategic change. But choosing the right time tactically to promote change is vital. For example:

● The greater the degree of change needed, the more it may be useful to build on actual or perceived *crisis*. If members of the organisation perceive a higher risk in maintaining the status quo than in changing it, they are more likely to change. For example, the management of a company threatened by takeover may be able to use this as a catalyst for transformational strategic change. Indeed, it is said that some chief executives seek to elevate problems to achieve perceived crisis in order to galvanise change.

● There may also be *windows of opportunity* in change processes. For example, the period following the takeover of a company may allow new owners to make more significant changes than might normally be possible. The arrival of a new chief executive, the introduction of a new, highly successful product, or the arrival of a major competitive threat on the scene may also provide such opportunities. These windows of opportunity may, however, be brief; and the change agent may need to take decisive action during these periods.

● It is also important that those responsible for change do not provide conflicting messages about the timing of change. For example, if they see that rapid change is required, they should avoid the maintenance of procedures and signals that suggest long time horizons such as maintaining the same control and reward procedures or work practices that have been in place for years. So the *symbolic signalling of timeframes* becomes important.

● Since change will be regarded nervously, it may be important to choose the time for promoting such change to avoid unnecessary fear and nervousness. For example, if there is a need for reduction in personnel or the removal of executives (see below), it may make sense to do this before rather than during the change programme. In such a way, the change programme can be seen as a potential improvement for the future rather than as the cause of such losses.

Job losses and delayering

Change programmes are often associated with job losses, from the closure of units of the organisation, with hundreds or thousands of job losses, to the removal of a few senior executives. As indicated above, the timing of such job losses in relation to the change programme can be important. There are other considerations which can affect a change programme:

● The tactical choice of where job losses should take place related to the change programme may be important. For example, it could be that there is a layer of management or particular individuals who are widely recognised in the organisation as *blockers* of change. Their removal may indicate powerfully the serious nature and intent of the change. The removal of one layer of management may also provide perceived opportunities to management below. As one chief executive commented: 'If I have to lose people, then I will choose the most senior levels possible: they're the ones most usually resistant to change; and it provides a wonderful incentive for those below.'

● It may also be important to avoid 'creeping' job losses. If the change programme is continually associated with a threat to security, it is less likely to be successful. The same chief executive continued: 'It is better to cut deeply and quickly than hack away remorselessly over time.'

● It is also important, however, that if job losses are to take place, there is a visible, responsible and caring approach to those who lose their jobs. Not only are there ethical reasons for this, but tactically it signals to those who remain that the organisation cares. There are now many examples of companies which have successful redeployment, counselling services, outplacement arrangements, retraining facilities and so on.

Visible short-term wins

The implementation of strategy within a change programme will require many detailed actions and tasks. It is important that some of these tasks are seen to be put into place and to be successful quickly. This could take the form, for example, of a retail chain quickly developing a new store concept and demonstrating its success in the market; the effective breaking down of old ways of working and the demonstration of better ways; the speeding up of decisions by doing away with committees and introducing clearly defined job responsibilities; and so on. In themselves, these may not be especially significant aspects of a new strategy, but they may be visible indicators of a new approach associated with that strategy. The demonstration of such wins will therefore galvanise commitment to the strategy.

One reason given for the inability to change is that resources are not available to do so. This may be overcome if it is possible to identify '*hot spots*' on which to focus resources and effort. For example, William Bratton (see Illustration 10.3), famously responsible for the Zero Tolerance policy of the New York Police Department, began the process by focusing the efforts on narcotics-related crimes initially. These were estimated to represent or underlie 50–70 per cent of all crimes but had only 5 per cent of the resources allocated by NYPD to tackle them. The success in this field led to the roll-out of his policies into other areas and to gaining the resources to do so.[35]

Illustration 10.7 shows how a new chief executive in the long-ailing knitwear manufacturer Pringle employed tactics and symbolic changes to galvanise change in line with the new strategy for the business.

There are then a variety of change levers that change agents may choose. What they choose will depend on the context they face (see section 10.2.2) and their skills and styles (see section 10.3.1) of managing change. For example, to take the extremes, if the need is to overcome resistance to achieve fast results, then the emphasis may have to be on achieving behavioural compliance to a change programme. On the other hand, if there is a need and the time to 'win hearts and minds' then there will need to be a focus on changing people's values and a much greater emphasis on their involvement in changing the culture of the organisation. Choosing the appropriate levers rather than following a set formula for managing strategic change is critically important.

Illustration 10.7

strategy into action

Tactics for strategic change at Pringle

In achieving strategic change it may be important to ensure that short-term actions signal long-term intentions.

Pringle, the long-established cashmere knitwear manufacturer, had endured a decade of losses and seen its workforce decline from over 2,000 in the early 1990s to 180 by 2000: the result of adverse exchange rates, an unsuccessful move into mass market sportswear and a decline in manufacturing quality. In 2000 the company was acquired by Hong Kong-based Fang Brothers for just $6m (€9m). The new owners recruited Kim Winser, a senior executive from Marks & Spencer, as chief executive.

The new chief executive decided Pringle's range was too big and poorly designed; and sought to reposition it away from its rather staid, middle-aged image towards a designer fashion brand. This was a major challenge, but the current situation, whilst of crisis proportions, nonetheless provided an opportunity. Her arrival, together with the state the company was in, ensured that everyone knew there was the need for radical change.

She decided on a relaunch of the fashion range of knitwear in just twelve weeks, a target that had never been achieved before – and one that was later reduced to nine. This, she argued, was essential in order to present a new range at the forthcoming Italian trade fair.

Most of the workforce that was left expected the factory to close, perhaps with manufacturing moving to the Far East. Instead she confirmed that manufacturing would remain in Hawick in Scotland. She further reinforced the Scottish link by branding the fashion merchandise 'Pringle Scotland' and explained: 'I have added Scotland to the name because in a lot of countries worldwide, it is definitely a bonus – people trust Scottish cashmere.'

New young designers were recruited; and the design function moved from Scotland to London. She also moved the company headquarters from the prestigious Savile Row in London to a new, more modern building.

Others left the company. The contract of the existing manufacturing director was terminated: and the contract of Nick Faldo, the golfer, who had been Pringle's celebrity face for almost 20 years, was not renewed: instead the merchandise was shown on young and trendy models.

The process of change was helped with the visit of the Princess Royal to the Hawick factory at around the same time as the redesigned sweaters were seen worn publicly by David Beckham, the internationally famous football star.

The target of the Italian trade fair was met, one-sixth of the existing retail outlets were dropped and new retailers recruited, including Harvey Nichols and Selfridges. By the end of 2000 sales were increasing, the workforce had been increased and there had been investment in new machinery at Hawick and 2001 sales were 30 per cent up on the previous year.

By 2003 commentators were reporting the new found success of Pringle. Having consolidated its position in the UK, plans were underway for retail expansion in the USA and Hong Kong. And Sophie Dahl was the 'new face' in Pringle's advertising.

Sources: Adapted from *Trouble at the Top*, BBC2, 28 February 2001; *Financial Times*, 24/25 February 2001; and 'Pringle look goes with a swing', *Brand Strategy*, April 2003.

Questions

1. Referring to section 10.4.7, identify the tactics used by Kim Winser.

2. In what ways were the short-term tactics in line with the longer-term strategy?

3. Using frameworks and concepts from the rest of the chapter, consider other ways in which Kim Winser might manage strategic change at Pringle.

10.5 POTENTIAL PITFALLS OF CHANGE PROGRAMMES

A great deal can be learned by understanding what goes wrong in change programmes. In an extensive study Lloyd Harris and Emannuel Ogbonna[36] identified a number of unintended outcomes of change programmes:

● *The ritualisation of change and 'initiative overload'*: change agents may recognise that change is not a one-off process; that it might require an ongoing series of activities, maybe year after year. However, the risk is that change programmes come to be seen by people in the organisation as a ritual signifying very little.

● *Hijacked processes* of change: another danger is that well-meaning change efforts generate the opportunity for others in the organisation to hijack them for different purposes. For example, in an insurance firm, the introduction of computerised telephone systems with the intention of improving customer service became a vehicle for reducing the number of personnel dealing with customer enquiries. The result was no improvement in service and a workforce highly sceptical about that and future change initiatives.

● *Erosion*: here the original intention of the change programme becomes gradually eroded by other events that are taking place within the organisation. For example, it is difficult to maintain the impetus of a change programme in a situation with a high turnover of staff or if reward systems are out of line with the intended change. The purpose of the change becomes masked by events or activities out of line with the intentions of the change programme.

● *Reinvention*: here the attempted change becomes reinterpreted according to the old culture. For example, a retail clothing company tried to create a customer-focused culture within an organisation which had long been a product-focused business. However, this became reinvented such that 'customer service' became translated as 'service quality' equally acceptable to those who remained loyal to the old product orientation within the firm and requiring no change in behaviour or assumptions on their part.

● *Ivory tower change*: here the proponents of the change – perhaps senior executives – are not seen by others in the organisation to understand the realities of change on the ground, in terms of either the needs of the marketplace or the views of people in the organisation. They are removed from reality and are therefore not credible.

● *Inattention to symbols of change*: change agents fail to link the big messages about change to the day-to-day and symbolic aspects of the organisation. There can be two results here. First the people in the organisation again see the change as removed from their reality. Second, since the change agents may not understand the power of symbolic change, they may inadvertently signal quite the wrong messages. Harris and Ogbonna give the example of a family firm, keen to bring in professional management which, by doing so at CEO level, inadvertently signalled that the previous family-dominated management was unprofessional and diminished what had been loyalty to the family and firm.

Illustration 10.8

The management of change from top to bottom

Strategic change has always been seen as the responsibility of top management: to what extent and how can top managers manage change?

John Kotter, a professor at the Harvard Business School, is one of the world's foremost authorities on leadership and change. In 1995 he published a paper in the *Harvard Business Review*[1] about the problems of transformational strategic change. He argued that problems of strategic change could be put down to top executives failing to recognise the necessary sequence required to manage such changes. His 'eight steps to transforming your organisation' are:

1. Establish a sense of *urgency* on the basis of market and competitive realities, clear discussion about potential crises or major opportunities.

2. Form a powerful *guiding coalition*: they are likely to be senior managers but might include other key stakeholders; and encourage this group to work together as a team.

3. Creating a clear *vision* to direct the change effort and developing clear strategies to achieve that.

4. *Communicate* the vision, using multiple communication vehicles, and ensure that the behaviour of the guiding coalition is in line with the vision.

5. *Empower* others to act on the vision: remove obstacles to change, change systems or structures that undermine the vision; encourage risk taking and non-traditional ideas, activities and actions.

6. Plan and create *short-term wins*: strategic transformation may take years but people need to see some results fast.

7. *Consolidate* improvements and produce still more change: when credibility of change has been established, then change more structures, systems and policies and promote those who can implement the vision: reinvigorate the process of change.

8. *Institutionalise new approaches*: as change takes form and establishes itself, show how it has helped performance and ensure the next generation of top management personifies the new vision.

However, in their paper in the *Academy of Management Journal*, Julia Balogun and Gerry Johnson[2] questioned the extent to which top managers can really manage change in a top-

● *Uncontrolled and uncoordinated efforts*: here the practices introduced in organisations, for example in terms of change systems and initiatives, are out of line with the intentions of the change as understood by the people in the organisation who therefore experience inconsistency.

● *Behavioural compliance*: finally there is the danger that people will simply appear to comply with the changes being pursued in the change programme without actually 'buying into' them. Change agents may think they see change occurring, when all they see is superficial compliance especially when the change agent is around.

The overall conclusion from this is that change programmes are difficult and complex. But there are more specific managerial implications:

● *Monitoring of change*. It is unlikely that change can be planned in such coherent detail from the top down that it can be put into place in specific detail without some aspects of the programme not going the way the proponents of the change intend. This emphasises the need to pay special attention to

down fashion. They studied the progress of a top management change initiative over time but from the point of view of how it was understood and interpreted by middle managers. They found that, whilst top management believed they were being clear about the intended strategy, change actually took place as follows:

- Middle managers make sense of change initiatives in terms of their own *mental models* in relation to their *local responsibilities and conditions* through discussion with their peers, and on the basis of rumour and local responses to top-down initiatives.

- Top managers could not be expected to understand or intervene in these dynamics in specific ways. They were inevitably too far removed from them.

- It is therefore not possible for top managers to directly manage how middle managers make sense of new strategic intent and change initiatives, particularly in large geographically dispersed or decentralised organisations.

- The reality is that these middle managers, in effect, *create* change locally as distinct from just implementing change as directed from above.

- They concluded that top managers may have to accept the inevitability of such interpretation and place greater emphasis on:

– Establishing clarity of *overall vision* with an acceptance that this will be variously interpreted.

– Paying attention to understanding the 'translation processes' at middle manager level.

– *Monitoring change* outcomes and responding much more to change 'initiatives' coming up from below.

– Being prepared to *adjust the strategic intent* in line with the emerging strategy.

Notes:
1. J. Kotter, 'Leading change: why transformation efforts fail', *Harvard Business Review*, March–April (1995), pp. 59–67.
2. J. Balogun and G. Johnson: 'Organizational restructuring and middle manager sensemaking', *Academy of Management Journal*, vol. 47, No. 4, pp. 523–549, 2004.

Questions

1. **What are the problems associated with top-down or bottom-up views of change management?**

2. **If you were a senior executive which approach would you take and in what circumstances?**

3. **Are the two views irreconcilable?**

(You will find the perspectives on the management of strategy in the commentaries useful background reading.)

the monitoring of change[37] as it takes place and the need to be flexible enough to change the emphases and tactics within the change programme as it develops.

- *Understanding the culture.* Forces for inertia should not be underestimated. There is a high likelihood that change programmes will run foul of the power of existing cultures. So underpinning a change programme with an understanding of the existing culture and its likely effects is vital (see section 10.2.3).

- *Involving people.* There are likely to be benefits in involving people throughout the organisation in times of change rather than regarding them just as recipients of change.

- *A major challenge.* Change agents need to be wary of over-inflating their own abilities to achieve change within organisations. Quite simply, it may be more difficult than the optimistic change agent may think.

Many of these problems and challenges of managing strategic change are reflected in Illustration 10.8, the key debate for this chapter.

Summary

A recurrent theme in this chapter has been that approaches, styles and means of change need to be tailored to the context of that change. Bearing in mind this general point, this chapter has then emphasised a number of key points in the management of strategic change:

- There are different *types of strategic change* which can be thought of in terms of their *scope* – the extent to which they involve paradigm change or not – and their *nature* in terms of whether they can be achieved through incremental change or require urgent, immediate action (the 'big bang' approach). Different approaches and means of managing change are likely to be required for different types of change.

- It is also important to diagnose wider aspects of organisational context such as *resources and skills that need to be preserved*, the degree of *homogeneity or diversity* in the organisation, the *capability, capacity and readiness* for change and the *power* to make change happen.

- The *cultural web* and *forcefield analysis* are useful as means of identifying blockages to change and potential levers for change.

- The management of strategic change is likely to involve different *roles in the change* process, including those of strategic leaders, middle managers and outsiders.

- Different *styles* of managing strategic change are likely to be necessary according to different contexts and in relation to the involvement and interest of different groups.

- *Turnaround strategies* require a focus on speed of change.

- Levers for managing strategic change need to be considered in terms of the type of change and context of change. Such levers include surfacing and *questioning the paradigm*, the need to change organisational *routines* and *symbols*, and the importance of *political processes*, *communication* and other change *tactics*.

Recommended key readings

- J. Balogun, V. Hope Hailey (with G. Johnson and K. Scholes), *Exploring Strategic Change*, Prentice Hall, 2nd edition, 2004, builds on and extends many of the ideas in this chapter. In particular, it emphasises the importance of tailoring change programmes to organisational context and discusses more fully many of the change levers reviewed in this chapter.

- For a discussion of styles of managing strategic change, see D. Dunphy and D. Stace, 'The strategic management of corporate change', *Human Relations*, vol. 46, no. 8 (1993), pp. 905–920.

- For a discussion of effective strategic leadership, see D. Goleman, 'Leadership that gets results', *Harvard Business Review*, March–April 2000, pp. 78–90, and C.M. Farkas and S. Wetlaufer, 'The ways chief executive officers lead', *Harvard Business Review*, May–June 1996, pp. 110–121.

- In many ways the most interesting book on political management remains Niccolo Machiavelli's sixteenth-century work, *The Prince* (available in Penguin Books, 2003). It is also the basis of a management book by Gerald Griffin, *Machiavelli on Management: Playing and winning the corporate power game*, Praeger, 1991.

- The paper by John Kotter, 'Leading change: why transformation efforts fail', *Harvard Business Review*, March–April (1995), pp. 59–67 (also see Illustration 10.8) provides a useful view of what a change programme might look like.

- The study of change programmes by L.C. Harris and E. Ogbonna, 'The unintended consequences of culture interventions: a study of unexpected outcomes', *British Journal of Management*, vol. 13, no. 1 (2002), pp. 31–49 provides a valuable insight into the problems of managing change in organisations.

References

1. Many books and papers on strategic change build on the idea that the current state of the organisation is likely to be one of inertia or resistance to change; and that there is, then, a need to 'unfreeze' this situation. The dominance of this idea can be traced back to the work of K. Lewin; see 'Group decision and social change', in E.E. Maccoby, T.M. Newcomb and E.I. Hartley (eds), *Readings in Social Psychology*, Holt, Reinhart and Winston, 1958, pp. 197–211.

2. For an explanation of strategic drift also see 'Re-thinking incrementalism', *Strategic Management Journal*, vol. 9, (1988), pp. 75–91.

3. See E. Romanelli and M.L. Tushman, 'Organisational transformation as punctuated equilibrium: an empirical test', *Academy of Management Journal*, vol. 37, no. 5 (1994), pp. 1141–1161.

4. *Exploring Strategic Change* by J. Balogun and V. Hope Hailey, 2nd edition, Prentice Hall, 2004, is a sister text to this book; this part of the chapter draws on their Chapter 3 on the context of strategic change.

5. For an interesting example of how different contexts affect receptivity to change, see J. Newton, J. Graham, K. McLoughlin and A. Moore, 'Receptivity to change in a general medical practice', *British Journal of Management*, vol. 14, no. 2 (2003), pp. 143–153.

6. See reference 3 above.

7. See J.-L. Denis, L. Lamothe and A. Langley, 'The dynamics of collective change leadership and strategic change in pluralistic organizations', *The Academy of Management Journal*, vol. 44, no. 4 (2001), pp. 809–837.

8. Approaches to how to use the cultural web for the purposes outlined here are dealt with in detail in the chapter, 'Mapping and re-mapping organisational culture', in V. Ambrosini with G. Johnson and K. Scholes (eds), *Exploring Techniques of Analysis and Evaluation in Strategic Management*, Prentice Hall, 1998, and the similar chapter in G. Johnson and K. Scholes (eds), *Exploring Public Sector Strategy*, Prentice Hall, 2000.

9. A discussion of different styles is provided by D. Dunphy and D. Stace, 'The strategic management of corporate change', *Human Relations*, vol. 46, no. 8 (1993), pp. 905–920. For an alternative framework see R. Caldwell, 'Models of change agency: a fourfold classification', *British Journal of Management*, vol. 14, no. 2 (2003), pp. 131–142.

10. For evidence of the effects of involvement in the strategy development process see: N. Collier, F. Fishwick and S.W. Floyd, 'Managerial involvement and perceptions of strategy process', *Long Range Planning*, vol. 37 (2004), pp. 67–83.

11. The intervention style is discussed more fully in P.C. Nutt, 'Identifying and appraising how managers install strategy', *Strategic Management Journal*, vol. 8, no. 1 (1987), pp. 1–14.

12. Evidence for this is provided by D. Dunphy and D. Stace (see reference 9 above).

13. This definition of leadership is based on that offered by R.M. Stodgill, 'Leadership, membership and organization', *Psychological Bulletin*, vol. 47 (1950), pp. 1–14. For a more recent and more comprehensive discussion of leadership, see G.A. Yukl, *Leadership in Organizations*, 5th edition, Prentice Hall, 2001.

14. For this evidence see D.A. Waldman, G.G. Ramirez, R.J. House and P. Puranam, 'Does leadership matter? CEO leadership attributes and profitability under conditions of perceived environmental uncertainty', *Academy of Management Journal*, vol. 44, no. 1 (2001), pp. 134–143.

15. For fuller explanations of the distinction between charismatic and instrumental and transactional leadership see M.F.R. Kets de Vries, 'The leadership mystique', *Academy of Management Executive*, vol. 8, no. 3 (1994), pp. 73–89, and the paper by Waldman *et al.* (reference 14 above).

16. The discussion on different approaches of strategic leaders and evidence for the effectiveness of the adoption of different approaches can be found in D. Goleman, 'Leadership that gets results', *Harvard Business Review*, March–April 2000, pp. 78–90, and C.M. Farkas and S. Wetlaufer, 'The ways chief executive officers lead', *Harvard Business Review*, May–June 1996, pp. 110–112.

17. See S. Floyd and W. Wooldridge, *The Strategic Middle Manager: How to create and sustain competitive advantage*, Jossey-Bass, 1996.

18. Turnaround strategy is more extensively explained in D. Lovett and S. Slatter, *Corporate Turnaround*, Penguin Books, 1999, and P. Grinyer, D. Mayes and P. McKiernan, 'The Sharpbenders: achieving a sustained improvement in performance', *Long Range Planning*, vol. 23, no. 1 (1990), pp. 116–125. Also see V.L. Barker and I.M. Duhaime, 'Strategic change in the turnaround process: theory and empirical evidence', *Strategic Management Journal*, vol. 18, no. 1 (1997), pp. 13–38.

19. See the 'Sharpbenders' study (reference 18 above).

20. For an example of this approach see J.M. Mezias, P. Grinyer and W.D. Guth, 'Changing collective cognition: a process model for strategic change', *Long Range Planning*, vol. 34 (2001), pp. 71–95.

21. For a discussion of the psychological context, thinking flaws, and the impact that these have for managers as they consider the future see K. van der Heijden, R. Bradfield, G. Burt, G. Cairns and G. Wright, *The Sixth Sense: Accelerating organisational learning with scenarios*, John Wiley, 2002, chapter 2.

22. T. Deal and A. Kennedy refer to 'the way we do things around here', in *Corporate Cultures: The rights and rituals of corporate life*, Addison-Wesley, 1984. Routines have, however, also become the focus of much discussion by researchers who take a resource-based view (see Chapter 3) because they are, arguably, the bases of organisational competences. See, for example, A.M. Knott, 'The organizational routines factor market paradox', *Strategic Management Journal*, vol. 24 (2003), pp. 929–943.

23. For a full explanation of 'core rigidities' see D. Leonard-Barton, 'Core capabilities and core rigidities: a paradox in managing new product development', *Strategic Management Journal*, vol. 13 (Summer 1992), pp. 111–125.

24. This quote is on page 135 of R. Pascale, M. Millemann and L. Gioja, 'Changing the way we change', *Harvard Business Review*, November–December (1997), pp. 127–139.

25. For a more extensive explanation of these processes see G. Johnson, S. Smith and B. Codling, 'Micro processes of institutional change in the context of privatization', *Academy of Management Review*, Special Topic Forum, vol. 25, no. 3 (2000), pp. 572–580.

26. For a fuller discussion of this theme, see G. Johnson, 'Managing strategic change: the role of symbolic action',

British Journal of Management, vol. 1, no. 4 (1990), pp. 183–200.

27. For a discussion of the role of rituals in change see D. Sims, S. Fineman and Y. Gabriel, *Organizing and Organizations: An introduction*, Sage, 1993.

28. See H.M. Trice and J.M. Beyer, 'Studying organisational cultures through rites and ceremonials', *Academy of Management Review*, vol. 9, no. 4 (1984), pp. 653–669; H.M. Trice and J.M. Beyer, 'Using six organisational rites to change culture', in R.H. Kilman, M.J. Saxton, R. Serpa and associates (eds), *Gaining Control of the Corporate Culture*, Jossey-Bass, 1985.

29. The importance of the language used by corporate leaders has been noted by a number of writers, but particularly L.R. Pondy, 'Leadership is a language game', in M.W. McCall, Jr and M.M. Lombardo (eds), *Leadership: Where else can we go?*, Duke University Press, 1978. See also J.A. Conger and R. Kanungo, 'Toward a behavioural theory of charismatic leadership in organizational settings', *Academy of Management Review*, vol. 12, no. 4 (1987), pp. 637–647.

30. This discussion is based on observations of the role of political activities in organisations by, in particular, H. Mintzberg, *Power in and around Organisations*, Prentice Hall, 1983, and J. Pfeffer, *Power in Organisations*, Pitman, 1981. For a fuller explanation of the different ways of explaining power in organizations, see S.R. Clegg, *Frameworks of Power*, Sage, 1989.

31. See D.M. Schweiger and A.S. DeNisi, 'Communication with employees following a merger: a longitudinal field experiment',

Academy of Management Journal, vol. 34 (1991), pp. 110–135.

32. See R.H. Lengel and R.L. Daft, 'The selection of communication media as an executive skill', *Academy of Management Executive*, vol. 2, no. 3 (1988), pp. 225–232.

33. See S. Fox and Y. Amichai-Hamburger, 'The power of emotional appeals in promoting organizational change programs', *Academy of Management Executive*, vol. 15, no. 4 (2001), pp. 84–95.

34. Research by E. Ogbonna and B. Wilkinson in a major UK grocery retailer concluded that it was direct managerial monitoring and control rather than changes in values and culture that accounted for change. See 'The false promise of organizational culture change: a case study of middle managers in grocery retailing', *Journal of Management Studies*, vol. 40, no. 5 (2003), pp. 1151–1178.

35. For a fuller discussion of this approach by Bratton and other change agents see W.C. Kim and R. Mauborgne, 'Tipping point leadership', *Harvard Business Review*, April (2003), pp. 60–69.

36. The observations and examples here are largely based on L.C. Harris and E. Ogbonna, 'The unintended consequences of culture interventions: a study of unexpected outcomes', *British Journal of Management*, vol. 13, no. 1 (2002), pp. 31–49.

37. The monitoring of change programmes is discussed more fully in L. Gratton, V. Hope Hailey, P. Stiles and C. Truss, *Strategic Human Resource Management*, Oxford University Press, 1999.

An extensive range of additional materials, including audio summaries, weblinks to organisations featured in the text, definitions of key concepts and multiple choice questions, can be found on the *Exploring Corporate Strategy* Companion Website at **www.pearsoned.co.uk/ecs7**

WORK ASSIGNMENTS

✳ Denotes more advanced work assignments.   * Refers to a case study in the Text and Cases edition.

10.1 Drawing on sections 10.2.1 and 10.2.2 assess the key contextual dimensions of an organisation (e.g. as for the case example on Compagnie des Services Pétroliers) and consider how they should influence the design of a programme of strategic change.

10.2✳ Draw up a cultural web and use forcefield analysis to identify blockages and facilitators of change for an organisation (e.g. one for which you have considered the need for a change in strategic direction in a previous assignment). Redraw the web to represent what the organisation should aspire to given the new strategy. Using the cultural webs and forcefield analysis, identify what aspects of the changes can be managed by a change agent and how.

10.3 Identify and explain the styles of managing change (section 10.3.1 and Exhibit 10.5) and approaches to strategic leadership (section 10.3.2 and Exhibit 10.6) employed by different change agents (e.g. Kim Winser in Illustration 10.8, David Bills at the Forestry Commission* or Luc Vandevelde of Marks & Spencer*.

10.4 Using Exhibit 10.8, give examples of changes to rituals which could signal change in an organisation with which you are familiar.

10.5✳ Consider a process of strategic change that you have been involved in or have observed. Map out the steps in the change process in the following terms:
(a) new rituals introduced or old rituals done away with, and the impact of these changes;
(b) the means of communication employed by change agents, and how effective they were.

10.6✳ In the context of managing strategic change in a large corporation or public sector organisation, to what extent, and why, do you agree with Richard Pascale's argument that it is easier to act ourselves into a better way of thinking than it is to think ourselves into a better way of acting? (References 23 to 27 will be useful here.)

10.7✳ There are a number of books by renowned senior executives who have managed major changes in their organisation. Read one of these and note the levers and mechanisms for change employed by the change agent, using the approaches outlined in this chapter as a checklist. How effective do you think these were in the context that the change agent faced, and could other mechanisms have been used?

Integrative assignments

10.8 Consider how the power relationships in an organisation (section 4.3) and in particular the power/interest matrix (Exhibit 4.5) might help understand blockages to change and ways of managing change in a public sector organisation (e.g. a university).

10.9 What would be the key issues for the corporate parent of a diversified organisation with a multi-domestic international strategy (see Chapter 6) wishing to change to a more related portfolio? Consider this in terms of (a) the strategic capabilities that parent might require (Chapters 4 and 6), (b) the implications for organising and controlling its subsidiaries (Chapter 8), (c) the likely blockages to such change and (d) how these might be overcome (Chapter 10).

The Compagnie des Services Pétroliers (CSP)

Frédéric Fréry and Hervé Laroche, ESCP-EAP European School of Management

In 2004 The Compagnie des Services Pétroliers (CSP) was a French oil services company with approximately 3,500 employees and a turnover of €500m. It had been founded in the 1950s and its headquarters were located near Paris.

CSP activities

Of CSP's sales, 75 per cent consisted of conducting field studies for oil exploration. These studies helped locate and evaluate hydrocarbon reserves both inland and at sea. Since 1997, CSP had also developed an industrial activity: it designed and manufactured very specialised equipment that was necessary for conducting such studies. Selling this equipment accounted for 25 per cent of CSP turnover.

Technology

Conducting a study had two phases: (1) data gathering, through a very large number of on-site measurements; this phase required specialised tools and quite a large workforce (around one hundred people for each site); (2) data processing, in order to obtain maps and graphics that could be interpreted by oil exploration experts; this phase required powerful and specialised computer tools (hardware and software).

Market and competition

Customers were mainly oil companies. The market was global and CSP was located almost everywhere in the world, through a network of local branches that were used as base camps for on-site missions. With a 20 per cent market share, CSP was the only French company in this industry. Its two main competitors were American, each of them also with roughly 20 per cent of the market. Other competitors were much smaller and generally specialised in one region.

Structure

CSP was organised in four main departments: Service, Equipment, Research & Development and Administration. A deputy CEO managed each of these departments. The Service department gathered all activities that were involved in conducting and selling studies, managed the network of local branches and had several computer labs. It was also responsible for two specialised ships that were necessary for sea measurements.

The Equipment department included subsidiaries involved in designing, manufacturing and selling of a whole range of electronic and electromechanical devices that were used for field studies. This equipment was sold inside CSP to the Service department, but also to competitors. It was an industrial activity.

Personnel

CSP employed a high proportion of managers and engineers: roughly one thousand out of 3,500 employees. Among non-managers, technicians comprised the vast majority. Approximately one third of the workforce was made up of 'prospectors', that is to say employees dedicated to on-site studies, generally in remote locations. In addition, CSP temporarily employed a local unskilled workforce during field missions.

Senior executives

Out of nine members of the executive committee, six were alumni of the most prestigious French school of engineering, the Ecole Polytechnique. Almost all of them had worked mainly for CSP during their career, starting as 'prospectors'. The CEO and the Deputy Director General – who had been designated as the next CEO – both had external experience, one in the Ministry of Industry, and the other in an oil company.

CSP achievements

CSP headquarters had a very unsurprising look: ordinary architecture, classic offices, minimum interior design, etc. Even senior executives' offices were neutral and functional. The only posters on the walls were huge maps of the world. Discretion was a highly respected virtue at CSP. However, the company was proud to be the only non-American company in its industry. It also took pride in being the only independent company in its sector: all its main competitors were parts of large integrated groups offering a complete range of services in oil exploration and exploitation. CSP was also proud to have survived the crises that periodically shook out the industry.

CSP senior executives willingly conceded that this success derived from the technical excellence of the company, particularly at the level of 'prospectors' and mission managers. Thanks to a high human and technical capacity for adaptation – and to a special resourcefulness – CSP specialised in operating in difficult areas (uneven land, deep forest, etc.). In contrast, American competitors seemed more efficient in areas where their organisation and procedures could easily be implemented. 'As long as it consists of driving a truck in a plain or a desert – for instance in Egypt – the fully automated American system works perfectly', said a senior executive.

Boldness and technical resourcefulness, belief in the virtue of local and fast action, contempt for hierarchy, liking for direct and convivial human relations constituted what was called the 'prospector spirit'. This spirit was built 'in the field' during 'missions'. Field experience was also used to select young engineers and technicians: on the one hand it eliminated those who were not sincerely attracted by the job and on the other hand it made it possible to spot high potentials. 'The key profile at CSP', explained a senior executive, 'is the mission leader who is able to adapt with 20 French pros (prospectors) and 200 Gabonese workers, in Gabon. When he survives, he is very good . . . Not everyone survives.' On this point, according to its senior executives, CSP differed again from its big competitors: 'American brains are not in the field. In the field there are only underlings.'

Senior executives acknowledged the quality and devotion of their employees in the field. They submitted to very hard working conditions and accepted a very high level of availability: 'A pro who's in the field in Indonesia on Monday, you tell him: Thursday you are in Alaska. He catches his flight, he goes to Alaska . . . Another who's on vacation, you tell him: sorry, you have to be there immediately. He packs his things and he goes there. Sometimes he grumbles, but he goes there. The company owes a lot to these people, who are generally very attached to the company.'

Salaries were considered as relatively low, but career was guaranteed: after a variable number of years in the field, prospectors were offered a sedentary job and worked at the head office. Obviously, some of them could become senior executives. Very few prospectors quit the company: there was no job market for these highly specialised engineers and technicians.

It was probably because of this special relation between the company and its employees that CSP could cope with a light administrative infrastructure. Hierarchy and procedures were denigrated. Trust, built over the years, enabled a high level of decentralisation, in spite of a large geographical spread: 'People are simultaneously highly autonomous and perfectly tied. The managing director at the Singapore branch, because of his training, because of his future, he is actually tied to the head office, not to his environment, his customers, or his Singaporean subcontractors. You need people like this to manage large operations.'

Concerns about the future

However, at the beginning of the new millennium some changes in the environment and the industry began to create tensions and raised questions. Repeated losses of some activities (in particular studies at sea) regularly raised the issue of redefining the portfolio of businesses. In the opinion of some senior executives, the answer was clear: 'We do any business in our industry, anywhere in the world. And we stick to it. It is certainly not the most profitable method. But experience has proved that it is the safest approach if you want to stay in the business. If each time an activity loses money you stop it, then in ten years you have nothing left, because everything is cyclical. What you need is a positive integral in the life cycle (i.e. during the whole life cycle, the average profit must be positive). If you have more products, you are able to mitigate these cycles and to get some regularity in your profit.'

Conversely, CSP considered diversifications in order to broaden its portfolio of businesses. There were some ongoing tests from the technologies used by the Equipment department and from the Service department. Again, the reaction to these possible diversifications was mixed. 'We are testing a whole range of ideas, but it takes too long', said the CEO. 'Ok, we could take over a competitor. But in our industry, a hostile takeover is impossible. In our business, people are the key, and if people disagree, they go somewhere else and you remain with nothing left but empty offices. You really need people to share your goals.'

Some executives were very pleased with this: 'It is much wiser to sell our services in Mexico than to sell socks in Singapore.' For others, mainly among younger executives, CSP top managers were culturally unable to consider diversification outside the oil industry. 'Is it wise when future CEOs of the company are people who have spent three quarters of their career in the Company? People who have seen nothing else? People who are totally submerged in oil? Do people who have been trained in the oil service at the Ministry of Industry have the right profile to consider large diversifications? They are not financiers either: they are all engineers. As a result, we go around in circles.'

Even inside CSP's core business, significant changes were underway. Whereas for ages the key phase of CSP business had been on-site measurements, data processing was becoming more and more crucial: because of the investments it involved (both hardware and software), because it was absolutely necessary to be competitive at this level (oil companies now signed separate contracts for data processing), because of constant evolution of methods and tools, and finally because it was necessary to hire top-level computer analysts, whereas traditionally CSP used former prospectors converted into computer experts.

In addition, because of the global scope of the business, and because CSP was now listed on the Paris stock exchange, high-level competences in accounting, finance, tax and law were required. The CFO felt this need very deeply. Other members of the executive committee were less concerned.

The first indication of these changes was the difficulty to hire – or retain – these specialists. They immediately asked for higher salaries than former prospectors who had similar positions. They also demonstrated a lower commitment and a lower loyalty to the company. Offering a long and progressive career was not enough to retain them. In the Service department, young engineers and young technicians showed the same tendency.

The last concern was the lack of potential top executives, mainly people able to renew the existing executive committee and above all to manage strategic development. Was it still possible to rely on internal promotion to select managers and senior executives?

According to one of the top executives, the future was worrying: 'After all, our Service department employs mainly former prospectors. And among our taken-for-granted assumptions, there was the secure redeployment of prospectors. This is probably something we will not be able to do in the future. We will not find a job for all prospectors at the head office. An experience in the field is undoubtedly a plus, but an experience in the field with no external adaptation or expertise is a dead-end.' Another senior executive also give a warning: 'The main risk is to have young up-and-coming managers and old veterans, and nothing in-between.'

Amongst senior executives there was no consensus on these concerns. According to some of them, with proper attention and a smart management of demographic evolutions, it was possible to guarantee a positive outcome while preserving the core values of the company. For others, a much deeper change was to be actively prepared.

Two change programmes at stake

When sales and profits were at their lowest in the life cycle of the industry the CSP share price plummeted. Believing that something had to be done, the CFO decided to appoint a consulting company specialised in the management of change.

In order to diagnose the change situation, these consultants drew up the cultural web of CSP. According to this diagnosis, they claimed that the CSP context was deeply unfavourable to change: taken-for-granted assumptions, routines and procedures, by blocking necessary changes, were exposing CSP to a deadly strategic drift. During their final presentation to the executive committee, they recommended a radical transformational change programme, using a series of levers:

- Stop the rite of passage of 'in the field' experience for newcomers.
- Hire fewer engineers and more managers and computer analysts.
- Make the hierarchy more explicit and build a more structured organisational chart.
- Diversify the profile of the executive committee members, for example by appointing a CIO and by replacing the current senior HR manager – a former prospector – by a professional HR manager, preferably a woman.
- Appoint the CFO – who was not a former prospector but an MBA graduate – as Deputy Director General. He was considered to be the main change agent.
- Replace the name of the company by an updated brand name that would be both more modern and less dependent on oil services.

Consultants also recommended two strategic directions intended to force a reconstruction of the culture of the company:

- Transform the Equipment department into a separate company, with a dedicated management structure and fully redesigned procedures.
- Consider alliances with competitors – or possibly a takeover – and/or partnerships with oil companies and software/hardware manufacturers.

Whereas some members of the executive committee considered these recommendations as sound and useful, others claimed that consultants were unable to understand the true meaning of CSP values. The Deputy Director General, in particular, was strongly against a radical transformation. He explained that

an evolution – or an adaptation at the very most – was preferable and that the main aspect of the change programme was careful timing: the drop in share price provided a good window of opportunity for incremental evolutions. He argued that the 'in the field' experience was the most powerful integration mechanism in the company. Stopping this rite would expose CSP to a very high risk of dilution: employees would no longer accept work conditions and salaries; technical expertise would be reduced. Adopting an 'American' approach – with hierarchical structures, formal procedures and limited on-site involvement – would kill CSP differentiation. What would be CSP competitive advantage in front of its powerful competitors without its unique spirit and implicit management routines? According to him, CSP achievements were rooted in its employees' commitment. He agreed to the use of some symbolic processes in order to facilitate the evolution of the culture, for instance adopting a new brand name or appointing a CIO. He also proposed to split the Service department into an Operations department, which would perform all on-site measurements, and a Computing department, fully dedicated to data processing. This new organisation would enable preservation of the specificities of the prospector spirit – and consequently the 'CSP way' – while amending the management of computer analysts, accountants or financiers towards a more market-based approach. In order to diversify the national origin of the workforce and to increase flexibility in HR management, the CFO also proposed to hire prospectors in CSP local branches through local contracts, instead of hiring them centrally from the head office with French contracts.

Questions

1. What is your diagnosis of the change situation of CSP? Build the current cultural web of CSP.

2. In order to fit its new environmental conditions, what could be the future cultural web of CSP?

3. What are the pros and cons of the consultants' change programme? What problems do you think CSP would face with this programme and how might CSP seek to overcome them?

4. What are the pros and cons of the Deputy Director General's change programme?

5. Make your own recommendations on what should be done.

Strategy into Action

In Chapter 1 a framework for this book was presented (see Exhibit 1.3). The subsequent structure of the book has been based on that model. The different parts of the book have discussed how the *strategic position* of the organisation can be understood (Part II), what *strategic choices* might be made (Part III) and in this part (Part IV) how organisations might translate *strategy into action.* Chapter 1 explained that, although these themes are dealt with separately and sequentially in this book, it may be an artificial divide. This is a theme taken up in this commentary.

This commentary focuses on Part IV of the book and is therefore concerned with reviewing the chapters on *organising, enabling and change* through the three lenses of design, experience and ideas. However, in so doing, a question that needs to be borne in mind is whether the translation of *strategy into action* should or can be seen as quite separate from, or the outcome of, other aspects of strategic management. Understanding the strategic position of an organisation, insofar as it is about making sense of issues in the environment, an organisation's capabilities or stakeholder expectations may very well take place in the day-to-day activities of management as much as through formal analysis. Similarly, strategic choice might take place in action, by people trying things out and experimenting.

Designing strategic action

For some managers a linear, sequential view of strategic management is seen as *the* logical approach to managing strategy. The design view of strategy encapsulates this linear view. Putting strategy into action is seen as an extension of the planning process; it is to do with *planning implementation* of strategy. A strategy is first formulated and then it is implemented. The emphasis is on getting the *logic* of the strategy right and then *persuading* people of that logic; designing *structures and control systems* appropriate to the strategy and using them as mechanisms of change; putting in place the *resources* required; and planning the *timing and sequencing* of changes required. *Control* mechanisms and feedback systems also need to be in place so that the strategies can be refined, amended and so on, but nonetheless the linear sequence remains. It is a conception of strategic management based on the notion that thinking precedes organisational action.

There are associated assumptions about who does all this. There are those who are responsible for the formulation of strategy, usually seen as top management. They determine what the strategy should be through careful analysis of their internal and external organisational context, they carefully evaluate strategic options and then they translate those into implementation plans. Other more junior managers then implement these plans.

Much of what was discussed in Chapters 8, 9 and 10 could be seen as providing the bases for this approach. Chapter 9 was concerned with organising. The design lens would suggest that 'structure follows strategy'. Indeed there is evidence that structures of organisations have indeed changed following significant shifts in organisational strategies. For example, Alfred Chandler showed how multidivisional structures followed the development of multi-product firms.[1] Control systems need to be designed to monitor how the implementation of strategy is progressing. These are likely to include financial systems such as budgets, reward systems and other ways of ensuring that the behaviour of those in the organisation corresponds to the strategy. So they need to focus on measures that are vital to strategy delivery. As section 8.5, Chapter 8, on *configurations* argues, an organisation's structure and its control systems therefore need to be appropriate to deliver the strategy: if they are not, the effectiveness of the strategy will suffer.

A lesson that might be drawn from Chapter 9 is that it also matters that what goes on within major resource areas corresponds to the overall strategy. So strategies for areas such as finance, technology, HR and information should correspond to the overall plan. And the priorities and key tasks being pursued in these areas, as well as people's behaviour, should be in line with overall strategy.

Chapter 10 provides frameworks whereby a strategic change programme might be designed. Such design presupposes that there is a designer, the change agent, who will carefully think through which style of change management and which levers for managing change are most appropriate and will have most effect in what organisational context.[2] There are then others, the rest of the organisation, who will be the subject of this programme of change.

To repeat, much of this is what has been explained in the previous chapters of this book and it makes a lot of sense. Without it an organisation and those within it could find themselves in a state of confusion with no clarity of direction, no way of knowing whether they were being successful and quite probably with a disenchanted group of shareholders and demotivated workforce. Some clarity of strategic direction and matching of overall strategy to the day-to-day workings of the organisation is clearly important. However, there are other lessons to be drawn about the links between the development of strategies and organisational action. The previous chapters and commentaries have raised some of these already but using the experience and ideas lenses to consider some of the issues in Part IV of the book can help emphasise their importance as well as provide additional insights.

Strategic action and experience

Throughout this book there has been an attempt to explain strategic management both in terms of concepts and frameworks and in terms of the behaviours and assumptions associated with individual experience, organisational cultures and institutionalisation. This highlights a point that is obvious when stated, but all too easy to overlook. Ultimately the success of translating strategy into action depends on the extent to which people are committed to it. This raises significant challenges.

Strategic inertia

The first challenge relates to the problem of strategic inertia and drift. Chapter 1 (section 1.5.3) raised this problem initially and the discussion of the experience lens in the commentaries to Parts I, II and III has continued to emphasise it. There is a very real danger that people in organisations become captured by their collective experience rooted in past success and organisational and institutional norms. Chapters in Part IV of the book have flagged up related problems.

Chapter 8 points out that organisations can become captured by their structures and systems. Some organisations, such as accountancy firms, universities, large public sector bureaucracies and arguably even some e-businesses of the new millennium, have become as much defined by the *way* they are organised as by what they do. In a sense in such organisations it is not so much that structure follows strategy as that 'strategy follows structure';[3] they pursue strategies constrained or informed by their structures and systems. This is the issue that forms the key debate for Chapter 8 (Illustration 8.8). Similarly, Chapter 9 points out that organisations may be captured by their resource legacy;[4] or by assumptions people make about what resource priorities really matter. A high-technology company becomes fixated on technology as the driving force of its business; a financially oriented chief executive focuses on financing issues to the detriment of wider issues; the HR function sets up 'state-of-the-art' HR systems without ensuring that they are compatible with the strategic direction of the organisation. The explanation of how strategies develop in organisations that follows in Chapter 11 makes a similar point: it may well be the resource allocation routines (section 11.4.2) or the culture (section 11.4.3) driving the strategy rather than the other way round.

Viewing strategic change (Chapter 10) through this lens emphasises the challenge of overcoming such inertia: indeed, much of the analysis of change needs and change context suggested in section 10.2 is about seeking to establish the nature and extent of inertia. For example, is it the result of passive inertia through embeddedness in the existing culture, or more active, perhaps politicised resistance to change? The rest of that chapter suggests that managing change is about finding ways of overcoming this.

Many frameworks for designing change programmes have started from the position that breaking down cultural inertia and overcoming resistance to change are key requirements for putting strategy into action. Some argue that there is a need to 'unfreeze' the organisation before a new strategy can be followed;[5] and that this involves challenging the prevailing paradigm so that inertial constraints on following a new strategy are reduced. The organisation will therefore go through processes of change in which the mechanisms discussed in this part of the book may play a part.

- A change in the environment of the organisation – new technology, changes in customer tastes, or the entry of new competitors leading to a deteriorating market position – may act as an *unfreezing* mechanism. However, in the absence of a clear and dramatic external force for change, there may be other ways to achieve the unfreezing process. Managers may emphasise, even exaggerate, external signs of problems or threats, make structural changes, set up different control systems, remove long-established management or switch resources to different priorities as ways of signalling that existing ways of doing things are under challenge.

- There may develop a situation of *flux* in the organisation, in which competing views surface about causes of, and remedies for, the problems. It is likely to be a time of high political activity. Not least, there is likely to be a defence of boundaries and investment in resources, perhaps controlled by functional departments.

- The way forward might be resolved by planned strategic direction coming from the top. Or it may be that individuals or groups within different parts of the organisation start to try new ways of doing things – a process of *experimentation*. This might be because a change agent is deliberately using a change style of participation or intervention (see section 10.3.1 of Chapter 10) or perhaps because people in a department see themselves potentially benefiting from structural change in the organisation. The result could be that there is growing commitment to a new strategy direction. It might also mean that managers trying to instigate the new strategy learn from such experiments and refine the strategy they had planned.

- Members of the organisation, faced with a new strategy, may require a 'safety net' for the future. *Refreezing* processes may be needed to confirm the organisational validity of the new strategy, so managers may need to consider ways of signalling this: for example, by changing organisational structures (see Chapter 8), investment in resource areas central to that strategy (Chapter 9), by changing everyday routines (section 10.4.4) or by symbolic signalling of the changed strategy (see section 10.4.5).

So here the whole emphasis of managing strategic change is how managers can utilise the sorts of processes discussed in Part IV of the book to overcome the inevitable inertia which exists.

The experience of middle management

The important role of middle management was discussed in Chapters 9 and 10. Imagine a situation where the top management of an organisation are trying to develop a new strategic direction. If they take the design view literally, they could assume that they can plan strategy implementation such that it will cascade down through the organisation. They will see middle management as part of this cascade, responsible for doing what the plan instructs them to do and monitoring its progress. There is another way of looking at this, however. If strategy is viewed as coming down through the organisation from the top, it is inevitable that those below top management must make sense of any intended strategic direction in terms of their existing experience, both individual and collective: they will translate the strategic intention through their own experience.[6] Indeed, they must do this in order to try to put the new strategy into effect, since it is impossible for a top-down strategic plan to cover every detailed aspect of the operations of any organisation. It has to be translated into action within the organisation; and usually by managers responsible for resource areas of the organisation. This provides the focus for the key debate (Illustration 10.8) in Chapter 10. If this is recognised, it throws a different light on the idea of putting strategies into action.

- *Top managers cannot plan everything.* Many strategic leaders recognise that the meaning and significance of strategies decided at the top are bound to be interpreted differently to a greater or lesser extent within the organisation and that these interpretations will influence action. They therefore adopt approaches to managing strategy and styles of strategic change which explicitly take this into account (see section 10.3 of Chapter 10). They may work through key subordinates whom they believe will closely align with them on what they are trying to achieve; or they may involve subordinates in strategy development so that they become so aligned. Or they may manage through being clear about overall strategic intent and simple rules (as suggested by the ideas lens) and be prepared to allow considerable latitude for interpretation down the line.

- *Organising for involvement*. Indeed, a second lesson is that it may be important that the interpreters of strategy – mostly the middle management – are involved in developing strategies. If they are not, they must find themselves in the position of interpreting those plans on a different basis from those formulating them. Arguably this accounts for attempts to flatten organisational hierarchies and do away with layers of management each of which interpret differently the intent of the other.

- *Relating to organisational realities*. The more managers do, indeed, see their role as planning the detail of implementation, the more they need to find ways of relating the desired strategic direction to the everyday realities of people in the organisation. They need to build a bridge between their intentions and the experience of those who will carry out those intentions in operational terms. This is why it is important to ensure that organisational routines and operating processes, day-to-day control systems and HR systems are in line with the intended strategy. Again, it is unlikely that top management can do all this; it is therefore vital that middle managers are engaged with and committed to such strategies so that they can perform this translation process.

Desirable as all this may be, however, it also needs to be recognised that such perfection of translation is not likely. What is intended from the top rarely comes about in action in its entirety, or in the form in which it was originally conceived. This 'imperfection' moves the discussion forward to the ideas lens.

Strategic action and ideas

An emphasis on organisational activities

The ideas lens accepts imperfections in organisational systems and highlights the importance of diversity and variety. In drawing on evolutionary theory and complexity theory it sees strategies as the emergence of patterns of order from that variety. Here the division between strategy formulation and strategy implementation disappears. Strategies are seen as developing from ideas that bubble up from within and around an organisation. They may arise because people are interacting with a changing environment which itself promotes new ideas; or they may arise because diverse, even maverick, ideas become attractive. These ideas may become absorbed or be post-rationalised into strategic plans, but their origins are not from the planning process. The ideas themselves are created and emerge in the everyday activity and social interaction that goes on in organisations and the world that surrounds those organisations. Strategies emerge and the potential for strategic change comes from what people do within organisations, not just at the top.

This raises questions about issues raised in this part of the book and some of the insights of both the design and experience lenses.

- The emphasis here is on the *importance of interaction* within organisations and across the boundaries of organisations. The greater such interaction, the more will new ideas and innovation come about. Whilst organisational structures and systems are unavoidable necessities, they tend to build barriers and boundaries and, consequently, reduce such interaction. The ideas lens suggests that this is one of the reasons why inertia and resistance to new ideas and new strategies take place.

- The potential for new ideas, innovation and change is already there in an organisation. *Ideas need to be released*. Far from seeing lower levels in the organisation as blockages to new strategies, they should be seen as the potential source of innovation.[7] It is the formalised systems (the result of a design approach) and the experience embedded in culture that get in the way.

- *Fostering innovation*: Top managers therefore have choices. They may block ideas, perhaps because they are not seen to fit with their experience of the current business idea (see the commentary to Part II), or they may encourage variety and tolerate those who do not conform. They may champion what might at first appear to be mavericks, or demand that they conform. They can set up rigid hierarchies which ensure conformity, or create the conditions which will encourage new ideas and tolerate apparent inefficiencies and the failure of new ideas. They can set up control systems solely concerned with measuring variance against plans and budgets, or they can monitor what happens to ideas, when they succeed and fail, and so help the organisation learn from them.

- The ideas lens highlights the *limitations of formal planning*: that the notion of a planned strategy being translated in such a prescriptive and precise way that it will be replicated in the detail of organisational action is unrealistic. Such planned intentions will be translated differently by people in the organisation; this is *imperfect copying* and, whilst the design lens would see it as inefficient, the ideas lens sees it as a source of new ideas and originality.

- There is, however, a recognition of the *need for guidelines and rules*. Without these there would be chaos. Those who are thinking about the direction of strategy should recognise the importance of clarity in overarching strategic purpose or intent and a few key guiding principles, around which measurement and monitoring might be built. However, they should avoid making these so prescriptive and constraining as to prevent interaction, sharing, questioning and innovative behaviour.

- Organisations in particularly *dynamic environments* are learning such lessons because environmental forces are changing so fast that traditional ways of organising and an embeddedness of culture do not exist in the same way as they do in more stable environments. Here there is no need for *unfreezing* mechanisms because the organisation is in a state of continual change.

All of this reflects the sort of arguments put forward by those that promote the idea of the *learning organisation* which is discussed in section 11.6.2 of Chapter 11: that organisations need to be capable of continual regeneration from the variety of knowledge, experience and skills of individuals through a culture which encourages mutual questioning and challenge around a shared purpose or vision.

A note on strategic change

The ideas lens – or more specifically the field of complexity theory it builds on – also offers two views of change processes. These are the 'edge of chaos' view and what is technically referred to as a 'dissipative structures view'. Each has a somewhat different perspective on extent to which managers might be able to manage change.

The concept of an organisational *edge of chaos*[8] is linked to that of 'adaptive tension' (see Exhibit I.v) was explained in the commentary to Part I: innovation (or change) is: 'most likely to occur when the organisation never quite settles down into a steady state or equilibrium' (page 45). The resulting volatility gives rise to new ideas whilst forces for organisational inertia are minimised. Systems on the edge of chaos appear constantly to adapt, self-organising again and again to ensure compatibility with an ever-changing environment. 'You can always explore the patterns of order that are available and try them out . . . you should avoid becoming stuck in one state of order which is bound to become obsolete sooner or later.'[9] The role of management here is to establish the context or conditions for change.

Whereas the edge of chaos notion suggests a situation of constant change – or at least volatility – a *dissipative structures* view offers a more episodic explanation of change. The original research on dissipative structures was conducted in the fields of physics and physical chemistry[10] and sought to explain the emergence of order from seemingly chaotic systems. Again the condition necessary for such change is an unstable rather than stable state. In such unstable states any system, including an organisation, becomes susceptible to signals that might have had little impact if it were in a state of equilibrium. Processes of positive feedback – perhaps from the market or from inside the organisation – can turn these tiny changes into 'gigantic structure breaking waves'.[11] For example, it is said that when Greg Dyke replaced John Birt as chief executive at the BBC (see Chapter 8 case example) that trigger released huge pent-up creativity and enthusiasm that had not been able to express itself. Typically what follows these major episodes of change are more stable conditions.

Robert MacIntosh and Donald MacLean[12] adopt a dissipative structures view of strategic change. They use this as a means of understanding how change happens and to suggest what role managers can play before and during change. They argue that change involves establishing conditions of sufficient disequilibrium (e.g. through the use of simple rules; see page 45) and encouraging and managing positive and negative feedback processes during such episodes of change. Their emphasis is, then, not only on managers being able to establish a context for change, but also on using the sort of levers for change described in section 10.4 to promote, guide and direct change.

Our view

As in two of the previous commentaries, we argue that these lenses are not mutually exclusive.

At its extreme, the design lens does indeed place too much emphasis on top-down management: all-knowing top executives who determine strategy and the idea that strategy can be masterminded from on high. However, there is a need for strategic direction and care in thinking through the structuring of organisations, the management of key resource areas or the role of managers in promoting change. Even if the insights from the other lenses stand, there is the requirement to marshal the energy for change and direct it meaningfully. In all this, the design lens has much to offer.

However, the importance of individual experience and organisational culture is certainly of central importance. The experience lens therefore provides important lessons and insight into managing day-to-day aspects of strategy. However, it does more than this. In explaining barriers to change, it provides insights into how those barriers might be removed or overcome and therefore into how change can be managed.

The ideas lens highlights the potential for new ideas and innovation, but it also argues for the relevance of the other lenses. Certainly individuals are captured within their own experience and their own cultures, but they also differ. They are the source of potential variety, and the challenge is to release the energy of that variety. However, the ideas lens also points to the importance of clarity of overall direction and the importance of a sufficiency of rules. Innovation in organisations does not occur because of unbridled and anarchic individuality, but because of a balance between diversity and variety and a necessary minimum of direction and control.

Our argument is that understanding strategy into action requires the three lenses, not that one is more important than another.

References

1. The evidence that 'structure follows strategy' was provided in the historical studies of strategy development and organisational structures by A.D. Chandler, *Strategy and Structure*, MIT Press (1962).

2. *Exploring Strategic Change* by J. Balogun and V. Hope Hailey (Prentice Hall, 2004) specifically acknowledges that it takes this design approach to change.

3. For an argument and evidence that strategy may follow structure, see D. Hall and M.A. Saias, 'Strategy follows structure', *Strategic Management Journal*, vol. 1, no. 2 (1980), pp. 149–163.

4. For an exposition of a 'resource dependency' approach see J. Pfeffer and G.R. Salancik, *The External Control of Organisations: A resource dependence perspective*, Harper and Row, 1978.

5. The unfreezing model of change is widely used. It has its origins in the work of K. Lewin, 'Group decision and social change', in E.E. Maccoby, T.M. Newcomb and E.L. Hartley (eds), *Readings in Social Pschology*, Holt, Reinhart and Winston, 1958, pp. 197–211; but, for example, also see L.A. Isabella, 'Evolving interpretations as a change unfolds: how managers construe key organisational events', *Academy of Management Journal*, vol. 33, no. 1 (1990), pp. 7–41 which uses the model to explain change.

6. For an explanation and example of the role middle managers play in translating strategic intent, see J. Balogun and G. Johnson, 'Organizational restructuring and middle manager sensemaking', *Academy of Management Journal*, vol. 47, no. 4 (2004), pp. 523–549.

7. This theme of strategies and change developing from within the organisation, and of formal structures potentially inhibiting strategic change, is discussed by H. Tsoukas and R. Chia in 'On organizational becoming: rethinking organizational change', *Organization Science*, vol. 13, no. 5 (2002), pp. 567–582.

8. See S.L. Brown and K.M. Eisenhardt, 'The art of continuous change: linking complexity theory and time-paced evolution in relentlessly shifting organizations', *Administrative Science Quarterly*, vol. 42 (1997), pp. 1–34 and *Competing on the Edge: Strategy as Structured Chaos*: Harvard Business School Press. 1998.

9. This is a quote by Brian Goodwin from P. Coveney and R. Highfield, *Frontiers of Complexity*, Faber and Faber. 1995.

10. For example see E. Jantsch, *The Self-Organising Universe*, George Braziller Publishers, 1980 and I. Prigogine and I. Stengers, *Order out of Chaos: Man's new dialogue with nature*, Bantam, 1984.

11. See Prigogine and Stengers, reference 10, page xvii.

12. See R. MacIntosh and D. MacLean, 'Conditioned emergence: a dissipative structures approach to transformation', *Strategic Management Journal*, vol. 20 no. 4 (1999), pp. 297–316.

Part V

How Strategy Develops

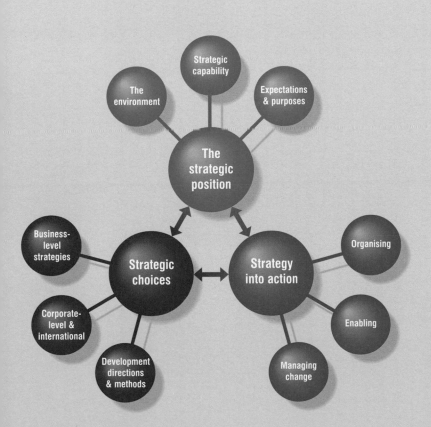

Introduction to Part V

In the book so far there have been chapters on understanding the *strategic position*, making *strategic choices* and translating *strategy into action*. Together they have provided concepts, frameworks and tools that are useful in thinking about the problems of strategic management. However, strategies followed by organisations do not come about solely as a result of managers thinking about strategic issues and carefully designing strategies for their organisation. So having a fuller understanding of how strategies do come about and how strategic management actually occurs in organisations is important.

Chapter 11 takes up this theme. It provides different explanations of how strategies develop in organisations. First it considers different explanations of how strategy might come about in an intended, deliberate way. This represents, perhaps, the conventional way of thinking about how strategies develop. However, the second part of the chapter considers other explanations of how strategies develop in a less intended, more emergent, way in organisations. Under these two headings of *intended* and *emergent* various explanations of strategy development are considered. They are not mutually exclusive and, indeed, the chapter goes on to argue that many of them will be found together in organisations. The underlying argument is that, if the concepts, frameworks and tools introduced in the rest of this book are to be useful, they have to be understood and applied in the context of how strategies actually develop in organisations. So this chapter helps the reader apply what is covered in the rest of the book.

In many ways the chapter also builds on and brings together arguments that have been made in the commentaries to the different parts of the book so far. These commentaries have consistently raised the question of how strategy development can be understood, not only as *design* but also as the *product of experience* and *ideas*. So Chapter 11 can also be seen as related to the commentaries. Indeed, the three lenses are used again in the brief commentary at the end of Chapter 11 to reconsider strategy development processes.

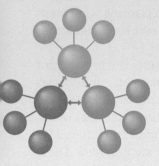

11

Understanding Strategy Development

Learning outcomes

After reading this chapter you should be able to:

● Explain what is meant by *intended* and *emergent* strategy development.

● Explain intended processes of strategy development in organisations such as:
  – strategic planning systems;
  – strategy workshops and project groups;
  – the role of strategy consultants;
  – externally imposed strategy.

● Explain emergent processes of strategy development such as:
  – logical incrementalism;
  – resource allocation routines;
  – cultural processes;
  – organisational politics.

● Consider how different processes of strategy development may be found in *multiple forms* and in *different contexts.*

● Explain some of the issues managers face in strategy development including:
  – the challenge of *strategic drift*;
  – the development of the *learning organisation*;
  – strategy development in *uncertain and complex conditions.*

Photo: Getty Images

Photo: Corbis

Photo: Digital Vision

11.1   INTRODUCTION

It is important to distinguish between the concepts and ideas that help explain what strategies are and the processes by which strategies come about in organisations. Most of the book so far has been concerned with explaining what strategies are and how they might be considered. This chapter provides explanations of how strategies come about in organisations.

The next section of this chapter (11.2) provides a background to different explanations of how strategies develop in organisations. In particular, it discusses the distinction between *intended strategy* as deliberately planned or conceived in organisations and the *emergence of strategy* in organisations in other ways. The orthodox view is that organisations' strategies are *intended*. In section 11.3 explanations of processes of intended strategy development are provided. These include the use of *strategic planning, strategy workshops, strategy project groups, strategic leadership, strategy consultants* and *externally imposed strategy*. However, the evidence is that often in organisations strategies do not so much develop on the basis of some grand plan as emerge from within the organisations. This is the notion of *emergent strategy*. Again there are different explanations for this and these are considered in section 11.4. The section begins by considering what has become known as *logical incrementalism*. It then descibes how strategies could be the outcome of *resource allocation processes* in organisations. The influence of *cultural processes* in organisations and their *political processes* are then discussed.

Section 11.5 of the chapter argues that, in fact, these different explanations of strategy development should not be seen as independent or mutually exclusive. Indeed it is likely that they could all be seen within organisations at the same time, or at different times to different degrees. So the third section of the chapter considers *multiple processes of strategy development* in organisations and how these may be context dependent.

The final section of the chapter (11.6) builds on this review of processes to raise some *implications for managing strategy development* including:

● How processes of strategy development may account for the phenomenon of *strategic drift* (briefly explained in Chapter 1) and how this raises challenges for managers.

● The challenge of developing what has become known as the *learning organisation*.

● How different approaches to strategy development may be more or less well suited to *stable, dynamic or complex* environments.

Exhibit 11.1 summarises the coverage of the chapter.

11.2   INTENDED AND EMERGENT STRATEGIES

In the previous chapter Illustration 10.2 and the discussion in sections 10.2.3 and 10.2.4 outlined some problems of strategic change in a local government

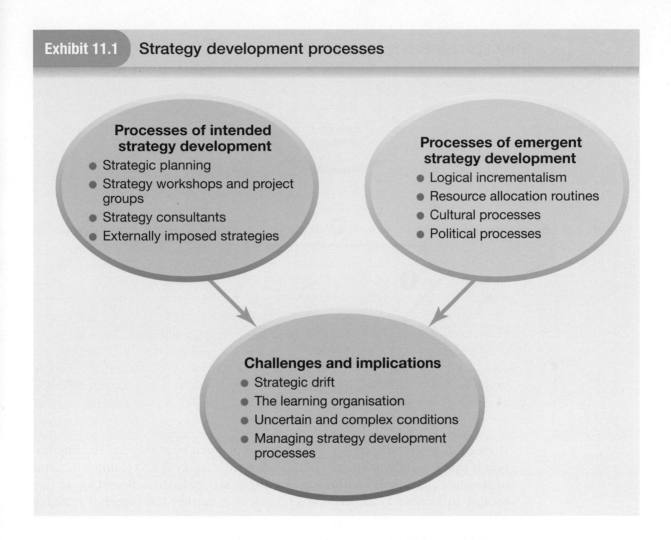

Exhibit 11.1   Strategy development processes

Processes of intended strategy development
- Strategic planning
- Strategy workshops and project groups
- Strategy consultants
- Externally imposed strategies

Processes of emergent strategy development
- Logical incrementalism
- Resource allocation routines
- Cultural processes
- Political processes

Challenges and implications
- Strategic drift
- The learning organisation
- Uncertain and complex conditions
- Managing strategy development processes

department. The chief executive had a clear intended plan. It was based on an analysis of the community's needs, it had been discussed with other senior executives and with the elected councillors and it was expressed in a formal document explaining that intended strategy in detail. There was no lack of careful thought behind this; it had been drawn up in a systematic way and the explanations underpinning it were well argued and documented. The intended strategy involved prioritising a number of local issues and delivering coordinated services to solve pressing social issues. However, this was not the strategy being followed by the organisation. Despite the fact that most of the senior executives said they agreed with the intended strategy, what was happening in practice was the persistence of a fragmented set of services based on the separate priorities of each department, as had always traditionally been the case.

This is not an unusual set of circumstances: the existence of an *intended strategy* from the top that is different from the strategy actually being delivered – or the *realised strategy* – that emerges from within the organisation. This fairly common pattern needs rather more explanation.

Typically, strategy has been written about as though it is developed by managers in an *intended*, planned fashion. **Intended strategy** is an expression of desired

Intended strategy is an expression of desired strategic direction deliberately formulated or planned by managers

Exhibit 11.2   Strategy development routes

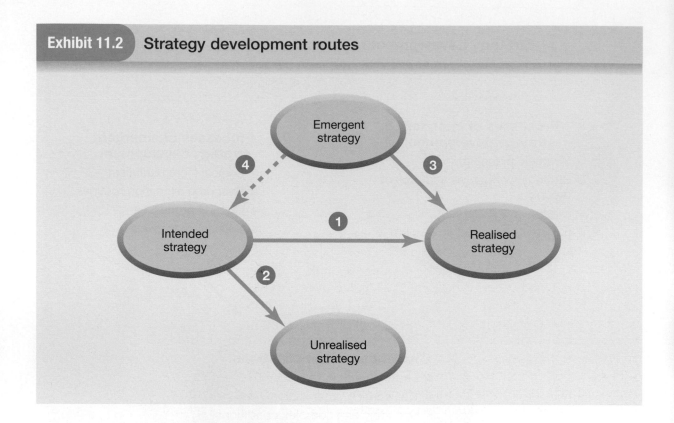

strategic direction deliberately formulated or planned by managers. The implication is that the implementation of this intended strategy is also planned in terms of resource allocation, control systems, organisational structure and so on (see route 1 in Exhibit 11.2).[1] Section 11.3 discusses further the processes typically associated with the development of intended strategy.

However, in many organisations that attempt to formulate detailed intended strategies, much of that which is intended follows route 2 in Exhibit 11.2 and is *unrealised*; it does not come about in practice, or only partially so. There may be all sorts of reasons for this. The plans are unworkable, the environment changes after the plan has been drawn up and managers decide that the strategy, as planned, should not be put into effect, or people in the organisation or influential stakeholders do not go along with the plan. (Also see the discussion of the drawbacks of planning systems in section 11.3 that follows.)

As illustrated above, it could also be that the intended strategy, whilst existing in the form of a plan of some sort, is not the **realised strategy**: that is, the strategy actually being followed by an organisation in practice. If strategy is defined as the long-term direction of the organisation, which develops over time, then it can be *emergent* (route 3 in Exhibit 11.2) rather than planned upfront. **Emergent strategy** comes about through more everyday routines, activities and processes in organisations that, on the face of it, may not be directly to do with development of strategy but nonetheless can play an important role. Such processes are explained in section 11.4.

It should also be noted that if strategic plans exist they might not perform the role of formulating strategies (route 2) so much as the useful role of monitoring

Realised strategy: the strategy actually being followed by an organisation in practice

Emergent strategy comes about through everyday routines, activities and processes in organisations

the progress or efficiency of a strategy which emerges (route 4 in Exhibit 11.2). This is discussed further in section 11.3.1 below on strategic planning systems. Indeed, such plans may do little more than pull together the views and 'wisdom' built up over time in the organisation. Whilst this too may be useful, it is often a complaint of chief executives that the planning systems in their organisation have degenerated into little more than post-rationalisations of where the organisation has come from.

If historical patterns of strategy development in organisations are examined, a pattern of what has become known as incremental strategy development is apparent. Strategies do not typically change in major shifts of direction. They typically change by building on and amending what has gone before. Prior decisions tend to affect future directions giving rise to the sort of pattern described in Exhibit 11.3. An apparently coherent strategy of an organisation may develop on the basis of a series of strategic moves each of which makes sense in terms of previous moves. Perhaps a product launch, or a significant investment decision, establishes a strategic direction which, itself, guides decisions on the next strategic move – an acquisition perhaps. This in turn helps consolidate the strategic direction, and over time the overall strategic approach of the organisation becomes more established. As time goes on, each move is informed by this developing pattern of strategy and, in turn, reinforces it.

In many ways this is to be expected. It would be strange and, arguably, dysfunctional for an organisation to change its strategy fundamentally very often. Moreover, if it has embarked on an overall strategic direction, it is to be expected that strategic decisions would be taken in line with that. So such a pattern is

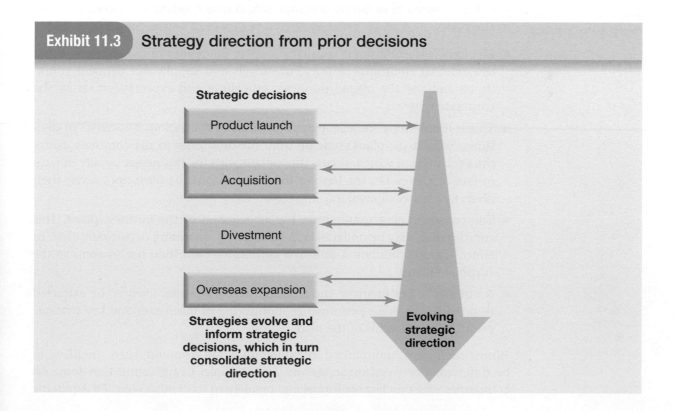

Exhibit 11.3 **Strategy direction from prior decisions**

Strategic decisions

Product launch

Acquisition

Divestment

Overseas expansion

Strategies evolve and inform strategic decisions, which in turn consolidate strategic direction

Evolving strategic direction

consistent with a view of strategy development as an intentional, considered and deliberate process. However, it is also possible to account for the same pattern as a persistent application of the familiar – organisations repeatedly taking decisions based on where they have come from, rather than a considered view of their future.[2] Arguably this is how many firms ended up being as diversified as they were in the 1980s and early 90s. Once they took the first acquisitive steps, each succeeding acquisition was justified on much the same grounds. The results were too often over diversified and near unmanageable conglomerates, nonetheless justified in annual reports and press releases as a 'grand strategy' of synergistic-related diversification.

To understand such incremental patterns of strategy development it is, therefore, useful to have a better understanding of different explanations of intended and emergent strategy development processes.

11.3   INTENDED STRATEGY DEVELOPMENT

11.3.1 Strategic planning systems

Strategic planning may take the form of systematised, step-by-step, chronological procedures to develop or coordinate an organisation's strategy

Often, strategy development is equated with formalised **strategic planning** systems.[3] These may take the form of systematised, step-by-step, chronological procedures involving different parts of the organisation. For example, in a study of strategic planning systems of major oil companies, Rob Grant[4] noted the following stages in the cycle:

● The cycle's starting point is usually a set of guidelines or assumptions about the external environment (e.g. price levels and supply and demand conditions) and also the overall priorities, guidelines and expectations set by the corporate centre.

● This is followed by strategic plans drawn up by the various businesses or divisions. So strategic plans come up from the businesses to the corporate centre the executives of which discuss those plans with the businesses usually in face-to-face meetings. On the basis of these discussions the businesses revise their plans for further discussion.

● The corporate plan results from the aggregation of the business plans. This coordination may be undertaken by a corporate planning department that, in effect, has a coordination role. The corporate board then has to approve the corporate plan.

● A number of key financial and strategic targets are then likely to be extracted to provide a basis for performance monitoring of businesses and key strategic priorities on the basis of the plan.

Whilst such steps, summarised in Exhibit 11.4, are common, there are likely to be differences between organisations. For example, Grant found that some oil companies were much more formal and regularised than others (e.g. Elf Aquitaine

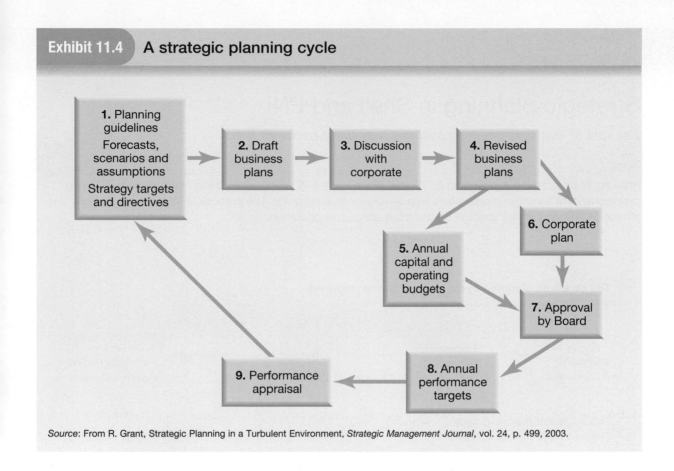

Exhibit 11.4   A strategic planning cycle

1. Planning guidelines
Forecasts, scenarios and assumptions
Strategy targets and directives

2. Draft business plans

3. Discussion with corporate

4. Revised business plans

6. Corporate plan

5. Annual capital and operating budgets

7. Approval by Board

9. Performance appraisal

8. Annual performance targets

Source: From R. Grant, Strategic Planning in a Turbulent Environment, *Strategic Management Journal*, vol. 24, p. 499, 2003.

and ENI), with greater reliance on written reports and formal presentations, more fixed planning cycles, less flexibility and more specific objectives and targets relating to the formal plans. Where there was more informality/flexibility (BP, Texaco and Exxon), companies placed greater emphasis on more general financial targets. Central corporate planning departments also played different roles. In some organisations they acted primarily as coordinators of business plans (e.g. Amoco and ENI). In others (e.g. Shell) they were more like internal consultants. Illustration 11.1 provides examples of the planning cycles of Shell and ENI.

It is important to note that major strategic decisions may not, themselves, be made within or as a direct result of such planning processes. For example, the decisions about competitive strategy in a business-level strategic plan will quite likely be taken in management meetings perhaps dominated by the chief executive and perhaps influenced by any of the processes – for example, organisational politics – explained in section 11.4 below. Such decisions may *then* be built into the formal plan.

Nonetheless a strategic planning system may have many uses. First, it may indeed play a role in how the future organisational *strategy is determined*. For example, it might:

● Provide a structured means of *analysis and thinking* about complex strategic problems.

Illustration 11.1   strategy into action

Strategic planning in Shell and ENI

The role of strategic planning systems may differ between firms.

Shell

Shell strategic planning is based on (a) 20-year plans every 4–5 years on the basis of its scenario planning process and (b) annual business plans with 5–10-year time horizons. The purpose is to enhance business unit strategies and coordinate strategy across the multinational operation.

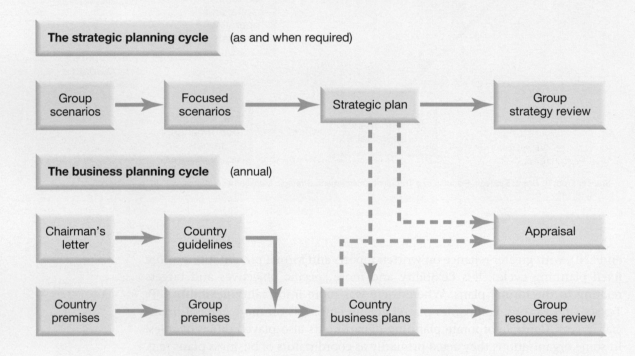

- Encourage managers to *question and challenge* the received wisdom they take for granted.
- Encourage a *longer-term view* of strategy than might otherwise occur. Planning horizons vary, of course. In a fast-moving consumer goods company, 3 to 5-year plans may be appropriate. In companies which have to take very long-term views on capital investment, such as those in the oil industry, planning horizons can be as long as 15 years (in Exxon) or 20 years (in Shell). However, in some oil companies, too, planning horizons can be just 4–5 years.[5]
- Provide a means of *coordination*, for example by bringing together various business-level strategies within an overall corporate strategy.

ENI

ENI has an annual planning cycle with a four-year time horizon embracing each business unit, sector and the whole group. The first year of the plan forms the basis of the annual budget and performance objectives. The emphasis is on central corporate control of business units and pressure on them to achieve greater efficiencies.

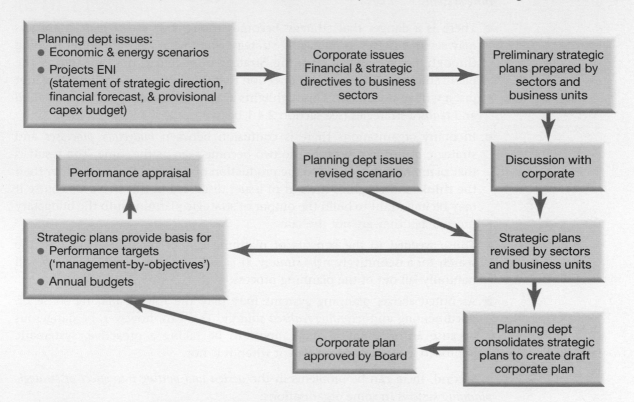

Source: From R. Grant, Strategic Planning in a Turbulent Environment, *Strategic Management Journal*, vol. 24, p. 498.

Questions

1. Explain the main differences between the two planning systems.
2. What other processes of strategy development are likely to be found in a major oil company?

A planning system may also facilitate converting an intended strategy into organisational action by:

● *Communicating* intended strategy from the centre.
● *Providing agreed objectives or strategic milestones* against which performance and progress can be reviewed.
● Ensuring the *coordination of resources* required to put strategy into effect.

A planning system may also have psychological roles. It can:

● Be a way of *involving people* in strategy development, therefore perhaps helping to create *ownership* of the strategy.

- Provide a *sense of security* and logic for the organisation and, in particular, senior management who believe they *should* be proactively determining the future strategy and exercising control over the destiny of the organisation.

Henry Mintzberg has, however, challenged the extent to which planning provides such benefits, arguing that there are dangers in the way in which formal systems of strategic planning have been employed.[6]

First there are problems associated with misunderstanding the *purposes of planning systems*:

- There is a danger that strategy becomes thought of as *the plan*. Managers may see themselves as managing strategy when what they are doing is going through the processes of planning. Strategy is, of course, not the same as 'the plan': strategy is the long-term direction that the organisation is following, not just a written document. This highlights again the difference between *intended* and *realised* strategies (see section 2.4.1 below).

- In many organisations there is confusion between *budgetary processes* and strategic planning processes; the two become seen as the same. The result is that planning gets reduced to the production of financial forecasts rather than the thinking through of the sort of issues discussed in this book. Of course it may be important to build the output of strategic planning into the budgetary process; but they are not the same.

- Those wedded to the benefits of planning can become obsessed with the search for a definitively *right strategy*. It is unlikely that a 'right' strategy will naturally fall out of the planning process.

- As noted above, planning systems may play the role of making sense of, documenting and *recording realised strategy*. This can, however, be dangerous because an organisation may appear to be taking a proactive, systematic approach to strategy development when it is not.

Second, there can be problems in the *design and putting into effect of strategic planning systems* in some organisations:

- The managers responsible for the implementation of strategies, usually line managers, may be so busy with the day-to-day operations of the business that they *cede responsibility* for strategic issues to specialists or consultants. However, these rarely have power in the organisation to make things happen. The result can be that strategic planning becomes an *intellectual exercise* removed from the reality of operation. As General William Sherman said in 1869 in the context of the American Civil War: 'I know there exist many good men who honestly believe that one may, by the aid of modern science, sit in comfort and ease in his office chair and, with figures and algebraic symbols, master the great game of war. I think this is an insidious and most dangerous mistake.'[7]

- There is a danger that the process of strategic planning may be so cumbersome that individuals or groups might contribute to only part of it and *not understand the whole*. This is particularly problematic in very large firms. One executive, on taking over as marketing manager in a large multinational consumer goods firm, was told by his superior: 'We do corporate planning in the first two weeks of April, then we get back on with our jobs.'

- Strategic planning can become over-detailed in its approach, concentrating on extensive analysis which, whilst sound in itself, may miss the major strategic issues facing the organisation. For example, it is not unusual to find companies with huge amounts of information on their markets, but with little clarity about the strategic importance of that information. The result can be *information overload* with no clear outcome.

- Highly formalised and rigid systems of planning, especially if linked to very tight and detailed mechanisms of control, can result in an inflexible, hierarchical organisation with a resultant *stifling of ideas and dampening of innovative capacity*.

Finally strategic planning systems may fail to gain *ownership* of the strategy:

- The strategy resulting from deliberations of a corporate planning department, or a senior management team, may not be *owned* more widely in the organisation. In one extreme instance, a colleague was discussing a company's strategy with its planning director. He was told that a strategic plan existed, but found it was locked in the drawer of the executive's desk. Only the planner and a few senior executives were permitted to see it!

- Planners can come to believe centrally planned strategy determines what goes on in an organisation. In fact it is what people do and the experience they draw on to do it that are likely to play a much more significant role. If formal planning systems are to be useful, those responsible for them need to draw on such experience and involve people throughout the organisation if planning is to avoid being *removed from organisational reality*.

The evidence of the extent to which the pursuit of such a systemised approach results in organisations performing better than others is equivocal[8] – not least because it is difficult to isolate formal planning as the dominant or determining effect on performance. Certainly there has been a decline in the use of formal corporate planning departments. For example, the study of corporate planning in the oil industry found that, between 1990 and 1996, corporate planning staff had declined from 48 to 3 in BP, 42 to 17 in Exxon, 38 to 12 in Mobil and 49 to 17 in Shell.[9] In the oil industry, as elsewhere, there has been a shift to line managers taking responsibility for strategy development and planning. This has been accompanied by a growing informality in the planning process and a greater emphasis on discussions of a few key underlying issues as distinct from details of plans. This goes hand in hand with a growing emphasis on planning trying to establish clarity of overall strategic direction rather than detailed programmes of action.

11.3.2 Strategy workshops and project groups

As it has become recognised that a purely top-down planning process in which the rest of the organisation is simply expected to implement the plans from the top is unrealistic, strategy workshops have become more common. These usually take the form of intensive working sessions of a few days, perhaps away from the office, by groups of executives addressing the strategy of the organisation. They may employ analytic tools and techniques, as well as drawing on participants' experience, to develop strategic recommendations to the senior executives.

A strategy workshop may be for the top management team of the organisation itself – perhaps the board of directors. It could be for a different level of management, perhaps the heads of departments or functions in an organisation. Or, again, it may consist of different levels of management and staff across the organisation. Indeed organisations may set up *project teams* to tackle particular issues with the specific intent of involving groups of managers or staff with familiarity of those issues. The aim is, therefore, to devolve responsibility whilst also accessing expertise.

The configuration of such workshops and project teams is likely to differ according to what their purpose is. Such purposes might include:

- To *reconsider or generate the intended strategy* of the organisation. In effect, here, a strategy workshop may be performing the role of strategic planning and may undertake, commission or receive reports based on extensive analysis for consideration. This type of workshop is likely to include most if not all of the top management team of the organisation.

- To *challenge the assumptions* underlying the existing strategy: to examine its continued relevance. Again this could be the top management team; but it may well include others, such as outsiders (e.g. consultants) or lower levels of management. Such challenging of existing strategy may be undertaken more or less formally. Certainly there exist systematic ways of questioning and challenging such assumptions.[10]

- To *plan strategy implementation*, i.e. to translate the intended strategy from the top into workable strategies down through the organisation. Top management may realise the likelihood is that they will not, themselves, be able to identify all the issues relevant in strategy implementation; so they may involve other levels of management in doing this.

- To *examine blockages to strategic change* and how to overcome them. Again, this is likely to involve people throughout the organisation and in particular those with specific responsibility for overcoming the major barriers to change. And, again such events may involve outsiders, perhaps skilled facilitators in the management of strategic change.

- To *undertake strategic analysis*. For example, the sort of competence analysis discussed in Chapter 3;[11] or perhaps the analysis of organisational culture using cultural webs as explained in Chapter 10.[12]

- To *monitor the progress of strategy*: it may be important for top management to get feedback on the development of strategy in the organisation. Again strategy workshops could be used for this purpose and might well involve multiple levels from within the organisation.

- To *generate new ideas and solutions*. Increasingly it is being recognised that, if innovation is to be fostered, it may be necessary for people in an organisation to step outside their work routines and be given the opportunity to make explicit and discuss ideas they may have but which may not normally get surfaced.

There are, then, many reasons why strategy workshops and project groups could be used. An example is shown in Illustration 11.2 of a series of workshops with different but related purposes.

Illustration 11.2   strategy into action

Strategy workshops at ESB Power Generation

Strategy workshops may have a variety of purposes relating to strategy development and strategic change.

The managing director of ESB Power Generation, responsible for the running of power stations in Ireland, was concerned that impending deregulation and possible future privatisation would inevitably mean thatthe business would face a very different future. There would be pressure to reduce market share as well as costs, and the business could find itself in a competitive situation for the first time in its history. It was necessary to examine the future strategy of the businessand he decided to do this through a series of strategy workshops involving different levels in the organisation.

Top team workshop

The process began with a two-day top team workshop which addressed a series of questions:

- What might be the key macro-environmental forces to affect the business in the next five years? Deregulation certainly but that could take different forms. New technologies and raw material costs were also identified as major unknowns that could have significant impact.

- What form might future competition take? This was less likely to be local and more likely to be from the entry of power generators from other European Union countries.

- So what might the possible future scenarios be?

- What competitive advantage might the business have over possible new entrants and what strategic capabilities could these build on? Given the different types of power stations ESB had in Ireland, an advantage it should have was flexibility in its offering to the market compared with potential competitors.

- What were the strategic options to compete in a deregulated environment? The strategy would have to change significantly whichever scenario came about and more emphasis would have to be placed on the differential advantages ESB had and might further develop.

Workshops with middle managers

The next level of workshops spread the discussion to managers who reported to those in the top team,

together with specialists from other functions. These reviewed the deliberations of the top team, going through the same process in order to establish whether they would come to similar conclusions. The managing director confirmed that the process was also about ensuring that they saw the need for change themselves and checking that they would be 'on board' with a very different strategy from the past.

Two such workshops were held and they did, indeed, endorse the strategy of the top team. They also examined just what a strategy emphasising flexibility would mean in terms of operational priorities in the various business functions.

Involvement throughout the organisation in planning change

There remained the problem of strategic change. Changing from a public sector utility to a competitive strategy of differentiation built on flexibility would require changes in the organisation from top to bottom. It was decided that these should be considered by means of workshops to consider the culture change necessary. The aim was to ensure that, not just the physical resources, but the people in the organisation and the way they dealt with customers and each other could deliver the flexibility that would be required. Workshops were held at levels varying from senior executives to supervisors in the production units to examine just what a culture of flexibility meant, the changes needed in detail and the priorities for action.

Questions

1. What frameworks of analysis might the different workshops have used to tackle the issues?

2. If you were a consultant facilitating the workshops what potential problems might you foresee for each level of workshop?

3. What benefits (or disadvantages) might such workshops have in comparison with other approaches to strategy development for such an organisation?

It is argued that whilst the effectiveness of such events depends on the quality of the data and the analysis of those data, success is also dependent on the extent to which there is top management support for such events, not least in ensuring participants can surface issues with confidence and have 'honest conversations'[13] about issues. Of course the effectiveness of workshops and project teams also depends on the capabilities participants have to manage the political agendas and personal biases that are bound to exist in such arenas.[14]

11.3.3 Strategy consultants

External consultants are often used in the development of strategy in organisations. There are large consultancy firms that focus on strategy such as McKinsey and Bain. Most of the large general consultancy firms also have operations that provide services in strategy development and analysis. There are also smaller 'boutique' consultancy firms specialising in strategy.

The reasons for organisations using such consultants vary. It could be that executives feel the need for an external, more objective view of issues relating to the strategy of their organisations. This could be related to the need to cut through internal disagreements within the organisation. External consultants also play a symbolic role since it is often seen that their involvement – and their cost – signal the importance of the work they are doing and conclusions they come up with.

Consultants may play different roles in strategy development in organisations:[15]

- *Analysing, prioritising and generating options.* Strategic issues may have been identified by the executives, but there may be so many of them, or so much disagreement about them, that the organisation faces a lack of clarity on how to go forward. Consultants may analyse such issues afresh and bring an external eye to help prioritise them or generate options for executives to consider. This may, of course, involve challenging executives' preconceptions about their views of strategic issues.

- *Knowledge carrier.* Consultants play a role in disseminating views, insights and the conclusions drawn from their analysis within organisations in meetings and discussions and in disseminating knowledge between organisations. In effect they are the carriers of knowledge and best practice between their clients.[16]

- *Promoting strategic decisions.* In doing all this consultants themselves may exercise strategic choice. They may play a powerful role in influencing the decisions that organisations eventually take. There is of course a risk here and a number of major consultancy operations have been criticised in the past for undue influence on the decisions made by their client organisation that has led to major problems. For example, *Business Week* ran a cover story critically examining the role of McKinsey consultants in companies such as Enron and Swissair. 'At Swissair Group, McKinsey advised a major shift in strategy that led the once highly regarded airline to spend nearly $2bn [€2.3bn] buying stakes in many small and troubled European airlines. The idea was for Swissair to expand into aviation services, providing everything from maintenance to food for other airlines as a way to increase revenues and profits. The strategy backfired, causing massive losses and bankruptcy filing (in October 2001).'[17]

● *Implementing strategic change.* Consultants play a significant role in project planning, coaching and training often associated with strategic change. This is an area that has seen considerable growth, not least because consultants were criticised for leaving organisations with consultancy reports recommending strategies, but taking little responsibility for actually making these happen.

11.3.4 Externally imposed strategy

There may be situations in which managers face what they see as the imposition of strategy by powerful external stakeholders. For example, government may dictate a particular strategic course or direction as in the public sector, or where it exercises extensive regulation over an industry; or it may choose to deregulate or privatise a sector or organisation currently in the public sector. Businesses in the private sector may also be subject to such imposed strategic direction, or significant constraints on their choices. A multinational corporation seeking to develop businesses in some parts of the world may be subject to governmental requirements to do this in certain ways, perhaps through joint ventures or local alliances. An operating business within a multidivisional organisation may regard the overall corporate strategic direction of its parent as akin to imposed strategy.

Whilst an imposed strategy may not be developed by the managers in the organisation concerned, the strategy may well have been 'designed' elsewhere. Indeed, it might be argued that such imposed strategy is a way of deliberately forcing strategic change in areas where management themselves have been reluctant or unable to do so. Increasingly governments have been doing just this through programmes of deregulation or privatisation of state-owned corporations. In the UK public sector a more direct interventionist approach began to be used in the early 2000s. So-called 'special measures' were employed for schools or hospitals deemed to be underperforming badly, with specialist managers being sent in to turn round the ailing organisations.

11.4 EMERGENT STRATEGY DEVELOPMENT

Section 11.2 explained how strategies may be intended or emergent. There have been many studies which show that the realised strategies of organisations are probably better accounted for as emergent. In other words, rather than thinking of strategies as resulting from top-down plans and intentions, they may well come about as a result of activities and processes within the organisation giving rise to decisions that become the long-term direction – the strategy – of an organisation.[18] These cumulative decisions may then subsequently be more formally described, for example in annual reports and strategic plans, as the strategy of the organisation. This section explains the organisational processes that might account for such emergent strategy development.

11.4.1 Logical incrementalism

In a study of major multinational businesses, Quinn[19] concluded that the strategy development processes he observed could best be described as *logical incrementalism*. **Logical incrementalism** is the development of strategy by experimentation and 'learning from partial commitments rather than though global formulations of total strategies'.[20] Quinn observed a number of processes that characterise this:

Logical incrementalism is the deliberate development of strategy by experimentation and learning from partial commitments

- Managers have a *generalised rather than specific view* of where they want the organisation to be in the future and try to move towards this position incrementally. There is a *reluctance to specify precise objectives* too early, as this might stifle ideas and prevent experimentation. Objectives may therefore be fairly general in nature.

- Effective managers realise that they cannot do away with the uncertainty of their environment by trying to 'know' about how it will change. Rather, they try to be sensitive to environmental signals through *constant scanning* and by testing changes in strategy in small-scale steps.

- They do this by attempting to ensure the success and development of a strong, secure, but flexible core business, building on the experience gained in that business to inform decisions about its development and *experimenting* with 'side bet' ventures. Commitment to strategic options may therefore be tentative in the early stages of strategy development.

- Such experiments cannot be expected to be the sole responsibility of top management. They emerge from what Quinn describes as '*subsystems*', in the organisation. By this he means the groups of people involved in, for example, product development, product positioning, diversification, external relations, and so on.

- Top managers may then utilise a mix of *formal and informal* social and political processes (see section 11.4.4 below) to draw together an emerging pattern of strategies from these subsystems.

Given the inevitable uncertainties of all this, it is not possible to predict the precise end results in terms of an overall strategy for the organisation. Nonetheless Quinn argues that logical incrementalism can be 'a conscious, purposeful, proactive, executive practice' to improve information available for decisions and build people's psychological identification with the development of strategy. In a sense, then, Quinn is describing processes that bridge intention and emergence, in that they are deliberate and intended but rely on social processes within the organisation to sense the environment and experiments in subsystems to try out ideas. Whilst this does not give rise to a clear and specific or detailed intended strategy, if what Quinn argues is to be accepted, it is nonetheless a deliberate process.

This view of strategy making is similar to the descriptions that managers themselves often give of how strategies come about in their organisation. Illustration 11.3 provides some examples of managers explaining the strategy development process in their organisation as they see it. They see their job as 'strategists' as continually, proactively pursuing a strategic goal, countering competitive moves and adapting to their environment, whilst not 'rocking the boat' too much, so as to maintain efficiency and performance.

Illustration 11.3

strategy into action

An incrementalist view of strategic management

Managers often see their job as managing adaptively: continually changing strategy to keep in line with the environment, whilst maintaining efficiency and keeping stakeholders happy.

● 'You know there is a simple analogy you can make. To move forward when you walk, you create an imbalance, you lean forward and you don't know what is going to happen. Fortunately, you put a foot ahead of you and you recover your balance. Well, that's what we're doing all the time, so it is never comfortable.'[1]

● 'The environment is very fast changing. You can set a strategic direction one day and something is almost certain to happen the next. We do not have a planning process which occurs every two years because the environment is stable, but a very dynamic process which needs to respond to the unexpected.'[1]

● 'I begin wide-ranging discussions with people inside and outside the corporation. From these a pattern eventually emerges. It's like fitting together a jigsaw puzzle. At first the vague outline of an approach appears like the sail of a ship in a puzzle. Then suddenly the rest of the puzzle becomes quite clear. You wonder why you didn't see it all along.'[2]

● 'The real strength of the company is to be able to follow these peripheral excursions into whatever . . . one has to keep thrusting in these directions; they are little tentacles going out, testing the water.'[3]

● 'We haven't stood still in the past and I can't see with our present set-up that we shall stand still in the future; but what I really mean is that it is a path of evolution rather than revolution. Some companies get a successful formula and stick to that rigidly because that is what they know – for example, [Company X] did not really adapt to change, so they had to take what was a

revolution. We hopefully have changed gradually and that's what I think we should do. We are always looking for fresh openings without going off at a tangent.'[3]

● 'The analogy of a chess game is useful in this context. The objective of chess is clear: to gain victory by capturing your opponent's king. Most players begin with a strategic move, that assumes a countermove by the opponent. If the countermove materialises, then the next move follows automatically, based on a previous winning strategy. However, the beauty of chess is the unpredictability of one's opponent's moves. To attempt to predict the outcome of chess is impossible, and therefore players limit themselves to working on possibilities and probabilities of moves that are not too far ahead.'[4]

Sources:
1. Quotes from interviews conducted by A. Bailey as part of a research project sponsored by the Economic and Social Research Council (Grant No.: R000235100).
2. Extract from J.B. Quinn, *Strategies for Change*, Irwin, 1980.
3. Extracts from G. Johnson, *Strategic Change and the Management Process*, Blackwell, 1987.
4. From a manager on an MBA course.

Questions

1. With reference to these explanations of strategy development, what are the main advantages of developing strategies incrementally?

2. Is incremental strategy development bound to result in strategic drift (see section 11.6.1)? How might this be avoided?

It can be argued that if strategies are developed in such a way, it has considerable benefits. Continual testing and gradual strategy implementation provides improved quality of information for decision making, and enables the better sequencing of the elements of major decisions. Since change will be gradual, the possibility of creating and developing a commitment to change throughout the organisation is increased. Because the different parts, or 'subsystems', of the organisation are in a continual state of interplay, the managers of each can learn from each other about the feasibility of a course of action. Such processes also take account of the political nature of organisational life, since smaller changes are less likely to face the same degree of resistance as major changes. Moreover, the formulation of strategy in this way means that the implications of the strategy are continually being tested out. This continual readjustment makes sense if the environment is considered as a continually changing influence on the organisation.

11.4.2 Resource allocation routines

*The **Bower–Burgelman explanation** of strategy development is that strategy develops as the outcome of resource allocation routines in organisations*

Strategies may also emerge in organisations through the more formalised routines and systems of the organisation itself. This is sometimes known as the **Bower–Burgelman explanation** of strategy development after two US professors – Joe Bower and Robert Burgelman[21] – who identified similar processes in their different studies, as have others later.[22]

All organisations have within them systems and routines for undertaking the operations of the business. These include day-to-day decision making processes about resource allocation across businesses. The Bower–Burgelman explanation is that strategy develops as the outcome of these resource allocation routines in organisations. For example, it could be that a manager within an organisation wishes to pursue a project and puts forward a proposal to do so. This may take the form of an argued case supported by a set of financial projections and measurements. In so doing that manager will be competing with other proposals for the resources available. The procedures for deciding between competing proposals will include financial yardsticks and benchmarks, the argued case by the competing managers and the extent to which those making the decision see it as fitting within an existing strategy and meeting the needs, in turn, of their own financial objectives and targets. The point is that, whilst the context for decisions may be established at the top, much of the resolution of what proposals go forward and what do not is happening at a much lower level than what would be conventionally thought of as 'strategic'. It is much more a day-to-day or month-to-month set of activities. However, the cumulative effects of such decisions will guide the strategy of an organisation. For example, if every new proposal for some new product development is turned down in favour of the development of new markets, then the outcome will be a strategy of market development across the business and a de-emphasis of product development. Or perhaps the proposals (and eventual performance) put forward to support one type of product development consistently seem to do better than proposals for another type. In such circumstances the overall strategy of the firm will begin to focus on that product type since resources will increasingly tend to be allocated in that direction. In effect what is going on is an internal market for ideas, rather like the ideas lens would suggest.

It may not be, however, that this resource allocation process necessarily favours the existing strategic direction. The Intel case at the end of this chapter makes this clear. In the 1980s the top management of the firm were wedded to Intel as a memory company, in the business of DRAMs – Dynamic Random Access Memories. Its major strategic switch to becoming a microprocessing company at that time did not come about because of top management direction, but because of the internal resource allocation processes going on within the firm much as described above.[23]

11.4.3 Cultural processes

Elsewhere in the book the importance of culture has been discussed. Organisational culture can be understood in terms of the taken for granted in an organisation. That includes the basic assumptions and beliefs that are shared by members of an organisation, in this book termed the paradigm (see Chapter 4, section 4.5). It also includes the taken-for-granted ways of doing things and structures that are encapsulated in the outer rings of the cultural web. The important thing to stress here is that this taken-for-grantedness works to define, or at least guide, how the people in an organisation view that organisation and its environment. It also tends to constrain what is seen as appropriate behaviour and activity. Some examples of this were given in Chapter 4 (section 4.5.3) and in section 10.2 of Chapter 10. It is important to realise the impact of this on the emergent and incremental development of strategy, and the potential consequences. So a **cultural explanation of strategy development** is that it occurs as the outcome of the taken-for-granted assumptions and behaviours in organisations.

The observed pattern of incremental strategy development of organisations can be explained in terms of, for example, deliberate logical incrementalism (see section 11.4.1 above). However, it can also be explained in terms of the outcome of the influence of organisation culture.[24] The influence of the paradigm and 'the way we do things around here' is likely to mean that, faced with forces for change, perhaps because of changes in the environment, managers try to minimise the extent to which they are faced with ambiguity and uncertainty, by defining the situation in terms of that which is familiar. This is not necessarily a conscious process; indeed arguably it is the perfectly natural process of understanding issues in terms of past experience and that which is familiar.

Exhibit 11.5 shows how this might occur.[25] The top line suggests that it is organisation culture that is driving the strategy and how it is put into effect; but that this is a self-reinforcing pattern. Faced with a stimulus for action, such as declining performance, managers first try to improve the effectiveness and efficiency of existing strategy. This could be through tightening controls and improving accepted ways of operating. If this is not effective, a change of strategy may occur, but a change in line with the existing culture. For example, managers may seek to extend the market for their business, but assume that it will be similar to their existing market, and therefore set about managing the new venture in much the same way as they have been used to. Alternatively, as shown in

A cultural explanation of strategy development is that it occurs as the outcome of the taken-for-granted assumptions and behaviours in organisations

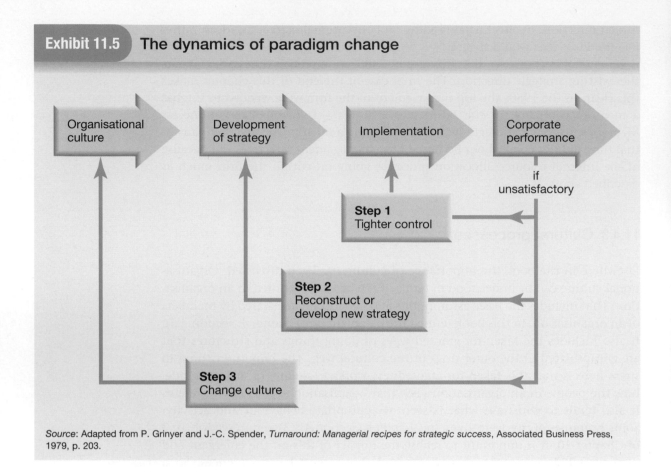

Exhibit 11.5   The dynamics of paradigm change

Source: Adapted from P. Grinyer and J.-C. Spender, *Turnaround: Managerial recipes for strategic success*, Associated Business Press, 1979, p. 203.

Illustration 11.4, even where managers know intellectually that they need to change, indeed know technologically how to do so, they find themselves constrained by taken-for-granted routines, assumptions or political processes (see section 11.4.4). What is occurring is the predominant application of the familiar and the attempt to avoid or reduce uncertainty or ambiguity. This is likely to continue until there is, perhaps, dramatic evidence of the redundancy of the paradigm and its associated routines.

As observed earlier, this is also an explanation of incremental strategy development. Indeed, it could be that changing the strategy within the culture makes sense: after all, it does encapsulate the experience of people in the organisation, and permits change to take place within what is familiar and understood. However, the outcome of processes of this kind may not keep strategy in line with environmental change. Rather, it may be adaptation in line with the experience enshrined in the organisational culture. Nonetheless, the forces in the environment will have an effect on performance. Over time, this may well give rise to the sort of **strategic drift** identified in Chapter 1 and shown in Exhibit 1.4 as a major strategic challenge in which the organisation's strategy gradually moves away from relevance to the forces at work in its environment. Even the most successful companies may drift in this way. Indeed, there is a tendency for businesses to become victims of the very success of their past in just such a way, a tendency that Danny Miller has called the Icarus Paradox.[26]

Strategic drift is where strategies progressively fail to address the strategic position of the organisation and performance deteriorates

Illustration 11.4 strategy into action

Technological change and organisational inertia in the computer industry

An organisation's 'Achilles heel' can often be found in the routines and processes which were the bases of past success.

In a fast-moving, technologically complex and innovative industry dominated by small firms with well-developed communication and technology transfer, one firm's inability to keep pace with innovations in manufacturing processes forced it out of business.

Kasper Instruments produced photolithographic alignment equipment, used to manufacture semiconductor devices. Their manufacture required the transfer of small, intricate patterns on to the surface of a wafer of semiconductor material such as silicon. This transfer process, called lithography, required only certain areas of the wafer to be exposed to light, with masks used to provide the appropriate shield.

Contact aligners were the first form of mask to be used commercially and, as the name suggests, these made contact with the wafers. Kasper Instruments' position as industry leader was because of its expertise in the contact alignment technique. However, as technology became more advanced, proximity masks were able to be used which did not come into contact with the wafer, so the risk of damage was reduced. Technology within the industry continued to develop incrementally until a quite different process of electron beam alignment was developed in which a focused beam wrote directly on to the wafer. Yet the industry leader was unable to make the technological transition; in the switch from contact to proximity aligners Kasper Instruments lost its position of industry leader to Canon and was ultimately forced to leave the industry.

The technological change needed for Kasper to keep pace with Canon and introduce the more efficient proximity alignment technique was, in technological terms, relatively minor; and the top team at Kasper were keenly aware of the need to change. However, they seemed unable to rise to Canon's challenge, refusing to accept the obsolescence of their own expert knowledge in the contact technique. Whilst Kasper continually held on to the past, trying to modify its own production technique to include some elements of Canon's innovative procedures, with no success, its market share slipped away. When the engineers at Kasper were given a Canon proximity aligner to take apart with a view to producing their own model, they dismissed it as a mere copy of their own (very different) contact.

What seemed to be a small incremental development in technology required Kasper to totally rethink the way it did business, from its production processes to its sales and marketing strategies. In its failure to translate its technical understanding of the need for change by changing the routinised processes existing in the organisation, it was not alone. Throughout the history of technological change within this industry, each innovation has been a harbinger of doom for the market leader.

Prepared by Phyl Johnson, Graduate Business School, University of Strathclyde.

Source: Adapted from R. Henderson and K. Clark, 'Architectural innovation: the reconfiguration of existing product technology and the failure of established firms', *Administrative Science Quarterly*, vol. 35 (1990), pp. 9–30.

Questions

1. Which processes of strategic management described in this chapter might have helped to avoid Kasper's problems?

2. Would these processes be suited to organisations facing less innovatory or changing environments?

11.4.4 Organisational politics

Managers often suggest that the strategy being followed by their organisation is really the outcome of the bargaining and power politics that go on between important executives. Such executives are continually trying to position themselves such that their views prevail or that they control the resources in the organisation necessary for future success. The **political view**[27] of strategy development is, then, that strategies develop as the outcome of processes of bargaining and negotiation among powerful internal or external interest groups (or stakeholders). This is the world of boardroom battles often portrayed in film and TV dramas. Illustration 11.5 shows how the interests of different stakeholders and the protection of their interests can influence strategy development.

The **political view** of strategy development is that strategies develop as the outcome of processes of bargaining and negotiation among powerful internal or external interest groups (or stakeholders)

Political activity is usually seen as an inevitable but negative influence on strategy development getting in the way of thorough analysis and rational thinking. A political perspective on strategic management suggests that the rational and analytic processes often associated with developing strategy (see section 11.3.1 above) may not be as objective and dispassionate as they appear. Objectives that are set may reflect the ambitions of powerful people. Information used in strategic debate is not always politically neutral. Rather information and data that are emphasised or de-emphasised can be a source of power for those who control what is seen to be important. Indeed one manager may exercise power over another because that manager controls important sources of information. Powerful individuals and groups may also strongly influence the identification of key issues and the strategies eventually selected. Differing views may be pursued, not only on the basis of the extent to which they reflect environmental or competitive pressures, for example, but also because they have implications for the status or influence of different stakeholders.

It is not surprising that in approaching strategic problems, people in organisations seek to be protective of their views in the face of different views. This may be linked to the exercise of power. It is not surprising that the conductor in Illustration 11.5 takes a different position from the marketing director and others in the organisation. They are approaching the problem with different backgrounds, from different cultural influences and different experience bases and are interested in preserving or enhancing the power of their positions.

Political activity may be seen as resulting in emergent or incremental patterns of strategy development. Emergent in the sense that it is this bargaining and negotiation that gives rise to strategy rather than carefully analysed, deliberate intent. Incremental for two reasons. First, if different views prevail in the organisation and different parties are exercising their political muscle, compromise may be inevitable. Second, it is quite possible that it is from the pursuit of the current strategy that power has been gained by those wielding it. Indeed it may be very threatening to their power if significant changes in strategy were to occur. In such circumstances it is likely that a search for a compromise solution which accommodates different power bases may end up with a strategy which is an adaptation of what has gone before.

There are, however, alternative ways of considering the influence of political processes. Arguably, the conflict and tensions that manifest themselves in political activity, arising as they do from different expectations or interests, can be the

Illustration 11.5   strategy into action

ASO: UK Symphony Orchestra

Stakeholders' interests and expectations can create problematic circumstances for the development of strategy.

Developing an artistic strategy for the ASO was a complex process, due largely to the interests and involvement of its numerous stakeholders. The process was prompted by a critical report from the Arts Council, the orchestra's main funder, in late 1996. Commenting on the 'audience resistance to new initiatives' brought in by the Conductor, the report argued that the organisation needed 'clearer artistic and audience focus'. It called for a change in strategic leadership, recommending 'that the CEO should take overall responsibility for the artistic direction'. The Conductor defended his previous decisions, arguing that he had been criticised both for having programmes that were too conservative and too adventurous. At the same time, his Artistic Advisor suggested the confusion over strategic focus was partly due to a 'clash of ideals' with the previous Marketing Director, who 'went off in her own direction'.

Other individuals expressed concerns about the orchestra's artistic direction, including members of the management, board, and the orchestra itself. The musicians' representative, for example, expressed the need for a change from 'churning out Tchaikovsky', but felt they had now gone too far the other way, playing lesser known repertoire which was neither the orchestra's strength, nor popular with their audiences.

Despite the widely shared concern over the orchestra's artistic direction, developing a strategy proved difficult. In late 1997, the CEO responded to the widespread disquiet with an announcement that he intended to appoint an Artistic Director who would 'own the artistic policy in future'. In the meantime, the Chairman commented, 'We haven't got an artistic strategy . . . the people struggling to find one are the conductor, the CEO, the Artistic Advisor, and the band.' He said that some months earlier he had also produced a 'strategic framework' document, which he had discussed with the orchestra because 'it was terribly important that it was owned by everybody'. The Board of Directors sought to contribute their views too and so an Artistic Sub-committee was formed. When the Artistic Director was appointed some months later, however, he decided that it was impractical to involve a committee in repertoire issues and instead worked with the Conductor on artistic planning.

Because of the number and diversity of stakeholder groups seeking input to the artistic strategy, the process was drawn out, with some difficult dynamics. Six months after his appointment, the Artistic Director still believed the big issue was 'to get the policy together', and at the Board's away-day in early 1999, he announced, 'I've been here for one year and I don't think I've made any impression at all.' At the same meeting, the Chairman said, 'We're accused of losing coherence in what we do and who we are. A compromise of what the Conductor wants and what's financially possible is what happens. It's impossible to create good concerts and certainly a long term strategy.' He concluded, 'We need agreement, even if it's not exactly to everyone's liking.'

Source: Adapted from S. Maitlis and T. Lawrence, 'Orchestral manoeuvres in the dark: understanding failure in organizational strategizing', *Journal of Management Studies*, vol. 40, no. 1 (2003), pp. 109–140.

Questions

1. Write a brief report to the chief executive explaining what the problem is and what he should do.

2. How important is a written strategic plan in such circumstances? Why?

source of new ideas (see the discussion on the 'ideas lens' in the commentary sections of the book) or challenges to old ways of doing things.[28] New ideas are likely to be supported or opposed by different 'champions' who will battle over what is the best idea or the best way forward. Arguably, if such conflict and tensions did not exist, neither would innovation. Similarly, as Chapter 10 (section 10.4.6) showed, the exercise of power may be critically important in the management of strategic change.

All of this suggests that political activity has to be taken seriously as an influence on strategy development. The problems of the orchestra in Illustration 11.5 are unlikely to be resolved by relying solely on a formalised planning system. Whatever thinking goes into the strategy will need to go hand in hand with activity to address the political processes at work. This is addressed in other parts of this book, in particular sections 4.3.3 and 10.4.6 as well as in the commentaries at the end of each part of the book.

11.5 MULTIPLE PROCESSES OF STRATEGY DEVELOPMENT

The discussion of different strategy development processes in sections 11.3 and 11.4 raises some further important general points:

● It has to be recognised that there is *no one right way* in which strategies are developed. This is discussed more fully below but it is sufficient here to point out, for example, that the way in which strategies develop in a fast-changing environment is not likely to be the same as in an environment in which there is little change; nor should it be. (See section 11.6.3 below.)

● It may also be that processes of strategy development *differ over time* and in *different contexts*. An organisation that is going through rapid change, perhaps the result of environmental turbulence or the need for internal strategic change, will very likely have different strategy development processes from an organisation in a more steady state. The chapter-end case study for this chapter shows this for Intel from the 1980s through to the turn of the century. Different strategy development processes tended to be more pronounced at one stage in its development than another and, apparently, beneficially for the organisation. Exhibit 11.6 shows how different processes may take form in different organisational contexts.

● It is also likely that the *perceptions of how strategies develop* will be seen differently by different people. For example, as Exhibit 11.7 shows, senior executives tend to see strategy development more in terms of intended, rational, analytic planned processes whereas middle managers see strategy development more as the result of cultural and political processes. Managers who work for government organisations or agents of government tend to see strategy as more imposed than those in the private sector.[29] People who work in family businesses tend to see more evidence of the influence of powerful individuals, who may be the owners of the businesses. Managers in public sector organisations tend to see strategy as externally imposed more than managers in commercial businesses, largely because their organisations are answerable to

| Exhibit 11.6 | Some configurations of strategy development processes |

Dominant dimensions	Characteristics	Rather than	Typical contexts
Planning Incrementalism (Logical incrementalism)	Standardised planning procedures Systematic data collection and analyses Constant environmental scanning Ongoing adjustment of strategy Tentative commitment to strategy Step-by-step, small-scale change	Intrusive external environment Dominant individuals Political processes Power groups	Manufacturing and service sector organisations Stable or growing markets Mature markets Benign environments
Incremental Cultural Political	Bargaining, negotiation and compromise amongst conflicting interests of groups Groups with control over critical resources more likely to influence strategy Standardised 'ways of doing things' Routines and procedures embedded in organisational history Gradual adjustments to strategy	Deliberate, intentional process Well-defined procedures Analytical evaluation and planning Deliberate managerial intent	Professional service firms (e.g. consultancy or law firms) Unstable, turbulent environment New and growing markets
Imposed Political	Strategy is imposed by external forces (e.g. legislation, parent organisation) Freedom of choice severely restricted Political activity likely within organisation and between external agencies	Strategy determined within the organisation Planning systems impact on strategy development Influence on strategic direction mainly by managers within the organisation	Public sector organisations, larger manufacturing and financial service subsidiaries Threatening, declining, unstable and hostile environments

The findings above are based on a survey of perceptions of strategy development processes undertaken at Cranfield School of Management in the 1990s.

government bodies. Illustration 11.6, the chapter's key debate, showes different accounts of strategy development for a highly successful stategy.

- Indeed, it is likely that *no one process describes strategy development* in any organisation. There will be multiple processes at work. For example, if a planning system exists, it will not be the only process at work in the development of strategy. There will undoubtedly be some level of political activity; indeed the planning system itself may be used for political purposes. Or, again, if strategy emerges on the basis of prior decisions, nonetheless those decisions may have been subjected to the scrutiny of consultants or strategy workshops and have been built into planning processes. Indeed there is evidence that those organisations that employ multiple processes of strategy development may perform better than those that take more singular approaches.[30]

| Exhibit 11.7 | Managers' perceptions of strategy development processes |

	Level in organisation		Environmental stability	
Perceptions that there exists:	**CEO**	**Middle management**	**Higher**	**Lower**
Precision of objectives	Yes	No	Yes	No
Detailed planning	Yes	No	Yes	No
Systematic analysis of environment	Yes	No	Yes	–
Careful evaluation of strategic options	Yes	No	–	–

These findings are based on a survey of perceptions of strategy development processes undertaken at Cranfield School of Management in the 1990s. The findings indicate statistically significant differences.

11.6 CHALLENGES AND IMPLICATIONS FOR STRATEGY DEVELOPMENT

The discussion in this chapter raises some important challenges and has implications for how managers manage the strategy development process.

11.6.1 The challenge of strategic drift[31]

One of the major strategic challenges facing managers was identified in Chapter 1 as the risk of strategic drift (see section 1.5.1). The discussion in section 11.4 of this chapter shows that there are strong forces at work that are likely to push organisations towards this pattern. Incremental strategic change is a natural outcome of the influence of organisational culture, individual and collective experience, political processes and prior decisions. However, if changes in an organisation's environment are at a greater rate than that rate of incremental strategic change, the organisation will get out of line with its environment. There is another danger: that organisations become merely reactive to their environment and fail to question or challenge what is happening around them or to innovate to create new opportunities; in short, that they become complacent.

All this suggests that strategy development processes in organisations need to encourage people in organisations to have the capacity and willingness to challenge and change their core assumptions and ways of doing things. This leads to the idea of the 'learning organisation' discussed in the next section. Desirable as this may be, the evidence is that it does not occur easily, as section 11.4 also shows. It also emphasises the delicate balance that an organisation faces in developing its strategy. For example, it has internal cultural forces for inertia that tend to constrain strategy development, yet potentially behaviours and routines within its culture that might provide the capabilities for competitive advantage (see Chapter 3, sections 3.4 and 3.6.2). It faces environmental forces, not least in terms of its markets, which it has to try and understand and address, yet the experience rooted in its culture makes it difficult to establish an objective and dispassionate view of those forces.

The key lesson for management is to recognise and accept the challenge; that in the absence of proactive steps to overcome the forces at work leading to such strategic drift, over time it is very likely to occur. How managers might do so is a central theme of this book of course, at least in terms of key questions that need to be tackled. However, the overriding lesson in terms of strategy development processes is that it is very unlikely that any one of the processes described in this chapter should be dominant. The likelihood is that there will be benefits from cultivating multiple processes of strategy development. This is discussed more fully in the next three sections.

11.6.2 The learning organisation

Traditionally, organisations have been seen as hierarchies and bureaucracies set up to achieve order and maintain control; as structures built for stability rather than change. Arguably, this conception of the organisation is not suited to the dynamic conditions for change of the 21st century. A **learning organisation** is one capable of continual regeneration from the variety of knowledge, experience and skills of individuals within a culture which encourages mutual questioning and challenge around a shared purpose or vision. It emphasises the potential capacity and capability of organisations to regenerate themselves from within, and in this way for strategies to emerge from within.

> The **learning organisation** is capable of continual regeneration from the variety of knowledge, experience and skills of individuals within a culture which encourages mutual questioning and challenge around a shared purpose or vision

Advocates of the learning organisation[32] point out that the collective knowledge of all the individuals in an organisation usually exceeds what the organisation itself 'knows' and is capable of doing; the formal structures of organisations typically stifle organisational knowledge and creativity. They argue that the aim of management should be to encourage processes which unlock the knowledge of individuals, and encourage the sharing of information and knowledge, so that each individual becomes sensitive to changes occurring around them and contributes to the identification of opportunities and required changes. Information flows and relationships between people are lateral as well as vertical. This emphasises the importance of seeing organisations as *social networks*,[33] where the emphasis is not so much on hierarchies as on different interest groups that need to cooperate with each other and potentially learn from each other. So as ideas bubble up from below, the risk of their fizzling out because of lack of interest from other parts of the organisation is reduced. Managers would be playing a less directive and more facilitative role. Arguably, an organisational form such as adhocracy, explained in section 8.5.1, aspires to this rather than to the more traditional notions of stability and control. The learning organisation is, then, one inherently capable of change and with a capacity for *organisational learning*.

The central tenets of organisational learning reflect the notion that there is a need to recognise the value of multiple processes of strategy development within a learning context. Such a context is likely to have the following basic characteristics:

● There is a need for organisations which are *pluralistic*, in which different, even conflicting ideas and views are welcomed, surfaced and become the basis of debate.

● *Experimentation* is the norm, so ideas are tried out in action and in turn become part of the learning process.

In many respects *organisational learning*[34] therefore corresponds to aspects of logical incrementalism described in section 11.4.1, especially insofar as it starts with the argument that the uncertainty and complexity of the world of organisations cannot readily be understood purely analytically. However, the idea of organisational learning is not restricted to fast-changing environments. Its emphasis on the importance of questioning and challenging that which is taken for granted is applicable to any organisation that seeks to avoid strategic drift and corresponds to the call by Gary Hamel for 'resilient' organisations that continually reinvent themselves by refusing to take their success for granted and building the capability to imagine new business models.[35]

The challenge, then, is for managers to recognise the potential benefits of different processes of strategy development so as to build learning organisations capable of adapting and innovating within a changing environment yet achieving the benefits of more formal processes of planning and analysis to help this where necesssary.[36]

11.6.3 Strategy development in uncertain and complex conditions

Not all organisations face similar environments and they differ in their form and complexity; therefore different ways of thinking about strategy development and different processes for managing strategy may make sense in different circumstances. Since one of the main problems of strategic management is coping with uncertainty, it is useful to consider this issue in terms of organisations facing different contexts.[37]

Exhibit 11.8 shows how organisations may seek to cope with conditions which are more or less stable or dynamic, and simple or complex.

● In *simple/static* conditions, the environment is relatively straightforward to understand and is not undergoing significant change. Raw materials suppliers and some mass-manufacturing companies are examples, at least from the past. Technical processes may be fairly simple, and competition and markets remained the same over time. In such circumstances, if environmental change does occur, it may be predictable, so it could make sense to analyse the environment extensively on an historical basis as a means of trying to forecast likely future conditions. In situations of relatively low complexity, it may also be possible to identify some predictors of environmental influences. For example, in public services, demographic data such as birth rates might be used as lead indicators to determine the required provision of schooling, health care or social services. So in simple/static conditions, seeing strategy development in formal planning terms may make sense. It might also be tempting to rely on past experience and prior decisions since little is changing. The problem

| Exhibit 11.8 | Strategy development in environmental contexts |

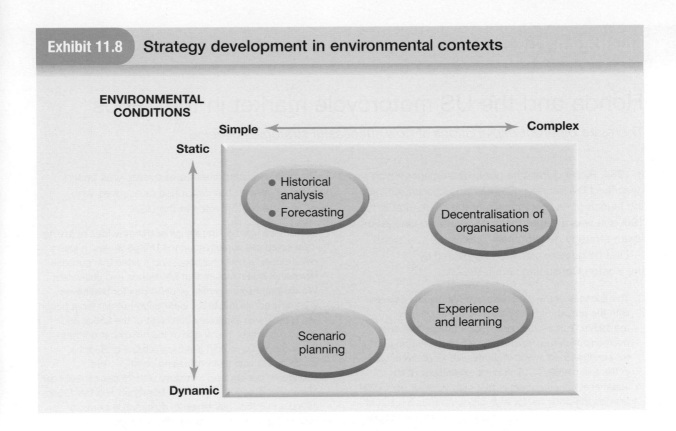

here is that all organisations may end up following the same strategies; and this could be a recipe for high degrees of competition and low profits (see Chapter 5).

- In *dynamic* conditions, managers need to consider the environment of the future, not just of the past. The degree of uncertainty therefore increases. They may employ structured ways of making sense of the future, such as *scenario planning*, discussed in Chapter 2 (see section 2.2.4), or they may rely more on encouraging active sensing of environmental changes low down in the organisation where change is seen as normal and not reliant on lengthy reference up and down decision-making hierarchies. The emphasis is on creating the organisational conditions necessary to encourage individuals and groups to be forward-thinking, intuitive and challenging in their thinking about possible futures, approximating to *logical incrementalism* and *organisational learning* described above.

- Organisations in *complex* situations face an environment difficult to comprehend. They may, of course, face dynamic conditions too, and therefore a combination of complexity and uncertainty. With more and more sophisticated technology, there is an increasing move towards this condition of greatest uncertainty. The electronics industry is in this situation. A multinational firm, or a major public service such as a local government authority with many services, may also be in a complex condition because of its diversity, whilst different operating companies within it face varying degrees of complexity and dynamism.

Illustration 11.6

Honda and the US motorcycle market in the 1960s

There are different explanations of how successful strategies develop.

In 1984, Richard Pascale published a paper which described the success Honda had experienced with the launch of its motorcycles in the US market in the 1960s. It was a paper that has generated discussion about strategy development processes ever since.

First he gave explanations provided by the Boston Consulting Group (BCG).

> The success of the Japanese manufacturers originated with the growth of their domestic market during the 1950s. This resulted in a highly competitive cost position which the Japanese used as a springboard for penetration of world markets with small motorcycles in the early 1960s . . . The basic philosophy of the Japanese manufacturers is that high volumes per model provide the potential for high productivity as a result of using capital intensive and highly automated techniques. Their market strategies are therefore directed towards developing these high model volumes, hence the careful attention that we have observed them giving to growth and market share.

Thus the BCG's account is a rational one based upon the deliberate building of a cost advantage based on volume.

Pascale's second version of events was based on interviews with the Japanese executives who launched the motorcycles in the USA:

> In truth, we had no strategy other than the idea of seeing if we could sell something in the United States. It was a new frontier, a new challenge, and it fitted the 'success against all odds' culture that Mr. Honda had cultivated. We did not discuss profits or deadlines for breakeven . . . We knew our products . . . were good but not far superior. Mr. Honda was especially confident of the 250cc and 305cc machines. The shape of the handlebar on these larger machines looked like the eyebrow of Buddha, which he felt was a strong selling point. . . . We configured our start-up inventory with 25 per cent of each of our four products – the 50cc Supercub and the 125cc, 250cc and 305cc machines. In dollar value terms, of course, the inventory was heavily weighted toward the larger bikes . . . We were entirely in the dark the first year. Following Mr. Honda's and our own instincts, we had not attempted to move the 50cc Supercubs. . . . They seemed wholly unsuitable for the US market where everything was bigger and more luxurious . . . We used the Honda 50s ourselves to ride around Los Angeles on errands. They attracted a lot of attention. But we still hesitated to push the 50cc bikes out of fear they might harm our image in a

It is difficult to handle complexity by relying primarily on formal planning. There may be ways of designing the organisation to help, however: for example, complexity as a result of diversity might be dealt with by ensuring that different parts of the organisation responsible for different aspects of diversity are separate, and given the resources and authority to handle their own part of the environment. So *organisational design* is important (see Chapter 8). More likely, though, the organisation has to *learn* to cope with complexity. This may entail top management's recognising that specialists lower down in the organisation know more about the environment in which the organisation operates than they do and have to have considerable influence; that this strategic competence based on *experience* may provide competitive advantage (see Chapter 4); that there are not 'right ways' of doing things and that the taken-for-granted has to be challenged.

heavily macho market. But when the larger bikes started breaking, we had no choice. And surprisingly, the retailers who wanted to sell them weren't motorcycle dealers, they were sporting goods stores.

Two very different accounts, yet they describe the same market success. Since the publication of the paper, many writers on strategy have hotly debated what these accounts actually represent. For example:

Henry Mintzberg observed: 'the conception of a novel strategy is a creative process (of synthesis), to which there are no formal techniques (analysis)'. He argued any formal planning was in the implementation of the strategy: '. . . strategy had to be conceived informally before it could be programmed formally'. He went on to add: 'While we run around being "rational", they use their common sense . . . they came to America prepared to *learn*.'

Michael Goold, the author of the original BCG report, defended it on the grounds that 'its purpose was to discern what lay behind and accounted for Honda's success, in a way that would help others to think through what strategies would be likely to work. It tries to discern patterns in Honda's strategic decisions and actions, and to use these patterns in identifying what works well and badly.'

Richard Rumelt concluded that '. . . the "design school" is right about the reality of forces like scaled economies, accumulated experience and accumulative

development of core competences over time . . . but my own experience is that coherent strategy based upon analyses and understandings of these forces is much more often imputed than actually observed'.

And Pascale himself concluded that the serendipitous nature of Honda's strategy showed the importance of learning; that the real lessons in developing strategies were the importance of an organisation's agility and that this resides in its culture, rather than its analyses.

Sources: This case example is based on R.T. Pascale, 'Perspectives on strategy: the real story behind Honda's success', *California Management Review*, vol. 26, no. 3 (Spring 1984), pp. 47–72 and H. Mintzberg, R.T. Pascale, M. Goold and R.P. Rumelt, 'The Honda effect revisited', *California Management Review*, vol. 38. no. 4 (1996), pp. 78–116.

Questions

1. Are the different accounts mutually exclusive?

2. Which of the different explanations of strategy development explained in the chapter do you discern in the Honda story?

3. Do you think Honda would have been more or less successful if it had adopted a more formalised strategic planning approach to its launch?

11.6.4 Managing strategy development processes

Sections 11.5 and 11.6.3 suggest that strategy development processes should, very likely, differ according to the circumstances the organisation faces. As this chapter explains, it is also likely that different processes play different roles and have different effects. There are a number of points here:

● It is likely that an organisation will need *different processes for different purposes*. Quite likely it will need to coordinate strategies across business units and for this purpose a systematic strategic planning system may be needed. It may need to develop the strategic understanding and competences of managers if they are going to contribute to the strategy debate. For this they might need to be involved in strategy workshops or project teams. If the challenge of strategic drift is to be taken seriously, there will need to be some way of challenging taken-for-granted assumptions and raising strategic options that might not otherwise be raised. This may require workshops tailored for this purpose, the introduction of new management or strategic leaders with different experience bases or perhaps the use of external consultants. The need is to consider which processes are appropriate for which purposes.

● Managers might therefore ask themselves if they are *emphasising the most important processes* with regard to strategy development. To take some obvious examples: if management effort is being dedicated to designing sophisticated planning systems, this could be dangerous in times of rapid change. If highly participative strategy workshops or development projects are being emphasised at a time when clarity of leadership and direction is required, there could be negative effects. If innovation and creativity are to be fostered, diversity of views and the challenging of assumptions could be crucial.

● Senior executives, in particular, need to consider what the *top management role* in strategy development is. Do they see themselves as the detailed planners of strategy throughout the organisation; as the ones who set broad strategic direction and cultivate managers below them who can develop more detailed strategies; or as developing their own capabilities to detect strategies and strategic ideas as they emerge from within the rest of the organisation? All of these are significant strategy development roles.

● There may be *different strategy development roles at different organisational levels*. A study of corporate parents' relationship to their business units or subsidiaries[38] found that there were distinct differences in the strategy development approaches and roles at these different levels. The business units/subsidiaries were playing the experimental role. Highly reliant on informal contacts with their markets, decisions were made largely on the basis of managers' experience. (Illustration 11.6 also shows how this was the case in Honda.) The executives at the centre were more concerned with the search for order throughout the business and therefore on planning and analysis, building on existing resources and refining existing strategy. Whilst this study was industry-specific – the telecommunications industry – it does make the point that it is unlikely that the different levels will play the same roles. What matters is that the different levels appreciate and understand that they do play different roles and have different contributions to make. The building of dialogue between the different levels in which the value of the different contributions can be learned may be very important.

● The complementary point is that *different managerial levels need to acknowledge and value different roles*. For example, if top managers see middle managers as merely the 'implementers' of top management strategy, they are likely to undervalue and underplay their potential role in helping develop the strategy of their organisation. It is becoming increasingly clear that the role of middle managers in organisations as contributors to the strategy development process needs to be taken seriously (see Chapter 9, section 9.2.3).

Summary

This chapter has dealt with different ways in which strategy development occurs in organisations. The main lessons of the chapter are now summarised.

- It is important to distinguish between *intended* strategy – the desired strategic direction deliberately planned by managers – and *emergent strategy* which may develop in a less deliberate way from the behaviours and activities inherent within an organisation.

- Most often the process of strategy development is described in terms of intended strategy as a result of management design through *planning systems* carried out by top management objectively and dispassionately. There are benefits and disbenefits of formal strategic planning systems. However, there is evidence to show that such formal systems are not an adequate explanation of what occurs in practice. There is a need for other explanations of strategy development.

- Intended strategy may also come about on the basis of *strategy workshops, project groups*, the intervention of *strategy consultants* and the *imposition of strategies* by external stakeholders.

- Strategies may emerge from within organisations. This may be explained in terms of:
  - How organisations may proactively try to cope through processes of *logical incrementalism.*
  - The *resource allocation* routines currently employed in the organisation which may favour certain strategy development projects over others.
  - The taken-for-granted elements of *organisational culture* favouring certain strategies.
  - The outcome of the bargaining associated with *political activity* resulting in a negotiated strategy.

- The *challenge of strategic drift* suggests that a key requirement of strategy development processes in organisations is to encourage and facilitate the *challenge of taken-for-granted* assumptions and ways of doing things.

- *Multiple processes of strategy development* are likely to be needed if organisations wish to create a *learning organisation* and cope with *increasingly dynamic and complex environments*.

This chapter has highlighted the importance of viewing the processes of strategy development in different ways. This is also shown in the key debate in Illustration 11.6. The commentary on Part V that follows more fully develops this point by examining the processes discussed in this chapter in terms of the three strategy lenses.

Recommended key readings

- A much quoted paper that describes different patterns of strategy development is H. Mintzberg and J.A. Waters, 'Of strategies, deliberate and emergent', *Strategic Management Journal*, vol. 6, no. 3 (1985), pp. 257–272.

- The changing role of strategic planning is explained on the basis of the study carried out by Rob Grant; see 'Strategic planning in a turbulent environment: evidence from the oil majors', *Strategic Management Journal*, vol. 24 (2003), pp. 491–517.

- For an explanation of logical incrementalism, see J.B. Quinn, *Strategies for Change: Logical incrementalism*, Irwin, 1980; also summarised in J.B. Quinn and H. Mintzberg, *The Strategy Process*, 4th edn, Prentice Hall, 2003. Compare this with the different explanations of incremental change and the explanation of strategic drift by G. Johnson, 'Rethinking incrementalism', *Strategic Management Journal*, vol. 9, no. 1 (1988), pp. 75–91.

- A fascinating case study of the effects of resource allocation routines on the developing strategy of Intel is provided by Robert Burgelman in 'Fading memories: a process theory of strategic business exit in dynamic environments', *Administrative Science Quarterly*, vol. 39 (1994), pp. 34–56.

- Insights into the importance of multiple processes of strategy development can be found in S. Hart and C. Banbury, 'How strategy making processes can make a difference', *Strategic Management Journal*, vol. 15, no. 4 (1994), pp. 251–269.

- For a good discussion and review of literature on the idea of the learning organisation, see J. Coopey, 'The learning organization, power, politics and Ideology', *Management Learning*, vol. 26, no. 2 (1995) pp. 193–213.

References

1. The framework used here is, in part, derived from the discussion by H. Mintzberg and J.A. Waters, 'Of strategies, deliberate and emergent', *Strategic Management Journal*, vol. 6, no. 3 (1985), pp. 257–272.

2. For a fuller discussion of different explanations of incremental strategic change see G. Johnson, 'Re-thinking incrementalism', *Strategic Management Journal*, vol. 9 (1988), pp. 75–91.

3. In the 1970s and 80s there were many books written on formal strategic planning approaches to strategy development. They are less common now but, for example, see R.W. Bradford and J.P. Duncan, *Simplified Strategic Planning: A no-nonsense guide for busy people who want results fast*, Chandler House Press, 1999; J.M. Bryson, *Strategic Planning for Public and Nonprofit Organizations: A guide to strengthening and sustaining organizational achievment*, rev. edn, Jossey Bass, 1995; and S. Haines, *The Systems Thinking Approach to Strategic Planning and Management*, St Lucie Press, 2000.

4. 'Strategic planning in a turbulent environment: evidence from the oil majors' is a study carried out by Rob Grant. See the *Strategic Management Journal*, vol. 24 (2003), pp. 491–517.

5. Again from Grant's research; see reference 4 above.

6. Many of these dangers are drawn from H. Mintzberg, *The Rise and Fall of Strategic Planning*, Prentice Hall, 1994.

7. Sherman's quote is taken from B.G. James, *Business Wargames*, Penguin, 1985, p. 190.

8. Studies on the relationship between formal planning and financial performance are largely inconclusive. For example, see P. McKiernan and C. Morris, 'Strategic planning and financial performance in the UK SMEs: does formality matter?', *Journal of Management*, vol. 5 (1994), pp. S31–S42. Some studies have shown benefits in particular contexts. For example, it is argued there are benefits to entrepreneurs setting up new ventures; see F. Delmar and S. Shane, 'Does business planning facilitate the development of new ventures?',

Strategic Management Journal, vol. 24 (2003), pp. 1165–1185. And other studies actually show the benefits of strategic analysis and strategic thinking, rather than the benefits of formal planning systems; e.g. see C.C. Miller and L.B. Cardinal, 'Strategic planning and firm performance: a synthesis of more than two decades of research', *Academy of Management Journal*, vol. 37, no. 6 (1994), pp. 1649–1665.

9. See reference 4 above.

10. For example, see J.M. Mezias, P. Grinyer and W.D. Guth, 'Changing collective cognition: a process model for strategic change', *Long Range Planning*, vol. 34 (2001), pp. 71–95. Also C. Eden and F. Ackermann, *Making Strategy: the Journey of Strategic Management*, Sage, 1998.

11. For example, see C. Eden and F. Ackermann, 'A mapping framework for strategy making', pp. 173–195 and P. Johnson and G. Johnson, 'Facilitating group cognitive mapping of core competencies', pp. 220–236 in Anne S. Huff and Mark Jenkins (eds), *Mapping Strategic Knowledge*, Sage, 2002.

12. Workshop analysis using culture webs is explained by G. Johnson in 'Mapping and re-mapping organisational culture', in V. Ambrosini (ed.) *Exploring Techniques of Analysis and Evaluation in Strategic Management*, Prentice Hall, 1998 and in 'Strategy through a cultural lens: learning from managers' experience', *Management Learning*, vol. 31, no. 4 (2000), pp. 429–452.

13. See M. Beer and R.A. Eisenstat, 'How to have an honest conversation about your business strategy', *Harvard Business Review*, vol. 82, no. 2 (2004) pp. 82–89.

14. A good analysis of the work of project teams and their politicised agendas can be found in F. Blackler and S. McDonald, 'Organizing processes in complex activity networks', *Organization*, vol. 7 no. 2 (2000), pp. 277–300.

15. The roles of consultants are identified by M. Schwartz in 'The role and contribution of consultants in strategy-making – how

consultants and managers work together in strategy-making', in the *Proceedings of the International Conference European Group for Organization Studies (EGOS)*, Copenhagen Business School, 2003.

16. For a discussion of how consultants, business schools and others act as 'carriers' of knowledge see E. Abrahamson, 'Management fashion', *Academy of Management Review*, vol. 21, no. 1 (1996), pp. 254–285.

17. This quote is from 'Inside McKinsey', by John A. Byrne, *Business Week*, 8 July 2002, p. 59.

18. Two of the early extensive case studies showing how cultural and political processes give rise to the emergence of strategies are A. Pettigrew, *The Awakening Giant*, Blackwell, 1985; and G. Johnson, *Strategic Change and the Management Process*, Blackwell, 1987.

19. J.B. Quinn's research involved the examination of strategic change in companies and was published in *Strategies for Change*, Irwin, 1980. See also J.B. Quinn, 'Strategic change: logical incrementalism', in J.B. Quinn and H. Mintzberg, *The Strategy Process*, 4th edn, Prentice Hall, 2003.

20. See J.B. Quinn, *Strategies for Change*, reference 19, p. 58.

21. The original studies are J.L. Bower, *Managing the Resource Allocation Process: a Study of Corporate Planning and Investment*, Irwin, 1972, and R.A. Burgelman, 'A model of the interaction of strategic behaviour, corporate context and the concept of strategy', *Academy of Management Review*, vol. 81 no. 1 (1983), pp. 61–70; and 'A process model of internal corporate venturing in the diversified major firm', *Administrative Science Quarterly*, vol. 28 (1983), pp. 223–244.

22. For example, see T. Noda and J. Bower, 'Strategy as iterated processes of resource allocation', *Strategic Management Journal*, vol. 17 (1996), pp. 159–192.

23. The Intel case is also written up by Robert Burgelman, see 'Fading memories: a process theory of strategic business exit in dynamic environments', *Administrative Science Quarterly*, vol. 39 (1994), pp. 34–56.

24. This is explained by Gerry Johnson more fully in 'Re-thinking incrementalism' (see reference 2 above).

25. This figure is based on that shown in P. Grinyer and J.-C. Spender, *Turnaround: Managerial recipes for strategic success*, Associated Business Press, 1979, and *Industry Recipes: The Nature and Sources of Management Judgement*, Blackwell, 1989.

26. See D. Miller, *The Icarus Paradox*, Harper Business, 1990.

27. There has been relatively little published which has examined strategic management explicitly from a political perspective, but it is a central theme of D. Buchanan and D. Boddy, *The Expertise of the Change Agent: Public performance and backstage activity*, Prentice Hall, 1992.

28. This is the argument advanced by J.M. Bartunek, D. Kolb and R. Lewicki, 'Bringing conflict out from behind the scenes: private, informal, and nonrational dimensions of conflict in organizations', in D. Kolb and J. Bartunek (eds), *Hidden Conflict in Organizations: Uncovering Behind the Scenes Disputes*, Sage, 1992.

29. For a discussion of the differences between strategy development in the public and private sectors see N. Collier, F. Fishwick and G. Johnson, 'The processes of strategy development in the public sector', in G. Johnson and K. Scholes (eds), *Exploring Public Sector Strategy*, Pearson Education, 2001.

30. See S. Hart and C. Banbury, 'How strategy making processes can make a difference', *Strategic Management Journal*, vol. 15, no. 4 (1994), pp. 251–269.

31. For a detailed explanation of strategic drift see 'Re-thinking incrementalism' (reference 2).

32. See, for example, J. Coopey, 'The learning organization, power, politics and ideology', *Management Learning*, vol. 26, no. 2 (1995), pp. 193–213.

33. The concept of the organisation as a set of social networks is discussed by, for example, M.S. Granovetter, 'The strength of weak ties', *American Journal of Sociology*, vol. 78, no. 6 (1973), pp. 1360–1380, and G.R. Carroll and A.C. Teo, 'On the social networks of managers', *Academy of Management Journal*, vol. 39, no. 2 (1996), pp. 421–440.

34. The concept of the learning organisation is explained in P. Senge, *The Fifth Discipline: The art and practice of the learning organisation*, Doubleday/Century, 1990. Also M. Crossan, H.W. Lane and R.E. White, 'An organizational learning framework: from intuition to institution', *Academy of Management Review*, vol. 24, no. 3 (1999), pp. 522–537.

35. See G. Hamel and L. Valikangas, 'The quest for resilience', *Harvard Business Review*, September (2003), pp. 52–63.

36. This idea of a balance between analytic rigour and intuition and imagination is the theme of G. Szulanski and K. Amin, 'Learning to make strategy: balancing discipline and imagination', *Long Range Planning*, vol. 34 (2001), pp. 537–556.

37. R. Duncan's research, on which this classification is based, could be found in 'Characteristics of organisational environments and perceived environmental uncertainty', *Administrative Science Quarterly*, vol. 17, no. 3 (1972), pp. 313–327.

38. See P. Regner, 'Strategy creation in the periphery: inductive versus deductive strategy making', *Journal of Management Studies*, vol. 40, no. 1 (2003), pp. 57–82.

WORK ASSIGNMENTS

✱ Denotes more advanced work assignments.   * Refers to a case study in the Text and Cases edition.

11.1 Read the annual report of a company with which you are familiar as a customer (for example, a retailer or transport company). Identify the main characteristics of the intended strategy as explained in the annual report, and the characteristics of the realised strategy as you perceive it as a customer.

11.2 Using the different explanations in sections 11.3 and 11.4 characterise how strategies have developed in different organisations (e.g. Intel, Ericsson,* Sabhal Mòr Ostaig*).

11.3✱ Planning systems exist in many different organisations. What role should planning play in a public sector organisation such as local government or the National Health Service and a multinational corporation such as Dell (see Illustration 1.1) or The News Corporation?*

11.4 If you had to design a strategy workshop (a) to re-examine the strategy of an organisation and (b) to gain commitment to intended strategic change, suggest who the participants on the workshop should be and what they should do.

11.5 With reference to the explanations of incremental strategy development in the chapter and Illustration 11.3, what are the main advantages and disadvantages of trying to develop strategies incrementally?

11.6✱ Incremental patterns of strategy development are common in organisations, and managers see advantages in this. However, there are also risks of strategic drift. Using the different explanations in sections 11.3 and 11.4 suggest how such drift might be avoided.

11.7 Suggest why different approaches to strategy development might be appropriate in different organisations such as a university, a fashion retailer and a high-technology company.

Integrative assignments

11.8 To what extent and why would you agree/disagree with the statement that 'Most strategy development processes organisations employ are unlikely to achieve truly innovative strategies'?

11.9 How does the concept of the 'learning organisation' relate to (a) that of strategic capabilities (Chapter 3), (b) organisation culture (Chapter 5) and (c) organisational knowledge (Chapter 3)? Bearing this in mind, what would be the challenges of developing a 'learning organisation' in a large international corporation?

An extensive range of additional materials, including audio summaries, weblinks to organisations featured in the text, definitions of key concepts and multiple choice questions, can be found on the *Exploring Corporate Strategy* Companion Website at **www.pearsoned.co.uk/ecs7**

<table>
<tr><td>

CASE
EXAMPLE
</td><td>

Strategy development at Intel*

Jill Shepherd, Segal Graduate School of Business, Simon Fraser University, Canada
</td></tr>
</table>

Intel (an abbreviation of Integrated Electronics) is a digital company operating in, having arguably created, the semiconductor industry. Over thirty years the company has achieved strategic transformation twice.

Epoch I

Between 1968 and 1985, during which the CEO was mostly Gordon Moore, Intel was a memory company. Founded by Gordon Moore and Robert Noyce, Intel was the first company to specialise in integrated circuit memory products. Noyce co-invented the integrated circuit, whereas Moore, a physical chemist, saw the potential of metal oxide semiconductor (MOS) process technology as a way of mass-producing semiconductors at low cost. Both managers left Fairchild Semiconductors, the subsidiary of Fairchild Camera and Instrument Corporation they had helped found. According to Noyce, senior management at Fairchild were unsupportive of innovation, perhaps because they had become too complex and big an organisation. In turn, Andy Grove joined Intel, thinking that the departure of Moore and Noyce left Fairchild fatally bereft of middle management. Their aim was not to transform the industry, but to make memory chips which did not compete directly with Fairchild and others because they were complex.

Two events were critical in these early days. Firstly, the first Intel memory chip was static (SRAM), but was soon replaced by a dynamic chip (DRAM). Secondly, the traditional strategic choice of second sourcing manufacturing 'failed' as the chosen company could not deliver a new generation manufacturing process. Intel was obliged to do all its own manufacturing, but also retained all the profits. This

Photo: Courtesy of Intel Corporation

early success and 'luck', according to Gordon Moore, lasted nearly 20 years. Although this good fortune can be construed as luck, perhaps Intel was ahead of the silicon technology competence game – maybe without knowing it – and was expecting too much of its supplier.

Developing, manufacturing and marketing DRAMs involved an approach to management which was structured, disciplined and controlled. Technical excellence was married with goals stipulated by senior management, which needed cross-functional discipline if they were to be reached on time. An ethos of top-down financial rigour was balanced by a culture in which those who knew what was needed to achieve the goals were never crowded out because they were junior. Knowledge was more powerful when associated with technical excellence than hierarchical position, creating an Intel ethos of constructive

---

* Intel is one of the most researched companies, courtesy of a highly productive partnership between once CEO and subsequent Chairman of Intel, Andy Grove, and Robert Burgelman, a Professor of Management at Stanford University Graduate School of Business.

debate. Insofar as it existed, strategic planning was fairly informal: ideas bubbled up from engineers and marketers which top management assessed and allocated funds to. Recruitment processes focused on hiring staff suited to the Intel culture, and rewards were associated with high performance.

Epoch II

Come the early 1980s Intel moved towards a different era, courtesy of a more crowded marketplace. Over ten years, the big earner, DRAM, lost market share from 83 per cent to 1.3 per cent and amounted to only 5 per cent of Intel's revenue, down from 90 per cent. Innovation moved towards the equipment manufacturers away from the chip suppliers and professional buyers sought much tougher deals. Competition had heated up with choices having to be made as to which technical areas to excel in.

At this time Intel made a decision to geographically distance its three main product development areas, DRAM, EPROM (its most profitable product in the mid 1980s) and microprocessors. In the case of microprocessors, the development of which had begun in Epoch I, the new basis of advantage increasingly became chip design rather than manufacturing process as it was in the other areas.

Over time DRAM lost manufacturing capacity within Intel to the unplanned microprocessor area. A rule, created by the first Financial Director and designed to maintain Intel as a technological leading-edge company, stipulated that manufacturing capacity was allocated in proportion to the profit margins achieved in the different product sectors. The emphasis within the DRAM group was on finding sophisticated technical solutions to DRAM's problems; it was, however, innovation in markets where innovation was no longer commerically viable. DRAM managers nonetheless fought to have manufacturing capacity assigned purely to DRAM, proposing that capacity be allocated on the basis of manufacturing cost. Senior management refused.

Once this decision was made to keep the resource allocation rule, the strategic freedom left to corporate managers to recover the founding businesses, SCRAM and DRAM, to which they were very attached, diminished as market share fell beyond what could be deemed worthwhile recovering. DRAM managers had to compete internally with the technological prowess of the other product areas

where morale and excitement were at high levels and innovation was happening in an increasingly dynamic market. And as microprocessors gradually became more profitable, manufacturing capacity and investment was increasingly allocated away from memory towards them. Eventually corporate managers realised that Intel would never be a player in the 64K DRAM memory game, despite having been the creator of the business. In 1985, top management came to realise they had to withdraw from the DRAM market. In 1986, Intel made a net loss of \$173m (≈ €150m) and lost nearly a third of its workforce.

However, lingering resistance to the exit continued. Manufacturing personnel ignored implications of exiting from DRAM by trying to show they could compete in the marketplace externally, by explaining failure in terms of the strong dollar against the Japanese yen and battling with poor morale. Eventually Andy Grove, CEO from 1987, took the executive decision to withdraw from EPROM, leaving no doubt that microprocessors now represented Intel's future strategic direction. The subsequent exit from EPROM was rapidly executed. Staff associated with EPROM left and set up their own start-up.

The period pre and post the exiting of DRAM was turbulent. Although seemingly messy, it gave rise to a great deal of new thinking. A new link was created between manufacturing and technology, trying to rid the company of the rivalries established in the era of internal competition between DRAM and other technology areas and return to the era of collaboration. The approach to technology was also rethought and moved away from being so product-based. Product definition and design as well as sales and marketing became more important, manufacturing less so. Corporate strategy came into line with market developments and middle management priorities; and formal strategic planning processes and corporate management's statements of strategy began to champion microprocessors.

That said, the potential of the PC was not recognised immediately. Indeed, a presentation made by a newly recruited manager on that potential failed to grab the attention of managers. Later Intel managers reflected this was because the presenter, although enthusiastic, appeared to be 'an amateur'. Had that same analytical content been presented by a 'smooth-talker', perhaps the importance of the PC market would have been taken on board sooner by corporate management.

By the mid-1990s the relatively informal processes of strategy development were becoming difficult in what had become a huge corporation. More formal strategic long-range planning were introduced where each business unit had a subcommittee which on a yearly basis developed a business plan to be submitted for approval to corporate. Whilst this added discipline, the problem was that these plans became repetitive and lacked the innovation and renewal that had driven Intel's success.

Epoch III

Intel's performance as a microprocessor company was financially spectacular. In 1998 Andy Grove became Chairman and Craig Barrett took over as CEO. Both were aware that, once again, Intel was facing new challenges. After 10 years of 30 per cent per annum compound growth, 1998 saw a slowdown. The era of the internet had arrived and the company needed to broaden its horizons. Not only did Intel need to maintain its competence in design and product development alongside continuing manufacturing competence, but it also needed to understand more the needs of the user and develop competences in corporate venturing, allowing part or full ownership of companies with strategically important technologies. After a period of adhering strongly to its focus on microprocessors, it needed ways of regaining the entrepreneurial flourish of its former days. In any case, the business had become more complex, requiring as many chips as possible to be put along the whole value chain of the internet moving it towards wireless and the digital home.

Barrett launched a series of seminars for Intel top management aimed at getting them to dream up new businesses and a New Business Group (NBG), with different processes and values, was founded with the brief to kick start new internal business ventures. A framework was created to handle the interface between the NBG and the rest of the company to establish whether any proposed new business was not only strategically important externally but also built on, or required, the development of new competences internally.

The early years under Barrett saw a flourish of activity and new ventures. In the first two years these included: buying DEC's chip unit with rights to the zippy StrongARM processor, which Intel adopts for some mobile and networking products; dozens of new products in 1998, including routers and switches; the

launch of the cheap Celeron chip; the establishment of a home-products group to develop web appliances and internet-enabled TVs and set-top boxes; the acquisition of networking chipmaker Level One, specializing in chips that connect network cards to wiring; and of Dialogic, a maker of PC-based phone systems, giving Intel technology for the convergence of voice and data networks; and a home networking kit to send data over phone wiring in homes. 1999 saw the launch of 13 networking chips and Intel's first web-hosting centre, with capacity for 10,000 servers and for serving hundreds of e-commerce companies; the acquisition of DSP Communications, a leader in wireless phone technology, and IPivot, a maker of gear for speeding up secure e-commerce transactions. And in 2000 the launch of seven server appliances, called the NetStructure family, to speed up and manage web traffic.

In 2002 efforts were directed at promoting wireless technology development through an investment fund which was extended in 2004 to fuel the advance of the Digital Age into people's homes making the transfer of photos, music, documents, films between various devices. The fund backed start-ups working in the area and was also aimed at expanding interest in the area, both technological and consumer oriented. Intel believed that PCs would be needed for storage in the digital home but saw its future in all kinds of semiconductors, not just those for PCs. For example, Intel invested in three companies: BridgeCo which designs chips to link devices within the home; Entropic which designed chips for networking over coaxial cable; and Musicmatch selling software that records, organises and plays music. By how much digital appliances would complement or substitute for PCs remained to be seen but by 2003 Intel had determined to establish itself as a leader in the design, marketing and selling of chips.

In 2004 it was announced that in 2005 Paul S. Otellini, who does not have the engineering background of Barrett, would take over from Craig Barrett as CEO, who would take over as Chairman, making Andy Grove Chairman Emeritus. *Business Week* commented: 'In this new age of "Think Intel Everywhere", not just inside the PC, Intel will face tough competition, as it enters the communication, entertainment and wireless sectors whilst also defending its flank from other microprocessor companies such as AMD. . . . Whilst remaining driven by innovation Barrett and Otellini have spent time trying to learn from past mistakes, to become more market savy, forging closer relationship with customers to avoid designing products no one desires, becoming more cooperative and less arrogant whilst also investing in five new factories in 2005.'

Sources: R.A. Burgelman, *Strategy as Destiny: How strategy-making shapes a company's Future*, Free Press, 2002; R.A. Burgelman, 'Strategy as vector and the inertia of coevolutionary lock-in', *Administrative Science Quarterly*, vol. 47 (2002), pp. 325–358; *Business Week*, 13 March 2000, pp. 110–119.

Business Week, online (http://www.businessweek.com/technology/content/) (7 January 2004); Kharif, O. (2004) 'Intel bets big on the digital home', *Business Week*, 7 January 2004; *Business Week*, online (http://www.businessweek.com/technology/content/jan2004/tc2004017_7492_tc057.htm) (2nd March 2004).

'What is CEO Craig Barrett Up to? Hint: It's about much more than computers', *Business Week*, 8 March 2004, pp. 56–64.

Questions

1. Identify the different strategy development processes operating in Intel. How different/similar were these processes within and between the different epochs?

2. How effective were these different processes? What effect did these processes have on Intel's performance?

3. What were the tensions between processes within each epoch?

4. What proposals would you make as to the most appropriate strategy development processes that should exist as Intel moves into a more and more diversified business model?

Strategy Development in Organisations

This final commentary in the book has three parts. The first employs the strategy lenses again to review the explanation of strategy development processes in Chapter 11. However, rather than taking the approach adopted in the other commentaries of taking each lens in turn, here the different processes covered in the chapter are briefly reviewed through all three lenses. This is to emphasise the theme that the commentaries have consistently made: that the different ways the lenses provide to view strategy are relevant to all aspects of strategic management – even to processes that would appear on the face of it to exemplify one of the lenses. The second part emphasises this same theme by summarising research that has looked at how the tools of strategy analysis – many of which have been explained throughout this book – are actually used in practice. Finally there is a brief review to the use of the lenses throughout the book

Strategy development processes

This first part of the commentary briefly revisits the processes discussed in Chapter 11 and considers them and the concept of 'strategic leadership' in the light of the three strategy lenses of *design, experience and ideas.*

Strategic planning

On the face of it, planning is most obviously explained through the design lens; it can certainly take the form and appearance of a logical system of objective setting, analysis and evaluation leading to clearly articulated intentions from the top management in an organisation. However, the research by Rob Grant[1] reported in Chapter 11 (section 11.3.1) makes it clear that strategic planning is likely to perform the roles of communicating, controlling and communicating strategy rather than formulating the strategy itself. The other lenses also help explain the roles planning may play in organisations.

The experience lens suggests strategy actually develops on the basis of more informal sensing of the environment on the basis of people's experience or through the cultural systems of the organisation. Here planning is not seen as directing the development of strategy so much as drawing together the threads of a strategy which emerges on the basis of that experience. So the strategy comes to look as though it has been planned. In so doing the exercise of planning may help make sense of such emerging strategy, may provide a more coherent form to it, or indeed may help challenge some of the assumptions or biases on which it is based. So even if the role of planning is seen through this lens, it can be argued it performs an important role.

The ideas lens also emphasises the emergence of strategy from within the organisation rather than from the top; so again planning may be seen here as making sense of that emergent strategy. Planning systems can also be seen as one of the mechanisms by which ideas that emerge from within an organisation are selected and retained. Such ideas have to compete for their survival, or prove their worth against other ideas.

Strategy workshops

The design lens suggests that strategy workshops have the purpose of helping managers logically think through the strategy of an organisation. However, the experience lens tells us that, whilst they may employ the tools and techniques of such logical analysis and planning, such workshops consist of individuals who also exercise their experience and play out their political agendas. Indeed, arguably, strategy workshops become even more reliant on the experience of individuals precisely because they are relatively short timescale events in which the people taking part cannot always readily access all the information that may be relevant to the topics they are considering. So they may have to rely on their experience and judgement.

However, in some organisations such workshops or project teams are used specifically to generate the variety of insights and ideas that the ideas lens suggests is necessary for innovation. This might be by using brainstorming workshops, for example. Or, as with some organisations, by establishing multiple workshops or project teams with similar briefs as a way of stimulating different ideas and insights.[2]

The use of consultants

Consultants, too, are often portrayed as the objective, dispassionate counsellors of management the design lens would suggest. However, they may also be used to provide a different view – and hence increased variety – in deliberations on strategy. So they play a role in idea generation. However, whilst objective analysis and an outside or novel perspective may well be key roles, consultants also have to know who the most influential executives are or who are likely to be able to get a decision made – or indeed stand in the way of getting a decision made.[3] And consultants are often used to provide political muscle for the executives who bring them in. As the experience lens suggests, there is an undoubted political role for the consultant too.

Logical incrementalism

The experience and ideas lenses help provide an understanding of incremental strategy development. Both these lenses emphasise the importance in strategy development of the activities and contribution of people throughout the organisation, rather than just at the top. Sensing of environmental changes is done by drawing on the experience and sensing of people at different levels and in different roles in the organisation. The variety of these people's experience, emphasised by the ideas lens, is critical because it ensures sufficient diversity in the way the complexities of the environment and organisational capabilities are understood and interpreted. The top management role of providing overarching vision rather than tight control is also in line with the ideas lens.

However, the experience lens suggests another interpretation of logical incrementalism. As explained in Chapter 11, logical incrementalism is a bridge between intended and emergent strategy. Quinn describes it as 'conscious, purposeful, proactive, executive practice'.[4] On the other hand Johnson has argued 'whilst managers may describe strategy development processes in much this way, the driving force behind incrementalism is the development of strategies on the basis of managerial experience and organizational culture'.[5] Just as formal planning systems often make sense of or post-rationalise such experience, so too may the tag of 'logical' post-rationalise what are essentially cultural and cognitive processes.

Resource allocation routines

The design lens sees resource allocation routines as part of the logical, systematic processes associated with the planned processes of organisations; they are, indeed, deliberately designed to help make sensible decisions through an organisation. The experience lens, on the other hand, suggests that such routines become embedded in the culture of an organisation; they become 'the way we do things around here'. A good example is the resource allocation routines set up by government to reward UK universities for research quality. The Research Assessment Exercise (RAE) was set up to encourage good research (a *design* view). Over the years the criteria of the RAE have become so embedded, so taken for granted as important (an *experience* view), that they have become *the* driving force behind what academics in many universities see themselves about. Indeed when talking about research such academics may use the terminology of the RAE to describe the standard of a piece of research. The *ideas lens* provides further insight. The guidelines and criteria of the RAE have become the routine equivalent of simple rules and strategies start to develop on the basis of them. Research strategies have grown up around particular sorts of research that can be published in particular journals in order to perform well in the RAE and therefore generate the sorts of resources required for universities and the promotional opportunities for academics. The RAE and its criteria are changing university strategies in ways which may or may not be as intended.

Cultural processes

The cultural processes in organisations clearly align with the insights the experience lens provides. Yet, as intimated in terms of resource allocation routines, many of the more formal systems (e.g. planning systems) that would typically be associated with strategic intent and a design view of strategy have also become culturally embedded in organisations. How the strategic planning process is undertaken, how budgeting is done, the common use of strategy workshops, or indeed of consultants for strategy development purposes, have themselves become taken-for-granted, institutionalised ways of doing things. They are the way in which organisations work. Similarly, other writers have pointed out that the very language of strategy has come to take on symbolic significance. The ability to use the right strategic rhetoric, the right buzz words, refer to the appropriate tools and so on has come to take on significance in terms of the reputation, authority or the power of individuals within organisations.[6]

Organisational politics

Arguably the root of the negotiation and bargaining that characterises the political activity in organisations is the different experience base and therefore the different views of individuals and groups within organisations. The reconciliation of these differences is through political means. However, the political processes in organisations can also be understood through the other lenses. The ability to be able to use the strategy tools associated with a design view, or the language associated with such tools, can provide power and prestige in an organisation. There is therefore a link between apparent objectivity and rationality of design, analysis and planning and the politics of decision making.

The ideas lens also suggests that organisational politics can be seen as a manifestation of the sort of conflict that may be part of the context that generates innovation and new ideas. The variety and diversity that exists in organisations takes form in new ideas supported or opposed by different 'champions'. In this sense such battling over what is the best idea or the best way forward is to be expected as an inevitable manifestation of innovatory organisations. Indeed, arguably if such conflict and tensions did not exist, neither would innovation.

Strategic leadership

Within all these processes individuals are often seen as playing an important role in strategy development. Individuals such as chief executives may be personally identified with and central to the strategy of their organisation. Their personality or reputation may result in others willingly deferring to such an individual and seeing strategy development as his or her province. In other organisations an individual may be central because he or she is its owner or founder – often the case in small businesses. Or it could be that an individual chief executive has turned round a business in times of difficulty and, as such, personifies the success of the organisation's strategy. The design lens would suggest that such individuals take a considered and deliberate view of future strategic direction either by using the sorts of technique associated with strategic planning and analysis or by consciously, systematically and on the basis of their own logic worked through issues their organisation faces.

There are, of course, other explanations of how a strategic leader influences strategy. The strategy advanced by the individual could be formed on the basis of that individual's experience, perhaps within the organisation or perhaps from some other organisation. The strategy advanced by a chief executive new to an organisation may be based on a successful strategy followed in a previous organisation. The strategy of an organisation might also be associated more symbolically with an individual, for example the founder of a business, who may come to embody the strategic direction of the organisation. This is often the case in family-controlled businesses.

Whilst the ideas lens de-emphasises top-down design, it suggests the importance of an overall vision, mission or intent and the (perhaps few) guiding rules associated with these are recognised as important. Indeed, it is a role for which successful strategic leaders are often applauded because such a vision can provide sufficient clarity within which the discretion of others in the organisation can be exercised. Such visionary capacity is sometimes explained in terms of the intuition of top managers. However, more widely, research is beginning to show that the intuitive capacity of managers generally, perhaps together with more formal approaches to decision making, plays an important role in strategy development.[7]

The role of analytic tools

It is undeniably the case that the strategy tools of analysis so commonly associated with the development of intended strategies are used. They are used in formal planning systems, consultants use them, they are used in strategy workshops. Indeed in some organisations they have now been built into computer systems that individuals can employ. They have also been employed and explained in this book. However, the evidence is that such analytic tools are used to different extents and for different purposes in different organisations. Insights from such research serves to emphasise some of the observations made above.

Ann Langley[8] studied three organisational settings similar to the organisational types described in section 8.5.1 of Chapter 8: an artistic production organisation, rather like the loosely organised *adhocracy* type of organisation; a hospital as a *professional bureaucracy*; and a more *machine bureaucracy* setting within the public sector. When it came to use of formal tools analysis in these organisations there were three broad categories of usage that differed by type of organisation:

● What she termed '*armchair*' and 'short' studies involved relatively little data and largely intuitive argument. These were most common in the adhocracy type of organisation but also found extensively in the hospital she studied – a professional bureaucracy. They were, however, much less common in the more machine bureaucracy setting.

● '*Medium*' intensity studies were more extensive in their use of 'hard' data; perhaps a few pages of tables based on analytic tools employed. These were found commonly in the professional bureaucracy and machine bureaucracy type organisations, but less so in the adhocracy.

● When it came to *major* studies involving complex or multiple quantitative techniques these, too, were most prevalent in the machine bureaucracy and much less so in the adhocracy.

So the extent of use of analytic tools and techniques varied by type of organisation.

Langley also found differences in the role played by such analytic tools and techniques similar to those identified above in relation to strategic planning. These roles included:

● *Information gathering* for the purposes of establishing new knowledge, seeking information to back up preconceived ideas, checking out information provided by other sources or seeking opinion within the organisation. This role might involve outside specialists in analytic techniques (e.g. consultants) and was more often initiated from the top of the organisation.

- *Communication and coordination*, where analysis was used for a variety of purposes:
  - To *persuade* others on a point of view: here such analysis might be undertaken by managers within the organisation or commissioned from outsiders (for example, from consultants) where enhanced credibility was important.
  - To *educate or sensitise* people to issues through analysis. Top managers might involve subordinates in analytical processes to get them to understand a particular issue.
  - To *build consensus* around a particular issue by getting people involved in analysis – and therefore in understanding it.
  - *Conditioning*: using analysis to establish and justify a position on an issue, often taking the form of 'armchair' studies.
  - For *symbolic purposes*. Analytic tools might be used: (a) to establish the perception that arguments are rational and therefore to justify a decision; (b) to symbolise action, i.e. the use of the analytic tool itself to represent another stage in a process of strategy development; (c) to symbolise participation and concern where analytic tools involve others and encourage (or appear to encourage) new ideas.
- *Procrastination*: here analytical tools are employed to delay action or to delay a decision. They take on a political role.

Langley's research therefore helps to show the multiple roles of analytic tools and techniques and how they play different roles in different organisational contexts.

Reviewing strategy

At the end of this book, it is timely to review the subject of strategy as a whole; and again useful to do so by employing the three lenses.

The book began by emphasising that the management of strategy is distinctly different from operational management in its complexity. Because it is to do with the management of the future direction of the organisation, the coping with uncertainty, the competition of potentially irreconcilable influences, complexity is perhaps its most distinguishing feature. When people talk about strategy or strategic management that is what they imply.

Our encouragement in this book has been to cast a critical eye on understanding the management of strategy. The dominant influence of the design lens can be put down to its perceived potential to simplify, or at least place order on, that complexity. In this book we recognise the attraction and value of that. In *thinking through* this challenging topic, the design lens is especially useful. It draws on models and explanatory frameworks which allow for analysis and build on empirical findings from research. However, the challenge is not just to think about strategy but also to manage strategy. Managers and students alike should not delude themselves that a model which provides order means that the complexity is done away with.

It is because of this complexity and the importance of strategy as a management activity that the other two lenses are also important. The experience lens helps explain how managers actually cope with complexity, helps explain barriers and blockages to change and in so doing sheds light on how change might be managed.

However, by themselves neither of these two lenses says enough about innovation; and that is where the ideas lens is especially useful. It provides concepts that allow managers to consider how they can create and foster the organisational context for innovation. In so doing the ideas lens also provides a useful counterbalance to the design lens in that it questions some of its central premises, not least those of top-down planned strategy and linear processes of strategy development.

To repeat our message from other commentaries, we do not argue for the superiority or rightness of one lens over another. We do argue that by considering the subject through the different lenses more insightful questions will be asked, more important challenges will be acknowledged and, potentially, more useful solutions will emerge.

References

1. See R. Grant, 'Strategic planning in a turbulent environment: evidence from the oil majors', *Strategic Management Journal*, vol. 24 (2003), pp. 491–517.
2. This situation of overlapping or similar briefs appears to underlie the situation that Blackler and McDonald studied in their work on strategy project teams; see F. Blackler and S. McDonald, 'Organising processes in complex activity networks', *Organization*, vol. 7, no. 2 (2000), pp. 277–300.
3. This point is made by Mirela Schwartz in her research on consultants: see M. Schwartz in 'The role and contribution of consultants in strategy-making – how consultants and managers work together in strategy-making?', in *Proceedings of the International Conference European Group for Organization Studies (EGOS)*, Copenhagen Business School/Denmark, 2003.
4. J.B. Quinn, *Strategies for Change*, Irwin, 1980, p. 58.
5. G. Johnson, 'Re-thinking incrementalism', *Strategic Management Journal*, vol. 9 (1988), pp. 75–91.
6. For example, see C. Hardy, I. Palmer and N. Phillips, 'Discourse as a strategic resource', *Human Relations*, vol. 53, no. 9 (2000), pp. 1227–1248.
7. See I. Clarke and W. Mackaness, 'Management intuition; an interpretative account of structure and content of decision schemas using cognitive maps', *Journal of Management Studies*, vol. 38, no. 2 (2001), pp. 147–172. Also the discussion on intuition in chapter 6 of G.P. Hodgkinson and P.R. Sparrow, *The Competent Organization*, Open University Press, 2002.
8. See A. Langley, 'In search of rationality: the purpose behind the use of formal analysis in organizations', *Administrative Science Quarterly*, vol. 34 (1989), pp. 598–631.

Case Studies

A guide to using the case studies

The main text of this book includes 84 short illustrations and 11 case examples which have been chosen to enlarge on specific issues in the text and/or provide practical examples of how business and public sector organisations are managing strategic issues. The case studies which follow allow the reader to extend this linking of theory and practice further by analysing the strategic issues of specific organisations in much greater depth – and often providing 'solutions' to some of the problems or difficulties identified in the case.

The case studies are intended to serve as a basis for class discussion and not as an illustration of either good or bad management practice. They are not intended to be a comprehensive collection of teaching material. They have been chosen (or specifically written) to provide readers with a core of cases which, together, cover most of the main issues in the text. As such, they should provide a useful backbone to a programme of study but could sensibly be supplemented by other material. We have provided a mixture of longer and shorter cases to increase the flexibility for teachers. Combined with the *illustrations* and the short *case examples* at the end of each chapter (in both versions of the book) this increases the reader's and tutor's choice. For example, when deciding on material for Chapter 2, the case example *The European Brewing Industry* tests a reader's understanding of the main issues influencing the competitive position of a number of organisations in the same industry with a relatively short case. For a case that permits a more comprehensive industry analysis, *The Pharmaceutical Industry* and the associated case study on the *GlaxoWellcome/SmithKline Beecham* merger could be used. However, if the purpose is more focused – illustrating the use of 'five-forces' analysis – the illustration on *The Mobile Phone Industry* could be used.

Some cases are written entirely from published sources but most have been prepared in cooperation with and approval of the management of the organisation concerned. Case studies can never fully capture the richness and complexity of real life management situations and we would also encourage readers and tutors to take every possible opportunity to explore the *live* strategic issues of organisations – both their own and others.

The following brief points of guidance should prove useful in selecting and using the case studies provided:

- The summary table that follows indicates the main focus of each of the chosen case studies – together with important subsidiary foci (where appropriate) – and a brief headline summary of each case. In general, the sequence of cases is intended to mirror the chapter sequence. However, this should not be taken too literally because, of course, many of these cases cover a variety of issues. The 'classification' provided is therefore guidance only. We expect readers to seek their own lessons from cases, and tutors to use cases in whichever way and sequence best fits the purpose of their programmes.

- In addition to the cases published here, there are additional cases on the website: (**www. booksites.net/ecs**)

- Where cases have been chosen to illustrate the issues of strategic choices and strategy into action covered later in the book, it will normally be a prerequisite that some type of analysis of the strategic position is undertaken, using the case material. When planning the use of these cases within programmes, care needs to be taken to balance the time taken on such strategic analysis so as to allow the time required to analyse the main issues for which the case has been chosen.

- Where the text and cases are being used as the framework for a strategy programme (as we hope they will), it is essential that students are required to undertake additional reading from other sources and that their 'practical' work is supplemented by other material as mentioned above.

Guide to the main focus of cases

PAGE NUMBER IN THE BOOK	CASE	Introduction to strategy	Business environment	Capability analysis	Corporate governance	Stakeholder expectations	Social responsibility	Culture	Competitive strategy	Corporate-level strategy	International strategy	Strategic options	Diversification	Acquisitions and alliances	Global management	Organising	Enabling	Managing change	Strategic leadership	Strategic management process	Public sector/not-for-profit management	Public sector management	Small business strategy
617	**Ministry of Sound** – rapid growth but a questionable future in the music industry.	●●																					●
620	**The global pharmaceutical industry** – the global forces at work in the ethical pharmaceutical industry.		●●			●					●												
637	**Airlines post-9/11** – reshaping strategies and planning for the future in the wake of a global shock.		●●	●							●												
647	**Amazon** – long term planning of a successful dot.com.			●●								●	●										
673	**The Formula One constructors** – developing the capabilities for competitive success in a hi-tech industry.			●●					●								●						
685	**Baan Company** – enterprise and ambition, success and failure in the business software industry.	●	●●						●														
697	**Premier Oil and Hermes** – corporate governance and strategy: the responsibilities of companies and investors.				●●		●		●														
703	**Sheffield Theatres** – strategy formulation for a wide audience of public and commercial stakeholders.					●●		●													●●		●
717	**Salvation Army** – strategic challenges for a global non-profit organisation on a Christian mission.					●●					●●					●					●●		
725	**Eurotunnel** – clash of cultures threatens to derail Anglo-French rail link.							●●															
734	**BMW** – driving organic growth through market development in the automotive industry.	●	●						●●														
742	**The VSM Group** – the development of global competitive strategy in a declining market.	●	●						●●		●	●				●	●	●					
750	**Thorntons** – a variety box of strategies in the manufacture and retail of chocolates.			●					●●			●											
760	**The News Corporation** – corporate logic and corporate management in a worldwide media business.				●	●	●			●●	●								●				
776	**Allied Irish Banks** – competing in the global banking industry: the challenges for a mid-size bank.		●						●	●●	●												
789	**Mantero Seta** – an Italian textile company cottons on to opportunities in China.									●●													
797	**Coopers Creek** – developments in domestic and international collaboration for a New Zealand winery.			●						●●				●	●●								●
807	**SABMiller** – an African brewer takes on the world: learning to thrive in difficult circumstances.			●					●	●●					●								
819	**Xelibri** – Siemens launches an innovative phone into sophisticated international markets.									●●	●												
832	**Ryanair** – competitive challenge and strategic choice in the budget airline industry.		●	●					●		●●									●			

Key: ●● = major focus   ● = important subsidiary focus

PAGE NUMBER IN THE BOOK	CASE	Introduction to strategy	Business environment	Capability analysis	Corporate governance	Stakeholder expectations	Social responsibility	Culture	Competitive strategy	Corporate-level strategy	International strategy	Strategic options	Diversification	Acquisitions and alliances	Global management	Organising	Enabling	Managing change	Strategic leadership	Strategic management process	Public sector/not-for-profit management	Public sector management	Small business strategy
853	**Wimm-Bill-Dann** – where from here for a high growth diversified Russian conglomerate.								●			●●	●●										
863	**KPN** – the Dutch organisation surviving the crisis in the telecommunications industry.		●									●●											
876	**Coors** – an American brewer moves into the UK market.								●		●	●●											
886	**Barclaycard** – a market leader's strategic options for maintaining market dominance.											●●											
901	**Brown Bag** – strategy development and strategic choice for a small business in an international market.											●●											●●
908	**Community safety** – strategic partnership in the public sector reflects consortia developments in the private sector.													●●								●●	
913	**GlaxoSmithKline** – the wisdom of mergers for a global pharmaceutical giant.									●				●●									
924	**Sony** – a diverse hi-tech multinational responds to change with repeated reorganizations.										●					●●		●					
937	**Arts Council** – changes in structure and responsibilities in funding the arts in the UK.															●●						●●	
941	**SerCom Solutions** – the role of technology in positioning a global supply chain management company.														●		●●						
948	**Forestry Commission** – from forestry management to service provider: the challenge of managing change.					●		●●										●●			●	●	
966	**Marks & Spencer** – can new initiatives and new management reverse a decline?								●	●								●●	●				
979	**Eden Project** – inspiration, innovation and entrepreneurship to create a new 'wonder of the world'.																	●●	●●	●			
990	**Ericsson** – innovation from the periphery: the development of mobile telephone systems.																			●●			
1000	**Sabhal Mòr Ostaig** – strategy development for a small niche business.																		●	●●	●		●
ON THE COMPANION WEBSITE at www.booksites.net/ecs	**Corus** – the Anglo-Dutch manufacturing giant steels itself for mergers, acquisitions and strategic challenges.	●●																					
	Jordan – the challenge of building capabilities for success in Formula 1.			●●					●											●			
	HomeCo – wrestling with governance and strategy in the boardroom; a role play.				●●					●	●												●
	Fed-Ex – packaging new business models to deliver competitive advantage.														●		●●						
	Chem Tech – innovative strategy development in the flavours and fragrances industry.																			●●			

Key: ●● = major focus   ● = important subsidiary focus

Ministry of Sound

Richard Whittington

The Ministry of Sound went from start-up to maturity in little over a decade. The case raises issues concerning both business strategy, particularly regarding sustainable competitive advantage and resources, and corporate strategy, particularly regarding diversification and internationalisation. There are also issues of ownership and organisation. In the end, the fundamental question is: what future for the Ministry?

● ● ●

In 1991, 28-year-old James Palumbo invested £225,000 (≈ €340,000) of his own capital into a new dance club located in an old South London bus depot. As an old Etonian (the UK's most elitist private school), a graduate of Oxford University and a former merchant banker, Palumbo was an unlikely entrant into a dance culture that was still raw and far from respectable. He actually preferred classical music. The club's name, the Ministry of Sound, ironically recalled Palumbo's father, a former Minister in the Conservative government of the day. Yet within just ten years, Palumbo built the Ministry of Sound into a music and media empire worth nearly £150m. Two years later, Palumbo had quit as chief executive and the Ministry of Sound was looking for a new strategic direction.

The Ministry of Sound's start had been difficult. Dance music had its origins in 'acid house', itself with its roots in the futuristic, electronic music of the gay clubs of Chicago and New York. The new style had been picked up by British DJs in Ibiza, who combined it with the drug Ecstasy to create a new 'blissed-out' sound. Dance music arrived in Britain during 1988, the so-called 'Second Summer of Love', strongly associated with recreational drugs. By the early 1990s, drug-dealing in its most ugly sense had become part of the dance culture. Palumbo recalled:

Photo: © S.I.N./Corbis

When I came into this business, with my bonuses and my nice City suits, I was completely naïve. Just a joke. I found that every Friday and Saturday night my door was taking £30,000 and the security team was making £40,000 on Ecstasy. It happens everywhere in the UK leisure business. There are all these fat bastards running chains of discos and bowling alleys, and none of them admits it. We went through a really traumatic time at the club.[1]

Palumbo changed his security team, bringing in security professionals from the North of England with no links to the local drugs gangs. He even hired a psychoanalyst to cope with the gangland threats that followed his drugs crack-down:

> If they say 'we're going to kill you', you know what you're up against. But the threats [from London's East End drugs gangs] are much more sinister. The word is fed back that if the business is cut off, they will follow you home, go for your family, stab you or murder you.[2]

But Palumbo persisted in making his club a safer, cleaner environment. During the 1990s, he campaigned nationally against the use of drugs in youth venues.

Thus the Ministry of Sound led in the transformation of club culture from an underground movement associated with 'acid house' into a mainstream youth market activity. An illuminated sign on Palumbo's office wall read:

> We are building a global entertainment business based on a strong aspirational brand respected for its creativity and its quality. The Ministry of Sound team will be more professional, hard-working and innovative than any other on the planet.[3]

The Ministry established a distinctive logo and brand and invested heavily in club facilities and sound equipment. It was a leader in developing the new 'super-clubs', fronted by 'super-DJs' earning six-figure sums for playing other people's music. By 2001, over two and a half million clubbers had visited Ministry of Sound nightspots and that same year its first festival weekend attracted 55,000 people at Knebworth.

The business developed in many directions during this period. A magazine aimed at clubbers, *Ministry*, was launched in the mid-1990s and achieved a readership of 300,000. The Ministry of Sound radio show was broadcast in London and Central Scotland, besides being syndicated in 38 countries worldwide. The Ministry's Relentless joint venture became the largest independent record-label in the United Kingdom, with its Chill

Out Sessions 1 and 2 reaching number one in the album charts and its So Solid Crew reaching the top of the singles charts. Large supermarket chain Asda was distributing the Ministry's albums to shoppers around the United Kingdom. The Ministry's distinctive logo had become the basis for a large merchandising business, mostly for clothing. By 2001, the Ministry's touring division was hosting 300 events worldwide, including China and India, and had regular summer residencies in Ibiza, Ayia Napa and Benidorm. A Ministry of Sound superclub opened in Bangkok. By this point, the Ministry's original nightclub only accounted for about 3 per cent of a total turnover reaching around £100m per annum.

As a mark of the Ministry's success, in the summer of 2001 venture capitalist company 3i acquired approaching 20 per cent of the Ministry's equity for £24m. James Palumbo was quoted as saying: 'With 3i's support, we are now poised to spread the dance music gospel worldwide'. In its Rich List 2001, *The Sunday Times* estimated Palumbo's total fortune as £150m. A spokesman for 3i said:

> We had obviously heard a lot about the Ministry and James [Palumbo] has had a lot of good press. We were impressed by how successful the brand has become and by how fast it has grown . . . Ministry has a phenomenal skill in helping new acts hit the big time. The more successful it became, the more people wanted to become associated with it . . . When making an investment, you have to be totally comfortable and confident that you are backing an A1 team. With James we found the perfect deal. James is the sort of person VCs [venture capitalists] can make money out of.[4]

The Ministry of Sound was aiming for a stock-market listing within a couple of years.

Then things started to go wrong. The dance music on which the Ministry was based was going out of fashion. Dance music (including house, trance, techno, breaks and drum'n'bass music) saw its share of the UK singles market fall to 15.4 per cent in 2002, down from 34 per cent in 1991. Dance clubs were closing or down-sizing, while live music audiences were growing. Malik Meer, deputy editor of *New Musical Express* commented in early 2004:

> The dance culture as a whole got lazy. It came to be perceived as one thing: this cheesy, superclub,

---

[1] *New Statesman*, 5 September 1997.
[2] Ibid.
[3] *Marketing*, 4 December 1997, p. 3.

[4] *European Venture Capital Journal*, September 2001, p. 1.

larging-it lifestyle . . . Dance music came from an underground culture and was about being edgy and anti-establishment. At the height of superclub-dom, a club would be £25 to get in and be full of slightly-older people, glammed up and wearing crap labels. If you are young and want to be cool, you are not going to buy into that.[5]

For many aficionados, the last straw was when the Sugababes got crowned the 'Best Dance Act' of 2003.

At the end of 2002, Palumbo was obliged to close down his flagship magazine, *Ministry*. Ministry of Sound then worked with publishers Condé Nast to launch a new style magazine, *Trash*, which would be able to share expertise and economies of scale. *Trash* was closed after just one issue. The recording joint venture Relentless went out of business, owing £3m. Bangkok's Ministry of Sound closed after a change in local laws restricted late-night attractions. In February 2003, James Palumbo quit as chief executive to become chairman of the company of which he was still the largest shareholder. Rumours that he was forced to stand down by venture capitalist investor 3i were dismissed.

Ministry's 36-year-old marketing director, Mark Rodol, took over as chief executive and launched a strategic review of the whole business. Rodol commented on Palumbo's exit:

> James is an entrepreneur – but what is going to make this business great is a focused, long-term brand strategy. To his credit James has had the foresight to step aside and let the people who understand and believe this run the company. It's about a difference in style.[6]

As to the strategic review, Rodol observed:

> Over the years, we've pursued a number of opportunities that we shouldn't have done. The intention we have over the next couple of months is to examine what the core of Ministry of Sound actually is.[7]

Ministry of Sound was not, however, abandoning all initiatives. Rodol saw large potential in continued merchandising in areas such as branded clothing, specialist holidays and consumer hi-fi products, with turnover targeted to reach £5m by 2006. On top of this, Ministry was starting to sell branded DJ equipment and offering branded mobile phone games. A Ministry PlayStation game allowing gamers to mix their own dance music was being launched too. An advertising-supported online broadcast music channel was launched, with potential for streaming over mobile phones. As a spokesman put it, 'this will be just like MTV, only on the Web'.[8] A new superclub was also opened in Taipei, Taiwan, in the second half of 2003 and Rodol declared an ambition to have a Ministry of Sound club in every big city in the world.

Rodol also reorganised the Ministry, leading to several management departures. As well as the continuing record business and club activities, there would be three divisions: an international arm, encompassing radio, touring and record compilation; a brand division, focused on retail, product licensing and the Ministry website; and a marketing division, aiming to form long-term relationships with brands such as Philips and Bacardi. Rodol denied that the reorganisation was motivated by simple cost considerations, and underlined its importance for moving the brand forward towards long-term goals.

Central would be keeping the brand cool in the eyes of its customers. Ministry of Sound was perceived by many as having lost its 'edginess'. Mark Rodol insisted:

> That's what we're working on. It is possible to be big and cutting edge – there are big mass market brands like Nike and PlayStation that manage to retain an edge despite their size. That's what we intend to do.[9]

---

[5] *The Independent*, 2 January 2004, p. 10.
[6] *Financial Times*, 30 April 2003, p. 13.
[7] *Financial Times*, 28 February 2003, p. 22.

[8] *New Media Age*, 13 November 2003, p. 24.
[9] *Financial Times*, 30 April 2003, p. 13.

The global pharmaceutical industry

Sarah Holland and Bernardo Bátiz-Lazo

The case looks at the development of the ethical pharmaceutical industry. The various forces affecting the discovery, development, production, distribution and marketing of prescription drugs are discussed as are issues of corporate social responsibility in the industry and the strategies being followed by major pharmaceutical companies. Readers are then invited to consider trends for the future.

● ● ●

In late 2003, Britain's *Guardian* newspaper commented that, on the face of it, the global pharmaceutical industry 'looks like the epitome of a modern, mature industry that has found a comfortable way to make profits by the billion: it's global, hi-tech, and has the ultimate customer, the healthcare budgets of the world's richest countries.'[1] Pharmaceutical manufacturers certainly did not appear to be faced a looming crisis, yet, declared the newspaper, that was the alarming conclusion of a research report by analysts at investment bank Dresdner Kleinwort Wasserstein. The analysts argued that the world's largest drugs companies were operating a business model that was unsustainable and 'rapidly running out of steam'. The treatment they prescribed was further industry consolidation. This case explores some of the trends affecting the '*ethical*' (research-based) sector of the industry and invites readers to prepare their own analysis and prescription.

Industry evolution

As described in Box 1, the pharmaceutical industry is characterised by a highly risky and lengthy research and development (R&D) process, intense competition for *intellectual property*, stringent government regulation and powerful purchaser pressures. How has this unusual picture come about?

The origins of the modern pharmaceutical industry can be traced to the late 19th century, when dyestuffs were found to have antiseptic properties. Roche, Ciba-Geigy and Sandoz all started out as family dyestuff companies based near the Rhine in Basel, Switzerland, which moved into synthetic pharmaceuticals and eventually became global players. Penicillin was a major discovery for the emergent industry, and during the 1940s and 1950s R&D became firmly established within the sector. The industry expanded rapidly in the 1960s, benefiting from significant new discoveries with permanent patent protection. Regulatory controls on clinical development and marketing were light and healthcare spending boomed as economies prospered.

The pharmaceutical market developed some unusual characteristics. Decision making was in the hands of medical practitioners whereas patients (the final consumers) and payers (governments or insurance companies) had little knowledge or influence. As a result, medical practitioners were insensitive to price but susceptible to the sales efforts of individual representatives. This enabled numerous 'me too' drugs to achieve satisfactory returns on investment. Imitating a known drug reduced R&D risk considerably, while the market-

_____

[1] *The Guardian*, 12 September 2003.

This case was prepared by Sarah Holland (Manchester Business School) and Bernardo Bátiz-Lazo (London South Bank University). It is intended for class discussion rather than as an illustration of either good or bad management practice. Comments from Christopher Berry, Simon Ling, Stella Richter, Justin Boag and MBA graduates of the Open University are gratefully acknowledged. © K.S. Holland and B. Bátiz-Lazo, 2004. Not to be reproduced or quoted without permission.

Photo: AstraZeneca UK Ltd

there is effectively only one powerful purchaser, the government. In the 1980s, governments around the world began to focus upon pharmaceuticals as a politically easy target in their efforts to control rising healthcare expenditure, although drugs typically accounted for less than a tenth of that expenditure. Many countries introduced some form of price or reimbursement control. The industry lacked the public or political support to resist these changes.

Entering the 1990s, worldwide economic recession reduced cash for provision of healthcare through tax-funded systems (Canada, Italy, Spain and UK); social security supported systems (France, Germany and Japan), as well as employer/privately-funded systems (US). Payers could no longer tolerate spiralling healthcare costs and created incentives for decision-makers to seek better value for money. In Germany in 1993, overall pharmaceutical sales fell by 11 per cent while the four leading generics manufacturers increased their sales between 10 and 63 per cent. Pressure was put on the industry to deliver genuine product innovation rather than '*me too*' drugs.

place was open to products offering minor advantages such as a more convenient dosage form or fewer side effects, but with much the same therapeutic outcome.

There were two important developments in the 1970s. Firstly, the Thalidomide tragedy (where an anti-emetic given for morning sickness caused birth defects) led to much tighter regulatory controls on clinical trials. Secondly, legislation was enacted to set a fixed period on patent protection – typically 20 years from initial filing as a research discovery. This led to the appearance of '*generic*' medicines. Generics have exactly the same active ingredients as the original brand, and compete on price. The impact of generic entry is illustrated by Bristol Myers Squibb's brand Glucophage, a treatment for diabetes, which generated US sales of $2.1bn in 2001. Following loss of the patent in January 2002, brand sales plunged to $69m for the first quarter. Generics legislation had a major impact on the industry, providing incentives for innovation and a race to market. The time during which R&D costs could be recouped was drastically curtailed, putting upward pressure on prices. The introduction of generics, however, was very beneficial for society: valuable medicines became extremely cheap. Indeed, health economists have estimated that the social returns from pharmaceutical R&D exceed that appropriated by firms by at least 50 to 100 per cent. By the end of the 1970s generic entrants and more stringent controls on clinical trials had led to substantial increases in R&D spending.

The pharmaceutical industry is unusual in that in many countries it is subject to a 'monopsony' –

A new type of industry player appeared in the 1980s – small biotechnology start-ups backed by venture capital to exploit the myriad opportunities opened up by molecular biology and genetic engineering. By 2003 there were more than 600 publicly traded *biotechs* worldwide. However, biologicals were more complex to produce than traditional pharmaceuticals, causing a global shortage in production capacity. This drove up prices and often limited biotech applications to low-volume, high-need areas. Although sales doubled in the five years to 2002, at $27bn biologicals contributed only 7 per cent of global market value. Many biotechs originally planned to integrate and perform all functions from research to sales. However, most biotechs lacked the finances to cope with the huge risks involved and by 2003 only three companies had achieved this goal, namely, Amgen, Biogen and Genzyme. Moreover, only 40 out of 1,466 biotech companies in the US were trading profitably. Amgen was the only serious global player, ranking number 17 in terms of sales during 2002. The other leading biotechs (Genentech, Chiron, Genetics Institute) were partly owned by larger firms. Biotechs had thus largely abandoned attempts to market drugs themselves (although

BOX 1 The drug development process

The pharmaceutical industry has long new product lead times, with the period from discovery to marketing authorisation typically taking almost 12 years (Exhibit 1). New product development can be divided into distinct research and development phases. The research phase produces a *new chemical entity* (*NCE*) with the desired characteristics to be an effective drug for a targeted disease process. Development encompasses all of the formulation, toxicology and clinical trial work necessary to meet stringent regulatory requirements for marketing approval.

During all of these phases 'attrition' occurs, as promising agents fail particular hurdles, so most R&D projects never result in a marketed drug. Of those that do, 80 per cent fail to recoup their R&D investment. The cost of developing and commercialising a new drug is now estimated at $500–800 million. When the costs of all the projects that do not reach fruition are considered, it becomes clear that pharmaceutical R&D is a very high stakes game.

Given the enormous risks and considerable investment involved, it is not surprising that pharmaceutical companies compete fiercely to establish and retain *intellectual property* rights. Only by securing a patent that can be defended against imitators can the value of all this R&D be recouped. The patent clock starts from the moment that a promising agent is identified in pre-clinical tests and its chemical structure and synthesis filed with patent offices worldwide. Once the patent application is made public, other companies are likely to try to create improved, patentable versions. Where genuine discoveries or inventions are made, patents can also be obtained for manufacturing method and even mode of administration. All of these supplementary applications can extend patent life and the earnings period for a new drug.

Pre-clinical development involves testing new agents against the target – for example, lowering cholesterol – to select the most promising leads. After further tweaking, these best candidates are evaluated in animal disease models to find the one with the best trade-off between efficacy and tolerability. Finally the lead agent is put through a battery of toxicology tests in animals and if successful put forward for clinical development in humans. Clinical development is usually divided into three phases. Phase I trials determine whether the product is safe to use in humans. Phase II trials aim to select dose and demonstrate efficacy. Phase III trials are conducted versus the best current treatment, with the goal of proving superiority. Typically only 1 in 10 molecules survive from Phase I to launch, with late failures (Phase III) being more costly.

The industry is subjected to rigorous regulatory scrutiny. Government agencies such as the *Food and Drug Administration* (*FDA*) in the USA thoroughly examine all of the data to support the purity, stability, safety, efficacy and tolerability of a new agent. The time taken is governed by legislation and is at least six months. Every regulatory authority is different and while FDA endorsement is very helpful it does not guarantee approval in other countries. Companies must address varied geographic requirements as regulatory authorities wish to ensure that the

they often sought to retain US marketing rights) and instead used the global reach of the research-based multinationals to leverage return on R&D through out-licensing and strategic alliances. As stock market funding dried up,[2] the sector began to consolidate to marry revenue streams with promising pipelines. In the UK, for instance, British

Biotech merged with drug company Vernalis, while Celltech acquired Oxford Glycoscience.

Industry sectors

At the turn of the millennium, prescription-only or *'ethical'* drugs comprised about 80 per cent of the global pharmaceutical market by value and 50 per cent by volume. Ethical products divide into conventional pharmaceuticals and more complex

---

[2] US stockmarket flotations of biotechs fell from 40 in 2000 to only 4 in 2001–2.

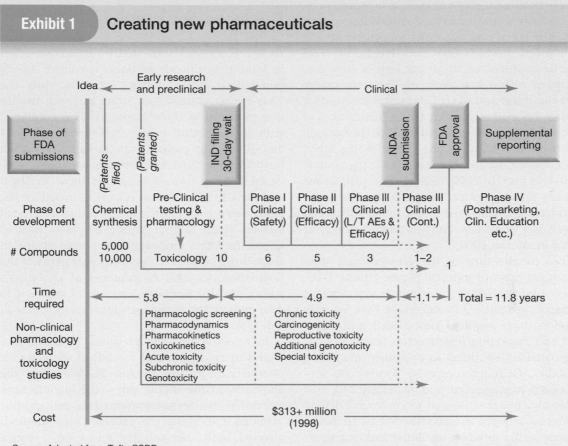

Exhibit 1   Creating new pharmaceuticals

Source: Adapted from Tufts CSDD.

product is suitable for their population – for example, some Japanese people may metabolise the drug differently from Western subjects – and delivers improved health outcomes when compared with the standard of care in their country. Obtaining marketing approval is no longer the end of the road in many countries, as further hurdles must be overcome in demonstrating the value of the new drug to justify its price and/or reimbursement to cost-conscious payers.

'biological' agents and vaccines. The remainder were '*over the counter*' (OTC) medicines, which may be purchased without prescription. Both ethical and OTC medicines may be branded or 'generic'.

The typical cost structure at ethical pharmaceutical companies comprises manufacturing of goods (25 per cent), research and development (12 to 21 per cent), administration (10 per cent), and sales and marketing (25 per cent). The key strategic capabilities at these companies are R&D and sales and marketing, and manufacturing historically

suffered from low utilisation, high fixed costs and low productivity. Growing pressure on margins became an incentive to restructure manufacturing, rationalising the number of production sites and placing them in strategic locations offering tax advantages (e.g. Puerto Rico, Republic of Ireland). Companies also improved supply chain management to release the value trapped in high inventories.

However, manufacturing and distribution efficiency at research-based companies was not comparable with that of generics manufacturers, who competed on price. During the late 1990s, there was a collapse of generics prices in the US and a shakeout to determine cost leadership. In this environment, economies of scale proved decisive and the sector underwent consolidation. As a result the speed and aggression of generic attacks on branded products increased sharply. By 2002 generics captured 65 to 80 per cent of new prescriptions within five weeks of US patent expiry on major drugs and overall accounted for nearly a third of US market volume. Given the number of major global brands with patent expiries looming and markets with untapped potential (e.g. Italy, Spain, France, Japan), the outlook for the generic sector was rosy. In 2002, nine of the top 10 fastest growing pharmaceutical companies were generics manufacturers and predicted compound annual growth rate of 12 per cent was forecast to deliver $30bn in sales in 2004.

Thus by the turn of the century there were four broad types of industry player: ethical, OTC, generic and biotech. Each required very different strategic capabilities. Producers of branded prescription drugs required strong R&D and global sales and marketing infrastructure. Branded OTC drugs demanded direct-to-consumer marketing capability. Generics companies focused on supply chain management and manufacturing cost leadership. Biotechs needed to create and defend *intellectual property* in specialised research fields. Because of the different attributes and cost structures involved, multinationals which owned OTC and generics businesses generally operated them separately, frequently using another company name. Similarly, those that had acquired biotechs normally left them to operate fairly autonomously.

Business environment

As key economies stagnated in 2002, challenges in funding healthcare advances remained. Ageing populations created further pressures, since the 'over-65s' consumed four times as much healthcare per head as those below 65. This combined with more expensive high technology solutions and increasing patient expectations created an unsustainable situation. On the one hand, universal coverage systems (such as those in Spain and the UK) were slow or unable to introduce the latest treatments. On the other, insurance-funded systems (such as that in the US) were able to afford the latest innovations but were unable to share those benefits with an increasing part of the population. In 2002 the number of US citizens without health insurance rose by 5.7 per cent to 43.6 million, the biggest single annual increase in a decade.

In response to these pressures, payers used a wide variety of methods to control spending on pharmaceuticals (see Exhibit 2). Some put the emphasis on the supply side – the manufacturer and distributor. Some emphasised the demand side – the prescriber and the patient. Other methods affected both. No country relied on a single approach. Types of control reflected deep-rooted cultural differences with supply-side measures

---

Exhibit 2 Methods used to control pharmaceutical spending

Controls on suppliers	Mixed effect	Controls to influence demand
Negotiated prices	Partial reimbursement at price negotiated with manufacturer	Patient co-payments*
Average pricing		Treatment guidelines
Reference pricing	Generic substitution	Indicative or fixed budgets
Positive and negative lists		Incentives to prescribe or dispense generics or parallel imports
Constraints on wholesalers and pharmacists		Transfer from prescription-only to OTC

* Where the patient pays some of the drug cost.

favoured by more centralised, less market-oriented economies. The choice of strategy was also affected by the importance or otherwise of the national pharmaceutical industry as a contributor to GDP, balance of trade and employment.

In countries with supply-side controls, negotiating price or reimbursement approval could take as long as six months or a year. In countries with demand-side controls, there were similar delays in achieving market penetration, because of the need to negotiate product inclusion in formularies, or endorsement by bodies such as the *National Institute for Clinical Excellence* (*NICE*) in the UK.

Generics posed a particular threat. Several important markets (Japan, France, Spain, Italy) featured low volume use of generics – no more than 6 per cent. However, generics were being actively encouraged in all EU markets and rapid penetration was anticipated. Computer systems enabled prescriptions to be printed in their generic rather than branded form, enabling the pharmacist to supply the cheapest generic drug.

Pharmaceutical spending controls were designed to reward genuine advances. Price premiums and/or reimbursement levels were based on perceived innovativeness and superiority, penalising 'me too' drugs. As a result, there was a race to market with each new drug class, since only the first to market would benefit. Competition was waged most fiercely at the level of drug class and being late to market with an undifferentiated product was a recipe for failure.

The industry adopted a number of strategic responses to these challenges. Many pharmaceutical companies introduced '*disease management*' initiatives.[3] Another common response was to conduct pharmacoeconomic evaluations, studies that aimed to demonstrate the added value offered by a new drug as a result of improved efficacy, safety, tolerability or ease of use.

Government price controls created another challenge for the industry in the form of 'parallel trade'. The principle of free movement of goods across the Single European Market meant that distributors were free to source drugs in low price markets (Spain, Portugal, France, Italy and Greece) and ship them to high price markets (Germany,

the UK, Sweden and the Netherlands), pocketing the difference. There was minimal benefit to governments or consumers, but a significant loss for the industry. Instead of being ploughed back into R&D, this arbitrage profit went to the parallel importers. Parallel imports were exacerbated when pharmaceutical wholesalers consolidated internationally through cross-border mergers and acquisitions, making it even easier to buy in one country and distribute in another. By 2002, parallel imports had gained 17 per cent of the UK market, 7 per cent of the German market and were estimated to account for €3.5bn of revenues a year across the EU. Furthermore, the enlargement of the European Union was expected to exacerbate parallel trade, as prices in Central and Eastern Europe tended to be low.

Parallel trade was also prevalent in the Far East and there was even a latent problem in the crucial US market given the price differentials with Canada. Canada had one of the toughest environments worldwide for the industry, with stringent and inflexible pricing and reimbursement criteria. In contrast, the US had no formal price controls and price increases were customary. Over time, this led to a wide disparity in prices (best-selling cholesterol-lowering drug Lipitor was $3.20 per pill in the US in 2003, compared with just $1.89 in Canada) that exposed the industry to sensationalist newspaper headlines such as 'Canada's Rx drugs pouring into USA'.[4] Cross-border trade was driven by the rapid rise in medication cost, the 25 per cent of US seniors with no drug coverage, the economic slowdown, the ease of long-distance commerce over the internet and increased awareness of price disparities. By 2003, state governors and Congress representatives were proposing to institutionalise and promote imports, despite opposition from the FDA and the Justice Department. Storefront import pharmacies and drug-sale parties in care homes were appearing all over the US and grass-roots activism was rife. The real threat to the industry was not the actual level of imports ($800m in 2002), but the risk posed to free pricing in the US from the public backlash. FDA commissioner Mark McClellan declared that there was an impending global crisis. The situation where US citizens bore the lion's share of the global cost of pharmaceutical R&D through high prices appeared unsustainable. Either US prices would fall, damaging R&D

---

[3] These involved understanding the goals of the healthcare system in addressing a specific disease. The firm then aligned itself with the healthcare providers, trying to offer an integrated service that improved eventual disease outcomes, positioning its drugs as one part of the solution.

[4] *USA Today*, 7 October 2003.

BOX 2   Globalisation

A number of factors contributed to the globalisation of the pharmaceutical industry. Chief among these was the international convergence of medical science and practice under the influence of modern communications technology and increased travel and information exchange. Well-funded US universities and hospitals generally led their fields, while conferences and specialist seminars in the US were the most prestigious platforms to learn about new discoveries. This may account for the fact that drugs first launched in the US gain far greater global market share and achieve twice the sales of those first launched elsewhere.

Regulatory processes were also undergoing international harmonisation. In Europe the European Medicines Evaluation Agency (EMEA) was established to enable more rapid regulatory approvals across Europe through the 'centralised' procedure, which granted regulatory approval in all member states simultaneously. The creation of EMEA offered great benefits in terms of reduced costs and accelerated time to market for pharmaceutical companies, but also increased risk as more was at stake on one decision. There was also a move towards global harmonisation of standards for drug approval through the International Conference on Harmonisation (ICH).

Further evidence of globalisation could be found in the tripling of the number of blockbuster brands between 1998 and 2003. There were also clear signs that leading corporations were 'globalising'. Most had a presence in all significant markets, with overall sales reflecting the market size of each country. Production sites had a global mandate and were selected by worldwide screening. R&D was sourced from best place worldwide regardless of location, and that often meant the US. In 1990, the industry spent €8bn on research in Europe and €5.3bn in the US. By 2001, the US was receiving €26.4bn of spending compared with €18bn in Europe. GlaxoSmithKline, Europe's biggest drugs company, was being run from Philadelphia, while Novartis, the second largest, announced it was moving its research headquarters to Boston.

In 2003, the leading global industry players all originated from Triad countries – predominantly the US and Europe, as Japanese companies lagged behind. The strong US market enabled US companies to grow faster than their competitors and provided a springboard in achieving global ambitions. Pfizer, Merck and Johnson & Johnson recorded 2002 growth at or above 15 per cent, while Novartis and Roche languished at around 7 per cent. US companies even outdid their rivals in the EU market – of the seven top 20 companies that achieved double-digit growth in 2002, five were US firms. Multinationals from the US and EU also developed presence in Japan through acquisitions and in 2003 occupied four of the top 10 positions, where they were significantly outperforming domestic firms.

investment, or other wealthy countries, such as Germany and Canada, needed to shoulder a fair share of the burden. But with their domestic pharmaceutical industries in decline, there was scant incentive for other governments to change their practices.

Key markets

As described in Box 2, the majority of global pharmaceutical sales originate in the 'Triad' (US, EU and Japan), with ten key countries accounting for over 80 per cent of the global market. The US has been by far the largest pharmaceutical market by volume and value ($192bn in 2002 – half of global sales), with the strongest growth among key markets, contributing 65 per cent of global market growth. In 2002, the US accounted for a staggering 70 per cent of blockbuster sales, compared with only 4 per cent from Japan and 12 per cent from the EU. Projecting out to 2007, the US was predicted to increase its share of the global market, while the shares of Japan and the EU would decline. Non-Triad countries were expected to retain around 11 per cent share between them.

Overall, the world market was set to become even more US-centric, leaving the industry heavily exposed to fluctuations there.

Following regulatory changes in 1997, pharmaceutical companies were permitted to market directly to US consumers. *Direct-to-consumer (DTC)* advertising transformed the marketplace and fuelled rapid sales growth. However, the US operating environment was getting tougher. Managed care, in which plan administrators set cost and reimbursement limits on healthcare services, was also changing market dynamics. In 1990, 63 per cent of prescriptions were paid in cash by patients, but by 2001, 73 per cent were paid by managed care plans. As companies' cost for providing drug benefits to employees increased from 19 to 20 per cent annually, MCOs began to encourage the use of generics through schemes where the consumer paid less if a generic was prescribed and extra for newer drugs. Furthermore, powerful bulk purchasers, such as the Veterans Administration with 6.9 million members, were able to extract prices even lower than those in Canada, so that average US prices paid were actually significantly lower than headline figures in the popular press suggested.

Japan had traditionally been the second largest market for pharmaceuticals, with sales of $47bn in 2002. The Japanese operating environment had historically been very different from that of the US or the EU. This divergence occurred at all levels, from medical practice, healthcare delivery and funding, to regulatory requirements, higher prices, the lack of generics, distribution, and the accepted approach to sales and marketing. Not surprisingly, relatively small domestic companies dominated the market. The Japanese pharmaceutical industry experienced significant environmental turbulence in the 1990s. Following a number of scandals, the system controlling clinical trials and regulatory approvals underwent a major modernisation programme, and many domestic companies were ill equipped to operate to the new standards. The economic recession caused tax revenues to fall, while the cost of treating the world's most rapidly ageing population was rising. This resulted in unprecedented price cuts, changes to healthcare funding and the introduction of stringent price controls. The upshot was very low pharmaceutical market growth of only 1 per cent in 2002.

Europe made up the third part of the Triad, with the top five markets (Germany, France, Italy, UK, Spain) predicted to continue contributing around three quarters of EU sales out to 2007. European markets each had their own unique operating environments but they were generally characterised by strong payer pressures and consequently lower prices than the US or Japan. Combined with slowing economies, these pressures constrained EU market growth to 8 per cent in 2002. Expansion of the EU, however, provided opportunities for growth, especially in Poland and central Europe, but also brought new challenges from generics and low-priced parallel imports.

Although growth prospects for emerging markets were considered modest in 2003, their enormous populations and high levels of unmet need offered significant long-term potential. Many had strengthened patent protection and liberalised equity controls. The pharmaceutical markets in Latin America had proved highly volatile, reflecting underlying economic trends. Nevertheless they had large numbers of wealthy consumers who were able to afford branded drugs.

Pacific Rim countries were becoming more important. Copy products were traditionally a significant issue in these markets, where patent protection was absent or very difficult to police. Pharmaceutical companies focused particularly on China, which had one of the fastest growing pharmaceutical markets. While Chinese herbal medicine remained a core part of healthcare, the use of Western medicines was on the increase, especially in booming coastal cities such as Shanghai.

Although least developed countries were not in a position to offer a significant market opportunity, they did present the industry with important strategic choices in the area of corporate social responsibility which had global ramifications. This is discussed further below.

Innovation

Ethical pharmaceutical companies establish competitive advantage by developing products that are innovative and differentiated, patentable, can be developed rapidly; and marketed globally. Moves away from the pharmaceutical 'core' have been made by various firms in the past, the results of which were mixed at best and usually weakened earnings and stock market performance. Companies with consistently high levels of R&D spending and productivity became industry leaders. For this reason, stock market valuations place as much importance on the R&D 'pipeline' (i.e. the

BOX 3   Genomics

Genomics is the study of human genes and through a joint multinational effort known as the Human Genome Project (HGP) has delivered a complete list, in order, of the chemical 'letters' making up the DNA in human cells, discovering the location and composition of all human genes. But sequencing the genome did not equate to fully understanding the function of the genes. It was essential to understand what genes were actually doing – so-called 'proteomics' – in order to identify new targets for pharmaceutical intervention. The total number of drug targets discovered up to the year 2000 amounted to well under 1,000. Proteomics had the potential to increase this by orders of magnitude, offering immense promise in the search for more effective and less toxic therapies.

The HGP provided only the 'plain vanilla' version of the genome, reflecting one individual's genetic make-up. Variations in genetic make-up (Single Nucleotide Polymorphisms or SNPs) were also of great interest. Understanding genetic susceptibility to disease could deliver improved screening tests and earlier intervention. Furthermore, 'pharmacogenetics' exploited

genetic knowledge to understand why some patient populations benefited more than others from a therapy, or why some experienced specific side effects. A senior R&D executive at GlaxoSmithKline explained that 90 per cent of drugs only work in 30–50 per cent of people, and claimed that 'by eliminating the people that we predict will be non-responders we'll be able to do smaller, faster and cheaper drug trials.'* As a consequence, 'we will have better and better targeted drugs, better and fewer side effects', enthused a CEO.** This was likely to appeal to payers.

Some commentators predicted a dramatic increase in productivity at the early stage of research, and argued that while output would dip in the short term because of increased costs, it would soon take off again. Others believed that the HGP had led to irrational investor exuberance in 1999–2000 and driven biotech valuations to an unsustainable peak.

* Allen Roses of GSK, quoted by the *BBC News*, 8 December 2003.
** Matthew Emmens, CEO of Shire Pharmaceuticals, quoted in *The Guardian*, 15 November 2003.

products in development) as on the currently marketed products.

Basic research is vitally important to probe into the causes of disease and identify new potential targets for pharmaceutical intervention. As well as conducting in-house research, many companies sponsored academic research, although it was becoming much more difficult and expensive to secure intellectual property rights from academia. Companies also sought research alliances with biotechs and *genomics* companies (see Box 3).

The holy grail of pharmaceutical R&D is the *'blockbuster'*. Like 'killer applications' in the software market, blockbuster drugs are genuine advances that achieve rapid, deep market penetration. Because of their superlative market performance, blockbusters often determine the fortunes of individual companies. Glaxo went from being a small player at the beginning of the 1980s to the world number one, with a presence in 50 countries, on the strength of a single drug – Zantac for

stomach ulcers. A blockbuster drug is typically a long-term therapy for a common disease that offers a step change in efficacy or tolerability and is marketed globally. Annual sales must normally exceed $1bn for a drug to earn this accolade.

While blockbusters made immense contributions to company fortunes and provided tremendous returns on R&D investment, they were few and far between. In 1998, only 40 products achieved over $1bn sales worldwide, while the average for all drugs was put at $186m. However, blockbusters rapidly increased in importance and by 2002 this number had tripled. Seeking a blockbuster was clearly a high risk R&D strategy, but was fast becoming the only game in town, exposing an already high-stakes industry to even greater levels of risk. The 1995 industry pipeline had 450 drugs with average estimated peak year sales of $260m, while the 2001 pipeline had 209 with average estimated sales of $634m. However, over-dependence on blockbuster sales rendered companies highly vulnerable to generic competition at patent expiry. Between 2003 and 2008, 20 blockbuster drugs were due to lose patent protection. By 2002 global exposure to generics was already around $40bn, of which over 60 per cent affected the top eight pharmaceutical companies. So even if the risky R&D pipeline delivered a blockbuster, blockbusters vastly exacerbated the volatility of the corporate sales line.

Unfortunately for the industry, development times were lengthening and R&D productivity was arguably in decline. The time taken for drugs to move from laboratory to market increased by nearly seven years from 1960 to 2000. Most of this increase occurred in the clinical development phase. The average number of trials and number of patients for each new drug application increased enormously, from 26 trials involving 1,500 patients in 1980, to more than 65 trials involving over 4,000 patients by 1995. As a consequence clinical trials became, by far, the most expensive element of the development process.

As clinical trials became ever more complex and costly, there was a sharp rise in R&D expenditure. The average fully capitalised resource cost (including research on abandoned drugs) to develop a new drug was estimated to be $1.4bn in 2003. The corresponding figure in 1987 was $231m and would have grown to under $500m by 2003 at the pace of general inflation. R&D spending by the major corporations reached $35bn in 2001, double the figure for 1997 and nearly triple the 1992 investment. But despite increasing average R&D spend from 11 to 12 per cent of annual sales to 16 or even 17 per cent, pharmaceutical companies had not much more to show for it. The launch of 24 genuinely new drugs in the US in 2001 was considered poor and the 2002 figure dropped further to 17, the lowest for 20 years. The European Medicines Evaluation Agency received only 31 applications, down from 58 in 2001. While this could have been a natural consequence of blockbuster focus, half of the applications were for treatment of diseases with a limited commercial market.

Pharmaceutical companies endeavoured to be both creative and efficient. Some argued that the secret of successful R&D lay in organisational competencies such as team-working, knowledge management and close relationships with external opinion leaders. Others emphasised 'lean and flexible' operations and outsourcing of all but core competencies. Some large companies attempted to rekindle innovation and productivity by reorganising their R&D so as to create smaller and more nimble units – like internal biotechs. Others sought external innovation, entering alliances where technology was emerging, and only acquiring in-house capability once the technology was proven. For example, Aventis prided itself on managing a complex web of alliances with more than 300 universities and biotechs. In such companies, the management of alliances itself became a key competency. Not surprisingly, biotechs were contributing an increasing share of the industry's new products – a record 35 per cent in 2001.

The organisational infrastructure required to deliver a new drug application had become large and complex. However, because of high attrition in new drug development, company pipelines could often be 'lumpy'. Many companies concluded that maintaining a high fixed-cost clinical development capacity did not make sense. Instead, they outsourced some clinical development to *Contract Research Organisations* (*CROs*). Typically it would cost more to conduct a trial *via* a CRO, but capacity could be switched on or off at will.

As the needs of patients with common chronic diseases became increasingly well satisfied by existing treatments, companies sought new research arenas. Some chose to pursue areas of high unmet need, such as cancer and Alzheimer's disease. Others focused on so-called 'lifestyle' conditions such as impotence, obesity and hair loss. It was not surprising that with drug targets becoming more challenging, increasing time to market and tougher regulatory hurdles, fewer new products reached the market.

Some questioned whether the levels of R&D investment could be sustained. For example, in 2002 there were 340 cancer drugs in development. With pressures on payers growing it seemed improbable that such enormous aggregate R&D investment could ever be recouped. Overall the industry arguably faced substantial R&D over-capacity. Financially-tight biotech firms offered acquisition opportunities for cash-rich pharmaceutical firms. In 2003 Novartis acquired a 51 per cent stake in Idenix, a biotech that had been forced to abandon plans to float. Licensing deals also provided an important source of promising new products. Two-thirds of the industry's total pipeline resided in small companies with 67 per cent available for licensing. Alliances, however, required some sacrifice of sales margins and late stage deals (i.e. those where the product was close to reaching the market) were rare, costly and competitive.

Sales and marketing

Sales and marketing capability became an increasingly important source of competitive advantage. A company that developed a strong global franchise with its customers could maximise return on its in-house products and was in a good position to attract the best in-licensing candidates. For example Bristol-Myers Squibb built the world's leading cancer business based entirely on in-licensed compounds.

The traditional focus of drug marketing was the personal '*detail*' in which a sales representative (rep) discussed the merits of a drug in a face-to-face meeting with a doctor and often handed over free samples. Pharmaceutical promotion was subject to industry self-regulation. For example, in the UK, sales reps had to pass an examination testing medical knowledge within two years of going on the road. In some countries, government regulatory agencies checked that promotional claims were consistent with the data.

Payer efforts to influence prescribing in the 1990s gave rise to a belief that large salesforces were becoming obsolete and could be replaced by small numbers of specialist payer liaison salespeople. However, companies that also continued to increase their conventional salesforce size and resulting 'share of voice', such as Pfizer, found that it paid off handsomely. Experience taught firms that the more sales reps they deployed, the higher their sales. As a result the number in the US almost tripled from 1995 to 2002, reaching around 90,000, while the number of doctors rose only 20 per cent to 850,000. However, doctors had less time to see sales reps with the average call lasting less than five minutes. More reps selling fewer drugs resulted in returns from every dollar invested in marketing falling from $22 in sales in 1998 to $17 by 2001. Although cutting salesforce numbers would have made sense overall, firms were caught in a classic 'prisoners dilemma' – no one was willing to call off the arms race.

Given the resulting squeeze on margins, maximising salesforce effectiveness became crucial. Pharmaceutical companies became more sophisticated in the tools they gave reps and in the targeting of their selling efforts. Novel communication channels such as e-detailing, where the doctor heard a presentation over a computer link, suited busy doctors' schedules and saved costs.

There were important differences in the marketing of 'primary care' and 'specialist' products. Office-based practitioners generally prescribed primary care products, whereas treatment with specialist products was typically initiated in hospitals. Sales volume, marketing spend and skills required differed for the two segments. Product-led muscle marketing was the name of the game in the primary care sector, while specialist products involved targeted relationship marketing. A small number of companies built their strategies around under-served specialised customer groups, aiming to satisfy their needs on multiple dimensions. In other words, they developed a franchise. An example was Elan Corporation, which built a profitable niche business by targeting the needs of the neurology market.

In 2002, firms spent nearly $9.4bn on marketing in the US. A key factor that drove up costs was the growth in DTC advertising, where spending reached $2.7bn by 2002. Companies recognised that well-informed patients were prepared to ask for drugs by name, creating a powerful new 'pull' strategy. DTC could be very costly because of the vast target audience and expensive television advertising. It also required new marketing skills – both Pfizer and Novartis employed consumer marketers to smarten up their DTC promotion and branding. DTC also rendered drug advertising much more visible and risked creating a backlash against the industry.

Successful drug launches correlated strongly with product superiority, high prices and high promotional spend. An interesting trend began to emerge where drugs that were second to market were more successful than the original pathfinder drug. Evidently, it proved relatively easy to identify flaws in the first drug and deliver a follow-up positioned as 'best in class' or targeted at specific sub-populations. Exhibit 3 illustrates that the period of *market exclusivity* for first in class drugs was also shrinking fast.

The term 'high compression marketing' was coined to describe the approach adopted by leading companies to launch global brands. This involved simultaneous worldwide launches, global branding, and heavy investment in promotion and share of voice at time of launch. High compression marketing aimed to create a rapid take-off curve that would maximise return by creating higher peak year sales earlier in the product life cycle. A good example was the launch of Celebrex in 1999, which netted $1bn sales in the first nine months. Truly global branding was vital, with consistent brand name, messages, and visuals used around the

Exhibit 3   Number of years of market exclusivity enjoyed by selected drugs, 1965–99

Innovative drug/launch year

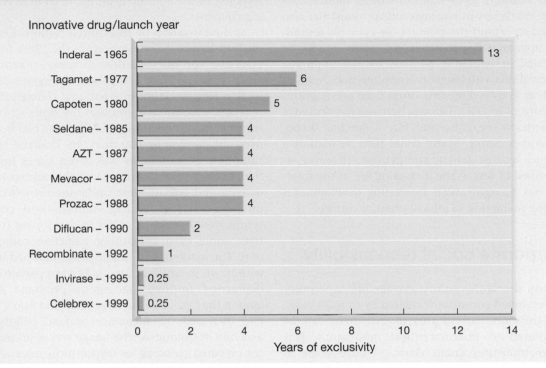

Years of exclusivity

BOX 4   Consumers and the net

Increasingly vocal, well-informed and demanding consumers seemed inevitable. As the convergence of telephone, information technology and television accelerated, it was difficult to envisage how a ban on DTC in the EU could be maintained. Patients with internet access could obtain information on new products directly themselves. It was easy for non-US citizens to access US websites, and information on new drugs reached consumers via both company and independent web sites and through distribution of press releases to PR services. Health was one of the top two reasons for people to conduct searches on the internet. In the US, up to 75 per cent of those that searched for health-related information were likely to discuss that information with their healthcare providers (44 per cent on average in the EU).

This trend was likely to increase patient demand for new effective, better-tolerated therapies, particularly in litigious countries such as the US. However, the internet also had the potential to raise awareness of international price disparities. Consumers were even beginning to purchase across borders, but with no guarantee that the drugs they received had been stored and shipped correctly and were not adulterated, contaminated, or counterfeit. The US FDA estimated that fake drugs accounted for over 10 per cent of the global medicine market, generating annual sales of more than $32bn, with fake Viagra being an internet best-seller. More worrying, it was easy to purchase addictive painkillers and other potentially harmful drugs over the internet, and rogue websites even offered miracle cures for cancer and AIDS. The pace of change was outstripping the capabilities and powers of regulators.

world for maximum impact. Blockbusters launched between 1998 and 2003 typically reached $2bn in sales within 3.5 years, at least twice as fast as historical norms.

In addition to seeking an earlier, higher sales peak, marketers in pharmaceutical companies also aimed to extend the product life cycle. As a product approached patent expiry, effort might be invested in switching patients to new improved formulations with longer patent protection. Another strategy involved moving drugs from prescription-only status to OTC. The aim here was to encourage patients to recognise and buy a familiar brand. Consumer brand loyalty could then be used as a defence against generic competition. However, as described in Box 4, the increasing use of the internet has brought about interesting developments for the marketing of ethical pharmaceuticals.

Corporate social responsibility

During the 20th century average life expectancy in developed countries increased by over 20 years. A significant part of this improvement can be attributed to pharmaceutical innovation. Few other industries could claim to have done as much for the well being of mankind. So how did an industry that had delivered such enormous benefits acquire such a tarnished image and become an easy target for unpredictable government intervention?

One problem is that the market for pharmaceutical innovation has the characteristics of what economists describe as a 'public good' – i.e. expensive to produce but inexpensive to reproduce. The manufacturing cost of drugs is usually tiny compared with the amortised cost of R&D that led to the discovery. Setting prices that attempt to recoup R&D therefore looks like corporate greed in comparison with the very low prices that can be charged by generic manufacturers.

Some companies in the US and Europe acted in ways that damaged the industry's overall reputation. Sales details in particular were under increasing scrutiny. In Italy in 2003, 40 company staff and 30 doctors were under investigation for *comparaggio* – the prescribing of drugs in exchange for gifts such as computers and lavish trips. Many EU countries restricted the value of such gifts and voluntary industry codes of conduct were increasingly augmented with formal regulation. Similar problems emerged in the US: Pharmaceutical firms paid over $2bn in fines between 2000 and 2003 in cases brought by the US Justice Department, principally for pricing and marketing crimes. The industry also faced growing condemnation of its response to the enormous unmet need in developing countries.

An investigation by the United Nations Centre on Transnational Corporations in the 1980s found evidence for questionable industry practices.[5] Twenty years later campaigning organisations such as Health Action International claimed those practices were still rife and that the types of drugs consumed did not correspond with the real health needs of developing countries. In Thailand, consumption of antibiotics was seven times higher than necessary, while drugs to combat tuberculosis, malaria and leprosy were under-used. Ineffective products such as tonics, vitamins and cough syrups were firms' best sellers in developing countries, some even containing addictive components. The marketing of unsafe drugs that had been withdrawn in developed markets was a particularly depressing finding. Dangerous products were among the best sellers in Argentina and Brazil and had increased the incidence of fatal childhood anaemia in Colombia. The image was of an industry prepared to break its own ethical rules when not properly policed on the fringes of the global economy.

Lacking adequate sanitation, nutrition and primary health care facilities for much of their population, developing countries relied on pharmaceuticals as the first line of defence against a wide range of infectious and parasitic diseases. Although for many diseases affecting millions of people, effective drugs and vaccines already existed, often their cost was beyond the means of the people who needed them. It was argued that leading pharmaceutical companies could make a significant contribution such as reallocation of R&D efforts in favour of major tropical diseases, the sale of low-priced essential drugs and technology transfer. According to a report by the International Federation of Pharmaceutical Manufacturers Associations (IFPMA), some global firms were rising to the challenge.[6] IFPMA claimed

---

[5] United Nations Centre on Transnational Corporations (UNCTC), *Transnational Corporations in the Pharmaceutical Industry of Developing Countries*, UNCTC, New York, 1984.
[6] *Building Healthier Societies Through Partnerships*, IFPMA, August 2003.

that in sheer size, spending by pharmaceutical companies rivalled that of the World Health Organisation (WHO) and programmes benefited tens of millions of people in over a hundred countries. Examples included Pfizer's commitment to provide its antifungal medicine Diflucan free of charge and without time limits to people in the least developed countries living with HIV/AIDS and with cryptococcal meningitis and/or oesophageal candidiasis.

Questions around the purpose and ethics of the global pharmaceutical industry gained a high public profile as disputes over access to modern antiretroviral therapies for AIDS patients reached crisis point and threatened to jeopardise broader world trade agreements. AIDS was killing 3 to 4 million people annually, 2.3 million of them in Africa. The humanitarian efforts of major corporations were inadequate in the face of this immense need and according to campaigners, often came with unacceptable strings attached. Countries began taking matters into their own hands. Brazil halved the number of people dying of AIDS by providing patented anti-retroviral drugs to 150,000 people free of charge. It either made cheap, generic versions of the drugs itself, or obtained them cheaply from the patent-holder by threatening to do so. However, multinationals worried that supplying drugs free or at very low prices would flood higher priced markets with parallel imports. When the South African government proposed legislation to allow generic imports, a coalition of 39 firms took legal action. Given the tragic AIDS epidemic and the saintly figure of Nelson Mandela, this wasn't one of the best examples of corporate public relations.

Between 2002 and 2003 the CEO of GlaxoSmithKline (GSK), Jean Paul Garnier, helped negotiate the industry out of the South African court case and established clear principles of operation for GSK. The company would supply critical drugs to poor countries on a no-loss, no-profit basis. As for investing in research into 'not-for-profit' diseases, Garnier declared:

> We'll go after it. It's just that we've got to be street smart about the funding . . . There's plenty of money . . . to fund those initiatives and we've never been turned down. I talk to Bill Gates all the time.[7]

By early 2003 other companies were under pressure to follow GSK's example. A group of powerful investors stated publicly that the industry risked becoming the 'new tobacco' unless it cleaned up its act. Firms were accused of failing to prioritise cures for diseases prevalent in poor countries while concentrating on lucrative 'lifestyle cures' for prosperous ones. The group, with combined investments totalling $940bn, said if the industry did not shape up, its reputation would be destroyed and future profits put at risk. 'The statement came from a concern about the impact on shareholder value in the long term,' commented one industry analyst.[8]

At the Doha trade talks in 2001, ministers stated that patents could be broken in cases of national emergency, such as AIDS or tuberculosis epidemics. Intellectual property rights should not prevent efforts to 'promote access to medicines for all'. The industry negotiated safeguards so that generic drugs would be labelled, packaged, shaped or embossed differently from the patented original, and importation could only be 'in good faith to protect public health' and not in order to 'pursue industrial or commercial-policy objectives'. However, corporations feared a broader threat to the hard-won intellectual property at the heart of their business model. Garnier portrayed the battle as an 'economic war' in which unscrupulous generics companies were using AIDS as a 'Trojan horse' to undermine the patent system. His concern was that those companies sought to pirate hard-won pharmaceutical discoveries and supply them to countries such as China and India, accounting for around 80 per cent of the world's population. 'If the patents go away in those countries it's the end of the pharmaceutical industry as we know it.'[9] The agreement valiantly attempted to balance the interests of the global industry with the public-health needs of the world's poor, but it remained to be seen whether it offered a workable solution.

Strategic responses

While the pharmaceutical market remained relatively fragmented, with very large numbers of domestic and regional players, it was consolidating at the global level. No company held more than a 7.5 per cent market share in 2002, but Pfizer's acquisition of Pharmacia took this over 10 per cent in 2003. The top 10 players accounted for nearly

[7] *The Guardian*, 18 February 2003.

[8] *BBC News*, 24 March 2003.
[9] *The Guardian*, 18 February 2003.

Exhibit 4	Leading global pharmaceutical companies, 1997 and 2002

(Top worldwide sales, retail market share and major drug mergers in the late 1990s)

1997		2002			
Company	Total sales ($bn)*	Company	Total sales ($bn)*	Share within global retail	Sales growth (2001 to 2002)
Glaxo Wellcome[1] (UK)	11.6	Pfizer[5] (US)	29.5	7.3%	11.4%
Merck (US)	11.4	GlaxoSmithKline[6] (UK)	27.9	7.0%	7.0%
Novartis[2] (CH)	11.0	Merck (US)	20.0	5.0%	6.6%
Bristol-Myers Squibb (US)	9.3	Johnson & Johnson (US)	18.6	4.6%	16.1%
Johnson & Johnson (US)	8.7	AstraZeneca[4] (UK/Swe)	18.1	4.5%	8.6%
American Home Products (US)	8.4	Novartis (CH)	16.6	4.1%	12.8%
Pfizer (US)	8.4	Aventis[3] (Ger/Fra)	14.3	3.6%	10.0%
Roche (CH)	8.0	Bristol-Myers Squibb (US)	14.3	3.6%	–7.4%
SmithKline Beecham (UK)	7.4	Roche (CH)	12.5	3.1%	6.5%
Hoechst (Ger)	7.4	Pharmacia (US)[7]	12.2	3.0%	8.1%

Notes:

Number	Created	Originating companies	
1	1995	Glaxo (UK)	Wellcome (UK)
2	1996	Sandoz (CH)	Ciba-Geigy (CH)
3	1998	Hoescht (Ger)	Rhône-Poulenc (Fra)
4	1998	Astra (Swe)	Zeneca (UK)
5	2000	Warner-Lambert (US)	Pfizer (US)
6	2000	Glaxo Wellcome (UK)	SmithKline Beecham (UK)
7	2000	Monsanto (US)	Pharmacia (US)

* $US1 = approx. €0.83.

Sources: The Economist, 21 November 1998; *Financial Times,* 6 April 2000, and own estimates.

half of global pharmaceutical sales and significantly only two blockbuster drugs were held outside the top 20 corporations. A strong trend was for previously diversified conglomerates to divest their non-healthcare businesses (e.g. agrochemicals), to focus purely on high-margin pharmaceuticals.

Although the overall market appeared fragmented, this disguised the true level of concentration. Since both R&D and commercial franchises divided naturally along therapeutic lines, competition was fought at the level of therapeutic area and most intensely within specific product classes. The market leader within a franchise might hold a share as high as 28 per cent (AstraZeneca in Gastroenterology & Metabolism in 2002) and 20 per cent was not uncommon. The more successful companies led key franchises and competed in product classes that were large, fast-growing or had high unmet need. In 2002, the top 10 classes grew at 37 per cent compared with overall market growth of 8 per cent.

There was a strong belief that companies needed critical mass in R&D and global marketing presence in order to compete effectively. However, there were notable exceptions such as Sanofi-Synthelabo from France, and US-based Amgen, which ranked at 17 in terms of sales but grew at over 20 per cent in 2002.

Exhibit 4 shows how the industry response to the need for critical mass had been a wave of mergers and previously unheard-of hostile acquisitions leading to amalgamation.

Mergers had resulted in the formation of Novartis, Aventis, AstraZeneca and GlaxoSmithKline, while Pfizer acquired Monsanto (Warner-Lambert) and then Pharmacia. Exhibit 4 also shows how Pfizer overtook Merck, which followed an organic growth strategy throughout the 1990s. Leading companies were under pressure to consider further mergers after Pfizer's acquisition of Pharmacia. Eliminating duplicated costs remained one surefire way to keep profits relatively healthy. But there was little conclusive evidence that mergers enhanced revenue or R&D productivity. Successful mergers were based on strategic purpose and fit, rather than exacerbating weaknesses, and managing the process effectively had itself become a strategic capability.

A key rationale for mergers and acquisitions was to combine a company with a strong pipeline but weak sales and marketing with its converse. For example, the acquisition of Warner-Lambert gave Pfizer full marketing rights to the cholesterol-lowering agent Lipitor, which Pfizer then built into the world's best-selling drug.

Another argument for increasing size was to improve R&D productivity, since it rested at least partly on 'technology platforms'. Companies had to invest in expensive new capabilities (such as High Throughput Screening) to keep pace with the industry leaders in speed to market. The larger the total R&D programme, the greater the number of individual projects that could benefit from the new capability, and amortise these costs. Pfizer's acquisition of Pharmacia gave the new entity an R&D budget of nearly $7bn, 50 per cent greater than its nearest rival.

Others argued that mergers actually reduced R&D productivity: more management layers resulted in greater bureaucracy, less freedom to innovate and a reduced research output. The success of biotechs in drug discovery suggested creativity was greater in small R&D organisations. Portfolio management could also be problematic in merged companies. Cutting too many projects in the search for blockbusters could exacerbate risk. Cutting too few meant under-resourcing potential winners and risked an over-stretched and unfocused organisation. In one analysis, the median number of projects at merged firms fell from 85 in both pre-merger companies, to 56 by three years post-merger. Companies were either removing duplication and focusing on winners, or becoming less productive. Definitive evidence was years away.

Another argument for increasing size was to invest in larger sales-forces to secure greater 'share of voice' and to acquire global reach. Pfizer's acquisition of Pharmacia took the new entity from no. 4 in Europe and no. 3 in Japan to no. 1 across the Triad. Companies which lacked presence in key markets were obliged to make use of licensing deals, sharing the profit with another company. A strong global marketing capability was also vital in attracting the best in-licensing candidates and

co-marketing deals, to strengthen the product pipeline. Supporters of organic growth claimed that marketing success came from combining the right skills, resources and competencies rather than sheer sales force size, pointing to the success of smaller 'franchise' players.

Some advocates of further industry consolidation emphasised that its purpose should be to create dominance in just a few therapeutic franchises, with non-core activities being sold off, making these huge corporations more manageable, and focusing R&D and sales and marketing efforts. Others proposed that the R&D and commercial functions could operate autonomously. The commercial organisation would develop a product portfolio based on therapeutic franchises, using clearly defined business relationships with external R&D partners. In turn, this would free in-house R&D to discover and to develop innovations beyond the commercial portfolio strategy.

An intriguing response to environmental change was adopted by managers at Roche, who positioned themselves as operating a new 'integrated healthcare' business model. Roche had a strong diagnostics division, owned much of the relevant intellectual property, and Roche's managers portrayed it as a complex business with high barriers to entry. Their strategic vision was to move from seller of instruments and reagents to a health information provider, offering value through better targeting of treatments, convenience and 'peace of mind'. Roche claimed to be the only company embracing these principles, having both requisite experience, and all the necessary tools to lead the paradigm shift in healthcare offered by genomics and diagnostics.

Summary

Many large pharmaceuticals companies are facing their toughest outlook in a decade. The industry has made a tremendous contribution to human well being, yet is vilified in the media and targeted by governments in their efforts to curb spiralling healthcare costs. R&D and sales and marketing costs have risen sharply, while the product life cycle has shortened. Product approval, pricing and promotion are subject to increasingly onerous regulation, yet free trade allows wholesalers to extract a large chunk of value from the chain without adding anything back. Companies must balance shareholder return against the huge unmet need of developing nations. Exciting opportunities do still exist – more educated consumers, advances in genomics, regulatory harmonisation and of course unmet medical need. Industry consolidation is driven by the dominant belief that size is what counts, although a few players prefer to build focused franchises or offer integrated healthcare solutions. Ultimately, meaningful innovation is what matters most, but it is not clear that a business formula based on inventing and selling blockbuster drugs can continue to sustain double-digit growth rates.

Chaos in the skies – the airline industry pre- and post-9/11

Gary J. Stockport

The case provides an opportunity to analyse the Airline Industry both pre- and post-9/11. It shows how one major event in the business environment can reshape many aspects in both the macro and competitive environment of an industry. In turn this requires a reshaping of strategies for most of the individual companies in the industry in order to cope with this new environment. It also provides an opportunity for students to recommend how airlines might better plan for, as well as react to, disruptive events such as 9/11 happening in the future.

● ● ●

This is a true story from the many stories of 11 September 2001. It was a typically routine early morning flight home. United flight 890 had left Narita Japan several hours earlier, and the sun would be coming up any minute. Captain Jim Hosking was looking forward to getting home to see his wife in LA. Suddenly a message from the cockpit teleprinter came in from the US Federal Aviation Authority (FAA). Such messages were routine, advising of bad weather or maintenance requirements. However, this message was different and it read:

UA890 NRTLAX –

–MESSAGE FROM CHIDD–

THERE HAS BEEN A TERRORIST ATTACK AGAINST UAL AND AAL AIRCRAFT. WE ARE AT HIGH ALERT. WE ARE ADVD[a] THERE MAY BE ADDTL[b] HIGHJACKINGS IN PROGRESS.

SHUT DOWN ALL ACCESS TO FLIGHT DECK.

UNABLE TO ELABORATE FURTHER.

[a] ADVD – Advised
[b] ADDTL – Additional
Source: USA Today, 12 August 2002, p. 1A.[1]

Ironically, it was the United Nations (UN) International Day of Peace. At 8:46 am, American Airlines flight 11 (a fully fuelled Boeing 767) crashed at a speed of roughly 490 miles per hour into the north side of the northern tower of the World Trade Centre (WTC) in New York, approximately between floors 94 and 98. This was the start of one of the most deadly terrorist attacks in the history of the world occurring concurrently in New York City, Washington DC and near Pittsburgh, all in the US. Four passenger jets were hijacked and three were deliberately crashed into the WTC and the Pentagon. Moments before the second crash, a passenger on Flight 175 called his father from the plane, reporting that hijackers were stabbing flight attendants in order to force the crew to open the cockpit doors. At 9:02:54 am, United Airlines flight 175 (another fully fuelled Boeing 767) crashed with a speed of about 590 miles per hour into the south side of the southern tower, banked between floors 78 and 84. Parts of the plane continued through the building at its east and north sides, falling to the ground some six blocks away.

At 9:59:04 am, the south tower of the WTC collapsed and then at 10:28:31 am, the north tower

---

[1] A. Levin, M. Adams and B. Morrison, 'Four hours of fear: decision-making in a crisis', *USA Today*, 12 August 2002, p. 1A.

---

collapsed. New York was the scene of a nightmare as people on fire jumped in terror from the towers just before the buildings collapsed. At the Pentagon, part of the building was destroyed in the ensuing fire. The fourth hijacked plane crashed in a Pennsylvania field after passengers and crew tried to retake control of the plane from hijackers. Casualties were in the thousands: 265 on the planes, 2,650 people at the WTC, including 343 firefighters who had rushed into the towers, and 125 at the Pentagon.

At 9:24 am, President George W. Bush had been interrupted with the news of the second crash as he participated in a class with Florida schoolchildren. He waited out the lesson, and then rushed into another classroom commandeered by the Secret Service. Within minutes he made a short statement, calling the developments 'a national tragedy', and was hurried aboard Air Force One.

At 9:40 am, US airspace was cleared and no civilian aircraft were allowed to take off. The US military around the world was immediately put on *Def Con Delta* – its highest state of alert. Aircraft carriers and guided missile destroyers moved to locations near New York City and Washington to provide air defence and National Guards across the US were mobilised. US financial markets were closed and trading did not resume until 18 September, a week after the terrorist attacks. President Bush was protected by fighter jets as he and his closest advisers flew on *Air Force One* from Florida to Washington. On the ground, at Barksdale Air Force base, the President was protected by US Air Force servicemen in full combat gear, armed with M-16 rifles. His motorcade was additionally protected by a military humvee vehicle armed with a machine gun turret. The White House, Congress, Treasury, and other departments were shut down and evacuated. Landmark buildings across the US were also evacuated.

Immediately, international flights to and from North America as well as all domestic US and Canadian flights were paralysed. Under orders from the FAA, all 5,000 airports across the country halted all outbound flights while keeping their runways open for incoming aircraft. NavCanada, the Canadian air traffic control service, had been ordered to stop all departures until further notice. Aircraft crossing the Pacific and Atlantic en route to the US were re-directed into Canadian airports. Most passengers were not immediately allowed off the aircraft. Generally, air travel around the world was severely disrupted. British Airways (BA) diverted 21 UK outbound aircraft either back to the UK or towards Canada or Bermuda.

At the time of the hijackings, the US accounted for around 40 per cent of the world air travel market, with about 37,500 flights a day departing from US airports on both domestic and international flights. The groundings lasted three days until 14 September. Every day that the industry was totally grounded, it lost over US$300m (≈ €250m).[2] During this time, military and medical flights continued.

The timing could have not been worse. Year 2000 had seen the dot-com bubble burst and stock markets collapsing in sympathy around the world. The New York Stock Exchange, which remained closed for the longest period since the 1930s Depression, reopened for business on 18 September. As expected, sectors such as airlines and insurance were quickly decimated. Continental Airlines led the large US carriers down, with a 49 per cent drop in their share price. It had been seen as the most financially healthy of the US carriers until the attack, but it subsequently announced that it could not make US$70m in aircraft financing payments. AMR, the operator of American Airlines, was down 39 per cent while UAL, the owner of United Airlines, was down by 43 per cent. The world's third largest airline, Delta, fell 46 per cent. Southwest Airlines, the world's leading low-cost carrier, fell 34 per cent. Smaller players were especially hard hit and America West fell 65 per cent amid fears for its financial survival. The damage went beyond US financial markets and Swissair shares fell more than 40 per cent since 11 September. British Airways (BA) was down 33 per cent from its level before the US attacks.

Global airline industry before 9/11

Fundamental economics

Air travel is essentially a commodity with service being the only differentiator. Once a flight takes off, a seat or place has been consumed and those not sold are lost forever. In economic terms, these considerations pointed to the achievement of a breakeven load factor as crucial for survival. After breakeven had been achieved, the marginal cost of

---

[2] J. Oberstar, (19 September 2001), *T&I Committee Considers Airline Assistance*, [Online], Congressman Oberstar Press Release, Available from: <http://www.house.gov/oberstar/airasst.htm> [15 October 2003].

carrying an extra customer in a designated flight was very low.

There had been significant structural changes within the global airline industry for many decades. For example, since the 1960s, there had been significant ongoing advances in the efficiency of jet engines that allowed much longer routes to be served. As newer and larger aircraft were introduced, airlines were forced to compete at an ever-increasing pace. Several of the contributing factors to structural change included: globalisation; deregulation; consolidation; technology improvements including aircraft and communications, and the high costs associated with the Full Service Carrier (FSC) business model.

Demand

The demand for air transport was a derived demand for some final activity such as business or leisure. Passengers fly because they wanted to go some place, and freight or mail was moved to a certain destination. The many drivers for the increased demand had been: the rise of world GDP; increasing world trade and investment; the liberalisation of markets, as well as the growth in the number of retirees. Between 1990 and 2000, the global number of tourist passengers increased from about 450 million to 700 million, with a large proportion of this rise linked to an increase in the number of retirees. Around 55 per cent of passenger air travel was for leisure, which was a function of income and wealth.

Cost factors

There were variations in the cost structure of different airlines that could be partially explained by factors such as geography, the market in terms of the length of haul or by currency exchange rates. Furthermore, variations also related to the protection afforded, and consequently, perhaps, the complacency of management as well as the power of labour unions. Airline costs had been rising quite rapidly through 2000. Fuel prices rose more than 50 per cent from 1999 to 2000. Typically, labour costs accounted for between 25 per cent and 40 per cent of an airline's revenue and 75 per cent of its controllable costs. Labour prices had been rising at a rate substantially above inflation. Large US domestic trunk carriers were 50 per cent more efficient with considerable cost advantages compared to European airlines. However, despite these efficiencies, the US airline industry only earned an average 1–2 per cent net profit compared to the US industry average of 5 per cent as a whole.

Returns (yields – RPKs)

Despite air travel increasing since deregulation, with US passenger travel increasing by over 160 per cent from approximately 250 million in 1978 to almost 660 million in 2000, and the continuous drive towards achieving better margins through cost cutting, there had been a gradual and steady decline in the real value of airline yields throughout the US as measured by RPKs (the average revenue per passenger kilometre). Since 1970, airline yields had fallen at a rate of about 2.5 per cent per annum.

Globally, in the short-haul market, the highest 5 per cent of fare payers accounted for 8 per cent of airline revenues in 1992 and by 1998 this had grown to around 18 per cent of revenues. Many travellers also needed hotels, car rental and other auxiliary services that may or may not have been supplied by the airline. During the 1970s, a number of airlines broadened their service offerings to encompass this whole experience. Nevertheless, by the 1990s many had moved back to their core business and had divested or outsourced their non-core activities.

Full service carriers (FSCs)

Typically, the business model for a Full Service Carrier (FSC) (also known as a networked carrier) focused on networks and product quality, and had an emphasis upon providing service to as many cities as possible, with high levels of frequency and interconnectivity. Examples of FSCs included American Airlines, Singapore Airlines and Qantas. FSCs typically had a variety of aircraft and support systems to support the complex itineraries within and between airlines and destinations. Another feature of this connectivity included the hub-and-spoke airport network structure.

Extra service features such as in-flight catering, entertainment, leg-room and loyalty programmes provided differentiation. This differentiation was discriminated by the class of travel and this class of travel through market price segmentation relied upon restrictive ticket conditions such as time of purchase, limited travel times and purchasing channels such as travel agents. This segmentation allowed airlines to leverage some passengers'

Exhibit 1	Cost advantages of low cost carriers on short haul routes

Cost item	Cost per seat reduction (as % discount from the operating cost per seat of a conventional scheduled carrier)
Operating advantages	
Higher seating density	−16%
Higher aircraft utilisation	−3%
Lower flight and cabin crew salaries/expenses	−3%
Use cheaper secondary airports	−6%
Outsourcing maintenance/single aircraft type	−2%
Product/service features	
Minimal station costs and out-sourced handling	−10%
No free in-flight catering	−6%
Marketing differences	
No agents commissions*	−8%
Reduced sales/reservations costs	−3%
Other advantages	
Smaller administration costs	−2%
Total cost reduction	−41%

* Assumes 100% direct sales and none through agents.

Source: R. Doganis, *The Airline Business in the 21st Century*, Routledge, London, 2001.

willingness to pay a premium for better classes such as business class or urgent or unexpected travel.

The FSC model entailed high costs, many of which were fixed, and relied on economies of network size and traffic density to bring unit costs down. High fixed costs, with a need for complex pricing in addition to the highly income elastic nature of air travel, had led FSC profits to become highly cyclical. For example, BA went from record profits in 1998 to only a £5m profit in 2000. Other factors such as changes in fuel prices and foreign exchange rates also significantly influenced profits.

Even when FSCs did have market oligopolies, few destination pairs supported more than two carriers. Economies of scale and density essentially through the ability to attract a higher share of business travel had forced FSCs that lacked capital and financial depth out of most routes. Passengers wanted convenience such as the interlinking of 'smooth' connections between airports or terminals. The FSC model provided passengers with high interconnectivity within and between airlines with relatively low passenger transaction costs. This offered passengers requiring a complex or flexible itinerary high value.

Low cost carriers (LCCs)

Long before September 11, structural changes within the industry had seen the emergence of a new business model for airlines, the Low Cost Carriers (LCCs). The LCCs focused upon the management of costs (Exhibit 1), and were successfully eroding the FSC's market share with the changes in patterns of passenger demand with what represented a value for money fare, providing simple point-to-point itineraries.

The growth of LCCs had changed the nature of airline competition. The most common features of the LCC business model included:

- simple point-to-point services with no or limited interconnectivity in short-haul routes;
- fewer in-flight or on-ground amenities, leading to lower costs (especially as a result of having more seats on the aircraft through the space saving);
- single class operations with greater seat density and lower costs per seat;
- uniform fleet, leading to lower operating and maintenance costs;

- in the US and Europe, utilising secondary, less congested and cheaper, airports;
- lower labour costs (compared with the FSC model);
- high aircraft utilisation;
- lower cost distribution channels, especially the internet; and
- a different and simpler form of price discrimination based upon the time of purchase.

The US-based LCC, Southwest Airlines, had 29 years of continuous profit up to September 11, and offered a successful model for other LCCs such as Westjet (Canadian) and Ryanair (EU). In 2002, Ryanair unveiled record pre-tax profits of €172m, up 40 per cent from 2001. LCCs had been able to win significant market share from even the most efficient FSCs and outperform them on the critical performance measures of profitability and market capitalisation. It was suggested that this performance by the LCCs has led to inbred complacency. According to Pearse Reynolds, General Manager of Corporate Travel in the UK and Ireland at American Express,

> Many (LCCs) are starting to behave like traditional airlines, and that's where they are facing problems. Instead of flying to secondary airports, which have a quicker turnaround time and lower costs, and scheduling flights at odd hours, many are now serving primary destinations and so have lower profitability because their aeroplanes stay on the ground for longer.[3]

Fragmentation

The global airline industry was fragmented primarily from the constraints of national and international regulations and politics as well as public ownership. These limiting effects were usually in the form of landing rights and associated competitive restraints. Generally, even larger FSC airlines were only able to achieve a regional dominance at best.

Open markets

Since the late 1970s, the deregulation of the air passenger transport industry in both the US and globally had brought about major structural changes within the industry. Most notable was the 1978 US *Open Markets* policy. The *Open Markets* policy effectively removed barriers to entry and enabled new competitors to enter the industry. Deregulation brought the freedom to choose routes, set prices in accordance with market demand and increased competition from new entrants.

Market concentration soon followed deregulation as many FSC carriers had merged to gain the benefits of economies of scale and scope in order to remain competitive. In the US, concentration had led to the emergence of mega-carriers such as American Airlines and United Airlines. The top eight airlines accounted for 90 per cent of the US market in 1990, whereas 15 airlines had around 90 per cent in 1984. However, the increased competition led to lower prices and this had eroded the bottom line profitability of most airline companies. Consequently, airlines were forced to focus upon reducing costs in order to arrest the price increases and maintain margins.

Hub-and-spoke

Starting in the US, the cost cutting measures led to the rationalisation of many route structures. Additional efforts to increase efficiency saw the formation of the hub-and-spoke networks develop during the 1980s, whereby the aircraft traffic feed was brought to a central place (the hub) from other areas within the vicinity of the hub (the spokes). This inconvenienced some passengers as they had to change aircraft at the hub. However, for most passengers there were many benefits such as single tickets and lower prices. With the cheaper ticket prices as a trade-off for the inconvenience, the hub-and-spoke networks gained acceptance from most travellers.

The economics of the emerging hub-and-spoke systems were powerful. A hub with 20 spokes could theoretically provide a one-stop service to 190 different city-pairs and could service these markets with fewer planes, fewer staff and more frequent service. This allowed the airlines to fully maximise their resources and resulted in substantial savings for the incumbent airlines. Some of these hubs developed over time into fortress hubs i.e. a particular carrier or alliance dominated the hubs. For example, the Washington Dulles airport hub was dominated by US Airways/United Airlines to monopoly levels i.e. above 70 per cent of passenger traffic. The creation of fortress hubs that integrated

---

[3] C. Hayward, 'Uneasy jets', *Financial Management*, March 2003 pp. 16–19.

Exhibit 2	OneWorld™, Star™ and SkyTeam™ as of 2000	

Star™	OneWorld™	SkyTeam™
Combined revenues: US$69.3bn Combined profits: US$2.0bn Aircraft in fleet: 2002	Combined revenues: US$49.1bn Combined profits: US$2.2bn Aircraft in fleet: 1481	Combined revenues: US$31.0bn Combined profits: US$0.8bn Aircraft in fleet: 1047
Air Canada Air New Zealand ANA Ansett Austrian Airlines BMI Lauda Lufthansa Mexicana SAS Singapore Airlines Thai Tyrolean United Varig	Aer Lingus American Airlines British Airways Cathay Pacific Finnair Iberia LanChile Qantas	AeroMexico Air France Alitalia CSA Czech Delta Korean Air

Source: www.oneworldalliance.com, www.star-alliance.com, www.skyteam.com, www.atwonline.com

both domestic and international routes resulted in increased international competitiveness, as the incumbents were able to leverage feeds to international operations.

Alliances

Airlines gained economies of scope by forming alliances with other airlines that utilised such strategies as code sharing, block spacing and franchising. Under code sharing, an airline offered services on another airline under its own flight codes. A derivative of code sharing was block spacing, which was an agreement whereby one airline allocated a certain amount of seats on its own flights to another airline, who could then sell the allocated seats through their own marketing and distribution systems. Franchising occurred when an airline sold the rights to use its name and image. All three types of alliances allowed airlines to earn revenues without the need to own and operate aircraft in a particular region, and conversely shielded them from unprofitable operations if they undertook them alone. Furthermore, marketing advantages could be leveraged by all the partners.

Internationally, the renegotiation of bilateral agreements led to more freedom and ultimately to the rise of alliances that had global reach. Alliances such as OneWorld, Star Alliance and SkyTeam linked many large airlines around the world with, for example, common frequent flyer benefits, lounge access and code-shared flights (Exhibit 2).

Some airline predictions before 9/11

In 2001, before 9/11, analysts were predicting that the US airline industry would lose some US$2.5bn because of the slowing economy combined with the surprising large decline in business travel. Globally in June 2001, business travel declined 41 per cent from its levels in 2000, with an overall 11 per cent reduction in ticket purchases compared to 2000. Customer price sensitivity was increasing and there was a steady shift from business and first-class services to economy fares. Instead of paying top dollar for the most convenient but expensive flights available on the major carriers, many business travellers started behaving like vacationers through, for example: purchasing cheaper tickets in advance; flying discount airlines, as well as searching websites for deals. They also started to use their cars more often for shorter trips.

Global airline industry after 9/11

Demand

In the first four days after September 11, US domestic airline bookings fell by 74 per cent and bookings in the rest of the world were down 19 per cent. In addition to the temporary but complete shutdown of the commercial aviation system, the attacks caused many travellers to reduce or avoid air travel altogether as they were wary of the increased personal risk associated with flying. The longer queues and check-in times at major airports had increased passenger door-to-door travel time and influenced the not-to-fly decision. This resulted in some passengers seeking alternatives such as: video conferencing; driving for distances under 500 miles; and using high-speed rail where available.

9/11 had resulted in both a negative transitory shock of over a 30 per cent reduction in passengers that dissipated roughly five months after the attack, and a persistent negative demand shock amounting to roughly 7–8 per cent of pre-September 11 demand.

Cost factors

In the US, many large FSC carriers focused upon dramatic cost-cutting programmes and staff cost reductions were the main focus (Exhibit 3). United Airlines and US Airways sought relief by filing for Chapter 11 bankruptcy. United Airlines continued to trade under bankruptcy provisions but still lost money in spite of reducing employees from over 100,000 to less than 70,000 after September 11. America's bankruptcy code allowed it to continue operating even though it stopped servicing its debts. This code, in effect, allowed defunct airlines to price flights at marginal cost and created unfair competition. United's network coverage had also been reduced by 24 per cent since 9/11 but despite this, in 2003, United still suffered from the highest costs and lowest productivity within the US airline industry.

American had also shed over 30,000 jobs to 2003, and decreased operating expenses by over 3.8 per cent or US$804m. The cost savings implemented from late 2001 and 2002 drove this. American had identified that it needed to further reduce annual operating costs by US$4bn to remain viable but had only been able to identify US$2bn in additional cost reductions through a number of initiatives. These included: scheduling efficiencies; reducing hub peaks; fleet homogenisation; streamlined customer interaction; distribution modifications; in-flight product changes; operational changes; and headquarters/administration efficiencies.

For passengers that flew in the aftermath of the terrorist attacks, the new realities of civil aviation meant that there were other types of cost that now had to be incurred. For example, the new check-in time for international flights had increased to three hours from the previous two hours.

The stiffened security measures around the world also led to higher operating costs for air traffic systems. At US airports, next to every metal

| Exhibit 3 | Airline industry layoffs after September 11 |

Company	Announced layoffs	Comment
AA	20,000	20% schedule reduction
America West	2,000	20% schedule reduction
BA	7,000	10% reduction of flying time through frequency and route cutbacks
Boeing	20,000 to 30,000	Layoffs by year-end 2002
Continental	12,000	20% schedule reduction
UAL	20,000	20% schedule reduction
US Air	11,000	23% reduction of available seat-miles
Virgin Atlantic	1,200	20% schedule reduction

Source: 'Airlines slash workforces', *Air Transport World*, October 2001.

detector station stood two military policemen in addition to the airport personnel. After September 11, there was also a general global consensus to adopt an assortment of initiatives such as: strengthening cockpit doors; increasing the flow of sensitive criminal and national security information from Federal Agencies to airlines; updating airline and airport employee identification credentials; conducting detailed employee background checks; deploying federal air marshals on certain routes; modifying airline computer software to better identify passengers who could pose a security risk; and restricting access to parked aircraft and secure areas within airport terminals. US policymakers viewed such initiatives as necessary, but by no means sufficient, for ensuring public safety.

During late 2001, President Bush signed into law the Aviation and Transportation Security Act that resulted in the appointment of 28,000 security screeners as federal employees. This legislation was funded with a statutory US$2.50 per passenger security tax, per flight leg, to help pay for additional security measures. By September 2003, the US Air Transport Association estimated that the additional security cost to the industry as a result of 9/11 was about US$4.15bn. Of this total, US$1.5bn came from the controversial new security tax levied on tickets.

Following 9/11, insurers withdrew liability coverage for war and terrorist attacks. New legislation had to be introduced in the US and Europe and governments had to assume some responsibility for war risk claims. When insurers re-entered the market, the premiums rose between 200–500 per cent. Although insurance costs previously accounted for some 1–2 per cent of operating costs, this increased to 5–10 per cent following 9/11. Airlines were forced to pass these costs onto passengers.

In September 2003, a US District Court judge ruled that the hijacking of commercial jets was the kind of 'foreseeable risk' that the airline industry should have guarded against. This gave the families of the people who had died in the terrorist attacks of September 11 the go-ahead to sue the airline industry for negligence based upon the fact that they had been negligent in failing to carry out the proper security checks that might have prevented the hijackings. Boeing, it was argued, could have designed a cockpit door that hijackers could not break into. Potentially the costs for this could run into several US$bns in claims.

Returns (yields – RPKs)

Following 9/11, record losses were posted (Exhibit 4). In Q3-2001, US Air reported losses of US$766m, the biggest quarterly loss in its 61-year history. The results included the US$331m the airline had received from the federal government to compensate

Exhibit 4 **US airline earnings in Q3-2001**

Southwest 151
Northwest 19
Continental 3
−32 America West
−259 Delta
−414 AMR
−766 US Air
−1,159 UAL

US$m

Source: www.businessweek.com

for losses resulting from 9/11. For the same quarter, AMR posted losses of US$414m. However, the worst quarterly loss ever in the history of the industry was posted by UAL which had already been in difficulties prior to the terrorist attacks. UAL posted losses of US$1.16bn just for Q3-2001.[4] UAL CEO James Goodwin warned employees that the company 'will perish sometime next year [in 2002]'[5] if drastic measures were not taken. But the US aviation market had the worst month-on-month drop of its history, as revenue-passenger-miles dropped 32 per cent in September 2001 versus September 2000. For the same period, load factors for US airlines decreased from 70 to 59 per cent.

On 21 September, President Bush and Congress passed US$15bn in emergency assistance to help the US aviation industry. The US Air Transportation Safety and System Stabilization Act provided airlines with US$10bn in federal loan guarantees and credits, plus an additional US$5bn in reimbursements for direct losses. By mid 2003, the US airline industry had lost US$18bn since the 9/11 attacks, despite the US$15bn bailout. Against advice from the White House that felt the industry deserved only limited aid of around US$900m and that such support would reduce the airlines' resolve to solve their own problems, Congress voted to award the airlines more than US$3bn in special wartime subsidies.

Within the highly fragmented European market, Sabena made history by becoming the first European flag carrier to file for bankruptcy which threatened the loss of thousands of jobs. Sabena flights were grounded amid chaotic scenes at Brussels airport and remained suspended for days. The European Commission (EC) told member governments they could only come to the aid of their crisis-struck airlines to the extent of helping out with the immediate and direct consequences for the industry of the 9/11 attacks. They could not use the crisis as an excuse to bail out already failing national airlines. European carriers had a collective loss of more than US$3bn for 2001.

Full service carriers (FSCs)

Travel patterns changed after 9/11. For example, the transatlantic market collapsed as Britons

decided to holiday closer to home. Traffic to North America from London's three main airports fell by more than a third whilst traffic to other faraway destinations served by Gatwick, Heathrow and Stansted fell by 14 per cent. Airlines such as BA and Virgin Atlantic, which had based most of their profit on long-haul flights, felt the pinch. The corporate market had also suffered as businesses quickly cut back on travel spending. As mentioned earlier, FSCs tended to use business class to subsidise the rest of their operations but the net effect of 9/11 for the FSCs was that people wanted to travel business class but they did not want to pay the price differentials compared with economy class.

Low cost carriers (LCCs)

Within the US, there was a persistent and pronounced fall of around 44 per cent in the short-haul air travel segment (less than 500 miles) in June 2002 compared to 2001. This was attributed in part to the increased 'hassle factor' associated with increased security procedures (notwithstanding the increased perception of the flying risk) which added to the total travel time. Nevertheless, LCCs such as Southwest Airlines were still able to generate a profit. How the airlines have fared has largely depended upon how they quickly responded to 9/11. According to Toby Nichol, Corporate Communications Manager at EasyJet, a UK-based LCC,

> The aviation world reacted in two different ways: Traditional airlines started crying into their balance sheets and put up fares to deal with the predicted drop in revenue. Low cost airlines reacted in the opposite way. They launched, independently of each other, a 'let's get flying again' campaign and cheap seats abounded in the last quarter of 2001. People were still prepared to travel, but didn't want to pay as much as they had before.[6]

In Europe, some LCCs also expanded their markets to capture some of the elements of business travel. For example, package holiday segments including weekend breaks as well as longer distance 5–7 hour point-to-point routes at lower prices (compared with their former 1–2 hour services). This consequently led to dramatic LCC passenger growth rates. For example, Ryanair reported a 37 per cent

[4] 'UAL posts record net loss, also sees 4th-qtr loss', *Reuters*, 1 November 2001.
[5] www.chicagotribune.com, October 2001.
[6] Ibid.

increase in passengers in 2002, against the overall generally slow recovery or declining passenger travel for the FSCs.

Alliances

September 11 had also adversely affected alliances. For instance, United Airlines played a pivotal role in the Star Alliance, a group of 15 airlines that shared reservations information and some revenue, jointly marketed products and services, and redeemed one another's frequent-flier miles. As the only US carrier in the alliance that included Air Canada, Lufthansa, Singapore Airlines and Varig, amongst others, United's ability to 'funnel' customers to its foreign partners was crucial and that ability had been curtailed as United had scaled back routes following the attacks.

Thinking ahead

In 2003, the global airline industry had an annual turnover in excess of US$3.5 trillion with 1.83bn passengers flying nearly 3.3 trillion RPKs. The global industry directly employed some 1.77m people and almost 18,000 aircraft including freighters were in service.

9/11 had been a major disruptive event within the industry that some airlines felt had been impossible to forecast. However, others within the airline industry felt differently and argued that future success may lie in the ability of the airlines to properly assess the probability of future shocks occurring as well as being able to react quickly and effectively to them. Developing future strategy for an airline was probably about strategic thinking and planning for ongoing chaos in the skies.

Amazon.com – from start-up to 2004

Gary J. Stockport

This case analyses the changes in Amazon.com from its early first-mover advantage through to the technology bubble crash in 2000, the introduction of a cost discipline, and its eventual emergence into what seems to be a profitable company. The case highlights the strategic thinking behind adopting a long-term approach to developing an e-commerce business model that incorporated substantial growth, global expansion and an ever-widening range of products and services.

• • •

Introduction

The CEO of Amazon.com, Jeff Bezos found himself in a unique position in the closing months of 2003. The company he founded in 1995 was finally making a profit, and although the amount of the profit was only modest, seven of the last eight quarters had been profitable. Sales and profits were expected to reach record levels in the fourth quarter of 2003 as Amazon.com maintained a strategy emphasis of widening the reach within its business model by expansion and customer innovation.

In 2003, Amazon.com was one of the most recognised brands in the world and was the number one global online service. The company had six websites serving over 32 million customers that were located in 150 countries. It had an associate programme with 900,000 members linking up with Amazon.com through the internet or by putting the company's content on their own websites, and it had unique patented software technology driving its delivery of products and services.

Since 1995, online commerce had established itself as a legitimate commerce vehicle with turnover by 2003 exceeding $93.1bn (≈ €77bn) in online spending and a further $137.6bn spent offline after first seeking information online. The United Nations forecasted worldwide spending at $22 trillion by 2006 (UN Ecommerce Report 2002) and there were several reasons behind this phenomenal growth rate. New customers come online every year as connection rates to the internet grow and economies develop. Existing internet users become more confident of

Photo: Amazon.co.uk

This case was written by Professor Gary J. Stockport and MBA student, Mark Ivory, at the Graduate School of Management, University of Western Australia, Perth, Australia. It is intended as a basis for class discussion and not as an illustration of either good or bad management practice. The authors would like to acknowledge David Street, MBA student, University of Cape Town for his work on earlier published Amazon.com case studies. © Gary J. Stockport, 2004. Not to be reproduced or quoted without permission.

transacting over the internet as security and safety systems are improved. Also, existing online businesses develop new products and categories and get better at displaying and presenting these, creating more choice and convenience for online consumers.

A central tenet of Amazon.com's strategy, therefore, had been customer-focused innovation designed to improve the convenience of the online shopping experience. These had included offering the world's biggest collection of goods and services where customers can find and buy anything they want online. Amazon.com lists millions of products and services in a vast array of categories. Importantly, filtering this choice, finding products, services and information content as well as providing transaction safety for customers had been driven through technology development. Jeff Bezos argues:

> By building new technologies ourselves, we get to offer a better customer experience for millions of people. Does that give us an advantage? Absolutely [But] you have to continue to innovate. This is something that has to be refreshed every day, every week, every year.
>
> (*BW Online*, 25 August 2003)

As 2003 drew to a close and Jeff Bezos' vision was turning into reality there were a number of strategic issue questions that he had to think about. For example:

- Is the Amazon.com business model the right model looking ahead five or more years?
- Should they continue to try to be all things to all people?
- How can they continue to constantly innovate and enhance the customer experience?
- Is the logical end game scenario being the Wal-Mart of the internet?

The founder – Jeff Bezos

At the age of 14, Bezos, the stepson of a petroleum engineer, admitted to wanting to become an astronaut or a physicist, or something that would allow him to use cutting-edge technology. During his high school years he founded his first venture, DREAM Institute, which was a summer school programme aimed at stimulating creative thinking in youngsters.

By age 30, Jeff Bezos, the Princeton summa cum laude graduate with a bachelor degree in elec-

trical engineering and computer science, was the youngest senior vice-president of D.E. Shaw, running a Wall Street hedge fund. While working at Shaw, Bezos came up with the statistic that the electronic world, known as the World Wide Web, would grow at the incredible rate of 2,300 per cent monthly. Bezos, stunned at these growth figures felt driven to act quickly saying:

> . . . I decided that when I was eighty I wouldn't regret quitting a Wall Street job when I was thirty, but when I was eighty I might really regret missing this great opportunity . . .
>
> (quoted in Saunders, 1999, p. 8)

After quitting his job, Bezos drove his wife, MacKenzie, and their dog across the US in a Chevy Blazer that his stepfather had donated, arriving in Seattle on 5 July 1994. Bezos had already selected books as his preferred product due to their low price point and the size of the global market estimated at over $80bn (Dessauer, 1997). He believed web-based technology would provide customers with a larger range of titles within the nine key segments (see Exhibit 1), and also through better organisation and presentation.

Seattle was the logical choice because it was close to Ingram Books, the largest US book distributor, and it had access to computer software talent. The state of Washington also had a more favourable sales tax climate. Over the next 12 months, whilst operating from the garage of his rented home, Bezos, his wife, and three others established relationships with shippers and wholesalers, developing the software and raising money. The system went live with an online store in July 1995.

Early start-up – 1995 and 1996

Bezos believed the power of the internet lay in continuous communication and word of mouth, which made branding even more important. As a result, he chose to name his site after the world's largest river, believing Amazon.com would become the biggest bookstore in the world. In 1995 Amazon.com had no significant online rivals and although Barnes and Noble had a 14 per cent market share of traditional retail bookstores, they had no online presence. Once launched, it took less than a year for Amazon.com to be recognised as the Web's largest and best online bookstore with over one million titles.

Exhibit 1 **US book market segment expenditures in 1996**

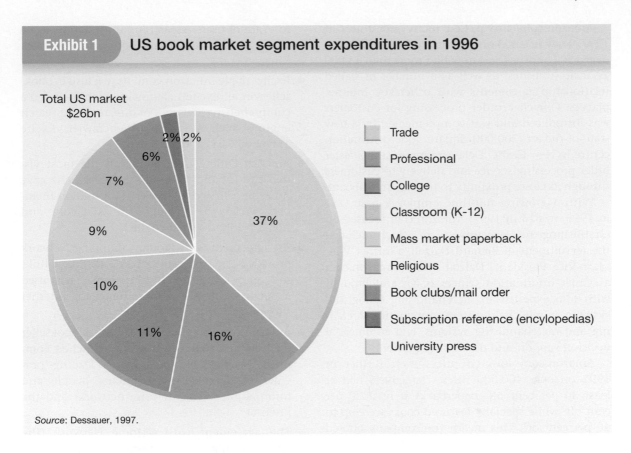

Total US market
$26bn

- Trade
- Professional
- College
- Classroom (K-12)
- Mass market paperback
- Religious
- Book clubs/mail order
- Subscription reference (encylopedias)
- University press

Source: Dessauer, 1997.

Despite the rapid growth of the business, the first few months found Bezos doing the manual work, loading and unloading packages in the back of his Blazer and delivering them to the post office himself. Unable to raise critical funds needed to grow from his existing contacts in New York's money market, Bezos relied on private investment of $1.2m and Silicon Valley funding of a further $8m.

From the outset, Amazon.com provided a powerful search facility through a series of customer initiatives that included:

- a Personal Notification Service consisting of an e-mail notification when a book you want comes out in paperback or when your favourite author releases another book;
- a recommendations section exceeding 20 categories;
- an awards section where books that have won various prizes are listed;
- an Associate Programme where other sites can link to Amazon.com where they sell selections from Amazon.com's database and receive a commission for each sale.

Whilst large numbers of physical bookstores were launching their own websites as marketing extensions of their retail outlets, no large competitors existed during these years and few retail sites on the internet had recouped their start-up costs. This included Amazon.com and Bezos warned investors in the prospectus and in subsequent financial reports each year that they needed to be in for the long term (Amazon.com Prospectus and Annual Report, 1997). Analysts also warned of a highly volatile sector where strategic plans and business models were constantly being revised.

From early growth to IPO – 1997

The Initial Public Offering (IPO) comprised three million Amazon.com shares that raised $50 million which enabled a more aggressive expansion of the business. This was important because the first-mover advantage that Amazon.com had been able to exploit so far was now being met with increasing competition, particularly from Barnes and Noble who went online in February 1997, supporting their 431 retail superstores.

Amazon.com also passed many milestones in 1997. They reached one million new customers in over 150 countries and now had more than 15,000 associate websites, as well as a number of signed relationship agreements with other key internet players. One-click order processing for customers was introduced and was complemented by a new state-of-the-art 200,000 square foot distribution centre in New Castle, Delaware, promising a faster order processing service and delivery to customers through its closer proximity to the eastern seaboard.

With a growing full-time employee base (151 in 1996, to 614 in 1997) Amazon.com focused on establishing their executive team, which included the recruitment of Richard Dalzell, a former Wal-Mart Vice President. Dalzell joined Amazon.com as Chief Information Officer (CIO) and brought with him expertise in merchandising & logistics systems, supply chain systems, international retailing and merchandising systems, and commercial decision support and data mining systems.

Amazon.com lowered prices even further in 1997 on over 400,000 titles. Hardcovers had at least 30 per cent off, paperbacks at least 20 per cent off, while specially featured books were up to 40 per cent off. This meant the company offered the lowest book prices anywhere in the world, online or off. Additional discounts were also available on all audio books as well as calendars in all categories. These price reductions encouraged more repeat purchasing online as cumulative customer accounts grew to over 1.5 million at year end, a growth of over eight-fold from 180,000 customer accounts at 31 December 1996.

Amazon.com's editorial ability and technological development enabled new and unique features to be launched during 1997, which included:

- a state-of-the-art Recommendations Centre, including customer-to-customer recommendations for those with similar tastes;

- 22 subject browsing areas;

- An innovative Gift Centre augmenting its powerful recommendations centre.

Extensive promotional relationships with emerging internet players reinforced Amazon.com's momentum as the leading online bookseller through the generation of substantial brand awareness and customer flow for the business. Some of these are explained below:

- Yahoo.com (the world's largest internet navigational guide) provided a seamless transition

for Yahoo! users researching information to be able to purchase relevant books directly from Amazon.com;

- Excite made Amazon.com its exclusive book-seller on all Excite's channels which included a comprehensive network of directory and search engines such as Excite, Webcrawler, Excite Travel by City, and Magellan;

- America Online (AOL.com) was the most visited site on the web, and an agreement gave Amazon.com access to over eight million members worldwide through the AOL.com and AOL's NetFind search engines;

- An agreement with Prodigy Shopping Network provided Amazon.com access and direct links to Prodigy's large and loyal customers that used a database of over 20,000 items for internet shopping;

- Amazon.com became the exclusive bookseller on Netscape Netcentre's newly launched commerce section. Netscape was a leading provider of open software, linking people and information over enterprise networks and the internet;

- The agreement with @Home Network (the leader in high-speed internet services) made Amazon.com the premier bookseller throughout the @Home service;

- Amazon.com was incorporated throughout GeoCities 39 themed communities, offering its members and visitors new book features and services. GeoCities was the world's largest and fastest growing community on the Internet.

Amazon.com also completed a US$75m credit facility providing the company with substantially increased resources to execute its long-term strategy. This was aimed at enhancing Amazon.com's flexibility and it allowed them to pursue their goal of extending their market position.

Fast growth – 1998

By the end of 1998, Amazon.com had served a cumulative 6.2 million customers, exceeded the cumulative US$750m revenue level, had more than 60,000 members in their Associate Programme, launched music, video and gift stores in the US, and expanded operations into the UK and Germany. Sales grew from US$148m in 1997 to US$609m and new customer growth was complemented with repeat customer orders that grew to 64 per cent of sales.

Staff increases from 614 in December 1997 to around 2,100 in December 1998 included the strengthening of the management team with the appointment of Jimmy Wright who joined as Vice President, Chief Logistics Officer. A former Wal-Mart senior manager, Jimmy Wright had more than 25 years of experience in logistics management. He took over the responsibility for all global supply-chain activities at Amazon.com, including product purchasing, distribution centres and shipping.

New product rollouts continued with the introduction of *Amazon.com Advantage* that increased the visibility and sales of titles from independent publishers by ensuring their books appeared more often and more prominently throughout Amazon.com's catalogue of titles. *Amazon.com Kids* was also launched, which became the most comprehensive resource for children's and young adult books on the World Wide Web. The expansion programme also included acquisitions and strategic relationships with other dominant internet players, reinforcing Amazon.com's number one position. Some of these relationships included:

- An agreement with Intuit meant Amazon.com was promoted on the desktop within select Quicken software. Intuit, a financial software and web-based services company, developed and marketed Quicken, the leading personal software; TurboTax, the best-selling tax preparation software; and QuickBooks, the most popular small business accounting software.

- During 1998, Amazon.com linked up with Yahoo!'s globally branded network of world properties including web guides in Japan, Korea, Canada, Australia and New Zealand, France, Germany, UK and Ireland, Denmark, Sweden, Norway and Italy. It also included language-based websites, *Yahoo! Chinese* and *Yahoo! En Espanol*, as well as an English-language site based in Singapore, *Yahoo In Asia*. This gave Amazon.com the capacity to reach a huge worldwide audience.

Amazon.com also expanded by acquiring *Bookpages* (one of the largest online bookstores in the UK), and *Telebook* (Germany's no. 1 online bookstore) was acquired to support expansion into the European marketplace. The sites provided a vast selection, guaranteed safety of transactions, unparalleled convenience, and electronic gift certificates for worry-free gift giving.

Amazon.de (Germany) featured 335,000 titles from German publishers, fast and easy access to 374,000 US titles, swift delivery, as well as an array of recommendation features to better serve book buyers, including instant recommendations. German editors were used to develop reviews and recommendations of German-titled books. Amazon.co.uk carried a complete catalogue of 1.2 million UK titles in print, fast and easy access to 200,000 US titles, and speedy delivery. UK editors provided recommendations and reviews.

Internet Movie Database (www.imdb.com) was also acquired. Launched in 1990, it offered a comprehensive repository for movie and television information on the internet and would support Amazon.com's eventual entry into online video sales.

Planetall and Junglee were acquired for e-commerce. Planetall had just under 1.5 million members and provided a unique web-based address book, calendar and reminder service. Junglee was the leading provider of advanced web-based virtual database technology assisting shoppers to find millions of products on the internet.

New distribution and customer service centres were opened in the UK and Germany, and a 323,000 square feet property was leased in Fernley, Nevada for a mechanised distribution centre. The Fernley centre more than doubled Amazon.com's distribution capacity and it was hoped would offer additional improvements in delivery times to its customers.

1998 also began the first of many product expansions with the launch of Amazon's hugely successful music store, offering over 200,000 CDs of which 42,000 were classical. The CDs were priced with a 40 per cent discount and the selection represented some 25 times more CDs than a typical retail store. The venture achieved number one status in its first full quarter of launch. Video and Gifts were added in November with Video achieving number one status in only six weeks.

The growing product lines caused inventories to rise from US$9m at the beginning of the year to US$30m by year-end, enabling improved product availability and improved product cost through direct purchasing from manufacturers. The economies of scale and scope of the online business model was changing the nature of retailing and the company received top honours in the prestigious Computerworld Smithsonian Award competition, taking first place in Business and Related Services.

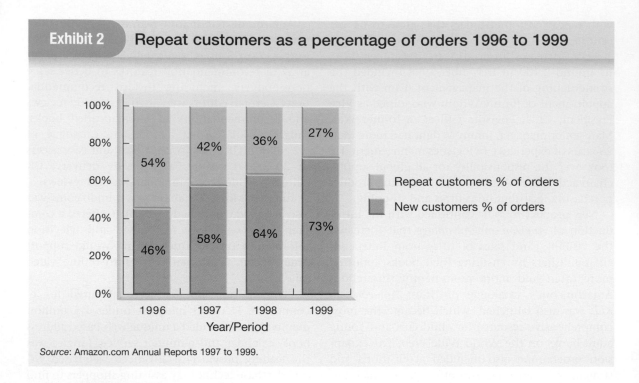

| Exhibit 2 | Repeat customers as a percentage of orders 1996 to 1999 |

Source: Amazon.com Annual Reports 1997 to 1999.

Ever faster growth – 1999

By 1999, the company had built a leading global brand with cumulative customer accounts exceeding 17 million in over 150 countries and repeat customer business representing 73 per cent of orders (see Exhibit 2). Repeat business was linked to improved customer experience through the ease of one-click purchasing and as a consequence of the expanded and diversified product range. This assisted in helping to develop the brand and dispelling concerns about a lack of internet customer loyalty because competitors were only one click away.

The company continued to build on its management strength, naming Warren C. Jenson as its Senior Vice President and Chief Financial Officer (CFO). Jenson had been CFO at Delta Airlines and before that, CFO of NBC. The position of Vice President-General Manager of Operations was awarded to Jeffrey A. Wilke, formerly Vice President and General Manager of AlliedSignal's Pharmaceutical Fine Chemicals unit. Wilke had extensive experience in multiple distribution centre management in the US, Europe and Asia. Also, Joseph Galli Jr was named President and Chief Operating Officer (COO) after a distinguished career building the resurgence in Black and Decker's fortunes. Galli Jr was elected onto Amazon.com's Board of Directors the same year but resigned from the Board in 2000 citing personal reasons.

New products during 1999 included toys, games and a full electronics store featuring a range of popular products and brands. Amazon.com also launched a range of home improvement products as well as *Amazon.com Advantage* for video where customers had access to hard-to-find books, CDs and videos. Another innovation during this year was the introduction of *zShops* and Auctions allowing any individual or business to access Amazon.com's 13 million experienced online shoppers. With the launch of *zShops*, Amazon.com introduced Amazon.com Payments, which allowed individuals to pay for purchases with credit cards using Amazon.com's 1-Click payment feature.

Auctions allowed customers to discover and buy anything online with innovative and time saving features such as Bid-Click[SM] for hassle-free bidding. To enhance customer safety, the Amazon.com Auctions Guarantee covers purchases of up to US$250 in the event that a buyer did not receive what a seller promised. Other product innovations included:

● *Amazon.com Cards* which consisted of a free electronic greeting-card service. Cards could be sent by visiting www.amazon.com and clicking on the e-cards tab;

● *Amazon.com Anywhere*, a wireless e-commerce service that allowed customers to shop and check the status of auction items when they were away from their desktop;

- *Wish List*, an online gift registry which became the no. 1 request in the 1998 vacation season and had one of the fastest adoption rates for any Amazon.com feature;

- *All Products Search* placed on the welcome page that helped shoppers to find anything for sale on the net;

- *Recommendations Centre* offered music fans authoritative guides to the best CDs in more than 100 music styles, and located music by CD, artist, style or year;

- *Purchase Circles*™ featured thousands of best-seller lists for hometowns, workplaces, universities, and more;

Amazon.com also extended its strategic relationships, with a deal leading to the co-branding of Dell Computers and Amazon.com home pages on their respective websites. Amazon.com also announced strategic investments in the following companies who they believed were aligned to offering customer value through selection, service, convenience, and community. These included:

- *Drugstore.com*, an online seller of brand-name health, beauty and wellness products. Amazon.com had approximately 46 per cent of the company's shares;

- *Pets.com*, the leading internet pet-store, specialising in popular and rare pet accessories, products, and food for all types of animals;

- *Della & James' wedding-gift registry* was made available enabling Amazon.com's customers to find wedding registries and purchase wedding gifts;

- A 35 per cent stake in *HomeGrocer.com* that allowed the online grocer serving customers in the Seattle and Portland areas to accelerate its national rollout;

- *Gear.com* gave its customers access to the only Internet store to offer 100 per cent closeout merchandise in all sports categories;

- 100 per cent acquisition of *Exchange.com*, a provider of hard-to-find, antiquarian books. This added more than 12 million books and music items for sale and auction;

- 100 per cent acquisition of both *Biblinfind.com* for used books and *Musicfile.com* for hard-to-find recordings and music memorabilia;

- LiveBid's technology expanded the breadth and types of items customers could find, improving Amazon.com's accessibility to local and regional auction houses.

This year also saw the total leased space of Amazon.com exceed five million square feet, which included five new distribution centres in the US and one each in the UK and Germany. Employees had jumped to 7,600 and the associates programme involving other websites numbered 430,000, an increase of some seven-fold over the previous year. The year concluded with Bezos named *Time Magazine*'s 'man of the year' and Amazon.com collecting a range of awards by independent survey companies (see Exhibit 3).

Exhibit 3   Amazon.com's survey ratings

Survey company	Awarded in segment or service
Gomaz Advisors	No. 1 in online bookstores
Greenfield Online Study	Most visited music store online
Interbrand, Newell & Sorrell	57th most valuable brand worldwide
Media Metrix	No. 1 in online shopping site No. 7 web property
Microsoft Survey (MSNBC)	No. 1 in toys
Opinion Research Corp	Most widely recognised e-commerce brand in US No. 1 as best place to save money
PowerRankings™	No. 1 in books, videos, toys and music

Source: Various.

Exhibit 4	M&A activity and shutdowns and stock price comparisons

(a) M&A activity and shutdowns

Year	Acquired	Shutdown
2000	1,446	283
2001	1,283	501
2002	1,085	170
2003	78	8
TOTAL	3,892	962

Source: Webmergers, Inc.

(b) Company stock prices 1999–2000*

	Year of the bubble burst		
	Jun 99	**Jan 2000**	**Dec 2000**
Amazon	$58.47	$64.56	$15.56
Barnes	$18.00	$11.62	$1.31
EBAY	$37.85	$37.51	$16.50
Priceline	$693.39	$348.01	$7.88
Yahoo	$86.12	$161.03	$30.06

* $US1 = approx. €0.83.
Source: www.yahoo.com (prices adjusted for stock splits).

The bubble bursts – 2000

At the commencement of the new millennium Jeff Bezos was greeted with increasingly sceptical financial markets as investors became jaded with the mounting losses within Amazon.com and began to question whether there was a real business there at all. The technology bubble eventually burst in April 2000, creating across-the-board falls in the NASDAQ index as well as stock markets around the world. Amazon.com's share price began to fall in March and by the end of 2000 over 75 per cent of shareholder value had been wiped out as the stock price fell from $64.56 to $15.56, adjusted for previous stock splits. Exhibit 4 shows the number of US companies acquired and shutdown between 2000–2003 as well as Amazon.com share price comparisons 1999–2000.

However, despite the bubble bursting, Amazon.com moved through 2000 with a similar momentum to 1999. The company celebrated its five-year anniversary having served over 20 million customers up from 17 million the year before, and the associates programme exceeded 530,000. Jeff Bezos was quoted as saying:

> Our vision remains being Earth's most customer-centric company, the best place for customers to find and discover anything they want to buy online. While we continue to see improvements in all of our businesses, we are especially pleased with the profitability in our US segments.

(Amazon.com Company Report
3rd Quarter 2000)

A large number of initiatives were introduced in 2000, both within the US as well as in Amazon.com's global operations. While some were new, others were additions to existing services and features. For example, Amazon.com and Amazon.co.uk extended access to Amazon.de using the Wireless Application Protocol (WAP).[1] The global Amazon Anywhere initiative underscored Amazon.com's commitment to enhancing the customer buying experience with the convenience, safety and speed of state-of-the-art wireless commerce. Other key expansion initiatives during 2000 included the following:

- Amazon.com launched Amazon.fr, a French language site offering books, music CDs, DVDs and videos dedicated to customers in France and to French speaking customers around the world;

- The launching of Amazon.co.jp with a comprehensive catalogue of Japanese and foreign books for Japanese and Japanese speakers worldwide;

- Toysrus.com, launched a co-branded toy store with Amazon.com to bring customers the best toy buying experience available online;

- Apple Computers announced it had licensed Amazon.com's 1-Click patent for its Online Store, as part of an e-commerce cross-licensing agreement;

- The Computer & Video Games store was opened in the US offering the largest selection of computer and video games and accessories available;

---

[1] Wireless Application Protocol (WAP) is the first open, licence-free standard which allows any brand of wireless device to talk to another across all networks worldwide.

- Within the third quarter, Amazon.co.uk added Software and Video Games to its store;

- the German website added a Video Games and later a Software store;

- a Camera and Photo store were introduced, offering cameras, optical gear and accessories, and announced an alliance with Ofoto Inc for online photography;

- Amazon Kitchen store featuring thousands of culinary products and accessories including product reviews, recipes, and entertaining tips;

- Home Living store commenced, allowing its customers to shop for furniture, decorative accessories, bed and bath linens, lighting and rugs;

- a new car buying service was launched providing customers with a network of premier auto dealers affiliated with its partner Greenlight.com;

- the company also partnered with Stephen King to provide online payment services for instalments of *The Plant*, a new episodic novel on the website.

In addition to the growth in employees from 7,600 to over 9,000, the company continued to recruit to add to its management strength, naming Paul Misener Vice President of Global Public Policy. Misener was a partner in a law firm and chairman of the e-commerce and internet practice group. He had degrees in electrical engineering and computer science from Princeton as well as a law degree from George Mason University. Amazon.com also named Diego Piacentini Senior Vice President and General Manager (International). He had been General Manager of Apple Computer with responsibility for operations in Europe, the Middle East and Africa for over three years, and had spent nearly 14 years in various roles with Apple. He had a degree in economics from Bocconi University in Milan, Italy.

During this year, Amazon.com announced strategic investments in Ashford.com and eZiba.com. These investments were different in that the products being sold online were not traditional discount items. Ashford.com was an online retailer of luxury and premium products offering new and vintage watches, fragrances, leather accessories, sunglasses and writing instruments, while eZiba.com was a leading online retailer of hand-crafted products from around the world. However, Amazon.com believed the fit was good because both these businesses had a desire for bringing customers value through selection, service and convenience.

At the end of 2000, net sales were $2.76bn with a gross margin of 23.7 per cent. Income losses from operations were $864m, and total net losses exceeded $1.4bn, which represented over 50 per cent of the net sales figure. These losses combined with the aftershocks from the April 'tech wreck' continued to wipe value from investors' portfolios and in response Amazon.com began cutting costs in 2000.

Good news and bad news – 2001

2001 saw two contrasting stories emerge about Amazon.com. The good news involved further sales increases to over $3.12bn, a rise of 13 per cent on 2000, and the associate programme continued to grow to approximately 700,000. International net sales were proving very successful with more than a three-fold increase from $198m to $661m as the expansion into France and Japan began to prove successful. International sales now represented over 25 per cent of all company sales. Amazon.com served 25 million customers and inventory turns increased to 16 per year.

The cost-cutting response to losses continued in 2001 but on a much larger scale. Employees were reduced by 1,200, the warehouse in McDonough, Georgia was closed as was the service centre in Seattle, and the company also announced that the service centre in The Hague, Netherlands would also be closed. Other closures or scale-downs were being considered as the company's financial reports noted unoccupied warehouse, service and office space. Despite the cost cutting, the market remained unimpressed as stock prices fell to a weekly low of $5.97 on 24 September 2001 from a weekly high of $106.69 on 6 December 1999 (see Exhibit 5).

However, the lower stock prices did not deter the ongoing rollouts of categories, products and innovation. Some of these included:

- Electronic store upgrades that increased the selection over seven times to more than 45,000 items.

- Kitchen selections were increased to three times the level of the previous year.

- Instant order updates that warned busy customers they had already bought the item and

| Exhibit 5 | Amazon stock prices – weekly highs and lows since 1998 |

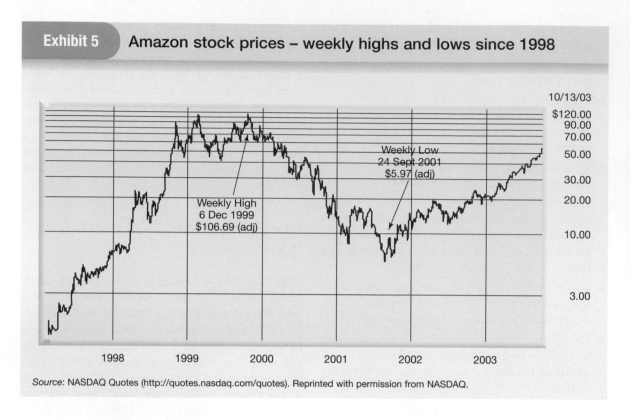

Source: NASDAQ Quotes (http://quotes.nasdaq.com/quotes). Reprinted with permission from NASDAQ.

also allowed customers to find, cancel or modify existing orders.

- Look Inside the Book allowing viewing of the front, back, inside cover, index, and some content of over 200,000 books (twice the number of items in a typical retail book store selection).
- Computer and magazine subscription stores where customers could purchase for themselves or buy subscriptions as gifts for others.
- Amazon Access was launched for visually impaired users enabling them to log on to pages with less text that used screen access software to read aloud the page.
- An Amazon.com credit card that provided a virtual credit card enabling customers to buy online and pay later when shopping on Amazon.com.
- Opening a travel store with leading online travel company Expedia featuring booking services and online travel status information.
- A co-branded website with Borders.com that offered books, music, videos and CDs on a joint site with Amazon.com but also linked into Borders physical stores.

- Amazon.co.jp, now the number one online bookstore in Japan, offered music, video, CDs, DVDs as well as Japanese editors and film and music critics.
- BabiesRUS.com and Amazon.com launched a co-branded baby store that offered a huge range of baby books, parenting guides, toys, music, videos and other merchandise.
- MGM Home Entertainment and Amazon.com partnered, enabling customers to purchase over 100 sought after movies from the MGM vault.
- A non-cash investment in CatalogCity.com, a California-based company that operated easy access to leading catalogue products and merchants.
- Amazon.com launched Marketplace in November which allowed used products to be listed on the same page as new items and gave access to thousands of used merchants and private sellers.

During this year, L. Michelle Wilson, an internal employee who had worked at Amazon.com since 1999, was promoted to Senior Vice President, Human Resources, General Counsel and Secretary. Prior to joining Amazon.com, Ms Wilson was a partner in a law firm earning her JD from the University of Chicago Law School and she held a BA in Finance from the University of Washington. Mark S. Hansen, aged 47, who was Chairman and CEO of Fleming Companies, Inc, joined the Amazon.com Board in November but left the following year. He became the sixth Board member, the fifth outside of Amazon.com.

By the end of 2001 some positive signs had begun to emerge. Gross profit had risen to just under $800m on a margin of 25.6 per cent. Although income losses from operations were $412m, this was half the previous year's total, whilst net losses were only 40 per cent of the previous year. This was the first time in Amazon.com's history that losses reduced as sales grew. Most importantly, fourth quarter sales were over $1bn, the highest quarter sales figure recorded, and the company posted its first ever pro-forma operating profit for a quarter of $59m and its first ever net profit of $35m. Bezos noted in the annual report of 2001 that:

> After four years of single-minded focus on growth, and then just under two years spent almost exclusively on lowering costs, we reached a point where we could afford to balance growth and cost improvement, dedicating resources and staffed projects to both.

Everything comes together – 2002

This year represented a turning of the corner for Amazon.com as the company made its first annual profit, although it was only a modest $64m. On a quarter by quarter basis, the company's income from operations was $2m (Qtr 1), $1.5m (Qtr 2), –$9.6m (Qtr 3) and $70.5m (Qtr 4). This meant the company had shown an income profit in four out of its last five quarters. Sales for 2002 were $3.93bn with increases in the four key groupings reported in the financial accounts (see Exhibit 6). International net sales was again the star performer nearly doubling to $1.17bn, which represented approximately 30 per cent of all net sales. Further, if International was combined with orders in other segments that came from overseas customers, over 35 per cent of sales were coming from outside the US. The investors gained some relief from the savaging of the past two years as the stock prices rose from $10.96 during 2002 to $18.89 (adjusted). Appendices A, B, C, and D provide extracts from financial reports for years 1997 to 2003.

There was a changing of the guard on the Board and in the executive management this year. Warren Jensen resigned as CFO and Scott Cook resigned from the Board. Tom Szkutak was appointed Senior Vice President and CFO in November after several positions at General Electric in a variety of business units. Thomas Ryder was appointed to the Board. Mr Ryder was Chairman and CEO of Readers Digest Association, Inc. Mark Peck was appointed Chief Accounting Officer (CAO) and Udi Manber was made Vice President and Chief Algorithms Officer. A further reduction in full-time employees by 300 was made bringing the total down to around 7,500.

Amazon.com expanded its international sales base with the opening of a website in Canada, Amazon.ca. This was the company's sixth website and, when combined with over 900,000 other websites participating in the associates programme, gave Amazon.com unparalleled economies of scale and scope in its ability to reach customers that now numbered over 32m. The company announced other initiatives throughout 2002 that included:

- The launching of Web Services allowing web developers to incorporate some of Amazon.com's unique content and features into their own websites.
- The Apparel and Accessories store was launched providing Amazon.com's customers with access to over 400 leading brands of clothing, shoes and accessories.
- Target announced its target.com online store would deliver four brands, Amazon.com, Target, Marshall, Fields and Mervyns, with Amazon.com providing technology and fulfilment for the Target website.
- Office Depot and Amazon.com announced a strategic e-commerce alliance involving 50,000 Office Depot products at Amazon.com/officedepot.
- A strategic alliance was formed with the Virgin Entertainment Group whereby Amazon.com would power the internet web page engine for Virgin Megastores and its e-commerce in the US and Japan.
- Amazon.com expanded its Magazine, Newspaper and Subscription service adding more than 50,000 new editions.
- Amazon.de launched Magazines and Periodicals on the German site.
- Bank One and Amazon.com announced a Platinum Visa Card.

| Exhibit 6 | Net sales and customer growth (total and by segment) 1996–2002 |

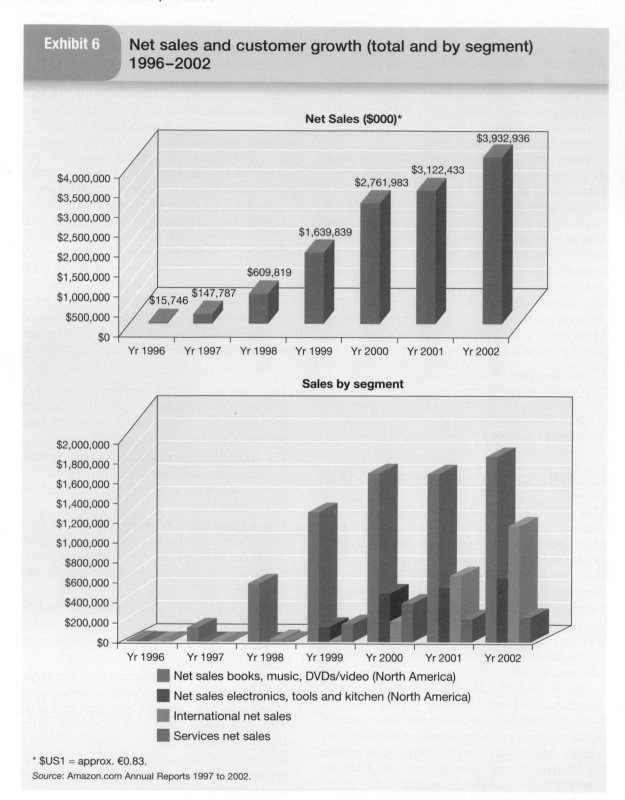

Net Sales ($000)*

- $15,746
- $147,787
- $609,819
- $1,639,839
- $2,761,983
- $3,122,433
- $3,932,936

Yr 1996, Yr 1997, Yr 1998, Yr 1999, Yr 2000, Yr 2001, Yr 2002

Sales by segment

- ■ Net sales books, music, DVDs/video (North America)
- ■ Net sales electronics, tools and kitchen (North America)
- ■ International net sales
- ■ Services net sales

* $US1 = approx. €0.83.

Source: Amazon.com Annual Reports 1997 to 2002.

Amazon.com also entered into a deal with Borders Group (mimicking the deal with Waldenbooks later in November) that enabled Amazon.com customers to collect their books, music and CDs at Borders book stores across the US. In addition, the company announced numerous deals that extended or renewed its marketing and alliance relationships with key players. This included a renewal of its relationship with drugstore.com, the re-launching of CDnow.com website, and extensions of partnership arrangements with travel businesses Hotwire and Cruise Vacation. Amazon.co.uk and Amazon.de also launched Marketplace that allowed 'used' items, such as books and collectables, to be listed alongside new products. This service was proving extremely popular and represented 15 per cent of Amazon.com's total orders in the fourth quarter of 2002.

During the year, Amazon.com settled its lawsuit against Barnesandnoble.com that had commenced in 1999 over illegal copying of its one-click technology. Amazon.com was also suffering from an increasing number of e-mail forgeries where small companies would send e-mails with Amazon.com's name and content in it. Customers that responded thought they were transacting with Amazon.com but found instead they were dealing with an entirely different company. This resulted in a number of lawsuits being filed during 2003.

Success continues – 2003

By perhaps any measure, 2003 was Amazon.com's most successful year to date. Sales by the third quarter were $3.3bn, up $814m on the same time last year. In the third quarter over 37 per cent of sales came from outside the US whilst income from operations remained positive in each quarter and totalled $133m. Despite lower prices and a free shipping offer, margins were stable at around 25 per cent. The result was that seven of the last eight quarters had been profitable.

William B. (Bing) Gordon was elected to the Board of Directors in April adding artistic and marketing experience as co-founder of Electronic Arts, Inc. Jason Kilar was promoted to Senior Vice President of Worldwide Application Software in June 2003. Mr Kilar had joined Amazon.com in 1997 and worked in senior management and vice-president positions. He had an MBA from Harvard Business School.

During the early part of 2003, huge customer interest developed in the fifth Harry Potter book that Amazon.com offered for immediate pre-order. As part of its company tradition in offering customer-focused solutions, on Saturday 21 June Amazon.com made e-commerce history by teaming up with the US postal service and FedEx to deliver more than 789,000 copies of *Harry Potter and the Order of the Phoenix* the same day the book

was released. Other 2003 initiatives around customers, alliances, products or categories included:

- Amazon.co.jp launched an Electronics store.
- An e-commerce agreement with Target Corporation was extended until 2008.
- The company teamed up with Jamie Oliver (London's famous cook) to launch a Cookware Line of products with 15 per cent of proceeds going to the Oliver restaurant that develops young talented cooks.
- A Sporting Goods Store was launched offering more than 3,000 brands in over 50 sports.
- Introduction of Search Inside the Book that extended on the popular Look Inside the Book which enabled customers to identify books by searching and previewing the actual text.
- Amazon.de opened a new shop for Kitchen and Housewares and Amazon.co.uk expanded into Kitchen and Home Ranges.
- Amazon.com powered the internet web page engines for basketball stores, NBA.com and WNDBA.com on behalf of the US National Basketball Association.

Amazon.com was also determined to stop e-mail forgery (called spoofing) that it believed was undermining consumer confidence and involved fraud. On Monday 25 August 2003, Amazon.com filed 11 lawsuits in the US and Canada against what it termed deceptive online marketers who forged e-mail to make it look as though it was from Amazon.com. The action had early success as Cyebye.com entered into an agreement to stop the practice and paid Amazon.com $10,000 in penalties. Additional steps involved Amazon.com opening an anti-spoofing site on their website to encourage customers to lodge complaints so it could pursue other companies engaging in the practice.

Defining the business

The vision behind Amazon.com had changed progressively since it started in 1995. What began as a goal to become the world's biggest and best online bookstore developed into a store that customers could buy 'anything with a capital A'. By 2003 the company earned over 37 per cent of its revenues outside the US, nearly 20 per cent comes from used items, and e-commerce was growing at a rate that

Bezos believed may make it the main source of revenue in his vision of the future. When asked what the main difference was between retail and his business, Jeff Bezos stated:

> The three most important things in retail are location, location, location. The three most important things for our consumer business are technology, technology, technology. That's what takes the place of real estate in our business.
>
> (Quoted in *BW Online*, 25 August 2003).

The key components of Amazon.com's offerings to customers purchasing its products included:

- *Browsing*. The Amazon.com site offered visitors a variety of features arranged in a simple, easy-to-use fashion intended to enhance product search and selection;

- *Searching*. Provision of interactive, searchable catalogues of books, music CDs, videos, DVDs, computer games and other titles. The company offered a selection of search tools to find products based on keyword, title, subject, author, artist, musical instrument, label, actor, director, publication date or ISBN. Customers could also use more complex search tools such as Boolean search queries.

- *Reviews and content*. Amazon.com stores offered numerous forms of content to enhance the customer's shopping experience and encourage purchases. Various types of content were available for particular titles, including cover art, synopses, annotations, review by editorial staff and other customers, and interviews by authors and artists.

- *Recommendations and personalisations*.
Amazon.com personalises its product and service offerings including greeting customers by name, and provided instant and personalised recommendations, bestseller and chart-topper listings, personal notification services and other related features.

- *One-click technology*. Amazon.com offered a streamlined ordering process using 1-Click technology. If a customer had previously activated one-click functionality, a customer could place an order by clicking one button without having to fill out an order form. Their shipping and billing information was automatically referenced on the company's secure server.

- *Secure credit card payment*. Amazon.com utilised secure server software for secure commerce transactions. It encrypted all of a customer's personal information, including credit card number, name and address, in order that it could not be read as the information travelled over the internet.

- *Availability and fulfilment*. Most of the company products were available for shipment within 24 hours, others were available within two to three days and the remainder within four to six weeks.

Despite observable changes in services, categories, products, and physical assets plus the economies of scale and scope, Amazon.com has continued to print its 1997 Letter to Shareholders inside every annual report. Jeff Bezos believed that the core of what defines the business was contained within this letter and that Amazon.com had remained true to it. The letter contains a series of core commitments and extracts from it are reproduced in Exhibit 7.

Since 2001, the company organised its operations into four principal groupings and it provided financial information on each of these segments. They comprised:

- Books, Music, Video, DVDs (BMVD) segment – which included retail sales from Amazon.com and Amazon.ca of books, music, DVD/video products and magazine subscription commissions. Also included were commissions from sales of these products through Amazon Marketplace, Merchants@ program and Syndicated Stores.

- Electronics, Tools, Kitchen (ETK) segment – which included retail sales from Amazon.com of electronics, home improvement, home and garden, mail order. Sales and commissions from sales of these products through Amazon Marketplace, Merchants@ and Syndicated Stores were also included.

- International segment – which included sales from Amazon.co.uk, Amazon.de, Amazon.fr, Amazon.co.jp. Sales of any product or service going through these stores was included as well as any overseas sales through Amazon Marketplace, Merchants@ and Syndicated Stores.

- Services segment – which included all sales for services through the Merchant@ program that are not offered through other stores, and also included Auctions, zShops, Amazon Payments and so on.

Whilst these principal segments provided a financial analysis tool it was also possible to divide the

Exhibit 7	Extract of 1997 letter to shareholders reprinted in 2002 Annual Report

1997 LETTER TO SHAREHOLDERS
(Reprinted from the 1997 Annual Report)

From the 6th Paragraph
Because of our emphasis on the long term, we may make decisions and weigh tradeoffs differently than some companies. Accordingly, we want to share with you our fundamental management and decision-making approach so that you, our shareholders, may confirm that it is consistent with your investment philosophy:

- We will continue to focus relentlessly on our customers

- We will continue to make investment decisions in light of long-term market leadership

- We will continue to measure our programs and the effectiveness of our investments analytically, to jettison those that do no provide acceptable returns, and to step up our investment in those that work best. We will continue to learn from both our successes and our failures.

- We will make bold rather than timid investment decisions where we see a sufficient probability of gaining market leadership advantages. Some of these investments will pay off, others will not, and we will have learned another valuable lesson in either case.

- When forced to choose between optimising the appearance of our GAAP accounting and maximising the present value of future cash flows, we'll take the cash flows.

Source: Amazon.com 2002 Annual Report.

company into three (not necessarily equal) functional areas. These were:

- *Product development.* Departments within this area included editorial, marketing, product feasibility, pricing, as well as website design and site navigation, e-commerce solutions.

- *Technology development.* Software and technical production along with databases, information technology systems, engineering and computer science.

- *Supply chain and distribution.* Distribution centres, business-to-business client relationship management, supply chain management.

Industry, market size and competitors

The online commerce industry relied on internet penetration rates within countries to provide its customer base and these numbers typically reflected the industrial development of a region or country, as well as education levels and the general tendency of the country to embrace technology (see Appendices E and F). Statistics showed that the top 20 countries had on average a 57.5 per cent penetration rate, with the US featuring fifth at 63.2 per cent. However, the next 213 countries had only an average of 4.5 per cent penetration rates and world data indicated the rate on average was only 10.7 per cent of the global population. Further, a review of US Retail to E-tail (online retail sales) figures showed that on average only around 1.5 per cent of all retail sales were being conducted on the internet although separate research suggested that up to 30 per cent of some industry sales were being influenced by online websites prior to a physical transaction occurring (see Exhibit 8).

Competitors

As noted earlier, in the past rivals such as Barnes and Noble were considered by many to be a major threat to Amazon.com because they had a physical infrastructure, supported by an online arm.

Exhibit 8 — Industry sector and market size data (million people)

Internet World Usage Statistics

World Regions	Population 2003 (est)	Usage Oct-03	Penetration Oct-03
Africa	880m	8m	0.9%
Asia	3.59bn	211m	5.9%
Europe	723m	200m	27.6%
Middle East	259m	12m	4.6%
North America	323m	201m	62.2%
Latin America	541m	35m	6.6%
Oceana	32m	15m	47.9%
Total	6.38bn	682m	10.7%
Projection for online pop. in 2004 709m (*eMarketer*)			
Projection for online pop. in 2004 945m (*Computer Almanac*)			

Top 10 Countries in Internet Usage

Country	Population 2003 (est)	Users Oct-03	Penetration Oct-03
United States	292m	184m	63.2%
China	1.31bn	68m	5.2%
Japan	128m	59m	46.4%
Germany	82m	44m	53.9%
UK	59m	34m	58.2%
South Korea	47m	26m	56.1%
France	59m	22m	37.2%
Italy	56m	19m	34.2%
Canada	32m	17m	53.1%
India	1.07bn	17m	1.6%

Source: InternetWorld Stats.com (Updated statistics on 26th Oct 2003).

Exhibit 9 — Competitor revenue comparisons

Revenue ($000)*	1997	1998	1999	2000	2001	2002
Amazon.com	$147,758	$609,996	$1,639,839	$2,761,983	$3,122,433	$3,932,936
Barnesandnoble.com	$11,949	$61,834	$202,567	$320,115	$404,600	$422,830
Ebay	$5,744	$47,352	$224,724	$431,424	$748,821	$1,210,000
Priceline.com	N/A	$35,237	$482,410	$1,235,396	$1,171,753	$1,000,000
Yahoo	$67,411	$203,270	$588,608	$1,110,178	$717,422	$953,070

* $US1 = approx. €0.83.

However, a review of Barnesandnoble.com's online revenues in 2003 shows they were less than 12 per cent of Amazon.com, or around 23 per cent of Amazon.com's US Books, Music, DVD/Video segment. Exhibit 9 gives a comparison of revenue between the major online competitors to the end of 2002.

In 2003, Amazon.com's competitors multiplied as the range of categories and products grew but it could be suggested that few presented a serious challenge to the company's dominance in the online world at this time. Wal-Mart, whilst a giant in traditional retailing with revenues of $246bn and around 1.4m employees in 2003, had progressively developed an online presence. However, their website, www.walmart.com, was supporting their physical stores rather than seeking to develop a dedicated stand-alone e-commerce site and the company did not separate its online sales in its financial reporting. eBay, once touted as 'so far ahead of its competitors that it currently enjoys a class by itself' (Brand, 1999), has now had its revenues exceeded by Amazon.com that might also beat it on profit in the near future. However, as Exhibit 10 shows, eBay had been able to convert customers and the time they spend on their website into earnings, although its business model concentrated on auctions, which was only a small part of Amazon.com's business. Appendix G shows gross profit, income and net profit as a percentage 1996–2003. A revenue per employee comparison is shown in Appendix H.

Exhibit 10	Bubble chart of EBITDA, time spent on website and number of shoppers

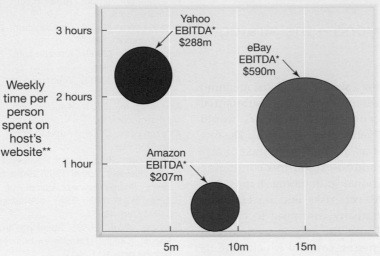

* EBITDA is a financial reporting measure of Earnings Before Interest Tax, Depreciation and Amortization used.
** Weekly figures used are for week ending August 3rd, 2003.

Sources: Greenspan, 2003, CyberAtlas, 2003, Yahoo.com, 2003.

Strategic choice – balancing quality and cost

Bezos' stated strategy in his 2002 letter to shareholders was to offer 'both world leading customer experience *and* the lowest possible prices.' Bezos acknowledged this apparent paradox and added:

We transform much of customer experience – such as unmatched selection, extensive product information, personalized recommendations, and other new software features – into largely a fixed expense. With customer experience costs largely fixed, our costs as a percentage of sales can shrink rapidly as we grow our business.

Amazon.com received the highest score ever recorded in customer satisfaction from the American Customer Satisfaction Index in 2002, considered as one of the most authoritative surveys of customer satisfaction. Bezos points out that this was not just online and not just retailing, it was the highest

score ever recorded in any service industry. At the same time, the company had continued to lower prices and now offered free shipping for orders over $25 in the US (this offer was slowly spreading to other countries), while customers, repeat customers and sales had all grown consistently.

In 2002, the company distribution infrastructure was still less than it was in 1999 indicating the changing nature of customer delivery, particularly as service revenues grow. E-commerce and especially web development and technology sharing were experiencing significant growth and although these figures were not separated in the accounts, Bezos suggested they accounted for around 20 per cent of revenues (*BW Online*, 25 August 2003). He also stated that this may become the major part of their business over time.

Amazon.com's main strategy since 1995 had centred on customers by constantly improving customer innovation. As such, the company had developed key competencies in technology development, computer science and software. It had also shown a willingness to form strategic alliances, invest or acquire other companies that offered developed technology, applications, products or services that fitted its existing business model.

2004 and beyond – the strategic issues

The internet was now a significant global medium, particularly in the western world, and a substantial and growing percentage of consumers would engage in an ever diverse range of services. The fact that Amazon.com was the best positioned of any company in the world to exploit this continuing switch from traditional purchasing habits was not just luck. However, risks and uncertainties remained as the company continued to enhance its business model and the way it serviced end users and also businesses, some of which were its competitors. Bezos added:

> It's like the early days of electrical appliances. The internet and the things that will come out of it are around the level of the 1908 Hurley washing machine. The electric outlet hadn't been invented yet. Nor had the on-off switch.
> . . . What we're doing really is new. And if we followed that second rule – follow and don't lead – we would be in serious trouble very quickly.
> (Quoted in *BW Online*, 25 August 2003)

It was early 2004 and Bezos reflected upon the great progress the company had made. Appendix I shows the timeline of company growth. He also pondered the future and questioned whether his vision would turn into reality. Amongst the many strategic issues that he considered were:

- Is the Amazon.com business model the right model, looking ahead five or more years?
- Should they continue to try to be all things to all people?
- How can they continue to constantly innovate and enhance the customer experience?
- Is the logical end-game scenario being the Wal-Mart of the internet?

Sources

Alexa.com (1999) www.alexa.com.

Amazon.com (1997) Amazon.com *1997 Annual Report*, Amazon.com, Inc.

Amazon.com (1998) Amazon.com *1998 Annual Report*, Amazon.com, Inc.

Amazon.com (1999) Amazon.com *1999 Annual Report*, Amazon.com, Inc.

Amazon.com (2000) Amazon.com *2000 Annual Report*, Amazon.com, Inc.

Amazon.com (2000) Amazon.com *3rd Quarter Report*, Amazon.com, Inc.

Amazon.com (2001) Amazon.com *2001 Annual Report*, Amazon.com, Inc.

Amazon.com (2002) Amazon.com *2002 Annual Report*, Amazon.com, Inc.

Amazon.com (2003) Amazon.com *1st Quarter Report*, Amazon.com, Inc.

Amazon.com (2003) Amazon.com *2nd Quarter Report*, Amazon.com, Inc.

Amazon.com (2003) Amazon.com *3rd Quarter Report*, Amazon.com, Inc.

Amazon.com (2003) Investor Relations Press Releases.

Boston Business Journal (1999) 'Bezos on Business, Books and Bears', *Boston Business Journal*, vol. 19, no. 19, pp. 3–4.

Business Week (1999) 'EBay vs Amazon.com', *Business Week*, 31 May, pp. 49–51.

Business Week (2003) 'Speaking out: Amazon.com's Jeff Bezos' [Online], http://www.businessweek.com/magazine [access date 1/11/2003].

Corcoran, E. (1999) 'On-line: Amazoned', *Forbes*, March, p. 22.

Cox, J. (2003) 'Amazon dives into technology services', IDG News Service [Online] http://www.arnnet.com.au/ [access date 30/10/2003].

CyberAtlas (2003) 'Populaton Explosion' [Online], http://cyber-atlas.internet.com/big_picture/geographics/article [access date 2/11/2003].

Dessauer, J. (1997) *Book Industry Trends*, Book Industry Study Group Inc. (Statistical Service Centre), New York.

Gibson, P. (1999) The sharp rise of e-commerce', *Information Today*, vol. 16, no. 7, pp. 28–33.

Greenspan, R. (2003) 'Small biz worried about success', [Online] http://cyberatlas.internet.com/markets/smallbiz/article [access date 2/11/2003].

Haylock, C.F. and Muscarella, L. (1999) *Net Success: 24 Leaders in Web Commerce Show You How to Put the Web to Work for Your Business*, Adams Media Corporation, Massachusetts.

Hof, R.D. (1998) 'A new chapter for Amazon.com', *Business Week*, vol. 3591, pp. 39–41.

Koselka, R. (1999) 'A real Amazon', *Forbes*, vol. 163, no. 7, pp. 50–53.

MSN (2003) [Online] http://news.moneycentral.msn.com [access date 19/9/2003].

Nucifora, A. (1999) 'Despite the hype, marketing internet's numbers adding up', *Business Press*, vol. 12, no. 8, pp. 13–14.

Porter, M.E. 'The value chain and competitive advantage', in Porter, M.E. (1985) *Competitive Advantage: Creating and sustaining superior performance*, The Free Press.

Roth, D. (1999) 'Meg muscles eBay uptown', *Fortune*, vol. 140, no. 1, pp. 81–87.

Sacharow, A. (1998) 'Amazon calling', *Adweek*, vol. 48, no. 24, pp. 70–71.

Saunders, R. (1999) *Business the Amazon.Com Way: Secrets of the World's Most Astonishing Web Business*. Capstone Ltd, Washington.

Schwartz, N.D. (1999) 'The tech boom will keep on rocking', *Fortune*, vol. 139, no. 3, pp. 64–67.

Stockport, G.J. and Street, D. (2000) 'Amazon.com: from startup to the new millennium', European Case Clearing House, 38pp, No. 300-014-1.

Stone, B. (1999) 'Amazon's pet projects', *Newsweek*, vol. 133, no. 25, pp. 56–57.

Tadjer, R. (1996) 'Redefining inventory', *Communications Week*, vol. 626, pp. 513–514.

United Nations (2002) *World Population Data Sheet of the Population Reference Bureau*.

United Nations (2002) *E-commerce and Development Report*.

US Census Bureau (2003) 'Service sector statistics: gateway to the service economy' [Online] http://census.gov/mrts/www/current.html [accessed 13/10/2003].

USA Securities and Exchange Commission (1999), Washington DC.

Webmergers.com (2003) 'Internet Companies Three Years After the Height of the Bubble' [Online] http://www.webmergers.com/data [accessed 29/10/2003].

Yahoo!Finance [Online] http://finance.yahoo.com/.

APPENDIX A

Consolidated Balance Sheet

Consolidated Balance Sheets*	Yr 1996	Yr 1997**	Yr 1998**	Yr 1999	Yr 2000	Yr 2001	Yr 2002	Qtr 1 2003	Qtr 2 2003	Qtr 3 2003
Assets ($000)										
Cash and cash equivalents	$6,248	$109,810	$25,561	$116,962	$822,435	$540,282	$738,254	$495,773	$641,728	$666,418
Marketable securities			$347,884	$589,226	$278,087	$456,303	$562,715	$586,779	$347,044	$398,242
Short-term investments	$0	$15,256								
Inventories	$571	$8,971	$29,501	$220,646	$174,563	$143,722	$202,425	$173,030	$178,107	$241,667
Accounts receivable, net and other current assets						$67,613	$112,282	$88,914	$84,375	$103,873
Prepaid expenses and other	$321	$3,298	$21,308	$85,344	$86,044					
Total current assets	$7,140	$137,335	$424,254	$1,012,178	$1,361,129	$1,207,920	$1,615,676	$1,344,496	$1,251,254	$1,410,200
Fixed assets, net	$985	$9,265	$29,791	$317,613	$366,416	$271,751	$239,398	$228,279	$221,674	$221,459
Goodwill, net			$174,052	$534,699	$158,990	$45,367	$70,811	$70,811	$70,811	$69,121
Deposits	$146	$166								
Deferred charges	$0	$2,240								
Other intangibles, net			$4,586	$195,445	$96,335	$34,382	$3,460	$2,548	$1,635	$659
Investments in equity-method investees***			$7,740	$226,727	$52,073					
Other equity investments			$0	$144,735	$40,177	$28,359	$15,422	$13,453	$12,764	$12,949
Other assets			$8,037	$40,154	$60,049	$49,768	$45,662	$46,346	$38,716	$35,297
Total assets	$8,271	$149,006	$648,460	$2,471,551	$2,135,169	$1,637,547	$1,990,429	$1,705,933	$1,596,854	$1,749,685
Liabilities ($000)										
Accounts payable	$2,852	$32,697	$113,273	$463,026	$485,383	$444,748	$618,128	$393,696	$445,098	$499,189
Accrued expenses and other current liabilities	$920	$6,167	$34,413	$126,017	$272,683	$305,064	$314,935	$234,194	$232,231	$236,184
Accrued advertising	$598	$3,454	$13,071							
Accrued product development	$500	$0	$0							
Unearned revenue				$54,790	$131,117	$87,978	$47,916	$42,979	$38,733	$40,843
Interest payable			$10	$24,888	$69,196	$68,632	$71,661	$16,632	$45,179	$44,476
Current portion of long-term debt and other	$0	$1,500	$808	$14,322	$16,577	$14,992	$13,318	$11,078	$8,143	$6,058
Total current liabilities	$4,870	$43,818	$161,575	$738,935	$974,956	$921,414	$1,065,958	$698,579	$769,384	$826,750
Long-term debt and other		$76,521	$348,140	$1,466,338	$2,127,464	$2,156,133	$2,277,305	$2,296,418	$2,074,306	$2,080,969
Long term portion of capital lease obligation		$181								
Stockholders' deficit ($000)										
Preferred stock, $0.01 par value;	$6									
Authorised shares – 500,000										
Issued and outstanding shares	159	239	3,186	3,452	3,571	3,732	3,879	3,916	3,967	4,004
Additional paid-in capital	$9,873	$63,792	$298,537	$1,195,540	$1,338,303	$1,462,769	$1,649,946	$1,714,616	$1,790,835	$1,852,308
Note receivable for common stock	-$612	-$1,930	-$1,099	-$1,171						
Deferred stock-based compensation			-$1,625	-$47,806	-$13,448	-$9,853	-$6,591	-$5,420	-$4,201	-$3,525
Accumulated other comprehensive income (loss)			$1,806	-$1,709	-$2,376	-$36,070	$9,662	$17,655	$25,708	$36,761
Accumulated deficit	-$6,025	-$33,615	-$162,060	-$882,028	-$2,293,301	-$2,860,578	-$3,009,710	-$3,019,831	-$3,063,145	-$3,047,582
Total stockholders' equity (deficit)	$3,401	$28,486	$138,745	$266,278	-$967,251	-$1,440,000	-$1,352,814	-$1,289,064	-$1,246,836	-$1,158,034
Total liabilities and stockholders' deficit	$8,271	$149,006	$648,460	$2,471,551	$2,135,169	$1,637,547	$1,990,449	$1,705,933	$1,596,854	$1,749,685

* $US1 = approx. €0.83.

** 1997 & 1998 figures reflect restatement for 1998 business acquisition accounted for under the pooling of interest method.

*** Consolidated with other equity investments in 2001.

Source: Amazon.com Company Reports 1997 to 2003 (Annual and Quarterly Reports).

APPENDIX B

Consolidated Statement of Operations

Consolidated Statements of Operations ($000)*	Yr 1996	Yr 1997**	Yr 1998**	Yr 1999	Yr 2000	Yr 2001	Yr 2002	Qtr 1 2003	Qtr 2 2003	Qtr 3 2003
Net sales	$15,746	$147,787	$609,819	$1,639,839	$2,761,983	$3,122,433	$3,932,936	$1,083,559	$1,099,912	$1,134,456
Cost of sales	$12,287	$118,969	$476,155	$1,349,194	$2,106,206	$2,323,875	$2,940,318	$812,977	$825,984	$848,635
Gross profit	$3,459	$28,818	$133,664	$290,645	$655,777	$798,558	$992,618	$270,582	$273,928	$285,821
Operating expenses:										
Fulfilment	$6,090	$40,077	$132,654	$237,312	$414,509	$374,250	$392,467	$103,705	$107,455	$107,057
Marketing	$2,313	$13,384	$46,424	$175,838	$179,980	$138,283	$125,383	$28,227	$25,326	$28,943
Technology and content (product development)	$1,035	$6,741	$15,618	$159,722	$269,326	$241,165	$215,617	$50,088	$52,135	$53,775
General and administrative				$70,144	$108,962	$89,862	$79,049	$21,102	$21,823	$22,393
Stock-based compensation		$1,211	$1,889	$30,618	$24,797	$4,637	$68,927	$27,323	$24,453	$20,936
Amortisation of goodwill and other intangibles			$42,599	$214,694	$321,772	$181,033	$5,478	$912	$913	$786
Restructuring-related and other			$3,535	$8,072	$200,311	$181,585	$41,573	$0	$0	$0
Total operating expenses	$9,438	$61,413	$242,719	$896,400	$1,519,657	$1,210,815	$928,494	$231,357	$232,105	$233,890
Income (loss) from operations	–$5,979	–$32,595	–$109,555	–$605,755	–$863,880	–$412,257	$64,124	$39,225	$41,823	$51,931
Interest income	$202	$1,901	$14,053	$45,451	$40,821	$29,103	$23,687	$6,540	$5,761	$4,324
Interest expense	$0	–$326	–$26,639	–$84,566	–$130,921	–$139,232	–$142,925	–$36,511	–$34,367	–$29,802
Other income (expense), net	$0	$0	$0	$1,671	–$10,058	–$1,900	$5,623	$2,859	$3,685	$252
Other gains (losses), net (PEACs & other)	$0	$0	$0		–$142,639	–$2,141	–$96,273	–$21,798	–$60,216	–$11,142
Net interest expense and other		$1,575	–$12,586	–$37,444	–$242,797	–$114,170	–$209,888	–$48,910	–$85,137	–$36,368
Income loss before equity in losses of equity-method investees	–$5,777	–$31,020	–$121,641	–$643,199	–$1,106,677	–$526,427	–$145,764	–$9,685	–$43,314	$15,563
Equity in losses of equity-method investees, net	$0	$0	–$2,905	–$76,769	–$304,596	–$30,327	–$4,169	–$436	$0	$0
Loss before change in accounting principle	–$5,777	–$31,020	–$124,546	–$719,968	–$1,411,273	–$556,754	–$149,933	–$10,121	–$43,314	$15,563
Cumulative effect of change in accounting principle	$0	$0	$0	$0	$0	–$10,523	$801	$0	$0	$0
Net loss	–$5,777	–$31,020	–$124,546	–$719,968	–$1,411,273	–$567,277	–$149,132	–$10,121	–$43,314	$15,563
Basic and diluted loss per share:										
Prior to cumulative effect of change in accounting principle	–$0.31	–$0.12	–$0.42	–$2.20	–$4.02	–$1.53	–$0.40	–$0.03	–$0.11	$0.04
Cumulative effect of change in accounting principle	$0.00	$0.00	$0.00	$0.00	$0.00	–$0.03	$0.01	$0.00	$0.00	$0.00
Cumulative effect of change in accounting principle	–$0.31	–$0.12	–$0.42	–$2.20	–$4.02	–$1.56	–$0.39	–$0.03	–$0.11	$0.04
Shares used in computation of basic and diluted loss per share	18,544	260,682	296,344	326,753	350,873	364,211	378,363	388,541	393,876	397,912

* $US1 = approx. €0.83.

** 1997 & 1998 figures reflect restatement for 1998 business acquisition accounted for under the pooling of interest method. Some figures were changed by the company in subsequent years during this period.

Source: Amazon.com Company Reports 1997 to 2003 (Annual and Quarterly Reports).

APPENDIX C

Consolidated Statement of Cash Flows

Consolidated Statements of Cash Flows ($000)*	Yr 1996	Yr 1997**	Yr 1998**	Yr 1999	Yr 2000	Yr 2001	Yr 2002	Qtr 1 2003	Qtr 2 2003	Qtr 3 2003
Cash and cash equivalents, beginning of period	$804	$864	$110,119	$71,583	$133,309	$822,435	$540,282	$738,254	$495,773	$641,724
OPERATING ACTIVITIES										
Net loss	–$6,246	–$31,020	–$124,546	–$719,968	–$1,411,273	–$567,277	–$149,132	–$10,121	–$43,314	$15,563
Adjustments to reconcile net loss to net cash provided by (used in) operating activities:										
Depreciation of fixed assets and other amortisation	$296	$3,442	$9,421	$36,806	$84,460	$84,709	$82,274	$19,750	$19,003	$18,338
Stock based compensation	$0	$1,354	$2,386	$30,618	$24,797	$4,637	$68,927	$27,323	$24,453	$20,936
Equity in losses of equity-method investees, net			$2,905	$76,769	$304,596	$30,327	$4,169	$436	$0	$0
Amortisation of goodwill and other intangibles	$0	$0	$42,599	$214,694	$321,772	$181,033	$5,478	$912	$913	$786
Non-cash restructuring-related and other			$1,561	$8,072	$200,311	$73,293	$3,470		$0	$0
Gain on sale of marketable securities, net			$271	$8,688	–$280	–$1,335	–$5,700		–$5,272	–$141
Other losses (gains), net (PEACs)				$0	$142,639	$2,141	$96,273	$21,798	$60,216	$11,142
Non-cash interest expense and other	$0	$64	$23,970	$29,171	$24,766	$26,629	$29,586	$7,877	$3,532	$1,343
Cumulative effect of change in accounting principle				$0	$0	$10,523	–$801	$0	$0	$0
Changes in operating assets and liabilities:										
Inventories	–$554	–$8,400	–$20,513	–$172,069	$46,083	$30,628	–$51,303	$30,625	–$2,479	–$62,147
Accounts receivable, net and other current assets			–$16,758	–$54,927	–$8,585	$20,732	–$32,948	$27,233	$5,914	–$14,844
Accounts payable	$2,756	$30,172	$78,674	$330,166	$22,357	–$44,438	$156,542	–$226,605	$45,486	$49,535
Accrued expenses and other current liabilities	$1,603	$5,274	$31,232	$95,839	$93,967	$50,031	$4,491	–$87,065	–$7,138	–$5,109
Unearned revenue				$6,225	$97,818	$114,738	$95,404	$22,968	$25,752	$29,932
Amortisation of previously unearned revenue				–$5,837	–$108,211	–$135,808	–$135,466	–$27,905	–$29,998	–$27,816
Interest payable			–$167	$24,878	$34,341	–$345	$3,027	–$55,028	$28,956	–$701
Net cash provided by (used in) operating activities	–$2,010	$687	$31,035	–$90,875	–$130,442	–$119,782	$174,291	–$251,782	$126,024	$36,817
INVESTING ACTIVITIES										
Sales and maturities of marketable securities and other investments	$0	$4,311	$227,789	$2,064,101	$545,724	$370,377	$553,289	$208,955	$350,068	$21,988
Purchases of marketable securities	–$5,233	–$122,385	–$504,435	–$2,359,398	–$184,455	–$567,152	–$635,810	–$233,055	–$109,259	–$71,880
Purchases of fixed assets, including internal-use software and Web site development	–$1,335	–$7,603	–$28,333	–$287,055	–$134,758	–$50,321	–$39,163	–$6,394	–$7,141	–$15,982
Investments in equity-method invested and other investments			–$19,019	–$369,607	–$62,533	–$6,198	$0	$0	$0	
Proceeds from sale of subsidiary and other										$5,072
Net cash provided by (used in) investing activities	–$6,568	–$125,677	–$323,998	–$951,959	$163,978	–$253,294	–$121,684	–$30,494	$233,668	$60,012

FINANCING ACTIVITIES

Proceeds from exercise of stock options and other	$195	$509	$14,366	$64,649	$44,697	$16,625	$121,689	$38,555	$53,042	$41,235
Proceeds from issuance of common stock, net of issuance costs	$0					$99,831				
Proceeds from long-term debt and other	$75,000		$325,987	$1,263,639	$681,499	$10,000				
Repayment of long term debt			−$78,108	−$188,886	−$16,927	−$19,575	−$14,795	−$3,221	−$277,249	−$3,437
Repayment of capital lease obligations and other	−$2,309		−$7,783	−$35,151	−$16,122	$0	$0		−$3,669	
Financing costs										
Net cash provided by financing activities	$8,638	$126,002	$254,462	$1,104,071	$693,147	$106,881	$106,894	$35,334	−$227,876	$37,798
Effect of exchange-rate changes on cash and cash equivalents	$0	−$35	$489	−$37,557	−$15,958	$38,471	$4,461	$14,139		$10,087
Net increase (decrease) in cash and cash equivalents	$60	$1,012	$38,536	$61,726	$689,126	−$282,153	$197,972	−$242,481	$145,955	$24,690
CASH AND CASH EQUIVALENTS, END OF PERIOD	$864	$1,876	$71,583	$133,309	$822,435	$540,282	$738,254	$495,773	$641,728	$666,418

SUPPLEMENTAL CASH FLOW INFORMATION

Fixed assets acquired under capital leases and other financing arrangements	$442					$5,597	$9,303	$25,850	$415	$1,572
Fixed assets acquired under financing agreements	$3,021						$5,608	$3,023		
Equity securities received for commercial agreements				$217,241	$54,402	$106,848	$331			
Stock issued in conjunction with business acquisitions and minority investments	$1,500.00			$774,409	$32,130.00	$5,000.00	$0.00			
Cash paid for interest	$26,629.00	$30,526	$67,252	$112,184	$111,589				$2,601.00	$30,019

* $US1 = approx. €0.83.

** 1997 & 1998 figures reflect restatement for 1998 business acquisition accounted for under the pooling of interest method. Some figures were changed by the company in subsequent years during this period.

Source: Amazon.com Company Reports 1997 to 2003 (Annual and Quarterly).

APPENDIX D

Consolidated Statement of Reportable Segments

Reportable Segments*	Yr 1996	Yr 1997	Yr 1998	Yr 1999	Yr 2000	Yr 2001	Yr 2002	Qtr 1 2003	Qtr 2 2003	Qtr 3 2003
Sales ($000)										
Net sales books, music, DVDs/video (Nth America)	$15,747	$147,787	$588,013	$1,308,292	$1,698,266	$1,688,752	$1,873,291			
Net sales electronics, tools and kitchen (Nth America)	$0	$0	$0	$150,654	$484,151	$547,190	$645,031			
Total net sales in North America	$15,747	$147,787	$588,013	$1,458,946	$2,182,417	$2,235,942	$2,518,322	704,712	$702,523	$709,271
International net sales	$0	$0	$21,806	$167,743	$381,075	$661,374	$1,168,935	378,847	$397,389	$425,185
Services net sales	$0	$0	$0	$13,150	$198,491	$225,117	$245,679			
Consolidated net sales	$15,747	$147,787	$609,819	$1,639,839	$2,761,983	$3,122,433	$3,932,936	1,083,559	$1,099,912	$1,134,456
Gross profit ($000)										
Gross profit books, music, DVDs/video (Nth America)	$3,459	$28,818	$128,710	$262,871	$417,452	$453,129	$527,542			
Gross profit electronics, tools and kitchen (Nth America)	$0	$0	$0	–$20,086	$44,655	$78,384	$89,863			
Total gross profit in North America	$3,459	$28,818	$128,710	$242,785	$462,107	$531,513	$617,405	186,832	$190,057	$201,121
Gross profit international	$0	$0	$4,954	$12,285	$116,234	$140,606	$249,089	83,750	$83,871	$84,700
Gross profit services	$0	$0	$0	$35,575	$77,436	$126,439	$126,124			
Gross profit consolidated	$3,459	$28,818	$133,664	$290,645	$655,777	$798,558	$992,618	270,582	$273,928	$285,821
Income (loss) ($000)										
Pro forma income (loss) from operations books, music, DVDs/video (Nth America)	–$6,443	–$31,384	–$35,534	–$31,000	$71,441	$156,753	$211,363			
Pro forma income (loss) from operations electronics, tools and kitchen (Nth America)	$0	$0	$0	–$163,827	–$269,890	–$140,685	–$73,220			
Pro forma income (loss) from operations in North America	–$6,443	–$31,384	–$35,534	–$194,827	–$198,449	$16,068	$138,143	51,661	$54,598	62,515
Pro forma income (loss) from operations international	$0	$0	–$25,498	–$78,321	$26,519	–$103,112	–$640	15,799	$12,591	11,138
Pro forma income (loss) from operations services	$0	$0	$0	–$79,223	–$145,070	$42,042	$42,599			
Segment operating income	–$6,443	–$31,384	–$61,032	–$352,371	–$317,000	–$45,002	$180,102	67,460	$67,189	$73,653
Net sales US vs outside US										
Net sales inside the US	100%	75%	80%	78%	78%	71%	65%	65%	64%	63%
Net sales outside the US		25%	20%	22%	22%	29%	35%	35%	36%	37%

* $US1 = approx. €0.83.

Source: Amazon.com Company Reports 1997 to 2003 (Annual and Quarterly).

APPENDIX E
Average Web Usage, US and UK in September 2003

	US Home	US Work	UK Home/Work
Number of sessions/visits per month	31	68	25
Number of domains visited per month	53	98	50
Time spent per month	26:14:45	75:59:47	13:37:10
Duration of a web page viewed	00:00:56	00:01:01	00:01:05

Source: CyberAtlas staff (http://cyberatlas.internet.com/) Copyright © Jupitermedia Corporation and www.cyberatlas.com.

APPENDIX F
US Internet Users by Household Income and Usage

Income	Users	Use per Month	Monthly pages Viewed
$15,000–$24,999	11,422,000	23.3 hrs	2,292
$25,000–$39,000	18,144,000	26.4 hrs	2,526
$40,000–$59,000	37,719,000	26.4 hrs	2,670
$60,000–$74,999	23,206,000	26.4 hrs	2,577
$75,000–$99,999	24,654,000	27.5 hrs	2,636
$100,000 or more	25,793,000	27.6 hrs	2,964

Source: CyberAtlas staff (http://cyberatlas.internet.com/) Copyright © Jupitermedia Corporation and www.cyberatlas.com.

APPENDIX G
Gross Profit, Income and Net Profit as a Percentage 1996 to 2003

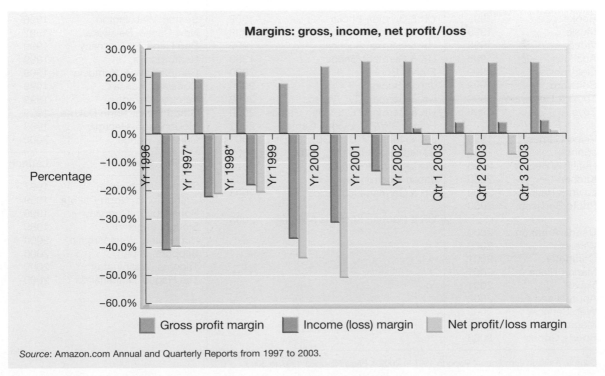

Source: Amazon.com Annual and Quarterly Reports from 1997 to 2003.

APPENDIX H

Revenue per Employee Comparison

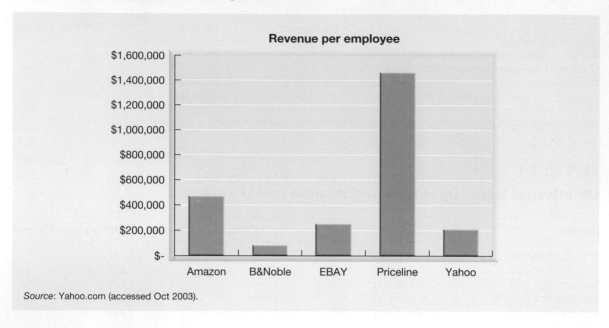

Source: Yahoo.com (accessed Oct 2003).

APPENDIX I

Timeline of Company Growth

Categories	Launch	International Categories	Launch	Distribution Centres	Launch
Books	1995	UK & German Books	1998	Seattle, Washington	1996
Music	1998	UK & German Music	1998	New Castle, Delaware	1997
Video	1998	UK & German Auctions	1999	Bad Hersfeld, Germany	1999
Auctions	1999	UK & German zShops	1999	Bedfordshire, UK	1999
Electronics	1999	France Books	2000	Campbellsville, Kentucky	1999
Software	1999	Japan Books	2000	Coffeyvill, Kansas	1999
Tools & Hardware	1999	UK & German DVD/Videos	2000	Fernley, Nevada	1999
Toys	1999	UK & German PC & Video Games	2000	Grand Forks, North Dakota	1999
		France SW/PC & Video Games	2001	McDonough, Georgia	1999
Video Games	1999	Japan Music, Video, CDs, DVDs	2001	Orleans, France	2000
zShops	1999	Canada Books, Music, DVD	2002		
Health & Beauty	2000	Marketplace International	2002	**Service Centres**	**Launch**
Kitchen	2000	Japan Electronics	2003		
Lawn & Patio	2000	UK & German Electronics	2003	Seattle, Washington	1997
Photo Services	2000			Grand Forks, North Dakota	1999
		UK & German Kitchens & Home	2003	Rogensburg, Germany	1999
Used@Amazon	2000			Slough, England	1999
Wireless	2000			Huntington, West Virginia	2000
Computers	2001			Sapporo, Japan	2000
Market Place	2001			Tacoma, Washington	2000
Travel	2001			The Hague, Netherlands	2000
Apparel and Acc	2002				
Web Services	2002				
Magazines	2003				
Sports Goods	2003				

Source: Amazon.com Annual Reports 1997 to 2002 & Press Releases 1997 to 2003.

The Formula One constructors

Mark Jenkins

This case describes four periods of dominance by particular firms in a highly competitive technological context. Formula One (F1) motorsport is the pinnacle of automotive technology and involves highly specialised constructors designing and building single-seat racecars to compete for annual championships which bring huge financial and reputational rewards. These four eras explore the stories of three contrasting companies, Ferrari, McLaren and Williams, each within a different competitive time period: in terms of how they both created and lost the basis for sustained competitive advantage.

● ● ●

Between two and four on a Sunday afternoon this is a sport. All the rest of the time it's commerce.

(Frank Williams, Managing Director, Williams F1)

In 1945 the Fédération Internationale de l'Automobile (FIA) established Formula A as the premier level of motorsport. In the years that followed Formula A became referred to as Formula One (F1) and a drivers' world championship was introduced in 1950. The first world champion was Giuseppe Farina of Italy, driving an Alfa Romeo. At that time Alfa dominated the racing along with the other Italian marques of Ferrari and Maserati. Drivers such as Juan Fangio, Alberto Ascari, Jack

Brabham, Jim Clark and Graham Hill were to take the championship during the 1950s and 60s, driving cars built by Alfa Romeo, Ferrari, Mercedes-Benz, Lancia, Cooper and Lotus. By the mid 1960s F1 had moved from being a basis for car manufacturers to promote and test their products, to a highly specialist business where purpose-built cars were developed through leading-edge technology to win a TV sporting event which enjoyed the third highest TV audience in the world, surpassed only by the Olympics and World Cup Soccer.

There have been between 10 and 14 race-car manufacturers or constructors competing in F1 at any one time. The constructors themselves can be grouped into a number of different categories. In 2003 the top three teams were Ferrari, Williams and McLaren, all medium-sized businesses turning over between $250 and $350 million per annum, with estimates suggesting that it took $30–$50m capital investment in research facilities to set up the minimum basis for being competitive. For the first three years of their entry into F1 in 2002 Toyota are estimated to have committed $1bn on capital and running costs of which only one fifth came from sponsorship. The top teams would typically have

Photo: © Michael Kim/Corbis

their own testing and development equipment, which would include wind-tunnels and other facilities. The larger teams would employ between 450 and 800 people in their F1 operations, a quarter of whom travel around the world attending Grand Prix every two to three weeks throughout the F1 season (March to November). Labour costs account for around 25 per cent of the budget. All the teams would have highly qualified technical staff which would include race engineers (who work with the driver to set up the car), designers, aerodynamicists, composite experts (to work with specialised carbon-composite materials) and systems specialists.

In addition to sponsorship, revenue is provided by prize money generated by winning championship points, in 2003 this was allocated on a sliding scale for the first eight places. The prize money is a way of dividing up the royalties earned from media coverage and other revenues negotiated, on behalf of the teams by Bernie Ecclestone's Formula One Administration (FOA). In 2003 Ferrari estimated that $30m (9.7 per cent) of their revenues would come from prize money.

In 2003 seven out of the ten F1 constructors were located in what has been referred to as 'motorsport valley', an area of the UK described by a broad arc centred around Oxford, stretching into East Anglia and down into Surrey. There were, however, other teams located outside this region such as Ferrari (Maranello, Italy); Toyota (Cologne, Germany) and Sauber (Hinwil, Switzerland). The focus on the UK has been attributed to the network of specialist engineering talent which is fundamental to success in F1, as summarised by the principal of the Renault team, Flavio Briartore: 'If you like proscuitto you come to Italy. If you like champagne, you come to France. For Formula 1 you come to England. I don't like the English weather, but the best engineering is here.'

The Formula One constructors provide a unique context to consider the competitive advantage of different multi-million pound organisations over time. The pace of change and the basis of advantage is constantly changing, shown by the fact that since the start of the world championships, only two constructors have won the championship consecutively more than four times (McLaren 1988–91; Ferrari 1999–2003) and only Ferrari (1975–77) and Williams (1992–94) have won for three consecutive years. The remainder of the case considers each of these periods of competitive dominance in chronological order.

Ferrari and its renaissance in the mid 1970s

The period 1975–77 saw a renaissance for the Ferrari team. Their previous F1 World Championship had been won in 1964, one of the few reminders of the glorious 50s and early 60s when the bright red cars of Ferrari dominated motor racing. In the mid 1970s they won 15 of the 45 races during 1975, 1976 and 1977.

Ferrari are the oldest of all the Grand Prix teams still racing. Their heritage gives them a special place in the hearts of all motor racing enthusiasts. Founded by Enzo Ferrari, an ex-driver and manager of the Alfa Romeo racing team in 1950, they and other Italian marques such as Maserati and Alfa dominated the sport during the 1950s. Ferraris have taken part in more than 550 Grand Prix (the next highest is McLaren with 440) and, despite the variable nature of the team's performance, drivers continue to view a contract with Ferrari as something very special. Perhaps this is why world champions such as Alain Prost, Nigel Mansell and Michael Schumacher have been attracted to the team at times when their cars have been far from the fastest or most reliable.

In an era when the majority of constructors are British specialists who buy in components such as engines and gearboxes, Ferrari have always done everything themselves. Engine, gearbox, suspension, chassis are all made at their Maranello factory, which enjoys the most up-to-date facilities in terms of designing, developing and building all the necessary components of a race-car. Whilst other constructors such as McLaren and Williams will paint their cars whatever colour required by their flagship sponsor, Ferraris always have been and, one assumes, always will be, bright red, the national colour of Italy, a throwback from the time when F1 cars were colour coded by country of origin. The cars have, until recently, very little evidence of sponsorship; it has always been the Ferrari emblem – a black prancing horse – which has the most prominent position. The Italian public see Ferrari as a national icon as observed by Niki Lauda:

> The Italians love you when you win and hate you when you lose and whatever you do, win, lose or simply break wind everyone in Italy wants to know about it!

The influence of Enzo Ferrari, or *Il Commendatore* as he was frequently known, was pervasive and the myths and stories surrounding him still permeate the team. It was legendary that Ferrari himself hardly ever attended a race and very rarely left the Maranello factory where his beloved cars were made. He relied on the media and his advisors for information which often created a highly political atmosphere in the team. Ferrari's first love was motor racing, despite having created a very successful range of road-going cars which he saw primarily as the source of funding for his racing. The merger between Fiat and Ferrari in 1969 provided Ferrari with a huge cash injection. Ferrari had sold 40 per cent of the company to Fiat and allowed Fiat to build the road cars. Enzo, who was then 71, would retain control of the racing operation however to concentrate on his first love, motor racing at the highest level: Formula One.

The resources which Ferrari have at their disposal have always been the envy of every other team. They had always built their own engines and have a large technical team dedicated to the task of engine design and development. In 1971 they opened their own test track at Fiorano, literally a few hundred yards from the Maranello factory. At the time it was the most advanced and sophisticated test circuit in the world, enabling the cars to be constantly tested and developed between the track and the factory. This effectively gave Ferrari their own grand prix circuit. All their competitors were obliged to hire a circuit such as Silverstone in the UK and transport their cars and equipment for a two- or three-day test. Ferrari himself attended most of the tests and would make sure he was kept informed as to exactly what was being tested and why. Enzo himself had always declared his love for the distinctive sound and power of a Ferrari engine as indicated by former Ferrari driver, Nigel Mansell:

> Enzo Ferrari believed that the engine was the most important part of the race-car. Colin [Chapman – head of Lotus] believed it was the chassis.

The early 1970s began shakily for Ferrari, the new ownership and influence from Fiat meant increased resources, but also increased pressure for results. At this time F1 was dominated by the Ford DFV engine. Built by Cosworth Engineering near Northampton and funded by the Ford Motor Company, the DFV was F1's first purpose-built engine – it was light, powerful and relatively inexpensive. In 1968 the engines were available for £7,500 each and were fully capable of winning a Grand Prix. This enabled the British constructors, who specialised in chassis design, to become increasingly competitive. In 1971 and 1973 every Grand Prix was won by a car using a DFV engine.

In 1971 the Ferrari race-cars were very fast, but not reliable. It got worse in 1972 and 1973 with cars only finishing every other race and rarely in the points. Enzo himself had been suffering poor health and the team seemed unable to turn around, despite having the huge resources of Fiat at its disposal. However through 1974 things began to change. A few years earlier Ferrari engineers had commissioned a small firm in the UK, TC prototypes, to build three chassis for the 1974 car using a monocoque structure, derived from aircraft design, and favoured by the English constructors. Mauro Forghieri had also been recalled to Ferrari in 1973 as technical director, Forghieri had been responsible for some of the more successful Ferraris of the 1960s, but had fallen from grace and spent the later part of the 1960s working on 'special projects'.

In addition to the arrival of Forghieri, a new team boss was also appointed to try and turn Ferrari fortunes around. At 25 years old, a qualified lawyer with connections to the Agnelli family who owned Fiat, Luca di Montezemolo, was an unlikely right-hand man for *Il Commendatore*. However he was given a relatively free hand by Ferrari and brought much-needed management discipline to the team. Whilst there had always been a huge supply of talent at Ferrari, particularly in the design and development of engines, gearboxes and suspension systems, it had not always reached its collective potential. Enzo's autocratic style of 'divide and rule' had created much confusion and rivalry within the team. Montezemolo defined strict areas of responsibility in order to reduce the amount of interference and internal politics. This created a situation where the various technical teams (chassis and suspension; engine; gearbox) concentrated on, and were fully accountable for, their own area. Montezemolo was also instrumental in the recruitment of driver Niki Lauda. Lauda was of Austrian aristocratic descent, but was totally committed to his racing. He had been very successful in Formula Two but was having a torrid time with the ailing BRM team in F1. In 1973 Enzo Ferrari told Lauda he wanted him to drive for Ferrari, an offer which very few drivers have ever refused.

In 1974 Lauda and the design team had embarked upon an exhaustive testing and development programme at the Fiorano test track. The new car, the 312B, was very fast; however, there were still reliability problems and although Lauda was leading the championship at the British Grand

Prix, the lead was lost through technical problems which resulted in Emerson Fittipaldi in a McLaren taking the eventual honours.

In 1975 the fruits of Forghieri's creative ideas and the intensive testing at Fiorano were exemplified in the new 312T which featured a wide low body with a powerful 'flat 12' 12-cylinder engine and a revolutionary transverse (sideways mounted) gearbox which improved the balance of the car, making it handle extremely well. Whilst the new car was not ready until the season had already started, Lauda, with the support of teammate Regazzoni, was able to easily secure both the drivers' and constructors' world championships. The Ferraris dominated the 1975 season. With their elegant handling and the power advantage of the engine, they were in a class of their own. Because the majority of the competition all had the same engine gearbox combination (Ford DFV and Hewland gearbox), they were unable to respond to a chassis/gearbox/engine combination which was unique to Ferrari.

1976 continued in much the same vein, with Lauda and Regazzoni winning the early races. The intensive testing did not let up and new ideas and innovations, such as a revised rear suspension system, were constantly being tried out. On the management front, Montezemolo had been promoted to head up Fiat's entire motorsport operation, which included the Lancia rally programme as well as Ferrari. Daniele Audetto was moved from managing the rally team to Sporting Director at Ferrari. However, things were not to go as smoothly as in 1975. At the German Grand Prix Lauda lost control of the car in the wet and crashed in flames. He was rescued by four other drivers, but not before suffering severe burns and inhaling toxic fumes. His life was in the balance for some weeks whilst the grand prix series continued with James Hunt (McLaren) reducing Lauda's lead in the championship. Miraculously Lauda recovered from his injuries and although still badly scarred, he returned to race for Ferrari. He and Hunt went into the last Grand Prix of 1976 (Japan) with Lauda leading by three points. There was heavy rain and Lauda pulled out of the race leaving the drivers' championship to Hunt, although Ferrari still collected the constructors' championship. Whilst on paper it was a good year, by rights Ferrari should have dominated 1976 as they had 1975. Audetto who, perhaps not surprisingly, had been unable to live up to the role created by Montezemolo and had failed to develop a strong relationship with

Lauda, returned back to the world of rallying. Ferrari went into 1977 in a state of disarray.

In 1977 Ferrari were still the team to beat, although the testing and development lost through Lauda's six-week convalescence had undermined the crushing dominance which the team had earlier shown. The competition were beginning to find ways of catching up. The Brabham team moved away from the Ford DFV and used an Alfa Romeo 'flat 12' similar to the Ferrari engine. Tyrrell launched the revolutionary P34 six-wheeled car which seemed to be the only car able to stay with the Ferrari. Ferrari themselves were not standing still and launched the 312T2 in 1976 which was a significant development of the original 312T. Ferrari won the 1977 drivers' and constructors' championship, but this was the end of the partnership with Niki Lauda; the relationship had never been the same since the Nurburgring accident. Lauda left to join Brabham, but did not regain the world championship until he drove for McLaren in 1984. Whilst Lauda was not perhaps the fastest racer on the track he was always able to develop a car and build relationships with the design team which enabled Ferrari to translate the driver's senses into reliable technical solutions.

The unprecedented run of Ferrari success continued in 1978 with the 312T3 car driven by two highly talented drivers: Argentinean Carlos Reutemann was joined by the flamboyant Gilles Villeneuve and whilst they were not able to win the constructors' championship they achieved a very strong second place. In 1979 Reutemann was replaced by South African Jody Scheckter whose consistency contrasted with Villeneuve's erratic speed. Scheckter won the drivers' championship, with Ferrari taking the constructors' championship. Their greatest moment was when Scheckter and Villeneuve finished first and second at the Italian Grand Prix at Monza.

However, 1979 was the last time that Ferrari were to win a drivers' world championship for 21 years. 1980 was something of a disaster for Ferrari. Scheckter and Villeneuve were totally uncompetitive in the 312T5 car which, whilst a significant development from the 312T4, was outclassed by the competition. New innovations in aerodynamics brought the 'ground effect' revolution, pioneered by Lotus and quickly adopted by Williams and Brabham. Here the underside of the car featured two 'venturi', or channels either side of the driver. These were aerodynamically designed to create a low pressure area under the car which sucked the car to the track allowing faster corner-ing. Sliding strips of material or 'skirts' were used to create a seal for the air flowing under the car. Whilst the Ferrari's engine was one of the most powerful it was a 'flat 12', meaning that the cylin-ders were horizontal to the ground, creating a low and wide barrier which gave no opportunity to create the ground effect achieved with the slimmer V8 DFV engines. In 1979 Alfa Romeo had launched a V12 engine to replace their flat 12 for this very reason. No such initiative had been taken at Ferrari who were concentrating on a longer term project to develop a V6 turbocharged engine. Autosport correspondent Nigel Roebuck commented on this change of fortune: 'Maranello's flat-12, still a magnificent racing engine, is in-compatible with modern chassis. Villeneuve and Scheckter were competing in yesterday's cars.' The lowest point came in the Canadian Grand Prix when the reigning world champion, Jody Scheckter, failed to qualify his Ferrari for the race, a bit like Italy failing to qualify for the soccer World Cup. Once again the full wrath of the Italian press descended on the team.

McLaren and Honda domination in the late 1980s

The period from 1988 to 1991 was unusual in the hyper-competitive world of F1, where the pace of change is rarely matched in any other competitive environment. This period was notable because of the dominance of one constructor. In one year the McLaren team won 15 of the 16 races. Such dominance had not been seen before and will almost certainly never be seen again.

Founded by New Zealander and F1 driver Bruce McLaren in 1966, the McLaren team had their first victory in the Belgian Grand Prix of 1968. Tragically McLaren himself was killed two years later while testing. Lawyer and family friend Teddy Mayer took over as team principal. The team con-tinued to develop and in 1974 secured a long-term sponsorship from Philip Morris to promote the Marlboro brand of cigarettes. This was a partner-ship that was to last until 1996, probably the most enduring relationship between a constructor and a 'flagship' sponsor. However in the late 70s McLaren found itself left behind by some of the new aerodynamic advances. In September 1980 Ron Dennis became joint team principal with Mayer, a position which he took over solely in

1982, when Mayer was 'encouraged' by Philip Morris to take a less active role in the manage-ment of McLaren. In the previous year McLaren moved from their modest site in Colnbrook to a modern facility at Woking in Surrey, south of London.

Dennis had been a mechanic for the highly successful Cooper and Brabham teams, but left to set up his own Formula Two (a smaller, less expen-sive formula) team in 1971. By the end of the 70s he had built up a reputation for professionalism and immaculate presentation. His Project Four com-pany brought in designer John Barnard who had some radical ideas about using carbon fibre, rather than metal, as the basis for a race-car chassis. These ideas were to provide the basis for the radical MP4 car. Both Dennis and Barnard were perfectionists, with Dennis's obsession with immaculate pres-entation and attention to detail complemented by Barnard's uncompromising quest for technical excellence. As John Barnard observed in an inter-view, the entire nature of the organisation shifted:

> We changed from being mechanic led to a team which was totally controlled by the drawing office. Ron used to tell everyone time and time again, 'I don't care if we're the last two cars on the grid, we'll be the smartest and the best presented' and that attitude built into the company once it was launched.

In 1986 John Barnard left to join the strug-gling Ferrari team. Barnard was considered by many to be the reason for McLaren's developing dominance. The partnership between Dennis and Barnard had been stormy, but a huge amount had been achieved through the energy of these two individuals. Dennis providing the managerial and commercial acumen and Barnard highly innov-ative design skills. To replace Barnard, Brabham designer Gordon Murray was brought into the team, perhaps best known for developing the innov-ative 'fan car' for Brabham in 1978. Murray, like Barnard, was at the leading edge of F1 car design.

A further factor in McLaren's success had been their relationship with engine suppliers. In the mid-1980s turbo-charging became the key tech-nology and in 1983 they used a Porsche turbo engine which was funded by the electronics com-pany TAG, a sponsor which had previously been with the Williams team. However, the emerging force in engine development was Honda who had re-entered F1 in 1983 in partnership with Williams. Importantly the engines were supported by a significant commitment from Honda in both people and resources. Honda used the relationship as an opportunity to develop some of their most talented engineers and to transfer F1 design and development capabilities to their production car programme. In the mid 1980s the Williams/Honda partnership was very successful, but following Frank Williams' road accident in 1986, Honda began to have doubts about the future of the Williams team and agreed to move to supply both McLaren and Lotus for the 1987 season.

Halfway through 1987 McLaren announced that they had recruited two of the top drivers in F1 to their team for the 1988 season: Alain Prost and Ayrton Senna. This was unusual as most teams tended to have a clear hierarchy with a lead driver being supported by a 'number two' who was either regarded as less skilful and/or less experienced than the lead driver. However McLaren appeared to feel that they would be able to deal with the potential problems which such a structure could cause, as reported in *Motorsport*:

> Ayrton Senna is being moved from Lotus to McLaren to join Prost in one of the most professional and well balanced teams of all time. Prost and Senna have been announced as joint number one drivers, and McLaren International has shown in the past that it is well capable of handling two top drivers, which few other teams have managed.

Ayrton Senna, the young Brazilian, had made a name for himself as being extremely talented and totally committed, but very difficult to manage. In his previous team, Lotus, he is alleged to have blocked the recruitment of second driver Derek Warwick as he regarded him too great a threat and persuaded the team to bring in the less experienced and younger Johnny Dumfries instead. Prost and Senna were real contrasts. Senna was fast, determined and ruthless; Prost was fast too, but a great tactician and adept at team politics, making sure that the whole team was behind him. It was rumoured that a key reason for Honda moving to McLaren was that they now had Alain Prost. However, it was ultimately Senna who was able to win the psychological battle and change the balance of power within the team.

In 1988 the Honda-powered MP4 car was without question the fastest and most reliable car on the circuit. This meant that effectively the only real competition for Prost and Senna was each other. This competition between two highly committed and talented drivers resulted in one of the most enduring and bitter feuds the sport has ever known. In 1988 Senna swerved at Prost as they raced wheel to wheel at 190 mph. Prost told him, 'If you want the world championship badly enough to die for it, you are welcome'. In 1990 the acrimony with Senna culminated in Prost moving to Ferrari. Senna now had the team to himself. But the battle between them continued, reaching a dramatic climax at the Japanese Grand Prix when Senna forced Prost's Ferrari off the road, and as a consequence became world champion.

Ron Dennis and his professional management style was synonymous with the success of McLaren, indicating that the era of the 'one man band' Formula One constructor was past. His record since taking over in 1982 has been unsurpassed. Eddie Jordan, principal of the Jordan team, made the following statement when planning to enter F1 in 1990:

> I know it sounds far fetched, but I want to emulate Ron Dennis. He's won that many Grand Prix, he's won that many championships, he's been on pole that many times and he's got the best drivers. Everyone hates him; but they only hate him because he's the best. I believe I'm as good as he is: I believe I'm in the same league, but only time will tell.

Dennis's negotiating and marketing abilities were legendary throughout Formula One. McLaren also created their own marketing consultancy operation where the smaller teams engaged them to find sponsors. In 1991 *Management Week* had Ron Dennis on the front cover with the question: 'Is Ron Dennis Britain's best manager?' Dennis likens the management of McLaren to that of a game of chess: '. . . you've got to get all the elements right, the overall package, the budget, the designer, the engine, the drivers, the organisation'. John Barnard once likened working with Dennis as: 'being in a room with a hand grenade rolling about without its pin, about to go off and make a horrible mess.' Dennis is renowned for being hyper-competitive and once chastised a driver who was delighted with finishing second with the comment – 'remember, you're only the first of the losers'. Dennis's ambitions went beyond F1 and in 1988 began a project to build a road-going car, the McLaren F1. In many ways this mirrored the development of Ferrari who had made the progression from producing dedicated race cars to also develop road-going cars. The McLaren F1 was launched in 1994 and with a price tag of £634,000 with a top speed of 231 mph became the most expensive and fastest road-going car in the world.

The McLaren–Honda combination had dominated F1 from 1988 through to 1991, and it was difficult to see what more could be achieved. In September 1992, following widespread speculation, Honda confirmed that they were pulling out of F1 racing. Honda's reasons were simple, they had been hugely successful and achieved all of their objectives; it was now time to stand back from F1 and find some new challenges. Whilst Dennis had been told about Honda's thinking in late 1991, it appeared that he hadn't taken it seriously enough and the team had no real engine alternatives. This meant they lost valuable winter development time as they tried to find a new engine supplier. In 1993 they competed with 'off-the-shelf' customer Ford engines available to any team who had the cash to buy them. Senna's skills still gave McLaren five victories, despite having a less than competitive car. However at the end of 1993 Senna left the McLaren team to move to Williams, whom he saw as having the superior car and engine combination. Former world champion and advisor to Ferrari, Niki Lauda saw this as the terminal blow: 'Senna was a leader. He told them exactly what was wrong with the car. Hakkinen [Senna's replacement] is not in a position to do that, so the reaction time is much longer. Senna motivated the designers.' John Hogan VP of European marketing for Philip Morris and holder of the McLaren purse strings saw the problem as design leadership and was advocating that Barnard be brought back to McLaren.

The mid 1990s were a particularly difficult period for McLaren. Having tried Peugeot engines in 1994 they moved to Mercedes in 1995. However, 1995 was perhaps best remembered for the debacle at the start when neither Nigel Mansell or Mika Hakkinen could fit into the new £50m MP4/10 and then Mansell's alleged £4.5m contract to race for the year fell apart when neither he nor the car came up to expectations. On a more positive note 1995 was significant in that it heralded a new partnership between McLaren and Mercedes. Mercedes had been considering a major commitment to F1 and in 1995 they concluded a deal which involved their taking equity stakes in McLaren (40 per cent) and also in specialist engine builder Ilmor Engineering, based near Northampton (25 per cent, increased in 2002 to 55 per cent), who were to build the Mercedes engines used in F1. This relationship was not just about F1 and would ultimately lead to the design and manufacturer of the new Mercedes SLR sportscar using F1 technology and materials.

Williams and the technological revolution: the mid 1990s

If the McLaren MP4 was the dominant car in the late 1980s, the Williams FW15 & 16 powered by a Renault V10 was the car to beat in the early 1990s. During the period 1992–94 Williams' cars won 27 out of 48 races; they secured the F1 constructors' title for all three years and the world championship for drivers was won in a Williams in 1992 (Nigel Mansell) and 1993 (Alain Prost).

Like most of the founders of the Formula One constructors, Frank Williams began as a driver, perhaps not of the same standing as Bruce McLaren or Jack Brabham, but nonetheless someone who lived, breathed and loved motor racing. His desire to remain in the sport led him to develop a business buying and selling racing cars and spare parts and in 1968 Frank Williams (Racing Cars) Ltd was formed. A series of triumphs, tragedies and near bankruptcies led up to the establishment of Williams Grand Prix Engineering in 1977 when Frank Williams teamed up with technical director Patrick Head. Frank Williams' approach and style owes a lot to the difficult years in the 70s when he survived on his wits and very little else, including at one time operating from a telephone box near the workshop when the phones were disconnected as he hadn't been able to pay the bill. His style could be described as autocratic, entrepreneurial and certainly frugal, despite the multi-million pound funding he managed to extract from the likes of Canon, R.J. Reynolds and Rothmans. Williams saw his role as providing the resources for the best car to be built. His long-standing relationship with Head was pivotal to the team and brought together a blend of entrepreneurial energy and technical excellence needed to succeed in F1.

The first car from this new alliance was the FW06, designed by Patrick Head and with support from Saudi Airlines. The team enjoyed some success in 1980/81 by winning the constructors' championship both years and with Alan Jones winning the drivers' title in 1980. Jones was a forthright Australian who knew what he wanted and was not afraid to voice his opinions. His approach to working with the team was very influential and coloured Frank Williams' view of drivers:

I took a very masculine attitude towards drivers and assumed that they should behave – or should be treated – like Alan.

A further success occurred in 1986/87 with Nelson Piquet winning the drivers' title in 1987 and Williams the constructors' title in both years. This was despite the road accident in 1986 which left Frank Williams tetraplegic and confined to a wheelchair. However 1988 was Williams' worst season; with Honda having switched to supplying McLaren, they were forced to suddenly switch to 'off-the-shelf' Judd V10 engines which were available to anyone who wanted one. Williams didn't win a single race, whilst McLaren won 15 out of the 16 Grand Prix of 1988 and a disillusioned Nigel Mansell left and went to Ferrari. Frank Williams had to search frantically for a new engine deal which he found in 1990 with Renault. At the end of 1985 Renault had withdrawn from Formula One as a constructor, having failed to win a world championship over the previous eight seasons. However, they continued their engine development activities with the aim of building a new F1 engine to meet the new non-turbo standards due to be introduced in 1989. Frank Williams was able to form an agreement for Renault to supply him with the new V10 engine. This relationship became a far-reaching and durable one, with Renault putting human and financial resources into the project with Williams. They also sought to develop the relationship further and extended their activities with Renault by running their team of saloon cars for the British Touring Car Championship, and also provided engineering input and the Williams name for a special edition of the Renault Clio.

In 1990 a lack of driver talent meant that the team were only able to win two races. In 1991 Nigel Mansell was persuaded to return from retirement by Frank Williams and narrowly missed taking the 1991 title, but in 1992 the team dominated the circuits, effectively winning the championship by the middle of the season. Nigel Mansell went into the record books by winning the first five consecutive races of the season. This was a phenomenal achievement and emphatically demonstrated that McLaren were no longer at the top; Williams most certainly were. However, deterioration in the relationship between Williams and Mansell led to the driver's retirement from F1 at the end of the year.

The Williams approach to design and development of a car was always the highest priority. Patrick Head had always been one of the more conspicuous of the technical directors in Formula One, a role which is often put into the shade by the team principal and driver. In a sport where personnel change teams frequently, the stable relationship between Williams and Head provided enviable continuity compared with the rest of the field. Whilst Head's designs had often been functional rather than innovative, he had always been able to take a good idea and develop it further. These have included ground effect (originally developed by Lotus), carbon-composite monocoque (McLaren), semi-automatic gearbox (Ferrari), and active suspension (Lotus). The car development process was always a top priority at Williams and Head was supported by many junior designers who then went on to be highly influential in Formula One, such as Neil Oatley and Adrian Newey (McLaren), Frank Dernie (Ligier, Lotus and Arrows) and Ross Brawn (Benetton, Ferrari).

This focus on developing the car and engine combination sometimes meant that the driver took second place in the Williams philosophy, despite the fact that a good test driver, who could tell the technicians what needed to be done to the car to improve its performance, was essential to the development process. There had been a number of high profile disputes between drivers and Williams which had, in part, been attributable to Frank Williams' 'masculine' approach to dealing with drivers. Controversy broke out when the relationship between Williams and two top British drivers broke down. In 1992 Nigel Mansell left when he felt his 'number one' driver position was threatened by the recruitment of Alain Prost for 1993 (although Prost himself left the following year for the same reason regarding the hiring of Ayrton Senna). A similar situation arose when the 1996 world champion, Damon Hill was not retained for the 1997 season and was replaced with Heinz-Harald Frentzen. In an interview with *The Sunday Times* Patrick Head set out the reasons for the decision not to hold on to Hill:

> We are an engineering company and that is what we focus on. Ferrari are probably the only team where you can say the driver is of paramount importance and that is because [Michael] Schumacher is three-quarters of a second a lap quicker than anyone else.

This emphasis on the driver being only part of the equation was not lost on Paul Stewart who was concentrating on developing the Stewart Grand Prix entry to F1 in 1996:

> If you haven't got the money none of it is possible, so money is one key to success – but what makes a

difference is how the money is used. It's not down to any one thing like a driver or a engine, but the interaction that matters. If you look at the Williams team, they rely on a solid framework, their organisation, their engine, their car design is all amalgamated into something that gives a platform for everyone to work on. They don't believe putting millions into a driver is going to make all the difference.

Williams' emphatic dominance in the 1992 season was due to a number of factors: the development of the powerful and reliable Renault engine was perfectly complemented by the FW15 chassis which incorporated Patrick Head's development of some of the innovations of the early 90s, namely semi-automatic gearboxes, drive-by-wire technology and their own active suspension system. As summarised by a senior manager at Williams F1:

> I think we actually were better able to exploit the technology that was available and led that technology revolution. We were better able to exploit it to the full, before the others caught up . . . it wasn't just one thing but a combination of ten things, each one giving you another 200/300th of a second, if you add them up you a get a couple of seconds of advantage.

However, other teams were also able to use these innovations and in 1993 the Benetton team made a great deal of progress with both the gearbox and suspension innovations largely attributed to the development skills of their new driver, Michael Schumacher. Williams' technical lead coupled with the tactical race skills of Alain Prost, supported by promoted test driver Damon Hill (due to Mansell's sudden exit) secured the 1993 world championship and constructors' championship for Williams F1.

1994 was a disastrous year, but not for reasons of performance as Williams won the constructors' championship for the third successive year (this was always their declared primary objective, with the drivers' championship very much a secondary aim). Frank Williams had, for some time, regarded Brazilian Ayrton Senna as the best driver around, with the obvious performance advantage of the FW15 chassis and the Renault V10 engine, Senna was keen to move to Williams. The problem was that a bitter and prolonged feud between Senna and Prost, originating from their time together at McLaren, meant that if Senna arrived Prost would leave. This was exactly what happened. Prost decided to retire (though he returned to run his own team) and Ayrton Senna was partnered by Damon Hill for the 1994 season. However, tragedy struck in the San Marino Grand Prix at Imola on 1 May 1994 when Senna was killed in an accident, an event which not only devastated the Williams team but the sport as a whole. Also due to the accident having occurred in Italy key members of the Williams team along with the organisers of the race were charged with manslaughter, a case which was only recently dropped by the Italian authorities.

For the remainder of the season Hill found himself as lead driver supported by the new test driver David Coulthard and a couple of 'comebacks' from Nigel Mansell. Whilst Williams lost the drivers' title to the rising star of German driver Michael Schumacher, despite these huge setbacks Williams retained the constructors' title for 1994.

In 1995 the Benetton team was eclipsing the Williams domination. Benetton had developed a car using many of the technological innovations used by Williams (with the help of ex-Williams designer, Ross Brawn). In addition Renault's ambitions to match Honda's previous domination of the sport as an engine supplier from 1986–91 led them to supply Benetton with their engines as well as Williams, a decision which incensed Head and Williams. 1995 was the year of Benetton and Michael Schumacher, breaking the three-year domination of the Williams team. However, in 1996 Schumacher moved to the then uncompetitive Ferrari team for £27m, putting him in third place in the Forbes chart of sports top earners. This left the way clear for Williams to dominate the season, with Benetton failing to fill the gap left by Schumacher.

Ferrari: the return to glory: 1999–2003

In the mid 1980s more and more investment was poured into the Italian facilities but with no effect on performance. A key problem was that new developments in aerodynamics and the use of composite materials had emerged from the UK's motorsport valley. Ferrari had traditionally focused on the engine as their key competitive advantage, which made perfect sense given that, unlike most of the competition who outsourced their engines from suppliers such as Cosworth, Ferrari designed and manufactured their own engines. However it appeared that these new technologies were effectively substituting superior engine power with enhanced grip due to aerodynamic downforce and improved chassis rigidity.

In 1984, in an effort to introduce a greater understanding of aerodynamics in Ferrari, British designer Harvey Postlethwaite became the first non-Italian Technical Director of Ferrari. In 1986 British designer John Barnard was recruited to the top technical role. However Barnard was not prepared to move to Italy as he felt that his technical team and network of contacts in the UK would be essential to the success of his position. Surprisingly Enzo Ferrari allowed him to establish a design and manufacturing facility near Guildford in Surrey that became known as the Ferrari 'GTO' or Guildford Technical Office. It seemed that rather than being a unique and distinctively Italian F1 team, Ferrari were now prepared to imitate the British constructors who Enzo had once, rather contemptuously, referred to as the 'Garagistes'. The concept of the GTO was that it was concerned with longer-term research and development and would concentrate on the design of the following year's car, whereas in Maranello, under Postlethwaite, they would focus on building and racing the current car. However the fact that Barnard was defining the technical direction of Ferrari meant that he became increasingly involved in activities at both sites.

Enzo Ferrari's death in 1988 created a vacuum that was filled by executives from the Fiat organisation for a number of years. It was written into the contract that on Enzo's death Fiat's original stake would be increased to 90 per cent; this greater investment led to attempts to run Ferrari as a formal subsidiary of the Fiat group. Barnard became frustrated with the interference and politics of the situation and left to join Benetton in 1989. However in 1992 Fiat reappointed Luca di Montezemolo, this time as CEO with a mandate to do whatever was needed to take Ferrari back to the top. Montezemolo, who had been team manager for Ferrari during the successful period in the mid 1970s, had subsequently taken on a range of high-profile management roles including running Italy's hosting of the soccer World Cup in 1990. One of Montezemolo's first actions was to reappoint John Barnard as technical director and re-establish GTO. He was quoted in *The Times* as follows: 'In Italy we are cut away from the Silicon Valley of Formula One that has sprung up in England.' With an Englishman heading up design he followed this up with the appointment of a Frenchman, Jean Todt, to handle the overall management of the team. Both appointments were clear signals to all involved in Ferrari that things were going to change. Todt had no experience in F1 but had been in motorsport management for many years and had recently led a successful rally and sports-car programme at Peugeot.

However the physical separation between design and development in Guildford and the racing operation in Maranello led to increased problems and eventually Barnard and Ferrari parted company in 1996, this time for good. This opened the way for Ferrari to recruit driver Michael Schumacher and a number of the key individuals in the Benetton technical team which had helped him to his world titles in 1994 and 1995. Todt and di Montezemolo also chose not to make a direct replacement for the role of technical supremo who would both lead the design of the car and the management of the technical activity. They split the role between a chief designer, Rory Byrne, who had overall responsibility for designing the car, and Ross Brawn who managed the entire technical operation; roles which both had undertaken in working with Schumacher at Benetton. However the contractual arrangement with John Barnard had been one where the GTO designers were paid through his private company. When he left they all went with him and Byrne and Brawn faced the task of building up from scratch a new design department – around 50 people, based in Italy.

As part of their recruitment of Michael Schumacher in 1996 Ferrari entered into a commercial partnership with tobacco giant Philip Morris to use their Marlboro brand on the Ferrari cars. In a novel arrangement Philip Morris, rather than Ferrari, would pay Schumacher's salary, and would also make a significant contribution to Ferrari's annual operating budget. In addition to Marlboro, Ferrari also entered into a long-term partnership with Shell to provide both financial and technical support to the team, a departure for Ferrari who had previously worked with Italian petroleum giant Agip. In these kinds of arrangements Ferrari led a trend away from selling space on cars to long-term commercial arrangements, with coordinated marketing strategies for commercial partners to maximise the benefits of their investments.

This rejuvenated team provided the basis for Michael Schumacher's dominance of F1. In 1997 they raced the Barnard-developed Ferrari and finished second in the constructors' championship. Their competitiveness continued to improve and in 1999 they won their first constructors' championship for 12 years – although the drivers' championship went to Mika Hakkinen in a McLaren-Mercedes. However in 2000 Ferrari secured both championships and it was at this point that they felt they had truly returned to the glory of the mid 70s, having been 21 years since their last drivers' world championship. In 2002 Schumacher and Ferrari were so dominant that a series of regulation changes were introduced to try and make the racing more competitive. These changes were also prompted by Ferrari's approach of having a lead driver, which meant that often the second driver was asked to move over in order for the lead driver to maximise his world-championship points. This happened in a particularly blatant manner at the 2002 Austrian Grand Prix when Ferrari number 2, Rubens Barrichello, moved over just before the finish line to allow Michael Schumacher to win. This produced an angry reaction from fans worldwide and made both the governing body – the FIA – and Ferrari reflect on the wisdom of such a blatant use of team orders.

Whilst Schumacher's talent as a driver and a motivator of the team (he learnt Japanese to converse with an engine technician recruited from Honda) was clearly critical, another key aspect in Ferrari's advantage for 2002 had been their relationship with Bridgestone tyres. In 2000 Bridgestone had been the sole supplier to all F1 teams and therefore tyres were no longer a source of advantage. However in 2001 Michelin entered F1 and Ferrari's main rivals – Williams, McLaren and Renault – switched to Michelin. At the time the regulations stipulated that each manufacturer could create only two specific tyre compounds. For Bridgestone, who now only supplied Ferrari and a number of less competitive teams, the choice was clear: they had to design and develop their compounds specifically for Michael Schumacher and Ferrari. Everyone else would have to make do with this specification. For Michelin the problem was more complex with many top teams and drivers vying for a compound that specifically suited their car and driving style. Inevitably the Michelin solution was a compromise across many drivers and teams. However in 2003 the regulations were relaxed and they were able to develop specific compounds for each team/driver. Despite stronger competition from Williams, McLaren and Renault in 2003 Ferrari were able to secure a record-breaking fifth consecutive constructors' title and Michael Schumacher a sixth world championship, breaking Juan Fangio's record which had stood since 1957.

Conclusion

Tempting as it was in 2004 to see Ferrari as the dominant force in the industry, commentators who knew it well pointed to history and suggested that the Ferrari era of success would undoubtedly come to an end at some time. But this raised interesting questions: who would take over and how would they achieve it? How and why does the basis for success shift over time? Is it possible for a team to sustain success for long periods and if so, how?

APPENDIX

Summary of World Champions

Year	Driver	Car/Engine	Constructor's Cup
1950	Giuseppe Farina	Alfa Romeo	
1951	Juan Manuel Fangio	Alfa Romeo	
1952	Alberto Ascari	Ferrari	
1953	Alberto Ascari	Ferrari	
1954	Juan Manuel Fangio	Maserati	
1955	Juan Manuel Fangio	Mercedes-Benz	
1956	Juan Manuel Fangio	Lancia-Ferrari	
1957	Juan Manuel Fangio	Maserati	
1958	Mike Hawthorn	Ferrari	Vanwall
1959	Jack Brabham	Cooper/Climax	Cooper/Climax
1960	Jack Brabham	Cooper/Climax	Cooper/Climax
1961	Phil Hill	Ferrari	Ferrari
1962	Graham Hill	BRM	BRM
1963	Jim Clark	Lotus/Climax	Lotus/Climax
1964	John Surtees	Ferrari	Ferrari
1965	Jim Clark	Lotus/Climax	Lotus/Climax
1966	Jack Brabham	Brabham/Repco	Brabham/Repco
1967	Denny Hulme	Brabham/Repco	Brabham/Repco
1968	Graham Hill	Lotus/Ford	Lotus/Ford
1969	Jackie Stewart	Matra/Ford	Matra/Ford
1970	Jochen Rindt	Lotus/Ford	Lotus/Ford
1971	Jackie Stewart	Tyrrell/Ford	Tyrrell/Ford
1972	Emerson Fittipaldi	Lotus/Ford	Lotus/Ford
1973	Jackie Stewart	Tyrrell/Ford	Lotus/Ford
1974	Emerson Fittipaldi	McLaren/Ford	McLaren/Ford
1975	Niki Lauda	Ferrari	Ferrari
1976	James Hunt	McLaren/Ford	Ferrari
1977	Niki Lauda	Ferrari	Ferrari
1978	Mario Andretti	Lotus/Ford	Lotus/Ford
1979	Jody Scheckter	Ferrari	Ferrari
1980	Alan Jones	Williams/Ford	Williams/Ford
1981	Nelson Piquet	Brabham/Ford	Williams/Ford
1982	Keke Rosberg	Williams/Ford	Ferrari
1983	Nelson Piquet	Brabham/BMW	Ferrari
1984	Niki Lauda	McLaren/Porsche	McLaren/Porsche
1985	Alain Prost	McLaren/Porsche	McLaren/Porsche
1986	Alain Prost	McLaren/Porsche	Williams/Honda
1987	Nelson Piquet	Williams/Honda	Williams/Honda
1988	Ayrton Senna	McLaren/Honda	McLaren/Honda
1989	Alain Prost	McLaren/Honda	McLaren/Honda
1990	Ayrton Senna	McLaren/Honda	McLaren/Honda
1991	Ayrton Senna	McLaren/Honda	McLaren/Honda
1992	Nigel Mansell	Williams/Renault	Williams/Renault
1993	Alain Prost	Williams/Renault	Williams/Renault
1994	Michael Schumacher	Benetton/Ford	Williams/Renault
1995	Michael Schumacher	Benetton/Renault	Benetton/Renault
1996	Damon Hill	Williams/Renault	Williams/Renault
1997	Jacques Villeneuve	Williams/Renault	Williams/Renault
1998	Mika Hakkinen	McLaren/Mercedes	McLaren/Mercedes
1999	Mika Hakkinen	McLaren/Mercedes	Ferrari
2000	Michael Schumacher	Ferrari	Ferrari
2001	Michael Schumacher	Ferrari	Ferrari
2002	Michael Schumacher	Ferrari	Ferrari
2003	Michael Schumacher	Ferrari	Ferrari
2004	Michael Schumacher*	Ferrari*	Ferrari*

* Unconfirmed at time of writing.

Note: Constructors' championship is based on the cumulative points gained by a team during the season. Currently each team is limited to entering two cars and drivers per race.

The rise and fall of Baan Company

Henk A. Post

Baan Company became one of the outstanding vendors of enterprise business software in the 1990s. It developed an ambitious strategy to speed up its growth. But initial successes turned into failure and the company lost its leading position in the market – culminating in its takeover by Invensys in 2000. The case describes the characteristics of the industry in the 1990s and Baan's strategy to become the winner of the global competition game.

● ● ●

Introduction

In May 1978 Jan Baan started as an entrepreneur with his own consultancy firm. By accident, in 1979, Baan developed its first financial software product. At that moment, the firm started the transition into a software firm. As a consequence, the first application was followed by a number of others. Two years later, it undertook the task of developing broadly applicable, enterprise-wide information systems. These were based on a modular approach to make them readily adaptable to changing technologies and end user needs. Baan sold its first information system in the Netherlands in 1981. Since then it has introduced several new generations of products and expanded its operations to encompass most major markets around the world. By the end of 1989 Baan started distributing the world's first ERP (Enterprise Resource Planning) package for client/server architectures. Companies used this software to tie together and coordinate internal operations like manufacturing, purchasing and logistics and to replace old-fashioned functional systems.

During the 1990s, Baan became one of the leading global vendors of ERP software. Its corporate mission was to provide companies with innovative business software solutions which were aligned with the company's organisational structure, business practices, and operational procedures. Baan's objective of being on the leading edge spilled over into marketing and implied targeting early adopters, or what it called 'innovators'. These customers tended to be larger, less price-sensitive, and capable of committing to large transactions. The resignation of the founder Jan Baan in July 1998, a disappointing order flow in 1998, and mistakes of the leadership team greatly weakened the competitive and financial position of the company. As a result, in 2000 it was taken over by the British firm Invensys. The founder and former CEO Jan Baan left the Board in 1998 and sold his minority stake in the company in 2000 to Invensys.

The industry

The ERP industry is rooted in the control automation market of the 1960s. In the 1970s, MRP (Materials Requirement Planning) brought about the integration of purchasing and stock control. During the 1980s, the MRP package was expanded to include functionality that took capacity into account in the planning process. This planning facility enabled manufacturers to optimise their existing capacity whilst at the same time working to fulfil their customers' wishes. This generation became known by the name of Manufacturing Resource Planning (MRP-II). Because larger companies in particular had been experiencing increasing

Dr Henk A. Post has held several management positions in Baan Company. He has written this case study in his capacity as a professor of strategic management at the Erasmus University Rotterdam. It is intended as a basis of class discussion and not as an illustration of good or bad management practice. © Henk A. Post, 2004. Not to be reproduced or quoted without permission.

Exhibit 1	The ERP vendors in 1994

Vendor	1994 ERP Revenue (in US$m)*	1994 Licences	1994 Installed Base
SAP	723	654	3,600
Computer Ass.	410	2957	10,000
System S/w Ass.	290	540	10,000
J.D. Edwards	157	427	1,644
JBA International	120	200	1,500
Baan Company	120	372	1,800
Oracle	113	121	216
Andersen Cons.	103	91	937
Marcam Corp.	102	353	13,000

* US$1 = approx €0.83.

difficulties in coordinating their activities, demand developed for IT packages that transcended departmental boundaries. The ultimate aim was to enable companies to optimise their processes both internally and externally using a new generation of business software, called ERP software. An important push for installing an ERP system was the advent of the client/server architecture. This type of architecture promised a very considerable decrease of IT costs and a drastic increase in system flexibility when it was combined with the implementation of standard off-the-shelf software. This was promoted by UNIX as the operating system, the first operating system that made vendors and users of standard software independent of hardware technology. The client/server architecture implies that every user has their own computing power on the desktop, instead of working with a dumb terminal connected to a big mainframe system. This results in flexibility and independence for the IT user. During the 1990s, the demand for ERP systems with a client/server architecture grew very strongly, in particular among the large companies. Especially in the years 1995–97 the second major reason for buying such a system was to solve the Y2K problem because the old systems were not millennium proof.

Demand for Unix-based ERP systems was, in the first half of the 1990s, among the strongest in the technology sector. According to the market research organisation AMR, the overall ERP market grew by 39 per cent in 1994 to about $3bn (≈ €2.5bn) worldwide. More impressively, the UNIX portion grew by 63 per cent. When markets grow at these rates, it is expected that most vendors will participate. In 1994 Baan outpaced the market, racking up 372 new accounts. In the UNIX market, Baan's performance was second only to SAP (645 new accounts). Baan crossed a significant threshold by moving beyond the $100m mark in 1994. The twin towers of Oracle and SAP loomed heavily over this marketplace, however. SAP was already a billion-dollar class company and Oracle then finished its fiscal year just shy of the $3bn mark. The potential of being overshadowed by the rivalry between the two was real (see Exhibit 1). More importantly, both of these companies had significantly greater resources at their disposal, as well as significant and mature distribution channels. In a market where size matters, this should not be overlooked.

Market expectations were still high in the second half of the 1990s. In 1997, according to Gartner Group, the market for ERP packages was estimated to be $5.4bn. The year before the market showed a 41 per cent growth compared to 1995. In the coming years the ERP market was expected to grow between 30–40 per cent a year. In the ERP market the large client/server ERP vendors had 54 per cent of the market – Baan Company, Oracle,

Exhibit 2	ERP large users matrix

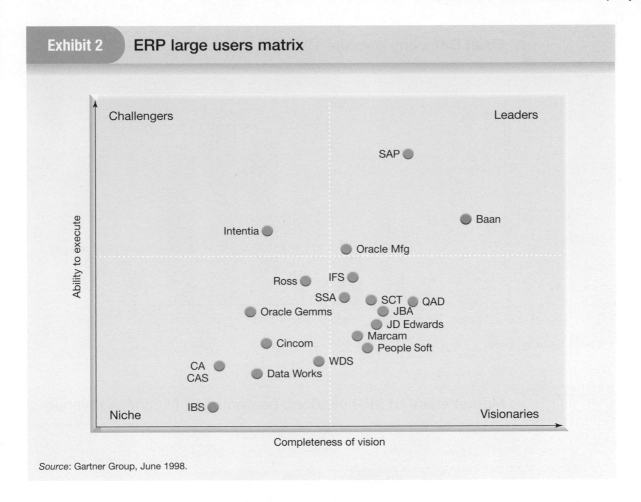

Source: Gartner Group, June 1998.

PeopleSoft and SAP or, as they were usually called, BOPS. Their strengths differed somewhat. Initially, Baan was especially strong with its manufacturing module, SAP with its finance module and PeopleSoft with its HRM module. Later on, the differences in strengths and weaknesses became smaller. Every vendor was in a continuing process of product improvement, imitation and innovation. The Gartner Group systematically carried out research on the players in the ERP market, and evaluated them on their vision and their ability to execute. The results of one of its surveys shows that SAP was strong in its ability to execute its strategy, while Baan was the most visionary of the ERP vendors (see Exhibit 2).

Outpacing market growth

From 1978 up to 1997, Baan Company went through a period of strong growth both in revenue and in number of employees. Exhibit 3 shows the rapid growth of the revenue from 1993 until 1997 and Exhibit 4 the growth in market share in the years 1995 to 1997. Baan gained market share in spite of the fierce competition.

To be successful in the marketplace, Baan needed to have in place a variety of alliances or partnerships. Most important were the consultancy and software service firms which did implementations and developed customisations for buyers of the standard product. The other important category of partners was the technology firms, including hardware vendors (such as IBM, Hewlett-Packard and Compaq), database vendors (such as Oracle) and Microsoft (as the vendor of Windows NT™, an alternative to UNIX™ from 1993 on).

Service firms partnering strategy

From the early 1980s, Baan positioned itself as a software manufacturer. Offering services was of secondary importance. To satisfy the needs of its customers and to strengthen its competitive position, from 1990 on Baan developed a partnership strategy. The company collaborated in a systematic way with service partners to expand and internationalise the services for its software package. It

Exhibit 3   Baan Company revenue 1978–99 in US $*

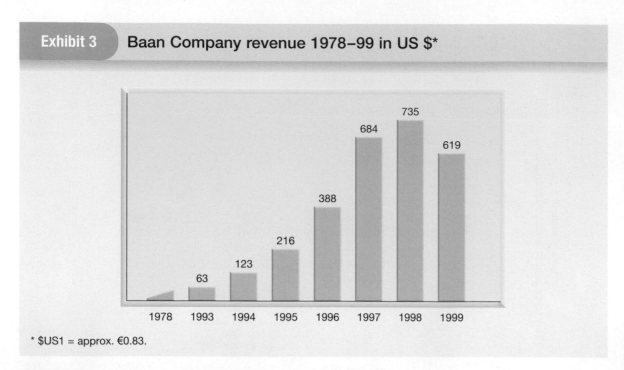

* $US1 = approx. €0.83.

Exhibit 4   Market share of ERP vendors: percentage of licences revenue

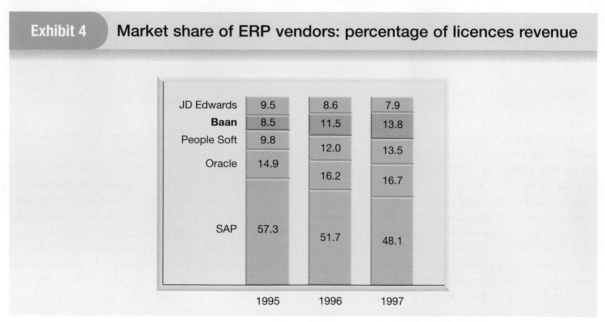

worked with four service partners on a global scale: Cap Gemini, Ernst & Young, KPMG and Origin. In addition to these global partners, Baan collaborated with a large variety of regional and local partners. A partner programme was designed to structure the cooperative processes. As a vital element, a service product suite – called Orgware – was developed as a methodology and a package of standardised services. In 1995, Baan launched a new phase with the implementation of a new

service model. The service model distinguished three types of services: (1) support services, (2) implementation services, and (3) partner services. The first type included installation, helpdesk, and integration and benchmark services. These services were offered primarily by Baan's international support centres. The second type included project management, implementation, consultancy and training. This category of services was offered by the local Baan operations in cooperation with service partners. The third type covered the services that Baan did not provide itself: support in the field of business process redesign, management consultancy, and project management for large-scale system integration projects, technical integration and customised software. In the meantime the level at which Baan offered services was changing. Its role was increasingly becoming that of project manager or project auditor. This helped the company to keep a good grasp of projects and to show commitment, which was important for its customers.

Licence revenue

A software vendor such as Baan had several revenue sources. Customers had to pay a licence fee to use the software. Licences are in general a main source of income for a software vendor. Additionally, the customers needed support from the vendor in several respects. First, the installation of the software at the customer's site required installation or implementation services from the software vendor and/or a services firm. Service revenues were a primary source of income for an ERP software vendor too. Second, smaller but still outstanding were the revenues from ongoing support to the customers and maintenance services.

Baan's growth in licence revenue was very strong. The revenue went from $17m in 1992 to $224m in 1996. In 1996 licence revenue grew 98 per cent, which was faster than the market (41 per cent), signalling a growing market share. It is important to notice that the margin on licence sales is extremely high because only the cost of media and freight, royalty of third party software and the amortisation of capitalised R&D costs

are included. Baan's margin on licence was above 90 per cent.

Baan chose a licence revenue growth strategy because of the strategic importance of market share and of growth of the installed base. A growing market share is a characteristic of a winning player. This attracts new customers. They prefer to buy from a market leader because they sense that the product is better and the risk of a failure is smaller than with another vendor. Growth in terms of revenue and market share influences the market capitalisation in a positive way. All the customers together form the installed base. A customer may have a varying number of users of the software, ranging from just a few to thousands of users. For example, customer Boeing Aircraft Corporation had in the early 2000s more than 40,000 users of the Baan software. Every new customer of the software enlarges the installed base which is attractive raw material for future exploitation. A new customer becomes locked in because ERP software is very expensive. No one customer of this software will consider replacing it within ten to twenty or even thirty years. This opens a window of revenue opportunities, such as complementary products (now and later), implementation and support services, maintenance services and future product versions.

Baan's Business Model is presented in Exhibit 5. A major difference between Baan and other players was the revenue composition as in Exhibit 6.

The licences market is more volatile than the services market, but the profit margin is much higher. Most important is that there were no growth limitations to selling licences for Baan. The customers paid up-front, and delivering the software took very little effort from the vendor. The

| Exhibit 5 | Baan Company Business Model (determined in 1997, 1998–2000 prospective) |

	1995	1996	1997	1998	1999	2000
Revenue $	200	370	670	1,100	1,600	2,200
Operating Margin	11%	15%	18%	22%	25%	28%
EPS $	0.17	0.38	0.80	1.50	2.75	4.+
Licence	67%	67%	67%	64%	59%	55%

Exhibit 6	ERP vendors in 1998

ERP software vendors	Licences as % of revenue	Services as % of revenue
Baan	60	40
SAP	35	65
Oracle	25	75
People Soft	42	58
J.D. Edwards	37	63

implementation process afterwards would take six to twelve months with the help of partner firms.

The importance of revenue growth, especially licence growth, was made very clear by Baan's chairman. In May 1998, Jan Baan said:

> There is a reasonable chance that we will realise by the year 2000 revenue of $2 billion. For this year – 1998 – the analysts have expressed the expectation that we will achieve revenue of $1 billion. That means that we will have to grow by 50 per cent next year. That seems to be an enormous target, but in view of the development of the market that should be possible. If that doesn't work we have to ask ourselves whether we are not jeopardising our own independent position. We should try in any case to be above the average growth of the market. Our market share has grown substantially to 14 per cent in the last few years. Our biggest competitor, SAP, on the other hand, went from two/thirds to 50 per cent. We expect this trend to continue. SAP will continue to reduce market share and we will be catching up, together with other players, such as PeopleSoft.

Baan was aware of the risks of playing the licences card, but the company deemed them acceptable. As a consequence of its business model, when the growth of the market of new software licences declined sharply in the second half of 1998, Baan was hit the hardest. Nobody had foreseen this dramatic slowdown of market growth, not even industry analysts.

Baan's breakthrough

In July 1994 Boeing placed an order with Baan for US$20m. To round off the contract negotiations Jan Baan and his people were invited for a 'power dinner' by John Warner, CIO (chief information officer) of Boeing. This was the biggest order ever placed in the ERP industry and was never to be surpassed. The order came to Baan at an important time. The financial position was not very strong – particularly owing to building up the size of the US operations during the previous year.

In 1995, Scott Griffin, the IT director of Boeing, explained why Baan secured the order ahead of Oracle or SAP:

> Boeing purchased the Baan software for various reasons. It supports our efforts to review the corporate processes and our transition to a centralised process management across a multitude of corporate units. When we asked Baan to collaborate with us at our restructuring of the corporate processes we got more than an ERP-software solution of world class. Baan also brought in two complementary concepts – a model for transfer of knowledge and their implementation methodology.

At Boeing Baan carried out the biggest software implementation in the history of both Baan and ERP systems. Boeing cleared out some four hundred old – 'legacy' – systems, of which the oldest dated back to the 1950s. These involved all kinds of applications running on large so-called mainframe computers. It was not possible to adjust these: the maintenance costs were high and the knowledge required to maintain these systems had been lost. Actually, these systems no longer met their current demands, let alone the future ones.

In the second place, the Boeing order meant a breakthrough for Baan in America. It resulted in the company acquiring a prominent position in the ERP software market. In 1995, Kevin Calderwood, president of Baan America, said:

The contract with Boeing meant that everything Baan was doing was approved: its vision, strategy and product. Prior to this transaction only a few companies knew Baan. After Boeing had opted for us, the general feeling in the market was that the company must have something really good to offer. The press paid a lot of attention to the contract. A lot of people wanted to know more about Baan and about our product. Both the reputation of Boeing and the size of the contract helped us a lot. As a result we were not only able to sell to other businesses but also to attract highly qualified employees in the sales and support of customers. Since then we belong to the top players.

The contract with Boeing gave Baan wings, not just in America but worldwide.

Venture capital and IPO

From 1982 until 1993, the founder Jan Baan and his brother Paul jointly owned the Baan Company. In that year, they sold a minority interest to investment company General Atlantic Partners. Reflecting its growth from a small Dutch firm to a global enterprise, Baan Company conducted its initial public offering (IPO) in 1995 on the NASDAQ and Amsterdam Stock Exchanges. In May 1995 Baan acquired an official listing which appeared to be highly successful. It strengthened its position not so much financially as commercially. A young organisation had been accepted into the major league. This meant broad recognition and added new fuel to a vision that had been unfolding for 17 years. Within a year of the IPO, Baan's stock exchange value placed the company among the Fortune 500 in America. The company's high price/earnings ratio allowed it to make acquisitions if it wished to do so.

Prior to the flotation, the two brothers jointly transferred their shares in Baan to the newly set-up Oikonómos Foundation. At Baan's flotation and at the second issue, this foundation sold Baan shares, but still kept an interest of nearly 40 per cent. Oikonómos incorporated in 1995 the investment company Vanenburg Ventures (100 per cent ownership) with its mission to speed up the growth of Baan and to strengthen its market position. Paul Baan became the CEO of the new company. Full of energy and totally committed, he was in charge of creating a network of companies and small businesses. He did this by acquiring existing companies and by starting new ones. Investments were made in new technologies such as the internet.

Vanenburg was most successful with developing a product to ease the installation of Baan's ERP software.

A positioning document of Vanenburg Ventures explained:

> Baan Company had as its focus the development, marketing and distribution of a generic product. This is its ERP product. To strengthen the execution of its mission Baan Company has built up relationships with a variety of partners, in the areas of technology and services. All these firms have their own mission and collaborate with Baan Company to execute their mission. The relationships with Baan Company are not exclusive relationships. The relationship between the Vanenburg companies and Baan is comparable to the one Baan has with its other partners. The contractual conditions are the same. Vanenburg encourages collaboration between these partners and engages in activities through its companies that are not taken up by other firms within Baan's business web. The objective is to generate new business on a joint basis.

However, in practice, to the outside world the relations between Baan and Vanenburg were opaque, raising a corporate governance debate in 1998.

Changes in the mid-1990s

In the mid-1990s, Baan Company was ranked the sixth largest software company in the world, behind Microsoft, SAP, Computer Associates, Oracle and PeopleSoft. Moreover, Baan was number two in the ERP market segment. In those years, the market for ERP packages was very turbulent. The product life cycle of a software package was constantly shortening, while on the other hand the investments that ERP suppliers needed to make in R&D were increasing all the time. As a direct consequence, many of them attempted to make their products last longer. The result of this discrepancy was that the market was gradually thinning out. Furthermore, the different suppliers were increasingly having to cope with the heavier demands made by the market. A clear trend that emerged among ERP suppliers was the search for alliances. By entering into these they hoped to shorten the development time, so that more complete products could be offered while at the same time their implementation time could be cut. To satisfy market demands, ERP suppliers not only had to have a clear vision for the future, but they had to make sure that they could actually deliver what they promised. The expectation was that the

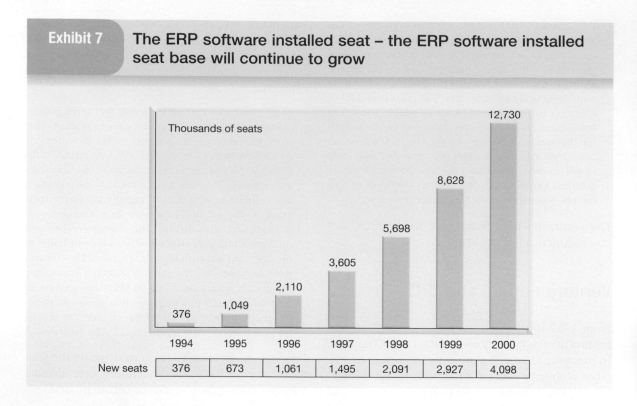

Exhibit 7 **The ERP software installed seat – the ERP software installed seat base will continue to grow**

New seats	376	673	1,061	1,495	2,091	2,927	4,098

market would grow enormously in the following years (see Exhibit 7).

A change in corporate strategy

The company's response to the changing market and the enormous growth opportunity was an ambitious strategy. Baan was seeking to expand dramatically its market share by becoming the undisputed market leader in the mid-market. To be successful and to achieve rapid growth in this emerging market, Baan had to extend its network of partnerships. The two main elements of the corporate strategy became the Baan Web and 'beyond ERP'.

The Baan Web

The Baan Web concept (see Exhibits 8 and 9) was developed by the Board assisted by McKinsey consultants serving Baan. These advisers were inspired by authors such as Brian McArthur and John Hagel III. It was expected that extending and intensifying Baan's business web would strengthen its competitive position, accelerate the growth and increase its market value. A growing web would make the

company highly attractive for partners. Baan would be able to offer a better, more varied, and more innovative product range. As a result, customers would be attracted by a broader product offering, which would eventually lead to additional sales – et cetera. The elements of the Baan Web were, in addition to Baan Company and Vanenburg Group, the customers and their partners. Baan was the shaper of the platform of the Baan Web by its ownership of the core technology and core applications. Vanenburg positioned itself as the growth accelerator and was as such the co-shaper of the web by investing in complementary businesses. Baan, Vanenburg and their partners would collaborate on a shared platform: architecture, tools, applications and brand name.

It is essential for the web dynamics that the share of the web builder in the web decreases in favour of the partners. In 1996, Baan's revenue was more than $400m and the web around it had total revenues of approximately $800m. A year later, Baan's revenue increased to almost $700m, and the revenues of the web partners to more than $1,300m. In January 1998, the president of Vanenburg, Sharman, announced: 'Our goal is to reduce our own [i.e. Baan's] share in the total value of worldwide Baan installations to about 20 per cent.'

Exhibit 8   Web dynamics: less is more

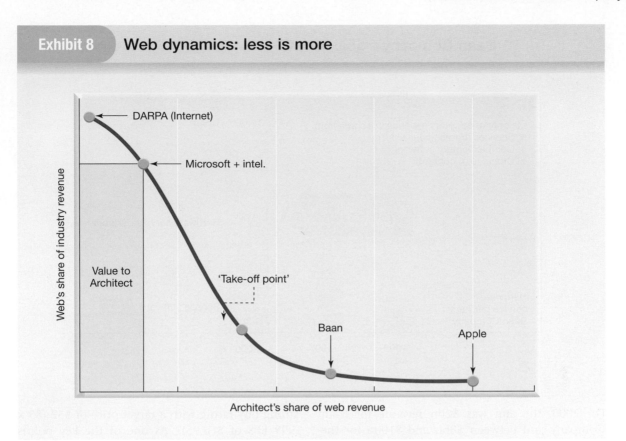

Exhibit 9   The Baan Web: a network of partnerships

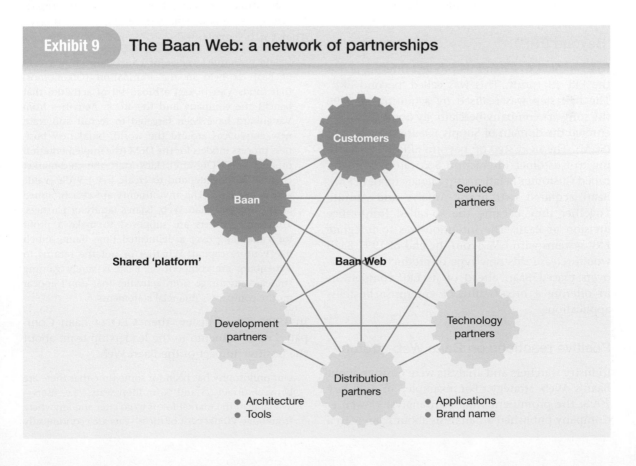

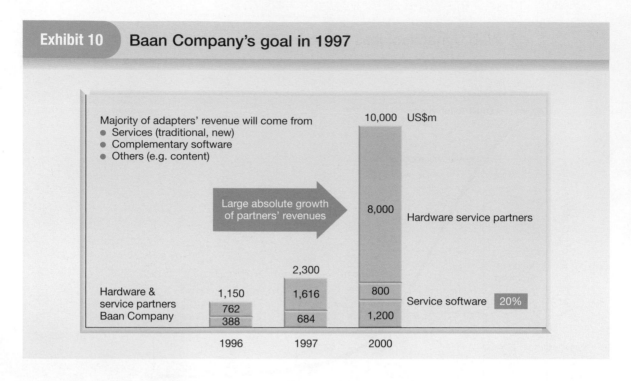

Exhibit 10   Baan Company's goal in 1997

For 2000, the aim was $2bn revenue for Baan Company and between $8bn and $10bn for the Baan Web partners (see Exhibit 10).

'Beyond ERP'

Baan wanted to extend its product offering across the ERP footprint. This was called 'beyond ERP'. The first step was realised by acquiring in 1996 the software company Berclain. By doing this Baan entered the domain of Supply Chain Management (SCM). The next step of 'beyond ERP' was stretching to Customer Interaction Software (CIS), later called Customer Relationship Management (CRM). Baan acquired two firms, Antalys and Aurum. Together they became the so-called front-office division of Baan. The intention was to integrate ERP systems with CIS. From the end of 1997 Baan would release this new type of product. The takeovers placed Baan ahead of its ERP competitors in offering a broad suite of enterprise business applications.

Positive reactions on Baan Web strategy

Industry watchers and analysts were positive about Baan's Web strategy. For example, in February 1998, the prominent American analyst Cowen & Company published an analysis about Baan with a 'strong buy rating with a target price of $52 (55 x 1999 EPS of $ 0.95).' As one of the key points it mentioned: 'Venture activity in Vanenburg is building the Baan Web around Baan Company.' They further explained:

Seeing powerful leverage of Vanenburg (40 per cent of Baan is held in the foundation (Oikonómos) that funds Vanenburg) a broad set of activities that benefit the company and the stock. Activities from Vanenburg have been targeted to recruit and train new employees around the world, build new business process models for the DEM (the implementation product suite Orgware), kick start the mid-market channel worldwide, and to create (>40) VARs (value added resellers). The investments are clearly aimed at growing the Baan Web, Baan's family of partners. These investments are supposed to make a profit for Vanenburg over a delineated time frame, much like venture capital. Whether or not the returns to Vanenburg are competitive, Baan is surely gaining strategic advantage from activities that don't appear on the company's financial statements.

In 1998, Tom Tinsley, then CEO of Baan Company, wrote a memo to the leadership team about the positive impact of the Baan Web:

Our philosophy has been for some time that there are between about 55 and 65 million seats – i.e. users – available in the market for us to go after and anywhere from 60 to 70 per cent of those seats are economically available to us by going to an indirect channel. So we began initiatives twelve, eighteen months ago with Baan Business Systems (a mid-market distribution company, 100 per cent owned by Vanenburg Ventures) and beyond that we now have created Baan Midmarket Solutions (owned by Vanenburg (80 per cent) and Baan Company (20 per cent)) which will effectively be the arm of the Baan group that offers the Baan product into our indirect channel partners. As we expand the technology footprint we are also expanding the way customers can receive the product whether it comes through a direct sales process or through an indirect channel partner or through a service firm offering.

The crisis of 1998

The lead-up to the crisis of 1998 took place some months before the departure of the Baan brothers from the Board. This was when the publication of the financial results of the first quarter of 1998 was postponed on account of adopting changed bookkeeping directives of the American stock market supervisor SEC. It was no longer allowed to include orders not invoiced to customers (users) in the declared revenue figure. This affected Baan's announced profit adversely. Then the second quarter was worse than expected. Moreover in the second quarter criticism from American securities houses arose about the financial accounting. In their eyes, the listed Baan Company was too interwoven with Vanenburg, the investment company of Oikonómos, a shareholder of Baan Company. The analysts thought the money flows between the various elements were unclear.

In order to provide the desired clarity, founder Jan Baan and his brother Paul retired in July 1998 from the management of Baan Company. Jan gave up his position as Chairman, Paul his position as Chairman of the Supervisory Board. However, the prospects for Baan seemed favourable then. Its market position was strong and promising, according to analyses by the Gartner Group (see Exhibit 2).

In his farewell letter Jan Baan wrote

Baan Company is in a stronger position than ever. (. . .) As Chairman, I say goodbye to Baan Company without any concerns in my heart. I am grateful to all those who have contributed to the success of the company for their efforts, inspiration and co-operation. Having worked for Baan Company for more than twenty years, I have experienced first and foremost a series of changes, the speed and breadth of which

have only increased. Being part of this has given me much pleasure. At first more as an active builder; during the last years more as someone stimulating the leadership team.

At that moment, Jan Baan could not suspect that in a couple of months there would be great unrest and serious concern.

On 12 October, CEO Tinsley sent a profit warning. The company pointed to the financial-economic situation in the world and the millennium problem which was making customers postpone their software investments. The losses at Baan gave investors a powerful signal to sell. The share price crashed by 30 per cent to €10. On 29 October, Baan announced a large-scale reorganisation. About 20 per cent of jobs were to disappear (from 6,000 to 4,800) and a number of offices would be closed. The total loss in 1998 then turned out to be $315m.

Baan was not the only vendor with disappointing results. The *Wall Street Journal* of 17 February 1999 reported: 'German software giant SAP AG, which has been an earnings juggernaut lately, stumbled in the fourth quarter amid delayed orders and payment problems in Japan and Russia. SAP missed its own forecasts, earning 712 million marks ($409 or €339 million) before tax, a 15 per cent drop from the year-earlier quarter. "We will have to start spending money more carefully if we can't drive revenues through the sky," says Hasso Plattner, SAP's co-chairman. "We are cautious."' More explanation was given by the *Wall Street Journal Europe* of 17 February 1999: 'All of Europe's enterprise software companies saw growth slow as customers tightened their information technology budgets to cope with pressures on spending, including the need to make their systems ready for the year 2000. "Slower economic growth as well as the Y2K issue is going to adversely impact licence sales more than anything else," warns Devika Malik, an analyst at J. P. Morgan in London."'

A week earlier *Computing Canada* (2.12.99) wrote:

CNET's *News.com* reported on JD Edwards' announcement that it disclosed earnings much lower than expected. The company's stock fell to a 52-week low following the news. Analysts commented that market factors had finally caught up with the company similar to other vendors. Baan, SAP, and PeopleSoft have all experienced dramatic drops in their share price in recent months as revenue growth had slowed. Worst hit was Baan Co., with dual headquarters in Barneveld, Holland and Reston, VA. Once nicknamed the 'Dutch darling of Wall Street' because of stellar growth rates, Baan recorded a fourth quarter loss of US$250m. The company responded by cutting 20 per cent of its staff worldwide. 'Baan's problems are linked to wrong strategy and execution and not indicative of a general market slump,' said Jim Shepherd, vice-president research at AMR Research, a Boston-based consulting firm.

Baan Company was confronted with severe operational problems. The newly appointed president of Baan, Mary Coleman, stated in an internal memo of February 1999 that cost cutting had a high priority. In an official press release the company said: 'In the memo, Ms. Coleman conceded that the company has let costs run out of control. Baan employees spent around $14,000 per person each year on travel, twice as much as competitors. To better keep control over expenses, Baan will give more responsibility for profits to nationally based country managers rather than global units. "We were too lax and did not have adequate controls or policies in place," she said.'

The collapse of the Web and Vanenburg

The disappointing results and the crisis for Baan in the second half of 1998 had very severe consequences for both Baan Company, the investment company Vanenburg and the Baan Web network of partner firms. Vanenburg operated fully in line with the Baan activities on account of the Web formula. The interests and activities were not spread. Service providers, who had directed a major part of their activities with Baan, also received a heavy blow. Vanenburg got into extra difficulties because for a large part of the investments the proceeds were only in the initial stage. Vanenburg had invested about US$1.0bn. It had borrowed US$0.5bn at various banks to finance the new activities with Baan shares as security. When in October 1998 the stock price crashed, the banks started selling the Baan shares. As a consequence, Vanenburg had to start a drastic reorganisation

that eventually was only rounded off in 2002. The Baan Web strategy was abruptly terminated in October 1998.

Officially, Baan Company made the decision to restructure the company. Actually, to get the company in good shape again, the Board preferred a merger with another company or the option of being acquired. This did not take place. The company did not become profitable again and lost much of its credibility with shareholders and customers. From 1995 to early 1998 Baan was the star of the Amsterdam bourse. The financial market said its problems stemmed from the damage done when its accounting practices were brought into question. The millennium issue dealt a further blow but also affected other companies marketing and supplying ERP systems. But unlike the mature rivals SAP and Oracle, Baan could not survive these difficulties.

After the crash

In an interview several years after the crash, Jan Baan commented:

> If there had been no Asia crisis, the company could have continued on the same footing for years. The problems of 1998 were not, in themselves, a disaster. Baan could have recovered. What should have been done was cutting costs and increasing the share of services in the revenue by retraining and redeploying staff. The company announced a drastic reorganisation but did not pursue it fully. If a merger/take-over had been successful, there would have been at that moment sufficient chances to correct things. As the saying goes: the cheapest reorganisation is a proper merger. In the old economy one would first choose a reorganisation and then a merger. Such rules do not apply to the kind of businesses such as Baan that belong to the new economy.

In 2000, nearly bankrupt, Baan was taken over by the British company Invensys. The company went through a period of restructuring, lay-off of employees, and cost cutting. In 2001, Baan recovered considerably and became profitable again.

Premier Oil and Hermes:
the responsibility of business

This case study is concerned with corporate governance and corporate social responsibility in the context of the engagement of a pension fund representative – Hermes – with Premier Oil, part of its investment portfolio. It raises the key question of what role shareholders and their agents, such as pension funds, should play in the strategic direction of businesses, and what responsibility the executives of such businesses have to shareholders.

• • •

Background

'Gin rummy behaviour (discard your least promising business at each turn).'

(Warren Buffet)

'The financial system encourages shareholders to walk away from problem companies.'

(Gordon Brown)

'We want to see shareholders sitting up and doing something.'

(HM Treasury)

It's called The Wall Street Walk. If you own a share in a company and you don't like the way the company behaves, you sell the share. Don't you? Well that certainly is the tradition of fund management in Britain and the USA. After all, how could you explain to your client that you held the share of a badly managed company? It's always easier to sell out of problems. So when Hermes first embarked on its shareholder engagement programmes, it was a pretty radical departure. 'If you are a shareholder,' said Alastair Ross-Goobey, Hermes CEO, 'you don't just own a security, you own a company. Companies with good owners will be worth more to their shareholders and are more likely to deliver for other stakeholders too.'

So it was that Ross-Goobey assembled a team of managers, strategists, investment professionals, lawyers and corporate financiers to address the performance of companies which lacked the necessary catalyst for change from their owners. By 2000 they had already been deeply involved in turnarounds of a number of companies such as Mirror Group, Smith and Nephew, Tomkins and Six Continents.

However, a number of them were keen that Hermes broaden its horizons, from issues of governance and strategy, to incorporate wider social issues. It was for this reason that David Pitt-Watson, a 20-year veteran of boardroom strategy, and Paul Lee, a committed young lawyer, suggested that Hermes should intervene in what seemed to be the intractable problems of Premier Oil.

By 2000, Premier Oil had become a cause célèbre amongst those concerned with governance and more particularly with the social, ethical and environmental responsibilities of business. Its share price was languishing, and it appeared unable to deliver on its stated strategy. For several years previously Hermes had communicated its concerns over the company's board structure and had voted against the re-election of several of the non-executive directors whom it did not regard as being independent. On the governance side, the fundamental issue was that the company was dominated by two major shareholders, Amerada Hess, a US company, and Petronas, the Malaysian national oil company, each of which held 25 per cent of the shares. Not content with the control and influence they wielded as such major shareholders, each of

---

them also had two non-executive directors on the board. Two further NEDs were also deemed non-independent by Hermes, one because he received substantial consultancy fees from the company alongside his fee as an NED, and one because he was a former executive.

These board problems were reflected in a failure by the company to address some of the severe problems that Premier was facing. The strategy was not clear. The strategy proposed in November 1999 when Petronas invested in the company (and on the basis of which independent shareholders had approved that investment) was to be a primary investment vehicle for Asian upstream investment by Amerada Hess and Petronas. It was not being followed, and it was not apparent to investors that an alternative had been developed. As Hermes saw it, the company was in a strategic hole: it was not large enough to compete in production and downstream work with the emerging super-major oil companies, but it was also not as fleet of foot as it needed to be, to fully exploit the exploration opportunities opened up by the super-major's focus on larger-scale fields. Its freedom of action was also limited by the company's high level of gearing.

In addition, the company had allowed itself to become exposed to major ethical and reputational risks as a result of being the lead investor in the Yetagun gas field in Myanmar. Myanmar, formerly known as Burma, was a country ruled by a military dictatorship which had refused to accept the results of democratic elections in 1990, where summary arrest, forced labour, and torture were widely reported, and which had therefore become a pariah state. Premier's involvement in the country had brought public criticism of the company from a range of sources including Burmese campaigners, Amnesty International, trade union groups and, not least, the UK government, all of whom viewed Burma as a problematic venue for inward investment (though notably the UK government refused to impose sanctions). It was not clear to shareholders that the company was effectively managing the reputational and ethical risks it faced as a result of its involvement in Myanmar.

To begin exploring these concerns, Hermes held a meeting in mid-2000 with Dr Richard Jones, Premier's corporate responsibility director, and the company's finance director John van der Welle. It was clear that Premier was undertaking considerable positive work on the ground in Myanmar – which included building schools, funding teachers, AIDS education and environmental remediation.

Nevertheless Hermes had continuing concerns. The board had not publicly stated that it believed it was effectively managing all the risks that were associated with its presence in Myanmar, and nor did Hermes have the confidence that the board as currently constituted could give shareholders the reassurance that they needed in that regard.

It was therefore no surprise to Hermes that, in the absence of a clear strategy, with a restrictive capital structure, with the lightning rod of its involvement in Myanmar not clearly being managed and a board which did not seem designed to address these issues in the interests of all shareholders, Premier's share price had dramatically underperformed and had done so for several years. (See Exhibit 1.)

Beginnings

With the combination of these issues, governance, strategic, capital structure, ethical and share price underperformance, Hermes concluded that it was appropriate for them, as representatives of shareholders, to ask for action to resolve the difficulties. As Ross-Goobey had said, Hermes believes it is in its clients' interest to become closely involved with companies where it perceives there to be problems. Such involvement is simply putting into effect the stewardship which Hermes' clients, as partial owners, should exercise over investee companies.

The engagement proper began in September 2000 with a letter to the chairman of Premier, Sir David John, requesting a meeting to discuss the full range of concerns.

While awaiting that meeting, Hermes was approached by two separate groups asking them to engage on the social, ethical and environmental (SEE) issues raised by Premier. The first group was Hermes clients, principally led by trade union pension fund trustees. The second was from NGOs who were focusing on disinvestment from Myanmar/Burma. As regards the trade unions, Hermes believes it is appropriate that they, as client trustee representatives, should take a keen interest in the stewardship of their investment, including investee companies' response to SEE issues. David Pitt-Watson was invited by Brendan Barber (now head of the TUC) to address the international body which coordinates trade union/shareholder campaigns. At that meeting he explained that Hermes could not support trade union campaigns based on a 'special interest'. Hermes would, however, be happy to engage

| Exhibit 1 | Premier Oil absolute (upper) and relative (lower) share price performance for 10 years to start of engagement (July 2000) |

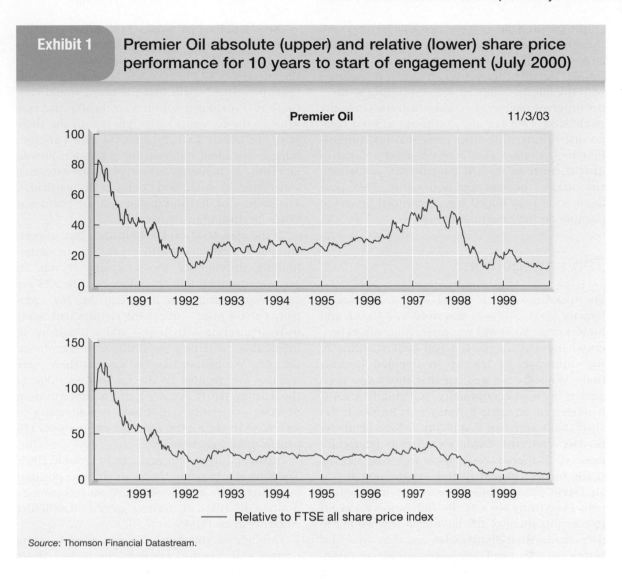

Source: Thomson Financial Datastream.

where failure to address SEE issues was as the result of poor governance, and threatened long-term shareholder value. Premier was one such case.

The second group who encouraged Hermes to take action were the NGOs. Hermes was invited to a meeting organised by other fund managers with representatives from the Burma Campaign UK and Amnesty International. Alongside the UK fund managers with strong ethical investment mandates, a US-based investor with a reputation for activism on social, environmental and ethical matters was represented at this meeting. Hermes were somewhat surprised to find that the purpose of the meeting was to discuss proposing a shareholder resolution criticising Premier for its involvement in Myanmar, something which most at the meeting seemed willing to countenance, despite the

fact that they had yet to meet the directors of the company to discuss this proposed plan of action. In any case, Hermes (by reason of its passive, index tracking mandates) was the only fund manager around the table that held a substantial stake in Premier Oil; indeed, most, in keeping with their ethical stance, held no shares at all.

At the meeting Hermes took what they felt was the responsible attitude of a part-owner of the Premier Oil business. They argued against the proposing of any immediate shareholder resolution, pointing out that there were much better ways to raise issues with the board which would not of themselves inspire confrontation. They volunteered to lead the engagement not only on behalf of Hermes, but with the tacit support of other fund managers.

The meeting did, however, provide Hermes with the opportunity to make contact with some of the NGOs active in Myanmar and among the Burmese people. Notably, Hermes began regular discussions with the Burma Campaign UK, explaining to them the different courses of action which the company might take. Paul Lee also continued to hold regular discussions with other interested institutional investors. Hermes also accessed other sources of insight, such as the UK government, academics, consultants, brokers and journalists. This gave them what they hoped was as rounded a view as possible on the Myanmar situation.

The engagement

The meeting with Sir David John took place in January 2001, and was described as a 'frank and honest one'. Sir David was an enormously experienced industrialist, with a real understanding of the difficulties of trading in troubled jurisdictions. While he pointed out that only a few years earlier, the world community, particularly ASEAN, had been encouraging investment in Burma, it was also rapidly apparent that he understood his shareholders' concerns. David Pitt-Watson later commented, 'If there is one person who deserves the credit for the success of this engagement it was Sir David John. While he may not have agreed with everything we said, he fully understood his role as Chairman of the Board and was willing to help ensure that shareholder concerns were put before the board and, where appropriate, resolved. Throughout he was entirely trustworthy in carrying out his role – even though we were not, and could not be a party to the private discussions the company was having with its two major shareholders and others about resolving Premier's problems.'

In December, the firm had already added a new, fully independent NED, in the person of Scott Dobbie, chair of Crestco and a director of the Securities and Futures Authority. Sir David also assured Hermes that further developments on the governance side were in train. While Hermes approved of these developments, they doubted that they would ultimately be adequate to address concerns. Sir David was also willing to discuss strategic and ethical concerns. Importantly, he agreed to Hermes' request personally to meet representatives of the Burma Campaign UK (until that point their contact with the company had only been through more junior staff).

David and Paul followed up this meeting with a detailed and direct letter outlining their concerns and asking Sir David to begin addressing them in the interests of all shareholders. Sir David's prompt response assured them that the board would continue to work for a solution to 'enable the true value of the company to be reflected in the share price'. In March 2001, Premier Oil added another fully independent non-executive. This was Ronald Emerson, a banking executive with extensive experience in Asia, and Malaysia in particular. The balance of decision making on the board was slowly beginning to change.

At the May AGM, Sir David made a very important public statement with regard to the shareholding structure of the company. It was an acknowledgement that the presence of two 25 per cent shareholders was a burden on the company's share price – the point Hermes had made in their meeting with him – and a statement of intent about seeking a resolution to this problem. He said: 'We believe that the current share price remains low relative to the underlying value of the business partly as a result of the concentration of share ownership. The board is continuing to seek ways to reduce the discount on assets for the benefit of all shareholders.'

Further positive steps occurred in October 2001. The company began to clarify its strategic position by selling assets in Indonesia and restructuring its position in Pakistan, having gained shareholder authority at an EGM.

Throughout this time Hermes were in close contact with pension funds in the United States who were engaged with Amerada Hess over their shareholding in Premier, and hence their involvement in Myanmar/Burma. Paul Lee recognised that Amerada's statements appeared to be at odds with UK law, and with statements made at the time of Premier Oil's shareholders' circular at the time of its refinancing. Separate discussions were thus begun privately with Amerada to progress these issues.

Over 2001, Paul Lee also worked with other institutional investors on their proposal for a statement on how investee companies should deal with any involvement in Myanmar. He argued that this document should follow the language of the guidelines Hermes had developed with other institutional investors, which were later published by the Association of British Investors in October 2001. This meant that Myanmar would not be singled out as an issue above all others – while the risks of involvement there were significant, there were other countries and other issues where risks were at a similarly high level – and Hermes was not keen to see companies overburdened with a variety of different 'codes' on a range of issues. Furthermore, Hermes believed that had it signed up to the sort of document that was being proposed it would have been harder for them to achieve the level of access and trust that had been achieved at Premier Oil. It therefore dropped out of the discussions on this document. The other institutions persevered and eventually published their statement in December.

Moving matters on

The first year of Hermes' engagement had brought some progress but had failed fully to address Premier's fundamental problems. Hermes met Sir David and Charles Jamieson, the CEO, in early 2002. This was an impressively frank meeting, where they were willing to be more open about the work they had been undertaking to resolve Premier's problems. Over the years since 1999, they had proposed a number of solutions to the company's strategic impasse, but each had been in some way barred by one or other of the major shareholders. They were, however, confident that both shareholders now had a different attitude and that a resolution in the interests of all investors could now be achieved – though it might take a number of months.

Following this meeting Hermes sent Sir David a further forthright letter expressing concern at the actions of the major shareholders and putting in writing its offer to lend him support in the negotiations, should that prove valuable. Hermes formally offered to call on their contacts at global institutions and share with them their concerns that certain of the directors of Premier had not proved themselves to be the friends of minority investors. They hoped that the implication of potential difficulties this might cause for fundraising by companies with which those directors were involved could bolster Sir David's hand in negotiations. They also raised again concerns that public statements by Amerada – that its investment in Premier was somehow ring-fenced from Myanmar and that its directors did not participate in any discussions on the company's involvement in that country – seemed out of line with UK company law and the fiduciary duties of directors to all their shareholders.

The company's preliminary results announcement on 13 March 2002 highlighted the positive progress the business was making operationally, but more importantly it detailed the progress being made in relation to the company's fundamental problems. It made clear the roadmap the company was using to solve its problems, talking about shedding mature assets in return for the exit of the major shareholders, and turning itself into a focused, fleet-of-foot exploration company once again. The statement read: 'We are in specific discussions with our alliance partners on creating a new Premier, better balanced to achieve our objectives. While the restructuring process is complex and involves careful balancing of the interests of all shareholders, we are committed to finding a solution before the end of this year and I am hopeful this will be achieved.'

As part of Hermes' usual series of financial analysis meetings following preliminary or final announcements, they next met representatives of the company – this time Jamieson the CEO and Finance Director, John van der Welle – on 27 March. This meeting gave further encouragement that genuine progress was being made, as they suggested that the major shareholders both now clearly understood that any deal that they agreed would have to be approved by independent shareholders without them having the right to vote. Therefore, any deal would have to offer minorities full value to be allowed to proceed. The implication was that negotiations were now on track to reach a resolution. That resolution was announced in September 2002. Premier Oil said that it was to 'swap assets for shares', with Petronas taking the Myanmar operation and a share of Premier's Indonesian activities, and Amerada a further segment of the Indonesian interest (in which Premier retained a stake). This, as well as a substantial cash payment from Petronas, was in return for cancelling their 25 per cent shareholdings, and losing their right to appoint NEDs. Thus the shareholding and governance issues were resolved in one step, and the cash was to be used dramatically to cut Premier's debt burden. By the same action, Premier reduced its oil and gas production activities and focused on 'fleet-of-foot' exploration. And finally it had withdrawn from Myanmar in a way which was fully acceptable to the Burma Campaign Group, other NGOs, and to the UK government.

But most critically, the share price of Premier Oil rose 10 per cent on the announcement. Indeed, news of Premier's change in direction had been

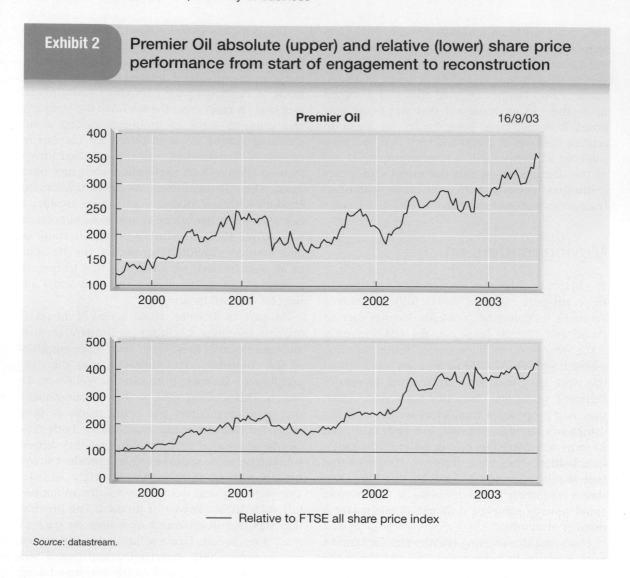

Exhibit 2 Premier Oil absolute (upper) and relative (lower) share price performance from start of engagement to reconstruction

— Relative to FTSE all share price index

Source: datastream.

anticipated by the market for many months. As a result, Premier Oil's share price doubled (relative to the oil and gas sector) during the period of Hermes' engagement, netting an excess return to Hermes clients of over £1m, and more than 50 times that sum to other minority shareholders (see Exhibit 2).

The price continued to rise thereafter until 12 September 2003 when the reconstruction was completed with the exit of the major shareholders and a 10:1 share consolidation. By 2004 Hermes saw Premier Oil as a strong independent E&P company with a real opportunity to continue to add value for its ongoing shareholders.

Sheffield Theatres Trust

David Brown and Kevan Scholes

The case study concerns a charitable trust which is responsible for two of the UK's leading provincial theatres – the Crucible and Lyceum Theatres in Sheffield. The Crucible Theatre first opened in 1971, and during the intervening 34-year period the theatre has seen many new developments and significant changes in its environment – particularly regarding its funding. The study provides an overview of the organisation from when it was extended to include the refurbished Lyceum Theatre in 1990, taking the reader through the subsequent difficulties faced by the theatre and its recovery to an award-winning arts organisation. The fact that the theatre complex has both commercial and public service objectives to pursue, illustrates that strategy formulation is not just a simple process of matching capabilities to environmental 'requirements'. Understanding the political context within which strategies are formulated leads to a process of balancing a variety of stakeholder interests whilst delivering and developing cultural and artistic ambitions.

●●●

Sheffield, a post-industrial city of 500,000 people in the north of England, has two distinct theatrical traditions: a profile of high-quality producing theatre and an extensive history and strong reputation for touring theatre. This distinction is fundamental: a producing theatre commissions and finances its own productions and employs its own artistes. By contrast, a touring theatre enters into contracts with touring companies who bring their productions (and their own artistes) to the theatre concerned. After a decade of working as a theatre complex, presenting both in-house performance arts productions and receiving touring productions across three stages, Sheffield Theatres received the prestigious accolade of Theatre of the Year 2001 in the Barclays Theatre Awards, presented by the Theatrical Management Association (TMA).

On completion in 1990, the restored Lyceum Theatre provided a superb example of a historic theatre, thoroughly refurbished to modern standards, and with seating for 1,100. The Crucible and Lyceum stand together overlooking a paved square, and for reasons of economy of scale, it was decided to form a new company, Sheffield Theatres, to run both venues. Outside London, Sheffield Theatres is unique in the UK in being able to produce, co-produce and present independent productions all in one complex. The distinctive role of each theatre was, however, to be retained, with the Crucible working largely as a producing house, and the Lyceum now hosting a new range of touring companies. The Studio theatre hosts a mixed programme of chamber music and drama and is the home of an international chamber music festival.

Until 1996, the board of the theatres was chaired by a Sheffield City Councillor but the pressure for further changes, which were forced on the company by The Arts Council of England, led to Norman Adsetts being asked to take over as chair of the board in summer 1996. A prominent business leader in the city, and the former chair of governors of Sheffield Hallam University, Norman Adsetts (subsequently Sir Norman) brought a new

emphasis on strategy and business planning. One of the first roles he had to perform was to recruit a new chief executive to replace Stephen Barry who left in 1996.

Grahame Morris was appointed chief executive in September 1997, bringing with him experience of combining production and touring theatre from Plymouth: one of the few other UK locations to work on that basis. His first task at Sheffield Theatres was to present a new business plan for approval by the board. The 1997 business plan, prepared with the support of an outside consultant, sought to unravel the various problems the theatres had faced. The plan proposed many modest but significant changes over a three-year period to make the complex more profitable. This would be achieved by developing the market further, increasing the number of co-productions with other theatres, strengthening the profitability of the catering function, and giving greater opportunities to the senior management team to manage the theatre as a single venture.

By 1998/99 a major decision was made to reverse the decline of the previous years by obtaining a commitment from stakeholders to a policy which recognised that the only way the theatres would succeed would be to invest in more significant productions which would attract sustainable audiences. This was a fundamental shift of thinking in that artistic quality and financial prudence were no longer to be seen as competing forces. In recognition of this, the appointment of Michael Grandage as associate director in 1999 brought to the forefront new and exciting productions – both in-house and touring – with some in-house productions transferring to London and around the UK, cementing the theatres' national profile. Sheffield Theatres receive regular recognition from national media and industry awards, most recently in the *Guardian* (media) Theatre Awards when the Crucible received the accolade of Theatre of the Year 2002.

Performing arts industry

There are two main branches of theatrical tradition: commercial theatre, whereby a theatre is owned outright by one or more owners and seek a profitable return on their investments, or producing theatre, whereby the company is a not-for-profit organisation producing theatre in repertory. Both traditions of theatrical production have an artistic remit, but producing theatre has an additional social remit utilising 'Art' as a tool to increase access to – and personal development from – the nation's cultural capital. As a result producing theatre receives the bulk of public funding for performing arts which enables companies to produce top quality productions at a reasonable price per ticket.

Many theatre buildings are used for a mixture of both theatrical traditions by playing 'host' to touring companies from commercial theatre, touring producing theatre or companies producing performing arts without a 'home' theatre base. Sheffield Theatres present all forms of performing arts, utilising three different forms of staging for maximum flexibility. The Crucible Theatre first opened in 1971 and seats 980 around three sides of a 'thrust' stage and the Studio Theatre is a flexible space which can seat up to 400, depending upon the style of staging of the production. The Lyceum Theatre is a traditional 'proscenium arch' theatre with 1,098 seats in the auditorium which mostly plays host to the touring companies, including musicals and other shows from the commercial theatre sector. The staging in the Lyceum is also the most suitable for Sheffield Theatres to produce theatre to tour around the UK, leading to some of Sheffield Theatres' in-house productions being developed at this theatre.

In 1977, the Crucible and Studio Theatres first played host to the World Snooker Championships and, with an expansion of the company to include the refurbished Lyceum Theatre in 1990, the company has been able to present a broad range of performing arts and hosts other sporting events alongside the snooker. As a result the theatre's main source of income is through the box office, supported by public subsidy from the local authority and Yorkshire Arts for the repertory productions, and special initiative grants for audience development or capital projects. In addition, the theatre receives bar and catering revenue, retail and programme sales, consultancy fees, royalties and box office revenue from tours of in-house productions, donations and sponsorship.

The product

The performing arts 'product' is developed, produced and presented to the audience (consumers) over a short period which makes production costs the heaviest financial burden for a producing theatre. Even productions which tour have a relatively short life span over a period of a few months. The social remit and the demands of the local audience to see a variety of shows at any particular theatre, requires producing and touring houses to change the productions regularly, even when the show has sold out for the allotted production run and could earn far more revenue for the company if the run was extended. Only commercial theatre, largely based in London, keeps a show running for a prolonged period, replacing casts regularly, reducing marginal costs over the life of the 'product' and maximising returns for the shareholders.

All live events utilise the audience as part of the product in that the event necessarily requires an audience to be present and with whom the production or event interacts to some degree. A theatre audience plays a vital role in their response to the material being communicated and as such forms a significant part of the level of artistic output. If attendance at a performance is low the quality of the product is directly affected by restricting interaction, lowering the quality of the experience and thus the perception of the quality of the production. Audiences are therefore vital not only for increased revenue purposes but also increased product quality. Sheffield Theatres are increasingly utilising audience (market) research and targeted marketing material for each production, and trying to draw positive media coverage to increase the likelihood of significant attendance figures.

Sheffield Theatres' season is planned and broadly budgeted in advance of opening in September, but there are many variables which make calculating costs difficult in advance of opening each production. These include the availability of cast members and production staff such as directors and designers, the total costs of the design of in-house productions, production costs of touring shows or the rate of return from hosting visiting companies. The 'uniqueness' of the product means that ticket sales forecasting for each production is problematic as projecting sales is generally based on past performance. Even when presenting something similar in the same slot as the previous year, Sheffield Theatres see variable results which are largely due to the audience demand at the time of the run. 'Star' casts, such as Kenneth Branagh in Shakespeare's *Richard III* staged in 2002 at the Crucible Theatre, are very popular but inevitably expensive. However, where the returns are generally low particularly at the end of the season in May and June, producing theatres will not risk programming an expensive show.

Performance: controversy and recovery

Prior to the reopening of the Lyceum, the Crucible had hosted some touring productions for up to

30 per cent of the year, but expanding into a theatre complex meant that Sheffield could play host to big-name touring productions of popular drama and musicals over most of the season. Seats at the Lyceum sold well, with average fill at over 60 per cent of capacity, and up to 100 per cent for some shows. This effectively freed up the Crucible Theatre to concentrate almost entirely on producing and developing its own work.

Controversy in the 1990s

A theatre that isn't controversial is dead. If people aren't talking about it and getting excited about the theatre, even if it includes criticism, then you are having no impact.

Claire Venables, Artistic Director,
Crucible Theatre, 1981–1990

Despite the positive public response to the reopening of the Lyceum, by 1991 it became clear a new crisis was emerging. An emergency meeting of the directors was called to discuss the drastic fall in Crucible box office receipts following the opening of the Lyceum. In October 1991, the *Sheffield Weekly Gazette* reported: 'The artistic director has resigned, attendances are down by 50 per cent, productions planned for the new year are cancelled, the company is heading for a £250,000 (≈ €380,000) deficit.' The then Chief Executive, Stephen Barry, insisted that the situation could be managed saying, 'We are not asking for more money, nor are we trying to take audiences away from the Lyceum. There are different types of audiences out there and we must look at ways of attracting them to the Crucible.' Two years later he reflected: 'In retrospect we were too defensive about the Crucible – narrowing our market appeal and attempting an over-specialist role. We did not capitalise on the single-site thinking brought about by the management structure. We knew the Lyceum would inevitably have an initial effect on the Crucible audiences – which was no doubt deepened by the recession.'

However, the crises in attendance levels were soon overshadowed by yet another, more significant financial crisis which emerged in 1993. A senior member of the finance staff had, over a period of two years, embezzled nearly £0.5m of funds from the various companies under the Sheffield Theatres umbrella. The person responsible was charged and convicted by the courts, and around a third of the money was subsequently recovered. But the events of the fraud created

a major trauma for everyone involved, exacerbating the overdraft in the theatre accounts with consequent ongoing interest charges. Box office revenue fell drastically from 1995 and, in 1995/96, the average capacity fill across all performances was only 57 per cent with a £353,000 deficit (≈ €530,000): considerably worse than the figure suggested in the shock headlines of 1991.

Fortunately, the charity has a major asset in the form of the Crucible building. Nevertheless, the accumulated deficit was such that there began to be some doubt as to whether the company was – in business terms – a 'going concern'. In the worst year, 1996/97, the accounts showed the company to have net assets of just £10,000, made up of a building worth £969,000 (≈ €1.5m) less accumulated deficits of £959,000. The severity of this was softened on a day-to-day basis, because theatres receive significant cash from ticket sales in advance of productions and at Sheffield Theatres this applies both for their own productions and for tickets sold for visiting productions. In addition, the predictable stream of revenue and capital grants, assist in the theatre's ability to remain active during periods of severe financial crisis. However, the burden of approximately £1m in accumulated deficits meant that the theatre had to make some very difficult strategic decisions.

Recovery

It's all about producing output of the highest quality – if you're not doing that, there's no point in being here.

Kay Ford, Finance Director, 2000

The resolve of the board to stick to its new strategy was severely tested.

Grahame Morris, Chief Executive of Sheffield
Theatres, 1997–2004

On arrival at Sheffield Theatres Trust, the new Chairman, Norman Adsetts, held crisis meetings in the summer of 1996 and a 'recovery plan' was agreed, which involved drastic cost-cutting. Productions were greatly slimmed back and key members of the permanent production staff were made redundant and offered purely seasonal contracts (the posts were eventually restored in 1999). The result was that artistic morale was extremely low and long-term planning seemed impossible: in order to control cash flow, budgets for each production could only be agreed once the outcome of preceding productions was known. The output

Exhibit 1	Performance figures and summary revenue accounts, 1990–2003*

Measure	1990	1991	1992	1993	1994	1995	1996	1997	1998	1999	2000	2001	2002	2003
Attendance (£000s)														
Crucible	173	180	110	139	131	92	84	88[5]	81	85	72	n/a[8]	80	83
Studio	13	5	10	9	15	28	22	–[5]	–	–	–	–	–	–
Lyceum	–	51**	316	288	299	253	219	268[5]	254	296	264	n/a[8]	203	220
Total (exc. snooker)	186	236	436	436	445	373	325	356	335	381	336	n/a[8]	283	303
Capacity fill														
Mean % capacity for in-house productions	58	65	41	64	63	49	40	48[5]	53	54	42	n/a[8]		
Financial														
Box office (£000s)	1,596	2,274[2]	4,051	3,929	4,599[1]	3,789	3,148	3,298	3,026	3,395	3,098	3,146	3,082	3,325
Annual grants (% of income)	40	36	25	27[3]	23	27	30	28	30	27	31	22	20	25
Surplus/ (deficit) (£000s)	(170)	98[2]	(31)	(36)	(115)	(219)	(353)	(164)[4]	10	87	19	195[6]	791	(4)[7]

Years shown relate to the financial year ending 31 March in the year shown – e.g. the column '1999' refers to performances for the year April 1998–March 1999.

* £1 = approx. €1.5.

** = part year only.

Notes:

1. The final surplus or deficit for each of the years 1991 to 1994 is affected to some extent by the fraud referred to in the text.
2. Accounting principles changed in 1991 to a basis similar to that used in 1985. The figures include box office sales and grants for the Lyceum (i.e. the figures from the Crucible Trust and Lyceum Trust have been amalgamated).
3. From 1993 the Lyceum site was the subject of a lease-back arrangement with the City Council – grants relating to lease payments are excluded from the calculation.
4. The figures given from 1997 onwards are for the consolidated surplus or deficit, covering both the charity (Sheffield Theatres Trust) and its trading subsidiary (Offstage Ltd.) in order to comply with the Statement of Recommended Practice on Accounting by Charities.
5. From 1997, when the company began using the three stages more flexibly, figures were analysed by *type of production* (in-house productions or visiting companies) rather than by the specific stage used. Hence the 'Crucible' line shows figures for all in-house productions and the 'Lyceum' line shows figures for all touring productions.
6. From 2001 the final surplus/deficit includes the funding from the stabilisation grants awarded to alleviate the burden of historical debts.
7. The marginal deficit recorded for the year reflects a reduction in the stabilisation grant and an increased investment in education work.
8. Figures not available at the time of compilation.

Source: Theatre records and published accounts.

began to be characterised by plays such as *Educating Rita* which could be mounted with two actors and a one-room set.

As a result, the reputation of the Crucible began to fall, with weak reviews and audiences less willing to travel to the theatre, resulting in even lower attendances. In its best year (accounting year 1994), Sheffield Theatres had achieved combined attendances across all three stages of 445,000 (see Exhibit 1). Just two years later in 1996 attendance had fallen by 27 per cent to 325,000. A clearer indication of the difficulties is shown in the figures for mean capacity fill for Sheffield Theatres' productions. In 1993 mean capacity fill was 64 per cent, but by 1996 this figure plummets to an unsustainable 40 per cent. The problems were compounded by a couple of poor Lyceum performances with box office sales below the level of the minimum guarantee given to the touring company.

The 1997 business plan bore fruit in the 1998 production of *Brassed Off* at the Crucible (based on the film of the same title), generating excellent box office sales in Sheffield and subsequently transferring to the National Theatre and then touring the UK. The production even returned to the Lyceum as a touring production, contributing to the substantial revenues that such spin-offs generate for Sheffield Theatres. Plans to invest in a high quality and ambitious artistic programme led to the appointment of Michael Grandage as associate director in 1999 with a brief to develop the range and scale of productions. Michael Grandage had already created a highly successful production of *Twelfth Night* at the Crucible as a freelance director in late 1998 and his proven capabilities as a director and national profile as an actor have since attracted very well-known actors including Joseph Fiennes, Kenneth Branagh, Amanda Donohoe and Sir Derek Jacobi. In turn the casts have generated substantial audiences to Sheffield Theatres and increasing critical acclaim.

As a testament to the boldness of the business plan, the financial position in 1997/98 showed a recovery to a small £10,000 surplus on the year, and in 1998/99 a very respectable surplus of £87,000 was achieved – well beyond the basic aim of a charity. In addition, by 2000 a production schedule could be planned and costed for a whole year ahead, enabling the theatres to market performances with long lead-times and to invest in high-quality, high-profile casts. As a result, in March 2002 the company had recorded five consecutive years of operating surpluses which is a measure of the new management philosophy and the timely arrival of additional investment funding.

Charity Commission guidance suggests that charities should have adequate reserves over and above their fixed assets to cover a reasonable period of expenditure, usually measured at three months. Sheffield Theatres would need a £2m increase in current assets for the charity to reach this level of financial security and, even with all the new funding agreed, the theatres would still be below this level. In 1999 ACE had announced the launch of its Stabilisation Programme, aimed at helping major arts bodies such as Sheffield Theatres to get on a stable footing, both in their financial structures and in their artistic output.

It was recognised, for example, that whilst good management would allow the theatres to balance their budgets each year and perhaps make a small surplus, there is no way they would recover the cumulative historic deficit of approximately £1m. By spring 2001 a total award of £1.7m was confirmed: the largest single injection of funds to Sheffield Theatres since the opening of the Lyceum. Although the majority of this money was targeted on debt clearance, £130,000 was for a new stage and lighting system and £140,000 for new IT infrastructure for the theatres, with the balance available as revenue funding up to 2003/04 (see Exhibit 1) to develop the artistic programme and educational work. This major injection of funds meant that by 2003, the burden of the historic deficit was swept away, giving the Trust the long-sought financial stability needed to develop.

Over the 1990s Sheffield theatres faced almost insurmountable problems, but, in response to a comprehensive business plan, the company was moving forward. Based on high levels of artistic investment, detailed research on audiences and ticket pricing, and a more strategic approach to maximising other income, the company continues to receive critical acclaim.

Operational structure

Serving the population of the fourth largest English city outside London, Sheffield Theatres had an annual income of around £5.5m in 2003, making it one of the 500 largest charities in the UK. But the aims of creating high-quality artistic work, filling sufficient seats, and working without deficits have created a constant challenge.

In the early days, all the work of the Crucible was handled by one Trust board. Then, from 1987, a separate Lyceum Trust was established alongside a further management company – Sheffield Theatres – providing the common support functions to both theatres. With three management bodies, it was clear that very few people (certainly very few board members) understood the overall financial situation. It was also found that grant aid might be increased to one company whilst being withdrawn from another, setting the two theatres in competition with one another. So, after extensive debate, it was agreed to transfer overall legal responsibility for the work of both theatres to one body, the Sheffield Theatres Trust in 1995. Sheffield Theatres Trust is a registered charity and a company limited by guarantee (with permission to omit the word 'Limited' from its title). As stated in its Memorandum of Association, its charitable objects are

● To promote, maintain, improve and advance education, particularly by the production of educational plays and the encouragement of the arts of drama, mime, dance, singing and music. . . .

● To receive, educate and train students in drama, dancing, music, and other arts, and to promote the recognition and encouragement of special merit in students. . . .

The board of Sheffield Theatres now operates in effect as one organisation, with overall responsibility for management of the whole complex. As trustees of the charity, board members are unpaid, but act in the capacity of both directors of the company and trustees of the charity. The full board takes responsibility for the entire work; the only sub-committees are an audit committee and a nominations committee responsible for seeking suitable candidates for replacing retiring trustees. All theatre staff, including the chief executive, are employees of the board: they are not actually directors of the company even where the job title 'director' is used.

Education

Sheffield Theatres has an extensive and highly regarded programme of work with young people. In 2003 there were 14,681 participants across six programmes, projects and initiatives. Additionally, the education website launched in September 2002 received 20,669 visits between going online and the end of March 2003.

Working with six partner primary schools and three secondary schools, 2002–2003 saw primary school pupils developing drama and literacy skills through work with playwright, Neil Druffield, developing a new play and a playwriting resource for Sheffield teachers written by Judy Marsh of the Crucible Youth Theatre. Sheffield Theatres also provided young people from the partner secondary schools with work experience opportunities, career workshops across the range of jobs in the theatre, Theatre-in-Education tours and participation, and workshops with touring companies. In addition, there were also 240 participants in the dedicated teachers' events.

In 2003, the Crucible Youth Theatre (CYT) continued to strengthen their work providing challenging drama workshops for their membership and also created a new series of projects. This programme included a new outreach project (Chaucer Youth Theatre) at one of the partner schools in the

---

Exhibit 2 **Summary of board membership, February 2004**

Directors / Trustees (12 persons):

Nominated by Sheffield City Council: 3 members (2 councillors + one other)

Elected: 9 members* including the chair

Observers:

Sheffield City Council Arts Department: 2 (officers of the Council).

Yorkshire Arts Board: 1

Officers in attendance:

Chief Executive
Associate Director
Finance Director
Marketing and Development Director

* These members serve for periods of three years after which they may be re-elected for one further three-year period. The board elects its own successors.

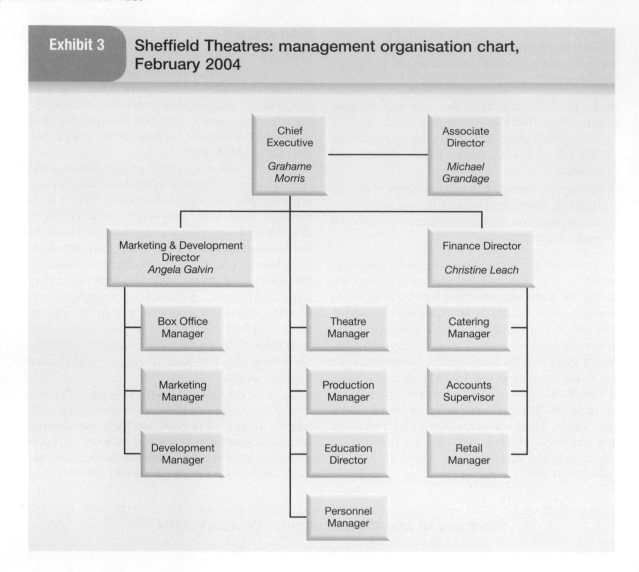

Exhibit 3 Sheffield Theatres: management organisation chart, February 2004

north of Sheffield and a number of training opportunities and theatre employment workshops.

An annual Children's Festival in June and July marks the culmination of the theatre's season of work and illustrates the commitment Sheffield Theatres have to the community and the trust's charitable objectives.

The company

Second only to production costs, staffing represents approximately 28 per cent of the annual expenditure of Sheffield Theatres Trust. However, as the difficulties of the late 1990s detailed below show, the effects of a hard-hitting financial plan led to low morale, reduced artistic output and a decreasing reputation for the theatre. Once the theatre stabilised and the seasonal staff were reinstated

to permanent positions, the performance figures show a good recovery (see Exhibit 1). Sheffield Theatres have regularly won national industry and media accolades, illustrating the extent of the contribution made by all employees.

Offstage Ltd

As with most charitable organisations of any size, it is necessary to have a trading subsidiary company to undertake non-charitable activities such as the sale of food and drink and commercial sponsorship: this is the role of Offstage Ltd. Offstage is wholly owned by Sheffield Theatres Trust, and at the end of each year, Offstage undertakes a gift aid payment to transfer all its profits to Sheffield Theatres Trust – this means no corporation tax is paid, and the theatres get the full

Exhibit 4	Employees at Sheffield Theatres, 2002

	No. employed
Technical (stage crew etc.)	41
Sales/front of house	69
Maintenance/security	23
Administration	13
Freelance cast/production	(av.) 17
Total	163
Offstage Ltd	56
Total	219

benefit of all associated activities undertaken on their premises.

The profits of the restaurant, bars and gift shop form an important source of additional income. Significant steps were taken from 1997/98 to increase the profitability of this side of the work, by altering staffing level, opening hours, menus and prices. Recent figures show that in 2001, for example, catering revenues were £43,000 rising to £54,000 in 2002 and £84,000 in 2003. Despite the success of these enterprises, there is little further scope for improvement due to design and location constraints. One of the longer-term aims of the major capital investments proposed for the Crucible will be a complete redesign of the front-of-house areas, relocating facilities to improve access and enjoyment of the theatre.

In addition to the catering and retail functions of Offstage Ltd, by the mid-1990s Sheffield Theatres became increasingly successful in attracting sponsors for many Sheffield productions, co-production deals and sponsorship for some touring productions, if not already sponsored through the touring company. In particular, from 1997/98 they received support through the DCMS-promoted Arts and Business Paring Scheme, and a further sponsor supported the education work. However, such income can be vulnerable in times of recession, as sponsorship of the arts is an obvious area for companies to reduce in times of difficulty. In 2000–2001, for example, sponsorship income from Offstage Ltd was £170,000, but in 2001–2002 this figure had fallen to £98,000, recovering marginally to £104,000 for 2002–2003.

Fundraising

As a charity, Sheffield Theatres has been active in various forms of fundraising over the years. A Programme Development Fund generated around £100,000 over four years in the mid-1990s, from individuals supporting the development of new Crucible productions. A number of charitable trusts make occasional grants to the theatres, but such grants are usually only for one-off projects. Certain capital projects have also been supported by fundraising, for example £400,000 was raised in 1994 for the enlargement of the Studio Theatre from 250 to 400 seats and improved auditorium access for disabled people. But the need for major upgrading of the Crucible building means that a new fundraising project in the region of £15m will soon be launched.

Snooker

The most long-standing source of external income has been from hosting the World Snooker Championships, and to many people in the UK the Crucible became synonymous with the World Snooker Championships which have been held there over three weeks every April/May from 1977. Although the snooker brought in substantial revenue including extra catering profits as well as the basic hire charge, this decision was not without its critics. One of the board members commented in 1996: 'I don't like snooker. I really object to my theatres being used as a snooker hall and it breaks up the theatre season. But it does mean that five or six times a day the *Crucible Sheffield* is mentioned on prime time TV. And we do need the money!' Although the net revenue from hosting the snooker has fallen over the years, the overall view of the board has been that the monies received remain important to Sheffield Theatres. It is uncertain whether the Crucible and Studio Theatres will continue to host the World Snooker Championships on a yearly basis as at present, but the Crucible is being used to near capacity for other sports events such as the Squash Championships.

Grant funding

Since the beginning of subsidised theatre in Sheffield in 1960–61, income had shifted from purely commercial sources towards a heavy dependence on grants, primarily from the Arts Council of Great Britain (as it was then known) and local authorities. In 1977 some 63 per cent of the income was in the form of grants; this declined to about 55 per cent by the 1980s, to 40 per cent in 1989, and to 27 per cent by 1995, though with some one-off grants for special initiatives the grant funding rose slightly to 31 per cent in 2000. In the accounting year ending March 2003, annual grants made up only 25 per cent of the theatre's income with box office receipts at 55 per cent (see Exhibit 1).

Arts Council England

The Arts Council does not give grants to touring theatres, but instead gives grants to certain touring companies towards the cost of their productions. The policy on public funding of the arts had changed substantially over the years. In 1985 there was an attempt to build up genuine 'centres of excellence' in the regions, and the Crucible was one of 13 regional theatres selected as a major beneficiary. Another important policy change in the late 1980s was the introduction of 'parity funding', by which the Arts Council aimed that the total public funding of any theatre should be shared equally between themselves and the local authority. However, Sheffield City Council was unable to reach an agreement with the Arts Council on this issue. David Patmore, Director of Arts for Sheffield City Council in 1992, stated that much of the problem was due to the internal structures of the Arts Council, which treated producing theatre and touring venues completely separately. As a result, the substantial money which the City Council was contributing to the Lyceum project was not recognised by the Arts Council in calculations of overall parity. The net effect was that the Crucible lost out substantially in the overall 'pecking order' of Arts Council grants, compared with other large provincial repertory theatres.

In the early 1990s, the Arts Council moved to a regional structure, which meant that most of the grant to Sheffield Theatres came from Yorkshire Arts Board rather than direct from the Arts Council of England (ACE). This change meant that the Crucible was no longer in direct competition for funds with as many other theatres as previously, there being only one other producing theatre in Yorkshire of comparable size. However, it also meant that the scope for Arts Council grants was influenced heavily by the initial split of the 'cake' into regional 'slices', over which the theatre had relatively little influence. As a result, the funding from Yorkshire Arts remained virtually static at around £650,000 from 1994 to 2000 – effectively a cut each year after allowing for inflation. But in 2001, a major shift in government policy towards the arts began to emerge, with new policies to support excellence in regional theatres, culminating in the announcement from Yorkshire Arts of an additional award to Sheffield Theatres of £247,500 for 2002/03, and £470,000 for 2003/04, as a reward for innovative output. This meant that over just two years the trust was due to receive a massive 72 per cent increase in its Yorkshire Arts core funding.

Sheffield City Council

Sheffield City Council has continued to see theatres as vital to the city for attracting commerce and investment, and relationships between the theatres and the Council are seen as good. Grant funding has been largely maintained despite heavy cuts elsewhere in the city's arts budgets: in 1999/2000 the City Council grant was worth £685,000 to Sheffield Theatres (excluding amounts related to the lease-back of the Lyceum site). However, in 2002 the grant had been reduced to £664,350 and this remained the same in 2003. With small cuts and the effects of inflation, the theatres continue to face year-on-year reductions in the net value of this support, and financial support from two other neighbouring local authorities (Rotherham and Barnsley) together worth around £23,000 was also withdrawn during the late 1990s. The squeeze on local authority funding must be set against the increase in the Yorkshire Arts Board grant as shown above, which directly rewards quality output at Sheffield Theatres. Local authority funding is restricted by the sources of its income and the performance indicators against which the whole range of the City Council's services are measured.

Special initiative grants

A large amount of time is spent securing additional funds for specific projects that are not included in the annual grants. All subsidised theatres access an array of sources dependent upon the requirements of each project. Since 1990, for example, Sheffield Theatres recognised opportunities arising from the following:

The launch of the National Lottery in 1994 meant a new possible source of support from the Arts Lottery Fund. Awards from the fund, administered by the Arts Council, are for specific initiatives, particularly for capital projects such as the proposed refurbishment of the Crucible Theatre. The fund would not normally award grants to support education and production development in a theatre as producing theatres receive annual government funding.

The election of the Labour government in 1997 saw some changes beginning to emerge in national policies towards support of the arts. The formation of the new Department of Culture, Media and Sport (DCMS) signalled new thinking and opened up new research into the role the arts play in the economy, health and the local community. Initiatives were set up specifically targeting the notion of 'social exclusion' and the role that the arts could play in its reduction in the local community. These initiatives enabled Sheffield Theatres to secure emergency funding from ACE of £100,000 per year for 1997–99, and a one-off grant of £300,000 for audience development work and the 'How Much?' research project on ticket pricing and the attendance constraints of young people. This research was conducted with Sheffield University and Sheffield Hallam University and was published in 2000.

As a result of the new political philosophy, the Stabilisation Fund launched in 1999 awarded Sheffield Theatres £1.7m over three years from 2001, the effects of which can be seen in the figures in Exhibit 1. The majority of the money was for debt clearance but the theatre was also awarded £270,000 for capital projects and there was an allowance of revenue funding for artistic and development work for 2003/2004.

Sheffield Theatres received a grant of £26,000 from the New Audiences programme (ACE) in the year 2001/2002.

With the financial support of the single regeneration budget a feasibility study and preliminary architectural plan was conducted in 2002 for a major redevelopment plan for the Crucible. An estimated £15m is urgently required for the refurbishment programme and from 2004 Sheffield Theatres will launch a capital fundraising project utilising a variety of sources – including Arts Council England and lottery funding – to complete the fund.

This is not an exhaustive list of sources of additional grant income, but serves as an illustration of the direction of strategic planning in theatre management, not only at Sheffield Theatres, but also on a national basis. The turnaround plan at Sheffield Theatres took into account the nature and availability of funds at the time rather than fighting for sufficient capital funds for the urgent repair and modernising of the Crucible Theatre.

Audiences: marketing and pricing

The Guardian Theatre Awards 2003. Best Theatre, Sheffield Crucible '. . . for its swagger, audacity and ability to lure the young away from the discos.'

Michael Billington, *The Guardian* theatre critic

Marketing

From 1996 a marketing director was added to the senior management team, and the roles of marketing and publicity, box office and development (fundraising) are now managed on an integral basis. A more systematic approach to marketing has seen attendances rise compared with the dire situation in 1996. Programming for each year includes an element of risk which is reflected in sales variations from year to year depending on whether the given season included any overwhelmingly successful productions. It is the job of the marketing team to identify target markets for each production and develop promotional material and bundling to enhance sales.

Both the Trust and its funding providers have long been concerned to extend the reach of the theatres to a wider audience. By 2000, the theatres had built a database of ticket purchasers running to some 250,000 names, but surveys in the past had found that around 70 per cent of all seats were sold to a core of around 20,000 regular theatre attenders, drawn largely from those living in certain middle class suburbs of Sheffield.

To help understand the audience issues more clearly, and especially to implement one of the Labour government's aims of making the theatre more attractive to young people, Sheffield Theatres successfully obtained a £300,000 Arts Council grant in 1998 for a two-year project entitled 'How Much?'. Theatre audiences are often dominated by middle-aged and older people: the obvious scope for audience growth is to attract more young people. Nationally, only 16 per cent of theatre audiences come from the 16–24 age group, and in Sheffield the figure was just 7 per cent, despite a large student population in the city. It was generally supposed that young people are cautious about theatre as a leisure activity, because of the twin problems of the cost of seats and unattractive programming for this age group. Cinema is widely regarded as being the main competitor for this target market and with a cinema situated directly behind the Crucible, marketing strategy had to be devised to combat preconceived ideas and test price constraints for young people. The 'How Much?' grant enabled the company to tackle this directly: 21 productions were publicised under the 'How Much?' banner with seat prices as low as £3.50 for those aged 16–24. Several new productions specifically tackled issues seen as relevant to young people, and others were marketed directly to them with headlines such as 'Sex . . . Violence . . . Brilliance . . . Shakespeare . . . all for £3.50'. With the support of the two universities in Sheffield, 'How Much?' was tackled as a major research project, also involving studies of those who do not attend theatre.

The net effect was a massive increase in seats sold to young people: for these 21 productions, 41 per cent of the audience was in the 16–24 age group, and overall, 29 per cent of the audience for these productions were new attenders. The box office coded all sales according to how the purchaser said they had heard of the production, so the marketing director knew exactly which sales came from which promotional medium. The results were seen as very exciting, but without further special grants, the theatres cannot continue to offer such low prices to young people (though student discounts and standby tickets continue to apply); there was also the problem that these productions were less attractive to some of the more traditional audience.

In May 2002, a research report was published by *Audiences Yorkshire* who had taken extensive data from the box office and other survey sources and formulated a detailed report on audience mapping and profiling. The catchment area was identified and bookers allocated by postcode, creating valuable information on where bookers were travelling from, which areas represent the core audience and which areas could be targeted to increase the theatre's penetration of the market. 'Mosaic' software also categorised bookers and households by 'lifestyle profiling' into 12 groups and 52 types.

Historically more often used by commercial organisations, customer profiling is increasingly being utilised by arts organisations like Sheffield Theatres, to enable them to better understand their audiences and demand patterns.

The research showed that the Studio has the most local audience with 75 per cent of bookers drawn from within a 20 minute drive. The Lyceum draws 67 per cent of its audience from this base and the Crucible has the lowest level of local audience with 57 per cent drawn from within a 20-minute drive time. A significant minority of 20 per cent of the audience for the Crucible travelled for 40 to 60 minutes to attend, making the Crucible audience the most geographically dispersed of the three stages.

The Lyceum draws the most loyal audience of the three theatres, with 75 per cent of its audience only booking for the Lyceum and just 3.5 per cent of its audience booking for all three venues. The audience of the Studio are the most likely to book for all three venues (21.2 per cent of the audience) with 49 per cent displaying loyalty to just the Studio Theatre. The Studio Theatre also diverges from the national trend in the profile of its audience where significant attendance has been identified from the Mosaic type categories of Bijou Homemakers, Bedsits and Shop Flats, College and Communal and Rejuvenated Terraces. Although all three theatres draw their core audiences from rather predictable groups such as High Income Families, Stylish Singles, Suburban Semis and Country Dwellers, the Studio has the most diverse audience, reflecting the breadth of the programming and perhaps an increased accessibility through having the lowest prices of the three venues. Investment in research of this nature develops long-term marketing strategies which should enable Sheffield Theatres to create accurately targeted audience development programmes and increased ticket sales. Core audience figures show an increase from 70,650 in 2001/02 to 75,760 in 2002/03 and broad programming and targeted marketing could continue to strengthen these numbers still further.

Whether productions are in-house or touring, it remains a real challenge to fill 2,500 seats of theatre capacity, across the three stages. Some local commentators have felt that Sheffield was simply unable to support this capacity of professional theatre (although there was no attempt to use all three stages for production for 52 weeks per year). But capacity fill remains the fundamental issue for

Ticket pricing

The largest part of Sheffield Theatres' revenues derives from ticket sales and this money must meet all the remaining costs not met by grants or ancillary income. Budgeting for this is dependent upon the three issues of how seats are priced, what proportion of seats for any production are sold, and to what extent seats are sold at concessionary prices.

After deducting VAT from the prices, and allowing for concessions, the average yield per seat in 2002 (i.e. the net revenue to the theatre's accounts) was around £9 for Sheffield productions and approximately £11 for performances mounted by visiting companies. In 2004, tickets for the Crucible ranged from £1 for the Public Dress Rehearsal up to £15 for a full adult ticket (£16.50 for the Christmas show). In the Lyceum, prices varied widely according to the production, but prime seats could be as much as £29.50 for a major touring musical or even £40 for an opera. Seats in the Studio theatre were normally priced in a similar range as the Crucible Theatre up to £10 for the theatre's own productions, but the Studio also hosts many musical concerts and smaller outside production companies. Concessions were also available to those over 60, children, students, registered unemployed, disabled people and their carers, with an additional 'Young People's Performance' priced at £5 for audience members aged between 16 and 26 for Sheffield Theatres' productions.

The theatre offers a range of discounts for regular theatre-goers who belong to one of seven categories of the *Square Circle* membership scheme which brings in an amount of regular committed income from the fees. In 2001/02 there were 1,467 members across the range of schemes and in 2002/03 this had risen to 1,678, drawing fee revenues of just under £47,000. These members purchased 19,459 tickets worth nearly £255,000, making the membership scheme a significant part of revenue building.

Since 1998 increasing emphasis has been placed on plays which originate at Sheffield Theatres but then transfer elsewhere as with *The Tempest* (2001), giving royalty income back to the company, or co-productions with other regional theatres where production costs are shared. The unique shape of the Crucible stage makes such transfers relatively difficult; but it becomes more viable if productions are developed at the Lyceum. For the same reason, the Lyceum is much more suitable than the Crucible for most touring companies. The ticket sales revenue from visiting productions is distributed between Sheffield Theatres and the touring company according to a contract which is negotiated individually for each production. However, with only 1,100 seats the Lyceum – which hosts most of the touring productions – is not quite sufficient to attract the very largest touring companies, especially those that bring their own sound and lighting equipment which occupies some of the seating area. In addition to these constraints, over 300 of the seats are in the balcony where visibility is limited.

In some cases quite complex formulae are used to allocate the box office sales for visiting productions, but a typical split is for 70 per cent of revenues to go to the touring company and 30 per cent to be retained by the theatre. However, it is not uncommon for the touring company to have a 'first call' on all sales up to a certain level, or even a minimum guarantee which the theatres have to commit before the touring company will agree to come to Sheffield. In terms of minimising risk, the best arrangement with visiting companies is 'hire only' where the touring company pays a fixed fee for use of the theatre, regardless of ticket sales – but then if such productions prove to be very successful, Sheffield Theatres has no share in the profits beyond the hire fee agreed.

The key question which remains is whether or not, on a long-term basis, the output of the theatres can be translated into a sustainable level of sales at the box office which would ensure the continued financial stability which Sheffield Theatres needs.

Looking to the future

Sheffield Theatres are beginning to fulfil our artistic potential for the first time in our . . . history as a complex. This is not an overnight success story, but one born of the changes at all levels beginning in 1996.
Sir Norman Adsetts, Chair, Sheffield Theatres Trust, 2001

There is real encouragement that the new government policies towards the arts are creating a potential where, for the first time in many years, Sheffield Theatres might really be able to move forward in the quality of its artistic output. By the end of the 2002 year review, Sheffield Theatres

Trust was free of debt for the first time in eight years. With the help of investment from the Arts Council England's Main Stabilisation Programme, the Theatre's enormous historical deficit was eliminated. This position has been hard won and is tremendously liberating for the company as we look to the future with both energy and optimism. But a strategy of high investment in production quality can only succeed in the long term if it leads to higher levels of attendance.

With this in mind, we intend to focus our attention on the physical redevelopment of the Crucible Theatre which is crucial to accessibility and the enjoyment of the audience. The Crucible represents the artistic heart of our work and needs better to reflect, in its fabric and facilities, the scale and quality of our artistic achievement and ambition for the people of Sheffield. A feasibility study was completed and the projected cost of modernising the facilities is now £15m. As a result, fundraising will continue to be a focus of business planning for the foreseeable future.

Grahame Morris announced that he will be stepping down from his position as Chief Executive of Sheffield Theatres in April 2004. In a press announcement he said 'My decision is timed to enable the company to consider its new leadership before embarking on the major, recently-announced project of redeveloping the Crucible buildings.'

Michael Grandage, Associate Director, said 'I have enjoyed working with Grahame enormously and shall miss his warmth and good humour. His sound judgement as Chief Executive has seen us reach a place where we are generously told by audiences, critics and awards juries that Sheffield is at the forefront of British theatre. I am pleased to count him as a friend and mentor. Now, our vision for the future is to go on exploring artistic excellence and innovation, to build our education programme, to continue our unique nurturing of young audiences and to offer our community the opportunity to engage with us at every level.'

Belief in action: The Salvation Army, a global not-for-profit organisation

Alex Murdock

The Salvation Army is a global not-for-profit organisation which has a number of quite distinctive characteristics. It adopted almost from its inception the military form and this has continued to be a distinguishing factor in its work. Its Christian mission and UK origin have not prevented it from working successfully across religious, language, national and ethnic divides. The growth and range of activities of the organisation have been remarkable. The resulting size and complexity pose a challenge to the organisation in respect of both how it acknowledges and incorporates the range of stakeholders and also in terms of how it confronts future choices.

● ● ●

Introduction

In August 2003 Alex Hughes, the UK Territorial Commander, wrote an open letter to all UK Salvation Army members. He began the letter with the words:

> As my wife and I travel around the territory, some people ask us, 'What will The Salvation Army be like in the future?' Although this is a good question, a simple answer is not easy. But this is a question we all need to grapple with, urgently!

The Salvation Army is a distinctive part of the universal Christian Church. Its message and the lifestyle it advocates are based on the Bible's teaching. Its work is to make known the good news about Jesus Christ and to persuade people to become his followers. Alongside this primary aim, the Army shows practical concern and care for the needs of people regardless of race, creed, status, colour, sex or age.

The Salvation Army was founded in 1865 in London. A quasi-military structure was quickly adopted and subsequently the organisation became a worldwide movement which is now to be found in 109 countries and operates in 175 different languages. This would be remarkable in any organisation whether in the private or not-for-profit sector. The long history of The Salvation Army and its associated steady growth have also marked it out as an organisation which has stood the test of time whilst remaining close to its original mission.

However the organisation is not static and one of the Commissioners observed, 'The twenty-first century ministry requires a mission-centred Salvation Army in continuous renewal' and averred that it was time for more bold initiatives pushing beyond what he described as the 'comfortable patterns of missioning behaviour'.[1] The actual mission statement of the Salvation Army in 2003–4 read as follows:

> The Salvation Army, an international movement, is an evangelical part of the universal Christian Church. Its message is based on the Bible. Its ministry is motivated by love for God. Its mission is to preach the gospel of Jesus Christ and meet human need in his name without discrimination.
>
> (Mission statement of The Salvation Army)

[1] Commissioner Israel L. Gaither quoted from *Salvation Army Yearbook*, 2004, p. 2.

The range of activities undertaken by The Salvation Army

The Salvation Army provides a very wide range of programme-based services in the global context. The Salvation Army's social service function has become very significant. The UK 2003 Annual Report asserted that it was the second largest provider of social services after the government. These can be divided as follows (Appendix 1 gives the precise breakdown of the range of provision offered).

Social programmes

Residential services are widely provided in a range of different forms. The single largest category are facilities for homeless people and in 2003 there were altogether over 600 separate facilities with a total capacity of nearly 32,000. However, The Salvation Army provided residential accommodation for almost every conceivable need group ranging from mother and baby through children to the elderly and disabled. They also provided remand and probation facilities. Day care was similarly provided for a wide range of client groups and needs.

Addiction dependency has long been a prime focus for the Army's work and this is reflected in the significant number of specifically targeted residential and day care resources. However due to the nature of the client groups it is reasonable to assume that addiction problems are likely to be found extensively through much of the clientele in both the residential and day care provision.

The armed forces provision has been very much a tradition from the long-established association of the Army with its 'armed counterpart'. The Salvation Army is, however, more akin to the Red Cross and has operated on both sides of conflicts. This apolitical approach is key to the ability of the Army to operate in a vast range of different countries.

Associated with this is the increased role the Army has come to play in disaster relief. This has often been undertaken in a similar manner to a range of other such organisations. The Salvation Army was a significant presence after September 11 in providing support and tangible sustenance to those affected and the rescuers.

The community services role has taken The Salvation Army into areas also peopled by probation and counselling services. There could have been potential areas of conflict here but The Salvation Army has traditionally been able to work in partnership with both statutory and voluntary agencies. These partnerships are often associated with the willingness of The Salvation Army to engage with clients whom other agencies are reluctant to assist, such as alcoholics and 'difficult clients'. The 'missing persons' service has been very highly regarded and (in the UK) has acquired a well-deserved reputation for successfully tracing a very high proportion of referrals.

Health care and hospital provision

The Salvation Army has developed a significant number of programmes in this area particularly associated with its work in the developing world. The development of mobile clinics and outpatient services has been significant and the Army has been active in responding to HIV/AIDS.

Education

Missionary-based organisations often see educational services as an important part of their role and it is hardly surprising that The Salvation Army has been active here. However the size of the provision is remarkable. The total number of pupils catered for globally was greater than the number of undergraduates in the whole of the UK.

The fundamental basis of The Salvation Army

As the name suggests, the basis of The Salvation Army which distinguishes from it from other aspects of Christian (and for that matter other) religious organisations is the adoption of a quasi-military form of structure. This was derived from the concept of 'spiritual warfare' and has been reflected in the use of ranks, uniforms and flags and indeed in its well-established publication 'The War Cry'.

However the actual work of The Salvation Army is not simply evangelistic but is heavily focused upon the relief of poverty and the provision of practical, cost-effective and skilled services. In some ways The Salvation Army anticipates the changing role of the traditional military which has had to adapt to new 'peace-keeping' and disaster assistance roles. However for The Salvation Army the service provision has been a long tradition. Previously the social service aspects were run in tandem with the missionary aspects but the organisational structure has changed to bring the two together.

The charity is well known for the modest salaries paid to its officers (ministers). When Commissioner Alex Hughes took on the Territorial Commander role in the UK in 2002 the newspapers noted his salary with a degree of astonishment. He was a chief executive managing a £161m budget (≈ €240m) and 5,600 staff. Yet he received a salary including benefits of £10,258 (≈ €15,000). This represented a minute fraction (about 15 per cent) of what chief executives of similarly sized charitable organisations might expect. A person working in the lowest clerical capacity in a charity in the UK would probably have received more.

Growth of The Salvation Army

In the tradition of many voluntary and missionary-focused organisations The Salvation Army draws much of its strength and vision from that of its founder, William Booth. Significantly for the Army the role of Catherine Booth, his wife, has been strongly acknowledged and the Army has had a long-established tradition of involving women in active and significant roles within the organisation.

In 2003 the Army had a General (John Larsson) whose wife, Freda, was also a Commissioner in the Army. In this respect The Salvation Army had reached a lot further than other faith-based organisations where the role of a spouse was seen as supportive but was not given full and potentially equal recognition.

The military form of the organisation does not mean that non-uniformed members are not important. Appendix 2 indicates that (as at 1 January 2002) there were a range of associations with The Salvation Army. Many non-officer employees held a number of significant posts and responsibility throughout the organisation. The rank of lieutenant was regarded as appropriate for someone who wished to become an officer on a temporary basis. It was somewhat akin to a 'short-service commission' in the regular army.

The discipline associated with the military mode of operation has been combined with a surprising degree of organisational flexibility. From its outset the organisation was very practically orientated. The provision of relief services to the poor led naturally to the evolution of a strong social service function. The organisation became able to respond to crisis and disaster. It increasingly became involved in international relief work.

The original focus upon poverty and the associated issues linked to alcohol and gambling has remained a strong part of the core of the organisation. The Salvation Army does not accept any donations or grants derived from these sources. Therefore it has not applied for monies from the UK National Lottery. However in other respects The Salvation Army has been relatively flexible about accepting money from a range of sources. The pragmatic view has been expressed that money can be cleansed by being put to good use.

However there were some concerns expressed following the acceptance of the American Territory of a bequest from Joan Kroc, wife of the founder of McDonald's restaurants in 2004. It was the world's largest single charity donation and had restrictions upon its use. A UK Salvation Army officer wrote in *The Guardian* in January 2004 referring to the US bequest:

> In the UK, where we run a vast array of services for vulnerable people, we rely on the support of the public and we would like to thank everyone who contributes. We don't need $1.5bn to make a difference to people's lives; £9 helps provide a homeless person with shelter for the night in a Salvation Army hostel, while £25 pays for one night's meal run, which can provide up to 60 people with soup and sandwiches.

Internationalisation and growth

From its beginnings in the UK The Salvation Army became a global organisation. The increase in countries was matched by an increase in the number of 'soldiers' and in 2003 there were over 1,024,000 senior soldiers worldwide. The organisation employed that year nearly 110,000 people. Appendix 2 sets out the make-up of The Salvation Army as of January 2002.

This growth was especially marked in developing countries and as the table below shows the number of soldiers was particularly high in Africa.

Table 1 Geographical distribution of soldiers

	Soldiers	% of total
Africa	438,483	43
Americas	127,460	12.5
Europe	71,888	7
South Asia	275,224	27
South Pacific & East Asia	107,082	10.5
		100

Source: Derived from Alan Read, 'The Salvation Army and government: Marching in step into the 21st century', unpublished master's thesis South Bank University, London.

The Salvation Army (unlike more conventional armies) has preferred to work in countries where they were legally recognised by the law of the country. In the UK The Salvation Army has enjoyed its own specific legislative provision, The Salvation Army Act of 1980. This is somewhat unusual in the charitable context. In part the legislation came about (in 1931) to deal with succession and to set a compulsory retirement age for the General.

The Army has sought to work alongside other faiths. Its website has stated:

> In many countries The Salvation Army co-exists with non-Christian faiths such as Islam, Hinduism and Buddhism. It respects the sincerely-held beliefs of devout non-Christians, and does not regard conflict or bitter controversy as suitable means to making known the good news of Jesus.

However the relationships with the governments of the countries in which it operates have not always run smoothly. The press made much of the attempts by the Moscow City Government to ban The Salvation Army in 2001 which led to a ban on The Salvation Army in Russia. The Salvation Army fought this through the Russian courts and was reinstated there as a charity in 2002. The Army has in fact been actively involved in Russia since 1913 and though banned by the communists re-established itself in 1992 with the fall of communism.

One researcher commented on this aspect of The Salvation Army work:

> That The Salvation Army relationship with governments varies so widely from country to country is a reflection not only of the internationalisation of The Salvation Army but also of the government frameworks, ideologies and policies within which it must work and it can also be conditioned by the work of

The Salvation Army in the lives of government leaders in their childhood.[2]

The governance and change process

The Salvation Army has differed in one important respect from its armed counterpart. There was not a global high command structure which determined local strategy and activities. The international HQ is in London but each Territory has a high degree of autonomy. Indeed each Territory is typically recognised through local legal provision in the country in which it operates. There are, however, several governance structures which have affected the operation of The Salvation Army globally:

- The High Council, constituted of all the Active Commissioners and Officers in charge of territories (some 63 in all), is called to deal with succession or when the General is unfit to continue. They can meet at any place in the UK, but normally meet at Sunbury Court (Sunbury on Thames) where there is a specific 'Conference Chamber' for the election of a new General.

- The Generals' Consultative Council comprises all the officers qualified to attend the High Council and advises on mission, strategy and policy. It meets more regularly (about four times a year) and operates electronically through the use of Lotus Notes.

- The International Management Council focuses on the efficiency and operation of the International HQ in London and meets monthly.

The Salvation Army has had some separation in its religious and social service functions with the latter being mainly run by professionals. There has been a move to integrate the social service provision into the religious part of Salvation Army activities. This has been greeted with a degree of apprehension by some of the professional staff.

The Salvation Army in the global context

The range and diversity of The Salvation Army activities means that the global organisation confronts

---

[2] Alan Read, 'The Salvation Army and government', unpublished master's thesis, South Bank University, London.

a very complex environment. The organisation primarily functions on a geographic basis through the Territorial Commissioners. However there is a considerable amount of local autonomy and the Commissioners are not to be compared in power and authority to their regular army counterparts.

Just as Generals in the regular army have to deal with politicians so The Salvation Army has to deal with the individual governmental bodies which affect its work. This presents an enormous degree of diversity. In the UK political leaders of almost all persuasions have been strongly supportive of The Salvation Army. In the USA it was built into the official post-9/11 response to disaster and was praised by *Forbes* magazine as one of the top 10 US charities.

However in Russia it encountered major problems and in areas of danger for western charities (such as Iraq or Afghanistan) The Salvation Army's values may offer it but limited protection. As an avowedly Christian organisation with a missionary element to its work the prospect of maintaining its global presence represents a major challenge. The development of the disaster relief work places it in a strong position and its particular competence and presence have made it one of the relatively few global charitable organisations.

The resourcing needs of The Salvation Army are likely to increase as the demands upon its services increase. The US bequest from the McDonald's heir raised some questions in the UK and it is possible that future fundraising strategies may test the limits of acceptability.

The apolitical stance of The Salvation Army may also be tested in the post-9/11 context. The Salvation Army's laudable desire to work in a non-conflictual way with other faiths may not sit easily with its involvement in homeland security in the USA.

The strategic review in the UK

In 2002 The Salvation Army in the UK completed a major strategic review – the first such exercise undertaken by The Salvation Army anywhere. The strategic review identified a number of factors which were regarded as critical for the future of the organisation. The review had commenced in 1999 and had involved the use of external consultants. The Henley Centre had undertaken a number of studies which examined changes in society which were relevant for The Salvation Army.

The Henley studies identified some major societal changes. They highlighted problems arising from prosperity whereby the gaps between the haves and the have-nots were growing yet the long-hours working culture put those who had apparently benefited from prosperity under greater stress. This was associated with increased family breakdown and increased alcohol and drug abuse. There were issues associated with what the Henley Centre referred to as a 'responsibility gap' whereby there was a lack of both informal and formal care for those who needed it whether they were young or old. The increasing pressures and expectations that society placed upon young people was associated with increased mental health problems and substance abuse as well as, in some cases, significant exclusion from society.

The Salvation Army faced the following problems:

- a declining and ageing membership;
- a growing demand for the services they provided;
- difficulties as an inter-generational organisation in relating to youth culture;
- whilst there were pockets of local innovation, there was an inherited 'top-down' culture that made it difficult to resource innovation;
- a move in social policy from the institutional care their social services had traditionally provided to more community-based provision.

However the strategic review identified the following strengths which The Salvation Army was seen to possess:

- a commitment to help the most needy;
- a willingness to undertake practical work as well as proclaim the gospel;
- trustworthiness and sincerity which made them an organisation people are comfortable to work with and contribute to;
- a strong caring ethos;
- an understanding of the needs of people today.[3]

The strategic framework stressed the need for The Salvation Army to focus upon the needs resulting from an increasingly fragmented society. The document did not set out the precise operational

---

[3] 'A strategic framework for the United Kingdom Territory with the Republic of Ireland', The Salvation Army, 2002.

requirements of the analysis. Rather it exhorted the reader to consider the implications in terms of people, buildings and financial resources and to develop further plans at a local level.

The implication of the review and the Henley report were significant for the focus of The Salvation Army in the UK. As Commissioner Alex Hughes commented:

> When The Salvation Army was founded over 130 years ago, it focused on helping the poorer sections of society. Now it is not only the poor who need our help. All sectors of society are at risk of suffering from the modern social condition – loneliness, stress and a deteriorating quality of life.

It can be argued that The Salvation Army in the UK has taken the lead in both taking a strategic view of the future of the organisation and also acknowledging that the circumstances that previously guided its work and directed it towards the poorest sectors of society have changed. In this respect the UK Territory may have broken the ground for the Territories in other developed countries. If the strategic framework initiated by the UK Territory is rolled out in other territories then The Salvation Army may move away from its original focus upon the poorest parts of society. The long-established practice of paying officers extremely modest salaries has been part of the values of the Salvation Army but will it be sustainable in the future if the Army extends its mission towards the wealthier sectors of society?

However the needs of the developing world remain as pressing as ever and were acknowledged and recognised in the 2003 Annual Report and literature of the UK Territory.

The future?

The Salvation Army has successfully grown over nearly 150 years to become one of the best known and widely respected organisations of its kind. It has been able to evolve and adapt its services whilst holding onto the core beliefs and practices associated with its founding. Peter Drucker, a well-respected authority on leadership, has suggested that The Salvation Army has three challenges:

- to avoid losing its soul (in this case through being too successful);
- to concentrate on areas where it can set the standard;
- to maintain the crucial balance between being a religious organisation and a social organisation.[4]

However it confronts an increasingly fragmented and uncertain world and as a global organisation it will need to negotiate its way. The pressure upon its services is likely to increase and The Salvation Army will be challenged to secure adequate resources to meet these demands within the constraints of its belief systems.

---

[4] *Salvationist Magazine*, 24 March 2001.

APPENDIX 1

Salvation Army programme activity

Social Programme

Residential	
Hostels for homeless and transient	539
Capacity	29,264
Emergency lodges	211
Capacity	11,507
Children's homes	202
Capacity	8,251
Homes for the elderly	212
Capacity	14,954
Homes for the disabled	39
Capacity	1,464
Homes for the blind	8
Capacity	369
Remand and probation homes	59
Capacity	941
Homes for street children	28
Capacity	567
Mother and baby homes	48
Capacity	1,588
Training centres for families	36
Capacity	877
Care homes for vulnerable people	45
Capacity	684
Women's and men's refuge centres	255
Capacity	2,035
Other residential care homes/hostels	246
Capacity	9,778

Day care	
Community centres	540
Early childhood education centres	218
Capacity	13,108
Day centres for the elderly	52
Capacity	1,456
Play groups	211
Capacity	5,811
Day centres for the hearing impaired	2
Capacity	70
Day centres for street children	18
Capacity	709
Day nurseries	112
Capacity	17,297
Drop-in centres for youth	178
Other day care centres	149
Capacity	2,644

Addiction dependency	
Non-residential programmes	92
Capacity	5,873
Residential programmes	128
Capacity	6,598
Harbour Light programmes	72
Capacity	6,543

Service to the Armed Forces	
Hostels for service personnel	10
Clubs and canteens	26
Mobile units for service personnel	44
Chaplains	50

Emergency response	
Disaster rehabilitation schemes (inc. civil unrest)	17,397
Participants	950,230
Refugee programmes – host country	5

Participants	7,860
Refugee rehabilitation programmes	1
Participants	7,000

Services to the community	
Prisoners visited	248,835
Prisoners helped on discharge	52,283
Police courts – people helped	137,184
Missing persons – applications	58,439
number traced	8,270
Night patrol/anti-suicide – number helped	42,798
Community youth programmes	61
Beneficiaries	7,872
Employment bureaux – applications	181,181
initial referrals	164,882
Counselling – people helped	442,769
Feeding Centres	1,039
General relief – people helped	17,693,151
Emergency relief	3,792,919
Emergency mobile units	757
Restaurants and cafes	25
Thrift stores/charity shops (social)	1,398
Apartments for elderly	1,938
Capacity	5,233
Hostels for students, workers, etc.	61
Capacity	3,511
Land settlements (SA villages)	10
Capacity	2,592
Other similar centres (farms, etc.)	18
Capacity	37,211

Health programme	
General hospitals	25
Capacity	2,704
Maternity hospitals	8
Capacity	250
Other specialist hospitals	4
Capacity	188
General clinics	131
Specialist clinics	72
Capacity	5,215
Mobile clinics	346
Number of inpatients	352,147
Number of outpatients	934,667
Number of doctors/medics	6,480
Invalid/convalescent homes	2
Capacity	67
Health education programmes	44
Beneficiaries	619,687
Eye camp – beneficiaries	30,101

Education programme	
Kindergarten/sub primary	643
Primary schools	926
Upper primary and middle schools	88
Secondary and high schools	187
Number of pupils	440,056
Number of teachers	13,698
Vocational training schools	89
Schools for the blind	6
Schools for the disabled	9
Colleges, universities, staff training and distance learning centres	746

APPENDIX 2

International statistics (as at 1 January 2002)

Countries and other territories where SA serves	109	Members	364,048
Languages used in SA work	175	Other women's ministries groups	3,546
Corps, outposts, societies, new plants		Members	69,505
and recovery churches	15,456	League of mercy groups	4,278
Goodwill centres	273	Members	110,774
Officers	25,662	SAMF members	8,973
Active	17,407	Over-60 clubs	1,651
Retired	8,255	Members	84,434
Auxiliary-captains	383	Men's fellowships	2,201
Lieutenants	144	Members	48,180
Envoys/sergeants, full-time	1,130	Young people's band members	13,957
Cadets	968	Singing company members	67,514
Employees	107,724	Other young people's music group	
Senior soldiers	1,010,829	members	35,369
Adherents	167,786	Sunday school members	668,237
Junior soldiers	398,500	Junior youth group members	140,441
Corps cadets	38,400	Senior youth group members	65,388
Senior band musicians	29,472	Corps-based community development	
Senior songsters	71,302	programmes	582
Other senior musical group members	41,094	Beneficiaries	546,414
Senior and young people's local officers	121,314	Thrift stores/charity shops (corps)	1,396
Home league groups	8,915	Recycling centres	16

Eurotunnel – how contrasting national cultures can affect strategy development

Geoff Goddin

This case summarises the key problems challenging Eurotunnel, the cross-Channel tunnel and shuttle service operator as it enters its 10th year of operations.

Eurotunnel's revenues look unlikely to be able to support its huge debt in the near future without a change of strategy.

The case illustrates the very different stakeholder and legal environment faced by managers of an Anglo-French enterprise and how this shaped strategy development.

● ● ●

A significant announcement

On 8 February 2004, Richard Shirrefs, Eurotunnel's CEO stated:

> Ten years after the opening of the tunnel it is clear that our structural problems, which are due to the strictly private-sector funding of the project, an excessively high debt level and insufficient rail traffic, cannot easily be resolved without a comprehensive and innovative approach to the problems faced by all the stakeholders of the cross-Channel rail industry.
>
> (February 2004 shareholder letter)

Eurotunnel was thus proposing its new 'Galaxie Project' by which access rates to use the tunnel paid by Eurostar rail service passengers and cross-Channel freight services were to be reduced heavily in exchange for a significant reduction in the debt and interest burden which Eurotunnel had to finance.

The plan was to be put to the rail operators, financing banks and the UK and French governments, even though the 1986 Treaty of Canterbury, which granted Eurotunnel the concession to build and operate the tunnel, forbade direct state aid to the enterprise at the insistence of the then UK Prime Minister, Margaret Thatcher. Eurotunnel however faced a complex web of stakeholder groups with quite different strategic perspectives due to its rather unique nature.

The constitution of Eurotunnel – a cross-channel and cross-cultural company

Eurotunnel is actually two companies, Eurotunnel plc (UK) and Eurotunnel SA (France). In February 2004 Charles Mackay was Chairman of the Joint Board and also of Eurotunnel plc, while Richard Shirrefs was Chief Executive of the combined group and President–Directeur Général of Eurotunnel SA.

The group was thus subject to two contrasting commercial law and governance systems. The lending banks in particular were 'secured creditors' under UK insolvency procedures, and stood above other creditors if they forced a foreclosure of loans, but under French legal procedures of *'redressment judiciare'* the interests of the enterprise, employees and shareholders ranked above them.

In 1996 this difficult legal position of twin jurisdiction was a useful lever in getting the banks to agree a moratorium on interest paid on certain of the debt till 2006, and to agree to swap some debt for share equity in the tunnel.

Shareholders also had additional rights of consultation and legal remedies under French law. Therefore in 1996 Eurotunnel set up two shareholder committees; this was unique for a UK company, and novel in France. These committees met quarterly with the Board in order to improve communication.

Higher debts, lower revenues

Eurotunnel's strategic problems related to a mismatch between higher than forecast debt levels and lower than forecast rail user revenues.

The debt position

The tunnel opened for business in autumn 1994. This was 18 months later than the planned date of May 1993, which cost it two summer seasons' revenues. The initial forecast cost of £4.85bn (≈ €7.3bn) had been increased by rising construction, fitting out, and commissioning costs to £7.85bn (≈ €11.8bn). But while the tunnel had been built largely on time, delays caused by commissioning and safety-testing caused interest roll-up, taking the debt to £8.54bn (≈ €12.8bn); interest of £700m (≈ €1.05bn) pa in 1995 dwarfed the £300m (≈ €4.5m) turnover. Thus on 14 September 1995 Eurotunnel simply announced that it would stop payment of interest for 18 months in order to negotiate a re-financing of the tunnel.

The 174 consortium banks had little option but to negotiate. Firstly, the then management had already managed growth in car and lorry traffic cross-Channel market shares to 34 per cent and 50 per cent respectively on the Eurotunnel-operated shuttle services, and the rail company Eurostar services were taking 40 per cent of London to Paris/ Brussels passenger traffic. Therefore replacing the management team looked unlikely to boost traffic receipts further.

Secondly, the tunnel's capital expenditure had been largely 'sunk' into infrastructure and specialised equipment; there was little prospect of a resale value that could meet more than a fraction of debt owed.

Thirdly, as noted, the Anglo-French tunnel enterprise was protected by *redressment judiciare* in the French Commercial Court, favouring the interests of the enterprise, employees and shareholders to a greater extent than US and UK banks were accustomed to (US banks held 24 per cent of debt).

On 12 February 1996 Eurotunnel groups auditors requested the Paris Commercial Court to appoint two mediators *'mandataires ad hoc'* to facilitate negotiations between Eurotunnel and its bank creditors. Thus, after lengthy negotiations there was a re-financing of the debt in 1998, incorporat-

ing £1.5bn of 'buffer zone' or 'stabilisation' finance available to cover unpaid interest on the core debt till 2006, £0.5bn of which could then be converted by the company from debt to new shares. The governments supported these negotiations and extended the life of the tunnel concession from 2042 to 2086, but did not offer financial assistance.

No debt repayments were due before 2006 on the core debt, but Eurotunnel had taken opportunities to reduce it by £1.2bn over five years, leaving total debt at 2003 at £6.4bn as set out in Exhibit 1.

Rail user revenues

Faced by the clause in the 1986 Treaty that forbade state assistance to tunnel finances, the then state-owned British and French railway operators, backed by their governments, had provided Eurotunnel with traffic forecasts that now look over-optimistic, both in order that the project looked financially attractive to private investors, and to ensure that it got built.

1987 forecasts of 21 million Eurostar passengers and 10 million tonnes of trans-Europe rail freight by 2003 (see Appendix) underpinned the agreement between Eurotunnel and the rail operators, that 50 per cent of the tunnel capacity would be reserved for the use of through rail services.

In exchange the train operators guaranteed a Minimum Usage Charge (MUC) for the first 12 years of operation to November 2006. Eurostar traffic growth was initially bugged by technical faults and an over-complex management structure drawn from the three rail owners – London and Continental (UK) 40 per cent, SNCF (France) 55 per cent, SNCB (Belgium) 5 per cent. More recently it has faced increasing competition from low-cost airlines. Thus by 2003 there were actually only 6.31m Eurostar passengers pa, although traffic grew 20 per cent after the much-delayed October 2003 opening of the first half of the UK high-speed Channel Tunnel Rail Link (CTRL) to Ebbsfleet, Kent (which cut 20 minutes from the journey time). When the CTRL opens through to St Pancras, London around 2007 a further 20-minute saving could reduce London–Brussels to 2 hours and London–Paris to 2 hours, 15 minutes. (The French and Belgian high-speed rail links were in place before the tunnel's opening in 1994.)

Through freight traffic growth had also been inhibited by the inability of Britain's rail infrastructure to carry the wider and higher continental wagons, and by the managerial and operational

| Exhibit 1 | Eurotunnel debt financing structure |

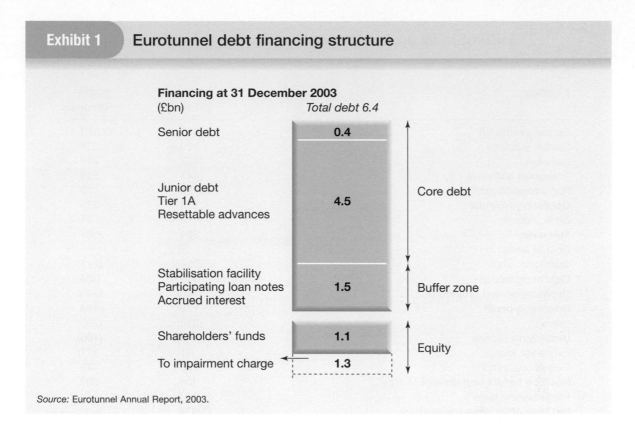

Financing at 31 December 2003
(£bn)   *Total debt 6.4*

Senior debt	**0.4**	} Core debt
Junior debt Tier 1A Resettable advances	**4.5**	
Stabilisation facility Participating loan notes Accrued interest	**1.5**	} Buffer zone
Shareholders' funds	**1.1**	} Equity
To impairment charge ←	**1.3**	

Source: Eurotunnel Annual Report, 2003.

disruptions resulting from the privatisation of Britain's rail network after 1996. Also services had been heavily disrupted by security measures to control pressures from asylum seekers trying to enter Britain clandestinely through the tunnel. Thus in 2003 only 1.74m tonnes of railfreight pa were carried through the tunnel.

These volumes of rail traffic were well below those envisaged when the MUC was negotiated, therefore the yearly MUC payment in effect became the floor charge paid by the rail operators to Eurotunnel. The MUC received in 2003 was £232m, equivalent to 10m Eurostar passengers pa and 5m tonnes of freight. In effect the MUC guarantee element was worth an extra £77m to Eurotunnel in 2003, but it also meant that charges made by rail operators to the actual traffic were higher than necessary (e.g. at £12 per passenger carried through the tunnel), these higher charges of course inhibited rail traffic growth.

Eurotunnel shuttle revenues

The Eurotunnel-operated 'shuttle' services for vehicles, terminal to terminal, rapidly came to dominate the cross-Channel vehicle shipment market, although the ferry companies unexpectedly maintained competitive pressure on the 'short' Channel crossing, rather than shift services to longer sea routes well to the east or west of Dover–Calais where the tunnel was not so convenient.

In 2003 Eurotunnel's services enjoyed cross-Channel market shares of 47 per cent of cars, 44 per cent of trucks and 33 per cent of coaches, however in that year a general decline in tourist crossings due to the Iraq conflict and low-cost airline competition, allied to intense price competition with ferry operators caused by excess capacity, led to a 11 per cent fall in shuttle revenues (see Exhibit 2). Whereas in 2002 for the first time Eurotunnel, thanks to exceptional profits on leasing and debt buyback operations, generated sufficient cash to pay debt interest, in 2003 lower revenues, profit and exceptionals gave a net loss after interest charges of £34m.

Because 2003 revenues lowered the forecast of future cash flows for the remaining 82 years of the concession, the net book value of assets was reduced by £1.3bn, thus a book-keeping 'impairment charge' of £1.3bn was added to the accounts in Exhibit 2, which created the 'headline grabbing' net loss of £1.334bn.

The real imbalance for Eurotunnel was the imbalance between profit on ordinary trading activities of £170m and interest charges of £318m, a situation that could not continue much longer.

Exhibit 2	Eurotunnel profit and loss account

£ million*	2003 actual	2002 reported
Exchange rate €/£	1.435	1.573
Shuttle Services	309	333
Railways	232	217
Transport activities	**441**	**550**
Non-transport activities	25	20
Operating revenue	**566**	**570**
Other income	18	11
Turnover	**584**	**581**
Cost of sales	(9)	
Operating costs	(259)	(247)
Operating margin	**316**	**334**
Depreciation and provisions	(146)	(140)
Operating profit	**170**	**194**
Interest	(318)	(299)
Underlying losses	**(148)**	**(105)**
Exchange losses	(1)	(21)
Exceptional profit	115	428
Net loss before impairment charge	**(34)**	**302**
Impairment charge	(1,300)	
Net loss after impairment charge	**(1,334)**	

Cash flow statement

	2003 actual	2002 reported
Exchange rate €/£	1.419	1.537
Net cash flow from operations	315	348
Capital expenditure (net)	(25)	(41)
Cash flow after capital expenditure	**290**	**307**
Net interest paid in cash	(278)	(248)
Net increase in financial assets	(1)	–
Net receipts from exchange rate hedging	–	2
Net receipts from financial operations	20	9
Net cash flow from change in financial assets and liabilities	(67)	10
Net equity receipts	–	1
(Decrease)/increase in cash balances	**(36)**	**81**
Interest cover before capital expenditure	98%	116%
Interest cover after capital expenditure	90%	102%

* £1 = approx. €1.5.

Source: Eurotunnel Annual Report, 2003.

Current problem – future crisis

KPMG and PricewaterhouseCoopers, the group's auditors, signed off Eurotunnel Group's 2003 accounts to year end 31/12/03 subject to two major reservations:

- The 'Going Concern' assumption for the business after 2006 was dependent upon its ability to negotiate a prior debt refinancing plan with creditors.

- Group asset valuation was dependent on assumptions about existing revenue contracts

Exhibit 3	Eurotunnel debt repayments

Year	Debt repayable (£m)
2006	4.1
2007	37
2008	70
2009	162.8

Source: Eurotunnel Annual Accounts, 2003.

and lowered levels of future debt, which were surrounded by considerable uncertainty; hence the 'impairment charge' of £1.3bn made.

The auditors were concerned that post-November 2006 the rail operators were released from the 12-year guaranteed MUC agreement, with a projected revenue fall of some £80m pa, while from January 2006 the debt stabilisation agreements of 1998 ended. From then Eurotunnel was due to service all debt interest and commence actual debt repayments as shown in Exhibit 3.

Clearly, with reduced rail revenues threatened, and shuttle revenues held back by intense competition, Eurotunnel management saw real difficulties in meeting debt interest and repayment obligations after 2006, hence the appeal to all stakeholders contained in the Galaxie proposals, the essential elements of which were:

● For rail operators and customers, large cuts in access rates (70 per cent) paid to put passengers or freight through the tunnel, thus enabling them to grow total through passenger and freight traffic.

● For bank creditors, a debt refinancing giving Eurotunnel a realistic prospect of paying a lowered level of debt interest and repayments, which would improve the credit-rating of those debts.

● For governments a better utilisation of under-utilised and expensive infrastructure; motorway and high-speed rail connections to the tunnel link had cost both governments some £15bn. Both governments and the EU were committed to transport strategies that encouraged increased use of rail for passengers and freight.

● For shareholders a more sustainable debt–revenue balance would improve the security

of their shares and permit a dividend. (In 1997 Chairman Patrick Ponsolle had suggested that the tunnel could start paying dividends after 2006, but this date had constantly receded.)

For UK analysts the real importance of 'Galaxie' was that the Eurotunnel Board had at last recognised that its financial problems were structural in nature rather than purely a matter of debt scheduling, i.e. its remaining debt was simply too large to be serviced by foreseeable revenues.

However, because of the cross-cultural ownership, governance and regulatory frameworks under which Eurotunnel operated, stakeholder perceptions of their power over its strategy development, and their analysis of strategic priorities, differed greatly.

Eurotunnel shareholder dissent and rebellion

Eurotunnel managers were coming under increasing pressure from the unusually high proportion of individual shareholders, particularly French shareholders of the *Association des actionnaires d'Eurotunnel* (ADACTE) who had been coordinating the campaign against the Board's strategy.

Many of these shareholders bought shares at 350p when the company floated in 1987; the shares briefly touched 800p in 1989 spurred by encouraging traffic and revenue forecasts (see appendix) but by March 2004 they were less than 40p.

At the May 2003 AGM ADACTE tabled a resolution to dismiss the Board, but it was heavily defeated because due notice had not been given. ADACTE then went to the Paris Commercial Court in December 2003, having obtained mandates in France representing 8 per cent of the share capital. This led under L.225-103 of the *Code de Commerce* to the Court appointing a *Mandataire*, Mr Henri Chriqui, tasked to convene a General Meeting of Eurotunnel SA shareholders with an agenda of 'The dismissal of all of the members of the Board of Directors and the election of new members to the Board'.

Shareholders represented by ADACTE had become disillusioned with the Board's strategy. One of the rebels, Jacques Maillot, founder of Nouvelles Frontières, the French tour operator, who had agreed to stand as a replacement board member, commented on Richard Shirrefs and his team 'They are catastrophic! This company is

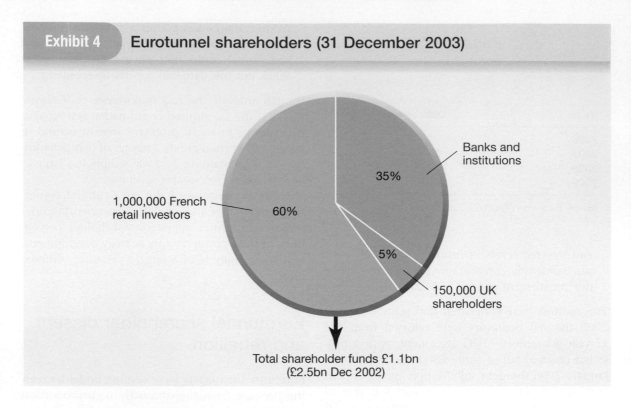

Exhibit 4   **Eurotunnel shareholders (31 December 2003)**

1,000,000 French retail investors — 60%

Banks and institutions — 35%

5%

150,000 UK shareholders

Total shareholder funds £1.1bn
(£2.5bn Dec 2002)

heading for the wall and they are unable to stop it, as they have become prisoners of their own systems!'

Eurotunnel management equally was very worried that ADACTE could succeed; they attacked ADACTE's contentions that revenues could be tripled as 'totally unrealistic', and asking bank lenders to write off debt as 'incredibly naïve'. The Board also dismissed the expectation that the UK and French governments, or Brussels (the EU authorities), would take over part of the debt as unrealistic because it contravened the Treaty of Canterbury.

The real worries of the Board ahead of the resolution were evidenced by Eurotunnel's attempted denigration of Nicholas Miguet, a colourful political candidate turned financier with past fraud convictions, who had spearheaded the campaign since the May 2003 AGM. In letters to all shareholders they warned that if the Board was dismissed and the company refused to pay creditors Eurotunnel shares would 'immediately lose all their value' and the banks would take control of all assets.

A different strategy perspective

ADACTE and the dissidents saw things differently: they criticised Eurotunnel's Board for a perspect-

ive of business governance that had a 'pro-British bias', with undue concern for creditors rather than the plight of shareholders, indeed both the Chairman, Charles Mackay and Chief Executive, Richard Shirrefs were British.

From the French cultural perspective of ADACTE the interests of the enterprise, its employees and shareholders were the most important. The banks were seen as locked into the project 'rather like a gaggle of holidaymakers strapped into the cars of a roller coaster' – an apt metaphor. They also realised that the crisis at Eurotunnel was a hot political debate in France, if not Britain. An advisor to Eurotunnel remarked 'This is a very emotive issue in France. We are talking about something that will play on prime-time TV and it is relatively easy for Miguet to say governments will pay.'

The French National Assembly had established a working party to examine the crisis and assembly centre-right deputies Pierre Cardo, Richard Mallie, and others had agreed to be nominated by ADACTE as replacement board members. By inclination French governments, even of the right, had a *dirigiste* attitude favouring state intervention in issues of transport infrastructure and prestige projects, and were mindful that Eurotunnel shareholders could influence 2–4 million votes in a French election.

ADACTE could claim three early victories once the *Mandataire* was appointed prior to the General Meeting:

- The company moved forward the AGMs of Eurotunnel plc and Eurotunnel SA from 13 May to 7 April 2004 to prevent the *Mandataire*-chaired General Meeting occurring before the AGMs.

- On 8 February 2004 the Eurotunnel Board launched its 'Project Galaxie' initiative, recognising that a serious structural problem threatened the tunnel, with debt too high for foreseeable revenues to meet interest on, let alone repay, which would have made Eurotunnel insolvent after 2005 – a situation that ADACTE said they should have been aware of much earlier due to the MUC ending November 2006 and the 'buffer zone' assistance of the debt stabilisation provisions ending December 2005.

- Finally, on 25 March 2004 Eurotunnel proposed the appointment of Philippe Bourguignon as Chairman-designate, Bourguignon was a French executive who had led the turnaround and financial restructuring of Euro-Disney Paris, 1993/97. He was seen as a considerably more (French) media-friendly Chairman, having the political savvy to do business with the different stakeholder constituencies – governments, local authorities, staff, unions and creditors.

The Board overthrown, 7 April 2004 – an earthquake in French company governance

The strategic dilemma for Eurotunnel was that it needed to grow traffic to satisfy all stakeholders. The enterprise and its staff would gain from better utilisation of capacity. The governments would gain from modal shift of passengers and freight to long-distance rail in line with EU transport policies, creditor banks would gain a more secure, if initially smaller, revenue stream underwritten by better long-term traffic growth (and elimination of ferry competitors who undercut tunnel access charges set too high), and long-suffering shareholders could hope for future returns on their past investment.

But to grow traffic by investing in new tunnel-operated England to Switzerland through freight services, or cutting tunnel access charges as proposed by Shirrefs, required either creditors to permit lower interest and debt payments, or the governments to provide aid. The growth in revenues would also take time that tunnel management did not appear to have.

But at the 2004 AGM only ADACTE appeared willing to confront the banks with the need for lower debt charges before meltdown, and to insist that the governments side-step the restrictions on financial support of the Treaty of Canterbury. The British-led Board had only recently announced the 'Galaxie' proposals which offered only a distant hope of a solution, and they did not appear to have engaged with the dissident stakeholders, offering only dire warnings if they lost office. It was ironic that despite having set up exemplary shareholder consultation structures, communication with at least the French shareholders seemed to have totally broken down.

Thus on the 7 April at a stormy AGM in Paris the French shareholders voted out the 'British Board' and installed Jacques Maillot as Chairman of a new and initially entirely French board, the first shareholder-led revolution in French corporate history!

However the new Board still faced the same financial realities, but with a different perspective, Herve Huas, once nominated Finance Director, proposed seeking a global restructuring of the debt, and finding cost efficiencies to increase profit. Before he had talked of the need to 'think out of the box' when presenting 'Project Avenir' (future), a compendium of proposals to increase tunnel fares, renegotiate debt, and canvass government aid. The new French-led Board was mindful that if they simply repudiated existing debt agreements then creditors could seek 'management substitution' and put in a professional management team. The French shareholder revolt led by the populist Miguet had put them in power, but the actual adoption of some of their wilder ideas could have quickly led to creditor intervention. It will be interesting to see the real difference between 'Project Galaxie' and 'Project Avenir' as a strategy to recast the future of the tunnel.

The creditors for their part realised that they had to engage with the new management, to find out their initial strategic intent, and to judge the attitude of the governments to the new team; they also had to keep in mind that legal steps to take over the tunnel would be complex and difficult.

The French and British governments, who had stood behind the project and their state railway traffic forecasts that had underwritten it, made it clear that the new management could expect no more state aid than the previous one, although Dominique Bussereau, the French budget minister, commented: 'The outgoing Board said it had done all it could to avoid the wholesale shake-up that is now likely.'

Closing the turbulent AGM Jacques Maillot read a communique signed by all the new directors, saying that the new Board would have to get to work to save Eurotunnel, pursue all the possible solutions it could think of, and take the necessary measures. 'Our ultimate goal is to restore the confidence of shareholders in the company'.

The construction of the tunnel required courage, imagination and a political will. It is an engineering triumph offering a smooth ride and reliable operations. Unless stakeholders sink confrontational differences, and negotiate with similar foresight strategic management of the asset will continue to be prone to extreme turbulence and stakeholders will continue to face considerable uncertainty of destination.

APPENDIX

The problems of traffic and revenue forecasting – Eurotunnel

Eurotunnel always expected one of the key users of tunnel capacity to be the UK and French state railways. In July 1987 Eurotunnel signed a user contract with British Rail and SNCF by which they anticipated that revenues from Eurostar passengers and freight tonnage would account for over 40% of total Eurotunnel revenues, with protected Minimum User Charges* for the first 12 years of operation.

However expected and actual figures have varied:

	Expected	Actual
Eurostar passengers in 1994	10.7m	4.9m
Eurostar passengers in 2003	14m	6.3m
Through freight tonnage 2003	5m tonnes	1.74m tonnes

* The MUC is equivalent to 10m passengers and 5m tonnes of freight.

Sources: www.Eurotunnel.com; Eurotunnel Annual Report 2003; past Eurotunnel reports, statements and shareholder communications; *Financial Times* 10.2.04, 6.4.04, 9.3.04, 8.4.04, and earlier archived articles; *The Business*, 28/29 March 2004.

BMW automobiles

Valeriano Lencioni

The BMW Group is a prominent European maker of prestige automobiles. Its operations also include motorcycles, software products and financial services: this case deals only with the group's automobiles. By 2004 it produced and sold over one million vehicles under three brands: BMW, by far the largest; MINI, a relaunch of the British icon small automobile from the 1960s; and the Rolls Royce, of which they relaunched the 'Phantom' model in 2003. Following the failure to grow market share and the range of models by acquiring the British group Rover, the Group in the early 2000s adopted an aggressive strategy of organic growth. The result was the launch of a large number of models across the price and class ranges, and a robust policy of market development.

• • •

The automobile industry in the mid 2000s

The first automobiles were produced in the late 19th century but the automobile industry became a significant employer and an economic force only after the Second World War, when national economies began to be rebuilt. With the end of the war, the industrial production and manpower that had fuelled the war effort were deployed to rebuild infrastructures and provide people with the consumer goods that were not available during the war. Automobile production was initially prominent in the US, but soon Europe, later Asia, especially Japan, became equally important forces. By the latter part of the 20th century, the automobile industry was global, mature and heavily consolidated: most of the world automobile production was concentrated in five companies – General Motors, Ford, Daimler-Chrysler, Toyota and Volkswagen (see Exhibit 1).

A number of environmental circumstances affected the industry in the first few years of the 21st century. The global economy experienced a sharp downturn in 2001, which lasted well into 2003 when some signs of acceleration were experienced, especially in the US economy. Equity prices had fallen until late in 2003: this, coupled with geopolitical tensions and concerns about oil supplies, added to the uncertainty about the economic and political environments. In this climate, sales in most automobile markets around the world declined, with the exception of the UK, some Scandinavian countries and China, which grew well above average. The

Photo: BMW

Exhibit 1	The automobile industry

BMW and the five major companies in 2003

Company	No of vehicles (m)	€ (bn)
General Motors	8.5	157.19
Ford	6.7	116.47
DaimlerChrysler	3.85	144.65
Toyota	6.25	125.30
Volkswagen	5.02	87.15
BMW group	1.12	41.52

decline in the automobile market in US was particularly severe.

From the mid 1990s automobile producers strove to improve engineering and quality of vehicles as a route to competitive advantage or, in many cases, to catch up with competitors, but ten years later there was very little to differentiate automobiles produced by many of the major companies. Therefore, in the first few years of the 21st century, players in the automobile industry as a whole stepped up price competition. A hefty overcapacity of around 30 per cent in the overall industry meant that 'a lot of metal chased little money', making low prices or incentives – mostly in the form of free insurance, zero per cent interest on hire purchase – the prevalent means to displace market share from competitors. However managers were fully aware that competing on price was not beneficial to anyone in the medium term, as it depressed the profitability of the whole industry: customers' expectations would become a very powerful barrier to increasing prices later. The result was that, as well as selling few cars, car companies sold them at a lower price; the consequent depression of profitability was likely to affect negatively their credit rating, thus increasing the cost of borrowing: a nightmare scenario. This was true especially with regard to the USA's 'big three', Ford, GM and DaimlerChrysler.

But the larger European car companies had also suffered from depressed demand and oversupply, with Volkswagen's profit falling by 49 per cent in the second quarter of 2003. Fiat was also trying hard to get out of a serious crisis by restructuring the company and renewing the dull model range under the guidance of the CEO who had turned around the fortunes of Pirelli, the tyre maker. In 2003, the jury was still out on Fiat's chances of comeback.

Changes in the basis of competitive advantage

By the mid 2000s the car market was teeming with good quality cars, but consumers found very few ways to distinguish between many of the available brands and models. Quality was no longer an issue in the industry: most models were well built and reliable. For example, the quality of US automobiles had improved 24 per cent from the late 1990s. 'The gap between the best and worst US performers, which was 212 defects per 100 vehicles in 1998, has narrowed to 53 defects.'[1]

Almost inevitably, the distinguishing elements, and customers' choice factors had become design and brand appeal, as demonstrated by the fact that companies that had given attention to the 'look' of their automobiles or had built powerful brands made small gains, rather than losing market share.

This realisation made design the first weapon in the fight for market share, as the feature that grabbed customers' attention. Naturally, boardrooms took up design as a major plank of their

---

[1] C. Dawson and K. Kerwin, 'Designer Cars', *Business Week*, 16 February 2004.

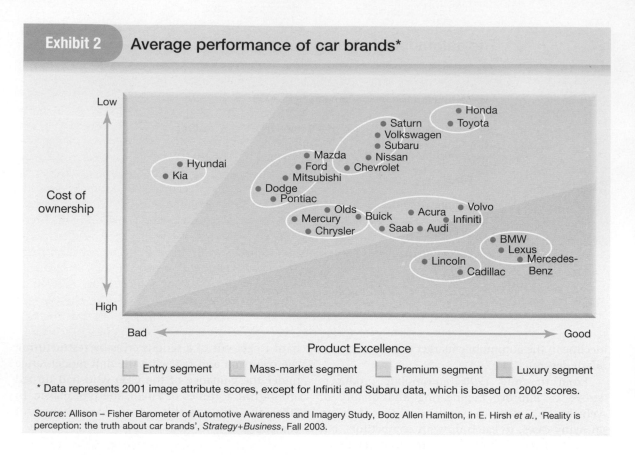

Exhibit 2   Average performance of car brands*

* Data represents 2001 image attribute scores, except for Infiniti and Subaru data, which is based on 2002 scores.

Source: Allison – Fisher Barometer of Automotive Awareness and Imagery Study, Booz Allen Hamilton, in E. Hirsh *et al.*, 'Reality is perception: the truth about car brands', *Strategy+Business*, Fall 2003.

strategy and sparked a hunt for top-level designers. The promised rewards were rich enough to lure the best talents, who were then provided with lavish high-tech design laboratories and art studios. This strategy was trodden by companies across price and vehicle type ranges.

However, pursuing quality and appeal in design was putting pressure on companies' resources. So was brand building and management, which was even more demanding and with less certain results. It had become clear that a brand identity was one of the most effective ways to be more competitive in an industry where more and more products came to the market. But simple advertising was not enough. In the US carmakers had spent more than $50bn (≈ €41bn) on marketing, equivalent to $2,900 for every car sold. Yet their combined US market share had fallen by more than 4 per cent, amounting to a $15bn loss.

Effective branding establishes emotional connections between customers on one side and products, salesmen, other users on the other. A prime example of successful branding was Toyota. It conveyed the perception of high quality and fuel economy, creating the emotional connections

of reliability and smart environmental awareness. BMW conveyed the image of the 'ultimate driving machine', even to those customers who bought models with small engines and automatic transmission, say a 3-series. The reason for this was that every model raised a set of general perceptions and emotional connections generated by the mother brand, as well as some specifically related to the model in question. The common theme of the brand conferred even to the least representative model a certain aura. This process had moved a long way from the concept of product as brand, for example Ford Model T.

This is not to say that the product was unimportant. Research conducted in 2003[2] demonstrated that consumers, based on their direct and indirect experience, measured different brands' performance against two overarching criteria: product excellence and cost of ownership. The researchers also added that 'the relative magnitude of product excellence and low cost of ownership

---

[2] E. Hirsh *et al.*, 'Reality is perception: the truth about car brands', *Strategy+Business*, Fall 2003.

determines a brand's value proposition in the marketplace'. The brands that are positioned in a crowded area of the competitive space suffer particularly from competition, and their profit is reduced. The positions reported in Exhibit 2 tend to be rather stable over time.

BMW Group

Origins

BMW was established during the First World War to manufacture engines; in 1945, the company was still Germany's leading manufacturer of aero-engines. Subsequently it diversified into what in 2000 were its main products, automobiles and motorcycles. By then BMW was one of Germany's largest and most successful companies. But BMW's road to sustained success was a troubled one and in 2000 the horizon was not all rosy. The group's activities were concentrated almost exclusively on two product ranges: high-performance saloon automobiles and motorcycles. The focus of this case is on automobiles.

The march to success

At the end of the Second World War, both its aero-engines market and its capital equipment were under serious threat. The demand for aero-engines, Germany having lost the war, had temporarily disappeared, and its main factory was now in the Soviet occupation zone. Therefore, whilst post-war West Germany experienced an economic miracle, BMW struggled. Uncertain of its destiny, the company concentrated on automobile production, but without a focus, its products ranging from small bubble cars, built under licence, to large limousines. In 1959 BMW faced bankruptcy, when it found a powerful shareholder, Herbert Quandt, who could see the company's inherent strengths beyond the current difficulties. The turning point came in 1961, when it launched the BMW 1500, which soon established the BMW automobile brand as one with a reputation for engineering excellence.

In the 21st century, the scarce resources that most influence national competitiveness are likely to be the skills displayed by the workforce. One of Germany's distinctive national resources was a highly qualified labour force that could be used by German manufacturers as a source of competitive advantage. Most of such advantage went to

companies that, like BMW, managed to build a perception of valuable differences in the minds of their buyers.

It was difficult to single out a specific resource that underpinned BMW's success: it was rather a series of factors, and the way they combined to sustain its competitiveness. BMW automobiles are powerful, reliable and luxurious, but not exceptionally so. BMW's technology had been advanced, but not exceptionally innovative (when compared, for example, with Citroën). Its automobiles were conventionally designed and traditionally styled, yet they were expensive, even considering the high level of specification offered by most models, with retail margins comparatively high. The company had tightly controlled its distribution network, to the benefit of brand management, communication and after-sales service. Being close to the buyers had also allowed them to segment the market effectively: for example, BMW automobiles have been positioned differently and priced differently in the various national markets. BMW also exercised a firm control on the supply chain and dealings and relationships with suppliers, who mostly had maintained a long association with the company. That combination, a system of production that gave the company advantage in its chosen segment, a reputation for product quality and a brand which immediately identifies the aims and aspirations of its customers, by the mid-1990s had built BMW into one of the most profitable automobile manufacturers in the world.

The BMW brand also acquired a distinctive identity as a symbol for young, affluent European professionals: most drivers perceived high-performance saloon automobiles as synonymous with BMW. They had been able to structure their production around an easy to summarise theme: 'The ultimate driving machine'. Ealey and Troyano-Bermudez wrote in 2000: 'When a person walks into a BMW showroom, the question isn't, "Which model do I want?" It's, "How much BMW can I afford?"'[3]

BMW's position in 2003

In 2003, Bayerische Motoren Werke (BMW), the group that owns the prestigious BMW brand, was one of Europe's top automakers. BMW automobiles

[3] L. Ealey and L. Troyano-Bermudez, '#The automotive industry: a 30,000-mile checkup', *The McKinsey Quarterly*, no. 1 (2000), p. 74.

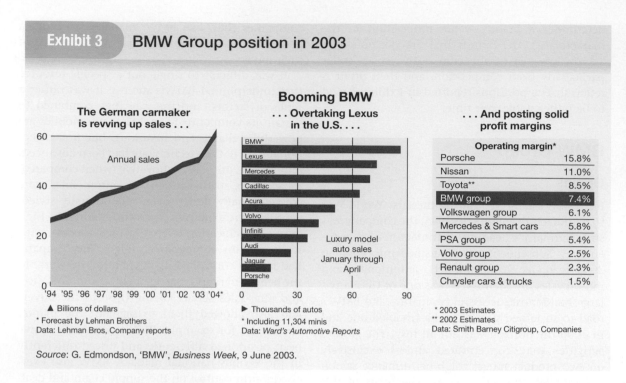

Exhibit 3 | **BMW Group position in 2003**

Booming BMW

The German carmaker is revving up sales . . .

Annual sales

▲ Billions of dollars
* Forecast by Lehman Brothers
Data: Lehman Bros, Company reports

. . . Overtaking Lexus in the U.S. . . .

BMW*
Lexus
Mercedes
Cadillac
Acura
Volvo
Infiniti
Audi
Jaguar
Porsche

Luxury model auto sales January through April

▶ Thousands of autos
* Including 11,304 minis
Data: *Ward's Automotive Reports*

. . . And posting solid profit margins

Operating margin*	
Porsche	15.8%
Nissan	11.0%
Toyota**	8.5%
BMW group	7.4%
Volkswagen group	6.1%
Mercedes & Smart cars	5.8%
PSA group	5.4%
Volvo group	2.5%
Renault group	2.3%
Chrysler cars & trucks	1.5%

* 2003 Estimates
** 2002 Estimates
Data: Smith Barney Citigroup, Companies

Source: G. Edmondson, 'BMW', *Business Week*, 9 June 2003.

accounted for about three quarters of the group's sales. The company's operations also included motorcycles, software and a growing financial services division. The turnover of the Group in 2003 was over €41.53bn (≈ £27.5bn), down 2.1 per cent over 2002 mostly due to the strength of the € over the US$ (discounting this effect, the growth in revenue over 2002 would have been 4.2 per cent). Gross margins, of €3.2bn, were down 2.8 per cent from 25.4 per cent of 2002, a reflection of the growing expenditure in product and market development. The group produced an annual surplus of €3.2bn, 3.6 per cent lower than 2002; the difference was mostly due to changes in the legislation for tax provision.

These results were even more remarkable if considered in the light of the generally downwards trend in the automobile industry's profitability.

BMW automobiles in 2003 employed over 104,000 workers in plants in Dingolfing, Munich and Regensburg in Germany, Spartanburg in the US, Rosslyn in South Africa, Oxford in the UK and in China. They produced over 1.1 million BMW, Mini and Rolls Royce cars. Of these, 928,000 were BMW automobiles, up 1.6 per cent on 2002.

In fact BMW had achieved some remarkably progressive agreements with the workers' unions, and were operating some of the most flexible and productive plants in the automotive industry. A

factory being built in Leipzig was planned to swing from 60 hours a week, when demand was slack, to 140 hours a week when demand grew. In the words of the Chief Financial Officer Stefan Krause, 'Our [machines] sweat more than other people's because they work longer hours'. However, given the pressure on prices generated by increasing competition in the premium car market, the most profitable in the industry, there was pressure on keeping cost down if an acceptable profit was to be realised. Moving production into growth markets achieved the double benefit of containing the costs and partially hedging against currency risks. The cost reduction resulted from an increased utilisation of the Spartanburg plant in the US, where they built the X5 and Z4, and the use of well qualified but much cheaper labour force in China. The strong rise of the euro versus the US dollar in the second half of 2003 demonstrated the wisdom of the policy.[4] BMW was planning to invest $480m by 2005, to take a 50 per cent share in a joint venture in China to produce 3-series cars, to be followed soon by 5-series cars. It aimed to achieve sales of 150,000 vehicles by 2008, from the present 8,000. The move was not a half-hearted one; up to 40 per cent of the parts used in

_____
[4] U. Harnischfeger, *Financial Times*, 26 June 2003.

Exhibit 4   Automobiles delivered by the BMW Group in 2003 (1,000 units)

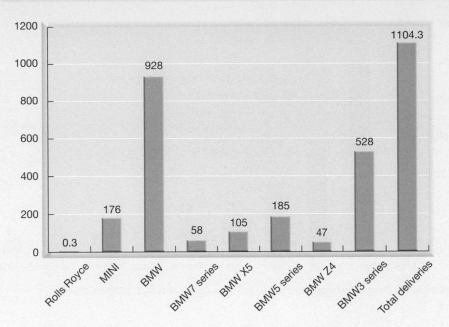

Source: Accounts Press Conference: Statement by H. Panke, CEO of BMW AG, 17 March 2004.

China would be sourced locally, according to CEO Helmut Panke.[5]

The markets

The main markets for BMW automobiles have been Western Europe, the USA, Japan and the Pacific region, with the markets of Germany and the US accounting for almost half the total car sales. Important markets have also been the fast-growing UK, and the Italian, French and Japanese markets. Sales in the USA market have been particularly successful, as they grew by over 8 per cent on the previous year to 277,000, becoming the biggest market for the group and overtaking the Lexus brand for the first time. At the end of 2003, the outlook for 2004 by group management and industry observers was upbeat. This view was supported by the successful launch of the new 5-series, the consolidation in Europe and Asia of the BMW Z4, and the introduction of the BMW X3. The new BMW 1 Series and the BMW 6 Series cabriolet were to be launched early in 2004. By far the most successful models were the MINI, the 3-series and the 5-series, but the other models were also in significant demand. In the Chinese markets there was growing demand for the higher end models of the range, specifically for 7-series and 5-series.[6]

Exhibit 4 shows the details of automobile deliveries in 2003.

The future

In the early 2000s, the size of the company and the range of models continued to be causes for concern. In the mid 1990s, they had tackled both problems by taking over Rover of the UK. However, the venture did not work and came to a sorry end five years later, when they had to sell the British company for the sum of £10 (≈ €8.30). The Quandt family had put pressure on the Group's managers to stop Rover's haemorrhagic losses: it is estimated they were in the region of €900m per year. The CEO, B. Pischetsieder, resigned after a stormy meeting with the shareholders. J. Milberg, the new CEO, had to deal with the messy acquisition and dispose of it. They retained the MINI

---

[5] J. Kynge, *Financial Times*, 28 March 2003.

[6] BMW Group Interim Report to March 2003.

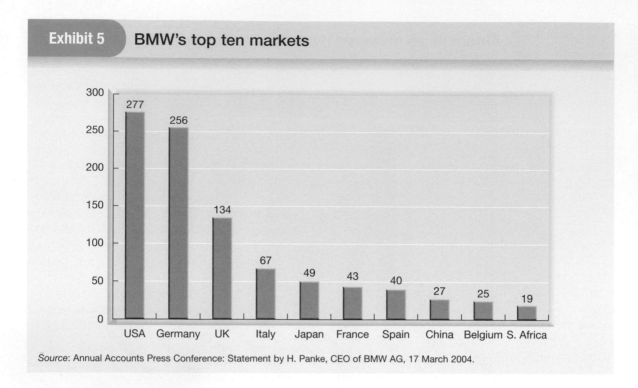

Exhibit 5   BMW's top ten markets

Source: Annual Accounts Press Conference: Statement by H. Panke, CEO of BMW AG, 17 March 2004.

brand and sold Land Rover, previously part of the Rover Group, to Ford.

The failure, as well as causing the loss of a great deal of money and of public face, had also left the group with two problems still unresolved. They were still little more than a niche player, competing with a handful of models. Also, their size was still modest when compared with that of the big five, and left them vulnerable to acquisition if the Quandt family were to decide to dispose of a sufficient amount of their shares.

In 2002, Helmut Panke, a nuclear physicist, had become the new Group's CEO, and started a strategy of internal growth through market and product development. In 2003, BMW was planning to launch a new model every three months through to 2005, providing a range of premium automobiles that ranged from the Mini to the Rolls Royce. The aim was to raise sales by 40 per cent a year for the next five years, and to achieve sales of 1.4 million vehicles. Mercedes-Benz would then become number two producer of premium cars, and BMW's long term ambition of being number one would be finally realised.[7]

To achieve the targets it had set itself, the company was pushing hard in the US and Asian markets to find buyers for the high-end models that they had found difficult to sell in the flat and saturated European market. Difficulties in dealing with labour cost control in the European political climate had also led BMW to expand its production facilities in the US, where the Spartanburg plant was not running at full potential, and China, where a well qualified labour force cost much less than in the West.[8] It was an ambitious plan that, if successful, as well as giving the group greater prominence and profitability would also effectively cure the problem of vulnerability to acquisitions.

But the strategy was not without risks. Three interconnected issues related to BMW's declared strategy.

First of all, increasing the output at the level planned by the company, could threaten the very reason for BMW's great success: a strong, but simple, theme summarised by the line 'the ultimate driving machine'. They had been able to exploit this brand identity very profitably and globally, wherever their niche could be found. There was no doubt that the brand could be extended and that the theme would still be recognisable and effective in the brand communication. However, how far it could go without causing damage was a matter of speculation. How would the launch of the 1-series be perceived by buyers, and perspective buyers,

---

[7] G. Edmondson, 'BMW', *Business Week*, 9 June 2003.

[8] U. Harnischfeger, *Financial Times*, 26 June 2003.

of the high-end BMW models? Would their perception of the value of the BMW brand be negatively affected? Related to this threat, there was also the risk that any model positioned in the proximity of a more expensive model could cannibalise it. For example, could the 1-series model cannibalise the 3-series?

Secondly, increasing the production of smaller cars could have the effect of reducing the historically high margins enjoyed by BMW (see Exhibit 3). Moving into smaller cars meant earning the lower margins that were typical of those market segments. But competitors in those segments were volume producers with lower costs than BMW. Would BMW be able to reap price premiums large enough to maintain their profitability level? The premium price automobile market, being one of the few profitable ones, was increasingly crowded, so new models came out, and new entrants nudged closer, all the time. The result was that price competition, which started when Lexus had entered the US market in the mid 1990s, was gaining pace. In such a competitive climate, the pressure was on to save costs by sharing components and platforms amongst models, for example between 3-series and X3. However, this sharing could lead to a flattening of the features of the different models, thus encouraging the cannibalisation of the more expensive model.[9]

A third concern was that of quality. With pressure on costs, the risk of quality lapses was bound to increase. The consequences of quality defects in the premium segments can be very heavy, as BMW learned when customers found it very difficult to use the iDrive they had installed in the 7-series. Expanding production with increasing contracting out of manufacturing processes could make quality control more difficult than it had been when a handful of models made BMW's reputation worldwide.

If H. Panke was mulling over any of these concerns, he did not show it at the *Annual Accounts of Press Conference* on 17 March 2004, when he said:

> We offer our customers emotional products, which, through the strength of the brand and the substance of the product, fulfil the customer's wish for individualisation and differentiation. The BMW Group will never build boring products.

---

[9] G. Edmondson, 'BMW', *Business Week*, 9 June 2003.

The VSM Group[1]

Jonas Dahlqvist and Anders Melander

This case describes the developing strategy of the VSM Group from 1997 to 2003, a time of considerable organisational and contextual change. During this period, the VSM Group became an independent company after being divested from a major industrial group. It also acquired a major competitor in distress. The case describes the strategic impact of these events in a situation of global competition in a declining market. The case provides an opportunity to consider the emerging strategic capabilities of an organisation, the bases and direction of competitive strategy, the integration of a major acquisition and issues of strategic change.

• • •

A new beginning

Sometimes, things just happen all at once. Electrolux's intention to divest its sewing business was well known, but the ownership question had been lingering for years before the deal was finally closed. It was not until 1997 that Electrolux actually did sell VSM AB to the investment fund Industri Kapital.[2] The deal was concluded on 6 February 1997, exactly 125 years after a decision was taken by the board of directors at Husqvarna AB to start manufacturing sewing machines.

During 1996, the Electrolux Group worked actively to find a buyer for their sewing machine business. During this period, the then CEO of VSM, Jörgen Johansson, resigned and a new CEO, Svante Runnquist, was appointed. Mr Runnquist had worked in a number of different positions, mainly in marketing, with Volvo for over 25 years. He had also held the position as CEO of Volvo Germany for five years.

A new direction

VSM AB developed, manufactured, marketed and sold household sewing machines. Electronic and computerised models were manufactured at the Husqvarna plant in Sweden, while low-priced mechanical machines and over-lockers were sourced from Asian manufacturers. When Svante Runnquist came to VSM, much of his work was directed towards improving the company's market orientation. The number of concurrent changes in the company made for a window of opportunity to redirect the strategic focus of the company. An intense weekend meeting in April 1997 marked the beginning of a very busy period for the top management team. Mr Runnquist explained:

---

[1] This case was formerly known as the Viking Sewing Machines AB. The title was changed to reflect new developments in the case. Since this is an account of major organisational change in and around the focal business over a period of 15 years, names have changed on various points in time. On the 30 April 1998, Husqvarna Sewing Machines AB changed its name to Viking Sewing Machines AB. In 2002, the name was 'acronymised' to VSM Group AB. Before it was purchased by Electrolux in 1977, the company name was Husqvarna AB. For simplicity, we will use the name 'VSM Group' to denote the sewing machine manufacture that stems from Husqvarna AB. Additional information on the company's history and performance as well as the current owner is given in the appendices.

[2] The full name of the formal owner is the Industri Kapital 1994 Fund. However, we will refer to the owner as Industri Kapital. Further details on the activities of Industri Kapital can be found in an appendix.

We started off with a week-end meeting on a country resort. I didn't even bring in a consultant this time. I have done that in the past, but this time I was so fresh on the job that I was the one who could ask all those 'stupid' questions.

During the first meeting, the basic scope of the strategy document was laid out while further refinements and changes were made during the summer of 1997. The new mission statement[3] and the companion strategy document were presented to middle management in a series of seminars. The opportunity to participate in the strategy process was a new experience to most of the people involved. Some took a dim view of the amount of time spent away from more pressing matters such as low sales or the installation of a new accounting system. Nevertheless, the high involvement seemed to pay off. The strategy document was often referred to for guidance on operational matters and the mission statement was frequently promoted in the company's public relations. The physical appearance of the strategy document was very plain; it consisted of folded and stapled photocopies wrapped in a two-colour sleeve. This was a reflection of the concern that the VSM management had about setting in stone something that was inherently an ongoing process. The strategic conversation within the top management team continued with at least five off-site workshops a year, formally dedicated to assessing the company's current strategic position. Summing up this initial process, Mr Runnquist said:

The first attempts were very unstructured and people were complaining about how it was all empty phrases and buzz words. My point is that, it is only when you engage in that type of discussion that you may come to realize that your thoughts aren't that clear after all.

Making it happen

Retailers were very important to VSM in their new plans for future profitability. This crucial link to the customers became a targeted area for VSM with the arrival of the new CEO. One important effort in this direction was the programme to transform the retailers into 'Dealer-Partners'.[4] The concept included extended support for business development to encourage them to carry the Husqvarna Viking product line exclusively. Marketing Director Sofia Axelsson put it this way:

There have been tremendous changes in VSM since Svante [Runnquist] came here, there really have. But we may change all we want; the customer only meets the retailer and as long as the retailer doesn't change, the customer won't perceive any change at all.

In the US, VSM started to cooperate with Jo-Ann Fabrics & Crafts, a large retailer of fabrics with over a thousand stores nationwide, setting up small sewing machine outlets inside their fabric stores. By May 1999, VSM had opened 47 exclusive Husqvarna Viking shops in the US, many in cooperation with Jo-Ann Fabrics & Crafts. Mr Runnquist explained:

The US is our biggest market,[5] then comes Sweden. This country [Sweden] is the only country where we have had exclusive retailers for a long time. In the U.S. we only started this a couple of years ago. You can make a living on the Husqvarna Viking brand there. In most other parts of the world we have very few exclusive VSM retailers; we're a brand among many others in the shop. A retailer in Europe typically carries 3–4 brands. Unfortunately, that's often the type that just 'peddles' machines. We don't believe it's our future.

It was in the light of the expanding after-market that retailer integration became really important, since the company's strategy expanded the core product beyond the sewing machine. The 'after-market' included services, such as training in sewing techniques, software for embroidery construction and ready-made embroidery patterns, together with spare parts and auxiliary sewing equipment. But how did the average retailer respond to VSM's proposal to expand their activities? Mr Runnquist again:

You really can make money on training and that's what we are trying to teach the retailers. Our organisation in the U.S.A. is particularly successful. Over there, people willingly pay 5–600 dollars to be in on a three-day course with a sewing expert.

Supporting the strategy

Changes in organisational structure and routines accompanied the company's claims of a new commitment to think more about the customer

---

[3] Please refer to the mission statement in the Appendix.
[4] VSM's name for exclusive retailers under special contracts.

[5] About 45 per cent of the turnover.

and less about technical 'features'. The top management team was changed to incorporate the managers of the major national sales companies as well as the marketing vice president. The new management structure was not only a change at the top level. There were also changes in operating systems. One of these was the installation of a new accounting system in May 1999. Earlier, VSM had only a vague idea about how much they spent on marketing of *specific* products, let alone what their competitors spent. The old system may have seemed sufficient during the Electrolux period when worries tended to end at the factory gate. However, as an independent company, VSM needed to assess the accounting information in new ways to keep track of the various activities in the value chain.

The marketing and the technical development department also moved into the same office building in January 2000. Earlier, Production and Technical Development had always been in the same building away from other departments. Perhaps it was no surprise that the turn-around programmes launched during the 1980s mainly focused on streamlining production efficiency, rather than developing customer value by innovative functions.

Into cyberspace by design

When VSM presented their new top-of-the-line Husqvarna Viking in early 1999, it was meant to be a 'world's first' in several respects. The *Designer I* came out as an engineering *tour-de-force*, retailing at a hefty $5,000.[6] The new model made extensive use of software to control the machine and contained no less than eight motors to cater for all functions. Several features were logical developments and refinements of existing solutions but the new sensor control for the needle plate with an automatic thread cutter, the built-in disk drive and a 'flash' memory made for a re-definition of what a sewing machine really is.

Each of these innovations was important for the overall impact of the final product. The construction of the new needle plate sensor made it possible to control all its functions by a microprocessor running proprietary software. The 'flash'

memory could be upgraded by the end-user by just inserting a floppy disc into the sewing machine. Not only the stitches or embroidery pattern could be upgraded in this way, but also the more fundamental characteristic of the sewing machine.

Since all the functions of the *Designer I* were now controlled by a microprocessor, it opened up completely new ways of customer support. One illustration was the way VSM started to make new versions of the operating system available to download via the internet, free of charge. The customer downloaded the upgrade from the internet site, saved it onto a floppy and slid it into the built-in disk drive of the *Designer I*. This method of upgrading performance and introducing new functions was well developed in the computer business, but was new for sewing machines.

The great e-business shakeout during the late 1990s and the plethora of 'dotcoms' raised serious doubts about the internet as a viable medium for the distributive trades. VSM's position on this was uncompromising and followed the lines developed in their strategy document. Since VSM tried to promote exclusive 'Dealer-Partners', there could be no parallel channels of distribution of Husqvarna Viking sewing machines. However, VSM did start a web-shop for low bulk accessories and software on their website. As a tangible sign of VSM's intention to stay on good terms with their exclusive retailers, a bonus clearing system on internet sales was instigated. Each customer was given a unique identification code linked to the area retailer. The area retailers were given a bonus based on web sales to clients within their assigned area. The information on the customer was not passed on to the retailers, only the money. As Anne Jansson, a manager of internet marketing, put it:

> Up till now, we haven't had one single complaint from the retailers. I think they rather like the idea of getting a bonus automatically without any work involved.

VSM and Embroidery Networks Ltd (Emnet) had started to cooperate in 1993 to develop software for embroidery. In March 1999, VSM declared that they had acquired this small British producer of software for PC-controlled professional sewing. CEO Svante Runnquist commented:

> The idea is not that strange if you think about the fact that we want the after-market to grow more than the total business. We cannot do that by selling more spare parts; we will probably be selling fewer . . . It's

---

[6] In 2004, the Designer I retailed for approx. $5,900 on the US market.

by selling more auxiliary equipment and developing new products for the after-market that we will grow and then software will be an important part for our computer-controlled machines.

With the breakthrough of the web, distribution of software and embroidery files took a new turn. People could exchange embroidery patterns through the internet or download them at the VSM websites. In the period 2000 to 2003, VSM expanded the number of software engineers from 3 to 17, not counting the new R&D director that was also hired from the software industry.

Competing in an international arena

The sewing machine industry lacked the market transparency normally associated with a mature manufacturing industry. Very little information was collected by official bodies and VSM cooperated with competitors to collect figures on volume in different price brackets through a third-party intermediary. VSM also collected information on competition through the sales companies and retailers. In addition, the R&D department as well as Marketing and Sales regularly compared their own machines to the ones manufactured by competitors. To the CEO Svante Runnquist the lack of market information came as a surprise:

> For me, coming from the car industry, all this lack of information is very frustrating. That was one of my first questions [when I came to VSM]: what does it [the market] look like? The industry is rather poorly monitored as to market shares. You know what models and specifications exist, but there are actually rather few that start from the customer and develop the product definition that way.

The volume manufacturers of sewing machines were located in the Far East. They mainly consisted of a number of medium-sized manufacturers, primarily acting as OEMs[7] for established brands in the lower price bracket. However, there were three competitors that set themselves apart. Brother, Janome and Juki were all major competitors to VSM. Janome alone produced over 1.5 million units in 2003. Not only were these companies high-volume manufacturers with complete product

ranges but, more importantly, they also sported their own R&D facilities capable of developing sewing-embroidery machines. Being Japanese, their location gave them access to low-cost production facilities in, for example, Taiwan, Thailand and Korea. However, this seemed to be a mixed blessing since the competition from local low-cost brands was fierce for modestly priced mechanical sewing machines.

The largest competitor by volume was Janome of Japan. Their main activity was domestic sewing machines, although they maintained some side activities in small industrial robots. They had no manufacturing of industrial sewing machines. Janome had introduced several important industry innovations such as touch-screen controls.

Brother was a well-known manufacturer of office machinery such as labellers, typewriters, faxes and copying machines. However, they were also very active in the sewing industry, both in the consumer and industrial markets. Their total production was an estimated 1.3 million machines in 2003. In addition, they continued to produce innovative products coupled with prices that undercut VSM by 20–30 per cent.

Another big player was the Juki operation. Being more specialised on sewing machines than Brother, they manufactured and marketed both industrial and domestic machines. After the Singer reconstruction, Juki made the entire range of computer-controlled machines for Singer, including their top-of-the-line embroidery models. Juki did not market these expensive models under the Juki brand in the US. Rather, the Juki models were very modest in features. After entering the embroidery segment, Juki had also been less aggressive in pursuing product development.

In Europe, the VSM Group and Bernina Fritz Gegauf AG were the only remaining independent manufacturers. Bernina was a fourth-generation family company located in Switzerland, enjoying a solid reputation and actively demonstrating their Swiss heritage. Their product range resembled that of VSM and their top model accepted embroidery files developed for other brands, including VSM. The relative geographical proximity and a similar corporate situation made Bernina an important quality benchmark for VSM. However, during the first years of the new millennium, Bernina had shown signs of lagging behind in product development. Although a competitor, Mr Runnquist deplored the fact that Bernina seemed to be losing ground.

---

[7] Original Equipment Manufacturer.

They have a good brand and a good reputation, but we think they have started showing signs of lagging in product development. To make a market you need each other – Mercedes needs BMW and BMW needs Audi and together they make a market. So nobody would be happier than I if Bernina were more active. Don't get me wrong though – I would still like to take over some of their retailers. But they are not helping us much today to create demand for creative sewing.

The demand for sewing machines in the western hemisphere had been declining for more than two decades in terms of units sold. As a result, industry profitability had deteriorated. This downturn had been particularly hard on manufacturers of industrial machines and low-price mechanical machines for domestic use. In Europe and in the US, the manufacturers competing on the professional side were severely affected by the sharp drop in demand for industrial sewing machines. Firms such as Pfaff, with production of domestic and industrial machines bundled together in the same company, experienced major difficulties in the 1990s. Pfaff, with about two-thirds of the sales in the professional market, went bankrupt in September 1999. A week later, the almost mythical Singer was on the brink of bankruptcy and filed for a Chapter 11, partly as a result of their 80 per cent ownership in Pfaff's industrial division. After a reconstruction, Singer was up and running again but with little or no in-house manufacturing. However, their huge global network of retailers was severely reduced.

The aftermath of the Pfaff/Singer bankruptcy proved to be very important for the development of VSM. When news about the demise of Pfaff reached VSM, it posed new and intricate challenges to the owner, Industri Kapital. Their original plan for VSM was to set a good track record over a five-year period in order to make a profitable exit through an IPO. The choice facing Industri Kapital in 1999 was to go ahead as planned or to support a bid for Pfaff's domestic sewing machine division. However, the latter alternative would necessitate a postponement of the planned exit on VSM. In the past, Industri Kapital had been known to seek out structural deals to develop companies in their portfolio. True to form, they decided to give the green light on the acquisition of Pfaff and the deal was closed on 2 May 2000. The combined company was renamed the VSM Group to avoid any confusion with the group's brand names and a new company slogan was coined – 'Changing the World of Sewing'.

Back to square one

The review process of the Pfaff acquisition started over a year before the closing of the deal. Deciding what had to go and what would stay was a daunting task. Based on the strategic plan of the VSM Group, it was clear from the beginning that VSM was only interested in the household part of Pfaff. But where was the value for VSM in their former competitor? In early 2004, Svante Runnquist commented:

> Looking back on May 2000 . . . Well, our main interest was of course the brand – it was a deal breaker. We said 'If we're not getting the full rights to the brand, we'll simply take the next flight home. No deal.' And we got it alright. But the legal stuff really takes longer than you would expect. I think I signed for Surinam just last week! But we're getting there.

The VSM Group was now in possession of two strong brands that partly competed for the same market space. Solving this threatening strategic conflict became a top priority – it was back to square one. A new process for crafting the strategic positions for Husqvarna Viking and Pfaff was launched and it would last two years. A basic premise was not to change the strategy that had turned VSM into a profitable operation. Mr Runnquist recollects:

> We wouldn't change Husqvarna Viking because that had been really successful and it was the one that generated good money. So, we asked ourselves: what is the soul in Pfaff? Frankly, there wasn't many left that could tell. But we just went head on and it took us two years to chisel it out. We held workshops with retailers in different markets; workshops with our staff; workshops with designers that had worked with Pfaff; with co-workers that had left us; with co-workers that had just been hired . . . We really worked it. And then we had this meeting in London . . . It was bloody war! That meeting was the first time we presented our new strategy. Whoa . . . it was fun! Half of the people were really upset and against it. But we just thought: Great! We're on the right track! There was just this huge involvement.

But what was it that so upset some people, and pleased others? Having two strong brands made for some interesting choices on how to separate the former competitors. It seemed to call for some sort of subordination of the Pfaff brand – at least when thinking only in terms of quality and price. However, it was not an idea that appealed to the VSM top management team; Pfaff was a very strong brand, and it did not seem like a good idea to buy it only to use it for simple medium- and low-priced models.

The solution was to pull the brands apart on other dimensions than price and quality. This meant keeping a full product range under each brand. To illustrate the difference in market offer, VSM developed dedicated key words for each brand. While Husqvarna Viking kept their 'innovative', 'family', 'caring' and 'fun', Pfaff's new keywords were 'elegant', 'individual' and 'sophisticated'. While the Husqvarna Viking brand sported pictures of families in the warm colours of red and yellow, Pfaff portrayed young professional women in cool surroundings in blue and green hues.

Another deal breaker was the production capacity in Karlsruhe, Germany. VSM's analyses showed that the German plant had fundamental problems with cost. In fact, VSM decided not to buy a single bolt from the German suppliers. The effect of this decision was of course drastic: 140 years of German sewing machine manufacturing came to an end. Only a handful of R&D engineers stayed on.

Moving production from Karlsruhe to the Swedish Huskvarna plant was no small feat. Through a deal with the German receiver, VSM continued buying manufacturing capacity from the Karlsruhe plant for another year while preparing to move production. Despite this period of grace, moving the production proved to be more complicated than expected since German and Swedish engineering principles were fundamentally different. The machines produced under the Husqvarna Viking brand were explicitly designed to take advantage of their single-loop manufacturing line and machines were assembled, tested and approved by a single team of workers. The Pfaff machines were manufactured in a double-loop line. The machines were first assembled but were then routed to a second line where *Meisters* adjusted and tweaked each machine into compliance. In the long run, this incompatibility needed major re-engineering, but in the short run, the Huskvarna plant had to solve these problems as they went along. In addition to this, the rejection rates on some German-made parts were soaring and this caused recurring hiccups in the production system.

Luckily, the VSM Group had an ace up their sleeve: the Zetina plant. A well-kept secret by Pfaff, the Zetina production plant located in Brno in the Czech Republic had produced over a million machines for Pfaff since 1992; only a few special models were still produced in Karlsruhe. Although the Czech plant was very cost-efficient, Pfaff had not used it to its full potential. The Czech operation had functioned purely as an assembly line. Parts sourced from high-cost German suppliers were sent in brown boxes to be assembled in the Czech Republic for a fixed price per machine and then shipped back to Germany. No development or sourcing was done locally.

The Zetina plant was an independent Czech company and the VSM team realised that controlling it was crucial to the production of Pfaff machines since the Husqvarna site could not produce even a fraction of the volume needed. Before the Pfaff deal was closed, the owners of Zetina were secretly invited to the Husqvarna site for a meeting and an offer they could not refuse. The VSM group offered to buy the Czech company, take over all personnel, and hire the owners as managers for the new company. The production facilities would be leased long-term by VSM, sweetening the deal even further. Having dealt with the withering Pfaff for years, this was all the Zetina owners could wish for. The purchasing function was now partly decentralised to the Brno plant, with some central coordination provided by VSM on the group level. Parts were now sourced locally or from suppliers in the Far East common to both brands. Compared to Pfaff's former suppliers, cost was cut up to 50 per cent on key parts concurrent with large improvements in quality and rejection rates.

Although the VSM team remained unimpressed with the cost of Pfaff's manufacturing organisation, marketing and distribution were all the more appealing. Pfaff dominated the German-speaking markets (Germany, Austria and Switzerland), and had higher market share and brand awareness than Husqvarna Viking pretty much everywhere else except for the Scandinavian markets and the US. However, as the process of integrating Pfaff into the VSM Group unfolded, an unpleasant discovery was made: Pfaff was losing money in its home market in a big way. In an effort to defend its market share in all segments, Pfaff had successively lowered their prices to meet the competition from Asian manufacturers. In order to keep their retailers alive they had had to lower the prices to German retailers to a level where they started to undercut the internal transfer prices to Pfaff's own sales companies. It turned out that Pfaff had grossly underestimated the costs associated with the German market and had incurred substantial losses for years. Even though production costs on the Pfaff products were cut by the VSM Group, margins were still inadequate and only one course of action remained: raising prices. This was tough medicine indeed and not something that VSM was expecting – the Pfaff marketing network was believed to be an asset, not a liability. Within three years, sales were down some 20 per cent by volume and a number of Pfaff retailers had chosen not to stay exclusive with Pfaff any more and were now carrying competing brands.

VSM had previously incurred losses for five years in a row on the German market and market penetration was going nowhere. Now they understood why; the market leader had been subsidising its home market. When Pfaff was declared insolvent, Germany had the lowest price level in the world on sewing machines. In February 2004, the pricing in Germany of the Pfaff and Husqvarna Viking ranges were back on a level with the rest of the European markets.

Looking back into the future

In 1999, VSM's focus was to nurture their relations between the company and its retailers in what they referred to as the Dealer-Partner programme. In 2004, that still topped their agenda, but with the addition of the Pfaff brand VSM needed to rethink their marketing strategy. The VSM effort to expand in the US market by setting up store-in-stores for the Husqvarna Viking brand in collaboration with Jo-Ann Fabrics had expanded rapidly.

By the end of 2003, the number of store-in-stores run by VSM in the US had reached 120.

A lot of energy was also being devoted to the integration of Pfaff and the problems in the German market. When VSM decided to continue Pfaff and Husqvarna Viking as two separate brands with separate product programmes, they also created potential for a clash especially when trying to cut costs by coordinating marketing and distribution activities. Svante Runnquist openly acknowledged that their struggle to strike a balance between exploiting synergies while safeguarding the integrity of their two global brands was partly a trial-and-error process.

We announced from the beginning that there was only going to be one sales company with two brands for each market. And we did make substantial savings in our European sales companies – they reached the critical mass needed to make money. Maybe we went too far on some functions, like retailing support and education – it hasn't delivered all the benefits that we had hoped for. But at the retail level, we prefer to have exclusive Pfaff or exclusive Husqvarna Viking retailers. At first, we were at bit unclear on this: should we combine Pfaff and Husqvarna Viking in the same store? Well, we did in our stores in Germany because we didn't have much to lose there . . . But on the other hand, I don't know if we gained anything either. It's just too much – too many new things for the retailers to keep track of. Frankly, we can hardly keep track of everything ourselves with the speed of development that we are experiencing in the company.

APPENDIX 1
Company history of VSM

An unbroken tradition of engineering and manufacturing since 1689 is something that is often emphasised in the company's own presentations of VSM Group AB. In 1846, a machine that could sew a lock stitch, using an under-thread and a shuttle, was patented by the American engineer Elias Howe. The sewing machines of today basically use the same principle. Towards the end of the 19th century, Husqvarna AB, then a manufacturer of guns for 200 years, needed something to support the company's declining sales and the new invention was seen as a solution that matched their skills in machining and precision casting. The company's first sewing machine appeared in 1872 but was relatively unsuccessful. In 1883, the engineers of Husqvarna AB presented a new model, the 'Freja'. It was an instant success and was manufactured for over 40 years.

In more recent times, the Husqvarna Company was early to investigate the possibilities of sintered metal technology in the 1950s and held the European patent rights for this special technology. Using sintered metal, the Husqvarna engineers were able to make the moving parts of a sewing machine permanently lubricated, thereby eliminating the need for oiling and greasing.[8] OEM production of sintered metal parts is still part of VSM's business.

---

[8] A sintered metal is made from a blend of metal powders that is compressed under high pressure and temperature to form a solid metal. A sintered metal can be given a number of properties (e.g. controlled porosity) that are not obtainable through traditional methods such as cast alloys. A porous metal can be permanently impregnated with oil, which gives a self-lubricating effect.

APPENDIX 2

Brief description of Industri Kapital

The owner of Industri Kapital Fund 1994 was a mutual capital fund, managed by Industri Kapital AB. This company was originally created in 1989 and specialises in unglamorous but well-kept companies with moderate annual growth. The funds for investments come mainly from large institutional investors such as banks and insurance companies.

The strategy of Industri Kapital is to buy companies where they think they can contribute to increase the value of the company, either by providing management know-how or by merging companies or parts of companies in their portfolio. Industri Kapital does not run companies indefinitely; they typically seek an exit either by an IPO[9] or by selling to another company. When Industri Kapital buys a company, the top management group of the target company is offered to engage financially in the buy-out. In the case of VSM Group AB, top management and other employees hold about 8 per cent of the shares.

APPENDIX 3

Mission Statement VSM

- To develop, produce market and sell consumer sewing machines and related products which enhance the joy of creative sewing.
- To grow our business by creating demand for more creative uses of sewing and being active in selected areas within the total sewing industry.
- To be a consumer-driven company, securing growth, profitability and success by providing superior satisfaction to the Consumer and our Dealer-Partner, and by continuously adding value to our brands.
- To provide valued employees growth opportunities in an environment of which they can be proud.
- To be recognised as the leading premium company in the world of sewing.

APPENDIX 4

Financial Overview*

Basic stats (fiscal year 2003, actual figures)

Average number of employees: 1,689
Net sales: 2.393 billion SEK
Operating profit (EBITA): 270 million SEK
Operating cash flow: 235 million SEK
Total numbers of sewing machines and overlockers sold: 549,000 units.

Historical data 1997–2003

Year	Sales (MSEK)	Gross margin	Cashflow	Profitability (ROC)
1997	954	51.3%	N/A	34.1%
1998	974	52.5%	99	25.2%
1999	1,185	55.1%	162	33.8%
2000	1,931	50.4%	152	30.5%
2001	2,543	50.0%	84	27.0%
2002	2,760	55.3%	239	36.5%
2003	2,393	59.4%	235	33.4%

* 1 SEK = approx. €0.11.

---

[9] Initial Public Offering: when a company sells stock to the public for the first time.

Thorntons plc: corporate and business strategy

David Jennings

The case concerns the growth and development of Thorntons, the UK's largest manufacturer and retailer of specialist chocolates. Throughout its history the company had followed a strategy of in-house manufacture, retailing largely through the company's own shops and, to a lesser extent, through franchising. This policy presented the company with the difficulties of economically meeting seasonal demand variations in the chocolate and gift markets. The case includes the company's attempts at diversification into the US market and Europe and their disappointing conclusion and later attempts to widen the product base and markets served.

● ● ●

Introduction

In September 2003 Thorntons, the UK's largest manufacturer and retailer of specialist chocolates, completed a three-year planning period aimed at achieving a turnaround in the company's performance. While company turnover had been increased to £167m (≈ €250m) providing Thorntons with an 8 per cent share of its core market, boxed chocolates, profit after tax had declined to the lowest level for seven years (Exhibit 1). During that time Thorntons had set out to follow a series of strategic initiatives involving the reorientation of the company towards becoming a retail-focused business, increasing the scale of the company's manufacturing and retailing operations and developments that would affect the company's product range, the markets served and product positioning.

For Thorntons' core products, the ranges of boxed chocolates, certain key manufacturing and selling activities are conducted in-house with the quality of the boxed chocolate selections assured by the use of quality ingredients and through the manufacturing expertise the company has developed. In addition in-house manufacture is felt to protect the exclusivity of Thorntons' principal recipes. None-core products, such as solid chocolate bars, are largely supplied by outside producers.

Similarly the manufacture of basic liquid chocolate, a capital intensive process, is by an outside supplier, the supplier achieving buying and processing economies of scale beyond those that would be available to Thorntons. Packaging, which accounts for a large part of the product's perceived value, is also manufactured by outside suppliers.

The majority of the company's sales are made through company-owned shops. The company's own retail outlets provide a good quality of service and offer the inclusion of personalised messages, written in icing, on such gifts as Valentine's Day chocolate hearts and Easter eggs. At extra cost products can also be purchased gift-wrapped. The company's shops have become a part of the UK high street. In an independent market research survey, consumers asked to rank their typical high street, included Thorntons in fifth place. Establishing and maintaining the company's shops requires a considerable commitment of resources. For a new shop the average cost of fitting out often exceeds £100,000. Once established shops need further expenditure to cover wear and tear. The layout and appearance of Thorntons' own shops are frequently altered, with the changes developed and evaluated in the company's mock shops in Derbyshire and the south of England prior to their high-street introduction. The company also

| Exhibit 1 | Thorntons Group: selected company information |

					(£m)*					
	1994	1995	1996	1997	1998	1999	2000	2001	2002	2003
Sales	96.6	95.6	97.6	111.3	132.8	141.3	153.4	159.9	163.8	167.1
Operating profit	12.6	10.1	5.8	11.3	12.9	13.1	10.5	10.1	10.4	9.4
Profit after tax	7.8	6.7	(15.1)	8.6	9.0	9.7	5.2	4.5	7.3	4.4
Fixed assets	51.0	50.4	45.1	52.1	86.2	109.1	104.4	96.7	88.8	83.2
Net assets	47.3	50.1	33.3	38.4	44.8	48.1	49.1	40.0	43.0	43.0
Gearing ratio (%)				16	71	105	130	111	86	67
Number of UK outlets										
Own Shops	243	263	269	300	344	390	410	400	395	389
Franchised	189	150	129	202	151	110	127	163	181	198

* £1 = approx. €1.5.

makes use of franchised outlets that have occasionally prompted concern regarding the quality of particular outlets or through their occupying a major location or an inappropriate location.

The freshness of the product is a distinctive feature of Thorntons chocolates. For many other manufacturers, addressing the wider chocolate market, the greater use of vegetable fat (other than cocoa butter) results in products with a shelf-life of over a year. Although Thorntons' own research had indicated that freshness is not the first concern for consumers when purchasing a gift of chocolates, the company believes that it is essential to maintain the customer's experience of a fresh product. As a consequence many retail outlets, corner shops, garages, and some of the supermarkets have at times been seen as not suitable for the product, even if the company wished to achieve sales through those outlets.

The demand for Thorntons boxed chocolates follows a strongly seasonal pattern: 35 per cent of sales are in the seven-week period before Christmas, a further 10 per cent are for Easter, including three million Easter eggs. The combination of providing a fresh product together with the need to meet a seasonal pattern of demand places particular pressures upon the company's manufacturing facilities. A proportion of the Christmas product is produced several months in advance, maintaining freshness through chilled storage. However Thorntons chocolates are enrobed in chocolate, rather than moulded. Their hand-made appearance makes the process of packing boxed chocolates less open to automation than is the case

for moulded chocolates (with their more uniform shape and size) produced by companies such as Cadburys. The seasonal demand for packing staff requires the increased use of casual workers, with consequent falls in efficiency. Seasonal demand also requires the use of temporary staff in the retail outlets to meet a sales pattern that can within a few days increase tenfold; typically the company sells £10m of chocolate in the last 72 hours of Christmas trading. At times the company has sold ice cream (self-manufactured or bought in) as an attempt to offset the effect of low, off-season, chocolate sales.

In certain respects Thorntons' strategy, with its emphasis upon vertical integration and product differentiation, can be traced back to the company's origins.

Development into a public company

Thorntons was founded in 1911 by Joseph Thornton, a commercial traveller engaged in selling confectionery. Tired of travelling, he opened his own shop in the city of Sheffield. His two sons, Norman and Stanley, joined him to combine their abilities in retailing, devising recipes, and manufacture, to provide freshly-made confectionery, manufactured in the shop it was sold in.

The benefits of self-manufacture and product innovation were soon to become apparent. During the 1920s several product lines were established that have continued to the present day. In 1925 a recipe for Special Toffee, based upon cream, butter and eggs, gave the business an outstanding product. The self-manufacture of Easter eggs, decorated in the shop to include names and messages, added to the range of freshly made and fresh-tasting confectionery.

In 1953 Stanley and Norman Thornton visited Switzerland to find out how Thorntons could make what was regarded as the very best of chocolates. The visit included the Basle School for Swiss Chocolatiers and the recruitment of an outstanding student, Walter Willen, who created the original recipes for Thorntons' Continental chocolates, a range that was to become the largest-selling specialist assortment of chocolates in the UK.

Thorntons began to develop sales outside the UK and by 1982 the value of Thorntons' exports to Europe and Australia had reached £300,000. Attracted by the prospect of further non-UK sales the company decided that the massive potential of the US market offered the best vehicle for expansion. Thorntons opened two shops in Chicago, with the longer-term intention of operating a 100-shop chain throughout the USA.

By the late 1980s Thorntons operated the largest chain of quality confectionery shops in the UK, 170 company-owned shops and 100 franchised outlets operating in towns too small to merit a Thorntons owned shop. Thorntons believed that there was scope in the UK for a further 130 retail outlets with the expansion concentrated in the south east, away from the company's heartland in the Midlands and the north, and that the time had arrived for the stock market flotation of Thorntons; this was achieved in 1988 at a flotation price of 130p per share. With the offer of shares eight times over-subscribed, share trading began at a good premium.

European and UK developments

Although Thorntons was achieving success in the UK, the venture into the US was showing little prospect of profit and was closed. However further opportunities for growth were anticipated through acquisitions in Europe, where markets were believed to be more similar to the UK than had proven to be the case with the venture in America. Within three months of flotation Thorntons had made its first European acquisition, Gartner, based in Antwerp, a specialist in high-quality chocolate

and fresh cream products with sales of £1.7m mainly made through patisseries. Thorntons established an integrated manufacturing and retail operation, distributing Gartner's products through Thorntons retail network as well as selling its own confectionery to the Belgium company's customers. In the following year Thorntons acquired two French confectionery retailers, Candice-Martial SA and Societe Nouvelle de Confiserie (SNC) for a total of £8.65m. Candice had 55 retail outlets based mainly in the Paris area selling confectionery and ice cream. SNC had 11 confectionery outlets in the Normandy and Brittany region. The French and UK factories were to contribute to the supply of each other's markets.

In the UK Thorntons had a 1 per cent share of the daily confectionery market and a 6 per cent share of the confectionery gift market; as a consequence sales were highly dependent upon a number of seasonal events. The six weeks before Christmas provided 30 per cent of turnover. Easter, Valentine's Day and Mothering Sunday accounted for a further 25 per cent of sales. The concentration of sales into short periods of time made the company particularly vulnerable to market conditions at those times. The comparatively short shelf life of the company's products exacerbated the problems of seasonality.

Thorntons continued to develop the products and packaging within its core chocolate gift ranges. The Continental range, the best-selling specialist chocolates in the UK, was developed to include a 'French' dark chocolate selection and a 'Belgian' milk and white chocolate selection. A new Classics traditional assortment and a Premier Selection of hand-finished chocolates were established to top the company's range.

While the majority of Thorntons' sales were made through the company's own shops, use was also made of other forms of distribution, including franchising. In certain respects franchising provided a cost-effective way to achieve distribution coverage, however it did not provide the customer with the same experience as shopping in a Thorntons-owned shop and occasionally it could be difficult to maintain standards. Franchising could also provide surprises. In 1995 the company lost 15 franchised outlets following their takeover by Clinton Cards, a company that did not normally sell confectionery. The retailing of greetings cards represented the principal business of a high proportion of Thorntons' franchisees. Thorntons itself owned Mary Morrison, a small chain of greeting card shops in Scotland; however the chain was not considered to be central to Thorntons' core business and in 1990 Mary Morrison was sold to Hall of Cards for £2m.

Progress was made in developing the company's commercial customers. Thorntons had a long-standing supply arrangement with Marks and Spencer and in 1991 Sainsbury's was added to Asda as a supermarket outlet for the company's products, with the range of chocolate products broadened to suit supermarket shelves. Commercial customers' products differed by style and recipe from those provided through Thorntons' own outlets and regular customers could not be sure they were made by Thorntons.

The attempt by the group to enter the European market began to show disappointing results. Marked differences became apparent between the UK and French markets both in consumer tastes, with the French consumer preferring bitter chocolate, and through seasonal sales being less important gift occasions. In 1993 Thorntons (France) made a loss of £1.8m – the accumulated cost of the French initiative had reached £20m. Thorntons began to plan for the conversion of some of the shops to the Thorntons brand, with the aim of increasing the synergy with the UK business.

A change of direction

John Thornton, the son of Norman Thornton, had joined the company in 1966, becoming Chairman and Chief Executive in 1987. During the latter part of 1995 the company announced that it was seeking a new person for the position of Chief Executive. In January 1996 Roger Paffard became the first non-family Chief Executive of Thorntons with John Thornton as Chairman. Roger Paffard's previous position was that of Managing Director of Staples UK, the office supplies superstore joint venture between Kingfisher and Staples, where he had presided over the expansion of the out-of-town superstore business. Announcing the appointment, John Thornton described Mr Paffard as 'energetic with a strong retail background'. Roger Paffard demonstrated his faith in the company by purchasing 73,000 shares at 135p. Further changes to the board of directors included the appointment of the company's first Marketing Director.

The new management team undertook a comprehensive review that resulted in a number of changes to the group. To improve efficiency and

cut costs, packaging was to be concentrated at the Belper packing and manufacturing site, providing annual savings of £250,000. The Belgium business, Gartner Pralines, was to be sold for a nominal sum. The 30 per cent of Gartner's output that had been produced for the UK would be replaced by production at the group's main plant at Alfreton. Within the year a buyer was found, again for a nominal sum, for the remaining shops in France.

With regard to UK operations the new Chief Executive concluded that the company's existing shops were 'tired and increasingly off-pitch', many of the shops were too small and in poor locations. The Chief Executive concluded that the group had become over-focused upon manufacturing to the comparative neglect of its retailing activities and the development of the product range. Mr Paffard had initially doubted whether Thorntons should continue manufacturing, however a review convinced the board that the company was the only possible manufacturer for 70 per cent of its product lines. With the aid of retail consultants Thorntons undertook a review of its UK market, concluding that there was still significant potential to increase the UK retail chain.

By the end of October 1996 the company's three-year plan had been developed to include the closure of 126 shops and the opening of 216, to take the total from 269 to 359 shops. There was to be an emphasis on developing larger and better, prime location sites, in such locations as malls, shopping centres and small market towns. Expansion was particularly targeted towards London and the south. The aim was to provide a 60 per cent increase in total floor space by the year 2000, with annual sales per shop of £350,000. In addition the product range would be developed to provide a wider range of products. Achieving these targets would require an ambitious programme of investment, averaging £17m a year for three years. Over the next three years the group invested a total of £53m in new factory, warehousing and till systems. The manufacturing investment tripling the level of potential output.

Targeting growth and innovation

By the late 1990s the company's senior management had come to see Thorntons as a market-led, retail-driven business, selling into a market that could be defined in a number of ways. Within the confectionery market Thorntons core products

Exhibit 2 — UK boxed chocolate market (% market share)

	1999	2002 (estimated)
Cadbury	24	24
Nestlé Rowntree	22	19
Masterfoods	13	16
Kraft Jacob Suchard	13	13
Thorntons	8	8
Ferrero	6	5
Other brands	10	9
Own-label	5	5
Total value of sales	£713m	£699m

were within the boxed chocolate market, a market in which four companies, Cadbury, Nestlé Rowntree, Masterfoods and Kraft Jacob Suchard, accounted for 72 per cent of sales (Exhibit 2).

(Appendix 1 provides an overview of the UK confectionery market that includes the boxed chocolate market.)

As a gift Thorntons' boxed chocolates competed with a wide range of products in the £5–10 price range, provided by high street specialist retailers such as Body Shop and KnickerBox. The same market was also addressed by postal gifts such as flowers and wine.

Thorntons' plans were revised to achieve further growth. Thorntons' channels of distribution were targeted for further expansion to increase the total of wholly owned shops to 507 by 2001 together with 200 franchised outlets. Overall the company's sales growth was targeted to increase by 15 per cent a year. At the same time greater importance was given to product development. Thorntons markedly increased the rate and scope of product innovation, repackaging and relaunching the Classics range, adding 'Swiss' and 'Austrian' selections to the core Continental range and introducing an Awesome American range. In 1997 27 new countlines (wrapped chocolate bars designed for one person to consume) were introduced, providing a five-fold increase in the range available. The ice cream range was expanded and a children's range introduced, with product themes including dinosaur eggs, fossils and dalmatian spots. In 1998 a further 132 new and updated products were introduced. Widening the product range to include a greater emphasis on countlines, which acted as a snack or impulse buy, attracted a wider range of customers but it also brought Thorntons into competition with the products of such companies as Nestlé and Cadburys.

Sales from the new ranges were over £5.5m (4 per cent of turnover) in 1998, but not all of the new products were to prove successful. Within the year 15 new products were discontinued due to their failing to reach an acceptable level of sales. Losses from the discontinued products were increased due to a lack of timely performance information; in 1998 the company had only begun a £3m programme to install EPOS in the shops.

During 1998 Thorntons' sales increased to £133m, with sales in the company's own shops growing to £105.9m. Sales to commercial customers had reached £17.4m, the main customer remaining Marks and Spencer. However, profits fell short of the company's own target.

The company continued to develop responses to the problem of seasonality. Through product development and shop relocation initiatives Thorntons sought to attract a wider range of customers thereby increasing the importance of impulse and everyday snack purchases. The effectiveness of these initiatives in smoothing demand was limited. In 1997–98 the tonnage produced at the low point of production remained half of that achieved at peak. The requirements of Thorntons' main commercial customers were seasonal and similar to their own.

The introduction of new products had achieved a number of beneficial effects, increasing the number of male customers, children and teenagers and lowering the overall age profile of the customers, although 50 per cent of turnover was still derived from the 12–16 weeks of sales involving Christmas, Easter, Valentine's Day, Mother's and Father's Day. The development of mail order provided an economic response to a seasonal pattern of demand while new forms of outlet, such as Café Thorntons (combining aspects of a café and a confectionery store), offered the possibility of developing outlets with a less seasonal pattern of sales. Seasonal demand remained difficult to meet. During the Christmas 1998 period consumers had tended to delay their seasonal purchases with the result that sales for the Christmas season were down by 3.8 per cent on a like-for-like basis. Roger Paffard explained 'Christmas came very late and our shops couldn't cope, which meant people were dropping off the queues rather than waiting to buy. If we had had one more day before Christmas at those busy levels we would have seen a like-for-like increase'.

Sales for Easter 1999 and Mother's Day were also disappointing leading to a warning of a reduction in profits. The Chief Executive announced that the group had underestimated the amount of new product necessary to stimulate sales over Mother's Day and Easter, advertising spending and new product launches were to be increased to raise the momentum of sales. The Chief Executive believed a slow-down in product development during 1999 had been 'lethal' in a situation where consumers constantly expected new offerings. For the coming spring (year 2000) new products and relaunches would make up 92 per cent of items on sale for Valentine's Day, 100 per cent for Mother's Day and 91 per cent for Easter Sunday. New products for Valentine's Day were to include chocolate-scented T-shirts and underwear, and for Easter eggs on sticks that could be hidden in the garden. New and relaunched products were to be in place for the 1999 Christmas sales period, including a relaunch of the best-selling Continental selection and a range designed for the millennium celebrations that included a chocolate champagne bottle.

The three phase turnaround plan (2000–2003)

In March 2000 the company announced that it was unlikely that it would achieve even the 1999

pre-tax profit of £10.5m let alone meet stock market expectations of £12m for the year to late June 2000. By mutual agreement with the board, Roger Paffard left Thorntons. Within a month the appointment of a new Chief Executive, Peter Burdon, had been announced. Peter Burdon's career included Esso, McKinsey & Co and the Boots retail group. The new Chief Executive announced that 'in the past Thorntons has focused a little bit too much on store openings and less on driving sales growth'. In his view the company needed to exploit its strong brand through marketing and advertising campaigns but did not need immediate changes in its product range: 'Thorntons is, and will remain, chocolate and toffee'. The core Thorntons customer was described as a 'thirty year old, Daily Mail reading woman'. However the company's deteriorating performance was prompting a revision of its strategic development. A new three-year plan was introduced aimed at achieving a turnaround in the company's performance. The plan consisted of a sequence of three, year-long, phases.

- Year One: stabilisation of the business.
- Year Two: the creation of organic growth.
- Year Three: the development of new growth options, possibly through the acquisition of rival confectionery brands.

Despite product developments Easter 2000 proved disappointing. Although like-for-like sales increased by 6 per cent the increase was not as much as expected, leaving the company with an excess of 300,000 chocolate eggs, subsequently sold off at half price or less. Expensive adult eggs, costing more than £15, proved difficult to sell and the market for novelty eggs, such as one that contained a CD, was also weak. After taking account of marketing expenditure the overall loss amounted to £5m.

Thorntons intensified their efforts to lessen their dependence on seasonal sales. New product development was focused towards day-to-day sales and the brand's advertising would no longer focus upon the company's heritage, typified by the advertising slogan 'Chocolate heaven since 1911', but upon the promise of 'There's lots in store for you'. In the financial press a number of analysts commented that consumers most often looked to the supermarkets for mass-market confectionery.

Over time product innovation had led to duplication within product ranges. New rules were to be followed to avoid cluttered product displays, including withdrawing products as new ones were introduced. The policies would eventually result in a 15 per cent reduction in the product range. Opportunities to increase commercial sales were also to be explored. The capital expenditure programme was to be reduced and focused more clearly on profit enhancement. The roll-out of new stores was to be slowed, however agreement had been reached for a number of joint venture shops, selling chocolates and cards, to be developed with the Birthdays Group (a 500-strong chain of greetings card and novelties outlets) as an experiment in serving small catchment areas. The lower rents and the attractiveness of the joint offer were to prove profitable and by 2001 the joint shops accounted for 40 of Thorntons' total of 400 'own' shops.

Thorntons' sales accounted for about 50 per cent of the market for premium boxed chocolates. Further research by the company had revealed that gift purchase was a key strength of the Thorntons business. It was announced that the company intended to reposition many of the company's products so that they were associated not only with such gift occasions as Christmas and Easter but with 'every occasion when people want to give a small gift' such as birthdays, exam success or job changes. The store environment was to be altered to gain more effective gift display. The product range and advertising messages were changed from 'there's lots in store for you', and the implication of personal indulgence, to focus on gift giving. Further growth was anticipated for the franchise network, despite its association with lower margins, and also for mail order distribution.

By mid 2001 the stabilisation phase of the plan was seen as having been completed on time with the company experiencing improved stock levels and reductions in selling and distribution costs. In addressing the second phase Mr Burdon stated in the 2001 Annual Report that Thorntons' vision was to become 'The UK's leading retailer and distributor of sweet special food' with the intention of markedly increasing their manufacturing and distribution to other retailers through Thorntons branded products as well as 'own brand', provided the product was 'indulgent and connected to chocolate and toffee'. Thorntons was to develop ranges of branded desserts, ice cream, sponge puddings, cakes and cheesecakes, biscuits and chocolate bars under the 'Thorntons Pure Indulgence' brand for sale through supermarkets. Licences would be arranged with suitable third-party food manufacturers. Further targeted outlets were to include pubs and restaurants. Thorntons' boxed chocolates and toffee would only be sold through the company's shops and franchise outlets, however impulse bars would also be sold through multiple grocers, initially with a 12-month exclusive supply arrangement with the Tesco supermarket chain.

Seasonal sales performance improved. For Christmas 2001 sales were 8 per cent higher than for the rather disappointing previous Christmas season. The internet, telephone and mail order service (which included options for combining chocolates with a bouquet, wine, perfume, cologne and toiletries, for individuals, weddings and corporate gifts) reported a 100 per cent increase in sales for the half year, with an average order value of £25 as against the average shop purchase of £7.

The annual report for 2002 focused upon the need to 'profitably lever . . . our greatest asset, the Thorntons brand'. Reflecting on the three-year turnaround plan Mr Burdon concluded that opportunities remained for significant organic growth and that future development should have this as its focus. Thorntons no longer intended to initiate the third year of the original three-year plan, the development of new growth options. The new strategic agenda would emphasise:

- *Brand values.* The clarity and consistency of all elements, such as product, packaging, shop environment and staff uniforms.

- *Support for retail activities.* Freeing store managers' time by simpler stock and planning systems; separate management structures for the cafés and the Birthdays joint-venture stores; developing the relationships and opportunities presented by third-party distribution.

- *Faster new product development.*

- *New café concept.* Aimed at doubling the number of cafés (from a total of 25) within two years.

- *Long-term shareholder value.* Through seeking new opportunities.

Seasonal sales continued to dominate Thorntons' revenue. In early 2003 the company's seasonal sales performance appeared to improve. In the two weeks' run-up to Valentine's Day 2003 the company sold 350,000 boxes of chocolates including 70,000 boxes of Eden. Directed towards younger women Eden combined such exotically named flavours as Forbidden Fruit, Grand Passion and All About Eve with chic packaging, pink lettering on a black box that was closed by a pink elastic 'garter'. Gross profit margins widened as new products were priced to encourage customers to trade up and poor selling products continued to be withdrawn.

However by Easter 2003 the UK chocolate market and Thorntons' sales became affected by what was to become the hottest summer in 30 years. Year end results to June 2003 revealed that like-for-like sales by the company's own stores had increased by only 0.9 per cent (1.6 per cent for the first half of the year). The Chief Executive's report stated that such vulnerability was expected to recede as the company increased its sales through other outlets. The ending of the exclusive supply agreement with the Tesco supermarket chain had been followed by further agreements being gained with other major confectionery retailers. Branded sales through other retailers had grown by 94 per cent during the year to a total value of £3.1m. Similarly royalties from licensed products had increased from £0.2m to £0.5m, commercial sales had grown by 25 per cent and sales by the Gift Delivery Service by 26 per cent to £5.3m. Long-term success, Mr Burdon stated, would best come from being a branded manufacturer operating through multiple channels to the customer.

New management and new directions?

The disappointing results for the year ending June 2003 brought critical comment from a financial press that had already become accustomed to Thorntons announcing warnings that profit targets were not being achieved. Questions addressed the longer-term failure of the company to develop its profitability and also the company's strategy, including the continued use of an extensive chain of own shops in a market where the supermarkets had developed their sales to account for over 50 per cent of UK confectionery sales. Within a few weeks the ownership of the company, in which the Thorntons family continued to control 29 per cent of the shares, was also opened to question by the proposal of a management buyout led by Peter Burdon and financed by a private equity firm. The intention was to return Thorntons to being a private company. On announcement of the news the company's share price rose 20.5p to 155.5p, its highest value for more than three years.

However, the price for control of the company was higher, 180p a share. By February 2004, with potential bidders unwilling to meet the required price, talk of a bid for Thorntons had disappeared. Two months later John Thornton signalled the end of 90 years of family management of Thorntons by announcing his retirement as the company's executive chairman.

APPENDIX

The UK confectionery market

UK per capita consumption of confectionery is one of the highest in the world. Within the UK market chocolate confectionery is viewed as an affordable treat, as part of snacking or a gift. The UK confectionery market is highly competitive with a great deal of product and packaging innovation. Manufacturers have tended to focus effort upon the chocolate sector, with its higher margins. The chocolate market after a period of steady growth has since 2000 shown signs of decline in both the volume and value of products sold.

UK confectionery sales (£m)*

	Total	Chocolate	Sugar
1993	4,415	3,038	1,377
1997	5,167	3,496	1,671
1999	5,462	3,750	1,712
2002 (estimate)	5,179	3,494	1,685

* £1 = approx. €1.5.

Mintel observes (November 2002) that compared to other food categories chocolate confectionery is 'highly indulgent', combining creamy chocolate taste, interesting textures and ingredients (such as caramel and nougat) to complement the chocolate content. The connotation of indulgence is often increased by the brand created for the product.

Chocolate market: sub-sectors

	Value share	
	1999 (%)	2002 (estimate) (%)
Countlines	45	43
Moulded bars	15	15
Boxed chocolates	19	20
Seasonal products	11	10
Bagged selflines	10	12
Total Value	£3,750m	£3,494m

Countlines: Wrapped chocolate bars designed for one person to consume. The sector is dominated by Kit Kat (Nestlé Rowntree) 16 per cent of countline sales value (advertising expenditure in 2002 £6.3m), Mars Bar 12 per cent. Between 1997 and 2002 this sector has experienced a slight decline in value of sales, partly due to the inability of new product development to counter the increasing attractions of alternatives for consumer expenditure (such as for teenagers, mobile phones and fast food) and the retail strength of the multiple grocers reducing daily opportunities for impulse buying.

Moulded bars: Chocolate as slabs or segmented, the product can be separated to be shared.

Boxed chocolates: The market for boxed chocolates is largely driven by gift giving for such occasions as Christmas, Easter and Valentine's Day. Since 1997 the value of the luxury/premium market has grown by 13 per cent. Within the boxed chocolates market brands occupy particular positions, Black Magic associated with romance, Roses informal expressions of thanks, Celebrations with sharing. Sales increases have been achieved by brands that emphasise sharing.

Within this sector competition to Thorntons is provided not only by the larger manufacturers, whose resources can sustain investment in product support (an average advertising to sales ratio of 3 per cent in 2000) and relaunch activity, but also smaller more specialist chocolate brands. The company Elizabeth Shaw, following success with their Famous Names range of liqueurs, launched Vodka Shots in 2001, designed to appeal to younger customers. Its success was followed by Mexican Tequila Shots and Imported Schnapps shots and The Collection, a sliding box of liqueurs launched in 2002, designed to appeal to ABC1 consumers aged 30–50. Certain retailers, for example Marks and Spencer, have high quality images that support the sale of own-label boxed chocolates as gifts. While a supermarket brand may not normally be appropriate for more than a casual gift occasion, retailers have addressed this deficiency by developing their own premium brands, such as Sainsbury's Taste the Difference. Often these products are innovative, for example Waitrose Chocolate Blueberries launched for Christmas 2000.

A number of international companies operate largely outside of the UK market. Leonidas, a Belgian manufacturer, has over 1,750 independently owned stores throughout the world (19 in the UK). The retailers receive supplies, at least weekly, from the company's three factories in Belgium. The retailer is allowed to add products of suitable quality produced by other companies to broaden the range of products available in the shop.

Seasonal products: This sector of the market includes all items that are packaged with a seasonal theme and are available for only a limited period. In 2000 Easter chocolate confectionery accounted for 66 per cent of the sales of seasonal chocolate, Christmas 23 per cent, followed by Valentine's Day 5 per cent, and Mother's Day 4 per cent. Value for money is becoming of less importance than the recipient of the gift liking the gift and the gift providing an appropriate celebration for the occasion. Recently manufacturers have found it difficult to present an increasingly sophisticated consumer with new items that will attract purchase.

As manufacturers Cadburys have market leadership in both the Easter and Christmas seasonal markets. Woolworths sold 20 million Easter eggs in 2003. Consumers showed themselves willing to purchase luxury Belgian chocolate eggs from Woolworths, but avoided the store's 'commodity' products.

Bagged selflines: Smaller chocolates sold in bags, examples include Smarties, M&M's, Mars Miniatures and more recently Toblerone.

Distribution

In 2002, 43 per cent of chocolate confectionery sales were through multiple grocers (1997, 39 per cent), CTNs 11 per cent (1997, 16 per cent), department stores 9 per cent (1997, 9 per cent), petrol forecourts 11 per cent (1997, 7 per cent). Despite the predominance of sales through multiple grocers brand sales account for over 90 per cent of chocolate confectionery sales.

Impulse sales are important in the chocolate confectionery market and are reflected in where confectionery is displayed in retail outlets. The growth of sales through petrol stations can be related to this factor and the absence of parking problems. Industry research has found that men tend to be associated with last-minute shopping and that impulse outlets such as petrol stations are an ideal place to attract them.

Source: Marketing data sources, Euromonitor, Mintel.

The News Corporation

Aidan McQuade

The case examines the corporate logic, business portfolio and corporate control style of News Corporation, which at the beginning of the twenty first century is one of the world's largest and most international media companies, in the main the creation of one man, Rupert Murdoch. It gives the opportunity for readers to consider if the bases of growth and the corporate management approach employed by Murdoch are sustainable in the future.

• • •

Introduction

'Family, religion, friendship: these are the three demons that you must slay if you're going to succeed in business'.

(Mr C. Montgomery Burns' advice to Lisa, The Simpsons)

Since its emergence as a national organisation in Australia and its subsequent emergence onto the world market, the activities of NewsCorp have been intrinsically linked with the motivations, personality and perceptions of Rupert Murdoch. He has described the ethos of the company as follows:

[W]e have always welcomed change. In fact, I like to think that we have helped to define the new world of media and entertainment. Our own evolution from a single newspaper to a multi-media, multi-platform global media company reflects our adaptability and agility; our constant search for new frontiers; our relentless pursuit of new and better products to serve our customers; our refusal to become complacent. Ours, indeed, is an entrepreneurial spirit.

For the year ending 30 June 2003, after two years of recorded losses, revenues at News Corporation (NewsCorp) reached over A$1.8bn (€1.04bn), and assets were stated as A$67.7bn (€39.27bn). Both the successes and failures over the years of NewsCorp and its subordinate businesses had almost entirely been the result of the strategic choices made by Rupert Murdoch.

NewsCorp – corporate logic

In a speech to the International Institute of Communications in September 1988, Rupert Murdoch suggested that he did not have a very detailed strategic plan:

If in 1980 we had attempted to chart on paper the destiny of our company, we would never have anticipated the 30 very diverse acquisitions we made on four continents, almost all of which arose from unique and unanticipated events. Business situations and business opportunities simply change too quickly for there to be much point in loading ourselves down with piles of strategic speculation.

Whether there was a formal corporate strategy or not, however, the expansion was plainly the product of Rupert Murdoch's strategic vision. Writing in the 2003 annual report, perhaps with the benefit of hindsight and reflection, Rupert Murdoch outlined a somewhat different vision of NewsCorp:

Throughout News Corporation's evolution our goal has been to create a Company as unified, as logical

This case was prepared by Aidan McQuade, University of Strathclyde, based on work by Julie E. Cooper, University of Reading, and with additional research and analysis by Delia Dias, Laura Greatrex, Anil Pandita, Dan Ridge and Matt Schneider, University of Strathclyde. It is intended as a basis for class discussion only and not for investment purposes or as an illustration of either good or bad management practice. © Aidan McQuade, 2004. Not to reproduced or quoted without permission.

of its affairs set against the actual figures for the week, and then compared with the same week in the previous year. Each Thursday it was passed to headquarters, with Rupert Murdoch studying it over the weekend. Control was also achieved by detailed telephone briefings and unannounced 'parachuting-in' trips to check in person on the details of a business's activities and management, or to take personal control at key moments. As one financial manager confirmed:

> He really is the driving force and most major decisions are made by him . . . even relatively minor decisions – like whether we start our TV burst of advertising now or do we put it back three weeks. Those are the sorts of thing that would be discussed with him before the final timings are decided. He does like leading from the front and where there's likely to be a bit of excitement he'll wade in. . . . I think his biggest advantage is understanding the businesses that he's in. He can get down to the core of the business and has a lot of vision as to where that business ought to be going.

and as creative as possible. Our vision has been one of a media company that is as well-integrated as it is international; one capable of delivering short-term results as well as building long-term value. We have worked to build a company with the agility to seize strategic opportunities when they arise, with the foresight to anticipate challenges and with little patience for conventional wisdom.

It was perhaps this effort 'to seize strategic opportunities' provided by 'unique and unanticipated events' that was most striking about Murdoch. One Australian financial analyst described him as 'an expansion-minded person, he's wanted to buy assets, he's wanted to take over, to move around the world, to build his media empire. But he also wants to retain control.'

Certainly such a high level of control has been central in the company's early growth and development. In NewsCorp's annual report for 1980, Rupert Murdoch noted:

> Over the years, expansion has been both by original start-up and acquisition. Typically, acquisition has been followed by a mobilisation of energies and talents to transform both the professional quality and the market performance of old or failing publications. . . . In virtually every market where [NewsCorp] operates, it has achieved its position by first purchasing the weakest existing publication and slowly restoring its viability.

He was known to have 'a proprietorial finger in every pie and on every pulse' (*Financial Times*, 24 April 1998); his management style was supported by an extremely efficient reporting system. This focused on a weekly document known as the 'Flash', for which each operating unit had to provide a summary of its operating results. These had to include the budgeted figures for every aspect

In more recent years, this retention of control of the business may be seen to be central in his ability to maintain his 'strategic agility' determining the priorities and focus of corporate development across the globe, frequently flouting conventional wisdom regarding the industry's driving forces.

Maintaining control also required that Rupert Murdoch looked outside of the business to the regulatory environment that might constrain his activities. Most governments believed that the media was an industry whose importance required regulation, particularly regarding foreign ownership, cross-ownership and concentration. Controlling a business with a global reach, with several media products, Rupert Murdoch was likely to find himself affected by national regulatory systems. Many commentators have suggested that his political friendships have bought him influence in this area.

For example, in 1979 the Australian government amended the rules regarding the foreign ownership of television stations, from a requirement that an owner be resident in Australia to one requiring only that an owner be an Australian citizen. This enabled Rupert Murdoch to acquire Channel 10 in Melbourne although he was no longer resident in Australia. These amendments were christened 'the Murdoch amendments' by the Australian press. Again, it was suggested that the support of Murdoch's newspapers for Margaret

Thatcher in the 1979 UK general election helped ensure that his acquisition of Times Newspapers in 1981 was not referred to the Monopolies and Mergers Commission, and certainly the government called a three-line whip to stop any referral.

However, as one commentator has put it: 'his personal politics are right-wing . . . but he's opportunistic in his business dealings. He doesn't support only right-wing leaders – he supports winners. And he supports people who are going to promote his business interests'. Hence his closeness to Bob Hawke, the former Labour Prime Minister of Australia, and support of Tony Blair, the British Labour Prime Minister from 1997.

Many have, however, doubted that Murdoch is guided by purely rational business motivations. In 1996 Ted Turner, a long-time business rival of Murdoch's, contrasted him with the executives of Time Warner. Where Time Warner 'just wanted to make money', Murdoch 'wanted to rule the world'.[1] One biographer, Neil Chenoweth, also noted how often Murdoch has been prepared to gamble the entire company, and occasionally his own personal wealth, on the success of his business deals. Chenoweth styled Murdoch 'a crisis junkie', implying that Murdoch may have followed such an ambitious and risky strategy of expansion partly because he enjoyed the buzz from successfully competing.

'There are two rules for negotiating with Rupert Murdoch. The first is that he is never quite where you think he is. The second is that there is a deal running underneath the main deal, with another deal running simultaneously underneath that'.[2] Chenoweth compared Murdoch to a poker player, but the breadth and complexity of his corporate dealings and the approach to business that Chenoweth described suggests that comparison with a chess master may be more apt.

Development of News Corporation

The origins of NewsCorp lie with the establishment in 1923 of a local newspaper, *The News*, in Adelaide, Australia, by Rupert Murdoch's father, Sir Keith. By 1980, Rupert Murdoch and NewsCorp had created that country's only national newspaper, *The Australian*, two national magazines and over twenty provincial newspapers. Interests in book publishing and television broadcasting had also been acquired, along with film making, record production, farming and transport interests.

The profitability of this Australian base was the springboard to multinational status. It provided the financial backing for the 1968 purchase of the UK-based News of the World Organisation, publishers of the *News of the World* (NOTW) Sunday newspaper. By 1980 the UK subsidiary was publishing not only the NOTW but also the *Sun*, both newspapers with consistently the largest circulation in the UK, and had interests in magazine and book publishing, printing, warehousing and transport. In 1981 NewsCorp added to its newspaper stable with the acquisition of Times Newspapers Ltd, publishers of *The Times* and *Sunday Times*. During the early 1980s, this UK subsidiary, with its newspaper interests, was the major contributor to NewsCorp profits, though at the price, according to many commentators, of driving downmarket the quality and standards of the print media in Britain, as he had already done in Australia.

From 1973, with the purchase of the Express publishing company of San Antonio, Texas, NewsCorp also operated in the United States. During the 1970s, expansion there occurred in the areas of local newspaper publishing (for example, the *New York Post* was acquired in 1976) and in magazine publishing (the *Star*, a national magazine, was founded in 1974; *New York Magazine* was acquired in 1977, as was, briefly, the *Village Voice*, a left-wing journal).

The 1980s saw NewsCorp accelerate its development. Early expansion continued to focus on traditional product areas of newspapers and magazines and by 1984, revenues had reached nearly A\$2bn. However, 1984 saw the beginnings of a major geographical and product shift. This expansion was US-focused. It aimed to transform NewsCorp into a vertically integrated global media group, with a place in all parts of that industry from newspapers to television, from magazines to film. In 1984, NewsCorp acquired the film company Twentieth Century Fox for US\$575m (€477m), and in 1985 paid US\$1.9bn (€1.58bn) for the six television stations of the Metromedia broadcasting group. These acquisitions provided the company with access to studios for making films and television programmes, to a film library of more than 2,000 titles, and to a distribution platform for that content. This was the basis of

---

[1] Chenoweth, N., *Virtual Murdoch*, Vintage, 2001.
[2] Ibid.

the Fox Broadcasting Company, which with its affiliated local stations managed to establish in the late 1980s a fourth national television broadcaster in the United States.

This expansion into the US had two significant implications for NewsCorp. Revenues and operating profits increased but so too did debt levels. Rupert Murdoch had to be careful that his acquisition, and the debt associated with them, did not breach private bank loan agreements, which required total borrowings not to exceed net assets by more than 10 per cent. Furthermore, as US law prevented foreign citizens from holding more than 25 per cent of any company with a broadcasting licence, in 1985 Rupert Murdoch became a US citizen, though NewsCorp itself remained an Australian company until in 2004, when Murdoch indicated his intention of making it American as well.

For Rupert Murdoch, this consolidation confirmed that:

> The News Corporation is now a multi-national, multimedia company . . . at the forefront of global marketing, ready to encourage the cross fertilisation of ideas between continents, and the different media within them. . . . The News Corporation is a citizen of the global village.

Writing in the 2003 annual report Murdoch identified what he saw as the advantage of such a position:

> One of the greatest advantages of a well-integrated worldwide company is our ability to respond to events with international strength: to share expertise, resources and personnel across platforms and across the globe.

Murdoch cited NewsCorp's coverage of the Iraq war (2003–) as evidence of this but such an approach has been characteristic of NewsCorp for years. For example, NewsCorp papers frequently promote NewsCorp satellite channels and vice versa. NewsCorp produced films, such as *Behind Enemy Lines*, have heavily promoted Sky News. Murdoch himself has even obtained a much-coveted cameo role in *The Simpsons*.

Entry into satellite broadcasting

During the second half of the 1980s, NewsCorp continued to expand and develop its traditional product and market areas. Significant acquisitions included the US book publishers Harper & Row and Triangle Publications, and the Australian *Herald and Weekly Times* (HWT). Although the issue of convertible notes (classified as equity finance) largely funded the acquisition of HWT, the increased debt involved with the acquisition of Triangle Publications was of such magnitude that Rupert Murdoch was obliged, in 1988, to commit NewsCorp to a significant debt reduction programme following a little reported financial crisis in 1987 that was only overcome by Murdoch guaranteeing the company with his own personal wealth.[3] This commitment, however, did not restrain the company from the launch in the UK on 5 February 1989 of Sky Television, a direct-to-home (DTH) satellite broadcasting television network. Satellite broadcasting represented a new approach to the distribution of programme material. Particularly, it provided the opportunity for any broadcaster to increase the 'footprint' (distribution) of any channel, allowing, for the first time, the distribution of programmes to more than one country.

Sky Television's origins went back at least as far as 1983 when, in his annual report, Rupert Murdoch disclosed that,

> In the past year, we have given careful study to the Company's options for the future, particularly in relation to the fast, emerging opportunities in electronic and satellite-assisted communications. . . . While we have every intention of continuing to build and strengthen our publishing enterprises we have reached the conclusion that at the same time we are advantageously placed for a strategic move into satellite broadcasting at an early stage in the development of that medium.

Following this, NewsCorp took a controlling interest in Satellite Television plc (SATV) which distributed English-language television programming by satellite to cable systems in Europe. SATV was first planned to function essentially as a distribution system with programming purchased from outside sources. The acquisition of Twentieth Century Fox and the restructuring of the US subsidiaries provided the opportunity for SATV to acquire entertainment and information programming from within the group. By 1988 the company broadcast four channels and was received by over 12 million viewers in 15 European countries.

In July 1988 Murdoch announced the launch of a new four-channel Sky service to be transmitted

---

3 Chenoweth, N., *Virtual Murdoch*, Vintage, 2001.

via a new satellite system called Astra based in Luxembourg. At the time, Sky was operating from slum offices in Foley Street in London's West End, the new Sky Broadcast Centre in Isleworth still a construction site. As for the staff involved, Murdoch 'had chosen to launch a multi-million pound venture with a handful of Australian TV cronies he had known for years – and not much else' (Andrew Neil, *Full Disclosure*, 1996).

Chenoweth, writing in 2001 of the decision to launch this initiative, commented that 'It is difficult [now] to appreciate just how knuckle-headed this decision must have seemed at the time' – given that all its experience in broadcasting thus far had been free to view and NewsCorp did not appear to have appreciated the particular difficulties associated with a direct to subscriber operation. Furthermore the decision exacerbated an already parlous financial situation for NewsCorp, following on the heels of the 1987 financial crisis. Hence the decision to launch such a costly venture seemed foolhardy.

To launch Sky ahead of its rival British Satellite Broadcasting (BSB), Murdoch brought in managerial talent from across NewsCorp. Andrew Neil, editor of the *Sunday Times*, became executive chairman in November 1988. Two further arrivals from Fox, Gary Davey, a creative programmer, and Pat Mastandrea, who knew about selling advertising in a competitive environment, strengthened the team. Tough targets were agreed and regularly monitored. The 24-hour news channel on which most of Sky's original (as opposed to bought-in) programming would appear was hastily put together:

> I insisted we take some of the programme formats of CNN and give them a British spin: they had already invented the wheel and I had no time to reinvent it. We took their popular *Crossfire*, a political debate show, and turned it into our *Target*, and CNN's *Larry King Show*, a talk/phone-in programme, and made it our *Frank Bough Show*. I also copied ABC's *Nightline* and called it *Newsline*. Formats that would have taken the BBC or ITV months or even years to launch were being piloted within weeks.
>
> (Andrew Neil, *Full Disclosure*, 1996)

The launch target of 5 February 1989 was met, but it was a low-key affair – it had been a rush, no one was sure it would work on the day and workers were still painting and fixing wires to the end.

Initially, the new Sky Television offered three of the 'own-brand', free-to-air, advertiser-supported channels that had been on SATV (with Sky Sports replaced by Eurosport). As before, these were distributed to cable systems throughout Europe. What made Sky Television different related to consumer hardware developments that had recently taken place. Individual satellite receiving dishes were now available at a price and size that made them affordable and usable by millions of households across Europe. This and new encryption technology to protect the content from the receivers of non-Sky subscribers opened up the possibility of a viable business model for Sky Television in the immediate future. Without such technology it is unlikely that they would have obtained any premium quality programming, particularly Hollywood movies.

UK media regulations barred national newspaper proprietors from owning more than 20 per cent of a television company. Even though Sky's programming was aimed mainly at a UK audience, Murdoch was able to evade this by beaming Sky's programmes from channels rented from the Luxembourg-controlled Astra satellite, though this technicality might not have been sufficient were it not for the close relationship that Murdoch maintained with the then British government of Margaret Thatcher.

There were fewer subscribers than expected, resulting in lower revenues. Although stringent cost reductions were implemented (one of Rupert Murdoch's maxims being that it was easier to take a million off costs than add a million to revenues), the performance of Sky Television had marked financial consequences for NewsCorp. In the year to 30 June 1990, £134m (€199.7m) had been invested in the venture, yet losses of nearly £10m (€14.9m) per month were being incurred.

Some respite was gained by November 1990, when Sky Television merged with its UK satellite rival, British Satellite Broadcasting (BSB). BSB had missed its launch date, commencing broadcasting in March 1990. Start-up costs here had also been higher than expected and the purchase of satellite dishes lower than expected. The merged company, BSkyB, was jointly owned by NewsCorp and BSB (although because BSB was a consortium, the next largest individual shareholder after NewsCorp held only 11 per cent). However, the new company came to be dominated by Sky Television. The Astra satellite channels and the technology used by Sky Television were adopted, redundancies following the merger occurred mainly among the BSB staff, and Sky executives came to dominate senior management, giving it operational and editorial control of the new company.

Financial chickens come home to roost

The financial risks that NewsCorp's radical expansion threatened finally overtook the company in 1990. These were exacerbated by a a protracted strike at the 50 per cent owned Ansett Airlines and a poor year at Twentieth Century Fox. NewsCorp was also investing £500m (€745m) in new printing presses in the UK. This was a heavy cash drain at a time when there was a slowing of the economies of each of NewsCorp's three main markets. These problems resulted in a gap in working capital financed by highly expensive short-term borrowing. At the same time, banks worldwide experienced a liquidity crisis that resulted in NewsCorp facing difficulty in refinancing maturing bank debt and in meeting working capital requirements. NewsCorp's market value fell to less than one-fifth of its 1990 A$11bn (€6.38bn) net asset value, while borrowings rose to five times stock market capitalisation. It became clear that, without some form of restructuring, the company would default on loans due for repayment in 1991.

In October 1990, the financial strain on NewsCorp finally came to a head when they called in Citibank of New York and began negotiations for the refinancing of its debt. At the time it was the largest and geographically most diverse corporate restructuring sought from international banks. Agreement to the restructuring was not automatic. The majority of problems developed following the discovery that original lenders had, quite legally, passed on some of their exposure to NewsCorp to other banks, without NewsCorp's knowledge. The result was that the company had to obtain unanimous agreement to the restructuring from a total of 146 banks. In February 1991, NewsCorp finally entered into a three-year, near A$9bn (€5.22bn) debt restructuring and A$700m (€406m) bridging loan agreement.[4]

Following this crisis by October 1991, NewsCorp had raised A$2bn (€1.16bn) through asset sales, and had announced plans for the flotation of 55 per cent of its Australian printing and magazine interests to raise a further A$700m (€406m). By the end of 1991, most of the A$1bn (€580m) debt repayment due in February 1992 had been paid, and it appeared that further obligations could be met from existing cash flows without raising new money. A

major restructuring of borrowing took place. This resulted in short-term private bank debt as a proportion of total debt falling from 80 to under 10 per cent, and the average maturity of public debt being extended from less than three years to over ten years. Debt repayments due in 1994 under the restructuring agreement were made early.

Lessons from BSkyB

BSkyB's main revenue is generated from subscriptions (74 per cent) totalling, from 7 million subscribers, over £3bn (€4.47bn) year ending June 2003, and there remained strong growth prospects in a UK market of over 25 million households.

Sky and BSB (and the subsequent merged company, BSkyB) were first marketed primarily as movie channels, for films receiving their first-time television screening, with Sky Movies becoming the first of the BSkyB channels to be subscription based. This was still seen as important, with BSkyB securing exclusive pay-TV rights to all major Hollywood films until 2002. However, in September 1992, BSkyB launched the Sky Sports channel, having secured exclusive rights to broadcast English football Premier League matches for five years. In less than six weeks, a million new subscribers were added. Rights to broadcast golf, cricket, rugby union and rugby league were subsequently acquired. A gap in the market had been identified that was to revolutionise the nature of sport, the finances of BSkyB and the broadcasting strategy of NewsCorp.

The unique value of sport was that it was inexpensive and easy to produce and best viewed live. It was therefore ideal for subscription and pay-per-view-based programming. Moreover, it was ideal for advertising, as it attracted those 'with the fattest wallet: man in the prime of life'.[5]

However, for a subscription-based broadcaster such as BSkyB it was important to be able to control the content that was received by the consumer to ensure receipt of all revenues due. Set-top decoder boxes and the use of encryption technology to securely 'scramble' and 'decode' the satellite signal, essential to enable Sky to launch in the first place, were again essential to facilitate this business development. Without these the consumer would be unable to watch programmes that had

---

4 Shawcross, W., *Murdoch*, Touchstone, 1994.

5 *The Economist*, 10 February 1996.

not been paid for and a rival content provider was unable to gain a distribution outlet. In the UK, News Datacom (NDS), a subsidiary of NewsCorp, controlled the only established technology at the time. Using NDS's proprietary encryption code, BSkyB sent viewers a smart card which, when inserted into the decoder box, allowed programmes to be viewed.

This has ensured full and appropriate payment for services provided by BSkyB. Furthermore, as one industry executive pointed out, the company 'is in a position to skim off money from anyone who wants to start a satellite channel'. Control of encryption technology made BSkyB a channel 'gatekeeper'. This means that for any other channel operator to get through the gate required the payment of significant fees to BSkyB. Bypassing the 'gatekeeper' required any new channel to establish its own encryption and marketing systems. Apart from the high investment and running costs, this would require viewers to buy a new decoder box to sit on top of their television sets. As a result BSkyB distributed the programme channels of other media companies via a series of joint ventures, owning, for example, 50 per cent of Nickelodeon UK and 25 per cent of the Paramount Channel.

The success of BSkyB's sports strategy made the company the most profitable television broadcaster in the UK. What provided value was the fact that the majority of revenues came from subscription. For the future, analysts believed that the company's exclusive rights to key programmes – films and sports – would drive the subscriber base forward:

> As critical mass is achieved and additional advertising revenues obtained, the strong cash flow generated will put the group in pole position to secure further sports rights and renegotiate the movie contract, which will in turn further stimulate subscriber interests.
>
> (Barclay de Zoote Webb)

In December 1994, the company made a public offering of 20 per cent of its shares for over £4bn (€5.96bn). This reduced NewsCorp's interest to 40 per cent, but its share of the flotation funds was a useful £600m (€894m).

Developing the US market

In 1995, the printed world of newspapers and magazines still provided over half of NewsCorp's profits. Existing newspaper businesses in Australia and the UK benefited from the reduced production costs resulting from the completion of capital investment programmes for upgrading printing facilities. British newspapers added new sections, which offered better-targeted advertising, and initiated aggressive price competition. In Australia, the company was at the forefront of the introduction of colour printing.

But increasingly, profits were coming from the screen, from films and from television. The mid 1990s was a time of intense competition in the US media market. The prize, in the words of Chenoweth, was control of the '200-million-plus single-language media market in the US . . . whoever won the US mega media wars of the 1990s would create a juggernaut too big for anyone else in the world to handle.'

> Indeed the economics of programme production meant that the only way to create a worldwide brand was to succeed first in the huge US market. It was the only way to achieve economies of scale. So the more that Murdoch expanded around the world the more he needed to make it in the United States. And here distribution was much more of a problem.[6]

As a relative newcomer in the US media markets, outside the established networks of NBC, CBS and ABC, and the existing cable operators, Murdoch was in the peculiar position of having access to some of the most critically and commercially acclaimed programming of the decade, including *The Simpsons*, but with limited distribution channels of his own. At the time programming was the resource that other media players regarded as the key to commercial success. Instead the focus of NewsCorp's expansion in the mid 1990s was on obtaining distribution channels.

The strategy of sports-led programming was viewed by Murdoch as his 'battering ram' for entry into new markets as had been demonstrated by BSkyB. So in 1993 in the US, the Fox group outbid CBS and paid US$1.6bn (€1.33bn) to obtain the broadcast rights to the National Football League's NFC games for four years and the 1997 Super Bowl. Fox also spent US$350m (€280.5m) to purchase the LA Dodgers, Lakers and Kings baseball teams.

Fox had also become a dominant player in local sports by accumulating stakes in numerous regional cable sports networks that collectively owned local TV rights to 70 of the 76 major league baseball, NBA and NHL teams. Thus Fox built

---

[6] Chenoweth, N., *Virtual Murdoch*, Vintage, 2001.

a national network by stitching together regional sports channels that televised local teams, often outbidding competitors in the process. Fox then wrapped its national programming around these local programmes. This was an alternative strategy to that of Disney's ESPN channel, which was the market leader in sports programming, but which focused on national programme events. Fox was therefore able to offer advertisers a unique alternative, a customised package of regional advertising that could in aggregate reach an audience bigger than ESPN. Fox was also able to sell the kind of local and regional advertising that ESPN could not.

This central battle of the mid 1990s for media giants to purchase television rights to the most popular sports events – European professional soccer, the World Cup, the summer Olympics and the leading North American professional team sports – sent fees soaring. To offset some costs in 1996 Fox and Tele-Communications Inc. (TCI), the leading US cable operator, established a joint venture as equal partners to create a global sports television network.

By 2000 through its combination of outright ownership of local television stations and its affiliated network, bound together by the quality of Fox's programming, Fox Broadcasting had the ability to deliver its programming service to 98 per cent of the total US network. In the future, station ownership would increase Fox's distribution position as a result of all US television stations being required to convert to digital by 2005. Each analogue channel could convert to six digital channels, increasing station distribution potential overnight.

Satellite broadcasting services began in the US in 1995 and by 2000 had more than 15 million subscribers (cable subscribers numbered 60 million). In 1996 NewsCorp and MCI paid US$682m (€566.1m) for the last unclaimed frequency and set up a new satellite television company, ASkyB. Through an alliance with Echostar in January 1997 Murdoch let it be known that he intended to eliminate the cable industry. This provoked a serious backlash by cable operators who threatened not to carry Fox's channels if NewsCorp began a satellite system in the US. In any event to carry out such a threat would have required a change in the US copyright laws to allow Sky to beam local television programming to all its customers across the US. When, by June 1997, it had become apparent that this would not be forthcoming NewsCorp backed out on its alliance with Echostar and

instead tried to forge an alliance with Primestar, a cable operator. When this deal was blocked by the Clinton administration as not being in the best interests of consumers, Murdoch was forced to sell ASkyB's assets to EchoStar for a deal that would have initially gained NewsCorp 37 per cent of the shares in Echostar but only 9 per cent of the votes. However the deal was structured by Echostar, bitter at what was perceived as a betrayal by Murdoch on their original agreement, in such a way that as Echostar stock prices rose the proportion of stock that NewsCorp would receive declined. In the end NewsCorp received only 1.7 per cent of voting rights and a proportionate decline in other stocks.

By June 2000 the company had the means to distribute its television content to 75 per cent of the world's population but the importance of the US market remained intact. By June 2003 81 per cent of NewsCorp's stated operating revenue and 76 per cent of its stated revenue was obtained from its US operations.

2003 also saw Murdoch finally manage to establish a satellite foothold in the US through the acquiring of 34 per cent of Hughes Electronics including DirecTV, America's biggest satellite operation with more than 11 million viewers. This deal was characterised by Murdoch in the 2003 annual report as a major strategic achievement.

Harnessing the potential of the 'Juggernaut'

Having obtained reliable distribution in the US market and the economies of scale that that brought, NewsCorp has been able to maximise the potential of their production capabilities across its entire global operation.

Good content has become increasingly expensive to produce or to purchase. In this situation Fox has had a number of advantages over the established US networks. As a start-up network, Fox could own as much of its own programming as it wanted, unlike the other networks which were hamstrung by legal limits and therefore had to buy more programming. Also, the Fox group included Twentieth Century Fox, which provided television and film programming. However, while Fox had the advantage of acquiring first-run programming from Twentieth Century Fox (purchasing over 50 per cent of its television output), internal sourcing was not the only route to acquiring good programming, and costs at Twentieth Century Fox have risen significantly. Thus Fox has not been shielded from the increasing costs of programme acquisition.

Besides films and sport, the other programmes to gain audiences are news and animation. As with sports programming, Fox trailed one or two of the other global media giants. Global television news has been the domain of Time Warner's CNN, but in 1996 Fox introduced the Fox News Channel to the US (and later globally) to better utilise the resources of NewsCorp as a whole. Despite its tagline of offering 'fair and balanced' news Murdoch was clear that that it would stand in opposition to CNN's 'left wing bias' and has consistently promoted a right-wing position.

Time Warner and Viacom have led in the global market for children's television with their respective Cartoon Network and Nickelodeon. Again, in 1996 Fox launched Fox Kids Channel. In the realm of animated feature-length films, Disney has enjoyed a virtual monopoly on output. However, animated films are ideal products for the global media market. There are no royalties to pay stars, large cross-selling and cross-promotional possibilities exist and they are easily dubbed into any foreign language. Fox (and Time Warner) has constructed new state-of-the-art digital animation studios to compete with Disney in this market.

Asia and STAR

As early as 1993, NewsCorp moved into Asia with the acquisition of the Hong Kong-based satellite television company STAR TV, which broadcasted free-to-air over China, India and 51 other countries containing approximately two-thirds of the world's population.

Initially, STAR was planned as a pan-Asian, English-language service, which would have been cheap to produce. However the diversity of the region indicated that such a pan-Asian approach was not viable. With the possible exception of Hollywood feature films, regional programmes in local languages were needed to make any impact outside English-speaking elites. Murdoch's strategy therefore became a variant of the 'think global, act local' philosophy, which in media terms implied a strategy of 'narrowcasting'. To that effect, STAR acquired the world's largest contemporary Chinese movie library and entered into exclusive agreements with prominent Hong Kong film companies. NewsCorp has subsequently launched

separate satellite services with costly local programming for India, the Philippines, Indonesia and China.

It was also clear that STAR would not be profitable remaining as a free-to-air service. While in the UK Sky moved to being a pay-for-view network with surprisingly little difficulty, the costs of developing such a network in the immature Asian market was great. Other problems related to how to find a *modus vivendi* with Asia's political leaders. In September 1993, addressing an audience in London, Rupert Murdoch had claimed that 'advances in the technology of telecommunications have proved an unambiguous threat to totalitarian regimes everywhere'. A month after this speech the Chinese passed a law that virtually banned individual ownership of satellite dishes. In response, Murdoch sold the anglophile *South China Morning Post* newspaper and STAR removed the BBC World Service from its northern Asia channel. Murdoch also offered authorities the opportunity of controlling satellite programming through NewsCorp's decoding technology. This would effectively allow censors to filter programmes to be broadcast.

Further problems arose in 2003 in India in a dispute with the Indian government over the ownership of Star India, a wholly owned subsidiary of NewsCorp. A 2002 Indian law limits any foreign partner in a media operation to 26 per cent of equity. Until the dispute was resolved Star News, a Hindi language TV news channel, was required to get Indian government permission to broadcast every seven days.

By June 2000 STAR was operating in 53 countries across 27 channels and reaching 80 million households and in 2003 NewsCorp reported that STAR posted its first full year of operating profitability. Writing in the 2003 annual report Murdoch attributed this to 'driving up both subscription and advertising revenues while improving efficiency'. Much of the new success of STAR was attributed to Murdoch's younger son James, who had headed up the operation until late 2003. Murdoch also anticipated further expansion in the Asian market with the development of Xing Kong Wei Shi, a Mandarin entertainment channel.

Elsewhere in Asia, by June 2000 NewsCorp owned 10 per cent of SkyPerfecTV!, which broadcast 168 digital television channels in Japan, reaching nearly two million subscribers. A little further afield, NewsCorp also has interests in pay-television services in Australia and New Zealand.

In November 1995, NewsCorp joined with three other television, programming and distribution groups to create a satellite service covering Latin America. These partners were Globo, Brazil's biggest media group; the Mexico-based Grupo Televisa, the biggest Spanish-language programming provider in the world; and TCI International, a subsidiary of Tele-Communications Inc. of the US. By June 2000 Sky Latin America had over one million subscribers.

Technological developments

BSkyB launched the UK's first digital service in 1998 delivering an increased range of channels and services to the subscriber using their culture to drive through the first mover advantage. It was the world's first television company to have switched all of its subscribers to digital. The transfer to digital was regarded as a costly gamble, involving the business giving away millions of set-top boxes worth over US$320 each. However operating profit for the year 2003 was estimated as reaching £321m (€478.3m), a 68 per cent increase on 2002.

By 2004 BSkyB's direct-to-home platform was fully digital, enabling a variety of added services. Essentially, this technology allowed for the distribution of significantly more data. However it is a technology that could be utilised by all the currently established distribution platforms – satellite, cable and terrestrial land-based. This would allow them to offer more programme channels (creating further demand for quality programming). By the end of 1997 most parts of the world had the opportunity to tune into at least 150 channels of digital television; in Europe the figure was over 500. Secondly, it allowed for the addition of new services such as video-on-demand and interactive television, allowing the consumer to decide what to watch and when. Thirdly, it allowed for the development of new products by offering internet access via the television.

Tony Ball, chief executive of BSkyB until 2003, suggested the future for the company:

> Sky has built a digital platform on which many different revenue-creating services can be delivered. Pay television is merely the first. . . . Sky's New Media Strategy is to develop and distribute our content across multiple devices and platforms and monetise the traffic through e-commerce, advertising and subscription.

Richard Freudenstein, COO of BSkyB, put a different perspective on the strategic direction for the company. 'Ten years ago in the analogue world, the thing that drove our business was the right to premier league soccer. Then we went digital and what you find is that the reason customers subscribe is choice'.

Technological development drove many of the competitive changes within the media industry throughout the 1980s and 1990s as traditional terrestrial systems of television distribution via aerial found themselves in competition with satellite and cable systems. NewsCorp has been involved with both of these new systems, fighting and generally winning, (albeit sometimes at great financial cost and risk to the company), distribution channels for the corporation's content. These technological changes went hand in hand with political changes in certain parts of the world that encouraged liberalisation and deregulation of national broadcasting monopolies or oligopolies.

For the future, unforseen technological developments may well be a driver of competitive change in the 21st century. However another plausible possibility may be that the development of broadband internet technology along with the rolling out of digital technology would mean that distribution channels become a given and the strategic focus of all media moves squarely back to content, and particularly gaining the rights to major sporting events. Whether technology would facilitate greater access to reliable information, international understanding and diversity of opinion in the mainstream media remains to be seen.

This may however give rise to yet another possible future where regulation catches up with technology and the advantages of 'gatekeeper' status given to NewsCorp by its encryption technology become substantially watered down in the name of ensuring competition and restricting the power of media barons such as Murdoch. It is perhaps with a eye on the restrictions that regulation might impose upon NewsCorp that its British papers have become vocal critics of the European Union and have begun to suggest that Britain should pull out.

The situation in 2003/04

In 2001 NewsCorp recorded a loss of A$746m which it attributed to a change in accounting policy which resulted in a 'one-off pre-tax charge to profit of A\$1,107m (€642m), with an associated tax benefit of A\$421m (€244.2m) in the fiscal year 2001'. The motivation for this change in accounting policy was stated as to ensure 'continued consistency with United States generally accepted accounting principles for producers and distributors of films'. Such a change may have been prepatory towards making NewsCorp an American company. However it may also have been an effort to secure investor confidence in the wake of the raft of corporate scandals in 2001.

NewsCorp's publicly disclosed finances had long been considered with some scepticism, and it was believed that their principal purpose was to facilitate corporate tax 'efficiency'. In the four years up to June 1998 NewsCorp and its subsidiaries paid only 6 per cent corporate tax, but a fraction of the 31 per cent by Disney for the same period. However by 2003, presumably as a result of the changes in accountancy practice, tax was stated as 25.8 per cent of overall profit on ordinary activities.

In 2002, NewsCorp recorded an even bigger loss of almost A\$12bn (€7bn). The company explained that this was principally the result of three factors. Firstly the company had been forced to write down the value of American football, baseball and motor racing contracts, which had been signed at a time when advertising was more buoyant. Secondly investments made in a German business Kirsch Media by NewsCorp, and KirschPayTV by BSkyB, were rendered worthless when the German company was declared bankrupt. Third there was a fall in the share price of two other businesses NewsCorp invested in, Gemstar TV Guide (a 44 per cent owned print, electronic and interactive programme listings company), and Stream, a 50 per cent owned Italian pay television service, leading to NewsCorp having to write down their book value. In addition, *The Sun*, a large-selling tabloid paper in Britain, became involved in a price war, additionally reducing NewsCorp's revenues.

While some of these problems, such as the loss of the value of the sports contracts, may have been unforeseeable, and the 'sports battering ram' had proven successful in the past, it was reported that it was Rupert Murdoch himself who insisted on BSkyB's US\$1.5bn (€1.2bn) investment in KirschPayTV reportedly against the wishes of Alan Ball, the then CEO of BSkyB.

NewsCorp recorded a profit of A\$1.8bn (€1bn) in 2003, and along with acquiring DirecTV also established a new Italian venture Sky Italia, with more than two million new subscribers and hence significant profit potential. NewsCorp transferred its stake in DirecTV to its subsidiary Fox Entertainment Group along with US\$4.5bn (€3.7bn) of debt and associated interest payments.

The future

NewsCorp's management structure has often been described as very informal by one aide, and as 'an emotionally driven and bonded company, where executives don't spend time guarding territories because nobody has one nailed down'. Another suggested that Rupert Murdoch's idea of management was to put in a manager and put in someone beside him, and not quite tell either of them what they were doing. A company executive confirmed 'I think he does do that. I don't think he does it to undermine the original person. I think he thinks that if the two can work off each other things will improve'.

Some have commented that he appears to be using just this approach with his two sons in determining who will succeed him as CEO of NewsCorp. In 1996, aged 65, Murdoch was asked which of his two daughters and two sons he would like to succeed him. He was quoted as saying: 'I hope we can work it out between us'; adding, however, that he would probably make a judgement about his successor in about twenty years. Until late 2003 Murdoch's elder son Lachlan appeared to be the heir apparent as deputy chief operating officer of NewsCorp and head of the unprofitable, but it is said beloved of Rupert, *New York Post*. In late 2003 however Murdoch, despite loud shareholder criticism, seemed to indicate a favouring of his younger son James by imposing him as CEO of BSkyB. Because BSkyB's shareholding is large and fragmented, fund managers were unable to prevent the appointment and James attempted to quell some criticisms by stating 'I work for BSkyB's shareholders and they are my only concern'. However, given that the single largest shareholder was NewsCorp, many shareholders remained concerned that in a situation where there was not a commonality of shareholder interests Murdoch junior might feel obliged to privilege some of Murdoch senior's more risky ventures to the detriment of the shareholders in the subsidiary business. This had already happened before James Murdoch's appointment in BSkyB, with the decision to invest in KirschPayTV paid for by suspension of dividends to BSkyB shareholders. It had also happened in Fox with it having to assume the debt of DirecTV. The digital change-over in BSkyB was also funded by the suspension of dividends.

Whatever Murdoch's feelings regarding the hereditary principle in NewsCorp, Andrew Neil, a former editor of the *Sunday Times* and Executive Chairman of BSkyB, has predicted that both NewsCorp and its founder would die together. Another biographer, Bruce Page, has suggested that there may be no adequate theory to explain Murdoch or his empire. 'NewsCorp may be the sprawling edifice of a hyperactive and authoritarian personality who has no overall objective other than constant activity and the wielding of power'.[7] Murdoch himself has stated that, 'For better or for worse, our company is a reflection of my thinking, my character, my values' (*Financial Times*, Profiles). Some thought that given such an intrinsic relationship between company and owner may indeed mean that NewsCorp is unable to be sustained in his absence and instead be broken up into its component parts.

Sources

Baker, R., 'Murdoch's mean machine', *Columbia Journalism Review*, vol. 37, no. 1 (May/June), 1998.

CBS News, 'Murdoch's News Corp on the move', 6 April 2004.

Chenoweth, N., *Virtual Murdoch*, Vintage, 2001.

Freedman, C., 'Citizen Murdoch – a case study in the paradox of economic efficiency', *Journal of Economic Issues*, vol. 30, no. 1 (March), 1996.

The Economist, 'Why Rupert Murdoch is polite', 9 April 1998.

The Economist, 'Rupert laid bare', 18 March 1999.

The Economist, 'Rupert's misses', 1 July 1999.

The Economist, 'Tangled webs', 23 May 2002.

The Economist, 'Rupert the invisible', 15 August 2002.

The Economist, 'Still rocking', 21 November 2002.

The Economist, 'Sky's the limit', 30 January 2003.

The Economist, 'Murdoch's twinkler', 24 July 2003.

The Economist, 'A man, a plan', 28 August 2003.

The Economist, 'Star turns', 25 September 2003.

The Economist, 'Like father, like son', 6 November 2003.

The Economist, 'A family affair', 6 November 2003.

Henriques, D.B., 'How the emperor got his clothes', *Columbia Journalism Review*, vol. 41, no. 4 (November/December), 2002.

Hickey, N., 'Is Fox news fair', *Columbia Journalism Review*, vol. 36 no. 6 (Mar/Apr), 1998.

Mehta, V., 'What's Murdoch up to?', *Nieman Reports, Fall*, vol. 50, no. 3, 1996.

Neil, A., *Full Disclosure*, Macmillan, 1996.

Strategic Direction, 'Forgotten people in News Corp success story', March, p. 151.

Shawcross, W., *Murdoch*, Touchstone, 1994.

---

[7] 'A man, a plan', *The Economist*, 28 August 2003.

APPENDIX

The News Corporation Ltd: financial data*

Statement of financial performance

FOR YEAR ENDING 30 JUNE
(A$ MILLIONS EXCEPT PER SHARE AMOUNTS)

	2003	2002	2001
Sales revenue	29,913	29,014	25,578
Operating expenses	(25,561)	(25,472)	(22,485)
Operating income	4,352	3,542	3,093
Net loss from associated entities	89	(1,434)	(249)
Borrowing costs	(1,000)	(1,291)	(1,268)
Investment income	209	291	333
Net borrowing costs	(791)	(1,000)	(935)
Dividend on exchangeable securities	(94)	(93)	(90)
Other revenues before income tax	679	5,627	3,335
Other expenses before income tax	(1,057)	(17,601)	(4,609)
Change in accounting policy before tax			(1,107)
Profit (loss) from ordinary activities before income tax	3,000	(10,959)	(562)
Income tax (expense) benefit on			
Ordinary activities before change in accounting policy and other items	(989)	(640)	(428)
Other items	215	(15)	19
Change in accounting policy			421
Net income tax (expense) benefit	(774)	(655)	12
Net profit (loss) from ordinary activities after income tax	2,228	(11,614)	(550)
Net profit attributable to outside equity interests	(418)	(348)	(196)
Net profit (loss) attributable to members of the parent entity	1,808	(11,962)	(550)
Net exchange (losses) gains recognised directly in equity	(4,064)	(3,021)	3,309
Items recognised directly in equity	152	(267)	1,060
Total change in equity other than those resulting from transactions with owners as owners	(2,104)	(15,250)	3,623
Basic earnings per share on net profit (loss) attributable to members of the parent entity			
Ordinary shares	$0.307	$(2.170)	$(0.174)
Preferred limited voting ordinary shares	$0.368	$(2.604)	$(0.209)
Ordinary and preferred limited voting ordinary shares	$0.344	$(2.431)	$(0.192)
Diluted earnings per share on net profit (loss) attributable to members of the parent entity			
Ordinary shares	$0.305	$(2.170)	$(0.174)
Preferred limited voting ordinary shares	$0.366	$(2.604)	$(0.209)
Ordinary and preferred limited voting ordinary shares	$0.342	$(2.431)	$(0.192)

* 1A$ = approx. €0.58.

Statement of financial position

FOR YEAR ENDING 30 JUNE (A$ MILLIONS)	2003	2002
Assets		
Current assets		
Cash	6,746	6,337
Receivables	5,701	5,809
Inventories	1,931	1,935
Other	483	566
Total current assets	14,861	14,647
Non-current assets		
Cash on deposit	698	
Receivables	1,219	796
Investments in associated entities	5,526	6,875
Other investments	1,195	1,712
Inventories	4,103	4,232
Property, plant and equip.	6,299	6,671
Publishing rights titles and television licences	32,724	35,348
Goodwill	377	455
Other	745	705
Total non-current assets	52,866	56,794
Total assets	**67,747**	**71,441**
Liabilities and Shareholders' Equity		
Current liabilities		
Interest bearing liabilities	33	1,856
Payables	8,298	8,073
Tax liabilities	714	848
Provisions	258	228
Total current liabilities	9,303	11,005
Non-current liabilities		
Interest bearing liabilities	12,396	13,585
Payables	3,545	4,054
Tax liabilities	666	434
Provisions	1,032	1,205
Total Non-Current Liabilities excluding exchangeable securities	17,639	19,278
Exchangeable securities	2,084	1,690
Total Liabilities	29,026	31,973
Shareholders' equity		
Contributed equity	28,427	28,239
Reserves	2,760	6,351
Retained profits	1,137	1
Shareholders' equity attributable to members of the parent entity	32,324	34,591
Outside equity interests in controlled entities	6,397	4,877
Total Shareholders' equity	38,721	39,468
Total liabilities and shareholders' equity	**67,747**	**71,441**

Statement of cash flows

For year ended 30 June 2003	CONSOLIDATED (A$ MILLION)		
	2003	2002	2001
Operating activity			
Net profit (loss) attributable to members of parent entity	1,808	(11,962)	(746)
Adjustment for non-cash and non-operating activities:			
Associated entity earnings, net of dividends	194	388	242
Outside equity interest	421	278	196
Depreciation and amortisation	776	749	706
Other items, net	90	13,179	1,342
Change in accounting policy after tax			686
Change in financial position:			
Receivables	(559)	(51)	(410)
Inventories	(206)	515	(889)
Payables	(657)	(396)	(395)
Tax liabilities and provisions	616	378	188
Cash provided by operating activity	2,483	3,078	920
Investing and other activity			
Property, plant and equipment	(551)	(505)	(1,113)
Acquisitions, net of cash acquired	(644)	(1,770)	(51)
Investments in associated entities	(794)	(942)	(1,714)
Other investments	(145)	(667)	(1,288)
Repayment of loan by an associate	170		
Proceeds from sale of non-current assets	167	4,284	2,387
Cash (used in) provided by investing activity	1,797	400	(1,779)
Financing activity			
Issuance of debt and exchangeable securities	3,172		1,496
Repayment of debt and exchangeable securities	(3,673)	(2,181)	(63)
Cash on deposit	(698)		
Issuance of shares	1,927	133	56
Repurchase of preferred shares			(91)
Dividends paid	(272)	(278)	(205)
Leasing and other finance costs	——	(7)	(5)
Cash provided by (used in) financing activity	456	(2,333)	1,188
Net increase in cash	**1,142**	**1,145**	**329**
Opening cash balance	6,337	5,615	4,638
Exchange movement on opening cash balance	(733)	(423)	(648)
Closing cash balance	6,746	6,337	5,615
Gross cash flows from operating activity			
Cash from trading operations			
Receipts	29,361	28,970	25,176
Payments	(25,561)	(24,423)	(23,120)
	3,800	4,547	2,056
Dividend and distribution receipts	48	38	86
Interest receipts	207	247	302
Interest payments	(1,084)	(1,324)	(1,225)
Income tax payments	(394)	(337)	(209)
Dividends paid on exchangeable securities	(94)	(93)	(90)
Cash provided by operating activity	2,483	3,078	920

Operating income by industry segment: 2003 versus 2002

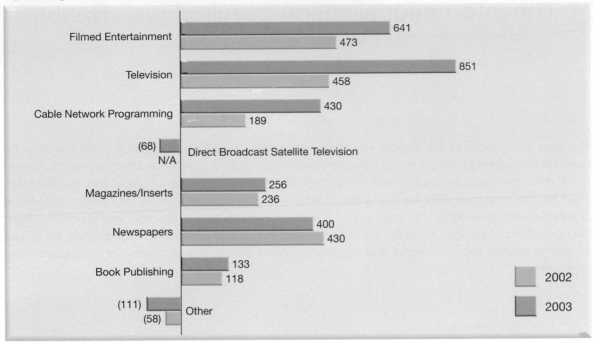

Revenues by industry segment: 2003 versus 2002

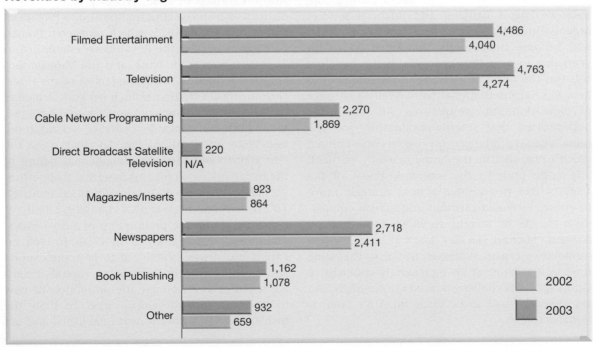

Note: These financial highlights are taken from the Concise Financial Report.

The internationalisation of Allied Irish Banks

Denis G. Harrington and Thomas C. Lawton

This case study explores the choices and challenges facing Allied Irish Banks (AIB) in their strategy for international market growth. It shows how the company diversified its revenue streams through international investment and acquisition and the limitations of international market expansion and management control for a bank with low brand recognition outside of its home market and limited experience of international operations. The case may be used to explore several strategic management issues: the competitive challenges faced by mid-sized companies in globally consolidating industries, the choice of foreign market entry strategies and the challenges of organisational control for internationalising companies.

• • •

Introduction

Soon after his appointment in 2001 as chief executive of the Allied Irish Banks (AIB) group, Ireland's largest banking and financial services organisation, Michael Buckley noted that revenues had become increasingly diversified in recent years due to overseas expansion. In his opinion, this was the result of a clear and resolute plan to be a top tier international bank. Well in advance of most domestic competitors, AIB executives had realised that internationalisation was the most effective strategy for expansion. Limited growth potential in the home market – particularly acute prior to the economic boom of the 1990s – had necessitated a bold strategic move to ensure increased earnings and market competitiveness. As he sought to move the company forward, Michael Buckley knew that he had to capitalise on past successes while at the same time take account of an increasingly competitive landscape. New challenges faced the company and key decisions had to be made on AIB's international activities.

The emergence of Allied Irish Banks

AIB was formed in 1966, bringing together three distinctive Irish banking traditions: the Provincial Bank, founded in 1825, which pioneered branch banking in Ireland; the Royal Bank, established in 1836 as a mercantile bank; and the Munster and Leinster, formed in 1885, the largest of the three, with the most extensive branch network. A merger of these three banking companies would have previously been unthinkable. However, Ireland in the mid-1960s was changing fast. An alliance was the best way to overcome the fragmented nature of the Irish banking sector and to seize the opportunities of an increasingly internationalised industry. The Irish economy was also changing rapidly at this time, under the premiership of Seán Lemass. The genesis of change lay in the 1950s. In 1952, an Export Board was established to promote exports and the government introduced capital incentive schemes to encourage the promotion of new industries in underdeveloped areas. In 1958, the Irish Industrial Authority was established and tax

Dr Denis Harrington is Lecturer in Strategy and Leadership at The Business School, Waterford Institute of Technology. Dr Thomas Lawton is Senior Lecturer in Strategy and International Business at Tanaka Business School, Imperial College London. © Denis Harrington and Thomas Lawton, 2004. Not to be reproduced or quoted without permission.

incentives, grants and other inducements were offered to encourage foreigners to establish new industries or new plants for their existing industries in Ireland. Moving forward, Ireland's accession to the European Economic Community (EEC) in 1973 had a profound effect on Irish industry, as did the Irish Industrial Development Authority's decision in the early 1970s to pursue a policy of encouraging such high-growth sectors as electronics, light engineering and pharmaceuticals. In the 10 years between 1973 and 1983, industrial exports increased by more than 10 per cent per year and in 1983 Ireland achieved the remarkable growth rate of 15 per cent, a figure far in excess of EEC and US figures. To take advantage of these changing conditions and emergent strategic developments, an alliance of the three banking organisations appeared to be the most effective option. The move represented the best way to overcome a fragmented banking industry and seize possible opportunities in the evolving marketplace.

In advance of most domestic competitors, AIB executives realised that internationalisation would be an effective strategy for market expansion. Limited growth potential in the home market – particularly acute prior to the economic boom of the 1990s – had necessitated a bold strategic move to ensure increased earnings and market competitiveness. The creation of a branch network in Great Britain in the 1970s was followed by an investment in the US in the 1980s. Allfirst, a wholly owned subsidiary of AIB, emerged from a 1997 merger of First Maryland Bankcorp (FMB), and Dauphin Deposit Corporation of Pennsylvania, becoming one of the top 50 banks in the US. The growth of the AIB Group escalated during the 1990s. The merger of its interests in Northern Ireland with those of TSB Northern Ireland created First Trust Bank. In 1995, AIB acquired UK-based investment management company John Govett. In addition, having done due diligence, AIB Capital Markets established twinning arrangements in Central Europe, primarily in Poland. In 1995, AIB took a minority shareholding in the Polish bank, Wielkopolski Bank Kredytowy (WBK) and in 1997, increased its stake to more than 60.2 per cent (making it a subsidiary company). In mid-1999, AIB acquired an 80 per cent shareholding in another Polish bank, Bank Zachodni SA. The combined bank, merged in mid-2001 to become BZWBK, one of Poland's top five banks by assets.

By the start of the new century, AIB had established itself as a dynamic and successful international banking and financial services organisation. At the time of its formation through merger in 1966, AIB's aggregate assets were IR£255m (€323.8m).[1] By the end of 2002, the AIB Group had assets of €86bn and operated principally in Ireland, Great Britain, the US and Poland. It employed over 31,000 people worldwide in more than 1,000 offices and operated through six main divisions:

- AIB Bank (Republic of Ireland) – focused on retail and commercial activities and also included Ark Life, the group's life and pensions subsidiary and other specialist businesses offering products such as credit cards and car finance.

- AIB Bank (Great Britain and Northern Ireland) – offered retail and commercial banking services. Traded as First Trust in Northern Ireland.

- AIB Capital Markets – comprised the treasury and international, investment banking and corporate banking activities of the group. Based in Dublin.

- USA – included Allfirst[2] (with 250 branches in the mid-Atlantic region of the east coast) and AIB US outlets in major cities such as New York, Chicago, San Francisco and Los Angeles.

- Poland – majority shareholding in Bank Zachodni WBK, the bank formed from the merger of Wielkopolski Bank, Kredytowy based in Poznan and Wroclaw-based Bank Zachodni. The bank had more than 400 outlets.

- Enterprise Networks and eBusiness – this division brought together most of the AIB Group's information technology functions. Its objectives included the development of the organisation's eBusiness strategy and investment.

AIB's position in the home market remained strong, with just under 43 per cent of its 2002 profits made in the Republic of Ireland. The company was widely recognised as Ireland's leading financial services organisation, slightly ahead of its largest domestic rival, Bank of Ireland. Both banks reaped the benefits of a booming domestic economy and large increases in credit growth during the latter half of the 1990s and early 2000s.

---

[1] The exchange rate value of the Irish pound has obviously changed during the 1966–2002 period. Prior to its replacement by the Euro currency on 1 January 2002, the Irish pound was valued at US$1.12 and 0.79 pence sterling (exchange rates on 1 December 2001).

[2] The ownership structure of Allfirst changed in 2003 as AIB merged Allfirst with M&T Bank, becoming the junior partner in the new entity.

Competitive dynamics in retail banking

The Irish context

The nature of AIB's internationalisation strategy can be explained in part through an understanding of the bank's competitive context both in Ireland and internationally. Retail banking in Ireland is dominated by the main clearing banks, which provide a full range of financial services based on comprehensive nationwide accessibility and the integration of service provision across all sectors (small and large, business and personal, etc.). This contrasts with many countries where there is still a strong segmentation in the banking sector between retail and wholesale banks. In Ireland, a significant number of smaller banks and building societies also compete with the major banks for retail customers. The two largest Irish banks, AIB and Bank of Ireland, are both publicly quoted companies and have raised the bulk of their capital through the Irish Stock Exchange. In each case, ownership is widely diversified, with over 100,000 shareholders, most of whom are private individuals with relatively small holdings. In the case of AIB, 41 per cent of shareholders own fewer than 1,000 shares each, while in the case of Bank of Ireland this figure is 54 per cent. Irish Life and Permanent is recognised as the third largest indigenous financial institution in the country and with the acquisition of TSB Bank it should see its position further improved in the years ahead. Behind these key players lie the Ulster Bank, Anglo Irish Bank and the National Irish Bank. The Anglo Irish Bank, with assets in excess of €1bn, has performed very effectively in recent years, prompting commentators to suggest that it may become a serious player in the Irish banking market.

All of Ireland's leading banking institutions reported strong profits and growth in the late 1990s and early 2000s and capitalised on the buoyant housing market, booming business banking profits and much lower write-offs than in previous years. Such profitability and growth had a significant positive effect on the Irish economy. For instance, in 1998, banks spent more than IR£1.8bn (€2.3bn) within the domestic economy, paying over IR£640m (€813m) to the exchequer in taxes. Banks are also one of the largest employers in Ireland, providing over 30,000 jobs in total.

In addition to banks, building societies (organisationally similar to US savings and loan institutions) have also provided retail banking services to Irish customers. Recent years have witnessed a decline in the number of building societies from sixteen in 1980 to three in 2000. Demutualisation has involved the conversion of two institutions into public companies, First National Building Society (now First Active) and Irish Permanent. The main reason for these changes was the restriction which mutual status placed on the ability of these institutions to expand their capital base. In 1999, Irish Permanent merged with the largest life assurance company in Ireland, Irish Life, to form Irish Life & Permanent, the third largest financial institution in the country in terms of asset size.

While banking institutions provide an important service to Irish customers, their role has changed and continues to evolve due to wider changes in the business environment. In particular, customers can expect to receive a wider range of services from their banks and experience new ways of receiving such service. As Irish banks face increasing competition from international operators and non-traditional financial outfits such as retailing organisations (e.g. Tesco or Marks & Spencer), they have been forced to rethink their attitude and approach to product development in general and customer service in particular. This has been intensified by the ongoing process of financial liberalisation at a European level, combined with technological developments, particularly the advent of e-banking. These forces have enabled Irish banks to increase the range of services that they offer to customers and improve the speed at which they respond to client queries and concerns. This process has been accompanied by the creation – although, as of 2004, not completion – of a single EU market in financial services.

The introduction of the euro also facilitated the integration of markets for financial services and increased the transparency of pricing across member states. With technological advances facilitating entry into the Irish banking market, or particularly profitable segments of it, these developments have contributed greatly to increasing the competitive environment in which banks operate.

These changes within the market have attracted considerable attention, particularly given their strategic importance for banking organisations. In 1999, AIB commissioned Dublin-based Amarach Consulting to undertake a '2010 Vision Report'[3] in

---

[3] *Business 2010 Report*, available online at www.aib.ie (specialist services). Also available through Amarach Consulting (www.amarach.com).

an attempt to forecast likely future trends within the market and in society more generally. The results reinforced the company's own view of the industry as being intensely competitive. But the research also highlighted the domestic challenges that lay ahead for the organisation. The author of the report, Gerard O'Neill, revealed that customers will become ever more knowledgeable and discerning as offerings increase and other operators enter the market. He remarked in the report that businesses will have to deal with customers who will have unprecedented choice of alternative providers and who will be confronted with totally new ways of buying and paying for products and services. According to analysts at Prospectus, another Irish consultancy company, banks will have to become used to this new environment and will have to adopt innovative practices to protect their positions. Judging from the number of changes introduced in AIB, this was not an uncommon view. Indeed change will be the order of the day for companies wanting to attract new customers. As a Prospectus report on the financial services sector puts it:

> A company that focuses on defending its historical entitlement will gradually be worn down. And with the current pace of change, defeat may not always be gradual.[4]

In particular, the report pointed to a number of areas that required attention from executives:

Increased competition

The most immediate threat has come from UK providers targeting the Irish market to increase the volume of their low margin products, through low cost channels. The Royal Bank of Scotland has been in the Irish market for some time through ownership of Ulster Bank. More recently, Northern Rock, MBNA and Bank of Scotland have entered the Irish market and although offering different value propositions (ranging from phone-based deposits to low interest credit card services and mortgage packages), these companies have reported a strong uptake of interest from Irish consumers. Commentators believe a pan-European brand to be the biggest future threat; however, a telesales or internet banking service to Ireland could equally

operate from the US. Such competitors are developing new business models to compete in Ireland. This should be of concern to AIB as most of these new models include a clear cost advantage through selective distribution.

Radical change in the status quo

Irish financial companies will no longer be in a position to apply defensive strategies or tweak existing strategies. Relying on the status quo will no longer suffice. Managing competitive threats with quick fix responses is a short-term approach. In light of the new competition, Irish financial institutions will need to roll out robust strategies to defend market share well in advance of the launch of new entrants.

These market challenges occur against the backdrop of a slowdown in the growth of the Irish economy (Table 1).

Table 1 The Irish economic outlook

Growth %	2000	2001	2002
GDP	11.5	5.9	3.6
GNP	10.4	5.0	2.8
Inflation (average)	5.3	4.9	4.8

Source: Mr Alan Kelly, AIB head of capital and group investor relations, 2002 and Irish Department of Finance statistics, 2003.

The global context

These changes and developments in Ireland are in line with that occurring in the wider international banking environment. Across Europe and the US, industry consolidation has been ongoing and there has been a scramble by many mid-sized banks to acquire other institutions in an effort to grow bigger and play at a different level. In the US for example, the ten largest banks and thrift holding companies control over 60 per cent of all US banking assets (see Table 2). Many of these underwent merger or acquisition activity during the 1998–2001 period, including the top two banks (Citigroup's acquisition of Travelers and the merger of Chase Manhattan and J.P. Morgan).

In Europe the situation is slightly different in that regulatory barriers mean that large banking organisations have difficulty in operating at a pan-European level. By 2004, few companies had been able to build strong competitive positions within the European market. In this sense many of

---

[4] Prospectus Report (1999) *Future channel warfare – a threat to the status quo*, online report, www.prospectus.ie.

Table 2 Top ten US bank and thrift holding companies by assets on 31 December 2002. Published 15 April 2003

Rank	Organisation	Assets ($000)
1	Citigroup Inc.	1,097,190,000
2	J.P. Morgan Chase & Co.	758,800,000
3	Bank of America Corp.	660,458,000
4	Wells Fargo & Co.	349,259,000
5	Wachovia Corp.	341,839,000
6	Bank One Corp.	277,383,000
7	Washington Mutual Inc.	268,298,000
8	Fleet Boston Financial Corp.	190,453,000
9	US Bancorp	180,027,000
10	National City Corp.	118,258,415

Source: American Banker Online (www.americanbanker.com).

the European banks have retained national status. However, change was underway across the EU, particularly in relation to cross-border mergers and alliances. For example, liberalisation has freed financial institutions to increase the range of services they offer, thus removing barriers to competition and making it difficult to distinguish between institutions. In addition, technology advances have also facilitated entry into national banking markets and have altered significantly the competitive environment in which banks operate. There has also been a trend towards increasing international integration of trade and investment in the last decade. This has been facilitated by the strengthening of international trade agreements that in turn have implications for the ways in which banks can operate and compete.

For Maurice Crowley, former AIB head of capital and group investor relations and subsequent chief financial officer at US subsidiary, Allfirst, these immediate issues have been examined within the context of the group's internationalisation process.[5] The bank recognised the requirement to expand carefully in an effort to build market share within specific regions. This idea was in keeping with above trends within the global banking industry. An Irish Government Report on the banking sector (2000)[6] revealed that the future is

likely to see a continued consolidation in banking at the level of individual countries with likely consolidation at a regional level – such as among banks in the euro zone countries. So new competitors are entering the Irish market, which traditionally included three to four institutions.

AIB's internationalisation strategies

UK market entry

The depressed economic conditions of 1970s Ireland prompted AIB to consider alternative routes to growing its business. There was a general consensus that the bank would need to look abroad for growth opportunities. Some commentators argued that the company had neither the resources nor the strategic vision to acquire or develop substantial market presence overseas. The group did lack the scale to compete directly with larger banks in markets such as the UK. As Aidan McKeon, Managing Director of AIB (UK), explained:

> Retail banking in the UK is a scale business (price and efficiency driven) and AIB had neither the capabilities nor the competencies to compete in this area.

Other strategic avenues would need to be explored if the group were to compete effectively in the UK banking market. One such avenue was to exploit the Irish ethnic market in the UK. Through effective marketing and event sponsorship within the Irish expatriate community in Britain, AIB emerged as the bank of choice for many – both individual customers and Irish-owned businesses. In this way the group established a viable bridgehead within the UK banking market.

In considering the firm's options for further growth, AIB executives pointed to the value of pursuing a niche strategy and concentrating on particular markets where the bank might compete effectively. In this sense, the bank's UK strategy would emphasise organic growth and market differentiation. Being different was important for the organisation. AIB would work hard to prove itself as more customer-oriented than any of its competitors. They would strive to work with the values of clients and to innovate in terms of service and product whenever possible. As Aidan McKeon commented: 'AIB's business in the UK is largely

---

[5] Maurice Crowley was interviewed for this case at AIB headquarters in Dublin on 8 March 2001. Further e-mail communications occurred during 2001 and early 2002.
[6] Review of the Irish Banking Sector (2000), Government Publications, Dublin.

niche and concentrates on providing quality service to SMEs, professional customers and the not-for-profit sector'.[7]

The company specialises in the 'straightforward approach' to banking, tailoring services to meet customer needs and providing relationship banking. Strategy in the UK market was therefore differentiation focused – AIB did not attempt to compete on cost or price. AIB (UK) emphasised relationship banking, focusing on providing personalised, quality service to small and medium-sized enterprises (SMEs) and professional customers. This strategy appeared to be paying dividends for the company. Independent surveys of banking practices reinforced the success of the AIB formula. In Forum of Private Business (FPB) surveys,[8] AIB significantly outperformed all the main high street banks as a provider of banking services and expertise to business. In 2002, AIB (GB)[9] was voted 'Britain's Best Business Bank' for an unprecedented fifth time in succession. The FPB survey, produced in conjunction with the University of Nottingham, analysed the responses of more than 6,500 British business owners and was widely regarded as the UK's foremost benchmark of business banking. This was an important independent measure of the bank's strategic approach and provided the group with an opportunity to evaluate itself against key players in the market. Clearly, the differentiated, customer-focused approach was working for the company.

Aidan McKeon put the success down to the bank's ability to develop and sustain quality relationships with customers. The superior service of AIB (GB) was exemplified in the FPD surveys by fewer customers considering switching banks, much lower rates of complaint and a higher level of customer confidence in advice from the bank. AIB (GB), one of the forerunners in relationship banking, scores highest in the survey for knowledge and understanding. The bank also scored highly on efficiency, reliability and customer satisfaction.

Through its relationship-oriented approach, the bank has earned a reputation for quality service that has proved difficult for others to imitate. AIB has invested heavily in developing its staff to meet the requirements of a more diverse and knowledgeable customer base. The group has gradually developed a banking presence and model that others are eager to learn from. A key success factor has been that each AIB branch has operated as a full service local bank offering a full range of first-class banking products, predominantly catering for the SME market. The results have shown that AIB (Great Britain and Northern Ireland) has been a significant profit earner for the wider group. For the year ended 31 December 2002, it turned a pre-tax profit of €240 million, up 8 per cent on the previous year. This sum accounted for more than 17 per cent of total group profits.

US market entry

The second stage in AIB's internationalisation strategy came in 1983, when the bank took a minority stake (49 per cent) in the US regional bank, First Maryland. This stake moved to 100 per cent in 1989. This wider and more ambitious entry into the large and highly competitive US market emerged from a willingness amongst AIB's senior management to extend their overseas market formula into selected parts of the US market. Although AIB had established a foothold in the US market during the 1970s with the opening of a New York branch (primarily serving the Irish expatriate community), US expansion began in earnest in the 1980s. AIB first bought a stake in First Maryland Bancorp and later increased it to 100 per cent in 1989. It made further acquisitions in the Maryland, Pennsylvania, Washington DC, northern Virginia and Delaware regions before re-branding the entire US operations under the Allfirst banner in 1999. Allfirst Financial Inc. became a regional, diversified financial services company headquartered in Baltimore, Maryland, offering a full range of financial services including banking, trust, investment and insurance to retail, business and commercial customers. In 2004 Allfirst had 250 branches and employed almost 6,000 people.

Despite the increasing uncertainties and general slowdown in economic activities, Allfirst reported net income to common shareholders of $184.4m for the year 2000, representing a 7 per cent increase over the year 1999 figure of $172.3m. Revenue

---

[7] Aidan McKeon was interviewed at the head offices of AIB (UK) in Uxbridge, Middlesex on 29 November 2001.
[8] Established in 1977, the Forum of Private Business is a UK pressure group working on behalf of more than 25,000 private companies to influence laws and policies that affect businesses (www.fpb.co.uk).
[9] The award was given to AIB 'GB' and not AIB 'UK' as Northern Irish businesses are not included in the survey.

grew a further 6 per cent the following year.[10] In 2001, Allfirst benefited from strong growth of 8 per cent in non-interest income from core banking activities, most notably 17 per cent growth in electronic banking income and 14 per cent growth in corporate deposit fees. These income streams were driven by both the acquisition of new customers and increased penetration of the existing customer base. Allfirst did not experience loan growth due to a decline in indirect retail loans, but was buoyed by a 13 per cent growth in home equity lending activities. Deposit growth of 10 per cent was achieved in the period, which primarily reflected growth in commercial deposits and resulted in Allfirst achieving the number one market position for deposits in the Greater Baltimore region. At the end of 2001, the company had financial assets of $18.8bn (€21.4bn).[11] According to Susan C. Keating, president and CEO of Allfirst at the time, the success of the company could be explained by its ability to anticipate and respond to changing customer demands and to keep abreast of non-traditional banking formats.

Despite these positive signs, some analysts questioned the rationale behind AIB's ownership of Allfirst, given its relatively listless revenue growth and high operating costs.[12] However, investors were willing to allow the bank time to consolidate its mainstream US market beachhead, seeing it as a key element in AIB's strategy to gain competitive advantage over archrival, Bank of Ireland.

To its credit, AIB (Allfirst), along with the Royal Bank of Scotland (First Citizen) and ABN-Amro (La Salle), are the only foreign banks to have successfully penetrated the US retail market. The key to the success of each has been a focus on building market share within specific regions.

Polish market entry

Buoyed by the success of AIB's entry into the UK and US markets, and following on from the firm's World Bank consulting work in the early 1990s, the bank's senior executives saw an opportunity to enter emerging markets. The former Soviet bloc countries of central and eastern Europe held particular appeal. This decision was not without its detractors. Concern arose about the logic behind the move. Some commentators questioned the company's ability to manage the transition to fundamentally different markets. The challenges were clear. First, there was the issue of successfully applying western management practices in a former communist country. Second, there were the cultural issues that at that time loomed large. Michael Buckley, AIB Group CEO, explained that from the group's perspective, language and cultural issues were major challenges for AIB:

> Language in Poland is a major problem. A different language means different concepts, different ways of thinking and different ways of reaching consensus and communicating decisions.[13]

Independent accounts pointed to the strategic benefits of entering the Polish market. These included:

- A domestic market of 39 million people
- A developing middle class/affluent segment
- An estimated small and medium-sized enterprise (SME) segment of 650,000 companies
- Projected EU accession in 2004
- Significant levels of foreign direct investment into Poland
- Low banking penetration among the general public.

Even so, there was a slight air of opportunism about AIB's entry into mainland Europe/Poland. In the late 1980s, AIB had a surplus of senior managers and many were consequently 'hired out' to undertake consultancy projects – e.g. for the World Bank in the newly opened economies of central and eastern Europe (particularly Poland, Hungary and the Czech Republic). These managers reported back to AIB Head Office on market opportunities in these countries. In 1993 the World Bank and the European Bank for Reconstruction and Development (EBRD) provided AIB with an opportunity, when they asked them to twin with a Polish bank. A common practice at this time was to twin

---

[10] These figures are prior to the February 2002 revelation that a trader at Allfirst had lost the company $691.2m as a result of fraudulent activities ongoing since 1997. As a consequence, Allfirst amended and refiled financial statements for 1998, 1999, 2000 and 2001 to account for the fraudulent foreign exchange trading activities. This put the restated net income to common shareholders at $197.8m for 1998, $141m for 1999 and $47.3m for 2000, with a net loss to common shareholders of $36.8m for the year ending 31 December 2001.

[11] Figures are prior to the 2002 fraud disclosure.

[12] Lina Saigol, 'AIB rules out any early disposal of Allfirst arm', *Financial Times*, 15 March 2002.

[13] Michael Buckley quoted in *Decision* magazine, February/March 2001, p. 38.

companies in the post-communist central and eastern European countries with a Western partner in order to tutor them in free market principles and practices. AIB had done due diligence on the Polish market and therefore chose WBK in Poznan. This twining led to AIB, in 1995, buying 16 per cent of the company for IR£16m (€18m). By 1997, they had increased their stake to 60 per cent, costing the company £95m (€114m). The remainder was quoted on the Polish Stock Exchange and proved difficult for AIB to purchase. The situation suited AIB in that they were happy to maintain the image of WBK as a Polish bank. By 1999, AIB had bought the ninth largest bank in Poland, Bank Zachodni, based in the southwest of the country. This move further strengthened its 'local branding, local profile' approach. AIB subsequently acquired permission to merge Bank Zachodni with WBK. The new entity was called Bank Zachodni WBK, or 'BZ WBK'. To reinforce their strategy of 'local brands for local markets', AIB chose not to put its name on the newly merged organisation. The merged Bank Zachodni WBK is a top tier bank in Polish financial services. Its major shareholder by 2004, with 70.5 per cent of shares, was Allied Irish Banks plc. The new bank has its head offices in Wrocław, while its corporate centres are located in Wrocław, Poznań and Warsaw. Post-merger, AIB became the fifth largest bank in Poland, with 7 per cent of the market. The group consequently hoped to further develop its services for customers. Gerry Byrne, head of operations for Poland, pointed to the following benefits for customers:

> Bank Zachodni WBK stakeholders can now look forward to benefiting from the combined scale, strong uniform product offering and focused quality service to customers.

The banking system in Poland was regarded as having considerable room for growth. Savings deposits, mortgage lending and credit card usage rates in Poland lagged well behind other former eastern bloc countries such as Hungary and the Czech Republic. Market analyst projections estimated a 40 per cent increase in mortgage applications coupled with a 36 per cent rise in credit card holders in the five years from 2000. Consumer lending was also expected to rise by at least 25 per cent, moving from 4 to 5 per cent of the population. Competition was intensifying as other companies recognised the potential of the Polish market. UniCredito was the biggest foreign bank in Poland. Bank Austria, ING and Citigroup also had Polish operations. In competition with these providers, the merger of WBK and BZ established a very strong business base for AIB in the west and south of Poland.

As in other regions, the Polish acquisitions underscored the nature of the bank's internationalisation strategy: to be a top tier *regional* – not national – operator in overseas markets. Notwithstanding the company's ability to compete in this market, there would be challenging times ahead for AIB in Poland. In 2001, gross domestic product grew by just 1.1 per cent – down from 4 per cent in 2000. Unemployment hit a record high at the end of 2001, reaching 17.4 per cent (3.1 million people). Also, domestic demand fell by 2 per cent, with the overall figure being kept in positive territory only by strong exports. However, the Polish economy stabilised during 2002 and BZWBK strengthened its market position. As a result, performance improved by 71 per cent, with pre-tax profit of €61m by the end of 2002, up from €36m the previous year.[14]

Entering and exiting Singapore

While AIB placed considerable emphasis on developing its UK, US and Polish operations, management was also keen to establish a presence in East Asia. Market developments suggested that locations in East Asia represented strong growth opportunities and AIB was eager to capitalise on this opportunity. AIB had treasury asset management and private banking operations in Singapore since the mid-1980s. The bank entered the Asian market in earnest in 1999 through a strategic alliance with Singapore-based Keppel Tat Lee Bank, acquiring one per cent of shares with an option to buy a further 25 per cent. The bank's holding company, Keppel Capital Holdings, was a financial services group offering a comprehensive range of services including consumer banking, corporate finance, international banking, treasury, asset management, capital market activities, stockbroking, bullion/futures trading and insurance.

In line with its strategic approach in other foreign markets, AIB was interested in Keppel Tat Lee due to its niche business in the mid/high-end consumer and SME markets. The Singaporean bank was also committed to providing innovative

---

[14] All figures are derived from AIB's Annual Report and Accounts 2002, for the year ended 31 December 2002.

quality products and good customer service. These market positions and organisational competencies coincided with those of AIB's operations in the UK, US and Poland.

AIB's initial premise for taking a stake in Keppel Tat Lee was to investigate whether or not the AIB banking model would work in Singapore. Due to impending government-backed consolidation of the Singaporean financial services industry, they realised that they may have to withdraw from the market at a relatively early stage. CEO Buckley explained the reasons for withdrawing from the Singaporean market:

> In reaching our decision to accept the offer [from rival bank OCBC to buy AIB's stake in Keppel], we were mindful of the trend towards consolidation in the Singapore market and believe acceptance to be in the best interests of AIB's shareholders. We have enjoyed a very good relationship with KCH and look forward to continuing a strong commercial relationship with them and OCBC into the future.

AIB withdrew from direct involvement in the Singapore banking market in mid-2001. In doing so, the company gained a substantial profit of €93m, from a minimal initial capital investment. The group maintains an investment management presence in Singapore.

Challenges ahead: overcoming the Allfirst fraud

The Allfirst/John Rusnak affair was the most visible example of control problems at AIB. In February 2002, AIB uncovered fraudulent activities in the foreign exchange trading operations at the Baltimore headquarters of its US subsidiary, Allfirst. John Rusnak, an Allfirst trader, had accrued huge losses on currency options over a five-year period.[15] The total pre-tax loss figure as of 8 February 2002, the end of the week the fraud was discovered, was $691.2m (€789m). That amount consisted of $291.6m in bogus assets, $397.3m in unrecognised liabilities, as well as $2.3m in legitimate trading losses incurred in 2002.[16] The crux

of the problem was that the bank failed to detect very large sums passing through the books of a tiny foreign exchange trading business. Although definitive responsibility rests with Allfirst's treasury unit management, ultimately responsibility resided with AIB group headquarters in Dublin.

The fraud dealt a severe blow to the bank's stakeholders. In and of itself, the financial damage was heavy, though absorbable. Unlike the Nick Lesson fraud that brought about the fall of Barings Bank in 1995, AIB was sufficiently large and financially robust to sustain the losses. More damaging was the way in which the episode preoccupied and undermined AIB's management for a considerable time afterwards. In particular, questions were asked both from within and outside the bank about how a mid-sized bank, not known as a major player in treasury markets could have made losses of this order.[17] Furthermore, shareholders needed to be reassured of the bank's continued viability as an independent organisation. Speculation abounded during 2002 of merger with archrival Bank of Ireland and even a possible takeover by non-Irish companies such as the Royal Bank of Scotland.

Once the fraud story was released to the markets, senior management began the daunting task of restoring credibility and repairing the damage done to the bank's brand image. A core task was to rapidly overhaul the internal controls set up by the group to monitor its subsidiaries. As Allfirst chief executive, Susan Keating admitted in a press statement: 'Clearly, controls broke down and we don't wholly understand how these broke down'.[18]

The then AIB Chairman, Lochlann Quinn, acknowledged the scale of the problem, suggesting that the Allfirst debacle was a blow to the bank and to its credibility. However, the problem as he saw it was even wider than the financial losses involved. He noted that the people who were really annoyed were the staff, most of whom were extremely dedicated and took pride in their company.[19] Mr Quinn argued that these people had been badly damaged. The company could rebuild credibility over time and by the fact that the actions taken were seen to be appropriate and fair

---

[15] At the time of writing there is no evidence to suggest that Mr Rusnak actually stole any money. Rather, it appears that he defrauded the bank by developing a scheme to cover up losses he had incurred.

[16] These figures are derived from the report of the independent investigation (the so-called 'Ludwig Report') commissioned by the Boards of AIB and Allfirst, March 2002.

[17] *Financial Times*, 'When Irish eyes are crying', 7 February 2002.

[18] Susan Keating cited in John Murray Brown, 'Internal controls to be scrutinised', *Financial Times*, 7 February 2002.

[19] Lochlann Quinn interviewed by John Murray Brown, 'The man at the centre of a gathering storm', *Financial Times*, 26 February 2002.

but it would be an altogether different task to regain the trust of employees.[20]

On 12 March 2002, the independent report commissioned by AIB's board was released.[21] Dubbed the 'Ludwig Report' after Eugene A. Ludwig, former US Comptroller of the Currency and the report's principal investigator, its findings exonerated the bank's senior management of any culpability but reproved them for failing to detect Mr Rusnak's fraudulent activities at an earlier stage. The report stated that:

> Allfirst's treasury missed some critical opportunities to detect Mr. Rusnak's fraud . . . Beyond this, Allfirst treasury personnel failed to give sufficient attention to issues about Mr. Rusnak's trading that were identified . . . There is no evidence that the front office supervisors scrutinized each of Mr. Rusnak's trades. And the back office did not always confirm the end of day prime settlement. All of these control failures would be exploited by Mr Rusnak. (pp. 19–21)

According to the Ludwig Report, there were a number of reasons why the fraud occurred and why it was not discovered for a period of years:

- The architecture of Allfirst's trading activity was flawed. The small size of the operation and the style of trading, produced potential risk that far exceeded the potential reward.
- Senior management in Baltimore and Dublin did not focus sufficient attention on the Allfirst proprietary trading operation.
- Mr Rusnak was unusually clever and devious.
- Treasury management weaknesses at Allfirst also contributed to the environment that allowed Mr Rusnak's fraud to occur.
- The proprietary currency trading business was inadequately supervised.
- Risk reporting practices should have been more robust.
- No policy and procedures review existed.

The report made it clear that the AIB Group, including Allfirst personnel, deserved credit for having taken immediate corrective and responsive action after discovering the fraud. Overall though, the report concluded that a flawed control environment existed at Allfirst's treasury operations department. A key recommendation was that AIB should conduct a careful and thorough review of risk management architecture throughout the group. The report findings and recommendations were accepted and rapidly acted upon by the AIB Group Board. Industry commentators argued that the scale of the breakdown in management control revealed by Eugene Ludwig's report presented AIB's chief executive with a serious strategic dilemma.[22] Was AIB's international presence sustainable, particularly in the US, or had the organisation over-stretched its resources and competencies? The implications for AIB's internationalisation strategy were likely to be significant and far-reaching.

Within a year of the Allfirst debacle becoming public knowledge, it was apparent that AIB's 'Main Street USA' market presence was on the wane. The *de facto* acquisition of Allfirst by US regional banking firm, M&T Bank, was approved by both M&T and AIB shareholders in December 2002. The US$3.1bn deal created a top-20 US bank with pro-forma combined assets of approximately $49bn. AIB management described this deal as an alliance allowing AIB to 'reposition and strengthen' its involvement in US regional banking. However, AIB emerged as very much the junior partner in the new combined company (controlling just over 22 per cent of the shares), indicating that AIB appeared in fact to be gradually withdrawing from large-scale US retail banking. AIB had learned a costly lesson with Allfirst that forced them to realise the management control limitations that can arise for mid-sized international companies. This resulted in a partial de-internationalisation, with the group's top management team preferring to concentrate resources and effort on more lucrative and less risky elements of their international operations.

---

[20] Mr Quinn interviewed in the *Irish Sunday Times*, 10 March 2002.

[21] *Report to the Boards of Directors of Allied Irish Banks, plc, Allfirst Financial Inc., and Allfirst Bank Concerning Currency Trading Losses*, submitted by Promontory Financial Group and Wachtell, Lipton, Rosen and Katz, 12 March 2002.

[22] Lina Saigol, 'AIB rules out any early disposal of Allfirst arm', *Financial Times*, 15 March 2002.

APPENDIX
Financial Data

Profit and Loss account

2001	€m	2002	Change %
3,751	Total operating income	3,930	5
2,284	Total operating expenses	2,318	1
1,467	Group operating profit before provisions	1,612	10
204	Total provisions	251	23
1,263	Group operating profit on continuing activities	1,361	8
1,366*	Group profit before tax	1,375	1

* includes profit on disposal of Keppel TatLee

Operating income

2001	€m	2002	Underlying change %*
2,258	Net interest income	2,351	7
67	Other finance income	62	–7
1,426	Other income	1,517	6
3,751	Total operating income	3,930	6
39.8%	Other income ratio	40.2%	

- 15% increase in banking fees and commissions
- Challenging year for Ark Life – underlying operating profit down 4%

* excludes the impact of currency movements and acquisitions

Risk weighted asset and loan growth*

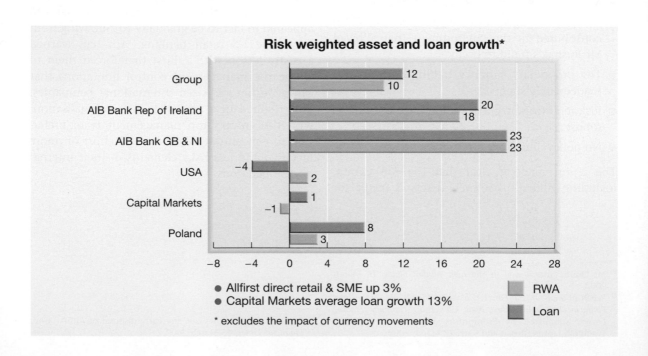

- Allfirst direct retail & SME up 3%
- Capital Markets average loan growth 13%

* excludes the impact of currency movements

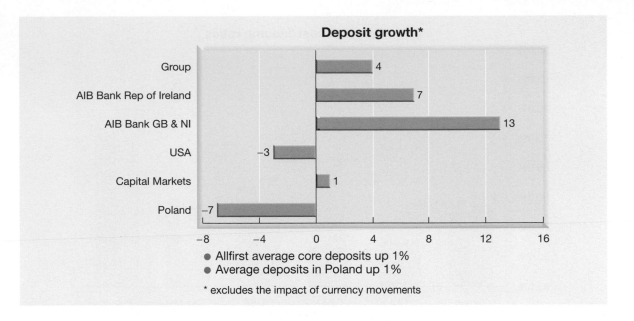

Deposit growth*

- Allfirst average core deposits up 1%
- Average deposits in Poland up 1%

* excludes the impact of currency movements

Operating expenses

2001	€m	2002	Underlying change %*
1,348	Staff costs	1,391	4
703	Other costs	707	3
195	Depreciation & amortisation	207	8
2,246		2,305	4
38	Integration costs	13	
2,284	Operating expenses	2,318	3
59.0%	Tangible cost/income ratio	57.8%	

* excludes the impact of currency movements and acquisitions

Performance by division

2001	€m	2002	Change %
562	AIB Bank Rep Ire	590	5
223	AIB Bank GB & NI	240	8
355	USA	308	-13
194	Capital Markets	209	8
36	Poland	61	71
(4)	Group	(33)	
1,366	Group profit before tax	1,375	1

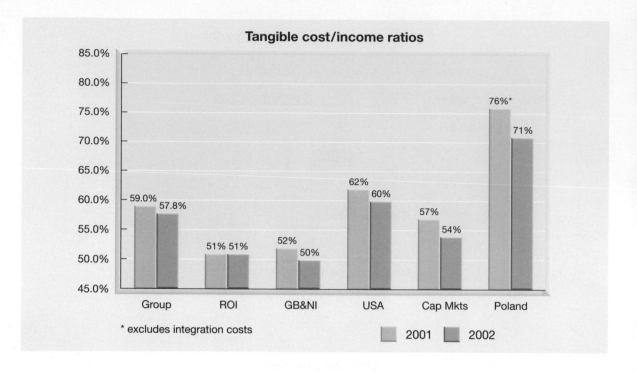

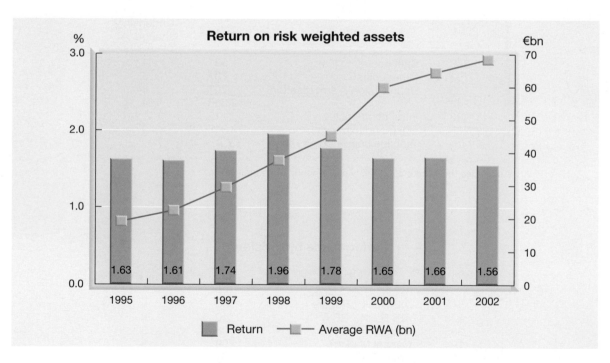

Mantero Seta Spa: a strategy for China

Valeriano Lencioni and Daye Zhang

Valeriano Lencioni and Daye Zhang

Mantero Seta Spa, a textile company from northern Italy, was a leading player in the silk area for the production of high-end fashion accessories and garments. They were a business-to-business operation, and sold their products to the best fashion houses in the world. In the mid 2000s, however, geopolitical factors and industry structure had severely affected their profitability and they were looking for new markets and new buyers. One option they were considering was entering the Chinese market to distribute products on licence, with a view to becoming later a business-to-customer operation that would market its own brands. This case looks at some of the circumstances surrounding the plan.

• • •

Background

One Friday evening in January 2004, the executive team of Mantero Seta Spa, who met weekly to discuss top management matters, was in session far longer than usual. On the agenda, only one item: 'A strategy for China'. The discussion was animated, even heated. Something had to be done. Mantero, a leading player in its area, had been badly affected by the crisis that had hit the world textile industry following the terrorist attacks in 2001 and the SARS crisis. This was coming on top of a global economic slowdown that had shown few clear signs of improvement. The changed circumstances had led Mantero's managers to radically reconsider their strategy in relation to the products they sold, the markets they served and the buyers to whom they sold their products.

They all agreed that it was essential for the success, perhaps even for the survival of the company that they entered new emerging markets: China seemed the natural choice, as they already had an office there that dealt with the supply of silk fibre and yarn. What they could not agree on was how to do it.

A number of options were put forward by the directors: each was found to have some attractive advantages, but also some serious disadvantages.

None was seen collectively as a clear-cut option. The CEO, on calling the meeting to a close, asked each of the colleagues to work out a full proposal on the method of entry into the Chinese market, initially to distribute products under licence, later as a business-to-customer operation marketing Mantero's own brand.

The fashion business in the mid 2000s

Overview

Fashion was defined by Paul F. Nystrom as 'nothing more or less than the prevailing style at any given time'.[1] Two important facts can be derived from this concise definition: a style is not fashion unless it is commonly accepted (prevailing); fashion is transient (at any given time). These characteristics of the fashion phenomenon had profound implications for the supply chain, the product life cycle and the complexity of the markets served by the industry.

[1] P.F. Nystrom, *Economics of Fashion*, New York: Ronald Press, 1928, p. 4.

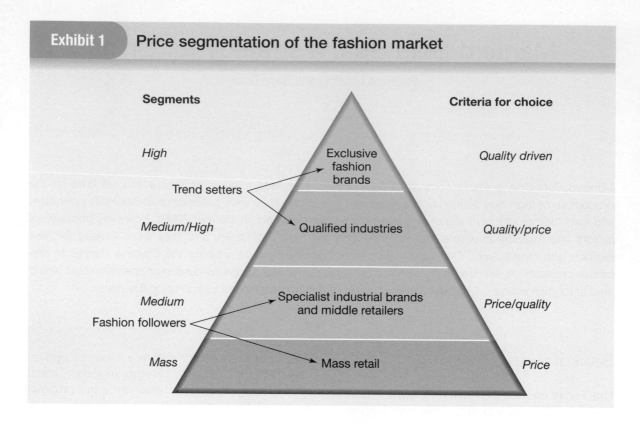

Exhibit 1   Price segmentation of the fashion market

The supply chain

The textile and clothing industry was very diverse and heterogeneous, with activities ranging from the production of raw materials (i.e. natural and man-made fibres) to the manufacture of a wide variety of semi-finished and finished products.[2] Textile specialists worked two years ahead to shape the general trends for each fashion season, for the coherence of new products with existing stylistic identities and for the coordination of collections and their marketing. Large fibre associations provided information on trends in colours, yarns, and fabrics at least 18 months ahead of the season. This information was then related to fabrics (in wool, silk, cotton, linen) and used as a guide for buyers.

Product life cycle

The speed at which clothing markets changed was high, with very short product life cycles. Many fashion items had product cycles as short as half a year, or even a few weeks. Consumers' preferences depended on the season, on the social and cultural

_____
[2] 'The textile and clothing industry in the EU, a survey', *Enterprise Papers*, no. 2, 2001.

environment and on the effects of previous marketing communication for fashion items or substitute products. Responding in a timely way to these changing demands was vital for success.

The market for fashion products

The characteristics of the fashion industry required companies to make strategic choices about factors such as quality, speed, technology, price, and flexibility: these factors defined the positioning of a company. Price segmentation was articulated as *high*, *medium/high*, *medium* and *mass* segments. The distinction was driven by the quality and price of the products. (See Exhibit 1.)

Fashion trend-setters were the customers in the high and medium/high market segments: they demanded products with innovative styles, realised in exclusive fabrics with top-level craftsmanship by fashion designers that had built the reputation of powerful brands. The haute couture and well-known designer brands occupy this segment. Examples of players in these segments are Christian Dior, Chanel, Yves St Laurent, Gianni Versace and Givenchy.

Some fashion houses, given the high quality expected of their products and the short product life cycle prevailing in fashion, adopted a vertical integration, which afforded them a full control of quality and operations.

Fashion followers crowded the medium and mass market segments, and purchased products from The Gap, Zara, H&M, Benetton and the like. To satisfy the needs of fashion followers, who sought value for money and shopping convenience, companies in the medium and mass segments had to follow the trends in the higher segments and reinterpret them for the crowd of followers. Effective and efficient distribution channels were necessary to handle the volume of goods, and sufficient flexibility was required to respond promptly to changing demand.

In the textile industry, the bargaining power of the suppliers was moderate: fibres and yarns were basically commodities, displaying little or no differentiation beyond the relative quality of the goods. Also, it was unlikely that suppliers had a credible ability to integrate forward. Competitive advantage was gained by using various suppliers and seeking new sources, in an attempt to reduce the bargaining power. The power of buyers was greater: the concentration at the fashion houses level, however, had raised the bargaining power of buyers from suppliers of the likes of Mantero. They had the ability to appropriate part of their suppliers' profits. This was a very important issue for every business-to-business operation in the supply chain, because it depressed the profitability of all the operators upstream of the fashion houses. The houses too were coming under pressure from changing consumer spending pattern and motivation. The intensity of rivalry between competitors in the fashion industry normally was high because of the over-capacity in the industry and because of the pressure on prices. In particular, in the high and medium/high segments, due to the high cost of production capability and high exit barriers, the competition was high, increasingly also on price.

Due to macro-economic pressures, the strategic management of clothing companies had undergone considerable changes, starting in the mid 1990s, and many fashion companies had chosen to establish joint ventures with lower cost manufacturers, mostly in developing countries.

Fashion markets in China

China's market for luxury goods, unlike western markets, was not mature. In the mid 2000s, stable economic growth had brought substantial income to many groups of people, and with it a growing demand for the satisfaction of higher level needs. They sought a high quality of life with entertainment, good health and a comfortable environment. Upper-class and middle-class people became increasingly interested in their social life, and chose to spend money to better enjoy their spare time. There was a huge potential to sell luxury goods to these groups: 2 per cent of the 1.3 billion people living in China (about 600,000 people in Shanghai alone) were potential buyers. These consumers displayed a desire to spend their money on everything that could make them stand out from others, in a confident and even ostentatious display of wealth. Consumers able to purchase luxury goods chose established brands marketed by foreign companies, mostly European. This explains why, in 2000, almost 80 per cent of the world's international luxury brands had moved into China's markets.

The old theory of the State managing the State-owned companies was being dismantled step by step: the companies that were replacing them adopted a corporate strategy with emphasis on profit-maximisation, and concentrated on developing a competitive advantage. More and more private companies grew under the new system, with fresh perspectives and an open mind policy. This was especially so in the fashion industry, because of its relatively low entry barriers.

China's accession to the World Trade Organisation (WTO) opened the doors to foreign companies, with new legislation to attract investors. As a whole, the worries in western countries that China would play unfairly on the road to reforms were revealing themselves unfounded: China's imminent full accession to the WTO would guarantee its accountability to a system based on western rules.[3] A distinct advantage deriving from operating in the Chinese market was represented by the lower cost of raw materials, labour, internal transport, energy and communication. For example the average labour cost in China was €1.5 per person per hour; in Europe it was €13.

But there were also some threats. At the end of the first quarter 2004,[4] the GDP growth was 9.7 per

---

[3] S.S. Roach, 'Why we ought to be thanking the Chinese', *Fortune*, vol. 149, no. 5, March 2004.

[4] B. Bremner *et al.*, 'Headed for a crisis?', *Business Week*, 3 May 2004.

cent, inflation 2.8 per cent (up from 0.9 per cent a year earlier) and GDP per head $1,120 (≈ €930). China, with its 1.3bn population, had a vast reserve of well-qualified labour force. The level of inflation was relatively low but growing fast, raising some concern about the sustainability of the high level of economic growth and consumption. A further threat was the undervalued currency: it was difficult to envisage how long China could keep its currency fixed to the dollar at such a low rate. If the financial authorities were unable to manage a gradual and painless adjustment, the resulting currency turbulence could badly affect foreign companies' profitability. Further, SARS had created havoc in 2003, and sporadic cases were still occurring in the mid 2000s. The government was adopting a policy of openness that would help clarity of information, if not public health, in the case of an epidemic reoccurring.

Fake fashion luxury products were appearing almost everywhere in Asia in the fashion market, and in China the practice had become a threat that worried greatly all foreign companies. Some fashion houses, for example Valentino and Yves St Laurent, had had to withdraw from the Chinese market to save their brand identity and reputation. The Chinese government was very concerned about this problem and was introducing legislation to protect the Register of Companies and patented brands. But China was a huge market, largely regulated by rather autonomous local authorities: this made it difficult to ensure a full protection. Companies that planned to enter the Chinese market had to devise their own strategy to cope with this threat. The increasing earning differential between city and country dwellers, capable in principle to lead to civil unrest, and to revive Tiananmen Square memories in investors, was generally seen as a distant threat. Finally, the banking structure in China was inefficient and the services provided were limited.

The level of technology and techniques used in China's textile industry in the mid 2000s were still at the level western textile industries had been in the 1970s and 1980s. Great attention was paid to the technical training of workers and to R&D. CAD tools had been introduced in China in the mid 1990s from Japan but only limited use had been made of them by small and medium companies or self-employed designers. In very few Chinese fashion companies was it possible to find a strong product R&D team. Innovation and creativity were therefore weak.

Fashion retail distribution in China

Retail identity was embodied in a company's offer to the market: it derived from the chosen distributive concept, i.e. location, channel, assortment, points of sale, communication and level of service. The government had adopted a series of policies to propel the retail industry through a process of fundamental transformation. The move had sparked dramatic changes in Chinese retailing, with market growth reshaping purchasing habits. As a result in the mid 2000s there were many different types of retailing methods, based on different products and market strategy. Affluent consumers had become mature and rational through the exposure to a wide range of products, and had grown keen on consumption of high quality products. These factors affected both markets and consumers, and encouraged innovation of retail formats. In the mid 2000s, the retail network in China included department stores, franchised services or chain-store outlets, warehouse discount stores, supermarkets, convenience stores and specialty stores, shopping centres, catalogue sales, TV home shopping and e-commerce. In particular chain stores, starting from the early 1990s, had enjoyed a substantial growth, primarily in Beijing, Tianjin, Shanghai, Guangdong and other coastal cities whilst catalogue sales, TV home shopping and e-commerce were not yet significant trends.

However, as lifestyles had become more dynamic, more and more people, especially from younger generations, accepted these new retail formats, notwithstanding obstacles such as payment methods.

In China, most international companies linked up with independent agents or local partners who, it was hoped, adopted an appropriate retail identity and, through high commitment and entrepreneurial flair, made possible the implementation of the company's expansion. Anecdotal but growing evidence suggested that this was not always the case, making the choice of a local partner a crucial issue.

Geographical differences

History, customs, culture and attitudes had caused different features to emerge in different regions, particularly between the north and the south of China, divided by the Yangzi River, with the north and south of the country offering different prospects to the retail industry. The reasons for the differences were various. In northern China, the nature of the four seasons was marked, with very cold winters and hot summers, so consumers made choices based on seasonal factors: they chose fur, leather jackets and the accessories to protect them from the cold; lighter and cooler fabrics, such as silk, linen and cotton were chosen for the summer season. In spring and autumn, knitwear, cashmere, wool and other kinds of heavy fabrics were used. Values and beliefs of people in north China were based on their imperial history and social traditions, with clear distinctions between different social groups and classes. The distinction was underlined in many ways, including clothing. People in the north were aware of their appearance, and wanted others to recognise their wealth and ability. In the south the climate was temperate; therefore consumers chose lighter, more comfortable and durable material for everyday wear. Lifestyle was more relaxed; social attitudes were more reserved than in the north: they were aware of others, but kept themselves to themselves. The majority of people dressed simply and casually, which made it difficult to tell their class and wealth. Those who could afford to pay high prices still liked to spend on good quality clothing from well-known brands, albeit, often, of a casual kind.

About 20 per cent of consumers in large cities occupied the high and medium/high market, and purchased products that were distributed in department stores, hotels, boutiques and franchise stores. Cities with more than one million population had one or two department stores that covered an area over 20,000 square metres and sold more than 80,000 varieties of products. These large department stores, with products ranging from designer label brands to local well-known brands and including fashion accessories, cosmetics and food, were known as the first line stores, and affluent customers enjoyed shopping there. In these major cities, there were also two or three second-line department stores, less well-known than the first-line department stores. Most of the five star or four star hotels displayed in their elegant shopping halls well-known brands that attracted resident customers as well as a small percentage of non-resident wealthy consumers. These attractive locations were also used as showrooms to reinforce brand images and establish their stylistic identities. Specialty stores and franchise stores were not mature enough in China to support a distribution strategy.

Marketing communication

Communication processes in the fashion business focused on the brand image and the values embodied in the product, rather than on the product itself. Processes included photographs, shows, showrooms, models, displays, videos and sample collections. Fashion companies used internal and external agents to manage their communication process, which involved the coordination of public relations agencies, event agencies, advertising agencies, press offices, art directors and specialised agencies for artistic sponsorship. Great effort was put into making each of the expensive communication tools enhance the companies' competitive advantage and stamp their products in the consumers' minds.

In the Chinese fashion market, communication had grown remarkably in the five years to the mid 2000s: many newspapers had fashion sections; news stands were overflowing with glossy fashion magazines and periodicals; more and more communication channels dealt with the fashion industry. However, compared with the global fashion industry, Chinese fashion communication was still at a rudimentary stage.

Channels of communication

Fashion shows and fairs

In general, fashion shows were a most important communication tool. They were the visible exhibitions that allowed designers to present their innovations, creations and their interpretation of current trends. Fairs were traditionally most important for the business-to-business function, but because of the emerging availability of alternative communication tools, fairs were increasingly used to connect more closely with the final consumer.

In China, fashion shows had had great appeal since the 1990s: every year in Beijing, Shanghai and Dalian there were well-attended and widely publicised fashion weeks that involved a vast range of communication activities. The results were obvious: some brands, such as Baoxi Bird, Lanbao and White Collar, had acquired solid identities and strong competitive advantage from their presence in the fashion shows and exhibitions.

Media

Worldwide, a wide range of media were used for effective communication. The press was the most important due to its widespread readership and advertising impact. Most of the daily newspapers had a fashion section of information related to fashion goods. The press had the advantage of targeting specific social groups. Advertisements in newspapers provided a durable, impressive coverage, particularly if it was linked to authoritative editorial content. Magazines were becoming more focused on specific groups of buyers. There were many specialised fashion magazines, and their content was not just clothing, but also accessories and furniture: all of great interest to those who like to follow the changing fashions. Trend setters, due to their habit of reading newspapers and magazines, purchased products advertised in the press more than others.

Television and videos, both on tape and compact disc, were the direct and shortcut processes that, due to their visual power, delivered the message straight to the mind of the consumer. Many television channels had fashion programmes including a few fashion channels dedicated to clothing, e.g. FashionTV. Videos were very effective in presenting and promoting products: they were played in showrooms, stores, fashion shows and fashion education establishments. The use of videos was particularly suitable for business-to-business communication.

In the mid 2000s Chinese people spent much of their spare time in front of the television set, so television was a very important tool for marketing communication. Also most consumers still perceived the information received from television as authoritative and useful to decide on their purchases. In recent years they had learned about fashion and started to follow the trends, usually based on the messages put across on television. Advertising on television was very expensive but effective and some large companies such as Seven Wolves and Baoxi Bird had realised considerable profit by investing in a few minutes of advertisements.

Potential for communication in terms of channels, information technology, editing capabilities and targeting, was promising, and in the five years to the mid 2000s many advertising companies had been established. They took in many ideas from the global market, eager to import and practise the knowledge and technology practised by western firms.

Catalogues and the internet

In China, as elsewhere, catalogues had been a traditional communication tool in fashion. They were originally used in the relationship between manufacturers and distributors to show collections. In the mid 2000s, companies rarely printed catalogues, apart from a few to display in the store: the main reason was their high cost. Media based on information technology such as the internet had replaced them. Regular consumers preferred to visit the internet or to receive personal service before examining a new collection in the store.

Mantero Seta Spa

Overview

Mantero Seta Spa, in the mid 2000s, was an Italian textile group leading the silk area in the design, production and distribution of fabrics and accessories. They employed 921 people, had a turnover of €133m and exported just over 70 per cent of its products. They produced quality fashion accessories and some garments, mostly in silk but also in other materials. They produced under contract for fashion houses or under licence which also included distribution. Their clients were some of the top fashion houses in the world. Mantero had a century-old history of partnership with top designers and international fashion chains. Due its extensive R&D activities, advanced technology, superior craftsmanship and dedicated consultation with its customers, it realised top quality products that displayed the company's capability for innovation and creativity. The company started in the early 20th century as a family business, and the family still largely owned and controlled it more than a hundred years later, in the mid 2000s. However, in the early 2000s, the CEO hired a team of highly capable professional managers, who modernised and enhanced the management processes. That management capability was instrumental in introducing the changes that were needed to cope with the rapid evolution of the global fashion industry. One of such changes was the company structure, which had grown into a number of largely autonomous divisions difficult to coordinate and often in competition with each other. The result of the review was a unitary structure largely based on functional lines.

The company

Mantero in the mid 2000s was a highly integrated company that performed most of the operations

Exhibit 2   Investment in 2003–2004

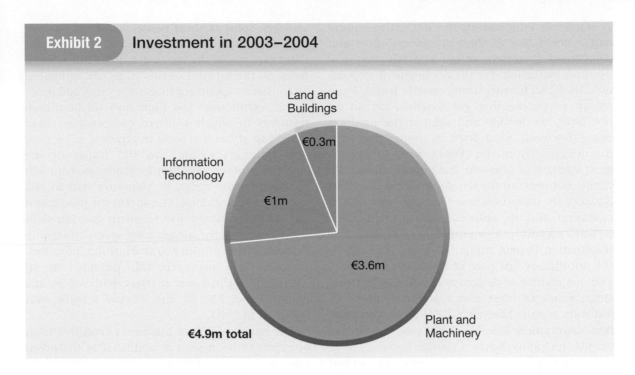

Land and
Buildings

Information
Technology

€0.3m

€1m

€3.6m

€4.9m total

Plant and
Machinery

that were needed to turn silk (and some other) fibres into the very desirable products that were sold at very high prices in glittering establishments around the world. It played a superior role in the supply chain of many companies operating in the high and medium/high segments of the fashion market. Some small-scale, more specific, operations were contracted out to a network of small highly specialised companies.

Starting from the early 2000s, Mantero's buyers, albeit competing in the exclusive market segments that were associated with significant price inelasticity, were affected by a number of geopolitical factors: a global economic slowdown, terrorist activities and SARS in the Far East. The combined effect of these factors was a marked pressure on their profits, a situation that lately had been further exasperated by a strengthening of the euro. So fashion houses, which often were part of large groups of companies, used their centralised purchasing departments, capable of very high bargaining power, to obtain favourable purchasing conditions from suppliers. This issue represented a real problem for Mantero, which saw its profit squeezed by the buyers despite the excellence of the products it created and despite the efficiency of its operations.

The company had an office in Paris and one in New York for sales. Starting from the mid 1980s, it also kept an office in China for the supply of raw materials.

Mantero had built a well-developed sales network of its finished licensed products. It had 69 agents and 1,800 doors (points of sale) for men's accessories and 36 agents and 2,200 doors for women's accessories all over the world.

It combined its manufacturing expertise and vast experience with constant investment in state-of-the-art technology and a remarkable production capacity. In the early 2000s, most companies, textile or not, reviewed their financial strategy to cope with the economic crisis: Mantero reacted by reducing investments in the production process, especially the dyeing technology. However, to maintain the high standard of 'Made-in-Italy' and its ability to keep its position in the fashion supply chain, Mantero transferred the investments to the finishing machinery, warehousing and market development, also including a modest investment for the future development of the Chinese market. As a result, the company allocated an investment or €4.9m for the year from August 2003 to August 2004. Exhibit 2 shows the distribution of the investment.

Mantero's resources and competences

The resources and competences possessed by Mantero were centred on three main areas: reputation, design, production methods.

Mantero's long history and distinctive culture had fostered two of their unique resources and competences: creative design and effective relationship marketing. For the development of products, they had formed strong creative teams: loose groups of people that got together, on an ad hoc basis, to develop and support the products being processed, most often in conjunction with the designers from the client's firm. This was a great strength of Mantero: the teams could advise clients not only on the design of the product, but also on its harmonisation with the rest of the collection and its coherence with the house's stylistic identity. A sophisticated Management Information System supported a fast response to the notoriously fast pace of the fashion industry. The rich archive of designs and models was a precious source of ideas and a powerful means to innovate within Mantero's 'DNA'. The company had distribution licences with very prestigious brands, including *Kenzo, Christian Lacroix, Emilio Pucci, Celine, Gianfranco Ferre, Trussardi, Ungaro* and *Cacharel*. Some of these houses had been on contract with them for over ten years. Mantero provided expertise at the top end of the textile market, based on the superior quality of its silk, enhanced by constant experimentation with yarns and innovative techniques. The high and medium/high segments in which Mantero competed required individual styles that were interpreted to propose new solutions focused on the reality of the customer's needs: constant feedback on them was provided by the ability of Mantero's staff to talk and listen to customers. To support the production process the company had excellent drawing skills and colour artistry; a high level of craftsmanship supported the printing and finishing processes. Education for managers was provided at all levels, and an in-house Masters delivered by the Politecnico di Milano, the 'Pegaso' scheme, was launched in 2003.

The next meeting of Mantero's executive team promised to be at least as animated as the previous one.

Coopers Creek and the New Zealand wine industry

Heather Wilson and Maureen Benson-Rea

This case describes the growth of a medium-sized New Zealand winery – Coopers Creek. It is concerned with the changing collaborative arrangements employed by Coopers Creek to service domestic and international markets since its inception. These changes are set against the background of a small, rapidly internationalising industry within a global market environment. Readers are encouraged to analyse Coopers Creek's value chain configuration over time in the context of the changing value system/ network in order to consider future strategic options.

● ● ●

Background to Coopers Creek

Between 1990 and 2004, Coopers Creek and the New Zealand wine industry experienced significant environment, industry and organisation change resulting in shifting network arrangements to meet domestic and international demand. Supermarkets were emerging as a major buying force for the industry, although consumer demand appeared to be fragmenting around new grape varietals and wine styles. New Zealand wineries continued to achieve strong growth in international markets but operated under the constraints associated with variable grape volume and exchange rate fluctuations. In addition, while Coopers Creek maintained its independent status, most of the larger and many of the medium-sized New Zealand wineries were being sold to global liquor companies. As Andrew Hendry, the owner and managing director of Coopers Creek commented: 'There are only a few New Zealand owned wineries left in West Auckland. . . . And there are companies overseas moving around wanting to buy medium-sized wineries, and quite a few have sold, so one day I guess something interesting will turn up.' It was against this background that Andrew Hendry was seeking to position Coopers Creek for the future.

The Coopers Creek winery was established in 1982 on four hectares of land in West Auckland

Photo: Coopers Creek

Photo: Alamy

---

using a 40 per cent bank loan, 20 per cent equity capital from Andrew and 40 per cent equity from a combination of the original winemaker, grape suppliers and former colleagues of Andrew's from Coopers and Lybrand. All but one of the grape-supplier shareholders have since sold their interests, despite experiencing capital gain, deciding that they could no longer operate on both sides of the fence; as suppliers they wanted to negotiate the highest price, but as shareholders they wanted to bargain for the lowest price. Meanwhile, the remaining grape-grower shareholder, with a focus on producing Chardonnay, was still supplying Coopers Creek. Apart from the original winemaker selling his shareholding to Andrew when he returned to the US, most of the other shareholders had retained or increased their shareholdings. In 2004, Andrew's family trust owned 72 per cent of Coopers Creek.

Coopers Creek acquired an additional vineyard in the Hawkes Bay, North Island, in the 1980s and, in the 1990s, the phenomenal export-led growth (see Table 1) led to the purchase of additional land for its own plantings in West Auckland and the Hawkes Bay, as well as buying grapes from independent growers in Marlborough, South Island, and Gisborne, North Island. This meant that, by 2000, the company had managed to spread the risk of adverse weather conditions in any of the four major New Zealand growing regions. Andrew further diversified the Hawkes Bay land interests by leasing another vineyard and developing a joint venture with the owner-grower of another. While interested in purchasing land in Marlborough, Andrew was content to continue leasing land and purchasing under contract for 2004 until prices stabilised: 'Currently the Marlborough prices are a bit crazy and it is likely there's going to be a bit of oversupply down there so I think, at some point, land will become available. . . . Some of the smaller blocks aren't particularly economic and, if the price of grapes goes down, they're going to want to sell. So, at that point, we'll be able to buy some there as they're good, proven areas.'

The land purchases and leasing arrangements supported a changing varietal focus, away from the over-supplied Chardonnay and to new plantings of Syrah, Pinot Gris and Viognier alongside existing emphases on Pinot Noir, Merlot and Cabernet Franc. According to Andrew, the Hawkes Bay was the best area for growing Syrah, and some of the best New Zealand red wines were of that variety. While Syrah would, in time, be sold in the US, the other new varietals were destined for the local market. The varietal emphasis was also consistent with a developing market focus on supplying restaurants (on-premise segment) which were '. . . always wanting something new, something different.' However, the company still supplied liquor outlets and sought to gain a presence in supermarkets, employing a diversified branding strategy in the process. Not only were wines marketed under the Coopers Creek name, the company had also developed a range of wines selling at different price points as exclusive labels for retail chains in the UK, USA, Australia and Holland. In addition, the whimsically-named Cat range had been established in both the domestic and international markets; *Fat Cat* Chardonnay, *Cat's Pee on a Gooseberry Bush* Sauvignon Blanc, *Tom Cat* Merlot and *Glamour Puss* Pinot Noir.

Coopers Creek's annual production was in the range of 900,000 litres, around 96,000 cases, and

Table 1 Comparative export figures

NZ wine industry figures	1992	1993	1994*	1995*	1996	1997	1998	1999	2000	2001	2002	2003
Total exports (NZ$m)**	34.7	48.3	41.5	40.8	60.3	75.8	97.6	125.3	168.6	198.1	246.4	281.8
% increase	37.4	39.2	−14.1	−1.7	47.8	25.7	28.8	28.4	34.6	17.5	24.4	14.4
Exports as % of sales (vol.)	13.9	18.7	21.7	20.2	23.6	25.2	28.5	30.2	31.7	34.7	41.4	44.1
% increase	15.8	35	16	−6.9	17	6.8	13.1	6	5	9.5	19	6.5
Coopers Creek figures	**1992**	**1993**	**1994***	**1995***	**1996**	**1997**	**1998**	**1999**	**2000**	**2001**	**2002**	**2003**
Total exports ($m)	.36	.76	1.1	1.0	1.2	1.8	2.0	2.3	2.1	2.1	3.1	3.8
% increase	65.0	111.1	44.7	−9.1	20.0	50.0	11.1	15.0	−8.7	0	47.6	22.6
Exports as % of sales (vol.)	22.4	42.9	48.9	42.4	49.2	63.3	57.9	61.5	49.1	49.1	57.8	67.4
% increase	97.3	91.5	14.0	−13.3	16.0	28.7	−8.5	6.2	−20.2	0	17.7	16.6

* Less wine available for export due to low cropping years (real effect of which covers 18 months).
** $NZ1 = approx. €0.53.
Source: Statistics New Zealand and Coopers Creek.

the production system at Coopers Creek was set up to produce in 25–30 tonne batches, a modular approach based on grape truck-load capacities. The company had the capacity to crush 100–120 tonnes of grapes a day, giving it a major competitive advantage: for example, in one year in five wineries may have to crush all of their grapes over a short period, as Coopers Creek did in the bad cropping year of 1995. The cost difference when installing the crushing plant was insignificant so it made sense to Andrew Hendry to install the larger machinery, and one person could operate this machinery alone if necessary. Despite this, the company contracted with a growers' cooperative crushing plant in Gisborne, essentially duplicating this operation. According to Andrew, while there were minor savings relating to staff costs, effluent disposal and wear and tear, the contract crushing involved higher costs but offered the opportunity to attain better quality by crushing close to the source. For example, in 2002, '. . . we managed to make a reserve [higher quality wine] from Gisborne Chardonnay which possibly we may not have if the grapes had all been trucked to Auckland.'

Coopers Creek also had the capacity to juice for other wineries, and was involved in occasional production-based collaborations with a group of local West Auckland wineries. As well as grape crushing at key times, the wineries swapped grapes, shared equipment and jointly purchased key inputs; for example, Coopers Creek shared the costs of container-loads of barrels with three other wineries. This local collaborative grouping had changed significantly in its lifetime; originally comprising five local and New Zealand-owned small and medium-sized wineries, by 2004 one had dropped out, a new one had taken its place with its relocation to the West Auckland area, one was taken over by another in the grouping and, in turn, this combined winery was taken over by an Australian winery. Thus of the current six West Auckland wineries in this local network, Coopers Creek was the third largest, behind two owned by overseas interests.

The New Zealand wine industry

All New Zealand winemakers had to belong to the New Zealand Wine Institute. In order to sell wine, companies were legally obliged to acquire a licence and take out membership of the Institute. The Institute acted as a self-regulatory body for the wine industry. Among its regulatory activities the Institute administered the Ministry of Health's export certification procedures, which involved chemical testing and blind tastings. Andrew Hendry was elected to the Board of the Wine Institute in 1986 as a representative of small producers (the wineries were categorised according to size by annual litre sales). By 1993, however, Coopers Creek was categorised as a medium-sized company. In 1995, there were 204 members of the Wine Institute comprising 4 large producers, 12 medium-sized companies and 188 small, 'boutique' wineries; by 2000, there were 358 members of the Wine Institute, with 4 large, 23 medium and 331 small companies. Table 2 shows the winery membership status of the Wine Institute as at 2003. The Wine Institute merged in 2002 with the body representing grape growers, the Grape Growers Council, to form Winegrowers of New Zealand, thus institutionalising the close cooperative relationship and common membership which had developed over the last 15 years of the industry.

Table 2 Size breakdown of New Zealand wine companies

Company sales	2003
Annual sales < 200,000 litres	388
Annual sales between 200,000 and 2,000,000 litres	30
Annual sales > 2,000,000 litres	3
Total number of NZ wineries	421

Source: WGNZ (2003).

Some Institute members with export interests in specific markets had established special interest groups: the Wine Guild had been formed by those wineries either already established in the UK export market or interested in entering this market; and another four groups, termed Country Action Groups, had been established to share information, experiences and promotional activities relating to Germany, the US, Canada and Australia. The groups developed marketing plans to explore and, ultimately, exploit export opportunities within the chosen markets, and these were implemented through a semi-formal funding arrangement whereby individual companies contributed to costs on a project-by-project basis. For example, only those companies interested in a particular promotion contributed to the costs of mounting it. Countries were split into Tier 1 markets, where New Zealand had a strong and growing presence (UK, US and Australia) and Tier 2 markets, where there was a smaller presence and growth potential (Canada, Germany, Ireland and Japan). These markets received differential attention and funding. As well as the UK Wine Guild, Coopers Creek was actively involved in the Canadian and US Country Action Groups in terms of joint promotional efforts.

In 1996, the UK Wine Guild involved around 53 full members and about 25 associate members. Generally, the associate members were very small producers not currently exporting but intending to at some stage and 15 could be termed active participants of the network targeting the UK. Trade New Zealand (the New Zealand government body concerned with promoting overseas trade) provided a third of the Wine Guild's funds in order to facilitate New Zealand wine exports. The members of the Wine Guild provided the additional two thirds funding, which was calculated as a percentage levy on sales (a one per cent levy on free on board sales). The Guild, originally organised on an informal basis, became more formalised once government funding ran out in 1997 and carried on with Wine Guild membership funding only. By 2004 the levy system had three tiers based on number of cases sold (Coopers Creek was in the middle tier). The levy covered the basic overheads of running a London office, which fulfilled more of a generic promotional role, with all other events being funded on a user-pays basis.

The overall Wine Guild administration, based in the offices of the Wine Institute in Auckland, was controlled by a Board of Directors, of which Andrew Hendry was Deputy Chairperson from 1996–1998. At that time there were also two Trade New Zealand representatives (one based in Auckland, the other in Wellington) as well as a rotating Chairperson. Another director on the Board of the Guild was the Executive Officer of the Wine Institute. In addition, the Wine Institute had seconded a half-time employee to work on behalf of the Wine Guild. These links with the Wine Institute facilitated information sharing, although the Institute had no voting rights in how the Wine Guild operated. Essentially, the Board provided financial and marketing expertise for the successful operation of the Guild, as well as ideas for future developments. Although a voting system was in place, decisions were usually made by consensus. However, with the end of government funding, the board of directors was disbanded and control

of the Wine Guild came under the function of the Wine Institute, dropping the 'Guild' name in the process. The Institute moved to a system of presenting UK promotion initiatives to members and inviting participation and payment, which, according to Andrew Hendry, resulted in the loss of feeling of involvement in the Guild: 'Whereas, in the older days, there was a committee of wine makers who decided what was to be done and then put that to the rest of the members and they said yes or no, now it's more of a bureaucracy that tells us.'

In those markets where collaborative efforts have been employed, the principal aim has been jointly and effectively to sell the New Zealand label ahead of individual wine company labels. Promoting the generic New Zealand brand in this way was seen as a way of benefiting all New Zealand exporters. The UK Wine Guild established an office in London with two full-time employees to promote and support sales of New Zealand wines. Basically, the agents of this Guild provided organised tastings of New Zealand wines, an information bureau, placement of advertisements, and travel arrangements for local wine writers and trade buyers to visit New Zealand. In the UK market, sales and distribution remained the responsibility of the exporting firms and, typically, they used exclusive agreements with established agents and distribution networks. However, these relationships evolved from more cooperative structures. For example, in the UK, one firm was agent for several New Zealand wine companies initially until the volume of business became too large for the agent to handle. Subsequently, the wineries had to find agents able to handle increasing volumes, and the agency/distributor relationships began to fragment. In the German and US markets, where growth was at an early stage, the New Zealand companies tended to share the same agents. The Wine Institute and the Guild played a role in facilitating distribution processes by hosting visits by groups of agents.

The wine industry's strategy meant that New Zealand wine producers obtained the highest average prices for wines in the UK market. Whilst the emerging global wine companies in the US, Australia and Europe[1] sought to supply reliable, consistent supermarket sales, the New Zealand

---

[1] For example, LVMH, Castel Freres, Pernod Ricard in France; E&J Gallo and R Mondavi in the US; and Southcorp and Mildara Blass in Australia.

producers aimed for the 'fine wine', connoisseur niche market. That said, 2003 saw a French wine company buy bulk New Zealand Sauvignon Blanc, which it then branded as New Zealand wine and sold as a three-litre bag-in-a-box of wine in the Tesco supermarket chain in the UK. The New Zealand brand was also affected by the increasing proportion of New Zealand wine companies becoming wholly or partially owned by offshore interests. Large scale wine corporations, focused on ownership-driven vertical integration, combined production and marketing of New Zealand wines with other overseas wineries.[2]

The issues facing the New Zealand wine industry in 2004 included some critical challenges arising from the global market and local responses to these. Among these was the gap between falling or steady consumption and increased global production. A major issue for New Zealand producers would be managing the growth of processing facilities and the marketing and promotional efforts which would be required. Whilst overall demand was declining, demand in non-traditional wine drinking regions was growing, especially for New World wine and high-quality single varietal wines, such as New Zealand Sauvignon Blanc. The New Zealand industry was studying demand structures in its international markets and was planning in order to control supply to maintain the price premiums it achieved from quality and differentiation. This trend increased pressures to reduce margins to achieve or maintain retail positioning. Thus, the New Zealand industry could expect increasingly fierce competition in its target markets, with the risk that New Zealand's position as a quality niche producer could be emulated and challenged by other new entrants. This was especially the case in the UK and US where New Zealand winemakers and their wines were seen as new and innovative. Consistent with the growing trend of branding in the wine market, New Zealand winemakers were developing a generic promotional programme. This aimed to continue to build awareness of the umbrella brand 'New Zealand wine', with the logo of 'the riches of a clean, green land' and thus to focus the marketing activities of industry participants.

---

[2] For example, Nobilo was purchased by BRL Hardy of Australia, which was, in turn, purchased by Constellation Brands Inc and, in 2004, Montana was wholly owned by Allied Domecq.

Coopers Creek – domestic market

In 2004, Andrew Hendry observed that the New Zealand domestic market had become increasingly competitive, with over 400 New Zealand producers and cheaper imports from Australia. Coopers Creek serviced the three segments of on-premise, liquor store and supermarket sales in the domestic market. Between 1998–99, the winery took the step of employing three sales representatives, one concentrating on restaurant sales, and the other two focusing on retail sales in Auckland and local country areas. By 2004, Coopers Creek was dealing directly with a number of larger Auckland-based restaurants and was able to offer them a more competitive price as a result, but Andrew did not foresee that such relationships would grow: '. . . it would be just Auckland based; it would be too difficult to organise it otherwise.' The company also had representation in the country's largest supermarket chain consisting of Woolworths and Foodtown, with the *Cat* brand in one and the Coopers Creek brand in the other; no mean feat when, as Andrew points out: '. . . supermarkets play a big part. You can't get your whole range in, you can only get, if you're lucky, three or four wines.' Elsewhere in the country, Andrew continued to use commissioned sales representatives and non-exclusive distributors.

On a more local level, Andrew had taken the initiative to form joint advertising and promotion relationships with a group of local West Auckland wineries after observing some Australian winemakers collaborating locally. For example, over Easter weekends three of the companies arranged tours, special wines, meals and music, with the aim that visitors should sample a different food course at each vineyard. This initiative promoted custom, getting a larger proportion of people to visit the wineries than on normal weekends. The grouping has also collaborated on trade tastings, when they emphasised current releases and invited retailers, restaurant owners and wine vendors to sample the wine. Since 1990, these companies have regularly gathered together as a group in an informal committee to decide on their next collaborative efforts. The situation has arisen where only two or three companies in the group have gone ahead with a particular promotion. Other times, all companies have been involved. However, as noted above, this local grouping had experienced significant change due to industry restructuring.

Coopers Creek – international markets

In 1987, less than one per cent of Coopers Creek produce was exported (mainly to Australia). The first export market was Australia which, according to Andrew, was a hard market in which to sell. This opportunity arrived almost by chance, or certainly ahead of Andrew's original export schedule. Entry to the marketplace was facilitated by the company's relationship with the Wine Institute of New Zealand, which coordinated a Wine Expo in Melbourne in 1985. At the time, the opportunity to venture into this market proved irresistible because it coincided with the devaluation of the New Zealand currency and the resulting value for money prices in the Australian marketplace. Despite some initial difficulties associated with new market entry, this exporting experience proved to be invaluable in overcoming problems associated with selling New Zealand wines abroad.

Coopers Creek initiated a serious export strategy in 1989, having delayed for one year because 1988 was a bad season for the production of grapes. The

UK was the next market targeted by the company, again in partnership with the Wine Institute (from which the UK Wine Guild evolved). This was followed two years later by excursions into other European countries (Holland, Belgium and Switzerland) and North America, principally because Andrew Hendry did not want to become too reliant on the UK market. Asian markets had not been a strong focus for Coopers Creek. However, by chance, Andrew met a Taiwanese agent in the Coopers Creek winery shop and a small shipment was sent to Taiwan in 2003. In addition, Coopers Creek was the New Zealand supplier to the state-owned supermarket chain, Fair Price, in Singapore. In terms of volume in 1995, 65 per cent of exports were sold in the UK market, with around 5 per cent each for Australia, Canada, Holland and the US (East Coast states). By 2004, 9 per cent by value was sold in the UK, 35 per cent in the US, 11 in Australia, 33 in Canada and 3.5 in Holland. Exhibit 1 illustrates the changing export sales in principal markets for the New Zealand wine industry and demonstrates the increasing focus on the US market, while Exhibit 2 illustrates Coopers Creek's export market emphasis relative to the New Zealand wine industry for 2003.

Andrew Hendry visited his overseas importers on a regular basis, spending 12 weeks per annum

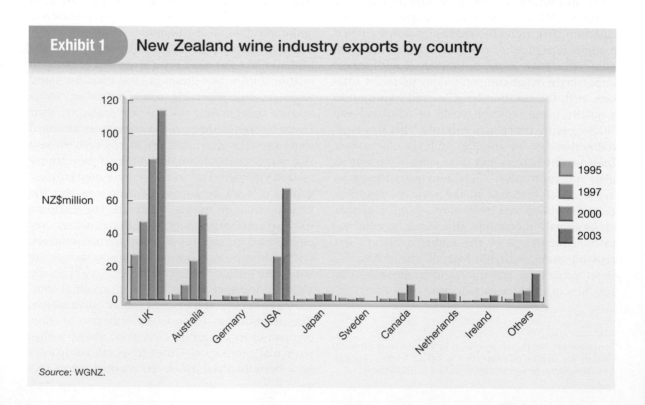

Exhibit 1   New Zealand wine industry exports by country

Source: WGNZ.

| Exhibit 2 | Coopers Creek export markets compared with NZ industry |

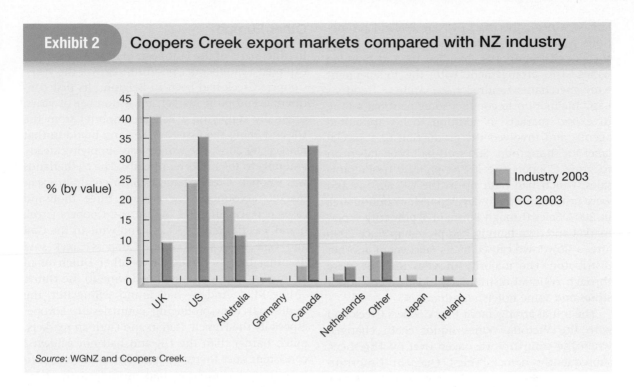

Source: WGNZ and Coopers Creek.

overseas, as much overseas contact as any other New Zealand winery regardless of size. The visits were usually linked to wine trade shows in the UK, France and the USA. Apart from the exchange of views on the state of the market, details of latest vintages and discussions on prospective new customers, the visits had proven successful in providing a constant reminder that the winery was committed to the market, encouraging the agent to focus attention on the Coopers Creek brand and making sure export customers were very clear about the amount of product they could expect from the winery in coming years.

Coopers Creek's focused export strategy involved differing combinations of collaborative and individual efforts. Collaboratively, Coopers Creek entered and developed the Australian, UK, US and Canadian markets, although considerable individual effort had also been expended in the process. Markets which Coopers Creek had essentially developed on its own included Holland, Belgium, Ireland, Hong Kong, Singapore and Switzerland, among others.

United Kingdom

The changing nature of the UK Wine Guild in New Zealand coincided with a change of staff in the London office and the perception that there were fewer attendees per winery at organised tastings. Coopers Creek was not alone in its concerns about the changes to the UK Wine Guild. A number of wineries had reduced their involvement in the Guild, including Coopers Creek, and a knock-on effect was experienced with lost support for other Country Action Groups and initiatives of the Wine Institute. In addition, the makeup of Coopers Creek exports to the UK, with 85 per cent comprising buyers' own brands, meant that the original Guild levy system caused some concern to Andrew Hendry. Essentially, the winery was in a high fees category, given the total volume of sales, but only a small percentage of these sales promoted the Coopers Creek label. These changes led to discussions in 2000 with two other New Zealand wineries to undertake some joint promotions, possibly in the UK and other markets, taking advantage of Trade New Zealand funding that was available to groups of applicants rather than individual applicants. However, the initiative faltered when one of these wineries was taken over by an Australian firm.

By 2004, Coopers Creek was dealing with three UK importers: a buying consortium represented 60 independent wine merchants; Stratford Wine Agencies carried the regular Coopers Creek range alongside wines from two other New Zealand companies whereby, although Coopers Creek was the largest winery, the costs of New Zealand promotions were equally shared; and Ehrmanns Group, their original importer, handled the *Cat* branded wines. The arrangement with the independent wine merchants resulted from Andrew Hendry's basic inclination to conduct some personal selling in export markets in addition to his appointed agents, and involved the production of a special label for that group. Stratford had been taken on to grow Coopers Creek's on-premise (restaurant) sales, which had built up in the UK regions and were just beginning to develop in the London area in 2004. Sales through Ehrmanns, primarily supermarket and own-brands, had picked up since 2000 after a slowdown caused by its takeover of another distributor. The majority of sales in 2004 were through regional distributors, independent liquor stores and some hotels/restaurants.

The initial arrangement that Coopers Creek had with the Victoria Wines liquor chain changed when the company was taken over by Threshers, subsequently named Thirst Quench. Unfortunately the takeover coincided with Coopers Creek being out of stock for six months as a result of the runaway success of the *Cat* label. This stockout, combined with the rationalisation of stock following the takeover, led to the Coopers Creek brand being dropped. Coopers Creek had subsequently entered an agreement to sell the *Cat* range in the UK through the Londis chain of independent retailers (a group which includes over 2,200 convenience, neighbourhood, supermarket and forecourt stores).

The winery's relationship with the Tesco supermarket chain ended in 1999. For nine years Coopers Creek had produced wine for the supermarket's specific own-label requirements. The winery had been actively involved in the promotion of new vintage releases through the supermarket chain, with Tesco carrying two own-labels and two Coopers Creek labels. Even though the wines were selling well, Tesco took a policy decision to drop the more expensive New Zealand wines and buy in bulk from a grower's cooperative in Marlborough. According to Andrew: '. . . they [Tesco] wanted a 33 per cent margin and we were only getting 13 per cent, so it just couldn't go on.' Although discussions with other supermarket chains Aldi and Co-operative did not result in sales, Andrew maintained: 'There's always the possibility of doing another label into some other group, if I need to, but in the meantime I'd prefer to do that business in the States.'

Other Europe

In other parts of the European market Andrew had explored a number of opportunities over the years. Coopers Creek had been in Belgium, its first continental European market, for a number of years, originally supplying a Belgian importer from the UK and being the first New Zealand brand in that market. By 2004, the winery was supplying steady amounts to the importer directly. The Netherlands was Coopers Creek's largest continental European market, accounting for around three thousand cases per year in 2004, where the Coopers Creek brand was the only New Zealand wine in the Gall and Gall wine store chain. Coopers Creek sold its other brands through two other Dutch retail chains. In addition, it supplied wine to the Dutch airline KLM. Andrew had found selling into the traditional wine-producing countries in Europe, especially the French, Italian and German markets, much harder than the UK and had not achieved consistent sales there. He had sold some wine into Italy, but the importer had misjudged the time needed to move that stock. He had had a similar experience in Germany, where a small distributor to specialist wine shops had flooded his network with Coopers Creek wine, without re-ordering sufficient to keep up with the demand that had generated. Through contacts made at the major European wine trade fair, Vinexpo, held biannually in Bordeaux, Andrew had sold wine to Greece – again to a specialist importer – and to Poland, and was in discussion with a French importer, though he saw this latter market as a long-term challenge. Finally, Andrew was targeting the Danish market, noting that Swedish sales had all but disappeared. Reflecting on the wider European market, Andrew remained open to opportunities but noted that it was difficult to compete in countries with their own traditional local wine industries. Moreover, in the price-conscious UK, Holland and Germany, South American and South African wines were seen as better value than New Zealand wines.

United States

Andrew Hendry had first entered the US market between 1991–94, when he sold wine in six East Coast states through a broker he had made contact with as a result of a trade fair in Las Vegas. This business had 'faded away', as Andrew put it, because of strained relations between the retailers and the broker. However, Hendry entered an agency agreement with the distributor Winebow, again on the East Coast, in 1995 and this was followed by a major New Zealand promotion the following year. In 1996 Coopers Creek and eight other wineries, under the auspices of the Wine Institute, jointly took a New Zealand stand at the Boston Wine and Food Show where wine was promoted alongside seafood, venison and other produce. This led to the winery developing a network of distributors and conducting regional tastings on a state-by-state basis, mainly focusing on the East Coast, but also Colorado and Wisconsin. Crucially, in 2000, Coopers Creek changed to a larger distributor with expertise in on-premise representation, being one of the top three distributors in New York servicing some 2,000 restaurants in Manhattan alone. Andrew Hendry considered an on-premise focus critical because, in the retail sector, Australian and New Zealand wines were marketed together and Australian wines were cheaper due to the ability to achieve scale economies. In 2004, Coopers Creek exported directly to New York and New Jersey, shipping roughly one container every two months for this specific geographical segment, and other states were beginning to buy direct given increasing volumes.

A collaborative arrangement in 1999, with a Chilean winery, a Californian winery and a US importer, saw Coopers Creek share the costs of employing a brand manager in the US, with the importer paying half of the manager's salary and the other half being split between the three wineries on the basis of cases sold. The brand manager had begun by organising all of the US promotions and going out with the importer's sales representatives, essentially doing the same sort of job that Andrew Hendry did on his overseas visits. Following this arrangement, Coopers Creek's sales trebled, growing from 1,500 cases in the late '90s to 6,000 in 2000 and rising to 10,000 cases in 2001. The arrangement worked well as the wineries produced different portfolios of wines and did not compete directly with each other. For a brief three-month period in 2002, the brand manager worked solely for Coopers Creek and increased his role, essentially cutting out the importer and distributing across 15 states from warehouses in California and New Jersey. By cutting out the intermediary, Coopers Creek had been able to reduce the cost to restaurants by 35 per cent, making its wine extremely competitive in the critical on-premise segment. However, the volume at that time meant

that the full-time status was not viable, so the brand manager started selling wines for Chilean, Australian and South African wineries. By 2004, Coopers Creek was experiencing an approximate 30 per cent increase in sales in successive years and had representation in 33 states. With the Australian winery thinking of dropping out of the cooperative agreement, the exclusive arrangement with the brand manager was back on the table at the time of writing.

In addition, with a lot more grapes about to come on stream, Andrew was in negotiations to supply own label wines to a number of US supermarkets, which was all new business for the winery. In 2003, Coopers Creek supplied a special label Marlborough Sauvignon Blanc to Trader Joe's 26 stores on the East Coast. With a warehouse in California but little business, Coopers Creek was negotiating to do something with the Californian-based Cost Plus supermarket chain. Andrew was also looking to employ a broker in the California area in order to cut out the importer and supply directly from the warehouse to the end customer.

Canada

Ontario was, perhaps, the toughest market in the major economies served by Coopers Creek since a 100 per cent margin is imposed on liquor prices by the state monopoly. In the mid 1990s, it took Andrew six months of negotiations with the Ontario Liquor Control Board to gain their agreement to distribute his wines to all of the Board's then 630 stores throughout Ontario. Special labels and cartons had to be developed to meet local requirements; and, because the wine could be shipped in the depths of the Canadian winter, when temperatures can be as low as minus 20°C, the wine was transported in heated containers. This effort was recognised by the award of a Trade New Zealand Export Commendation at the recommendation of the New Zealand Trade Commissioner in Canada. By 2000, Coopers Creek had two more listings by the Ontario board, which brought exports to 6,000 cases per year.

In 2004 Coopers Creek was the biggest New Zealand supplier in Canada, due mainly to its relationship with the Ontario Liquor Control Board. The *Cat* range was considered a core product and was carried by all of its 600 main stores, and its Marlborough Sauvignon Blanc was an essential product for about 40 specialist stores, making

Coopers Creek the only New Zealand winery represented on the stores' shelves year round. Andrew was expecting to sell close to 20,000 cases in this one market alone, and was beginning to realise sales in other Canadian provinces like Nova Scotia, British Columbia and New Brunswick and soon to be Alberta, Quebec and Manitoba.

The future

Andrew perceived that competition was greatest in the New Zealand market and that market growth was slowing considerably. He perceived that, although there was some growth in the UK market, it had been ceded to the larger lower priced New Zealand labels, many of which were no longer New Zealand owned and which guarded their supermarket and retail listings fiercely. Andrew considered China, Taiwan and Japan as future target markets, but pointed out that with '. . . the US market being so big, that's probably enough for us for now.' The decision to divert products from the UK to the US markets was considered appropriate given the speed with which that market was growing, leading to estimates that it would replace the UK market for New Zealand wines by 2007/8. However, Andrew acknowledged that, although on-premise sales represented a small but growing percentage of the winery's export sales, the supermarket and liquor store segments would continue to account for a significant proportion of revenue. He thought that this growth would be achieved by dealing direct with customers rather than through a broker.

Under these circumstances, can Andrew Hendry continue with the self-funded approach to growth? Will we continue to see Andrew's relationship-based approach impacted by the changing nature of the industry? Likewise, does increasing competition and powerful buyers mean that relationships will be less favoured than market-based transactions? Is Andrew positioning the company for potential sale in the near future?

SABMiller

Aidan McQuade

SABMiller grew on the basis of its strength in developing markets, first in Africa and then in other parts of the world. With its first acquisition in a developed market, Miller in 2002, it has become the second largest brewer by volume in the world and finds itself faced with a new set of challenges. This case study explains the business's development and the strategy of the firm. It shows how the strategy has changed with time and provides the opportunity to consider its future at both the corporate and competitive strategy levels.

• • •

Background

By 2004 SABMiller, the renamed South African Breweries following its acquisition of the American brewer Miller in 2002, had become the second largest brewer by volume in the world, described by its boss, Graham Mackay as 'a turnaround specialist'[1] with a record of returning breweries to profitability.

South African Breweries was registered in London by a syndicate of investors from the UK and South Africa in 1895, the same year it launched Castle Lager in Johannesburg to meet the demand of the burgeoning population of gold miners. It was listed on the Johannesburg Stock Exchange in 1897 and the following year was listed on the London Stock Exchange. As a company it is therefore older than the state of South Africa itself and has faced the challenge of doing business amidst the upheaval that country experienced during the 20th century. The most significant feature of this was the institution of the racist system of 'apartheid' introduced by the South African govern-

ment in 1948 and the subsequent internal and external opposition to this as part of the broader struggle to establish democracy. A central feature of the struggle was the campaign for economic sanctions on South Africa, aiming to restrict international business from investing in or trading with South Africa and restricting South African business from trading with international markets.

Photo: SABMiller

---

[1] 'The battle of big beer', *The Economist*, 13 May 2004.

In 1950 SAB moved its head office and seat of control from London to Johannesburg. Southern Africa was the focus of the majority of its business expansion during the subsequent four decades, principally in South Africa, but also in the occupied territory of Namibia, and in the states of its allies or economic dependencies in the region.[2] In 1970 SAB became fully incorporated in South Africa.

Aside from the growing external restrictions on market expansion during this period SAB also had to contend with restrictions placed upon it by the South African government. In 1955 excise duty structures were introduced favouring spirits over beer, making beer the most heavily taxed beverage in South Africa and until 1962 there was a general prohibition on the consumption of liquor by black South Africans.

SAB responded to these restrictions by focusing on dominating domestic beer production through acquisition of competitors and rationalisation of production and distribution facilities. SAB also expanded its product portfolio, obtaining control of Stellenbosch Farmers' Winery in 1960 and in the course of the rest of that decade obtaining licences to brew locally Guinness, Amstel and Carling Black Label. Further expansions followed within the beverage sector, principally through acquisition leading, by 1979, to SAB controlling an estimated 99 per cent of the market in South Africa as well as commanding positions in Swaziland, Lesotho, Rhodesia and Botswana.

Subsequently SAB, through a joint venture to diversify surplus investment funds, expanded into food, property, hotels, furniture, retail, clothing and footwear. In 1978 ground was broken on the Sun City casino resort, SAB's highest-profile development in hotels and gambling.

In the same year SAB published a code of non-discriminatory employment, one of the first industries in the country to do so. This did not immunise it against the growing pace of sanctions. In 1983 it was forced to decrease its interests in Zimbabwe to 25 per cent, though this was offset to some extent by the return on the company's first investments outside the Southern African subcontinent. These included Rolling Rock beer in the USA. However further pressures on business arose when in 1985 South Africa's short-term banking

facilities were called up, as part of the growing pace of the sanctions campaign. SAB established 'complex defensive investment structures' and continued to invest in diverse businesses in South Africa. For example in 1987 SAB became the leading safety match manufacturer in Africa, acquiring Lion Match Company from a disinvesting international investor.

By 1990 the pressure for change was so great that Nelson Mandela was released from prison and the process for the establishment of a multi-racial democracy was irrevocably in train. SAB decided that the time was right to expand its brewing capacity and invested in the development of three mega-breweries across the country. The change in the political system also eased SAB's return and expansion through the rest of Africa. In 1994 it was invited to participate in a joint venture with the Tanzanian government to revitalise the brewing industry there. It was also invited back to Zambia, Mozambique and later Angola.

By 2000 SAB had weathered the economic travails caused by apartheid to such an extent that 49 out of every 50 beers consumed in the country were brewed by them. Such market dominance provided a serious deterrent to potential competitors. However there remained little space for it to expand in Southern Africa, particularly in the beverage sector. Hence the company looked for other opportunities to expand beyond its traditional region. In 1993 it acquired Hungary's largest brewery, Dreher, in what it described as a 'beach-head move' into central Europe. The rest of the decade saw it establish operations in China, Poland, Romania, Slovakia, Russia and the Czech Republic. In 1999 SAB moved its primary listing back to London in order to make it easier to raise capital for expansion through the purchase of new acquisitions. Further expansion into Central America occurred in 2001.

By 2001, SAB was the fifth largest brewer in the world and the fastest-growing brewer from 1996 to 2000, with brewing operations in 21 different countries and an output of 77m hectolitres of beer.

Emerging onto the global market

The 1998 annual report of SAB explained the Group's strategy:

[2] Such as (until 1975) Portuguese-controlled Angola and Mozambique, and white-ruled Rhodesia (since 1980 Zimbabwe).

SAB's international focus has been on countries in which it believes it could use its expertise, which has been gained over 100 years in South Africa, to develop beer markets in emerging economies. SAB has invested significantly in its core businesses, and has commenced brewing operations in a further 5 African countries, 3 Chinese provinces, and 4 Eastern European countries since 1995. SAB intends to continue to protect and further develop its South Africa operations, while investing for growth in its international beer business, where a profitable base, with critical mass in selected developing markets and regions, has been achieved. Incremental growth, both organic and through acquisitions, is being pursued aggressively.

This was spelled out more fully by 2000:

In the less developed world, Africa and Asia and much of Europe, brewing remained highly fragmented, with beer drinkers supplied by breweries which were never more than small-scale and localised, often producing low-quality beer. This was also the case, even under the Communist regimes, in China, Eastern and Central Europe, despite their centralising and mass production strategy for most other industries.

This fragmentation presented the opportunity for SAB from the mid-1990s to create a profitable and fast-expanding business in emerging markets with huge potential. This opportunity involves, generally, taking a share in a brewery with a local partner and, while retaining the brand because drinkers tend to have fierce attachments to their local brew, transforming the business. This starts with upgrading quality and consistency to create a beer for which people are prepared to pay more and which can give us a healthy profit margin. Then comes improvement to marketing and distribution. Next we improve productivity and capacity.

In each country we have begun by acquiring an initial local stronghold from which we can advance into regions beyond the brewery's original catchment area. We then build critical mass in the region and progress, over time, to a national basis. This is often achieved by acquiring further brewing businesses and focusing the brand portfolio. An optimum brand portfolio gives us a better overall marketing proposition, increases total sales and delivers economies of scale in production and distribution.

This process demands, on one level, great political sensitivity in dealing with governments, partners, local communities and our workforce and, on another level, the deployment of expert operational management skills learnt in South Africa. At the same time we market and promote selected premium brands, either brewed locally or imported – often our own Castle Lager, which is the biggest selling beer in Africa. Our management structure is decentralised, reflecting the local nature of beer branding and distribution.

In most emerging markets, consumption of beer is directly related to the level of disposable income at consumer level. Attractive markets thus arise in developing economies as consumer spending increases. This is often accompanied by structural changes in society, such as increasing urbanisation and the development of more varied and sophisticated lifestyles, which also encourage beer consumption.

Our businesses do not all advance at the same speed, nor have the same potential. It is characteristic of emerging markets that growth can be variable, and we are accustomed to temporary setbacks. However, the spread of our international businesses provides a 'portfolio effect', thereby reducing the impact of setbacks in one or two individual countries. For example, last year adverse climatic conditions in Mozambique and Tanzania and economic problems in Romania were more than offset by spectacular growth in Poland and China, strong growth in Botswana and a steady improvement in more than a dozen other countries.

Since we embarked on our global expansion in 1994, the trend in sales and profits has been steadily upwards. We are confident that over time our returns will prove to be outstanding.

The culture that this approach nurtured was illustrated in an interview in 2002 when Julie Corkish, SAB's UK tax manager, emphasised the point that 'Emerging markets is our forte'.[3] SAB managers have the reputation for resourcefulness in managing their operations in countries in turmoil or where there is poor infrastructure. To illustrate this *The Economist* magazine in 2000 reported an incident when the water supply to one of its breweries in Mozambique failed. Rather than shut down production, SAB paid the local fire brigade to fetch water and hose it into the beer vats. This focus on emerging markets led by 2001 to SAB becoming the world's fifth largest brewer by volume with breweries in 24 countries across the globe.

Analysts noted a problem with this portfolio in that it meant that SAB earned most of its profits in 'soft' currencies. Hence a loss of confidence in emerging markets could hurt it badly if there were a resultant devaluation of the currencies of those markets which would in turn lead to a loss of profits in hard currencies. This could result also in a dip in its share price that would make it vulnerable to takeover. The situation was exacerbated with a slump in the value of the Rand in 2001 and there were fears it could be further effected by the devastating impact of the HIV/AIDS pandemic on

---

[3] 'Tax gets a look in as SAB goes global', *International Tax Review*, vol. 13, no. 3, March 2002.

the workforce, which aside from the human cost, is causing a decrease in productivity through the chronic and debilitating effects of the illness, particularly in sub-Saharan Africa.

Many commentators believed that for a brewery of its size SAB needed to have a major brand in the developed markets. It had tried to do so. In June 2000 it had considered acquiring Bass Brewers in the UK but baulked at the price.[4] Instead Bass was taken over by Interbrew of Belgium. Kronenbourg had been acquired by Scottish & Newcastle. And it was known that SAB was on the lookout for such a major brand.

By 2000 the five major brewers still made up less than 30 per cent of world beer sales, which suggested that this share would grow dramatically in the future. However, the likelihood was that this would be through acquisitions. This further emphasised the need for SAB to make such an acquisition.

In 1999 SAB decided on listing on the London Stock Exchange (LSE). This was justified by SAB as follows:

> The Directors believed that the listing of the company on the LSE and the placing would put SAB in a strong position to pursue its strategy of growth by giving the group greater access to world capital markets and providing it with the financial resources and flexibility to pursue this strategy in an effective and competitive manner. This would enhance the ability of SAB to take advantage of increasing consolidation in the international brewing industry and to compete with other international brewers for development opportunities throughout the world. The Directors expected to use the proceeds of the placing due to the Company to continue SAB's strategy of growth worldwide and, in particular, to continue its investment in its Polish and Eastern European operations. In recent years, SAB has committed significant resources both to international acquisitions and to the reconstruction of acquired businesses. SAB intended to continue to protect and further develop its SA operations, while investing for growth in its international beer business, where a profitable base, with critical mass in selected developing markets and regions, has now been achieved. Incremental growth, both organic and through acquisitions, is being pursued aggressively.

However, the listing had its problems. It was reported that SAB's share price lost 15.55 per cent relative to the FTSE 100 in the year to end November 2000 (in the same period it lost 2.68 per

cent on the South African Stock Exchange). Analysts argued, again, that this was because of the failure to make a major acquisition of a first-world brand and its over-reliance on its developing markets.

The *Financial Times*[5] also believed that their reception in London had surprised SAB directors. They quoted John Clemmow, of the South African Investment Bank, Investec, as saying 'I think it came as a shock to them to come over here and discover how unimportant they were in the lives of the City.' The FT believed that, whilst in South Africa the firm was well known, it was necessary for SAB to spend a great deal more time explaining itself in London and that it was not sufficiently geared up to doing this. Indeed Graham Mackay, SAB's chief executive, was reported as being taken aback by the harshness of some of the comments: 'It's more picky, to the point of cynicism and hostility, than you encounter in South Africa'.

SABMiller

In 2002 SAB finally succeeded in acquiring a major brand in a developed market when it acquired 100 per cent of Miller Brewing Company, the second largest brewery in the United States, and becoming SABMiller in the process. SAB paid Philip Morris Co, US$3.6bn (€3.2bn) in stock of the merged company and assumed US$2bn (€1.7bn) of Miller's debt.

In the 2003 annual report the company explained this acquisition as follows:

> We acquired Miller Brewing Company in July 2002, giving the group access, through a national player, to a growing beer market with the world's largest profit pool, and at the same time diversifying the currency and geographic risk of the group.

This acquisition made SABMiller the second largest brewery by volume in the world. However the acquisition brought with it its own problems. James Williamson, an analyst at SG Securities in London, commented, 'They didn't buy it because they thought it was a strong growth business. They bought it because they needed a mature cash cow. Unfortunately it's been losing more market share than expected.'

[4] 'Big lion, small cage', *The Economist*, 10 August 2000.

[5] Michael Skapinker, 'A whole world away from Johannesburg', *Financial Times*, 23 November 2000.

Indeed following the first full year of SABMiller operating Miller, its market share had dropped from 19.6 per cent to 18.7 per cent and by September 2003 the share price of the company had dropped from 530 pence (€7.9) on the day of acquisition of Miller, to 456.5 pence (€6.8).

SABMiller appointed Norman Adami, previously head of its Beer South Africa business, as head of Miller, and introduced the traditional SAB system of employee performance rating, making clear that employees who consistently scored unsatisfactorily would be dismissed. This was a considerable change from Miller's previous system of performance rating which routinely rated all staff at the highest level. They also announced that there would be a rationalisation of Miller's product portfolio from 50 brands to 11 or 12, meaning that market share would go down before it could go up again.

Sources close to the company and business analysts were quoted in the press as saying that Miller was more badly managed than SAB executives had anticipated, and while the move into the US market made sense some questioned whether the company had chosen the correct brand. However some press reports[6] in 2004 suggested that this loss of market share may have been reversed with Miller Lite sales sent 'soaring' in response to the popularity of low carbohydrate diets.

The portfolio in 2004

The following extracts from SABMiller's annual reports and some press commentaries give a picture of the company's interests and operations around the world.

Africa (outside South Africa) and Asia

In 2003 SAB was able to report of its operations in Africa:

Clear beer growth of 3.2 per cent in our African businesses was achieved with strong performances from Tanzania, Mozambique and Ghana. Tanzania experienced a good agricultural harvest, beer market growth and additional volume from the restructuring of our East African operations; whilst Mozambique benefited from the Laurentina acquisition. Ghana enjoyed strong market share gains. Our soft drink volumes grew by 15.3 per cent as a result of the inclusion of

Zambia Bottlers following the February 2002 acquisitions and an outstanding performance from Angola, where we exceeded the one million hectolitre mark and achieved organic growth of 41.2 per cent following the end of the civil war and an improving economy. Traditional beer, however, ended below prior levels following the decision to exit the low margin bulk beer segment in Zambia.

The situation in Asia was reported as follows:

Within Asia, our Chinese joint venture performed well with a key area of achievement being the successful integration of the Wuhan and Blue Sword acquisitions. Volumes reached the 24 million hls mark for clear beer and total volumes exceeded 27 million hls. The Chinese beer market is now estimated to be the biggest in the world by volume. The roll-out of the Snowflake brand throughout our 30 Chinese breweries continues, with the brand achieving volumes in excess of five million hls during the year.

Organic volume growth for the year of 5.7 per cent was achieved against total volume growth of 45.3 per cent. EBITA growth in China more than doubled year on year.

In 2004 the possibility of SABMiller undertaking the first hostile takeover of a Chinese firm emerged, with SABMiller battling with Anheuser-Busch to gain control of the Harbin Brewery, listed in Hong Kong. 'SABMiller bought a 29 per cent stake in Harbin last summer [2003], but recently launched a bid for the rest of the company after Anheuser-Busch tried to grab another 29 per cent stake.'[7] *The Economist* reported that if the Anheuser-Busch purchase were to succeed then whoever won the ensuing takeover bid would have to pay at least US$550m (€456.5m), almost 40 times Harbin's earnings the previous year. However with the Chinese beer market growing at 6–8 per cent per year this price still appeared tempting. By June 2004, SABMiller had abandoned its attempt at the takeover in the face of a US$720m counter bid from Anheuser-Busch.

The situation in India was reported as follows:

In India we achieved our target of break even at the operating profit level in our first full year with the expanded base of four operating units, including the acquisition of the Rochees brewery in Rajastan which was finally completed towards the end of the period. During the year we launched Castle Lager in Mumbai, Bangalore and Delhi with encouraging early signs.

---

[6] 'The battle of big beer', *The Economist*, 13 May 2004.

[7] Ibid.

Beer South Africa

South Africa was the original market for SABMiller and remains centrally important. However, here, the company had experienced mixed fortunes. In 2000 it had suffered a 2 per cent decline in volume, but could report an increase in its margins as a result of continuing productivity initiatives. The main reason for the downturn was the domestic situation in South Africa, and in particular a switch in consumer spending. The annual report explained this as follows:

> The proportion of disposable income which the average South African spends on beverages and tobacco has fallen steadily since 1992. The 'normalisation' theory suggests that this shift in consumer expenditure will continue as a higher proportion of discretionary expenditure moves from immediate gratification to self-improvement. As home ownership is encouraged, townships are electrified and more schools are opened, so money is earmarked for mortgages, rents, consumer durables and education. Mobile phones have also become very popular with the potential to divert spending further from beer.
>
> However, the increasingly stable macroeconomic environment, which has encouraged many of these trends, provides a significant opportunity for SAB to grow volumes over the long term. Sound economic policies, which create wealth and higher employment, also result in increased consumer expenditure. We believe that absolute expenditure on beer will rise even if beer is taking a lower percentage of growing consumer spending.
>
> In the meantime, we continue to work hard to increase our market share in the total South African liquor market by making beer the alcoholic drink of first choice for more people primarily through better channel segmentation, distribution and promotions. Our percentage share of the total liquor market is in the mid-50s, so there is scope for further increase.

By 2003 volume had increased 1 per cent on 2002, however this still represented almost 5 per cent decline on sales from a peak in 1999 and there remained concerns by analysts over SABMiller's position in South Africa. According to HSBC and ING Barings, by 2001 beer volumes in South Africa were declining at an annualised rate of about 4 per cent and there were few signs that growth in the rest of Africa was holding up. There were also concerns that costs of raw materials would rise, which was indeed noted in the 2003 annual report. Other conditions in South Africa also seemed to be worrying. As well as consumer spending on beer being diverted into other products such as the lottery and mobile phones, there was real concern about the spread of AIDS. SABMiller was dependent for turnover growth either on price increases or volume growth in the market and neither seemed very likely. There were no signs that consumer spending would increase on beer and population growth was unlikely, especially given the impact of AIDS. In 2001 it was estimated that one in nine South Africans, just over 11 per cent of the population, were infected by HIV or full-blown AIDS. However this was less than the estimates of the World Health Organisation, which had forecast a rise in the disease in the population of around 30 per cent by 2010, and some estimates showed a slowing of the rate of new infections. Nevertheless the worry of a holocaust of AIDS-related deaths in the first years of the 21st century remained. Most of these would be young adults, who were the key market segment for SABMiller as well as being a significant element of the company's workforce. HIV/AIDS is almost certain to have a comparable impact on the rest of Africa.

North America

The 2003 annual report described the situation in North America as follows:

> In the nine month reporting period, US beer industry volumes were affected by low consumer confidence, a lacklustre economy, recent world events, and poor weather, resulting in industry volumes being level with those of the prior year. Total Miller volume, after adjusting for a distributor stock reduction programme implemented in March, was down 3.7 per cent with domestic volume falling by 4.5 per cent (6.2 per cent before adjustment). Certain of Miller's core brands have been losing market share for a number of years. However, the rate of decline increased over the past year and we believe this to be due to a combination of factors including loss of management focus on core brands following the introduction of four FMBs and some understandable disruption during the transaction and subsequent integration into SABMiller. Contract brewing volumes grew 3.6 per cent and international volumes grew by 6.6 per cent.
>
> EBITA, for the nine month period, of US$250m (€207.5m), before exceptional items of US$52m (€43.2m), reflects the impact of the volume decline, as well as negative brand, pack and geographic mix, increased cost of raw materials and greater energy costs, partly offset by higher selling prices. There were also a number of significant one-time restructuring charges including costs associated with the uplift and write-off of excess production of the FMB brands, Sauza Diablo and Stolichnaya Citrona, and the reduction of four and one half days of inventory held in

distributor warehouses, which together amount to US$40m (€33.2m). A further US$16m (€13.3m) of FMB launch costs, as reported in our interim results, were also expensed during the year. Before taking account of the exceptional and other costs referred to above, EBITA for the nine month period was US$306m (€254m).

. . . Exports and international sales of Miller brands, led by MGD, continue to provide volume growth and stable income. We expect to achieve further growth in this area through leveraging the distribution network across the SABMiller group during the current year.

Much work is being undertaken on rebuilding the Miller brands and reshaping the portfolio. We will reposition the Miller trademark based upon extensive in-depth consumer research and mapping, with the first elements of the new architecture becoming visible in autumn 2003. We will, during the next 18 months, also be implementing initiatives to strengthen sales and distribution based upon our experience in other parts of the SABMiller group. These initiatives include prioritisation of local markets, improved channel management, strengthening and reorganising our sales force and improved management of distributors.

It will take time for the benefits of the brand repositioning and sales and distribution initiatives to become evident. However, we have identified opportunities to reduce costs over and above those included in the US$50m (€41.5m) of synergies described at the time of the acquisition. Importantly, we are also upgrading the performance management systems across the organisation and will be taking appropriate actions to implement a productivity and cost reduction programme.

Miller profitability will be impacted over the next two to three years by the current volume declines, adverse mix effects and the ongoing restructuring and reorganisation necessary to establish our platform for growth, although we are confident that our efforts will deliver shareholder value in the medium term. For the current financial year, we expect that EBITA, pre exceptional and before restructuring and reorganisation costs, will be trending lower than comparable previous periods.

Europe

Progress in Europe was described as follows:

The division enjoyed another excellent year of profit growth with EBITA up 39 per cent. Lager comparable volumes grew 8 per cent assisted by good summer weather in our two key markets of Poland and the Czech Republic. Productivity (measured in hectolitres per person per annum) improved by 12 per cent and contributed to the 120 point expansion in EBITA margin. Currencies in central Europe have strengthened against the US dollar, and this has contributed to the improvement in reported results.

Growth in the Polish beer market was 5 per cent for the twelve months to March 2003. Kompania Piwowarska (KP) outperformed the industry with a volume increase of 10 per cent, reaching 32 per cent market share. A new brand Debowe, competing in the strong beer segment, had a highly successful launch capturing over 20 per cent of that segment within nine months. Recently, we announced the acquisition of Browar Dojlidy Sp. z.o.o. for US$38m (€31.5m). This acquisition was completed on 30 April 2003, after securing all regulatory approvals and provides us with an economy brand in the mainstream segment, adding a third production facility and improving KP's representation in the east of the country.

In the Czech Republic, the Pilsner Urquell group exceeded expectations. The overall market declined, as anticipated, by around 1 per cent this past year. However, we saw volumes grow by 4 per cent, signalling good market share gains. In particular, the premium Pilsner Urquell brand grew by some 12 per cent, assisting margin expansion. Local management is to be commended on rapid reaction to, and recovery from, the devastating floods in August.

Our international premium brand Pilsner Urquell continues to perform well in the key export markets of the USA, Germany, and the United Kingdom. Sales volumes in these markets are encouraging, with volumes up 13 per cent, 17 per cent and 60 per cent respectively on the prior year. In total, volumes of Pilsner Urquell outside the Czech Republic have increased by 17 per cent to 653,000 hls. The stand-alone Pilsner Urquell business in the USA was integrated with the Miller Brewing Company operations shortly after the financial year end and this will provide a strong platform for the future potential of the brand in this market.

In Russia, industry volumes were up some 9 per cent for the year and SABMiller enjoyed a sharp recovery in the second half to end the year with 27 per cent growth. This followed the introduction of cans, a new brand Tri Bogatyrya launched into the growing mainstream segment, and the newly licensed production of Kozel from our Czech brand portfolio. MGD, Holsten and Pilsner Urquell volumes all more than doubled and our share of the Russian premium segment is now over 10 per cent. Expansion to 3.5 million hectolitres at the Kaluga brewery is virtually complete and well within budget.

In Hungary, general price stability continued, assisting overall industry profitability. Our Dreher subsidiary's volumes were up 5 per cent against the industry's 3 per cent and profits and cash flow surged during the year. Romania's beer market continues to disappoint with virtually stagnant volumes. However, SABMiller's volumes grew organically by 12 per cent and this, together with ongoing synergy developments from the prior year's Timisoreana acquisition, boosted Romania's profitability albeit off a small base. Slovakia continues to benefit from management and marketing integration with the Pilsner Urquell group. Volumes were up 14 per cent and our market share is now 25 per cent. The Canary Islands have suffered from the decline in global tourism and the beer industry lost ground this past year; volumes were down by 3 per cent though profits improved slightly.

Within Central and Eastern Europe, consolidation of the brewing industry continues. SABMiller expects to maintain a leading position in the region, and to continue competing effectively.

Central America

From the 2003 annual report:

Sales declines have depressed the reported EBITA performance and reduced operating margins. However, the year has been one of major structural change. The restructuring of our Central American businesses has proceeded well. In each country we have merged the sales and distribution functions for beer and CSDs. We have rationalised packaging assets in the businesses and closed certain production and distribution sites. Across the region we have merged our back office operations and integrated our financial systems. This has resulted in significant headcount reduction in both countries' operations and will lead to substantial savings in future financial years. The El Salvadorian companies have been merged and we expect to do the same in Honduras in the current year.

The strategy is to continue the conversion of the company into a marketing focussed enterprise with a strong portfolio of relevant brands. A number of brand and packaging changes are planned, and these should support improved performance in the market place.

Initiatives are also in place to improve production efficiencies with the roll-out of the World Class Manufacturing initiative, continued rationalisation of surplus facilities and ongoing sales and distribution integration.

Hotels and Gaming

From the 2003 annual report:

Hotels and Gaming achieved good earnings growth with increased operational contributions from both segments. The transaction regarding the restructuring of SABMiller's Hotels and Gaming interests became unconditional on 31 March this year. This consolidated subsidiary will in future be accounted for as an associate. The new Tsogo Sun Group is now set to pursue an independent future with the expectation that SABMiller's 49 per cent shareholding will be reduced over time.

The hotel industry benefited from a significant increase in foreign visitor arrivals to South Africa which has driven strong operating profit growth for the period. Occupancies at 72 per cent were well up from the 66 per cent achieved last year. Average room rates increased by 19 per cent, translating into an overall revpar increase of 34 per cent to US\$32.10 (€26.6). The successful hosting of the World Summit on Sustainable Development and the Cricket World Cup were also contributing factors.

Gaming division's results were strongly influenced by the performance of Montecasino, the division's flagship casino and entertainment complex, which continues to trade well. The Gauteng casino market grew by approximately 15 per cent when measured against the previous financial year, with Montecasino marginally gaining market share. Phase one of the Suncoast casino development in Durban was successfully opened in late November at a capital cost of US\$95m (€78.9m).

Where from here?

In 2003 the company outlined its strategy as follows:

Our strategy to grow shareholder value remains focused upon four key elements.

The first is to drive volume and productivity. We were pleased that last year we saw volume growth in our South African beer business, which once again delivered operating margin improvement. In Europe, our businesses in virtually all of the seven countries in which we operate have grown volumes by more than the market increase and have achieved year-on-year market share gains. In Africa, we continue to see excellent volume and market share performances in key countries.

The second element of the strategy is to optimise and expand our existing positions through acquisitions. We continue to seek opportunities to achieve growth within individual countries or geographic regions, where we can build strong positions, leverage synergies and achieve economies of scale. The acquisition by our Polish subsidiary Kompania Piwowarska, of the Browar Dojlidy brewery, announced during the year, is a good example of this type of transaction.

The third area of our strategy is to seek value-adding opportunities to enhance our position as a global brewer. We continue to believe that economic development, converging customer taste and lowering of trade barriers will drive further consolidation of the beer market. Currently, the four leading brewers account for around only 33 per cent of the global market compared to between 50 per cent and 80 per cent for other consumer sectors. Companies with a global footprint will benefit from the economies of scale that consolidation will bring and will, we believe, deliver greater shareholder value in the medium to longer term.

Growing our brands in the international premium beer segment is the fourth, and so far, the least developed element of the strategy. Our portfolio of premium brands now contains Pilsner Urquell, Miller Genuine Draft, Peroni and Castle. We believe that there are real opportunities to increase sales in this growing segment through leveraging our distribution platforms around the world.

By pursuing this strategy we have built a business that delivered adjusted earnings per share growth of 11 per cent for the financial year ended March 2003. But we cannot be complacent. We will continue to focus relentlessly upon operational efficiency and work hard on strengthening our regional brands and market positions, pursuing acquisitive growth only where we can see the potential to add real value for shareholders.

The report went on to state:

SABMiller has portfolios of strong national and regional brands principally based on the mainstream segments of the market. Our challenge is to support these regional brands to ensure that we retain or, in the case of Miller restore, their brand health. We are also looking to build our positions in the premium or 'worth more' segments that are driving what volume growth there is in developed markets. Crucial to this is our international brand portfolio described earlier.

To strengthen marketing focus and coordinate the drive behind our international premium brands, we have created a new role of group marketing director.

In addition, we are focusing on innovation and have had some notable successes in South Africa with Brutal Fruit and Sterling Light, and with Redd's in Poland and East Africa.

Having survived and grown for over 100 years SABMiller had emerged onto the world market at a time when it appears that the 21st century may prove globally as turbulent as the 20th was in South Africa. The jury is still out on whether the culture and competences that the company acquired in South Africa and other emerging markets will equip it properly to meet the challenges of developed markets in this new century.

Sources

Chaloner, N. and Brotzen, D., 'How SABMiller protects its biggest asset – its reputation', *SCM*, vol. 6, no. 6, Oct/Nov, 2002. *The Economist*, Special report on doing business in violent or chaotic countries, 18 May 2000. 'Big lion, small cage', *The Economist*, 10 August 2000. 'The worst way to lose talent', *The Economist*, 8 February 2001. 'Lead boots', *The Economist*, 13 December 2001. 'The battle of big beer', *The Economist*, 13 May 2004. 'The China Brew', *Far Eastern Economic Review*, 11 June 2002. Michael Skapinker, 'A whole world away from Johannesburg', *Financial Times*, 23 November 2000. Hobday, N., 'Tapped out', *The Daily Deal*, 8 September 2003. Hal Lux, 'Miller time (Mergers and Acquisitions). (South African Breweries acquires Miller Brewing Co.)', *Institutional Investor International Edition*, vol. 28. no. 1, January 2003, p. 45. 'Tax gets a look in as SAB goes global', *International Tax Review*, vol. 13, no. 3, March 2002. 'Miller Brewing gets New CEO from New Owner, South African Breweries', *Knight Rider/Tribune Business News*, 15 January 2003. Reports on SAB by HSBC and ING Barings. South African Breweries annual reports and website.

APPENDIX

Five-year financial review for the years ended 31 March 2003

	1999* US$m**	2000* US$m	2001 US$m	2002 US$m	2003 US$m
Income statements					
Turnover (including associates' share)	6,184	5,424	4,184	4,364	9,112
Turnover (excluding associates' share)	4,923	4,390	3,624	3,717	8,295
Profit before interest and taxation (including associates' share)	717	844	700	704	933
Net interest payable	(117)	(80)	(54)	(98)	(163)
Taxation	(195)	(186)	(195)	(208)	(349)
Minorities	(85)	(94)	(99)	(105)	(125)
Profit for the year	320	484	352	293	296
Adjusted earnings	394	426	372	350	581
Balance sheets					
Fixed assets	2,600	3,510	3,667	4,758	11,060
Current asset inv./cash at bank and in hand	749	316	218	290	561
Other current assets	913	558	514	643	1,258
Total assets	4,262	4,384	4,399	5,691	12,879
Interest bearing debt	(953)	(602)	(1,053)	(1,535)	(3,523)
Other creditors and provisions	(1,445)	(1,223)	(1,054)	(1,102)	(2,377)
Total liabilities	(2,398)	(1,825)	(2,107)	(2,637)	(5,900)
Net assets	1,824	2,559	2,292	3,054	6,979
Shareholders' funds	1,703	2,161	2,006	2,309	6,201
Equity minority interests	161	398	286	745	778
Capital employed	1,864	2,559	2,292	3,054	6,979
Cash flow statements					
EBITDA	933	917	854	904	1,483
Working capital movements	(45)	(53)	5	71	85
Net cash inflow from operating activities	888	864	859	975	1,568
Net interest and dividends	(119)	(82)	(93)	(158)	(238)
Taxation	(166)	(175)	(179)	(179)	(286)
	603	607	587	638	1,044
Net capital expenditure	(544)	(401)	(331)	(250)	(429)
Net investments	(1)	(569)	7	(49)	(18)
Net acquisition of subsidiaries and associates	(273)	30	(700)	(768)	(54)
Net cash(shortfall)/surplus	(215)	(333)	(437)	(429)	543
Management of liquid resources	(419)	503	64	19	44
Net cash inflow from financing	256	72	491	699	(136)
Dividends paid	n/a	(50)	(177)	(173)	(203)
Increase/(decrease) in cash for the year	(378)	192	(59)	116	248
Performance per share (US cents per share)					
Basic earnings	43.9	64.3	50.4	40.7	27.5
Diluted earnings	43.8	64.1	50.3	40.3	27.8
Adjusted basic earnings	54.0	56.6	53.3	48.7	54.0
Net asset value	220.1	279.3	258.9	274.6	487.8
Share statistics					
Total number of shares (*million*)	773.7	774.3	775.0	840.9	1,271.2
Weighted average number of shares (*million*)	729.9	752.8	697.21	718.5	1,076.1
Weighted average number of shares (*diluted*) (*million*)	731.3	754.8	699.4	766.6	1,148.3

	1999* US$m**	2000* US$m	2001 US$m	2002 US$m	2003 US$m
Returns and productivity					
Return on equity (%)	23.1	19.7	18.5	15.2	**9.4**
Operating margin (%)	13.2	14.6	16.7	16.1	**11.0**
Cash operating margin (%)	19.9	20.9	23.6	24.3	**18.1**
Operating return (%)	45.1	47.1	42.6	37.5	**34.8**
Cash operating return (%)	24.7	25.8	22.2	17.9	**13.2**
Group turnover per employee ($000's)	100.3	91.3	115.7	111.8	**196.1**
Average monthly number of employees	49,099	48,079	31,327	33,230	**42,402**
Solvency and liquidity					
Net interest cover (*times*)	7.4	9.9	13.0	7.2	**6.1**
Total borrowing to total assets (%)	22.4	13.7	23.9	27.0	**27.4**
Cash flow to total borrowings (%)	93.2	143.5	81.6	63.5	**44.5**

* Partial deferred tax basis.
** $US1 = approx. €0.83.

	Turnover					Operating profit				
	1999 US$m*	2000 US$m	2001 US$m	2002 US$m	2003 US$m	1999 US$m	2000 US$m	2001 US$m	2002 US$m	2003 US$m
Business segment analysis										
North America	–	–	–	–	**3,473**	–	–	–	–	**75**
Central America	–	–	–	186	**514**	–	–	–	7	**10**
Europe	n/a	n/a	1,097	1,280	**1,646**	n/a	n/a	130	168	**239**
Africa and Asia	n/a	n/a	700	946	**1,209**	n/a	n/a	130	162	**219**
SABI	1,352	1,474				190	199			
Beer South Africa	1,609	1,608	1,365	1,112	**1,270**	380	407	343	287	**338**
Other Beverage Interests	967	954	816	676	**788**	117	120	106	95	**120**
Hotels and Gaming	276	263	206	164	**212**	42	40	25	28	**42**
Central administration	–	–	–	–	–	(18)	(35)	(34)	(35)	**(44)**
Continuing businesses – **excluding exceptional** **items**	4,204	4,299	4,184	4,364	**9,112**	711	731	700	712	**999**
PGSI	1,751	1,125				75	61			
Group – excluding **exceptional items**	5,955	5,424	4,184	4,364	**9,112**	786	792	700	712	**999**
Exceptional items										
Group including **exceptional items**										
North America	–	–	–	–	–	–	–	–	–	**(58)**
Central America	–	–	–	–	–	–	–	–	–	**(12)**
Europe	–	–	–	–	–	–	–	–	(8)	–
SABI	229	–	–	–	–	(50)	(11)	–	–	–
Hotels and Gaming	–	–	–	–	–	(9)	–	–	–	–
PGSI	–	–	–	–	–	(10)	(13)	–	–	–
Group – including **exceptional items**	6,184	5,424	4,184	4,364	**9,112**	717	768	700	704	**929**

* $US1 = approx. €0.83.
n/a: not available prior to 2001, information is only available in respect of the international, non-South African group, in total.

	EBITA					Net operating assets				
	1999 US$m**	2000 US$m	2001 US$m	2002 US$m	2003 US$m	1999* US$m	2000* US$m	2001 US$m	2002 US$m	2003 US$m
Business segment analysis										
North America	–	–	–	–	**250**	–	–	–	–	**5,147**
Central America	–	–	–	22	**56**	–	–	–	1,135	**1,089**
Europe	n/a	n/a	148	198	**275**	n/a	n/a	1,091	1,253	**1,446**
Africa and Asia	n/a	n/a	132	171	**233**	n/a	n/a	472	728	**866**
SABI	191	205			**781**	1,033				
Beer South Africa	380	407	343	287	**338**	539	509	415	263	**356**
Other Beverage Interests	117	120	106	95	**120**	600	601	520	355	**524**
Hotels and Gaming	42	40	25	28	**42**	134	169	159	140	**167**
Central administration	(18)	(35)	(34)	(35)	**(44)**	(61)	(27)	(148)	(193)	**(272)**
Continuing businesses – excluding exceptional items	712	737	720	766	**1,270**	1,993	2,285	2,509	3,681	**9,323**
PGSI	75	61	–	–	75	–	–	–	–	–
Group – excluding exceptional items	787	798	720	766	**1,270**	2,068	2,285	2,509	3,681	**9,323**
Exceptional items										
North America	–	–	–	(58)	–	–	–	–	–	–
Central America	–	–	–	(12)	–	–	–	–	–	–
Europe	–	–	–	(8)	–	–	–	–	–	–
SABI	(50)	(11)	–	–	–	–	–	–	–	–
Hotels and Gaming	(9)	–	–	–	4	–	–	–	–	–
PGSI	(10)	(13)	–	–		–	–	–	–	–
Group – including exceptional items	718	774	720	758	1,204	2,068	2,285	2,509	3,681	9,323

* Partial deferred tax basis.

** $US1 = approx. €0.83.

n/a: not available prior to 2001, information is only available in respect of the international, non-South African group, in total.

Xelibri – a Siemens mobile adventure

Florian Clemens, Henning Hagen, Fabian Hedderich and Hendrik Sassmann

On 3 October 2002, 10 am, George Appling, President of Xelibri, addressed his team at the weekly All Team Meeting at their Munich headquarters: 'Good morning. So let me give you my usual update on what happened last week. On Tuesday I had another session with the board. When you talk to the board, you should always take some toys with you. So I showed them our first prototypes and they got totally excited. I think we're beyond the point-of-no-return now and it's clear that we will launch the first collection of Xelibri fashion accessory phones this coming spring . . . and every spring and fall thereafter – forever. This team has done a tremendous job so far in building our network of partners and agencies and getting us where we are now. When thinking of the next steps towards our launch let me highlight four points that we need to focus on.

'One, we need a world-class PR campaign to build our brand and a concept for advertising to support it. Two, we need to finalise our country strategy for the initial roll-out. Three, we need to get clear which channels we want to address to sell our products, and four, we have to get our pricing right. I am very confident we have all the right experience and spirit in the room to get that done. Go team!'

● ● ●

Siemens AG

Based in Munich, Germany, Siemens AG is a global solutions company with a focus on electronics and electrical engineering. With products ranging from mobile phones and computers to trains and power plants, Siemens AG employed 430,000 people in 190 countries in 2002. Global sales for the fiscal year (FY) 2001/02[1] were €84bn, which includes €18bn sales in Germany alone. For a size comparison, General Electric's revenues in FY 2001 were €144bn (≈ £100bn).

History of Siemens

In 1847, Werner von Siemens founded the 'Telegraphenbauanstalt von Siemens & Halske',

---

[1] Siemens AG's fiscal year ends 30 September.

starting with a small precision-engineering workshop. In the following decades, the company was able to produce numerous innovations, including the first electric streetlights in Berlin, the first electric elevator and the electric streetcar. With the guiding principle to concentrate on the whole of electrical engineering, the company branched out into lighting, electric medical equipment, radio transmission technology as well as household appliances in the 1920s. After the Second World War, Siemens expanded into new business segments: data processing systems, automotive systems and semiconductors. It also reestablished its presence in traditional export markets, returning to its old strength in the global marketplace in the 1960s. In 1969, Siemens' main business segments were assigned to six independent operating groups, a structure that still persisted in 2003 (see Exhibit 1).

Florian Clemens, Henning Hagen, Fabian Hedderich and Hendrik Sassmann prepared this case under the supervision of Professor Lutz Kaufmann to provide material for class discussion. The authors do not intend to illustrate either effective or ineffective handling of a managerial situation. The authors may have disguised certain names and other identifying information to protect confidentiality.

Exhibit 1   Key financial data of Siemens' operations business segments

	Information and Communications						Medical		Lighting	
	Information and Communication Networks (ICN)		Information and Communication Mobile (ICM)		Siemens Business Services (SBS)		Medical Solutions (Med)		Osram	
Fiscal year ending	2002	2001	2002	2001	2002	2001	2002	2001	2002	2001
Total sales (€m)	9,647	12,882	11,045	11,299	5,773	6,034	7,623	7,219	4,363	4,522
New orders (€m)	8,697	12,639	11,538	11,866	6,256	6,303	8,425	8,444	4,363	4,522
Net cash from oper. and investing activities (€m)	711	−2,350	594	14	173	339	1,124	86	284	349
EBIT (€m)	−691	−861	96	−307	101	−259	1,018	808	365	462
EBIT margin	−7.2%	−6.7%	0.9%	−2.7%	1.7%	−4.3%	13.4%	11.2%	8.4%	10.2%
Employees	39,000	51,000	29,000	30,000	34,000	36,000	31,000	30,000	35,000	35,000

	Automation and Control							
	Automation and Drives (A&D)		Industrial Solutions & Services (I&S)		Siemens Dematic (SD)		Siemens Building Technologies (SBT)	
Fiscal year ending	2002	2001	2002	2001	2002	2001	2002	2001
Total sales (€m)	8,635	8,947	4,480	4,563	2,995	2,520	5,619	5,518
New orders (€m)	8,728	9,065	4,120	4,881	2,810	2,281	5,601	5,549
Net cash from oper. and inv. activities (€m)	1,019	533	−107	−39	−70	261	295	49
EBIT (€m)	723	981	−198	97	45	−59	195	132
EBIT margin	8.4%	11.0%	−4.4%	2.1%	1.5%	−2.3%	3.5%	2.4%
Employees	51,000	54,000	29,000	30,000	12,000	12,000	36,000	37,000

	Power				Transportation			
	Power Generation (PG)		Power Transmission and Distribution (PTD)		Transportation Systems (TS)		Siemens VDO Automotive (SV)	
Fiscal year ending	2002	2001	2002	2001	2002	2001	2002	2001
Total sales (€m)	9,446	8,563	4,199	4,053	4,367	4,021	8,515	5,702
New orders (€m)	10,586	12,219	4,429	3,887	5,247	5,647	8,515	5,702
Net cash from oper. and inv. activities (€m)	662	2,045	149	−331	95	752	224	−89
EBIT (€m)	1,582	634	109	96	247	186	65	−261
EBIT margin	16.7%	7.4%	2.6%	2.4%	5.7%	4.6%	0.8%	−4.6%
Employees	26,000	26,000	17,000	21,000	17,000	14,000	43,000	44,000

Source: Siemens Annual Report 2002.

year. Most of the turnaround can be accredited to the Mobile Phones division posting EBIT of €92m, compared to a negative €540m a year earlier, a period which included significant charges for asset write-downs, particularly for excess handset inventories.

Siemens Mobile Phones (MP)

The world market share of the Mobile Phones division was 8.3 per cent in 2002, making it the fourth largest player in the handset market, down from a number three position in 2001. In the first quarter of FY 2003,[2] it achieved a record sale of 11m mobile phones, up 22 per cent over the previous year's first quarter. The Mobile Phones division offers products for all segments of the market, from teenagers in the light-user segment to business users interested in feature- and application-rich products. The voice-centric segment (VC) focuses on simple and cheap mobile phones mostly used by operators for the pre-paid, light-user segment (e.g. A50). The user-centric segment (UC) develops phones along the C, M, S, CL and SL lines (e.g. S45, ME45, CL50 and S55). 3rd Generation and Convergence (3C) comprises the UMTS product line (to which, for example, the U10 belongs) and mobile phones combined with personal digital assistants (PDAs). The Accessory Devices division (AD) adds products such as headsets and car kits. Xelibri was the fifth segment of Siemens mobile phones. The individual segments are P&L owners.

The product portfolio of Siemens Mobile Phones is not only structured along the lines of technology and price as phones are also targeted at user groups: Siemens positioned the CL50 as 'a girl's best friend', or the ME45 as a 'sophisticated outdoor phone', for example. However, this positioning is only done once a phone has been developed – rather than the idea of a certain target customer triggering the development or design of a mobile phone. Overall, Siemens phones mostly have a reputation for being a symbol of German engineering skills rather than emotions or design.

Information and Communication Mobile (ICM)

Led by Rudi Lamprecht as Group President, ICM takes pride in being an end-to-end solution provider with products including mobile communication infrastructure technology, mobile end-user devices, wireless modules and mobile applications. This wide range of products makes ICM not only a leading supplier to network operators but also a major global player in the third-generation mobile market, supplying at least one leading mobile operator in every major Western European market where the third-generation wireless standard was introduced: the Universal Mobile Telecommunication System (UMTS or 3G). ICM's end-user devices consist of cordless phones based on digital enhanced cordless telecommunications technology and mobile phones for all market segments under the Siemens brand (see Exhibit 2).

In FY 2002, ICM was back in the black with EBIT of €96m compared to a €307m loss in the previous

---

[2] October to December. This 'Christmas Quarter' traditionally features the highest sales of mobile phones over the year.

Exhibit 2 · Excerpt from the organisational chart of Siemens AG

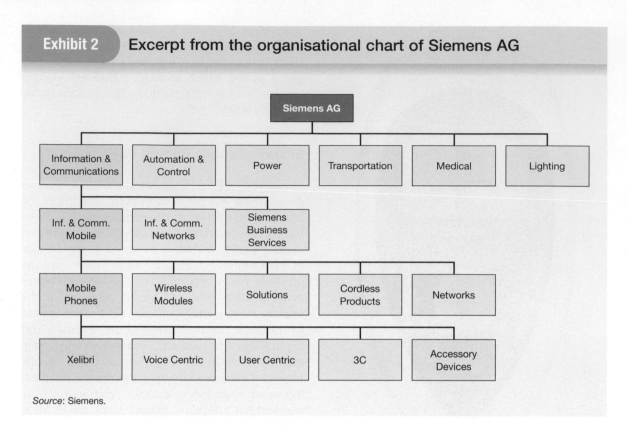

Source: Siemens.

Introduction to the mobile telecommunications market

In large parts of the world, mobile telecommunication as a mass product started with networks using the Global Standard for Mobile Communication (GSM). The first GSM network was launched by Finnish Radiolinja in cooperation with the handset and infrastructure producer Nokia in 1991. The next year, countries such as France, Germany, Portugal, Sweden and Great Britain followed. Once a mass market network was launched, penetration rates skyrocketed, growing faster than those of facsimiles, ISDN lines and even the internet in most countries. Within ten years, the mobile phone market was practically saturated (see Exhibit 3). The Japanese and South Korean markets not only used a different network technology, but also had always been ahead of the European and American markets in terms of new technology and new product development. Tech-savvy users in Japan made network operator NTT DoCoMo the symbol for profitable growth in a high-end mass market during the 1990s.

Competitiveness in the operator market

The enormous growth of the user base was achieved for several reasons: deregulation and liberalisation of most telecommunication markets helped new aggressive companies enter the scene, assuring ongoing competition. Moreover, as network operators incurred high fixed costs for the infrastructure but incrementally low marginal cost for additional traffic in their network, it was each operator's focus to attract new customers as fast as possible. Gigantic marketing campaigns, armadas of outlet stores and price wars for handset offerings became common in many countries. Another important factor was the introduction of prepaid services as a marketing concept: consumers bought a contingent of airtime minutes instead of entering into a long-term contract with the operator. Prepaid offerings were targeted at the light-user segment, mostly children and teenagers. In many countries, competition became so severe that, at the end of the 1990s, operators started to substantially subsidise handsets in order to further increase their subscriber base. Prepaid cards bundled with a handset would sell for as little as €35 – about

Exhibit 3 | **Penetration rates of information and communication technologies in Germany**

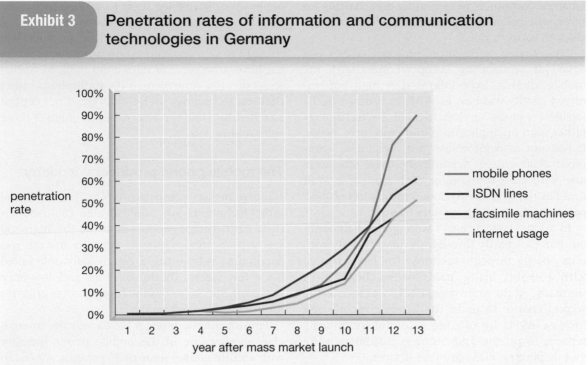

Source: Data derived from ITU Stat. Yearbook 2000, CIA World Factbook 2000, GfK, BA f. Statistik (data relative to specific target population within Germany).

40–50 per cent of handset production costs. This was at a point in time when many stock analysts thought the number of subscribers was more important for company valuation than an operator's costs or profits. Mobile phones bundled with a contract were given away 'for free' in some countries – with a minimum monthly fee guaranteed to earn back at least part of the sales subsidy.

Having entered the phone retail business with their outlets, network operators bought millions of handsets from all price categories, making their own stores the main point of sale. This way, the handset makers' contact to the customer was mostly through the operators, as phones were much cheaper when bought in a bundle compared to the device alone bought from an electronics retailer. This purchasing and market power gave much impact to the operators in terms of defining prices and functionalities of the handsets.

The evolution of products and services

Originally, GSM was thought to deliver universal availability of voice communication. One of its protocols, the short message service SMS, was the

first so-called killer application, i.e. an application that by its intelligent design and utility becomes indispensable for millions of people. Experts say it has remained the only one in European markets so far. SMS started out as a network control messaging application and was initially not marketed for end-consumer use. Nevertheless, the comparatively uncomfortable and in many countries expensive way of sending 160-character long texts was used by consumers and developed a growth that was never thought of: global SMS traffic was estimated to be around one billion messages every day by the end of 2002.

At the beginning of the new millennium however, network operators needed further growth to earn back their massive investments. As there were increasingly fewer people without a mobile phone, average revenue per user (ARPU) had to increase. At this point, voice and SMS were practically the only services European customers paid for while Asians were adding new services based on mobile internet to their daily life. Puzzled by the never-ending success stories, especially of Japanese NTT DoCoMo, European operators felt much pressure and saw potential to go in the same direction.

Japanese consumers were gaming and chatting for hours when commuting to and from work or being stuck in metro traffic.

The wireless application protocol (WAP) was aimed at acquainting European users with the mobile internet. Expectations were high but perceived quality was low, as WAP, in contrast to the Japanese i-mode service, focused on technology rather than on applications and customers' needs. It was not as comfortable, fast, helpful or error-proof as advertised. Accordingly, usage rates were low, with users thinking of WAP more as a 'Wait And Pay' service, due to slow transmission of WAP pages and high prices for data transfer.

In 2000, UMTS licences were granted throughout Europe – partly through so-called 'beauty contests', partly through auctions. The latter peaked with €50.5bn being paid for six licences in Germany. At the same time, UMTS was seen as the second chance to make the internet mobile and increase ARPU by offering colourful multimedia services to private and business customers using mobile phones, PDAs or other devices.

Today, expectations about UMTS have been brought back to a more conservative level. Several players have declared they will not use their licence. The intermediate standard, the General Packet Radio System (GPRS or 2.5 G), was replacing GSM, offering Multimedia Messaging Service (MMS) – being marketed as the new killer

application. It enabled users to take pictures with an add-on or integrated mini-camera and to send and receive picture messages. Prices for what was thought to be a first step in educating customers to use innovative services started out high. Nevertheless, operators now focused on applications rather than on technology alone. In 2002, 4 per cent of sold handsets had cameras; nine out of ten of those were sold in Asia.

The mobile phone producers' industry

Handset makers competed on creating more and more technologically sophisticated handsets for their cutting-edge product lines in the high-end segment. In this segment, time to market was paramount as innovation gaps usually only lasted for a few weeks. In the medium and low-price segments, the same brands competed on price for mostly standardised products.

Finnish mobile pioneer Nokia was the unarguable number one in the mobile phone industry with a world market share of 36 per cent. American Motorola as number two had 17 per cent market share, Korean Samsung (10 per cent), German Siemens (8.3 per cent) and Japanese-Swedish SonyEricsson (5 per cent) followed (see Exhibit 4).

The large Chinese market had several domestic players focusing on low-price products often inspired by the larger producers. They grabbed one

---

Exhibit 4 | **Global market shares of handset producers**

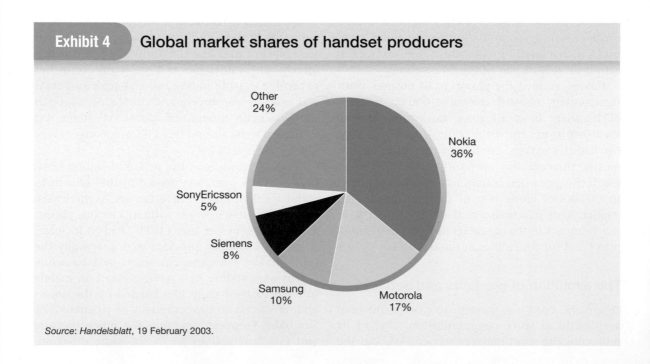

Source: *Handelsblatt*, 19 February 2003.

per cent of the domestic market in each month of 2002, challenging the big players. The domestic Chinese players in sum led the Chinese market for the first time in October 2002 with a combined market share of 27.7 per cent, taking over the number one position in that high growth market from Motorola. Analysts estimate that on average, retailers worldwide paid $155 for a Motorola handset, with production costs estimated to be around $70–90.

Outsourced manufacturing had been an industry trend for the last years: on the one hand, price competition caused pressure for cheap production and assembly. On the other hand, operators pressured handset makers to enlarge their product portfolios and to generate a constant flow of new products. Gaining or losing a big operator as a customer meant making profits or losses for almost all players, as only large volumes made the high research and development costs of a new handset worthwhile. There were two basic models of outsourcing: Electronic Manufacturing Services (EMS) companies, e.g. Flextronics, and Original Design and Manufacturing (ODM) companies like Finnish Microcell. The earlier type focused on production for handset makers, the latter took responsibility

for both development and production. Until 2000, many handset makers ramped up immense production capacities themselves. In 2001, they were then hit by much slower growth. Expected volume was much higher and even larger players turned considerable profits into severe losses within months. The next year, the world market barely recovered, growing 7 per cent to 422 million units.

The consumers and their local markets

While there was a considerable user group of price-insensitive, tech-savvy early adopters buying only the latest technology, many consumers cared only little about the newest features of the latest mobile phone. A large group of people just wanted a neat and reliable device to make phone calls, with the main purchasing reasons being design, price and quality (see Exhibit 5). In the early days of the industry, just having a mobile phone was a status symbol; later it was the technology, the applications it offered or just the style that mattered. Development and branding had changed from technology-driven to application-driven. Handset makers realised that another trend could lie in 'fashion-driven' phones. In August 2000,

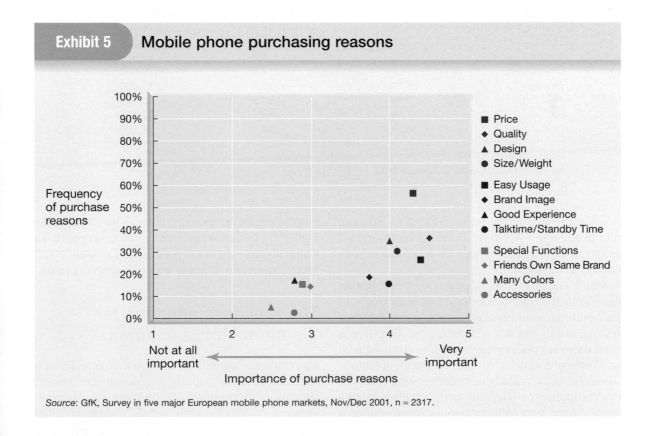

Exhibit 5   Mobile phone purchasing reasons

Source: GfK, Survey in five major European mobile phone markets, Nov/Dec 2001, n = 2317.

Exhibit 6	Country data

Country	Mobile Phone Penetration	Population (million)	GDP per capita (in purchasing power parity $*)
Australia	60%	19.3	23,200
Austria	82%	8.2	25,000
Belgium	70%	10.3	25,300
China	12%	1,273.0	3,600
Denmark	78%	5.3	25,500
Finland	82%	5.2	22,900
France	62%	59.5	24,400
Germany	69%	83.0	23,400
Greece	69%	10.6	17,200
Hong Kong	85%	7.2	25,400
India	1%	1,027.0	2,500
Indonesia	3%	228.4	2,900
Ireland	76%	3.9	21,600
Israel	80%	5.9	18,900
Italy	89%	57.7	22,100
Japan	60%	126.8	24,900
Malaysia	30%	22.2	10,300
Netherlands	74%	16.0	24,400
Norway	76%	4.5	27,700
Philippines	14%	82.4	3,800
Portugal	83%	10.1	15,800
Singapore	85%	4.3	26,500
South Korea	61%	47.9	16,100
Spain	72%	40.0	18,000
Sweden	81%	8.9	22,200
Switzerland	75%	7.3	28,600
Taiwan	97%	22.4	17,400
Thailand	12%	61.8	6,700
UK	77%	59.6	22,800
USA	53%	278.1	36,200

* US1 = approx. €0.83.

Source: ITU 2002, CIA World Factbook 2003.

Nokia made an attempt to introduce a fashionable phone when the Nokia 8210 model was marketed as the first phone developed in cooperation with fashion designers.

While consumers in Germany or Great Britain were used to heavily subsidised phones, users in Italy and many other countries had a much higher willingness to pay for a handset. In Asia, it was even more so: prices were very close to those paid in Western countries (usually without operators' subsidies), but especially in countries such as China, the Philippines or Thailand, people had to spend a much higher part of their disposable income on a mobile phone as average income was lower (see Exhibit 6). In China, about 65 million people had a yearly income of $5,000 ($\approx$ €4,200) or more in 2002. More than twice as many owned a mobile phone.

The business situation for Siemens Mobile Phones

In 2001, the growth of Siemens Mobile Phones had slowed down rapidly, mainly due to market saturation in the majority of Western countries. Siemens had sold 23.9m mobile phones in 2000 and 28.7m in 2001. Although this still translated into a growth rate of 20.1 per cent, the future looked uncertain. In 2001, there had been strong rumours about ICM top management considering completely abandoning the handset industry, since handset production was becoming a commodity business where only the biggest players could be profitable over time. The final decision was not to leave the industry, but to aim for becoming one of the top two players. In 2002, Siemens had to think about how they could deal with declining growth rates, diverging user groups and advancing technologies.

Heinrich von Pierer, CEO of Siemens, had announced minimum return goals for all business segments of 8–11 per cent for FY 2004. The Information and Communications segments, however, were granted one extra year to reach these results. Considering that last quarter's margin had only been around 2 per cent, this was still not an easy task for ICM. Looking at the situation, Rudi Lamprecht recognised that something had to be done in order to stabilise Siemens' mobile phone business.

'Go out and change the world!'

When further exploring the options, *designafairs*, an industrial design agency that was an ICM spin-off and designed – among other items – the mobiles phones for MP, came to mind: the designers had been complaining for some time that many of their creative ideas were not put into practice and that technology, not design, was determining the products' appearance.

In the beginning of 2002, Rudi Lamprecht met with George Appling, who had been working for McKinsey & Company, consulting Lamprecht on a turnaround strategy for Siemens Mobile Phones. Previous to that meeting there had been some discussions about George Appling taking over responsibility for MP's VC segment. Over breakfast at Munich's famous hotel Bayerischer Hof, Lamprecht explained to him the need for a different, unconventional project independent from MP's current operations: 'George, we need to do something bold, something nobody expects, and something that will reinvigorate growth in the mobile phone market.'

George Appling, who had expected to discuss managing the VC segment, was surprised and thrilled by this totally new possibility. Just recently he and Lamprecht had discussed several ideas to improve Siemens' performance in the mobile phone business. One scenario revolved around production optimisation through increased modularisation of components. Another possible approach was to put more emphasis on a design-based value proposition.

Reconsidering all options, Rudi Lamprecht and George Appling came to the following conclusion: if ICM was about to do something really bold, the only viable way of making it happen was to take the design-based approach and drive it forward independently from current operations. Lamprecht concluded: 'George, I will give you a budget, full responsibility for the financials, personnel, marketing, products, prices and distribution. All I want from you is to go out and change the world!' Appling agreed and quit his job as a consultant to start working as head of the project in April 2002.

The organisation

George Appling's first step in building what was then labelled 'X-Phones' was to convince MP employees and external people to join his ambitious project. A substantial number of people from MP's marketing department and many from other areas joined over the next months. They were all excited about taking the challenge of following the new approach and they were looking for a chance to develop their creativity and potential. The team soon also included external experts from different regions and with different backgrounds, such as fashion or design. By October 2002, the team had grown to 42 people from 17 nationalities.

Still being a part of MP, the team was allowed to function largely independently in order to foster the spirit of a start-up.

Defining the strategy

The first major task for X-Phones was to develop a comprehensive business strategy centred on a design-based value proposition. George Appling dug into the challenge and decided to focus 'his' start-up on making mobile phones a fashion accessory. To emphasise the idea of creating a totally new category – fashion accessory phones – and to set this category apart from current mobile phones, he decided to create a new brand: 'Xelibri'. The brand should have credibility to the fashion world, something Siemens did not have. He envisioned people associating mobile phones with watches, shoes, glamour and style rather than with computers, microchips or technological gadgets.

Xelibri was about to bring mobile phones to the fashion world, thereby turning the mobile phone industry on its head.

The team started to define key characteristics of the new design-oriented phones: the phones should only have proven technology in terms of market acceptance and availability. Design should be radically different from anything that had existed in the market. Launches should be timed according to the fashion industry's standards: two collections per year (spring/summer and fall/winter), defined by overarching themes. Also, each model was to be sold only for one year. Avoiding network operators' bundling policies could lead to freedom from subsidies and thus create the opportunity to establish constant prices, rather than seeing prices fall every quarter. George Appling believed that in order to create a successful brand, the best thing was to narrow the focus, especially when creating a completely new category.

The design-centred approach was based on the key insight that many consumers buy the phone that looks best. Appling believed that many people also had an interest in showing off their phones just like watches or handbags which they carried around all day. Thus, a phone had the potential to be turned into a fashion accessory. Fashion accessories were mostly bought based on their looks, not for their functionality, with many people thinking of them as collectables. 'So what should keep consumers from owning more than one

phone?' Appling asked. 'Actually, we will sell fashion accessories that make phone calls! This will then drive multiple phone ownership.'

The value chain

As Xelibri's main focus would be creating a brand and a new product category, it became obvious that it would need a unique approach to value creation. With mobile phone manufacturers at hand and Siemens GSM patents in stock, outsourcing of non-marketing-related steps of the value chain was clearly an option for Xelibri. 'It is in marketing where the value is,' George Appling explained to Lamprecht during one of their monthly review meetings. According to George Appling, the whole value chain should be marketing-driven, meaning that as the brand creator, Xelibri would provide industrial design agencies with marketing-driven briefings to design a collection of mobile phones. Designs would then be given to ODMs for development, sourcing and production. Outbound logistics should optimally be handled by a single external global provider. Marketing and sales would be Xelibri's core competence. Thus, the entire physical side of the business would be outsourced (see Exhibit 7).

'Dealing with fashion items is a risky business. It's a hit-or-miss market. How can we minimize the risk of demand fluctuations or disproportions in demand between the single models of a

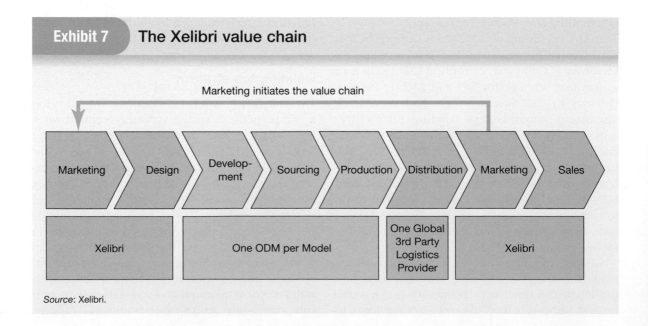

Exhibit 7   The Xelibri value chain

Marketing initiates the value chain

Marketing > Design > Development > Sourcing > Production > Distribution > Marketing > Sales

Xelibri | One ODM per Model | One Global 3rd Party Logistics Provider | Xelibri

Source: Xelibri.

Exhibit 8   **Xelibri's 'Space on Earth' Spring 2003 collection**

Xelibri 1

The first model in our range will change your life. Talk to people – wherever they are. Send electronic messages!

The world is your oyster.

Xelibri 2

Introducing our second Personal Communication Device (PCD). The written word is dead. Why not receive all your information in the form of live conversation. Don't believe us? Just try it!

Xelibri 3

Our tiny voice-controlled Personal Communication Device (PCD).

Particles in your voice are processed into instructions.

You say 'call', it 'calls'! Amazing but true.

Xelibri 4

Is the Personal Communications Device (PCD) for the man who cares about his appearance. Don't put it in your pocket!

Show it off 'future man'!

Source: Xelibri.

collection?' George Appling wondered. The targeted solution was based on an approach Dr Alfred Hauenstein, now VP Strategy and Innovation, had developed even before he joined Xelibri. The idea was to build every Xelibri model around the same core technology, put on a modular platform. If one of the models did not pull sufficient demand, the chips could be used for other models, thus avoiding scrap. This approach was to be implemented starting with the second collection.

On this basis, the team began institutionalising a new product development process. Together with Macron, a marketing strategy agency, Xelibri developed an overarching theme for the first three to four collections: retro-futurism. Derived from this, 'Space on Earth' was decided to be the design

inspiration for the first collection. From proposals presented by industrial design agencies, the Xelibri team would select models, aided by results from focus group discussions (see Exhibit 8).

The Xelibri agency network comprised as many as 15 agencies for brand building, industrial designs (ID), PR, corporate identity (CI) and events, many of them with a background in the fashion industry.

Branding and advertising in the fashion industry

Finding an optimal approach to brand building was a top priority on George Appling's agenda. The key aspects of the Xelibri brand personality had been clear since the earlier concept meetings: the new phones should be wearable, small and simple. They should be very fashionable and distinctive. Meant to be a fashion accessory, the brand needed an appealing image: Xelibri should be perceived as provocative and ironic, just like the idea of taking a technology product to a design industry. Observations from the fashion industry had shown that new brands are not established by direct advertising such as large TV campaigns. There had been startup companies from other technology-related industries spending enormous advertising budgets on large campaigns with no more than short-term effects. 'In the fashion industry, brands are not imposed on the consumer, they are found,' explained a fashion advisor to George Appling. 'If you want to build a brand that stands on solid ground, you will need to use a more grassroots-type of approach. You need people with influence in the fashion industry to believe in your brand and to spread your name by word-of-mouth. Their lifestyle will then be copied by other people.'

Advertising was considered a means of protecting existing market share, not as a way to build up a brand from scratch. 'PR has to play a crucial role in communicating Xelibri's identity to the market, yet we still lack a comprehensive PR strategy,' George Appling had noted at the last marketing meeting. 'We need to decide which communication channels work well with Xelibri's brand identity. We need to find veritable "messengers" for Xelibri even before identifying potential early adopters.' Special public events and focused sponsoring were considered important elements of a PR strategy as well. Xelibri and their agencies had to develop a holistic approach and a timeline taking all of that into account.

It was clear to George Appling that every communication activity would strongly affect brand perception and thus decide about success or failure of the project. 'How is it possible to combine the various communication requirements with the need to create desirability and a sense of scarcity while meeting our sales targets at the same time?' he wondered.

Distribution

Similar to communication, the choice of distribution channels would certainly affect brand perception. It was also obvious that Xelibri would have to come up with an adaptable strategy that would allow for national differences in the structure of distribution channels. Around which parameters should the strategy be built? 'We are not experts in local sales, we create the brand,' clarified Robert Kulewicz from Sales during a marketing meeting. 'We have to assure that our distributors fit with Xelibri's overall brand strategy. That means: will they play the Xelibri game? Will they accept our conditions of presenting the product? How can we assure that Xelibri keeps control over all brand-related aspects of distribution?' Furthermore, the necessary number of distributors per market, their coverage and the product profile of individual retailers were identified as key criteria for distribution strategy. Another important point was brought up: how should Xelibri treat Siemens' conventional distribution channels for mobile phones? Would network operators be allowed to offer Xelibri's fashion phones in their outlets? Would there be negative effects on Xelibri's brand perception from making sales along with regular mobile phones? Was subsidisation a good or a bad thing? Could it affect Xelibri's success? Xelibri was considering several distribution channels: retail outlets, fashion boutiques, Xelibri stores, shop-in-shop models, electronics retailers, operator outlets and others. But where and how could the desired value proposition and the required sales volume be realised?

Country selection

Xelibri's limited resources allowed only for a selective initial rollout. Among the candidates were some Western European markets and several markets in the Asia-Pacific region. Apart from a fit with the strategies concerning branding, distribution and pricing, which other selection criteria should be applied? How important were languages, demographics or income levels? Could concepts from other products and services be applied? In order to decide on countries that should be included in the initial rollout, the Xelibri team had to look at consumer behaviour and find out where the general ideas about branding, distribution and pricing could find a receptive market. During a meeting, several options came up. Should Xelibri focus on one continent first? Should they go for the biggest markets? Or for those that are known to be trendsetters? Thinking about the advantages of modular technology and resource constraints, it became clear that only one network standard could be covered with the first two collections. Where would people be willing to pay for a second or third mobile phone?

Pricing

Pricing was another complex issue. Historically, all mobile phone brands had offered products across all price categories. However, the fashion market was characterised by clearly defined 'price windows' for a brand. 'There is a reason why you would never get a real Rolex for $200. Price is an important landmark for brand identity,' George Appling pointed out. Another driver of the pricing decision was the fashion industry's expectations towards minimum margins per product, inventory turnover and sales per square metre. Additionally, Xelibri was expected to deliver profit contributions to raise MP's average rate of return in the medium term and to achieve break-even in FY 2002/03. Before focus groups would be questioned, a broad idea about a possible price range was required. What price would be needed to satisfy the demands of potential sales channels? What was an acceptable estimate of consumers' willingness to pay? Was there a minimum price required to establish Xelibri as a fashion accessory?

Getting things on the road

The ambitious goal was to get the first fashion phones into the stores early in the second quarter of calendar year 2003. But how could sufficient market pull be achieved right from the start? Could a staged rollout in terms of product availability be an option?

For sending a signal to the general public, an Xelibri birthday party was planned as the opening event of London Fashion Week for 15 February 2003. George Appling emphasised: 'Even though we'll have to give a pre-warning to the business press before that, this date will mark the start of our PR campaign. By then, we need to have solved the issues of brand building activities and marketing strategy with our agencies. We also need to find solutions for pricing, distribution, country selection and overall sales targets. Time is running short, we need to be specific and get things on the road.'

Ryanair

Eleanor R.E. O'Higgins

This case describes the strategic challenges faced by the budget carrier Ryanair in early 2004. Ryanair was the most successful airline in Europe in terms of profitability and market capitalisation. The case offers a chance to analyse the reasons for Ryanair's success and asks if Ryanair's strategic business model and its manner of implementation will be robust enough to withstand the challenges it faces in its competitive arena, the European airline industry. The case invites the reader to devise and evaluate strategic options for the company and its leadership.

• • •

A rough landing?

A shock profits warning

Early 2004 was not the best of times for Ryanair. On 28 January, the airline issued its first profits warning and ended a run of 26 quarters of rising profits. On that day, when the markets opened, the company was worth €5bn. By close of business, its value had shrunk to €3.6bn, as its share price plunged from €6.75 to €4.86. Investors were dismayed by the airline's admission that it was facing 'an enormous and sudden reduction of 25 to 30 per cent in yields', i.e., average fare levels, in the first quarter of 2004 (the last fiscal quarter of 2004).[1] This was on top of an earlier fall of 10 to 15 per cent in the first nine months.

Moreover, despite the low fares, the airline's load factor (the proportion of available seats that are filled) in January had fallen from 76 per cent to 70 per cent, year-on-year. In April 2004, Michael O'Leary forecast an 'awful' winter for European airlines, amid continuing fare wars and a shake-out among the many budget airlines. 'We will be helping to make it awful', warned Mr O'Leary, as he announced an 800,000 free seat giveaway.

The most difficult markets were predicted to be Germany and the UK regions where many new carriers, which were 'losing money on an heroic scale', had entered the arena.[2] O'Leary predicted that the company's 2004 profits would decline by 10 per cent, while 2005 profits would increase by up to 20 per cent with a 5 per cent drop in yields. However, if yields were to fall by as much as 20 per cent, the 2005 outcome would be break-even, at best.

The airline had certainly been punished by investors for its fall from grace. It was the second worst performer in the FTSE Eurotop 300 index up to the end of April 2004. So, had the famous profitable Ryanair low fare formula to fill seats finally run out of steam?

EU – competition or anti-competition

Investors (or 'disinvestors') were also put off by a decision from the EU Commission in February 2004, which ruled that Ryanair had been receiving illegal state subsidies for its base airport at publicly-owned Charleroi Airport (styled as Brussels South by Ryanair). Of course, it was not only the Charleroi decision but the precedent it could set

---

[1] Done, K., 'Ryanair's dream comes to an end', *Financial Times*, 29 January 2004.

[2] Done, K., 'O'Leary forecasts an "awful" winter for European airlines', *Financial Times*, 21 April 2004.

This case was prepared by Eleanor R.E. O'Higgins, University College Dublin, Republic of Ireland. The author gratefully acknowledges the assistance of Nico O'Higgins and Emmet O'Neill in compiling some of the data and exhibits. It is intended as a basis for class discussion and not as an illustration of either good or bad management practice. © Eleanor O'Higgins, 2004. Not to be reproduced or quoted without permission.

incentives of €1.92m for opening new routes, €768,000 in reimbursements for pilot training and €250,000 for hotel accommodation costs.

Ryanair and the Wallonian authorities staunchly defended the deal on various grounds. In an article in the *Financial Times*, Michael O'Leary asserted that the Ryanair deal at Charleroi complied with EU state aid rules because Ryanair paid a fee for every passenger, and the airline was not a net recipient of subsidies. The deal taken up by Ryanair was transparent and available to all its competitors. Many of those complaining, such as Virgin Express had shown no inclination to avail themselves of the Charleroi offer. Instead, they tried to protect their position at the costlier Zaventem Brussels airport by eliminating Ryanair from the competition equation through EU intervention. Michael O'Leary argued that the state aid rules allow the Wallonian government to stimulate traffic at an unused airport facility in exactly the same way that every private airport reduces its charges if it wishes to grow its business.[3]

At one point, Ryanair threatened to pull out of Charleroi, if the decision went against them. The airline had already shown itself willing to abandon an airport if terms and conditions do not work out in its favour. In August 2003, Ryanair ceased operations at Strasbourg after losing a court case brought by Air France. The verdict, under appeal by Ryanair, determined that Strasbourg had illegally provided Ryanair with €1m assistance to set up the service. Nevertheless, two months after the Charleroi verdict, Ryanair confirmed that it had agreed a new deal there. It would keep flying all its 11 routes from Charleroi, continuing existing airport and handling charges until the airport, which accommodates 1.8m passengers a year at present, reaches 2m passengers a year. The legality of the new arrangement was apparently underpinned by adjusting local taxes for all carriers. Ryanair maintained that the new arrangement was in line with private investor principles applied by the Commission. Meanwhile, the Walloon authorities intended to ensure that the discounted levies would be made available to other airlines too. However, the EU Commission was not readily convinced and initiated an investigation of the new settlement.

that was of concern. Other deals with public airports would come under scrutiny, although the vast majority of the airline's slots were at private airports. Also, it was estimated that Ryanair would have to repay between €2.5m and €7m to the regional government. Ryanair appealed the decision, but also threatened to initiate state aid cases and complaints against every other airline flying into every state airport which offer concessions and discounts. Airport fees comprised 19 per cent of Ryanair's operating costs and were deemed to be an inherent part of the airline's low-cost model. Thus, Ryanair warned that there was no mid-cost alternative model. Ryanair's sense of outrage about the EU ruling against the Charleroi deal and Michael O'Leary's opinion that it would set back low fares travel for customers was not shared by others in the aviation industry, as rival low fares carriers and full service airlines publicly welcomed the decision. Indeed, one could have concluded that other airlines took positive pleasure at the discomfort of their formidable foe.

The subject of the EU decision was based on non-discrimination legislation preventing airports from offering differential deals to different airline operators, and by an embargo on state subsidies to airlines. Incited by Ryanair rivals such as Air France, Virgin Express and Easyjet, Ryanair's deals with regional airports had caught the eye of the EU Transport Commissioner, Loyola de Palacio. An EU investigation was launched in late 2002 as to whether Ryanair had been in receipt of illegal state subsidies since its year 2000 establishment of a base at Charleroi. Apparently, the EU Commission had been shocked by alleged offers of a 50 per cent landing fee discount to €1 per landing passenger and an even larger handling fee discount to €1 instead of €8 to €13 charged to other airlines, pushing the fee below cost. The airport also provided a contribution of €4 per passenger for promotional activities for 15 years. This was on top of initial

---

[3] Michael O'Leary, 'In defence of the low-fare airline revolution', *Financial Times*, 20 November 2003.

On another front, the EU had devised new rules to cover overbooking that result in boarding denials to passengers by airlines. Air travellers bumped off overbooked flights by EU airlines would receive automatic compensation of between €250 and €600. Compensation might also be claimed when flights are cancelled for reasons that are the carrier's responsibility, provided the passengers have not been given two weeks' notice or offered alternative flights. Passengers would also be reimbursed when they face a delay through cancellation of at least five hours, receiving hotel accommodation when cancellation forces them to stay overnight, and meals and refreshments for shorter delays. The Association of European Airlines (AEA) was concerned that the new rules would increase the burden on EU carriers, especially in relation to US airlines that continued to receive subsidies from Washington, post-September 11. Ryanair declared that the new rules would not have a big impact on its operations, as it did not overbook its flights, and had the fewest number of cancellations and best punctuality record in Europe. It suggested that if the EU is serious, it should just outlaw the practice of overbooking.

One thing after another

A few days prior to the EU decision, on 30 January, at the Central London County Court, a disabled man won a landmark case against Ryanair after it charged him £18 (€25) for a wheelchair he needed at Stansted to get from the check-in desk to the aircraft. The passenger was awarded £1,336 (€2,400) in compensation from Ryanair, as the UK based Disability Commission said it may launch a class action against the airline on behalf of 35 other passengers. Ryanair's immediate reaction was to levy 70c a flight on all customers using the affected airports. Of the 86 airports served by Ryanair, only four – Stansted, Gatwick, Dublin and Shannon – do not provide a free wheelchair service. In defence of the levy, Ryanair pointed out that the fare of the litigant passenger had been just half of a wheelchair fee. The carrier contends that it should be the responsibility of airports to provide free services to disabled passengers.

As if these issues were not enough, pilots at Ryanair were examining ways of forming a trade union, so as to be in a more powerful position when their collective contract expired in 2005. It was understood that they hoped to pursue a change in their remuneration terms with less

emphasis on share options since the collapse in the share price. However, the pilots' case was unlikely to be helped by the fact that rival Aer Lingus was overstaffed with pilots; 46 of them had not worked for six months on full pay, and it was estimated that the airline would have to retrain or redeploy 100 pilots during 2004.

Overview of Ryanair

Ryanair was founded in 1985 by the Ryan family to provide scheduled passenger airline services between Ireland and the UK, as an alternative to the then state monopoly carrier, Aer Lingus. Initially, Ryanair was a full service conventional airline, with two classes of seating, leasing three different types of aircraft. Despite a growth in passenger volumes, by the end of 1990, the company had flown through a great deal of turbulence, disposing of five chief executives, and accumulating losses of IR£20m. Its fight to survive in the early 1990s saw the airline restyle itself to become Europe's first low fares, no frills carrier, built on the model of Southwest Airlines, the highly successful Texas based operator. A fresh management team was appointed by Tony Ryan, headed up by Michael O'Leary. The new formula effected a turnaround in the fortunes of the company, and by 1997, the company was floated in an IPO on the Dublin Stock Exchange and on Nasdaq. In July 1998, the company placed 9.1m shares on the London Stock Exchange, while the principal shareholders (the Ryan family, Michael O'Leary and Irish Air) disposed of 12.6m shares, thereby reducing the percentage of shares held by them from almost 62 per cent to 51.4 per cent. In 2002, the company was admitted to the Nasdaq-100.

The financial arrangements which surrounded the public offering were highly advantageous to Tony Ryan, his three sons, Cathal, Declan and Shane, and to Michael O'Leary. In effect, the Ryan family had sold the company for IR£56.7m and repurchased a 61 per cent stake for only IR£3.1m. Michael O'Leary was allowed to purchase 17.9 per cent of the company for IR£0.9m, partly to compensate him for the cessation of an executive bonus scheme which had netted him IR£17m over three years. Another investment group led by David Bonderman invested IR£1m in equity and an IR£24m loan to Ryanair through a vehicle company, Irish Air, for a stake of 19.9 per cent. Bonderman, an entrepreneur from Texas, Chairman of Continental Airlines and a partner in a Washington law firm, provided credibility for the company in the USA and was made Chairman of Ryanair at its flotation. The proceeds of the flotation of IR£58m for just under 35 per cent of the shares were used to repay loans and to purchase aircraft. It left the Ryans with 33 per cent of the company, Irish Air with 14.7 per cent and Michael O'Leary with 14.1 per cent.

Since then, over the years, the Ryan family has been successively selling off shares in Ryanair, raising close to €400m. Tony Ryan, founder and one-time chairman remains a non-executive director and the only family member on the board, with a 1.42 per cent stake while sons Shane, Cathal and Declan held 2.9, 2.57 and 2 per cent stakes, respectively. However, investors were not amused when members of the Ryan family sold 6.4m shares at €6.90 a share, pocketing €44.2m, just a fortnight before the announcement of the profits warning that set off the freefall in the share price. The matter has come under investigation. Michael O'Leary, too, has been selling Ryanair shares every year since flotation, realising close to €200m, but he remained the company's largest shareholder with a 5.4 per cent stake.

Ryanair's objective is to maintain its position as Europe's leading low fares airline, operating frequent point-to-point short-haul flights, mainly out of regional and secondary airports. The heart of its strategy is based on providing a no-frills service with low fares designed to stimulate demand, particularly from budget conscious leisure and business travellers, who might otherwise have used alternative forms of transportation, or who might not have travelled at all.

From the outset, as a budget carrier, Ryanair set itself vigorous but steady growth ambitions. In 1997, in the Ireland-UK market, Ryanair overtook Aer Lingus as the number one carrier on flights between the Republic of Ireland and the UK with 4m passengers and a 37 per cent market share. The entry of Ryanair into the Ireland-UK market, originally dominated by Aer Lingus, was followed by more competitors, which led to substantially lower fares and significantly increased traffic on the routes serviced by Ryanair. At first, Ryanair's successful growth was based on a perception that it was an Irish ethnic airline, relying on reciprocal visits between the large Irish population in the UK and their relatives and friends in Ireland, availing of low fares to travel more often. In fact, the term 'Ryanair generation' was coined to describe the younger educated Irish emigrant population in the UK. However, by 2001 less than 20 per cent of passengers originated from Ireland. By the end of 2003, Ryanair's route system had expanded from its primarily Irish-UK emphasis to serve 86 destinations on 133 routes across 16 countries. At one stage, Ryanair put in a bid with the Irish government to carry civil servants to EU meetings in Brussels, offering an annual IR£1m service contract instead of the IR£3m it claimed Aer Lingus charged. This bid received no response.

The carrier claimed that it generally made its lowest fares widely available by allocating a majority of seat inventory to its two lowest fare categories. According to the company, this meant that its no frills services allowed it to prioritise features important to its clientele, such as frequent departures, advance reservations, baggage handling and consistent on-time services. Simultaneously, this eliminated non-essential extras that interfered with the reliable, low cost delivery of its basic flights. These were advance seat assignments, free in-flight meals, multi-class seating, access to a frequent flyer programme, complimentary drinks and other amenities. When the catering firm which supplied Ryanair withdrew the provision of free ice, the airline sent a memo to cabin staff advising them that ice would no longer be available for passengers' drinks, a measure that would save the airline IR£40,000 (€50,000) a year.

In 1997, Ryanair dropped its cargo services, at an estimated annual IR£400,000 (€500,000) in revenue. With no need to load and unload cargo, the turnaround time of an aircraft was reduced from 30 to 25 minutes. It claimed that business travellers, attracted by frequency and punctuality, comprised 40 per cent of its passengers, despite often less conveniently located airports and the absence of pampering.

The company continued to incur significant capital expenditures in expanding its aircraft fleet to realise its growth ambitions. The aftermath of September 11 had proved traumatic for the mainstream European airlines. By contrast, in the no-frills airline sector, traffic climbed sharply, buoyed by strong sales promotions and heavy discounting. Importantly for Ryanair, the mainstream airlines' losses were the budget airlines' gains, strengthening their bargaining positions with respect to aircraft procurement, airport deals and staff recruitment. Ryanair renegotiated its contract order with Boeing. Not only were new aircraft available at bargain prices, but also nearly-new ones were being offloaded by airlines curtailing their route programmes. It was estimated that the world aircraft surplus in 2002 comprised 13.2 per cent of the total fleet.[4]

In 1998, Ryanair ordered 45 new Boeing 737-800 aircraft (189-seat capacity) worth $2bn, taking delivery of five aircraft a year. The newest aircraft would augment Ryanair's existing fleet of 20 used 130-seat capacity Boeing 737-200s, with an average age of over 15 years, and a life expectancy of 25 years. The average age was considerably higher than that of the fleets of Ryanair's current or potential competitors. Older aircraft entailed higher maintenance costs and were less fuel-efficient. Moreover, 14 of Ryanair's airplanes required the installation of hushkits to comply with an EU directive on noise requirements by 1 April 2002, at an estimated total cost of $19.6m. The increased weight of the hushkits would result in a higher level of fuel consumption.

The Ryanair fleet grew from 22 aircraft in 1999 to 54 at the end of 2003. A rolling programme would deliver a further 125 new Boeing 737s to the Ryanair fleet by 2009, with further options on another 125 planes. However, the airline was negotiating with Boeing to delay some of the deliveries from its first 125 aircraft order. Ryanair has always owned rather than leased all its aircraft, but in a departure from this policy, the airline intends that in the long term about a third of its fleet will be leased. Owning rather than leasing aircraft allows maintenance costs to be capitalised on the balance sheet, rather than to be reflected in variable costs. A large number of older fully depreciated aircraft in its fleet, bought secondhand when Ryanair converted to a budget airline, allowed the company to benefit from relatively low depreciation costs. Even a growing balance toward new aircraft would not add significantly to depreciation costs since they would be depreciated over a long period (23 years) to 15 per cent of the original cost, a low figure anyway, thanks to the excellent deal negotiated by the company.

Ryanair's operating expenses and revenues as well as assets and liabilities are denominated in the euro. This provides some stability, thanks to its increasing operations in euro pact countries, and the denomination of air traffic control charges in euro. The group engages in some foreign exchange hedging in transactions involving the euro, UK

sterling, and the US dollar. The company's fuel risk management policy is to hedge between 70 and 90 per cent of the forecasted rolling annual required volumes, to lock in the price against any short-term adverse movements in world jet fuel prices.

Too good to be true?

Although not a complacent man, at the end of 2003 Michael O'Leary would have had much to be satisfied about as he looked back on the events of the past eighteen months or so, and as he contemplated how the company should build on its success. Among the highlights were:

● Ryanair had become the most profitable and the most highly valued airline in Europe, surpassing the giant German flag-carrier Lufthansa and doubling in value over British Airways.

● In September 2002, Ryanair had issued a charter on customer service.

● In April 2003, it had completed the takeover of Buzz, the budget airline subsidiary of KLM, the Dutch national airline.

● Ryanair had engaged in several episodes of free seat giveaways on its routes, converting itself, in part, from a 'low-fares' to a 'no-fares' airline.

Ryanair flying high

When reporting on Ryanair's results for 2003 in September of that year, Chairman David Bonderman pointed out what an awful year it had been for the airline industry, what with war in Iraq, and an outbreak of Severe Acute Respiratory Syndrome (SARS). This compounded previous setbacks like the foot-and-mouth epidemic in cattle of spring 2002 and of course, the tragedy of 11 September 2001. Yet, Ryanair had delivered its 13th consecutive year of increased profitability. Its net margin had increased by 4 per cent to 28 per cent, surpassing its own long-term net profit margin target of 20 per cent. The staff efficiency ratio (passenger per employee) had improved by 15 per cent. (See Exhibit 1 for Ryanair's financial statements.)

Meanwhile, the group's market capitalisation had grown from €392m in 1997 to €4.73bn by 1 July 2003, as its profitability was seen to be unique among airlines worldwide. Many of Ryanair's European counterparts were struggling with financial losses, for example, Lufthansa, KLM, SAS and British Airways, while Swissair and

---

[4] Peter Costa, Doug S. Harned and Jerrold T. Lundquist, 'Rethinking the aviation industry', *McKinsey Quarterly*, no. 2, 2002.

Exhibit 1a — Ryanair Profit and Loss Account (full year March 2002 & 2003)

	€m 2003	€m 2002	% % Growth
Scheduled Revenues	732	551	32.8%
Ancillary Revenues	111	73	52.1%
Total Revenues	843	624	35.0%
Operating Expenses			
Staff	93	78	
Airport Charges	108	85	
Route Charges	68	47	
Fuel	129	104	
Maintenance	30	26	
Aircraft Rentals	0	4	
Depreciation	77	59	
Other	74	58	
Total Operating Expenses	579	461	25.5
Operating Profit (Loss)	263	163	61.3
Net Profit	239	150	59.3
Net Margin	28.4%	24.0%	18.3

Exhibit 1b — Ryanair Consolidated Balance Sheet (2002 & 2003)

	€000 2003	€000 2002
Fixed Assets		
Tangible assets	1,352,361	951,806
Current Assets		
Cash and liquid resources	1,060,218	899,275
Accounts receivable	14,970	10,331
Other assets	16,370	11,035
Inventories	22,788	17,125
Total Current Assets	1,114,346	937,766
Total Assets	2,466,707	1,889,572
Current liabilities		
Accounts payable	61,404	46,779
Accrued expenses and other liabilities	251,328	217,108
Current maturities of long term debt	63,291	38,800
Short term borrowings	1,316	5,505
Total current liabilities	377,339	308,192
Other liabilities		
Provisions for liabilities and charges	67,833	49,317
Accounts payable due after one year	5,673	18,086
Long term debt	773,934	511,703
Total other liabilities	847,440	579,106
Shareholders' funds – equity		
Called up share capital	9,588	9,587
Share premium account	553,512	553,457
Profit and loss account	678,628	439,230
Shareholders' funds – equity	1,241,728	1,002,274
Total liabilities and shareholders' funds	2,466,507	1,889,572

Exhibit 1c	Ryanair Profit and Loss Account (3rd Quarter Dec 2003 vs. 3rd Quarter Dec 2002)

	€000 Qtr End Dec 2003	€000 Qtr End Dec 2002
Scheduled Revenues	216,424	157,407
Ancillary Revenues	38,575	28,497
Total Revenues	254,999	185,904
Operating Expenses		
Staff	29,506	21,822
Airport Charges	38,123	26,224
Route Charges	27,442	15,944
Fuel	43,128	29,355
Maintenance	8,796	6,197
Marketing and Distribution	1,045	2,865
Aircraft Rentals	2,730	–
Depreciation	25,009	19,014
Aircraft Retirement Costs	6,773	–
Other	19,083	15,772
Total Operating Expenses	201,635	137,193
Operating Profit	53,364	48,711
Profit before taxation	44,813	47,795
Profit for the period	40,961	43,152

Sabena had met their demise the year before, their fundamental weaknesses exposed by the aftermath of September 11.

In fiscal 2003, Ryanair had delivered extraordinary growth in fleet, routes, traffic, revenues and profitability. For example, passenger volumes increased by 42 per cent to 15.7m, and seat numbers expected to grow by 60 per cent in fiscal 2004. Yet, average fares had seen a decline of 6 per cent to €46 and was expected to fall further, although part of this decline was due to currency fluctuations. Rapid expansion was also accompanied by a fall in the load or seat occupancy factor, which declined from 82 to 77 per cent in the first half of fiscal 2004. This seemingly paradoxical result, juxtaposed with the record profits, was made possible only by a continuing decline in unit costs. Also, CEO Michael O'Leary warned that the carrier should and would temper its expansion to return to a growth rate of between 20 to 25 per cent in the next couple of years.

The airline was committed to establishing a new hub each year up to 2008 to join the nine already existing at the end of 2003: Brussels South/Charleroi, Dublin, Frankfurt Hahn, Glasgow/Prestwick, Luton, Milan Bergamo, Shannon, Stansted, Stockholm/Skvasta. In December 2003, Michael O'Leary, flamboyantly dressed as the Pope for the occasion, announced that Rome Ciampino and Barcelona Girona would become the airline's tenth and eleventh bases in 2004. However, Ryanair's expansion plans excluded establishment of routes into any of the 10 states that joined the EU in 2004.

In line with its expansion, Ryanair beefed up its senior management team in 2002 and 2003 by creating two deputy chief executive positions, to be filled by company veterans, Michael Cawley, formerly chief financial officer, and Howard Millar, director of finance. The decision to appoint two deputies in a company renowned for cost prudence seemed out of character. At the time, a company spokeswoman pointed out that the establishment of deputy chief executive posts was in no way indicative that CEO Michael O'Leary was considering stepping down in the near future. The company had also recently appointed a director of communications and a director of treasury.

Ryanair's passenger charter and service

In its 2003 Annual Report, Ryanair declared itself to be 'No.1 for Customer Service'. The airline claimed to be Number 1 for punctuality, fewest cancellations, fewest lost bags and fewest complaints per 1,000 passengers flown.

The airline's claims of attention to customer service are encompassed in its Passenger Charter, which embraces a number of doctrines:

- sell the lowest fares at all times on all routes and match competitors' special offers;
- allow flight and name changes with requisite fee;
- strive to deliver on-time performance;
- provide information to passengers regarding commercial and operational conditions;
- provide complaint response within 7 days;
- provide prompt refunds;
- eliminate overbooking and involuntary denial of boarding;
- publish monthly service statistics;
- eliminate lost or delayed luggage;

- Ryanair will not provide refreshments or meals or accommodation to passengers facing delays. Any passengers who wish to avail themselves of such services will be asked to pay for them directly to the service provider;
- Ryanair facilitates wheelchair passengers travelling in their own wheelchairs. Where passengers require a wheelchair, Ryanair directs those passengers to a third party wheelchair supplier at the passenger's own expense. Ryanair is lobbying those airports which it serves that do not provide a free wheelchair service.

Exhibits 2, 3, 4 and 5 provide some independent comparisons of Ryanair with other airlines on fare levels, punctuality, customer recommendations and complaint numbers. Exhibit 5 relates to complaints lodged with the Air Transport Users Council (ATUC), a UK based consumer watchdog for the airline industry. Apparently, Ryanair has

---

Exhibit 2   Comparative fare levels (same booking date and approximate departure times)

Route: Dublin: to London return 1 night

Airline	From:To	Total:
Ryanair	DUB:STN	€152.52
Aer Lingus	DUB:LHR	€195.19
BMI	DUB:LHR	€98.12

Route: Dublin: to London return 3 nights

Airline	From:To	Total:
Ryanair	DUB:STN	€112.52
Aer Lingus	DUB:LHR	€159.19
BMI	DUB:LHR	€121.12

Route: London to Stockholm 1 night

Airline	From:To	Total:
Ryanair	STN:VST	€53.83
BMI	LHR:ARN	€440.61

Route: London to Stockholm 3 nights

Airline	From:To	Total:
Ryanair	STN:VST	€53.83
BMI	LHR:ARN	€440.61

Route: London to Biarritz/Bordeaux 1 night

Airline	From:To	Total:
Ryanair	STN:BIQ	€68.19
British European	LGW:BOD	€163.16

Route: London to Biarritz/Bordeaux 3 nights

Airline	From:To	Total:
Ryanair	STN:BIQ	€68.19
British European	LGW:BOD	€163.16

Route: London to Venice 1 night

Airline	From:To	Total:
Ryanair	STN:TSF	€61.01
easyJet	STN:VCE	€104.12

Route: London to Venice 3 nights

Airline	From:To	Total:
Ryanair	STN:TSF	€61.01
easyJet	STN:VCE	€104.12

Exhibit 3	Punctuality statistics – departures and arrivals (September 2003)

Reporting Airport / Airline	Origin/ Destination	No. of Flights	% early to 15 minutes late	Average Delay (minutes)	Planned Flights Unmatched
Birmingham – Ryanair	Dublin	180	88	6	0
Birmingham – Aer Lingus	Dublin	299	89	7	2
Birmingham– MyTravel	Dublin	4	50	20	0
Heathrow – Aer Lingus	Dublin	785	71	16	2
Heathrow – BMI British Midland	Dublin	432	71	14	0
Stansted – Ryanair	Dublin	727	79	11	1
Gatwick – British Airways	Dublin	180	82	9	0
Gatwick – Ryanair	Dublin	298	87	8	2
Heathrow – BMI British Midland	Brussels	354	73	13	1
Heathrow – British Airways	Brussels	452	84	9	2
Heathrow – BMI British Midland	Palermo	8	25	37	0
Heathrow – Alitalia	Milan (Linate)	174	63	15	0
Heathrow – British Airways	Milan (Linate)	178	80	10	0
Heathrow – BMI British Midland	Milan (Linate)	172	68	13	0
Heathrow – Alitalia	Milan (Malpensa)	298	48	24	0
Heathrow – British Airways	Milan (Malpensa)	180	80	10	0
Stansted – Ryanair	Bergamo	172	76	10	0
Stansted – EasyJet	Bologna	60	70	14	0
Stansted – EasyJet	Milan (Linate)	60	42	39	0
Stansted – EasyJet	Rome (Ciampio)	120	76	12	0
Stansted – Ryanair	Rome (Ciampio)	356	79	9	0
Stansted – EasyJet	Edinburgh	327	60	20	0
Stansted – EasyJet	Nice	120	70	24	0
Stansted – Virgin Express	Nice	1	0	184	0
Stansted – Ryanair	Montpellier	59	76	14	2
Stansted – Ryanair	Prestwick	562	87	6	4
Stansted – EasyJet	Glasgow	276	87	8	0
Glasgow – Aer Lingus	Dublin	176	80	9	4
Glasgow – BMI British Midland	Dublin	2	100	0	0

refused to deal with the Council since a disagreement in 1999 over the way Ryanair allegedly denied responsibility for damaged or lost luggage.[5] The airline explained that it did not enter into correspondence with ATUC because they 'duck out of addressing any of the real serious issues affecting consumers . . . service fees, travel agency commission, anti-consumer increases in airport charges and the publication of airline punctuality statistics'.[6]

---

[5] Marianne Brun-Rovet, 'Mishandled baggage lifts complaints about airlines', *Financial Times*, 20 August 2002.

[6] ANANOVA website (http://www.ananova.com/business/story/ sm_653699.html?menu=).

Buzz – A low-price purchase?

On 1 February 2003, Ryanair announced that it was acquiring Buzz, the loss-making (more than €1m loss per week) budget subsidiary of KLM, based at Stansted. The Dutch carrier was selling in some distress, since it was losing money overall, and had been struggling in vain to make Buzz a viable entity ever since its inception in early 2000. The agreed purchase price of €23.9m was later reduced to €20.1m, after Ryanair had completed due diligence. Since Buzz had €19m cash on hand, the final consideration of €370m, paid out of Ryanair's cash reserves, was negligible.

While perceived as a departure from its organic growth model, the deal was nevertheless greeted as

Exhibit 4a Airline ratings

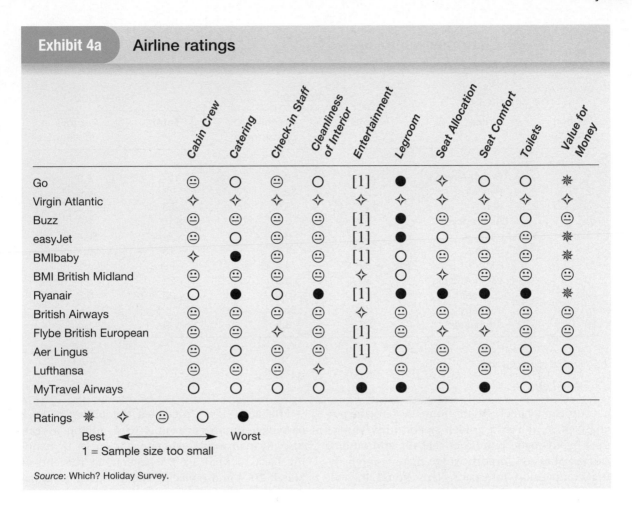

	Cabin Crew	Catering	Check-in Staff	Cleanliness of Interior	Entertainment	Legroom	Seat Allocation	Seat Comfort	Toilets	Value for Money
Go	☺	○	☺	○	[1]	●	✦	○	○	❋
Virgin Atlantic	✦	✦	✦	✦	✦	✦	✦	✦	✦	✦
Buzz	☺	☺	☺	☺	[1]	●	☺	☺	○	☺
easyJet	☺	○	☺	☺	[1]	●	○	○	☺	❋
BMIbaby	✦	●	☺	☺	[1]	○	☺	☺	☺	❋
BMI British Midland	☺	☺	☺	☺	✦	○	✦	☺	☺	☺
Ryanair	○	●	○	●	[1]	●	●	●	●	❋
British Airways	☺	☺	☺	☺	✦	☺	☺	☺	☺	☺
Flybe British European	☺	☺	✦	☺	[1]	☺	✦	✦	☺	☺
Aer Lingus	☺	○	☺	☺	[1]	○	☺	☺	☺	○
Lufthansa	☺	☺	☺	✦	○	☺	☺	☺	☺	○
MyTravel Airways	○	○	○	○	●	●	○	●	○	○

Ratings   ❋   ✦   ☺   ○   ●

Best ◄————————► Worst

1 = Sample size too small

Source: Which? Holiday Survey.

Exhibit 4b Would you recommend the airline to a friend?

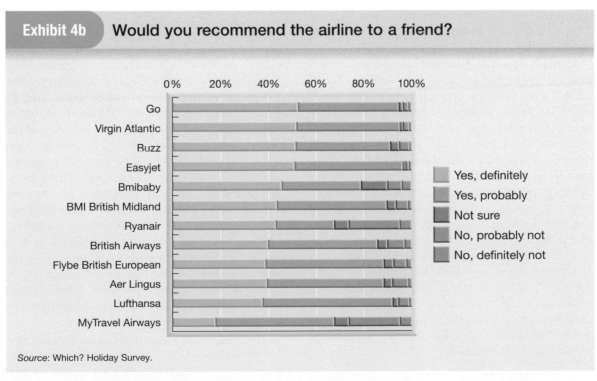

Legend:
- Yes, definitely
- Yes, probably
- Not sure
- No, probably not
- No, definitely not

Go
Virgin Atlantic
Buzz
Easyjet
Bmibaby
BMI British Midland
Ryanair
British Airways
Flybe British European
Aer Lingus
Lufthansa
MyTravel Airways

Source: Which? Holiday Survey.

Exhibit 5	Customer complaints

Position 2002/03	Airline	2002/2003		2001/2002	
		Total*	Per million passengers[†]	Total*	Per million passengers[†]
1	British Airways	257	6.8	117	2.9
2	Ryanair	201	12.7	77	6.9
3	KLM	140	5.9	53	3.3
4	Air France	139	3.6	110	2.8
5	easyJet	106	9.3	74	10.4
7	Iberia	39	1.6	18	0.7
9	BMI	33	4.2	29	4.2
10	Virgin Atlantic	30	7.9	22	5.4
12	Lufthansa	27	0.6	23	0.5
15	bmibaby	25	53.7		
19	Aer Lingus	20	3.2	9	1.4

* *Source*: Air Transport Users' Council website
[†] *Source*: Derived by author

a coup for Ryanair. Apart from the bargain purchase price, it was a golden opportunity to pick up a ready-made bundle of take-off and landing slots at Stansted Airport, where there is intensifying competition for space. This would increase Ryanair's share of slots at Stansted from 33 to 49.5 per cent for the summer of 2003. In late 2003, the British government announced that Stansted Airport had been designated for expansion and development.

Ryanair expected that the acquisition would produce profit by the fiscal year end of March 2004, thanks to restructuring measures. This would entail job losses, as Ryanair retained only 170 of Buzz's 610 staff and only 10 of its 24 routes. Moreover, the company said it would only meet the cost of statutory redundancy payments of less than €1m, while KLM would be responsible for meeting any additional contractual severance payments. A vast majority of those Buzz staff offered contracts by Ryanair accepted, and it was revealed that pilots and cabin crew being retained would be earning at least 14 per cent more than under their existing contracts, but would be flying more hours, up from 700–750 a year to 800–820 a year. Buzz pilots would still be earning 10–15 per cent less than Ryanair pilots on the basis that they were less productive. It was intended that the Buzz brand would disappear eventually.

Michael O'Leary predicted a doubling of Buzz passenger numbers, from 2 to 4 million a year. Also, Ryanair would generate efficiencies by handing back to KLM six BAe aircraft at the end of March 2004 and replacing them with larger capacity, more efficient Boeing 737s.

The no-fares airline?

Half of Ryanair's passengers will be flying for free by 2009, pledged Michael O'Leary in August 2003, in an interview with a German newspaper. The CEO predicted that Ryanair's fares would drop by an average of 15 per cent in 2003, with one out of every five tickets sold at no charge. He said that the average ticket price would fall by an average 5 per cent a year over the next five years, as passenger numbers grew by 5m annually. One analyst speculated that Ryanair's pronouncements on free seats 'is designed to put the wind up potential competitors in the hotly contested German market'.[7]

Meanwhile, the company confirmed that it would introduce a number of both revenue enhancing and cost-cutting new features on its flights. It was hoped that these modifications would enhance Ryanair's margins to compensate

---

[7] Una McCaffrey, 'Ryanair says 50% of seats will be free by 2009', *Irish Times*, 19 August 2003.

for falls in fare yields. For instance, the Ryanair fleet would heretofore be devoid of reclining seats, window blinds, headrests, seat pockets and other non-essentials. Leather seats instead of cloth ones would allow faster turnaround times since leather is quicker and easier to clean. More controversially, Michael O'Leary hoped eventually to wean passengers off checked-in luggage, eliminating the need for baggage handling, suitcase holding areas and lost property.

Ryanair continuously aimed to enhance its revenue through ancillary services offered in conjunction with its core airline business, because ancillary revenues would increasingly be used to subsidise falling airfares. This includes the availability of satellite television and internet services on flights, allowing passengers to watch their favourite television programmes or play arcade games for a fee. Market research suggested that these services would generate at least €1.25 per passenger, in addition to the average spend of €5 already being achieved from other ancillary sources. The introduction of an in-flight magazine and the on-board sale of travel insurance on flights from Ireland and the UK offer further ancillary revenue sources, in addition to on-board sales, charter flights, travel reservations, car rentals, website and in-flight television and magazine advertising, and advertising outside its aircraft, whereby a corporate sponsor pays to paint an aircraft with its logo. For example, passengers might have been surprised to find themselves flying inside a giant beerglass when Kilkenny, a Guinness Group beer brand, turned a Ryanair airplane into a flying billboard. Advertising on Ryanair's popular website also provides ancillary income.

The company believes that longer flights encourage higher per passenger revenues from in-flight sales, which should enhance such sales on newer routes to destinations in continental Europe, compared to the shorter Ireland-UK or within UK routes. The EU abolished duty-free sales on intra-EU travel from 1999, contending that it was a tax distortion. This could have been a triple blow to Ryanair – a direct loss of revenue, a drop in incentives to flight attendants who could earn as much as one-third of their compensation from commission on the sale of beverages and duty-free goods, and increased landing charges, since some Irish and UK airports increased landing charges by up to 20 per cent to make up for their loss of revenue from duty-free sales. Yet, despite the abolition of duty free sales on intra-EU

travel in 1999, Ryanair's revenue from duty paid sales and ancillary services continued to rise, from 11.7 per cent of operating revenues in fiscal 2002 to 13.12 per cent in fiscal 2003.

Costs and operations

To quote Michael O'Leary, 'Any fool can sell low airfares and lose money. The difficult bit is to sell the lowest airfares and make profits. If you don't make profits, you can't lower your air fares or reward your people or invest in new aircraft or take on the really big airlines like BA and Lufthansa.'[8]

The company realises that the maintenance of its leading position among no-frills airlines in Europe depends on being the lowest cost airline. This demands a continuous concentration on driving down costs to sustain low fares and remain profitable, even on low yields. Ryanair's cost reduction strategy focuses on five areas:

- fleet commonality;
- contracting out of services;
- airport charges;
- staff costs and productivity;
- marketing costs.

Fleet commonality

Ryanair's fleet consists principally of a single aircraft type – Boeing 737s, currently the most widely flown commercial aircraft in the world. Thus, the company is able to obtain spares and maintenance services on favourable terms thanks to economies of scale, limit costs of staff training and offer flexibility in scheduling aircraft and crew assignments.

Contracting out of services

Other than Dublin Airport where it maintains its own staff and services, Ryanair contracts out aircraft handling, ticketing, baggage handling and other functions to third parties. The company obtains competitive rates and multi-year contracts at fixed prices, limiting exposure to cost

8 Ryanair Annual Report, 2001.

increases. Third party service outsourcing also limits Ryanair's direct exposure to employee relations responsibilities and potential disputes.

While Ryanair engineering staff carry out routine maintenance, repair services and checks on aircraft, engine and heavy maintenance are contracted out to third parties. The carrier is able to strike hard bargains with outside contractors because of the size of its fleet. Contract work is carried out under the supervision and planning of Ryanair engineering staff, enabling the company to retain control of quality and safety without incurring the cost of a specialised labour force for a modestly sized fleet. The in-house maintenance and supervision costs are included under staff costs in the profit-and-loss accounts.

Airport charges and route policy

Airport charges include landing fees, passenger loading fees, aircraft parking fees and noise surcharges. Ryanair reduced these fees by avoiding congested main airports, choosing secondary and regional airport destinations, which are anxious to increase passenger throughput. Most of these airports are significantly further from the city centres they serve than the main airports. For example, Ryanair uses Frankfurt Hahn 123 kilometres from Frankfurt, Torp 100 kilometres from Oslo, Charleroi 60 kilometres from Brussels, and Beauvais 35 kilometres from Paris. In December 2003, the Advertising Standards Authority rebuked Ryanair and upheld a misleading advertising complaint against it for attaching 'Lyon' to its advertisements for offers on flights to St Etienne. A passenger had turned up at Lyon Airport, only to discover that her flight was leaving from St Etienne, 75 kilometres away. The airline dismisses the ruling on the basis that Lyon is only written in small print underneath St Etienne, and is not misleading.

Since Ryanair has been typically able to produce high volume for airports, it has negotiated favourable access fees. Less expensive gate locations and outdoor boarding stairs rather than jetways (which also consume more turnaround time) help to keep costs down. Generally, less congested airports can be expected to provide higher rates of on-time departures, faster turnaround times, and fewer terminal delays, all of which maximise aircraft utilisation and ease restrictions on slot requirements and on the number of allowed take-offs and landings.

Consistent with its policy of point-to-point flights on short-haul routes, Ryanair does not interline with other airlines. This allows the airline to offer direct non-stop journeys, avoiding the costs of providing through service (baggage transfer, passenger assistance) for connecting passengers, as well as delays often caused by the late arrival of connecting flights. Unavoidable services are contracted out and charged to passengers.

The carrier asserted that it would quit any airport location that raised its charges to an unacceptable level when contracts are renegotiated. Although Ryanair initially obtained 90 per cent rebates from the Irish Airports Authority, Aer Rianta, Michael O'Leary continues to publicly attack the Irish airport operator. This centres on a number of issues, including an increase in airport charges, and inadequate congested amenities at Dublin Airport, with parking facilities described as 'a joke'. Ryanair claims that these inadequacies stifle its growth plans. The airline submitted a plan to build its own €25m terminal at Dublin Airport, or alternatively, it would support another consortium with a proposal to build a second terminal. In late 2003, the Irish government indicated that it would probably open tenders to build a second terminal at Dublin Airport to enhance budget airline traffic. By then however, Ryanair had moved its centre of gravity away from Dublin toward the UK and mainland Europe.

Staff costs and productivity

Since employee compensation costs are typically the most important component of total airline costs, Ryanair controls these costs through a performance related pay structure. The company believes that its labour costs are lower than those of many established airlines. Nevertheless, despite modest base salaries, pilots and cabin crew can earn total remuneration in excess of industry norms by, for example, maximising the number of sectors flown daily within regulation limits. In May 1998, Ryanair announced an employee share option scheme worth up to 5 per cent of the shares of the company. In 2001, Ryanair pilots and in-flight employees received an apparently generous five-year pay, productivity and share options package. The agreement narrowly averted a threatened strike by pilots over working schedules and conditions.

Although EU legislation abolished intra-EU duty free sales, Ryanair cabin attendants still make commission on duty-paid sales and in-flight refreshments. The absence of 'free' in-flight service normally provided by full service airlines, has several beneficial spin-off effects – the opportunity for staff to earn commission for paid service, and a reduction in the extent to which the aircraft need cleaning between flights, so cabin crew can tidy up the cabin and allow a quicker turnaround time between flights.

Ryanair has been a newsworthy and controversial company in Ireland with respect to its employment practices, most specifically in its refusal to recognise trade unions. Ryanair asserts that it will only recognise trade unions when a majority of workers opt to join. The company regards the heavily unionised nature of employment in its rival Aer Lingus as a huge contributory factor to the state airline's historic lack of competitiveness. Ryanair's stance over union recognition aroused strong feelings on both sides of the issue. The company was criticised by the EU Commissioner for Social Affairs, by members of the Irish legislature and in the press. Editorials and government ministers' statements were made to the effect that Ryanair's behaviour posed a threat to the series of tripartite agreements involving trade unions, employers' organisations and government that had created industrial peace in Ireland for over a decade, deemed to be an important factor in the creation of a vibrant and growing economy. However, those on Ryanair's side claimed that Ryanair was simply leading the way in facing the realities of international competitiveness and the alleged growing irrelevance of trade unions to effective enterprise and workers' rights. In the face of controversy over the carrier's employment conditions, Ryanair employees issued a statement asserting that they were happy to work for the company.

Marketing costs

Ryanair advertises its low fares, primarily on its website, in newspapers, and on radio and television. In 1997, Ryanair was one of the first European airlines to cut its rate of commission to travel agents, from 9 per cent to $7\frac{1}{2}$ per cent. Since then travel agents' commissions have been further reduced to negligible rates by Ryanair and other airlines have followed suit by reducing travel agents' commission. In a move to capture more value from its operations and improve contact with its customers, Ryanair established Ryanair Direct Limited in Dublin in 1996, transferring its reservations operations from two locations in Dublin and London.

The company benefited from a package of government grants and incentives in setting up Ryanair Direct. Ryanair Direct enabled management control over customer service quality and consistency and increased sales of ancillary services.

In January 2000, Ryanair launched its www.ryanair.com website. This has had the effect of saving money on staff costs, agents' commissions and computer reservation charges, while significantly contributing to growth. By 2003, www.ryanair.com accounted for over 95 per cent of bookings. It provided substantial extra revenue from advertising and selling ancillary services directly, such as travel insurance, car rental, and connecting rail services, and commission on sales of other services such as hotel reservations. Ryanair's website is acclaimed as being one of the most user-friendly and visited travel websites in Europe.

Exhibit 6 details some operating statistics for Ryanair.

The European airline industry

Although the shock of 11 September 2001 was blamed for the crisis the airline industry suffered in 2002, the industry had already been deteriorating beforehand, thanks to a slowing of passenger growth rates and over-capacity which was putting pressure on yields and margins. September 11 did, however, highlight the contrast between the fortunes of the mainstream carriers and the budget airlines, as the latter continued to capture a growing share of the aviation market, and were the only operators to make a profit. Traffic in the sector climbed sharply, buoyed by strong sales promotions and heavy discounting, with all budget airlines adding capacity. In hard times demand for premium service tends to decline as more passengers seek less expensive travel alternatives. The European budget sector is regarded as being in its infancy with just 7 per cent penetration, versus 25 per cent in the US. In the expanding European Union, the potential is seen to be even greater with its larger population base, higher fares environment, and weaker competition.

Budget airlines were making inroads, not only on the territory of mainstream airlines, but also on charter airlines and car ferries. In the case of charters, which relied traditionally on the package trade provided by tour operators, they have been deserted by travellers who prefer to make their

| Exhibit 6 | Ryanair operating statistics 2002 and 2003 |

	2003	2002	Change %
Total aircraft	54	44	22.7%
Average aircraft age	9.6	10.7	−10.3%
Average seats per aircraft	161	155	3.9%
ASK	14,097	9,730	44.9%
Average daily aircraft hours	8.03	7.28	10.3%
Passengers	15.74	11.09	41.9%
Revenue passenger kilometres (RPK)	11,139	7,209	54.5%
Average length of haul	708	650	8.9%
Revenue per RPK	€0.076	€0.087	−12.6%
Revenue per ASK	€0.060	€0.064	−6.3%
Operating costs per ASK	€0.041	€0.047	−12.8%
Break-even load factor	54.3%	54.7%	−0.7%
Load factor	85.0%	81.1%	4.8%
Average staff	1,952	1,531	27.5%
Average staff per aircraft	40.1	43	−6.7%
Passenger per employee	9,013	7,169	25.7%
Average staff cost	53,306	50,575	5.4%
Airport charges per passenger	€6.86	€7.65	−10.3%
Marketing costs/scheduled revenue	2.0%	2.2%	−9.1%

own holiday arrangements using cheaper scheduled flights. Meanwhile, falling passenger volumes on car ferries are blamed on the availability of low fare flights.

The pattern of competition in the low cost segment shows that a winner-takes-all dynamic favours early entrants which have established themselves. Indeed, most budget airlines lose money and/or are eventually taken over. The exceptions tend to be those which were early entrants, like Ryanair or Southwest. Nowhere is this better illustrated than in Go's foray into Dublin, which was seen off easily by Ryanair, less than four months after it had launched flights between Dublin, and the two Scottish cities, Edinburgh and Glasgow.[9] Ryanair, which had flown only between Dublin and Glasgow/Prestwick up to then, launched an all out war in response to this incursion into its own home base, by instituting flights to Edinburgh and increasing frequency to Prestwick at prices that Go could not match.

Barbara Cassani, the then CEO of Go, reminisces about the episode and regrets having launched 'world war three', claiming that Michael O'Leary saw Go's move into Dublin as a 'personal affront'. Ms Cassani also learned a crucial lesson about discounting. 'You can't take on someone with lower costs because they dig deeper than you to lower their prices and still make money while you're bleeding.'[10]

By 2002, some warning bells were being sounded lest the European budget airlines got too optimistic about their prospects.[11] Since head-to-head competition is so damaging, sustainable new routes could be scarce, especially out of London. Moreover, it is debatable whether continental locations are as viable as London. French and Southern Europeans travel much shorter distances to reach sunny locations and may find it more convenient to go by car. Experts argue that the longer holidays of continental Europeans, as long as 30 working days, allow them to take their time when travelling. Thus, it suits a family to pack up the car and drive to a holiday destination. Continental Europeans also have the alternative of high-speed trains, subsidised by the state in France and Germany. As well, budget carriers may find it increasingly hard to retain their low-cost positions

---

[9] Go, originally launched by British Airways as a budget airline subsidiary in 1998, was spun off in 2000, and eventually acquired by easyJet in 2002.

[10] Emmet Oliver, 'Former Go boss offers lessons in high flying', *Irish Times*, 28 November 2003.

[11] Urs Binggeli and Lucio Pompeo, 'Hyped hopes for Europe's low-cost airlines', *McKinsey Quarterly*, no. 4, 2002.

as the scarcity of appropriately located airports increases their power over the airlines, and initially favourable deals, struck to stimulate airport development, begin to run out. The attraction of business travellers to switch away from mainstream airlines is dependent on a high daily frequency of flights between certain destinations, something that budget airlines cannot offer on most of their routes whilst still retaining a critical high passenger load factor.

Erstwhile charter and mainstream airlines are not standing still either; some charter companies are starting their own airlines. An example is Birmingham based MyTravelAir which has inaugurated MyTravelLite, a no-frills scheduled service, and Hapag-Lloyd Express, owned by Tui of Germany, the world's biggest travel group. Regional carriers, already used to point-to-point travel, are also joining the budget airline fray by adapting their business model.

The mainstream carriers, such as British Airways, Lufthansa, Scandinavian Airlines and BMI have reacted in a number of ways. One is to cut fares on a range of short-haul routes and scrap conditions, such as a Saturday night stay to get low fares. They also decreased costs on domestic flights by flying larger aircraft with one passenger class, reducing in-flight service, and introducing internet booking. The suggestion was that they could extend this low cost model to international flights and take on the budget airlines. While in 2000 the reduced fares offered by traditional carriers were still higher than those of budget airlines, some believed business passengers might be inclined to pay up to €100 more for a return fare, knowing they could get on to another flight or be given a bed for the night if their flights were cancelled or seriously delayed. Another response by traditional carriers was to set up low-fares subsidiaries. Despite the short-lived experiments by British Airways with Go and KLM with Buzz, other airlines were attempting to establish budget airlines, run separately to the main airline. In Germany, Bonn/Cologne airport is the base of a new budget carrier, Germanwings (which was planning low-fares flights to Dublin in 2004) backed by Lufthansa.

The stance of the European Commission also threatens budget airlines, not least because of compulsory compensation for cancelled flights but also because of an impending imposition of a 'climate protection charge' on aircraft taking off and landing in the EU. The effect on budget airlines with their frequent take-offs and landings on many short-haul routes would be disproportionately greater than on the mainstream airlines which combine long and short-haul flights within and outside the EU. It is conjectured that the environmental fee would have the effect of doubling many no-frills operators' fares.

In response to various EU issues, Ryanair promoted the formation of a budget airline lobbying group, the European Low Fares Airline Association (ELFAA). Other than Ryanair, the members of ELFAA are relatively tiny lightweight newcomers – Flybe, Volare Web, Scandinavia's Sterling and Slovakia's Sky Europe. Other low-fares carriers – Easyjet, bmibaby, Air Berlin, Virgin Express and Germanwings – have decided to remain out of the group. EasyJet regards the Association simply as a means for Ryanair to promote its own agenda by campaigning its own concerns as industry-wide issues. Additionally, it is suggested that Ryanair will use ELFAA to reduce its lobbying bill.

Ryanair's competitive arena

The following section describes Ryanair's budget airline competitors and some selected other carriers. See Exhibits 7 and 8 for financial and operational comparisons with competitors and benchmark airline operators.

easyJet

Stelios Haji-Ioannou launched easyJet in 1995 with two leased aircraft operating two routes to Glasgow and Edinburgh from its London Luton base. The airline has grown organically and by acquisition since, servicing 39 airports in the UK and continental Europe, from 8 hubs at the end of 2003. The company floated on the London Stock Exchange in 2000, and in 2002, acquired Go, the budget airline originally set up by British Airways. In 2002, the flamboyant Stelios was replaced by a professional team consisting of Sir Colin Chandler, non-executive chairman and CEO Ray Webster.

The business model of easyJet is somewhat different to Ryanair in that it uses more centrally located airports, thus incurring higher airport charges, but more actively courting the business traveller. For example, Schiphol in Amsterdam and Orly Airport in Paris are hubs, while the airline also flies into Charles de Gaulle Airport in the French capital.

Exhibit 7 Comparative airline financial statistics

	Aer Lingus 2003 (€m)	British Airways 2003 (£m)	easyJet 2003 (£m)	Lufthansa 2003 (€m)	Southwest 2003 ($m)	Virgin Express 2002 (€m)
Total Revenue	888.3	7,688	931.8	15,957	5,937	227.3
Operating Costs:						
Employee costs	250.1	2107		4,612	2,224*	
Sales & marketing	79.9	706	41.4	1,017		19.7
Airport charges		576	149.3		372	
Ground handling		961	95.2			
Fuel		842	120.6	1,400	830	25.3
Maintenance		566	89.1	617	430	
Lease charges	43.3	189	84.8		183	
Depreciation	69.7	676	19.9	1,930	384	1.7
Total operating costs	814.2	7,309	883.4	16,742	5,454**	224.7
Operating profit (loss)	74.1	379	48.4	−785	483	3.4
Net profit (loss)	69.2	72	32.4	−984	442	0.4
Net margin	0.08	0.01	0.03	−0.05	0.07	0.0017

Sources: Annual reports.

* Figure made up of salaries and benefits.

** Figure includes $48 of agency commissions and $983 of other operating expenses.

Exhibit 8 Comparative airline operational statistics (scheduled passenger service)

	Aer Lingus 2003	British Airways 2003	easyJet 2003	Lufthansa 2003	Southwest 2003	Virgin Express 2002
Aircraft	30	233	74	218	388	11
Average aircraft age			5.1 years			
Average daily aircraft hours			11.1			
Capacity		139,172 ASK(m)	21,024 ASK(m)	124,000 ASK(m)	71,790.4 ASM(m)	4,080 ASK(m)
Passengers	6.6m	38.02m	20.3m	45.4m	65.7m	2.53m
Revenue passenger distance units		100.11 RPK(m)	17,735 RPK(m)	90,700 RPK(m)	47,943.1 RPM(m)	3,302 RPK(m)
Average length of haul			869km		730miles	
Revenue per passenger			£43.28		$87.42	
Revenue per revenue passenger distance unit		6.52p/RPK		11.3c/RPK	11.97c/RPM	7.61c/RPK (2002)
Revenue per capacity unit		4.73p/APK	4.43p/APK	8.4c/APK	8.27c/ASM	6.15c/APK (2002)
Operating cost per capacity unit			4.19p/APK		7.60c/ASM	
Break-even load factor		63.70%	73.2% (2002)	61.80%		83.6% (2002)
Load factor	81.00%	71.90%	84.10%	73.10%	66.80%	81.30%
Average staff	4,476	51,631	4,142	34,559	32,847	870
Destinations	43	215	39	148	58	15

In 2003, easyJet was being compared unfavourably to Ryanair on various counts. Investors watched the airline underperform on the FTSE all-share index by 26 per cent in 2003, while Ryanair outperformed it by 6 per cent. Contrasting easyJet's acquisition of Go with Ryanair's takeover of Buzz, it was observed that Ryanair paid barely a net €1m for an airline that will carry 4m passengers, while easyJet paid €400m for circa 5m potential passengers. Moreover, easyJet had to terminate an option, costing €9.3m, to buy Deutsche BA, after it failed to reach a workable deal with the German airline's pilots and cabin crew that would allow it to introduce its business model. At about the same time, Ryanair convinced Buzz pilots to agree to its tough employment terms, enabling it to open 13 new routes, including ones to Germany.

The summer of 2002 saw easyJet plagued by logistical problems as it tried to integrate Go and to introduce a new flight crew roster while dealing with the volume and complexity of the summer schedule. It ended up with stranded and dissatisfied passengers and had to invoke flight cancellations to get its operations under control. In the middle of this, a critical report by an anonymous air traffic controller reprimanded low-cost airline pilots for their 'growing tendency to challenge and sometimes ignore instructions from the ground to save time', because of 'an aggressively commercial ethos that exists within some airline companies'.[12] Stelios tried to draw Ryanair into a controversy by suggesting that the Irish carrier's older aircraft are riskier than newer aircraft. On the one hand, there was a negative reaction to Stelios' behaviour as analysts regarded his attack as ill-judged, since 'you never know when it may happen to you'.[13] However, it did bring the safety culture of low-cost airlines into question for a period.

In late 2002, easyJet announced a controversial decision to order 120 aircraft plus 120 options from Airbus, apparently in response to an offer from Airbus that could not be refused, so desperate was the aircraft manufacturer to secure the deal. It means that easyJet will operate a mixed fleet and will incur extra training costs on its new aircraft. This is in contrast to Ryanair and Southwest Airlines, which both remain committed to the tried-and-tested Boeing 737 aircraft that have become the workhorse of budget airlines. EasyJet hopes to mitigate some of the complexity of operating both Boeing and Airbus aircraft types by separaing them between its various bases, and Airbus is providing support for crew training and the supply of spares and maintenance costs in the early stages. Nonetheless, the airline will incur £5m on training on the new aircraft.

By 2004, easyJet appeared to be over the worst and was being compared favourably to Ryanair. For instance, its load factor of 77 per cent for January 2004 was unchanged from the year before. Days after Ryanair's profits warning, easyJet issued a confident trading statement, declaring that the carrier had slowed its capacity growth to 20 per cent, enabling it to maintain its yields. The airline was accelerating its penetration of continental Europe, especially in Germany where it had decided to grow organically after the abandonment of its takeover of Deutsche BA. The easyJet share price rebounded in early 2004, reaching a 12-month peak of €5.75 from a low of €2.45 in June 2003. However, in May 2004, easyJet's share price fell by 25 per cent after CEO Ray Webster announced a slight adjustment in its profits forecast for the year and warned about intensifying competition, with more than 50 budget airlines operating in Europe. Many observers considered the drop in the share price as a nervous overreaction. The airline had increased its yields and had cut its losses from £24m to £18m for the first six months of its fiscal year and expected an overall improvement in earnings per share for the full year, since it ordinarily made its profits in the second half.

The EU ruling against state aid from airports did not affect easyJet as badly as Ryanair, thanks to easyJet's concentration on primary airports that were less likely to need to do 'sweetheart deals' to get customers. Ray Webster, easyJet CEO was positively crowing about it, perhaps in retribution for Michael O'Leary's remark describing easyJet as 'not the brightest sandwich in the picnic'.[14]

Virgin Express

Virgin Express grew out of EuroBelgian Airlines (EBA). EBA had been mainly a charter carrier until it was acquired by Richard Branson's Virgin Group in 1996. Run entirely separately from the Virgin Group, the airline has converted itself into a

---

[12] Kevin Done, 'Lifting the lid on a Pandora's box of aviation safety', *Financial Times*, 22/23 June 2002.

[13] Ibid.

[14] K. Done, 'Ryanair talks of disaster, but the low-cost revolution flies on', *Financial Times*, 7/8 February 2004.

mainly scheduled services budget airline, based in Brussels. Like easyJet, Virgin Express flies into main airports in major cities. In 2000, the airline established a secondary hub at Shannon, Ireland, but pulled out after only an 18-month operation there. Since its inception as a budget airline, Virgin Express has struggled to make a profit. Its operating margin has never exceeded 4.4 per cent (1997), and its performance has been deteriorating, with losses of €6m and €60m in 1999 and 2000 respectively. Although it recovered in 2001 and 2002, it posted a loss of €19m for 2003. Yields had fallen by 21 per cent while costs had been reduced by only 11 per cent.

Its problems arose partly from the demise of Sabena in late 2002, with which it had had a contractual arrangement whereby Sabena purchased a fixed number of seats on certain Virgin Express routes from Brussels, reselling them as its own Business and Economy classes, with appropriate services provided by Virgin Express. In fact, Virgin Express blamed its own languishing performance on overexpansion and underpricing by SN Brussels Airlines, the carrier that replaced Sabena, but it confirmed in March 2004 that it had tentatively agreed to be taken over by its erstwhile rival, in a deal to be completed in September that year. Certainly, Virgin Express was in a position where it had to protect its home territory in Brussels. It had very few options to expand beyond this base. Attempts to grow in France, out of Orly, and in Germany, proved too risky. A merger between Air France and KLM and high-speed rail plans in the Benelux region would put further pressure on Virgin Express. Virgin Express was among those fighting hard to have Ryanair's deal with Charleroi/Brussels South Airport repealed.

bmibaby

In March 2003, bmi British Midland began operating its low-fares subsidiary, bmibaby from its own base at East Midlands Airport. By the middle of 2004, bmibaby had expanded into 29 airports in various UK cities, Ireland, Spain, France, Italy and the Czech Republic, and it had 14 Boeing 737s in service.

Its parent company, bmi was the UK's second largest scheduled service operator serving domestic, European and American routes. By 2003, bmibaby had yet to make a profit. It was a competitor on the Dublin–London Heathrow route.

flybe

In the summer of 2002, British European Airways, a UK regional carrier, restyled itself as flybe, incorporating aspects of the budget airline model. These included: a change in its booking practices away from travel agents to the internet, so that 80 per cent of its seats are sold on the internet at the end of 2003, a reduction of travel agent commission rates from 10 per cent to 1 per cent, passenger payment for on-board services, no ticket refunds, a charge for itinerary changes and credit card booking. The network was also redesigned to focus on more leisure-type destinations. However, it does provide an economy-plus product offering frequent flyer points, a lounge, priority check-in and complimentary onboard service, alongside the standard product.

By 2004, Flybe served 29 destinations in the UK, Ireland, France, Spain, Austria, Switzerland and the Czech Republic from six bases across the UK and Channel Islands. It chose primary airports, such as London Heathrow and Paris Charles de Gaulle. The carrier was planning to standardise its fleet to Bombardier Dash-8 Q400 turboprop jets. The average seat costs of the sub-120 seat capacity of these aircraft are higher than those of the larger 737s, but flybe CEO Jim French argued that the airline competed not on seat costs but on higher frequencies than 737s. However, the airline may add mainline jets to its fleet to cater for further continental routes, beyond the economic range of some of its current aircraft. French predicted that the consolidation of the European airline industry would reduce the number of hubs. Former hubs are ideal for take-up by low-fares airlines. An example is Amsterdam–Schiphol where former KLM slots were expected to be freed up after the Air France–KLM merger.

French acknowledged that the adoption of the low-cost model has been a cultural challenge. He also described flybe as not in the same low-cost bracket as Ryanair. In terms of fare and service levels it was just ahead of easyJet, but below the mainline carriers, similar to the ground formerly occupied by Go.

MyTravelLite

Birmingham-based MyTravelLite began operations in October 2002 as a budget airline subsidiary of MyTravel, the loss-making tour operator. It serves Dublin, Belfast, Geneva, Alicante and Malaga, using four Airbus A320s. The founder of the airline, Tim Jeans is the former sales and marketing director of Ryanair. Although the group has budgeted to lose its €5m investment, Jeans predicted that it would break even in 2004.

In autumn of 2003, MyTravelLite inaugurated flights between Birmingham and Dublin, selling seats from €1.99, in direct opposition to Ryanair and Aer Lingus on the same route. Jeans is a veteran of Ryanair wars against its competitors and was at the forefront of the assault that forced Go out of Dublin. He claims that an in-depth knowledge of Ryanair tactics will stand to him. 'It will get bloody, but this is not some sort of testosterone contest. I think there is a sound business opportunity.' When Ryanair lowered its Birmingham fare to 99 cents, Jeans saw this as an advantage for MyTravelLite, since it generated publicity. He admitted, 'Ryanair will not give in easily. They will not roll over. I'll be like a boil it wants to lance. The only issue is can we make enough noise and create enough local awareness in the market to make our presence felt . . . It is not just about big advertising spends, it's about being controversial if needs be, and taking the fight to Ryanair. We will roll the tanks on the enemy lawns.'[15]

Aer Lingus

Aer Lingus is the national state-owned airline of Ireland, operating domestic and international services, with a fleet of 30 aircraft. The events of September 11 were particularly traumatic for Aer Lingus, as the airline teetered on the verge of bankruptcy. It put paid to plans for a flotation which had already been postponed several times. In late 2001, the choice was to change, or to be taken over or liquidated. Led by a determined and focused chief executive and senior management team, the company set about cutting costs. One ingredient of its cost reduction was a severance programme, costing over €100m, whereby 2,000 of its 6,000 employees left the group. Another element was a reduction of 26 per cent in distribution costs, due to an increase to 32 per cent of bookings made on the company's internet site. Fuel costs fell owing to a reduction in capacity and in fuel prices. Other one-off costs were incurred for share issues

to remaining employees and the rationalisation of the aircraft fleet. By the end of 2002, Aer Lingus had turned a 2001 €125m loss into a €33m profit, and it improved still further in 2003 with a net profit of €69.2m.

In essence, Aer Lingus claims that it has transformed itself into a low-fares airline, and that it matches Ryanair fares on most routes, or that it is only very slightly higher. The airline's chief operating officer says that 'Aer Lingus no longer offers a gold-plated service to customers, but offers a more practical and appropriate service . . . it clearly differentiates itself from no-frills carriers. We fly to main airports and not 50 miles away. We assign seats for passengers, we beat low fares competitors on punctuality, even though we fly to more congested airports, and we always fulfil our commitment to customers – unlike no frills carriers'.[16]

In May 2003, Aer Lingus won the Best Overall Value Award from the Air Transport Users' Council of Ireland, displacing Ryanair, the traditional winner. Ryanair, the winner for Best Online Services failed to turn up for the award ceremony, because of a board meeting clash. After declaring the Aer Lingus award 'bizarre' the Ryanair Communications Manager, John Rowley went on to add that 'only a bunch of complete idiots could possibly vote Aer Lingus as best value airline . . . If this is what passes for best value for money among the top 1000 chief executives in the survey, then maybe they're still drinking too much free champagne on Aer Lingus's overpriced flights'.[17]

Leading Ryanair into the future

Although Michael O'Leary consistently praised his management team, Ryanair is inextricably identified with its dynamic chief executive. He is credited with single-handedly transforming European air transport. The airline has won various international awards, such as Best Managed Airline. In 2004, The *Financial Times* named Michael O'Leary as one of 25 European 'business stars', who are expected to make a difference. The newspaper described him as personifying 'the brash new Irish business elite' and possessing

---

[15] Siobhan Creaton, 'MyTravelLite set for combat with Ryanair', *Irish Times*, 15 August 2003.

[16] Siobhan Creaton, 'Aer Lingus's new model airline takes off', *Irish Times*, 8 August 2003.

[17] Emmet Oliver, 'Ryanair finds rival's award bizarre', *Irish Times*, 27 May 2003.

'a head for numbers, a shrewd marketing brain and a ruthless competitive streak'.[18]

Present and former staff have praised O'Leary's leadership style. 'Michael's genius is his ability to motivate and energise people . . . There is an incredible energy in that place. People work incredibly hard and get a lot out of it. They operate a very lean operation for a company of its size. It is without peer', says Tim Jeans.[19] Another former Ryanair director, Charlie Clifton has been charged with starting a new budget airline in Singapore, Tiger Airways, majority owned by Singapore Airlines, with a 40 per cent stake by Indigo Partners, a joint vehicle of the Ryan Family and David Bonderman. When asked about the type of person who would make a good chief executive for the new airline, Clifton replied, 'We would be delighted if we could get someone of the calibre of Michael O'Leary. Michael has got a very personal way of doing business that might work down here or people might be highly insulted by it . . . If a potential candidate comes in cursing, roaring and shouting, that doesn't mean they will get the job.'[20]

O'Leary's publicity seeking antics earned him a high profile. These included his declaration of war on easyJet when, wearing an army uniform, he drove up in a tank to easyJet's headquarters in Luton Airport. In similar vein, he flew to Milan Bergamo when Ryanair opened its hub there aboard a jet bearing the slogan 'Arriverderci Alitalia'. He has also dressed up as St Patrick to promote ticket offers.

It is O'Leary's outspokenness which has made him a figure of public debate. 'He is called everything from "arrogant pig" to 'messiah'.[21] He has certainly made investors very happy, and even detractors would credit Ryanair with opening up the era of inexpensive air travel. At the same time, he is a reviled figure among trade unionists, and he has antagonised Irish government circles with his continuous attacks on the state airport authority. In late 2002, when the government announced plans to break up the state monopoly, the minister involved was accused of cowtowing to Michael O'Leary. Michael O'Leary is very personally involved in Ryanair's battles with the EU, and some pundits believe that his abrasive style has only served to annoy the Commissioners. Indeed, the Belgian Commissioner, Philippe Busquin, denounced Michael O'Leary as 'irritating . . . and insists he is not the only Commissioner who is allergic to the mere mention of the name of Ryanair's arrogant chief.'[22]

An *Irish Times* columnist, John McManus has suggested that 'maybe it's time for Ryanair to jettison O'Leary'.[23] McManus claims that O'Leary has become a caricature of himself and that he fulfils all 15 warning signs of an executive about to fail. Professor Sydney Finklestein of the Tuck Business School at Dartmouth, US identified 15 signs under five headings – ignoring change, the wrong vision, getting too close, arrogant attitudes and old formulae. After allegedly demonstrating how well O'Leary fits the Finklestein criteria, McManus nonetheless concluded: 'So, is it time for Ryanair to dump Mr O'Leary? Depends whether you prefer the track record of one of the most successful businessmen in modern aviation, or the theories of a US academic from an Ivy League school.'

Perhaps the last words should go Michael O'Leary himself: 'We could make a mistake and I could get hung' he said in June 2003. He reiterated a point he had often made before: 'It is okay doing the cheeky chappie, running around Europe, thumbing your nose, but I am not Herb Kelleher (the legendary founder of the original budget airline, Southwest Airlines in the US). He was a genius and I am not.'[24]

In what might appear to be his darkest hour, O'Leary was irrepressible: 'This is the most fun you can have without taking your clothes off. It is much more fun when the world is falling apart than when things are boring and going well', he declared on the day he announced the shock profits warning.[25]

[18] B. Groom, 'Leaders of the new Europe: Business stars chart a course for the profits of the future', *Financial Times*, 20 April 2004.

[19] Graham Bowley, 'How low can you go?', *Financial Times Magazine*, no. 9, 21 June 2003.

[20] Siobhan Creaton, 'Son of Ryanair aims to realise eastern promise', *Irish Times*, 12 December 2003.

[21] Ibid.

[22] S. Creaton, 'Turbulent times for Ryanair's high-flier', *Irish Times*, 31 January 2004.

[23] John McManus, 'Maybe it's time for Ryanair to jettison O'Leary', *Irish Times*, 11 August 2003.

[24] Graham Bowley, 'How low can you go?', *Financial Times Magazine*, no. 9, 21 June 2003.

[25] S. Creaton, 'Turbulent times for Ryanair's high-flier', *Irish Times*, 31 January 2004.

Wimm-Bill-Dann: a decade of growth

Nadia Shchegrova

Wimm-Bill-Dann: history at a glance

On February 2002, Wimm-Bill-Dann (WBD) became the first Russian consumer company to list level 3 ADR[1] on the New York Stock Exchange and the third Russian company to have ever floated on NYSE. It was a remarkable achievement for the company that made its first carton of juice only 10 years earlier.

● ● ●

In 1992, five entrepreneurs came to Moscow's leading Lianozovo Dairy Plant to launch production of juices under a lease agreement. By 2003, publicly listed food conglomerate WBD Foods Open Joint Stock Company (WBD) was the largest producer of dairy products and juices in Russia, with a portfolio of some 1,100 types of dairy products and over 170 types of juice employing over 17,000 people. It consisted of 24 manufacturing facilities in 20 cities in Russia and the Commonwealth of Independent States (CIS), as well as distribution centres in 26 cities in Russia and abroad. The company distributed its products in Canada, Israel, the Netherlands, the UK, and the USA through both its own distribution network and independent distributors. In Moscow alone, over 2,000 shops worked directly with WBD, offering its wide range of products to consumers.

Independent studies reported that in 2002 WBD Dairy was the leader in many packaged dairy markets in Russia with a market share, in terms of sales volume, of 33 per cent in traditional milk products, 41 per cent in enriched products, and 46 per cent in yoghurt and dessert dairy products. More than 50 per cent of the sterilised milk consumed in Russia was made by WBD. In 2003, WBD's estimated share in the juice market was 32 per cent.

Economic conditions in Russia

For over a decade after the implosion of the Soviet Union in 1991, the Russian economy experienced tremendous stress as it moved from a centrally planned economy to a free market system. To eliminate the distortions of the Soviet Administrative Command System, the government launched a 'shock therapy' programme that included cutting subsidies to money-losing farms and industries, decontrolling prices, moving toward convertibility of the ruble and restructuring the largely state-owned economy. However, these changes took place before other vital structures that govern private property, regulate financial markets and enforce taxation were functional.

By 1998 the government fell into a debt crisis, not able to pay off the interest on the loans it had taken. Over the period of the reforms, the government had raised cash through foreign borrowing, high interest-bearing domestic bonds, privatisation, and especially oil revenues. Due to falling

---

[1] Rather than issuing shares directly in the United States, foreign companies generally issue American Depositary Receipts (ADRs). These are claims to the shares of the foreign company that are held by a bank on behalf of the ADR owners.

Exhibit 1   WBD: Operating and financial indicators: 1999–2002

	1999	2000	2001	2002
Sales volumes, 000 tons	N/A	N/A	1174.3	1422.7
	US$m*	US$m	US$m	US$m
Turnover	357.7	465.4	674.6	824.7
Gross profit	64.0	116.3	181.6	245.0
Selling and distribution expenses	(22.4)	(34.1)	(62.2)	(109.5)
General and administrative expenses	(29.3)	(43.0)	(54.5)	(63.0)
Operating income	9.2	37.9	60.5	66.0
Financial income and expenses, net			(10.6)	(14.1)
Net income		21.4	31.8	35.7

* $US1 = approx. €0.83.

world oil demand as a result of the East Asian crisis, by August 1998, the state could not meet its debt obligations, declaring a moratorium on these debts. No longer able to prop up the value of the ruble at an artificially high exchange rate, its value collapsed against the dollar, losing two-thirds of its value overnight. Inflation rose to an average 86 per cent in 1999, compared with a 28 per cent average in 1998. Between August 1998 and the end of 1999, ordinary people found their wages falling by roughly 30 per cent and their pensions by 45 per cent.

The economy, however, recovered due to the devaluation, which greatly reduced the costs of production in Russia. But by 2004 it was still in a precarious state, supported largely by high oil prices. Over 2000–2003, the economy grew by nearly 29 per cent and industrial production increased by 30 per cent. The most considerable achievement was the level of inflation, which in 2003 was only 12 per cent. However, despite the fact that people's real income grew by 60 per cent, the Russian citizens, especially those living outside the capital, did not feel that their well-being had improved substantially. After over a decade in transition, roughly half the population in Russia had become impoverished in a country where poverty had been largely non-existent. In terms of the structure of the economy, Russia remained heavily dependent on exports of commodities, particularly oil, natural gas, metals, and timber, which accounted for over 80 per cent of exports, leaving the country vulnerable to swings in world prices. Russia's industrial base was increasingly dilapidated.

The situation in the food industry

Russia, with a population of some 145m people, is one of the biggest consumer markets in the world both in volume and in growth potential (5–7 per cent every year, with some sub sectors growing at a rate of 15–20 per cent per annum). In 2003, the capacity of the Russian food market was $47.5bn with the dairy market being some 10 per cent of the total food market. While the Russian dairy market was the eighth in the world in terms of value, average consumption of the dairy products was about one-fifth of that in other European countries.

A similar pattern could be observed in the juice market. Average consumption of juices in Russia was very low until the 1990s. Many Russian consumers tried orange, pineapple and grapefruit juices for the first time in 1991. Since then juice consumption has been gradually increasing up until the financial crisis in 1998, when imported products became unaffordable for the average consumer. By 2001, the Russians were drinking as much juice as they used to before the crisis, but still much less than other Europeans.

Economic reforms that followed the collapse of the Soviet Union, eased import of juices, which enabled foreign companies to occupy significant share of the Russian juice market. The financial crisis of 1998, however, forced many of them to leave the country, whereas domestic producers either significantly reduced or completely terminated juice production. The beginning of the new millennium was marked by a substantial growth in sales of juice. According to Tetra Pak, the world leader in packaging, in 2001 alone the Russian juice

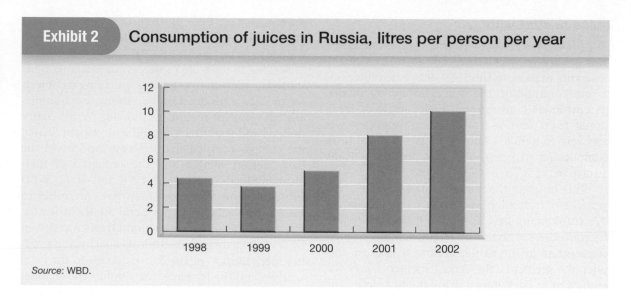

Exhibit 2 Consumption of juices in Russia, litres per person per year

Source: WBD.

market grew by 65 per cent (see Exhibit 2). By 2003, some 95 per cent of the juice market was occupied by domestic producers with the remaining share represented by premium-range imported juices.

Overview of the dairy industry

The dairy sector in Russia at the beginning of the 90s was region or city-centred. The typical product range of a local dairy included traditional products: packaged milk, kefir,[2] soured cream, butter, cream, and cottage cheese. Packaging technologies were not able to provide long shelf life of the products, which dictated the necessity to have production close to the sources of raw materials and to the consumers. For producers that would be able to expand product range and ensure longer storage period and thereby reach wider markets the liberalised economic environment offered abundant business opportunities.

Availability of raw milk, however, became the weakest link in the supply chain. High fuel and grain prices over several years, combined with overall gross inefficiency of agricultural production almost halved livestock in some regions and resulted in a considerable drop in production and quality of milk as a whole. The widespread practice of regional dairies to search for suppliers as far as 500km away from the production facilities resulted in higher prices of the end produce, underutilisation of processing facilities and poor efficiency. Steady

demand on dairy produce in the late 1990s posed producers with the problem of a weak resource base, which became a crucial factor of competition.

Other factors of competitive rivalry were access to financial resources, wider product range and efficient distribution. Regardless which route dairy producers chose to follow – building new facilities or upgrading existing dairies – high value added products such as yoghurts and dairy desserts required massive investments in production and packaging equipment. Given the economic circumstances in the country and the fact that 35–80 per cent of a family budget was spent on food, the necessity to keep prices low posed producers with tough challenges. Among these were to get production and distribution costs under control, and to reach wider markets, especially in the regions, where the total purchasing power of the population was much lower than in Moscow, the epicentre of competitive battle among WBD, Danone, Campina, Ehrmann and Parmalat.

Wimm-Bill-Dann – new player on the market

WBD was created in 1992, when a group of entrepreneurs came to the Lianozovo Dairy plant to launch production of juices. The team's aspiration was to create Russia's leading nationwide food producer. The implementation of the idea began in many directions simultaneously: product development, distribution, quality, packaging, and marketing.

---

[2] Fermented dairy drink.

Juice to start with . . .

At the outset of the project, the team saw branding and quality control as the key to success in the emerging market. In the 1980–90s, when juice was a rare commodity, the domestic market offered its customers conventional juices made of traditional fruits and vegetables. The packaging was awkward to handle (3-litre glass jars or metal tins), complicated to open, and was not aesthetically attractive.

WBD entered the Russian market with seven varieties of fruit juices and nectars under the brand 'J7', introducing new tastes and quality to domestic consumers. Cargill, the largest supplier of juice concentrate in the world, became a strategic supplier of ingredients; the Tetra-Pack technology was employed to pack juices, using bright colours and foreign-sounding labels to attract attention. The *J7* juice series quickly became a benchmark for any domestically produced juice in Russia. Despite the lack of a juice-consumption tradition and an unfamiliarity with the new type of product (nectar), by 1997 WBD increased annual sales of juice from 6m litres to more than 100m litres and to 165.4m in 2000. With 25–40 per cent annual growth of the juice market over 2000–2003, WBD remained the absolute leader with an estimated market share of 32 per cent in 2003.

. . . and then milk

After the initial two years of only making juices WBD expanded its product portfolio by including milk and other dairy products, which became possible after the takeover of the Lianozovo Dairy, one of the biggest dairies in Europe. By 1997, the volume of production at the plant increased by 500 per cent and the dairy became the stronghold of the company and the major provider of funds for further expansion. In the same year, WBD acquired majority stakes in the Baby Food Plant and in two more dairies in Moscow, which made WBD the leader in the dairy market in Moscow and the region and allowed it to add new types of products to its portfolio.

Whereas Russia's population is spread over a large territory, the concentration of population in Moscow and the fact that the total purchasing power in Moscow is 19 times higher than in the outlying regions, meant the capital was a logical place to start. This emerging market attracted big international players, such as Danone, Campina, Parmalat and Erhmann, who had entered the

Russian market by importing dairy products and later by opening their own production facilities in the Moscow region.

Seeking to replicate its success in Moscow, WBD started expansion into regions, pursuing its objective to have a production base in every economically developed region in Russia. While dairy desserts and yoghurts were still a novelty in Russia, the company anticipated the vast capacity of the dairy dessert market and the potential of their local production. Between 1998 and 2002, WBD gained control over more than ten enterprises in the Far East, Siberia, Central and Southern Russia. The selection of the acquisition targets was driven by several factors: the technical capacity and product specialisation of the dairies, access to the local markets and the resource base. Prominent regional dairies had well-developed distribution systems, which helped to ensure that these plants, when modernised, maintained leading positions in their regions. Raw materials played another important role. WBD aimed to settle in the most resource-rich regions. For instance, about 15 per cent of all raw milk in Russia was produced in four regions where WBD had production facilities.

Earlier than its competitors, WBD established its own distribution network. The company opened or acquired trade branches in 26 cities in the regions where it did not have production facilities and acquired distribution companies in more than 40 Russian cities.

In 2000, WBD continued its expansion beyond Russia's boundaries by acquisition of majority stakes in dairies in Ukraine and Kyrgyzstan. The Ukrainian market of yoghurts grows by 25–30 per cent every year; and Kyrgyzstan has abundant natural resources, namely fruits (peaches, apricots, and tomatoes) that can be processed into juice concentrates. In addition to this, Kyrgyzstan is a member of the World Trade Organisation, which eases exports from the country, especially to other states in Central Asia. The acquired dairy, Bishkeksut, produced hard cheeses – capability that WBD had not had until then.

WBD's increasingly competitive environment

In the dairy market

Political changes of the 1990s in Russia opened the country to foreign companies attracted by the capacity of the emergent market. Having started with traditional products, such as milk, cottage cheese, soured cream and kefir in the late 1990s WBD introduced new product lines, including yoghurts and dairy deserts, to match the assortment of the Western rivals importing the goods. Market growth in food sectors in Russia was largely determined by changes in disposable income, therefore most of the products were positioned by price and not by distinctive qualities. WBD enjoyed obvious benefits of local production, so it was able to offer the same range of products in the same quality package at a lower price. As one of the founders put it, 'due to the very nature of the business – the food industry – prices need to be affordable because our consumers represent 100 per cent of the population'. While every city in Russia has a dairy plant, often local production and particularly packaging technologies were not able to ensure a long storage period, which led to very low-price products targeted on tight budgets. WBD occupied a niche of long-life goods that competed with imported analogues in the range and, due to lower transport and production costs, was price competitive.

The consequences of the financial crisis in 1998 had various implications for producers, processors and consumers. When the national currency lost 75 per cent of its value and consumers became extremely price conscious, the switch to cheap domestic goods was inevitable. Russian dairies faced a better situation than their Western competitors: access to local raw materials, low labour and production costs gave an edge that importers found difficult to achieve. WBD was one of few companies that managed increased sales at the height of the crisis with a slight reduction in profitability. Active regional expansion, growth of product portfolio and continuous advertising resulted in the capture of 30 per cent of the national dairy market and 30 per cent of the juice market.

Competition, however, also saw the attractiveness of low production costs and the expanding market. Western producers faced the necessity of relocating their production to Russia: in 2000, Ehrmann and Danone launched yoghurt production facilities in Moscow region; Parmalat and Campina started production of packed milk.

With new entrants the yoghurt market experienced its boom stage. According to some marketing studies, yoghurts accounted for more than 31 per cent of the entire dairy market. This segment was growing by some 20 per cent every year and perceived to be far from saturation: in 2003 about one third of all yoghurts was consumed in Moscow.

Up to 2001, WBD was seen as the absolute leader of the sector with a total share of 50 per cent of the market. In 2001, the share shrunk due to a reported lack of yoghurt producing capacity. While WBD was increasing production of milk and juices, its Western competitors were focusing on yoghurts. Ehrmann, for instance, doubled sales volumes in 2001 and by 2002 reached the leading position in the yoghurt market with a share of 36 per cent. However, WBD was one of the few companies investing in yoghurt production in the regions. The other one was Danone that already had processing facilities outside the Central region and in 2003 started construction of another pant in Novosibirsk.

Having recovered from the consequences of the 1998 financial crisis, in the new millennium consumers were becoming wealthier, spending more money and changing their purchasing patterns. Yoghurt, for example, was initially perceived as a tasty product rather than a healthy one. Consumers preferred it creamy, with lots of fruit and high fat content. The trend soon started changing. First in Moscow where the population is more 'westernised' and then gradually in other European regions. Customers were becoming increasingly

Exhibit 3	Market share in Russia by June 2000		
Company	**Yoghurt**		**Dairy products**
Wimm-Bill-Dann (Russia)	33%		30%
Campina (Netherlands)	16.9%		10.6%
Ehrmann (Germany)	8.6%		3.1%
Danone (France)	17.4%		12.4%

Exhibit 4	Market shares in the juice market		
	2001	**2002**	**2003**
WBD	28%	31.4%	32.4%
Multon	27%	22%	25.1%
Lebedyansky	15%	22%	27.5%
Nidan-Ecofruct	N/A	11%	13.1%

interested in healthy diets and started buying more products with biologically active ingredients, vitamins and a lower fat content. Special product lines for children, with various supplements and multi-vitamins became another rapidly expanding niche in the market.

Changes in consumption patterns were taking place in the regions as well, although at a slower pace and in a different way. A double-digit growth in real incomes resulted in the emergence of middle-class consumers and gradual growth of the consumer's requirements for quality products. An average shopping list would now include less traditional, low cost products and more juices, and 'high-tech' yoghurts and desserts.

In the juice market

The dynamics of the juice market resembled those of the dairy market. From 2000–2003, total juice consumption grew from 750m litres to 1,800m litres, which attracted new players who invested heavily in production, distribution and marketing. By the end of 2003, the juice market was dominated by four domestic producers: WBD, Multon, Lebedyansky and Nidan-Ecofruct. Together, they occupied more than 90 per cent of the national market.

By 2004, the growth of the juice market had gradually slowed down. In 2002 it showed 26 per cent increase in volume, in 2003 the growth was 19 per cent and projected increase in 2004 was only 15 per cent. By the beginning of 2004, average consumption of juice in Moscow and St Petersburg nearly reached saturation: 24–30 litres per customer per year, whereas average juice consumption in the rest of the country was only 11 litres. High price sensitivity of customers in the regions also resulted in the rapid growth of low and medium price juices. The target customer displayed little loyalty to any particular brand, so producers had to find new marketing solutions especially when the room for price wars was so limited. WBD, for instance, changed packaging of J7 from cartons to aseptic plastic bottles, arguing that the new package appealed to the customer and allowed for quick and inexpensive changes in branding. Multon replaced its orange nectar *Kind* with 100 per cent orange juice with no changes in price; Lebedyansky managed to increase sales of its juice *Fruit garden* by 50 per cent merely by repositioning of the brand.

Despite its overall leading position in the juice market, at the end of 2003 WBD reported reduction of produced juice by 0.6 per cent. Moreover, it started losing its positions in some segments. Market studies conducted in the 11 biggest cities in the regions showed that WBD's market share was only 26.5 per cent losing its leadership to Lebedyansky. Industry observers commented that WBD was too slow to react to the increased competitive pressure in the middle and low price segments. They also suggested that the delayed launch of the new packaging, the reformation of the distributing network, and the shift of the focus to new projects were some of the factors affecting the deteriorating performance.

On the resource side, all producers were highly geared to imported ingredients: up to 90 per cent of any juice (with the exception of apple and tomato) were of foreign origin.

Changes in corporate structure and flotation

Up until 2000, WBD's corporate structure was vague and complicated, with an unclear ownership structure adopted to minimise taxes. Effectively, WBD was a group that consisted of separate companies and enterprises, where a newly acquired dairy was buying another, and then the latter would become a parent to the next acquisition target. Among shareholders, there were private people, investment groups and banks, food companies and local governments – overall over 1,300 individuals and organisations.

The prospective flotation made the management team revise and restructure the business by making it transparent to the prospective investors. WBD was transformed into a holding company and became the first Russian company that disclosed its ownership structure, including private shareholders. Independent experts with international reputation were also introduced into the Board as non-executive directors.

The management structure also underwent serious transformation. The seven directors of WBD were the team that had been with the company since 1992 with responsibilities allocated on the principle of 'everyone does what he can do best'. By 1999, the managers realised that the existing structure had stopped being effective to cater for needs of the evolving business. In his interview Pavel Dudnikov, then CEO, explained: 'now we understand that our dream was not daring enough. Tomorrow for WBD is not limited by the territory of our country. Now we have a new dream of becoming a world-scale corporation. That means there is a new phase of the development, new objectives and goals, and more importantly, new requirements for the management'. One of the key changes that took place was formalisation of the management structure, where owners of the holding represented by the Board decided to focus on strategic management and control leaving operations to managers and directors of the production facilities.

The Initial Public Listing of 11m of WBD's ADR took place on 8 February 2002. One month after the IPO, the share price rose by $4 ($24.9 per share).

Further product development and diversification

Production of drinks was one of the most dynamic industries in Russia in 2000–2003. Sales of beer were increasing by 16 per cent, bottled water by 23 per cent and juices by 25–40 per cent per annum. WBD saw this as a possibility for diversifying its product portfolio and for utilising the full potential of the existing distribution network. Further to the initial success of J7 juices, which by 2003 included 22 different flavours and occupied 22 per cent of the national market, other brands of juices, nectars and juice-based drinks were added to target customers in both premium and low medium segments.

In 2001, WBD launched one of the first in Russia juice and dairy umbrella brand *Ginger up!* Aimed at children aged 5–9, *Ginger Up!* came complete with its own magazine, games and comics. Juices and nectars *Ginger Up!* were based on the technology of J7 but priced 10 per cent higher than J7 and enriched with vitamins, which was the core message in advertising. It was planned that an additional revenue stream would be developed from licensing the brand to producers of chocolate bars and board games.

Products with a higher added value, such as mousses, fruit-flavoured milk and kefir, puddings and fruit-flavoured cottage cheese were added to the extensive portfolio of traditional dairy products. This area was identified as one of the major strategic directions to follow with the purpose of meeting changing customer preferences, keeping competitive edge and improving operational efficiencies. A new line of health-oriented enriched products *Neo* included drinks, fruit and milk cocktails enriched with vitamins and live bacteria. *Neo* was priced 25 per cent above retail average and targeted consumers with high income. To support this direction of product portfolio diversification, WBD set the promotion of dairy and juice consumption culture as one of its strategic objectives for its business activity.

WBD also entered the mineral water and cheese markets. The decision to move into the water sector was prompted by the rapid growth of this sector and by the opportunity to level out revenues during summer when consumption of dairy products reduces. The size of the mineral water market in retail prices was some $800m in 2002. Volume was growing by 23 per cent annually with total production estimated to be from 1,800m litres to 2,300m litres in 2003 (see Exhibit 5), which is bigger than the volume of the juice market (1,800m litres in 2003). The growth was attributed to the increasing income and gradual drift of consumers towards drinking bottled water instead of tap water and to the interest in the sports life style. In 2003, WBD launched its own table mineral water *Sanctuary Valdai*, which became possible with acquisition and modernisation of a plant in

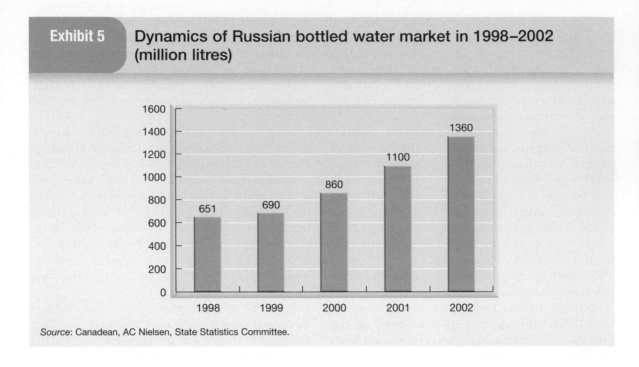

Exhibit 5 Dynamics of Russian bottled water market in 1998–2002 (million litres)

Source: Canadean, AC Nielsen, State Statistics Committee.

the Novgorod region near the Valdai National Preserve. The upgraded plant had the largest production capacity of bottled still and sparkling mineral water in the European part of Russia. Industry observers were cautious about the chances of it becoming a leading producer as the Russian bottled mineral water market had long been divided among Coca-Cola (*Bon-Aqua*), Pepsi-Cola (*Aqua-Minerale*) and Nestlé (*Saint Spring*).

Nevertheless, WBD persisted in attempts to expand into this sector. In September 2003, the Company acquired Healing Spring Ltd, a producer of *Essentuki* brand mineral water, and Geyser Ltd, the owner of the *Essentuki* water wells. By doing so WBD entered a very saturated market. More than 150 enterprises bottle and market Caucasian mineral water. However, only a few enterprises had licences for the production of mineral water. As a result, there was abundance of various *Essentukis* in shops and supermarkets. One benefit was that WBD did not have to invest in promotion of the brand, which was famous from Soviet times: some 21.2 per cent of Russians drink *Essentuki*. On the other hand, as commentators pointed out, WBD's water could get lost in this 'sea' of *Essentuki*. As of the end of 2003, no one had exclusive trademark rights on *Essentuki*.

The cheese sector had long been divided between imported products positioned in the premium and upper middle price segments (60 per cent of the national market) and domestically produced cheeses (40 per cent of the market, low price segment). WBD identified a gap in the market for domestically produced high quality cheese at reasonable prices. By targeting this segment WBD was intending to compete with imported analogues in the upper medium price segment that accounted for 22 per cent of the total cheese market.

In mid-2003 WBD started production of processed cheese followed by the launch of hard cheese production under the *Lamber* trademark. The *Lamber* brand offered high quality at a reasonable price, a convenient 1kg size and attractive packaging. A dedicated advertising campaign of the new brand aimed at promoting greater consumption of cheese was launched on Russian national television in November 2003. Per capita cheese consumption in Russia was a fraction of European consumption levels.

Continued diversification

In 2000, attracted by the fast growth of the beer market in Russia, the company acquired interests in several breweries across the country. The original plan was similar to that in the acquisition of regional dairies: investments in modernisation, extensive marketing and distribution via existing channels. The move provoked a number of sceptical comments from industry observers and producers:

the beer market is one of the most saturated in the country, with well-established players, both foreign and domestic, abundant promotion spending, prominent brands and extensive local production facilities. With not much explanation given to the public, in 2001 the acquired breweries were handed over to the specially created Central European Brewery Company (CEBC). Officially WBD and CEBC operated separately, sharing only distribution channels, although major individual shareholders of WBD controlled more than 75 per cent shares of the CEBC. By June 2003, CEBC consisted of four breweries and accounted for 2.6 per cent of the domestic bottled beer market.

Another project in the food sector was a joint venture with Hungarian cannery 'Globus'. However, jars of pickled vegetables under WBD's brands did not enjoy much of consumers' attention and got stuck in supermarkets.

The beer and cannery projects were not the only ones that were developed outside the core business. In 2003 and 2004 the directors of the company used proceeds from selling small portions of their shares to invest into a real estate complex in Moscow region (initial investment of US$10m) and in the development and production of anti-smoke hoods aimed at reducing the number of people dying from inhaling smoke and poisonous gases in case of fire. The real estate project included construction of 200 elite houses, 400sq m each, that were going to be offered to the market for US$0.6m per house. Upon the launch of the anti-smoke hoods project at the beginning of 2004, the entrepreneurs argued that this individual protection device could reduce the death toll by as much as 80 per cent and with a largely unexplored market they expected a good return on the initial US$30m investment. Among the first corporate customers there were transport and construction companies, oil- and gas-producing companies and utilities.

Potential acquisition by Danone and losses of 2003

In 2003, speculations that Danone might buy WBD appeared in the press. The French producer was consistently increasing its share in WBD's stake and by 2003 held 7.2 per cent. Over almost two years, shareholders of WBD were exploring a variety and number of potential combinations, joint ventures or partnerships with Danone.

At the end of 2003, it was announced that the two-year negotiations were terminated by mutual agreement. Reportedly, the parties failed to reach agreement on at least 20 clauses of the contract relating to the strategy for the company, price of the shares, future and structure of the management team.

Danone's interest in the company lied primarily in WBD's milk business, its regional network of distributors, processing facilities and strong brands. If the $1bn takeover had been successful, Danone's total share of the Russian yoghurt and kefir markets could have reached 70 per cent. WBD's juice and water processing facilities would have to be disposed though, as they were not part of Danone's core business. At WBD's dairies, production of packed milk and juices were technologically connected, which would have made the separation costly. In addition to this, substantial financial resources would have been required to upgrade the existing production facilities up to Danone's standards.

Another important issue was the price of the deal. The French attempted to buy the company that had been investing heavily in marketing, distribution and promotion but with a little return, given increasing competitive pressures. The press implied, that given WBD's weaker commercial performance in 2003, and the declining sales in the juice sector, Danone tried to negotiate a lower than expected price. The results of the nine months of 2003 showed that WBD's personnel, advertising, marketing costs and other commercial expenses increased by 34.3 per cent when compared to the same period in 2002, but net profit decreased by 36 per cent. Moreover, the Russian producer projected losses in the fourth quarter of 2003.

Commenting on the figures, Sergei Plastinin, CEO of WBD, identified lower than anticipated sales in both juice and dairy segments and higher raw milk prices as additional reasons contributing to the weakened performance. But he also added: 'We believe that, with our in-depth knowledge of the Russian market, and a skilled management team, we will continue to grow our business successfully, despite increasing competition and growing costs. In the Dairy Segment we are concentrating on productivity increases and on launching more value added products, especially in the regions, while our efforts in the Juice Segment are focused on introducing innovative products and strengthening our distribution system. Our

	Exhibit 6	Key operating and financial indicators for nine months of 2003 and the full year 2003

	9m '03	9m '02	Change	FY '03	FY '02	Change
Sales volumes, thousand tons	1,104.0	1,029.8	7.2%	1,484.5	1,422.7	4.35%
	US$m*	US$m		US$m	US$m	
Sales	**684.6**	**592.4**	**15.6%**	**938.5**	**824.7**	**13.8%**
Dairy	479.5	406.6	17.9%	662.3	563.0	17.6%
Juice	203.8	185.7	9.7%	274.5	261.7	4.9%
Water	1.2	–	–	1.6	–	–
Gross profit	**208.4**	**182.2**	**14.4%**	**273.4**	**245.0**	**11.6%**
Selling and distribution expenses	(100.2)	(74.6)	34.3%	(140.7)	(109.5)	28.5%
General and administrative expenses	(57.7)	(45.1)	27.9%	(76.0)	(63.0)	20.6%
Operating income	**44.8**	**58.4**	**(23.3%)**	**49.2**	**66.0**	**(25.5%)**
Financial income and expenses, net	(13.1)	(9.2)	42.4%	(15.3)	(14.1)	8.5%
Net income	**20.8**	**32.5**	**(36.0%)**	**21.2**	**35.7**	**(40.6%)**

* $US1 = approx. €0.83.

key goal looking ahead is to improve our bottom-line while reducing operational expenses in the near future.'

The stock market reacted with a 20 cent increase in WBD's share price once the termination of the deal was announced. Commentators interpreted it as a good sign, signalling investors' confidence in the company and their hope that WBD's management team would start dedicating more time to the development of the business. But there were others that said that Danone's interest in the leading Russian producer was far too strong and the talks might resume in 2004.

Sources

Isvestia, 19 June 2000, 5 December 2001, 24 April 2002.
Gazeta.Ru, 25 February 2004.
Financial Izvestia, 24 June 2003, 10 September 2003.
The Financial Times, 31 May 1999.
Kompania, 27 February 2003, 24 February 2004.
Moskovskie Novosti, 22 August 2000, 19 September 2000.
Vedomosti, 5 December 2001, 16 July 2003, 15 August 2003, 30 September 2003.
The Voice of Russia, 19 December 2003.
www.wbd.com. www.wikipedia.org. The World Factbook, www.cia.gov

KPN – surviving the crisis in the telecommunications industry

D. Jan Eppink

On 1 November 2003, Ad Scheepbouwer had been CEO of KPN for two years. He was appointed when banks and financial institutions indicated they no longer had confidence in his predecessor. Decisions in the years before had led to an enormous increase in debt. Vast amounts had been spent in acquiring mobile operators abroad as well as in obtaining UMTS licences.[1] The expected high growth in mobile revenues, however, did not materialise. The share price dropped from a high of €73.46 in the first half of 2000 to a low of €2.21 in 2001. Turning around the company was an enormous challenge.

● ● ●

Background

KPN was born out of the public sector Post and Telecommunications corporation in the Netherlands. On 1 January 1989 the legal form of the PTT was changed from a department of the Ministry of Transportation and Public Works into a plc – initially 100 per cent government-owned. The mission of the new company called KPN (Koninklijke PTT Netherlands) was stated as:

> Royal PTT Netherlands is a company that within and outside of the concession it has been granted will deliver to the business and private market a complete set of high quality products and services, concentrated around the national and international transportation of information, goods, and valuables.

The change from government department into government-owned company was not just a legal one. Government decided that in view of the liberalisation of the markets and the expected increase in competition, a change of management style was also required. After a short transition period the whole executive board consisted of

newcomers. The new CEO of KPN came from Unilever and another director was lured away from

Photo: Royal KPN N.V.

[1] UMTS is a third generation (3-G) mobile communication system which can deliver voice, text, music and animated images at high speed.

IBM. Also top managers for the two divisions (Mail and Telecom) were attracted from outside. The new CEO of KPN Telecom was recruited from the Dutch subsidiary of Alcatel, a French company supplying to the telecom industry. One of his main challenges was to change the culture from a bureaucratic one into an entrepreneurial one.

The 1989 annual report stated:

> External conditions change at high speed. Because of this, our company is continually confronting new challenges.

Rather than seeing these changes as threats, the company applauded them:

> PTT telecom is in favour of this deregulation, provided it is based on international reciprocity and on equal terms for all suppliers of telecom services. (Annual report 1994)

When the company was quoted on the Amsterdam Stock Exchange in 1994, about one third of the shares that had been held by the government were sold to the public.

In June 1998 KPN was split up into two companies. Of these, PTT Telecom would carry the name KPN in future, whereas the mail and courier activities would be named TPG. Both companies were quoted on the Amsterdam Stock Exchange. The cable company Vision Networks was internally demerged.

In the years after the privatisation, the environment had changed dramatically for a number of reasons. First was the gradually increasing deregulation in the international market. This was a particularly important factor. Until the early 1990s international calls were handled on the basis of bilateral agreements between countries. Deregulation meant that the exclusive rights of the national operators would progressively disappear and that operators would need to find cheaper ways to route traffic. Second, deregulation had as an objective to stimulate competition. National governments had to make it possible and attractive for new companies to enter their markets. For companies that for decades had been monopolists this meant an enormous change of the playing field. Some entrants were relative newcomers in the telecom business, but had had quite an impact in those parts of the market they had chosen to enter – for example, Vodafone. Other entrants were telecom operators from other countries, such as France Telecom, British Telecom and Deutsche Telekom. Often they used new brand names.

A third cause of changed environment was the technological developments that enabled the rise in the use of the internet. Particularly important in this respect were methods of increasing the speed of the data transmission and data processing (microprocessors and routers). KPN started giving internet-related issues serious top management attention in the second half of the 1990s.

Fourth was the initially surprising growth of mobile communications. Also in the last years of the 20th century, the development of third generation mobile communication (UMTS) gave rise to unprecedented expectations of growth. To become a player in this business required equally unprecedented level of investments in licences and equipment. The money for these investments could not be generated internally and had to come from outside, either from the issue of new shares or an increase in debt.

Strategy

In order to face all these challenges the strategy of the company was stated as follows in the 1999 annual report:

> In 1999 KPN has identified its core activities: fixed telecommunication; mobile telecommunication; data communication (IP/data) and Internet, call centre, and media services (ICM) (abbr. added, DJE). In all these fields KPN wants to excel. That means: in three of the four sectors (mobile, IP/data, and Internet, call center and media services) KPN aims for fast growth and a position in the European top three.

The activities identified above had quite different characteristics. Fixed telecommunications, for instance, is basically a service for the domestic market. IP/data is very international and requires fast global or at least pan-European infrastructures. Mobile telecommunications is a business with many new entrants, where branding is important as well as the kind of services (camera phones, messaging) that can be provided. The call centre business is partly based on outsourcing by large companies of customer contacts to a third party, and therefore is a business-to-business market.

In the annual report for the year 2000, the foreword by the Chairman of the Board of Management stated that expansion would be mainly realised in Germany, the Netherlands and Belgium.

> KPN will continue to grow, but the emphasis is now on organic growth in the countries I have mentioned.

In order to intensify our focus in relation to our business operations, we will dispose of our non-core assets . . .

In his first foreword as Chairman and CEO, Ad Scheepbouwer remarked in the 2001 annual report:

In the first few months after my appointment there was not much inclination or time for exploring strategic horizons. But it was precisely during this period that – under pressure of circumstances – we had to make some fundamental choices, both in terms of activities and geographical focus . . .

The Dutch Fixed Network is still KPN's backbone and cash generator, but we expect growth above all in the mobile and the Data/IP segments.

Customers

Historically KPN had two groups of customers in its home market: private individuals and small businesses (which did not spend large amounts on telecommunications), and big companies whose telecommunication bills could run into tens of millions of euros. The latter group was especially important for future success for two reasons. First, it was expected that because of the ongoing internationalisation of business, telecommunications needs would increase. Second, developments such as just-in-time deliveries, enterprise resource planning systems, the internet, and increasing size of companies (through mergers and acquisitions) were also expected to have an impact on the demand for telecommunication and the competitive situation.

In the course of the 1990s the strategy of the company changed, not only to include more and new services (mobile and internet), but also in a geographical sense. The market was no longer just the familiar home market, but also other countries both nearby and far away. The following paragraphs will describe the major steps in the process of internationalisation, that is, before the decison was made to invest heavily in UMTS operations.

Strategic alliances: Unisource

One of the initial pillars of becoming a large international player was the formation of strategic alliances. In 1991 the alliance with Televerket from Sweden (now Telia) was announced just before the international Telecommunication Exhibition in Geneva. Both companies would eventually join their international activities in a new company called Unisource. Unisource would offer worldwide network and advanced fax services for larger international companies. Depending on the area and the service, Unisource would seek appropriate additional partners. In 1992 Swiss PTT Telecom announced it would join Unisource. In that year an agreement was also signed between Unisource and USA-based Sprint for the distribution of worldwide network services. In late May 1996 Telefonica, the Spanish Telecom operator, became the fourth equal partner in Unisource.

The formation of Unisource had two aims for the partners. The first was to achieve economies of scale. To give an idea of the relative size of the companies in the international arena: KPN was in 1991 the sixth largest company in the field of international telecommunications, but only one tenth of the size of the fifth largest. The other aim was to make possible 'one-stop-shopping' for international businesses.

In December 1994 the perspective was broadened when USA-based AT&T and Unisource decided to start a joint venture named Uniworld. The new entity targeted large internationally operating companies with an integrated package of worldwide data and voice services. The company offered its services via its own offices or through local providers. In Europe Uniworld also represented World Partners (the alliance of Unisource, AT&T, KDD from Japan and Singapore Telecom). In 1996 the name Uniworld was changed into AT&T-Unisource Communication Services (AUCS), in which Unisource had a 60 per cent share and AT&T a 40 per cent share.

The alliance between Unisource and AT&T was not the only worldwide telecom alliance aimed at multinational companies. Global One had been formed in early 1996 by US-based Sprint and Europe's Atlas, which was formed by Deutsche Telekom and France Telecom (each 50 per cent). Another major alliance was Concert, formed in 1994 by British Telecom and MCI from the USA. In November 1996 BT and MCI announced that they had entered into a merger agreement. BT would offer $20bn for the shares of MCI.[2]

In April 1997 Telefonica, BT and MCI announced they had formed a new strategic alliance. To compensate for the damage this caused to Unisource,

---

[2] In fact the merger never took place – it was overtaken by other events.

Telefonica had to pay several hundreds of millions of dollars to the three other Unisource partners. Finally Worldcom made a far higher bid ($37bn) in October 1997 for MCI's shares and won the contest with BT. Telefonica was, for the time being, left without a partner. In March 1998 Telefonica, WorldCom and MCI announced a new partnership, which later was dissolved. WorldCom and Sprint announced a merger in 1999: WorldCom offered $129bn for the shares of Sprint (including debt) but anti-trust authorities on both sides of the Atlantic Ocean blocked this in July 2000. After the Telefonica, BT and MCI partnership fell apart, BT teamed up with AT&T to form the Concert global equity joint venture. Concert aimed at the business customer with complex telecommunication needs.

Breaking up Unisource

In the course of 1998 there were fundamental discussions within Unisource about the strategy the company should follow. The financial results were still negative (1998 loss of dfl 382m on revenues of dfl 2.610m) and the interests of the original partners seemed to be diverging. The 1998 Unisource annual report made the newly developed strategy look like a 'leap forward' rather than a split up of Unisource:

> Unisource made a thorough analysis of what had been achieved since 1992, against the background of the rapidly changing telecommunications market. This resulted in a new strategy in which Unisource will concentrate on the segment of small- and medium-sized enterprises with a full range of products and services, but with a special focus on data services and Internet protocol (IP) services in the largest telecommunications market in Europe. We can realise this ambition only from an independent position.

Observers within KPN would remark later that Unisource missed a compelling strategic *raison d'être* and that the alliance model was not working any longer. Stronger links between companies were required. Moreover decision making was very time consuming, which sometimes hindered quick reactions to changes in the market.

It was decided that the three owners of Unisource would each buy the Unisource business networks that served their home market. KPN bought the Belgian network as well. Later, other parts of Unisource were sold to other operators and parties.

In the course of 1998 AT&T decided it would withdraw from WorldPartners. This again weakened the position of what was left of Unisource. In the same period other strategic alliances were dissolved also. Global One fell apart after France Telecom and Deutsche Telekom fought over a participation in Italy.

Joint venture: KPNQwest

In 1998 KPN and Qwest from the USA decided to establish KPNQwest, a new jointly owned company which was quoted on exchanges in the Netherlands and USA in November of the next year. By 2001 this company was a leading pan-European provider of data-centric services based on the internet protocol (IP). It had an advanced 20,000 km fibre-optic network, which connected 50 cities in Europe. It was one of the largest business ISPs in Europe, operating in 15 countries. The company was developing a network with a large capacity, the so-called EuroRings, which could connect 50 cities. In 18 of these locations Cybercenters would provide hosted customers with unlimited bandwidth. The first CyberCenter was opened in Munich in July 2000, whereas Paris and London were ready for service at the end of 2000. Milan, Frankfurt and Stockholm were offered services in 2001. KPNQwest wanted to become the highest-quality and lowest-cost fibre-optic network in Europe.

In 2001 KPN sold 10 per cent of its 44.3 per cent stake in KPNQwest for €102m and reduced it to 39.9 per cent. The reason given in the 2001 annual report was that

> . . . KPN's entanglement in a network of international partners . . . reduces its room for manoeuvre.

During the year 2001 there were many announcements about new customers or new services for existing customers, among others for AOL Time Warner. In early 2002, after accounting problems with Worldcom and Global Crossing became world news, there were rumours in the press that similar things had occurred with KPNQwest as well. The company denied any wrongdoings on 13 February 2002, stating that all transactions were in compliance with US GAAP. On 31 May 2002 KPNQwest filed for bankruptcy, after a failed attempt to restructure financially.

Together with other parties KPN kept KPNQwest's network operational for a period of time, which made sure customers could migrate to other operators without significant disruptions. Many telecom operators tried to buy at bargain prices parts of the advanced infrastructure KPNQwest had built in the aftermath of the bankruptcy. KPN itself bought the German network in August 2002. The UK network and the transatlantic sea cable capacity were bought in September of the same year.

Equity participations

Through the 1990s the internationalisation of KPN was also pursued in another way – through direct equity participation in existing or newly formed telecom operators in other countries (see Exhibit 4 for more details).

The political changes in Central and Eastern Europe of the late 1980s were a trigger to explore the market possibilities in that part of Europe. Important investments were made in the Czech Republic, Slovakia, Ukraine and Hungary.

Besides Central and Eastern Europe the focus was also on other areas. Some ventures were in small markets, such as Antillean Telematics that was established in 1991 to provide telematic services in the Caribbean area. Other targets were large and fast-developing markets such as Indonesia.

In most cases the investments were made in developing countries outside of Europe or in Eastern Europe. One exception to this rule is Ireland. In 1996 KPN formed a consortium Comsource with its Swedish Unisource partner Telia to acquire a 20 per cent stake in Telecom Eireann. The growth opportunities in Ireland were good and considerable possibilities for synergy existed.

On many of these participations a former member of the management board commented:

> They have in common that as a minority partner we do not have much influence. Moreover the initial capital outlays are very high with value creation expected on the longer term. It is very difficult to achieve synergies and cost savings if you do not have management control.

All the above-mentioned equity participations were sold when the financial situation became untenable. In the foreword to the annual report the CEO had already mentioned that although the ambition to strive for a leading position in Europe had not changed, the focus had been intensified:

> . . . we will mainly realize growth in this period in Germany, the Netherlands and Belgium.

The emergence of UMTS ('3-G' mobile telecommunication)

In the second half of the 1990s many people expected an enormous increase in revenues from transactions that could be made via the internet. Amazon.com was an example of the almost limitless growth that could be achieved. Based on new technological developments it would become possible to make these internet transactions via mobile telephones as well. Moreover with the new technology, called UMTS or 3-G, completely new services could be offered to the public, ranging from on-line mobile contact with your stockbroker to sending pictures of a grandchild to its grandmother at the other side of the world. Telecom operators would profit from all these transactions by the expected increase in the volume of traffic and/or by a percentage of the amount of money involved in each transaction.

In many countries, not all, governments decided that selling licences for the new kind of mobile telecommunications would be a nice source of revenue. Therefore they organised auctions in which telecom operators could make bids for such licences. In many cases consultants were hired to find ways to extract the most money from these telecom companies. In the Netherlands academic game theory specialists were involved in the process. The sums involved were enormous. KPN, a relatively small player in Germany, paid in 2001 €8.7bn for the UMTS licence for its subsidiary E-Plus. Moreover it had already paid €10.6bn for its stake in that company. These investments in Germany alone were equal to 150 per cent of KPN's turnover in 2000. In absolute and relative terms this is an enormous amount of money. Most of it had to be borrowed and added to the company's debt. Other telecom operators made similarly large investments. But more investment was also needed to roll out the 3-G networks. KPN expected that in the years 2003 through 2005 an additional amount of €1.4bn would be needed in its three core markets. Hutchison's subsidiary 3-G[3] mentioned it needed to invest €18.2bn to roll out its network in 10 countries. The delay it encountered in 2003 because of the limited availability of mobile 3-G phones added another €2bn to the amount still

---

[3] Hutchison Whampoa is a Hong Kong-based conglomerate that has also invested in mobile telecommunications in various countries.

to be financed, which increased to €7bn. It was expected that UMTS/3-G mobile telephony would be introduced in the second half of 2004 in European countries.

In hindsight it is clear that expectations of the bidding process were unrealistic. The auction of the licences in the Netherlands did not generate the amounts politicians had hoped for. Since the earlier auctions in UK had generated much higher sums per potential user, the junior minister responsible for organising the auctions nearly had to step down under pressure from parliament because of the disappointing result. In the meantime KPN had written off its investment in licences. It was not just the telecom operators that overestimated the short-term potential of 3-G.

The introduction of third generation mobile telephony in many countries of continental Europe was behind schedule because of the enormous write-offs that were necessary. These caused a financial crisis for many companies in the industry. Also the economic recession played a role since the public might be less willing to spend large amounts of money on such services.

The following paragraphs describe the deals that KPN made to position itself in its foreign core markets Belgium and Germany. KPN obtained a licence for mobile telephony in Belgium well before it decided to bid for a 3-G licence also. In Germany the mobile operator E-Plus was bought some months before the bidding for the 3-G licence.

Relationship with NTT-Docomo and Hutchison

On 9 May 2000 KPN Mobile announced an agreement with NTT-DoCoMo, the immensely successful Japanese mobile operator. NTT-DoCoMo would not only provide financial resources, but also advanced technology for future generations of mobile telecommunications. It was decided that NTT-DoCoMo would acquire 15 per cent of the shares in KPNMobile in exchange for several billion euros. NTT-DoCoMo would also have influence on certain decisions. As a consequence of this cooperation KPN Mobile was able to introduce in 2002 i-mode, an advanced technology for mobile communications, which makes possible the introduction of new services. The introduction was achieved in the three main markets. In 2003 KPN started marketing domestically a new generation

of i-mode handsets with which photos can be sent and received, and Java games played. I-mode technology is a further step in the convergence of mobile telephony and internet. For the foreseeable future a further step is the introduction of UMTS, which NTT-DoCoMo had already introduced in Japan.

For NTT-DoCoMo the agreement is a step forward in its strategy of building a global presence and taking full advantage of its technological advantage. In the annual report for 2001 Ad Scheepbouwer was very enthusiastic about the cooperation with the Japanese company.

In 2000 NTT-DoCoMo also bid for German UMTS licences together with KPN-Mobile. Initially Hutchinson Whampoa from Hong Kong was also involved, but it withdrew from the bidding. KPN's share in the licences is estimated at €6.5bn. KPN expected another €3.5bn would have to be invested before the network would be operational.[4]

Mobile in Belgium: the origin of BASE

In July 1998 the third mobile licence in Belgium was granted to a joint venture of KPN and France Telecom, in which each shareholder had a 50 per cent stake. The mobile operator started services in the second half of 1999. In that year turnover was €6m. In 2000 turnover increased to €58m. In February 2001 the parents agreed that KPN would buy the shares of France Telecom for €399.5m as well as pay back a shareholder loan that France Telecom had given KPN Orange. Turnover in 2001 totalled €232m and in 2002 €289m. By the end of 2002 BASE (as it was renamed) had 1.1 million subscribers, which meant a market share of 14.5 per cent.

In March 2001 KPN Mobile acquired a Belgian UMTS licence for the amount of €150m.

Mobile in Germany: E-Plus

On 9 December 1999 KPN announced it had come to an agreement with BellSouth to buy 74.49 per cent of its shares in the mother company of E-Plus, the third German mobile operator (market share

---

4 Research agency Forrester had a much higher estimate: between €4–6bn for the infrastructure and another €2–3bn for marketing efforts.

16 per cent; 3.8m subscribers). This move gave KPN an entry into the large German market of some 80m inhabitants; €9.1bn was paid in cash. BellSouth was given the right to convert (between 9 June 2001 and 8 December 2003) their remaining 22.51 per cent in E-Plus into shares of KPN or KPN Mobile; BellSouth could also continue to hold the shares. To this end KPN gave BellSouth a warrant. Upon conversion, BellSouth would be entitled to approximately 499.6m Class A shares in KPN Mobile, or 100m shares in KPN. In order to expand its room for manoeuvre, KPN reached an agreement with BellSouth in January 2002 for the exchange of the remaining 22.51 per cent in E-Plus. BellSouth would receive 234.7m ordinary shares in KPN for its interest in E-Plus. Furthermore, Bell South gave back the warrant. BellSouth sold the KPN shares to various institutional investors some weeks later. From March 2002, KPN had full control of E-Plus.

Merger attempts

The investments in UMTS-services had dramatically increased the amount of KPN's debt. (See Exhibit 1.) It was originally planned to have KPN Mobile quoted on the Amsterdam stock exchange in mid 2000. In view of the general investment climate at that time it was decided it was better to delay the introduction until stock prices increased again. Therefore the financial situation did not improve.

In the first months of 2000 negotiations had started about forms of close cooperation or even merger with Telefonica from Spain, the former partner in Unisource. If it was successful this would take some of the pressure off KPN. A KPN press release of 8 May 2000 stated that although a majority of the Telefonica Board of Management was in favour of the cooperation, they could only proceed with the full commitment of the entire board. It was rumoured that differing political views in Spain were behind the split in the Telefonica Board. The tight financial situation continued.

In the summer of 2001 discussions started between KPN and Belgacom on the possibility of a merger. The advantage for KPN was that Belgacom had a strong balance sheet, which could take some of the financial pressure off KPN. In view of the market environment at that time the two companies decided to cease discussions on a possible merger. This decision was announced on 31 August 2001. No doubt also such issues as who would get what position, and the percentage of shares each company would receive, played a role. Since Belgacom was not under financial pressure from its creditors, it had time to play its cards prudently.

| Exhibit 1 | Some data about KPN (in €m if not otherwise indicated) |

	1998	1999	2000	2001	2002	2003
Turnover	8,041	9,132	13,511	12,859	12,784	12,907
Operational result (EBITDA)	2,986	3,355	5,756	3,381	4,671	5,643
Depreciation, amortization and impairments	1,412	2,302	3,039	17,817	10,252	2,535
Operating profit (–loss)	1,575	1,053	2,717	–14,436	–5,581	3,108
Income from participating interests	42	253	249	–81	–1,700	161
Net profit after tax	687	828	1,874	–7,495	–9,542	2,731
Total investment	2,711	3,800	35,513	4,165	2,495	1,612
Total assets	13,629	17,991	53,465	41,122	25,161	24,125
% of total assets	19.9	21.1	66.4	10.1	9.9	6.7
Long term debt	3,474	5,411	20,149	16,896	12,680	9,230
Bank loan	736	329	5,508	5,724	2,360	952
Average collection period (days)	58	48	54	51	41	41
No of employees (average fte)	36,073	38,550	41,305	45,720	40,195	31,267
No of employees (as per December 31)	36,073	38,850	45,151	49,121	38,118	29,668

Source: Euronext website, KPN annual reports.

Exhibit 2	Segmentation of turnover, EBIT, investment of KPN (in €m), and customer bases

	1998	1999	2000	(segmentation changed in 2000)	2000	2001	2002	(segmentation changed in 2003)	2003
Turnover									
Fixed network services	6,308	6,738	5,353	Fixed networks	6,371	6,500	6,632	Fixed	7,399
Mobile	1,274	1,748	5,861	Mobile	5,861	4,673	5,312	Mobile	5,379
IP/data			1,286	Business solutions	2,075	2,068	2,047	Other	1,364
ICM			683	Other activities	1,879	2,148	1,264	Intercompany sales	−1,235
Other			1,551	Inter-division revenues	−2,675	−2,530	−2,471		
International	1,018	1,572							
Inter-division revenues	−656	−926	−1,223						
Total	7,944	9,132	13,511		13,511	12,859	12,784		12,907
Earnings before interest and taxes									
Fixed network services	1,316	383	1,437	Fixed net	1,129	533	1,095	Fixed net	1,713
Mobile communications	114	234	1,603	Mobile	1,603	−14,130	−6,254	Mobile	1,047
IP/data			−16	Business solutions	197	−18	−100	Other	348
ICM			−132	Other activities	−212	−821	−322		
International activities	145	436							
Other			−175						
Total	1,575	1,053	2,717		2,717	−14,436	−5,581		3,108

	1998	1999	2000	2001	2002	2003
Investments in						
Immaterial fixed assets	596	1,019	28,052	809	1,270	6
Material fixed assets	1,949	2,524	3,847	2,949	1,137	1,499
Financial fixed assets	226	257	3,614	407	88	107
Total	2,771	3,800	35,513	4,165	2,495	1,612
Customer bases			**(millions)**			
KPN Mobile						
The Netherlands			4.8	5.2	5.0	5.2
E-Plus Germany			6.7	7.5	7.3	8.2
BASE, Belgium			0.6	1.0	1.1	1.3

Source: KPN Annual Reports.

Financial crisis and the new CEO

In 2000 total assets rose from €17.991 at the beginning to €53.465 at the end. This increase was for the most part due to the UMTS licences acquired in Germany (€6.5bn) and the Netherlands (€0.7bn) and the goodwill paid in the acquisition of E-Plus (€20.3bn). Other investments were in plant and equipment related to these deals (€3bn) and loans to participating interests (€2bn). The investments had been financed by an increase of shareholder equity (€10bn), long-term liabilities (€15bn) and €7.5bn Exchange Right related to BellSouth's right to exchange its 22.51 per cent interest in E-Plus into shares of KPN or KPN Mobile. Roughly, KPN's debt was twice its turnover.

Already in the year 2000 KPN's debt was far higher than acceptable to investors and banks. Attempts to bring back the debt to more normal proportions had not delivered adequate results. The flotation of KPN Mobile, which was expected to bring in €8–10bn, had been cancelled in 2000. Moreover the merger attempts with Telefonica and Belgacom were without result as well. Again the balance sheet could not be strengthened. Moreover it became clear that the enormous investments in UMTS would not deliver the revenues that were initially promised, therefore debt had

Exhibit 3	Some information on competitors

(year 2002 and €bn; BT and Vodafone and mmO2: £1 = approx. €1.5)

Belgacom

Turnover	5.2
Net profit after taxation	0.9
Total assets	6.6
Creditors	2.3
No. fixed lines	4.8m
No. mobile customers	4.3m
No. internet customers	0.83m

British Telecom (2002–2003)

Turnover	26.9
Net profit after taxation	3.9
Total assets less current liabilities	26.6
Creditors > 1 year	19.4
No. UK exchange line connections	29.4m
of which: business	9.1m
of which: residential	20.2m
of which: service providers	0.1m

Note: BT no longer operates a mobile network. This network was spun off in November 2001 and is now mmO2.

Deutsche Telekom

Net revenue	53.7
Net profit after taxation (– = loss)	–24.6
Total assets	125.8
Debt and other liabilities	74.3
No. fixed-network lines	57.5m, of which 51.3 in Germany
No. mobile subscribers	81.7m, of which 24.6 in Germany
No. internet subscribers	12.2m, of which 10 in Germany

France telecom

Net revenue	46.6
Net Income	–20.7
Total assets	106.6
Total debt	106.8
No. fixed-line clients	49.4m, 34.1 in France, 13.8 rest of Europe, 1.6 ROW
No. mobile clients	49.9m, of which 19.2 in France, 26.7 rest of Europe, 3.9 ROW
No. internet clients	10.1m, of which 3.9 France, 6.1 rest of Europe, 0.085 ROW

Vodafone (2002–2003)

Turnover	43.776 Europe 18,883, ROW 8,659, other operations 2,833
Net income (loss)	14,139 Europe –5,718, ROW –4,982, other operations –469
Balance sheet total	189,409 (creditors substracted from assets, merger reserve of 98,927)
Creditors (all)	40,392 (20,581 due within one year, 19,811 due after one year)
Mobile customers worldwide	295m, in all wholly and partially owned operators
Mobile customers Europe	108

mmO2 (2002–2003)

Turnover	7,019
Retained loss for the year	14,613
Total assets	19,257
Creditors (all)	4,353
Mobile customers	19,372 (UK, Germany, Netherlands, Ireland, Isle of Man)

Sources: Annual reports, Company Websites.

to be reduced dramatically – a huge task for the executive board.

In January 2001 Standard & Poor's, the credit rating agency, lowered KPN's rating from single A minus to triple B. In response to this news the Management Board emphasised that it would aim at getting back to a single A status in the medium to long term.

In the summer of 2001 it became clear that the banks that had financed the enormous investments with medium-term loans had lost their patience. No visible improvements in the financial structure had been made by the CEO and his board. KPN's stock prices had dropped by the end of June 2001 from a year high of €55.50 to €6.50. An article in *Het Financieele Dagblad* in September 2001 characterised the debt of KPN as being of junk-status. The company had to renew loans in December 2001 and in June 2002 and it was unlikely that banks would want to do that unless fundamental measures were taken. Some of the credit lines could only be used if debt had been reduced to less than €17bn, whereas at that moment it was still around €23bn. The company had its back against the wall and its CEO had lost his credibility with the banks and investors.

On 11 September 2001 Ton Risseeuw, chairman of the supervisory board, announced that the CEO would step down and would be succeeded by Ad Scheepbouwer, CEO of TPG, the former sister company of KPN, and member of KPN's supervisory board. This change in leadership convinced the banks that a new wind would blow. A consortium of eight banks gave a new loan of €2.5bn with strings attached. The banks had claimed a right to veto certain strategic decisions. Based on earlier agreements other parties also had a say in decision making: Dutch government (golden share), NTT-DoCoMo (15 per cent in KPN Mobile) and BellSouth (E-Plus deal). This made restructuring far from easy.

Financial restructuring

The financial restructuring followed two main directions. One was the disposal of assets, the other was reducing costs and increasing cash flow.

The minority equity participations in many countries were sold in the year 2000 and after. This brought in much-needed cash and eliminated further investment in these companies. Moreover,

---

Exhibit 4   Major entry and exit decisions

Country	Services offered	Year of entry	Year of exit
Czech Republic	GSM and fixed	1990	2003
Ukraine	GSM and fixed	1992	2003
Hungary	GSM	1993	2002
	Fixed	1994	1999
Indonesia	GSM	1996	2001
Ireland	Fixed	1996	2002
	GSM	1996	2002
Belgium	GSM	1998	BASE
	UMTS licence bought	2001	BASE
Germany	GSM	2000	E-Plus
	UMTS licence bought	2000	E-Plus
UK	3-G	2000	2002

Discussions and negotiations not leading to investments with:

Bulgaria	India
China	Rumania
Dutch Antilles	Slovakia
France	

Source: KPN Annual Reports, KPN Press releases.

Exhibit 5	Major disposal of assets

Asset	Amount €m	Comments
2000 KPN Mobile 15% NTT DoCoMo	2,312	Sold to NTT DoCoMo as part of an alliance agreement
SNT	20	KPN share in SNT Public Offering
Infonet	21	KPN share in Infonet's Public Offering
D-Plus, Arcor	147	Revenue of winding-up Unisource Germany and sale of Arcor
2001 Indonesia: participation in Telkomsel 23%	668	Sold to Singapore telecom
Ireland: Eircell, 21%	572	Sold to Vodaphone
Ireland: Eircom, 21%	632	Sold to Valentia, a consortium of investment funds
KPN Datacenter	163	Sold to Atos Origin, an IT company
KPN Lease	161	Sold to Lage Landen, a subsdiary of Rabobank
KPNQwest, 10%	102	Sold to Qwest:deconsolidation effect on debt: €106m
Real estate	100	Various parties
2002 End User Services	29	Transferred to Atos Origin
Teleprofs, temporary labour company, 50%	6	Sold to Vedior a temporary labour company
Hungary: Pannon GSM, 44.66%	603	Sold to telenor SA; deconsolidation effect on debt: €106m
KPN Network Construction, 55%	14	Sold to construction company KWS, rest will be transferred in 2004
Vision Networks: Cable activities Czech Republic and Poland	n.a.	Reconsolidation effect: €630m less debt and €700m more equity
2003 Cesky Telecom: 6.5% direct participation	226	Sold to Credit Suisse First Boston
Cesky Telecom: indirect participation via Telsource NV, a J V with Swiss telecom	347	Sold by means of a quick 'book built' transaction
Telephone directories	500	Sold to 3i and VSV, two venture capital firms
Ukrain: Utel, UMC	73	Sold to Russian telecom operator MTS
Total amount	6,696	
2003 Hungary: Pantel		Investor AIG and GMT Communications have shown interest

Source: KPN press release and annual reports, Euronext website, *Het Financiëele Dagblad*.

management attention would be much more focused on the core problems. In some cases it was not just the cash proceeds that improved the financial structure. In a few cases the companies sold had been consolidated before the sale. In selling the equity stakes KPN no longer had to put their debt on its balance sheet.

A large number of non-core assets were disposed of as well. These ranged from financing activities to the sale of the telephone directories. (See Exhibit 5 for more details.)

Because of such divestments net debt had been lowered from €22bn at the end of 2000 to €15.5bn by the end of 2001. At the end of 2002 net debt had been further reduced to €12.35bn.

In 2001 and 2002 KPN had to write off large amounts because the goodwill paid in acquisitions and the UMT's licences had a much lower market value. In 2001 the amount was €14.1bn and in 2002 €7.3bn.

The reduction of debt was not only achieved by selling non-core activities, but also by increasing productivity and cash flow. In 2000 the restucturing plan Vision was launched. It aimed at improving infrastructure, business processes and the quality of the services. One of the key elements of Vision was the reduction of the workforce by some 8,000 jobs. At the end of 2001 the company agreed a social plan with works councils and trade unions to reduce the workforce by a maximum of 5,200 jobs in the Netherlands, of which approximately 2,300 were voluntary redundancies and some 2,900 forced redundancies.[5] Employees that voluntarily left the company were entitled to the existing retirement scheme. For the forced redundancies the company opened 'mobility shops' to help them find a new job. For 2001 KPN took €676m in restructuring charges. The effect on productivity was that in 2002 almost the same turnover was realised with over 10,000 employees (22 per cent) less by year's end than the year before. The impact on cash flow was substantial.

Other contributions to debt reduction came from such actions as cost reductions other than labour costs, reduction of working capital and a decrease in capital expenditures. Total operating revenues in 2002 were €75m (some 0.6 per cent) lower than in 2001. Yet many costs were significantly lower. Some examples are: costs of work contracted out and other external expenses were €480m (10.5 per cent lower), other operating expenses were €504m (30 per cent lower). Interest payments were €279m (15 per cent lower). Current assets were reduced from €10.9m at the end of 2001 to €5.2m at the end of 2002. Over the same period property, plant and equipment were decreased from €11.1bn to €9.9bn (10 per cent).

The efforts to improve the financial structure of KPN paid off. On two occasions Moody's, one of the well-known credit rating agencies, improved its rating: first in April 2003 from Baa3 to Baa2 and on June 23 to Baa1.

The aim stated in the 2002 annual report was to further reduce net debt to approximately €10.5bn by the end of 2003. This meant a reduction by another €2.35bn. Capital expenditure, however, is expected to rise to an estimated €1.6–1.8bn in 2003 (2002: €1.1bn). In a meeting with investors and analysts on 10 December 2003 Ad Scheepbouwer announced that net debt by the end of 2003 would be reduced to €8.6bn, well ahead of earlier targets. Capital expenditure for 2004 would be at the same level as in 2003, but would increase in 2005 to €1.8–€2.0bn. Free cash flow for 2004 and 2005 was expected to be above €2bn each year.

Strategic options at the end of 2003

In Ad Scheepbouwer's view KPN had two main options by the end of 2003. The first was to remain the type of player it was now, with its activities fixed and mobile telephony, and data communication on a regional base (Netherlands, Belgium and Germany). Such a company could play an important role. There were some risks attached to that option. In the longer run, margins might come under pressure. A risk was also that such a regional player might not be able to attract the right kind of personnel. Furthermore, large international companies might find such a company not able to take total care of the worldwide telecommunications needs of its present and potential customers.

The second option was to become an important international player. Then the margins over time could be higher; the company would be a very attractive employer for the kind of personnel it needed. Also, it could fulfil the telecommunication needs of large companies.

Looking from the outside, one might say that KPN in 2003 had similar choices to make as it had had some ten years earlier. Would it choose the option with the lowest down-side risk in the short term, or would it go for the more adventurous and more risky international option? How could it learn from its experience since 1991?

---

[5] The social plan also stipulated that during the period it would be in effect, the remuneration of the members of the Management Board would be reduced by 15 per cent.

Exhibit 6	Glossary of abbreviations

ADSL	Asymmetric Digital Subscriber Line: an advanced technology to increase the capacity of normal copper telephone lines. Increases the speed of web-surfing. Can reach speeds of up to 1,000 kbps.
BD	Business development: in the mid-1990s this department was responsible for creating new business opportunities for KPN.
DSL	Digital subscriber line. Allows transfer of digital information only. Used for customers wanting to transfer large quantities of data.
GSM	Second generation technology for mobile telecommunication in use in many parts of Europe and Asia. Not used in the USA.
ICM	Internet, Call centres and Media services: a 'division' of KPN.
i-mode	Mobile data service developed and launched by NTT-DoCoMo.
IP	Internet protocol: a standard for sending messages over the internet.
IP/Data	Divison of KPN responsible for data transmission for corporate customers.
ISP	Internet Service Provider: company that provides access to the internet. May also provide additional services, such as content.
ISDN	Integrated Services Digital Network: an early technology to increase the capacity of telephone lines. Can carry data and voice at a speed of 64 kbps.
UMTS	Universal Mobile Telecommunication System. One of the major new third-generation (3-G) mobile communication systems being developed. UMTS is suited to deliver voice, text, music and animated images. Through UMTS data can be sent at a speed up to 334 kbps, comparable to an ADSL connecton. In future, higher speeds may be possible.
VPN	Virtual Private Network: for instance an intranet that is operated by a telecom operator.

Coors – a move into the UK brewing industry

Mike Blee

This case commences with a brief overview of Bass Plc and evaluates its subsequent acquisition. In 2002 Bass was split between two companies: Interbrew of Belgium and Coors, the American Brewer. The case gives a background to the US and UK brewing industry and examines the acquisition undertaken by Coors and Coors Brewers' subsequent strategy in the UK.

• • •

Background

Bass plc

Bass's origins date back to 1777 when William Bass set up a brewery in Burton upon Trent, UK. By the mid 1990s Bass was a widely diversified leisure UK company. Under the chairmanship of Sir Ian Prosser, it incorporated brewery operations, a soft drinks company, hotels, public houses, bingo halls, betting shops and gaming machine manufacturers.

In strategic terms the 1990s were a major turning point for the company. The strategy took an emergent focus as the company changed direction several times. In 1996 there was a proposed merger between Bass Brewers and the British arm of the Carlsberg-Tetley brewery in Burton upon Trent. At this point, Bass should have approached the UK government for confirmation that the merger would not breach its guidelines on competition within the brewing industry. This needed to be accompanied by the launch of a campaign to gain acceptance for the idea. The company failed to undertake this crucial step before the merger discussions had taken place and as a result the monopolies and mergers commission (now the Competition Commission) blocked the deal. It cost Bass an estimated £60m (≈ €90m) in losses and restructuring costs.

The 1997 accounts emphasised the growing importance of leisure to the company, their book-makers Coral were showing growth with excellent margins and this resulted in Bass launching a take over bid for one of Coral's competitors, William Hill. The company was unsuccessful in this acquisition, being outbid on this occasion by a Japanese investment company Nomura. During this same period Bass disposed of the majority of their independently managed public houses and their bingo division. The major branded chains of the public house estate were retained. Press comment at the time was that Bass were very good at disposal but very poor at acquisition and growth.

1998 was to see a major change of strategy involving acquisition and disposal. In this respect Bass were reacting to City pressure to counter their lacklustre performance in the UK share market. During 1998 Bass acquired Inter Continental Hotels to add to their Holiday Inn chain and at the same time announced the disposal of the majority of its leisure interests. It became a three-division company with a focus on brewing, hotels and public house chains.

Strategic direction changed again in the year 2000 and this was opposed to the 1996 strategy of trying to grow the brewing business. It resulted in the lower margin brewing operation being offered for sale. Brewing was the cash cow of the Bass company and seen as unfashionable by what was rapidly becoming a much more focused company.

Following an intense bidding war Interbrew of Belgium won control of the Bass-brewing sector

Mike Blee of the Bournemouth University, Institute of Business and Law prepared this case Spring 2004. The author is indebted to Paul Hegarty, External Communications Manager, Coors Brewers Ltd for his assistance in providing the supporting information.

Photo: Coors Brewers Limited

The US beer market

In 2003 there were a number of key factors in the US that differentiated the market from that in the UK. The three major brewers in this market hold 80 per cent of the total volume.

- US beer sales were still growing – although slowly;
- beer was generally sold through wholesalers not direct from the breweries;
- 75 per cent of the beer was sold in the off-trade;
- legal age of drinking is 21 – penalties for being caught are severe;
- women drink 25 per cent of beer volume;
- alcohol laws differ from state to state;
- one company (Anheuser-Busch) brews 50 per cent of all US beer.

with an unconditional bid. The Bass Company retained their hotel and pub chain business. Initially these traded under a new company name Six Continents but this rebranding was very short lived as demerger followed splitting Six Continents into two groups, Inter Continental Hotels with the retail pub estate trading as Mitchell and Butlers.

However in 2001/02 the UK Competition Commission again intervened and decided to examine the acquisition of Bass brewing by Interbrew. As a result they subsequently ordered Interbrew to dispose of this acquisition. Following an appeal Interbrew were allowed to retain the Bass brand and the Tennents Scottish brands (see brewing industry case, Chapter 2). The Carling Brewing Company in Burton upon Trent was again offered for sale.

Unlike 2000 there were few bidders for this brewery and Coors, the third largest brewer in the US market, much to the surprise of UK industry observers, launched a successful bid.

The Anheuser-Busch 2003 annual report showed that they were the market leaders in the US with sales revenues up 4 per cent in a mature market. In volume terms the company recorded 0.8 per cent growth in the US market with an overall sales figure of 111m barrels of beer, 102m of which were sold in their domestic market, giving them a US market share of 50 per cent. In addition the company sold overseas a further 19m barrels brewed through its arrangements with its equity share partners.

The second placed brewer in the US in volume terms was SABMillers, purchased in 2002 by South African Breweries. In their first nine months of operation they achieved a sales volume of 28 million barrels which gave them a US market share approaching 20 per cent. In 2003 the introduction

Exhibit 1	US beer sales (in US barrels)

	2001	2002	% Change
Total US tax paid malt beverages	180,647,000	181,842,000	0.7%
Sale of imports in US	21,755,000	23,070,000	6.0%
Total US beer sales	202,402,000	204,912,000	1.2%
US beer exports	2,163,314	2,059,279	(4.8%)

Source: www.beertown.org.

of a turnaround management process began: this consisted of rebuilding the brands, modification of sales and distribution networks, organisational restructuring and cost cutting. In 2003 volume of sales by SABMillers fell in the US market by 4 per cent.

Coors brewery in 2004 was the third position US brewer in volume terms. It was a family-owned brewery founded in 1873 with the voting shares tightly controlled by the owners. The Coors brewery had grown in the period 1983–93 from a previously held fifth position in volume terms. This was due to its policy of widening distribution of its product to 50 North American states, though its main sales occur in the southern states. Volumes at Coors in the three years from 2000–2002 had been fairly static at 22.7m barrels giving them an 11 per cent market share. In order to grow it appeared that Coors would have little option other than to look overseas for expansion. However previous expansion in Europe had been less than successful with their brewing operation ceasing in Spain in 2000 with the accounts that year showing $20m exceptional costs which were directly related to this disposal.

Sales volume continued to decline in Coors' home market during 2003 by 1.4 per cent. Overall the 2003 company results showed an increase in revenue and sales volume, however this was due to the success of their operations within Canada and the UK. Competition in the North American market was extremely high with the dominant market leaders giving Coors a fairly low market share. Their 2002 annual report states 'that they had not grown in their American market in the way that they had wanted to' and the 2003 report adds 'overall 2003 was a tough year for Coors Brewing Company'.

The Beer Institute, which represents the US beer industry, reported that the growth in the North American market would pause in the 2000–2010 decade. In 2003 the major brands dominated with the only real high-growth products being the introduction of low carbohydrate beers; the alcoholic flavoured beverage market entered a steep decline.

Coors did not launch their low carbohydrate product until 2004 leaving Anheuser-Busch in the brand leader position. Anheuser-Busch had first mover advantage in this segment with the leading brand of Michelob Ultra. This brand with its low calories and low carbohydrates appeals to people who are engaged in an active lifestyle and has taken market share of 2 per cent of the total US beer market in its first year of launch.

The UK brewing market

The UK alcoholic drinks market in 2002 was worth £34bn (≈ €50bn) (see Exhibit 2), bigger than the

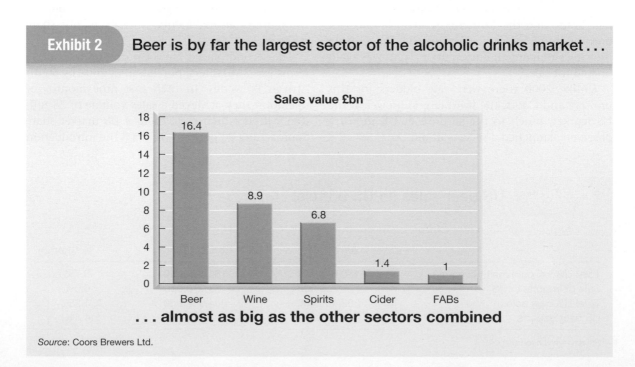

Exhibit 2   **Beer is by far the largest sector of the alcoholic drinks market ...**

Sales value £bn

Beer	Wine	Spirits	Cider	FABs
16.4	8.9	6.8	1.4	1

... almost as big as the other sectors combined

Source: Coors Brewers Ltd.

Exhibit 3   The UK beer market 1980–2002 (with projections to 2007)

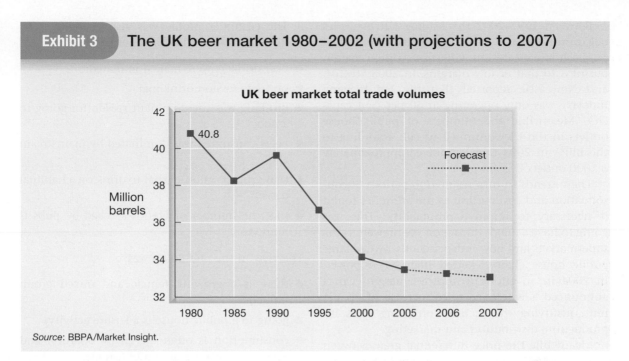

UK beer market total trade volumes

Source: BBPA/Market Insight.

Exhibit 4   The shift from the on-trade to the off-trade

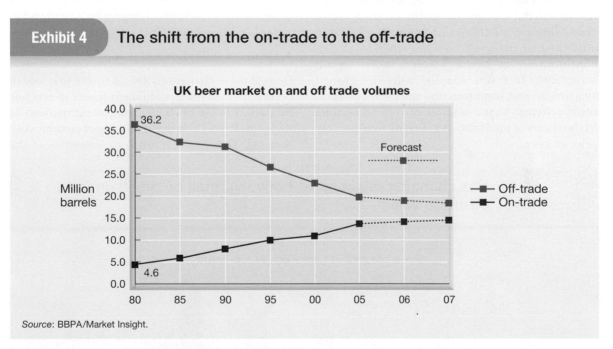

UK beer market on and off trade volumes

Source: BBPA/Market Insight.

market for clothing, motor vehicles, tobacco and six times that of the confectionery market. It is very valuable to the UK government in economic terms giving high revenues through the collection of taxes and excise duty.

The Office for National Statistics, however, shows that expenditure on alcohol is reducing as a proportion of consumer expenditure. In 1976 it accounted for 7.8 per cent of the total of all consumer expenditure, by 2000 this figure had reduced to 5.4 per cent. Volumes of beer sold had also significantly reduced with 34m barrels being traded in 2000 against 40.8m barrels in 1980 (see Exhibit 3).

In the period 1980–2000 there had been a major shift from the on-trade (trade in public houses) to the off-trade (the take-home market – trade in shops and supermarkets). (See Exhibit 4).

Between 1997–2002 the leading UK breweries began to dismantle their previously controlled public house estates, moving from a high margin business to that of low margins. In 2003 Scottish and Newcastle reported that the UK brewing industry was only operating at 50 per cent capacity. Meanwhile the numbers of public house outlets in the UK continued to fall; according to the BBPA in 2003 they numbered approximately 60,000 outlets.

These trends in turn resulted in periods of consolidation and cost cutting as the breweries found it necessary to improve profitability. This was going to have a major impact on the brewers as the supermarkets and now independently owned large public house chains exerted high buyer power. In 2004 in an effort to improve margins Coors announced a wholesale price increase of 5p per pint, justifying the increase on rising costs for production, distribution and marketing.

Meanwhile the price differential grew between the on and off trade which was one of the many factors driving this growth in the on trade sector. (See Exhibit 5.) Other contributing factors were attributed to changing lifestyles whereby alcohol consumption at home became more socially acceptable. This was coupled with the growth, availability and sophistication of home entertainment systems. As the amount of volume declined in the on trade public houses steadily increased the price of beer.

The customer profile was also changing. The traditional view of the consumer had been:

● beer drinkers were male dominated;
● on trade session drinking;
● drinking was the dominant reason for going to a pub;
● beers consumed was dominated by mainstream ales;
● that drinkers choose what to drink on a habitual basis;
● that the number of brands stocked by pubs is limited.

The view in the mid-2000s was:

● there is a growing female and mixed group influence;
● going to a public house is a leisure activity;
● consumption is often driven by occasion and events in both the on- and off-trade;
● premium beers are becoming an important sector;
● there is a wide choice of outlets;
● there is a wide choice of brands.

Despite these changes Exhibit 6 shows that sale of beers remained the single largest source of revenue for pubs, the UK on-trade still generating most of its profitability from the sales of beer (source: A.C. Nielsen). Due to the control by breweries of the

Exhibit 5   The changing relationship between retail prices in on- and off-trade sales

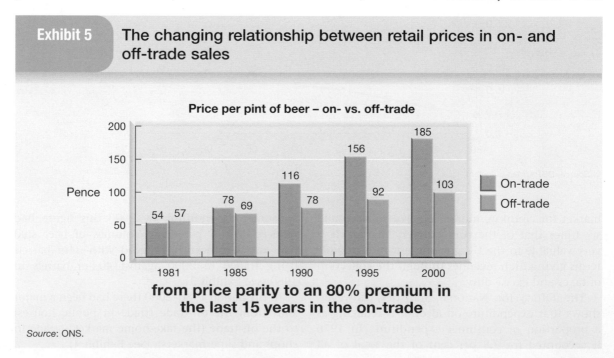

Price per pint of beer – on- vs. off-trade

from price parity to an 80% premium in the last 15 years in the on-trade

Source: ONS.

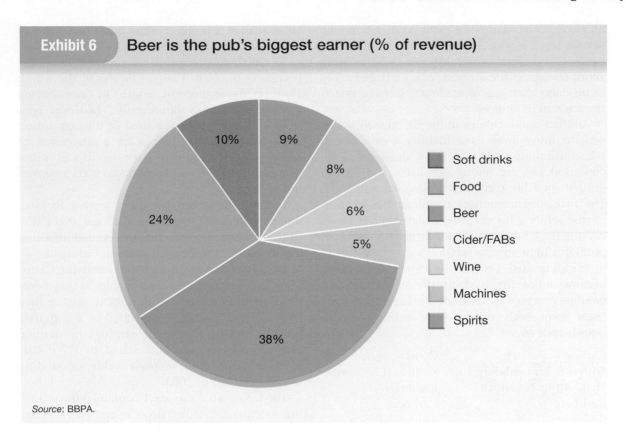

Exhibit 6   **Beer is the pub's biggest earner (% of revenue)**

- Soft drinks
- Food
- Beer
- Cider/FABs
- Wine
- Machines
- Spirits

10% 9% 8% 6% 5% 24% 38%

Source: BBPA.

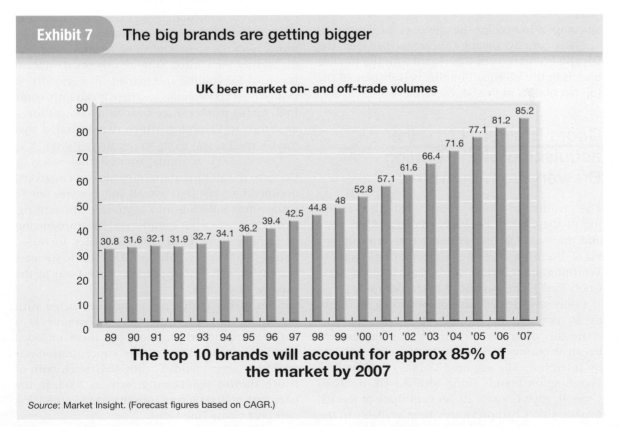

Exhibit 7   **The big brands are getting bigger**

UK beer market on- and off-trade volumes

Year	Value
89	30.8
90	31.6
91	32.1
92	31.9
93	32.7
94	34.1
95	36.2
96	39.4
97	42.5
98	44.8
99	48
'00	52.8
'01	57.1
'02	61.6
'03	66.4
'04	71.6
'05	77.1
'06	81.2
'07	85.2

The top 10 brands will account for approx 85% of the market by 2007

Source: Market Insight. (Forecast figures based on CAGR.)

on-trade outlets until the early 2000s few public houses stock a wide range of competing brands; however consumer demand should begin to bring about change. If the off-trade offers a large variety of products then the on-trade will have to match the amount of choice.

Another major change in the UK brewing sector was the move away from traditional cask ales to the consumption of light beers and lager. Cask condition ales are highly perishable and have a limited shelf life compared to keg ales and lager. The mainstream younger consumer has demonstrated a liking for the much higher profit lagers causing the UK brewer to concentrate on this more profitable high volume sector.

Branding had become important as brewers become more involved in the marketing and volume process (see Exhibit 7). Lager and light beers form high competition within the UK; brands such as:

Carling & Grolsch	Coors
Fosters & Kronenbourg 1066	Scottish & Newcastle
Stella Artois & Labbatts	Interbrew
Carlsberg	Carlsberg
Budweiser	Anheuser-Busch
Harp	Diageo
Heineken	Heineken

all compete to become the choice of the consumer.

There are significant differences between the UK and US markets in this regard with the top five brands in the US equalling the market share of the top ten brands in the UK.

Coors Brewers Ltd – the acquisition of the Carling Brewery from Interbrew

The creation of Coors Brewers Ltd (the renaming of the Carling Brewery) commenced in 2002 and the main UK brands under this ownership or via a licensing agreement are Carling, Grolsch, Worthington, Caffreys and Reef. Late in 2003 Coors Fine Light was added to the portfolio.

Coors saw their acquisition of Carling at £1.2bn as an opportunity as they were able to purchase this company for what they considered to be an economic price due to the enforced sale by Interbrew. The acquired Carling, Caffreys and Worthington brands along with the UK rights to Grolsch, gave Coors a 20 per cent share of the UK market. Coors had previously been available in the

UK market as a licensed brand but it had failed to capture a brand presence.

In 2002 this acquisition resulted in Coors becoming the eighth largest brewer in the world. However the acquisition resulted in Coors having to increase its debts significantly. The Coors' consolidated accounts at the time of the acquisition show an additional borrowing arrangement of $1.55bn increasing the debt to capital ratio. (Consolidated five-year accounts to 2003 are given in the Appendix.).

Initially the policy by Coors tended to leave much of the decision making at a local level under its UK management structure rather than imposing a heavy control from head office in Colorado.

In 2003 trade in the UK increased for Coors. This allowed them to return capital payments more speedily on the acquisition debt that they had incurred. They also benefited at a corporate level by having significant earnings in sterling. The consolidated accounts stated in US dollars benefited from the increase value of sterling towards the end of 2003.

The Coors' accounts 2001 contained the following statement: 'Getting stronger and more global. In 2002, the Carling Brewery acquisition proved to be a very good fit. It added to our talent and contributed immediately to Coors' revenues and profit, creating a stronger, more solid business by broadening the sources of those revenues and profit. Further the United Kingdom shows significant potential for volume and market share growth'. If this growth and volume are there it can only come from taking market share away from competitors – as shown in Exhibit 3, which demonstrated that the UK market was likely to remain fairly static.

Coors' 2003 accounts showed that sales by Coors to the all-important off-trade (supermarkets) declined by 5 per cent overall and this was due to competitors entering into aggressive discounting. However due to a hot summer and the introduction of Carling Extra Cold, on-trade sales increased during 2003. Coors' policy in 2003 was to increase margin though this appears to have been at the expense of volume.

Sales of the traditional brands associated with British brewing were dropping in volume as a national trend and at Coors UK these included Worthington & Caffreys. Coors' concentration was on its key lager brands Carling & Grolsch both of which showed significant growth in 2003. In the later part of 2003 Coors introduced into the UK a new beer Coors Fine Light.

In 2003 Carling was the UK's top selling beer with sales of 5m barrels annually. However, unfortunately for Coors opportunity for market expansion of the Carling brand was limited as they only held the rights to the Carling name within the UK. Different companies own this brand name across the world.

Although the brand sales grew rapidly in 2003 the distribution coverage was limited. The parts of the Bass Company purchased from Interbrew had traditionally had weak representation in London, the South East of England and Scotland. It is estimated that the Carling brand was only stocked by approximately 30 per cent of all UK outlets.

A major concern for Coors was to ensure that their various brands did not cannibalise each other and therefore brand positioning becomes very important. The Coors key brand portfolio is positioned as follows:

- Carling – an everyday mainstream lager brand
- Grolsch – a premium lager brand
- Coors Fine Light – a speciality light beer
- Caffreys – a differentiated beer – an Irish ale
- Worthington – traditional British bitter
- Reef – flavoured alcoholic beverages

When Bass Plc sold their brewing business, supply agreements accompanied the deal. This gave the Carling Brewery the rights to brew Bass until the mid 2000s with an agreed distribution deal for Carling products through Mitchell and Butlers to a similar date. In 2003 the first of the licensed brewing agreements expired causing a volume drop at the Burton brewery. The Bass draught brand brewed by Coors in Burton however was now owned by Interbrew and they had spare brewing capacity elsewhere. Although it is technically possible to brew Bass to the same taste at another plant, it must be questioned if it would prove acceptable to Bass devotees to move production. This key decision by Interbrew might impact upon Coors' future brewing capacity at the Burton site.

Coors' UK strategy

In the mid-2000s the key elements of Coors' strategy were as follows.

1 Cutting costs and rationalising production

The initial strategy from Coors had been to consolidate brewing activities and costs with the large Cape Hill brewery in Birmingham being closed and the land being made available for redevelopment opportunities.

2 Changing the perception of beer

Exhibit 8 compares the differences in consumers' perceptions of the beer and wine industries in the UK. Coors used this comparison as a basis of staff and industry communication and concluded that the wine industry was much better at promoting its attributes. Given the importance of beer sales to the company the in-house philosophy at 2004 was that their staff must be trained to have a respect for the product and treat it with a deserved reverence.

3 Marketing and brand introduction

The marketing and promotion mainstream spend was on the Carling brand with a Carling Cup being

Exhibit 8	Consumers' perceptions of the beer and wine industries

The Beer Industry	The Wine Industry
Beer is seen as a chemical product made in big factories	A sophisticated crafted rural product
A session drink	A drink of moderation
An unhealthy drink	A healthy drink
A poor partner for food	An excellent partner to food
A male drink	Equally sold to men and women

Source: Coors.

Exhibit 9   The overlap in strategies

Brewers
- More people drinking our brands
- More people drinking in on trade
- Surprising and delighting consumers with quality

?

Retailer
- Consumers spending more – Transaction building
- More traffic into pubs
- Improving the image and quality of business

Source: CBL.

awarded in the football league and a move into live music. As at 2004 Carling was the sponsor of the Leeds and Reading music festivals and the 'Coming Back Home' events which concentrated upon taking the biggest popular music artists back to their roots by their appearing at venues near their home towns. They had a relationship with leading music promotion company, the Mean Fiddler Organisation. In the latter part of 2003 the company introduced Coors Fine Light, a new beer, in the hope of attracting the devoted Budweiser consumer.

4 The off-trade

At the close of 2003 Coors chose to concentrate on profit margins rather than volume. This was a difficult policy for Coors to pursue unless the other brewers decided to follow them with a similar strategy. In the busy period to Christmas that year the accounts show that Grolsch market share had fallen against competitors. Merchandising would become critical to reinforce the consumers' brand awareness.

5 The on-trade

The key thrust of Coors' UK strategy was towards the on-trade. Although this still accounted for the majority of industry sales this was perhaps sur-

prising given the overall trends within the industry (as previously shown in Exhibit 4). Coors stated in 2004 that there was an overlap in strategies between the brewers and the on-trade. Brewers needed pubs and pubs needed brewers (see Exhibit 9). The UK business realised that its US parent was renowned for its service culture and this approach needed to be reinforced in the UK through partnership between Coors and on-trade outlets. Strategies were therefore focused upon building brand loyalty, improving the perception of beer and the realisation that the public house had neighbours and was part of the community.

6 Social responsibility

Sensible drinking is high on the agenda with anti-alcohol attitudes and litigation. Coors are promoting self-regulation working in partnership to encourage moderate drinking and reduction in alcohol abuse. The industry needs to change so that it promotes responsible beer drinking and the major brewers are recognising that the industry needs to undergo a major change if it is to stand any chance of growth. Government regulations in Sweden and self-regulation in Germany are very strong and as the UK moves towards liberalisation of the licensing laws this will become an important governance issue for the industry.

Challenges for the future

The American parent had already stated that the UK offered opportunities for volume and market share growth. However, in a static market this may be difficult to achieve. There was a potential for a number of issues to arise regarding the parenting style between the US and its UK subsidiary. At the time of writing management power was devolved and the cultures of the two parts of the company remained largely independent of each other.

APPENDIX

Consolidated accounts

Selected financial data

Following are selected financial data for each of the five years in the period ended 28 December 2003.

(In thousands, except per share data)	2003	2002[1]	2001	2000[2]	1999
Consolidated Statement of Operations					
Gross sales	$5,387,220[3]	$ 4,956,947	$2,842,752	$2,841,738	$2,642,712
Beer excise taxes	(1,387,107)	(1,180,625)	(413,290)	(427,323)	(406,228)
Net sales	4,000,113	3,776,322	2,429,462	2,414,415	2,236,484
Cost of goods sold	(2,586,783)	(2,414,530)	(1,537,623)	(1,525,829)	(1,397,251)
Gross profit	1,413,330	1,361,792	891,839	888,586	839,233
Marketing, general and administrative	(1,105,959)	(1,057,240)	(717,060)	(722,745)	(692,993)
Special charges, net	–	(6,267)	(23,174)	(15,215)	(5,705)
Operating income	307,371	298,285	151,605	150,626	140,535
Interest (expense) income, net	(61,950)	(49,732)	14,403	14,911	6,929
Other income, net	8,397	8,047	32,005	3,988	3,203
Income before income taxes	253,818	256,600	198,013	169,525	150,667
Income tax expense	(79,161)	(94,947)	(75,049)	(59,908)	(58,83)
Net income	174,657	$ 161,653	$ 122,964	$ 109,617	$ 92,284
Net income per common share – basic	$ 4.81	$ 4.47	$ 3.33	$2.98	$ 2.51
Net income per common share – diluted	$ 4.77	$ 4.42	$ 3.31	$2.93	$ 2.46
Consolidated Balance Sheet Data					
Cash and cash equivalents and short-term and long-term marketable securities	$ 19,440	$ 59,167	$ 309,705	$ 386,195	$ 279,883
Working capital	$ (54,874)	$ (93,995)	$ 88,984	$ 118,415	$ 220,117
Total assets	$4,486,226	$ 4,297,411	$1,739,692	$1,629,304	$1,546,376
Current portion of long-term debt and other short-term borrowings	$ 91,165	$ 144,049	$ 88,038	$–	$–
Long-term debt	$1,159,838	$ 1,383,392	$ 20,000	$ 105,000	$ 105,000
Shareholders' equity	$1,267,376	$ 981,851	$ 951,312	$ 932,389	$ 841,539
Consolidated Cash Flow Data					
Cash provided by operations	$ 544,138	$ 258,545	$ 193,396	$ 280,731	$ 211,324
Cash (used in) investing activities	$ (229,924)	$(1,584,338)	$ (196,749)	$ (297,541)	$ (121,043)
Cash (used in) provided by financing activities	$ (357,393)	$ 1,291,668	$ (38,844)	$ (26,870)	$ (87,687)
Other Information					
Barrels of beer and other beverages sold	32,735	31,841	22,713	22,994	21,954
Dividends per share of common stock	$ 0.820	$ 0.820	$ 0.800	$ 0.720	$ 0.645
Depreciation, depletion and amortization	$ 236,821	$ 227,132	$ 121,091	$ 129,283	$ 123,770
Capital expenditures and additions to intangible assets	$ 240,458	$ 246,842	$ 244,548	$ 154,324	$ 134,377

[1] Results prior to 2 February 2002 exclude Coors Brewers Limited.
[2] 53-week year versus 52-week year.
[3] $US1 = approx. €0.83.

Barclaycard: still the king of pla$tic?

Bernardo Bátiz-Lazo and Nurdilek Hacialioglu with contributions
by Jarunee Wonglimpiyarat and Douglas Wood

The case study looks at milestones in the UK credit card market. It then focuses on how a long-standing market leader maintains a position of advantage and develops its business in a fast-moving industry undergoing significant change. There are many different strategic options open to Barclaycard, but which will be most suitable? Will all the options be acceptable, not only in terms of the likely risk and returns but also to the major stakeholders? Will the options be feasible? The case invites readers to evaluate and compare a range of strategic options and to choose the best way forward for Barclaycard.

• • •

One of the biggest blunders in recent corporate history took place in 2003 when Matt Barrett, CEO of the Barclays Group, publicly stated:

> I don't borrow on credit cards because it is too expensive . . . [I do] not recommend to anyone they chronically borrow on their credit card.[1]

He was the first bank executive who talked about credit cards openly – or bluntly. Although his comments led to a public relations fiasco, they also reflected growing concern around who should be in charge of advising consumers to borrow responsibly. Banks and regulators were concerned that credit card borrowing had doubled between 1999 and 2003 to £168bn (≈ €250). At the same time, interest rates had fallen by two-thirds since 1992 while rates charged for unpaid credit card balances had only declined by a third in the same period and some store cards charged up to 32.5 per cent. Managing over 10m UK customers, 85,000 retailers, 5,000 staff and offering one of the highest-priced card products it was not surprising that Barclaycard was under close scrutiny as the inquiry into the credit card industry evolved.

Photo Barclaycard

The origins of credit cards and Barclaycard

Credit cards emerged in the first half of the 20th century. Initially credit cards were used for identification purposes against non-cash purchases.

---

[1] *The Guardian*, 17 October 2003.

This case was prepared by Bernardo Bátiz-Lazo (London South Bank University) and Nurdilek Hacialioglu (Open University) with contributions by Jarunee Wonglimpiyarat (The National Science and Development Agency of Thailand) and Douglas Wood (Manchester Business School). It is intended for class discussion rather than as an illustration of either good or bad management practice. Comments from Jill McGavock, Gregory Reece-Smith and MBA graduates of the Open University are gratefully acknowledged. The contribution by Professor Douglas Wood (1942–2003) was published posthumously.

The launch of Travel and Entertainment (T&E) cards by Diners Club in 1950 was a turning point because bills from places such as hotels, restaurants and airlines were reimbursed by the issuer and then billed to be paid in full by the customer. T&E cards, thus, merely functioned as a charge card.[2] Diners' T&E cards led to the establishment of similar cards by American Express and Carte Blanche.

It was around this time when the Franklin National Bank (based in New York) developed what is recognised as the first real credit card. This innovation considered offering rollover credit up to an authorised credit limit. Managers at Franklin National Bank also recognised the competitive potential of issuing credit cards to other banks' customers. Due to regulatory constraints, however, branch banking in the US was highly localised. At the same time, there was an increasingly mobile population across the country as a whole. A franchising system developed when trying to find ways to facilitate customer purchases anywhere in the US and, at the same time, increase credit card usage. Under this system banks acquired the right to issue branded cards in a particular city that customers could use with collaborating merchants locally and elsewhere in the US.

In 1958 the Bank of America, with the advantage of its huge West Coast network, launched the blue, white and gold *BankAmericard*. By 1965 and alongside its own branch network, Bank of America had established a successful franchising system owing to high promotional activities and considerable effort in establishing a large merchant network. In this way BankAmericard customers were provided with a national (and eventually international) network of service points which was later to become Visa International. Unlike the T&E card, which was basically a charge card, credit cards expanded rapidly.

In subsequent years marketing activities for credit cards exploded. At the same time the merchant network was widened and the right to issue Visa cards extended to an increasing number of banks as well as non-banking institutions. Alongside these developments, Visa and MasterCard evolved as independent payment organisations owned by issuing banks.

Duality was introduced in 1988, whereby banks could issue both Visa and MasterCard credit cards. However, both Visa and MasterCard prevented their members from issuing American Express or Discover cards, a practice that was challenged at the end of the 1990s in the US by both the Federal government and a powerful group of retailers (who wanted to promote their own cards).

In any event, duality further enhanced the potential for scale economies since banks could process all the Visa and MasterCard transactions of their merchants. As illustrated in Exhibit 1, payment associations have no direct contractual contact with customers or merchants. Instead, they provide all the mechanisms that enable card transactions. Moreover, payment associations are not directly exposed to card fraud as it is the issuing bank that bears the incidence of the misused cost of fraud. The growth of payment associations thus relied on advances in the technology to settle payments and on the growth of their members' customer and merchant base.

Barclays was the first UK bank to recognise the potential of credit cards. After evaluating the operations of BankAmericard in the US, Barclays Bank negotiated a franchise from Bank of America at the end of 1965. A small team was set up to plan a UK launch under the *Barclaycard* brand. After six months 30,000 retailers were signed up. Early promises to retailers to publish the name and address of every shop accepting Barclaycard led to what is still believed to be one of the largest ever press advertisements. It appeared in the *Daily Mail* on 29 June 1966 extending over eight pages and carrying all the 30,000 names and addresses of participating retailers. Successful acceptance of Barclaycard by the British adult population meant that by the end of 1966 Barclays Bank had passed the milestone of one million Barclaycard holders.

Information technology

During the 1980s and 1990s, Barclaycard continued to benefit from being the 'first mover' in many aspects of the banking business including:

● issuing the first credit card in the UK,
● being the first credit card company to have an institutional presence on the internet,
● starting the first loyalty scheme in the UK,

---

[2] In a *charge card* all transactions for a given period (often monthly) are expected to be paid in full at the settlement date. In a *credit card* there is rollover credit as the cardholder may choose to pay any amount over the minimum required and is charged interest on the outstanding balance. In a *debit card* payment is linked to a customer's current account. There is no credit facility unless it is a feature of the underlying bank account.

Exhibit 1   The five players in the plastic card game

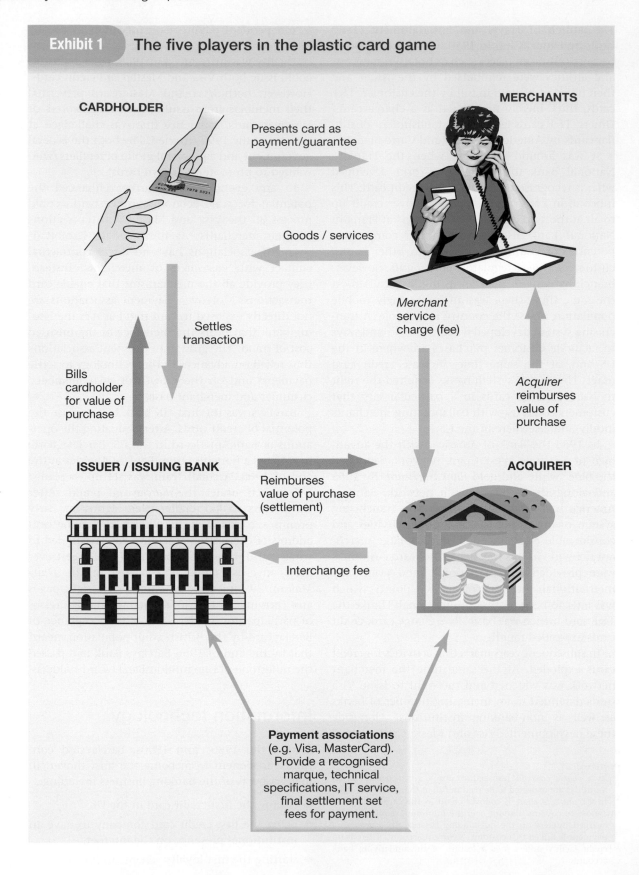

- being the first bank to enable credit card payments over the internet.

Clearly, the use of IT applications and computer technology in particular were critical for implementing Barclaycard's strategy. Excluding marketing costs, the initial investment of Barclays in the Bank of America franchise was low. Barclaycard's management team was able to migrate the entire operation from the US. This included Bank of America's computer programs, and the terms and conditions of service to both retailers/merchants and cardholders. Only minor modifications were required for the UK purposes as stated by a senior executive at Barclaycard:

> From Barclaycard's viewpoint, it envisaged that the complexities of adopting a US system for UK use were for example integration with feeder systems for capturing voucher details, customer payments (as the US had a radically different banking system), authorization (which was then an intense manual process), Country Club Billing (where individual transaction slips were matched and sent out with the statement) and address formats/postcodes which were very different from the United States model.

Although some customisation was required, the original system (like its paper or cardboard-based predecessors), relied primarily on carbonless duplicate paper vouchers imprinted with details embossed on the plastic card. Credit control was then managed using floor (merchant) limits combined with telephone authorisation. Growth in card usage convinced Barclaycard that automation through a fully computer-based transaction system was required. One was thus commissioned in 1974 to eliminate much of the paperwork, to speed up the authorisation process, and also to provide narrative statements for cardholders. The need to accelerate service delivery time eventually led to the formation of a platform for 'real time' operations: in other words, an array of IT applications that allowed automatic credit authorisation and speeded funds transfer from the merchant or retailer to the bank. This was achieved through a well-developed infrastructure developed by Visa and MasterCard. In particular, using extensive communications networks to link Visa's and Mastercard's electronic fund transfer protocols as well as their 24-hour-a-day and 7-day-a-week credit authorisation systems.

Alongside the developments in the credit cards market, banks also issued cash/cheque guarantee cards, and installed automated teller machine (ATM) networks to lower the costs of basic banking services. Barclays Bank led the world with the first operational ATM in 1967 while IBM introduced the first magnetic stripe plastic cards in 1969. Together these innovations marked the birth of electronic banking. Bank systems then developed to implement 'real time' transactions through ATMs.

Barclays' early adoption of ATMs was in parallel with the extended use of credit cards. Initially, the heavy investment required to build an ATM network was seen as a major source of competitive advantage for large banks, so interconnection was slow to develop. But after 30 years the absurdity of terminals connected to different networks and of ATMs located side by side was recognised only after terminal density had reached saturation point. This eventually resulted in a single interconnected UK network in 1999. Barclays then announced that it would charge non-customers for using its machines – a proposal that was withdrawn after being vilified in the press.

Given the slowness with which banks integrated their networks it was not surprising that standards developed within Visa and MasterCard were adopted for debit cards. In the UK, banks were again split between the Switch and Visa/Delta formats. Debit cards were a new source of growth for card issuing banks during the late 1980s to the extent that in 1991 MasterCard, with its European partner Europay International, launched their global online direct debit system to provide immediate (i.e. real-time) transfers from customers' accounts against transactions (branded *Maestro*). Shortly after that a system to support direct debit for ATM cash withdrawal (branded *Cirrus*) was developed worldwide.

In summary, developments in the 40 years that followed the launch of credit cards in the UK by Barclaycard were marked by the continuing improvement of the industry standards, interconnecting and interoperating hardware and software, and overlapping membership of the two technology platforms for payment systems (namely Visa International and MasterCard) as well as by almost identical functionality between cards. Barclaycard's achievement over this period was that it retained the advantage that was gained through early entry and remained as the market leader, not just with the basic credit card services but also in many aspects of card business. From scratch, Barclaycard grew to be the largest credit card business in the UK, with a presence in other European countries and also in parts of Africa.

Transaction processing

The transition from paper to electronics introduced large scale economies in card processing. Due to the dominant market share of Visa and MasterCard cards, processing of credit card transactions is determined by these two networks. Such processing is also characterised by relatively high one-off investments, such as setting up the interface with a global communications infrastructure. Software, equipment and operating staff are relatively independent of volume and therefore offer economies of scale. In order to take advantage of such scale economies and as had been the case in other countries, Barclaycard used electronic processing heavily in its cards business to facilitate the transition from paper to electronic processing. In 2003, with 9m cards issued in the UK alone, Barclaycard had 27 per cent of total credit market when its nearest rival, Lloyds TSB, only had 5m cardholders.

Although outsourcing was favoured by small-scale issuers, Barclaycard rejected the potentially profitable opportunities of servicing other card issuers until 2003 and, thus failed to take full advantage of scale economies. Rival issuers including Bank of Scotland, Royal Bank of Scotland and National Westminster provided card services on behalf of other institutions such as building societies and retailers. Outsourcing of card services including plastic card issuing, statement printing or even customer services became more favoured with the entrance of US 'mono-lines' in the UK market. For instance, MBNA had over 16m cardholders in the US at the time of its entry into the UK market. MBNA, therefore, brought a good deal of experience in terms of managing a credit cards business and eventually became very active in providing its services to other potential issuers in the UK (such as department stores and retailers).

The strength of banks' links with their customers was increasingly being tested by other businesses, such as utility companies and petrol retail companies, who have frequent close contact with their customers and could offer direct incentives for customers to take their card rather than the banks' card. Barclaycard again found a way forward. By 2003 most retailers no longer dealt directly with card associations such as Visa. Rather an acquirer consolidated the electronic readings on the cards through their own multi-card reader, which would be rented to the merchant. The reader could be provided by Barclaycard or a third party such as Streamline (who in turned was owned by HSBC, another UK-based multinational bank). Thus instead of the need for the old system needing one reader for each card, the retailer accepted the acquirer provided these links through its own software. The system as portrayed in Exhibit 1 became more diffuse as card issuers knew of their own customers whilst the acquirer could know about the merchant's customer base. Barclaycard was the only bank card which was a card issuer as well as an acquirer and hence, was in a position to gather information about its own and merchants' customers.

Another technological development which affected card processing was the introduction of smart or chip cards. The initial benefit of chip was to reduce counterfeiting and to increase security for internet and other remote transactions (see Exhibit 2). For instance, its introduction in France a decade earlier reduced card fraud by customers to

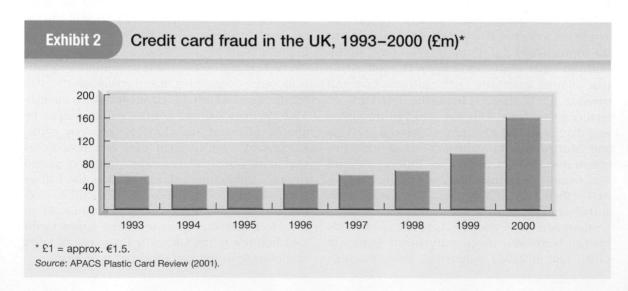

Exhibit 2   Credit card fraud in the UK, 1993–2000 (£m)*

* £1 = approx. €1.5.

Source: APACS Plastic Card Review (2001).

a tiny fraction of previous levels. Smart cards can store a vast amount of transaction data without the need to access multiple networks as required by a typical credit card transaction. The on-board chip in smart cards can handle complex security features including biometrics, which reduces card delinquency for banks switching to the new technology.

The UK's nationwide roll-out for chip cards started in late 2003. This move aimed to cut down credit card fraud by two-thirds. By the roll-out date, Visa member banks had already issued 23m chip cards and were offering e-commerce transactions which were supported by Visa's Secure Electronic Transaction platform. At the same time, Mastercard had developed similar capabilities through its purchase of Mondex, the smart card based electronic wallet developed by National Westminster Bank.

The chip roll-out originally presented issuers, retailers and end consumers with technological and user educational challenges. In another technological twist, innovations in information technology also offered the potential for transactions between personal or commercial customers and retailers to be handled directly and securely without the need to contact their banks. For instance,

mobile phone companies were experimenting with the use of bar codes (similar to those used in food wrapping) displayed on the handset's screen. Using systems such as those for text messaging (SMS) they effectively turned a mobile phone into a payment mechanism when interacting with a device (already in use by all supermarkets) that could scan and store transaction details.

Card profitability

Exhibit 3 summarises the revenue stream for card issuers. These comprise seven potential sources of income including: annual card fees charged to cardholders, cash withdrawal fees, income from interest charged on outstanding balances which are rolled over, income from proceeds emerging from the use of the card abroad, late payment charges, commissions received from acquiring banks (i.e. interchange income) and other sources of income (such as printing additional statements).

Despite being the initial and for a considerable period the only credit card issuer in the UK, Barclaycard made losses for the first decade of its operations as it built up its card and merchant

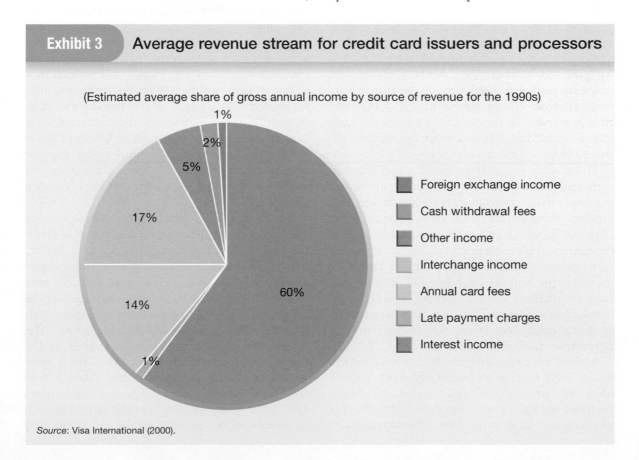

Exhibit 3 **Average revenue stream for credit card issuers and processors**

(Estimated average share of gross annual income by source of revenue for the 1990s)

- Foreign exchange income
- Cash withdrawal fees
- Other income
- Interchange income
- Annual card fees
- Late payment charges
- Interest income

1%
2%
5%
17%
14%
1%
60%

Source: Visa International (2000).

Exhibit 4	Barclaycard financial results, 1999–2003 (£m)*

					Half-year ended				
	30.6.99	31.12.99	30.6.00	31.12.00	30.6.01	31.12.01	30.6.02	31.12.02	30.6.03
Net interest income	241	247	344	341	392	415	431	455	498
Net fees and commissions	231	249	255	269	281	298	320	376	380
Total income	472	496	599	610	673	713	751	831	878
Total costs	(195)	(202)	(229)	(210)	(253)	(236)	(256)	(296)	(292)
Provisions for bad and doubtful debts	(82)	(88)	(136)	(168)	(164)	(210)	(181)	(221)	(205)
Operating profit	195	206	234	230	254	266	312	312	381

* £1 = approx. €1.5.

Source: Barclays PLC, Interim Results.

volumes. As the market leader it consistently priced Barclaycard at a premium. As late as 2001 Barclaycard still charged a discretionary annual card fee as well as the highest interest rate on credit card debt (annual percentage rate or APR) in the market. The result of the pricing strategy, however, was a healthy financial contribution to the parent organisation as illustrated in the financial summary in Exhibit 4.

Cards have delivered a high proportion of non-interest income and are, therefore, attractive to banks which have to provide regulatory capital to back interest bearing assets. Actually, the growth of credit cards has been part of the reason why both international and British banks have been able to more than double the proportion of their income earned as fees and commissions over the last 30 years.

The decade to 2003 reflected a period when competition between UK card issuers intensified and was characterised by extending activities and product development, thus vastly increasing the range of products and services available to final consumers. A plethora of competitors in the credit card market emerged on the back of the open membership policies of Visa and MasterCard. New competitors tried to develop market share through low rates (including a zero interest rate as introductory offer) on outstanding balance transferred from other providers.

Most of the new card entrants, however, experienced high level of customer disloyalty because once the introductory offer ended, customers switched to other issuers. But even with a flood of new entrants during the 1990s, Barclaycard kept its defection rates below 5 per cent per annum. Defection rates for established participants were low thanks to the inertia of bank customers, which was historically high. Even for credit cards, where the formalities of changing suppliers are minimal, customer retention rates were also high historically. For instance, according to some industry estimates the average adult Briton was four times more likely to divorce than to change credit card supplier.

Acquisition of new customers was a different story. By 1995 Barclaycard's share of new cards issued dropped down to 15 per cent of total new acquired customers: well below their ongoing market share of 30 per cent of the market. The drop in new acquired customers thus reflected how card processing specialists such as MBNA or Royal Bank of Scotland gained ground at the expense of participants which had grown organically and issued cards only to their own customer base. See Exhibit 5.

At the same time and in spite of customers at the turn of the millennium having access to credit far easier and more cheaply than ever before, the UK government considered that interest rates charged for outstanding credit card balances were still far higher than the level they deemed as acceptable. This led to a government inquiry that included chief executives of big card issuers. The aim was to establish why interest charges on UK credit cards had declined by only a third since 1992 when Bank of England had taken LIBOR (i.e. the main reference rate) to two-thirds of its 1992 value (and the lowest in the last 40 years!). As a result of the inquiry, banks and credit card

Exhibit 5	Total number of credit cards issued in the UK, 1996–2002 (in 000)		

Year	No. of credit cards in the UK	No. of Barclaycards	Market share %
1996	32,541	9,000	28
1997	36,565	9,400	26
1998	40,106	9,400	23
1999	43,459	7,100	16
2000	49,705	7,900	16
2001	54,778	8,200	15
2002	60,802[e]	9,700	16[e]

e = estimates

issuers agreed to make credit card charges more transparent and easier to understand and to introduce so called 'honesty tables'.[3]

With around £9.7bn pounds of outstanding balances in 2003, Barclaycard was required to provide £480m of regulatory capital. So profits of £615m in 2002 provided a return of close to 100 per cent on equity, a vivid contrast with a British bank's typical return on equity (ROE) of 15 per cent per annum. This was also an indicator that, despite claims of increased competition, credit cards remained a remarkably profitable component in a bank's portfolio. For example, the profitability of the card business within Citibank was such that it had been estimated to be worth 50 per cent more as a stand-alone business than the entire value of the bank.

Another element in the profit equation is the average value of balances settled outside the 'free interest period'. If a customer pays off the outstanding balance in full, then the issuing bank earns only interchange income and commission fees. As seen in Exhibit 6, the percentage of interest bearing credit card balances was at around 75 per cent as of December 2001, which was much lower than 1998 and 1999 averages. This was due to introductory offers such as low or zero interest rates for balance transfers and reflected the widespread use of such offers by cardholders between 1998 and 2003.

In parallel to the industry average, Barclays aimed for its customers to have at least 70 per cent of interest earning balances outside the free interest period. Thus, card issuers provide medium-term consumer finance. But to be able to grow credit card balances profitably issuers must entertain the possibilities under which credit risk might increase. For instance, in 2000 Barclaycard's transaction volume grew by 12 per cent while charges for bad and doubtful debts increased by 34 per cent. As the economy slowed down in 2002, however, transaction volume grew by 8 per cent while bad debt charges also grew by 8 per cent. Financial performance thus suggests that the aim of credit card managers is to find customers who need rollover credit but will not default on repayments. Barclaycard's in-house skills in measuring and monitoring credit risk have, therefore, been crucial to their strategy.

Challenges to Barclaycard's strategy

Barclaycard's strategy aims to develop and maintain market leadership by differentiating its product range: for instance, designing a comprehensive benefits package to potential and existing cardholders as described in Exhibit 7. Products and services were sometimes introduced independently from those at the Barclays Group while, at the same time, not all offers were available to all cardholders: they were linked to the customer's banking relationship with Barclays (e.g. Barclaycard

---

[3] Called the Schumer box in the US, they draw together information traditionally in 'the small print' of an application into a single table, making loans and credit card offerings from different providers easier to understand and compare.

Exhibit 6 | Monthly credit card outstanding balances in the UK and percentage of interest-bearing balances in outstanding balances, 1998–2000*

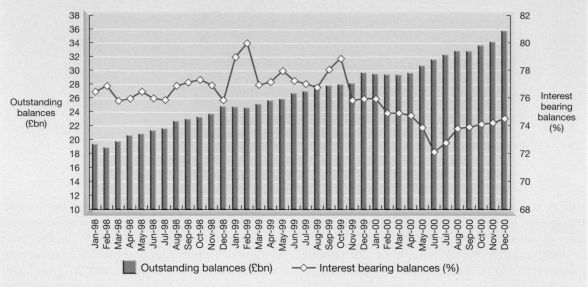

Outstanding balances (£bn) — *Interest bearing balances (%)*

* £1 = approx. €1.5.
Source: APACS.

Exhibit 7 | Barclaycard products and services, 2003

Credit cards	• *Standard credit cards:* Classic Card, Student Card, Graduate Card, Premiership Card • *Special privilege cards:* Barclaycard Gold, Barclaycard Platinum, Barclaycard Open Plan (By linking a customer's current account, savings and mortgages, the new card offers 0 per cent interest on purchases for 3 months) • *Company Cards:* Corporate Card (e.g. BTI Corporate Card), Purchasing Card (e.g. HM Government Card), Business Card.
Free user benefits	• *Barclaycard Purchase Protection:* Goods are protected against theft and accidental damage for 60 days after purchase. • *Barclaycard Extended Warranty:* Free 12 months extended warranty. • *Travel Accident Insurance:* Free Travel Accident Insurance worth of £50,000 for each adult. • *Nectar Points:* Rewards programme that allows cardholders to collect points from retailers. • *Barclaycard Price Promise:* Find any item purchased on the card cheaper elsewhere and Barclaycard will refund the difference. • *Internet Delivery Protection:* Goods purchased online are protected from loss or damage during transit. • *Online Fraud Guarantee:* Online purchases are guaranteed against fraud.
Advice	• *International Rescue:* 24-hour emergency advisory service including lost card replacement and emergency cash advances.
Online services	• *Online Account Management:* Keeping track of spending; settling bills; requesting a credit limit increase; applying for a new PIN, cheque book or new card; contacting customer services.

Exhibit 8	Growth of transactions in the UK card market, 1991–2001 (million of transactions per year)

	1991	1992	1993	1994	1995	1996	1997	1998	1999	2000	2001
Debit cards	359	522	659	808	1,004	1,270	1,503	1,736	2,062	2,337	2,696
Credit & charge cards	699	724	748	815	908	1,025	1,128	1,224	1,344	1,452	1,558
Store cards	46	70	82	100	109	118	128	134	131	125	117
All card purchases	1,104	1,316	1,488	1,723	2,023	2,413	2,759	3,094	3,537	3,914	4,381
Cash withdrawals by cards	1,112	1,199	1,277	1,372	1,512	1,656	1,809	1,917	2,025	2,102	2,269

Source: APACS.

Exhibit 9	Outstanding balances on UK credit cards, 1993–2001 (£000)*

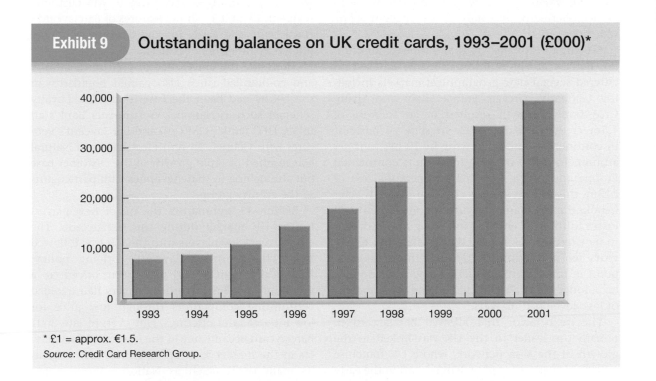

* £1 = approx. €1.5.
Source: Credit Card Research Group.

Open Plan). At the same time, other UK retail banks would tailor the marketing of their credit cards as bundled with other banking products.

Barclaycard's strategy in the cards market has been associated with a number of major factors. The first is the continued growth of the credit card market as shown in Exhibits 8 and 9. Over the period of 1991 to 2001 the volume of credit card transactions grew by 9 per cent per annum, while debit cards transactions grew by 31 per cent. Outstanding balances, on the other hand, tripled between 1993 and 2001.

Despite increases in credit card and transaction numbers, the average number of annual transactions per credit card fell in 2000 whereas the average annual spend per credit cardholder went up. These trends sat alongside a switch in individual expenditure patterns moving from cash transactions to credit cards. Also, multiple card holding became an important feature of the UK cards industry, with over 50 per cent of all cardholders having two or more credit cards (and 5 per cent six or more!). However, there was still a long way to go for the 'cashless society': for instance, only 4 per cent of all payments were made by credit cards in the UK, compared with 25 per cent in the US. Industry estimates elaborated by APACS projected that by 2011 half of the adult UK population (expected to be 26m cardholders) would be regular credit card users, compared to 18m regular users in 2001.

The use of debit and credit cards, however, showed significant differences between North America and Europe. The US accounted for 40 per cent of the cards issued and a massive £340bn credit card spending in 1995 whereas the same figure in the UK and Italy was £44bn and £6bn respectively. The potential for growth in continental European markets was also highlighted by figures from the Credit Card Research Group showing that credit card payments in 1997 in the UK were equivalent to 8.5 per cent of GDP while in France, Germany and Italy the equivalent figure was 1 per cent.

Seeking to capitalise on that business opportunity, Barclaycard grew internationally. Barclaycard entered several new geographical markets including Germany, Greece, France, Italy and Spain. Cross-border growth resulted in an increase of 1.3m credit cards by 2002. In spite of business in continental Europe growing by 10 per cent per annum, in 2002, as a business unit, continental Europe and Africa recorded an operating loss of £13m, this followed a loss of £20m in 2001. Peter Crook, the UK managing director, attributed such losses to the cost entailed in setting up businesses in new territories – noting that it takes four to five years for new entrants to reach the break-even point in the mature UK market, and it would take even longer in the more challenging environment of less developed markets.

The next factor that allowed Barclaycard to remain the leader in the UK was linked to the growth of the Visa network, whose UK franchise was exclusively enjoyed by Barclaycard in the early years. By 2000, Visa secured its position as the world's most widely used plastic card accounting for US$1.9bn of transaction volume or 60 per cent of the global market. Yet, Visa itself did not seem much satisfied with this outcome. A senior executive at Visa International expressed their ambition in this respect as:

> When I can go out of a hotel and tip the porter using a Visa card and he'll accept it, that's when we'll have succeeded.

Another factor was the ability of Barclaycard's managers to avoid price competition – that is until

recently – by emphasising brand and product development. The introduction of gold cards represented a good example of how Barclaycard articulated their branding policy. Although MasterCard introduced their gold card in the US in 1981 and by 1992 there were similar offerings in the UK (such as those supplied by American Express or the Co-operative Bank), Barclaycard did not introduce its Barclaycard Gold until 1995 but immediately acquired 90,000 Gold customers. The launch pushed its market share to 30 per cent of total new credit cards issued. The gold card also aimed to segment its customer base and to customise card features. Apart from pricing, non-price features such as extended purchase warranties, purchase protection insurance and travel accident cover were also rearranged according to the customer segment. Exhibit 10 shows features of Barclaycard's *classic* and *gold* cards in comparison with those offered by other major issuers.

Alongside the emergence of gold cards affinity and co-branded cards also gained popularity in the UK as had been the case in the US. Loyalty schemes such as National Westminster Bank's air miles, HFC Bank's GM card and Barclaycard's ventures with Cellnet, Eastern Electricity and Natural Gas resulted in rapid growth of the customer base but also having to share revenues with participants in the affinity group.

Exhibit 11 summarises the major new players in the UK market during the last decade. The entrance of new players into the UK was followed by a change in Barclaycard's pricing policy. Historically, Barclaycard had been priced at a premium and Barclaycard managers had avoided confronting competitors through low price (or low interest rate) offerings. However, in late 2001 Barclaycard became one of the last traditional players in the market to scrap its annual fee, whereas its main rivals (such as National Westminster, Lloyds TSB and Bank of Scotland) had abolished annual fees as early as 1999.

Card issuers (and banks in particular) realised that the same technology that supported retail credit cards could also support business to business transactions. Europay estimated that in the 1990s European businesses spent £100bn per year on routine business expenses, which were paid mostly by cash or cheque. Corporate cards offered a cost-effective alternative to such transactions as the technology was already in place to provide detailed reports and cost centre consolidation for travel and subsistence costs. The same was true for company

Exhibit 10 Credit card competitors, 2003

Issuer	Card Type	Annual Fee	Interest-free Days	APR on Purc. %	Bal.Trans. Int.[1] APR %	Bal.Trans. Int.[1] Period Days	Insurance Purchase Protect.Days	Insurance Travel Accident	Loyalty Scheme[2]
Classic credit cards									
Barclaycard	V,M	0	56	11.9	0–6.9[3]	Life[4]	60	£50k	Cashback, Nectar
HSBC	M	0	45	15.9	3.9	180	0	none	none
NatWest	V,M	0	56	17.4	4.9	Life[4]	0	£50k	Air Miles
LloydsTSB	V,M	0	56	17.9	5.9	Life[4]	0	none	none
HBoS	V,M	0	57	16.9	0	150	100	£100k	none
RBS	V,M	0	56	16.9	0	180	0	£50k	Air Miles
Goldfish	M	0	52	14.9–17.9[5]	0–4.9[5]	180	0	none	Goldfish
Tesco	V, M	0	56	14.9	0	Until 01/04	50	£50k	Clubcard Points
Egg	V	0	45	13.9	0	Until 03/04	0	none	Cashback
Smile	V	0	46	9.9–10.5[5]	N/A	N/A	0	none	Cashback
MBNA	V,M	0	59	15.9	0	180	0	£50k	none
Amex Blue	Amex	0	56	18.9	9.9	Life[4]	90	£50k	Moneyback
Gold credit cards									
Barclaycard	V	0	56	11.9	0–6.9[3]	Life[4]	60	£50k	Cashback, Nectar
HSBC	V	0	56	14.9	3.9	180	90	£100k	none
NatWest	V,M	0	56	16.4	4.9	Life[4]	100	£100k	Air Miles
Lloyds TSB	V,M	0	56	15.9	5.9	Life[4]	120	£100k	none
HBoS	V,M	0	57	14.9	0	150	100	£250k	none
RBS	V,M	0	56	16.9	0	180	100	£100k	Air Miles

[1] The balance transfer rates and periods refer to the preferential rates offered to new customers with outstanding balances brought across from a different card issuer.

[2] Additional benefits such as purchase discounts, medical insurance, extended warranty and personal liability are not included for reasons of space.

[3] 0% APR applies only to customers who spend a minimum of £50 per month on their new Barclaycard. Those who do not use their Barclaycard during a particular month pay 6.9% APR on that month.

[4] For the life of the balance.

[5] These card issuers customise the card features according to customers.

Source: Website of each issuer; accessed on 15 September 2003.

procurement. American Express launched their Corporate Purchasing Card in the US in 1993 and in 1995 in the UK, while Visa International introduced their corporate purchasing system to the European market in 1994. Purchasing cards were attractive to business organisations by allowing paperless 'order to payment' purchasing, itemised transaction reports as well as consolidated reports by employee, supplier or purchase category.

In the late 1990s, Barclays introduced both company charge cards and purchasing cards under the Visa-marqued *Company Barclaycard*. In a relatively short period of time, Barclaycard gained market leadership in corporate charge cards in the UK. Four Barclaycard corporate cards, all Visa marqued, offered a combination of travel discounts and insurance, extended purchase warranties and supplier discounts as well as providing detailed reports. Again Visa marqued Company Barclaycard *Purchasing Card* allowed customers to nominate a monthly statement date and provided opportunities to extend credit as well as detailed reports. Barclaycard's leading position in this market was underlined by their success in securing the account for a Government Procurement Card with variants provided to the Ministry of Defence, Customs and Excise, the Ministry of Agriculture, Fisheries and Food and the Environment Agency.

Marketing has traditionally been an area where the management team at Barclaycard invested heavily. Indeed, to sustain its position extensive advertising and promotional campaigns were

| Exhibit 11 | Selected new players in the UK credit card market, 1990–2003 |

Type of players	New Players in the UK market	
Foreign entrants	American Express	Bank One[1]
	Citibank	GE Capital Bank
	MBNA	Providian
	HFC Bank	Morgan Stanley
	Capital One	
Non-financial institutions (Processed by)	Virgin (MBNA) GM Card (HFC Bank)	Accucard (London Scottish Bank)
Retailer credit cards (Marquee, processed by)	Tesco (Visa, Royal Bank of Scotland)	Marks & Spencer (MasterCard, Marks & Spencer)
	Sainsbury (Visa, Bank of Scotland/HBoS)	Harrods (MasterCard, GE Capital Bank)
Internet based card suppliers (Parent organisation)	Egg (Prudential)	Cahoot (Abbey National)
	Marbles (HFC Bank)	IF (Halifax/HBoS)
	Smile (Co-operative Bank)	Goldfish (Lloyds TSB[2])

[1] US-based Bank One sold its UK credit card business to the Halifax in June 2000.
[2] Gas and electricity supplier Centrica sold its UK credit card business to Lloyds TSB in October 2003.

launched. For example, in 1995 and 1996 Barclaycard spent over £12m on advertising compared with National Westminster's £1.5m and American Express's £3m. As a result, Barclaycard was the most recognised financial brand in the UK. Shaun Powell, a commercial director of Barclaycard, was typically opposed to anything that would dilute Barclaycard's brand: '. . . branding is a discipline, it is all about sustaining your premium price.'

Few in the UK will not be familiar with the long-running television advertisement series featuring Rowan Atkinson (a.k.a. Mr Bean) playing the role of an accident-prone diplomat, which even led to a Hollywood movie! The message in the advertising encapsulated the essence of Barclaycard's strategy and how it planned to differentiate itself from competitors. The advertisements emphasised peace of mind – in case of an emergency such as losing the credit card or passport, experiencing medical problems while on holiday or losing goods purchased with Barclaycard. By 2003 marketing was directed into sponsorship which included six key areas, namely education, the disadvantaged, people with disabilities, the arts, the environment (through the Young People's Trust for the Environment) and a three-year sponsorship of the English Football Association's Premier League. Yet, as illustrated in Exhibit 12, Barclaycard was having difficulty in keeping a differentiated offering in the debit and credit card market: the four biggest card issuers accounted for nearly three quarters of the cardbase in 1993 while their share fell to 50 per cent in 2001, with Barclaycard falling from almost 30 per cent in 1993 to 18 per cent of the market share in 2001.

Until 2002 Barclaycard had developed its customer base through a combination of organic growth and alliances. These alliances included companies in telecommunications such as BT and Cellnet and food retailers such as Marks & Spencer and Sainsbury's. Managers of Barclaycard, however, abandoned plans to develop its own loyalty scheme when Barclaycard aimed to differentiate itself from its competitors by establishing *Nectar* in conjunction with Sainsbury (food retailer), Debenhams (department store) and BP (retail petrol) late in 2002. Within a year Nectar became the biggest loyalty scheme in the UK with over 12m active users. New partners were quickly

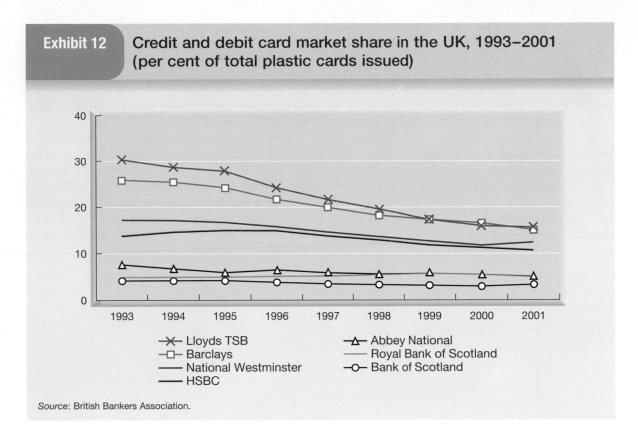

Exhibit 12 Credit and debit card market share in the UK, 1993–2001 (per cent of total plastic cards issued)

Lloyds TSB — Abbey National
Barclays — Royal Bank of Scotland
National Westminster — Bank of Scotland
HSBC

Source: British Bankers Association.

added such as Vodafone (mobile telephony), First Quench (retail wine merchants) and Adams (children's clothes retailing).

Alliances, however, were unable to stop a significant dilution of Barclaycard's market share. Also in 2002, Barclaycard performed its first ever acquisition with the purchase of the UK operations of Providian (the eighth-largest credit card provider in the US in terms of assets). The acquisition helped Barclaycard enter a new market segment (that of lower income customers) and brought with it half a million new customers with balances of around £400m, that is, a 14 per cent increase in interest income, 6 per cent increase in provisions and 9 per cent increase in credit balances. Moreover, the newly acquired expertise in the low income segment encouraged Barclaycard to agree with Littlewoods Ltd (a leading retailer in the low income market) the supply of credit cards and other financial products to Littlewoods' customer base. After Providian, in May 2003 Barclaycard also acquired the point of sale business of Clydesdale Financial Services, further enhancing its merchant network.

White paper or whitewash?

When the government introduced its 'white paper' on credit card borrowing in 2003, Barclaycard was criticised by the Office of Fair Trading after advertising a 'zero per cent forever' card deal which was nothing of the kind. Customers actually had to pay off existing balances first before they could get the offer. There was thus support for claims of a whitewash in the credit card industry: issuers included 'hidden' charges (levied for late payment or early repayment) that consumers were often not aware of.

This was worrying as consumer debt had mushroomed from £429m in 1969 (equivalent to £5.25bn in 2003) to £168bn in 2003. A poll by Mori said that 76 per cent of people found consumer credit advertising confusing and 84 per cent found the language of the paperwork unintelligible. The poll also found the term APR, used by credit card providers and other loan companies to describe the rate of repayment, confusing (while 59 per cent would not describe APR as an annual percentage rate). At the same time, 83 per cent of consumers would look at the APR when deciding which of the 1,300 credit cards in the UK to apply for.

Ministers ruled out any cap on interest rates for credit cards, relying on consumer pressure to reduce rates. Checks on companies applying for credit licences were to be tightened up. New fines were introduced as well as new powers for regulators. Ministers were to pressure for a reduction in interchange fees and consultants at PricewaterhouseCoopers expected the move would cost the industry over £450m in lost revenue per year. Some feared this would lead to higher charges for credit card issuers and fewer reward programmes for consumers.

The same day the white paper was published, concerns for Barclaycard were also prompt in-house: John Varley, Finance Director of the Barclays Group and heir apparent to Matt Barrett, put investors on edge by warning of the risks further interest rate increases posed to Britain's debt-saddled consumers.

Developments in the UK were worrying for managers at Barclaycard, particularly as other European countries were contemplating regulatory changes along the lines of those in the UK. Managers wondered whether these developments might result in return to cash-only transactions and thus, would they be beheading the king of plastic?

Brown Bag

John Cullen

This case study charts the development of an Irish animation company from small, unambitious beginnings to becoming an award-winning, globally recognised company with a growing list of international clients. It describes how the enterprise emerged at a time of demographic and cultural change in Ireland, and how the withdrawal of significant investment created entrepreneurial opportunities for animators. Having charted the issues that underpinned Brown Bag's early success and acclaim, the case ends with a focus on the strategic decisions which the directors faced eight years after their accidental beginning in 1994.

• • •

In the mid-1990s Cathal Gaffney and Darragh O'Connell knew nothing about running a business. In fact, they didn't want to know anything about running a business. They had never outgrown a childhood fascination with comics and graphic novels and considered themselves artists working (infrequently) on the small Dublin animation circuit. By 2003, they were running Brown Bag Films, an award-winning, Oscar®-nominated Irish animation powerhouse with a large and growing number of Irish and international clients for whom they produce television series, feature films, commercials and digital media. Brown Bag Films was typical of many Irish 'Celtic Tiger' era start-up success stories. It was lean, innovative and heavily reliant on highly skilled staff using state-of-the-art technology. It was also at a juncture where strategic decisions about the future of the company had to be addressed.

Animation in Ireland

The story of the animation industry in Ireland over the last twenty years is one of boom-to-bust-to-new-beginnings. In 1992 *Business and Finance Magazine* reported that the Industrial Development Authority (IDA) 'reckoned that Ireland could become a major world animation centre. [Ireland was] . . . to become the cartoon capital of Europe. Today the dream is over.'[1] Ten years later, two Irish films received nominations for the 2002 Academy Awards®; both were short animated films produced by small, young, Irish companies.

The 1970s saw a 'baby-boom' in Ireland; as birth rates reached, and surpassed, previous highs of the early 1950s, infant mortality rates dropped significantly. This new, young population was served by the first official state broadcasting agency, RTE, which had been established in the early 1960s. However, most of the animated content of children's television programming and on television advertising was produced by American companies (principally Disney) and home-produced animation was almost non-existent.

As the global recession worsened in the early 1980s, the IDA ('a state agency whose prime focus was to get industries with the highest job content for Ireland')[2] changed strategy. Their ten-year strategic plan directed that the agency:

[1] Gerald Luke, 'Mickey Mouse Job', *Business and Finance*, 20 August 1992.
[2] Padraic White, *The Making of the Celtic Tiger: The Inside Story of Ireland's Boom Economy*, Dublin: Mercier Press, 2001, p. 206.

. . . should focus on attracting industries that could achieve high output growth using the best technology available, while maximising their spending on Irish services and materials. In this way, the IDA would maximise the gains for the economy, both through jobs within the company and via the related service employment that would be created in consequence. Our judgement was that the most technologically advanced firms would be the most successful in the market place. We believed the jobs would follow that success. This marked a reversal of the IDA's traditional approach of attracting the most labour intensive industries, since labour was in abundant supply in Ireland.[3]

In the mid-1980s the IDA sought to attract large animation companies to Ireland and met with good initial levels of success, attracting three large American companies to set-up in Dublin: Sullivan-Bluth (later Don Bluth Entertainment), Murakami Wolf Swenson (later Fred Wolf Films) and Emerald City. When it emerged that Bluth initially employed American and European animators in most of the skilled positions in the company and Irish animators were employed in functional positions,[4] Bluth and the IDA looked seriously at the provision of serious training opportunities for Irish animators. The result was a two-year animation course in Ballyfermot College of Further Education (BCFE),[5] followed shortly afterwards by a course in Dun Laoighaire Institute of Art, Design and Technology.

These three companies employed 530 staff by 1990.[6] Three years later Emerald City had gone into liquidation, Don Bluth Entertainment closed and Fred Wolf Films laid off two thirds of its workforce; it too would later close its Irish operation. The biggest blow to the sector was the closing of the Bluth operation which resulted in 380 (over 70 per cent of the 'big three' animation companies) jobs being lost. By 1998 employment in the Irish animation sector had shrunk to 70 full-time and 30 contract/freelance employees.[7]

At the time many reasons were given for the retreat and collapse of the US companies. The period of economic fallout in the aftermath of the first Gulf War and competitive pressures within the international animation industry contributed to a situation where locating in Ireland was no longer a viable option for companies in the sector.[8,9] North America was the spiritual home of commercial animation and Dublin in the early 1990s offered little tangible strategic benefit in locating a production facility in Dublin.

Ironically, the attraction of large American companies, and their subsequent withdrawal had sown the seeds of a healthy indigenous industry. When the foreign investment bubble burst, a community of young, talented film-makers remained behind. They were skilled creatives who had worked on large commercial productions for the big three animation houses. They had energy, experience and a drive to succeed on their own terms, but little money or business experience.

Beginning Brown Bag

Cathal Gaffney had an idea: the idea was a short animated film which would lampoon a classic of Irish language literature, *Peig*, an autobiographical account of island life at the start of the 20th century. *Peig*, was a staple of school curricula and was widely disliked by students forced to read the text.

Darragh O'Connell was from Leixlip, a satellite town of Dublin in County Kildare which had mushroomed as a result of large-scale migration from rural areas in the late 1960s. His original interest in the field was encouraged by the emergence of a new wave of science fiction comics such as *2000 AD* which began to be widely distributed in Ireland in the late 1970s. He began writing and drawing his own graphic sci-fi novels with distribution limited to a close group of friends.

Gaffney's original interest was in the more sedate area of fine arts. He also grew up in an area which experienced population growth in the late 1960s; the Navan Road area of Dublin. They had both attended secondary school at a time when unemployment was a pressing reality for everyone in Ireland, the concept of return-emigration was inconceivable, and the value of employment was universally appreciated. Employment for visual artists is never assured, and the opportunity to

[3] Ibid.

[4] Paul Farren, 'Irish Animation: A Brief History', *Film Ireland*.

[5] Then, Ballyfermot Senior College.

[6] A 1992 Coopers and Lybrand Report cited in a 1998 Industry and Business Employers Confederation Position Paper: *Realising the Potential of the Animation Sector: Position Paper* (Dublin: IBEC Audiovisual Federation, June 1998), p. 2.

[7] Ibid.

[8] Luke, op. cit.

[9] Farren, op. cit.

train and work in a field they enjoyed was welcomed by both of them after they left school.

Following stints at Bluth and BCFE, O'Connell and Gaffney met while unemployed and developed Gaffney's idea for the best part of a year. Eventually, they pitched the idea to the newly formed Independent Productions Unit (IPU) at RTE.

RTE had created the IPU in response to the Broadcasting Authority (Amendment) Act 1993. It aimed 'to enhance the service to viewers by expanding the range and diversity of Irish-made programmes on our screens and to foster new sources of creativity and energy within the independent television production sector.'[10]

At the time the IPU were not interested in the idea of a short film, and instead commissioned a series of 7 × 3.5 minute short animated pieces based on the proposed concept. At this time, the partners were interested in bringing the *Peig* project to fruition and were not interested in developing a business. Animator friends were brought on board to assist in the production (a mixture of hand-drawn cell-animation and stop-motion models). The work was expensive, labour intensive and time-consuming. Although listed on the IPU's web-archive as a 'Young Peoples' television programme, the content was directed towards an Irish adult late-night TV market.

When aired on RTE, the *Peig* series achieved critical acclaim (the *Irish Times* reviewing it as 'one of the best and funniest Irish productions in ages'). One of the more tangible benefits of the experience for the directors was the establishment of working roles: Gaffney as producer and O'Connell as director.

Having completed their project, they discussed dividing their remaining assets. Gaffney soon secured a contract from a UK-based company to develop another project, once again asked O'Connell to come on board, and Brown Bag Films were officially established in 1994. Existing assets were invested in procuring expensive state-of-the-art animation technology and training.

Growing the enterprise

At this initial stage the directors of Brown Bag were still very 'art-oriented' as opposed to having a business drive. Much of this was due to the fact that they were following their primary interest and expertise. Gaffney and O'Connell realised to continue to work in the field that they would have to grow their understanding of business. Following their initial small-scale success, capital was almost non-existent and no offers for work were forthcoming. The need to effectively market their services became paramount as business was quiet, perhaps as a result of a loss of faith in the Irish animation sector. Some business training was undertaken and a show-reel was developed and pitched at festivals and trade-fairs.

With little work available in the television sector, Brown Bag pursued other markets and contracted animation work with CD-ROM production companies. In the mid-90s this field had a high-book worth to the company and helped alleviate many of their early financial difficulties. They also began to work on television commercials for advertising agencies which proved to be a highly lucrative field (see Appendix 1 for a list of key company milestones). Their client list included Aer Lingus, SmithKline Beecham, 11850, the Department of the Environment and Local Government, RTE, TG4 and Saudi Arabian State television.

A major departure for the company in the late 1990s was securing the contract to coordinate the animation work for a major Warner Brothers production, *The King & I*, which involved utilising groundbreaking virtual animation studio technology and resulted in a significant boost to the company's profile.

Over the following years Brown Bag worked for and with a variety of production companies, mainly outside Ireland. A production/promotion momentum had begun for the company and the directors became increasingly involved in moving between sourcing contracts and delivering completed projects.

In 2002 Brown Bag was nominated for an Oscar for their short film 'Give Up Yer Aul Sins'. The award proved instrumental in establishing Brown Bag at the vanguard of independent film production in Ireland. 'Give Up Yer Aul Sins' became the first Irish short film to receive an extensive nationwide theatrical release and was screened in over 100 cinemas.

By 2003 the work volume of Brown Bag broke down as shown in Exhibit 1. The two main areas of work were TV production and TV commercials. TV production is based on large formats and involves extensive research and development; TV commercials are high-profit and quick turnover. The

---

[10] http://www.rte.ie/tv/ipu/.

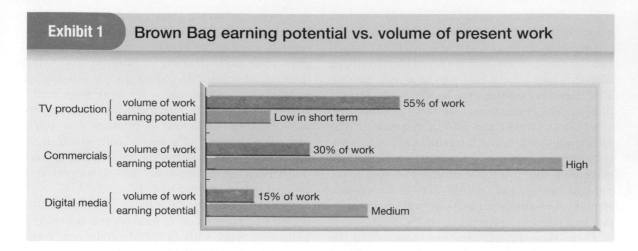

Exhibit 1   Brown Bag earning potential vs. volume of present work

TV production { volume of work — 55% of work
               earning potential — Low in short term

Commercials { volume of work — 30% of work
              earning potential — High

Digital media { volume of work — 15% of work
                earning potential — Medium

directors remain focused on television production as Brown Bag has a proven track record in this area, and achieved international recognition with their nomination for an Academy Award® in 2002, which generated international interest in the company. Markets for television animation are large and continue to expand. An example of this is the phenomenal success of *The Simpsons*. It began in 1987 as a series of animated inserts in a now defunct comedy show, but its contract with Fox till 2005 would make it the longest running TV comedy series ever.[11]

The company had become increasingly aware of the potential for long-term revenue generation through the development of a library of intellectual property as revenues could be increased by distributing series developed in one setting to international markets. In the late 1990s, Brown Bag developed a 24-part series ('Why?') for pre-school children which was sold in over 20 countries.

The directors had reached a point where their primary interest was in achieving long-term business growth and were in no doubt that they were first and foremost business people rather than artists.

Future challenges

Gaffney and O'Connell realised that Brown Bag was at a watershed and they were entering a key period for business growth. They were conscious of needing to address several concerns, as outlined below.

Capital

. . . animation is a labour-intensive and costly process. On average an animated series costs between $300,000–$600,000[12] a half hour to produce. A live action children's programming can be produced far more cheaply (for as little as $15,000 an episode). Development time for a show is usually one year but can take far longer.[13]

This creates considerable difficulties for small firms and places limits on productivity. 'While the promise of advance sales helps, there appears to be major cash flow problem for small firms without the sort of clout, distribution deals, capital reserves and networks of the Disneys of this world.'[14]

Animation does have some advantages over live-action production, however. It has a longer shelf-life than live-action productions; it can be dubbed into foreign languages with greater ease; merchandising opportunities are greater; and it is easier to repurpose it into different media (internet, wireless, etc.).

The cost of technology is often prohibitive, but can help in turnaround time (see below). Irish animators in general were critical of the lack of support received from Irish broadcasting agencies, but most animation companies acknowledged the assistance of state support. Agencies such as the Irish Film Board, were critical of the finance plans of production companies and state agencies such as Enterprise Ireland encouraged and assisted

[11] Zoe Williams, 'Homeric Epic', *New Statesman*, 21 April 2003, p. 42.

[12] In Ireland this is estimated to cost in the region of €250–450,000 a half-hour to produce.
[13] Dominic Schreiber (1998) *Television animations: Opportunities in the Global Marketplace* (London: FT Media & Telecoms), 4.
[14] Luke, op. cit.

many production companies looking to create full time employment and produce work for international markets.

Like other animation companies, Brown Bag focused on producing high-quality material for international audiences. However, Brown Bag needed significant investment. Gaffney and O'Connell had reinvested all profits made to date to meet project research and development costs. A significant injection was required if Brown Bag was to break out of the production/promotion loop (see 'Staff' below).

By way of comparison, Pixar Films (the creators of *For the Birds*, the eventual winner of the 2002 Academy Award® for best animated short), had the resources necessary to develop high quality state of the art product. In partnership with animation giant, Disney, it had produced four animated feature films (*Toy Story, Toy Story 2, A Bugs Life* and *Monsters Inc.*) since 1995, which had earned over $1.5bn. The story of its emergence features the names of some of the creative and commercial titans of the computing and cinema sectors. Steve Jobs (chairman and CEO) purchased the computer graphics division of George Lucas Lucasfilm in 1986 and established Pixar as an independent company with 44 employees. By 2003 Pixar had 600 employees and produced films (short and feature length), commercials and logos. It had also developed ground breaking animation software and had its own animation-training facility. Pixar went public in 1995 and was the biggest IPO that year.[15]

Business development

Gaffney and O'Connell admitted that growth had been slow, but they did not regret this as it has enabled them to become expert in their field and establish a sound national and international profile.

Brown Bag's strategy by 2003 was: to develop slates of projects through its sister development company (Brown Bag Development Ltd) and enhance its television output; develop a slate of feature films for TV and DVD markets; develop a commercials production arm of the company with international representation; promote expertise in Flash animation to digital media markets.

Staff

One of the competitive advantages that Dublin had enjoyed as a location was a steady supply of newly-trained and experienced freelance animators. During its original start-up phase Brown Bag had 19 animators on its payroll. The company quickly restructured to a small core staff and a floating pool of contract staff. While this enabled Brown Bag to run a necessarily tight operation, it meant that the energies of key staff were often tied into administrative and developmental duties which affected securing new business. The balance between sustaining development activities in tandem with production work is a factor which all production companies struggle with.

International markets

The Irish national television market is small. The Film Industry Strategic Review Group reported:

> Small innovative film companies will remain critical to this industry. But they are not sufficient alone to drive the next phase of strategic development. It needs companies with sufficient scale, capitalisation, business/management expertise and editorial discipline to sustain a strategic focus in the international market. An increasing ability to retain rights and build or acquire libraries will be an important component of their future economic strength as will the ability to market and sell more effectively.[16]

Brown Bag had had some success outside Ireland. The international prestige of an Oscar® nomination had opened some possible markets for them. They were also involved in an ongoing business partnership with a middle-eastern company to develop commercials and had successfully engaged agents in Saudi Arabia. A significant development had been the creation of a strategic alliance with Klasky Csupo, a major US animation firm and commercials producer, which in 1999 became the first non-Disney studio to break the $100m US domestic box-office with an animated feature film.[17] This was important because Klasky Csupo's was one of the major animation growth companies and innovators in the important US animation market and was producing three of the most watched television series for children.

[15] http://www.pixar.com/companyinfo/aboutus/index.html.

[16] *The Strategic Development of the Irish Film and Television Industry 2000–2010.* Film Industry Strategic Review Group, 1999. http://www.iftn.ie/strategyreport/index.htm.
[17] www.klaskycsupo.com.

Technology

Brown Bag used a range of software packages including Avid, Animo, 3-D Studio Max, Maya, Flash, Photoshop and After Effects. This technology was often expensive, but speeded up the animation process to huge effect. This meant that smaller teams of animators were necessary to bring projects to fruition.

They showcased their expertise in Flash animation on a separate web domain and had recently formed an alliance with a web development company to develop interactive cartoons. They were also producing content for wireless applications such as WAP mobile phones.

Competition

By 2003 Brown Bag was one of the largest animation companies in Ireland. They had achieved peer and industry recognition for producing high quality work. The larger players to emerge in the post-Bluth era also included TerraGlyph and Magma Films. By virtue of the fact that there were two Irish animated shorts nominated for Oscars® there was growing evidence of the continual emergence of new Irish talent. Although the Irish animation sector was competitive, its size meant that the competing interests knew each other's work and often undertook projects for or with each other (for example, Brown Bag had previously completed work for TerraGlyph).

Conclusion

Brown Bag Films was one of the animation success stories to emerge from the ashes of the first phase of development of the animation sector in Ireland, which failed as a result of the collapse or withdrawal of large US employers. Brown Bag began almost by accident in 1994 and by 2004 had to make key strategic decisions and secure investment to lever profitability. Following eight years of business, numerous awards and a high national and international profile, Gaffney and O'Connell faced the considerable challenge of capitalising on their successes, and growing and developing their business internationally.

APPENDIX 1

Key Brown Bag milestones

December 1994	Established by producers/directors Cathal Gaffney and Darragh O'Connell.
	First production was *Peig* for RTE, Ireland's state-owned broadcasting company.
1995	Brown Bag worked on the co-production of the series 'Wolves, Witches and Giants' for Honeycomb animation (UK).
	Designed/directed animation on 'Fun Trucks' CD-ROM for Maris Multimedia (London). The project involved leading a team of 30 Russian animators.
1995–97	Co-produced CD-ROM titles 'Witches Academy', 'Ghost Castle' and 'Robin Hood' for Pixel Magic and Ravensburger.
1996	'Cartoon times': a series of political animations for RTE running every day for three weeks prior to the 1996 Irish general election.
1997	36 x one-minute pre-school series, 'Aesop's Fables', produced for RTE.
1998	Co-ordinated animation for 'The King and I' (Warner Brothers). Project involved coordination of work produced in studios throughout Europe, Korea and the US.
1998–99	Produced 24-part pre-school series 'Why?', which has sold to nearly 20 territories from China to the UK.
	Produced 'Barstool', a 7-part adult series for RTE.

1999–2000   Produced 'Taxi', 7 × 3-minute adult animation series for RTE.

Brown Bag Development Ltd established to develop slate of television and cinema projects with an international outlook.

1997–2001   Produced animation for TerraGlyph on CD-ROM titles: 'Looney Toones' (Warner Brothers), 'Hansel and Gretel' and 'Rumpelstiltskin'. Other titles with TerraGlyph included 'The Little Mermaid' and '102 Dalmations' (Walt Disney Interactive). Also produced over 30 TV commercials for Ireland and the Middle East. Undertook various digital media and e-Learning contracts.

2001 onwards   Produced award-winning 'The Last Elk', a six-minute film charting the decline of the last herd of Irish elk. Each elk is represented as a separate musical instrument. The last elk is hunted, and as it dies the music fades and the elk are extinct. It has featured in over 20 international film festivals.

'Racism' has received theatrical release in Irish cinemas through Buena Vista distribution. It is a tongue-in-cheek infomercial advertising a product heretofore unavailable in Ireland: 'Racism'.

'Give Up Yer Aul Sins' nominated for Best Short Animated Film award at the 74th Academy Awards. Based on real audio recordings of children in an inner-city Dublin school over 30 years ago. Shot as an animated documentary recording in sepia tones, it has won widespread acclaim for its innovative approach; one national Sunday newspaper described it as 'the most brilliant programme on RTE . . . a work of genius'.

Producing a second series of 'Why?' (28 × 2 min) for Channel 5 (UK).

Developing a slate of productions including 'Ronan Long Gets It Wrong', a 26 × 11-minute series based on the best-selling book for children and narrated by Ardal O'Hanlon.

Invested heavily in new media, website production and Flash animation. See www.brownbagfilms.com.

Continue to work on co-productions with Irish and European companies.

APPENDIX 2

Organisational structure

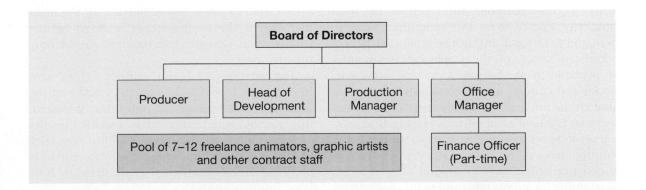

At the start of 2003 the Board of Directors comprised the Producer, Head of Development and a business consultant acting as Business Development Manager.

West Dunbartonshire Community Safety Partnership

Mik Wisniewski and Anna Frost

This case looks at an example of a strategic partnership in the UK public sector. Although the case is UK focused, it is interesting to observe the strategic pressures and changes starting to occur in other economies and sectors. This is occurring both in the public sector, where consortia developments are increasingly the norm, and in the private sector, where globalisation frequently requires more joint venture approaches either with other private sector companies or with public sector organisations.

● ● ●

From the banks of Loch Lomond to the shores of the Clyde

Scotland conjures up a variety of familiar images to tourists and visitors. Mountains and heather. Moorland and open-countryside. The lochs (lakes) and glens. Whisky! Rain! Sheep and hairy cows!

Without doubt, Scotland enjoys some of the best scenery in the world characterised in the lyrics of the famous traditional song 'The bonnie, bonnie banks of Loch Lomond'. In 2002 around 2.5 million visitors saw Loch Lomond and its surrounds. And yet most of those visitors would have seen little beyond the majestic scenery. The southern banks of Loch Lomond form part of the local authority area of West Dunbartonshire Council. Scotland's 32 local authorities (councils) have a significant impact on the people and communities of Scotland in most areas of political, economic, social and cultural life. The councils are responsible for the provision of a wide range of public services to Scotland's 5m citizens ranging from education to street cleaning to housing to leisure and cultural services to welfare services. Their combined net expenditure is around £7bn (€10bn), accounting for almost one third of the public sector expenditure and they employ almost 300,000 people amounting to about 15 per cent of the total Scottish workforce. The West Dunbartonshire council area stretches to the outskirts of Glasgow – Scotland's largest city with a population of around 600,000 – and covers an area of around 260 square kilometres with a resident population of around 93,000.

The area has much to commend it. Loch Lomond and the neighbouring Trossachs area was designated Scotland's first National Park in 2002 and provides a gateway for those wishing to enjoy the diversity of the landscape and the abundant wildlife. The Forth and Clyde Canal, re-opened in 2002, and the River Clyde Waterfront provide opportunities for both recreation and for economic development and urban renewal. The area is also strategically well-positioned with the main highway to the north-west of Scotland cutting through and Glasgow International airport only minutes away.

And yet the area is not without its problems in large part linked to its industrial past and the decline of those traditional industries. Shipbuilding, marine engineering, glass making, textiles are now long gone and the jobs and income they created leaving behind long-term socio-economic problems in the community. To illustrate, in 2001 West Dunbartonshire had:

This case was prepared by Mik Wisniewski, Senior Research Fellow, Strathclyde Business School & Anna Frost, formerly Community Safety Coordinator, West Dunbartonshire Council. It is intended as a basis for class discussion and not as an illustration of either good or bad management practice. © M. Wisniewski and A. Frost, 2004. Not to be reproduced or quoted without permission.

- the third highest number of single parents in Scotland;
- unemployment levels at 6.7 per cent, considerably higher than the Scottish average of 4.1 per cent;
- an estimated half of all children coming from households that suffer poverty;
- the lowest proportion of adults in Scotland obtaining secondary school (high school) qualifications;
- the fourth highest premature death rate in Scotland;
- an above-average number of adults classed as problem drug users.

Unsurprisingly, these problems impact on the perceptions of the local community as to how safe are their neighbourhoods. Local surveys in 2001 indicated that:

- there were increasing concerns about vandalism, theft and violence and street disorder;
- around a quarter of the community were very worried about becoming a victim of crime;
- domestic abuse was a major concern for many.

Community safety

West Dunbartonshire was not alone in having such problems in its community and this is one of the reasons why in the late 1990s the issue of community safety became an important one for both national and local government. Local councils were strategically well placed to address their community's concerns over safety given the range of activities they were involved in and their local base. However, it was also widely recognised that councils could not deliver safer communities by themselves given their limited resource base and the complex environment of community safety. Making communities safer is a key task for a whole range of agencies in the public, voluntary and private sectors and councils were encouraged to form community safety partnerships (strategic alliances) to bring relevant organisations together to develop an integrated strategic approach. The need for this can be illustrated with an example. A local community had recently been plagued by petty vandalism involving young people: graffiti was being spray-painted on walls, windows in empty properties were being broken, street lights were

being vandalised. Understandably the community was concerned. At first it might appear that this is down to the local police service to deal with, after all crimes and offences are being committed. However, the police by themselves may not be able to provide a long-term solution to the problem, other organisations also will need to contribute. The council may need to involve several of its services. Leisure services may need to be involved if there is a perceived shortage of leisure facilities and activities for young people in the area. Education services can help promote appropriate behaviour as part of the educational curriculum. Social services may need to support young offenders. Technical services may need to ensure a speedy repair service to vandalised property. Voluntary sector organisations such as youth organisations also have a role to play as do local businesses which need to try to ensure spray paint is not sold to under-age groups.

Clearly a strategic alliance is necessary between relevant organisations to ensure that everyone recognises community safety as a key strategic objective. It was for this reason that in 1999, the Scottish Executive published a document 'A Safer Scotland' which described government strategy for tackling crime and its causes, and identifies the way forward for building public confidence and safer communities. (The Scottish Executive is effectively the regional government for Scotland under the UK's devolution arrangements.) The Executive based the principles of 'A Safer Scotland' on the premise that 'public safety is of paramount concern and that everyone should feel safe in their community and their own home'. 'A Safer Scotland' was preceded by a partnership strategy for action on community safety, 'Safer Communities through Partnership', published following two consultative conferences involving local authorities, voluntary organisations and the business community. That strategy encourages local authorities and the police to take the lead in building safer communities by establishing local strategic partnerships involving public organisations, the private sector and voluntary bodies. Clearly, at a local level a number of opportunistic alliances were already in place, usually at an operational level and usually because of initiatives taken by a small number of individuals. The local police and the council's roads departments might be collaborating at reducing road traffic accidents. The local health service and the council's social services department might be working together to tackle drug abuse. The Executive's intent was to build on these informal, local partnerships at a more strategic level. The Executive also published good practice guidance on the key factors that would contribute to the success of such strategic partnerships. Amongst these were:

● developing a shared strategic vision between the partners;

● clarity of strategic goals and objectives;

● trust and openness between partners;

● equality between partners;

● clarifying roles and responsibilities so that expectations are clear and attainable;

● maintaining motivation and commitment.

The Partnership in West Dunbarton

West Dunbartonshire developed its first community safety strategy in 1997 and established a Community Safety Forum in 1999 (later renamed as the Partnership). The Forum was formally supported by the four key public sector agencies (the council, the police service, the fire service and the health service) and supported by a variety of other groups. However, the meetings of the Forum were sporadic and usually held to discuss specific and individual issues of concern that had arisen and there was no set work for partners arising out of Forum meetings. Ensuring continuity of attendance at Forum meetings was also difficult to achieve. In 2002 the Partnership appointed a Community Safety Officer with specific responsibility for coordinating the work of partners. It was recognised at this time that the Partnership was not working as effectively or as strategically as it needed to. Meetings frequently turned out to be 'talking shops' with little agreement on actions or the way forward. When decisions were taken they tended to be about operational issues rather than strategic. There was no shared view of strategic priorities across the partner agencies. Accordingly, the Partnership decided to undertake a strategic review of community safety in West Dunbarton and the Partnership itself. An external facilitator was used with experience of working with public sector strategic alliances. The overall purpose was to critically review the Partnership's plans, activities and performance. The primary outcome was to agree, and plan for, the key actions the Partnership

needs to take to ensure its continuing success particularly in the context of ensuring:

● all partners had a clear understanding of their respective roles and responsibilities from a strategic perspective;

● a clear decision-making process for setting strategic priorities;

● agreed criteria for the management and dispersal of funding;

● an agreed framework for evaluation and measurement of both operational and strategic performance.

The review process utilised a number of key strategic questions shown in Exhibit 1 with the main visible outcome being an agreed set of key actions for the Partnership to take forward. A less visible, but arguably more important outcome, was that the Partnership had been able to reach a consensus on the way forward. One of the key actions agreed was the need to review the existing Partnership strategy. This took place around an overall strategic process as illustrated in Exhibit 2. The Setting Direction stage involved the Partnership in considering its overall role and purpose and agreeing a new vision/mission statement, 'Working together for a safe and confident West Dunbartonshire', that all partners felt they could contribute to. This confirmed one of the observations made in the published guidance on community safety partnership working: 'Given the very different organisational styles and backgrounds of partnership staff, establishing a common vision of what the partnership aims to achieve . . . is vital. It should not be assumed that this will happen automatically.'

The Partnership also agreed key strategic goals based on stakeholder mapping and the strategic analysis that had already been completed. These were:

● to reduce crime and the fear of crime in our communities;

● to reduce substance misuse and related harm within our communities;

● to reduce accidents within our communities;

● to improve our strategic community safety partnership.

The first three goals were clearly externally facing – focusing on the needs of the community. The fourth goal was felt to be strategically important in terms of continuing to improve the strategic

Exhibit 1   Strategic review questions

Where are we now?

Deliverables

- What were the key deliverables the Partnership was set up originally to produce?
- What impact were we expected to have?
- What successes have we had?
- How do we know we've been successful in these areas?
- Why were we able to achieve success in these areas?
- What are the key areas where we have been less successful than we would have liked?
- What are the main reasons for our lack of success in each of these areas?

The Partnership

- Why are we still needed?
- Who are our main customers? What do they want/expect from us? Do we deliver what they expect? How can we do better?
- Running the Partnership: What do we do well? Why are we able to do these things well? What needs improvement?
- What are our key processes and how well do we do them?
- What value do we add as a Partnership?
- Who should our partners be? Why do we need them? Why do they need us?
- What does a SWOT of the Partnership look like?
- Which of these are critical to our future?

Where do we want to be?

- What do we see as the main challenges facing the Partnership in the future?
- What should our future role be? (Do we have/need a mission statement?)
- What impact do we want to have in the future?
- What do we have to get right for this role/impact (what are our critical success factors)?
- What will the indicators of our success be? How will we know we are successful?
- What will stop us achieving this impact?
- How do we manage/avoid these blocks and barriers?

How do we get there?

- Based on our discussions, what are the key changes the Partnership needs to make happen?
- How will we do this? Who will do this?

alliance between partners and to continue to improve common processes and systems necessary for effective Partnership working. The second stage of the process focused on 'Putting plans together' an area in which historically the Partnership had been weak. The Partnership members were introduced to the concept of strategy mapping and used this approach effectively to identify the overall strategic plan designed to achieve the strategic goals that had been established. Strategy maps are an integral part of developing a Balanced Scorecard and show visually the key strategies linked to the overall goals that have been set. Such maps can be highly effective at ensuring a robust strategic plan is developed and, importantly in this context, they allow the responsibilities and contributions of individual partner agencies to be identified. The strategy map also proved useful at showing the

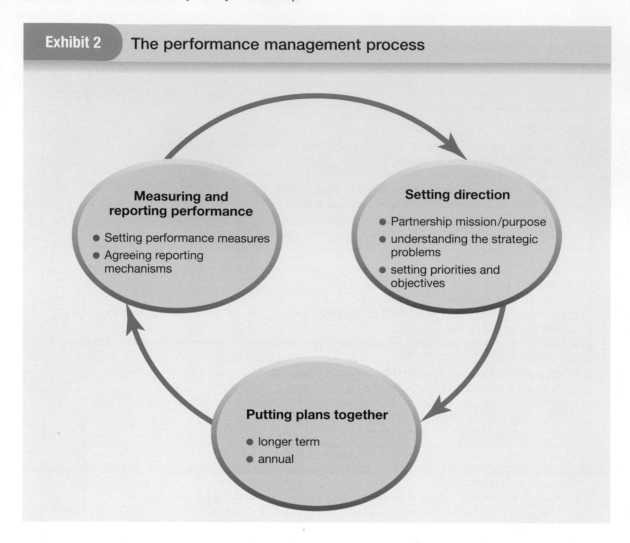

Exhibit 2   **The performance management process**

linkages and dependencies between the partner strategies, something that had been previously missing. The final stage involved 'Measuring performance' and the Partnership adopted a Balanced Scorecard approach to establishing a set of strategic performance measures visibly linked to its overall strategy. The Partnership also agreed the reporting mechanisms that should be in place so that the Partnership and the community could regularly review performance.

The process proved a challenging – yet productive – one for the Partnership. Many of the Partnership members had little formal experience of strategic thinking and strategic planning particularly on a partnership basis. However, the introduction of a robust, but flexible, approach to strategic planning proved very useful. It provided a

focus for discussion, it enabled a set of consensus agreements to be finalised and it provided an integrated framework for linking the different stages of the strategy process. As a number of the partners commented, this had been the first time the partnership had really had the opportunity or focus to share aspirations, ideas and concerns in an open and honest manner. The Partnership commented that there was now a real commitment to joint working in an atmosphere of trust and cooperation. The Partnership has continued to build on this approach and has achieved considerable success in terms of integrating strategic performance across the partners, delivering initiatives intended to improve community safety on the ground and attracting additional funding from the Scottish Executive.

GSK – a merger too far?

Bernardo Bátiz-Lazo

This case describes events leading to the creation of a global pharmaceutical giant and the early years of its performance while inviting readers to consider the process of growth through mergers and acquisitions as a general strategy. The case also looks at the expectations, deliberations and motivation of managers and stakeholders in doing so. The case invites readers to reflect on whether more mergers are to be the future of GlaxoSmithKline.

• • •

After a first round of merger talks collapsed acrimoniously in 1998, renewed interest in a merger between Glaxo Wellcome and SmithKline Beecham emerged when Jan Leschly announced his retirement from SmithKline Beecham in mid-1999. The announcement effectively removed a major barrier to the merger. Sir Richard Sykes, head of Glaxo Wellcome and destined to become chairman of the new colossus, said about his company's determination to do a deal:

> This is where two big successful organisations come together, not to protect future earnings growth but actually to increase critical mass to really outperform the industry. . . . The more effort, the more money, and the more power you can put to research, the stronger the company is going to be.[1]

Sykes's statement summarised how Europe's pharmaceutical companies have been locked in a high stakes multibillion dollar struggle with their US rivals to stay in business in the 21st century. This struggle is associated with increased takeover activity and pharmaceutical companies seeking economies of scale to finance escalating research and development budgets. For instance, at the time of the creation of GlaxoSmithKline in 2000, the Association of the British Pharmaceutical

Industry (ABPI) estimated the cost of bringing a new drug to market to be in the region of £350m (≈ €525m). Three years later that estimate had ballooned to £500m. Not surprisingly the slowdown in new drugs coming to market was a major concern. In 2001 only 24 genuinely new drugs were launched in the US, considered a poor outcome of so costly an investment by so many companies. The year 2002 was even worse with only 17 genuinely new drugs introduced. Poor returns to R&D

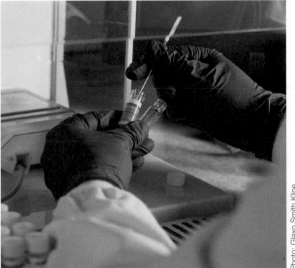

Photo: Glaxo Smith Kline

---

[1] *Pharmaceutical Executive,* May 1999, p. 37.

This case was prepared by Bernardo Bátiz-Lazo, London South Bank University. It is intended for class discussion rather than as an illustration of either good or bad management practice. Research assistance from Alicia Arribas and comments from Simon Ling, Stella Richter and MBA graduates of the Open University are gratefully acknowledged. © B. Bátiz-Lazo, 2004. Not to be reproduced or quoted without permission.

investment came despite sharp increases in spending on research and development by the main companies, which according to Goldman Sachs, the US investment bank, reached $35bn in 2001. This was double the figure for 1997 and nearly triple the 1992 investment.

Pharmaceutical companies on both sides of the Atlantic had been trying to finance spiralling research and development budgets through amalgamation. In the endless race to keep up with transatlantic rivals, Pfizer announced a $60bn take-over of US-based Pharmacia. This created a new world pharmaceutical giant, as the deal rocketed Pfizer's share of world market sales from 6.7 per cent to just over 10 per cent, compared with GlaxoSmithKline's 6.9 per cent. Green light for the amalgamation was given in 2003. As a result Pfizer's share of the lucrative US market increased from 10 per cent to almost 15 per cent. With this move Pfizer effectively became the market leader in the US as well as in Europe (where it was previously fourth), Japan (previously third) and Latin America.

Merger activity took place while pharmaceutical companies were seeking economies of scale in research and development at the same time that associated marketing costs of new products were growing quickly. However, little evidence had emerged to suggest bigger research programmes were better (least of all after a merger) to replenish the pipeline. Indeed, the Pharmacia deal put Pfizer way ahead of GlaxoSmithKline at a time when many questioned the ability of the latter to generate and sustain revenue growth. GlaxoSmithKline was struggling with patent expiries and a lack of new drugs. There were some 125 promising compounds in the pipeline but in the short term the company was being forced to increase the number of licensing agreements.

In fact, between 1998 and 2003, GlaxoSmithKline had bought licences to market 40 drugs from other companies (effectively doubling the number of licences acquired between 1988 and 1997). This compared negatively with the average for the industry's top 20 companies which was 31. Not surprisingly in the second quarter of 2003 GlaxoSmithKline's share price slumped to its lowest level in five years (when considering pre-merger stock market valuations or its lowest ever as a standalone company). See Exhibit 1.

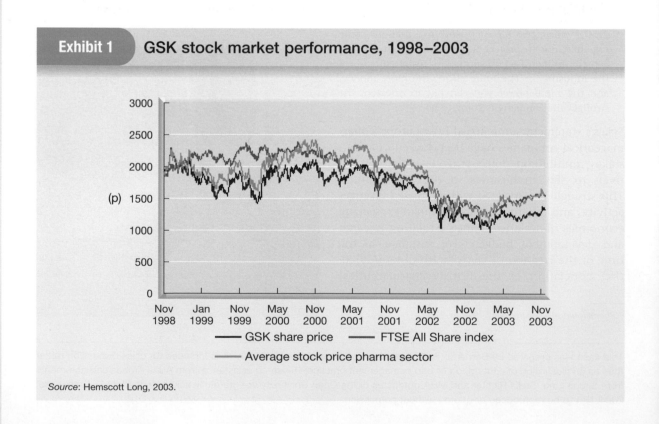

Exhibit 1   GSK stock market performance, 1998–2003

Legend: GSK share price — FTSE All Share index — Average stock price pharma sector

Source: Hemscott Long, 2003.

Growth through amalgamation

The companies giving birth to GlaxoSmithKline themselves resulted from amalgamation. On the one hand, SmithKline Beecham was created in 1989 through the merger of Beecham and SmithKline Beckman. On the other hand, Glaxo and Wellcome amalgamated in 1995.

SmithKline Beecham

The creation of SmithKline Beecham (SB)[2] resulted from two companies running out of internal options: SmithKline Beckman (SKB) had failed in its efforts to replace the income stream of its main blockbuster drug (Tagamet) but had an aggressive sales force in the US. Beecham was essentially a consumer goods company that had been successful in early research on antibiotics. Beecham was very 'old school British': for example, some buildings had separate dining rooms for different grades of staff and managers and there was even a 'members only' bar at Beecham House (i.e. head office). Beecham had neither the mass nor the competencies to become a serious pharmaceutical player but both Beecham and SKB felt threatened as potential takeover targets.

The amalgamation of Beecham and SKB was lengthy and relied on a combination of benchmarking (i.e. continuous improvement efforts) and process re-engineering. Top management invested substantial time and effort to create a new culture (under the 'SB Way' banner, also called the 'simply better way'). This initiative introduced new methods to measure and reward individual performance. At the same time, managers worked together saving the best of each group: for instance, the more street-wise and marketing-orientated Consumer Healthcare people (largely from Beecham) were encouraged to cross-fertilise with their pharma colleagues. The 'Leadership and Development Review' was set up to facilitate that this sort of cross-fertilisation sat nicely alongside the career development plans of staff. Throughout this process the more laid-back British approach of the Beecham group was replaced by a process-orientated way of working.

By 1994 there was a real feeling of success about SB. Processes, procedures and corporate culture had come together in harmony. There was a 'reward and celebrate' culture and SB people in general were genuinely proud to work for their company. The company had grown and developed critical mass in new geographical markets, especially Central and Eastern Europe. The amalgamation really felt like a merger of equals and the company went to great lengths to show this to the outside world. The share price just rocketed. This also benefited employees that had taken advantage of the very generous 'buy one get one free' share plan. Indeed, the canteen at headquarters even had a screen with the share price and people talked about it obsessively.

Through amalgamation both Beecham and SmithKline Beckman tried to keep up with critical mass in R&D, as the combined research budget doubled, but total R&D expenditure still lagged behind the likes of top firms such as Glaxo, which was outspending them two to one. At the same time, some managers felt the SB Way initiative was running out of steam.

Glaxo Wellcome

Glaxo Wellcome resulted from the merger of two leading UK pharmaceuticals in 1995. In the mid 1970s, Glaxo was a small British firm with its origins in the dried milk business and had most of its sales in antibiotics, respiratory drugs and nutritional supplements. During the 1980s Glaxo grew organically and rapidly thanks to the commercial success of its R&D efforts. By 1994 Glaxo had reached the top industry position in sales as they totalled £5,656 million or 3.6 per cent of the world market with earnings emerging from a strong presence in Europe and the US. Glaxo managers effectively engineered a takeover of Wellcome, as the Wellcome Foundation (the largest non-profit medical institution in the UK) owned a 40 per cent stake in Glaxo's Zantac and 39 per cent of Wellcome's share capital. Zantac was an anti-ulcer blockbuster product and the world's best selling drug, commanding 35 per cent of the antiulceran market and achieving record sales of £2.4bn in 1994. Zantac had been launched at the beginning of the 1980s and became the top product even though it was second to market and 60 per cent more expensive than SmithKline's Tagamet.

---

[2] When SmithKline Beecham was created the 'official and 'correct' abbreviation for the then new company was 'SB'. Reference to just 'SmithKline' was avoided as this gave the impression that Beecham had been taken over. Preventing the alienation of Beecham people was also why the abbreviation was a new 'SB' rather than the old 'SKB' used by SmithKline Beckman.

Zantac contributed 43 per cent of Glaxo's revenues, resulting in a large part of Glaxo's growth being based on its success. The problem was that Zantac's patent expired in 1997. At the same time, the Wellcome Foundation was amenable to the merger as it offered possibilities to dissipate risk and to ensure that resources would be available for basic research.

Wellcome was known for its 'academic' approach to pharmaceuticals, with strong science but weak marketing. In 1996 and six months after the merger of Glaxo with Wellcome, managers claimed that the newly created Glaxo Wellcome was fully integrated. Its sales volume ranking was the first in the world, it was the third largest company by market capitalisation in London and the world's largest pharmaceutical research firm with 54,000 employees.

But the reality was that a severe clash had occurred: on the one hand, Wellcome had rather *laissez-faire* or laid back management style, that is, it was oblivious to budget control but focused on science and medical applications. A style that Wellcome people saw as positive in fostering innovation. On the other hand was Glaxo's hard-nosed, commercial and control-driven culture. Whereas the styles of Beecham and SmithKline Beckman co-existed in the formation of SB since both had a corporate/team approach, Glaxo's culture predominated and obliterated Welcome's benevolent style. Things worsened by the fact that few former Wellcome executives survived the takeover to serve the new Glaxo Wellcome. Top managers endeavoured to rationalise the overall organisation and introduce economies of scale in R&D activities. But the truth was, however sad, that in spite of complements in the product portfolio top executives had great difficulty holding the new company together.

By the end of the 1990s, some analysts were sceptical on whether the merger of Glaxo with Wellcome had produced any synergies at all. It was true that sales of revitalised Wellcome products through Glaxo's marketing muscle had helped to avoid slipping in the rankings, but it was also true that the drugs pipeline was unimpressive and many new products had failed to live up to expectations. The merger had, indeed, brought Glaxo presence in therapeutic areas that it had not exploited before (e.g. antivirals), while Wellcome benefited from greater financial discipline and focus. This resulted in analysts wondering whether costs had really been brought under control, whether Glaxo Wellcome had relied too much on disposals to flatter its earnings performance and, on balance, many were disappointed that augmented R&D facilities had done little to replenish the pipeline by producing new potential blockbusters.

The birth of GlaxoSmithKline (GSK)

The marriage of Glaxo Wellcome and SmithKline came at a time when the overwhelming industry response to the need for critical mass in R&D and global marketing presence was a wave of mergers and previously unheard-of hostile acquisitions leading to amalgamation. The frenzy of takeover activity included the amalgamation of Hoechst (Germany) and Rhône-Poulenc (France) into Aventis, a merger which reported a meagre 13 per cent annual increase in profits between 1999 and 2000. Aventis' financial performance was amongst the lowest in the industry but typical for a drug company that had merged and had realised as much cost-saving as possible. Other products of amalgamation in the late 1990s included Novartis (1996), AstraZeneca (1999) and Sanofi-Synthélabo (1999) in Europe. Amalgamation in the US included the creation of Pharmacia & Upjohn (1995), the acquisition of Monsanto by Pharmacia & Upjohn to create Pharmacia (2000) and the acquisitions of Warner-Lambert (2000) and Pharmacia (2003) by Pfizer.

In 1998, the merger between the two top British drug companies seemed virtually complete with Glaxo Wellcome shareholders having 59.5 per cent of the new group, leaving 40.5 per cent to SmithKline Beecham (SB) shareholders. With a market capitalisation of US$110bn, the deal would create the biggest pharmaceutical company and the world's third biggest corporation. The chief executive for the new group was going to be Jan Leschly, a former international pro-tennis star turned pharmaceutical executive and SB's CEO. The new chairperson would be Sir Richard Sykes, CEO of Glaxo Wellcome. But after a weekend meeting of intense negotiations and to everyone's surprise, the deal was called off. The following trading day $6.6bn or 10 per cent of SB's market capitalisation was knocked off while the stock price of Glaxo Wellcome lost 13 per cent.

Formally, Glaxo Wellcome's directors indicated that they were not prepared to proceed on the agreed basis. Informally, SmithKline Beecham directors claimed that Glaxo Wellcome reneged on the original agreement that Leschly would be leader of the new colossus. Glaxo Wellcome executives never challenged this version of the events. Sykes also rejected Leschly's suggestion of spinning off the entire research effort into a separate capital raising company. Sykes and his team considered the plan too radical as it would sacrifice innovation in the pursuit of short-term cost reductions.

Both Leschly and Sykes had worked together in the past and some sort of rivalry seemed to have emerged since then. Leschly's patriarchal management style and SB's financial rigour and performance-related culture seemed to have clashed with Sykes's passionate (sometimes even messianic) belief in science. But it appears that if Leschly and his colleagues had retreated on the CEO issue, the merger would have gone through, and Leschly would have been $100m richer – the value of his shares and stock options in SB, according to an estimate published in *The Economist*.

Another explanation offered for Leschly's bitter reaction against the possibility that he might not be the chief executive of the new group was based on matters of principle and dignity. As CEO of SmithKline Beecham and before that as the CEO who delivered Squibb to Bristol-Myers, Leschly had done well financially. With or without the merger with Glaxo Wellcome he had already amassed enough for him and his family to fulfil any conceivable material wants. At the same time, Sykes and his management board disliked Lechly's management style and feared the merger would turn into a takeover by SB people. Glaxo Wellcome's management board also wanted to break with tradition (as Skyes had not led the initial move to merge) and claim the top post, because Glaxo Wellcome was the biggest of the proposed partners in terms of market capitalisation, products, and R&D expenditure.

The fact remained that after the failure to merge SmithKline Beecham still lacked the R&D funds to pursue its many leads for new drugs. Other major drug companies continued with their plans and merged. Later that year Glaxo Wellcome still remained without partner as managers also failed in their talks to amalgamate with Bristol-Myers Squibb while SB's had two other unsuccessful merger attempts (including one with American Home Products).

After a first round of merger talks collapsed acrimoniously in 1998, renewed interest in a merger between Glaxo Wellcome and SmithKline Beecham emerged after Jan Leschly announced his retirement as SB's CEO in mid-1999. The announcement effectively removed a major barrier to the merger. As part of the deal in the year 2000, Sir Richard Sykes agreed to become non-executive Chairman, a post of influence but with little management responsibilities.

Jean-Pierre Garnier was appointed the Chief Executive of GSK (as the company was commonly referred to in the industry). Known simply as 'JP', he had been raised in Normandy, where he grew steadily on a diet of British and US movies and music (he still claims Jimi Hendrix as a patron saint). Garnier gained a master's degree and a doctorate from France's Université Louis Pasteur before accepting a Fulbright scholarship to pursue an MBA at Stanford University. Except for a few years in various parts of Europe, Garnier's career had kept him in the US ever since. He joined SB in 1990 as president of the pharmaceutical division. Although his early training in France was in pharmacology, he made his name in marketing, and was credited with much of the success of SB's leading products, specifically Paxil, taken for depression, and Augmentin, an antibiotic.

Garnier had been Leschly's right hand man for three years as Chief Operating Officer and was clearly seen as a 'bad cop' or hatchet man with Leschly playing the 'good cop'. Garnier's style could not have been more different than that of Jan Leschly. Although externally Leschly was perceived as 'patriarchal', he managed to keep good relations with the City. Leschly was also good at communication internally but he was more than that: he was truly charismatic and managed to engage people. He was popular with staff and endeavoured to 'make the job fun'. His oft repeated mantra was 'if you're not keeping score, you're not practising', echoing the performance driven culture. In contrast Garnier was known to be tough with people, highly attentive to detail and was perceived as cold and sometimes even arrogant. Garnier moved to number one after Leschly announced his retirement and was an acceptable candidate for the management team at Glaxo Wellcome.

British and European regulators were swift to give clearance to the emergence of GSK. However the Federal Trade Commission (FTC), the US competition regulator, forced the divestiture of medicines for chemotherapy-induced nausea and herpes with annual sales of almost $400m. At that point managers felt the most substantive issues had been dealt with. However, the FTC continued to have concerns on the merged company's perceived domination of the US smoking-cessation market and this caused a second delay in taking the merger forward. The concerns of the FTC were based on the fact that, at the time, SB had the leading over-the-counter brand and Glaxo Wellcome the only approved prescription drug to help smokers quit. Two key products which the FTC felt would give the combined company control over 90 per cent of that market.

For some observers, managers at GlaxoSmithKline failed to envision that creating the world's biggest pharmaceutical firm could involve a complex regulatory submission process. Others argued that the arrogant approach by the new company management team to the FTC was to blame. Yet others felt that regulators were burdened with the increased number of mega-mergers (in pharmaceuticals and elsewhere) taking place at the end of the 1990s. The influence of the run-up to the US presidential election in 2000 was also felt as candidates put the spotlight on healthcare spending.

Managers thought that some regulatory delays were anticipated but not that regulatory concerns in the US over monopoly power of the new group in certain therapy classes would consume more than 10 months of negotiations and backtrack the merger process twice. Furthermore, lengthy negotiations with US regulators prevented the early implementation of the new organisational structure. Executives were prevented from specifying how economies of scale in labs would be achieved, how performance would improve or how cooperation across business units would be implemented. Delays in getting regulatory clearance also prevented managers from stopping speculation that the company could eventually split up into separate business or announce how they would reckon with incompatible information technology platforms. All this, in turn, threatened staff's morale and increased the potential of a 'brain drain' of middle managers. These developments were worrying for a corporation which had yet to be born and which was already involved in a process full of mishaps.

A new structure for R&D

Cost reductions

In January 2000, when Glaxo Wellcome amalgamated with SmithKline Beecham at the height of the merger boom, the move was explained in visionary terms. As one of the key points of the merger, managers considered building operational headquarters in the US while corporate headquarters would remain in the UK. The new company's increasing tendencies to a US management style and reliance on US markets puzzled many, as Britain was home for both originating companies and the UK was one of the world's leading centres for the research, development, and manufacture of prescription medicines. However, Garnier argued that GSK had 99 manufacturing sites in 44 countries (including the UK). Moreover, ever since the merger was announced, Garnier maintained that whilst the new company was proud of its UK roots:

> . . . a world-class competitor cannot operate all its functions from a market that represents only 6 to 8 per cent of its existence. The US, by contrast, accounts for 45 per cent of the global pharmaceutical market.[3]

As with any other merger of companies in related areas there was potential for cost reductions. Top executives anticipated the combined company would save an annualised £1bn after three years. These savings would come on top of previously announced restructuring at both companies, expected to cut a combined £570m a year. Initially analysts of pharmaceutical companies at investment banks were disappointed by the planned savings. Most estimated the figure to be between £1.1bn and £1.5bn, and expected some sort of immediate disposal of factories, reduction of intermediate capacity or outsourcing plan. After two and half years cost savings had in fact amounted to £1.8bn and measures taken two years earlier were beginning to bear fruit. By 2003, cost reductions had taken GSK's trading profit margin to 35 per cent, although it remained close to the 2002 level when excluding £87m from disposals. Continued enthusiasm for cost savings as the main fuel for increasing pre-tax profits in 2002 and 2003 resulted in Jean-Pierre Garnier hinting that he was considering a second stage of cost cutting.

Breaking up the 'pipeline'

Combining Glaxo Wellcome with SB also promised to deliver the most cost efficient research organisation in the pharmaceutical industry. Expected savings of £250m from combined R&D operations were destined to be ploughed back into

---

[3] *Chemical Market Reporter*, January 2000, p. 24.

R&D efforts. The company would kick off into life with an annual research budget of £2.4bn, the largest in the world after that of Pfizer. Analysts were encouraged by potential pay-offs that could come from the complementary research skills of the two companies. In other words, Glaxo Wellcome's investment in technology to automate the chemistry of developing drugs combined well with SB's leadership in genomics[4] (which promised a wealth of drug development opportunities). In fact, SmithKline Beecham had an existing pipeline of four promising drugs in the final stages of development. This was indeed very attractive to Glaxo Wellcome, who relied heavily on the generic sales of its blockbuster drug Zantac.

The new company then revealed plans to re-engineer its R&D and marketing operations. At the time, Garnier considered that organising 15,000 scientists across several time zones, with an annual budget of billions of pounds, would require a radical new structure. However rivals such as Pfizer, Novartis or Aventis, which had already restructured their core operations, questioned how radical Garnier's plan really was. Garnier was philosophical about such struggles, he considered that the ultimate success in the pharmaceutical industry lay in innovating for the future, not fighting over the past. He also frankly admitted that his company's approach was not guaranteed to deliver, but he was absolutely certain that the old way would no longer do.

The plan considered breaking up discovery efforts through a combination of centralisation and decentralisation. Investments to generate new chemical entities (NCE) would concentrate on traditional activities and genetics while aiming to develop economies of scale. Discovery efforts would then be broken into six autonomous sub-units, aiming to maintain the excitement of a small discovery outfit. They were to remain small enough to be creative and innovative, without the dead-weight associated with the bureaucracy of a large global player. Drug development (including clinical trials) and marketing would again be coordinated by the central organisation.

Maintaining a single effort to discover NCEs sought to apply scarce skills and expensive equipment across a range of diseases, two administrative

divisions were created, one in Genetics Research and the other to look at the traditional Drug Discovery Research. The emphasis on genetic research followed the new company inheriting substantial investments in the use of genomics in drug discovery: at its formation, GlaxoSmithKline had over 500 patent filings for genomics-based drugs. Actually, just as merger proceedings evolved, SmithKline Beecham brought to clinical testing a genomic-based drug to treat obesity and one to treat hypertension.

As mentioned, out of the middle section of the pipeline six sub-units were created in 2000 (one in Italy, two in the UK and three in the US). A seventh Centre of Excellence for Drug Discovery (CEDD) was created in 2003 to concentrate on bio-pharmaceuticals, a field where GSK was progressing a growing number of chemical compounds in the early stages of the pipeline. The CEDDs effectively organised the efforts of the 24 R&D sites across the world in existence prior to the merger. They worked semi-autonomously and competed to attract financial resources from head office (and eventually from venture capitalists and even the stock market).

The seven sub-units were empowered to use compounds discovered within internal early research divisions, brought in from academia or from external biotechnology groups. It was hoped that as a result of the plan, the CEDDs would avoid the hassle of bureaucracy, associated with a large global player, while maintaining agility, creativity, entrepreneurial spirit and individual accountability in a key part of the drug discovery process. There was an expectation that talent would be attracted by emulating the culture at biotechnology firms, including the introduction of big share option packages through which scientists receive royalties on the sale of medicines they helped to invent.

GSK's structure also considered clinical trials and marketing had to be undertaken on a massive scale, often across continents, and simultaneously complying with strict regulatory conditions. Scale at this last stage of the pipeline aimed to achieve corporate control and uniformity as well as capitalise on global reach. For instance, shortly after the merger was announced, two licensing agreements were signed by SmithKline Beecham while looking to strengthen links with the Japanese pharmaceutical sector. Since marketing partnerships were seen as the only way to enter some markets (particularly for non-Americans to enter

---

[4] Genomics, the study of genes and their function, promised to increase treatment effectiveness while limiting side effects by identifying people who would definitely respond to a specific medicine.

the US or for non-Japanese to enter Japan) the deals could become very important to make the best of the new organisation. Alliances expanded in markets outside the US and Europe. For instance in India, where a deal was signed in 2003 to collaborate with a local company, called Ranbaxy, in the development of NCEs. Interestingly, Ranbaxy and GSK often came head to head in the sales of generics in the US market.

From plan to action

Effectiveness of R&D

For all its efforts and fanfare the jury was still out on the relative success of the new R&D and marketing structure. (See financial performance in Appendix.) There had been little time between 2000 and 2003 for 'the dust to settle'. Nevertheless, from the start observers were sceptical as to actual degree of autonomy that would be granted to the seven 'internal biotech units'. There was also scepticism that the CEDDs plus the global platforms for drug discovery, clinical trials and marketing would actually deliver increased productivity.

At the time of the creation of GSK there was significant overlap in the product portfolio of the amalgamating companies (both being weak in cancer and cardiovascular diseases but strong in gastrointestinal, antibiotics and nausea prevention drugs). Only 7 per cent of Glaxo Wellcome's sales depended on drugs whose US patents expired before 2006 as compared to SB's 33 per cent. GlaxoSmithKline was therefore born with assured income streams given patent protection and the fact that no single drug accounted for more than 12 per cent of sales. Thanks to this, GSK was confident to avoid the 'sudden-death syndrome' that afflicts some companies when their blockbuster loses protection. Assured income streams also gave GSK managers some slack time to test the efficacy of the 'radical' new organisational structure. In 2002, however, GSK only had 42 new chemical compounds in early-stage clinical trials. Few of these would actually make it to the market and questions were being raised as to whether the company might or might not maintain its growth rate while (eventually successful) drugs slowly made their way to market.

Between 2000 and 2003, the company did launch a few interesting medicines but an increasing number of them were licensed from other firms, and none were considered blockbusters. Internally, during the first two to three years R&D people had felt as if in limbo. The number of re-organisations in the way of implementing the new structure effectively meant absence of direction: for instance, the forming and reforming of teams, changes in location, alterations and delays in plans associated with the new global organisational structure only lengthen the time to take products to market.

In 2003 the company held a *research day* to discuss promising drug candidates with analysts and investors – the first time it had done so since the merger in 2000 that created the company. The meeting was crucial for GSK's management team as it needed to reassure investors, anxious about its long-term growth prospects, that GSK had potential blockbuster drugs in the pipeline. While GSK's management team had been adept at cutting costs since the merger, questions remained about its ability to convert exciting research into marketable drugs after a history of disappointments.

During the *research day* GSK declared that it had 147 projects in clinical development, spanning a variety of therapeutic areas and encompassing a number of pioneering approaches to treating patients in need. The 147 projects included 82 new chemical entities (NCEs), 45 product line extensions (PLEs), and 20 vaccines. The company had 30 more NCEs in the pipeline than in 2001, and had increased the number of NCEs in Phase II and III/registration from 23 in 2001 to 44 in 2003. GSK's goal was to bring more than 20 NCEs to Phase III development between 2004 and 2007, leading to an anticipated record number of filings between 2004 and 2009 many of which, the company said, with the potential to reach blockbuster status.

The risk for GSK, however, was that investors remained unconvinced. According to Max Hermann, analyst at ING Barings, during the presentation GSK's management had '. . . four or five interesting products to talk about . . . and in the past, they had a bad record at taking drugs from phase III trials to market.'[5]

The spirit of GSK

In spite of promises that synergy in R&D would 'turn the corner' of decreased productivity plaguing

---

[5] *Financial Times*, 3 December 2003.

the industry, three years on there was little evidence of success. Indeed, because of a thin late stage pipeline GSK had become dependent on licensed products such as Levitra – Bayer's impotence treatment – and cost savings to lift short-term growth. Not surprisingly Garnier was increasingly being asked by the media as to whether his company might consider another merger. He would shrug off these questions alleging his company already had everything needed to succeed:

> Miracles don't exist, but you will see that R&D has changed at GlaxoSmithKline. It has taken hard work and painful choices.[6]

Garnier and the senior management team had made an effort to come close to employees: e-mails could be sent directly to him while responses were placed for all to read in the company's intranet. They felt efforts to combine both cultures under the *Spirit of GKS* banner had been successful. Other initiatives included an improved benefits package (internally called *Total Reward*) which brought all forms of remuneration under one programme – including a favourable share purchase scheme and links between performance to pay and bonus.

Some managers and particularly those outside the US and the UK, however, felt there was evidence that, after three years, the company was still in desperate need of a distinctive identity: the different management philosophies of the two merged companies were still much alive. So much so that specific advice was often at hand on how to deal with the former Glaxo or former SB employee. Getting people to work to common processes was also a 'problem': managers, for instance, would agree on a way forward during a meeting but on returning to their sites would carry on as before and allow people to stick to their Glaxo or SB way of doing things.

Some felt that the added time needed to dissipate differences in management style plus other teething problems was allowing bureaucracy to run rampant and all this was getting in the way of long term change. Gossiping about potential further cost cuts, possibilities of more business units were turned into autonomous companies and indeed the phantom of a new merger were all very distracting for some employees. In spite of internal differences and unease, people got on with the job. GSK did portray a coherent image

to the outside world thanks to consistency at the business unit level. Moreover, to the eternal question of 'How to respond to increased competitive pressure?' (that is, whether after each new merger deal respond with matching amalgamations or risk falling behind in the race for market share) GSK people retorted:

> Where would we be if we hadn't merged? Would we be able to do all the things we do today?[7]

At the same time, GSK's choices in the areas of corporate governance and corporate social responsibility had acted in ways that both enhanced and damaged the company's overall reputation. See Box 1.

Commentators wondered if the shareholders of GlaxoSmithKline would continue to endure disappointing results. Should GSK look for a new amalgamation? And if so, who? Accounting anomalies followed by a government investigation ruled out a number of potential partners in the US (including Bristol-Myers Squibb, Elan Corporation, Merk & Co and Eli Lilly's). Another possibility was looking in Europe: for instance considering amalgamating with AstraZeneca, the Anglo-Swedish pharmaceutical. But AstraZeneca's share price was at least 30 per cent overvalued (trading at 23 times earnings, compared with an industry average of 15 and GlaxoSmithKline's 13 times earnings). Switzerland's Roche was a poor alternative because Roche had been approached by different potential suitors, both formally and informally, but Roche's in-built defence mechanism had repeatedly spurned merger attempts. However Novartis, the other Swiss giant, could be attractive as in 2004 was outbid by a medium-sized French drugs group, Sanofi-Synthélabo, in a bitter, highly politicised and very public battle for its Franco-German rival, Aventis.[8]

In light of mounting pressure to amalgamate yet again, Jean-Pierre Garnier, the chief executive of GlaxoSmithKline, pointed out that his company made profits of £3.7bn in the first six months of 2003, up 9 per cent on 2002, or 18 per cent if the effects of the depreciating dollar versus sterling were stripped out. Turnover was up 6 per cent in constant currency terms, with disappointment

[6] *Financial Times*, 1 May 2003.

[7] Personal interview, 30 October 2003.
[8] The deal effectively created a 'French champion' by placing the new company ahead of Novartis but behind Pfizer and GlaxoSmithKline as the deal created the world's third-largest pharmaceuticals company by sales.

BOX 1 Governance and social responsibility

Between 2000 and 2003, the corporate governance and corporate social responsibilities were a mixed bag of good and bad news for the top team at GlaxoSmithKline (GSK). On the bright side the company had developed and met very specific goals for global corporate environmental standards. Another positive development came in 2003 when, for the second consecutive year, GSK was recorded as giving the largest amount to global good causes of any FTSE 100 company. This as GSK's programme of involvement in the community was worth at least 2.4 per cent of pre-tax profit in 2002.

On the less bright side, ineffective public relations left GSK open to accusations of profiteering. The company held the patent for a key drug in the treatment of HIV/AIDS. The issue of how best to provide treatment in Africa resulted in a very public and very long clash between GSK managers and the South African government, Aids-Africa relief activists (including Nelson Mandela) and even some of GSK's institutional investors.

Even more damning, however, was the whole issue of the ultimate pay awarded to Garnier in 2003. A pay package (including severance payment and pension entitlements) worth at least £11m resulted in a long and highly publicised row with both small and institutional investors. After suffering an unprecedented defeat in the annual general meeting, Sir Christopher Hogg referred the matter for independent advice to ensure recommendations for remuneration were in line with best practice. Garnier argued that pay recommendations should be similar to those at other 'blue-chip' companies in the US and highlighted that the deal would also affect the remuneration of hundreds of managers throughout the company. At the same time, institutional investors complained that the proposed targets for Garnier were too lenient and wanted them explicitly linked to GSK's performance compared with that of other pharmaceuticals, rather than to the economy as a whole. The independent advisors eventually found a formula that satisfied shareholders, Garnier and other managers at GSK.

only in the consumer goods business. Moreover, GSK was strengthening its presence in the global market for over-the-counter (OTC) drugs, was confident on its portfolio of new drugs and hoped the letter would reassure investors. Garnier expected the immediate future of GSK would see a string of announcements describing a drug development pipeline positively alive with exciting new products. However, somehow that message had proved hard to sell.

APPENDIX
Summary of Financial Performance, 2000–2003

	Annual Turnover (Sales year ended 31 December)			
	2000 £m*	2001 £m	2002 £m	2003 £m
Region				
Pharmaceuticals				
US	7,705	9,037	9,797	9,410
Europe	4,268	4,561	4,701	5,114
Rest of the world	3,456	3,607	3,497	3,657
Total	15,429	17,205	17,995	18,181
Therapy class				
Pharmaceuticals				
Central nervous system	3,279	4,007	4,511	4,455
Respiratory	2,789	3,537	3,987	4,417
Anti-virals	1,899	2,128	2,299	2,349
Anti-bacterials	2,472	2,604	2,210	1,815
Metabolic and gastro-intestinal	589	875	960	1,079
Vaccines	842	948	1,080	1,123
Oncology and emesis	710	838	977	1,001
Cardiovascular	463	591	661	771
Other pharma	1,939	1,677	1,310	1,171
Divested products	447	n/a	n/a	n/a
Total	15,429	17,205	17,995	18,181
Consumer health				
Over the counter medicines	1,454	1,603	1,586	1,556
Oral care	642	1,106	1,052	1,082
Nutritional healthcare	535	575	579	622
Divested products	19	n/a	n/a	n/a
Total	2,650	3,284	3,217	3,260
Turnover	18,079	20,489	21,212	21,441

* £1 = approx. €1.5.

Source: Annual reports.

Restructuring Sony

Vivek Gupta and Konakanchi Prashanth

The electronics and media giant Sony was struggling through the late 1990s and early part of the 21st century. With each disappointment, it seemed that Sony's management launched another restructuring of the company. By 2003, commentators were beginning to ask whether restructuring was part of the solution or part of the problem. How should Sony be managing its strategic renewal?

• • •

As conditions change, Sony has to change accordingly, because their conventional strategy won't transcend to the Internet-enabled model.[1]

Mitchell Levy, author of
The Value Framework

Introduction

For the first quarter ending 30 June 2003, Japan-based Sony Corporation (Sony)[2] stunned the corporate world by reporting a decline in net profit of 98 per cent. Sony reported a net profit of ¥9.3 million compared to ¥1.1 billion for the same quarter in 2002. Sony's revenues fell by 6.9 per cent to ¥1.6 trillion for the corresponding period. Analysts were of the opinion that Sony's expenditure on its restructuring initiatives had caused a significant dent in its profitability. In the financial year 2002–03, Sony had spent a massive ¥100bn on restructuring (≈ £500m; ≈ €750m). Moreover, the company had already announced in April 2003

about its plans to spend another ¥1 trillion on a major restructuring initiative in the next three years.

Analysts criticised Sony's management for spending a huge amount on frequent restructuring of its consumer electronics business, which accounted for nearly two-thirds of Sony's revenues. In 2003, the sales of the consumer electronics division fell by 6.5 per cent. Notably, Sony's business operations were restructured five times in the past nine years. Analysts opined that Sony's excessive focus on the maturing consumer electronics business (profit margin below 1 per cent in 2002–03), coupled with increasing competition in the consumer electronics industry was severely affecting its profitability.

However, Sony's officials felt that the restructuring measures were delivering the desired results. According to them, the company had shown a significant jump in its profitability in the financial year 2002–03. Sony reported a net income of ¥115.52bn in the fiscal 2002–03 compared to ¥15.31bn in 2001–02. (See Table 1 for Sony's key financials in the past 13 years.) A statement issued by Sony said, 'The improvement in the results was partly due to the restructuring of its electronics business, especially in the components units.'[3]

---

[1] 'Sony Analyzed via the Value Framework', Mitchell Levy, posted on www.ecmgt.com, October 2002.

[2] Sony was established in 1946. The company invented the video recorder, walkman and mini-disc recorder. It is a leading manufacturer of audio, video, communications and information technology products. Sony has also forayed into diverse fields like music, television, computer entertainment and motion pictures. The company is engaged in five main lines of business – electronics, games, music, pictures and financial services.

[3] 'Financial Results for the Second Quarter, FY 2002', posted on www.sony.net, 28 October 2002.

Table 1 Sony's financials (1991–2003)

Year ended March 31	Sales & Operating Revenue (¥bn)*	Operating Income/loss (¥bn)	Net Income/loss (¥bn)
1991	3695.51	302.18	116.92
1992	3928.67	179.55	120.12
1993	3992.92	126.46	36.26
1994	3744.28	106.96	15.30
1995	3990.58	−166.64	−293.36
1996	4592.56	235.32	54.25
1997	5663.13	370.33	139.46
1998	6755.49	520.21	222.07
1999	6804.18	338.06	179.00
2000	6686.66	223.20	121.83
2001	7314.82	225.35	16.75
2002	7578.26	134.63	15.31
2003	7473.63	185.44	115.52

* ¥100 = approx. €0.75.

Source: Annual Reports 1991–2003, www.sony.net.

At the beginning of the new millennium, Sony faced increased competition from domestic and foreign players (Korean companies like Samsung and LG) in its electronics and entertainment businesses. The domestic rivals Matsushita and NEC were able to capture a substantial market share in the internet-ready cell phones market. Analysts felt that the US-based software giants like Microsoft and Sun Microsystems and the networking major Cisco Systems posed a serious threat to Sony's home entertainment business.

Background

On 7 May 1946, Masaru Ibuka (Ibuka) and Akio Morita (Morita)[4] co-founded a company called Tokyo Tsushin Kogyo Kabushiki Kaisha (Tokyo Telecommunications Engineering Corporation) with an initial capital of ¥190,000 in the city of Nagoya, Japan. They gave importance to product innovation and decided to offer innovative, high-quality products to their consumers.

The founders introduced many new products like the magnetic tape recorder, the 'pocketable radio', and more. By the 1960s, the company had established itself in Japan and changed its name to Sony Corporation. During the 1960s, the company focused on globalisation and entered the US and European markets. In the 1970s, Sony also set up manufacturing units in the US and Europe. During this period, Sony developed and introduced the Walkman, which was a huge success. It significantly boosted Sony's sales during the 1980s. By the mid-1980s, Sony's consumer products were marketed in Europe through subsidiaries in the UK, Germany and France.

In 1989, Norio Ohga (Ohga) took over as the chairman and CEO of Sony from Morita. Under Ohga, Sony began to place greater emphasis on process innovations that improved efficiency and controlled product costs. By 1994, Sony's businesses were organised into three broad divisions – Electronics, Entertainment and Insurance and Finance (see Table 2). Each business division was in turn split into product groups. The electronics business division was split into four product groups, which produced a wide variety of products. The entertainment division, which consisted of the music group and the pictures group, made music videos and motion pictures. The finance division consisted of Sony's life insurance and finance business. The company's growth was propelled by the launch of innovative products and by its foray into the music and films business.

Restructuring of electronics business (1994)

Under Ohga's leadership, Sony witnessed negligible growth in sales during 1990 and 1994. Sales

---

[4] Akio Morita was a graduate in physics, while Masaru Ibuka had a degree in electronic engineering. When Morita joined the Japanese navy as a Lieutenant, he met Ibuka at the navy's Wartime Research Committee.

Table 2 Sony's businesses (1994)

Business	Product Groups/Companies	Details
Electronics	Video equipment	Comprises 8mm, VHS, and Beta-format VTRs, laserdisc players, broadcast and industrial use video equipment, Hi-Vision-related equipment, and videotapes.
	Audio equipment	Comprises CD players, Mini Disc system, headphone stereos, personal component stereos, hi-fi components, digital audio tape recorders/players, radio-cassette tape recorders, tape recorders, radios, car stereos, car navigation systems, professional-use audio equipment, audio tapes, and blank MDs.
	Television	Comprises colour TVs, Hi-Vision TVs, computer displays, professional-use monitors, satellite broadcast reception systems, projector systems, and large colour video display systems.
	Others	Comprises semiconductors, electronic components, cathode ray tubes (CRTs), telephone and telecommunications equipment, computers, computer peripherals (including floppy disk systems and CD-ROM systems), home video game systems, batteries, and FA systems.
Entertainment	Music Group – Sony Music Entertainment	Includes Columbia Records Group; Epic Records Group; TriStar Music Group; Sony Music International; Sony Classical; Sony Classical Film & Video; Sony Wonder; Sony Music Entertainment (Japan) Inc.
	Pictures Group – Sony Pictures Entertainment Inc. (SPEI)	Includes the Columbia TriStar Motion Picture Companies; Sony Television Entertainment; Columbia TriStar Home Video; and Sony Pictures Studios and The Culver Studios. Sony Retail Entertainment includes Sony Theatres.
Insurance and Finance	Sony Life Insurance and Sony Finance International	Comprises the insurance business of Sony Life Insurance Company Limited and the finance operations of Sony Finance International.

Source: Sony Annual Report 1995, www.sony.net.

and operating revenues improved by only 2 per cent during that period. However, the net income and operating income registered a drastic fall of 87 per cent and 67 per cent respectively. Analysts felt that the stagnation in the electronics industry coupled with factors such as the recession in the Japanese economy and the appreciation of the yen against the dollar led to the deterioration in the company's performance.

It was noticed that in the electronics business (see Table 3), the revenues of the video and audio equipment businesses were coming down or were at best stagnant, while the television and 'Others' group were showing signs of improvement. The 'Others' group, which consisted of technology intensive products such as computer products, video games, semiconductors and telecom equip-

ment, was performing very well and had a growth rate of nearly 40 per cent. In order to focus on the high growth businesses, Sony announced major changes in the structure of its electronics business in April 1994.

Sony's management felt that the 'Group' structure, which had fuelled the company's growth in the 1980s, was proving to be redundant in the dynamic business environment of the 1990s. In the new structure, the product groups of the electronics businesses were regrouped into eight divisional companies. The eight companies were the Consumer Audio & Video Products Company, the Recording Media & Energy Company, the Broadcast Products Company, the Business & Industrial Systems Company, the InfoCom Products Company, the Mobile Electronics Company,

Table 3 Sales performance of the electronics business (1991–95) (in ¥bn)*

Year/ Business	Video Equipment	Audio Equipment	Televisions	Others
1991	928	882	552	619
1992	896	948	593	793
1993	828	928	634	772
1994	669	841	618	817
1995	691	899	709	909

* ¥100 = approx. €0.75.

Source: Sony Annual Report 1995, www.sony.net.

Table 4 Five main goals of the new system

- To further enhance core businesses while developing new ones.
- To introduce an organisational structure in which sales and production work closely together and respond quickly to market changes.
- To simplify the structure to clarify responsibilities and transfer authority, thus ensuring quick responses to external changes.
- To reduce the levels of hierarchy in the organisation.
- To encourage the entrepreneurial spirit in order to foster a dynamic management base for the 21st century.

Source: 'From a Business Group System to a Divisional Company System', posted on www.sony.net.

the Components Company, and the Semiconductor Company. The restructuring exercise laid special focus on the products that formed the 'Others' group.

Each divisional company had its own goals and was responsible for all its operations (production, sales and finance). The presidents of the divisional companies were authorised to decide upon the investments to be made up to a prescribed limit. They could also take decisions regarding the HR issues for all employees up to the level of divisional director. In addition, they were made responsible for the financial performance of the companies headed by them. Sony's presidents were expected to perform a role similar to that of CEOs and were accountable to shareholders.

The restructuring of Sony's electronics business was aimed at improving the company's focus on high potential products and expediting the decision making process to make the company more responsive to changing market conditions. Following the restructuring, the number of layers in the decision-making process was reduced from six to a maximum of four layers. Commenting on his responsibilities within the new structure, Ohga said, 'First of all, I would like for the divisional presidents to run their companies as if they were reporting to shareholders once a year at a shareholders' meeting. My role will be to review their

strategies, examine any points I feel should be questioned and provide advice when and where necessary.'[5]

The main goals of Sony's newly formed organisation system were explained in a memorandum entitled 'The Introduction of the Company within a Company System' (see Table 4). Explaining the rationale for the new system, Ohga said, 'By revitalising its organization, Sony aims to introduce appealing products in the market in a timelier fashion while further strengthening cost-competitiveness companywide.'[6]

In 1995, after the implementation of the divisional company structure in the electronics business, changes were announced in Sony's management structure. Under the new framework, Sony was to be led by a team of executives at the top management level. The team included the Chairman & CEO, Vice Chairman, President & Chief Operating Officer (COO), Chief Officers and the presidents of divisional companies. Analysts felt that Sony's management took this measure to reduce the company's reliance on a single leader. In March 1995, Nobuyuki Idei (Idei) was appointed the President and Chief Operating Officer of Sony.

---

[5] 'From a Business Group System to a Divisional Company System', posted on www.sony.net.

[6] As quoted in the 1995 annual report, posted on www.sony.net.

Despite the organisational changes, the financial performance of Sony deteriorated in 1995. For the fiscal year ending March 1995, Sony reported a huge net loss of ¥293.36bn. The write off of goodwill during 1994, the poor performance of the Pictures group and the strength of the yen were regarded as major reasons for this loss. During 1994, the yen was at an all-time high against the dollar, making Sony's exports uncompetitive. Analysts also felt that Sony's consumer electronics business lacked new, innovative products.

Given this poor financial performance, the top management of Sony decided to integrate the company's various domestic and global business functions such as marketing, R&D, finance, and HR. The functions of its numerous divisional companies were thus brought under the direct purview of headquarters. Idei also decided to strengthen the existing eight-company structure and to lay more emphasis on R&D in the IT field. He felt that Sony needed to focus on developing IT-related businesses. Accordingly, Sony's management reorganised the existing structure to create a new ten-company structure.

The ten-company structure (1996)

In January 1996, a new ten-company structure was announced, replacing the previous eight-company structure (see Table 5). Under the new structure, the previous Consumer Audio & Video (A&V) company was split into three new companies – the Display Company, the Home AV Company and the Personal AV Company. A new company, the Information Technology Company, was created to focus on Sony's business interests in the PC and IT industry. The Infocom Products Company and the Mobile Electronics Company were merged to create the Personal & Mobile Communications Company. The other companies formed were the Components & Computer Peripherals Company (formerly called the Components Company), the Recording Media & Energy Company, the Broadcast Products Company, the Image & Sound Communications Company (formerly called the Business & Industrial Systems Company) and the Semiconductor Company.

In order to devise and implement the corporate strategies of the Sony Group, an Executive Board was created. The board was chaired by Idei. The other members of the board included the Chief Human Resources Officer, the Chief Production Officer, the Chief Marketing Officer, the Chief Communications Officer, the Chief Technology Officer, the Chief Financial Officer, the Executive Deputy President & Representative Director and the Senior Managing Director.

In an attempt to consolidate the marketing operations of Sony, the marketing divisions that belonged to the previous organisational setup were spun off to create three new marketing groups – the Japan Marketing Group (JMG), the International Marketing & Operations Group (IM&O) and the Electronic Components & Devices Marketing Group (ECDMG). The JMG was responsible for all marketing activities in Japan for five companies – the Display Company, the Home AV Company, the Information Technology Company, the Personal AV Company and the Image & Sound Communications Company. The IM&O was responsible for supporting all overseas marketing efforts for these companies. The ECDMG oversaw the worldwide marketing operations for the Semiconductor Company and the Components & Computer Peripherals Company. Analysts felt that this consolidation was done to separate Sony's Japanese marketing operations from its worldwide operations

Table 5 Basic features of the ten-company structure

- A new company structure to promote quicker, more effective operations that better reflect market changes.

- The establishment of an Executive Board to reinforce headquarters and corporate strategy and management functions.

- The appointment of new companies and groups for entering into the IT and telecommunications businesses.

- The consolidation of marketing functions.

- The establishment of Corporate Laboratories for new business development.

- The training of promising young talent to foster future managers.

Source: 'Sony Announces a New Corporate Structure', posted on www.sony.net, dated 16 January 1996.

so that the company could operate in a focused manner.

To centralise all the R&D efforts of Sony, the previous R&D structure (in which each company had its own R&D division) was revamped and three new corporate laboratories were established. The laboratories were the Architecture Laboratory (responsible for carrying out R&D for software, network and IT-related technologies), the Product Development Laboratory (R&D for product development in AV businesses) and the System & LSI Laboratory (R&D for LSI and system design, the basic components of hardware products). In addition, a new D21 laboratory was established to conduct long-term R&D for future oriented technology intensive products.

Sony also gave emphasis to grooming young, talented people to take up top management positions. The company also introduced the concept of 'virtual companies' – temporary groups consisting of people from different divisions for launching hybrid products. Sony applied this idea when developing the latest generation Mini Disk players. For the financial year 1995–96, Sony registered a 15 per cent increase in revenues and became profitable again.

In April 1998, a new organisation, Corporate Information Systems Solutions (CISS), was established to realign and upgrade Sony's information network systems and its global supply chain. The CISS comprised an advisory committee of individuals from management consultancy firms and Sony's CISS representatives. The committee members advised the President on technological and strategic issues related to CISS. Representatives of the CISS were placed in all divisional companies to accelerate the implementation of corporate IT projects.

During early 1998, Sony formed Sony Online Entertainment in the US to focus on internet-related projects. In May 1998, Sony changed the composition of its board of directors and established the new position of Co-Chief Executive Officer (Co-CEO). Idei was appointed Co-CEO. Idei reshuffled the management system to facilitate speedy decision making, improve efficiency, and provide greater role clarity to managers. The new system separated individuals responsible for policy-making from those who were responsible for operations.

Under the new system, Idei was responsible for planning and designing Sony's strategies and supervising the growth of e-business. Along with Ohga, he had to supervise the performance of the entire Sony group. President Ando was made responsible for overseeing Sony's core electronics business, while Chief Financial Officer (CFO) Tokunaka was made responsible for the company's financial strategies and network businesses. In addition, the top management positions of Sony's global subsidiaries, which were previously called Corporate Executive Officers, were redesignated Group Executive Officers. Explaining the rationale for these changes, a Sony spokesman said, 'These changes are aimed at making Sony's management more agile'.[7]

The implications

From 1995 to 1999, Sony's electronics business (on which the restructuring efforts were focused) grew at a compounded annual growth rate (CAGR) of 8.55 per cent (see Table 6). The music business had a CAGR of 10.5 per cent while the pictures business had a CAGR of 17 per cent. Significant gains were, however, recorded by the games and insurance business. The games business registered a CAGR of 215 per cent, while the insurance business registered a CAGR of 31 per cent.

---

[7] 'Sony Names Management Team', by Yoshiko Hara, *EE Times*, 9 May 2000.

Table 6 Sales performance of Sony's businesses (1995–99) (in ¥bn)*

Year/Business	Electronics	Game	Music	Pictures	Insurance	Others
1995	3027	35	481	282	113	52
1996	3283	201	506	317	207	78
1997	3930	408	570	439	228	88
1998	4377	700	660	643	291	84
1999	4355	760	719	540	339	81
CAGR (4 years)	**8.55%**	**215%**	**10.5%**	**17%**	**31%**	**11.7%**

* ¥100 = approx. €0.75.

Source: Sony Annual Report, 1999, posted on www.sony.net.

In the late 1990s, Sony's financial performance deteriorated. For the financial year 1998–99, its net income dropped by 19.4 per cent. During that period, Sony was banking heavily on its PlayStation computer game machines. It was estimated that the PlayStation (Games business) accounted for nearly 42 per cent of Sony's operating profits and 15 per cent of total sales for the quarter October–December 1998.

In the late 1990s, many companies across the world were attempting to cash in on the internet boom. At that time, Sony's management felt the need to establish a link between its electronics business (TVs, music systems, computers) and its content-related businesses (music, video games, movies and financial services) by making use of the internet. The management felt that in future, the revenues generated by internet-related businesses might even surpass those earned through the consumer electronics business. It wanted to use the internet as a medium for selling its electronic products as well as its content (music, movies and so on).

In order to achieve this, Sony announced another reorganisation of business operations.

Analysts felt that Sony was in a good position to exploit the opportunities offered by the internet since the company already had an established position in the electronics and content-related businesses.

The unified-dispersed management model

In April 1999, Sony announced changes in its organisational structure. Through the new framework, the company aimed at streamlining its business operations to better exploit the opportunities offered by the internet. Sony's key business divisions – Consumer Electronics division, Components division, Music division and the Games division – were reorganised into network businesses. This involved the reduction of ten divisional companies into three network companies, Sony Computer Entertainment (SCE) Company and the Broadcasting & Professional Systems (B&PS) Company (see Exhibit 1). SCE Company was responsible for the PlayStation business while

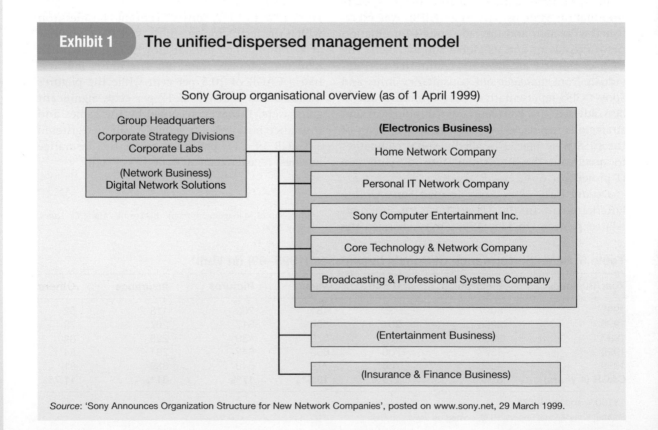

Exhibit 1   The unified-dispersed management model

Source: 'Sony Announces Organization Structure for New Network Companies', posted on www.sony.net, 29 March 1999.

the B&PS Company supplied video and audio equipment for business, broadcast, education, industrial, medical and production related markets. The restructuring aimed at achieving three objectives – strengthening the electronics business, privatising three Sony subsidiaries, and strengthening the management capabilities. The restructuring also aimed at enhancing shareholder value through 'Value Creation Management'.[8]

Strengthening the electronics business

The three network companies created were the Home Network Company, the Personal IT Network Company and the Core Technology & Network Company. Each network company was governed by a network company management committee (NCMC) and a network committee board (NCB). The NCMC was responsible for developing management policies and strategies. Its members included the officers and presidents of the concerned network company. The NCB was responsible for managing the day-to-day operations of the network company while keeping in mind the overall corporate strategy of the entire organisation. Each NCB was chaired by the concerned company's President & CEO, Deputy President, President and Representative Director, two Executive Deputy Presidents and Representative Directors, and Corporate Senior Vice President.

The new structure aimed at decentralising the worldwide operations of the company. The corporate headquarters gave the network companies the authority to function as autonomous entities in their corresponding businesses. To facilitate more functional and operational autonomy, the corporate headquarters also transferred the required support functions and R&D labs to each network company.

To give a further boost to Sony's electronics business, the management created Digital Network Solutions (DNS) under the purview of headquarters. The role of DNS was to create a network business model by charting strategies and developing essential technologies for exploiting the opportunities offered by the internet. The basic aim of creating DNS was to develop a network base that would provide customers with digital content (such as music and movies) and financial services.

Privatising Sony's subsidiaries

As part of its strategy to promote functional and operational autonomy and to devote more attention to units which contributed significantly to its revenues and profits, Sony decided to convert three of its companies – Sony Music Entertainment (Japan), Sony Chemical Corporation (manufactured printed circuit boards (PCBs), recording media and automotive batteries), and Sony Precision Technology (manufactured semiconductor inspection equipment and precision measuring devices) – into wholly owned subsidiaries of Sony. In addition, Sony converted SCE, which was jointly owned by Sony and Sony Music Entertainment (Japan), into a wholly owned subsidiary of Sony.

Strengthening the management capability

To strengthen the management capability, Sony clearly demarcated the roles of headquarters and the newly created network companies. Accordingly, distinction was made between the strategic and support functions. Sony's headquarters was split into two separate units – Group Headquarters and Business Unit Support.

The role of Group Headquarters was to oversee group operations and expedite the allocation of resources within the group. The support functions, such as accounting, human resources and general affairs, were handled by the network companies so that they could enjoy more autonomy in their operations. Significant long-term R&D projects were directly supervised by the headquarters, while the immediate and short-term R&D projects were transferred to the concerned network companies. In order to evaluate the performance of the network companies, a value based performance measurement system[9] was introduced.

The implications

While pursuing its restructuring efforts, Sony started developing products which were compatible with the internet. Its electronic products, such

---

[8] It aimed at creating value by dividing the group into networked autonomous business units such that the resources within the Sony Group complemented each other.

[9] A system that helps in effectively determining the cost of capital. The measurement is based on economic profit, which is calculated by subtracting the cost of debt and equity from the operating profit after tax. Sony planned to use this system of measurement to set targets and evaluate business unit performance. The performance was to be linked, in future, with management compensation.

as digital cameras, personal computers, music systems, and Walkman, were made web compatible. Through its website, www.sony.net, consumers could participate in popular television game shows, listen to music, and download songs and movie trailers. Sony also ventured into e-business with the acquisition of Sky Perfect Communications.[10] While focusing on offering internet-enabled products, Sony also attempted to increase internet penetration by offering internet connection at lower cost and higher speed to consumers in urban areas.

Sony's restructuring efforts in 1999 were well received by investors. Following the announcement of the restructuring programme, Sony's stock prices nearly tripled. This positive trend continued even in 2000. By March 2000, its stock prices were at a high of $152. Having already offered its PlayStation game console on the internet, Sony successfully launched its PlayStation 2 (PS2) video game console in Japan in March 2000. The PS2 sold 980,000 units within the first three days of its launch.

However, Sony still faced problems since its other businesses, including electronics, movies, personal computers, and mobile telecommunications, were not performing well. Analysts felt that the low internet penetration rate in Japan (estimated to be 13 per cent in 1999) was proving to be a major hurdle for Sony.

Consequently, Sony's financial performance deteriorated by the end of 1990s. For fiscal 1999–2000, Sony's net income fell to ¥121.83bn compared to ¥179bn in the fiscal 1998–99. This resulted in a major fall in its stock prices. By May 2000, Sony's stock prices fell by 40 per cent to $89. Analysts were quick to criticise Sony's efforts towards transforming itself into a web-enabled company. They commented that the company had created more hype rather than taking a few significant steps in this regard.

In response to these financial problems, Sony announced a reshuffle in its top management. Idei became the Chairman and Chief Executive Officer of Sony. Ando, who headed Sony's PC division, was made the President, while Tokunaka, who previously headed the PlayStation unit, was made the Chief Financial Officer of Sony.

Sony also undertook a massive cost-cutting exercise. Its global manufacturing facilities were reduced from 70 in 1999 to 65 in 2001. Sony planned to further bring down the number of manufacturing facilities to 55 by the end of 2003. This move would result in the elimination of 17,000 jobs. While implementing these measures, the company had to deal with severe resistance from employee unions and local governments (in areas where jobs would be eliminated).

Despite the above measures, Sony's financial condition did not show any significant improvement in 2001. The company was severely affected by the slowdown in the IT industry during 2000–01, which led to a decline in the demand for its computer-related products. As a result, in spite of a 9.4 per cent increase in revenue in the fiscal 2000–01 (mainly due to the improved sales of the PlayStation games console) Sony's net income dropped significantly from ¥121.83bn in the fiscal 1999–2000 to ¥16.75bn in the fiscal 2000–01. Analysts commented that Sony required a new business model. The company had immediately to take concrete measures to increase its net income.

Sony's management also felt that with the emergence of net-compatible devices like cellular phones, audio and video gadgets and laptops, PCs were losing their charm. It felt that in the emerging age of 'broadband'[11] the demand for the above products was likely to increase in future. Sony's management felt that in order to boost profitability and exploit the opportunities offered by the broadband era, there was a need for yet another organisational restructuring.

Restructuring efforts in 2001

Sony announced another round of organisational restructuring in March 2001. The company aimed at transforming itself into a Personal Broadband Network Solutions company by launching a wide range of broadband products and services for its customers across the world. Explaining the objective of the restructuring, Idei said, 'By capitalising on this business structure and by having businesses cooperate with each other, we aim to

---

[10] A popular satellite broadcasting company in Japan which owned Sky Perfect TV and had successfully ventured into the internet service provider (ISP) business by launching the website, www.so-net. This website enabled online shopping, interactive games, fortune telling as well as stockbroking.

[11] An acronym for broad bandwidth, it is a high-speed, high-capacity data transmission channel that sends and receives information on coaxial cable or fibre-optic cable (which has a wider bandwidth than conventional telephone lines). This channel can carry video, voice and data simultaneously.

| Exhibit 2 | Sony organisational chart: electronics-related business (as of 1 April 2001) |

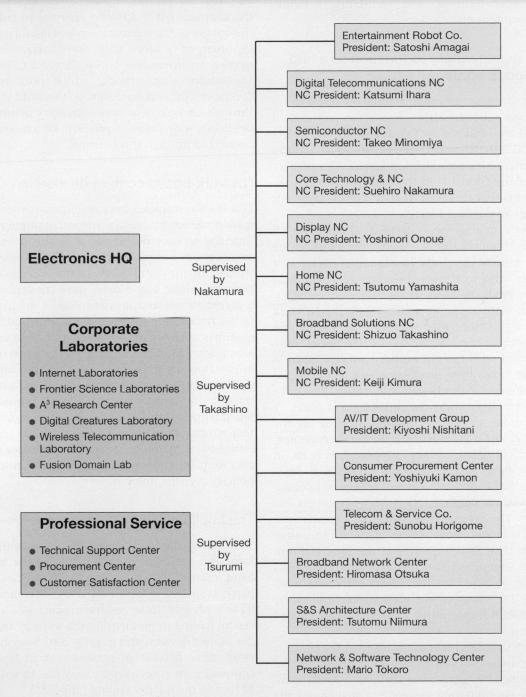

Electronics HQ

Corporate Laboratories

- Internet Laboratories
- Frontier Science Laboratories
- A³ Research Center
- Digital Creatures Laboratory
- Wireless Telecommunication Laboratory
- Fusion Domain Lab

Professional Service

- Technical Support Center
- Procurement Center
- Customer Satisfaction Center

Supervised by Nakamura

Supervised by Takashino

Supervised by Tsurumi

Entertainment Robot Co.
President: Satoshi Amagai

Digital Telecommunications NC
NC President: Katsumi Ihara

Semiconductor NC
NC President: Takeo Minomiya

Core Technology & NC
NC President: Suehiro Nakamura

Display NC
NC President: Yoshinori Onoue

Home NC
NC President: Tsutomu Yamashita

Broadband Solutions NC
NC President: Shizuo Takashino

Mobile NC
NC President: Keiji Kimura

AV/IT Development Group
President: Kiyoshi Nishitani

Consumer Procurement Center
President: Yoshiyuki Kamon

Telecom & Service Co.
President: Sunobu Horigome

Broadband Network Center
President: Hiromasa Otsuka

S&S Architecture Center
President: Tsutomu Niimura

Network & Software Technology Center
President: Mario Tokoro

Source: 'A New Group Structure for the Next Stage of Integrated, Decentralized Management', www.sony.net, 29 March 2001.

become the leading media and technology company in the broadband era.'[12] The restructuring involved designing a new headquarters to function as a hub for Sony's strategy, strengthening the electronics business, and facilitating network-based content distribution.

New headquarters to function as a hub for Sony's strategy

Under the new structural framework (see Exhibit 2), Sony's headquarters was revamped into a Global Hub centred on five key businesses – electronics, entertainment, games, financial services and internet/communication service. The primary role of the Global Hub (headed by the top management) was to devise the overall management strategy of the company.

Sony's management decided to integrate all the electronics business related activities under the newly created Electronic Headquarters (Electronics HQ). In order to achieve the convergence of Audio Video Products with IT (AV/IT convergence), Sony devised a unique strategy called '4 Network Gateway'. Under this strategy, the games and internet/communication service businesses were combined with the electronics hardware business so that innovative products could be developed and offered for the broadband market. The three businesses were under the supervision of Ando.

In order to provide support services for the entire group, a management platform was created, which consisted of key support functions in diverse fields such as accounting, finance, legal, intellectual copyrights, human resources, information systems, public relations, external affairs and design. The management platform was later split into the Engineering, Management and Customer Service (EMCS) Company and the Sales Platform (which comprised the regional sales companies and region-based internet direct marketing functions). The management platform was headed by the Chief Administrative Officer, a newly created position.

Sony's management also converted the product-centric network companies into solution-oriented companies by regrouping them into seven companies. Group resources were allocated among the network companies on the basis of their growth potential.

Strengthening electronics business

To enhance the profitability of the electronics segment, Sony's management decided to give emphasis to product development efforts. The management felt it was also essential to enhance the quality of the electronic devices manufactured. In order to achieve this, Sony's management devised an innovative business model called the Ubiquitous Value Network,[13] which connected the company's existing hardware, content and services through an agency of networks. Sony planned to develop a wide range of products which could be connected through this network.

Network-based content distribution

Like the electronics, games and internet/communication service businesses, the entertainment and financial services businesses were also developed in a network compatible manner to facilitate electronic content distribution. In the entertainment business, music and movies were converted into a digital format and distributed over the internet (apart from being distributed through traditional channels such as music stores and theatres). In Japan, Sony Music Entertainment launched online music through its website. This website allowed customers to download popular songs for a fee. In the financial services business, Sony Life Insurance Japan launched the 'Life Planner' consultancy system which offered personalised financial services online to its customers. Sony Life Assurance Japan also went online and started selling its insurance policies over the internet.

The implications

Soon after the reorganisation, Sony launched some innovative products to cater to the broadband market. For instance, in 2001, the company launched a series of internet-compatible mobile phones. However, the product was unsuccessful (owing to problems in the software used in the mobile devices) and in early 2002 Sony had to recall three batches of phones sold to Japanese companies. In consequence, Sony had to write off $110m in the quarter ending June 2002.

---

[12] As quoted in the Annual Report 2002, www.sony.net.

[13] The Ubiquitous Value Network is an environment in which PC and non-PC consumer electronics devices are seamlessly connected to each other and to the network, giving users access to all types of content or service, from anywhere across the globe.

Exhibit 3	Sony organisational chart (as of 1 April 2003)

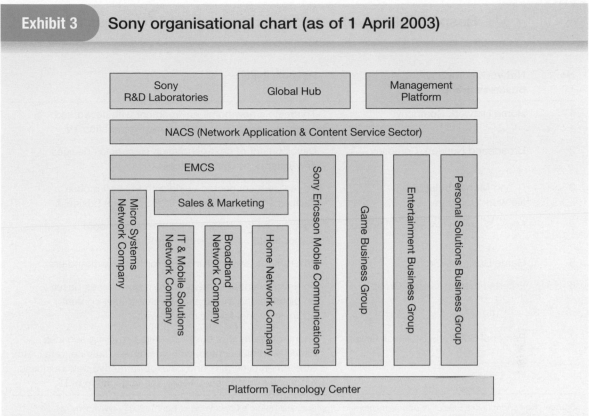

Source: 'Sony Announces Executive Appointments and Organizational Reforms Effective as of April 1, 2003', www.sony.net, 31 March 2003.

In April 2003, Sony announced another major restructuring exercise (to be carried out in the next three years) in order to strengthen its corporate value (see Exhibit 3). Following this announcement, Sony was reorganised into seven business entities – four network companies and three business groups (see Exhibit 4). These business entities were given the authority to frame short-term and long-term strategies.

According to analysts, the company's financial performance did not improve in spite of the frequent restructuring by Sony's management. For the financial year 2001–02, Sony's operating income fell by a significant 40.3 per cent while its revenues registered a marginal increase of 3.6 per cent. According to a *BusinessWeek* report, sales of Sony's most profitable products – the PlayStation and the PS2 game consoles – were likely to fall (see Exhibit 5).

Due to Sony's poor financial performance, the management planned to further reduce the number of manufacturing facilities and shift some production activities out of Japan. Analysts also criticised Sony for being a diversified business conglomerate engaged in several businesses from semiconductors to financial services. They felt that the company should focus on a few highly profitable businesses like games, insurance, and audio-video equipment and hive off the unprofitable businesses.

Analysts felt that spending huge amounts of money on restructuring was not justified, particularly since the restructuring exercises had not yielded the expected results. In 2001, restructuring efforts had cost the company ¥100bn; and the proposed restructuring in April 2003 was expected to cost another ¥140bn.

Analysts also felt that the convergence of consumer electronics, PCs and the internet was not only opening up new opportunities for Sony but also creating more competition for its core businesses. As Sony took steps to strengthen its networking capabilities, the company faced new forms of competition in both domestic as well as foreign markets. For instance, in the US, software giants like Microsoft and Sun Microsystems (as

Exhibit 4	**Responsibilities of network companies and business groups**

No.	Network company/ business group	Responsibility
1	Home Network Company	To create a new home environment with networked electronic devices centred on next-generation TV
2	Broadband Network Company	Development of next-generation electronics devices and linkages to Game devices
3	IT and Mobile Solutions Network Company	To realise a connected world with PC and mobile devices and strengthen the B2B solutions business
4	Micro Systems Network Company	To enhance key devices and modules as core components of attractive set products
5	Game Business Group	To promote Game businesses for the broadband era
6	Entertainment Business Group	To develop entertainment content businesses based on pictures and music and develop a new content business model for the network era
7	Personal Solutions Business Group	To integrate various business units providing services based on direct contact with customers (finance, retail, etc). Strengthen synergies and develop attractive new business models for customers through the application of IT.

Source: 'Sony Announces Executive Appointments and Organizational Reforms Effective as of April 1, 2003', www.sony.net, 31 March 2003.

Exhibit 5	**Break-up of Sony's businesses (31 March 2002)**

Business	Sales ($bn)	Operating profits ($m)
Electronics	35.6	125
Games	7.4	578
Insurance	3.7	91
Films	4.6	147
Music	4.5	203
Others	0.6	NA

Source: 'Can Sony Retain the Magic', by Irene M. Kunii & Cliff Edward, *BusinessWeek*, 11 March 2002.

well as a few startups) were planning to enter the home entertainment market. Even Cisco Systems, which provided network solutions, had started manufacturing consumer electronics products. A *BusinessWeek* report said that Sony lacked any distinctive competencies in the internet-related businesses. It was neither an aggregator of content like Yahoo!, nor a limited-product vendor with an efficient distribution network such as Dell.

Arts Council England – new structures for new challenges

Kevan Scholes

Funding the arts has always created controversy. In England since 1946 the responsibility for public funding of the arts has rested with the Arts Council. This case describes how the responsibilities within the Arts Council – between the centre and the geographical regions were changed from 2003 – together with the stated strategic reasons for these structural changes.

● ● ●

Background

Arts Council England went live on 17 February 2003. Its birth was reported in several press releases such as this one from the East Midlands region:

. Arts Council England is the newly launched development agency for the arts, which replaces all the Regional Arts Boards and the Arts Council of England. This combined organisation will see an increase in funding to the arts from £230 million (≈ €380m) in 2002/03 to around £300 million (≈ €450m) in 2005/06. The merger of the Regional Arts Boards and Arts Council England will also mean expected savings of at least £20 million over the next three years. The new organisation . . . will bring about big changes in the arts funding world including a new streamlined application process with a particular new emphasis on increased funding for individual artists. . . . Laura Dyer, Executive Director of Arts Council England East Midlands, said: 'This is not just the case of the arts having a corporate face-lift, all the changes are for the good of artists and arts organisations both within the East Midlands and nationwide. The arts have the power to transform people's lives as well as cross all language barriers and cultural differences. Our ambition is to place the arts at the heart of national life and we are planning a bold programme of investment to achieve that aim.'

The original Arts Council of Great Britain was set up in 1946 to manage the public funding of the arts. It allocated money to many diverse activities included under the rather ill-defined heading of 'the arts'. Initially the Arts Council operated as a single organisation covering Great Britain – although it allocated about 20 per cent of its funding to Regional Arts Associations throughout Great Britain. In the early 1990s it was decided to make radical changes to shift the balance and control of arts funding to the geographical regions. Independent Regional Arts Boards were created (10 for England) whilst the national activities became the responsibility of the Arts Council of England (ACE). ACE was based in London and managed the large slice of money that went to national arts companies (such as Opera, Dance and The Royal Shakespeare Company). However, by the end of the 1990s there was growing dissatisfaction in government with the way this fragmented approach was working. For example, it was difficult to develop a truly national policy for the arts or to deliver consistency in the way that funding to recipient organisations was managed by these separate independent Regional Arts Boards. As a consequence, the Department for Culture, Media and Sport (the government department with responsibility for the arts) asked ACE for proposals for restructuring the system. The Culture Secretary, Tessa Jowell, commented on their proposals in a letter to Gerry Robinson, the Chairman of ACE in July 2001:

I think the model you propose, of a new single organisation with Regional Arts Councils and enhanced levels of Local Government involvement is an excellent one and I am happy for you to consult now on operational detail. I am glad to see the regions at the centre of the new proposals, with a clear intention that decision making should be as devolved as possible. I think it is important to emphasise that this is a new organisation with the regions at its heart – not just a re-invented Arts Council. The new organisation must work differently, must work well, and must attract and retain the best people. I see this transformation as a key piece of public service reform.

I wanted to see proposals which:

- created a dynamic new organisation, streamlined in operation and responsive at regional level;
- brought the regions into the heart of the funding system instead of being independent supplicants to a central body;
- delegated real decision making to regional level informed by regional priorities;
- set challenging targets for administrative savings;
- was simpler and more consistent for those applying for funding.

I think your new proposals will deliver this. I note your target for savings of between £8 and £10 million to be ploughed back through the Regions to the arts – I would like to see these savings realised and my Department will be monitoring this and the other intended effects of the reorganisation very closely.

Ambitions

In preparation for the launch of Arts Council England their publications and the website explained the ambitions of the new organisation. These are extracts:

Arts Council England is the national development agency for the arts. Between 2003 and 2006 we will invest £2 billion of public funds in the arts in England, including funding from the National Lottery.

We believe in the transforming power of the arts – power to change the lives of people throughout the country. Our ambition is to place the arts at the heart of national life, reflecting the country's rich and diverse cultural identity as only the arts can. We want people throughout England to experience arts activities of the highest quality. We believe that access to the arts goes hand in hand with excellence. This is the start of a new era of significant expansion for the arts in England. The financial case for the arts is being won with Government. In 2002's spending round, we achieved a major increase in public investment in the arts. Now we intend to capitalise on that success by

backing the country's artistic talent and winning further support for the arts.

From 2003 to 2006 we will:

- prioritise individual artists
- work with funded arts organisations to help them thrive rather than just survive
- place cultural diversity at the heart of our work
- prioritise young people and Creative Partnerships
- maximise growth in the arts.

The website went on to explain the ambitions in its priority areas:

The Arts Council and 'the arts'

We will adopt a more modern definition of the arts, one that is open to current trends in emerging (and often challenging) arts practice, in arts and technology, and in breaking down the boundaries between art forms, and between the arts and other disciplines . . . We will promote our artists internationally, encourage international exchange and co-production, and do all we can to ensure that audiences and artists in this country benefit from the best of the arts from outside the UK.

Placing artists at the centre

The artist is the 'life source' of our work. In the past, we have mainly funded institutions. Now we want to give higher priority to the artist. We can do this indirectly through training, legislative change, or in stimulating the economy for artists. Or we might provide direct assistance through more funding, or help with spaces to work, with equipment, time, or travel and opportunities for international exchanges. We believe artists, at times, need the chance to dream, without having to produce. We will establish ways to spot new talent; we will find ways to help talent develop; we will encourage artists working at the cutting edge; we will encourage radical thought and action, and opportunities for artists to change direction and find new inspiration.

Our relationship with arts organisations

Most of our funding will continue to go to our portfolio of 'regularly funded organisations'. We are looking for a new, grown-up relationship with arts organisations; one that is based on trust, not dependency. We will expect hopes, aspirations and problems to be shared openly with us. We consider this new relationship to be fundamentally important to the future of the subsidised arts. Arts organisations provide the foundation for the arts in this country. Because of this, these organisations must play a leadership role in terms of artistic innovation and experimentation, as well as in how they are managed and governed. They are crucial to all our priorities and we will ask them to make a major contribution to our ambitions in cultural diversity. At the same time, we will not ask them to take on any agendas that are not consistent with their fundamental purpose and ambition. We want to lighten rather than add to their burden.

Cultural diversity

The arts provide spaces to explore differences. The results can be greater understanding and tolerance or, at their best, a sense of shared excitement and celebration of the miraculous richness and variety of cultural identity and endeavour. We can achieve much in cultural diversity through persuasion, illustration and by identifying and sharing good practice. But we also need to take positive action if we are to share our riches and achieve greater equality of opportunity. We will at the very least make more funding available specifically for culturally diverse arts. We will also take steps to change the employment profile, governance and activities of both the Arts Council and the funded arts sector.

The arts and young people

We recognise the transforming power of the arts in relation to young people. We value the wealth of arts and education activity that has taken place and will continue to take place in schools and other settings up and down the country. We see Creative Partnerships as a highly valuable extension of our previous arts and education work, and embrace the Creative Partnerships initiative with much excitement and enthusiasm. Creative Partnerships can bring about profound change in how education relates to the arts and vice versa. We will give it a very high priority, evaluate it thoroughly and we will do all we can to turn it from a pilot into a mainstream activity.

Growth in resources for the arts

As an organisation, we will be focused on growth. We will bring the transforming power of the arts to bear on issues of health, crime, education and inclusion. Many artists are naturally drawn to those fields.

Without compromising our main purpose – the arts – we will make the most of growth by establishing healthy and effective partnerships with a range of national, regional and local organisations. Nationally, these include government departments for health, education, trade & industry, and the Home Office as well as agencies such as the Youth Justice Board and national broadcasters. Regionally and locally, these include regional development agencies, regional government, regional government offices, local strategic partnerships, regeneration agencies and, of course, local authorities. We will draw up a plan for growth nationally and regionally, with some clear and challenging targets.

We will place added emphasis on marketing and communicating the value of the arts. This will include marketing of the 'transforming power' of the arts – all the arts, not just the arts we fund – and more specific marketing, for example, in relation to new opportunities to raise extra resources for the arts.

The Council and Regional Arts Councils

The move to a single corporate entity from 11 separate organisations required changes in the structures of both governance and management as explained on the website:

Our governing body is the Council, selected in the summer 2002. It comprises up to 15 people, including the Chairman and nine members who also chair the regional arts councils. Each of our nine regional arts councils is also made up of up to 15 members, except the South East Regional Arts Council, which has 20 members.

The Council

Members of our national Council are appointed by the Secretary of State for Culture, Media and Sport. Council members are usually appointed for four years, and may be reappointed for a further term of four years. Council meets approximately five times a year. Each member is appointed because of their special interest in, or experience of, the arts as practicing artists or arts administrators; as senior academics; or as public or private sector executives. Council members are responsible for ensuring the achievement of Arts Council England's objectives, which are to develop and improve the knowledge, understanding and practice of the arts, and to increase the accessibility of the arts to the public. They do this by deciding on policy and priorities, and investing money in artists and arts organisations directly and through the regional arts councils.

Regional Arts Councils

The nine regional arts councils consist of 15 members. Six members on each of the councils are representatives of local government or regional government.

The regional arts councils are responsible for:

● agreement of regional strategies, plans and priorities for action within the framework of national policies and priorities
● approval of three year regional investment plans
● agreement of detailed regional annual budgets (including all grants over £25,000 for named, funded organisations)

Executive structure

The management consisted of a chief executive, 9 regional executives, one executive for national policy and national companies and three 'functional' executives (finance, development & external relations).

The future

The website also painted a vision of the future:

Investment in the arts
Our grant-in-aid will increase from £335 million in 2003/04 to £410 million in 2005/06. (In addition there were funds from the National Lottery for capital projects for the arts.) In a radical new budget that covers the entire country, many organisations will receive a step change in their funding to help them realise major ambitions. There is substantial investment in new ground-breaking organisations and the previously less recognised arts.

A modern, dynamic Arts Council
In order to fulfil our ambitions we need a dynamic and effective Arts Council . . . Overall, we will improve our operational performance and responsiveness, for example through our much simplified grants for the arts [replacing 100 separate, regionally-based, funding programmes with five national programmes – used by all regions].

In summary, we believe that the new Arts Council will be able to:

- position and market the arts publicly throughout the country so that the case for government funding in future will be immeasurably stronger
- make operational changes that deliver a much improved service to the arts at considerably less cost
- lever resources for the arts from a wide variety of national and regional sources at a level far greater than was possible previously
- work to one agenda, joining up our programmes and policies with action, and delivering against clearly stated ambitions

Arts Council England will be bold and set ambitious targets in order to maximise these advantages. Where there are major gains to be made, we will take risks and encourage the arts community to take risks.

In the past, the Arts Council had many policies and strategies. Now we have this manifesto. It states clearly what we want to do and replaces other general policy statements. Now is the time for action.

The website also explained how the organisation expected its performance to be judged:

How we will measure our success (examples only):
- more people saying that the arts play a valuable role in their lives
- an enhanced reputation for England and the UK as a world centre for critically acclaimed art
- significant growth in the number of artists who have previously received direct funding from us now enjoying an ongoing economic return from their work
- cultural institutions more open to people from diverse backgrounds as performers, audiences and staff
- more teachers, health professionals, probation officers, youth workers, social workers and carers reporting the value of the arts in their work
- the arts community reporting that we have broadened our range to show a clear interest in new and emerging arts practice
- the arts community recognising that we speak up more effectively for artists and for the value of the arts

We invite artists, organisations, partners and colleagues to join us in this bold adventure.

Sources

Arts Council England website (www.artscouncil.org.uk); press releases.

SerCom Solutions: outsourcing options

Eleanor Doyle and Frédéric Adam

This case study focuses on SerCom Solutions Ltd located in Dublin, Ireland. SerCom's business evolved substantially since its establishment in 1978 and by 2004 focused on the provision of supply chain management (SCM) services. Its business strategy is built around its competences in anticipating and meeting the supply-chain needs of its customers across a range of sectors, particularly the Information and Communications Technology (ICT) sector, where demands evolve constantly.

The case describes the evolution of the company as it decided to position itself as a global SCM company and how this decision had implications for the role of technology, specifically Information Technology (IT) systems within the company. The history of the company is described and relates the reaction of the company over time to different opportunities perceived in its market. The industry characteristics driving the growth in SCM activities, particularly the role of changing technology, is relevant for understanding the evolution of the SCM industry broadly and the implications of such industry evolution for SerCom Solutions.

The case can be used to explore the relationship between Strategy and Actions of the organisation and how these two aspects change and interact over time.

● ● ●

Company evolution

Confidential Report Printing (CRP) was founded in 1978 as a commercial print company, which became Printech International Group in 1983 and SerCom Solutions in 1999. By 2004 SerCom Solutions was one of the world's leading global providers of supply chain management (SCM) services to the IT and telecommunications sectors.

In the late 1970s, Brian Stokes's job involved having reports printed on behalf of *RTE* the national Irish broadcasting company. In the face of poor levels of service provided by printing companies Brian perceived an opportunity to set up in business for himself and Confidential Report Printing was born. The company was quickly successful based on a strong customer focus, a niche market and investment in modern equipment.

Winning a contract in the early 1980s from Digital Equipment Corporation to print computer manuals represented a key point in CRP's history and required numerous versions of each manual in different languages. Successful delivery of the order to required standards and an understanding of business-critical timelines resulted in follow-on business from DEC. From a timing perspective this success with DEC was fortuitous since by this time Ireland had become the second largest computer software exporter in the world (and a major PC assembly centre). Demand from Irish-based information technology (IT) companies for computer software and hardware manuals boomed and in 1983, the company decided to focus exclusively on this market, and changed their name to Printech.

The focused strategy required substantial additional investment in printing equipment and

This case was prepared by Eleanor Doyle and Frédéric Adam, University College Cork, Ireland. It is intended as a basis for class discussion and not as an illustration of either good or bad business practice. The authors are grateful for the contribution of Rose McCarthy, Group Supply Chain Manager, SerCom Solutions to the case. © E. Doyle and F. Adam, 2004. Not to be reproduced or quoted without permission.

improvements in quality and production control. As the company grew, additional equity was required and in 1984 Development Capital Corporation (DCC plc) took a minority stake in the company. DCC became the parent company in 1986 and is one of Ireland's leading public companies. Printech generated sustained growth and profitability over 20 years as a supplier of printed material to IT companies. The company prided itself on a commitment to adapt to the rapid changes taking place in its market.

With growth in the number of IT companies contracting out regionalisation and packaging of manuals and CDs, Printech responded by, again, diversifying its business model. This process, *fulfilment*, also involved the translation of manuals, packaging and boxing. Fulfilment refers to a process that supplies a finished manufactured product directly from a manufacturing facility to a distributor or end user *without* the finished product going back through the company that has created the product. It became necessary for Printech to expand its warehouse facilities and install packaging lines, in addition to strengthening its procurement and production management skills.

In 1993 Printech established a turnkey operation in Scotland: a turnkey business includes everything required to immediately start running a business and could include any mix of tangible assets – such as inventory and equipment – through intangibles, such as a previously established reputation and goodwill. The company considers that it was around 1995 that their repositioning within the SCM market began in earnest. Another turnkey business followed in Limerick in 1999 accompanied by another name change to SerCom Solutions as the company graduated to providing full supply-chain management services and attempted to rebrand itself as a major player in the SCM market.

In January 2004 Kuehne & Nagel (K & N) and SerCom Solutions established a strategic partnership to combine their respective capabilities in global logistics and supply chain management solutions, which increased SerCom's international reach into 600 locations across 96 countries. Headquartered in Cloverhill Industrial Estate Clondalkin, SerCom employed 400 staff across their two facilities in Cloverhill and Limerick. SerCom Solutions' evolution into a provider of supply chain management services to the computer industry resulted in it becoming one of the leading suppliers of high quality, outsourced supply chain management solutions to blue chip IT and telecommunications corporations in Ireland, Europe and the US. The merger with K&N was a critical move as the new global status it conferred on SerCom meant it could address a much broader range of customer needs. Its core activities included:

- Supply chain activities, i.e.:
  - demand forecast management
  - sourcing/procurement
  - warehousing/inventory management
  - consigned stocks
  - component quality management/screening
  - live feed into clients' assembly process
  - logistics management
  - hubbing/bundling of components
  - website development and hosting
- Manufacturing activities:
  - printing
  - software replication
  - regionalisation
  - programming
  - assembly and sub-assembly (including software).

Industry evolution

Logistics involves providing the appropriate physical environment, tools, equipment, labour and materials required for business operations to run smoothly. It involves the management of flows of all materials into, within and out of an organisation to meet its business goals. Pressure to focus on logistics has emerged from many quarters as discriminating customers increasingly demand tailored services while new technology and internet adoption facilitate freer and faster dissemination of information. Having come through a period of rationalisations and business process re-engineering, many companies are now focusing on logistics and how to better manage their inventories as factors to contribute to increasing their value-adding potential.

How this might be achieved varies. Some companies simplify inputs by reducing the number of parts required through redesign. Others outsource and buy in sub-assemblies rather than individual components. Another option chosen by some companies is to adopt a built-to-order model (BTO) in cases where they could reduce their lead time to a level that was acceptable to their customers (eliminating build up of inventories of inputs or finished goods but requiring comprehensive and flexible provision of required inputs). Specialist companies such as SerCom Solutions have chosen to build their competencies in logistics and are a 'third party' to which many companies now turn to meet the challenges of supply-chain organisation, one component of which is logistics.

In an environment where workers in one location supply to consumers in far distant locations, supply-chain management is a global phenomenon requiring careful logistics management. Standard decisions about which products to produce and how production should best be organised are now often less important than the decision on how to coordinate delivery of inputs from various locations and how to move finished products to the target market which could be on the other side of the world. Providing solutions to such problems is sometimes called *hubbing*, which is an area where SerCom has specialised.

Estimates of the size of the logistics market are not easily available although McKinsey assess that the US market is worth about $1 trillion (≈ €0.83tr) per year (2002 estimate) and was growing at approximately 4 per cent pa – making it a mature industry. However, focusing on the third party market alone, the value of the industry was $50bn and growing by 15–18 per cent pa. The corresponding European third-party market was estimated to expand to $213bn by 2005.[1]

The contribution of logistics companies consists of analysing of how best a supply chain should be structured or configured in order to optimise deliveries in a logically sequenced manner to meet production and assembly requirements and get products to customers as required. Considering that an average car has 10,000 separate parts for which many alternative suppliers exist, the impression of complexity in international supply-chain organisation is clear to see. By outsourcing elements of supply-chain management companies aim to achieve greater efficiencies and improve time to market so that core business activities can become their focus. They are also able to take substantial volumes of costs off their books by relying on a partner such as SerCom to hold such inventories. In the case of non-production items (which are sometimes not monitored by firms), some of SerCom's customers achieved substantial savings by simply asking SerCom to control the allocation of stocks.

In a world where the procurement and distribution functions of businesses have superseded the production side in terms of complexity and value added, companies such as SerCom play the role of global outsourcing partner to some of the world's leading edge companies which are happy to increasingly allow SCM specialists handle key aspects of their supply chain in order to achieve a number of key objectives including:

- shorter lead times to market
- reduced inventory levels
- more cost effective and efficient distribution.

The benefits of greater efficiencies and improvements in time to market allow businesses that outsource to reorient their focus towards their core business activities.

Understanding outsourcing

Outsourcing as a strategy for sourcing key resources or services had become commonplace by the late 1970s and early 80s. IT outsourcing in particular, quickly became an important area for managers and throughout the 1990s many firms entered outsourcing agreements instead of setting up their own IT departments in-house to reduce costs on activities they no longer perceived as essential to their business.[2]

However, recent research has observed more and more activities being considered as potential targets for outsourcing. In the past, outsourcing was regarded as a way to reduce costs and eliminate non-value adding activities, which enabled the firm and its managers to focus on their core competencies. Recent developments have seen firms electing to outsource even core activities and establish virtual companies where they act as a hub and use a number of partners to carry out manufacturing activities, distribution of their products or, more recently, their entire procurement activities.

Initially, the theory of outsourcing was that only non-critical activities should be outsourced and managers would have been quite worried about creating any kind of dependence vis-à-vis an external partner in a domain of importance.

[1] 'Special Report: Logistics', *The Economist*, 7 December 2002.

[2] Mary C. Lacity and Rudy Hirscheim, 'The information systems outsourcing bandwagon', *Sloan Management Review*, vol. 35, no. 1, Fall 1993, pp. 73–87.

Nowadays, the thinking has moved to a vision of outsourcing as an opportunity of finding a partner who specialises in a narrow activity and has obtained more efficiency gains than any other firm could obtain without significant investment. Organisations such as SerCom, which specialise in providing supply chain solutions can derive substantial economies of scale from printing and packaging activities, for instance, and can deliver services to their clients for a fraction of the potential cost clients would incur without SerCom's input.

In modern outsourcing agreements, managers try to ensure that they retain control over the core activity e.g. the design of the products and the brand name – and find reliable partners to execute the rest of the work. This more selective approach to outsourcing enables organisations to 'pick and choose' activities from which they can derive revenues and which they can safely outsource.

In the case of SerCom, firms are offered a variety of supply chain solutions involving varying degrees of integration with the client's own systems, from simple outsourcing arrangements focusing on one simple step in a process to taking over an entire process and delivering directly to their client's own customers. Thus, they are able to offer very flexible solutions to their clients. As Rosemary McCarthy (Group Supply Chain Manager) put it, 'No activity is too small for us, we are not proud!'

This type of outsourcing has become known as *Business Process Outsourcing*.

SerCom strategy and technology

Competition in the Supply Chain Management market forced SerCom to re-evaluate its strategy and in 1999 they commissioned a feasibility study of the electronic fulfilment market. Fulfilment requires reliable, quality controlled distribution to individual consumers and companies. A 'fulfilment cycle' may include receiving customer orders, configuring the products to order, shipping and invoicing products to distribution outlets or end users anywhere in the world. SerCom was concerned that internet development represented a viable substitute for its core business – physical fulfilment. Technological support via electronic commerce to facilitate the fulfilment process was being adopted by SerCom's competitors, some of whom:

- offered new services, aimed at managing core functions for their clients – smoothing the links in the supply chain on one hand and facilitating optimal provision of products to customers on the other;
- used already-proven technology platforms and applied them to the supply-chain management market.

However, few competitors offered comprehensive business solutions opting instead for providing fragmented or component services of supply-chain management. SerCom saw this as an opportunity it could exploit and set about establishing a position as a global provider of e-business solutions, specifically – 'everything behind the buy button'. Formulating and implementing such a strategy was easier said than done!

An e-commerce approach had wide-ranging implications for how business should be conducted and some immediate issues emerged:

- SerCom's customers had limited access to information regarding the progress of components, products or customer orders in the supply chain. Faxed and/or e-mailed reports were manually produced on a periodical basis. Increasing complexity of fulfilment programmes as well as SerCom's desire to reposition itself in its market demanded that the information flow process be altered.
- Rising fulfilment orders signalled SerCom's success but again, pointed to the need for an information system that could facilitate more effective monitoring and management of order status in the supply chain for each company and each product.
- The diversity and complexity of fulfilment orders received indicated that bulk orders were declining and concurrently sales were moving to a more demand-driven, customisation model.
- Web-based ordering was increasingly demanded by customers. Furthermore, in the case of the manuals/CD products, Electronic Software Delivery (ESD) as an additional technological development had to be embraced. ESD allows software to be delivered via the internet, saving on production and distribution costs. Slow adoption of broadband communications limited the take-up of this technology but the general consensus was that it was the way forward. Anything less than state-of-the-art ordering services

for customers would compromise SerCom's new strategy.

In 1999 SerCom's own Manufacturing Resource Planning (MRP) system that had been used to manage order processing, procurement and logistics incorporated neither a web-based facility for customers nor a facility to handle diverse orders. The consensus was that the system was outdated, provided inadequate functionalities, and did not facilitate required cross-docking (checking) of supplies with orders. To deliver its new strategy, SerCom itself required a technological leap forward in the form of an information systems upgrade that would increase the probabilities for SerCom of providing value-added services to its customers. The company did not want to simply supply components, and thereby compete mainly only on the price attribute but rather supply more strategic activities that addressed logistics and supply-chain needs on as comprehensive a basis as customers demanded.

A detailed description of the implementation of an Enterprise Resource Planning System (ERP) at SerCom between January 2000 and June 2001 is documented by Enterprise Ireland in its E-Business Case Studies series.[3] An ERP system is an integrated enterprise-wide software package designed to support the key functional areas of the organisation.[4] In SerCom's case the implementation covered all financial aspects as well as Supply Chain Operations, Human Resources Management, Customer Relationship Management and Business Intelligence (including traditional scheduled reporting, more ad-hoc decision support systems and data mining – i.e. finding trends and connections in data to inform and improve competitive performance and identify future strategic direction/position). Many well-documented examples exist of failed attempts to implement ERPs, however, in SerCom's experience the ERP was delivered to the standard required to contribute to the desired strategy and played a role in the successful establishment of the strategic partnership in 2004 between SerCom and Kuehne & Nagel. Some of the

reasons proposed to explain the success of this information systems implementation by SerCom were:

● the drawing up a comprehensive and robust blueprint mapping out the critical functionality of the SAP application and its implications for SerCom's business processes to which the company adhered strictly;

● confidence in the blueprint based on the diligence given to detailed planning – this was paramount in the successful and timely roll out of the ERP;

● successful training of 'super-users' from the implementation team. Skills were kept in the team and training was delivered from staff who not only knew the product, but also new the requirements and idiosyncrasies of their relevant departments;

● selecting the best people from each department for the planning and implementation phase. However, the difficulty of this phase can be considerable if managers are reluctant to 'give up' their best people. It is also critical to minimise the impact of this redeployment of staff on the everyday business activity of the firm. This requires backfilling the position occupied by team members by equally qualified staff, which may prove elusive or costly to find.

SerCom strategy and the customer

A range of types of strategic alliance (or partnership as SerCom classifies them) exists and a range of motives underlie the development of such inter-business relationships. Key factors determining alliances include the main features driving an industry's profitability.

One key challenge for SerCom in implementing its e-commerce strategy was to generate trust with their clients. Such trust is often built up only over time and must be carefully managed to generate the optimal benefits to all parties concerned. In practice, many of SerCom's customers began with small-scale contracts and expanded their business relationship as trust grew based on SerCom's ability to deliver as promised resulting in significant unit cost savings. Their customer base included companies such as Apple, Canon, Dell, IBM, MascSoftware, MapInfo, Medtronic, Nortel Networks, Palm, Symantec, and The MathWorks.

[3] SME E-business Case Studies, SerCom Solutions, Enterprise Ireland, http://www.enterprise-ireland.com/documents/uploaded/Sercom.pdf

[4] For more on ERPs generally and for a specific implementation example of ERP see F. Adam and E. Doyle, 'Enterprise Resource Planning at Topps International Ltd', case study in G. Johnson and K. Scholes (eds), *Exploring Corporate Strategy*, 6th edn, Prentice Hall, 2002, pp. 984–94.

A key issue for any Supply-Chain Management company is to deal with the fear faced by potential customers – that of losing control in 'handing over' some of their business processes to an 'outsider'. In 2004, the Group Supply Chain Manager at SerCom, Rose McCarthy explained that 'customers can retain as much or as little control as they require' and argued that a key issue for SerCom was their focus on quality, which should help to allay such fears. In terms of their Quality Assurance SerCom have been ISO-registered since May 1988 through NSAI (National Standards Authority of Ireland), one of the first indigenous companies to be awarded both ISO 9001: 2000 and ISO 14001. The NSAI reviews the Quality System through twice-yearly audits. Ongoing internal audits of the entire system were conducted frequently and provided the facility for customers to carry out audits of the system and its processes when requested. As reported on the company website (http://www.sercomsolutions.ie):

> In December 2000 the ISO standard was revised from ISO 9002: 1994 to ISO 9001: 2000 and all companies must now undergo a re-registration in order to be certified to ISO 9001: 2000. The quality group within SerCom Solutions actively pursued the implementation of this revised standard and as part of this a gap analysis was completed on all sections of the revised standard. This identified areas which we needed to address in order to comply with ISO 9001: 2000. SerCom Solutions have set a target date for certification to the new standard of January 2002. In April of 2002 we were audited against all elements of the revised standard by NSAI and we were awarded registration to the revised standard with no non-compliances received during the assessment.
>
> As part of our ISO accreditation we are required to have a documented Quality System and this is done in the form of a detailed Quality Manual which outlines how we operate and maintain our Quality System, in the implementation and control of quality related documentation and also in the control of documented operating procedures. Operating procedures are in place for all our processes and other Quality related areas of our business.

In 2004 SerCom stated it was happy to operate from customers' Approved Vendor Lists or provide vendors/suppliers from its own book of business, as required. Over 3,000 suppliers were on their books with 90 being identified as key. To ensure confidence in the suppliers, SerCom monitored all its suppliers to ensure that deliveries arrived on time and were of the requisite quality. Monthly meetings were held with key vendors and weekly summary quality reports were provided to each supplier.

A Supplier Corrective Action Report was initiated in cases where any problems were identified. Rose McCarthy's views on quality and the need to adapt to changes in the market are clear:

> A supply chain is only as good as its weakest link . . . careful monitoring of performance and communication . . . is vital in guaranteeing ongoing conformance . . . The marketplace is constantly changing and we have to change with it. That means being flexible in everything we do. It also means constantly re-assessing what we do to see how we can improve. Each and every project we undertake is re-assessed on an ongoing basis to ensure that savings and other targets are being met in the timescale agreed. If not we do something about it immediately – we are happy to embrace change.

The company used the same criteria for the initial supplier selection process as used in its ongoing feedback to suppliers, namely: quality, delivery, continuity, support and cost. Quality includes areas such as supplier systems, investment and technical expertise and quality represented 40 per cent of the overall marking in the feedback process. Weekly senior management meetings at SerCom reviewed reports of 37 different criteria monitored along the supply chain.

The information system in SerCom (SAP based) was accessible by all customers who, by using a browser, could view their account and product information at any time. Some customers preferred to use their own systems to view data and SerCom had to ensure both systems were integrated to support provision of data in the required formats to customers' own systems. Such free access to the rich information resources affords SerCom's customers an accurate perspective on how their company is performing in terms of which products are being shipped to whom and when.

SerCom achieved its goal of offering e-fulfilment to their customer base. For example, if a customer wanted SerCom to ship out software to an end user via the customer's website, SerCom was able to redirect the request to SerCom's own server and automatically fulfil the online order. The objective of offering 'everything behind the buy button' had been reached.

From SerCom's perspective better integration between their internal information systems, including their warehouse, has brought about complete automation in the supply chain management. A radio-frequency supported technology employed in the warehouse allowed the company to accurately keep track of stock and production in a wireless environment! The increased efficiencies generated as a result within their organisation allowed SerCom to reduce the number of employees by 25 so far (the majority by attrition). Also, the integration with a transport company has afforded tighter controls on shipping and delivery.

SerCom views their e-business strategy as a continuing process. Every three months the ERP project team meets to discuss any new requirements and functional additions or changes to the system. As a result, lists of new projects are generated and the company sets about prioritising and undertaking as many as possible. Whether such continual assessment and incorporation of changes keeps SerCom ahead of its competition and in a position to attract more business will be proven and tested in the marketplace.

SerCom strategy and the bottom line?

Focusing on sales revenues (1989–2003) – see Exhibit 1 – there was a clear upward trend in SerCom's sales figures. However, operating profits at SerCom have declined since 2000 (operating profits of €3.8m in 2000 declined to €2.8m in 2001 and to operating losses of €114,000 in 2002). The decline in 2001 was attributed to what the parent company DCC described as 'developmental investment in IT systems, skilled personnel and management resources' (DCC Annual Report, May 2001). More recently, there has been an increasing trend

for the traditional customer base of SerCom, i.e. technology companies, to locate manufacturing activities in Eastern Europe and Asia. As a result, SerCom has had to try to broaden its own customer base beyond the IT industry and attempt to reduce its own cost base.

Looking to the future in 2004, SerCom considered that while manufacturing trends in its main ICT (Information and Communications Technology) customer segments focused on mass production or 'job shop' i.e. customised solutions, such emphasis would shift to a greater focus on demands for niche production on the one hand and mass customisation on the other. To meet the trends they predicted in the ICT market, SerCom argued that the Irish SCM sector was 'world-class' but operating under capacity. To enhance development of the SCM sector implies supporting an environment increasingly conducive to virtual manufacturing for the largest multinational companies. Logistically, suppliers in locations such as China for example, which provides a substantial and rising proportion of manufactured goods, would be targeted by SerCom through its Irish base to meet the requirements of the substantial cluster of ICT companies already profitably serving their European needs.

In addition, to strengthen its position SerCom may seek a change in policy by Ireland's Industrial Development Authority (IDA) towards providing the same incentives for multinationals to use Irish based SCM specialists (because they create local employment opportunities even when they don't open facilities in Ireland) as they currently offer to firms who open a base in Ireland.

| Exhibit 1 | SerCom Solutions annual group revenues |

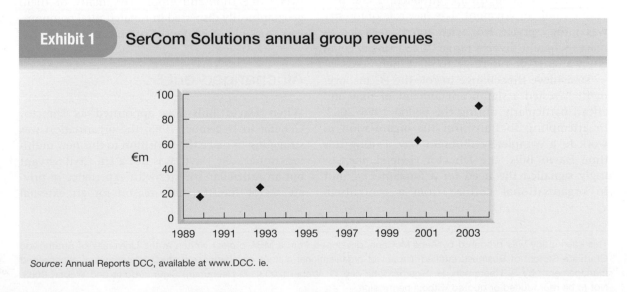

Source: Annual Reports DCC, available at www.DCC. ie.

The Forestry Commission: cultural change to deliver a new strategy

Anne McCann

This case illustrates the Forestry Commission of Great Britain's strategic response to society's changing expectations about what forestry should deliver. The case is primarily concerned with how the strategic change processes were managed during the period from 1995 to 2003. It contains detailed descriptions of some of the change programmes that were implemented and accounts by the people involved describing the challenges they faced. The case provides a context in which to consider the extent to which these change programmes succeeded in effecting strategic change.

● ● ●

Forestry can only survive if it is relevant and meets community aspirations.

(David Bills, Director General, Forestry Commission of Great Britain, 2003)

By 2003, the Forestry Commission of Great Britain (FC) was a devolved organisation working in partnership with many other agencies to deliver local solutions so that communities could enjoy and make use of forests and woodlands for a wide range of recreational pursuits. It was also responsible for developing policies in support of sustainable forestry development to deliver social, economic and environmental goals. This modern multifunctional role represented a significant change from the traditional economic role of forestry, which was primarily about timber production and providing rural employment. The new role of forestry was more 'service led' with forests regarded as places where a diverse range of consumers could enjoy a range of 'offerings' to meet their needs.

To achieve this change in role the FC management invested a significant amount of time and effort, particularly during the period 1996–2002, in attempting to transform the organisation to work in a completely different way. During this time David Bills, the Director General, increasingly signalled the need for a fundamental shift in organisational culture from a centralised, hierarchical organisation implementing standard solutions, towards devolved decision making to deliver local solutions through greater consultation and participation with local communities and other partners. For example, in October 2001, he stated:

When the remit of the Forestry Commission was simpler it was possible for templates or procedures to be issued from the centre, and for common solutions to prevail. But now as we work closer to communities and with a broad range of funding and implementing partners we have to be prepared to allow decisions to be taken closer to the action.

However, it was no simple task to implement changes on this scale across an organisation with over three thousand employees, many of them geographically dispersed in isolated rural communities throughout England, Scotland and Wales.

All changed out

When David Bills was appointed as Director General in December 1995, the organisation was struggling to make the transition to this new multifunctional role. David was not a UK Civil Servant but an Australian forester with experience in private sector forestry. One reason for an external

Photo: Forestry Commission\Crown Copyright

appointment was that the Board were concerned that the FC was still rooted in the old mechanistic ways of handling its employees and activities.

When he arrived he found a challenging task ahead of him. 'When I came to this organisation, there was low morale and many thought it was a sinking ship'. He felt the organisation was 'a bit bruised and battered' and had 'lost its confidence'. The Board wanted him to help restore that confidence and to get the organisation into a 'healthy shape to be able to respond to the challenges that lay ahead'. David also realised that although the organisation had already proved that it could respond effectively to change, he had a difficult task ahead: 'When I arrived the staff seemed all "changed out". They seemed to think that the only solution was no more change! It took time to make people recognise that it is better to grab the initiative rather than having changes imposed upon us.'

David Bills also had a major challenge to persuade civil servants in Whitehall that his role was not that traditionally expected of a Director General, which he had been advised was '. . . keep the ministers out of trouble, stay within budgets and make good policies . . .', but rather that of managing the FC and its people to facilitate a move from the 'old-fashioned' inwardly focused organisation to a more progressive, flexible and outward looking organisation. The FC Board of Commissioners were strongly supportive of this agenda.

Proud tradition of forest stewardship

The FC was established as a government department in 1919 with the passing of the Forestry Act. This was a direct response to gradual deforestation that had taken place throughout the Industrial Revolution, which was exacerbated by increased timber demand during the First World War when shipping blockades limited imports. The government wanted to create a timber industry to secure future timber supplies in the event of another war: also high on the political agenda was a need to create rural employment for large numbers of British soldiers returning from the war.

The FC's principal aim was to rebuild and maintain future timber reserves. The original organisational structure was influenced by the hierarchical military systems of the time and the use of military language; 'Forest District Officers' wore uniforms and 'orders' were issued down through the 'chain of command'.

A primary task in these early days was afforestation, which involved forest design, large-scale plantings and care of young saplings. The organisation gradually built up a body of research knowledge and developed a reputation for its skills and expertise in forestry: FC staff were regarded as 'forestry experts' and stewards of the nation's forests. There was a strong sense of ownership of the forests and the public were sometimes regarded as 'getting in the way' of the real business of timber production.

The traditional culture

Forestry was traditionally a 'man's world' with a hard work ethic. The FC were strong in applying professional and specialist skills to technical problems related to the tasks of timber production, harvesting, fencing and planting new trees. The organisation was good at getting on with the job and delivering results: received wisdom was that effective timber production meant growing large numbers of a chosen species, i.e. planting 'Sitka Spruce' in tight ranks so that the trees grew tall with few branches in order to produce the type and quality of timber required. This resulted in forests that could be harvested efficiently but were lacking in variety, unattractive and impenetrable for social use.

The FC played an important role in creating employment in rural communities: low staff turnover, particularly in the Forest Districts, eventually created an ageing workforce imbued with a hard work ethic and fairly traditional views on how forests should be managed. To quote a forest worker: 'We're all long-term employees so the past affects us'.

'Them and us'

In the early days the FC had militaristic influences and these continued to be reflected in many structures and practices. The organisation structure was hierarchical with a high power distance between top and bottom. Power and status were based on grand job titles, rank, expert knowledge and political influence. Typically, HQ management sat at the pinnacle of the organisation structure: policy, planning, procedures and funding flowed from this central source 'down' through the organisation and outwards from HQ towards the districts. This led to a 'them and us' split between HQ and Forest Districts, who felt they were on the receiving end of 'inappropriate' centralised decisions and 'unnecessary' bureaucracy.

The management style was autocratic, top-down, with an emphasis on 'command and control'. The management decided what, when and how things had to be done: they rigorously controlled the execution and outcomes of timber production. In response, 'workers' just did as they were told: they did not tend to use their own initiative as this was seen as a risk; workers feared that they would be 'blamed' in cases of failure; they also perceived that if their initiatives turned out to be successful no reward or acknowledgement was given. Equally this situation meant that workers could blame management decisions whenever things went wrong.

The workforce was divided between 'non-industrials' (management, office, technical and professional staff) and 'industrials' (field staff). These groups had significant differences in terms and conditions of employment and pay structure. For example industrials were paid weekly in cash for work completed and non-industrials received a monthly salary paid directly into a bank account. Very few industrials were promoted across this invisible divide, which reinforced perceptions of 'them and us' between staff in HQ and field staff in the Forest Districts.

The various perceptions of 'them and us' combined with the opaque decision making and lack of clear communication, led to a culture where there was low trust and a tendency to blame others, described by one executive manager 'as symptomatic of a culture where we have not been very good at confronting issues and being honest with each other.'

Changes in the operating environment

During the 1960s and 70s productivity increased due to mechanisation. Guaranteed timber supply resulted in major investment in 'timber using' industries (e.g. sawmills and pulp), which created new markets and further increased demand for timber.

The 1970s saw a growing trend in conservation awareness. In addition, changes in legislation meant that the public were given the 'right to roam' (allowed to enter and enjoy the forest). In response to these trends, conservation and amenity issues were increasingly considered within FC policy and planning.

In the 1980s Thatcher's Conservative government began the shift to the 'market model' by embarking on their privatisation programme, which involved selling off public sector organisations and land. This represented quite a threat to the FC and what it stood for, because purely commercial timber production does not necessarily equate with the ethos of stewards of the nation's forests.

During the early 1990s the FC was under assault from several quarters: it had narrowly missed being sold off; the political agenda had become even more focused on efficiency of public services; the government were pushing very hard for industrial efficiency through a whole range of imposed targets. Meanwhile public sector reform was being driven through, aimed at improving accountability and reducing bureaucracy.

In response to these kinds of pressures, the Forestry Review in 1994 took an in-depth look at the rationale for the FC and its policies. This led to an internal split to form Forestry Authority (FA) which had a regulatory role, and Forest Enterprise (FE) which became the commercial arm of the organisation. FE embarked on a drive for operational efficiency and the combined effects of increased mechanisation and outsourcing of certain activities to contractors (e.g. harvesting) led to significant reductions in the numbers of field staff. This also had the effect of increasing the pressure on the remaining staff as they struggled to cope with the imposed changes and at the same time meet demanding new targets for efficiency and public sector reform.

During the period 1996/97 world timber prices collapsed as a result of over supply '. . . because of large-scale and swift increases in timber harvest'[1] in Eastern European countries (largely the Baltic states) desperate to generate revenue. This was not foreseen and this, with the strong British pound, had the effect of dramatically reducing income from timber sales, which put even further pressure on organisational resources.

A different approach to forestry

The Rio Earth Summit[2] and the Kyoto International Convention[3] were global initiatives that raised environmental concerns and began to influence government policy for 'sustainable forests'.[4] Around this time, different external stakeholder groups also accused the FC of lack of awareness of various environmental and animal rights issues.

It became increasingly crucial to the FC's economic survival for it to be skilled at balancing the conflicts between the harsh economic realities of a commercial enterprise with the valuable 'not-for-profit' contributions it made to society. The relatively straightforward tasks of timber production and forestry management developed into the increasingly complex role of managing sustainable forests to take account of environmental issues whilst also providing public access for recreational activities.

In 1997 the new Labour government's Social Inclusion Agenda placed an emphasis on social forestry issues such as public access, health and recreation. This meant that the FC's policies and practices had to incorporate this agenda by providing public access to woodland walks, cycle trails etc.

This also meant that the FC had to become a more consultative organisation, working closely

> When David Bills was asked what significant changes had taken place within the Forestry Commission during the period of his tenure, he gave the following reply:
>
> > Foresters used to think about the trees in the forest. Now we are thinking more of the spaces between the trees, because it's what happens in those places which makes the forest really live and work, socially as well as environmentally.
>
> (David Bills, Director General, Forestry Commission of Great Britain, 2003)

with conservation groups and local communities alike, and actively conveying its mission to the public by facilitating a diverse range of recreational, educational, and conservational activities as well as supporting the development of timber related industries. Whilst the FC was always recognised as authoritative, it had to become more forward thinking and more accommodating to the needs of working in partnerships with others. In order to develop these new ways of working, the FC had to become a more flexible and adaptive organisation where people achieved things through networking internally and by working in partnership with external stakeholders.

The implications for staff were that they had to learn to work in completely new ways – in many cases this meant 'surviving' internal restructures, taking on new roles, learning new skills and behaviours, and being empowered through taking greater responsibility for making decisions locally.

Change programmes

How did the FC manage to make the shift away from the traditional, hierarchical, command and control type culture towards being a more networked, responsive, and flexible organisation? Reflecting on their journey, David Bills and other members of the Executive admitted that 'there was no Grand Master Plan' but that it was more of a process of asking questions, listening and responding by trying some things out, learning from them, and using external partners as a sounding board. One of the consultants explained why, despite culture change being a difficult process, it has worked so well in the FC's case: '. . . because there was a

---

[1] F.H. Faustman, 'Forest economics in Eastern Europe', *Journal of Forest Economics*, vol. 5 no. 3, 1999, p. 2.

[2] Rio (1992): the United Nations Conferences on Environment and Development, aiming to work towards international agreements, which respect the interests of all and protect the integrity of the global environment and developmental system.

[3] Kyoto (1997): 110 industrialised nations committed to making substantial reductions in their emissions of greenhouse gases during the period of 2008–2010.

[4] Sustainable forests: forest management that contributes to the long-term ecological and economic well being of forest-based communities.

recognition from the top down that it takes time, there was a willingness to invest in supporting change and accept that there's no simple easily installed solution.'

Prior to the appointment of the new Director General in December 1995, the FC had already been working hard to address the challenges that were imposed on it by changes in government policy. It had become very focused on economic survival, which involved reducing costs and attempting to deliver a wide range of government imposed targets. To do this, the organisation had undergone a series of restructures to streamline operations and improve efficiency through reducing resources and simplifying work processes. This involved investment in new labour saving machinery, increasing centralisation of power structures and outsourcing many activities to contractors, all of which reduced the work force in the field. Many Forest Districts were amalgamated and in some cases re-amalgamated; some of these changes involved redundancies and were described as 'painful'. As a result, by December 1995 morale was low.

Therefore David Bills felt that rather than immediately imposing too many changes, he had to try to 'find the pulse of the organisation' and 'understand what made it tick', before he could facilitate more sustainable changes in the way things were done. He set about visiting different parts of the organisation and asking questions to find out what people thought and how they felt about how the organisation conducted its activities. These informal discussions led to a number of formal reviews of existing processes and practices.

One of the first requirements was to slim down the organisation, with a costly voluntary early retirement scheme, which involved a significant number of people. This did not help to rebuild morale and trust amongst the workforce but it did provide an opportunity to refresh the Executive Management Team and appoint a Change Management Team. These groups were to play a major part in the future change interventions which were many and varied, with some more successful than others. The four different change programmes outlined below were directed, influenced and supported by these groups.

'Unification'

In 1996 David Bills decided to investigate the process of unifying the two-tier workforce within the

---

Main aims and outcomes of unification

The main aims of unification were to create a united workforce by defining a common set of terms and conditions and removing the 'them and us' barriers by treating all staff equally. In practical terms it required the abolition of industrial wage structures, allowances and pension funding.

Post-unification, there was no artificial demarcation – all employees shared common structures for pay and grading, communication, and training and development.

Quote: 'The attitude became if you are qualified you can do the job.'

FC. This was partly in response to what he heard during his informal discussions around the organisation, and partly in response to the requirements of public sector reform[5] aimed at reducing bureaucracy in the Civil Service.

Traditionally there had been a massive gulf between 'industrials' and 'non-industrials': industrials were often looked down upon as 'manual labourers' and non-industrials were perceived to have higher status within the organisation. It was a structure akin to officers and ratings, a hangover of the past militaristic influences.

The feedback from an earlier communication review had heightened senior management's awareness of the importance of keeping people informed. Therefore in 1997 the Unification Working Group was established to facilitate the unification process. This group consisted of experienced field staff and trade union representatives. This was described as 'the first genuine attempt to approach change in a different way' by communicating with staff face-to-face and by working in collaboration with the trade unions as partners in the process of change.

The Unification Working Group coordinated the unification process by conducting road shows to consult with staff and to inform them about all of the issues involved in harmonising the terms and conditions for both staff groups. Unification meant significant personal change for many people

---

[5] Public sector reform: includes changes within central and local government, i.e. a drive to reform public services by including and expanding the role of the private sector.

and the team worked hard to make the road shows 'informative and inclusive of employees and their families, with two way communication'. They consisted of short presentations followed by a question and answer session and further one-to-one sessions where required. The group also travelled to every Forest District and ran surgeries to provide advice and guidance in response to individual queries. In addition, newsletters were sent out regularly to employees and a helpline was installed to answer individual questions.

Three years after the decision to tackle unification, it was accepted in a vote by staff (60 per cent of eligible staff voted and 67 per cent of them voted in favour of unification), and the revised structure took effect from July 2000.

Many employees viewed unification positively as it symbolised a significant shift away from the old 'them and us' hierarchy. However, despite all the efforts to communicate with employees, there were mixed views on unification and the implementation of the new structure. Some found the one-to-one sessions useful as they helped to decrease anxieties pertaining to the new wage structures. However, others expressed frustration from feeling inadequately informed about how unification would be implemented and how it would affect them. Some were cynical about the process: one employee said, 'I voted for it, not that it would have mattered – it had been decided already.'

This outcome indicated that whilst the approach had been helpful and had achieved a successful outcome, there was still a good deal of work to be done to improve two-way communication and build trust with all staff.

The leadership programme

In response to the feedback from their first staff survey, senior management decided that the way forward was to enhance the leadership skills of approximately 250 senior and middle managers. A steering group was established to produce a brief and select an external partner to conduct the training. The steering group was led by the Change Manager but also comprised a broad range of managers representing different parts of the organisation.

A small group of consultants were chosen primarily because they had a challenging approach to the change process, which recommended more depth and breadth than the FC had initially requested. As a senior manager recalled: 'They were pretty good at not saying "this is your brief – we will deliver it" but at saying "have you thought about the brief – are you sure it is what you want to do?"' From the consultants' point of view it was evident that what FC were asking for was different from what they needed: 'They weren't so clear about articulating that they wanted to change the culture; their solution was to ask for a training programme.' The consultants' understanding of their brief was to help develop 'internal change agents' who could take ownership of the change to lead and support it from inside the organisation.

The consultants worked in partnership with the steering group to design leadership events that helped managers to be more aware of the changes that were taking place around them and of people's emotional responses to change and how these might create resistance. They were also designed to help managers to reflect on their own responsibilities for leading and supporting people through change and to develop a better understanding of how their own leadership behaviour impacted upon their staff. The events also provided managers with tools and techniques for leading change.

Each leadership event lasted three days and hosted up to 20 managers. They were designed to help managers explore the organisational culture in a strategic context to make sense of and articulate the required changes, then decide what actions they should take to support the changes 'in their own patch'. During the period January to December 2001, a total of 13 events were held with the voluntary attendance of around 250 senior and middle managers. David Bills and the members of the Executive Management Team attended many of the events to participate in the discussion and listen to the views expressed.

The leadership events were initially targeted at all senior and middle managers, but not the executive group. However, after the first three events the executive group requested their own event: one of the executives explained how they started to feel obliged to understand what was being discussed at the leadership events, '. . . it became quite difficult for us dealing with managers who had been [to the leadership events] as we didn't always have the answers.'

The outcomes from this series of events were summarised in the past and future cultural webs (see Exhibits 1 and 2 below). The web shown in Exhibit 1 characterises the managers' perceptions of the traditional culture and the web in Exhibit 2

Aims and outcomes of leadership programme

The main aims of the leadership programme were to create a large group of 'internal change agents', who could lead and support their people through the implementation of strategic change.

The cultural webs were used to help these senior and middle managers explore the strategic context for change and consider the implications for 'the way things are done around here'.

The main outcomes were that managers felt that the process helped them to consider what they needed to do differently to help their people adapt to new ways of working. The second staff survey reported significant improvement and there was also a lot of qualitative feedback indicating that things were changing.

Quote from a middle manager: 'A lot has changed as a result of the leadership events; there's definitely more commitment from senior staff. I see it in my boss and his boss and they are far more committed to involving people. They have become less autocratic and are involving me more in their decisions, and also more open to involving the rest of my staff. I find that a very positive development.'

Exhibit 1   Past cultural web – description of 'traditional FC culture'

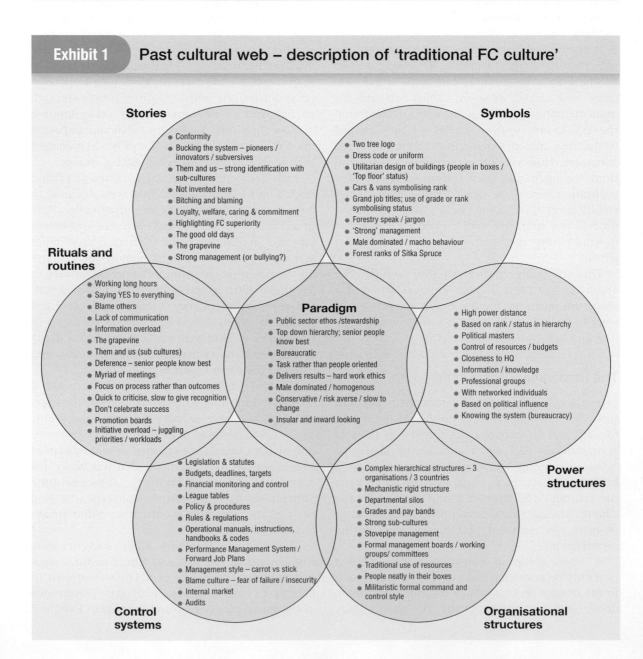

Stories
- Conformity
- Bucking the system – pioneers / innovators / subversives
- Them and us – strong identification with sub-cultures
- Not invented here
- Bitching and blaming
- Loyalty, welfare, caring & commitment
- Highlighting FC superiority
- The good old days
- The grapevine
- Strong management (or bullying?)

Symbols
- Two tree logo
- Dress code or uniform
- Utilitarian design of buildings (people in boxes / 'Top floor' status)
- Cars & vans symbolising rank
- Grand job titles; use of grade or rank symbolising status
- Forestry speak / jargon
- 'Strong' management
- Male dominated / macho behaviour
- Forest ranks of Sitka Spruce

Rituals and routines
- Working long hours
- Saying YES to everything
- Blame others
- Lack of communication
- Information overload
- The grapevine
- Them and us (sub cultures)
- Deference – senior people know best
- Myriad of meetings
- Focus on process rather than outcomes
- Quick to criticise, slow to give recognition
- Don't celebrate success
- Promotion boards
- Initiative overload – juggling priorities / workloads

Paradigm
- Public sector ethos / stewardship
- Top down hierarchy; senior people know best
- Bureaucratic
- Task rather than people oriented
- Delivers results – hard work ethics
- Male dominated / homogenous
- Conservative / risk averse / slow to change
- Insular and inward looking

Power structures
- High power distance
- Based on rank / status in hierarchy
- Political masters
- Control of resources / budgets
- Closeness to HQ
- Information / knowledge
- Professional groups
- With networked individuals
- Based on political influence
- Knowing the system (bureaucracy)

Control systems
- Legislation & statutes
- Budgets, deadlines, targets
- Financial monitoring and control
- League tables
- Policy & procedures
- Rules & regulations
- Operational manuals, instructions, handbooks & codes
- Performance Management System / Forward Job Plans
- Management style – carrot vs stick
- Blame culture – fear of failure / insecurity
- Internal market
- Audits

Organisational structures
- Complex hierarchical structures – 3 organisations / 3 countries
- Mechanistic rigid structure
- Departmental silos
- Grades and pay bands
- Strong sub-cultures
- Stovepipe management
- Formal management boards / working groups / committees
- Traditional use of resources
- People neatly in their boxes
- Militaristic formal command and control style

Exhibit 2

Future cultural web – description of 'new culture to which FC aspired'

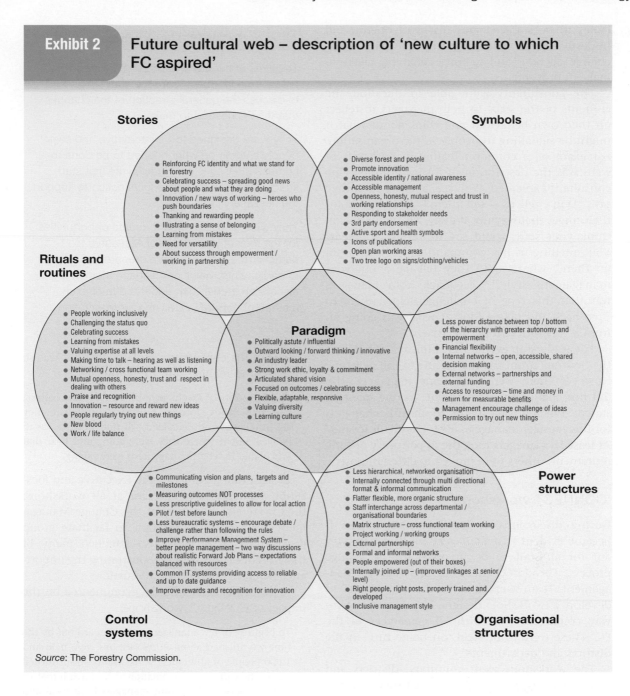

Stories

- Reinforcing FC identity and what we stand for in forestry
- Celebrating success – spreading good news about people and what they are doing
- Innovation / new ways of working – heroes who push boundaries
- Thanking and rewarding people
- Illustrating a sense of belonging
- Learning from mistakes
- Need for versatility
- About success through empowerment / working in partnership

Symbols

- Diverse forest and people
- Promote innovation
- Accessible identity / national awareness
- Accessible management
- Openness, honesty, mutual respect and trust in working relationships
- Responding to stakeholder needs
- 3rd party endorsement
- Active sport and health symbols
- Icons of publications
- Open plan working areas
- Two tree logo on signs/clothing/vehicles

Rituals and routines

- People working inclusively
- Challenging the status quo
- Celebrating success
- Learning from mistakes
- Valuing expertise at all levels
- Making time to talk – hearing as well as listening
- Networking / cross functional team working
- Mutual openness, honesty, trust and respect in dealing with others
- Praise and recognition
- Innovation – resource and reward new ideas
- People regularly trying out new things
- New blood
- Work / life balance

Paradigm

- Politically astute / influential
- Outward looking / forward thinking / innovative
- An industry leader
- Strong work ethic, loyalty & commitment
- Articulated shared vision
- Focused on outcomes / celebrating success
- Flexible, adaptable, responsive
- Valuing diversity
- Learning culture

Power structures

- Less power distance between top / bottom of the hierarchy with greater autonomy and empowerment
- Financial flexibility
- Internal networks – open, accessible, shared decision making
- External networks – partnerships and external funding
- Access to resources – time and money in return for measurable benefits
- Management encourage challenge of ideas
- Permission to try out new things

Control systems

- Communicating vision and plans, targets and milestones
- Measuring outcomes NOT processes
- Less prescriptive guidelines to allow for local action
- Pilot / test before launch
- Less bureaucratic systems – encourage debate / challenge rather than following the rules
- Improve Performance Management System – better people management – two way discussions about realistic Forward Job Plans – expectations balanced with resources
- Common IT systems providing access to reliable and up to date guidance
- Improve rewards and recognition for innovation

Organisational structures

- Less hierarchical, networked organisation
- Internally connected through multi directional format & informal communication
- Flatter flexible, more organic structure
- Staff interchange across departmental / organisational boundaries
- Matrix structure – cross functional team working
- Project working / working groups
- External partnerships
- Formal and informal networks
- People empowered (out of their boxes)
- Internally joined up – (improved linkages at senior level)
- Right people, right posts, properly trained and developed
- Inclusive management style

Source: The Forestry Commission.

how it needed to change if it was to deliver the emerging strategy.

The cultural webs provided a structure for shared discussion with the facilitators encouraging debate amongst the managers. Managers described this process as 'valuable, really important, and thought-provoking', because it produced many insights about the strategic direction of the FC and their own role in leading and supporting the required change. One manager said it had struck

him how much 'everybody wanted the same thing . . . to improve communication, to be more involving . . . to be fair to people.'

Yet there were some major contradictions in how different groups of managers interpreted various aspects of the culture. For example what was considered to be 'strong management' further up the hierarchy was perceived as 'bullying' or 'harassment' further down. However the facilitated discussions provided opportunities for these issues to be surfaced and discussed openly and honestly, which meant they became part of the change agenda, and actions could be taken to make improvements.

The consultants were able to question the contents of the webs to help managers to reflect on their own behaviour and think about what it might be signalling to people in the organisation. For example, a common feature in both sets of webs was the description of 'blame culture'. One consultant explained: 'You see, at every level they say: "Don't tell us – tell them." And they point their finger that way up. We say "Ok, what do you think your staff would say if we talk to them? You're telling us it's 'command and control from up there', what would they tell me about your management style?"' Feedback from managers was that this type of challenge helped them to 'step back and take a look at what was going on from a very different perspective'.

The leadership events were aimed at facilitating the 'journey' from the old culture to the new one. However there were still some managers who did not change their behaviour. As one manager stated: 'I'm too long in the tooth, this change is for the younger managers, it's too difficult for me.' At least 15 managers took the opportunity of early retirement; others were moved to different posts.

'CONNECT workshops'

During discussions at the leadership events it became evident that managers felt it was important for all staff to be involved in the change process. To address this issue the Change Management Team worked with the consultants to develop a workshop designed to improve two-way communication with all employees in the FC. These were to be held 'on home turf' in the districts and departments.

The workshops were voluntary: districts and departments were invited to request them if interested; employees' participation was not compulsory. These workshops were named CONNECT.

One member of the Change Management Team described the purpose of CONNECT workshops:

> We wanted to become an organisation which would use its people in a more effective way and would be more flexible and adaptable for the future . . . that's about realising people's talents, recognising them in the process and giving them a chance to grow . . . we now have more pockets of that happening.

Aims of 'CONNECT' workshops

The aims of the CONNECT events were to present the feedback from the staff survey and to discuss the general direction of the changes that the FC needed to make.

They were designed to be interactive and seek people's views on what needed to be done to address the issues arising from the first staff survey, and also to initiate local action to support the necessary changes.

They were also designed to create opportunities for the Executive and Senior Managers to demonstrate that they were prepared to *listen* to participants' views and engage them in discussion, rather than adopt the traditional method of 'telling' i.e. making a presentation.

One of the consultants explained why it was so important to include staff in the process:

> There are lots of bright people right at the coalface, who actually love forestry . . . they are articulate, they are intelligent and dedicated. All they needed was to be clear about where they were going and hear that articulated in what management were saying.

At least one member of the Executive and local Senior Managers were present at all workshops; there were also members of the Change Management Team and a consultant to facilitate group discussions. David Bills also attended many of these events as a way of demonstrating the importance he placed upon these discussions.

A senior manager from HQ commented on the impact of CONNECT workshops:

> To begin with few managers came forward but by the time we finished about 40 workshops were held and 1,600 people of all grades, skills and locations turned up. Each workshop was facilitated by an internal or external person and senior managers both local and from HQ attended and took an active part. It was a huge effort and it started to convince staff that this culture change programme was going to last.

One of the most significant benefits of the CONNECT workshops was the opportunity for senior staff to have direct face-to-face communication with all employees. One of the consultants explained:

> They heard a lot of negative things, people got an opportunity to get things off their chest . . .

Unification, what happened in 1919, things to do with money, its all the things that people see as grievances and the important thing is that people were allowed to express them.

Similarly David Bills described receiving the feedback in this way

Sometimes it is difficult for senior managers to listen to the criticism because some of the criticism perhaps feels unjust or unfairly biased. But that doesn't matter. It is the fact that the feeling is out there that is import-ant. And we need to understand why it is and what we can do to make things better.

A feature of many of the CONNECT events was to provide an opportunity for groups that work together to discuss particularly difficult issues, which were directly impacting their workplace. They were invited to work on a plan of action to tackle this issue and to take it to their managers for discussion before implementation. This way groups could see how they could be empowered to improve their workplace without retreating to the traditional response of 'why don't *they* fix it?' Where these home actions took place there was perhaps the most rapid and significant cultural change.

Although 1,600 employees took part in CONNECT, the events were voluntary and some districts did not participate. One executive said, 'I feel that there are some parts of the organisation that for historical reasons feel like outsiders and feel a bit left out. They will be the late adopters.' Another senior manager commented, 'Some who really needed them didn't have them.' Sub-sequently, some of these late adopters began to hold CONNECT-type events, either because of upward pressure from staff or because senior man-agers identified that there were some issues that needed to be addressed.

Feedback from those attending the CONNECT events was mixed: they were seen by many as a symbol of openness and a genuine attempt by senior managers to really listen to what was being said. One district manager explained the way things work in his district

We have a CONNECT event every year now – where the staff are thinking about the future and discussing the issues in the district. These have made people realise that they are partially responsible for their own future.

An executive explained that: 'the CONNECT banner has moved initially from communication to culture change'.

'The New FC Values'

Another feature of the CONNECT workshops was that they were designed to engage staff in discussions about the values of the organisation. These discussions built on earlier feedback from the first staff survey and leadership events and then led to further consultation, which resulted in a form of words to reflect what people felt the organisation 'stood for'.

In order to 'reaffirm the new organisational culture', the Director General communicated the new FC Values in May 2002. These were:

Teamwork – Professionalism – Respect – Communication – Learning – Creativity

The values were launched with the production of a booklet, which was sent to every individual member of staff and these still continue to be sent to every new recruit. A 'Values' version of the FC screen saver was developed and a calendar was sent out to all staff as a follow up reminder. The FC values are now the cornerstone of the culture change programme on the VSPC workshops (see next change programme, below).

However, there remained a level of mistrust. As one participant commented, 'There is some scepticism and cynicism about the new culture.' Many participants said, 'We want to see action. Will anything actually change as a result of all that had been said?'

In October 2001, another Executive event took place to review all of the feedback from the staff survey, the leadership events and the CONNECT workshops. The main issues arising from the feed-back were the need for clearer leadership, greater trust in people, better communications, improved people management and improved performance management. This event resulted in Senior Man-agement agreeing on a 'CONNECT Action Plan' to support further change based on the feedback that they had heard. Each member of the Executive was responsible for championing one key area of the plan with a timetable for solutions to be implemented.

The Change Support Team was established to provide dedicated resources and support for the detailed implementation of the Connect Action Plan.

The VSPC programme

Feedback from the Leadership events and CONNECT workshops indicated that there was a need to support all front line managers in 'leading the journey from the old to the new culture'. The steering group suggested developing another type of event, and senior management agreed to support these events after funding issues had been solved. This new programme replaced the Leadership events to become the main management development vehicle open to all levels of management within the FC. Many executives, senior and middle managers participated in these events, alongside front-line managers and supervisors.

One senior manager reflected on the process

> . . . in the beginning, we were saying 'Ok, target that middle management level' but then we realised this has to go all the way down to frontline supervisors and all the way up to the senior management. And that has happened. We have now got a series of courses which are called VSPC, which stands for 'Valuing and Supporting People and Change'.

These development workshops were a vehicle for helping all levels of managers to understand the changes taking place around them. By March 2004, 26 of these events had taken place, involving some 400 managers and supervisors, with about 150 people scheduled to attend future events as part of their Personal Development Plan.

The consultants designed the VSPC workshops in conjunction with a new steering group that included some front line managers.

Aims of the VSPC Programme

The aims were to help all frontline managers to:

- Understand the strategic context for the culture change.
- Challenge some of their deeply held assumptions and beliefs, often played out as 'old culture' behaviours.
- Consider whether the 'new culture' was being translated into action e.g. were the new FC Values being practised in daily working life?
- Reflect on their own behaviour and consider what kind of signals they were sending out to people e.g. to what degree was their own behaviour 'living' the FC values?

The consultants had previously used theatre '. . . to penetrate some of the most impenetrable recesses of people's thinking, to present them with pictures of themselves from different angles'. They had the idea of adapting elements of this method into an FC case study that could be used as the basis for helping people to understand what really needed to change in order for the new culture to become an everyday reality.

The steering group worked with the consultants and the Change Team to add contextual relevance and validity to the consultants' design of case study scenarios. These featured a number of fictitious but archetypal characters representing different aspects of the 'traditional' organisational culture. The case study placed them in a series of different scenarios representing the modern multifunctional role of forestry described earlier. Caricatures of these six exaggerated characters are illustrated in the Appendix.

The workshops provided a safe environment in which the participants could explore why some of the traditional behaviours were no longer appropriate and to consider what they needed to do differently in the future. The consultants also wanted to increase managers' awareness of people's emotional responses to change and provide some tools and techniques to help them develop skills to respond effectively in a range of different situations. A line manager reported that the VSPC course provided '. . . a good lesson in how to communicate and conciliate and get everybody on board.'

Throughout the three-day programme, the characters were placed in scenarios that represented real situations requiring new ways of working as described in the 'future cultural web', and reflected in the FC Values. As the scenarios unfolded, the characters increasingly had to overcome problems that they had largely created as a result of their earlier behaviour and actions. The delegates had regular opportunities to reflect on how the characters struggled with many of the situations they found themselves in because of their habitual attitudes, behaviours and approach to working with others. They also had a chance to debate with their colleagues many of the issues confronting the characters. Feedback from delegates indicated that this process helped them to understand and make sense of the changes taking place around them, and provided them with practical tools and techniques for operating more effectively in the changing context of their role.

One consultant observed:

Once they [participants] begin to understand the impact that change has on people and what they need to do to lead change it helps them to decide how they have to behave differently. We don't tell them how they have to behave differently – we just let them decide for themselves. All we do is just present them with scenarios.

One manager commented:

There were times in the course when you were asked as an individual to do things you probably wouldn't have wanted to – wouldn't normally have done. But that stimulated the thought process of 'Yeah, that's another way I could manage those situations.' And I tried to put some of it into practice.

Over 400 managers have attended these VSPC workshops, and many more have requested attendance at future workshops. This has enabled the FC to develop a critical mass of front line managers who understand the strategic imperative and core values of the organisation, and who have the awareness and skills to translate these into action on a daily basis.

One of the consultants observed that an outcome of the workshops was 'The organisation moved on to stop talking about culture and start talking about real behaviour'.

Change continues . . .

In August 2002 Ministers announced the Forestry Devolution Review (FDR), leading to an internal restructure within FC into three separate funding and delivery streams (England, Scotland and Wales) on 1 April 2003. It was a change that the organisation had seen coming as Ministers had declared a will to transfer responsibility for forestry to Scottish Ministers and the National Assembly for Wales in 1999. The aim was to achieve greater integration with rural policy work, whilst retaining the desirable opportunities for a collaborative approach to common issues.

Devolution changed the role of the Silvan House HQ in Edinburgh as decisions concerning public forestry were to be made in each country and no longer centrally managed the funding. The former HQ became known as 'Shared Services', offering services to the countries, which used to be centrally directed from HQ. David Bills commented on the change for the former HQ, 'We

are like a multinational governmental department now.' One manager expressed his concerns:

I'm not sure if the culture in Silvan House is going to work in the future . . . now that they are a Shared Service. They are no longer on the top of the tree, if you like; they are now servicing other parts of the organisation; that is a big cultural change for them.

Devolution was a significant change, although not a surprising one. David Bills explained the benefits of having gone through the culture change before devolution:

The work we have done to get the culture right . . . it's now much easier to handle devolution. Without having had this cultural change approach we would be struggling. . . . In a way we can talk about it [devolution] now and people are more open about it because of the work we have done on culture. They are not feeling so threatened by it.

Has the Forestry Commission changed?

Having invested so much time and effort in trying to change, a key question is 'what has actually changed?'

Changes in what the FC delivers

Today many forests look different from the traditional timber production sites of densely packed rows of Sitka spruce that were so typical of the economic drive for efficiency in past eras. The FC has developed numerous sites to meet the social and environmental agendas: these are mixed woodland, well signposted with car packs and picnic facilities, mapped out with footpaths, nature trails and cycle tracks. The FC is also increasingly involved in environmental projects to return land to its natural habitat, and urban forestry projects to build green networks and improve the quality of urban environments. There is less emphasis on a 'one size fits all' approach and more emphasis on solutions tailored to meet the needs of people and the environment.

Changes inside the organisation

There are not only changes in what is being delivered, but quantitative and qualitative evidence indicates that there are changes in people's perceptions of working within the FC. Employee feedback indicates that things have changed. A group of field staff stated: 'Our work is more acknowledged now, we are encouraged to work for ourselves, which makes us proud of what we do.' When asked for his views on what was different as a result of the change process, one manager summed it up, 'I think the FC is well placed for the changes it faces in future . . . because it has been able to embrace change, influence and actually initiate change in its own domestic sphere.'

In November 2002 a second staff survey was conducted to measure whether the change efforts had made any impact. This time 58 per cent of employees participated and their responses indicated many definite improvements. A summary of some of the key outcomes is presented in Table 1.

The following short extracts are based on interviews with staff at three different Forest Districts: these provide some evidence of the nature of the changes that have taken place.

Comments about change from within Forest District A

Whatever next!

Historically this district was very hierarchical and the FDM had an authoritarian management style, which meant that changes were introduced as dictates and this discouraged openness. Staff had become so used to trying to cope with the many and frequent changes that their normal response to one another was to shrug, shake their heads and ask with a sigh, 'whatever next!'

The most constructive change that they experienced was the appointment of a new FDM, whose management style was completely different to his predecessor. This seemed to have generated much more optimism towards change, as indicated by one employee: '. . . [the organisation] used to be led from the centre [but is] now leading from the front.' Such directly perceived benefits have positively influenced the atmosphere within the district, for example, the employees recognise the newly developed 'team' culture has replaced the traditional 'blame' culture. The overall feeling reflected within the district is summarised by: 'I'm more able to be myself, happier when I come to work.'

An increased feeling of being valued appears to have been developed by perceptions of increased empowerment and autonomy: 'My job allows me to be much more empowered', and people are perceived to '. . . put more of themselves into it . . . take more initiative.' Unification and increased openness have facilitated the beginning of improved communication, although it is acknowledged throughout the district that further improvements are still needed.

The FDM has noticed a visible increase in openness, stating that:

The biggest change for me is that everybody in the district has a right to speak to me as their manager. They always had that right before but there was that barrier that people just would not come in.

He also reported less of a blame culture amongst managers:

There is nobody looking over your shoulder . . . looking for any mistake . . . there is recognition that people are trying to do their best.

These changes enabled him to disseminate an open supportive culture within his district.

The FDM felt that one of the most significant personal benefits employees noticed as a result of the change process was:

[employees] do recognise that they are needed and that they are not just used for other people's benefits. It's a team that achieves rather than an individual that takes credits.

District staff also reflected this opinion and indicated that Unification had also positively influenced this viewpoint.

Another important factor the FDM noted was increased responsiveness and communication from senior management:

there is recognition [from senior management] that this might increase the work employees have to do in the district but for the forestry and for the following reasons it has to take place. If they at least explain themselves, that helps . . . it's these little things, not really the big things that you remember; it's just the wee things that are always repeated that help to change the mindset.

Table 1 **Excerpt from summary of results from staff surveys**

Statement	Survey 1 2000 [%]	Survey 2 2002 [%]	Change
I know how my work fits into the team . . .	92	93	+1
I would recommend the FC as a place to work . . .	49	67	+18
Morale is generally high . . .	33	45	+12
The FC takes training seriously . . .	38	59	+21
My pay is fair . . .	30	41	+11
Overall positive . . .	55	61	+6
But			
Well informed . . .	63	59	−4
Promotion is based on merit . . .	22	26	+4

Source: The Forestry Commission.

Comments about change from within Forest District B

The mavericks

Historically this district was also very hierarchical and when the FDM arrived in the early 1990s, his managerial characteristics fitted well with the old FC culture. He explained:

> I heard someone talking on the radio about treating people like adolescents when they come to work. I thought '. . . that's exactly how we have been treating people for years, having been a forest worker when I was a student I was treated like that; you came to work, you left your brain behind, because you weren't allowed to use it . . .'.

As a result he realised that he had to change himself to be able to create a team-based working environment.

The process of change included empowerment of staff, more open communication, regular team meetings, training, and a more inclusive management style involving staff in the decision-making process. One member of staff commented:

> '. . . it's been a gentle process because they [district employees] were very reluctant at first . . . although production hasn't changed . . . they're more in control of their own destiny.

Teamwork and open communication are core factors in this FDM's leadership style. In his own words: 'It's more important to get people involved in a way of working rather than a method of working, actually thinking and reacting to what they see.' To support teamwork the district tries to create and maintain team spirit. 'We organise events every now and then, for example white-water rafting, where everybody can join in. This brings us closer together . . .'. This closeness helps to improve working relationships with management as well as with people from other functions. 'The team is the whole district, which is then made up of sub teams' (Forester). This then facilitates the openness that has developed in the district over the years.

Despite having a team approach in the district, employees feel that even after the change process the FC as a whole is still quite hierarchical and quick to blame, as highlighted by one employee: 'I think there are some people I know who would say things that would benefit the organisation if their opinions were allowed to be voiced and they felt there was going to be no comeback.' Scepticism exists about the responsiveness of some senior management to the change process.

Some respondents mentioned that although the organisation had encouraged increased openness during the change process, many areas were not used to the level of openness existing in District C:

> . . . the difficulty is we are still working in a hierarchy based company, so this district is seen as relatively maverick, because we are so team based. That has led us into other issues where we are regarded with suspicion by some of the other districts because of the way we operate.

Some employees valued the change process events finding them empowering and/or informative, one forester describes the VSPC course as: 'It was a lesson in how to communicate and conciliate and get everybody on board.' The FDM appreciated the value of the change programme events, and has periodically commissioned the consultants directly to work for his district. When asked about the culture change within the district, he states that:

'We are not there yet, but we have come a long way and there is still a long way until we are all completely open and honest with each other. But it is a lot better than it used to be.'

It would appear that some significant changes have taken place, but are these changes universal across the organisation?

Comments about change from within Forest District C

One big happy family?

District C is a large district that traditionally made a considerable income from timber production, although it contains many historical sites and diverse wildlife. More recently there was an increasing need to balance timber production with nature conservation and recreational activities.

The district had its share of repeated amalgamations with neighbouring districts, leaving an un-bridged divide amongst employees in the combined district. A decision had to be made about where the district office should be located and this created a 'winner and a loser in the newly amalgamated district'. Regretting the divide among staff that this created, an employee stated (somewhat tongue in cheek): '. . . we were amalgamated, and now we are all one big happy family'. The FDM explained that there were fairly deep seated issues amongst staff:

I've often been dismayed by the territoriality. In fact it is very, very disturbing in some cases people talking about old management units that go back to forests of 20 years ago and gripes and groans and prejudices arising from as far back as that.

The district was geographically dispersed, which made it quite challenging to maintain good communication with all staff. Attempts had been made to increase awareness through holding regular team meetings and providing access to the internet. The employees seemed disinterested in the changes that had been occurring and there appeared to be a lack of willingness to be involved in decision making regarding the district and the FC as a whole. The district had a CONNECT event but as one employee stated: 'I was quite happy

that I wasn't involved.' This opinion appears to reflect the views of staff interviewed within the district, many of whom did not appear to feel strongly about the event.

The 'them and us' divide still existed, both in regard to staff in Edinburgh (old HQ), which is seen as external and out of touch with district issues and the old (now amalgamated) districts. Informal hierarchical order and ranking still appears to be preferred, as illustrated by one manager: '. . . it's a very hierarchical approach . . . but they rank themselves up against each other . . . and that's ok.'

When asked about the culture change programme the FDM reported:

You can't put a lot of pressure on them [staff] to conform to the new culture, or force them to go on courses . . . you've got to prove that the trust works . . . it doesn't happen overnight . . . people who have been doing a job for 20 years are not going to change their minds because they have been to a meeting.

As a result he saw his role throughout the process as: '. . . very complicated. We've organised a number of events, brought in external people from a change group in headquarters.'

The FDM reported that there are still some issues with trust within the district. Staff also indicated during interviews that there was a lack of trust in the organisation and expressed frustration at their experience of the way change was handled within the district. Although the FDM had tried to be responsive by implementing suggested initiatives such as computer e-mail training, he found it '. . . difficult to come up with new ideas that are fresh and alternative' within the district.

Clearly, people's experience of change and their responses to it have been different in various parts of the organisation.

Conclusion

In terms of the process, people initially had not truly conceptualised what exactly needed to change, although they had an idea of where they wanted to get to. The consultants noticed that in the course of the many discussions and debates with staff, the Director General's 'vision' of the future became more clearly articulated and shared. David Bills states that:

Culture is about behaviour. You cannot have one without the other. You can talk about values, you can talk about culture, but the ultimate thing is how you behave; how you behave when there is a challenge, when there is a difficult issue, when there is an opportunity. Run out and look for help or run away from it, all of that. Do you dial Head Office for direction or do you get on with it on a local level but with a willingness to share experience and learn from others' successes and mistakes. So, if we hadn't achieved behaviour change we hadn't achieved anything.

An outcome of the overall change process appears to be the acceptance amongst staff that change is inevitable, as one line manager stated:

At least the change process has made employees aware that change is a part of life now . . . it [change] will carry on even if you don't.

APPENDIX
VSPC characters[1]

The Traditionalist

Matt Grey represented the traditional Forest District Manager whose main aim was efficient timber production, based on the economic role of Forestry.

Matt couldn't really see the need for all this change, and didn't really want 'the hassle', after all the FC had been successful, so why change anything?

'Just Do It' Management

Richard 'Dick' Tator represented the traditional management style, sometimes referred to by staff as the 'just do it' approach.

This management style did not just refer to senior management – it permeated down through all levels in the organisational hierarchy.

Quote from a staff member in a Forest District: 'In the past the district was very hierarchical with an authoritarian management style and this discouraged openness: *that was the way things were, you didn't make waves*.'

The Maverick

Damian Sharp, the Forester 'with attitude', was a real maverick. Many of those attending the workshops could relate to this character. He represented the cynical response of many people to organisational changes within FC, because of the way they had experienced change during the 1980s and 1990s.

The character also represented the resentment felt by many people towards the autocratic management style. Damian reflected the rebellious response of many staff, who tended to blame management and take every opportunity to challenge, create conflict and resist change.

---

[1] Illustrations by graham@ogilviedesign.co.uk.

The Survivor

Joe Steadman represented those staff who had 'survived' the many restructures to Forest Districts during the 1980s and 1990s when change was synonymous with changing the structure and introducing a whole range of targets.

People had recounted their experiences of many different types of change: from major organisational structural changes and amalgamations with other forest districts to changes in the nature of their work related to recreational activity.

Quote from a staff member: 'The district has undergone many changes over the years, prompting us to ask each other: *"Whatever next!"*'

Action Man

John Keen represented the target/deadline driven response of many staff who felt overworked and under pressure as a result of the many restructures and targets that were introduced during the 1990s.

This character responded to the demands placed on him by working long hours. He was constantly trying to be efficient and stay on top of his workload, but he was so driven by deadlines and targets that he had begun to lose sight of the real priorities.

The New Role of Forestry

Vicky Smiley represented many aspects of the new multifunctional role of Forestry. She also represented the very gradual shift away from the homogenous 'macho' culture towards a more diverse organisation.

Marks and Spencer

Nardine Collier

Marks and Spencer became a household name internationally by the early 1990s. However, the last part of that decade began to see decline. This case examines successive attempts to reverse this decline, with many new initiatives and new managers over several years. These efforts appeared inadequate to turning round the company and culminated in the 2004 resignation of Marks and Spencer's chairman.

• • •

Michael Marks began what was to become one of the most recognised brands on the planet by establishing a penny bazaar in the late 1880s, it was a huge success with the majority of products only costing one penny. Marks rapidly expanded his business, and soon decided he needed a partner to help run the growing firm. Tom Spencer, a cashier of Marks' supplier, was recommended and from this partnership Marks and Spencer (M&S) steadily grew. A successful retail formula had begun to emerge surrounding this growth, but by the early 21st century, M&S's success was beginning to run out.

The M&S formula for success

Simon Marks took over the running of M&S from his father. He was aggressive with his ideas for the firm, and went to America to investigate how they ran their stores. On his return to Britain he made a number of changes to the penny bazaars, firstly by turning them into stores, establishing a simple pricing policy and introducing the 'St Michael' logo as a sign of quality. There was feeling of camaraderie and a close-knit family atmosphere within the stores, which was compounded by employing staff whom the managers believed would 'fit in' and become part of that family. The staff were also treated better and paid more than sales assistants in other companies. The family nature of this firm dominated the top management too: until the late

1970s the board was made up of family members only.

Marks was renowned for his personal control over the business and his attention to detail. According to a Channel 4 programme (25 February 2001) his was a style of top-down management which could often take the form of shouting and bullying. This concern for control was also manifested in the way Marks dealt with suppliers. He always used the same UK-based suppliers and meticulously ensured that goods were exactly to specification; a relationship designed to build reliance of the suppliers and ensure high and consistent quality.

Until the late 1990s M&S was hugely successful both in terms of profit and market share. It achieved this by applying a structured formula to all its operations and maintained it by establishing a set of fundamental principles which were held as core and used in all of its business activities. In his book on Marks and Spencer Tse (1982) described these principles:

1 to offer our customers a selective range of high-quality, well designed and attractive merchandise at reasonable prices under the brand name St Michael;

2 to encourage suppliers to use the most modern and efficient production techniques;

3 to work with suppliers to ensure the highest standards of quality control;

Photo: Marks and Spencer

for good quality clothing was built on basics, the essentials which every customer needed; for example in womenswear this included underwear, jumpers and skirts. As it did not have fitting rooms till the 1990s, all assistants carried tape measures and M&S would give a 'no quibble' refund to any customer who was unhappy with the product he/she had purchased. As its products remained in the stores all year round for most of its history it never held sales. It priced its goods at a 'reasonable' level while emphasising the products' high quality: a claim which it believed was accepted because of its insistence on using mainly British suppliers. (More than 90 per cent of the suppliers were British.)

The success of M&S continued into the 1990s, with ever-rising profits and share prices. Richard Greenbury, the CEO from 1991, explained this success as follows:

> I think that the simple answer is that we followed absolutely and totally the principles of the business with which I was embued . . . I ran the business with the aid of my colleagues based upon the very long standing, and proven ways of running it.
>
> (Radio 4, August 2000)

4 to provide friendly, helpful service and greater shopping comfort and convenience to our customers;

5 to improve the efficiency of the business, by simplifying operating procedures;

6 to foster good human relations with customers, suppliers and staff and in the communities in which we trade.

Other components of this formula were developed. Its specialist buyers operated from a central buying office from which goods were allocated to the stores: a formula which stood M&S in good stead for most of its years. The store managers followed central direction on merchandising, layout, store design, training and so on. Every M&S store was identical in the procedures it followed, leading to a consistency of image and a guarantee of M&S standards. However, it also meant conformity to central direction, with store managers being severely restricted in how they could respond to the local needs of customers.

During M&S's growth period there were few changes to its methods of operation or strategies. It stocked generic clothing ranges with a wide appeal to the public: buyers often made choices which would outlast the current fashion and trends seen in other high street retailers. Its reputation

This commitment from the very top to the M&S way of doing things had been evident since the time of Marks and for all the succeeding chief executives. Indeed, chief executives of M&S were renowned for their attention to detail in terms of supplier control, merchandise and store layout; and it had seemed to work. M&S's success under Marks was often attributed to his understanding of customer preferences and trends. However, because of this, it could also mean that buyers tended to select merchandise which they knew chief executives would approve of. For example, the BBC's *Money Programme* (1 November 2000) reported that since it was known Greenbury did not want M&S to be at the cutting edge of fashion, buyers concentrated on the types of product they knew he would like – 'classic, wearable fashions'.

The same programme also reported on the problems of centralised authority; on one occasion Greenbury had decided that to control costs there would be less full-time sales assistants. Although this led to an inability in stores to meet the service levels required by M&S, when Greenbury visited, store managers ensured they were fully staffed by bringing in all available employees so that it appeared the stores were giving levels of service that, at other times, they were not. It also meant there was little disagreement with directives sent down from the top, so policies and decisions remained unchallenged even when executives or store managers were concerned about negative effects. The *Money Programme* also claimed that customer satisfaction surveys showing decreasing satisfaction throughout the late 1990s (positive view of M&S: 71 per cent – 1995; 62 per cent – 1998; 45 per cent – 1999) were kept from Greenbury by senior executives, who felt he might be annoyed by the results. Responding to this Greenbury stated that he never saw customer surveys results, but used sales figures and visits to stores as the basis to make judgements on how M&S was operating.

A hitch in the formula

M&S's problems began to hit the headlines in October 1998 when it halted its expansion programme in Europe and America. The expansion programme had begun in the early 1990s when M&S had moved into a number of overseas markets, where it implemented its tried and trusted formula. In America M&S operated as Brooks Brothers, and in Canada opened 22 stores via a joint venture. It had stated it would spend £130m ($\approx$ €200m) a year on the expansion until 2001, as it was essential for the firm's long-term progress. However in 1998 it admitted having financial difficulties worldwide, having been hampered by tough trading conditions.

In November M&S announced a 23 per cent decline in first-half profits, causing its shares to fall drastically. Greenbury, chairman and CEO, blamed a turbulent competitive environment, saying that M&S had lost sales and market share to its competitors from both the top and bottom ends of the retail market. Competitors at the top end of the market were niche organisations such as The Gap, Oasis and Next, offering similarly priced goods, yet more design focused with up-to-date fashions, and from which obvious comparisons could be made against the more traditional M&S merchandise. Furthermore these stores were attracting customers who would have naturally moved on to become M&S customers. At the bottom end of the market there was competition from discount stores, such as Matalan, and supermarkets, such as the 'George' range at Asda. These stores were competing against M&S by offering essential and basic clothing, but at significantly lower prices. Moreover, Tesco and

Sainsburys moved into offering added value foods, which had been pioneered by M&S.

It was frequently reported in the press that M&S no longer understood or reacted to its customers' needs. It misread its target market, and could not understand that customers who purchased food or underwear might not want products from its home furnishings range.

> It was seen to have been too complacent and ignoring changes in the domestic market which have now caught up with it.
>
> (*Financial Times*, 16 January 1999)

Analysts commented that M&S had continued too long with its traditional risk-averse formula and ignored the changes in the marketplace. Its competitors, meanwhile, were being praised for improving their performance as they quickly reacted to the changes. Although Greenbury blamed the competitive environment for M&S's difficulties, a Channel 4 programme (25 February 2001) felt that it was his focus on the day-to-day operations of the firm rather than long term strategy that had been the problem. The programme also reported that M&S was firmly placed in the 'middle ground', and tied to a generalised view of the market, instead of trying to understand and tailor offerings to the various market segments.

Commentators tried to make sense of what had happened. M&S did not have a loyalty card at a time when almost every other retailer did. Although a large proportion of M&S customers were women and much of the merchandise was womenswear, top management was dominated by men. It was also accused of having an inward looking culture. Almost all M&S managers and executives were promoted internally, starting at the bottom of the organisation, and becoming immersed in the routines and established traditions of M&S, a culture that had been established, and continually reinforced, since its creation. There had never been a CEO of M&S who had not been a member of the founder's family or a lifetime employee. It was believed that the culture was also strongly reinforced by Greenbury and not helped by his autocratic approach:

> I would strenuously deny that I was autocratic, what I would say is that I was extremely demanding, I was considered to be tough but fair . . . I introduced to the business a method of discussion in the boardroom, and outside of the boardroom that was far reaching down the business in terms of discussing what we were doing. I was like any chairman, I had strong

views and if I could persuade people of my views then obviously I tried to.

(Greenbury, Radio 4, August 2000)

In November 1998, after months of speculation and boardroom arguments, Greenbury announced that he would be stepping down. There then ensued a series of heavily publicised arguments between Keith Oates, Greenbury's deputy, and another senior director, Peter Salsbury, whom the media suggested was Greenbury's favoured successor. The in-fighting at M&S came to a conclusion when Greenbury returned to Britain after a sudden end to his holiday. He held a five-hour long meeting with the board and non-executive directors to determine who would be the successor. However, when put to the vote, Oates did not attend and elected to take early retirement. Salsbury was appointed as CEO. This was poorly received by shareholders and the City, where M&S shares fell $25\frac{1}{4}$p. Analysts commented that, as Salsbury had only worked in womenswear, one of the worst-performing units in M&S, it might have been wiser to bring in an outsider (Channel 4, 25 February 2001).

During this period of boardroom scuffles, M&S's problems were compounded by its £192m purchase of 19 Littlewoods department stores, on the grounds that they were situated in prime locations and complemented the existing M&S stores. The stores were acquired with the aim of being refurbished (at a cost of £100m), so that a full range of M&S products could be stocked in city centre locations. However, not only were the Littlewoods stores being refurbished, but so were the existing M&S stores. The disruption caused by the double refurbishment had a far worse effect on customers than M&S had predicted, leading Greenbury to describe the clothing section as a 'bloodbath'.

In January 1999 M&S announced its second profits warning. This caused a rapid sell-off of M&S shares. M&S blamed customers who it believed had been unwilling to pay full price for products over the Christmas period, especially when they could buy similar items cheaper from competitors. Furthermore, it had over-estimated sales and bought £250m worth of stock. The excess stock then had to be heavily discounted for a quick sale so that there was storage space for the next season's stock. There were also problems with its European operations. M&S had been pursuing a series of rapid expansion initiatives in Europe, yet many of the countries were difficult to expand in.

These stores' performance had been worsening over the previous months, totalling a cost of £25m. As they continued to show no signs of improvement, a programme was put in place to gradually close most of the European stores.

New tactics

To overcome the difficulties M&S had been facing, and in an attempt to regain confidence, Salsbury implemented a restructuring strategy, splitting the company into three: UK retail business, overseas business and financial services. His plans also involved establishing a company-wide marketing department to break down the power of the traditional buying fiefdoms, which were established around product lines. Salsbury wanted the marketing department to adopt a customer-focused approach, rather than allowing the buyers to dictate what the stores should stock. M&S also launched new clothing and food ranges, reinforced by a large-scale promotional campaign, to attempt to restore its image as an innovative retailer offering unique, quality products. Salsbury also issued a memorandum explaining that he wanted to move M&S away from its bureaucratic culture, by creating a decision-making environment that was unencumbered by hierarchy. He wanted to challenge the traditional ways that M&S operated, as he believed these were the root cause of its problems.

However, by May 1999 Salsbury was forced to announce a severe drop in trading and a halving of profits. He then outlined more measures he would take to alter the perception of M&S. As well as stripping away further layers of hierarchy, M&S would take a lifestyle approach to buying and presenting products. For example, previously it had placed together all types of trousers, even to the extent of separating suits. One analyst commented:

> M&S has behaved more like a wholesale buyer of products . . . rather than thinking about the sort of person that was buying the item and what else they could sell to that customer.
>
> (*Financial Times*, 19 May 1999)

M&S also established a property division to enable it to charge rents to the individual stores, this was done to make store managers more accountable for their branches' actions.

In June Greenbury retired a year early; a decision which came just before the board entered a three-day meeting to discuss 'a few hundred pages of its new strategy'. Salsbury commented:

> What we are doing has moved away from his [Greenbury's] methodology and thought processes and decisions were reached without him being able to have an input.
>
> (*Financial Times*, 23 June 1999)

In another attempt to slow the profits decline, July saw the closure of six European stores, a reduction in the size of its head office, and the closure of all its Canadian stores, which had been operating at a loss for 24 out of 25 years of trading (*Financial Times*, 10 July 1999). In the UK market M&S implemented a costly store change strategy. It commissioned design consultants to create a new store image. The pilot store displayed new lighting and flooring to create a mood which 'looks to the future with the anticipation of creating change'.

. . . And more problems

In September 1999 M&S announced further changes as a result of a strategic business review conducted over the previous 18 months. It stated that it was in the process of overseas sourcing while severing links with UK suppliers, streamlining international operations, diversifying into home and internet shopping, and creating a department dedicated to identifying new business opportunities.

Shortly after these plans were announced there was yet another profits warning, despite major investments to make the stores more customer friendly, a new well-received fashion range, and more shop floor staff to improve customer service. Customers continued to voice their concerns regarding the clothing range, and customer comments were reported in the press:

> There are so many items here to find and they don't tend to segregate it out, so there's something I might like next to something my granny might like.
>
> (*Financial Times*, 28 September 1999)

By November M&S had more bad news for its shareholders when it revealed its shares had fallen to $250\frac{3}{4}$p, the lowest price since 1991. By December there were stories of companies being interested in acquiring M&S. Those interested included Tesco, American pension fund companies, and Philip Green, the retail entrepreneur. Yet observers believed that acquisition was not the answer. They felt there continued to remain deep structural problems in the marketplace, as there were high costs of entry and maintenance to remain in the clothing market. In an effort to counteract the acquisition rumours, and restore the wavering faith in the company, M&S implemented another management restructuring to become more customer focused. It attempted to achieve this by splitting into seven business units: lingerie, womenswear, menswear, childrenswear, food, home, and beauty. Executives were appointed at just below board level to head the units, reporting directly to Salsbury who believed the flatter structure allowed M&S to be more responsive to market changes and customer needs.

A new horizon

January 2000 did not just bring a new millennium, but also a new chairman for M&S. Belgian-born, 48-year-old Luc Vandevelde was appointed with a two-year contract, a £2.2m 'golden hello', and a salary of £1.3m a year plus share options. In taking the position at M&S, Vandevelde had left his managing director role at Promodés, the French food retailer. At Promodés he had achieved a six-fold increase in stock value, and finalised its sale to Carrefour, thus creating the second largest retailer in the world. This was the first time anyone from outside M&S had been appointed to the position of chairman. Vandevelde explained that he wanted to revitalise the domestic brand and then go overseas with an extensive expansion programme. Further, he wanted M&S to become a multi-format retailer, as was Promodés. Analysts observed that this would certainly require a major culture change for the organisation.

By February M&S promised an extra 4,000 staff to operate on the shop floor. By directly serving and helping customers, M&S felt it was offering a more personal service. It also entered into deals with two football clubs as part of its plan to tailor stores geographically, and unveiled an exclusive clothes collection designed by haute couture fashion designers. Purchasing of the clothing range was also shifted to almost 100 per cent Asian sources.

In March 2000 M&S declared a dramatic overhaul to its brand. It planned a new corporate image. It stopped using its famous green carrier bags and downgraded the once acclaimed, and seemingly invaluable, St Michael brand. The plans encompassed a complete overhaul of the firm, as the stores, uniforms, packaging and labelling all had to be altered to fit with the new image. However, Vandevelde said he thought the changes were 'evolutionary rather than revolutionary' (*Financial Times*, 13 March 2000). M&S explained that customers were confused about the differences between the St Michael and Marks and Spencer brands and felt that it needed to use one distinct brand which everyone could understand. The new-look M&S brand was launched in a range of colours each indicating different departments. The St Michael brand was relegated to inside clothing labels as a symbol of quality and trust.

Vandevelde also changed M&S's supply chain. He grouped the stores on the bases of demographic characteristics and lifestyle patterns, instead of operating with the old system which allocated merchandise dependent on floor space. This new move was widely accepted and received positively as one of the first major steps to becoming customer focused.

Vandevelde conducted numerous interviews in an effort to raise awareness and his and M&S's profile, mainly with the City, investors and shareholders. In an interview with the *Financial Times* (4 April 2000) he admitted that in the past M&S had lost its way in a fast-changing market where new competitors were making the rules. He argued that the strategies he intended to implement would not involve drastic changes to the board or the structure of the organisation, and added:

> I think in the glory days of M&S everybody felt proud to be associated . . . it drove our reputation and our share price up to levels that we may not have deserved. Whereas when things started going slightly sour I guess everybody just exaggerated and we probably were punished a bit more than we deserved as well. Understanding that is important . . .
>
> There is one general theme and that is that we are probably too 'push' and not enough 'pull' orientated . . . this is echoing a theme that the group was not focused sufficiently on the customers. Today it is much more difficult to come up with real unique propositions and customers are much more intelligent and have minds of their own, so they don't wait for a retailer to tell them to come by. We have got to start with the customer and work our way backwards.
>
> (*Financial Times*, 4 April 2000)

He also explained that because of their geographic distance and lack of influence from the atmosphere in the UK, the overseas stores had developed their own strategies which were tailored to the needs of the local market. Vandevelde hoped that the ideas and strategies they had experimented with would provide leverages that could be exploited in the UK.

In May 2000 M&S announced its figures for the year, reporting £8.2bn of sales, the same as in 1999, and a fall in profit of £71.2m. So despite new measures and strategies there was no visible improvement. M&S's shareholders were also unimpressed after receiving the first cut in their dividend, seeing it fall from 14p to 9p. Salsbury commented that M&S had slowed the sales decrease, and that customers had noticed a difference in the stores and products: the dividend cut was made so that future investment capacity was not compromised.

The grand plan

Vandevelde planned to stabilise M&S in the UK and then relaunch internationally. His strategy for the year focused on four overarching priorities, which again had the objective of moving the business closer to the customer: (1) creating clear profit centres; (2) creating a customer-facing organisation; (3) restoring overseas profitability; and (4) building the financial services sector. He was confident that this would start M&S on a path of sustained recovery. He aimed to achieve these objectives by a further restructuring of M&S into five operating divisions: UK retail; international retail; financial services; property and ventures. Within the UK retail division seven customer business units were established, and to ensure customer focus each unit would have dedicated buying and selling teams. M&S also created a Customer Insight Unit to perform in-depth research with customers to gain an understanding of shopping habits, demographics and their perceptions of the M&S brand. Vandevelde said that the in-depth research had already identified that one in five items from the clothing range was the wrong offering for the stores' local market.

As for the stores, a series of different formats would be launched; there would be further modernisation; more customer advisors on the shop floor; and the opening of three prototype stores where all new initiatives and concepts would be tested. In addition M&S disclosed its plans to offer clothes at a discounted price in factory outlet malls, which would be used to sell excess stock, something its more aggressive competitors had been doing for a number of years. Although space could be quickly cleared for new stock and money recouped from slow-selling items, commentators wondered what loyal customers would think when the clothes, to which they attributed a certain standard of quality and price, were being sold up to 50 per cent cheaper. Then, in September 2000, Salsbury retired from M&S.

In March 2001 M&S announced its plans to withdraw from its 38 stores in Europe and Brooks Brothers in America. Its stores in Hong Kong were sold to franchises. M&S also closed its 'Direct' catalogue operations at a cost of £300m. Vandevelde explained that the disposals were necessary so that M&S could focus on its core domestic clothing. However the European retrenchment did not proceed smoothly. The problems began in France, where 1,700 jobs were to be lost. At the announcement of M&S's plans French unions stepped in to represent the employees and organise strike action. Although analysts could see the wisdom of the withdrawal, consumers were concerned by the negative headlines and employee demonstrations through London. The situation was compounded by the French government who, after an investigation, determined that M&S had broken French employment law. The restructuring plans were suspended and M&S fined for 'manifestly illegal trouble-making'. This meant M&S had to completely restart the withdrawal process. Analysts were astonished that Vandevelde, formerly head of French group Promodés, had so seriously misjudged both the legal obligations and the extent to which French politics would unite to stop the closures. It was not until the end of 2001, when Brooks Brothers was sold for $225m (originally purchased for $750m in 1988), that the withdrawal process was completed.

In the midst of the store closure fracas, news broke that Vandevelde was going to be awarded a bonus worth £810,000, originally guaranteed when he joined M&S. As Vandevelde's strategic targets had all been met, M&S could not deny him his bonus. Yet that did not prevent a wave of hostile emotion, not only from the trade unions, but also from senior executives at Baker Street who were annoyed that Vandevelde would receive a bonus when they were unlikely to get one themselves, because they had failed to meet their financial targets. Following the controversy, and taking advice from the non-executive directors, Vandevelde decided to defer his right to the bonus for a year.

In reporting its end of year results, the comments continued to be negative. Discussing the results Vandevelde scaled back on the promises he had made at his arrival 15 months prior for recovery within two years. Although he remained confident that the group would recover, he admitted it was taking much longer than anticipated. The fall in underlying pre-tax profits was primarily blamed on intense high street competition, price deflation and a poorly performing core clothing range. Yet even though better purchasing had improved margins it had had little effect because, Vandevelde admitted, M&S was still resorting to heavy mark-downs to clear its stock. Commentators stressed that reducing the number of mark-downs necessary required better stock control and cooperation with suppliers, with whom M&S had only just begun to rebuild relations after shifting the majority of its sourcing overseas.

However Vandevelde was confident that he had the right recipe for recovery, it was just a matter of time. In an interview with the *Financial Times* (23 May 2001) he commented that turning M&S around was like making mayonnaise. You never know when the mixture of oil, eggs and vinegar will blend perfectly – but you know it will eventually if you keep beating it:

> There is nothing mechanical about this business – there is no one thing you can turn to make it go right. It is a synthesis of many things. The structure has to be right; the people have got to be right. At some point it will eventually turn positive.
>
> (*Financial Times*, 23 May 2001)

He also admitted that things were far worse at M&S than he had expected before he joined the group and had famously made himself hostage to fortune by predicting rapid upturns. Vandevelde refused to make further predictions for M&S's future performance. Instead he was said to be hoping for 'small pockets' of improvement that would restore confidence.

It was also at this time when some promising news emerged from the M&S camp. M&S planned to move out of its headquarters in Baker Street, London and into a new building in Paddington in Spring 2004. Commentators were delighted as they felt it showed M&S was interested in making meaningful changes and tackling the problems at its core, not just altering merchandise and store layout:

> In recent months much has been written about M&S's big portfolio of stores, but little, if anything, about

its HQ. The headquarters is the cultural centre of any company, a window on its soul. Anyone looking into Baker Street today will see a static environment with many closed offices and long corridors, redolent of a company that has not fully embraced modern management techniques and working methods – regardless of what the consumer on the high street is seeing . . . Until the heart of the organisation understands and lives the new values, the people who deal with the consumer will be unsure of the conviction behind any new direction that they are asked to take. The opportunity to relocate the headquarters, for any organisation, is a catalyst for real and deep-seated change that can yield benefits well beyond cost savings.

(*Financial Times*, 24 April 2001)

Analysts and the press hoped that the new headquarters would be redesigned to reflect the values M&S needed to emphasise, and that it signalled its intent to reform its culture.

For those who had worked in M&S's headquarters, the grey and imposing building symbolised much that had gone wrong with the retailer. Its endless corridors were described as Kremlin-like, and the small individual offices reflected the status of the occupant by the thickness of the carpet. Former managers described the building as 'oppressive', with facilities that were not conducive to modern working practices, few casual meeting rooms, and a highly structured hierarchy for the 4,000 employees who worked there. Fluid communication and the building of *esprit de corps* were felt to be prevented because executives and directors sat in offices which were separate from their staff.

Not long after this news the Annual Report was published. It explained that M&S's priority was to restore the confidence of its 'core' customer, the classically stylish woman who admired and relied on M&S, and would like to feel she could rely on it again. In addition the employee initiatives that had been implemented were described. In her book on M&S Bevan (2001) described these initiatives, a campaign entitled 'Fighting Back' was meant to be a rallying cry, encouraging staff to get behind M&S and make a difference in key areas of recovery. Posters appeared in staff rooms, with an accusing Kitchener-type finger pointing, asking what 'You' were doing to bring customers back. In the run-up to Christmas, over 2,000 head office staff, including Board members, directors and senior executives, were drafted to work one day in a local store, helping customers to pack or stacking shelves. The idea was to give an insight to those who usually operated 'behind the scenes', and to lift employee morale.

Vandevelde then spoke to shareholders about M&S's position:

Stories in the news often claim the M&S brand has lost its lustre, is no longer attractive, and that people don't want to shop with us any more. Naturally I disagree with this view. This is still a unique company, with unique fundamental strengths and the most dedicated staff of any retailer in the UK . . . In summary, we have made mistakes and have admitted them. We know that this year our most loyal customers haven't always found the clothes they want in our stores.

(Annual Report, 2001)

Shortly after, M&S unveiled its Autumn-Winter fashion collection presided over by Yasmin Yusuf, the new creative director. This was where it was aiming to achieve recovery because clothing sales remained in steep decline with most weeks showing double-digit falls in women swear. The new collection marked a return to M&S's roots with the main focus on classically styled clothing such as tweeds in neutral colours and classic knitwear, targeted at the group's more traditional shoppers. There was also a formally tailored range, evening wear and a new range entitled 'Perfect', a back-to-basics collection which included jeans, classic shirts and polo-necks. Analysts commented that the collection was more appealing for core customers than M&S's clothing had been for years.

More time

At the group's AGM in mid-July Vandevelde again told shareholders that he needed more time to turn M&S around. He explained that he was confident recovery was achievable, despite a further drop in group sales, but believed the only way to achieve this was by attracting and retaining the best people. To accomplish this he asked shareholders to double the share options available for key executives, to three times annual salary. Although given a tough time at the AGM shareholders praised him:

He was excellent really, I can't say I am happy about the performance of M&S or the outcome of the meeting, but that man could sell refrigerators to the Eskimos.

(*Financial Times*, 12 July 2001)

Vandevelde left the AGM again promising to significantly improve its clothing ranges' performance.

One way it attempted to do this was through a joint venture to design and source children's clothing with one of its leading suppliers, Desmond & Sons. Analysts suggested that this was a tacit admission that its children's range was not as good as it could be. Yet positively the analysts felt it showed they had begun to look at themselves radically. M&S hoped that the joint venture would allow them to deliver more fashionable clothes faster.

The other attempt to improve its clothing was a collaboration with George Davies, founder of Next and the creator of the 'George' clothing range at Asda supermarket. It was Davies' responsibility to design a women's range that would specifically cater for M&S's fashion-conscious customers. The new range, named 'Per Una', Italian for 'for one woman', targeted women aged 25–35 who wished to wear designer-style clothing, and attempted to compete with brands like Mango and Kookai. Davies had secured a deal whereby he owned Per Una, and retained the profits from supplying M&S. To operate so autonomously he had invested £21m of his own money. He was therefore designing, manufacturing and distributing the clothes independently of M&S.

Davies believed that to appeal to the twenty-something age group Per Una should be at the front of the store, and used as a mechanism to attract them into the store. He felt that M&S was too old-fashioned and sent too many different messages, and so decided his range needed its own separate, walled floor space and different shop fittings from the rest of the store; this was something M&S had never done before. Unlike M&S's traditional ranges Per Una was merchandised in 'fashion capsules', where jumpers were displayed with matching trousers.

One month after Per Una's September launch, M&S reported better trading figures to the press, and a rise in share price. Per Una was well received by customers, with sales running at more than double the original targets. However this resulted in demand outrunning supply, so M&S had to scale down its rollout programme. Critics commented that as well as M&S had performed it would have done better had it had more stock. Although analysts were pleased with M&S's results, some investors remained sceptical, preferring to wait for reassurance that Per Una's successful sales were not simply a result of cannibalisation of M&S's other clothing range's sales.

By October 2001 Vandevelde's initiatives seemed to be coming to fruition, as it produced its first quarter-on-quarter sales increase for three years. Even with this positive news Vandevelde refused to make any predictions for the future:

> Every retailer always hopes that next Christmas will be the best ever. But we'll let our customers judge (that) . . . Last year was a desperate cry – I needed to create enough emotional willingness from our customers and everybody else because we didn't have the ammunition from our performance.
>
> (*Financial Times*, 10 October 2001)

Per Una and M&S's own 'Perfect' range also continued to perform well, and as such shares rose 10 per cent. Vandevelde said it was a sign that customers were positive about the improvements to the core ranges. Yet in discussing the next interim results he commented:

> One quarter of positive trading is not good enough to talk about a turnaround . . . But we are seeing the first results of almost 18 months of very hard work which is coming together and convincing our customers.
>
> (*Financial Times*, 7 November 2001)

This news was compounded by the sale of shares in the group from M&S's two biggest investors and was heralded by analysts as a sign that M&S's recovery was on track.

A new style

At this time M&S employed Roger Holmes, who had been poached from the Kingfisher group, to be M&S's head of UK retailing. One of Holmes' first tasks was to implement a store refurbishment programme. In the stores beige walls were replaced with white ones, the floors and lighting updated, and 'shops within shops' created with the intention of giving customers an idea of how different styles worked together. Yet Holmes insisted that this was achieved at a cost of only £14 a square foot, previously M&S had spent up to £70 a square foot achieving their designs.

M&S was then rewarded with the news that it had the best performing stock on the FTSE100 for 2001. It also reported its strongest Christmas sales in years, although this was achieved in buoyant conditions. Analysts were impressed with the news:

> Through luck, judgement or building up the right team, Luc seems to have turned it round more quickly than people thought he would be able to.
>
> (*Financial Times*, 17 January 2002)

The strong Christmas figures were credited to increases from both Per Una and M&S's more traditional ranges. This resulted in Vandevelde receiving his £650,000 bonus for the year, plus the bonus he had previously deferred.

In March 2002 M&S closed its final salary pension scheme to new members. The pension had been regarded as one of the best in the UK. As well as being set to save M&S millions, it was seen as a symbolic move away from one of its last acts of corporate paternalism.

M&S then delivered its end of year results: although there had been a rise in pre-tax profits Vandevelde was keen to state that M&S was not secure in its recovery, but that it had 'turned the corner'. He stressed that the revival so far had been aided by buoyant trading conditions over the year. M&S then outlined its next steps. Its objectives were to maintain the revival of its core clothing and footwear departments, with a three-pronged approach to expansion in the UK:

● Development of its homeware department in existing stores and dedicated satellite outlets in out-of-town locations.

● Expansion of its 'Simply Food' convenience store format, targeted at high-traffic areas such as railway and underground stations.

● Leveraging of its financial services operations.

Although financial services had strong brand recognition and trust among customers, it was the most under-exploited part of M&S. Over the year its profits had fallen £12.1m with much of this blamed on M&S's decision to accept rival credit cards, as this had minimised usage of its own charge card. To attempt to leverage some of its 5m cardholders it launched a pilot scheme of its own combined credit and loyalty card. However less than a month later Vandevelde put financial services under strategic review. To solve the problems in financial services M&S considered joint venture, outsourcing and a partial flotation.

At the AGM in July Vandevelde announced his resignation as CEO, to become part-time Chairman. Unsurprising to many, Holmes was promoted to fill the vacant position. These moves worried some analysts who felt Vandevelde was leaving too early in the recovery process, whereas others believed it indicated he was confident about M&S's revival and were crediting Holmes for much of its recent success. The mood at the AGM was upbeat and friendly, something which shareholders reflected had not happened for a number of years.

Holmes had been credited with much of the responsibility for the recovery. He had spoken to the actual customers and walked with them around the stores:

> I was very struck by how inwardly focused the company had remained through the period of change. They had been through all this de-layering but they were still all looking backwards. Nobody seemed to be asking how many customers . . . were actually experiencing a difference.
>
> (Bevan, 2001)

His conclusion was 'we needed to get back to a passion for product' (Bevan, 2001). Holmes was seen as the driving force behind the revitalisation of women's clothing, specifically the collaboration with Davies, and the recruitment of Yasmin Yusuf to produce 'classic clothes that are not boring – classics with a twist' (Bevan, 2001). He injected innovation into the food ranges, with the popular 'steam cuisine' being protected by patent, and had been crucial in the overseas withdrawal.

It seemed as if M&S were pulling out all the stops for its recovery, as it forged a surprising alliance with England captain, and then Manchester United star, David Beckham. M&S negotiated a three year children's wear deal with Beckham, seen as a natural hero and role model for boys, who would also reflect the company's brand values. The boys range was launched in September 2002, and exceeded all sales targets. By October the jubilation surrounding M&S continued as in poor performing market conditions it had achieved an increase in first half sales. The only area continuing to lose market share was children's clothing. A month later and the problems with the children's range had worsened. Overstocking in both children's and women's wear had spoilt M&S's recovery story, where M&S admitted it had got its targets wrong, purchased too much stock, and had a vast number of items reduced for sale.

In December M&S achieved what many commentators regarded as a coup, when it poached Vittorio Radice with a £1.7m package from the chief executive position at Selfridges to head its home furnishings division. Analysts and investors alike were impressed by M&S's new found ability to attract such widely renowned creative talent, feeling that it was a sure sign of its recovery, further commenting that its rivals should be worried.

In the new year M&S reported on its Christmas trading period. It presented its second successful Christmas in a row, where sales had risen 6.7 per cent, which led it to outperform most of its competitors and beat the City's predictions. Holmes was pleased:

> I think there is a building confidence among our customers. In the end, it all comes down to product and in clothing we have got the core fashionability right.
> (*Financial Times*, 16 January 2003)

However in spite of this there were further markdowns, the full cost of which was 5 per cent higher than in 2001. Holmes blamed unseasonably warm weather for slow sales of winter coats and associated apparel. This resulted in a 6 per cent fall in its share price. Yet Holmes had been right about one thing, confidence was building with the customers. As such M&S was back in the rankings of the 'World's Most Respected Companies' after an absence of three years. It had regained its place because of the way it had restructured and refocused itself, and underlined the strength of the brand and culture.

To improve its recovery further M&S streamlined its general merchandise logistics by cutting its contractors from four to two, producing a saving of £20m per year. While in another move to strengthen its financial services arm, after successful pilot trials, it decided to launch a nationwide credit and loyalty card scheme, entitled '&more', which it hoped would make it one of the UK's biggest issuers. &more would allow card holders to earn points for purchases they made, redeemable as M&S vouchers. M&S also won a Queens Award for Enterprise for its washable suit, which had been on sale since 2001. In winning this award M&S was hopeful of instilling a culture of innovation through its workforce.

In May Vandevelde reported the end of year figures, where shareholders were pleased to hear him disclose both a rise in profits and an increase to the dividend. Holmes then promised that M&S would soon recover from its recent sales slowdown, and would begin winning back market share and customers from its competitors. To achieve this he vowed that the top priority would remain clothing and food. Radice also announced his growth plans for homeware. He intended to build 25 stand-alone stores, entitled 'Lifestores', which would only stock homeware products. The centrepiece of each store would be a house designed by an elite designer. The house would be fully functioning, designed so that customers could see the homeware range in situ. It was hoped that customers would not simply buy one item, but instead purchase the way of life.

June 2003 saw M&S take a further step away from its former image as a bastion of corporate paternalism. It introduced new staff contracts resulting in cuts to overtime pay. The press believed it was a sign that M&S was less concerned with staff retention than it used to be. However by July, after significant employee uproar, M&S decided to bow to staff opinion and concluded that reduced overtime pay would only be implemented for new staff.

At this time M&S also announced that it was considering opening food stores in motorway service stations, as an expansion of the Simply Food format. Although stressing that it would proceed cautiously with its new formula, it admitted planning to open 150 Simply Food stores by 2006. M&S explained that while operating smaller stores presented new challenges, they had delivered sales in excess of the average return per square foot for food.

Then followed more changes at M&S as Vandevelde further reduced his role of chairman, as he handed over chairmanship of financial services to Holmes. His contract was also altered so that he was paid entirely in shares:

> It is a vote of confidence in the team that my remuneration is closely tied to the value which we create for our shareholders.
> (Vandevelde, *Financial Times*, 9 July 2003)

In addition Vandevelde shocked investors because as well as his position as non-executive chairman at Change Capital Partners he had taken a similar role at Vodafone. The press were unimpressed by his decision, feeling that it was far too early in M&S's recovery to be distracted by other commitments.

Where from there?

By November 2003 there were concerns that M&S's recovery had seriously faltered. Both senior and middle management were reported to be increasingly disappointed with the organisation's lack of progress. Now Holmes was seen as the problem, being blamed for being too nice, taking too long to make decisions, and lacking relevant experience.

Everyone likes Roger, but he's really a management consultant, not a clothing retailer. Instead of taking a decision, there'll be another committee formed.

(*Daily Telegraph*, 3 November 2003)

M&S's complicated structure compounded these problems, where underneath the main board was a group operating committee made up of 19 members. An M&S insider commented:

Decision making is so slow. The bureaucracy hasn't really changed. They had a go at it, but now its gone back to the old ways. There's a lot of people who are fed up. There's a general level of frustration and discontent.

(*Daily Telegraph*, 3 November 2003)

In addition to these concerns, many employees talked about 'turf wars' between Davies and Yusuf regarding space and designs. Further, commentators were shocked to see M&S holding an unprecedented '20 per cent off' knitwear campaign, as a move to gain interest in its autumn sales. They felt that such severe discounts meant M&S must have sold new goods at less than cost price.

Yet in discussing the interim results, Holmes explained that he felt M&S had made a very solid performance because its profits had increased. Against the accusation that the recovery was running out of steam, Holmes stressed how much M&S had achieved over the last few years, most importantly he felt that it had regained customer trust. Childrenswear and women's formalwear continued to be a problem. To counter this Holmes explained M&S was planning to segment its offerings more attractively by introducing mix and match tailoring solutions. Anthony Thompson, a former M&S employee, rejoined as head of childrenswear, where he was optimistic that the range would soon be a success.

Problems with food also returned, where, although M&S continued to grow market share, it still underperformed the market. In response to this it announced an increase in the role of its Simply Food stores, as they were performing better than the main stores for sales per foot. In addition homeware was having problems. Holmes blamed this on a dependence on promotions and under-exploiting opportunities. He continued to feel confident for the future, explaining his intention to bring greater breadth and 'newness' to M&S's products and styles. M&S also reported the success of its &more card. After a massive advertising campaign prior to Christmas, M&S disclosed that it was on track with its plans. More than just revitalising financial services, it had given M&S an opportunity to build a relationship with what Holmes called its 'most important customers'. He explained that through &more M&S was able to build loyalty, understand its customers and open a lasting dialogue with them.

However, in January 2004 M&S issued its trading statement, which underlined the problems it was experiencing. Total sales were down, with the main area of concern again being clothing, where Holmes described the womenswear ranges as 'not strong enough', with 'the wrong products in place'. As a result of this David Norgrove stepped down from his position of Director of Clothing, and Holmes stated that he would be taking a more direct interest in womenswear, until the appointment of a new director. Holmes also reported that the home division had underperformed, and described food's performance simply as 'adequate'. Commentators agreed that despite some obvious changes that had been made to M&S, Vandevelde and Holmes had failed to make an impression on the culture.

Shortly after these results, in May 2004, Vandevelde resigned. The board were reported to be extremely concerned that Vandevelde had 'lost interest' in the job, because of the increasing time he was spending on the Vodafone and Carrefour boards, and running Change Capital, a private equity fund. One M&S executive remarked:

In retrospect, it's clear that what Luc did was to tart us up with a lick of paint.

(*Sunday Telegraph*, 9 May 2004)

Commentators felt that although quick results for sales and profits had been achieved, underlying structural problems had not been dealt with.

Sources

BBC2, 'Sparks at Marks', *The Money Programme*, 1 November 2000. BBC2, 'Marks and Spencer', *Trouble at the Top*, 6 December 2001. Beaver, G., 'Competitive advantage and corporate governance: Shop soiled and needing attention, the case of Marks and Spencer plc', *Strategic Change*, vol. 8, 1999, pp. 325–34. Bevan, J., *The Rise and Fall of Marks and Spencer*, Profile Books: London, 2001. Channel 4, 'Inside Marks and Spencer', 25 February 2001. Radio 4, Interview with Sir Richard Greenbury, 22 August 2000. Rees, G., *St Michael: A History of Marks and Spencer*, Weidenfeld and Nicolson, London, 1969. Tse, K., *Marks and Spencer: Anatomy of Britain's most efficiently managed company*, Pergamon, Oxford, 1985.

APPENDIX

Marks and Spencer Group financial record, 2003–1997

	2003 (£m)**	2002 (£m)	2001 (£m)	2000 (£m)	1999 (£m)	1998 (£m)	1997* (£m)
Profit and loss account							
Turnover	8077.2	8135.4	8075.7	8195.5	8224.0	8243.3	7841.9
Operating profit/loss before exceptional operating costs	761.8	643.8	467.0	543.0	600.5	1050.5	1700.2
Exceptional operating costs	−43.9	–	−26.5	−72.0	−88.5	53.2	–
Total operating profit/loss	717.9	643.8	440.5	471.0	512.0	1103.7	1037.9
Profit/loss on sale of property/fixed assets	1.6	41.2	−83.2	−22.3	6.2	−2.8	−1.8
Provision for loss on operations to be discontinued	–	–	224.0	–	–	–	–
Loss on sale/termination of operations	−1.5	−366.7	–	–	–	–	–
Net interest (expense)/payable	−40.5	17.6	13.9	14.2	27.9	54.1	65.9
Profit/loss on ordinary activities before taxation	677.5	335.9	145.5	417.2	546.1	1155.0	1102.0
Taxation	−197.4	−182.5	−142.7	−158.2	−176.1	−338.7	−346.1
Profit/loss on ordinary activities after taxation	480.1	153.4	2.8	259.3	370.0	816.3	755.9
Minority interests	0.4	−0.4	−1.5	−0.6	2.1	−0.4	−1.3
Dividends	−246.0	−238.9	−258.3	−258.6	−413.3	−409.1	−368.6
Retained profit/loss for the year	234.5	−85.9	−257.0	0.1	−41.2	406.8	386.0
Balance Sheets							
Fixed Assets	3466.6	3431.5	4177.2	4298.4	4448.7	4034.5	3646.5
Net current assets	3289.1	3760.7	3516.2	3717.1	3355.9	3401.5	3204.2
Short-term creditors	1610.2	1750.8	1981.6	2162.8	2029.8	2345.0	1775.1
Long-term creditors	1810.0	2156.3	735.1	804.3	772.6	187.2	495.8
Provisions for liabilities and charges	228.4	203.8	315.7	126.6	105.0	31.0	31.8
Net assets	3038.4	3081.3	4661.0	4921.8	4897.2	4872.8	4548.0
Equity shareholders' funds	3038.4	3080.9	4645.4	4905.3	4883.9	4853.7	4529.3
Statistics							
Earnings/loss per share	20.7p	5.4p	0p	9.0p	13.0p	28.6p	26.7p
Adjusted earnings/loss per share	22.2p	16.3p	11.4p	13.2p	15.8p	27.3p	26.7p
Dividends per share	10.5p	9.5p	9p	9.0p	14.4p	14.3p	13.0p

* Marks and Spencer altered its accounting practices in 1998 and therefore the figures for 1997 are not strictly comparable with those from the other years.

** £1 = approx. €1.5.

Eden Project

Roger Jones

This case describes how, initially, a small group of people became inspired to create and build one of the most unique and imaginative projects undertaken anywhere in the world in modern times. The Eden Project is a demonstration of how entrepreneurial ideas, action and ability fuse together to strategise. The result being the development and implementation of business strategies, which have produced an internationally acknowledged masterpiece of human innovation and achievement. The case provides examples of change and transformation, risks and opportunity, vision and regeneration. Through determination and perseverance, entrepreneurs persuaded international companies and national funding agencies to engage in a spirit of adventure, and to participate in the fulfilment of a dream. Dubbed 'the eighth wonder of the world' the Eden Project has been recognised with awards and accolades from around the world.

● ● ●

Regional background

The Eden Project is located at Bodelva, which is near the town of St Austell in Cornwall on the south-west coast of England. Eden was built in an old china clay mining pit which had almost exhausted its natural resource. China clay mining, tin mining, fishing and agriculture had been the mainstay of the Cornish economy over centuries. Although fishing and agriculture remain as continuing industries today, the mining of china clay and tin have almost disappeared from the Cornish economy. China clay mining in particular has left its historical testament in the shape of ugly spoil heaps which proliferate the landscape in the St Austell area. So big are these spoil and waste heaps, that locals often refer to the area as 'the Cornish Alps'. As a geographical region of the United Kingdom, Cornwall has been regarded as one of the poorer areas by the European Union and in need of regional regeneration. Since the demise of traditional industries, Cornwall suffered economic decline, becoming increasingly dependent on tourism.

Factual fast-track

The Eden Trust is a UK registered charitable trust and home to its wholly owned subsidiary, Eden Project Limited, the company which operates the Eden site. Cornwall's £86m (≈ €130m) Eden Project welcomed almost 2m visitors in its first year and 1.3m in the first six months of its financial year from 1 April 2002. Hidden from view, Eden has been constructed within a 60-metre deep, 15-hectare former china clay quarry, and is home to the two largest plant conservatories in the world, called Biomes. Eden is acknowledged as a 'living theatre of people and plants', dedicated to the appreciation and study of human dependence on plants and plant life. Visitors to Eden pass through a journey that tells the stories of human dependency on plants.

At 55 metres high and big enough to house the Tower of London, the larger of Eden's Biomes recreates the climate of the Humid Tropics, with plants from Amazonia, West Africa, Malaysia and the Oceanic Islands. The slightly smaller Warm Temperate Biome plays host to plants from the

Mediterranean, South Africa and California. Outside, the roofless Temperate Biome presents many displays of plants that thrive and live in temperate climates.

The scaffold structure created during construction of the Biomes became the world's largest freestanding scaffold structure. The lightweight steel roof of the Biomes uses ETFE foil (ethyltetrafluoroethylene) instead of glass. ETFE is not only strong and lightweight; it allows sunlight rays to easily pass through. The original site, a sterile wasteland in 1999, led to the pioneering development of recycled spoil heap waste into 85,000 tonnes of soil. An independent Economic Impact Survey has shown that in its first eight months Eden introduced an additional £111m (≈ €167m) million into the Cornish economy – annualised to a figure of £150m (≈ €225m). In the next ten years of operation, it is forecast that the Eden Project could generate £2bn (≈ €3bn) in revenue for the Cornish economy. Eden's unprecedented popularity has led to the Project employing more than 800 full-time staff. The Eden Project was part funded by a grant of £43m (≈ €65m) from the Millennium Commission together with a groundbreaking collaboration of private and public partners.

And in the beginning . . .

The personal strategiser

In 1987, after a successful career in the music industry spanning ten years, Tim Smit decided to locate to Cornwall with his young family. It was time to reflect and reconfigure his personal strategies: as Smit comments:

> Have you ever stood in a bar like I have, and heard yourself holding forth yet again about what you'd really like to do with your life? The pipe dream comes alive for a happy hour or two, but does it fade by morning, leaving that growing sense of self-hatred as you realise you haven't got what it takes to do the interesting or brave thing? If you're a successful barrister, or financier, or teacher and that's what you always wanted to do, fine, be happy. But suppose what you really wanted was to be a boat-builder, or explorer or a bug collector instead? How many times have you heard friends, even very successful friends, in despair at what they had made of their lives?

What Smit didn't know was that he was about to embark on not just one, but several life changing experiences. He intended building a recording studio at the farmhouse he had bought, when a friend and local builder, John Nelson, invited Smit to explore an old estate in the company of its new owner. Smit recalls the event as: 'On 16 February 1990, within minutes of cutting my way into what was later to become known as the Lost Gardens of Heligan, my life changed forever'. His personal strategies were being shaped and re-shaped in the boundaries of a very old walled garden set in an almost derelict Cornish estate.

The gardens at Heligan, a few kilometres from the future site of the Eden Project, had been a working example of Victorian productive horticulture until the outbreak of the First World War. However, Heligan became neglected, without maintenance, and was left for over seventy years to the ravages of nature. Over the next six years, Smit, Nelson and a group of willing volunteers set about restoring the Heligan gardens. It was during this period that Smit discovered his own fascination with plants and plant life, learning by experience and tutelage from two key influences with a vast amount of professional knowledge and experience – Peter Thoday and Philip McMillan Browse. Thoday and McMillan Browse have been horticultural professionals all their lives and later would play a huge role with Smit as his personal strategies evolved. Thoday offered the first of many challenges to Smit . . . 'Do you want to create a greatest hits record, or are you brave enough to perform the whole opera'? The challenge invited Smit and his Heligan colleagues to restore everything at Heligan to its full function; to run it exactly as it would have been in the middle of the 19th century – as a productive and successful business enterprise operated and managed commercially. Smit accepted the challenge and set about changing Heligan from dereliction to production. Philip McMillan Browse joined the Heligan enterprise as its first horticultural director.

The task of restoration commenced in 1991, presenting Smit with the opportunity to develop his own business skills and also to expand his knowledge of plants and plant life. By 1994, the productive gardens at Heligan were largely restored and became commercially self-supporting. Visitors to Heligan were growing, and an educational niche was established by virtue of the way in which plants and plant life was presented 'with a sense of theatre'. The Heligan message was to present plants and plant life with a feeling of awe and mystique. The success at Heligan was demonstrated through the productive gardens, when it was realised that most people had eaten what they saw, but had little idea where plant produce came from. Plant life education became central pillars of Heligan's success. The funding of Heligan's restoration required Smit to collaborate with a number of large institutions that held control of the mechanisms for financial support. In particular: the Countryside Commission had granted £400,000 and the Rural Development Commission had awarded £130,000. As Heligan progressed, Smit believed he had approached the end of his personal strategising – those attempts at realigning his personal strategies, giving purpose and direction. Renovating The Lost Gardens of Heligan had provided an ideal catalyst for Smit and the experience had been instructive and rewarding. A longer-term strategy had been set which would see Heligan become the number one visitor attraction of its kind in the UK. So what next?

The entrepreneur strategiser

Early in 1994, Smit and a few colleagues were discussing what to do with some spare space at Heligan that still required renovation. Several ideas were considered but they became convinced that a glass-house growing a range of plants 'that had changed the world', would generate great interest as well as being in keeping with the Heligan mission. In true entrepreneur style, a new vision was being shaped as conversation drifted to discuss spices, cotton, rice, exotic fruits, rubber, tea and coffee. In no time, they had a list that would more than fill the planned conservatory, so the intended new idea would have to go back to the drawing board – but the idea had taken root in Smit's imagination – 'where it would stay until we could find a pocket deep enough'. But the Eden Project idea had started. Although the idea was locked away in Smit's entrepreneur conscience, it would soon be revealed with a velocity, which would become unstoppable. The success of Heligan was showing economic benefits for the towns and villages nearby, and this became the prompt which triggered Smit's imagination towards regional regeneration on a much larger scale than Heligan. Smit comments, 'I believed something could be done in the china clay district around St Austell, but I didn't know what'.

Networking and drawing upon experiences became commonplace during the entrepreneur strategiser period, enabling ideas to be formed, strategy to be discussed, and the shaping of a culture of enthusiasm and determination for the emerging, yet unnamed, Eden Project. Along with

Thoday and McMillan Browse, Smit explored examples of regional regeneration which had been introduced in the 1980s by the then British Minister for the Environment, Michael Heseltine. Year-long garden festivals had been introduced as a catalyst of change in environmentally depressed areas. Smit recognised that St Austell was equally a deprived area and should also be considered for regeneration.

By May 1994 an outline strategic vision was formed by Smit and McMillan Browse. This included five glasshouses, or giant poly-tunnels, linked together for a walk-through experience, representing world climate regions and productive plants. The initial idea included rainforest, sub-tropical rainforest, Mediterranean, and a combination of savannah and desert. The first business mission was perceived to be a vague notion of 'celebrating floristic riches and the productivity of our planet, with a nod towards conservation – in essence a large-scale theme park fit for a garden festival that intended to make a case for permanence'. Ideas and concepts were developed, and discussions held with several government regeneration departments. However, enquiries about potential funding, and presentations about their early vision and strategy for Eden, were all politely rebuffed.

The founding team of Smit, McMillan Browse and Thoday were not organised into any formal business structure and were little more than entrepreneur enthusiasts with an idea – an idea which could possibly help regenerate the Cornish economy. However, they came to realise that their ambitions, and the scale of their early intentions, was beyond their collective experiences. Meanwhile, The Lost Gardens of Heligan continued to be a huge success and the media were generous in their coverage, featuring Heligan in a number of television programmes. Smit shared his new idea with Dr Jo Readman, a television producer and scientist – Readman became very excited about the idea, offering support and advice. Enthusiasm for the nascent Eden Project idea was becoming infectious. It was time to get serious, if the idea was to move forward.

Big time thinking – big time strategy

Tim Smit visited many china clay pits in the St Austell area in his search for a location for his vision, including the Bodelva Pit, near the village of St Blazey. Instinctively, Smit knew he had found his Eden – the site was perfect, but not yet available, and had a sale price of around £10m. However, Smit's team had no money, and they had no experience of large-project management. It would have been very easy for Smit to abandon his idea for Eden, as the concept looked beyond his business experience – but he persevered and, surprisingly, persuaded others to join him in his vision. Jonathan Ball, an architect based in Bude, north Cornwall, held strong views about regeneration in Cornwall and became very enthusiastic about Smit's ideas. Ball and Smit became the co-founders of Eden, with Ball using his network of professional contacts to create the right political climate of support, particularly at Westminster – the home of British government. Ball was also well connected to the world of architecture at a national level. He suggested that the venture needed a big-name architect to give it credibility, making contact with a wide range of people to create an important constituency of influence. Meanwhile, Smit quickly came to terms with the realisation of 'how much we didn't know or understand. We knew we had the bones of a good idea. We had no idea of cost, no operational business plan, no money and no site. Other than that, everything was perfect. Heligan's success fuelled our optimism and we were completely unfazed by our ignorance. We had to consider where to go for funding. We were well aware that we couldn't go to the big agencies immediately; our plan was so rudimentary that we would have been laughed out of the door. We needed to do a feasibility study'.

Cornwall's leap of faith – the first financial donation

Smit knew most of the councillors at his local borough of Restormel through his work at Heligan, but had to convince them, and the wider community, of his intentions to regenerate the Cornish economy. Smit and Ball encouraged local people to engage in the project, giving a sense of participation and ownership. Support was secured from the borough chief executive and councillors at Planning and Economic Development; and it was suggested to Smit and Ball that they apply for seed-corn funding to help the feasibility study. The Committee eventually awarded £25,000 towards the study, representing a lot of money for a small

Cornish community. This funding proved to be the catalyst for success, enabling the team to move forward with the backing of their local community and, at the same time, giving confidence to other agencies in the region to make donations. Interest spread, with many people making donations between £5,000 and £15,000. Local people, who had retained their anger at the lack of regeneration, saw the venture as a symbol of hope and a challenge to the region's disadvantage and lack of political muscle. In advance of the upcoming new Millennium, the British government launched the Millennium Fund in 1994.[1] Smit and Ball decided that the Millennium Fund would be their prime funding target and although they had no business plan, they submitted an application of intent. Through Ball's architect connections two leading design companies were suggested. Nicholas Grimshaw and Partners, who had recently completed the Waterloo International Rail Terminal, and Renzo Piano, the Italian who had just completed the Osaka Airport project. Both had international reputations for their work with transparent materials. However, a 'Buy British' policy was adopted and Grimshaw's were chosen as the lead architect. As the team developed their proposal for the Millennium Commission (MC), it became clear that the criteria for applications were being made more difficult. One particular setback came when the pioneering Millennium Project Cornwall (the name given to Eden in the early days), realised that the MC would advance no funds to cover 'setting up' costs.

The burden of risk, therefore, was placed squarely on the shoulders of those organisations applying for funding. The only solution open was to find funds, and link these to a strategy of carrying forward the costs incurred by the team and their partners, and regard this as an accepted risk to be redeemed at a later date against a successful outcome. All the major players in the project would therefore work for nothing in the early formative years. The MC required applications in the name of a legal Trust. This was formed and Trustees appointed. Confidence grew throughout the small team, when Nicholas Grimshaw and Partners confirmed that they were committing themselves to the venture and that they were bringing the entire design team who had worked on Waterloo International Rail Terminal. The early Eden business structure was being shaped from a founding group of entrepreneur enthusiasts and several professional companies who had been 'persuaded' to engage. Smit and Ball put together the bid for the MC – a bid which Smit later confessed as 'being able to drive a horse and cart through, particularly the financial costings'! The MC turned them down, rejecting their bid outright as it did not fit any of the MC categories.[2] Smit and Ball discussed the rejection at length, and Smit decided to be a 'little economical' with the truth: 'It's not over Jonathan; we're going to bluff it out. We are going to tell everyone that we have caught their imagination and have been asked to work it up (the proposal) a bit more. And what's more we are not going to take no for an answer'. This is precisely what they did, informing the media and their project partners. No one ever questioned them and they continued with the formation of the Eden Project idea.

Rites of passage for a growing team

Strategies for the Eden business had started to be shaped during the early years when Smit and his colleagues began forming and nurturing ideas. However, it was not until 1995 that strategic planning became serious. This was a period which saw the team go through a rite of passage; from amateur enthusiasm to the harsh realities of creating from nothing, the largest construction project in Cornwall's history. The professional companies set about preparing a detailed specification that would meet the MC criteria, and secure the grants that would enable the project to proceed. Guarantees of success and acceptance, however, could not be

---

[1] This formed part of the public-benefit provision under which Britain's national lottery had been set up. The Act of Parliament stipulated that a portion of all revenues generated by the lottery should be divided between sport, charities, heritage, the arts and the Millennium Fund. Each of the five sectors would have £1.5bn to spend. The MC had the responsibility to choose 12 Landmark Projects with a maximum £50m for each project or 50 per cent of total costs. The stipulation being, however, that each project had to find half its costs from elsewhere – what is called matched funding.

[2] The MC had three categories – Category A, which meant bids are being considered; category B, which meant bids were being rejected for now, but encouraged to resubmit. The Smit and Ball bid fell into category C, which meant their application was unacceptable and unrealistic. In other words, forget it!

underwritten and each of the professional companies undertook the risk of uncertainty and the potential of substantial financial loss. The project had very little money and no one was going to get paid until the MC agreed to give the project its financial support.

The outline strategic plan was constructed on three visitor scenarios – 500,000, 600,000 and 1 million. These forecasts were based upon market analysis extrapolated from tourist industry and regional projections. The project was going to cost £106m. With a maximum £50m grant from the MC and a potential £20m from other agencies in matched funding – the shortfall of £36m needed to be raised from private funding and sponsorship. The challenges facing Smit and his team looked insurmountable; and they only had an option to purchase the Bodelva pit. He summarised his position in one press interview, commenting: 'Site, maybe. Design, maybe. Money, no'.

Getting the right money . . . and the money right

The Eden Project team, assisted by their professional partners, continued their quest to arrange finance. During 1996, the embryo strategic plan would target two key funding agencies: Target 1: The MC for public sector grants available on a matched funding basis. Target 2: Government Office for the South West (GOSW) as the regional brokers for The European Development Fund (EDF). Cornwall had designated regeneration status, and been allocated £150m to assist infrastructure development. Although Smit and his team had very little money, they gained some encouragement when the project received a generous donation from Tarmac – a large UK-based construction company. Tarmac's financial donation was gratefully accepted but on the clear understanding that Eden were not obligated to choose Tarmac as their contractors. The MC and GOSW terms required that the appointment of contractors for the project had to be tendered in open competition. Tarmac did make a tender for the construction project but the contract was won by the McAlpine Joint Venture. Numerous financial institutions were approached to secure matched funding, mostly without success, until the Canadian Imperial Bank of Commerce (CIBC) agreed to become the first bankers.

A key role to meet the conditions of the various government and financial institutions was the appointment of an operator – an organisation who would run Eden on a daily basis. Although Smit and the Eden pioneers were concerned about this, they were left with no choice. Several organisations were interviewed but none were satisfactory. Eventually Eden chose Primary Management, which was represented by Evelyn Thurlby. Thurlby became seconded to the venture as the operator, and would profoundly influence the course of the project for the next two years. The fledgling Eden Project had secured:

- professional design and engineering teams of international repute;
- professional project management and construction teams;
- a major contractor to build and develop the site;
- an operator to manage and govern the new business through early stages;
- a banker with an interest to invest and meet matched funding;
- a formative green team to deal with plants and horticulture;
- an abundance of goodwill, commitment and energy, but still no money.

Everything was set 'in principle', waiting for the outcomes of their bid to the MC which was finally submitted in December 1996. Problems arose when the professional quantity surveyors advised that the project could not proceed based upon the current strategic plan. The plans for the Eden site had to be rigorously cut back, enabling financial forecasts to be more realistic. The total capital project bid to the MC was reduced to £74.3m, supported by considerable assumptions regarding funding from Europe and English Partnerships, and 'guesstimates' about sponsorship and private sector investment. Smit describes the bid 'as little more than an act of faith'; and the MC were pushing hard for much stronger evidence of matched funding from partners. Eden had logged its application for European funds but had received only a limited contribution towards the cost of the environmental impact survey. Time was rapidly running out for the project team to meet the MC matched funding criteria and, in the meanwhile, the local community were again demonstrating their displeasure at the prospect of the Eden Project being sited on their doorstep.

Celebration time

Smit and his colleagues believed it was essential to gather support from the entire Cornish community, in particular the local and county councils. All were regarded as primary stakeholders in the Eden venture. Many public meetings were held which addressed planning permission, infrastructure changes, road access and myriad social, civil and construction issues. Resistance and barriers to the Eden concept and strategy became legend in the community. As the seconded Operator, Thurlby took an increasingly proactive role with the various funding partners, as the potential revenue streams from operations became closely scrutinised by the MC. Confidence grew, however, when the local Training and Enterprise Council approved funds for Eden, further endorsing community support, and English Partnerships confirmed the offer of a grant amounting to £500,000.

Smit found himself in London for a book display.

> I was trying to park outside the book shop in the busiest street in London, blocking a bus lane and access to a construction site, when my mobile phone went. Flustered, I said I couldn't talk and could they ring back in a few minutes. A voice I recognised said, I think you'll want to hear this now. It was Doug Watson the MC project director. You've got it he said: the Millennium Commissioners have made a conditional grant of £37.15 million.

Delight and relief spread through the Eden team as Smit informed his colleagues of the news. The Eden Project, at last, had a real future, but the next two years would be even more difficult as the team wrestled with managing the strange and conflicting mix of its strategic portfolio.

The green team

Under the direction of Peter Thoday and Philip McMillan Browse, a highly qualified green team had been formed from people specialising in global horticulture. Thoday had drawn upon his elite group of former students from his days as Director of Horticulture at Bath University; they all joined the Eden venture without hesitation – and without pay. The green team task was to procure the Eden 'star attractions' – plants from around the world. With a grant of £450,000 an established plant nursery was purchased at Watering Lane, a site near the Bodelva pit. This would be the base for the storage and cultivation of exotic plant specimens from around the world, before planting into the relevant climate Biomes. International contacts were established with foreign governments, Universities, Research Establishments and Conservation Groups. The grant of £37.15m awarded by the MC still had to be match funded. This was before any money could be drawn down to pay for the Biome design and development costs, or provide capital for the huge real-estate and construction costs needed for reshaping the site at Bodelva pit. It was time for the maverick Eden team to get serious and, by some strange alchemy, change and transform into a professional business structure. As Smit reflects,

> there comes a moment in all great ventures when talking has to stop. We'd created the constituencies, we'd talked the hind legs off donkeys, we'd been snake-oil salesmen with attitude and we had a dream to peddle. However, turning a dream into reality needs iron in the soul, money in the bank and military organisation. Now we would have to crank up a gear. Now we had more to lose than our own time and money; we had the hopes of the region on our shoulders, and those are some heavy monkeys.

Corporate governance and egos in the mist

The conditional award from the MC in May 1997, heralded the beginning of the end of the old way of doing things. The Eden Project team was growing rapidly and the Trustees were under pressure from the MC and banks to take the responsibility of forming a corporate structure and governance chain which aligned to Eden's purpose and stakeholder expectations. Tensions arose, and friction began to creep in between individuals regarding the leadership of the Eden Project. Moreover, the Trust did not want the private sector to take equity in its operating company, seeing this as a dilution of control. The argument was presented that should the project have operational problems, there was a chance that they could lose control of a huge asset to a minority shareholder. A compromise was reached that required the Trust to proceed along the equity route, but with an option to buy out the investors should funding materialise from elsewhere.

The challenges to the Trustees increased as the Eden team passed through significant change very quickly – a large fund of money was becoming available and the design team was getting restless, having worked for almost nothing for over two years. Contracts had to be made and formalised between Eden and the professional 'Executive Officer' who would take the project forward and formulate governance over the day-to-day affairs of the newly formed Eden Project Limited. Smit was considered to have political, big-picture skills but delivered with a maverick-gusto style. However, the Trustees pursued a more traditional executive who could work within the rigorous governance requirements imposed by stakeholders. What became painful to the egos of the founding Eden pioneers was the need to establish organisational ergonomics – business governance and organisational paradigms which fitted the Eden strategies and culture; but also fitted with the policies of the major stakeholders. Evelyn Thurlby decided to offer herself as a candidate for the new Chief Executive post. Evelyn proved to be the best candidate and was appointed as the first Chief Executive of Eden Project Limited. The early ambassadorial roles adopted by the founding entrepreneurs had almost come to an end and tensions were arising between individuals who felt they were being distanced from the dynamics of rapidly changing Eden. Jonathan Ball in particular, felt he was becoming 'estranged and frozen out' from the project group, now working from offices at Heligan Gardens, whilst he continued his architect practice from Bude. Dissatisfaction deepened and was compounded by the Trust's reluctance to address past and future rewards for the efforts and risks individuals had taken over the previous three years. The euphoria of moving Eden from its early vision, to its present position, had overtaken all else. Fundamental risk and reward issues, along with compensation issues had been neglected, but were now rising to the surface. Dissatisfaction and key player tensions were mitigating with Eden's strategic plans, and Jonathan Ball presented an argument suggesting that 'if personal conditions were not sorted out before new people came into the project, it would only be a matter of time before the founders would be airbrushed out'.

Evelyn Thurlby set about restructuring management roles and establishing clarity of corporate governance herself undertaking all contract negotiations and liaison with the MC, banks, the constructor and other investors. Smit became Project Director and signed a contract with the company,

holding responsibility for creating the Eden culture and developing relationships with funding agencies. Ball, however, could not agree an acceptable role for himself and it was left for him to draft his own job description for Thurlby to consider. Ball's self-designed specification established himself with a very wide brief, which Thurlby rejected as she remained unconvinced that Ball had the requisite expertise. However, a compromise was reached and Ball became Corporate Affairs Director, in charge of various initiatives for promotion and fund-raising. Dissatisfaction stretched further, when the Trustees announced that Smit and Ball should no longer attend Trust meetings, since Thurlby was senior representative of the company. To compound problems, Jonathan Ball decided to register the name – The Eden Project – as a trademark belonging to him. The action was not challenged, as the new company hoped that the matter could be resolved amicably! Evelyn Thurlby quickly made her mark as CEO, demonstrating her management experience and strategic abilities across the entire Eden project. Her tough, no nonsense approach quickly earned her respect from all connected with the project. Although Thurlby had strong financial skills, the growing financial structure needed a full time qualified professional. Gaynor Coley had been used to 'big numbers' as Finance Director at Plymouth University and joined the Board as the Eden Project Limited first Finance Director. Eden needed a corporate image and worked closely with Imagination – a London corporate imaging company. Peter Hampel joined the Eden team, interpreting and directing the Eden message on site; David Meneer was recruited as Marketing Director; Dr Jo Readman gave up her TV job and joined as Education Director and Kary Lescure was appointed as Project Manager.

On the verge of collapse – and pressure is mounting

It was important that Eden secure the Bodelva pit and obtain planning permission for Eden to be built. In theory, Eden had got all the investors needed to enable the MC grant to 'go live', but as Smit recounts, 'getting them to commit to paper was like herding eels'. Pressure from the designers and contractors, who by now had committed several million pounds to the project, but without payment, meant progress was essential. The risk of key players pulling out was high on the agenda – but nothing could be done until the Bodelva pit was purchased from the Goonvean Company. Under the auspices of the Government Office for the South West a key meeting of all the major players was called to resolve the problems. The meeting consisted of:

- Government Office South West, representing European money;
- English Partnerships, representing regional investment;
- NatWest, representing National Westminster Bank interests;[3]
- McAlpine Joint Venture, representing the build contractor;
- Millennium Commission, representing public money;
- Eden Project Limited, representing the client;
- the Goonvean China Clay Company, owners of the Bodelva pit.

Smit's account of the meeting reflects the difficulty of Eden's position:

> The mood of the meeting was serious, and not for the first time NatWest and McAlpine's acted in concert, stating that the much vaunted private/public partnership, of which Eden was supposed to be a shining example, was on the verge of collapse. If the Bodelva pit could not be bought now, and the promised funds from the public sector were not released from the bureaucratic logjam, they were pulling out and the project was over.

By the end of the meeting Eden had guarantees from all parties that they were top of priority lists for immediate action. This became a massive vote of confidence, but the MC grant was still conditional, as all matched funding was not secured. To resolve the logjam a simple solution was found. The Goonvean China Clay Company, who already owned the Bodelva pit, lent Eden £5m (half the pit purchase price), which provided the matched funding; enabling the MC to release funds for the other half of the pit price. However, even this solution had a huge sting in the tail. The con-

tractual risk stated that: 'if Eden didn't complete the pit purchase transaction by a certain date, the deal would be forfeit and Goonvean would be able to keep the MC money and have the pit back'. Decommissioning was quickly sorted and Goonvean people assisted by managing the water pumping operations, transferring the waterlogged site from a lake, to a relatively dry hole in the ground. Eden took ownership of the Bodelva pit site on 17 October 1998, and this became their liberation.

Outline planning permission had been consented to in 1997, but Eden had to secure and raise a bond to create a new road, which was trapped in a tangled web of land tenure. Such was the commitment to the project that the McAlpine Joint Venture paid the bond for the road to the County Council, ensuring that it would be built as soon as planning permission was granted. This was achieved in November 1998. In February 1999, Thurlby and Coley signed an important funding deal with NatWest bank and eventually, Eden received a European funding grant of £12.5m. The full draw down of the MC grant could now be operational, as matched funding was now in place – and Eden had its site at Bodelva pit.

Acts of faith and the big build

Confidence grew as the final plans were prepared by Thurlby and Coley – plans which were built around solid financial foundations, enabling the important site development to proceed. McAlpine's were already several million pounds into the project and, for the first time in their history, were operating without a signed contract. McAlpine's reflected on their position: 'We are too far into the Eden project; beyond a point of no return, and felt inspired by an act of faith and belief that funding would come!' Similar acts of faith were becoming commonplace. Construction of the large greenhouses at the Watering Lane nursery had started in October 1998 and was later opened by the Lord Lieutenant of Cornwall. This connection introduced Eden to the Pennon Group who made a loan of £1m and sponsored the waterfall in the Humid Tropics Biome. During October 1998, the McAlpine Joint Venture invaded the Bodelva site, clearing the base of the pit in readiness for what was to become a building site for the next two years. However, early into the New Year (1999), the Cornish weather disrupted plans and

---

[3] NatWest became involved after CIBC withdrew their interest when Eden cut the project from £106m down to £74.3m, implying that such a sum was 'small beer' to CIBC operations.

work ceased for two months. The worst weather in Cornwall's history poured 43m gallons of water into the pit in January alone. The big build was on its way, despite Cornwall seeing 100 consecutive days of rain during the 1998/99 winter.

After two years of steering Eden through some of its most testing experiences, Evelyn Thurlby decided it was time to move on, leaving a substantial gap in Eden's management. Many of Eden's partners had come to see Thurlby as the outstanding executive at the Eden Project and openly expressed their concerns at her departure. However, after much debate, Tim Smit was appointed as Eden's second Chief Executive, with Gaynor Coley becoming Deputy Chief Executive and Managing Director. Smit describes himself as having 'a cavalier enthusiasm which can excite people about Eden, but lacking high level corporate experience'. Although Coley would become Smit's saviour at times, particularly when dealing with complex financial issues, they presented a formidable senior management duo.

Public preview and Eden's official opening

As national interest grew, the Board decided to offer the public a preview of Eden during its construction – a celebration of achievement called 'the big build'. The preview would last from May 2000 to January 2001 and visitors would be allowed to visit the proximity of the Biomes and observe what was happening at Eden. During the preview, Eden had almost 500,000 visitors, all curious to see what was happening in a redundant Cornish china clay pit. The event was an overwhelming success, but no one, as yet, had seen the star attractions – the plants in situ in their high-technology home. The Biome construction was almost complete, enabling the green team to commence many months of planting, and the artistic team to build their stories about human dependency on plants. Planning and logistics had to be precise when Smit decided that the Eden Project would officially open as a visitor attraction in Spring 2001. Coley negotiated a further £13m to cover ongoing operating costs, and McAlpine's handed over the site to Eden with a certificate of completion. The green team worked day and night to meet the official opening date, completing their

work with less than 12 hours to opening. The Eden Project officially opened to public visitors on 17 March 2001.

> With passion and commitment, thousands of 'small' people built this place as a symbol of hope – in action. We may all have feet of clay but that should not stop us trying to make a difference. Wouldn't we all rather look back and say, 'I'm glad I did', rather than 'I wish I had'? We make no apology for wanting to bring people of differing opinions together if, in doing so, we find solutions that will improve all our lives and make the world a better place for all living things. Some might smile at the naiveté of such ambition, believing it impossible . . . We say; Demand the impossible.
>
> (Tim Smit, Co-founder of the Eden Project, 17 March 2001)

Author's notes

1. It is impossible in this case study to describe the work undertaken by the so called 'muck shift people', and do justice to the enormity of the task they undertook. However, I recommend the video/DVD of Eden's construction as valuable teaching support material alongside this case. Video/DVD copies can be purchased direct from Eden Project.

2. A critical factor during Eden's phases of progress was that – although finance procurement, strategic planning, engineering and site construction tend to work within business time-plans and schedules – plants do not! Plants respond to growing seasons, and it became critical to closely manage the landscape and Biome construction programmes with that of plant growing seasons. With no home, 'on time', for the horticultural programme, several million pounds in plant investment would die. Timing was critical, as many species were being shipped to Watering Lane and the Bodelva site from all parts of the world.

Sources

Sources of information consulted to support this case study: Eden Marketing Department, *The Eden Effect*, 1 October 2002 (an overview of the Eden Project's Local and Regional Economic Impact). Eden Media Department, Media Pack, 1 October 2002. *Eden: The First Book*, Eden Project Books, Fifth reprint, July 2002. *Eden: The Second Book, Watch Us Grow*, Eden Project Books, 2002. *Eden Project: The Guide*, Eden Project Books, Revised 2002. Eden Project Video, Eden Project Books, 2001. Smit. T., *Eden*, Eden Project Books, Corgi, 2002. www.edenproject.com

Acknowledgements

The author acknowledges the valuable advice and cooperation given by David Meneer during the final reading of this case. My sincere thanks are given to Eden Project Limited for giving permission to release this case for publication. My thanks also to Gendall Design, Cornwall, for providing the photography.

Caveat

The author wishes to record that the events expressed in this case study are entirely based upon his own research and interpretation of information available in the public domain. Moreover, that any such interpretation has not, directly or indirectly, been influenced, suggested or offered by the Eden Trust, Eden Project Limited, or any past or present employee of Eden Project Limited.

Ericsson and the creation of the mobile telephony systems business

Patrick Regnér

The case describes the history of the Swedish telecommunications company Ericsson's entry into the mobile telephone systems market. It examines the characteristics of strategic change from a public telecommunication to a mobile telephony focus, and shows how strategic innovation may emerge from the periphery of an organisation. The case describes how a small and insignificant unit in Ericsson turned the company into the world's largest supplier of mobile telephone systems. The focus is therefore on the dynamics of strategy innovation from the beginning of the 1980s to the turn of the century.

● ● ●

Ericsson delivered the first commercial mobile telephone system in the world to Saudi Arabia in 1981. The company sold the system despite Saudi Tel, Saudi Arabia's PTT,[1] not specifying it at all in its order of telecommunication networks and equipment. Furthermore, Ericsson did not actually have a mobile phone system to sell or the required products for its infrastructure. This was, however, the first step towards making Ericsson the largest mobile telephony company in the world.

SRA – an autonomous and self-reliant company with a vision

It was a small and autonomous subsidiary of Ericsson, SRA, which insisted on selling a mobile telephone system to Saudi Arabia. SRA led a rather languishing life as a radio communication supplier at the time and, basically, was an independent company. The company's focus had been on radio products for military as well as civilian use (radio receivers, gramophones, TVs, radio systems for aviation and shipping, radar installations, etc.). From the 1960s the company had consolidated into communication and military radio equipment, leaving consumer goods. Its major business was in the military market. SRA's independence from Ericsson was not only due to its small size, unrelated technology and generally microscopic role in Ericsson, but reflected the fact that British GE-Marconi owned 29 per cent of the company at the time.

The president of SRA, Åke Lundqvist, was extremely enthusiastic about mobile telephony. He had joined SRA in the mid-1960s and had been in charge of the land-mobile radio division since 1970. He had been involved in mobile radio and mobile telephony since the end of the 1950s, when he worked for another company. He participated in the development of one of the early Swedish mobile telephone systems, MTB (which could handle only six telephone calls simultaneously in Stockholm). SRA also had a history in the system since they supplied its base stations and telephones.[2]

---

[1] PTT refers to Post, Telephone and Telegraph, which were the traditional government organisations or monopolies responsible for running a country's postal and telecommunications services.

[2] A base station is equipped with transmitters and receivers and covers a geographical area or a 'cell' with radio signals connecting to mobile telephones. Base stations are connected to mobile telephone switches, which in turn are linked to the fixed telephony network.

Lundqvist had an early vision of the importance of mobile telephony, a vision 'based on radio technology, to eliminate the wire from the regular telephony'. However, at Ericsson, SRA's vision was laughed at, and the company was considered a 'garage outfit', a 'bicycle repair shop' represented by 'cowboys'. As one manager in Ericsson's largest division, the Public Telecommunications Division put it: 'They were not really a part of us. They looked different and behaved differently.'

Ericsson – a public telecommunications company with AXE as the flagship product

The main products of Ericsson had traditionally been switching and transmission equipment. A switch, or telephone exchange, controls and operates telephone calls in a telephone network. In the early days it consisted of a manual system where an operator used pairs of plugs to connect people on a switchboard. All major R&D was invested in switching and Ericsson introduced its digital switching technology, AXE, at an early stage. It became widely known and well respected and contracts all over the world had been signed by 1980. The PTTs had historically been the principal markets for these products. Roughly a dozen telecommunications companies dominated the world market (AT&T, Ericsson, CIT-Alcatel, Fujitsu, Hitachi, ITT, NEC, OKI, Plessey, Siemens, Strowger). They competed for orders from the PTTs where markets were open. The US was still closed and the British PTT bought only from British companies. Similar arrangements prevailed in many other markets. Political considerations often played a larger role than commercial or technological ones. Once a relationship had been built with a PTT, it usually lasted for a very long time, with continuous follow-up contracts, and competition was limited. John Meurling, director of corporate relations and investor relations at Ericsson of the time:

> The vendor–customer relationship could often be described as marriage-like: once a PTT had made its system choice – or often vendor choice, which might go back to the beginning of the century – the relationship was expected to continue for a long time . . . Not many countries were supplied by one

manufacturer only, but very few countries had more than two or three. For most companies it was cozy.[3]

Even if Ericsson had one of the least 'cosy' positions, because the Swedish PTT manufactured most of its own switches, their culture and way of doing business reflected the prevalent stable and semi-competitive environment. However, SRA, although quite remote both in terms of technology and products, had spent its whole 60-year history in a less protected and quite competitive business environment. Most managers at Ericsson did not know much about SRA; it was a minor, independent and pretty unglamorous business. AXE was the flagship of Ericsson and Public Telecommunications was its captain. As John Meurling described it:

> We [Public Telecom] were the biggest, the most important, and the most beautiful part of the Ericsson Group – and we knew it.[4]

The Nordic mobile telephone network

The Swedish and other Nordic PTTs were pivotal in developing and establishing mobile telephony in Sweden and the Nordic countries. They joined forces in order to develop the Nordic Mobile Telephone (NMT) network. Telecommunication equipment manufacturers were asked in 1977 to submit proposals to provide the NMT network. Ericsson and SRA and their competitors – among them NEC, Motorola, Mitsubishi and Fujitsu – were invited to bid. Ericsson, however, was not particularly enthusiastic about mobile phone systems. Its Public Telecommunications unit was not interested in providing switches for mobile systems. They finally offered switches, but it was more in order to preserve old relations with its long-term partner, the Swedish PTT, than enthusiastically to enter a new market. Ericsson did not offer its latest technology (AXE) at first. An adjusted AXE switch for mobile telecommunication was simply seen to have a limited future. The company, however, subsequently did offer AXE at the insistence of the Swedish PTT, which indicated

---

[3] Meurling, J. and Jeans, R. (1995) *A Switch in Time: AXE – Creating the Foundation for the Information Age*, London: Communications Week International.

[4] Meurling, J. and Jeans, R. (1994) *The Mobile Phone Book: The Innovation of the Mobile Phone Industry*, London: Communications Week International.

that otherwise it might adopt the technology of NEC, the closest contestant.

Ericsson's lack of enthusiasm for mobile phone systems reflected its very small role compared with its other businesses and a belief that mobile telephony would continue to be of minor importance. Mobile telephony was seen as something more exclusive and directed towards professional use. Personal application was something not very serious – a service for the privileged. Ericsson was far from alone in its assessment of a limited mobile phone market. For example, the NMT network was initially thought to be complementary to manual mobile telephone systems. Bell Labs at AT&T, which originally invented mobile telephone networks, hired a major US management consultancy firm to study mobile telephony and its market potential around this time. The firm concluded that the potential was insignificant and firmly advised against involvement in mobile telephony. Another reason for Ericsson's resistance was that in radio the company's involvement was in closed radio systems and it was questionable whether SRA had the right competences for mobile telephony. In fact, the rest of Ericsson did not think much of the SRA personnel. As one SRA manager of the time explained: 'We were considered as lacking in knowledge, stupid and inexperienced.'

At SRA, enthusiasm for the NMT venture was greater and they did have some radio technology competences. However, their mobile systems competences were limited. SRA did not yet have its own base stations, a central part of a mobile system. At first SRA was more focused on the mobile telephone itself than on the entire mobile system, but its technology in that area was inferior as well. SRA had succeeded in developing a mobile telephone, but it was not the latest technology. Instead, one of SRA's main resources at this time was its entrepreneurial spirit and, perhaps, insight compared with the rest of Ericsson and competitors. As Åke Lundqvist put it: 'We had a vision to eliminate the wire in telephony, everybody laughed at us!'

The first commercial cellular mobile system in the world

In the end, Ericsson got the order to deliver switches for the NMT network in the Nordic countries and SRA became a sub-supplier of a base station control unit for Magnetic, a local Swedish radio technology firm. SRA also supplied mobile telephones or stations for the system.[5] Since SRA needed competence in this area they acquired Sonab in 1978, a rival in radio technology and the leader in mobile stations in Sweden at that time. That company had a land mobile terminal that was upgraded to a mobile telephone. Despite winning the NMT order there was still limited interest in mobile telephone systems at Ericsson and consequently little integration of Ericsson's and SRA's products, mobile telephone switches and radio equipment, respectively.

The first commercial mobile telephony system in the world was delivered in 1981, not to the Nordic countries, but to Saudi Arabia. The NMT in the Nordic countries was not in operation until a couple of months after the Saudi première. In the late 1970s Ericsson won a major order to supply Saudi Arabia with a fixed telecommunication infrastructure. Åke Lundqvist enthusiastically took the initiative on a mobile telephony system in Saudi Arabia. Lundqvist suggested to Ericsson's CEO, Björn Lundvall: 'Can't we try to sell a mobile telephone system to Saudi Arabia? They want the latest of everything else.' Lundqvist managed to convince both the CEO and the head of Ericsson's Public Telecommunications Switching Division, Håkan Ledin, to offer the Saudis a mobile telephone system. They were prepared to go along with Lundqvist's ideas; after all, any mobile phone deal would only be small compared with the fixed network that represented the main order. Ledin actually believed a system already existed. However, SRA and Ericsson did not have a complete system at that time; even some of the core products did not exist.

The first cellular mobile systems were not without problems. The Saudi order included 8,000 mobile stations, which put pressure on production sources – there were no terminals left to sell in the Nordic home market. Competitors naturally exploited the situation. Furthermore, there were important quality problems. Among other things, the telephone station keypads melted in the hot Saudi sun, and the armour-plated limousines and cars caused installation problems. In addition, as SRA tried to get its first generation of mobile phones into production on the Nordic market, the competitors were bringing out their second

---

[5] The correct terminology here is mobile stations or terminals. At this time these were based on land-mobile products and were large and heavy units to be installed in vehicles.

generation. Flemming Örneholm, SRA's Marketing Manager at the time, referred to the situation as a disaster:

> It was a mess . . . Quality was certainly not up to expectations . . . The competitors were beating the hell out of Ericsson [SRA].[6]

Trying to sell integrated mobile telephony systems

At the end of the 1970s and beginning of the 1980s more PTTs started to show an interest in mobile telephony. SRA began to see a sizeable potential market and started to penetrate more markets, 'shooting at everything they saw' as one manager put it. They wanted to provide a more coordinated and integrated mobile telephony *system* of Ericsson's switches and their own radio equipment to the operators. However, the initial orders were small, and the contracts were of modest size from the viewpoint of Ericsson's corporate management and switching division. Switching merely regarded mobile telephony as another way among many others to sell switches. Attempting to exploit mobile telephony applications was more trouble than it was worth and it was out of the question that SRA, with not quite 4 per cent of total sales, would be in charge of Ericsson's flagship product AXE for mobile systems. Furthermore, it was far from obvious that mobile telephony was a promising future market. There were no indications in terms of market investigations or any other indicators and few thought that mobile telephony would grow into a mass market. Forecasts continuously underestimated the number of subscribers during the 1980s. Mobile phone network operators, governmental bodies, mobile phone infrastructure providers and mobile phone manufacturers all underestimated the tremendous growth of mobile telephony. During these early years of mobile phone networks, Ericsson and SRA continued to submit separate offers. And the different views on mobile system integration resulted in increased tension between the two units. However, even if there was no coherent arrangement for mobile phone systems, SRA were finally given at least the marketing responsibility for them.

A contract in the Netherlands

SRA continued to fight dual battles for a more complete system concept, both internally, versus the Switching Division and corporate management, and in the market. This was apparent in the Netherlands, where both the Dutch PTT and Ericsson's corporate management and Switching Division had to be convinced of the advantage of the integrated system idea. From Ericsson there were separate offers as usual; the Switching Division offered switches, and SRA offered radio-technology. The PTT wanted Ericsson's AXE switch since it had a high capacity. However, Motorola was involved in the discussion as well and suggested a combination of AXE switches and its own base stations. The Dutch PTT supported this concept. So did Ericsson at first. The arrangement could eventually lead to further AXE orders to be filled jointly with Motorola. However, Åke Lundqvist strongly disapproved. He argued that Ericsson should be a provider of integrated systems in mobile telephony, and should furnish the whole package – switches and base stations – or nothing. Lundqvist's position brought matters to a head, causing considerable distress among managers at Switching. Ericsson would risk losing the entire order and would actually be declining an opportunity to sell its principal product. This was particularly frustrating since SRA were not ready either in terms of products – their base station was not fully developed – or in terms of competence. Since Switching also supplied switches to the PTT's fixed network, relations with this customer had to be handled with care. As one manager of the time explained:

> That is a thriller, it was terrible . . . They were absolutely lost . . . They did not really understand, they made base stations and there was not much to it . . . I wondered: Can this be true?[7]

The Netherlands PTT and Motorola considered that agreement had been reached on the arrangement, which would include Motorola's base stations and Ericsson's switch. However, Lundqvist did not give up, but tried to convince the parties involved. He managed to obtain the passive approval of Ericsson's new CEO, Björn Svedberg,

[6] Meurling, J. and Jeans, R. (1997) *The Ugly Duckling: Mobile phones from Ericsson – putting people on speaking terms*, Stockholm: Ericsson Mobile Communications AB.

[7] McKelvey, M., Texier, F. and Alm, H. (1997) *The Dynamics of High Tech Industry: Swedish Firms Developing Mobile Tele-communication System*, Working Paper No. 187, November, Linköping University.

and consent from some Switching managers. All in all, it was not a major AXE order; and they were more concerned with the relationship with the Dutch PTT because of the supply of AXE to their fixed network which, naturally, was larger. Prompted by Motorola, the PTT now required a 'small-cell concept' (a technology where the cells – the geographical area covered by a base station – are particularly small) to suit the topography and the density of population in the Netherlands. SRA lacked knowledge in the small-cell technology required. Nevertheless, Lundqvist continued to fight. He happened to know, and managed to recruit, one of the best US consultants in the area, Chan Rypinski. SRA and Lundqvist were playing a tough game with high stakes. First, he obtained partial consent from the CEO. Second, the Switching Division was convinced. The PTT's purchasing department, however, showed no interest in the proposal. Unconventional methods were required. When the PTT did not listen, Lundqvist became furious. He recalled: 'This was the only time I ever slammed my fist on the table while arguing with a customer.' With SRA playing the leading role, they and Ericsson finally managed to win the contract, which included a complete system of switches, base stations and cell planning services (the design and planning of the number of cells, base stations, etc.), but it was a hard sell to the PTT. Thus, SRA and Ericsson had begun to sell a more integrated system and not only separate parts of mobile telephony.

Later SRA thought that the integration had to be complete and that it had to be finally decided whether Public Telecommunications (including switching) should invest in mobile telephony or if this mission should be left to SRA alone. The discussions were heated. Although the Switching Division still saw only a limited future for AXE in mobile telephone networks, after much pressure and debate corporate management finally gave SRA the business and responsibility for the system as a whole, including base stations, switches and cell planning services. As one executive recalled: 'The reason was not lack of competence. They [Switching] simply did not believe in this.' The drive from SRA to coordinate proposals into a package deal and integrate the whole business had paid off. SRA and mobile telephony were now at least and at last 'an accepted, but not acceptable activity', as one SRA manager put it. However, the Switching Division was to be in charge of and manufacture the switches and sell them to SRA.

While mobile telephony now was central to SRA, it was still a peripheral and negligible business for the rest of Ericsson. The entire Radio Communications business area, of which SRA was part, only accounted for 5 per cent of Ericsson's sales in 1982 and mobile telephony was only a small part of that.

Entering the US

In 1983 Åke Lundqvist predicted that 'by the turn of the century, sales in Ericsson's mobile telephone business would pass those in public telecom'. John Meurling, director of corporate relations and investor relations at Ericsson of the time, replied: 'God help us, that's ridiculous!' Corporate management had their strategic focus on something completely different: information systems, the merger between computer and telecommunication technology, was the wave of the future. Ericsson was to participate in this vision in order to create the 'paperless office'. The company made a bold strategic change, forming an entirely new business area, Ericsson Information Systems (EIS), including four new divisions.[8] Beginning in 1981, EIS received considerable attention, resources, capital and manpower. Two main acquisitions were made to obtain the new technologies needed.

SRA continued its aggressive and ambitious ways of doing business. In order to acquire knowledge in mobile telephony, SRA had an active policy: 'We had a well-developed buying approach, we bought firms or consultancy services' (Åke Lundqvist). Through the consultant in the Netherlands case, Åke Lundqvist happened to meet another US-based consultant, Jan Jubon, who urged SRA to enter the US. Lundqvist was interested, and the consultant was hired to submit a market report. The SRA management made a decision to enter. The entry was initially a trial and error expedition. SRA thought the risks were reasonable in order to make a try. The organisation set up was small, in temporary offices and with staff commuting to the US. Its job was to get acquainted with the operators and present products and services. Lundqvist regarded the pioneers in the US venture as heroes:

---

[8] EIS initially had four divisions: Communication Systems (business switch from Ericsson, MD 100, and network communications), Business Systems (bank terminals and mini computers), Alfaskop Terminals (computer terminals) and General Terminals (voice, text and computer systems).

There were two or three persons in the US, making calls for hours. They made a superhuman accomplishment. EIS (Ericsson Information Systems) did the opposite, they had hundreds of salesmen.

SRA's US mobile system was marketed to various potential operators applying for licences to the Federal Communications Commission (FCC), the federal government body regulating public communication systems in the US. In 1982 it became clear that the SRA system had been used and specified in 30 per cent of the applications to FCC. This news did not mean that any contracts were assured, but it was positive, and somewhat surprising. The main competitors in the US market were Motorola, together with Northern Telecom, EF Johnsson, Harris Corporation and NEC. In fact, SRA and Ericsson were not awarded any contracts at first, but in May 1983 they obtained their first order for a mobile telephony network system in Buffalo in competition with Motorola and NEC. Later the same year, another important contract was won in Chicago. Subsequently the US organisation was strengthened in order to fulfil all requirements regarding planning, installation and testing. More contracts followed in other parts of the US. SRA competitors now had to take them seriously, but their market position was far from well established. Soon competitors were offering creative financing solutions, a challenge to SRA since the risks involved were high and financing was not one of the company' strengths. While this problem held SRA back at first, later a 'pay as you grow' strategy was implemented in which the operator repaid his loans as he obtained more subscribers.

SRA also experimented with various methods in order to gain contracts and they took considerable risks. In the competitive fight, Lundqvist brought up the idea of taking responsibility for filling the stock of subscribers, if the operators had not filled it themselves within a certain timeframe. It was initially quite successful, but some argued that in the end a large sum of money was almost lost. Besides entering into risky market ventures, daring actions were undertaken internally as well. When SRA entered the US they did not have the products. They developed a base station based on their prior knowledge in radio technology for the military. Åke Lundqvist recalls: 'Normally it takes 3–4 years to develop a base station. We took one that we used for military purposes; but we managed it; it had a good technical performance.' Furthermore,

since the AXE switch seemed too large, especially for small networks in the US, where competitors such as Motorola and AT&T had smaller and cheaper ones, they carefully thought about building their own switch. AXE was considered too costly anyway and the trouble with the switching division could be put aside if they had their own switch. SRA had product plans, even brochures, and developed prototype versions of switches. However, these plans had to be abandoned. Another undertaking was to go for mobile telephones. It was an area where SRA had started out, but where they did not have any large market shares and did not have any products at all to offer the US market. Motorola marketed mobile phones in the markets that were up for mobile system bids and had swung decisions its way. SRA set up a new research laboratory and tried to increase sales of mobile telephones. However, the business was quite small and unprofitable through the whole decade.

Because Marconi was owned by one of Ericsson's competitors in switching (GE), Ericsson bought Marconi's interest in SRA at the turn of 1982/83. However, they still did not pay much attention to SRA: they kept their focus on EIS. However, SRA became a wholly owned company under the name of Ericsson Radio Systems AB (Inc.). ERA became part of Radio Communications, one of seven business areas that were created.

Continued international expansion – new markets and new standards

An opportunity in the UK appeared at the same time as the US venture. Massive resources were required in the US. An additional attempt in another market where Ericsson had limited and mostly unpleasant experience would put even more pressure on the organisation, but they entered anyway. As one ERA manager of the time explained: 'We had to choose between the US and UK markets, we decided to take them both on.' This step was a bold venture by ERA as it involved expansion from a small sales organisation to a large manufacturing and R&D company in the UK. In addition, it meant working with a new mobile telephony standard, TACS (Total Access Communications System). In 1983 Vodafone, one of two British operators, chose ERA as infrastructure supplier. The company won the contract in competition with AT&T and Motorola and it was fulfilled in 1985. As ERA entered more and more markets in Europe and North America, the company faced an increasingly complicated environment, including various uncertainties about technologies and standards, and deregulated markets involving more and more multifaceted customers. The market potential was highly unpredictable and competition intensified. ERA encountered this complexity with a business and action-oriented culture, as one ERA manager of the time explained:

> We were independent entrepreneurs . . . hunting mobile telephone technology . . . fighting over markets . . . and firing at everything we saw.

The Nordic PTTs decided to upgrade the NMT system in 1983. ERA, which still lacked complete base station technology and products at this time, bought the Swedish radio technology company Magnetic the same year. The two companies received orders for base stations in Sweden. A strong competitor was Radiosystem, a spin-off from Magnetic. The new NMT system was opened in August 1986. Meanwhile expansion continued into other markets. ERA was successful in Canada in 1984 and additional contracts were won in Houston and major cities in Ohio the same year and in California in 1985/86. In 1987, ERA won a prestigious contract for a network infrastructure in New York City. By now ERA had definitely established itself as a serious competitor in North America. They were also able to enter markets in the Far East – Thailand and Indonesia – and also Australia in 1985. With the mobile telephony vision as a foundation, ERA aimed at gradually moving into different technologies, standards and markets in order to 'obtain as many customers as possible and then deliver', as one ERA manager put it. When they entered the Far East they had a proactive approach, according to another ERA manager:

> Often the Asian ministries answered that they did not have 450 MHz available [the required radio frequency for ERA's system]. Our people became acquainted with these engineers and located opportunities in their frequency plans. We were very proactive.

The entrepreneurial and independent culture of ERA caused frequent friction with the more methodical and bureaucratically oriented corporate management and switching division in the Public

Telecommunications business area. 'It was two completely different worlds. Ericsson was ignorant, there was animosity and competition', explained an Ericsson manager of the time. Despite their market success and growth, ERA was still regarded as a minor business and was treated accordingly by corporate management and, in particular, by managers in Switching, who 'considered us as something the cat dragged in', as one ERA manager put it. From corporate management's point of view ERA was not considered to have a strategy. The CEO of Ericsson criticised ERA's strategy for being 'completely absent'. One ERA manager of the time argued that there even seemed to be talks about getting rid of ERA altogether: 'It was most probably discussed . . . I am sure someone tried to strangle us.'

Corporate management had to keep their focus on the information systems venture (EIS), but now for reasons other than expansion. The new division, EIS, had expanded rapidly and met its goals in terms of company growth to 31 per cent of total sales in 1985, but the market growth predictions faltered immensely and so did profit expectations, and it reported a loss of SEK 806m (roughly $100m). The unit had to be fundamentally restructured, but it took several years to repair the damage. Understandably, this process required considerable attention from top management. Meanwhile, ERA and mobile telephony had been largely left aside, and when they were bothered, Åke Lundqvist, president of SRA, fought the botherers off. As one ERA manager recalls: 'He kept corporate management away when they troubled us.'

Recognition and success of mobile telephony

In 1986 Lars Ramqvist, former president of the Components business area, became one of three vice-presidents, and part of the Ericsson Corporate Executive Committee. He was assigned to examine Ericssons's corporate strategy. Ramqvist identified several core businesses. Among them all, mobile telephony was included, although the AXE switching system was clearly still the central product. As John Meurling put it:

> For the first time cellular [mobile telephony] was seen as a legitimate, worthwhile, even important, part of Ericsson's business. However, there was a great deal

of lack of understanding and distrust left, even if more people saw its importance. They said 'those damn cowboys' and at ERA they said 'those damn bureaucrats'.

In 1988 ERA succeeded in their long-term internal battle and the mobile telephony business was almost fully integrated. Sales in the area had increased substantially and market growth continued to increase as well. ERA was given responsibility for the entire mobile telephone system, including switches. Nevertheless, the Switch Division within the Public Telecommunications business area controlled the research and development of digital switching. Other technological and development responsibilities for mobile system switches were shifted to ERA. Controversies continued between parts of the switch division and ERA, but more people now seemed to realise the impact of ERA and mobile telephony. The same year the Swedish base station company Radiosystem was acquired. It increased ERA's market share in base stations considerably and together with strong market growth ERA gained almost 40 per cent share of the world market for mobile telephony systems. Also in the same year Åke Lundqvist, who was considered 'too wild and unstructured' by corporate management and whose ERA still ran into conflicts with the rest of the organisation, resigned. Lars Ramqvist became the president of ERA. He came from the four-man Corporate Executive Management team and the change indicated the increased importance of ERA in Ericsson. In addition, more structure and order in the organisation followed. As explained by one ERA manager:

> When Ramqvist arrived we got more freedom. There was a reorganisation and some people disappeared then. But it is unclear if it was a strategic undertaking even at that time.

An obvious problem with various national analogue mobile telephone networks (NMT, TACS, etc.) was that terminals or telephones could not be used across borders. The standardisation organisation of western Europe's PTTs had appointed a group, GSM (Groupe Spéciale Mobile), to work on a new common standard for mobile telephony in 1982. Ericsson had a strong position in the negotiations with its involvement in both NMT and TACS. A Nordic solution, close to the system on which ERA had been working, won in a referendum among the European countries in 1987. The German and French telecommunication companies

were clearly behind. Ericsson first obtained contracts in Germany, Sweden, Norway and Finland. By 1990 Ericsson had contracts with ten out of the 18 European GSM countries. Besides digital GSM, in which sales were increasing, analogue systems continued to be sold worldwide, in Mexico, eastern Europe, China, etc. Radio Communications sales, including ERA, increased by almost 70 per cent between 1988 and 1989; that year it accounted for 20 per cent of total Ericsson sales. It was a business to be taken seriously and more and more people did so, including corporate management. Lars Ramqvist was appointed new CEO of Ericsson in 1990. Kurt Hellström became the president of ERA. Some animosity continued between Radio and Switching, but it diminished after the entire responsibility for mobile telephony, including all switching development, including digital GSM, was transferred to Radio Communications and ERA in 1992. The two following years showed immense and sustained growth. 1993 was a turning point, since Radio Communications passed Public Telecommunication in sales with 40 per cent of total sales, compared with 32 per cent for PT. Mobile telephony alone (apart from other product areas in Radio Communications) had achieved sales equal to the total for Public Telecommunication, 32 per cent. Now there was no doubt that mobile telephone systems were a strategic and important part of Ericsson, as their 1994 annual report stated:

> Ericsson's success in mobile telephony is based on the very farsighted and advanced development work in the field of radio that was begun at an early stage within Ericsson Radio Systems [ERA].

Sales successes and expansion continued as ERA continued to enter into all standards as new digital ones were launched. Ericsson enjoyed repeated success when the digital standard in the US was adopted (Digital AMPS – Advanced Mobile Phone System). With digital mobile telephony in the US, Ericsson managed to increase its market share there considerably. The company also had similar successes in another digital system, the Personal Communication System (PCS), in the US. Moreover, Ericsson became a competitor in the segment based on the Japanese digital standard, Pacific Digital Cellular (PDC). In general the Asian markets expanded rapidly for Ericsson during the end of the 1990s, especially Japan and China. Other Asian markets included the Philippines, India, Indonesia, Taiwan and Korea. By 1994,

Radio Communication, including ERA, accounted for more than 50 per cent of Ericsson's sales and almost 30 per cent of its workforce. Radio Communications was the main product area and mobile telephone systems was its flagship. Later, mobile telephones and terminals were to be another flagship. The tremendous growth of Mobile Systems continued and in 1997 total mobile telephony sales had reached 70 per cent of the corporate total, and the number of employees had almost quadrupled since 1992. The same year the Radio Communication business area was divided into two new business areas: Mobile Systems, including mobile system infrastructure equipment, and Mobile Phones and Terminals, with 44 and 26 per cent of total sales, respectively. Sales increased by another 10 per cent in 1998 to more than twice as much as four years earlier. The introduction to the strategy section, 'The new world of Telecom', in the 1998 annual report illustrates the importance of mobile telephony:

> Ericsson is a world leader in mobile telephony. The corporation is the largest supplier of mobile systems, with ca. 30 per cent of the world market, in dollars. The corporation is also among the largest on the market for digital mobile telephones and public switches.

By the turn of the century Ericsson was completely dominated by the mobile telephony business. Meanwhile the Public Telecommunication business area, renamed Infocom, went through a restructuring process and some sections were outsourced and sold.

Epilogue

By 2001, after years of success, Ericsson was experiencing major difficulties. The *Financial Times* (29 May 2001) reported:

> The group's handset business is in crisis and its infrastructure arm is being battered by global economic slowdown . . .

To be sure, Ericsson was not the only telecoms group to be hit by global slowdown and a difficult transition to third-generation (3G) mobile telephony. But its problems were not just the market's making – and they were big enough to risk permanently damaging the group's competitive position.

The financial crisis hit Ericsson hard and there were even worries that the company would not survive. However, a very tough cost-cutting programme seemed to have been effective and the company signalled in July 2003 that the crisis was over with a return to profit during the year. The *Financial Times* (7 October 2003) reported:

> Carl-Henric Svanberg certainly knows a thing or two about timing. Six months ago, when he took over as chief executive of Ericsson, the world's leading maker of mobile phone infrastructure, the company was struggling with heavy losses, announcing job cuts and wallowing in the worst recession the telecommunications industry has seen. But it now appears that he joined just as the company's savage cost-cutting was beginning to bear fruit and the devastating three-year slump that has ravaged Ericsson and other telecoms infrastructure makers around the world was bottoming out. In July he was able to declare Ericsson's financial crisis over and give the first cautiously optimistic assessment that the market for telecoms networks was stabilizing . . .

The scars of the long downturn would be visible at Ericsson for a long time – by 2004 the company was half the size it was at the beginning of 2001 when it had 107,000 employees and would be down to 47,000 by the time its cost-cutting programme is complete at the end of that year. It lost SKr53bn (€58bn) in 2001 and 2002. There was still no evidence of growth in revenues – indeed in 2003 they were almost half the peak level of SKr221bn (€243bn) seen in 2002. Moreover, its debt was still rated as junk by the credit rating agencies and some credit analysts believed it might need to strengthen its balance sheet again . . .

In one sense, at least, the company had come through the trauma in good shape – it had managed to maintain its market share of 35 to 40 per cent for global system for mobile communications (GSM) and wide-band code division multiple access (WCDMA), its 3G successor. Mr Svanberg seemed happy with the shape of the company.

Ericsson's mobile telephony handset business had been even worse hit than their infrastructure arm. It had gone through a major crisis with decreasing market shares and design, quality and image problems. As reported by the *Financial Times* (29 May 2001):

> As recently as 1998, Ericsson's handsets business was almost neck-and-neck with Finland's Nokia and was the world's leading supplier of digital cellular phones. By 2002, it was making bigger losses than any other company in the handsets business – a total of SKr24bn (€26.5bn), SKr553 on each phone sold. Its market share in the first quarter of 2003 was a mere 7 per cent, while Nokia's had soared to nearly 40 per cent . . .

Ericsson was criticised for being too much of a technology-focused company and not enough of a consumer products company, which resulted in well-engineered phones, some even argued over-engineered – 'while failing on basics such as design, usability and battery-life'. The solution was a joint venture with Sony's mobile telephony handset division in 2001, but the former profit-ability and market share figures had not returned. The *Financial Times* (7 October 2003) reported:

> The one disposal that analysts have often expected Ericsson to make is its 50 per cent stake in Sony Ericsson, its handsets joint venture with Sony of Japan. But Mr Svanberg insists this will be kept. The venture has been in the red since it was set up in October 2001 but is now in sight of black figures, just like Ericsson itself.

'They have a number of interesting products com-ing out,' he says brandishing the company's new Z600 clam-shell, colour screen, camera phones. The venture has brought an excellent blend of skills from the two partners, he says. 'It's obvious the marriage is great. Our commitment to Sony Ericsson is as strong as it has ever been.'

Other sources

Ericsson Annual Reports 1978–1998. Mölleryd, B. (1999) 'Entrepreneurship in technological systems – The development of mobile telephony in Sweden', Dissertation, EFI, Stockholm School of Economics. Regnér, P. (1999) *Strategy Creation and Change in Complexity – Adaptive and creative learning dynamics in the firm*. Published doctoral dissertation. Stockholm: Institute of International Business, Stockholm School of Economics.

Sunshine and storms on the Isle of Skye:
Sabhal Mòr Ostaig and the Gaelic Renaissance[1]

Donald MacLean

This case study concerns the development of Scotland's only Gaelic-medium college, from its inception in 1973 through to 2004. Initially established as a small business school for Gaelic speakers, Sabhal Mòr Ostaig has evolved into the international focal point for the development of Gaelic culture and education. The case study provides opportunities to look at Sabhal Mòr Ostaig from a variety of perspectives: in terms of the strategic issues facing small to medium-sized enterprises (SMEs); in terms of the relationships between context, strategy and organisation; to consider how strategy and organisation develop hand-in-hand in a shifting context of key relationships, activities, resources and evolving intentions; to speculate about SMO's future challenges as viewed by senior figures in the college; and to reflect on implications for the strategic practices of individuals involved in the strategy process.

• • •

A view of the future

Professor Norman Gillies sipped his tea as he gazed out over the scene around him. In front lay the turbulent blue waters of the Sound of Sleat with the spectacular mountain scenery of the Knoydart peninsula on the Scottish mainland in the distance. Behind him stood the award-winning campus of Scotland's only Gaelic medium college, Sabhal Mòr Ostaig, a bold statement of confidence about the future of Scotland's ancient and distinctive culture.

The symbolism of his situation was not lost on him. From its humble beginning in an old barn, Sabhal Mòr Ostaig had grown into a vibrant institute of higher education and one that had attracted praise from the highest quarters. However, significant hazards and challenges lay in its way to the heart of a rejuvenated and growing Gaelic language and culture.

Part of the problem stemmed from the college's success, which had created a growing infrastructure and its apparently insatiable demand for funds. Increased staff costs, rising overheads, pressure on revenues and a looming funding gap were serious issues on the underside of progress.

Professor Gillies was not alone in his concerns. His head of studies, John Norman MacLeod was increasingly worried about the dwindling supply of suitably qualified staff as the demand for the college's offering increased in various parts of the world. Gaelic speakers were in short enough supply; add to that the need for educational ability, expertise in particular subject areas and the need for information technology skills for IT-enabled modes of learning, and one was looking into a rather small recruitment pool.

Likewise, Sabhal Mòr Ostaig's development manager, Archie MacLean, found the financial uncertainty hanging over the college both disconcerting and frustrating. With an investment cycle of at least one human generation (as is required when dealing with the development of language and culture), continuity of funds was essential for a robust planning process. Archie was also concerned about the mismatch that was beginning to open up between the college's own infrastructure

---

[1] See Table 1 for a guide to the pronunciation and meaning of Gaelic terms used in the case.

and that of its surrounding area – Sabhal Mòr Ostaig had all but exhausted availability of power, water and other services and was placing increasing demands on communication services such as transport and telephony.

Perhaps the most fundamental concern however, and one that united all three men, was the feeling that the success which was increasing the financial pressure on the college had also led them onto a new level of visibility and into more pressurised and bureaucratic areas of the Scottish establishment. What made this more difficult was Sabhal Mòr Ostaig's refusal to fit tidily into existing funding and regulatory categories just as the funding requirement were moving up a gear. In a mainstream that had difficulty in understanding, let alone supporting, the college's existence, this issue posed a serious operational challenge and obstacle to continued growth.

A breath of fresh air

Located on the Sleat peninsula to the south of the Island, the award-winning college campus makes a bold statement about the future of the culture which it represents. Innovative design and construction have created a unique space in which ancient tradition and state-of-the-art facilities combine to produce a light and relaxed atmosphere, laced with an almost tangible commitment to Gaelic education and cultural development.

The accommodation block, modelled on the ancient Scottish fortification known as a broch, is reminiscent of a large lighthouse and has been adopted by seafarers as a navigation mark; it stands symbolically as the beacon for a growing community of Gaelic learners and scholars throughout the world.

For a Gaelic community and culture which for many years had been declining and struggling to survive, Sabhal Mòr Ostaig (SMO) is a breath of fresh air. Gaelic, introduced to mainland Britain in the opening centuries of the Christian era by the Scoti tribe from Ireland, became the national language of the country to which its bearers gave their name. Although Gaelic was displaced by Broad Scots in the Lowlands in the later medieval period, it was the common tongue of the Highlands until the early part of the last century. Since then however, the numbers have been in continuous decline with approximately 59,000 individuals able to speak the language.

There were however, signs of a reversal of the downward trend and growing optimism with which SMO is closely identified. By 2003 almost 4,000 children were going through Gaelic medium playgroups and primary schools, with more than

Table 1 Guide to pronunciation and meaning of Gaelic terms

Term	Pronunciation	Meaning
Sabhal Mòr Ostaig	Sole more ostek	literally – the Big Barn of Ostaig
Gaelic	Galik	the Gaelic language
Gaidhealtachd	Geltachk	the Highlands and Islands area
Baile Ur Ostaig	Bal oor ostek	the new village of Ostaig
Arainn Chaluim Chille	Aren chalum chilu	the St Columba centre or place
Co as a tha thu/sibh	ko as a ha oo/shiv	where are you from
Co leis thu/sibh	ko laysh oo/shiv	to whom do you belong
Ciamar a tha thu/sibh	kimar a ha oo/shiv	how are you
Fàs	Faas	literally – growth
Leirsinn	Layrshin	literally – vision

(ch – as in loch)
(à – accent signifies long sound)

this number studying Gaelic in English-based primary and secondary education. The Gaelic broadcasting industry was expanding, employing 250 people and broadcasting 300 hours of TV and 2,000 hours of radio annually. Television programmes regularly attracted audiences of over 200,000 viewers. The college has played a key role in these developments through the activities of its Gaelic broadcast training unit and its educational software and learning-materials company, as well as increasing demand for such services through its normal educational activities.

In the beginning

In 1973, the Scottish merchant banker and entrepreneur Sir Ian Noble ended his search for a highland country estate with the purchase of 20,000 acres on the Sleat peninsula of Skye from the MacDonald estates, parts of which were being sold off. Some years later, observing that many of the island's young people were having to leave in order to study (often never to return) and that the Sleat peninsula, like much of Skye, suffered from a lack of entrepreneurial opportunity and infrastructure, Sir Ian and some associates identified possible benefits from the conversion of a dilapidated farm steading into a small, Gaelic-medium business school. The rationale for such a development included the perceived need to stem the island's 'brain-drain' by providing local further education facilities, whilst, by focusing on the area of business in Gaelic, allowing fluent speakers to learn, in their native tongue, key skills which

would contribute to the island's social and economic development. The idea of Sabhal Mòr Ostaig was thus born.

In the years that followed, a small team with the necessary experience, skills and connections obtained approval for its plans from key bodies and potential funders such as the Highland and Islands Development Board and the Scottish Education Department, whilst developing its first academic offering – an HND in Business with Gaidhealtachd Studies for fluent Gaelic speakers.

Viewed as a major innovation for the Highlands and Islands region, the support of powerful establishment contacts was key to sanctioning a development which might otherwise have floundered. Interestingly, key external stakeholders were more attracted to the notion of a highland business school as, at the time, business and business schools were seen as positive forces for renewal; its Gaelic orientation was seen by some as something of a secondary issue.

In 1983, the college became operational and started teaching its first HND cohort of seven students. Coincidentally in this year, the two individuals who later came to direct the college's activities arrived on the small teaching team – the Head of Studies, John Norman MacLeod and the Director, Norman Gillies.

Things carried on at this level until 1987 when a second course was added – Business Studies with Information Technology – in recognition of the growing importance of IT in business, and in response to a personal interest in computing of the then director. This perhaps paved the way for the important role which information and communications technology (ICT) was to play in the development of the college's distance-learning and internet based provision in later years.

In the early 1990s, by which time SMO had established itself as a small further education establishment, with a handful of staff delivering its two courses to around twenty students, another development was to occur which would have a major influence over the college in years to come. Television broadcast franchises were coming up for renewal in Scotland at a time when there was increasing political pressure to provide Gaelic broadcasting on a larger scale than ever before. There was thus a real pressure on TV companies to prove that they were taking Gaelic seriously. To SMO, this constituted a timely opportunity.

Keen to upgrade and enlarge the campus in order to facilitate growth, staff at SMO identified an opportunity in the development and provision of a Gaelic Broadcast training course. Such a course would strengthen the college's links with the media whilst allowing TV companies to demonstrate commitment to Gaelic. In practical terms, if SMO was to increase the flow of a critical and limited resource – skilled Gaelic-speaking personnel for TV companies – the companies in turn might invest in the development of such a resource.

In 1991, Scottish Television and Grampian Television donated £300,000 (≈ €450,000) and £100,000 respectively to SMO with no formal strings attached, but on the understanding that the college would use the money to progress its aspirations in relation to Gaelic broadcasting (a placement-based course was launched in 1991). By 1993, the money had been used to leverage access to other funds and in 1993, the college campus was upgraded to include more teaching and admin space, new student accommodation and an (as yet unequipped) TV studio. The studio was equipped later that year on the closure of the BBC studio in Aberdeen, at which point SMO became a provider of in-house Gaelic broadcast training, for which it has subsequently developed a very strong reputation.

A change of heart?

With the latest development now behind them, staff at the college began to think of the next phase of expansion. In the interim, it had become clear that one of the founding assumptions of the college was perhaps running up against its limits in that there simply weren't sufficient numbers of native Gaelic-speaking business students to sustain the college in the longer term. In contrast to this, there was growing interest in the Gaelic dimension of SMO's provision both in terms of studying the language and culture in-house, and in developing IT-enabled, access-level material for distance learning. In some senses, since SMO had exhausted availability of native language speakers, it was dedicating increasing resources to creation of a new supply, and in the process, was en-route from its origins as a Gaelic-medium business school to its position as the steward of, and campaigner for, Gaelic language and culture.

In 1995, Norman Gillies, together with leading figures in the local economic development agency, came to hear about the establishment of the Millennium Commission, which would distribute funds to worthy causes to mark the commencement of the third millennium. The news crystallised a desire to embark on an exciting new project in the hope that funding for it would come from the Millennium Commission. Norman Gillies, John Norman MacLeod and others came up with a plan and drawings for 'Baile Ur Ostaig' – The New Village of Ostaig. This was an ambitious £20m development of the current campus which would enable the provision of many more courses in the Gaelic language, developing some of these towards degree level, as well as scaling up the infrastructure to include enhanced student accommodation, state of the art teaching and learning facilities, a theatre, a new broadcast training unit, a research centre and other facilities. Whilst such a development may sound overly-ambitious for such a small college, staff had become accustomed to thinking on a 20-year time-frame since by then, the key concern of expanding the Gaelic language and culture, was viewed as something which occurred on the timescales of a human generation. Plans had to be laid for children who were just about to enter Gaelic-medium education at the pre-nursery level.

Commitment to and belief in 'Baile Ur Ostaig' was such that in 1995, a signpost was erected outside the college campus – indicating the impending development. In 1996, staff received news that the bid had been unsuccessful. Part of the reasoning was that SMO would not get the necessary planning consents to secure the development, and that even if this were not the case, the infrastructure around the current campus was simply not capable of dealing with such a development. Just as the SMO development was rejected by the Millennium Commission, the UHI project was given the go-ahead.

In many ways, the UHI development was like a much bigger version of the SMO concept, with a similar rationale but without the Gaelic focus. Leading eventually to the establishment of an IT-intensive University of The Highlands and Islands, the UHI-Millennium Institute bid envisaged the coalescence of numerous further education facilities in the Highlands into a networked provider of higher education. Since this would present an attractive local alternative to aspiring students who would otherwise have no option but to leave, the development was seen as key to arresting the processes of erosion of the cultural fabric (and future) of the region.

Whilst the rejection of the SMO bid was something of a blow in the short term, it nevertheless pointed to an alternative, longer-term development opportunity. If the college was to become an active part of UHI-MI, it would pave the way to its elevation to the status of higher-education institute (rather than remaining in further education) thus providing access to sources of funding and a higher standard of educational activity.

In the meantime, the organisation which owned the land around the campus confirmed that it could not sanction any development as it would run counter to its own constitution. However, in a generous move, its leader offered, for a nominal sum, a six-acre site less than a mile from the current campus, overlooking the sea with superb views of Knoydart and the Scottish mainland. He had purchased this site some time previously with a view to building a family home, but recognised, years later, that this was unlikely ever to happen. This site was undoubtedly one of the prime locations on the island, with views to rival any in the Scottish Highlands. With this fortunate and generous turn of events, resolve developed at SMO to show the Millennium Commission what a mistake it had made.

Arainn Chaluim Chille

By 1996, SMO had developed its reputation around the role of champion for the Gaelic language and culture. A course in Gaelic arts had been added in 1994, and the original course in Business

Studies though still running, was no longer central. In part, its reputation had been developed and sustained through a series of high profile annual lectures in which a senior public figure gave what has become known as the Sabhal Mòr Ostaig Lecture. As an indication of their significance, in recent years the lecture, which typically reflects on the value and future of the Gaelic language and culture, has been delivered by the architect of Scottish devolution and First Minister – the late Donald Dewar, and by the UK Chancellor of the Exchequer, Gordon Brown.

In 1997, the SMO lecture was given by the President of Ireland, Mary Robinson. A champion of the Gaelic cause, and the co-founder of the Columba Initiative which was launched to develop and nurture links between the Gaelic cultures of Ireland and Scotland, her lecture was regarded as a significant milestone in the development of the college. As a senior and internationally respected politician, she warmly endorsed the aspirations and intentions of SMO as a champion of the distinctive cultures of Scotland and Ireland:

> When I became President of Ireland, some six and a half years ago, I spoke of a province of our imagination, a fifth province, a common ground on which we could come together and celebrate what we share. Perhaps we can create an island space for ourselves to celebrate what Scotland and Ireland share.[2]

When President Robinson went on to plant a tree on the recently acquired site, the symbolism translated into solid conviction that this was 'the island space' of which she spoke. Interpreted as no less than a blessing from the leading figure in Ireland's Celtic revival, in the presence of the great and the good of the Scottish establishment, the high-profile endorsement galvanised renewed efforts to establish a new campus.

Development followed at rapid rate. A degree programme, which had been launched in 1996/7, signalled SMO's readiness to join the higher education firmament and aligned it for incorporation into the UHI-MI network. A funding package of £7m was secured from a variety of public and private sources (including the Millennium Commission), and building work for the new campus commenced in late 1997. A year later, the first building was opened and the new campus, Arainn

---

[2] Oraid Sabhal Mor Ostaig 1997, A lecture by President Mary Robinson.

Chaluim Chille, became operational in time for the millennium.

The organisation of Gaelic and the Gaelic of organisation

By 2003 Sabhal Mòr Ostaig, officially an independent educational charity, had a turnover of around £3m, approximately half of which came through public funds via the UHI-MI system, the Scottish Higher and Further Education Funding Councils and the Scottish Executive, whilst the other half was generated through activities such as running self-funding courses, hosting conferences etc. It employed around 70 people, including 16 in Canan, its independent publishing and educational software business. As such, the college was a major feature of the social economy of Skye.

In its 2003 strategic plan the college states (in English) its vision in the following terms:

> Sabhal Mòr Ostaig seeks continually to contribute to a revitalised, thriving and self-confident Gaelic community by inspiring and motivating students, staff and all those who interact with it to realise their potential in terms of Gaelic language, culture and heritage.

and its mission as

> Sabhal Mòr Ostaig is committed to being a centre of excellence for the development and enhancement of the Gaelic language, culture and heritage, by providing quality educational, training and research opportunities through the medium of Scottish Gaelic; and by interacting innovatively with individuals communities and businesses, to contribute to social, cultural and economic development.

The activities of SMO could be divided into four categories. The largest is its teaching and educational activities – with over 600 students each year, of which just under 100 are full-time students, just under 200 distance-learners and the remainder made up by summer-school and short-course students. It also has an independently run theatre company which hosts and stages cultural events, open to the public as well as students. It has an independent publishing and software company that developed the material for the televised 'Speaking our Language' programme and active in web-based learning and development technologies. It also has an embryonic research capability – which employes three people, but which is seen a key area for development in the future.

Table 2 Summary of key measures and trends

Year/Key Measure	Turnover (£m)*	No of students	No of Staff
1999	3.032	553	55
2001	2.877	531	60
2003	2.677	630	66

* £1 = approx €1.5.

Table 2 contains a summary of key measures in the early part of the millennium.

The organisation has a formal structure – broadly divided into academic and infrastructure development activities, the former directed by John Norman MacLeod and the latter by Norman Gillies.

However, although the college has all the structural attributes, documentation and jargon which typifies the modern organisation, there is a highly distinctive mode of managing and organising. The language of the college is Gaelic and this applies to its management and organisation as much as to its products and services. In reality the organisation works in a highly informal, conversational mode. Perhaps maintaining the flavour of its small origins or perhaps expressing an attribute of its distinctive culture, or both, the college is very much a community.

As such, the college has the feel of a focal point for what is almost an extended family. In the words of Archie MacLean, Development Manager:

> In Gaelic culture the two most important questions you can ask are, 'Co as a tha sibh?' (where are you from?) and 'Co leis thu?' (to whom do you belong?) – answers to these questions generate a sense of community. When someone asks, 'Ciamar a tha thu?' (how are you?), they want to know the answer in some detail – 'fine' or 'OK' won't do – its an important part of day-to-day work.

The working atmosphere is an unusual blend of almost evangelical focus, pride and relaxed informality. Staff members rarely stick to a single job, often involved in many projects at once. This approach has continued from the early days when there were simply more tasks than people and a general recognition that, if the college was to survive, then people had to be flexible and the 'system' had to search for ways of letting people do things that are both good for them as individuals and good for the college.

Whilst there are often disagreements about how to achieve a particular end, the ends themselves are rarely disputed in that they all relate to the development of the language and culture. The shared vision of a vibrant Gaelic community represents both the longing that justifies and galvanises action and the belonging which makes such actions meaningful and coherent. Such is identification with the future of Gaelic culture that for many now, the success of SMO is synonymous with the survival of the culture itself.

Three views of the past

Perhaps unsurprisingly, different views emerge when reflecting on the development of Sabhal Mòr Ostaig to date.   .

For Norman Gillies, the key features of the development process have been strong vision, determination, creativity, quality, powerful friends and important symbolic events. In his own words:

> We haven't gone down the conventional path. We've had to deal with things creatively and recognise that sometimes the shortest route isn't the one you take – sometimes we have to be a bit chameleon-like. We have to do things well; 'cheap and nasty' isn't an option as this would damage our culture . . . President Robinson planting the tree, in the presence of the great and the good, was an important and encouraging gesture – it seemed to say that we were that special place she alluded to in her speech and gave us a real endorsement . . . we have many helpful and generous friends who perhaps get some form of emotional payback from their connection with the college and what it stands for. It's a source of pride.

John Norman MacLeod focuses on a different set of features. For him, the strong sense of community and teamwork that brings together the varied staff members is the key. This community spirit is also an important aspect of the college's external partnerships – with its local community, the regional development agency and the UHI network. It works well with the college's style of leadership and direction, fosters involvement and participation at all levels and sustains commitment and energy.

John Norman also sees the commitment to quality and standards as a vital factor in the past fifteen years or so:

> In 1987, we failed a validation for a postgraduate course in entrepreneurship. There were big reverberations after this. Partly because of it, and partly because what we do is of questionable value in the eyes of the

mainstream, we now overdo the quality standards – if we've got something to do we do it well; failure is not an option.

Development Manager Archie MacLean sees SMO's success as an outcome of the commitment, energy and motivation of the staff, their identification with the college's vision, their preparedness to be flexible and to do whatever is necessary to succeed. As he puts it:

> All the people who work and study here care; they care that the college succeeds and that the Gaelic language and culture develop – and this gives us a real edge to our mission. I doubt if any other colleges have this level of commitment.

Whilst he sees the college as the achievement of everyone involved, he points out the critical role played by a succession of key individuals who have directed and orchestrated major developments internally and externally with passion, determination and skill.

All three men accept each other's interpretations, agreeing that they are 'coming at the same thing from different directions'. The also agree that they, their colleagues and SMO's various scholars and visitors share a common bond of belonging to something that is of immense worth and currently under some threat. Whilst, in a very real sense, their lives, those of their families and communities are bound up with the fortunes of the college, beyond that, the connection with the fate of the Gaelic culture and history imbues the whole enterprise with a sense of deeper social, cultural or spiritual significance.

They also agree that there are core principles or practices that seem to endure and underpin the somewhat unpredictable responses to unfolding circumstance. There is a kind of 'grow your own' approach where students become staff or return as private customers or external champions later on in their lives. There is a shared belief in the value of thorough preparation for all events and a determination to see things through to completion one way or another. Underpinning all of this is the view that everything counts, everything is an expression of the hopes and aspirations for the Gaelic culture, and so it must be done well as there is more than the college's fate riding on the outcome. Paradoxically perhaps, it is this identification with something older, bigger and beyond the college that may be the key to its success.

The future in view

Norman Gillies drained his cup and took one last look at the view. A large cargo-vessel punched its way through the waves, making sure if somewhat perilous progress up the Sound of Sleat. Turning the image over in his mind, the professor made his way back to his office and the multitude of tasks that awaited him.

Acknowledgements

The author would like to express his gratitude to Professor Norman Gillies and Messrs John Norman MacLeod and Archie MacLean for their help with the compilation of the case-study, and to everyone at Sabhal Mòr Ostaig for their hospitality during that process.

Glossary

Acceptability is concerned with the expected performance outcomes of a strategy (p. 361)

Acquisition is where strategies are developed by taking over ownership of another organisation (p. 349)

Backward integration is development into activities concerned with the inputs into the company's current business (p. 285)

Balanced scorecards combine both qualitative and quantitative measures, acknowledge the expectations of different stakeholders and relate an assessment of performance to choice of strategy (p. 418)

Barriers to entry are factors that need to be overcome by new entrants if they are to compete successfully (p. 81)

Black holes are subsidiaries located in countries that are crucial for competitive success but with low-level resources or capabilities (p. 327)

The **Bower–Burgelman explanation** of strategy development is that strategy develops as the outcome of resource allocation routines in organisations (p. 580)

Business-level strategy is about how to compete successfully in particular markets (p. 11)

A **business model** describes the structure of product, service and information flows and the roles of the participating parties (p. 462)

A **cash cow** is a business unit with a high market share in a mature market (p. 316)

A **change agent** is the individual or group that effects strategic change in an organisation (p. 519)

Coercion is the imposition of change or the issuing of edicts about change (p. 517)

Collaboration or *participation* in the change process is the involvement of those who will be affected by strategic change in the change agenda (p. 515)

Competences are the activities and processes through which an organisation deploys its resources effectively (p. 119)

Competitive rivals are organisations with similar products and services aimed at the same customer group (p. 85)

Competitive strategy is concerned with the basis on which a business unit might achieve competitive advantage in its market (p. 242)

An organisation's **configuration** consists of the structures, processes and relationships through which the organisation operates (p. 396)

Consolidation is where organisations protect and strengthen their position in their current markets with current products (p. 342)

Contributors are subsidiaries with valuable internal resources but located in countries of lesser strategic significance, which nonetheless play key roles in a multinational organisation's competitive success (p. 326)

Convergence is where previously separate industries begin to overlap in terms of activities, technologies, products and customers (p. 77)

Core competences are the activities and processes through which resources are deployed in such a way as to achieve competitive advantage in ways that others cannot imitate or obtain (p. 121)

Core values are the principles that guide an organisation's actions (p. 207)

Corporate-level strategy is concerned with the overall purpose and scope of an organisation and how value will be added to the different parts (business units) of the organisation (p. 11)

Corporate parent refers to the levels of management above that of the business units and therefore without direct interaction with buyers and competitors (p. 281)

Corporate social responsibility is concerned with the *ways* in which an organisation exceeds the minimum obligations to stakeholders specified through regulation and corporate governance (p. 191)

Critical success factors (CSFs) are those product features that are particularly valued by a group of customers and, therefore, where the organisation must excel to outperform competition (p. 96)

A **cultural explanation of strategy development** is that it occurs as the outcome of the taken-for-granted assumptions and behaviours in organisations (p. 581)

Cultural processes are concerned with organisational culture and the *standardisation of norms* (p. 416)

The **cultural web** is a representation of the taken-for-granted assumptions, or paradigm, of an organisation and the physical manifestations of organisational culture (p. 201)

Data mining is the process of finding trends, patterns and connections in data in order to inform and improve competitive performance (p. 459)

The **design lens** views strategy development as the deliberate positioning of the organisation through a rational, analytic, structured and directive process (p. 41)

Development directions are the strategic options available to an organisation, in terms of products and market coverage (p. 340)

A **development method** is the *means* by which any strategic direction will be pursued (p. 348)

Devolution concerns the extent to which the centre of an organisation delegates decision making to units and managers lower down in the hierarchy (p. 421)

A **differentiation strategy** seeks to provide product or service benefits that are different from those of competitors and that are widely valued by buyers (p. 246)

Diffusion is the extent and pace at which a market is likely to adopt new products (p. 481)

Direct supervision is the direct control of strategic decisions by one or a few individuals (p. 411)

Direction involves the use of personal managerial authority to establish a clear future strategy and how change will occur (p. 516)

The **directional policy matrix** positions SBUs according to (a) how attractive the relevant market is in which they are operating, and (b) the competitive strength of the SBU in that market (p. 319)

Diversification is a strategy that takes the organisation into both new markets and products or services (pp. 282, 346)

Dogs are business units with a low share in static or declining markets (p. 316)

A **dominant strategy** is one that outperforms all other strategies whatever rivals choose (p. 266)

A **dominated strategy** is a competitive strategy that, if pursued by a competitor, is bound to outperform the company (p. 266)

Dynamic capabilities are an organisation's abilities to develop and change competences to meet the needs of rapidly changing environments (p. 132)

Education and communication involve the explanation of the reasons for and means of strategic change (p. 515)

Emergent strategy comes about through everyday routines, activities and processes in organisations (p. 566)

Enabling success is concerned with the two-way relationship between overall business strategies and strategies in separate resource areas such as people, information, finance and technology (p. 446)

In game theory, **equilibrium** is a situation where each competitor contrives to get the best possible strategic solution for themselves given the response from the other (p. 266)

The **ethical stance** is the *extent* to which an organisation will exceed its minimum obligations to stakeholders and society at large (p. 189)

The **experience lens** views strategy development as the outcome of individual and collective experience of individuals and their taken-for-granted assumptions (p. 45)

A **failure strategy** is one that does not provide perceived value-for-money in terms of product features, price or both (p. 252)

Feasibility is concerned with whether an organisation has the resources and competences to deliver a strategy (p. 371)

In **financial control** the role of the centre is confined to setting financial targets, allocating resources, appraising performance and intervening to avert or correct poor performance (p. 424)

The **five forces framework** helps identify the sources of competition in an industry or sector (p. 78)

A **focused differentiation** strategy seeks to provide high perceived product/service benefits justifying a substantial price premium, usually to a selected market segment (niche) (p. 251)

A **forcefield analysis** provides a view of change problems that need to be tackled, by identifying forces for and against change (p. 514)

Forward integration is development into activities which are concerned with a company's outputs (p. 285)

A **functional structure** is based on the primary activities that have to be undertaken by an organisation such as production, finance and accounting, marketing, human resources and research and development (p. 398)

Game theory is concerned with the interrelationships between the competitive moves of a set of competitors (p. 264)

Gatekeepers are individuals or groups who gain power from their control of information (p. 466)

The **global–local dilemma** relates to the extent to which products and services may be standardised across national boundaries or need to be adapted to meet the requirements of specific national markets (p. 300)

Global sourcing: purchasing services and components from the most appropriate suppliers around the world regardless of their location (p. 297)

In a **global strategy** standardised products exploiting economies of scale and value-adding activities are typically concentrated in a limited set of locations (p. 300)

The **governance framework** describes whom the organisation is there to serve and how the purposes and priorities of the organisation should be decided (p. 165)

A **holding company** is an investment company consisting of shareholdings in a variety of separate business operations (p. 402)

Horizontal integration is development into activities which are complementary to present activities (p. 285)

A **hybrid strategy** seeks simultaneously to achieve differentiation and a price lower than that of competitors (p. 248)

Hypercompetition occurs where the frequency, boldness and aggressiveness of dynamic moves by competitors accelerate to create a condition of constant disequilibrium and change (p. 89)

The **ideas lens** sees strategy as the emergence of order and innovation from the variety and diversity which exist in and around organisations (p. 49)

Individual experience is the mental (or cognitive) models people build over time to help make sense of their situation (p. 46)

An **industry** is a group of firms producing the same principal product (p. 77)

Intangible resources are non-physical assets such as information, reputation and knowledge (p. 118)

Intended strategy is an expression of desired strategic direction deliberately formulated or planned by managers (p. 565)

Internal development is where strategies are developed by building on and developing an organisation's own capabilities (p. 348)

Intervention is the coordination of and authority over processes of change by a change agent who delegates elements of the change process (p. 516)

Key drivers of change are forces likely to affect the structure of an industry, sector or market (p. 69)

Key value and cost drivers are the factors that have most influence on the cash generation cability of an organisation (p. 469)

Leadership is the process of influencing an organisation (or group within an organisation) in its efforts towards achieving an aim or goal (p. 519)

The **learning organisation** is capable of continual regeneration from the variety of knowledge, experience and skills of individuals within a culture which encourages mutual questioning and challenge around a shared purpose or vision (p. 589)

Legitimacy is concerned with meeting the expectations within an organisational field in terms of assumptions, behaviours and strategies (p. 199)

Lock-in is where an organisation achieves a proprietary position in its industry; it becomes an industry standard (p. 256)

Logical incrementalism is the deliberate development of strategy by experimentation and learning from partial commitments (p. 578)

A **low-price strategy** seeks to achieve a lower price than competitors whilst trying to maintain similar perceived product or service benefits to those offered by competitors (p. 246)

Managing for value is concerned with maximising the long-term cash-generating capability of an organisation (p. 466)

Market development is where existing products are offered in new markets (p. 346)

Market penetration is where an organisation gains market share (p. 344)

Market processes involve some formalised system of 'contracting' for resources (p. 418)

A **market segment** is a group of customers who have similar needs that are different from customer needs in other parts of the market (p. 91)

A **matrix structure** is a combination of structures which could take the form of product and geographical divisions or functional and divisional structures operating in tandem (p. 402)

A **mission statement** is a statement of the overriding direction and purpose of an organisation (p. 209)

A **multidivisional structure** is built up of separate divisions on the basis of products, services or geographical areas (p. 399)

In a **multi-domestic strategy** value-adding activities are located in individual national markets served by the organisation and products and/or services are adapted to the unique local requirements (p. 300)

A **'no frills' strategy** combines a low price, low perceived product/service benefits and a focus on a price-sensitive market segment (p. 245)

Objectives are statements of specific outcomes that are to be achieved (p. 209)

Operational strategies are concerned with how the component parts of an organisation deliver effectively the corporate- and business-level strategies in terms of resources, processes and people (p. 12)

Organisational culture is the 'basic *assumptions and beliefs* that are shared by members of an organisation, that operate unconsciously and define in a basic taken-for-granted fashion an organisation's view of itself and its environment' (pp. 47, 196)

An **organisational field** is a community of organisations that partake of a common meaning system and whose participants interact more frequently with one another than with those outside the field (p. 197)

Organisational knowledge is the collective and shared experience accumulated through systems, routines and activities of sharing across the organisation (p. 133)

A **paradigm** is the set of assumptions held relatively in common and taken for granted in an organisation (p. 200)

The **parental developer**: a corporate parent seeking to employ its own competences as a parent to add value to its businesses and build parenting skills that are appropriate for their portfolio of business units (p. 311)

Performance targets relate to the *outputs* of an organisation (or part of an organisation), such as product quality, prices or profit (p. 417)

The **PESTEL framework** categorises environmental influences into six main types: political, economic, social, technological, environmental and legal (p. 65)

Planning processes plan and control the allocation of resources and monitor their utilisation (p. 412)

The **political view** of strategy development is that strategies develop as the outcome of processes of bargaining and negotiation among powerful internal or external interest groups (or stakeholders) (p. 584)

Porter's Diamond suggests that there are inherent reasons why some nations are more competitive than others, and why some industries within nations are more competitive than others (p. 71)

A **portfolio manager** is a corporate parent acting as an agent on behalf of financial markets and shareholders (p. 308)

Power is the ability of individuals or groups to persuade, induce or coerce others into following certain courses of action (p. 185)

Primary activities are directly concerned with the creation or delivery of a product or service (p. 136)

Product development is where organisations deliver modified or new products to existing markets (p. 344)

Profit pools are the potential profits at different parts of the value network (p. 141)

A **project-based structure** is one where teams are created, undertake the work and are then dissolved (p. 408)

Punctuated equilibrium is the tendency of strategies to develop incrementally with periodic transformational change (p. 28)

A **question mark** (or problem child) is a business unit in a growing market, but without a high market share (p. 315)

Realised strategy: the strategy actually being followed by an organisation in practice (p. 566)

A **recipe** is a set of assumptions held in common within an organisational field about organisational purposes and a 'shared wisdom' on how to manage organisations (p. 199)

Reinforcing cycles are created by the *dynamic interaction* between the various factors of environment, configuration and elements of strategy; they tend to preserve the status quo (p. 433)

Related diversification is strategy development beyond current products and markets, but within the capabilities or value network of the organisation (p. 285)

The **resource-based view** of strategy: the competitive advantage of an organisation is explained by the distinctiveness of its capabilities (p. 116)

Returns are the benefits which stakeholders are expected to receive from a strategy (p. 361)

Risk concerns the probability and consequences of the failure of a strategy (p. 369)

Routines are the organisationally specific 'ways we do things around here' which tend to persist over time and guide people's behaviour (p. 527)

Scenarios are detailed and plausible views of how the business environment of an organisation might develop in the future based on groupings of key environmental influences and drivers of change about which there is a high level of uncertainty (p. 76)

Processes of **self-control** achieve the integration of knowledge and coordination of activities by the direct interaction of individuals without supervision (p. 413)

Staged international expansion: firms initially use entry modes that allow them to maximise knowledge acquisition whilst minimising the exposure of their assets (p. 297)

A **stage-gate process** is a structured review process to assess progress on meeting product performance characteristics during the product development process and ensuring that they are matched with market data (p. 488)

Stakeholder mapping identifies stakeholder expectations and power and helps in understanding political priorities (p. 181)

Stakeholders are those individuals or groups who depend on the organisation to fulfil their own goals and on whom, in turn, the organisation depends (p. 179)

A **star** is a business unit which has a high market share in a growing market (p. 315)

A **strategic alliance** is where two or more organisations share resources and activities to pursue a strategy (p. 353)

A **strategic business unit** is a part of an organisation for which there is a distinct external market for goods or services that is different from another SBU (pp. 11, 241)

Strategic capability is the adequacy and suitability of the resources and competences of an organisation for it to survive and prosper (p. 117)

Strategic choices involve understanding the underlying bases for future strategy at both the business unit and corporate levels and the options for developing strategy in terms of both the directions and methods of development (p. 18)

Strategic control is concerned with shaping the *behaviour* in business units and with shaping the *context* within which managers are operating (p. 425)

The **strategic customer** is the person(s) at whom the strategy is primarily addressed because they have the most influence over which goods or services are purchased (p. 96)

Strategic drift is where strategies progressively fail to address the strategic position of the organisation and performance deteriorates (pp. 27, 582)

A **strategic gap** is an opportunity in the competitive environment that is not being fully exploited by competitors (p. 99)

Strategic groups are organisations within an industry with similar strategic characteristics, following similar strategies or competing on similar bases (p. 89)

Strategic leaders (in the context of international strategy) are subsidiaries that not only hold valuable resources and capabilities but are also located in countries that are crucial for competitive success (p. 326)

Strategic management includes *understanding the strategic position* of an organisation, *strategic choices* for the future and turning *strategy into action* (p. 16)

Strategic planning may take the form of systematised, step-by-step, chronological procedures to develop or coordinate an organisation's strategy (p. 568)

In a **strategic planning style** of control, the relationship between the centre and the business units is one of a parent who is the *master planner* prescribing detailed roles for departments and business units (p. 423)

The **strategic position** is concerned with the impact on strategy of the external environment, an organisation's strategic capability (resources and competences) and the expectations and influence of stakeholders (p. 17)

Strategy is the *direction* and *scope* of an organisation over the *long term*, which achieves *advantage* in a changing *environment* through its configuration of *resources and competences* with the aim of fulfilling *stakeholder expectations* (p. 9)

Strategy development processes are the ways in which strategy develops in organisations (p. 19)

Strategy into action is concerned with ensuring that strategies are working in practice (p. 19)

The **strategy lenses** are three different ways of looking at the issues of strategy development for an organisation (p. 32)

Substitution reduces demand for a particular 'class' of products as customers switch to the alternatives (p. 82)

Success criteria are used to assess the likely success of a strategic option (p. 357)

Suitability is concerned with whether a strategy addresses the circumstances in which an organisation is operating – the strategic position (p. 358)

Support activities help to improve the effectiveness or efficiency of primary activities (p. 137)

A **SWOT analysis** summarises the key issues from the business environment and the strategic capability of an organisation that are most likely to impact on strategy development (pp. 102, 148)

Symbols are objects, events, acts or people which express more than their intrinsic content (p. 528)

Synergy refers to the benefits that might be gained where activities or processes complement each other such that their combined effect is greater than the sum of the parts (p. 282)

The **synergy manager** a corporate parent seeking to enhance value across business units by managing synergies across business units (p. 310)

Tangible resources are the physical assets of an organisation such as plant, labour and finance (p. 117)

A **team-based structure** attempts to combine both horizontal and vertical coordination through structuring people into cross-functional teams (p. 406)

A **technological path** identifies the major factors that are influencing technological developments (p. 478)

Threshold capabilities are those capabilities essential for the organisation to be able to compete in a given market (p. 119)

A **tipping point** is where demand for a product or service suddenly takes off or declines – sometimes dramatically (p. 482)

A **transnational structure** combines the local responsiveness of the international subsidiary with the coordination advantages found in global product companies (p. 404)

In a **turnaround strategy** the emphasis is on speed of change and rapid cost reduction and/or revenue generation (p. 523)

Unique resources are those resources that critically underpin competitive advantage and that others cannot easily imitate or obtain (p. 121)

Unrelated diversification is the development of products or services beyond the current capabilities or value network (p. 288)

The **value network** is the set of inter-organisational links and relationships that are necessary to create a product or service (p. 140)

Vertical integration is backward or forward integration into adjacent activities in the value network (p. 285)

Virtual organisations are held together not through formal structure and physical proximity of people, but by partnership, collaboration and networking (p. 430)

General Index

S